Banks, Exchanges, and Regulators

Banks, Exchanges, and Regulators

Global Financial Markets from the 1970s

RANALD C. MICHIE

OXFORD
UNIVERSITY PRESS

OXFORD
UNIVERSITY PRESS

Great Clarendon Street, Oxford, OX2 6DP,
United Kingdom

Oxford University Press is a department of the University of Oxford.
It furthers the University's objective of excellence in research, scholarship,
and education by publishing worldwide. Oxford is a registered trade mark of
Oxford University Press in the UK and in certain other countries

First Edition published in 2021

Impression: 1

Published in the United States of America by Oxford University Press
198 Madison Avenue, New York, NY 10016, United States of America

British Library Cataloguing in Publication Data
Data available

Library of Congress Control Number: 2020947866

ISBN 978–0–19–955373–0

DOI: 10.1093/oso/9780199553730.001.0001

Printed and bound by
CPI Group (UK) Ltd, Croydon, CR0 4YY

I dedicate this book to my wife, Dinah Ann Michie, née Brooks. I owe my life to her and her prompt action on 28 December 2019. The NHS then did the rest.

Preface

My original intention for this book was to write a history of recent developments in the global stock market following on from the publication in 2006 of my book, *The Global Securities Market: A History*. When I was writing that book I became aware that I had collected a large amount of material relating to the period from the early 1980s onwards that I was unable to make full use of at that time. In particular the information I had already gleaned from the *Financial Times* (*FT*), and continued to do so on a daily basis, was adding a level of depth and breadth regarding more recent events that would completely unbalance a general account of the development of a global securities market from medieval times to the present. The decision I reached, reluctantly, was to put most of that material to one side, though not to ignore it completely, and pursue my original intention, which was to provide an account of the rise, fall, and recovery of the global securities market over the centuries but with an emphasis on the last 200 years. That is what I did. What then happened was the Global Financial Crisis, which had its beginnings in 2007, reached its crescendo in 2008 and continued into 2009 and beyond. That crisis forced a fundamental rethinking of the way I had been viewing the global securities market, especially from the 1970s onwards. In particular, I became much more conscious of the role played by regulators, the growth of the Over-The-Counter Market and the importance of a small number of banks with global operations. Though I had been collecting material on these subjects for some time I was not fully aware of their significance until the Global Financial Crisis. Clearly I could no longer write a book that would simply be a continuation of the history of the global securities market, as that would not suffice in the face of the revelations produced by the Global Financial Crisis.

However, as I began the process of researching and writing a book that would not only build on my history of the global securities market but also take account of all that the Global Financial Crisis had revealed, my academic work took a new direction. Under pressure from the university authorities to apply for and obtain external research funding I became involved in a bid to the Leverhulme Trust in response to their invitation to conduct research into Tipping Points. This bid was led by Professor Stuart Lane of Durham's Geography Department and Director of its Institute of Hazard, Risk, and Resilience. As my contribution I put forward the suggestion that I would lead a strand that looked at the financial crisis of 2007–9 as a Tipping Point in British banking history. Until the failure of Northern Rock Bank in 2007, followed by the rescue of the Bank of Scotland/Lloyds and the Royal Bank of Scotland/NatWest in 2008 there had been no banking crisis of this dimension in Britain since the collapse of Overend and Gurney in 1866 and the bank failures associated with that. I thought it would be an interesting diversion to explore what had happened to the British banking system prior to the crisis of 2007/8 that had transformed it from one of the most resilient in the world throughout the twentieth century to one of the most vulnerable. That proved a fascinating voyage of discovery whose fruits were published in 2016 by Oxford University Press in a book entitled *British Banking: Continuity and Change from 1694 to the Present*. In 1989 David Lascelles had observed that, 'It is a mystery to most people in the banking industry why those outside find it dull'[1] and I can only echo his views.

Nevertheless, my focus remained firmly on writing the more recent history of the global securities market in the light of the financial crisis of 2007–9. That plan was then disrupted by the shock of the Durham team winning the Leverhulme Trust mandate to undertake research into Tipping Points. This was a five-year collaborative research project lasting from 2010 to 2015, and it absorbed most of my research time. Neither the University of Durham nor the Department of History made any allowance for the work involved in the project through a reduction in my other duties, and so I continued with both a full teaching load and additional administrative duties, most notably acting as admissions tutor. I was also let down by the first Research Associate appointed. He used the post to concentrate on his personal agenda to the exclusion of the work required for the project. This placed the burden of the project on me until the appointment of a replacement Research Associate, Dr Matthew Hollow, who delivered far beyond what could be reasonably accepted, considering the circumstances under which he took the post.

Throughout the years of the project I continued to collect material relating to my planned book on the more recent history of the global securities market and to write the occasional piece on that subject. Eventually I finished my contribution to the Tipping Points Project with the publication of a book on the history of British banking in 2016. Once that had been done I begun the massive task of transforming my cuttings from the *FT* into a digital file that would provide me with the material I required in a form that could be used to write this current book. I had expected this to take me the whole of 2016, while seeing the banking book through the press. That would then leave me 2017 in which to write the book with publication in 2018. As I had been granted the academic year 2013–14 as delayed research leave, and then retired from the University of Durham on 30 September 2014, after a forty-year career, I envisaged that I would have plenty of time to finish the Tipping Points Project, assemble my *FT* notes, and then write the new book. This was a wholly unrealistic assumption. No sooner had I retired from Durham University but Newcastle University Business School asked me to contribute to a module, 'Accounting Change and Development', in which I could use my expertise in financial history. That module gave me an opportunity to apply my accumulated knowledge to a new audience and I eagerly accepted their offer. That teaching also put me in regular contact with Professor David McCollum-Oldroyd, whose module it was, and I have benefited enormously from discussing the progress of this book with him over the years. The result helped me to better formulate my understanding of recent financial history though the effort was far more absorbing of my time than I had expected. In addition I had totally underestimated how much material I had amassed from the *FT* and how long it would take to read it and extract what was both important and relevant. In total it took me twenty-two months to complete the examination of my cuttings and type the results into a digital file. By the end, as I kept adding new material from the *FT*, I had over 800,000 words. Converting that into a draft of the book of around 450,000 words took another twenty-two months with an additional four months required to produce a finished product of 300,000 words. Overall, this book took me four years to complete. My friend, Francis Pritchard, then helped with the copy-editing and compilation of the bibliography, for which I am extremely grateful.

[1] David Lascelles, 'Anything but dull', 25th September 1989.

Over that initial twenty-two-month period, in which I worked through my *FT* material, the scope of the book broadened to include not only all financial markets but also banks and regulators. Over time the idea grew of writing a book on the theme of the role played by banks, exchanges, and regulators in global financial markets from the 1970s to the present. This would take a holistic approach to the study of financial markets by attempting to incorporate those elements that did not take an institutional form, as was the case of exchanges. Why did some markets, such as stock exchanges, become highly institutional while others did not, puzzled me as there was no obvious answer. There was no clear trajectory over time from informal direct trading or a reliance on specialist intermediaries to highly-organized exchanges as much of what took place from the 1970s witnessed the reversal of that. In turn that led to questions concerning the role played by banks, as they had the capacity to internalize the market mechanism within a single business. I was also increasingly aware of the consequences of state intervention in the regulatory process as a supplement to or replacement of self-regulation. Writing a book on the history of the global securities market, completed in 2006, followed by one on British banking, finished in 2016, provided me with two fundamentally divergent views on the development of financial markets, especially in the light of the Global Financial Crisis of 2007–9. Writing the history of British banking had provided me with insights into the working of diverse financial markets, especially those for money, currencies, and derivatives and an appreciation of the position occupied by banks and their over-riding concern regarding liquidity. At the same time the need to gain an understanding of what had led to the Crisis, and the role played by central banks and their supervision of the banking system, led me to give far greater prominence to the role of regulators.

It was the work conducted for the Tipping Points Project, and the interdisciplinary nature of the research involved, that has framed this book and made it radically different from the one that I had planned in 2006. Prior to that time I was focused on the competition that had emerged between exchanges and the challenge they faced collectively from both electronic platforms and the internal markets operated by global banks. What I had not comprehended was how all this fitted into the convergence between different financial instruments, whether they were stocks, bonds, or derivatives; their relationship to other financial markets such as those for money and currencies; and the interplay between formal exchanges and Over-The-Counter (OTC) trading. In my defence all I can say is that these issues appeared to be little understood by others at the time, which is probably why there was a global financial crisis in 2007–9 and why lessons need to be learnt from what happened at that time. But these lessons need to be informed by past practice because nothing that happened in 2007–9 was that different from what had taken place in the past. Gillian Tett emphasized in 2018 how important it was to learn from the past so as to avoid the disasters of the future: 'Never before have those financial history books mattered quite so much.'[2] Past crises had led to solutions being devised that contributed to a more stable and more resilient global financial system. It was not only the British banking system that was remarkably stable from 1866 to 2007, for the world financial system was also remarkably stable from 1873 to 1913, or a period of forty years, before being subjected to the shocks of two world wars and an intervening world depression against which there was no protection. It was also stable again between 1945 and 1971 but in many ways that was a false position because it was achieved through the suppression of the market and the

[2] Gillian Tett, 'When the world held its breath', 1st September 2018.

compartmentalization of banking and financial systems rather than an acceptance of change within a changing world. The result was the crisis of the 1970s, followed by an ongoing series of mini-crises that finally erupted with the Global Financial Crisis of 2007–9.

This book is an attempt to merge my two experiences of approaching banking from the perspective of financial markets, as in the *Global Securities Market* book, and financial markets from the perspective of banking, as with the *British Banking* book, with the third dimension of regulation being added to the mix. The triangulation of analysis, the concentration upon the events of the last thirty years, and the need to explain the Global Financial Crisis are the driving forces behind this book. However, none of that would be possible without the information culled from the pages of the *FT*. The period covered by this book is the one during which the *FT* established itself as the authoritative voice of international finance rather than a London-based newspaper specializing in financial news mainly of interest to a British readership. It was this switch from a British business newspaper to a global financial newspaper that made this book possible. One example of that change was the printing of a European edition in Frankfurt in 1979 and the launch of a US edition in 1997.[3] Today the *FT* claims to be the 'World Business Newspaper'. Otherwise the collection of the relevant information would have been an impossible task. Important as data is in capturing global trends over time, especially for the recent past, it alone is insufficient to explain the decisions taken that were instrumental in determining the fate of different banks and exchanges and the policies followed by regulators. As the eminent statistician, Hans Rosling, reflected in 2018, 'The world cannot be understood without numbers. And it cannot be understood with numbers alone.'[4] Reading the *FT* has provided me with both the numbers and the information required to interpret them.

Nevertheless, this book is far more than a recycling of old stories or a summarizing of past analysis. It is an attempt to explain the revolution in global finance that has taken place over the last thirty-five years using the information that was being gathered daily by *FT* journalists, correspondents, and contributors from around the world, and then relayed to their readership through the regular columns of the newspaper and the supplements produced covering specific topics and countries. I have extracted what I deemed relevant from this mass of reporting. What exists in this book is my attempt to make sense of what I have discovered from this material in the light of my past work in financial history. In the process of collecting the information much has been ignored while also much was left out in selecting what to use in the book. While objectivity was the over-riding principle the final product was also the result of subjectivity that was both deliberate and inadvertent. It was deliberate that a choice had to be made about what to focus on. Hence the title of *Banks, Exchanges, and Regulators*, as well as the more recent past stretching back to the 1970s but biased towards the mid-1980s onwards, and especially the years of the Global Financial Crisis and its aftermath. It was also inadvertent in what appears here is not the views and analysis of the hundreds of *FT* journalists whose work I have used, and relied upon, but my interpretation of what they wrote at particular times, on particular subjects and under particular circumstances. Some of that turned out to be highly perceptive in the light of subsequent events while others have not stood the test of time being the product of a specific era or a personal mindset. The same verdict can be reached regarding this book, and almost certainly will, but it is my best effort.

[3] Lionel Barber, 'The world in focus', 13th February 2013.

[4] Hans Rosling, *Factfulness: Ten reasons we're wrong about the world—and why things are better than you think* (London: Sceptre/Flatiron Books, 2018).

Without this daily reporting of developments around the world by the *FT* it would be impossible to write a history of global financial markets over the last thirty to forty years. It was in those years that a revolution took place that transformed these markets and, luckily, the *FT* was there to report on what was happening around the world. However, this does not mean that this book is no more than a précis of that reporting. There is a completely different approach between a journalist reporting events as they unfold and an historian trying to make sense of those same events in terms of why they took place, the sequence that they followed, and the consequences that they had. In addition, the task of the historian is to make judgements with the aid of hindsight when trying to understand why the outcome was as it turned out rather than another. There was nothing predetermined in the revolution that occurred. The combination of a reading of my cuttings from the *FT* for a thirty-five-year period and the analysis derived from writing about the global securities market and British banking, brought home to me the accuracy of the comment that correlation was not proof of causation, though contemporaries, including journalists, were always too ready to make that assumption. To address the question of causation requires an understanding of the sequence of events and the context within which they took place. That is what I have been able to glean from the *FT*.

I began keeping cuttings from the *FT* regularly in 1982. While this initially focused on stock exchanges I was fully aware that a narrow institutional approach to the subject omitted the environment within which they existed and the interaction between them and other components of the financial system. Quite quickly that stock-exchange-focused approach was transformed into one in which financial markets became the focus with stock exchanges becoming only one field of study, and not always the most important. The material I was extracting from the *FT* broadened to include banks and regulators because of the key role each played in both shaping the financial system and being shaped by it. Throughout my scope was to cover the entire world, and it was a daily reading of the *FT* that made this possible. As an editor of the *FT*, Lionel Barber, so succinctly put it in 2008, 'Journalism, so the adage goes, is the first draft of history.'[5] So here is the second draft!

[5] Lionel Barber, 'How gamblers broke the banks', 16th December 2008.

Contents

1
Introduction
Chronology and Causality

General

A study of banks, exchanges, and regulators at any particular moment in time reveals a mixture of the new and the old. What is omitted is the deceased. Such a perspective is suggestive of inevitability as it ignores strategies that were unfulfilled but were of momentary importance, products that were of brief significance but were subsequently abandoned, businesses that flourished and then died, institutions that only fleetingly existed, and rules that were introduced only to be quickly repealed. By omitting these, what is lost are the banks, exchanges, and regulations that were instrumental in determining the eventual outcome, but are no longer present so that their contribution is ignored in the final reckoning. In contrast a perspective that recognizes change over time generates a deeper understanding as it captures all that had come and gone in the years before but had contributed to making the world of finance what it had become. Furthermore, the use of hindsight makes it possible to distinguish between the contribution made by long-term trends compared to major events. Without the richness of detail that narrative provides, the chronology that is essential in identifying cause and effect is absent. What is then revealed is that the outcome that emerged at any particular time was just one among a number of possibilities had different decisions been taken. Only by eliminating all alternatives can a convincing story of path dependency can be constructed linking the past to the present in a series of logical steps for which there is no other outcome. The problem with such an approach is that it assumes that the outcome that came about was the only one possible, and so selects the evidence that supports that conclusion. What is ignored is that evidence which points to a contrary outcome, and so leaves unanswered the question of why that alternative course was not followed.

It is equally important to trace what was not done and why as it is to plot those trends, events, and decisions that were instrumental in reaching a particular outcome. Otherwise it is impossible to plan a different future because the route forward has already been chosen. When all the possibilities are explored the conclusion that emerges is that the world was not trapped in a process that connected the changes that took place in the 1970s to the Global Financial Crisis of 2008 and its aftermath. Throughout the intervening period decisions were made within banks and exchanges and by regulators that influenced the pace, nature, and direction of change, but their importance can only be assessed if their existence is recognized. Contributing to the failure to recognize the significance of these decisions is the heavy reliance placed on statistical series and mathematical models to establish cause and effect and measure significance. Though mathematical models are an important aid to analysis, the degree of certainty they provide is only obtained through a process of selection and simplification that ignores the human element in decision-making. Humans react to the past and anticipate the future and this makes it difficult, bordering on impossible, to

Banks, Exchanges, and Regulators: Global Financial Markets from the 1970s. Ranald Michie, Oxford University Press (2021).

DOI: 10.1093/oso/9780199553730.003.0001

model their behaviour accurately through the use of numbers alone. After a lifetime's study the eminent statistician, Hans Rosling, reached the conclusion in 2018 that 'The world cannot be understood without numbers. And it cannot be understood with numbers alone.'[1] It is the combination of the two that produces true understanding.

There is another problem attached to making judgements without a full understanding of what preceded a particular outcome. That lies in the basis of comparison used. In the years leading up to the crisis it was the post-war era of control and compartmentalization that was regarded as untypical of global financial markets. Reflecting on that era in 2007 Martin Wolf wrote that 'We are witnessing the transformation of mid-twentieth century managerial capitalism into global financial capitalism. Above all, the financial sector, which was placed in chains after the Depression of the 1930s, is once again unbound.'[2] What this judgement reflected was a common view of the twentieth century which regarded the middle years as something of an aberration. As Martin Wolf himself reflected in 1999, 'The twentieth century began in 1914, with the First World War, and ended between 1989 and 1991, with the collapse of the Soviet Empire... By its end... the world had returned, in a modernised and modified form, to the economic liberalism with which it began.... What war and depression did for nineteenth-century laissez faire, inflation and then rising unemployment, notably in western Europe, did for the Keynesian consensus.'[3] Conversely, writing in 2015, in the years that followed the Global Financial Crisis of 2008, Philipp Hildebrand, the former head of the Swiss National Bank, viewed 'the 15 years running up to 2007'[4] as an aberration because it had led to financial markets unfettered by the chains of regulation. To him, normality was the era when central banks were able to exercise a high degree of control. Forgotten in any approach that uses a supposed Golden Age as representing normality was that each period was itself the product of a unique set of circumstances. For global financial markets there was never a period of normality against which all others could be judged, and to which a return could be made by undoing subsequent developments. As Larry Tabb, an expert observer of financial markets, said in 2011, 'Markets are living and breathing things that grow and change over time, reacting to external pressures slowly but surely.'[5] That is why a narrative account can be so much more revealing than either a snapshot or a model.

What a narrative account also provides is the context within which decisions were made, as these were the product of incomplete information and without perfect foresight. Globalization, liberalization, and the revolution in trading technology and business organization were major disruptive forces from the 1970s onwards and that made predicting the future especially difficult. Though the changes to the financial system after the 1970s owed much to the force of these global trends, combined with the actions of governments in removing barriers and forcing change, once begun they developed a momentum of their own. As Janet Bush observed in 1988, 'The financial world has a way of conducting its own post-mortems and prescribing its own cures before the regulators and public opinion get in on the act.'[6] Those actions were driven by bias, self-interest, and misconceptions and reflected a flawed assessment of the current situation, preparation for a future that never

[1] Hans Rosling, *Factfulness: Ten reasons we're wrong about the world—and why things are better than you think*, (London: Sceptre/Flatiron Books, 2018).
[2] Martin Wolf, 'The new capitalism', 19th June 2007.
[3] Martin Wolf, 'Painful lessons from a turbulent century', 6th December 1999.
[4] Patrick Jenkins and Martin Arnold, 'Lenders struggle to weather storms on all sides', 11th November 2015.
[5] Larry Tabb, 'Playing ostrich over high-speed trading is not an option', 14th July 2011.
[6] Janet Bush, 'Portfolio insurance loses its appeal', 10th March 1988.

came about, or a misplaced faith in the precision and certainty of mathematical models. In 2011 John Kay reflected in the aftermath of the Global Financial Crisis, that 'The belief that models are not just useful tools but are capable of yielding comprehensive and universal descriptions of the world blinded proponents to realities that had been staring them in the face. That blindness made a big contribution to our present crisis, and conditions our confused responses to it.'[7] Though fundamental forces were at work it was these decisions that were instrumental in determining which financial centres prospered, which banks emerged as the leading players, which exchanges discovered the formula that led to success, which regulations were introduced, and what markets and products thrived. Driving these decisions was not only a reaction to what had happened and what was current, but also attempts to anticipate what was to come, however misguided that turned out to be. Few prophesied, for example, that there would be a global financial crisis in 2008. As John Kenchington reflected in 2014, 'One of the most remarkable things about the 2008 financial crisis was the fact that almost nobody saw it coming.'[8] There was nothing predetermined in what took place in global financial markets from the 1970s onwards because they were the product of decisions taken for numerous reasons. To contemporaries, even the most informed, the future was hidden even if they believed otherwise, and they had to do their best with the knowledge they had available and the conclusions they drew from it. It is important to keep in mind the ancient Chinese proverb, 'We think too small, like the frog at the bottom of the well. He thinks the sky is only as big as the top of the well. If he surfaced, he would have an entirely different view.'[9] Contemporaries were no different from the frog at the bottom of the well and their actions need to be judged accordingly, especially at a time of considerable change.

What is uncontested is that world within which banks, exchanges, and regulators existed was transformed from the 1970s onwards, and contemporaries were increasingly aware of what was happening. Writing at the end of the twentieth century a number of commentators expressed their judgements on the degree of change that had taken place. One was Peter Martin who observed that:

> It has become much easier to run a global company. Falling communications costs, the existence of third-party logistics suppliers, lower trade barriers and internationally accessible financial markets—all these make it easier for any company, even a start-up, to operate on a global scale... Because there are advantages in operating at the largest possible scale, national companies appear to be rapidly losing out to those that operate around the world. More and more industries are moving... towards a situation in which there is merely a handful of global competitors, surrounded by a cluster of thousands of national or local niche players. The room left for substantial, mass-market national competitors is diminishing all the time: the choice is to seek to be global, or settle for a niche.[10]

Another was George Graham who applied his analysis of current trends to banks: 'One of the most striking effects of technological advance on banking has been to make it much easier for new entrants to break into a market, without going to the expense of building a new branch network. To confront these new entrants, and to keep pace with the efficiency

[7] John Kay, 'A realm dismal in its rituals of rigor', 26th August 2011.
[8] John Kenchington, 'Investors are being urged to stress test fixed income funds', 3rd November 2014.
[9] Often attributed to Mao Zedong.
[10] Peter Martin, 'Multinationals come into their own', 6th December 1999.

opportunities within the traditional banking industry, banks have embarked on a quest for scale.'[11] Jeffrey Brown traced the implications of these trends for financial markets, noting that 'Globalisation of equity markets looks unstoppable as trade and capital flows are increasingly liberalised and multinational companies continue to dominate the marketplace.'[12] An inescapable conclusion was that a transformation was underway and this had implications for all aspects of finance, forcing fundamental changes on the way each component operated and their relationship to one another. The certainties that had built up since the Second World War had ended in the 1970s. A world characterized by the compartmentalization along national and sectoral lines was being replaced by one involving the free movement of funds around the world, the inability of institutions to enforce market discipline, the disappearance of divisions between different types of financial businesses, and the declining power of governments to exercise direct control over financial systems.

Nevertheless, this was not a return to the pre-1914 era because government-appointed regulatory agencies and state-owned central banks had the authority to impose rules that governed the behaviour of banks and the operation of markets. At the same time new possibilities in finance had emerged because of the much greater volatility of prices, exchange rates, and interest rates and the degree of international integration made possible by the ability to communicate at speeds that came close to destroying the separation of markets. The response came in the form of global banks, international rules, and financial derivatives. The ending of fixed exchange rates created active foreign exchange markets. The ending of commodity controls and fixed-price regimes created active commodity markets. The ending of stock exchanges as regulated monopolies created active securities markets. The ending of bank cartels created active money markets. However, it was not simply the removal of controls that led to a flourishing of active markets. Human ingenuity also played a major role as can be seen in the exponential growth of derivatives. As business became organized in the form of ever-larger companies able to internalize the market so derivatives were created to provide a way of minimizing the risks that these companies were running whether it involved currency fluctuations or interest-rate volatility. In turn a market developed in these products so creating a new life for the commodity exchanges, whose role had been supplanted by the managed supply chains existing with multinational corporations. Alternatively, new exchanges were created in which these derivative products could be traded. At the same time banks turned to these products to cover the risks they were exposed to if one of their customers failed. It was not only the banks that were becoming 'too big to fail' but also the businesses that banks served, forcing them to seek ways of spreading the risks that they took which, in the past, would have come through a numerous and diverse customer base. However, the very growth in scale of banks allowed them to either internalize this market in derivatives or develop an Over-The-Counter (OTC) market in which they traded risks between each other, especially in terms of currencies and interest rates. To those who commented daily on the changes taking place, such as John Plender and Martin Wolf, the transformation of global financial markets was symbolized by the emergence and expansion of the financial derivatives market. The outstanding value of interest-rate swaps, currency swaps, and interest-rate options rose from nothing in 1970 to $3.5tn in 1990 before reaching $286tn in 2006.[13] It was the use made of these derivatives

11 George Graham, 'Cottages consolidate', 6th December 1999.
12 Jeffrey Brown, 'From slow start to relentless build-up', 1st January 2000.
13 John Plender, 'The limits of ingenuity', 17th May 2001; Martin Wolf, 'The new capitalism', 19th June 2007.

that was then held responsible for the Global Financial Crisis that followed. Writing in 2011 Patrick Jenkins, Brooke Masters, and Tom Braithwaite acknowledged that:

> With hindsight, it is clear the structure of the sector was an accident waiting to happen. Institutions had grown distorted in the pursuit of bumper profits. They held little equity capital to protect themselves—and what they did have was in many cases amplified by as much as fifty times with debt instruments. Vast profits were made from borrowing cheaply, often short-term, and assuming that the risks inherent in products from domestic mortgages to complex derivatives were negligible.[14]

Banks

In this changing world of finance banks, exchanges and regulators had to make decisions of what strategy to follow. Banking, in particular, was in a state of flux. Before the 1970s a number of distinctive types of banks operated, each seeking to maximize the profits that they could generate and minimize the risks they ran. All banks were exposed to two main types of risk. One related to liquidity and the other to solvency. As a bank made loans using borrowed money it could face a liquidity crisis caused by those from whom it had borrowed money demanding its return more quickly than its receipts from those to whom it had lent. When a bank was unable to meet withdrawals it would have to close, having lost the trust of those who had lent it money. As John Authers observed in 2018, 'Banks are fragile constructs. By design, they have more money lent out than they keep to cover deposits. A self-fulfilling loss of confidence can force a bank out of business, even if it is perfectly well run.'[15] A bank could fail due to a liquidity crisis even if it was solvent. It also faced a solvency crisis when its liabilities were greater than its assets, which could occur if those to whom it had lent money were unable or unwilling to repay. To survive a bank had to cover both liquidity and solvency risks while conducting a business that met its costs and generated profits. This meant it had to take risks in accepting money, which it promised to repay on demand, while making loans for a longer period. The income generated from doing this business came from the differential between the two rates of interest charged. One way of containing risk and generating income was to operate through an extensive branch network as this spread the business over numerous and diverse customers, provided it with the scale required to support the training and monitoring of staff, and allowed it to retain reserves necessary to meet a sudden rise in withdrawals and increase in losses. These banks collected deposits from savers and lent short-term to borrowers, adopting a policy of constantly matching liquid assets with liquid liabilities. They operated the lend-and-hold model of banking as loans were retained until maturity and, when expertly managed, these types of banks proved both stable and profitable though restricted in the range of activities they engaged in as they avoided making long-term loans despite the higher returns generated because of the liquidity risks they posed.

An alternative to branch banking was to operate as a universal bank. A universal bank provided the full range of financial services ranging from collecting deposits and providing short-term loans to making long-term investments and issuing and trading securities. These long-term investments in individual businesses did expose a universal bank to a

[14] Patrick Jenkins, Brooke Masters, and Tom Braithwaite, 'Hunt for a common front', 8th September 2011.
[15] John Authers, 'In nothing we trust', 6th October 2018.

liquidity crisis caused by the sudden withdrawal of deposits that had been used to fund assets that could not be easily liquidated or quickly repaid, especially fixed assets like property. To reduce this risk universal banks restricted long-term investment to a few carefully-monitored high quality assets, held a portfolio of securities that could be easily sold, had a large capital base, and kept extensive reserves. A universal bank used a mixture of the lend-and-hold model of banking and an originate-and-distribute one. With the originate-and-distribute model a bank made loans but then converted them into negotiable securities like bonds which were then sold to investors. In that way the bank could be repaid the money it had lent as well as freeing itself from the risk that the borrower would default. In addition to these types of banks there were numerous other variations, which specialized in particular types of the business. These ranged from banks which collected savings and invested in bonds, to the financing of property development using a mixture of retail deposits and wholesale borrowing. There were also the investment banks, which provided long-term finance to government and companies through the issue of securities. They specialized in the originate-and-distribute model of banking, using funds borrowed from other banks to finance loans, which were then repaid once the stocks and bonds had been sold to investors.[16]

These divisions between different types of banks had never been rigidly observed, unless enshrined in legislation, and began to break down from the 1970s onwards. The growing size of business enterprises forced banks to respond in terms of scale and scope if they were to provide the financial services now required. Those banks operating the lend-and-hold model were called upon to provide larger loans as a result. However, once a business reached a particular size it could move funds internally so as to provide themselves with the credit facilities that had been previously drawn from banks, which undermined the business of those following the lend-and-hold model. Conversely, large businesses often adopted the corporate form and that led them to issue stocks and bonds, which required the services of an investment bank, as that was where their expertise lay. This benefited those banks that had adopted the originate-and-distribute model. The emergence of an increasingly integrated global economy also encouraged banks to expand internationally so as to participate in the new opportunities that were emerging and meet the needs of their existing customers. As a result of these changes branch banks were forced to expand into long-term lending while universal banks responded by opening branches to engage more directly with customers as competition between them grew. Specialist banks were then caught in the middle, including savings, mortgage, and investment banks, as the territory each occupied was invaded by others. Within this increasingly competitive environment there was a switch to the originate-and-distribute model as this was increasingly favoured by regulators. The lend-and-hold model was ideal when a bank could rely on the stability of its depositor base and the limited risk attached to lending as this greatly reduced the chances of a liquidity or solvency crisis. These conditions had prevailed in the 1950s and 1960s but faded from the 1970s onwards with far greater volatility of interest and exchange rates, more uncertain business conditions, and increased competition for savings. Under these new circumstances the originate-and-distribute model was favoured as it provided a means of reducing both solvency and liquidity risks. Loans could be made, repackaged into bonds, and then either retained by the bank or sold to investors. If sold the bank was then freed from its exposure to a default while, if retained, the bonds could be sold so releasing funds to meet a liquidity crisis.

[16] Richard S. Grossman, *Unsettled Account: The Evolution of Banking in the Industrialized World since 1800* (Princeton: Princeton UP, 2010) pp. 3, 63, 72–6.

As the popularity of the originate-and-distribute model spread so the traditional but blurred divisions between different types of banks broke down. The result from the 1970s onwards was the growth of a small number of super-banks that covered the entire range of financial activity and had a presence in all major financial centres around the world. These super-banks, or global universal banks, then suffered a reversal with the Global Financial Crisis of 2008. A number had collapsed, most notably the US investment bank, Lehman Brothers, while others had to be rescued by governments before they experienced the same fate. Such was their size and connections they were considered to be too big to be allowed to fail because of the consequences that would have for the entire global financial system. In the aftermath of the crisis there were widespread calls for the break-up of the megabanks and the re-imposition of the divisions that had previously existed. As the impact of the Global Financial Crisis faded these calls became less strident, through demands to restrict the range of activities that the megabanks engaged in remained, along with requirements that they held more capital and reserves to cover liquidity and solvency risks. Despite the action taken to curb the megabanks it became increasingly apparent that the world required banks that were both global and universal, regardless of the risks they posed to the stability of financial systems. The Global Financial Crisis had left unaltered the direction of travel being taken by the global financial system. This was towards greater openness and integration, and these conditions that had favoured the emergence of super-banks. Nevertheless, that did not mean that all such banks benefited because only a few were in a position to take advantage of the conditions created by much greater regulatory intervention that followed the Global Financial Crisis.

Exchanges

With the global financial system in a state of flux from the 1970s it was not only the divisions between different types of banks that were disappearing. The distinction between banks and financial markets was also being blurred, especially as the lend-and-hold model gave way to the originate-and-distribute one. Whereas in the lend-and-hold model banks made loans which were then retained until maturity, under originate-and-distribute these were converted into bonds which were sold on to investors. For this a market was required. This was both a primary one, where initial sales were made, and a secondary one, through which existing investors could trade with each other. In the past public markets like stock exchanges would have played a role in providing the secondary market. However, super-banks that were simultaneously global and universal were able to internalize many financial transactions that had previously passed through the market. This included not only issuing stocks, bonds, and related securities but also providing a market where they either matched buyers and sellers from among their own customers or used their own resources to act as counterparties. Super-banks maintained huge holdings of negotiable securities from which they could meet demand as well as controlling vast funds that could be used to make purchases. This allowed them to bypass stock exchanges. The markets for money and currencies had long been inter-bank affairs and that for bonds had gone the same way. A similar process was happening to corporate stocks and that was the route followed by the financial products that were generated by the increasing use of the originate-and-distribute model. All manner of loans ranging from mortgages to credit payments were converted into negotiable instruments, or securitized, and then sold to investors by banks, which then took responsibility for providing the secondary market. This also meant that stock exchanges were increasingly bypassed. Commodity exchanges were also experiencing a similar fate as businesses internalized supply chains through horizontal and vertical integration both within countries and internationally. This left exchanges with residual roles as places where reference prices were set rather than supply and demand matched. Even the regulatory function of exchanges was increasingly undertaken by government-appointed agencies.

Not all financial instruments required the existence of an exchange to give them value and provide liquidity. Exchanges were designed to provide a market for standardized financial products traded through intermediaries on behalf of numerous buyers and sellers. What exchanges also provided was a means of coping with counterparty risk through a set of rules and regulations that governed who was allowed to participate, the standards they had to meet and the penalties for non-compliance. An exchange involved expenses and so the volume of trading had to be sufficiently large to justify those as well as providing the intermediaries involved with an income. Many financial products were not of this kind being issued in limited quantities or little traded, and this included a large number of bonds, derivative contracts, and the stock of smaller companies. Conversely, there were other financial products that were of a standardized nature and traded in high volumes that were also unsuited to exchanges. Numbered among these was money in all its forms, ranging for currency to short-term bills, as this was traded either directly between banks or through specialist intermediaries without the expenses involved in using an exchange. Those involved also constituted a closed group who were each responsible for the deals that they made and so had no need for the regulations imposed by an exchange. For those reasons only a subset of financial markets were provided by exchanges as they neither catered for customized products such as swaps nor the high-velocity trading in foreign exchange that was largely an inter-bank affair. These OTC markets were the ones that flourished most from the 1970s onwards despite the revival of exchanges. Stock exchanges benefited from the growing investor interest in corporate stocks and the mass privatization of state assets while those commodity exchanges that embraced financial derivatives experienced a boom. Nevertheless, more and more trading was of the OTC variety.

The growth of megabanks facilitated both the internalization of market activity and direct trading between them. A large bank was able to match sales and purchases between its own customers as well as being of a size that made it a reliable counterparty. The growth of a new species of intermediary, the interdealer broker, epitomized this change, as they provided banks with a network of connections that was previously only obtainable through an exchange. This trend towards trading gravitating to OTC markets was greatly facilitated by the increasingly important role played by statutory agencies, as they supplanted the self-regulatory authority that was once the exclusive privilege of an exchange. The desire to bypass exchanges had also been intensified by the way exchanges had used their regulatory powers to restrict access to the market they provided and so increase the charges levied on users. The authority vested in exchanges by governments had allowed them to monopolize trading in certain products, to the advantage of their members and the disadvantage of users. What happened from the 1970s onwards was that self-regulation was increasingly deemed inadequate to protect users of financial services and so increased power was given to statutory agencies, with a remit to promote competition while also maintaining stability. Such a trend played into the hands of the biggest banks, as they possessed robust regulatory mechanisms of their own and were already subject to external supervision. The result was a growth of OTC markets in which trading was conducted by these large banks either directly with each other or through the intermediation of interdealer brokers, and not through the exchanges.

During and after the 1970s the ability to create alternative market structures was also transformed through a technological revolution. The combination of near-instantaneous communication networks and the processing power of ever-faster computers with almost infinite capacity eventually produced a serious rival to the trading floor that had been at the centre of every exchange. These trading floors not only provided members of exchanges with the means of conducting sales and purchases but also gave exchanges the power to enforce rules and regulations. Those who refused to comply with the rules of an exchange were denied entry while those who broke them were expelled. With the dematerialization of trading and the rise of megabanks the exchanges lost control over the financial markets they had once almost monopolized. As this took place against a background in which government-imposed barriers that compartmentalized markets both internally and internationally were removed, the result was the emergence of global OTC markets, successfully challenging exchanges for business. The products of securitization, for example, were all traded on OTC markets and not exchanges as were most of the new derivative contracts. The Global Financial Crisis did raise the prospect that exchanges would, once again, return to a central position in the provision of financial markets. During the crisis it was a number of OTC markets that had caused difficulties by ceasing to operate, making it impossible to buy and sell the financial products traded there, or even obtain a price for valuation and collateral purposes. This had severe implications for those dependent upon the liquidity of the assets they held, such as the banks. In contrast, exchange-traded financial products continued to possess a market, which encouraged many to press for all financial markets to be placed under the control of exchanges. Quite quickly this course of action was exposed as impractical as it was recognized that exchanges could not provide the markets now required, whether it was little-traded swaps or much-traded currencies. A number of the most important OTC markets had operated without problems during the crisis, and those who participated in them resisted any attempt to force trading through exchanges. In a world where financial markets remained dominated by the buying and selling activity of global banks, international fund managers, and multinational corporations, the role played by exchanges remained confined to niche activities, such as corporate stocks and the pricing of key benchmark contracts.

Under these circumstances prevailing from the 1970s onwards those running exchanges had difficult decisions to make if they were to survive. One course was to pursue a national strategy that involved horizontal mergers, combining stock and commodity exchanges into a single multi-product institution. This institution would be in a position to monopolize what business there was, while spreading the costs involved over a large organization, especially those that necessitated a massive investment in the new trading technology that was becoming available. Another strategy derived from the use of electronic technology was to adopt the vertical-silo model, which combined trading with processing. Trading was moving from a reliance on face-to-face contact through the use of the telephone linking buyers and sellers to electronic platforms that matched orders automatically. At the same time computer-based systems handled clearing, delivery, and payment creating the possibility that the entire transaction, from placing of an order to final completion, could be handled as a single integrated operation. A final strategy was transnational mergers between exchanges that produced a single institution capable of providing a global market in whatever products they specialized in. Which of these strategies was the one most likely to succeed always remained open to doubt. It was never a foregone conclusion, for example, that the use of open outcry and voice broking were doomed to be replaced by electronic platforms. The vertical model was disliked by both banks and regulators because of the power it gave to exchanges to impose their charges on users. There was considerable opposition to horizontal mergers from those that wanted to remain independent. This made achieving any of these strategies hazardous because of the barriers to be overcome and the risks to be taken, though hindsight revealed the eventual winners and losers among exchanges that was not obvious at the time.

Regulators

Prior to the 1970s the way that regulation was conducted was to treat the financial system as a series of separate compartments. This worked when governments were able to exercise a significant degree of control through erecting barriers between national economies. With the removal of those barriers regulatory intervention on a national basis was at the mercy of being subverted externally through the movement of activity to a rival financial centre. The effect was to greatly reduce the power of national central banks and national regulatory agencies to dictate terms within their own financial systems. A similar process was taking place domestically as the divisions between banks and markets broke down. Conventional wisdom separated banks from financial markets or went even further in focusing on particular types of banks or on specific financial markets, ignoring the links that existed between them and the degree of overlap. However, as national barriers disappeared with the ending of exchange and capital controls, and governments themselves fostered competition in order to appease complaints from investors and savers over low returns and borrowers because of a shortage of finance, it was no longer possible to regulate through the principle of divide and rule. These changes taking place in the global financial system created difficult choices for regulators. In the era of compartmentalized financial activity and national barriers regulators had been able to rely on the policy of divide and rule as a means of exercising control. Increasingly that was not available from the 1970s onwards, forcing regulators to search for alternative means of exercising their influence. The need to do so remained as governments continued to expect that financial systems would continue to be monitored and supervised to a high degree, especially the protection of savers and investors from fraud and even loss. Tasked with implementing monetary policy on behalf of governments central banks also looked for ways of policing the behaviour of banks and financial markets. One option was to establish a single authority covering the entire financial system, and so capture the convergence of financial activity that was taking place. Another was to retain specialist agencies to meet the specific requirements of different types of markets, businesses and institutions because of the continuing diversity present in the system. In no case and at no time was it obvious which of these choices would produce the best result but decisions had to be taken on one or the other. The Global Financial Crisis of 2008 then altered the relationship between banks, exchanges, and regulators, forcing all to address a new set of choices. Underlying these choices, whether before or after the crisis, was the ever-present regulator's dilemma. If regulatory intervention was too intrusive and too draconian then financial activity was either suppressed or driven into channels that were beyond their remit. Neither of these outcomes was desirable as they undermined the ability of the financial system to deliver the services required of it in a safe and secure way. Conversely, if regulatory intervention was either non-existent or lax then users were left vulnerable to exploitation and the entire system rendered unstable. That was an equally undesirable outcome. Whatever decisions were taken they developed a momentum of their own which then influenced future regulatory intervention.

What did develop from the 1970s onwards was by government-appointed regulatory agencies placing increasing reliance upon large banks to act as their agents in supervising the financial system. With exchanges under suspicion because of the restrictive practices and all manner of OTC markets appearing, regulators found it easiest to operate through the largest banks. These banks were already subject to close supervision, not least by central banks, because of the risks they posed to national financial systems. This supervision also took place internationally through the co-ordinating role played by the Bank for International Settlements, as this acted on behalf of the world's central banks. Central banks acted as lenders of last resort to their national banks, ready to intervene if a liquidity crisis threatened. It was these banks that increasingly dominated financial markets, especially the inter-bank ones where money and foreign exchange were traded, while their control over those for bonds, stocks, and derivatives was also growing rapidly. These large banks already possessed internal controls because of their size and structure and the liquidity and solvency risks they were exposed to. For regulators the use made of banks posed a dilemma. The regulators wanted banks to take responsibility for market regulation but that was best achieved by large banks as they had the scale and resources to train and pay for the appropriate staff. These large banks were also considered too big to fail, and had reputations to preserve, and so were in the position of trusted counterparties, guaranteeing that every deal would be completed. Increasingly it was the large banks that became the trusted gatekeepers of the financial system under the overall supervision of statutory regulatory authorities. Neither central banks nor regulatory agencies had the means or expertise to monitor behaviour within the entire banking system or the transactions taking place in active financial markets. They had no alternative but to devolve responsibility to others and their chosen instruments from the 1970s onwards were the megabanks. As these banks extended their operations around the world and into different financial activities they became the ideal partners for central banks searching for ways of ensuring stability in an integrated global financial system and regulators tasked with supervising highly-complex and inter-connected national financial systems. The dilemma came because central banks and regulators also wanted the financial system to become more competitive as this would better meet the needs of users, whether they wanted to save and invest, borrow, or make and receive payments. This was tackled in terms of exchanges by removing the monopoly power they possessed which helped account for the proliferation of OTC trading and the fragmentation of the stock market, which exchanges had once dominated. The solution in banking was to stimulate rivalry between banks, including megabanks, and remove the barriers between different types of financial activity so as to encourage greater competition.

There had always been an uneasy relationship between regulated markets provided by exchanges and those that operated on an OTC basis, ranging from the internal matching of deals within banks and fund managers to the more public trading of bonds. What changed after the 1970s was the balance as off-exchange activity became the new normality even in those markets, such as those for stocks and derivatives, which had previously relied on exchanges and the rules and regulations under which trading took place. These rules governed such issues as counterparty risk and market mechanisms to ensure that sales, purchase, and payments were honoured, prices were free from manipulation, and liquidity was maintained. It was not until the Global Financial Crisis that the consequences of this shift were realized. Confident in the resilience of large banks, as exhibited during successive crises, governments and regulators forgot the central importance of leverage and liquidity as the twin keys to understanding how a bank operated. Increasingly banks were no longer regarded as special components of the financial system deserving of individual treatment.

Of even greater concern was the fact that bankers themselves also forgot that. Prior to the Global Financial Crisis of 2007–9 there was a belief that banking was becoming more resilient as a result of benign supervision, the application of sophisticated mathematical computer models, and the scale, spread, and diversity that came with size. However, by favouring large banks in the belief that they brought stability to the financial system, regulators affected the balance between the bank and its customers and this had consequences for financial markets. Rather than markets comprising numerous brokers trading between each other on behalf of numerous customers, trading became dominated by banks acting as both market-makers and intermediaries, trading for others and themselves. As these banks were closely supervised this was believed to eliminate the necessity for exchanges to regulate the market, especially as this had given them the power to further the self-interest of their members. There was a perennial problem in regulation, which was to balance the need to intervene to prevent abuses and allowing the system to adapt and evolve to meet changing needs over time. Prior to the Global Financial Crisis that balance had been lost.

The pre-crisis belief in the infallibility of the models, and the resilience of banks that were too big to fail, was shared by politicians, central bankers, and regulators. Such a belief left each free to pursue their own agendas. Politicians were convinced that they had discovered a magic formula in terms of monetary policy that would provide the financial system with the stability previously associated with an interventionist regime of control and compartmentalization. In this new world the excesses of the market had been tamed while its benefits were harnessed for the greater good of mankind, included the use of expanded tax receipts which democratically elected governments could collect, spend, and gain popularity as a consequence.[17] A belief in the self-correcting powers of the financial system also meant that central banks could drop any responsibility for direct intervention, as long as they created a stable financial environment for them to operate in. Individual bank failures would then be the result of mismanagement leading to insolvency. As illiquidity was not the cause of failure central banks were not required to provide support as doing so would only encourage a climate of risk-taking by removing the penalties attached to losses. This was the issue of Moral Hazard that central bankers fell back on when providing a reason for non-intervention prior to the crisis. A belief that the imposition of the Bank for International Settlement's Basel rules made banking safe meant that regulators could devolve responsibility for policing the financial system to the global banks, with their extensive in-house monitoring, supervision, and enforcement systems.

After the crisis there was a general recognition of the liquidity issues faced by banks, regardless of size. It was appreciated that banks were different from other financial institutions because of the contagious effects of a collapse of trust. Even the failure of one bank, if it was sufficiently large and inter-connected, could destabilize an entire financial system. In response central banks from all the leading economies agreed to co-operate in making the financial system safer through greater regulation. This still left the megabanks playing a key role as they had the ability to spread the costs of regulation and supervision across large income streams and asset bases. In turn, these banks gained a competitive advantage over their smaller rivals as the unit cost of providing internal systems for monitoring risks and policing behaviour was lower. Nevertheless, one effect of this regulatory intervention was to displace financial activity from the highly-regulated and systemically-important banks into the hands of other financial institutions that increasingly resembled banks, including

[17] John Plender, 'Originative sin', 5th January 2009; John Plender, 'Re-spinning the web', 22nd June 2009.

their exposure to liquidity crises. The greater the controls they placed on banks the more the financial activity they had undertaken was placed in the hands of those banks that were subject to little or no regulation. As Larry Tabb warned in 2011, 'Not all regulation is bad. However regulators need to weigh the risks of new rules against the costs and unintended consequences of change.... while regulation may provide a veil of protection, we must be careful that new rules don't create a market worse than where we started.'[18] Interventions by regulators to solve one problem had the potential to create a different problem that then posed more of the threat than the original because it took place in a less-regulated part of the financial system.

The problem was the difficulty in identifying with any accuracy the consequences of intervention in a financial system that was continuously evolving. What regulators gradually became aware of after the Global Financial Crisis was the risks to the stability of the financial system they were attempting to control by restricting bank lending, and especially high levels of leverage, had shifted to the shadow banking system. The reaction from regulators was not to reduce the restrictions placed on banks, so that they could resume lending to the customers they knew and understood best and in ways that they were long familiar with in terms of risks and rewards. Instead, regulators sought to extend their restrictions to those elements of the shadow banking system they could easily identify and police. However, as long as the demand from business for finance was there sources of supply would find mechanisms through which flows from the latter to the former could take place. The choice facing regulators was how to regulate the banking system in such a way and to such a degree that it could continue to meet the demands of borrowers, and so remove the need for alternative providers who escaped regulation entirely as these posed a far greater risk to financial stability because their activities took place away from the public gaze. Regulators had already achieved the same result in other financial markets with the regulations imposed on the stock market driving business away from regulated exchanges to dark pools. The implication of the above was that in trying to tackle one perceived abuse in the market, regulators destabilized markets whether to protect investors, as in the case of equities, or reduce risks, as in the case of derivatives. Markets are complex and evolving so that a change in one component has unforeseen consequences as users seek to adapt to the new conditions in order to capture the benefits they had previously enjoyed. The response by regulators to problems caused by regulation tended to be the extension and deepening of the regulatory boundaries and not a re-examination of the consequences of past regulation and an acceptance that the approach and shape needed to be addressed.

Conclusion

After the 1970s a new global financial system was put in place to replace the one that had failed. To all appearances this system seemed to combine resilience with dynamism as a number of crises were surmounted without causing a major banking or stock market collapse. These included sovereign debt defaults, bank collapses, and the bursting of a speculative bubble. These did not create systemic crises and caused only a brief interruption to the rapid pace of global economic growth. Trust was placed in megabanks to deliver and then maintain this new world. Unbeknown to most regulators were the risk-taking culture they

[18] Larry Tabb, 'Playing ostrich over high-speed trading is not an option', 14th July 2011.

were giving rise to as this extended far beyond the new financial products such as derivatives and securitized assets, new financial businesses like hedge funds and high-frequency traders, and new financial markets like electronic communication networks and dark pools. However, there was a fatal flaw in these pre-crisis beliefs and that was that the likelihood of serious and damaging liquidity crises had been ignored when calculating risks inherent in the financial systems of developed economies. It was only with the crisis that the vulnerability of global banks to a collapse of confidence was revealed, and the devastating consequences that could have. Reviewing the pre-crisis years Stephen Foley concluded in 2013 that 'One of the biggest shortcomings of traditional economic modelling was how little attention it paid to banks. Money was just assumed to find its way from those with capital to spare, to the businesses or households looking to borrow.'[19] Nowhere in these calculations was provision made for the need to ensure adequate liquidity if markets froze, and banks simply stopped lending to each other, because such an event was considered so unlikely to occur. The sophisticated models used by banks to direct the loans and investments they made ignored the possibility of extreme volatility in market prices, the swift evaporation of trading liquidity, and the role played by individual greed and self-interest in the decisions made.[20] Writing in 2014 Patrick Jenkins judged that 'Many constituencies must bear responsibility for allowing the system to get out of control—incompetent managers, lax regulators and conniving politicians among them.'[21]

The years since the 1970s had witnessed a revolution in global finance that was greater than any that took place in an equivalent period, in terms of pace, scale, and impact. That revolution in finance culminated in a Global Financial Crisis that took place between 2007 and 2009, the consequences of which were still felt some ten years later. That crisis was generated from within the global financial system because it cannot be attributed to outside forces unlike the Wall Street Crash, with which it has been compared. The Wall Street Crash was very much unfinished business stemming from the economic, financial, and monetary consequences of the First World War, which had not been resolved during the 1920s. In contrast, the Global Financial Crisis was preceded by thirty years of peace and prosperity. That being the case it is important to understand why such a transformation of global finance took place and what shaped it. To that end it is necessary to choose a focus so as to aid analysis and combine that with a deep knowledge of all that happened. A choice of the three elements of banks, exchanges, and regulation provides that focus as each was a key variable in the process of change, and contributed significantly to the crisis that eventually took place. Through an understanding of the changes that took place to banks, exchanges, and regulation, and how the relationship between all three was fundamentally altered from the 1970s onwards, an insight can be gained into why a crisis of such magnitude took place. To achieve that understanding it is essential to know what did not happen as well as what did. If the study of the past is confined to the outcomes that exist at the time such research is conducted the result is a belief in inevitability, which is of limited value in planning for the future. That future becomes no more than an extension of current trends, shorn of any understanding of what had determined that particular outcome and what alternatives would have existed if different choices had been made. Under those circumstances it becomes impossible to plan for the unexpected because all is already known. In financial markets this leads to the belief that either prices will always rise or always fall even

[19] Stephen Foley, 'How to stay on top of the wave', 19th October 2013.
[20] Patrick Jenkins, 'Humbled financiers reassess their culture', 17th March 2014.
[21] Patrick Jenkins, 'It's right for shareholders to share the pain', 13th November 2014.

though past experience proves that not to be true. It also leads to the belief that banks do not fail because only the survivors remain and those that have disappeared are forgotten. It also generates a view among regulators that only solvency is important and not liquidity because all counterparties can be relied upon to act rationally as they possess a full knowledge of the situation. A failure to investigate both what did not happen and that which did, but led nowhere, is essential if an explanation is to be found for why the Global Financial Crisis occurred in 2007–9.

2

Trends, Events, and Centres, 1970–92

Introduction

It is always difficult to disentangle the effects of trends from that of events when making judgements about the causes of long-term development. Evidence drawn from contemporary observers magnifies the significance of events, as they had no means of judging long-term consequences. Reliance on later commentators minimizes the importance of an event as they connect what preceded it with what followed, leading to a conclusion of inevitability, while dismissing the importance of the changes it produced. Beginning before the 1970s fundamental forces were already driving change in global financial markets, as governments struggled to maintain the controls and compartmentalization introduced after the Second World War. What had existed in the 1950s and 1960s was very much the product of the events that had preceded them, especially the international financial crisis of 1929–32, the world economic depression of the 1930s, and the global military conflict that had raged between 1939 and 1945. However, what took place in the 1970s and 1980s was not simply a product of long-term trends reasserting themselves. They were also conditioned by what had been in place and a reaction to the events that had brought about the collapse of the era of control and compartmentalization. Throughout the 1970s and 1980s governments, central banks, and regulators were being forced to search for new ways to exert influence and recognize the limitations of their power. The result was a mixture of intervention, driven by the need to react to crises, and deregulation as barriers to competition were removed because of the inefficiencies and abuses they created. As Nigel Lawson, one of the architects of financial reform in Britain in the 1980s, explained in 1992, 'Financial deregulation in no way implies the absence of financial regulation for prudential purposes.'[1] Under these circumstances both trends and events influenced the outcomes reached as the role played by government, either directly or through central banks and regulatory agencies, continued to exert a major influence, especially in responding to events and setting the agenda. There was to be no return to the financial world that had existed before the First World War while that in place in the 1930s was to be avoided at all costs, because of what it had contained and led to.[2]

Events

The years between 1970 and 1992 included a number of major financial crises. The early 1970s witnessed the collapse of the fixed exchange rate policy pursued since the end of the Second World War and the emergence of far greater volatility for prices and currencies.

[1] Nigel Lawson, 'Side effects of deregulation', 27th January 1992.

[2] Alexander Nicoll, 'A banker rather than a regulator', 20th January 1987; John Plender, 'The limits of ingenuity', 17th May 2001.

Banks, Exchanges, and Regulators: Global Financial Markets from the 1970s. Ranald Michie, Oxford University Press (2021).

DOI: 10.1093/oso/9780199553730.003.0002

There were also banking crises that threatened the stability of not only national financial systems but also exposed the risks posed through the web of inter-bank lending and borrowing. This was of sufficient concern to governments that in 1974 the Bank for International Settlement (BIS) set up a committee on Banking Regulation and Supervisory Practices, with responsibility for drawing up rules and making recommendations about the way banks should operate. In 1975 agreement was reached on how bank supervisors should divide responsibility for banks whose activities crossed national boundaries. One particular issue was to ensure that banks maintained sufficient reserves to cover their exposure to a liquidity crisis. Banks had been making loans on the basis of property, and when prices collapsed and borrowers defaulted they were left with assets they could not sell. As depositors became aware of the situation they withdrew their savings leaving even solvent banks facing a liquidity crisis. This forced central banks to act as lenders of last resort but this raised the issue of moral hazard, as the support provided rescued those banks that had been taking excessive risks as well as the more conservative ones. While anxious to avoid a systemic bank failure central banks did not want to encourage risk-taking and so looked for ways of forcing banks to make their own provision against not only the possible default of borrowers but also a liquidity crisis. The solution was the introduction of rules on the amount of capital and reserves systemically-important banks should hold.

Further intervention along these lines followed after the international debt crisis of 1982, as that also exposed the vulnerability of banks to a liquidity crisis, when Latin American governments defaulted on their loans. Increasingly the solution to bank exposure to a liquidity crisis was to recommend the adoption of the originate-and-distribute model rather than the lend-and-hold one. In this way banks would hold assets that could be sold if required, as they would be in the form of bonds not loans. Loans were non-transferable, or only with difficulty and delay, whereas bonds could be sold, even at a loss, so releasing funds which could be used to meet withdrawals and redemptions. At the same time banks themselves made much greater use of inter-bank markets to either employ funds that were surplus to immediate needs or to supplement a shortage of cash required to meet outflows. Through the use of the inter-bank money market, banks could also operate on the basis of much lower capital and reserves as they could top up supplies by borrowing from those banks with a surplus, as long as confidence was maintained that loans would be repaid. By 1984 Peter Montagnon reported that this inter-bank market,

> which is so central to the operation of the international banking system... has thrived and prospered on a very informal and unregulated basis. Hundreds of millions of dollars change hands by the minute on the basis of simple telephone calls between dealers. It only works because each participating bank has an inherent trust in other banks' ability and willingness to repay—and that trust has been sorely tested by the debt crisis.[3]

In the mid-1980s the next crisis that rocked the global financial system was the global stock market crash of 1987. Prior to that crash there had been a growing confidence that the recommendations from the BIS and the development of markets had made the financial system more efficient and liquid and so contributed to greater resilience. As well as banks holding more capital and reserves, the inter-bank money market allowed banks to lend and borrow among each other while the growth of active stock and bond markets contributed a

[3] Peter Montagnon, 'International powerhouse', 21st May 1984.

much greater degree of liquidity to financial assets. Finally, the development of financial derivatives from the early 1970s onwards provided banks with an additional means of covering the risks they were exposed to through the greater volatility of interest and exchange rates. However, what the stock market crash of 1987 revealed was how integrated financial markets could spread as well dissipate exposure, once sellers tried to unload assets once prices began to collapse. With financial data supplied on an almost instantaneous basis to 300,000 terminals located in over one hundred different countries around the world there were now no borders to impede the spread of panic. The lesson learnt at the time was that markets alone were not sufficient to remove the risk of a liquidity crisis as some securities could become unmarketable when a wave of selling overwhelmed some markets. The response was further interventions. The response in 1988 was for the BIS to set common standards for capital adequacy that were then followed by central banks around the world. Through a combination of central bank intervention at the national and international level, and the development of financial markets, solutions were devised during the 1970s and 1980s to the new problems that were emerging as the world moved on from the era of control and compartmentalization that had been in place during the 1950s and 1960s. This was not a planned return to an earlier era but a series of responses to an evolving situation and to meet the more immediate issues exposed by successive crises.[4]

Other changes that took place in the 1970s and 1980s were of a similar kind, and a number had significant consequences. One was the removal of fixed commissions by the New York Stock Exchange in 1975, as required by the Securities and Exchange Commission. This was called May Day at the time, because it was seen to overthrow the established order. Doubt was later cast on the significance of what had taken place. Some ten years after the event no less a person than William Schreyer, chairman and chief executive of one of the leading US investment banks, Merrill Lynch, downplayed its importance: 'In New York, on Mayday 1975, all we did was deregulate fixed commissions, and the rest of it has been evolutionary, a piecemeal crumbling of the Glass–Steagall Act that's taken ten years.'[5] It was the Glass–Steagall Act of 1934 that had forced through an artificial separation of investment and commercial banks in the USA, which was slowly undone from the 1970s onwards. Contributing to the unravelling of the division between investment and commercial banking in the USA was the removal of the requirement placed on all members of the New York Stock Exchange to charge the same fees, regardless of the efficiency of their business model or the volume of trading generated by individual clients. With the removal of that constraint investment banks like Merrill Lynch could aggressively compete for business, undercutting rivals and so able to grow their business. Such banks were ideally placed to capitalize on the growing popularity of the originate-and-distribute model, as increasingly recommended by regulators, as they already had the expertise and connections to not only issue stocks and bonds but also provide a secondary market. What May Day unleashed was the power of the US investment banks, undermining the divide imposed by the Glass–Steagall Act and forcing other US banks to respond by also adopting the originate-and-distribute model.

The impact of May Day was not confined to the USA as it led to the London Stock Exchange abandoning its regime of fixed charges in 1986. US investment banks aggressively

[4] David Lascelles, 'A New York–Tokyo–London axis', 7th April 1986; Richard Lambert, 'The new toys were fallible', 14th October 1988; Barry Riley, 'Home looked safest', 14th October 1988; Clive Wolman, 'London's weakness', 14th October 1988; Stephen Fidler, 'A franchise under stress', 2nd July 1990; David Lascelles, 'Reforms fail to keep pace with changes in the markets', 24th May 1991; Richard Waters, 'Progress seen in world settlement systems says G30', 17th December 1992; George Graham, 'BIS weighs expanded role', 9th June 1997.

[5] Barry Riley, 'London's the third leg of our stool', 27th October 1986.

competed for business from UK institutional investors, especially after the UK abandoned exchange controls in 1979. That led to increasing calls for the London Stock Exchange to end its policy of fixed charges, as that was making it uncompetitive as a market for the stocks of leading UK companies, especially those that were extensively held by foreign investors. Those calls were taken up by the UK government, keen to maintain the international competitiveness of the City of London as a financial centre. The result was a series of reforms in London's financial markets in 1986, labelled, at the time, 'Big Bang' or the 'City Revolution', because of the belief by contemporaries that they were of major importance. In turn, these reforms set off, according to David Lascelles in 1989, 'a seemingly unstoppable chain reaction of smaller bangs'.[6] The reforms introduced in the UK exposed stock markets across Europe to competition from London, including the US investment banks that were based there. Though the introduction of a single European market in financial services was not to take place until 1 January 1993 it was preceded by a series of European Council directives designed to achieve that objective. By imposing a common set of rules and regulations and removing barriers such as exchange controls, banks and financial markets were being forced to compete for business on an equal basis throughout the European Union. This was a boon to the universal banking model as it removed the restrictions placed on banks engaging directly with financial markets like stock exchanges. Added to the competitive pressures coming from New York since 1975 and then Big Bang in London in 1986 these changes across the EU, combined with the ending of exchange and other controls, forced stock exchanges around the world to abandon the fixed charges and restrictive practices that had long allowed them to monopolize domestic stock markets. The cumulative effect was a rolling revolution that removed the barriers that had prevented banks from dominating the stock market and so emulating the position they had already achieved across money, currencies, and bonds. This was to the great advantage of the emerging megabanks whose activities spanned the entire spectrum of financial activities and took place on a global basis. Though such an outcome might have been achieved without events such as May Day in the USA, Big Bang in London, and the moves towards a single market in the EU, each was an important stepping stone in achieving that objective though few of those involved recognized the consequences of what they were doing. When judged as part of a cumulative process, events possessed sufficient power to accelerate change and force a change but only when acting in harmony with the underlying trends, as was the case in the 1970s and 1980s.[7]

Trends

Powerful trends were at work in the 1970s and 1980s and these were visible to contemporaries, especially the combination of a technological revolution, global financial integration, and a transformation in the role played by government. Reflecting on what had taken place in the 1980s Stephen Fidler picked on the latter in 1990: 'At the beginning of the decade the world could be split into a handful of separate capital markets with little overlap among

[6] David Lascelles, 'The barriers are falling', 2nd May 1989.

[7] Barry Riley, 'The City Revolution', 27th October 1986; Barry Riley, 'London's the third leg of our stool', 27th October 1986; David Lascelles, 'A magnet for foreign banks', 27th October 1986; John Kay, 'Big Bang shows the power of competition to surprise', 24th October 2006; Nigel Lawson, 'We must not take London's success for granted', 23rd October 2006; Peter Thal Larsen, 'Hats off: Big Bang still brings scale and innovation to finance in London', 26th October 2006.

them.... But when government after government began to lift controls on the transfer of capital, the barriers between capital markets were removed and every financial intermediary, wherever based, became a potential competitor to every other.'[8] During the 1970s and 1980s the breakdown of centrally-imposed authority and the removal of barriers to the free movement of funds transformed the world within which banks and financial markets operated. In some cases the result was to disperse trading around the world, as with stocks and bonds, because of the strong gravitational pull of domestic markets due to their greatest depth of liquidity in individual securities. Sara Webb observed in 1991 that 'as the tentacles of deregulation have spread around the globe, international investors have found it easier to invest in a growing number of government bond markets'.[9] Conversely, trading in money and currencies tended to concentrate in a few locations around the world as only they could provide the depth of liquidity and the breadth of connections required by the banks that dominated this type of business. Those banks possessing international networks and established expertise, ranging across credit, currencies, stocks, bonds, and derivatives, were major beneficiaries of these trends in technology, integration, and deregulation. As Guy de Jonquières noted in 1988, 'After decades of operating along well-established lines, defined by the borders of their national markets and by traditional products and customer bases, commercial banks in almost every country are being forced to confront a confusing array of fresh challenges.'[10] Driven by fiercer competition, shifting patterns of demand, evolving government policies, and technological change the dividing lines both within banking, and between it and financial markets were becoming blurred, forcing each to restructure their operations if they were to survive.[11]

One example of the fundamental trends driving change was the rapid rise in international connectivity through advances in technology. Fibre-optics revolutionized telecommunications, providing cheaper and faster connections as well as increased capacity, while the removal of national monopolies brought these benefits to all users. In 1956 the cost of a transatlantic call was $2.53 per minute but this fell to $0.04 in 1988. At the same time capacity grew over 400-fold. Writing in 1991 Hugo Dixon and Greg Staple considered that, 'The one billion telephones linked together by networks of cables and satellites constitute the nervous system of the global market.'[12] Combined with this revolution in the speed, capacity, cheapness, and availability of global communications was a similar one taking place in the processing and transmission of financial information. In 1973 the Society for Worldwide Interbank Financial Telecommunications (Swift) was set up as an inter-bank co-operative, and in 1977 it introduced a messaging service that provided banks with a standardized, reliable, and secure way of quickly transferring money around the world. Robert Corzine visited its processing centres in 1991 and came away impressed: 'The only sound associated with the electronic transfer of several trillion dollars a day around the world is the background hum of high-speed computers at heavily-guarded centres in the Netherlands and the US run by Swift.'[13] By then Swift was processing

[8] Stephen Fidler, 'When family loyalties are placed under severe strain', 28th December 1990.

[9] Sara Webb, 'International investors find a silver lining', 22nd July 1991.

[10] Guy de Jonquières, 'Risk, opportunities and arduous negotiations', 18th May 1988.

[11] David Lascelles, 'The barriers are falling', 2nd May 1989; Stephen Fidler, 'When family loyalties are placed under severe strain', 28th December 1990; Simon London, 'Cedel's rise in turnover confirms trend', 5th February 1991; Richard Waters, 'Level playing field may not be open to all-comers', 14th February 1991; Leyla Boulton, 'Soviet oil and gas exchange opens this month', 11th June 1991; Norma Cohen, 'Clients move from global to local services', 24th September 1991; Lynne Curry, 'Heavy demand for shares', 16th June 1992.

[12] Hugo Dixon and Greg Staple, 'New perspective on patterns of power', 7th October 1991.

[13] Robert Corzine, 'Executives attempt to stretch Swift's wings', 4th December 1991.

1.5m messages daily between 1,885 banks in seventy-three countries, underpinning virtually every international trade deal, the cross-border trading in securities, and transactions in the foreign exchange market.

These advances in telecommunications and processing had major implications for banks and financial markets. In 1992 Barry Riley captured the pace and nature of the changes, when he noted that, 'Technology, in a tantalising way, is beckoning the investment management industry. A few high-powered personal computers or work stations with the right software and the right interfaces may be all that is needed to wrest control of important aspects of the trading and settlement process from the exchanges, the brokers and the custodian banks.'[14] Advances in technology were making it easier to develop alternative ways of connecting savers and borrowers, buyers and sellers, that challenged established banks and financial markets. For example the provider of global news, Reuters, was behind developments that were transforming the way both foreign exchange and derivatives were traded. In 1992 Reuters launched a system called Dealing 2000 for the foreign exchange market leading Dixon and Staple to suggest that 'the telecommunications network has become the market itself'.[15] The same year Globex was launched, and Reuters was also behind this initiative, along with Leo Melamed and the Chicago Mercantile Exchange which he led. Globex aimed to provide a global 24-hour screen-based electronic dealing system for futures contracts, connecting 250,000 users worldwide.[16]

Another long-term trend was the growing scale of business and its increasingly global nature. As companies became larger and more international they required different services from banks and financial markets, and even possessed the ability to bypass them entirely through the internal movement of funds. However, they were also exposed to greater risks and so looked to banks and financial markets to cover these, especially in the more volatile conditions that prevailed from 1970 onwards. The internationalization of business, for example, substantially increased the level of foreign exchange risk to which banks and companies were exposed. In response financial products were introduced designed to reduce the risks associated with currency fluctuations. Other products covered the risks related to the volatility of stock and bond prices as well as interest rates. Banks were constantly searching for ways to eliminate the risks they ran through their mismatch of assets and liabilities across time, space, currency, and interest rates, and their exposure to the default of major borrowers, and these grew during the more volatile conditions that prevailed in the 1970s and 1980s. The result was a proliferation of derivative products that built on the inter-bank arrangements that banks had long used, but had been somewhat neglected in the more stable conditions that had existed in the 1950s and 1960s.[17]

It was this combination of the growing scale of business, the process of globalization, and the increased volatility that produced the underlying conditions that drove innovation in financial markets. The same conditions also forced banks to become bigger, diversified, and

[14] Barry Riley, 'Move to join Swift is slow', 9th December 1992.

[15] Hugo Dixon and Greg Staple, 'New perspective on patterns of power', 7th October 1991.

[16] Hugo Dixon, 'Reconnecting charges with costs', 3rd April 1990; Hugo Dixon, 'The phone redraws map of the world', 8th June 1990; Joyce Quek, 'A revolution in the wings', 30th April 1991; Kenneth Gooding, 'Financial engineering tames the gold market', 26th July 1991; Peter Purton, 'Glass is at the heart of a revolution', 7th October 1991; Barbara Durr and Tracy Corrigan, 'The future comes into focus on screen', 25th June 1992; Richard Waters, 'Markets start to multiply', 10th November 1992; Barry Riley, 'Move to join Swift is slow', 9th December 1992; Andrew Adonis, 'Lines open for the global village', 17th September 1994; George Black, 'Challenges for Swift', 15th November 1994.

[17] Tracy Corrigan, 'Treasurers learn to hedge their bets', 28th March 1991.

more international to meet the needs of their customers. There was a steady convergence between the different types of banking, as business customers and institutional investors looked to banks for a growing range of services. The traditional divide between investment and commercial banking broke down as each invaded the territory of the other in the pursuit of profits and in order to retain the business of existing customers who no longer wanted either credit or capital and either savings and investments but both. These trends met the greatest resistance in those countries such as the USA and Japan where legal restrictions existed on what types of business banks were able to pursue. Even where such legal restrictions were absent others existed that impeded convergence, such as membership of stock exchanges. These institutional restrictions largely disappeared over the course of the 1980s and early 1990s, permitting the convergence of banking activities where legally permitted. The result was that banks became ever more powerful competitors, challenging exchanges, for example, especially as governments removed many of the barriers that had allowed them to resist the forces unleashed by the process of global integration and the transformation of the technology of trading.[18]

However, the response to these trends was neither simultaneous nor uniform across the world, being conditioned by national differences in the roles played by banks and financial markets in individual countries. There were huge differences between the importance of banks and financial markets in centrally-planned economies, like China and the Soviet Union, compared to those where capitalist enterprise dominated, as in the USA, Japan, and the countries of Western Europe. Even within Western Europe Guy de Jonquières observed huge variations in 1988: 'These differences cover a wide spectrum. At one end, Britain has a predominantly equity-based corporate finance system, an enthusiastic approach to most kinds of innovation and a commitment to international markets. At the other, West Germany's financial system is conservative, more inward-looking and built around the commercial banks, which are the main source of corporate finance.'[19] One measure of that disparity was the reliance upon the funds managed by private pension providers and life assurance companies to provide security against premature death and eventual retirement as compared to state provision. In 1987 the value of the assets held by pension funds and life assurance companies in the UK was 105 per cent of GDP and 72 per cent in the USA compared to 32 per cent in Japan, 29 per cent in West Germany, and 19 per cent in France. Trends underpinned the process of change but their impact was distorted by the diversity that existed between countries and the willingness and ability to resist the forces at work. The outcome was both piecemeal and gradual, spreading outwards from the USA and the UK to closely-linked countries like Canada, Australia, and member states of the EU but long delayed across Asia (including Japan), Latin America, and Africa. Even by the early 1990s much remained to be accomplished in the transition between the control and compartmentalization of the 1950s and 1960s though there had been a major transformation of global financial markets during the 1970s and 1980s, which can be traced in the development and relative standing of the world's financial centres during those decades.[20]

[18] David Lascelles, 'Reforms fail to keep pace with changes in the markets', 24th May 1991; Angus Foster, 'Future of stock exchange comes to a head', 16th August 1991.

[19] Guy de Jonquières, 'Risk, opportunities and arduous negotiations', 18th May 1988.

[20] Tim Dickson, 'Coming soon, the Euro pension', 12th July 1990.

Centres

As the sole financial superpower left standing at the end of the Second World War the USA should have supplied the dominant financial centre, which would have been New York. Important pre-war financial centres like Amsterdam, Berlin, Brussels, London, Paris, Shanghai, Tokyo, and Vienna had all been badly damaged by the conflict and took time to recover. Some never did, like Berlin, left marooned in a centrally-planned communist state. Alternatives to these financial centres did exist, located in countries that had been neutral during the war, such as Stockholm in Sweden and Zurich in Switzerland, but they lacked the scale, infrastructure, connections, and government-backed support to replace them. This left New York in a commanding position, though London did retain a residual, but fading, importance, being the centre of a sterling-based international currency system. However, the post-war era of control and compartmentalization was not conducive to the development of any international financial centre because of the barriers to the free movement of funds around the world and the operation of global markets. Inter-government transfers, managed currencies, state-controlled banks and regulated markets, along with national financial systems under the direction of central banks, were characteristic of the twenty-five years that followed the end of the Second World War. These conditions encouraged the internalization of commercial and financial activity within large multinational companies, not transactions on global commodity, money, and securities markets located in diverse financial centres. Those financial centres that did flourish in this era were those that could provide banks, businesses, and individuals with a means of escaping the controls in place, as well as evading or avoiding high taxes and oppressive regulations. Known as offshore financial centres they could attract businesses by providing them with an environment of low taxes, minimal regulations, and few controls. Among them were included the likes of Zurich, Geneva, and Luxembourg in Europe; Hong Kong in Asia; and a growing band of small states such as those in the Caribbean. As the world economy recovered from the ravages of the Second World War, generating increasing trade and financial flows between countries, these offshore centres flourished by providing a means through which money could flow unhindered by government-imposed barriers and taxes.

The need for financial centres to act as key interfaces in the world economy did grow steadily during the 1950s and 1960s as global trade and international investment not only recovered but grew strongly. At the very least a mechanism was required through which international payments and receipts could be handled and investment flows directed from areas of surplus to those in need of finance, while avoiding the controls imposed by governments. The development of the Eurodollar and then Eurobond markets from the late 1950s onwards was one example of the process at work. Hong Kong, for example, provided a means of linking the US$ and UK£ currency zones at a time when exchange controls applied to the latter, lasting until 1979. Zurich thrived as a low-tax location through which international funds could flow, and that attraction remained long after the era of government controls over external financial flows ended. London emerged as an offshore centre where transactions could be conducted on the basis of US$s without the restrictions imposed by the US government. During the 1970s and 1980s governments and central banks gradually abandoned their attempts to control international financial flows, fix the price of gold and other key commodities, and dictate the level of exchange rates and interest rates. This was accompanied by a higher degree of volatility in terms of such variables as commodity prices, exchange and interest rates compared to the past, requiring constant adjustments between banks as it was through them flowed not only payments and receipts but also the credit required to support the functioning of an integrated global economy. This all worked to the advantage of those financial centres with the depth and breadth to host these emerging global markets and provide a base from which internationally focused banks could operate. One example was the rapid rise of currency trading from the early 1970s onwards as the regime of fixed exchange rates in place since the end of the Second World War was abandoned. In turn this generated a demand for financial centres where these markets could be located, in which banks could settle transactions between each other, and through which funds could flow. This was taking place both domestically and internationally. It was in the 1980s, for example, that Sydney emerged as the dominant financial centre in Australia, as it became the interface between the domestic and the global economy.

Despite the removal of barriers to international financial flows within an increasingly integrated global economy there continued to be a role for offshore financial centres in the 1970s and 1980s, because of the lack of harmonization of regulations and equalization of taxes across the world. The continued existence of government controls, regulations, and taxes, as well as the restrictive practices employed by banks, exchanges, and regulators, continued to either compartmentalize financial activity or drive it to those centres offering lower taxes and/or limited disclosure requirements. Multinational companies and those conducting extensive international trading operations were in a position to choose where to generate their profits and so pay their taxes and reveal details of their income and expenditure.[21] This was the case even in the EU with Barry Riley observing in 1990, 'Ultimately, a single market in financial services makes no sense without fiscal harmonisation.'[22] Nevertheless, the main development in the 1970s and 1980s was the emergence of a tri-polar grouping among financial centres with New York serving the Americas, Tokyo representing Asia, and London catering for Europe. Whereas the position of the first two was largely secured by the relative standing of their domestic economies, that of London owed much to the role it already played internationally, along with its strategic positioning in the world's time zones, standing between Asia and the Americas. Historically London possessed a cluster of banks and markets of international importance and these were well placed to benefit from the global economy requiring a location where banks could trade with each other, as they matched assets and liabilities across time and currencies, and markets could operate free from barriers and restrictions. It was London that was able to provide such a place, especially after the UK abandoned exchange controls in 1979. In 1960 there were already seventy-five foreign banks directly represented in London and that number then grew strongly throughout the 1960s, 1970s, and 1980s reaching 514 by 1993, which was far more than any other financial centre, including New York. These included a growing number of US and Japanese banks as they discovered that by basing their international operations in London they could escape the restrictions imposed at home on combining investment and commercial banking.[23]

[21] Clive Wolman, 'Cuts and vigilance reduce appeal of secret money', 12th June 1987; David Lascelles, 'Euromarkets face uncertain fate', 1st March 1989.

[22] Barry Riley, 'A formidable task', 29th March 1990.

[23] Nicholas Colchester, 'A heavyweight sheds pounds', 8th April 1986; Barry Riley, 'A unique global background', 3rd July 1986; Michael Blanden, 'Leading players take the plunge', 2nd October 1986; Elaine Williams, 'Banking's unifying force', 16th October 1986; Bernard Simon, 'Obstacles yet to be surmounted', 28th November 1986; Stefan Wagstyl, 'Reforms on the way', 22nd June 1987; David Lascelles, 'Trying to end the City paperchase', 22nd September 1987; Evelyn Costello, 'The big engine shows its capacity', 3rd December 1987; Kenneth Gooding, 'A boost for the market', 13th June 1988; Sean Heath, 'City's stability appreciated', 26th September 1988; Marjorie Ritson, 'Some may prefer Europe', 26th September 1988; Stefan Wagstyl, 'Risk of missing the global bus', 2nd

That positioning of London, New York, and Tokyo along the world's time zones did not mean they were immune from competition. Each faced a growing challenge as the barriers that had compartmentalized the world were reduced or removed. For New York the challenge was domestic, coming from Chicago with its expertise in financial derivatives. In Asia both Hong Kong and Singapore benefited from the restrictions in place in Japan, which hindered the ability of Tokyo to emerge as the dominant financial centre of the region. London faced competition from Frankfurt, Paris, Amsterdam, and Zurich in Europe. This liberalization also opened up competition between Tokyo, London, and New York as each was in a position to expand the time zones it operated in as well as offer a home to those activities not permitted in the others.[24] One location where competition between financial centres was most intense was in Europe because of the existence of a number of possible locations, each of which had a claim to occupy a prime position, and progress was being made towards the creation of a single market in financial services, which would remove protective national barriers. Of those centres it was Paris that mounted the strongest challenge in the 1980s. By 1990 George Graham claimed that Paris was:

> perhaps the only European centre in a position to compete head-on with London. A conscious policy of deregulation, carried through by successive left-wing and right-wing finance ministers, has provided France with the tools for international financial operations. These include formal stock, bond and futures markets, liquid interbank markets in short-term instruments, foreign exchange and derivative products, and since the beginning of this year, free capital movements.[25]

December 1988; Ralph Atkins, 'Zurich's precious tradition', 19th December 1988; Hugo Dixon, 'Reconnecting charges with costs', 3rd April 1990; Kevin Brown, 'A gateway to Asia and the Pacific', 5th June 1990; Desmond MacRae, 'How depositories raise efficiency', 3rd September 1990; Kenneth Gooding, 'Havens of inertia', 22nd June 1992; Richard Mooney, 'At the tip of an iceberg', 22nd June 1992; Vanessa Houlder, 'A mountain of debt', 7th August 1992; Ian Rodger, 'Private banking provides fuel', 2nd December 1993; John Plender, 'City plays growing role in drawing investors', 2nd October 1995; Charles Pretzlik, 'US banks take Europe by storm' in *Europe Reinvented: The new rules of the game*, *Financial Times*, London 2000.

[24] D. Campbell Smith, 'Hunting for the gig game', 28th November 1983; Barry Riley, 'Well-placed centre with advantages', 28th November 1983; Barry Riley, 'Concentration of talent bolsters prominent role', 18th November 1985; Barry Riley, 'Foreign banks attracted by open policy', 8th January 1986; William Dullforce, 'Tax cuts urged to revive Swiss market', 14th March 1986; David Lascelles, 'A New York–Tokyo–London axis', 7th April 1986; Nicholas Colchester, 'A heavyweight sheds pounds', 8th April 1986; Barbara Casassus, 'Top-slot turnover has quadrupled', 27th May 1986; Michael Blanden, 'Leading players take the plunge', 2nd October 1986; David Lascelles, 'Foundations laid, but plans still vague', 23rd June 1987; Michael Blanden, 'A chance to move in on the stock market', 21st September 1987; Guy de Jonquières, 'Risk, opportunities and arduous negotiations', 18th May 1988; Marjorie Ritson, 'Some may prefer Europe', 26th September 1988; Sean Heath, 'City's stability appreciated', 26th September 1988; George Graham, 'Major reforms under way', 29th September 1988; Eric Short, 'Unit trusts gear up for a European challenge', 12th November 1988; Stefan Wagstyl, 'Risk of missing the global bus', 2nd December 1988; James Andrews, 'The latecomer has potential', 20th February 1989; Andrew Freeman, 'Spurred by the Americans', 20th February 1989; Michiyo Nakamoto, 'Domestic market loses out', 13th March 1989; Karen Fossli, 'Liberalisation helps to fuel interest', 30th March 1989; Karen Fossli, 'Liberalisation helps to fuel interest', 30th March 1989; David Lascelles, 'A potential financial capital for the EC', 25th September 1989; Robert Taylor, 'Sweden to axe bond turnover tax', 26th January 1990; Barry Riley, 'A formidable task', 29th March 1990; Stephen Fidler, 'W Germany may suffer withholding tax legacy', 18th May 1990; Kevin Brown, 'A gateway to Asia and the Pacific', 5th June 1990; David Lascelles, 'Banks seem set to move cautiously', 2nd July 1990; Lucy Kellaway, 'Many moves on the way to market', 21st November 1990; Richard Waters and George Graham, 'Birth of a market needs burial of differences', 28th November 1990; Richard Waters, 'Warning on European capital market', 14th December 1990; Lucy Kellaway and Tim Dickson, 'Painful birth of single market', 19th December 1990; Richard Waters, 'Securities firms look across borders', 7th January 1991; Jim McCallum, 'End of controls provides a lift', 11th November 1991; Ian Rodger, 'London is now a banker bet for the Swiss', 2nd December 1992.

[25] George Graham, 'Paris takes on London', 26th June 1990.

During the 1980s a major deregulation of the French financial system had led to a renaissance of its bond and equity markets while Paris also became a centre for trading foreign exchange and financial derivatives. The process through which this had taken place began in 1984 and was led by successive French governments intent on making Paris into the major financial centre of Continental Europe, if not in a position to compete with London on the global stage, though that was also an underlying ambition. In his first spell as Minister of Finance in the French socialist government, from 1984 to 1986, Pierre Beregovoy drove through a series of financial reforms. His initiatives were then taken forward by his conservative successor, Edouard Baladur, between 1986 and 1988 before being resumed by Beregovoy when he returned as finance minister. The result was that France moved from a bank-dominated financial system, under the control of the government, to one in which savers, investors, businesses, and markets were free to make their own decisions. This was achieved through a comprehensive package of reforms covering banking, the raising of capital for business, and the functioning of the markets for credit, currency, bonds, equities, and derivatives.

Though begun as a government initiative, these reforms took on a momentum and direction of their own. By 1990, again according to George Graham, 'Five years of reforms have left France with a completely modernised financial system. Monopolies have been broken, barriers demolished, and new structures created which, in areas such as settlements, payment systems or governments, are the envy of many countries.'[26] His words followed similar views expressed by bankers such as that of Jorgen Wagner-Knudsen, senior vice-president of the Paris branch of Morgan Guaranty, in 1989: 'In five years, France has moved from being one of the most highly-regulated markets in Europe to one of the most deregulated, in parallel with the UK.'[27] These reforms transformed Paris as a financial centre, with the result, according to George Graham in 1991, that 'France has undertaken over the past seven years a rapid and far-reaching overhaul of its financial markets that has placed it firmly in the front rank among the financial centres of continental Europe.'[28] Despite these laudatory remarks the success of Paris largely rested on serving the French domestic market. Paris as a financial centre continued to lack the depth, breadth, and connections possessed by London's financial markets. Instead, Paris remained a collection of separate markets and bank offices, reflected in their spread across the city, and they lacked the cohesion of London with concentration of financial activity in one particular location, the City. Only in a few derivatives contracts, as in that for sugar, was Paris of international importance, which meant that French banks continued to gravitate to London as it was only there that they could access the global market. As the London correspondent of the French business newspaper, Les Echoes, observed in 1990, 'France's leading banks have found the City of London an irresistible lure.'[29] Numerous French banks continued to either open offices in London or acquire British subsidiaries during the 1980s, suggesting that it possessed advantages, which Paris could not match despite the reforms, and that these were of growing importance in the 1980s.[30]

[26] George Graham, 'Creating a modern system', 22nd October 1990.

[27] David Lascelles, 'Important transformation', 7th November 1989.

[28] George Graham, 'In the front rank in Europe', 17th June 1991.

[29] Patrick de Jacquelot, 'London's irresistible lure', 22nd October 1990.

[30] George Graham, 'Faster growth than London's', 20th January 1987; George Graham, 'Paris adds to continuous market', 20th January 1987; Alexander Nicoll, 'Agreement among rivals', 19th March 1987; George Graham, 'Matif forges ahead', 19th March 1987; George Graham, 'Paris sugar market under siege', 13th August 1987; Stephen Fidler, 'Deregulate or risk being left behind', 21st October 1987; Paul Betts, 'Banks rush to buy French brokers', 9th December 1987; David Blackwell, 'London builds up lead in white sugar contest', 2nd February 1988;

Despite the advances made by Paris in the 1980s the most obvious alternative to London as a financial centre in Europe was Frankfurt, located as it was in the continent's largest and most successful economy, West Germany. However, as a financial centre Frankfurt was of relatively recent creation, having replaced Berlin, and had yet to establish itself even within Germany. As David Waller observed from the vantage point of 1992, 'Frankfurt has lost out when competing with other financial centres to provide a range of financial services, and the German equity market is especially underdeveloped.'[31] This was the result of a number of important factors. One was the federal structure of the German state from which encouraged political opposition to the centralization of the domestic financial system in any one centre. There were eight regional stock exchanges, for example, and each was supported and regulated by their respective Länder. All resisted the introduction of Federal regulation and supervision. Frankfurt's weakness as a financial centre was also a product of the structure of Germany's financial system itself, which was dominated by banks to the disadvantage of financial markets. Taxes and other regulations imposed by the German government also restricted the development of centralized financial markets. The turnover tax on securities transactions, for example, suppressed the growth of active markets in stocks, bonds, and money. These taxes even encouraged what trading there was to migrate to centres outside Germany, such as London. Conversely these taxes benefited the banks by removing potential competitors for the savings being generated by the German population. In contrast banks were either exempt from these taxes or could escape them by internalizing transactions.

It was only from the mid-1980s that the German government began to introduce measures designed to enhance the position of Frankfurt as a financial centre. Theo Waigel, when finance minister, embraced this cause which was shared by those running Germany's banks, who were aware of the slow erosion of business to other financial centres in Europe. One of those was Rolf Breuer, a main board director of Deutsche Bank and responsible for the bank's securities activities. Speaking in 1992 he made clear what the extent of Germany's aim was in terms of establishing Frankfurt as a financial centre: 'Our ambition is not to be better than London—we must stick with what is realistic, and it would be illusory to think we could overtake London given that city's traditional advantages. To be the leading financial centre on the continent is more realistic.'[32] The most visible example of this loss of business to London was Liffe developing a successful futures contract on German government bonds. The stimulus to change that came with the competition from London was compounded in the late 1980s by the moves towards a single European market for financial services. This directly threatened the business of the German banks as savers could now

George Graham, 'In need of ratings', 17th February 1988; Barbara Casassus, 'Report likely to allay anxiety', 10th March 1988; George Graham, 'Major reforms under way', 29th September 1988; George Graham, 'France launches search for new financial centre', 10th January 1989; George Graham, 'A rapid developer', 8th March 1989; George Graham, 'Year of quiet change', 2nd November 1989; David Lascelles, 'Important transformation', 7th November 1989; George Graham, 'A tale of two sugar markets', 16th February 1990; George Graham, 'New weapons for the global fray', 5th June 1990; George Graham, 'Paris takes on London', 26th June 1990; George Graham, 'Creating a modern system', 22nd October 1990; George Graham, 'Doubts about tax burden', 22nd October 1990; Patrick de Jacquelot, 'London's irresistible lure', 22nd October 1990; George Graham, 'Tuffier collapse highlights decline in commission rates', 22nd October 1990; George Graham, 'Foreign investment doubles', 22nd October 1990; George Graham, 'A battle with London', 22nd October 1990; George Graham, 'Sanctioned to protect', 22nd October 1990; George Graham, 'Worries over imbalances', 22nd October 1990; George Graham, 'In the front rank in Europe', 17th June 1991.

[31] David Waller, 'Going for the lion's share', 1st July 1992.

[32] David Waller, 'Bank chief's sights set on central role for Germany', 10th June 1992.

look elsewhere for more attractive rates of return including the opportunity to avoid German taxes. In the face of the loss of business to rival financial centres in Europe, the Federal government in Germany inaugurated a series of reforms to both the structure of German financial markets and to the taxation system from 1987 onwards. These reforms included a relaxation of the highly-restrictive anti-gambling laws, which had prevented the development of futures markets in Germany. It was not until 1990 that the financial derivatives exchange, the Deutsche Terminbörse (DTB), was launched. In 1991 the securities turnover tax was abolished and the cumbersome issuance approval procedures were removed, leading to the rapid growth of a domestic commercial paper market. However, it was only slowly that progress was made in introducing the reforms required to make Germany a more competitive location for financial services. In the words of David Waller in 1992, 'Steadily and surely... Frankfurt financiers are building the institutional infrastructure essential if Finanzplatz Frankfurt is to become on a par with London, New York and Tokyo—or even to achieve the more modest objective of establishing a clear lead ahead of the other continental European financial centres.'[33] Many commentators were of the view that it was all too late and that Frankfurt had lost the initiative not only to London but also Paris, because the degree of change required was too great. Those included David Waller who concluded in 1992, that 'it seems improbable that Germany can develop into a leading financial services centre without developing a financial culture as well'.[34] Nevertheless, foreign banks like Goldman Sachs were being attracted to Frankfurt as its status as Germany's financial centre became established, and the German government was mounting a strong bid for it to be the location of the European Central Bank.[35]

It was not only Paris and Frankfurt that were bidding to become the leading financial centre in continental Europe as there were those who made the case for Amsterdam. According to Laura Raun in 1989 the Dutch master plan was to develop Amsterdam as the 'financial gateway to continental Europe', taking advantage of the moves towards a single market and the limited progress being made in Germany.[36] To this end Dutch financial markets were liberalized, charges reduced, and new financial products introduced in a bid to attract both banks and business from elsewhere. Though that attempt was partially successful, with the likes of the Swiss Bank Corp and Citicorp opening offices in Amsterdam, the overall result was failure. Amsterdam could not compete with the liquidity of London's markets. In turn, that forced Dutch banks to shift their international business to London in order to compete successfully with foreign banks and their well-developed global networks.[37] The problem for Amsterdam was that Europe remained a collection of markets

[33] David Waller, 'Bonn has a change of heart', 26th October 1992.

[34] David Waller, 'Going for the lion's share', 1st July 1992.

[35] Haig Simonian, 'Thwarted by the tax', 17th February 1988; Haig Simonian, 'Liffe eyes D-Mark business', 18th February 1988; Guy de Jonquières, '1992: countdown to reality', 19th February 1988; Katharine Campbell, 'Liffe dilemma for German banks', 19th January 1989; Haig Simonian, 'A computer-based market', 8th March 1989; Haig Simonian, 'Quiet revolution for German securities', 13th September 1989; Katharine Campbell, 'Anxious parents await DTB birth', 26th January 1990; Katharine Campbell, 'No recipe for long-term success', 9th March 1990; Katharine Campbell and Deborah Hargreaves, 'Bund futures force pace of change', 4th May 1990; Stephen Fidler, 'W. Germany may suffer withholding tax legacy', 18th May 1990; Richard Waters, 'Banks compete for a share', 19th June 1990; Katharine Campbell, 'Risks and rewards of change in Frankfurt', 7th January 1991; Katharine Campbell, 'Roles are reversed for city of bankers', 28th October 1991; David Waller, 'Bank chief's sights set on central role for Germany', 10th June 1992; David Waller, 'Going for the lion's share', 1st July 1992; Leslie Colitt, 'Face to face with reality', 1st July 1992; Andrew Fisher, 'City flexes financial muscle', 1st July 1992; David Waller, 'Bonn has a change of heart', 26th October 1992.

[36] Laura Raun, 'Dutch master plan', 28th March 1989.

[37] Laura Raun, 'Loss of business stemmed', 21st April 1987; David A Brown, 'Capital market in those of big changes', 30th June 1988; Laura Raun, 'Dutch master plan', 28th March 1989.

divided by different taxes, laws, and cultures. This made it difficult for any financial centre, based in a small country like the Netherlands, to develop markets that were simultaneously broad and deep, and so able to attract banks from across the continent. Conversely, the Netherlands was too large to position itself as a tax haven, which was the course followed by Luxembourg, as that would require too many concessions to be granted to domestic business, and so deprive the Dutch government of revenue. As a financial centre Luxembourg focused on providing legal and administrative services for those banks and businesses that located there so as to take advantage of its favourable taxes.[38]

A convenient and alternative European financial centre to any located within the EU was Zurich in Switzerland. It could provide a large domestic base and offer a safe-haven/tax-free status. However, Zurich suffered from many of the same difficulties that undermined Frankfurt as a financial centre. The federal structure of the Swiss state created opposition to the centralization of financial activity in one centre. Hence the use of the collective term 'Finanzplatz Schweiz' to cover Zurich, Geneva, Basel, and Lugano. It was only in the 1980s that Zurich emerged as the dominant financial centre in Switzerland. Even then Geneva remained of major importance both for private banking and meeting the needs of the French speaking population. Also, as in Germany the connection between gambling and derivative contracts delayed the launch of the Swiss options and financial futures exchange (Soffex) until 1988 while the dominant position of a few universal banks similarly stunted the development of both the money and capital markets. This was compounded by a tax on financial transactions, which encouraged buying and selling to take place either within or between the banks. The effect was to limit trading in both Swiss franc-denominated bonds and the market in the shares of Swiss companies. As the barriers to free financial flows disappeared in the 1980s the market in both these gravitated to London. Until the 1980s Zurich had also been the pre-eminent European foreign exchange market but then lost out to London. In response Swiss banks shifted their foreign exchange trading to London. By 1992, according to Ian Rodger, 'The only sector in which the Swiss financial centre appears to be holding its own is in asset management, mainly in connection with private banking.'[39] Major Swiss banks like UBS and Credit Suisse found it easier to build up an international trading team from a London rather than a Zurich base. Nevertheless, unlike most offshore financial centres Switzerland was a sufficiently large economy to support both a number of large and globally-important banks and markets in gold, stocks, bonds, and foreign exchange.[40]

The European financial centre against which all others competed was London. In 1992 Robin Leigh-Pemberton, the governor of the Bank of England, could confidently state that 'London is one of the three major world financial centres, perhaps the only truly international centre and certainly the pre-eminent international centre in Europe, with a depth, variety and liquidity in its money and capital markets.'[41] Nevertheless, as a financial centre London was subject to a two-way pull in the 1980s and into the 1990s. On the one hand the

[38] James Buxton, 'Regional strategy for a second-tier alliance', 16th May 1991.

[39] Ian Rodger, 'Worrying outflow of funds', 7th May 1992.

[40] William Dullforce, 'Share registration rules under fire', 28th June 1988; Ralph Atkins, 'Zurich's precious tradition', 19th December 1988; John Wicks, 'A world leader must not be left behind', 25th April 1989; William Dullforce, 'Swiss under pressure', 29th March 1990; William Dullforce, 'How Geneva is still holding its ground', 9th October 1990; Barry Riley, 'A bridge between New York and Tokyo', 29th November 1990; William Dullforce, 'Squalls in a safe haven', 13th December 1990; Peter Martin, 'Bank feel the electronic impulse', 13th December 1990; Tracy Corrigan, 'The syndicate disbands', 13th December 1990; Ian Rodger, 'Worrying outflow of funds', 7th May 1992; Ian Rodger, 'London is now a banker bet for the Swiss', 2nd December 1992.

[41] Emma Tucker, 'The Square Mile stays out in front', 29th May 1992.

removal of barriers to the free flow of money around the world, and London's key location as a telecommunications hub, attracted business to the deep and broad markets London could provide in such products as foreign exchange, Eurobonds, and international equities. Writing in 1991 Hugo Dixon and Greg Staple concluded that 'The UK is a bridge between North America and Europe...'[42] Those conditions also favoured the centralization of specialist services in London, where so many banks already had offices and could benefit from the convenient time zone and support facilities it provided.[43] As Richard Lambert observed in 1989, 'Firms come to London because so many other firms are already there, and once they have gone to the expense of setting up shop they will not lightly switch their location.'[44] Conversely, the ending of punitive taxes and the decline of restrictive practices abroad removed a number of the causes that had driven business to London. London also suffered from increased regulations imposed by the EU, which harmed its ability to handle cross-border transactions and attract banks from around the world.[45] London was also an expensive location due to the high level of office rents and staff salaries. One solution to the question of cost was to move even more of the routine office functions to less expensive locations elsewhere in the UK, while retaining trading and specialist services in London.[46] However, there was a limit to what could be relocated because so many of the activities that took place in London's financial district were inter-connected, reliant upon the constant flow of information and transactions between offices.

What London was left with were those financial activities in which it possessed permanent and high-level advantages and so could justify the expense involved. Those that were the product of temporary conditions, or were no longer competitive, departed for other locations either within Britain or abroad. On balance London continued to prosper as an international financial centre, as reflected in the continued arrival of banks and brokers from other countries, despite the high cost involved in establishing and maintaining an office there. Arrivals outweighed departures with London becoming increasingly attractive to banks from Continental Europe, while the number from the USA declined.[47] Though the City of London was regarded domestically as 'a place of limited vision and selfish interests,'[48] according to Richard Lambert in 1987, it continued to be the mecca for banks and brokers because of its cosmopolitan environment and international outlook. As David Lascelles pointed out in 1990, London's 'strength has always been in the wholesale markets which operate without regard to borders'. That continued to be as true then as it had always

[42] Hugo Dixon and Greg Staple, 'New perspective on patterns of power', 7th October 1991.

[43] Richard Waters, 'Heated dispute', 18th December 1991; Emma Tucker, 'The Square Mile stays out in front', 29th May 1992.

[44] Richard Lambert, 'Finance grows into a threat to the City', 1st June 1989.

[45] Simon London, 'Cedel's rise in turnover confirms trend', 5th February 1991; Sara Webb, 'International investors find a silver lining', 22nd July 1991; Richard Waters, 'Heated dispute', 18th December 1991; Robert Peston, 'Invisible threats sighted to City's international status', 8th July 1992.

[46] David Lascelles, 'Trying to end the City paperchase', 22nd September 1987; David Lascelles, 'City sticks to a paper standard', 3rd August 1988; David Barchard, 'Putting down provincial roots', 27th January 1989; Richard Lambert, 'Finance grows into a threat to the City', 1st June 1989; David Lascelles, 'No room for complacency', 29th November 1990.

[47] David Lascelles, 'Foundations laid, but plans still vague', 23rd June 1987; Michael Blanden, 'A chance to move in on the stock market', 21st September 1987; Barry Riley, 'Critical mass works in the City's favour', 16th November 1987; Marjorie Ritson, 'Some may prefer Europe', 26th September 1988; Philip Coggan, 'Horses for bourses in the world race', 28th November 1988; David Lascelles, 'City bank branch costs £3m to set up', 24th April 1989; David Lascelles, 'Fortunes vary as recession bites', 29th November 1990; Richard Waters, 'In the shadow of Big Bang', 29th November 1990.

[48] Richard Lambert, 'A stain not easy to wash out', 17th October 1987.

been despite the increased competition in Europe coming from both Paris and Frankfurt.[49] Writing in 1991 Barry Riley continued to hold the view that 'London remains Europe's dominant centre in many aspects of international finance, but it is up against stiff competition.'[50] In 1970 the City of London's success as an international financial centre relied on the provision of insurance and commodity trading, which contributed 74 per cent of its external earnings compared to banking and securities dealing at 13 per cent. By 1992 the position had been reversed with banking and securities dealing on 56 per cent share and insurance and commodity trading down to 26 per cent.[51]

As the financial centre of the world's dominant economy at the time New York should have been unchallenged, even by London, in the 1980s. However, the slow pace of deregulation in the USA continued to hamper its competitiveness, whether that involved the mandatory separation of investment or commercial banking, the intrusive regulatory regime of the SEC, or the restrictions on trading practices imposed by the New York Stock Exchange. It was no accident that the most dynamic and competitive financial market in the USA was Chicago-based derivatives trading, as they were regulated by the more permissive Commodity Futures Trading Commission (CFTC) and operated by the likes of the Chicago Mercantile Exchange (CME). Whereas only 50,000 were employed in financial services in Chicago in 1978, ten years later in 1988 the figure had reached 330,000. In contrast, New York was continuing to export financial services employment to the surrounding areas such as New Jersey, driven by the need to reduce costs so as to stay competitive.[52] However, Chicago also faced growing competition from other financial centres as they copied the derivatives products that had underpinned its success and established their own futures exchanges. By 1991 Deborah Hargreaves was of the opinion that, 'The stranglehold Chicago once held on the derivatives industry has been loosened and business has spread more evenly throughout the world.' However, she added the caveat that 'electronic trading could concentrate that volume again on one screen.'[53]

Tokyo was the other heavyweight financial centre in the world in the 1980s but its competitiveness also continued to be hampered by limited deregulation. The statutory compartmentalization within banking, that went even further than in the USA, remained despite some blurring of the boundaries. Continuing restrictions also stifled the market in financial derivatives as, unlike the USA, these applied to all exchanges. Nevertheless, some progress was made in the development of a number of money and currency markets though there was a continuing prohibition on banks dealing in corporate bonds.[54] The restrictions under which both banks and financial markets continued to operate in Tokyo in the 1980s benefited rival financial centres in Asia. Despite the global importance of

[49] David Lascelles, 'Prospects look less certain', 29th November 1990.

[50] Barry Riley, 'Big three join battle for supremacy', 4th July 1991.

[51] David Goodhart, 'Economy's world standing given a frank assessment', 25th May 1994; Richard Lapper, 'A tale of two cities', 12th June 1996.

[52] David Lascelles, 'Why the transatlantic deal must be extended', 7th May 1987; Deborah Hargreaves, 'In need of a strong leader', 10th April 1989; Roderick Oram, 'Merrill Lynch joins Manhattan exodus', 29th June 1989; Deborah Hargreaves, 'Derivatives come of age', 13th March 1991.

[53] Deborah Hargreaves, 'Derivatives come of age', 13th March 1991.

[54] James Andrews, 'The latecomer has potential', 20th February 1989; Stefan Wagstyl, 'Signposts to expansion', 8th March 1989; Stefan Wagstyl, 'Suffering from insecurity', 13th March 1989; Michiyo Nakamoto, 'Domestic market loses out', 13th March 1989; John Ridding, 'New set of much-needed hedging instruments', 13th March 1989; James Andrews, 'Sphere of influence', 13th March 1989; John Ridding, 'Second fiddle's new tunes', 13th March 1989; Patti Waldmeir, 'Big four still recruiting', 13th March 1989; Michiyo Nakamoto, 'Portfolio-power provides lift-off', 25th May 1989; Stefan Wagstyl, 'A testing time for equities', 2nd July 1990; David Lascelles, 'Reforms progressing slowly', 9th July 1990.

Tokyo as a financial centre, it failed to dominate the continent in which it was located. To some, such as Garry Knight, chief executive of the Hong Kong Futures Exchange, the multiplicity of financial centres hosting separate financial markets was simply a reflection of the size and diversity of the Asia-Pacific region: 'The Pacific rim is bigger than the US market, and there's nothing to say we can't have three or more financial centres in the area.'[55] However, it was also a product of an underlying lack of financial integration in the region, as can be seen from trading in the foreign exchange market. Whereas London was the dominant location for trading in Europe and New York for the Americas, Tokyo shared its position in Asia with Singapore and Hong Kong.

Within Asia the rivalry between different financial centres was well established and intense, being backed by governments in the pursuit of national interests. In 1990 the cross-listing between the Stock Exchange of Singapore and the Kuala Lumpur Stock Exchange, for example, was ended because the Malaysian government wanted to promote Kuala Lumpur as a rival financial centre. The result was that across Asia financial centres were very domestically focused leaving the international arena rather neglected. That arena could have been occupied by Tokyo but its own domestic restrictions prevented it doing so. In contrast, with limited domestic bases to fall back on, both Hong Kong and Singapore moved to fill the gap left by Tokyo. Both strove to develop their foreign exchange, futures, and international equity markets so as to attract business from elsewhere in Asia. Hong Kong was most successful in establishing itself as a centre for international banking and fund management while acting as an interface between China and the rest of the world. Singapore became a major centre for both foreign exchange and financial futures trading as a way of compensating for the loss of the market in the stocks of Malaysian companies. Hong Kong had benefited from its political stability, location, good communications, and a favourable tax regime but even by 1992 all these advantages were being undermined by the uncertainty caused by the prospect of control passing from the UK to China in 1997. This uncertainty benefited Singapore as foreign banks and brokers established offices there in case they had to leave Hong Kong once the Chinese took over. The Chinese government also promoted Shanghai as a rival financial centre but it lacked the legal, accounting, and regulatory standards that most international banks and fund managers were accustomed to, and found in Hong Kong.[56]

By the early 1990s a hierarchy of financial centres had emerged in which both London and New York held relatively secure positions serving distinct regions, namely Europe and the Americas, as well as playing an important international role. In contrast, Tokyo was secure only in its command of the Japanese market because it was neither dominant in Asia nor was it the interface between that continent and the rest of the world. Both Hong Kong and Singapore could claim to occupy that position. There were then even a number who questioned whether the whole concept of financial centres occupying a physical location was rather old fashioned, and no longer reflected a world where national barriers had been removed and global communication was instantaneous. Barry Riley summed up this view in 1991: 'In theory there no longer needs to be financial centres at all. Modern information

[55] Philip Coggan, 'Exchange faces a Catch-22 situation', 20th November 1991.

[56] Barry Riley, 'A question of survival', 26th October 1988; David Waller, 'Not all gloom and doom', 12th June 1990; Joyce Quek, 'A blessing in disguise', 9th August 1990; Joyce Quek, 'Profits of big four leap by 30%', 9th August 1990; Charles Goodhart and Antonis Demos, 'The Asian surprise in the forex markets', 2nd September 1991; Angus Foster, 'Fear beneath the optimism', 20th November 1991; Philip Coggan, 'Exchange faces a Catch-22 situation', 20th November 1991; Simon Holberton, 'Foreigners join the queue for Shenzhen flotations', 3rd April 1992.

technology hooked up by satellites and optical cable can mean that a trader far away in the countryside can have all the screens and voice links required to be right in the middle of the electronic marketplace.' He then went on to critique that theory:

> You need a critical mass of salesmen and traders, a similar quantum of back-office staff...and all the programmers and technicians who make the equipment work....This focus on people explains why financial centres still have a strong geographical concentration. In such compact areas an efficient labour market can develop, so that people can pursue a career from firm to firm without necessarily uprooting families or even altering their route to work.

He was aware, though, of the disruptive influence that the removal of barriers and the revolution in technology was having on the location of financial markets: 'Firms no longer need to be quite so close to the stock market, the money market and the commodities exchanges because there is a smaller and smaller requirement for papers to be physically distributed. Such trends have encouraged the development of satellite centres.'[57]

What was happening in the world was that as barriers were removed and communication revolutionized it freed financial activities to either cluster or disperse according to which course suited them. There was a tendency for certain financial activities to cluster because of the need to access deep, liquid, and fast-moving markets. This applied especially to the world's largest financial market, as measured by turnover, which was that for foreign exchange. 'A financial market which never closes, knows no national boundaries and is beyond the control of governments' was how Jim McCallum described it in 1991.[58] The foreign exchange market was dominated by trading in the US$ against other currencies and was conducted between a small number of global banks with global operations. That trading was clustered in London, New York, and Tokyo, in that order, because that was where the liquidity was greatest. Together, these three centres accounted for two-thirds of total foreign exchange turnover in 1991. At the other end of the spectrum was fund management, which involved a huge range of assets and a large number of participants with deals customized to fit the needs of individual buyers and sellers. Based only on equities under management in 1990 Tokyo, New York, and London, in that order, again emerged as the most important financial centres, but there were also many more of major, though lesser significance. These included Geneva and Zurich in Switzerland; Boston, San Francisco, Philadelphia, Los Angeles, Chicago, and Hartford in the USA; Toronto in Canada; Paris in France; Frankfurt in Germany; and Edinburgh in the UK. In the business of fund management it was important to be close to customers, especially institutional investors, as well as the financial markets in which stocks, bonds, derivatives, and currency were traded and where funds could be easily borrowed and lent. This had the effect of producing a much more tiered financial system in which the relative importance of different financial centres was much more a product of domestic conditions than international flows of credit and capital.[59] For those reasons financial centres were in a constant state of flux as they simultaneously lost and gained particular activities. The inertia of the past had been associated with a controlled and compartmentalized world that was steadily disappearing after 1970, generating both challenges and opportunities as a result.

[57] Barry Riley, 'Big three join battle for supremacy', 4th July 1991.
[58] Jim McCallum, 'Big three battle it out', 29th April 1991.
[59] Barry Riley, 'Individualists seek a niche', 16th May 1991.

Conclusion

By the beginning of the 1990s the world was moving towards global 24-hour financial markets, driven by trends in technology and the removal of government-imposed barriers. However, such a world still remained some distance in the future. Much remained to be done in making the technology fit practical requirements and removing the numerous internal barriers that prevented integration. Nevertheless, it spelled the end of the nationally focused compartmentalized financial system that had been in place since the end of the Second World War. That world had begun to crumble during the 1960s and 1970s and the 1980s spelled its final demise. The new world that emerged had major implications for banks, exchanges, and regulators as globalization and technological change proved to be disruptive forces. For banks the business models that had sufficed in the past could no longer be relied upon as the divisions between different types of banks, and even banks and financial markets, were increasingly blurred. This posed a serious challenge for those banking systems in which divisions were enshrined in law, as that hindered the ability to respond. Conversely, this new situation created opportunities for those banks able to extend their operations into new areas including expanding internationally. During the 1970s and 1980s exchanges were also having to come to terms with the ending of the monopoly that they had long enjoyed. The once sacrosanct separation of commodity and stock exchanges, for example, was no longer applicable with the growth of financial derivatives and the links between cash and futures trading. The very future of exchanges was also in doubt with the ability of megabanks to internalize transactions, trade directly with each other or use the services of interdealer brokers. Also undermining the position of exchanges was the proliferation of government-sponsored agencies that regulated financial markets instead of leaving that role to the institutions themselves. The intervention of regulators also favoured large banks as they presented them with a business model that was tightly managed and resilient compared to either a numerous and disparate banking community or looser market organizations. Regulators could no longer rely on control and compartmentalization to make intervention effective but had to work with financial systems that were much less responsive to the dictates of national governments.

Despite the elimination of distance as an important variable in the location of financial markets clustering of activity remained important. Even global markets had to have a core. That was where contact was instant and liquidity greatest. There continued to be a need for human interaction when complex deals were being negotiated. The more complex the deal the more it relied on a range and depth of services that only existed where demand was most concentrated. Similarly, in fast-moving and inter-connected markets, sales and purchases could only be made quickly and at current prices in highly-liquid markets. For that reason it was centres such as London and New York that remained prominent, being favoured by the world's banks and brokers as locations from which they could conduct an international business. Those centres located in Europe were especially favoured by time-zone advantages as they linked Asia and the Americas. However, there was no single location to which financial activity naturally gravitated because all possessed both advantages and disadvantages and it was the balance between the two, in relationship to each other, which determined the ebb and flow of business. In determining this balance the relative freedom from controls and restrictions was a major consideration. These controls and restrictions extended beyond barriers to international financial flows as these were increasingly removed. Instead, they included the taxes levied on particular financial transactions and the restrictions placed on banks and financial markets that curbed the business that they could do and the way in which they were allowed to operate. Important as were the fundamental forces at work it was the decisions made in the 1970s and 1980s that shaped the new financial world that was emerging and determined the winners and losers among banks, exchanges, and financial centres. Though hindsight might suggest a future dictated by path dependency the reality that emerges from a careful reading of the evidence was one that was much less certain.

3

Banks, Brokers, Bonds, and Currencies, 1970–92

Introduction

Though the First and Second World Wars, along with the intervening years of crisis, had a major negative impact on the world's banking systems they were even more damaging for financial markets. Banks did collapse and even disappear but governments intervened to ensure that, collectively, the banking system survived because of the essential role it played in the financial system. Banks were so closely intertwined with the means of payment, the mobilization of savings and the supply of finance that no modern economy could operate without them. Under these circumstances it was only to be expected that governments after the Second World War would prioritize banks over markets within both national and international financial systems. The result was to alter the balance between banks and financial markets firmly in the direction of the former. Banks responded by expanding, reaching a size and scale that allowed them to internalize financial transactions within a single organization. That position then changed from 1970 onwards with an end to the era of control and compartmentalization. The process of change involved the gradual removal of the protection that national boundaries and segregated activities had provided banks with since the end of the Second World War. What it did not mean was uniformity between countries as the legacy of the past meant that there continued to exist major differences between countries, creating a complex environment that banks had to negotiate. One example was the diversity between owner-occupation and rented accommodation in the provision of homes. Whereas owner-occupation was the dominant form in the USA, UK, and Japan in 1990, that was not the case for Germany, even when only that portion in the West that had not been under communist control is considered. Another major difference between countries was the reliance of business upon debt finance through the issue of bills and bonds as compared to that raised through bank loans. In 1992 this was very high in the USA and much lower in the UK, Germany, and Japan. These were among the long-standing structural differences that affected the way both banks and financial markets operated in each country, regardless of the changes that took place after 1970.[1]

Nevertheless, whatever the particular environment, after 1970 banks, of whatever type, could no longer rely on the inertia of savers and borrowers, the stability of economies, and the immunity from competition that had existed since the end of the Second World War. Instead, they had to cope with much greater volatility and instability, a growing intensity of competition for savings, and a battle to attract borrowers. The nature of the customers they served also changed. As businesses grew in scale they became sufficiently large and diversified to dispense with banks as a source of credit, as this could be managed internally.

[1] John Gapper, 'Uncertainty over expansion plans', 29th November 1994; Adrian Coles, 'UK home ownership typical of EU', 10th July 1995; Norma Cohen, 'The remarkable fall and rise of Canary Wharf', 21st October 2000.

Banks, Exchanges, and Regulators: Global Financial Markets from the 1970s. Ranald Michie, Oxford University Press (2021).

DOI: 10.1093/oso/9780199553730.003.0003

Instead, they looked to banks for other financial services such as the issue of stocks and bonds, temporary finance to cover takeovers, foreign exchange facilities, and ways of minimizing exposure to fluctuations in prices. In turn that forced banks to become bigger and more diversified if they were not to lose these businesses as customers. Even the routine business of banking, which was to collect savings from the many and lend it short-term, was subjected to change after 1970. Such business was not without its risks, revolving around the sudden withdrawal of funds by savers, causing a liquidity crisis, and the default of borrowers on their loans, causing a solvency crisis. Both these type of crises did become more likely after 1970 as volatility returned to interest rates and exchange rates while fluctuating economic conditions increased the likelihood of borrower defaults. At the same time the increasing level of competition encouraged banks to explore ways of generating additional profits, as those obtained from the more routine business of accepting deposits and making short-term loans fell.

Among alternatives were ones that certain banks had long specialized in, such as providing long-term loans by way of mortgages on property or financing business through the issue of stocks and bonds. Both these had long offered higher profits than collecting savings and providing credit but at increased risks, and so had been shunned by those banks exposed to the sudden withdrawal of deposits. However, the incentive to engage in longer term lending increased as competition eroded the profits banks could make from sticking to those activities which involved fewer risks. What this situation led to was a search by banks after 1970 for ways of maximizing profits and minimizing risks. One outcome was the increasing adoption of the originate-and-distribute model in place of the lend-and-hold one. This strategy was also accompanied by the emergence of banks that were both global and universal, which meant that they operated regardless of national boundaries and were engaged across the whole range of financial activities. Writing in 1989 Patrick Henderson referred to 'the increasingly deregulated and competitive world of international banking'.[2] That was very different from the world of 1970 when the banks conducted business on a national basis and restricted themselves to particular activities. However, this transformation was accomplished only gradually and in a piecemeal fashion in the 1970s and 1980s, and remained far from complete by 1992.

Banking

Leading the way in the changes that took place in those decades was the USA, even though it had never embraced the lend-and-hold model to the extent that other countries had. In turn, it was developments in the USA that were then picked up on around the world as other banks looked to ways of generating higher profits and lowering the level of risk in the new environment they faced after 1970. Legislation passed in the nineteenth century had prevented the growth of nationwide branch banking in the USA while that of the 1930s stopped the creation of universal banks. The effect was to limit the size of US banks despite the opportunities presented because of the depth and breadth of the US economy. This meant that the move towards the lend-and-hold model of banking was arrested in the USA, preserving a much greater role for the originate-and-distribute one than in other countries. The originate-and-distribute model was then refined and developed in the USA so that it

[2] Patrick Harverson, 'Profit matters most now', 2nd May 1989.

reached a new level of sophistication. The operation of the originate-and-distribute model required the support of an entire financial system if it was to be accomplished successfully, which meant an avoidance of undue risk-taking. One example of that was the role played in the USA by credit-rating agencies. When banks provided funds directly to borrowers in the lend-and-hold model they conducted their own assessment of the risks that they were taking, informed by a close and long-term relationship. That relationship did not exist in the originate-and-distribute model through which loans were made through the issue of bills, bonds, and other financial instruments, handled by banks on a transaction by transaction basis. Those purchasing the securities generated under the originate-and-distribute model looked for a degree of reassurance regarding the ability of the borrower to service the debt and then repay on maturity, and this is what the credit-ratings agencies provided. Those who bought the securities generated under the originate-and-distribute model also looked for a means through which subsequent buying and selling took place. What this meant was an increased importance for financial markets as the process did not end after the securities that had been created and sold to investors.[3]

Not only was there a continued reliance upon the use of bills and bonds within the US financial system but banks themselves turned to a process known as securitization. With securitization existing loans were repackaged and either sold to investors, with credit-ratings agencies on hand to provide investors with the reassurance they required. After each crisis securitization grew in popularity both within the USA and around the world because it provided the solution to a bank as to how to increase profits and reduce risks. David Lascelles observed in 1986 that 'Banks are in the process of becoming altered creatures: deal-makers rather than loan-makers, and this raises all sorts of questions to do with their management, culture and regulation... Although this prospect is undoubtedly exciting, an honest banker will admit that nobody has yet fully grasped its implications, which must extend into the next century.'[4] The conversion of loans into marketable securities reduced exposure to borrower defaults if sold, while releasing additional funds for lending, allowing the business done by the bank to be expanded and further profits generated. If the securitized assets were retained by the bank they now existed in a form which made them easy to sell. The result was to provide a bank with greater protection from the increased solvency and liquidity risks that existed after 1970. Writing in 1991 Simon London reported on the 'changing relationships between banks and borrowers and the evolution of new styles of lending'.[5] The financial crisis of the early 1990s revealed the risks that the lend-and-hold model exposed banks to when holding property as collateral, and provided a further incentive towards a switch to the originate-and-distribute model. Banking regulators encouraged this switch seeing the combination of the originate-and-distribute model and securitization as a way of simultaneously increasing the stability of the banking system without the necessity of reducing the level of overall lending, and so dampen economic growth. While the originate-and-distribute model had been growing in popularity around the world after 1970 it was the crisis of the early 1990s that led to its greatly increased

[3] Simon London, 'Captains of industry search for impeccable ratings', 9th January 1991; David Lascelles, 'Reforms fail to keep pace with changes in the markets', 24th May 1991; David Barchard, 'Cut-throat business', 24th May 1991; Patrick Harverson, 'Back to normal after scares over prepayment risks', 19th June 1991; Bob Vincent, 'Market impetus drives through the credit crunch', 19th June 1991; John Plender, 'Uncertainty in a stable world', 22nd July 1992.

[4] David Lascelles, 'A time to map new strategies', 22nd May 1986; cf. John Plender, 'The risk of conglomerates slipping through the net', 25th September 1985; David Lascelles, 'The stampede to become global players', 2nd April 1986; John Plender, 'The dangers of deregulation', 9th May 1986.

[5] Simon London, 'Captains of industry search for impeccable ratings', 9th January 1991.

adoption. Forgotten in the process was the requirement to ensure that the securitized assets created as a result required markets if they were to possess the liquidity that their holders wanted, as this was left to the banks that had produced them in the first place. There was a growing confidence that banks were in a position to do this because of changes that were taking place within the structure of banking both within the USA and around the world.

At the same time as the popularity of the originate-and-distribute model and securitization process was spreading from the USA, that country was moving towards adopting both nationwide branch banking and universal banking. The prohibition on interstate banking, for example, was relaxed in the face of the crisis facing the savings and loans institutions. With greater volatility of interest rates after 1970, and the increased competition for savings, these institutions were caught between the fixed-interest rate charged on mortgage loans and the variable one paid to depositors, with some facing bankruptcy as a result. In response the government allowed out-of-state banks to acquire those likely to fail and then continue to operate them. The result was the slow emergence of nationwide branch banking. At the same time individual US states, including New York, had begun relaxing some of the more strict provisions imposed by the Glass–Steagall Act. Though it had to dispose of its retail branch network in 1977 the New York-based Bankers Trust, for example, began making long-term loans using short-term funds raised in the wholesale money market. These funds were then repackaged as bonds and sold to investors. In 1986 another New York commercial bank, Morgan Guaranty, merged its commercial and investment banking operations into a single corporate finance group. Conversely, Merrill Lynch, which had begun as a brokerage house, began offering customers in the 1970s an interest-bearing account and a means of making payment and obtaining credit. This was a direct challenge to the commercial banks, which were prohibited from paying interest above a regulatory maximum, dealing in stocks, and operating nationwide. By 1985 Merrill Lynch had converted itself into a bank in all but name with its money-fund account attracting 1.3m users. As yet these were only small chinks in the regulations that prohibited nationwide banking in the USA and prevented the combination of retail and investment banking operations. Elsewhere in the world banking was already moving in this direction with nationwide branch banks diversifying into the whole range of financial services while universal banks, which already offered the whole range, were spreading their operations through an expanding network of branches. Under these circumstances the largest US banks, especially those located in New York, the world's most important financial centre, looked abroad as a means of both evading domestic restrictions and a way of expanding the business that they did by attracting new customers.[6]

It was after 1970 that global banking became firmly established. Though there had long existed banks with offices and even branches located around the world most international banking was conducted through correspondent links. Under this system a bank in one country had a formal arrangement with others elsewhere in the world, through which it and its customers could make and receive payments, borrow and lend money, and exchange currencies. However, the huge advances made in both international communications and

[6] Paul Taylor, 'Major banks spearhead era of massive re-organisation', 21st May 1984; Margaret Hughes, 'Quest for new sources of finance', 29th May 1984; Paul Taylor, 'Bankers Trust breaks ranks—again', 15th July 1985; John Plender, 'Hard to pull off gracefully', 20th December 1985; David Lascelles, 'Global wrestling match hots up', 11th April 1986; John Plender, 'Deregulation gains that add up to zero', 29th August 1985; John Plender, 'Hard to pull off gracefully', 20th December 1985; David Lascelles, 'The stampede to become global players', 2nd April 1986; Bernard Simon, 'Obstacles yet to be surmounted', 28th November 1986; David Lascelles, 'Shift is mixed blessing', 28th November 1986; Clive Wolman, 'Shearson bounces back after its Big Bang shake-out', 8th November 1988.

the organization and management of multinational businesses was creating the possibility of global banking. In a global bank, correspondent relationships were internalized within the branch network with the full range of activities being managed centrally. Such banks were in increasing demand from multinational companies who looked to a single organization to provide them with the full range of services rather than rely on a multiplicity of different banks. Similar pressures were coming from large institutional investors who managed complex portfolios spread across different financial instruments and countries. Their needs were best met by banks with proven experience, a depth of resources, a range of expertise, and extensive branch networks. This favoured a combination of branch banking, as operated within many countries around the world that had followed the UK pattern, with universal banking, as practised in countries like Germany and Switzerland, rather than the more specialized systems found in the USA. Leading the movement towards global banking were the largest US banks. In the increasingly competitive environment that existed from 1970 onwards the largest commercial and investment banks in the USA recognized that they had to respond to the diverse needs of their customers if they were to retain their loyalty. The solution found by a number was to locate certain activities outside the reach of the US authorities, with London being a favoured location. In London a US commercial bank could expand into investment banking while an investment bank could follow the opposite direction. Having opened branches abroad it was then a short step to providing the service offered to US corporate customers to those from other countries, operating out of a London office.[7] In 1986 William Schreyer, chairman of the US investment bank, Merrill Lynch, claimed that 'No longer can we fool ourselves and say we're a US firm and the US is what counts. We have all to think in terms of a one-world market.'[8]

A US bank with a London branch could provide its customers with the full range of financial services.[9] In 1985 John Plender observed that London had become 'the adventure playground of the international banking system, in which foreign financial institutions can experiment with all the business and product combinations that are off-limits back at home'.[10] On the back of this international expansion, and using London as a base but with branches strategically placed around the world, US banks could leverage the advantages that a huge domestic market and direct access to the world's currency, the US$, provided them with. This made them highly competitive, forcing banks in other countries to respond or experience a loss of business from their largest customers. One of Britain's largest nationwide banks, the Midland, attempted to respond by acquiring the US commercial bank, Crocker National, in the 1980s, for example, but this was a disaster. It left the Midland with a portfolio of poorly performing loans and huge losses, forcing it to sell out to Wells Fargo Bank in 1986. The Midland was eventually acquired by HSBC.[11] A number of British merchant banks also attempted to establish themselves in New York in the 1980s but they lacked the scale required as well as the expertise necessary to navigate the complexities of US legislation.[12] What was happening in the 1970s and 1980s was the emergence of a small

[7] Dominique Jackson, 'Private investors are regaining confidence', 20th August 1988; John Edwards, 'Profiting from a small outlay', 20th August 1988.

[8] Barry Riley, 'London's the third leg of our stool', 27th October 1986.

[9] David Lascelles and Stephen Fidler, 'Morgan Stanley sticks to equities', 29th February 1987.

[10] John Plender, 'The risk of conglomerates slipping through the net', 25th September 1985.

[11] David Lascelles, 'Selectivity, not size', 2nd October 1986; David Lascelles, 'How Midland was struck by a Californian earthquake', 25th January 1988; David Lascelles, 'Midland storm-troopers fight to stem soaring losses', 27th January 1988.

[12] David Lascelles, 'Wall St lures UK merchant banks', 27th February 1985; David Lascelles, 'Morgan takes a flyer', 18th June 1986; David Lascelles, 'An enigma with a shrewd view of how to use capital', 15th December 1986.

number of megabanks that were able to offer both a universal and a global service, and it was an elite group from the USA that were best placed to do this. In addition to these US banks, also well positioned were a number of European universal banks, especially Credit Suisse and UBS from Switzerland and Deutsche Bank from Germany, as they already possessed the experience of being able to combine commercial and investment banking. Japanese banks were hampered by their own version of the Glass–Steagall Act, imposed on that country at the end of the Second World War, though there was no restraint on nationwide branch banking. This left them without the experience of universal banking and lacking the advantages possessed by US banks of operating on the basis of the US$ and a vast domestic market. Nevertheless, Japanese banks also expanded internationally using London as a base from which they could conduct a diversified business. These included brokerage houses like Nomura, that were then able to respond to the need of Japanese companies for a wider range of banking facilities.[13] These emerging megabanks were willing to invest huge amounts in staff and equipment in order to support their assault on the world market, which made them very competitive both within their own countries and internationally, slowly destabilizing banking systems around the world during the 1970s and 1980s.[14]

However, it would be a mistake to exaggerate the degree of change taking place in banking around the world in the 1970s and 1980s or attribute it mostly to the competition coming from the USA, and the examples that developments there provided. It took a long time for the controls and compartmentalization built up since the Second World War to be dismantled, especially as numerous external and internal barriers to financial flows and competition remained. What this meant was that the change that took place, or the lack of it, was largely the product of forces internal to countries over those years, with the consequences of globalization being largely delayed to the 1990s and beyond. This can be seen in the case of the UK which was not only a country most exposed to influences from the USA

[13] Barry Riley, 'Living by their wits without privileges', 29th May 1984; Margaret Hughes, 'Sector receives fresh lease of life', 29th May 1984; Maggie Urry, 'Profitability on the horizon', 12th September 1984; Barry Riley, 'Increased emphasis placed on taking a global view', 7th December 1984; Barry Riley, 'Cross-border phenomenon', 7th December 1984; Barry Riley, 'More aggression shown on a broader front', 18th November 1985; Barry Riley, 'It's going to be like New York', 3rd July 1986; Drexel Burnham Lambert Advertisement, 27th October 1986; David Lascelles and Stephen Fidler, 'Morgan Stanley sticks to equities', 29th February 1987; Alexander Nicoll, 'Agreement among rivals', 19th March 1987; Alexander Nicoll, 'Warning signs in global game', 21st April 1987; Stephen Fidler, 'More than a mere slogan', 7th May 1987; Alexander Nicoll, 'The rocky road to a global village', 27th May 1987; David Lascelles, 'Through the pain barrier', 21st September 1987; David Lascelles, 'New strengths and a ticket to the City's turf', 21st September 1987; David Lascelles, 'Thrive, merge or specialise', 21st September 1987; David Lascelles, 'Clearers look overseas', 21st September 1987; Alexander Nicoll, 'Liffe in search of greater liquidity', 30th September 1987; David Lascelles, 'Banking on an international status', 3rd November 1987; Deborah Hargreaves, 'Hybrids fight to escape regulation', 9th December 1987; Deborah Hargreaves, 'Regulators seek to protect retail customer in battle of look-alikes', 10th March 1988; Stephen Fidler, 'A force more respected than loved', 11th May 1988; John Paul Lee, 'Technology demonstrates its worth', 18th May 1988; Peter Montagnon, 'Securitisation can often be the key to the future', 18th May 1988; Steven Butler, 'Investment banks cash in on volatile oil prices', 1st July 1988; David Lascelles, 'Specialise if you're not a global player', 26th September 1988; Sean Heath, 'City's stability appreciated', 26th September 1988; Paul Taylor, 'Blow, not knockout', 28th September 1988; Janet Bush, 'Five banks with universal plans', 2nd May 1989; David Lascelles, 'Questions over the City's future', 22nd December 1989; David Lascelles, 'Cautious steps in the merchant bank forest', 2nd January 1990; Deborah Hargreaves, 'Chicago exchanges at variance', 9th March 1990; David Lascelles, 'The London cavern is the hub for Europe', 5th June 1990; Andrew Freeman, 'Tokyo institutions build up derivatives expertise', 25th July 1990; Martin Dickson, 'Now the Swiss call the shots', 17th December 1990; Tracy Corrigan, 'Treasurers learn to hedge their bets', 28th March 1991; Richard Waters, 'Intermediaries warned of tough challenges', 24th April 1991; Tracy Corrigan, 'Competition helps cut costs', 29th April 1991; Tracy Corrigan, 'Currency upheaval wins converts', 8th December 1992.

[14] Barry Riley, 'It's going to be like New York', 3rd July 1986; William Cochrane, 'A worldwide acceleration', 13th November 1986; Bernard Simon, 'Obstacles yet to be surmounted', 28th November 1986; Alan Cane, 'Pioneers pay a high price', 3rd December 1987.

but also possessed a financial system that shared many of the same features, especially the use of financial markets.[15] It was not until 1979 that the UK removed exchange controls, and many of the changes stemmed from that decision, as it destroyed the protection enjoyed by the British financial system from external challenges. One result was to remove the separation between banks, which financed businesses through loans, and building societies, which specialized in providing mortgages on property. Both relied on retail deposits gathered from nationwide networks of branches. As competition for these deposits intensified, the rate of interest paid was pushed up, while the move of banks into the mortgages drove down the rate paid by borrowers.[16] By 1986, according to Clive Wolman, building societies faced 'an onslaught from outside competitors on their two traditional markets, for savers' deposits and residential mortgages'.[17] The result was to drive both banks and building societies to contemplate a switch from the lend-and-hold model to the originate-and-distribute one.[18] Maggie Urry picked up on this in 1986:

> The use of the wholesale market to raise funds has contributed to the enormous changes which are sweeping through the building society movement. Quick and flexible access to cheaper and longer-term funds means that societies can function more readily as suppliers of finance to house buyers. But there could be even greater changes to come. Some bankers expect a market to grow up in the sale of mortgages. Building societies could become originators and administrators of mortgages. Working through their branch networks they could find house buyers, lend to them (and provide them with other financial services), and collect mortgage payments, but not hold the mortgages on their own books. By selling mortgages, probably in quite large packages, they could raise further funds to provide yet more home loans.

She added that, 'This has yet to happen in the UK, but it is a distinct possibility in the near future.'[19]

This battle between banks and building societies was a major feature of the British financial scene in the 1980s.[20] As Hugo Dixon put it in 1987, 'The gloves are off, the combatants are in the ring and the fight is about to start.'[21] A year later David Barchard reported that 'banks and building societies have made major inroads into each other's traditional preserves'.[22] Nevertheless, this increasingly competitive environment did not lead to the

[15] Ian Hamilton Fazey, 'The manager still matters', 1st April 1986; Mark Meredith, 'Heed the southern giants', 2nd July 1986; James Buxton, 'Action south of the border', 2nd October 1986; David Lascelles, 'Now it's the Big Five', 2nd October 1986; Nick Bunker, 'Escalating the war', 2nd October 1986.

[16] David Lascelles, 'Huge changes in progress', 21st May 1984; David Lascelles, 'UK mergers bring a conflict of interest', 29th May 1984; Barry Riley, 'Living by their wits without privileges', 29th May 1984; Stefan Wagstyl, 'Ultimate seal of approval', 30th January 1985; *Financial Times* Reporters, 'City well placed to benefit from banking trend', 10th July 1985; Maggie Urry, 'Two good years, now the crunch', 2nd October 1986; Michael Blanden, 'Leading players take the plunge', 2nd October 1986; David Lascelles, 'Now it's the Big Five', 2nd October 1986; Ian Hamilton Fazey, 'Sharper eye kept on progress', 2nd October 1986; William Dawkins, 'Buy-outs bring benefits', 2nd October 1986.

[17] Clive Wolman, 'Pace of game quickens', 8th February 1986.

[18] David Lascelles, 'Sidestepping the Big Bang', 15th January 1986; Clive Wolman, 'Pace of game quickens', 8th February 1986; Maggie Urry, 'Advantage to lending opportunities', 8th February 1986; David Lascelles, 'Rich field for bright ideas', 8th February 1986; Alexander Nicoll, 'Set to play a prime role in markets', 8th February 1986; Maggie Urry, 'Ingenuity of structures seems unlimited', 17th March 1986; Nick Bunker, 'Still evolving from the cartel', 2nd October 1986.

[19] Maggie Urry, 'Advantage to lending opportunities', 8th February 1986.

[20] Nigel Lawson, 'Side effects of deregulation', 27th January 1992.

[21] Hugo Dixon, 'Men of mutuality look to profits', 14th February 1987.

[22] David Barchard, 'Buyers have the whip hand', 23rd April 1988.

abandonment of the lend-and-hold model of banking in the Britain and its replacement by the originate-and-distribute one to any great extent. The UK's banks and building societies possessed the size and scale, with their nationwide operations, to support the lend-and-hold model of banking with only a residual reliance upon wholesale funding or use of securitization. Commenting in 1987 on the repacking of mortgage loans as securities, and their resale to investors, Richard Wheway, the finance director of the largest UK mortgage lender, the Halifax Building Society, stated simply that, 'The conditions for such a market just do not exist in this country as they did in the US.'[23] His assessment proved correct as those mortgage-backed securities in circulation in the UK were issued not by banks or building societies but by specialist finance companies, and these then got into difficulty in the early 1990s.[24] What this illustrated was that, outside the USA, the originate-and-distribute model made slow progress in the 1970s and 1980s because of the fundamental differences in banking systems. Those banks operating through nationwide branch networks or universal banking models could simultaneously tap the supply of savings and demand for loans and match the two internally, supplementing their funds, when required, by borrowing from the wholesale market. The lend-and-hold model involved a long-term relationship between lender and borrower, which securitization would disrupt, and so neither banks nor mortgage providers were keen to repackage loans and sell them on, as long as they were able to satisfy customer demand from retail deposits and wholesale borrowing. Some progress was made in Japan, where securitization offered banks an opportunity to repackage assets and then sell them directly to their own customers and so compete with the brokers. Elsewhere banks still favoured the lend-and-hold model.[25]

Bills and Bonds

One reason for the continuing reliance on the lend-and-hold model outside the USA in the 1970s and 1980s was the lack of deep and broad markets for the financial instruments generated by the originate-and-distribute model, and the implications that had for bank liquidity and solvency at a time of greater instability and volatility. The problem with the originate-and-distribute model was that it relied on the existence of sufficiently active markets to provide liquidity. These were little developed outside the USA before 1990, having slowly declined in importance due to the dominance of the lend-and-hold model and the controls imposed by governments. In the USA a number of different money markets had continued to flourish, benefiting from the restrictions placed on both inter-state and

[23] Clare Pearson, 'Wholesale success by Halifax', 15th July 1987.

[24] Tracy Corrigan and Richard Waters, 'Japan turns to securitisation', 20th March 1991; Simon London, 'The "credit crunch": hard fact or financial fiction', 24th May 1991; Simon London, 'Total amount in issue reaches £10bn', 19th June 1991; Tracy Corrigan, 'Specialist alive and well in nascent market', 19th June 1991; Barry Riley, 'Beginnings of a flight to safety', 24th July 1991; David Barchard, 'House in need of repair', 24th July 1991; Richard Waters, 'Securities industry capital rules move closer', 30th January 1992; John Gapper, 'The equation that didn't add up', 2nd February 1993; Vanessa Houlder, 'Weighed down with debts', 5th March 1993; Robert Peston, 'Silent launch of the lifeboat', 19th October 1993; Richard Waters, 'Talk of mergers is in the air', 12th August 1996.

[25] Norma Cohen, 'A home-loan hurdle', 27th March 1990; Tracy Corrigan and Richard Waters, 'Japan turns to securitisation', 20th March 1991; Simon London, 'The "credit crunch": hard fact or financial fiction', 24th May 1991; David Barchard, 'Cut-throat business', 24th May 1991; George Graham, 'An unusual path', 19th June 1991; Patrick Harverson, 'Back to normal after scares over prepayment risks', 19th June 1991; Bob Vincent, 'Market impetus drives through the credit crunch', 19th June 1991; Bob Vincent, 'Market impetus drives through the credit crunch', 19th June 1991; Tracy Corrigan, 'Europeans edge forward', 19th June 1991; Tracy Corrigan, 'An innovative way of raising money', 20th July 1992; John Plender, 'Uncertainty in a stable world', 22nd July 1992.

universal banking as well as the cap on interest rates. One was the commercial bill market, which grew from $10bn outstanding in 1966 to $322.6bn in 1986. Commercial bills were short-term unsecured promissory notes issued by businesses needing credit. They evaded the interest-rate ceiling imposed on banks and so allowed higher returns to be paid to savers.[26] As large corporations grew in importance, altering the balance between banks and their business customers, a growing number of them issued their own bills which were bought directly by investors. General Motors even formed a subsidiary company for this purpose, the General Motors Acceptance Corporation (GMAC), and this accounted for 10 per cent of the commercial bills in circulation in the USA in 1986. Commercial bills were popular with banks because they were able to closely match the duration of a bill to their liability to repay short-terms loans and so they were normally held until redemption, though the facility did exist to sell them on.[27] However, it was only slowly that the use of bills expanded elsewhere in the world, often meeting opposition from central banks keen to maintain their control over the money supply. The result was to leave these short-term money markets poorly developed outside the USA, even by the end of the 1980s, and so lacking in the depth and breadth that would support the liquidity that banks looked for.[28]

Another product of the unique nature of the US banking system was the existence of a market in mortgage bonds. In most countries the provision of finance for home ownership had become internalized within banks or specialized mortgage institutions, using retail deposits to fund long-term loans at variable rates of interest. Such was not the case in the

[26] David Lascelles, 'Green light for market in UK commercial paper', 30th April 1986; Roderick Oram, 'Banks fight for share of oldest market's growth', 28th November 1986; Peter Montagnon, 'Across the threshold of credibility', 28th November 1986; Alexander Nicoll, 'Europe is watching American programmes', 28th November 1986; Maggie Urry, 'A subtle equation between risk and return', 28th November 1986.

[27] Alexander Nicoll, 'UK commercial paper market on the way', 20th January 1986; Alexander Nicoll, 'Set to play a prime role in markets', 8th February 1986; Alexander Nicoll, 'London hopes for sterling paper market', 14th March 1986; David Lascelles, 'Green light for market in UK commercial paper', 30th April 1986; Barbara Casassus, 'Top-slot turnover has quadrupled', 27th May 1986; Peter Montagnon, 'Caution at the top end', 2nd October 1986; Roderick Oram, 'Banks fight for share of oldest market's growth', 28th November 1986; Stephen Fidler, 'Deregulation aids fledgling markets', 21st April 1987.

[28] Alexander Nicoll, 'UK commercial paper market on the way', 20th January 1986; Alexander Nicoll, 'Set to play a prime role in markets', 8th February 1986; Alexander Nicoll, 'London hopes for sterling paper market', 14th March 1986; David Lascelles, 'Green light for market in UK commercial paper', 30th April 1986; Roderick Oram, 'Banks fight for share of oldest market's growth', 28th November 1986; Stephen Fidler, 'Deregulation aids fledgling markets', 21st April 1987; Stephen Fidler, 'Rising demand for sterling CP', 2nd December 1987; Lisa Martineau, 'The rules need to be eased', 17th February 1988; Haig Simonian, 'Thwarted by the tax', 17th February 1988; Alexander Nicoll, 'Borrowers' confidence grows', 21st April 1987; Stephen Fidler, 'Deregulation aids fledgling markets', 21st April 1987; Michael Blanden, 'A chance to move in on the stock market', 21st September 1987; Stephen Fidler, 'Rising demand for sterling CP', 2nd December 1987; Janet Bush, 'A fragile monopoly', 17th February 1988; Alexander Nicoll, 'Confidence is growing though snags remain', 17th February 1988; David Waller, 'Three-way benefits', 17th February 1988; Alexander Nicoll, 'Profit for the few', 17th February 1988; Dominic Hobson, 'Wide appeal', 17th February 1988; Stephen Fidler, 'Europe slower to lighten balance sheets', 17th February 1988; Clare Pearson, 'Less fashionable, still useful', 17th February 1988; Alexander Nicoll, 'Higher risk, greater reward', 17th February 1988; Dominic Hobson, 'How the Continentals beat London on its home ground', 17th February 1988; Clare Pearson, 'A healthy niche operation', 17th February 1988; Lisa Martineau, 'The rules need to be eased', 17th February 1988; Haig Simonian, 'Thwarted by the tax', 17th February 1988; Bruce Jacques, 'Bonds shortage whets appetites', 17th February 1988; David Owen, 'Banks close the gap', 17th February 1988; George Graham, 'In need of ratings', 17th February 1988; Peter Montagnon, 'Securitisation can often be the key to the future', 18th May 1988; Stephen Fidler, 'Great leap forward', 29th June 1988; Dominic Hobson, 'Four banks dominate the market', 25th July 1988; David Lascelles, 'City sticks to a paper standard', 3rd August 1988; David Housego, 'A bull market far from being tamed', 20th December 1988; Katharine Campbell and Deborah Hargreaves, 'Bund futures force pace of change', 4th May 1990; Stephen Fidler, 'Money brokers step into the financial limelight', 22nd November 1990; Tracy Corrigan, 'Borrowers rush to tap newly-opened Paris market', 13th March 1991; Tracy Corrigan and Richard Waters, 'Japan turns to securitisation', 20th March 1991; David Owen, 'Old credit routes are back', 23rd May 1991; Christopher Parkes and David Waller, 'Politics comes to the Finanzplatz', 24th January 1992.

USA where funds were provided by numerous local savings and loans institutions at fixed rates of interest. These loans were repackaged, being often grouped with others into a portfolio, which was then labelled a bond, floating note, or other financial instrument, and sold to investors looking for returns higher than those obtained from a bank. This instrument could be subsequently traded. Securitization benefited the bank or mortgage provider, as it was free to go ahead with new lending using the receipts from the sale of the loan; the purchaser, who acquired a high quality marketable security; and the borrower, who received a more flexible loan with a lower rate of interest. It was also viewed favourably by regulators as a contribution to greater liquidity as a market in debt was created, so liberating the assets trapped in the lend-and-hold model. With these advantages and recommendations the practice of securitizing mortgage loans was then applied to other forms of debt.[29] Patrick Henderson, writing in 1989, described what was happening: 'Assets such as mortgages, credit-card, corporate and sovereign loans will be increasingly traded by banks on secondary markets in the search for a better return on assets.'[30] Despite concerns that borrowers would default on payments, securitization grew rapidly in the USA. By 1988 Stephen Fidler noted that 'The creation of securities out of financial assets, such as mortgage loans and credit card receivables, has been an important part of the changing face of financial markets in the 1980s.'[31] By then one-fifth of US mortgages had been securitized. Overall, the value of asset-backed securities in circulation in the USA hit $1,000bn in 1990. Though nominally liquid these securitized assets were little traded as their duration and security matched the requirements of long-term investors such as insurance companies and pension funds, though they were also held by banks, using a mixture of retail deposits and borrowing in the wholesale market to finance their purchases.[32]

Neither commercial bills nor mortgage bonds possessed the active markets that US banks required to safeguard against a sudden liquidity crisis, but US Treasury bills and bonds did. Trading in US Treasury bonds was conducted in enormous volume at tiny spreads over the telephone, either directly between banks or through specialist brokers, with the Federal Reserve Bank of New York providing settlement facilities. There was also a repurchase, or repo, facility through which a sale was accompanied by an agreement, specifying the price and date for repurchasing the Treasury bond. The result was a highly liquid market with a daily turnover of $100bn by 1988.[33] This volume of trading was sufficiently great to support a 24-hour market, making it attractive to banks wherever they were located, supported by the importance of the US$, which had become the world's vehicle currency for inter-bank transactions. Writing in 1987 Roderick Cram referred to the US Treasury Bill market as 'the largest, and most liquid, securities market in the world, with some $2,100bn of outstanding issues'.[34] Donal Magrath, from the United Bank of Kuwait,

[29] Stephen Fidler, 'Bank points to blurred boundaries', 8th February 1990.

[30] Patrick Harverson, 'Profit matters most now', 2nd May 1989.

[31] Stephen Fidler, 'Europe slower to lighten balance sheets', 17th February 1988.

[32] Alexander Nicoll, 'UK commercial paper market on the way', 20th January 1986; Alexander Nicoll, 'Set to play a prime role in markets', 8th February 1986; Alexander Nicoll, 'London hopes for sterling paper market', 14th March 1986; David Lascelles, 'Green light for market in UK commercial paper', 30th April 1986; Roderick Oram, 'Banks fight for share of oldest market's growth', 28th November 1986; Stephen Fidler, 'Bank points to blurred boundaries', 8th February 1990; Tracy Corrigan and Richard Waters, 'Japan turns to securitisation', 20th March 1991; Patrick Harverson, 'Back to normal after scares over prepayment risks', 19th June 1991; Tracy Corrigan, 'Europeans edge forward', 19th June 1991.

[33] Richard Lambert, 'Questions for the Gilt-Edged Market', 18th April 1984; David Lascelles, 'The backroom gets ready for Big Bang', 15th January 1986; David Lascelles, 'Round-the-clock bankers', 9th April 1986; Barry Riley, 'Strangers at the gilt-edged gate', 28th July 1986; Barry Riley, 'A big leap predicted', 27th October 1986.

[34] Roderick Oram, 'Japanese established as traders', 21st April 1987—see David Lascelles and Roderick Oram, 'Key link added to a global chain', 3rd March 1987.

explained in 1991 that 'We have about $2bn of funds under management, of which about eighty per cent are bonds such as US Treasuries. We aim to enhance the return on the portfolio by lending these out.'[35] What the existence of this repo facility in US Treasury bonds provided dealers with was certainty. Those selling bonds could deliver them by borrowing what they did not own. Those buying bonds could pay for them by borrowing, using them as collateral, if they lacked the means to do so. That situation contributed enormously to the liquidity of the US Treasury market as there were always ready buyers and sellers.[36] No other government debt market could match the liquidity of that of the USA. This was caused by either a lack of suitable issues, high taxes, restrictive regulations, or poorly developed markets. Changes were taking place during the 1980s onwards but nothing on a scale that could match that of the US Treasury market.[37] Large as the UK's government debt market was, for example, its turnover was estimated at £1bn per day in the 1980s. UK government debt was also denominated in £s, which was becoming of minor importance as a global currency. It was also under the influence of the Bank of England, which impeded progress towards the development of a repo facility on the grounds that it would damage the control it could exercise.[38] Generally, the intervention of governments and central banks prevented the development of broad and deep money markets capable of matching that provided by US Treasuries in New York. What was apparent in the 1970s and 1980s was that only the USA possessed the conditions required to support highly liquid domestic money markets, as they were a product of both the size and nature of its economy and the way that legislation had moulded its banking system.[39]

It was the existence of these markets that supported the popularity of the originate-and-distribute model of banking in the USA, while their absence discouraged such a move elsewhere in the world. Without such markets banks were left with unmarketable assets,

[35] Sara Webb, 'Repo traders fight their corner', 24th July 1991.

[36] Andrew Freeman, 'When clients ask for more', 20th February 1989; Andrew Freeman, 'Secondary market moves into first place', 7th June 1990; Simon London, 'Secretive market set to enter the spotlight', 26th September 1990; Stephen Fidler, 'Money brokers step into the financial limelight', 22nd November 1990; Sara Webb, 'Repo traders fight their corner', 24th July 1991; Andrew Freeman, 'Cross-border lending now big business', 24th September 1991; Sara Webb and Peter Montagnon, 'Losing its lustre', 27th November 1991; Tracy Corrigan, 'Dull can be dynamic', 27th May 1993; Philip Gawith and Richard Lapper, 'The new kid in the City', 1st March 1996; Richard Lapper, 'Clarifying a complicated subject', 1st March 1996; Graham Bowley, 'Troubled road to reform', 1st March 1996; Conner Middelmann, 'Domestic market is struggling', 1st March 1996; Norma Cohen, 'Learning lessons from the US', 1st March 1996; Andrew Jack, 'More liquid than London', 1st March 1996; Samer Iskandar, 'Safer lending of securities', 5th December 1997; Samer Iskandar, 'Definitions of a new financial instrument', 5th December 1997.

[37] Barry Riley, 'A question of survival', 26th October 1988; Katharine Campbell, 'Liffe dilemma for German banks', 19th January 1989; Michiyo Nakamoto, 'Domestic market loses out', 13th March 1989; Tracy Corrigan, 'Investors attracted by firmer currency', 2nd July 1990; David Lascelles, 'Reforms progressing slowly', 9th July 1990; Haig Simonian, 'Playing a waiting game in Milan', 11th July 1990; Tracy Corrigan, 'The syndicate disbands', 13th December 1990.

[38] P. M. Elstob, 'UK links with Tokyo houses', 14th February 1984; David Lascelles, 'System more accessible to outsiders', 19th March 1984; Alexander Nicoll, 'Hesitant steps on road to success', 11th December 1985; Barbara Casassus, 'Top-slot turnover has quadrupled', 27th May 1986; Sara Webb, 'Repo traders fight their corner', 24th July 1991.

[39] Richard Lambert, 'Questions for the Gilt-Edged Market', 18th April 1984; Barry Riley, 'A tough battle for survival', 10th July 1985; David Lascelles, 'The backroom gets ready for Big Bang', 15th January 1986; Alexander Nicoll, 'UK commercial paper market on the way', 20th January 1986; Alexander Nicoll, 'Set to play a prime role in markets', 8th February 1986; Alexander Nicoll, 'London hopes for sterling paper market', 14th March 1986; Barry Riley, 'Strangers at the gilt-edged gate', 28th July 1986; Clive Wolman, 'A shake-up in gilts', 2nd October 1986; Peter Montagnon, 'Caution at the top end', 2nd October 1986; Barry Riley, 'A big leap predicted', 27th October 1986; *Financial Times*, 'Investing in bonds: now back in favour', 9th November 1998; Edward Luce, 'Bankers and Brussels at odds over impact on London', 9th December 1998; Ivar Simensen, 'Branching out from their German roots', 29th November 2004.

exposing them to a liquidity crisis.[40] Liquidity was a perennial issue for banks and the problem with many of the new financial instruments being issued was that they lacked established markets through which they could be readily traded. Annual turnover in London's Eurocommercial bill market, for example, was estimated at only 5 per cent of the total outstanding in 1988, and these were among the most liquid of such securities. Many bills were little traded and so were almost as illiquid as the loans that underpinned them. The normal practice among investors was to hold bills and notes to maturity, matching assets with liabilities, as most were of short duration. The growing trend towards bank mergers encouraged this approach through the increased ability to match assets and liabilities internally.[41] This lack of liquidity also extended to many corporate bonds, and those financial instruments created through securitization. This was despite the efforts made by the bank issuing them to ensure that a secondary market did exist once they had been taken up by investors, including a commitment to repurchase them. Failing repurchase by banks, holders needing to sell were often reliant on brokers, who would attempt to arrange sales and purchases using their extensive network of contacts among potential investors. Even in the USA there was no public market for many of the smaller corporate issues while in many countries the whole corporate bond market was illiquid because of the entrenched position of the banks and a combination of taxes and laws. The Swiss bond market was small and illiquid, suffering from a tax on transactions. In Japan businesses had strong and lasting relationships with particular banks, and so continued to rely upon them for finance, while the alternative of issuing bonds faced legal restrictions that pushed up costs and reduced access. In some economies, such as Argentina, corporate bond issues were limited because the government absorbed what demand there was for financial instruments of this kind. Out of the global total of bonds in circulation in 1988, valued at $9,400bn, only a small number met all the criteria required to generate liquidity and then not all the time.[42]

A substitute for domestic bond markets was the London-based Eurobond market. Though its initial attractions lay in its ability to bypass the taxes and controls imposed by national governments, especially that of the US authorities on the use of the dollar, its popularity grew as the concentration of trading generated a degree of liquidity greater than most domestic markets. In 1988 David Lascelles claimed that, 'The UK's domestic markets are neither as big nor as important internationally as the Euromarkets, also based in London.'[43] A Eurobond was a debt security issued outside the country of the currency in which it is denominated. The most common Eurobonds were denominated in US$s and were issued in London, where they were not subject to the controls and taxes imposed by the US government. The first issue of a Eurobond took place in the late 1950s but, as the

[40] Stephen Fidler, 'Great leap forward', 29th June 1988; Tracy Corrigan, 'Borrowers rush to tap newly-opened Paris market', 13th March 1991; David Owen, 'Old credit routes are back', 23rd May 1991; Simon London, 'A squeeze in the interbank loans market', 16th October 1991; Robert Corzine, 'Executives attempt to stretch Swift's wings', 4th December 1991; Simon London, 'Slower pace pleases dealers', 27th March 1992; James Blitz, 'A top-hat tradition in the balance', 22nd June 1992.

[41] Stephen Fidler, 'Great leap forward', 29th June 1988; Tracy Corrigan, 'Borrowers rush to tap newly-opened Paris market', 13th March 1991; David Owen, 'Old credit routes are back', 23rd May 1991; Simon London, 'A squeeze in the interbank loans market', 16th October 1991; Robert Corzine, 'Executives attempt to stretch Swift's wings', 4th December 1991; Simon London, 'Slower pace pleases dealers', 27th March 1992; James Blitz, 'A top-hat tradition in the balance', 22nd June 1992.

[42] Tracy Corrigan, 'Finland opens doors to foreign investment', 11th January 1991; John Barham, 'Argentine dealers glimpse the future', 1st March 1991; George Graham, 'In the front rank in Europe', 17th June 1991; Simon London, 'Recession spurs bonds', 11th November 1991; Ian Rodger, 'This difficult year', 17th December 1991; Haig Simonian, 'Italians chase a futures fast track', 20th March 1992; Simon London, 'Slower pace pleases dealers', 27th March 1992.

[43] David Lascelles, 'City sticks to a paper standard', 3rd August 1988.

US$ became the preferred currency for international transactions, the volume of those in circulation expanded rapidly through the 1960s and 1970s. What these Eurobonds initially lacked was a market in which they could be bought and sold. Without such a market Eurobonds were less attractive to investors, as they had to be held until redemption, and possessed no mechanism for generating current prices, which was essential if they were to be used as collateral. A liquid secondary market was increasingly important for institutional investors as they adopted a strategy of generating returns by locking in capital gains through regular trading rather than the interest paid on long-term investment. That market developed during the 1970s and 1980s through direct dealing between banks and the activities of a group of interdealer brokers, who acted as intermediaries. Assisting the growth of the market was the formation of the Association of International Bond Dealers in 1969, with a head office in Zurich, as this provided the market with a set of rules and regulations. At the same time the establishment of Euroclear in Brussels in 1968 and Cedel in Luxembourg in 1970 provided the Eurobond market with a mechanism for dealing with transfers and counterparty risk. The result was a market that grew in volume and sophistication and so met the needs of the banks for certainty and liquidity.[44]

Even with the disappearance of exchange controls the popularity of Eurobonds remained because of differential taxation. The US withholding tax, for example, separated the domestic from the international bond market in the USA despite the use of the US$ for both. Because of the tax-free and bearer nature of Eurobonds US corporate borrowers could often borrow more cheaply from US banks in London than domestically. A similar position applied in Japan and, once free access to the international Euro-Yen market was permitted. Japanese borrowers, including companies and the government itself, also turned to them as a cheaper and more flexible source of finance, despite the abundance of domestic savings. The international debt crisis of 1982, which exposed the risks associated with syndicated lending as borrowers defaulted and banks were left with assets which produced no return and could not be sold, encouraged a switch to Eurobonds. Writing in 1985 John Makinson praised the Eurobond market for being 'cheap and efficient' but criticized it because it 'is almost entirely unregulated'.[45] It was this lack of government regulation that had made the Eurobond Market so attractive to banks before the 1980s but, subsequently, as the restrictions were removed and taxes harmonized, it retained its popularity because it had evolved into a liquid market in which the issues of regulation, transfers, and counterparty risk had been addressed. This meant it continued to be used by a mixture of governments and companies. Though many Eurobond issues were too small to generate active markets the overall market had an annual turnover of about $5tn by 1987, with trading taking place over the telephone, and often involved complex deals as brokers attempted to match buyers and sellers across price, instrument, currency, delivery dates, and other variables. Once the trade was completed virtually all transactions were then processed through the clearing systems maintained by Euroclear and Cedel. One indication of the continuing growth of

[44] Peter Montagnon, 'Profound changes in culture', 19th March 1984; Mary Ann Sieghart, 'Increasing reliance on innovation as market declines', 19th March 1984; David Lascelles, 'System more accessible to outsiders', 19th March 1984; Barry Riley, 'Equities develop global market', 23rd November 1983; Barry Riley, 'A unique global background', 3rd July 1986; Peter Montagnon, 'Pragmatic approach to City rules', 27th October 1986; David Lascelles, 'A propitious moment for the Bang', 27th October 1986; Bernard Simon, 'Obstacles yet to be surmounted', 28th November 1986; Stephen Fidler, 'A force more respected than loved', 11th May 1988; Andrew Freeman, 'Cross-border lending now big business', 24th September 1991.

[45] John Makinson, 'Advance of the Euroequity', 2nd November 1985.

the Eurobond market in the 1980s was that turnover on Cedel alone rose from $80.3bn in 1980 to $1,720bn in 1988.[46]

Foreign Exchange

Another market that boomed after 1970 was that for foreign exchange. There was a gradual build-up of foreign exchange trading after the Second World War but the explosion in the market came with the end of fixed exchange rates in the early 1970s. Following the move to floating exchange rates there was a boom in currency trading by the major international banks as they rushed to cover their positions by swapping commitments with each other. Those banks with extensive international connections were the main players, trading huge volumes of currency spot and forward in large individual amounts both for themselves and on behalf of smaller banks. As the US$ was the world's dominant currency US banks were the key players in this emerging foreign exchange market. However, those trading from New York faced restrictions on their freedom to operate in the foreign exchange market, as well as an unfavourable time zone location. Increasingly the centre of this market was London which also enjoyed a favourable location between Asia and the Americas. Trading in both New York and Tokyo was most active when each overlapped with London. Such was the depth and breadth of this London-centred foreign exchange market that it survived a major shock in 1974 with the collapse of the German Bankhaus Herstatt. That bank had been paid for currency that it had not yet delivered by the time it suspended operations. This exposed the risks in a 24-hour market in which payments and receipts were not instantly matched because of time-zone differences. In response banks themselves quickly devised ways of coping with counterparty risk, especially as the business was concentrated in the hands of a small number of active players.[47]

Daily turnover in the foreign exchange market rose from around $5bn a day in 1973 to $25bn in 1979. In the face of continuing currency volatility in the 1980s, combined with increasing trade and international investment, activity in the foreign exchange market expanded rapidly. By the 1980s the foreign exchange market had become an essential tool used by banks to match their assets and liabilities across currencies both for present and future commitments. It was also made use of by multinational corporations when managing their internal financial flows. At the same time a number of large banks saw the foreign exchange market as a profit-making opportunity by acting as counterparties to foreign exchange transactions made by others, which helped to drive up turnover.[48] By 1986 the

[46] Alexander Nicoll, 'Firms seek benefits of automation', 8th January 1987; Boris Sedacca, 'New trade-matching system launched', 10th November 1988; Simon Holberton, 'How hedging can help to trim the risk', 28th November 1988; Deborah Hargreaves, 'Value of Cedel deposits surges', 2nd January 1990; Andrew Freeman, 'AIBD rule fuels bond clearers row', 25th January 1990; Andrew Freeman, 'Weakness of Tokyo equities punishes Eurobond market', 2nd July 1990; Andrew Freeman, 'Eurobonds ride crest of a wave', 2nd August 1990; Clay Harris, '"Trailblazer" with vision for London's future', 8th November 1997; Daniel Dombey, 'Lack of growth signals need for reinvention', 7th June 2001; Daniel Dombey, 'Transatlantic invasion keeps industry thriving', 7th June 2001; Ivar Simensen, 'Inaugural issuer back after 40 years', 27th May 2004.

[47] Peter Montagnon, 'Novel offerings bring fresh edge to competition', 14th February 1984; Terry Dodsworth, 'Master of the game no longer', 27th May 1986; Barbara Casassus, 'Top-slot turnover has quadrupled', 27th May 1986; Jim McCallum, 'End of controls provides a lift', 11th November 1991; Ian Rodger, 'London is now a banker bet for the Swiss', 2nd December 1992.

[48] Peter Montagnon, 'Novel offerings bring fresh edge to competition', 14th February 1984; Alan Cane, 'Information systems play an integral role', 14th February 1984; Godfrey Hodgson, 'The race is on for the universal terminal', 28th November 1984; Raymond Snoddy, 'An information revolution', 24th March 1986; David Lascelles, 'A New York-Tokyo–London axis', 7th April 1986; Nicholas Colchester, 'A heavyweight sheds pounds',

average daily turnover was \$0.2tn, and this rose to \$0.9tn a day in 1992. Trading involving the US\$ dominated turnover was increasingly concentrated among the largest banks, as they were the most trusted counterparties, and in a few financial centres, which contained the deepest pools of liquidity. London was the most important of these, dominating the European time zone and attracting the business of US banks, which conducted much of their international trading out of London, where they had established international dealing rooms. New York was next in importance, dominating the Americas time zone. Though Tokyo was the most important Asian centre it was losing out to Singapore and Hong Kong. The development of the foreign exchange market in Tokyo was hampered by restrictions imposed by the Japanese government. Banks were prevented from directly participating in the foreign exchange market until 1985, for example, being forced to trade through the *tanshi*, or money brokers, who charged high commission rates. Even after that requirement was removed there remained a ban on Japanese securities houses directly participating in the foreign exchange market.[49]

Supporting the growth of a global 24-hour/7-day a week market were developments in both dealing technology and communications systems. Those banks that played a central role in the money and foreign exchange markets needed to keep in constant contact with their major trading partners. For that reason they were quick to adopt those technological advances that provided them with constantly updated prices. The major breakthrough came in 1973 when the news and information provider, Reuters, introduced its Monitor terminals with screens displaying foreign exchange rates with transactions taking place via the telephone.[50] The most significant feature of the 1980s was the development of interactive dealing systems. By 1986 Reuters hosted a network of 17,000 subscribers worldwide connected through 54,000 screens. The largest banks and brokers were in a position to trade foreign exchange between each other either via these terminals or through the

8th April 1986; George Graham, 'Rowing with the tide', 22nd May 1986; George Graham, 'Mercurial times in the market', 27th May 1986; Colin Millham, 'Caution is entering the market', 27th May 1986; Barbara Casassus, 'Top-slot turnover has quadrupled', 27th May 1986; Terry Dodsworth, 'Master of the game no longer', 27th May 1986; David Lascelles, 'An established profit centre', 27th May 1986; Jeffrey Brown, 'Major players in their own right', 27th May 1986; Alan Cane, 'Increasing quality and speed in dealing rooms', 27th May 1986; Richard Lambert, 'More products now need round-the-clock trading', 27th October 1986.

[49] Peter Montagnon, 'Novel offerings bring fresh edge to competition', 14th February 1984; Alan Cane, 'Information systems play an integral role', 14th February 1984; Godfrey Hodgson, 'The race is on for the universal terminal', 28th November 1984; Raymond Snoddy, 'An information revolution', 24th March 1986; David Lascelles, 'A New York-Tokyo–London axis', 7th April 1986; Nicholas Colchester, 'A heavyweight sheds pounds', 8th April 1986; George Graham, 'Rowing with the tide', 22nd May 1986; George Graham, 'Mercurial times in the market', 27th May 1986; Colin Millham, 'Caution is entering the market', 27th May 1986; Barbara Casassus, 'Top-slot turnover has quadrupled', 27th May 1986; Terry Dodsworth, 'Master of the game no longer', 27th May 1986; David Lascelles, 'An established profit centre', 27th May 1986; Jeffrey Brown, 'Major players in their own right', 27th May 1986; Alan Cane, 'Increasing quality and speed in dealing rooms', 27th May 1986; Richard Lambert, 'More products now need round-the-clock trading', 27th October 1986; Barry Riley, 'Hedging lifts the five-date contract', 19th March 1987; Lisa Martineau, 'Hedging helps the boom', 3rd June 1987; David Lascelles, 'Foundations laid, but plans still vague', 23rd June 1987; James Andrews, 'Trading likely to rise by a quarter this year', 15th July 1988; Andrew Freeman, 'Spurred by the Americans', 20th February 1989; Ian Rodger, 'London is now a banker bet for the Swiss', 2nd December 1992; James Blitz, 'All change in foreign exchanges', 2nd April 1993; James Blitz, 'New anxieties for the banks', 26th May 1993; Philip Gawith, 'Forex surge masks maturing market', 24th October 1995; Philip Coggan, 'It's just a small problem', 8th February 1996; George Graham, 'BIS outlines forex settlement risk strategy', 28th March 1996; George Graham, 'Forex dealers move to limit settlement risk', 5th June 1996; Richard Adams, 'Brokers alter shape of things to come', 25th June 1999; Jennifer Hughes, 'Where money talks very loudly', 27th May 2004; Jennifer Hughes, 'A veteran with a proud record of service', 27th May 2004.

[50] Godfrey Hodgson, 'The race is on for the universal terminal', 28th November 1984; John Plender, 'Deregulation gains that add up to zero', 29th August 1985; Charles Batchelor, 'Concern expressed over electronic equity dealing', 18th November 1985; Alan Cane, 'Expectations are now more realistic', 16th October 1986.

continuing use of direct telephone lines. As Alan Cane noted in 1986 'there is no central, physical market floor and dealing is carried out over the telephone. The calculations required are complex and the risks substantial. So quality of telecommunications and speed of connection between dealers or dealers and brokers are critically important.'[51] In the same year David Lascelles reported that 'Today's dealing rooms are high-technology nerve centres, bulging with the latest telecommunications equipment to girdle the globe, and packed with computers programmed to spot opportunity in a dozen currencies and in foreign exchange-based instruments like options and futures.'[52] This dependence upon technology for trading also extended to the settlement of transactions, which had been recognized as a serious issue since the Herstatt bank failure of 1974. Again, the solution to that problem was one of the foreign exchange market's own making. By 1986 eleven banks in London had set up a computer-based settlement system which netted off their positions at the end of each day so reducing the danger of losses caused by the domino effect of a single payment failure.

The result of all these developments was to make foreign exchange trading a global market with buying and selling conducted on a continuous basis. According to Peter Montagnon in 1984, 'Foreign exchange dealing is a 24-hour-a-day business, with major centres in the Far East dealing through the European night and European traders staying up late to catch the market in New York.'[53] This judgement was echoed in 1988 by Richard Huber, head of capital markets and foreign exchange at Chase Manhattan Bank. In his judgement foreign exchange trading had become 'The most global market' where trading took place 'seamlessly across national borders and time zones.'[54] This trading was increasingly driven by international financial flows and the need to cover the risks involved at a time of volatile exchange rates as Janet Bush explained in 1987, 'The development of ever more sophisticated markets, backed up by hedging mechanisms and a myriad of financial instruments, has meant that a large proportion of the flow of funds through the foreign exchange market can be traced to investment shifts rather than genuine trade transactions.'[55] For most banks, dealing in foreign exchange remained a service they provided for their customers, covering their risks through the spot and forward market. However, for the emerging megabanks foreign exchange was becoming a core business where large profits could be generated from taking a position in the market, acting as counterparties to the buying and selling of others. The effect was to drive up volume, making the foreign exchange market into one where liquidity was available virtually twenty-four hours a day, seven days a week. As Lascelles observed in 1988, 'The trading action moves with the clock from one centre to the next, and each centre is responsible for the positions it takes. As the Far East hands over to London, and London to New York, and New York back to Sydney, dealers brief each other about their sensitivities.'[56]

To maintain a position in the foreign exchange market required these megabanks to invest heavily in technology and staff and be able to offer a range of currency facilities to their customers. This had the effect of concentrating the business in their hands. According to Phillip Stephens in 1987, 'Turbulent markets, of course, are more often than not good news for the banks and brokers who dominate the 24-hour-a-day business of foreign

[51] Alan Cane, 'Increasing quality and speed in dealing rooms', 27th May 1986.
[52] David Lascelles, 'An established profit centre', 27th May 1986.
[53] Peter Montagnon, 'Novel offerings bring fresh edge to competition', 14th February 1984.
[54] Janet Bush, 'Low post crash volumes the major problem', 15th July 1988.
[55] Janet Bush, 'Pressure grows for freer markets', 3rd June 1987.
[56] David Lascelles, 'Trusting in local judgement', 15th July 1988.

exchange trading.'[57] Also encouraging concentration were the enormous risks being run and so banks confined their trading to those counterparties that could be trusted to meet their commitments. This requirement for a high level of trust also limited the switch to electronic trading that automatically matched buyers and sellers, though these systems were being developed by a number of information providers. By April 1992 Reuter's Dealing 2000-2 system was operational, developed at a cost in excess of $75m, but the thirty banks that took the service made limited use of it because they could not control for counterparty risk. Instead the banks largely stuck to current practice. When trading foreign exchange a trader in a bank contacted his equivalent in another bank directly, either by computer or telephone, and negotiated a bilateral deal. Alternatively, the business was placed in the hands of interdealer brokers who used their personal network to complete the transaction. In contrast, the electronic systems matched sales and purchases anonymously with no regard for the reliability of the counterparties involved. Despite the technical superiority of Reuter's dealing system it had failed to gain immediate acceptability in 1992, and there remained doubts over whether it ever would.[58]

Brokers

Contributing to the development of the various financial markets that grew enormously in importance after 1970 were a species of intermediary that became known as interdealer brokers. They did not take a position in the market but operated between the banks, which did. Hence the term interdealer brokers as they arranged sales and purchases between the banks. In many deals the banks did not want to trade directly with competitors as it revealed whether they were buying or selling, borrowing and lending. Interdealer brokers could also handle the deals where the bank lacked either the staff, expertise, or connections and so was happy to pay commission to those who possessed all three. There had always been different varieties of interdealer brokers in all major financial centres, servicing the needs of banks as well as trading on their own account. Sometimes they belonged to exchanges but often they did not, preferring to operate as free agents unconstrained by the

[57] Phillip Stephens, 'Living with turbulence', 3rd June 1987.

[58] Phillip Stephens, 'Living with turbulence', 3rd June 1987; David Lascelles, 'Earnings continue to increase', 3rd June 1987; Janet Bush, 'Pressure grows for freer markets', 3rd June 1987; Janet Bush, 'Calm follows squeezed margins', 3rd June 1987; Lisa Martineau, 'Hedging helps the boom', 3rd June 1987; Roderick Oram, 'Volatility spurs cross-trading', 3rd June 1987; Haig Simonian, 'Banking growth bolsters demand', 3rd June 1987; Alan Cane, 'Advantage from the third phase', 3rd June 1987; Philip Coggan, 'Lobbying clout grows', 3rd June 1987; Philip Coggan, 'Corporations are chary', 3rd June 1987; Stephen Fidler, 'A broader and safer market in a storm', 18th May 1988; David Lascelles, 'Trusting in local judgement', 15th July 1988; Patrick Daniel, 'B&C cliff-hanger still runs', 15th July 1988; Ralph Atkins, 'More join the risk business', 15th July 1988; Alan Cane, 'Deals system wins praise', 15th July 1988; Simon Holberton, 'Return of the large private player', 15th July 1988; Janet Bush, 'Low post crash volumes the major problem', 15th July 1988; James Andrews, 'Trading likely to rise by a quarter this year', 15th July 1988; Haig Simonian, 'Dealers welcome rise in volatility', 15th July 1988; Ralph Atkins, 'A sterling drama at the money theatre', 15th July 1988; Rachel Johnson, 'Reuters triumphs in the derivatives jungle', 21st December 1989; Peter Elstob, 'Anxious to become the Ecu centre', 29th November 1990; Jim McCallum, 'Big three battle it out', 29th April 1991; Charles Goodhart and Antonis Demos, 'The Asian surprise in the forex markets', 2nd September 1991; Jim McCallum, 'End of controls provides a lift', 11th November 1991; James Blitz, 'Forex dealers can buy time', 12th August 1992; James Blitz, 'All change in foreign exchanges', 2nd April 1993; James Blitz, 'New anxieties for the banks', 26th May 1993; Philip Gawith, 'Forex surge masks maturing market', 24th October 1995; Philip Coggan, 'It's just a small problem', 8th February 1996; George Graham, 'BIS outlines forex settlement risk strategy', 28th March 1996; George Graham, 'Forex dealers move to limit settlement risk', 5th June 1996; Richard Adams, 'Brokers alter shape of things to come', 25th June 1999; Jennifer Hughes, 'Where money talks very loudly', 27th May 2004; Jennifer Hughes, 'A veteran with a proud record of service', 27th May 2004.

rules and regulations imposed by the membership of institutions. However, the particular species of interdealer broker that begun to appear in the late 1950s and then flourished from 1970 onwards was a product of the post-war era of control and compartmentalization. In that era regulated markets like exchanges became much less accommodating in terms of new products, such as Eurobonds, encouraging non-members to take up the business of making a market in them on behalf of the banks. The switch from the lend-and-hold model to the originate-and-distribute one also benefited the interdealer brokers because they were on hand to provide a means of trading the securitized assets once they had been issued. Similarly, the explosion in foreign exchange trading also generated a need for intermediation to supplement the trading that took place directly between the banks. The result was the appearance and growth in the number of interdealer brokers ready to seize the opportunity to make a profit by matching supply and demand between banks. These interdealer brokers became established as major players in the financial markets that grew up in London and New York after 1970.

At first there were only a few of these interdealer brokers and they were very small. Some such as Cantor Fitzgerald in New York evolved out of trading in stocks and bonds to become interdealer brokers. Others were founded to take advantage of specific trading opportunities such as Tullet and Riley, which was set up in London by four men in 1971 to make and maintain a market in Eurodollar deposits and foreign exchange. During the 1970s these interdealer brokers established a network of offices that linked the emerging money and foreign exchange markets in London, Tokyo, and New York into a single global market. They relied on real time information supplied by the likes of Reuters to constantly monitor current prices and then used telephone links to banks to provide a trading forum. It was not only Reuters which spotted the profits to be made in supplying financial data. In 1969 Neil Hirsch introduced an electronic system, Telerate, to report money market rates in New York, and this was taken up by the interdealer brokers in the 1970s. It was the combination of screens displaying current prices and the telephone providing a means of communication that constituted the market for the financial products that began to be actively traded in the 1970s, with interdealer brokers acting as the intermediaries between the banks. These interdealer brokers replaced or absorbed those who had previously acted as intermediaries between the banks, such as London's bill brokers and discount houses, who had confined themselves to dealings in UK government debt and in UK£s. The Bank of England had tried to protect the discount houses from competition, because of the role they played in its management of UK monetary policy, but eventually abandoned them as it recognized that the London money market was becoming ever more diverse and international. In 1986 Derek Tullett, by then chairman of Tullett and Tokyo Forex International and representative of the Foreign Exchange and Currency Deposit Brokers' Association, observed that 'It is up to the markets to decide which companies it wants to deal with. Why should we have this restriction on us when it is the principals who should be taking the decision.'[59] The interdealer brokers acted as intermediaries across all the markets, including foreign exchange, bills and bonds, and inter-bank borrowing and lending, using the US$ in their transactions wherever they took place.[60]

[59] George Graham, 'Hopes of an end to O'Brien Rules', 27th May 1986.

[60] Terry Garrett, 'Giants head the broking league', 14th February 1984; John Burke, 'Tensions beneath the surface', 14th February 1984; P M Elstob, 'UK links with Tokyo houses', 14th February 1984; John Moore, 'Ultimate target is broad band of financial services', 14th February 1984; Alice Rawsthorn, 'Intermediaries' buy out', 27th May 1986; George Graham, 'Hopes of an end to O'Brien Rules', 27th May 1986; David Lascelles, 'When the walls come down', 23rd July 1986; David Lascelles, 'The competition will get tougher', 2nd October 1986; Stefan

By the early 1980s a group of influential interdealer brokers had emerged, trading across the whole range of financial instruments linking activity in foreign exchange to that in bills, bonds, stocks, swaps, futures, and options. What they provided was a service connecting banks together in a closely integrated network as they continuously bought from one and sold to another on commission while never taking a position on their own. These interdealer brokers competed aggressively for the business of the banks both against each other and the banks' own staff. By 1984 Tullet and Riley had a staff of over 1000, by which time there were significant barriers to entry as banks confined their dealings to a small number of brokers in whom they had confidence and possessed the expertise, connections, and technology to deliver the service they required. These interdealer brokers were responsible for around half of all trading in foreign exchange in the mid-1980s, for example, creating and maintaining liquidity through the depth and breadth they brought to the market. David Lascelles claimed in 1984 that 'Even the world's largest banks have nothing like the intelligence networks built up by the biggest money brokers: thousands of contacts all over the world, dozens of offices, highly-sophisticated and costly communications systems. At the height of trading a large firm like Astley and Pearce has twenty telephone lines permanently open between London and New York.'[61] There were around ten interdealer brokers running a global business spanning Tokyo, London, and New York and they were able to provide the 24-hour market that banks now required. These interdealer brokers operated as all-purpose money brokers, facilitating the constant borrowing and lending that took place between banks as they sought to maximize the use of the funds they had available and minimize the risks they ran. Though interdealer brokers were members of certain exchanges, as with CME and CBOT in Chicago and Liffe and the London Commodity Exchange in London, they were also rivals to these institutions, able to provide access to global markets on a 24-hour basis. A liquid 24-hour market enabled banks and their customers to complete transactions at the timing and price of their choice, without having to take risks on currency or interest-rate movements. With their operations in the London-centred foreign exchange and inter-bank markets, the New York-centred US Treasury bond market, and the Chicago-centred financial derivatives market these interdealer brokers could provide banks with the service they required.

Threatening the position achieved by the interdealer brokers in the 1980s was the ability of the megabanks, as they were able to internalize transactions and to trade directly with each other through computerized networks. These megabanks were in a position to hold positions for long periods, accepting the risk of large losses in volatile markets because of the possibility of equally commensurate gains. However, there remained numerous other banks with an increasing need to access the money markets, including that for foreign exchange, and they were reluctant to pass all this business on to a rival. For that reason alone there continued to be a role for the interdealer brokers, let alone the expertise and connections they could provide. Unless a bank was willing to invest extensively in the staff and technology already possessed by an interdealer broker it had little choice but to continue using the services they provided. The result was a sharing of the market between the interdealer brokers and an emerging group of global banks. The interdealer brokers fed the banks with current information and acted for them when their dealers wanted to buy and sell. As Robin Packshaw,

Wagstyl, 'Glint of change in the gold market', 5th December 1986; James Blitz, 'A top-hat tradition in the balance', 22nd June 1992; Robert Peston, 'Silent launch of the lifeboat', 19th October 1993.

[61] David Lascelles, 'Big business but competition keen', 14th February 1984.

chairman of International City Holdings, owner of the interdealer broker Charles Fulton, explained in 1987, 'A busy dealer simply can't look at too many screens. One, two, three or even four at a pinch is as much as one man can cope with.'[62] By the early 1990s an exclusive group of interdealer brokers had made themselves the market across a widening range of financial products. They could connect banks with separate pools of liquidity around the world, putting them in a position to constantly balance assets and liabilities and so either take or avoid risk, depending on the strategy to be pursued at any moment in time.[63]

Conclusion

Banking was in a state of flux after 1970 but this was mainly in North America and Western Europe, while the pace and scale of change elsewhere in the world was relatively subdued. Much of this flux was driven by the need banks had to respond to both deregulation and changing habits among savers and borrowers. Deregulation fostered a much more competitive environment as previously entrenched barriers between different types of banks were lowered or even disappeared. In this competitive environment the lend-and-hold model of banking, that dominated much of Western Europe along with countries such as Canada and Australia, was threatened. Instead, banks had to compete for custom by offering higher rates of interest to savers and lower rates of interest to borrowers. One effect this had was to increase the risks that they took. In response, banks employing the lend-and-hold model looked to the USA for alternative ways of conducting business. In the USA the effect of legislation had been to preserve the originate-and-distribute model of banking that had once been the dominant form. That model of banking was then refined and developed in the USA so that it reached a new level of sophistication. Not only did it continue to rely on the use of short-dated financial instruments, such as commercial bills, but it also introduced new variations in the process known as securitization. With securitization existing loans that banks and other financial institutions had made were repackaged as bonds. The effect was to introduce a greater element of marketability to bank lending as these bonds could be either sold to investors, and so release additional funds for the bank to lend, or held by the bank as an asset that could be easily disposed if required, such as to generate additional liquidity. Having been pioneered in the USA developments such as securitization gained popularity elsewhere in the world, but only slowly because of the entrenched position of those banks practising the lend-and-hold model. The financial crises of 1974, 1982, and 1992 had revealed the risks that the lend-and-hold model was exposed to when it involved long-term loans to governments and lending with property as collateral assets. In a crisis neither of these assets was easy to dispose of leaving banks with

[62] Janet Bush, 'Calm follows squeezed margins', 3rd June 1987.

[63] David Lascelles, 'Big business but competition keen', 14th February 1984; Terry Garrett, 'Giants head the broking league', 14th February 1984; Charles Batchelor, 'Wider range of contracts urged', 14th February 1984; John Burke, 'Tensions beneath the surface', 14th February 1984; P. M. Elstob, 'UK links with Tokyo houses', 14th February 1984; John Moore, 'Ultimate target is broad band of financial services', 14th February 1984; Charles Batchelor, 'Wider range of contracts urged', 14th February 1984; George Graham, 'Mercurial times in the market', 27th May 1986; Alice Rawsthorn, 'Intermediaries' buy out', 27th May 1986; George Graham, 'Hopes of an end to O'Brien Rules', 27th May 1986; Jeffrey Brown, 'Major players in their own right', 27th May 1986; Richard Lambert, 'More products now need round-the-clock trading', 27th October 1986; David Lascelles and Roderick Oram, 'Key link added to a global chain', 3rd March 1987; Janet Bush, 'Calm follows squeezed margins', 3rd June 1987; Stephen Fidler, 'Where British brokers rule world', 7th July 1987; David Lascelles, 'Another flurry in money brokers' world', 19th August 1987; Barry Riley, 'More interdealer brokers to open', 28th March 1988; Patrick Daniel, 'B&C cliff-hanger still runs', 15th July 1988; Stephen Fidler, 'Money brokers step into the financial limelight', 22nd November 1990.

a liquidity crisis leading to questions of solvency. In each case these crises provided an incentive to switch to the originate-and-distribute model, as that allowed banks to covert loans into transferable securities which they could either sell or retain as liquid assets. Banking regulators, in particular, saw in the combination of the originate-and-distribute model with the securitization of existing loans as a way of simultaneously increasing the stability of the banking system without the necessity of reducing the level of overall lending, and so dampen economic growth.

The problem with the combination of the originate-and-distribute model and securitization was that it relied on the existence of sufficiently active markets where the financial instruments created could be easily and quickly bought and sold. Without such markets the bills, bonds and other securities produced would lack the liquidity that made them so attractive to banks, investors, and regulators. However, these markets were still in their infancy even in the early 1990s, especially outside the USA. There were only a number of financial products that possessed the deep and broad markets that could guarantee liquidity. One was the market in US Treasuries as these could always be bought and sold at close to prevailing prices. For that reason it was beloved of banks searching for the ultimate liquid asset, especially as it was denominated in US$s, which was the world's preferred currency. Other government debt markets could also offer liquidity but not at the level of US Treasuries and not in US$s. The other markets that could provide liquidity were mainly inter-bank markets. One was the market through which banks lent to and borrowed from each other. This was very much confined to those banks that possessed the size and scale that meant that they commanded the trust of their peers as counterparties, and so other banks channelled their inter-bank activities through them. Another market that grew in both volume and liquidity was that in Eurobonds, having begun in the late 1950s. However, the market that grew exponentially after 1970 was that in foreign exchange, where banks were engaged continuously in balancing their assets and liabilities not only across different currencies but also over time. As with the inter-bank money market the foreign exchange market was also one dominated by a small number of very large banks with extensive international connections. The volume of trading and the speed of transaction made it vital that every participant could be relied on not only to complete the deal but also exactly as agreed as they were all linked. Much of the activity in these inter-bank markets was located in London though it operated on the basis of the US$.

What was emerging in the 1980s were integrated global markets which revolved round the activities of a small number of banks. These new markets relied not only on direct trading between banks but also the activities of a small group of interdealer brokers that developed after 1970. These interdealer brokers built up close contacts with banks and established a global network that linked the world's financial centres into a continuous market. Increasingly it was the links between interdealer brokers and their customers that became the market for a variety of financial products ranging from currencies and bonds through to bank deposits and derivatives. This market had no physical location as trading was conducted between the offices of the banks and interdealer brokers through the use of the telephone with screens displaying financial information that was constantly updated. Such was the success of these interdealer brokers that they displaced other long-established intermediaries, such as London's discount houses, despite the support the latter were given by the Bank of England. What these interdealer brokers had done was tap into the simultaneous phenomena of the dematerialization of trading, the globalization of the market, the use of the US$ as the world currency, and the emergence of megabanks that could be relied upon as trusted counterparties to any transaction.

4

Commodities, Futures, Options, and Swaps, 1970–92

Introduction

One of the most dynamic financial markets to appear after 1970 was the trading of derivatives. As Tracy Corrigan and Patrick Harverson reflected in December 1992, 'In the past 10 years, the most creative engineering in the world of international finance has been concentrated in the huge and rapidly growing market for derivative products.'[1] By then the estimated value of all futures, options, swaps, and related instruments traded on exchanges and Over-The-Counter (OTC) markets was put at $10,000bn. Prior to 1970 the fixed nature of both interest rates and exchange rates, because of government controls and central bank intervention, limited the need to cover risks in these areas. With the breakdown of the Bretton Woods system in the early 1970s both interest rates and exchange rates experienced rising volatility, forcing banks to turn to derivatives as one way to coping. Governments of countries ranging from France to India also began relaxing the prohibition on the trading of futures contracts that had been introduced in the past as a way of coping with destabilizing speculation.[2] The incentive to use derivatives was much greater among US banks because they lacked either the nationwide or universal structure that would have allowed them to cover such risks internally by matching the diverse needs of numerous customers.[3] As a result it was a number of US commodity exchanges that were the first to respond to the demand for a cheap and accessible means of covering the risks coming from increased volatility. What these commodity exchanges traditionally provided was a market for hedging against price rises and falls. Increasingly the contracts traded did not involve actual delivery, as that took place through organized supply chains and customized arrangements. Instead, these contracts compensated those who held them for any adverse price movements between the time an order was placed and delivery, so removing the risks attached to long-distance trade because of the delay between shipment and arrival. It was not only producers and consumers who used these contracts to cover such risks but also the merchants and dealers involved, as they were exposed through the stocks they held, and the banks who provided the credit, as the value of the collateral could fall. What was required after 1970 was to design contracts that served new areas of volatility covering not only additional

[1] Tracy Corrigan and Patrick Harverson, 'Ever more complex', 8th December 1992.

[2] John Plender, 'Through a market, darkly', 27th May 1994; John Plender, 'Out of sight, not out of mind', 20th September 1999; John Plender, 'The limits of ingenuity', 17th May 2001.

[3] Clare Pearson, 'Demand disappoints enthusiasts', 27th May 1986; John Ridding, 'New set of much-needed hedging instruments', 13th March 1989; Andrew Freeman, 'A business that has to perform', 2nd May 1989; John Plender, 'Through a market, darkly', 27th May 1994; John Plender, 'Out of sight, not out of mind', 20th September 1999; Special Correspondent, 'Poised for a comeback after 27 years', 12th April 1996; Andrew Jack, 'Paris market opens doors to wheat futures trading', 5th July 1996; Tony Tassell, 'Pepper futures exchange for India', 16th October 1996; Deborah Hargreaves, 'Future looks brighter for EU farm futures', 18th November 1996; James Kynge, 'China may form cotton exchange', 17th December 1998.

Banks, Exchanges, and Regulators: Global Financial Markets from the 1970s. Ranald Michie, Oxford University Press (2021).

DOI: 10.1093/oso/9780199553730.003.0004

commodities but also currencies, interest rates, and stock and bond prices. Without these contracts producers and consumers; buyers and sellers; and savers, investors, and borrowers were all reluctant to enter into commitments that exposed them to losses due to the volatility of prices, interest rates, and exchange rates. Conversely, there were others attracted by the possibilities of the profit to be made by acting as counterparties in such contracts.[4]

Aiding the design of new contracts was the advances made in collecting, disseminating, and modelling real-time financial information, as these allowed the price of future and option contracts to constantly reflect trends in the underlying market, whether for commodities, currencies, stocks, or bonds. Increasingly the users of derivative contracts could have confidence that they did provide them with a reliable means of hedging their risks.[5] The result was a proliferation of derivative contracts after 1970, each designed to tap into a particular source of volatility. With stock market indexes being calculated electronically and continually revalued a futures contract that tracked them became the quickest, cheapest, and safest way to change the weightings of an investment portfolio. Writing in 1985 John Edwards reported that 'Every month there are reports of proposed new futures contracts all over the world, ranging from Indonesia and the Philippines to Amsterdam, Paris and Montreal.'[6] These derivative contracts could take the form of an option, allowing the holder to either complete the deal or let it lapse; a future, which had to be concluded if only by a matching reverse deal; or a swap, which was a bilateral transaction in which each counterparty accepted an equal but reverse risk. The difficulty lay in designing a contract that met the requirements of all users, and success was only achieved through a process of trial and error. That difficulty was greatly magnified when the contract was not a bilateral swap, customized to suit both sides in terms of product, time, type, location, amount, and currency but a standardized product that appealed to the many. The problem with customized derivatives was that they took time to draw up and agree upon, and were inflexible once made, being ideal for long-term arrangements or specific circumstances. They also left little scope for third party involvement while their unique features made them difficult to trade. In contrast, future and option contracts contained standard features, involving a series of compromises, which broadened their appeal and so made them tradeable. Once it was possible to trade a derivatives contract it became more attractive to those willing to act as counterparties, as they could adjust their position quickly in response to changing circumstances. This made them ideal for banks, as they were required to constantly balance assets and liabilities across numerous variables so as to cover the risks they ran. As these risks grew in the more turbulent times after 1970 so the appeal of both bespoke and standardized derivatives grew. Whereas the appeal of a swap lay in its ability to match specific

[4] Barry Riley, 'The fight for Liffe', 12th September 1984; John Edwards, 'Fight ahead to maintain growth', 5th March 1985; Alexander Nicoll, 'Fast growth on back of market volatility', 11th December 1985; Alice Rawsthorn, 'Saving companies from erratic swings', 27th May 1986; A H Hermann, 'Lessons from the ITC debacle', 13th March 1986; Tracy Corrigan, 'Where innovation prevails', 13th March 1991; Jim McCallum, 'Institutional interest quickens after tax changes', 13th March 1991; Tracy Corrigan, 'Treasurers learn to hedge their bets', 28th March 1991; Tracy Corrigan, 'A broader tool found for hedging', 3rd April 1991; Tracy Corrigan, 'Competition helps cut costs', 29th April 1991; Simon London, 'Banks take expansive view', 19th March 1992; Tracy Corrigan, 'Diversification is the spur', 19th March 1992; Tracy Corrigan, 'End of rapid growth', 20th July 1992; Richard Waters, 'Gaps in information on markets', 11th November 1992; Tracy Corrigan and Patrick Harverson, 'Ever more complex', 8th December 1992; Laurie Morse, 'New law lifts uncertainty', 8th December 1992; Richard Waters, 'Higher return, no extra risk', 8th December 1992; Tracy Corrigan, 'Currency upheaval wins converts', 8th December 1992; Javier Blas, 'How it all came about', 25th November 2009.

[5] Barry Riley, 'Design stands test of time', 1st July 1985; Jeremy Stone, 'Yardstick by which to gauge success', 1st July 1985; Tracy Corrigan and Terry Byland, 'Stock market tail wags vigorously', 3rd May 1994.

[6] John Edwards, 'Broader base and wider choice', 5th March 1985.

conditions those of standardized futures and options was related to their liquidity. In turn that liquidity relied on the existence of an active market in which such contracts could be bought and sold. The breakthrough in financial derivatives came in 1972 when the Chicago Mercantile Exchange (CME), introduced a tradeable Eurodollar futures contract. This contract became popular with banks seeking to cover the foreign exchange risks they and their customers were increasingly exposed to. That contract from the CME was quickly followed by a contract on stock options in 1973, from the Chicago Board Options Exchange (Cboe), and another on interest rates from Chicago Board of Trade (CBOT).[7]

By 1989, according to Katharine Campbell, 'Futures and options have become accepted in professional circles as an integral part of the financial landscape.' She did add that the public had still to come to terms with this change: 'Still, the public perception of the denizens of the pits as wild speculators, whose antics easily spill over into and damage the sober process of capital accumulation elsewhere in the economy, is remarkably stubborn, and apt to resurface when anything at all goes wrong.'[8] Though derivatives could and were used for speculative purposes, and misused in different ways, their primary purpose was as a hedging tool for banks to be used to reduce or eliminate the risks inherent in their business rather than increase it. The invention of currency-based derivatives, for example, which allowed investors to hedge their underlying assets against exchange rate risks, transformed international investment in the 1980s at a time of currency volatility.[9] In 1992, one US bank, JP Morgan, advertised the importance of derivatives as part of the service it could provide to its customers:

> Derivatives don't make risk disappear, but they do make it possible to exchange a risk you'd rather not take for one you're more willing to accept. Options, swaps, and other derivatives are simple in essence, but since they're so versatile, evaluating their various uses can be complex. That's especially true with newer derivatives linked to commodity and equity indices. But it's not our style to magnify complexity. Our success has always been based on helping clients think through every situation fully and clearly. Then we draw on the technical resources of our global network to design the specific tactic that fits your particular strategy. By taking the mystery out of derivatives, we make it easier to take advantage of these important financial tools. It's a key reason we've become a global leader in the full range of risk-management products.[10]

Megabanks, in particular, were in a position to either design specific products to meet their customers' needs or access the standard ones traded on exchanges, through their membership of such institutions.[11] It took time for the use of these products to become accepted, understood, and then used in preference to the facilities traditionally provided through the

[7] Mary Ann Sieghart, 'Kick-off for US-style sport of financial futures trading', 3rd May 1984; Maggie Urry, 'The round the clock future', 7th December 1984; John Powers, 'Doors open for pin-striped pork bellies', 5th March 1985; John H Parry, 'Threat from over-complexity', 5th March 1985; John Edwards, 'Fight ahead to maintain growth', 5th March 1985; John Edwards, 'Why the future may not work', 26th July 1985; Alexander Nicoll, 'A new option for the corporate treasurer', 1st August 1985; Deborah Hargreaves, 'Sharp rise expected', 13th June 1988; Laurie Morse, 'New law lifts uncertainty', 8th December 1992; Tracy Corrigan, 'Currency upheaval wins converts', 8th December 1992.

[8] Katharine Campbell, 'They may kick the puppy-dog', 8th March 1989.

[9] James Blitz, 'An insurance or a threat to stability?', 26th May 1993.

[10] JP Morgan advertisement, 8th December 1992.

[11] Deborah Hargreaves, 'Derivatives come of age', 13th March 1991; Tracy Corrigan, 'Europe takes a bigger share', 19th March 1992; Laurie Morse, 'New law lifts uncertainty', 8th December 1992; Tracy Corrigan, 'US pioneers lured to new frontier by rich packages', 8th December 1992.

spot and forward market. Banks themselves turned to futures and options markets as the volatility of currencies and interest rates increased, and stock and bond prices fluctuated, in order to protect themselves against possible losses as well as for potential profit. Through the use of stock index contracts institutional investors could effectively trade a basket of stocks representing the whole cash market providing them with either a form of portfolio insurance or a way of speculating on the rise and fall of the whole market. It was the latter strategy that was blamed for accentuating the stock market crash of 1987 because of the level of selling generated by computer-based trading strategies. Due to the linkages between the futures and cash markets the primary influence on what happened to stock prices was the trend in stock index futures through the arbitrage that took place between the two. As long as both markets were liquid, adjusting positions on either could be done quickly without having much impact on the overall price level. However, when liquidity in the cash market dried up in the crash of 1987 the deluge of selling, driven by the need of those in the futures market to adjust their positions, pushed prices sharply down, sparking even more selling followed by further price falls and so the process went on. Conversely, the futures market could not absorb the selling pressure coming from the cash market without dramatic price declines, which put further pressure on the cash market. Despite the criticism made of the futures market in the wake of the 1987 crash, and the retreat of a number of participants, the continuing volatility of stock prices, interest rates, and exchange rates generated a growing demand for financial derivative contracts. One example was the recovery of the Hong Kong futures market, which had been almost destroyed by the 1987 crash, with megabanks such as Morgan Stanley and the Swiss Bank Corporation playing a central role. Financial derivatives were increasingly recognized by banks and fund managers as a means of reducing the risks that they ran, at least on a temporary basis, while for others they represented an opportunity to generate large profits by taking a position in the market.[12]

Commodity Exchanges

Despite the growing popularity of financial futures and options those related to commodities continued to dominate activity until the 1980s.[13] Increased price volatility in commodities drove up the volume of trading in existing contracts and encouraged exchanges to devise new ones. With the ending of the fixed price for gold in 1971 the New York Commodity Exchange (Comex) launched a successful gold futures contract in 1974, while the growing volatility in oil prices led the New York Mercantile Exchange (Nymex) to introduce a contract based on heating oil in 1978.[14] The inability of governments and multi-

[12] Alexander Nicoll, 'Agreement among rivals', 19th March 1987; Roderick Oram, 'Time to level with volatility', 19th March 1987; Roderick Oram, 'Innovators to cut global risk', 19th March 1987; Philip Coggan, 'A more flexible way to manage interest rates', 19th March 1987; Philip Coggan, 'New players speed trade', 21st April 1987; Richard Mooney, 'Unrivalled sector for volatility', 28th October 1987; Janet Bush, 'Strategists were a factor but not the cause', 10th March 1988; Simon Holberton, 'Two ways to shield profits', 10th March 1988; Dominique Jackson, 'Swaps keep in step with the regulators', 10th August 1988; Dominique Jackson, 'Private investors are regaining confidence', 20th August 1988; John Edwards, 'Profiting from a small outlay', 20th August 1988; Katharine Campbell, 'They may kick the puppy-dog', 8th March 1989; Deborah Hargreaves, 'Collars suit the UK', 2nd July 1990; Stephen Fidler, 'When family loyalties are placed under severe strain', 28th December 1990; Simon Davies, 'Focus on a dynamic present', 20th October 1993.

[13] David Owen, 'Farm futures in the shade', 23rd July 1986; David Owen, 'Exchanges look to diversification', 23rd July 1986.

[14] Charles Batchelor, 'BT helps to seal the future', 5th March 1985; Laura Raun, 'Gold contract initiative', 5th March 1985; John Edwards, 'Why the future may not work', 26th July 1985; Stefan Wagstyl, 'Glint of change in the

national companies to control commodity prices created opportunities for commodity exchanges to step in and provide contracts that allowed producers and consumers to hedge their exposure.[15] The prime purpose of most commodity exchanges was to provide protection, through future and option contracts, against unpredictable price fluctuations.[16] With trade increasingly taking place between and within large multinational companies, and being conducted on the telephone using information displayed on computer screens, there was little need for a physical marketplace in which commodities were traded apart from a few unique and expensive commodities, such as Antwerp and its diamond market.[17] Even gold bullion, which existed in a standardized form, was traded in a global 24-hour market.[18] According to Kenneth Gooding in 1992, 'It is a truly open market where buyers and sellers are brought almost directly into contact with one another by means of modern technology.'[19] Where exchanges played a role, including for gold, was to provide a benchmark price that was continuously updated, so allowing producers, holders, and banks to adjust their positions both relative to each other and their customers. The gold futures contract traded on Comex did this.[20] The role played by exchanges in establishing reference prices, and continuously updating them, was highly valued by the banks, as they financed the trade in commodities. What the banks wanted was a futures contract that reflected current prices, was easy to buy and sell, and was free from manipulation and counterparty risk and this is what commodity exchanges delivered.[21] Even on the London Metal Exchange (LME), which continued to combine the physical and the futures market, it was setting the reference price across a range of metals that was its principal function.[22] This need for reference pricing led to the establishment of new commodity exchanges, especially in developing countries and those in which central pricing was being replaced by market mechanisms.[23] Once a commodity exchange became the centre of liquidity for a contract that was where it stayed, unless circumstances changed. Trading in oil futures on New York Mercantile Exchange (Nymex) dictated the price at which oil changed hands, though it was vulnerable

gold market', 5th December 1986; Alexander Nicoll, 'Potential begins to be fulfilled', 11th December 1985; David Owen, 'Experience wins over Chicago', 3rd February 1987; Peter Caddy, Mark Schofield, and Chris Johnson, 'How the consumer outweighs Opec', 3rd February 1987; Stefan Wagstyl, 'Reforms on the way', 22nd June 1987; Kenneth Gooding, 'A boost for the market', 13th June 1988; Deborah Hargreaves, 'Sharp rise expected', 13th June 1988; Ralph Atkins, 'Zurich's precious tradition', 19th December 1988; Richard Mooney, 'At the tip of an iceberg', 22nd June 1992.

[15] Tracy Corrigan, 'A broader tool found for hedging', 3rd April 1991.

[16] Stefan Wagstyl, 'Living in the shadow of an avalanche', 21st November 1985; Andrew Gowers, 'International tin trading slows down to a trickle', 2nd December 1985; Stefan Wagstyl, 'Paying the price of the market's collapse', 12th March 1986; A. H. Hermann, 'Lessons from the ITC debacle', 13th March 1986; Kenneth Gooding, 'LME prepares for tin's rehabilitation', 12th April 1989; George Graham, 'Paris sugar market under siege', 13th August 1987; David Blackwell, 'Brighter prospects for a revival', 28th June 1988; Kenneth Gooding, 'Global regulation provides the immediate challenge', 2nd October 1989.

[17] Tim Dickson, 'Antwerp polishes up diamond sales', 22nd February 1989; Maurice Samuelson, 'International fur trade scurries away from the City', 7th August 1989; Vanessa Houlder, 'Meat and potatoes row', 11th August 1992.

[18] Kenneth Gooding, 'A boost for the market', 13th June 1988.

[19] Kenneth Gooding, 'Havens of inertia', 22nd June 1992.

[20] Kenneth Gooding, 'A boost for the market', 13th June 1988; Kenneth Gooding, 'Havens of inertia', 22nd June 1992; David Blackwell, 'Market hooked on hedging', 22nd June 1992; Richard Mooney, 'At the tip of an iceberg', 22nd June 1992.

[21] Kenneth Gooding, 'Shortage of stocks may threaten the return of tin', 1st June 1989; Kenneth Gooding, 'Global regulation provides the immediate challenge', 2nd October 1989.

[22] Kenneth Gooding, 'Metal traders start their mating season', 8th October 1991; Tracy Corrigan, 'Currency upheaval wins converts', 8th December 1992; Kenneth Gooding, 'From Calcutta clerk to metals magnate', 10th December 1992; Kenneth Gooding, 'Bagri sees wider horizons for LME', 17th December 1992.

[23] Leyla Boulton, 'Soviet oil and gas exchange opens this month', 11th June 1991.

to competition because its contract reflected US domestic conditions. However, it took until 1988 before the International Petroleum Exchange (IPE) in London came up with an alternative that reflected the world oil market, with its Brent Crude contract. What this indicated was the high degree of inertia that existed in the derivatives market.[24]

Nevertheless, what was happening in the 1980s was that in a world freed from barriers trading was gravitating to the market that could provide the greatest liquidity.[25] Faced with an increasingly competitive environment commodity exchanges were forced to abandon fixed charges, reduce costs, and improve the service provided in order to survive. One way chosen in order to gain an advantage was to replace floor trading with a computerized system because it was cheaper and more flexible. Governments were also forced to reduce taxes and exchange authorities to remove restrictive practices. Commodity exchanges also experimented with different contracts though it was estimated in 1992 that the chance of success was one in four. Unless a new contract generated a significant level of trading from the outset it failed to attract additional users, and so build up the momentum required to ensure its survival.[26] Those running commodity exchanges acknowledged that this was the situation. In 1986 Saxon Tate, chairman of the London Commodity Exchange (LCE), observed that 'People will now trade in the best market, and that's entirely right. They tend to look totally internationally. And if I'm trading I really don't like a thin market.'[27] Gilbert Durieux, managing director of France's derivative exchange, the Marché à Terme des Instruments Financiers (Matif), said in 1990 that, 'It is clear we will have to do battle until one of us yields.'[28] In 1992 Robin Woodhead, who was in charge of London's Futures and Options Exchange (FOX), and had played a central role in setting up the International Petroleum Exchange (IPE), admitted that 'At various times in the last 10 years all of the

[24] Lucy Kellaway, 'Opec hang on to control', 3rd February 1987; David Owen, 'Experience wins over Chicago', 3rd February 1987; David Owen, 'Pros and cons in WTI contract', 3rd February 1987; Peter Caddy, Mark Schofield and Chris Johnson, 'How the consumer outweighs Opec', 3rd February 1987; Lucy Kellaway, 'Futures contract proves popular', 3rd February 1987; Lucy Kellaway, 'Need and firmness brighten the year', 3rd February 1987; Steven Butler, 'Oil traders braced for the onset of regulation', 10th February 1988; Steven Butler, 'London's crude oil traders look to the futures', 25th January 1989; Laura Raun, 'Dutch aim to get in on the act', 25th January 1989; Laura Raun, 'Rotterdam oil futures challenge to London's IPE', 31st October 1989; Steven Butler, 'Mixed reviews for London oil futures late show', 19th January 1990; Barbara Durr, 'Nymex pipes in its natural gas contract', 4th April 1990; Edi Cohen, 'A change for the better', 12th June 1990;

Steven Butler, 'IPE budgets $1m in oil futures launch', 13th June 1990; Barbara Durr, 'Nymex plans 1992 launch for electronic trading', 8th November 1991; Barbara Durr, 'New products to hold the line', 19th March 1992; Kevin Morrison, 'Nymex relents and allows electronic trade', 12th June 2006.

[25] Bruce Jacques, 'Sydney sheds the casino image', 19th March 1987; David Owen, 'Chicago trading livens up', 27th May 1987; David Blackwell, 'London raw sugar to trade on screen from Friday', 9th January 1991; Vanessa Houlder, 'Many hurdles for Fox to jump', 8th February 1991; Barbara Durr, 'CBOT to launch first insurance futures', 26th February 1991; Barbara Durr, 'New futures exchange in US', 27th February 1991; Vanessa Houlder, 'FOX attempts to build on property futures', 10th May 1991; Tracy Corrigan, 'London Fox', 16th August 1991; Tracy Corrigan, 'Fox orders review of structure by year-end', 19th November 1991; David Blackwell, 'Fox tries to make up lost ground', 16th January 1992; Barbara Durr, 'New products to hold the line', 19th March 1992; David Blackwell, 'Fox tries to dig itself out of a hole', 1st December 1992; Laurie Morse, 'After-hours Globex has yet to live up to its promise', 1st December 1992.

[26] Bruce Jacques, 'Sydney sheds the casino image', 19th March 1987; David Owen, 'Chicago trading livens up', 27th May 1987; David Blackwell, 'London raw sugar to trade on screen from Friday', 9th January 1991; Vanessa Houlder, 'Many hurdles for Fox to jump', 8th February 1991; Barbara Durr, 'CBOT to launch first insurance futures', 26th February 1991; Barbara Durr, 'New futures exchange in US', 27th February 1991; Vanessa Houlder, 'FOX attempts to build on property futures', 10th May 1991; Tracy Corrigan, 'London Fox', 16th August 1991; Tracy Corrigan, 'Fox orders review of structure by year-end', 19th November 1991; David Blackwell, 'Fox tries to make up lost ground', 16th January 1992; Barbara Durr, 'New products to hold the line', 19th March 1992; David Blackwell, 'Fox tries to dig itself out of a hole', 1st December 1992; Laurie Morse, 'After-hours Globex has yet to live up to its promise', 1st December 1992

[27] Andrew Gowers, 'Lost business not yet returning', 23rd July 1986.

[28] George Graham, 'A tale of two sugar markets', 16th February 1990.

London futures exchanges have been described as being about to close.'[29] There was even an ambitious plan in 1992, proposed by David Burton, chairman of the London International Financial Futures Exchange (Liffe), to merge all London's derivatives exchanges into one, but this was never accomplished.[30] One commodity exchange that did successfully reinvent itself by following the path of the CBOT and the CME, and embrace financial derivatives, was the Sydney Futures Exchange in Australia.[31]

Financial Futures: Exchanges

Despite the increased trading of commodity derivatives, especially those related to oil and metals, it was trading in financial futures and options that expanded exponentially after 1970. Turnover of financial derivatives on US exchanges grew from 13.6m lots in 1970 to 149.4m lots in 1984.[32] By then John Edwards reported that a transformation had taken place in the US derivatives market: 'An industry that was devised to cater for the needs of traders in raw materials is now being dominated by a totally different set of participants—dealers in money and stocks, financial institutions and banks.'[33] Chicago was at the centre of this revolution having, according to John Edwards in 1985, 'emerged as the triumphant winner in financial futures'.[34] By then the CME and the CBOT dominated global trading of financial futures with 80 per cent of the total market, by volume.[35] A key reason for that success was the early initiative of Leo Melamed, who was behind the CME's move into financial futures. He explained why in 1985: 'Financial markets offered more potential in terms of investments and uses than did agriculture markets. More people can utilise financial markets, whereas a limited universe is going to utilise agricultural futures.'[36] These Chicago exchanges then gained an international following for their derivatives contracts, as they provided a cheap and convenient way for banks to hedge their exposure to volatile commodity prices and fluctuations in exchange rates and interest rates. In 1989 33 per cent of the trading taking place on the CME was coming from outside the USA, which drove up turnover and thus improved liquidity. As Katharine Campbell wrote in 1990, 'If there is a single key to a flourishing exchange, it is the task of amassing liquidity.'[37] In 1988 the three

[29] David Blackwell, 'Fox tries to dig itself out of a hole', 1st December 1992.

[30] Tracy Corrigan, 'Liffe merger improves outlook for equity options', 29th October 1991; Tracy Corrigan, 'A marriage made in the market place', 15th January 1992; Tracy Corrigan, 'A new Liffe together', 4th February 1992; Tracy Corrigan, 'Liffe and market makers resolve argument', 23rd March 1992.

[31] Bruce Jacques, 'Sydney sheds the casino image', 19th March 1987; David Owen, 'Chicago trading livens up', 27th May 1987; Nikki Tait, 'Sydney exchange sees future in commodities', 3rd January 1997.

[32] Charles Batchelor, 'Wider range of contracts urged', 14th February 1984; John Powers, 'Doors open for pin-striped pork bellies', 5th March 1985; Christopher O'Dea, 'Financial instruments hold sway', 5th March 1985; John Moore, 'Pension fund involvement will become commonplace', 5th March 1985; John H. Parry, 'Threat from over-complexity', 5th March 1985; Nancy Dunne, 'A bright spot in the gloom', 11th December 1985.

[33] John Edwards, 'Fight ahead to maintain growth', 5th March 1985.

[34] John Edwards, 'Fight ahead to maintain growth', 5th March 1985.

[35] Nancy Dunne, 'Innovation becomes basis for expansion', 5th March 1985; Alexander Nicoll, 'A boon for the corporate treasurer', 11th December 1985; Nancy Dunne, 'A bright spot in the gloom', 11th December 1985; David Owen, 'Exchanges look to diversification', 23rd July 1986; Nancy Dunne, 'A bright spot in the gloom', 11th December 1985; Lucy Kellaway, 'Opec hang on to control', 3rd February 1987; David Owen, 'Experience wins over Chicago', 3rd February 1987; David Owen, 'Pros and cons in WTI contract', 3rd February 1987; Deborah Hargreaves, 'Black box is on trial', 10th March 1988; Barbara Durr, 'New products to hold the line', 19th March 1992.

[36] Nancy Dunne, 'A bright spot in the gloom', 11th December 1985.

[37] Katharine Campbell, 'New Exchanges on trial', 9th March 1990.

Chicago exchanges accounted for over 70 per cent of global futures and options trading.[38] The US exchanges did experience growing competition in financial derivatives, especially as the contracts did not provide a perfect match to global markets and were only actively traded during the US working day. As John Edwards observed in 1985, 'Futures trading has been one of the big growth international industries during the past 15 years. New futures exchanges have spread all over the world, from Rio de Janeiro to Singapore and Auckland, spurred on by the development of the financial instruments contracts dealing in a universal commodity—money.'[39] Brazil's future exchange, the Bolsa de Mercadorias and Futuros (BM&F) began operations in 1985, dealing in financial futures.[40] One important exception was Japan where both the government and the stock exchanges succeeded in placing obstacles in the way of those trying to develop a derivatives market in that country. Such actions were a disappointment for Takao Tsutsumi, executive governor of the Osaka Securities Exchange, which had introduced a contract based on the Japanese stock index, the Nikkei 225: 'We have no proof that trading on the futures market has adverse effects on the cash market, but if additional restrictions are going to alleviate the fears of the individual investor, the futures market has to be sacrificed.'[41] The result of the heavy regulation imposed on the trading in financial futures in Japan was to drive trading to the Singapore International Monetary Exchange (Simex), which had launched in 1986 a contract based on the Nikkei 225. The average daily trading volume of Nikkei futures on the Tokyo Stock Exchange (TSE) fell from 87,980 in 1991 to 48,289 in 1992 while it grew from 3,045 in 1991 to 13,897 in 1992 on Simex.[42]

However, most of the early attempts to rival the success of the US commodity exchanges made little impact, such as those from the London Traded Options Market and the European Options Exchange in Amsterdam, both established in 1978.[43] In 1985 John Edwards remained confident that, despite the growing competition, 'The US exchanges, backed by American commission houses with branches in most countries, can expect to attract a large slice of the increasing international business.'[44] That confidence came from the fact that the US contracts were the most liquid in the world:

> Adequate liquidity to get in and out of the market easily without disturbing prices is of particular importance to larger operators in futures, so the trend has been for the big markets to get bigger, while the smaller markets are finding it increasingly difficult to survive. This trend towards the concentration of business into the biggest single marketplace has ominous implications for the rest of the world. With improved communications it is just as easy to trade on the big US exchanges as in London or Singapore. With

[38] David Owen, 'Expansion is the keynote', 19th March 1987; Deborah Hargreaves, 'Black box is on trial', 10th March 1988; Deborah Hargreaves, 'Supremacy battle hots up for on-screen trading', 10th November 1989; Barbara Durr, 'New products to hold the line', 19th March 1992.

[39] John Edwards, 'Fight ahead to maintain growth', 5th March 1985; David Marsh, 'Expansion seen for new French financial futures market', 28th February 1986; David Marsh, 'Cocoa butter melts away', 23rd July 1986.

[40] Nick Reed, 'Investors seek wider horizons', 22nd November 1996; Jonathan Wheatley, 'Small victory for exchange', 10th June 1997; Jonathan Wheatley, 'Ready for foreign flows', 27th June 1997.

[41] Emiko Terazono, 'Fears of new restrictions', 19th March 1992.

[42] Joyce Quek, 'A revolution in the wings', 30th April 1991; Emiko Terazono, 'Japanese futures activity soars', 17th December 1991; Emiko Terazono, 'Fears of new restrictions', 19th March 1992; Emiko Terazono, 'JGB futures stir bad memories', 20th October 1993.

[43] John Edwards, 'Fight ahead to maintain growth', 5th March 1985; John H Parry, 'Threat from over-complexity', 5th March 1985; Alexander Nicoll, 'Potential begins to be fulfilled', 11th December 1985; Alexander Nicoll, 'Bittersweet birthday celebrations for options', 12th April 1988.

[44] John Edwards, 'Broader base and wider choice', 5th March 1985.

> American commission houses drumming up business throughout the world and tending to favour the American exchanges, competition from the US is becoming stronger.[45]

Nevertheless, the proliferation of new exchanges and new contracts gradually picked away at the dominant position of the US incumbents.[46] By the late 1980s the US derivatives exchanges faced a serious challenge.[47] The problem all these new derivatives exchanges faced was reaching a level of liquidity that attracted customers, for without them they could not build up liquidity and so attract more customers as, according to Dominique Jackson in 1988, the US derivatives exchanges 'have established a virtually impregnable position in many financial instruments'. She went on to express the opinion, widely shared in the financial community, that 'Once an exchange established a liquid market, it is extremely difficult for others to dislodge it.'[48] Given the global importance of the US$, the US economy, US corporate enterprise, and US banks, dislodging these incumbents was deemed an impossible task. The solution adopted was to design financial contracts that did not simply duplicate what was already being done. When Liffe was established in London in 1982 it cloned the Chicago exchanges, from products to methods of trading, which made it difficult for it to compete with them. In the case of Liffe the breakthrough came with the restructuring of the UK government bond market. That presented it with an opportunity to design and trade a futures contract based on long-dated UK government debt because of the liquidity of the underlying market. This contract was attractive to local banks and investors and so they used it, leading to a build-up of liquidity that attracted further trading.[49] Based on that success Liffe absorbed the London Traded Options Market (LTOM) in

[45] John Edwards, 'Fight ahead to maintain growth', 5th March 1985.

[46] David Blackwell, 'Moving house broadens LCE's options', 22nd May 1987; David Owen, 'Chicago exchange to re-launch gold futures', 28th May 1987; Stefan Wagstyl, 'LME plans dollar switch for silver contract', 28th May 1987; Nancy Dunne, 'London scores sweet victory', 28th July 1987; George Graham, 'Paris sugar market under siege', 13th August 1987; David Blackwell, 'London builds up lead in white sugar contest', 2nd February 1988; Laura Raun, 'Amsterdam drops gold relaunch plan', 10th February 1988; Deborah Hargreaves, 'Sharp rise expected', 13th June 1988; David Blackwell, 'Brighter prospects for a revival', 28th June 1988; Ralph Atkins, 'Zurich's precious tradition', 19th December 1988; Deborah Hargreaves, 'A yoke for Japan's bull', 8th March 1989; Kenneth Gooding, 'LME zinc restrictions spark row', 22nd December 1989; David Blackwell, 'Going for a "buzz" at the Baltic Exchange', 16th February 1990; George Graham, 'A tale of two sugar markets', 16th February 1990; Barbara Durr, 'Comex chief talking himself out of a job', 22nd March 1990; Barbara Durr, 'Moscow marketeers stampede to Chicago', 13th June 1990; Richard Mooney, 'Members of Fox vote for restructuring', 20th July 1990; Kenneth Gooding, 'London Metal Exchange chairman resigns his post', 20th July 1990; Anne Steadman, 'A chance to manage risk', 23rd November 1990; David Blackwell, 'A ring of confidence in the market', 29th November 1990; Deborah Hargreaves, 'In pole position for Europe', 29th November 1990.

[47] Chris Sherwell, 'Many teething troubles', 5th March 1985; David Marsh, 'Higher profile being taken', 5th March 1985; John Edwards, 'Why the future may not work', 26th July 1985; Alexander Nicoll, 'Volumes rocket after Big Bang', 19th March 1987; Steven Butler, 'Simex is on target', 19th March 1987; Barry Riley, 'Hedging lifts the five-date contract', 19th March 1987; George Graham, 'Matif forges ahead', 19th March 1987; Bernard Simon, 'Pension boost to expansion hopes', 19th March 1987; Lisa Martineau, 'Hedging helps the boom', 3rd June 1987; George Graham, 'Paris sugar market under siege', 13th August 1987; Alexander Nicoll, 'Liffe in search of greater liquidity', 30th September 1987; Alexander Nicoll, 'New class of seat may appeal to locals', 10th March 1988; Barbara Casassus, 'Report likely to allay anxiety', 10th March 1988; Alexander Nicoll, 'Bittersweet birthday celebrations for options', 12th April 1988; George Graham, 'A rapid developer', 8th March 1989; Stefan Wagstyl, 'Signposts to expansion', 8th March 1989.

[48] Dominique Jackson, 'Futures scramble triggers global gold rush', 28th October 1988.

[49] Charles Batchelor, 'Wider range of contracts urged', 14th February 1984; Barry Riley, 'The fight for Liffe', 12th September 1984; John Edwards, 'Readiness to change becomes the most vital commodity', 12th September 1984; Charles Batchelor, 'Popularity matches that of future exchanges', 12th September 1984; Maggie Urry, 'The round the clock future', 7th December 1984; Charles Batchelor, 'BT helps to seal the future', 5th March 1985; Laura Raun, 'Exchange answers its critics', 19th March 1987; Dal Hayward, 'Computer dealing shows its value', 19th March 1987; Terry Byland, 'Contracts take a fivefold leap', 19th March 1987; Bruce Jacques, 'Sydney sheds the casino image', 19th March 1987; Bernard Simon, 'Pension boost to expansion hopes', 19th March 1987; Euromarkets staff, 'Irish futures market subscriptions on target', 30th September 1987; Olli Virtanen, 'Finnish

1992.[50] This pattern was then followed by other derivative exchanges, designing contracts that piggybacked on existing local cash markets, and so attracted trading despite a lack of initial liquidity. As Gerard de la Martinière, chairman of the French clearing house, Chambre de Compensation des Instruments Financiers de Paris (CCIFP), made clear in 1987, 'You cannot have a successful futures market when there is no underlying cash market.'[51] That year the Matif launched a French government bond future, on the back of an active local cash market. The Sydney Futures Exchange had a successful Australian government bond futures contract already in operation, dating from 1984. In 1988 the Swiss Options and Financial Futures Exchange (Soffex) was used by large Swiss banks to trade share options on the stock of the largest Swiss companies, as there was a robust underlying market.[52]

Bolstering this competition to the incumbent US exchanges was the adoption of trading systems that were cheaper and faster than the existing ones, as these relied on floor-based

options exchanges to merge', 18th January 1988; Alexander Nicoll, 'New class of seat may appeal to locals', 10th March 1988; Alexander Nicoll, 'Bittersweet birthday celebrations for options', 12th April 1988; Dominique Jackson, 'Liffe and LTOM fall into step', 12th October 1988; Katharine Campbell, 'They may kick the puppy-dog', 8th March 1989; John Wicks, 'A world leader must not be left behind', 25th April 1989; Katharine Campbell, 'Ifox set date for electronic trading', 3rd May 1989; Katharine Campbell, 'London traded options seeks to go it alone', 23rd May 1989; Deborah Hargreaves, 'Marriage plan surprises the guests', l Times 4th April 1990; Deborah Hargreaves, 'LTOM upgrades system', 18th May 1990; Deborah Hargreaves, 'Liffe aims at one exchange', 7th June 1990; Edi Cohen, 'Amsterdam trading buoyant', 12th June 1990; Edi Cohen, 'An early stage of development', 12th June 1990; Deborah Hargreaves, 'An exchange by any other name', 29th June 1990; Deborah Hargreaves, 'Chicago giants fight to keep their share', 2nd July 1990; David Blackwell, 'Price-fixing volatility attacked', 25th October 1990; Tim Dickson, 'Brussels braced for little bang reforms', 28th November 1990; Deborah Hargreaves, 'In pole position for Europe', 29th November 1990; Deborah Hargreaves, 'Time for players to take their pick', 12th December 1990; Barbara Durr, 'World market share shrinks', 13th March 1991; Tracy Corrigan, 'Competition helps cut costs', 29th April 1991; Jim McCallum, 'Few tears shed for open outcry', 25th April 1991; Jim McCallum and Tracy Corrigan, 'Outcry over screen trading plan', 14th June 1991; Tracy Corrigan, 'Liffe merger improves outlook for equity options', 29th October 1991; Tracy Corrigan, 'A marriage made in the market place', 15th January 1992; Tracy Corrigan, 'A new Liffe together', 4th February 1992; Emiko Terazono, 'Fears of new restrictions', 19th March 1992; Tracy Corrigan, 'Liffe and market makers resolve argument', 23rd March 1992; Richard Lapper, 'No longer the new kid', 21st March 1996.

[50] Jim McCallum and Tracy Corrigan, 'Outcry over screen trading plan', 14th June 1991.

[51] George Graham, 'Matif forges ahead', 19th March 1987.

[52] Alexander Nicoll, 'Agreement among rivals', 19th March 1987; Alexander Nicoll, 'Volumes rocket after Big Bang', 19th March 1987; Barry Riley, 'Hedging lifts the five-date contract', 19th March 1987; Steven Butler, 'Simex is on target', 19th March 1987; George Graham, 'Matif forges ahead', 19th March 1987; Kevin Hamlin, 'New contracts started', 19th March 1987; Terry Byland, 'Contracts take a fivefold leap', 19th March 1987; AP-DJ, 'Nagoya SE plans options trading', 29th September 1987; Alexander Nicoll, 'Liffe in search of greater liquidity', 30th September 1987; Clare Pearson, 'October's storm produces ideal trading weather', 10th March 1988; David Dodwell, 'Now for silver linings and tight rules', 10th March 1988; Barbara Casassus, 'Report likely to allay anxiety', 10th March 1988; Dominique Jackson, 'Futures scramble triggers global gold rush', 28th October 1988; Katharine Campbell, 'They may kick the puppy-dog', 8th March 1989; Stefan Wagstyl, 'Signposts to expansion', 8th March 1989; Chris Sherwell, 'A storm mars September', 8th March 1989; George Graham, 'A rapid developer', 8th March 1989; John Ridding, 'New set of much-needed hedging instruments', 13th March 1989; Andrew Baxter, 'Liquidity poses the greatest problem', 21st June 1989; Katharine Campbell, 'Still no substitute for skill', 26th October 1989; Stefan Wagstyl, 'Banks welcome Tokyo's infant', 9th March 1990; Sara Webb, 'Give the infants time', 29th May 1990; Deborah Hargreaves, 'Chicago giants fight to keep their share', 2nd July 1990; Joyce Quek, 'Profits of big four leap by 30%', 9th August 1990; George Graham, 'A battle with London', 22nd October 1990; Gary Mead, 'Outpost that refuses to die', 16th November 1990; Patrick Harverson, 'Leningrad exchange planned', 12th December 1990; Tracy Corrigan, 'Liffe aims for ECU contract success', 6th March 1991; Barbara Durr, 'World market share shrinks', 13th March 1991; Tracy Corrigan, 'Competition helps cut costs', 29th April 1991; Joyce Quek, 'A revolution in the wings', 30th April 1991; Barbara Durr, 'Plea for a level playing field', 13th June 1991; Tracy Corrigan, 'The heat is on for Italian bond futures', 19th September 1991; Richard Waters, 'Matif in Italian contract move', 11th October 1991; Barbara Durr, 'New products to hold the line', 19th March 1992; Tracy Corrigan, 'Small markets stock up', 19th March 1992; Emiko Terazono, 'Fears of new restrictions', 19th March 1992; Tracy Corrigan, 'Volatility demands ingenuity', 8th December 1992.

traders who were always ready to buy and sell in the expectation of gain. According to Tracy Corrigan in 1992, 'The market in futures and options and other so-called derivative products is at the forefront of technological development in the financial markets.'[53] Rapid progress was being made in creating networks directly linking dealers in their offices while a number of exchanges began experimenting with automated order matching by computer.[54] To Campbell and Hargreaves in 1989, 'Technology lies at the very heart of the fierce battle between futures and options exchanges to secure for themselves a bigger share of the global pie.'[55] In the same year Haig Simonian referred to 'Technology wars being waged by futures and options exchanges around the world.'[56] As Deborah Hargreaves observed in 1989, 'Technology has crept to the very edge of most of the world's physical markets and is now eroding the futures industry's long-preserved but anachronistic way of trading by open outcry.'[57] The results were systems that moved beyond the electronic display of current prices on screens, combined with trading over the telephone, to ones that either matched orders automatically or placed market-makers at the centre.[58] In 1989 Campbell identified the dilemma of which system to choose: 'Despite the fact that screen trading is a minefield of problems and unknowns, no exchange feels it can afford to be behind the game, if this is the way the industry is to develop. Perhaps the right technological formula has yet to be found, but there is an inevitability about the process.'[59] Nevertheless, many remained to be convinced that electronic systems would triumph, such as Dominique Jackson in 1988: 'So far, screen-based trading has worked reasonably well in small national markets where the participants are geographically dispersed like New Zealand or Sweden... the myriad technical problems, with such things as trading procedures, margin levels, daily price limits and contract guarantee consistency, imply that the industry may

[53] Tracy Corrigan, 'Europe takes a bigger share', 19th March 1992.

[54] John Edwards, 'Broader base and wider choice', 5th March 1985; John H. Parry, 'Threat from over-complexity', 5th March 1985; Alexander Nicoll, 'A new option for the corporate treasurer', 1st August 1985; Dal Hayward, 'Computer dealing shows its value', 19th March 1987; Deborah Hargreaves, 'Black box is on trial', 10th March 1988; John Burton, 'The web spreads', 9th March 1990; Jim McCallum and Tracy Corrigan, 'Outcry over screen trading plan', 14th June 1991.

[55] Katharine Campbell and Deborah Hargreaves, 'Liffe plans to put open-outcry pits on the screen', 2nd February 1989.

[56] Haig Simonian, 'Liffe accelerates the tempo in technology race', 23rd February 1989.

[57] Deborah Hargreaves, 'International regulators slow to tame the machines', 22nd December 1989.

[58] Katharine Campbell and Deborah Hargreaves, 'Liffe plans to put open-outcry pits on the screen', 2nd February 1989; Haig Simonian, 'Liffe accelerates the tempo in technology race', 23rd February 1989; Katharine Campbell, 'Suspicion lingers in the pit', 8th March 1989; Chris Sherwell, 'It's open all hours for Sydney futures', 23rd November 1989; Deborah Hargreaves, 'The new player arrives at work', 30th November 1989; Deborah Hargreaves, 'International regulators slow to tame the machines', 22nd December 1989; Deborah Hargreaves, 'More join the bandwagon', 9th March 1990; Deborah Hargreaves, 'Screens stretch time', 9th March 1990; Deborah Hargreaves and Barbara Durr, 'Computers threaten the futures pits', 29th May 1990; Deborah Hargreaves, 'Chicago giants fight to keep their share', 2nd July 1990; Jim McCallum, 'Footsie futures steps out', 15th February 1991; Deborah Hargreaves, 'Derivatives come of age', 13th March 1991; Katharine Campbell, 'Late starter tries to catch up', 13th March 1991; Jim McCallum, 'Few tears shed for open outcry', 25th April 1991; David Owen, 'In place of the pit', 23rd May 1991; Jim McCallum and Tracy Corrigan, 'Outcry over screen trading plan', 14th June 1991; Barbara Durr, 'Competition grows fiercer and spawns new alliances', 22nd July 1991; Tracy Corrigan, 'Uncertain future for stock option trading', 17th December 1991; Ian Rodger, 'Successful Soffex', 17th December 1991; Barbara Durr, 'Exchange stakes out fresh index territory', 12th February 1992; Tracy Corrigan, 'Europe takes a bigger share', 19th March 1992; Haig Simonian, 'Italians chase a futures fast track', 20th March 1992; Barbara Durr, 'A shrinking share of a larger pie', 11th June 1992; Barbara Durr, 'Expansion planned by Chicago Mercantile Exchange', 22nd June 1992; Barbara Durr and Tracy Corrigan, 'The future comes into focus on screen', 25th June 1992; Tracy Corrigan and Patrick Harverson, 'Ever more complex', 8th December 1992; Tracy Corrigan and Laurie Morse, 'A global game for allies and rivals', 8th December 1992; Ian Rodger, 'Soffex gets the real thing', 17th December 1992.

[59] Katharine Campbell, 'Technology wars ravage Chicago', 21st March 1989.

have to experiment with various systems before global futures and options trading...can be firmly established.'[60]

The first derivatives exchange to fully embrace the electronic route was the New Zealand Futures Exchange, which was opened in 1985 but it had only seventeen members and generated little activity. The system it employed had no guaranteed counterparty and left it short of liquidity. In 1987 the Swiss Options and Financial Futures Exchange (Soffex) unveiled a fully-electronic trading system but it suffered from breakdowns and it was not until 1988 that it could be relied upon. Even more ambitious was what was taking place in Sweden. Under the leadership of Olof Stenhammar the first fully-integrated electronic options exchange, the Stockholm Options Market (OM) was set up in 1985, capturing the Swedish derivatives market. The OM group then attempted to roll out a series of electronic derivatives exchanges across Europe, beginning in Paris (1988) and Madrid (1989) followed by London (1990). The Sydney Futures Exchange also launched a screen-dealing system. However, these electronic trading systems could not yet match the liquidity provided on the trading floors of the largest derivative exchanges and this discouraged their adoption.[61] The CME continued to see the future as one reliant on floor trading, with Barbara Durr reporting in 1992 that it was planning 'to bring into use an extra trading floor to cope with new business. The current floor has become so overcrowded that vertical boxes have been built so that brokers and traders can better see what's happening amid the mass of people in the pits.'[62]

[60] Dominique Jackson, 'Futures scramble triggers global gold rush', 28th October 1988.

[61] Alexander Nicoll, 'Agreement among rivals', 19th March 1987; David Owen, 'Expansion is the keynote', 19th March 1987; Bruce Jacques, 'Sydney sheds the casino image', 19th March 1987; Roderick Oram, 'Innovators to cut global risk', 19th March 1987; Dal Hayward, 'Computer dealing shows its value', 19th March 1987; William Dullforce, 'Soffex will eschew the ring's hurly burly', 10th March 1988; Barbara Casassus, 'Report likely to allay anxiety', 10th March 1988; Deborah Hargreaves, 'Black box is on trial', 10th March 1988; Dominique Jackson, 'Liffe and LTOM fall into step', 12th October 1988; Katharine Campbell and Deborah Hargreaves, 'Liffe plans to put open-outcry pits on the screen', 2nd February 1989; Haig Simonian, 'Liffe accelerates the tempo in technology race', 23rd February 1989; Katharine Campbell, 'Suspicion lingers in the pit', 8th March 1989; George Graham, 'A rapid developer', 8th March 1989; Katharine Campbell, 'Liffe and the Matif bare their knuckles', 21st April 1989; Deborah Hargreaves, 'Matif to join Globex electronic trading', 9th November 1989; Deborah Hargreaves, 'Supremacy battle hots up for on-screen trading', 10th November 1989; Chris Sherwell, 'It's open all hours for Sydney futures', 23rd November 1989; Deborah Hargreaves, 'The new player arrives at work', 30th November 1989; Deborah Hargreaves, 'OML opens London branch', 15th December 1989; William Dullforce, 'Prices ignore good forecasts', 19th December 1989; Deborah Hargreaves, 'International regulators slow to tame the machines', 22nd December 1989; Deborah Hargreaves, 'More join the bandwagon', 9th March 1990; Deborah Hargreaves, 'Screens stretch time', 9th March 1990; Janet Bush, 'A pointer from New York', 9th March 1990; John Burton, 'The web spreads', 9th March 1990; Sara Webb, 'Give the infants time', 29th May 1990; Deborah Hargreaves, 'Chicago giants fight to keep their share', 2nd July 1990; Deborah Hargreaves, 'Sydney FE to set up own clearing house', 14th December 1990; Jim McCallum, 'Footsie futures steps out', 15th February 1991; Deborah Hargreaves, 'Derivatives come of age', 13th March 1991; Katharine Campbell, 'Late starter tries to catch up', 13th March 1991; Jim McCallum, 'Few tears shed for open outcry', 25th April 1991; David Owen, 'In place of the pit', 23rd May 1991; Jim McCallum and Tracy Corrigan, 'Outcry over screen trading plan', 14th June 1991; Barbara Durr, 'Competition grows fiercer and spawns new alliances', 22nd July 1991; Tracy Corrigan, 'Uncertain future for stock option trading', 17th December 1991; Ian Rodger, 'Successful Soffex', 17th December 1991; Barbara Durr, 'Exchange stakes out fresh index territory', 12th February 1992; Tracy Corrigan, 'Europe takes a bigger share', 19th March 1992; Haig Simonian, 'Italians chase a futures fast track', 20th March 1992; Barbara Durr, 'A shrinking share of a larger pie', 11th June 1992; Barbara Durr, 'Expansion planned by Chicago Mercantile Exchange', 22nd June 1992; Barbara Durr and Tracy Corrigan, 'The future comes into focus on screen', 25th June 1992; Tracy Corrigan and Patrick Harverson, 'Ever more complex', 8th December 1992; Tracy Corrigan and Laurie Morse, 'A global game for allies and rivals', 8th December 1992; Ian Rodger, 'Soffex gets the real thing', 17th December 1992; Nicholas George, 'Stockholm legend has tough battle ahead', 31st August 2000.

[62] Barbara Durr, 'Exchange stakes out fresh index territory', 12th February 1992.

By the early 1990s a number of non-US derivatives exchanges had become important centres of liquidity in the global derivatives market.[63] In 1991 Deborah Hargreaves observed that 'The stranglehold Chicago once held on the derivatives industry has been loosened and business has spread more evenly throughout the world.'[64] According to Tracy Corrigan and Laurie Morse in 1992, 'The futures industry is becoming increasingly competitive, as new exchanges spring up around the world and competing exchanges launch rival products.'[65] Tracy Corrigan added in 1992 that, 'Futures business, once dominated by the large US exchanges, is shifting to Europe.'[66] Though the volume of trading continued to grow on the leading US derivatives exchanges the rate at which this was happening was much slower than on these newer exchanges.[67] Nevertheless, the depth of liquidity in the contracts traded on the CME, CBOT, and Cboe meant that Chicago continued to be the central force in global financial derivatives in the early 1990s, serving not just their home market but also international customers. These exchanges were intent on retaining the business of overseas customers through the design of new contracts, extended trading hours, and reduced charges. However, none of these responses was particularly successful. It was very difficult to design a contract that would have a universal appeal or was not already traded on an existing exchange. Various attempts were made and abandoned.[68] Another response was to extend the hours their trading floors were open. However, there was a limit to how long traders could maintain the physical effort required and so these moves to extend hours were strongly resisted.[69] Instead, the defensive weapon of choice was to embrace electronic trading systems, as this could lower costs, and thus charges, while expanding capacity and extend the trading day and so concentrate activity in Chicago, which was already the largest centre of liquidity.[70] In 1992 Barbara Durr suggested that 'The advent of worldwide electronic trading…could mean that derivatives volume is

[63] David Dodwell, 'Now for silver linings and tight rules', 10th March 1988; Kevin Hamlin, 'New contracts started', 19th March 1987; Dal Hayward, 'Computer dealing shows its value', 19th March 1987; Dominique Jackson, 'Futures scramble triggers global gold rush', 28th October 1988; Chris Sherwell, 'A storm mars September', 8th March 1989; Chris Sherwell, 'It's open all hours for Sydney futures', 23rd November 1989; Deborah Hargreaves, 'The new player arrives at work', 30th November 1989; Deborah Hargreaves, 'Chicago faces a strengthening challenge', 13th December 1989; Kevin Brown, 'A gateway to Asia and the Pacific', 5th June 1990; Barbara Durr, 'New futures exchange in US', 27th February 1991; Reuter Report, 'Slow start for Manila currency futures', 6th March 1991; Barbara Durr, 'World market share shrinks', 13th March 1991; Tracy Corrigan, 'Competition helps cut costs', 29th April 1991; David Owen, 'In place of the pit', 23rd May 1991; George Graham, 'In the front rank in Europe', 17th June 1991; Haig Simonian, 'Italian derivatives look towards a new future', 2nd August 1991; Peter Bruce, 'Downside emerges after fairy-tale beginning', 23rd October 1991; Tracy Corrigan, 'Small markets stock up', 19th March 1992; Barbara Durr, 'New products to hold the line', 19th March 1992; Eric Frey, 'Luring the local saver', 22nd May 1992; Tom Burns, 'Divided Meffsa looks both ways', 4th June 1992.

[64] Deborah Hargreaves, 'Derivatives come of age', 13th March 1991.

[65] Tracy Corrigan and Laurie Morse, 'A global game for allies and rivals', 8th December 1992.

[66] Tracy Corrigan, 'Small markets stock up', 19th March 1992.

[67] Deborah Hargreaves, 'Derivatives come of age', 13th March 1991; Tracy Corrigan, 'Small markets stock up', 19th March 1992; Barbara Durr, 'A shrinking share of a larger pie', 11th June 1992; Tracy Corrigan and Laurie Morse, 'A global game for allies and rivals', 8th December 1992.

[68] Alexander Nicoll, 'Agreement among rivals', 19th March 1987; David Owen, 'Expansion is the keynote', 19th March 1987; Bruce Jacques, 'Sydney sheds the casino image', 19th March 1987; Roderick Oram, 'Innovators to cut global risk', 19th March 1987; Deborah Hargreaves, 'Black box is on trial', 10th March 1988; Deborah Hargreaves, 'Hopes fade of Liffe-CBOT link', 22nd March 1988; Barbara Durr, 'Chicago lines up a link with Japan', 13th June 1990; Barbara Durr, 'Chicago lines up a link with Japan', 13th June 1990; Barbara Durr, 'Japanese derivatives approved by CBOT', 21st June 1990.

[69] Deborah Hargreaves, 'Hopes fade of Liffe–CBOT link', 22nd March 1988; Deborah Hargreaves, 'The new player arrives at work', 30th November 1989; Deborah Hargreaves, 'International regulators slow to tame the machines', 22nd December 1989; Deborah Hargreaves, 'More join the bandwagon', 9th March 1990.

[70] Deborah Hargreaves, 'Derivatives come of age', 13th March 1991.

still concentrated in the US.'[71] What was increasingly envisaged was a single global market for derivatives made possible by electronic trading systems accessible to all. Such was the judgement reached by Tracy Corrigan and Laurie Morse by the end of 1992: 'Technological advances have enabled traders around the world to come together on screen-based systems, while the breakdown of barriers between domestic markets has furthered the internationalisation of futures as well as cash markets.'[72] Such a situation would meet the needs of banks as Alexander Nicoll explained in 1987: 'Nowadays, the biggest users of futures are the big securities houses and banks. They need large, liquid markets in which they can trade cheaply at any time, from any of the major financial centres around the world. It is to their needs that exchanges are now increasingly responding, with a number of important implications for the industry as a whole.'[73] Banks craved liquidity from the contracts they used as that allowed them to continuously balance their assets and liabilities across a range of variables so allowing them to minimize risks and maximize profits. Maggie Urry claimed in 1984 that the derivatives market could deliver this as, 'The sun never sets on trading in financial futures and options.'[74]

In terms of liquidity the reality was different, being concentrated in separate pools spread around the world. For those contracts on the main US exchange liquidity was especially deep during the US trading day but shallow before and after. Banks were reluctant to trade when the market lacked depth because of volatile pricing as well as the possibility that deals could not be completed. In turn that suppressed volume and so prevented the required level of liquidity being reached.[75] The conclusion reached by Alexander Nicoll in 1988 was that 'The scope for liquid 24-hour markets in instruments other than currencies at present seems limited.'[76] That included derivatives.[77] The solution was to recognize the role played by individual derivatives exchanges as centres of liquidity for particular contracts and time zones, and to establish alliances that could provide customers with access to different liquid markets around the world. The conclusion reached by Barbara Durr in 1991 was that, 'As derivatives have become a more common financial tool, the competition among the exchanges that trade them has grown fiercer. But the competition has also spawned a new set of co-operative alliances, especially in the US, where financial futures began.'[78] Though agreements were signed formalizing co-operation none were successful. No exchange was willing to compromise the position it had created for itself by giving concessions that could undermine its own control over the pool of liquidity it commanded and

[71] Barbara Durr, 'Competition grows fiercer and spawns new alliances', 22nd July 1991.

[72] Tracy Corrigan and Laurie Morse, 'A global game for allies and rivals', 8th December 1992.

[73] Alexander Nicoll, 'Agreement among rivals', 19th March 1987.

[74] Maggie Urry, 'The round the clock future', 7th December 1984.

[75] Lachland Drummond, 'Closer Overseas Ties', 5th March 1985; Laura Raun, 'Gold contract initiative', 5th March 1985; Alexander Nicoll, 'A global defensive strategy', 11th December 1985; Alexander Nicoll, 'Hesitant steps on road to success', 11th December 1985; Alistair Guild, 'Clearing in line for development', 11th December 1985; Laura Raun, 'Campaign to lead in Europe', 14th April 1986; David Marsh, 'Cocoa butter melts away', 23rd July 1986; Alexander Nicoll, 'Time-span suits futures', 27th October 1986; Deborah Hargreaves, 'Black box is on trial', 10th March 1988; Laura Raun, 'Exchange answers its critics', 19th March 1987; Bruce Jacques, 'Sydney sheds the casino image', 19th March 1987; Laura Raun, 'Amsterdam drops gold relaunch plan', 10th February 1988; David Blackwell, 'Market hooked on hedging', 22nd June 1992; Tracy Corrigan and Laurie Morse, 'A global game for allies and rivals', 8th December 1992.

[76] Alexander Nicoll, 'A pendulum over the pit', 10th March 1988.

[77] Steven Butler, 'Simex is on target', 19th March 1987; AP-DJ, 'Nagoya SE plans options trading', 29th September 1987; Stefan Wagstyl, 'Banks welcome Tokyo's infant', 9th March 1990; Joyce Quek, 'A revolution in the wings', 30th April 1991; Emiko Terazono, 'Fears of new restrictions', 19th March 1992.

[78] Barbara Durr, 'Competition grows fiercer and spawns new alliances', 22nd July 1991.

jealously guarded.[79] By 1992 Tracy Corrigan observed that 'Talk of links between exchanges, common a few years ago, has faded.'[80] The result was a world that continued to consist of separate pools of liquidity.[81]

The CME did try a different approach in a bid to 'to position itself as the world's leading derivatives exchange,' according to Barbara Durr.[82] The instrument chosen to achieve this objective was Globex, which was the creation of the CME's chairman, Leo Melamed, 'acknowledged as the driving force behind the development of financial futures markets.'[83] The purpose of Globex was to provide a single electronic platform that linked these existing pools of liquidity into a single marketplace to which all members would have equal access. Janet Bush foresaw in 1990 a global market in which 'electronic trading on computer networks... match buyers and sellers around the world and around the clock.'[84] In that way banks and institutional investors would be presented with a single, seamless global derivatives market that was always liquid. According to Katharine Campbell in 1989 major users of derivatives exchanges 'Would prefer a single system giving them rapid access to as many markets as possible.'[85] In this new arrangement individual exchanges would retain control over their own markets, and the products traded there, while participating in a global network. That global network would allow the members of each exchange to trade on any other so giving them direct access to markets around the world. The expectation was that those exchanges that joined Globex would place their members in a privileged position to tap global liquidity.[86] 'If there is a single key to a flourishing exchange, it is the task of amassing liquidity',[87] was Katharine Campbell's assessment in 1990. Once the advantages conferred by membership of Globex became apparent other exchanges would join the organization further enhancing its appeal. Hargreaves and Durr predicted in 1990 that, 'It will be hard for other exchanges to resist the temptation to trade their products on the global club created by the new system.'[88] That certainly applied to the CME's great rival, the CBOT, as it agreed to join. William O'Connor, the chairman of CBOT, made clear why in 1992, 'Globex will become a tool that we will use to defend our market share.'[89] What Globex was expected to combine was the benefits of a global electronic network with those

[79] Alexander Nicoll, 'Agreement among rivals', 19th March 1987; David Owen, 'Expansion is the keynote', 19th March 1987; Bruce Jacques, 'Sydney sheds the casino image', 19th March 1987; Roderick Oram, 'Innovators to cut global risk', 19th March 1987; Deborah Hargreaves, 'Black box is on trial', 10th March 1988; Deborah Hargreaves, 'Hopes fade of Liffe–BOT link', 22nd March 1988; Barbara Durr, 'Chicago lines up a link with Japan', 13th June 1990; Tracy Corrigan, 'Europe takes a bigger share', 19th March 1992; Tracy Corrigan and Laurie Morse, 'A global game for allies and rivals', 8th December 1992.

[80] Tracy Corrigan, 'Europe takes a bigger share', 19th March 1992.

[81] Deborah Hargreaves, 'Mixed response to black box trading', 23rd October 1987; Deborah Hargreaves, 'Hopes fade of Liffe–CBOT link', 22nd March 1988.

[82] Barbara Durr, 'Exchange stakes out fresh index territory', 12th February 1992.

[83] Janet Bush, 'Wall Street wants to deal wholesale', 30th August 1988.

[84] Janet Bush, 'A pointer from New York', 9th March 1990.

[85] Katharine Campbell, 'Technology wars ravage Chicago', 21st March 1989.

[86] Deborah Hargreaves, 'Hopes fade of Liffe–CBOT link', 22nd March 1988; Chris Sherwell, 'It's open all hours for Sydney futures', 23rd November 1989; Deborah Hargreaves, 'The new player arrives at work', 30th November 1989; Deborah Hargreaves, 'International regulators slow to tame the machines', 22nd December 1989; Deborah Hargreaves, 'More join the bandwagon', 9th March 1990; Deborah Hargreaves, 'Screens stretch time', 9th March 1990; Deborah Hargreaves and Barbara Durr, 'Computers threaten the futures pits', 29th May 1990; Barbara Durr, 'Chicago lines up a link with Japan', 13th June 1990; Deborah Hargreaves, 'Chicago giants fight to keep their share', 2nd July 1990.

[87] Katharine Campbell, 'New Exchanges on trial', 9th March 1990.

[88] Deborah Hargreaves and Barbara Durr, 'Computers threaten the futures pits', 29th May 1990.

[89] Barbara Durr and Tracy Corrigan, 'The future comes into focus on screen', 25th June 1992.

of face-to-face trading.[90] Deborah Hargreaves was being told in 1989 that 'A screen may be speedy in its response, but the frenetic trading atmosphere of a futures pit is hard to reproduce on screen.'[91]

The CME was not acting alone in creating Globex as it was partnered by the global information provider, Reuters. In 1987 an agreement was reached between CME and Reuters under which CME contracts would be dealt on Reuters' screens when the CME was closed. By 1988 this was being transformed into an automated trading system. However, Globex was a technically demanding project while it proved very difficult to persuade other exchanges to participate, as it meant giving up a degree of independence. As a result proposed launch dates came and went. By the end of 1989 Reuters had orders for only 260 Globex terminals and these were confined to the USA (205) and the UK (55). Though some exchanges had expressed an interest in joining Globex, such as Nymex in New York, Matif in Paris, and the SFE in Australia, others had refused, like Liffe in London, which had ambitions of its own. By 1991 Globex had still not been launched and Deborah Hargreaves expressed the views of many when she said 'the world has become impatient with its repeated delays and many exchanges are pushing ahead with their own systems'.[92] In 1992 Barbara Durr was comparing it unfavourably to the progress made by Nymex, which had pulled out of the Globex project: 'Given the global and round-the-clock nature of the oil business, Nymex's Access may stand a better chance of success in drawing in new international business than Globex will for Chicago.'[93] By then she had become very disillusioned with Globex: 'Once heralded as the key to internationalisation of the futures market, Globex has suffered three years of delays and is beginning to look more like an adjunct to that process—and perhaps not even the most technologically advanced one.'[94] Later the same year she referred to Globex as 'long-awaited, and with its start postponed successively for three years'.[95] Its launch finally took place in 1992 after five years of development and a cost of $80m. Globex provided an order-matching system for the products traded in the pits after they closed but the only derivatives exchange to join the CME was the CBOT in Chicago and the Matif in Paris. This left Globex extremely short of the global reach that was such a key element in its appeal. By the end of 1992 Globex had attracted little custom, and was widely regarded as a failure.[96]

[90] Deborah Hargreaves, 'Mixed response to black box trading', 23rd October 1987; Deborah Hargreaves, 'Black box is on trial', 10th March 1988; Dominique Jackson, 'Futures scramble triggers global gold rush', 28th October 1988; Deborah Hargreaves, 'Chicago faces a strengthening challenge', 13th December 1989.

[91] Deborah Hargreaves, 'The new player arrives at work', 30th November 1989.

[92] Deborah Hargreaves, 'Derivatives come of age', 13th March 1991.

[93] Barbara Durr, 'New products to hold the line', 19th March 1992.

[94] Barbara Durr, 'New products to hold the line', 19th March 1992.

[95] Barbara Durr, 'A shrinking share of a larger pie', 11th June 1992.

[96] For Globex see Alexander Nicoll, 'Volumes rocket after Big Bang', 19th March 1987; Alexander Nicoll, 'Liffe in search of greater liquidity', 30th September 1987; Deborah Hargreaves, 'Mixed response to black box trading', 23rd October 1987; Deborah Hargreaves, 'Hopes fade of Liffe–CBOT link', 22nd March 1988; Katharine Campbell and Deborah Hargreaves, 'Chicago ready to give the go-ahead for Globex', 2nd February 1989; Katharine Campbell, 'Technology wars ravage Chicago', 21st March 1989; Deborah Hargreaves, 'Matif to join Globex electronic trading', 9th November 1989; Deborah Hargreaves, 'Supremacy battle hots up for on-screen trading', 10th November 1989; Chris Sherwell, 'It's open all hours for Sydney futures', 23rd November 1989; Deborah Hargreaves, 'The new player arrives at work', 30th November 1989; Deborah Hargreaves, 'International regulators slow to tame the machines', 22nd December 1989; Barbara Durr, 'Open outcry from Chicago's pits', 27th June 1990; Deborah Hargreaves, 'Derivatives come of age', 13th March 1991; Joyce Quek, 'A revolution in the wings', 30th April 1991; Barbara Durr, 'Competition grows fiercer and spawns new alliances', 22nd July 1991; Barbara Durr, 'New products to hold the line', 19th March 1992; Barbara Durr, 'A shrinking share of a larger pie', 11th June 1992; Barbara Durr, 'Expansion planned by Chicago Mercantile Exchange', 22nd June 1992; Barbara Durr and Tracy Corrigan, 'The future comes into focus on screen', 25th June 1992; Laurie Morse, 'After-hours Globex has

Underlying the failure of Globex as originally conceived was a fundamental division between the aims of the exchanges and information providers like Reuters and also Telerate. As Katharine Campbell described it in 1989, 'Globex is essentially one huge electronic order book which automatically matches orders at the best price as they come in.'[97] Information providers operated a business model that depended upon them selling data and dealing services to as many subscribers as possible, with no responsibility for ensuring that an orderly market was operating. In contrast exchanges operated a different model that involved controlling access to the market, enforcing an agreed set of rules and regulations, and creating an environment in which active buying and selling could take place in full confidence that all deals would be completed. Those who were members of exchanges paid fees that met the costs incurred and abided by the mutually agreed rules and regulations. In return they not only gained entry to the trading system but privileged access to current prices, which gave them an advantage over non-members. If the likes of Reuters and Telerate simply charged a fee for the use of the information and dealing service, then membership of an exchange would confer no advantage, making them redundant. As long as Globex was to confine itself to after-hours prices and trading then the different objectives between the CME and Reuters were of little consequence. However, as the project expanded to include working day trading then it threatened the survival of the exchanges involved and the livelihood of their members.[98] Deborah Hargreaves reported at the end of 1989 that 'Exchanges, information vendors and the OTC market are becoming linked in one large electronic market-place, with the boundaries between institutions ever more blurred.'[99] Through Globex Reuters would be gifted control of the global futures and options market as its network of interactive screens connected paying customers around the world. As the launch of Globex approached these fundamental divisions between exchanges on the one hand and banks and information providers on the other became more acute and unresolved.[100] The megabanks saw what was happening as an opportunity of freeing themselves from the charges and restrictions imposed by exchanges.[101] For those reasons member-controlled exchanges were very reluctant to sign up to Globex or even co-operate with the London-based clearing house, the International Commodities Clearing House (ICCH), in

yet to live up to its promise', 1st December 1992; Tracy Corrigan and Laurie Morse, 'A global game for allies and rivals', 8th December 1992; Tracy Corrigan, 'Exchanges fight for the future across Europe', 15th January 1993.

[97] Katharine Campbell, 'Technology wars ravage Chicago', 21st March 1989.

[98] Alexander Nicoll, 'Liffe in search of greater liquidity', 30th September 1987; Deborah Hargreaves, 'Mixed response to black box trading', 23rd October 1987; Deborah Hargreaves, 'Hopes fade of Liffe–CBOT link', 22nd March 1988; Katharine Campbell and Deborah Hargreaves, 'Chicago ready to give the go-ahead for Globex', 2nd February 1989; Deborah Hargreaves, 'Tighter regulation feared', 10th April 1989; Deborah Hargreaves, 'International regulators slow to tame the machines', 22nd December 1989; Deborah Hargreaves, 'Screens stretch time', 9th March 1990; Deborah Hargreaves and Barbara Durr, 'Computers threaten the futures pits', 29th May 1990.

[99] Deborah Hargreaves, 'International regulators slow to tame the machines', 22nd December 1989.

[100] Deborah Hargreaves and Barbara Durr, 'Computers threaten the futures pits', 29th May 1990; Barbara Durr, 'Potentially crippling attack', 25th June 1990; Barbara Durr, 'Open outcry from Chicago's pits', 27th June 1990; Barbara Durr, 'US exchanges race for 24-hour trading', 27th June 1990; Deborah Hargreaves, 'Chicago giants fight to keep their share', 2nd July 1990; Deborah Hargreaves, 'Derivatives come of age', 13th March 1991; Joyce Quek, 'A revolution in the wings', 30th April 1991; Jim McCallum and Tracy Corrigan, 'Outcry over screen trading plan', 14th June 1991; Barbara Durr, 'Competition grows fiercer and spawns new alliances', 22nd July 1991; Barbara Durr, 'New products to hold the line', 19th March 1992; Barbara Durr, 'A shrinking share of a larger pie', 11th June 1992; Barbara Durr, 'Expansion planned by Chicago Mercantile Exchange', 22nd June 1992; Barbara Durr and Tracy Corrigan, 'The future comes into focus on screen', 25th June 1992; Laurie Morse, 'After-hours Globex has yet to live up to its promise', 1st December 1992; Tracy Corrigan and Laurie Morse, 'A global game for allies and rivals', 8th December 1992.

[101] Deborah Hargreaves, 'Screens stretch time', 9th March 1990.

creating a global clearing system, as that would also erode the exclusive privileges provided to members.[102]

In contrast to Globex the new German derivatives exchange, the Deutsche Terminbörse (DTB), also launched in 1992, made a success of an electronic trading system. The DTB was located in Frankfurt, where derivatives trading had been non-existent, and faced strong competition from the Matif in Paris and Liffe in London. Liffe had already taken advantage of the lack of a German derivatives market to introduce in 1988 a successful contract based on German government bonds, the Bund. There had long been opposition to derivatives in Germany and this took the form of legal restrictions on their use. That position was not reversed until the late 1980s with progress towards establishing the German Options and Financial Futures Exchange (Goffex) being slow. Writing in 1989 Michael Jenkins, the chief executive of Liffe was rather dismissive of any challenge coming from Germany: 'It was clear to us right from the start that the Germans knew the cash market but had no experience of futures.'[103] The German government even had difficulty in repealing the tax and regulatory barriers to the development of futures and option trading. What helped the German government achieve its reforms of derivatives trading was the success of Liffe in introducing a German Bund contract. Its success threatened to erode the grip exercised by the German universal banks on their domestic financial system, including the cash market in German government bonds. The German banks also faced a threat from Matif in 1988 as it was working on an interest-rate contract denominated in Deutsche Marks. In the face of this external pressure Rolf Breuer from Deutsche Bank, pushed forward the plans for a German derivatives exchange, now called Deutsche Terminbörse (DTB). The DTB began trading options in 1989 but futures did not follow until 1990, giving Liffe and Matif time to get their contracts established. The consensus view in 1989 was that those behind the establishment of the DTB had left it too late. Faced with existing and popular contracts in the areas it hoped to enter, the DTB chose the risky route of opting for an electronic market, as its main competitors in Europe, Liffe, and Matif, remained committed to open-outcry pit trading.

The decision was taken to adopt the model in use by the Swiss Options and Financial Futures Exchange (Soffex), which was entirely computer-based without a physical trading floor. In a federal country like Germany an electronic market possessed considerable appeal, as it offered equal access to all rather than centralization in Frankfurt, and so reduced the level of opposition from individual German states. At a cost of $42m the DTB fully opened in January 1990, trading a mixture of options and futures on corporate stocks and government bonds. With the DTB and Liffe both trading an identical futures contract on ten-year German government bonds there was competition for the first time between an electronic platform—the DTB—and open-outcry trading—Liffe. The prospect intrigued contemporaries from the outset. Writing in 1990 Katharine Campbell and Deborah Hargreaves noted that 'The battle will mark the first time in the world futures industry that a traditional open outcry market has competed for business against an electronic system.'[104]

102 John Edwards, 'Broader base and wider choice', 5th March 1985; Alexander Nicoll, 'Hesitant steps on road to success', 11th December 1985; Alexander Nicoll, 'Underpinning the market's liquidity', 19th March 1987; Allison Maitland, 'Slow steps in the paper chase', 21st October 1987; Deborah Hargreaves, 'Mixed response to black box trading', 23rd October 1987; Deborah Hargreaves, 'Mixed response to black box trading', 23rd October 1987; Barbara Durr, 'Competition grows fiercer and spawns new alliances', 22nd July 1991; Laurie Morse, 'After-hours Globex has yet to live up to its promise', 1st December 1992; Tracy Corrigan and Patrick Harverson, 'Ever more complex', 8th December 1992.

103 Katharine Campbell, 'Liffe dilemma for German banks', 19th January 1989.

104 Katharine Campbell and Deborah Hargreaves, 'Frankfurt fights to regain bunds', 26th November 1990.

The expectation was a victory for Liffe as its own attempt to introduce an electronic trading system had not proved popular with its membership while Soffex, the model upon which DTB was based, had not yet proved a success. Alex Cooper, director of financial markets at Crédit Lyonnais, expressed the view of most users in 1990 when he said, 'What matters is the liquidity and the speed of execution... people don't care what medium they trade on as long as it has the business.'[105] As the home of the existing Bund contracts Liffe held the commanding position. Nevertheless, Rolf Bruer, who had become chairman of DTB, was convinced that the technological superiority of the German exchange would deliver it victory over Liffe. Michael Jenkins, chief executive of Liffe, disagreed: 'We think open outcry will work better than a screen in periods of intensive trading... with a computer system it takes a long time to key in bids and offers.'[106] However, the DTB's technological superiority was not confined to the trading system but also extended to other parts of the system. In 1989 the Inter Banken Informations System (IBIS) had been launched in Germany. This was an electronic price reporting system for stock and bond prices. What DTB had put in place by 1990 was an integrated trading and clearing system. In addition, the leading German banks were committed to supporting the DTB, and they dominated trading in both the cash and futures market in German government bonds. Rolf Breuer was not only chairman of the DTB but also a member of Deutsche Bank's board of management. As it was DTB gained market share from Liffe in the German Bund contract, making a significant breakthrough in 1991. The DTB share of trading in the German Bund contract rose from 6 per cent at the beginning of 1991 to 30 per cent a year later with German banks switching trading from London to Frankfurt. By 1992 the DTB was ready to expand its operations beyond Germany by placing terminals across Europe, including London and Paris. It was also engaged in a four-way alliance, First European Exchanges (FEX), between itself and other European derivatives exchanges, though this failed, like so many others. However, what the success of the DTB in the German Bund contract had demonstrated was the ability of an electronic market to compete with an open-outcry one and win.[107]

[105] Katharine Campbell and Deborah Hargreaves, 'Frankfurt fights to regain bunds', 26th November 1990.

[106] Katharine Campbell and Deborah Hargreaves, 'Frankfurt fights to regain bunds', 26th November 1990.

[107] Haig Simonian, 'Liffe eyes D-Mark business', 18th February 1988; Clare Pearson, 'October's storm produces ideal trading weather', 10th March 1988; Haig Simonian, 'Liffe hijacks the Bund-wagon', 21st September 1988; Katharine Campbell, 'Liffe dilemma for German banks', 19th January 1989; Katharine Campbell, 'OTC derivatives take up the running in equities', 9th February 1989; Haig Simonian, 'West German futures face tough debut', 23rd February 1989; Haig Simonian, 'A computer-based market', 8th March 1989; George Graham, 'A rapid developer', 8th March 1989; Katharine Campbell, 'Liffe and the Matif bare their knuckles', 21st April 1989; Haig Simonian, 'Quiet revolution for German securities', 13th September 1989; William Dullforce, 'Prices ignore good forecasts', 19th December 1989; Deborah Hargreaves, 'International regulators slow to tame the machines', 22nd December 1989; Katharine Campbell, 'Anxious parents await DTB birth', 26th January 1990; Deborah Hargreaves, 'More join the bandwagon', 9th March 1990; Katharine Campbell, 'New Exchanges on trial', 9th March 1990; Katharine Campbell, 'No recipe for long-term success', 9th March 1990; Katharine Campbell and Deborah Hargreaves, 'Bund futures force pace of change', 4th May 1990; Katharine Campbell, 'A call for support', 19th June 1990; Katharine Campbell and Deborah Hargreaves, 'Frankfurt fights to regain bunds', 26th November 1990; Deborah Hargreaves, 'Derivatives exchanges seeks tax reform', 12th December 1990; Katharine Campbell, 'German banks search for support for futures market', 19th December 1990; Katharine Campbell, 'Late starter tries to catch up', 13th March 1991; Katharine Campbell, 'Conservative investors find a taste for adventure', 17th July 1991; Barbara Durr, 'Competition grows fiercer and spawns new alliances', 22nd July 1991; Katharine Campbell, 'DTB announces launch of two options contracts', 16th August 1991; Katharine Campbell, 'Roles are reversed for city of bankers', 28th October 1991; David Waller, 'Lack of regulator stalls DTB expansion', 12th February 1992; Tracy Corrigan, 'Small markets stock up', 19th March 1992; Tracy Corrigan and Laurie Morse, 'A global game for allies and rivals', 8th December 1992; Tracy Corrigan, 'DTB and Matif in co-operation agreement', 14th January 1993; Tracy Corrigan, 'Swaps market may be bigger than estimated', 16th November 1993; Conner Middelmann, 'Domestic market is struggling', 1st March 1996.

The OTC Derivatives Market

Despite the proliferation of new options and futures exchanges, and the innovation they showed in terms of products and technology, the fastest growing component of the derivatives market from the 1980s onwards were those products traded directly between banks or through interdealer brokers. It was estimated that the size of the swap market in 1992 was $7,000bn rather than $4,500bn, as the focus had been on exchange-based products. By then the OTC market dwarfed the exchange-traded one in terms of contracts outstanding. As the use of derivatives expanded in volume and variety the standard products available from exchanges provided only an imperfect fit. The exchanges wanted contracts that could attract as wide an audience as possible, and so generate a high level of trading, if they were to occupy valuable space on the floor and the time of those who bought and sold them for a living. This meant a fairly generous specification making such contracts unsuitable when a more precise match was required. In contrast an OTC derivatives contract was designed to meet a specific requirement, customized to suit the interests of both parties. It was this match to requirements that won many converts to OTC derivatives. This was despite serious issues of counterparty risk because of their bilateral nature compared to exchange-traded ones, where clearing arrangements were in place, providing a guarantee that terms would be honoured and payments made. During the 1980s megabanks like JP Morgan, Banker's Trust, and the Swiss Bank Corporation were able to convince counterparties that they had the financial strength to be relied upon. By 1992 40 per cent of the swaps market was in the hands of ten of the world's largest banks led by US banks such as JP Morgan and European banks like Paribas. Swaps provided banks and companies with the flexibility to manage their assets and liabilities on a continuous basis or to construct a portfolio tailor-made to suit different exposures. Using swaps a bank could not only match assets and liabilities across different variables but also reduce their exposure to any single borrower, whether a large company or a sovereign country. In a competitive market a bank was always reluctant to refuse a loan to a long-standing borrower as that could result in the permanent loss of that customer if another lender provided them with the finance they required. Conversely, a bank was also reluctant to become over-exposed to an individual borrower as their default could endanger its survival by prompting a liquidity or even solvency crisis. By sharing commitments with each other a bank could reduce its exposure while maintaining a close relationship with that customer. What swaps also did was challenge the established divisions between different types of banks which suited those that had already followed the universal model, as with the Swiss. That encouraged US banks, in particular, to locate much of their swaps business in London where the Glass–Steagall act did not apply.[108]

The swap market began in 1981 in the corporate debt market in the USA where banks were exposed to large losses as the size of business borrowers grew while legislation restricted a matching expansion in the scale of banks. Swaps were then taken up

[108] John H. Parry, 'Threat from over-complexity', 5th March 1985; Alexander Nicoll, 'A new option for the corporate treasurer', 1st August 1985; Alexander Nicoll, 'A global defensive strategy', 11th December 1985; Alexander Nicoll, 'A boon for the corporate treasurer', 11th December 1985; Alexander Nicoll, 'Potential begins to be fulfilled', 11th December 1985; Alistair Guild, 'Clearing in line for development', 11th December 1985; Maggie Urry, 'Pru-Bache opens up a swaps warehouse', 16th December 1985; Yoko Shibata, 'Early setback for Tokyo bond futures', 11th December 1985; Peter Montagnon, 'A need for banks to watch extent of commitment', 17th March 1986; James Blitz, 'New anxieties for the banks', 26th May 1993; Tracy Corrigan, 'A short cut to domination', 20th October 1993.

internationally as the Latin American debt crisis made banks aware of the risks they were running even with sovereign borrowers. That was then followed by the 1987 stock market crash, which encouraged banks to turn to swaps as a way of covering the risks they were running. The notional amount outstanding in the swaps market grew exponentially, from an estimated \$3bn in 1985 to \$3.9tn in 1991, comprising 40 per cent of the total value of derivative contracts outstanding. Such was the exponential growth of the swaps market that an International Swap Dealers Association was formed in 1985 to develop standard contracts and agreed rules. While smaller banks sought to limit their exposure to risk through the use of OTC derivatives markets, the megabanks were willing to increase their exposure to risk as they could use their capital and reserves to act as counterparties in the expectation of exiting a deal at a profit.[109] As Marion Robinson, of Bankers Trust, noted in 1988, 'When the market first started, swaps were usually dismissed as little more than an exotic and dubious sideline. Now few financial institutions can really afford to ignore the market and most are still actively upgrading their swaps capabilities.'[110] By then interest rate and currency swaps had been transformed from 'rarefied and risky instruments' into 'routine and indispensable tools for exposure management', according to Dominique Jackson.[111] Exchange-traded and OTC derivatives were not alternatives to each other as Gerard Corrigan, chairman of the Federal Reserve Bank of New York, explained: 'It is exceedingly difficult for me to see how swaps could be traded on organized exchanges, given that so many swaps are custom-tailored for specific purposes and uses.'[112]

In the OTC markets bank customers could be provided with a bespoke product that covered their precise risk. In the exchange-traded market the banks themselves could obtain the cover they required to protect themselves from the risks they had taken on. Banks became increasingly experienced in using both exchange-traded and OTC contracts to reduce the risk they were exposed to through interest rate and currency volatility, especially the former. Some of these OTC contracts lacked the price transparency and liquidity provided by those quoted on an exchange making them difficult and expensive to unwind before maturity. This left a bank with a liquidity risk because the specific nature of the OTC contract made it difficult to trade. For that reason banks turned to exchange-traded derivatives for cover, as these were highly liquid. In that way the growth of the OTC market drove up turnover of exchange-traded futures and options. That then contributed to the expansion of the OTC market and so on.[113] As Alexander Nicoll reported in 1987, 'The biggest

[109] D. Campbell Smith, 'Hunting for the gig game', 28th November 1983; Peter Montagnon, 'International powerhouse', 21st May 1984; Alexander Nicoll, 'Risks yet to be tested', 17th March 1986; Peter Montagnon, 'A need for banks to watch extent of commitment', 17th March 1986; David Lascelles, 'A New York–Tokyo–London axis', 7th April 1986; Peter Montagnon, 'Downgrading of Libor', 22nd May 1986; Barbara Casassus, 'Top-slot turnover has quadrupled', 27th May 1986; Elaine Williams, 'Banking's unifying force', 16th October 1986; David Lascelles, 'Swaps market likely to last, says Bank', 12th February 1987; Philip Coggan, 'Regulators cramp market's growth', 21st April 1987; Philip Coggan, 'New players speed trade', 21st April 1987; Stephen Fidler, 'Loan market emerges from twilight', 21st May 1987; Alexander Nicoll, 'Liffe in search of greater liquidity', 30th September 1987; Dominique Jackson, 'Swaps keep in step with the regulators', 10th August 1988; Dominique Jackson, 'Private investors are regaining confidence', 20th August 1988; John Edwards, 'Profiting from a small outlay', 20th August 1988; Laurie Morse, 'A two-pronged development', 20th October 1993.

[110] Dominique Jackson, 'Swaps keep in step with the regulators', 10th August 1988.

[111] Dominique Jackson, 'Swaps keep in step with the regulators', 10th August 1988.

[112] Tracy Corrigan, 'End of rapid growth', 20th July 1992.

[113] David Lascelles, 'Swaps market likely to last, says Bank', 12th February 1987; David Owen, 'Over the counter, round the law', 19th March 1987; Philip Coggan, 'A worldwide stratagem', 19th March 1987; Alexander Nicoll, 'Warning signs in global game', 21st April 1987; Philip Coggan, 'Regulators cramp market's growth', 21st April 1987; Philip Coggan, 'Regulators take an interest', 3rd June 1987; Philip Coggan, 'Corporations are chary', 3rd June 1987; Alexander Nicoll, 'Liffe in search of greater liquidity', 30th September 1987; Philip Coggan, 'Just a simple idea', 29th June 1988; Steven Butler, 'Investment banks cash in on volatile oil prices', 1st July 1988; Katharine

players, who have increasingly sophisticated trading strategies developed with the aid of computers, are not over-concerned about whether they trade on exchanges or not, particularly if some alternative instrument, traded elsewhere, provides the same or even a better, tailor-made function more cheaply. Hence the growing threat of off-exchange trading to established exchanges.'[114] The megabanks had the capital to support the risk of OTC trades and the reputation, scale, connections, and size to be considered reliable counterparties, with a number specializing in particular areas.[115] David Owen observed in 1987 that these megabanks were 'introducing a fast-expanding range of financial products which bear an uncanny resemblance to futures and options—but are traded over-the-counter.'[116] Facilitating this OTC derivatives market were the interdealer brokers and information providers like Reuters. With banks taking responsibility for their own counterparty risk the interdealer brokers and information providers acted as electronic marketplaces. As Deborah Hargreaves wrote in 1989, 'In the competitive financial world, established exchanges are not only competing between themselves for a slice of the global pie but also with over-the-counter markets, where technology gives the edge to a cheaper market. Information companies such as Reuters and Telerate are already using their technological

Campbell, 'OTC derivatives take up the running in equities', 9th February 1989; Jeffrey Brown, 'More Players respond as volatility falls', 8th March 1989; Patrick Harverson, 'When gilts are sick there is a remedy', 8th March 1989; Katharine Campbell, 'Protection for the portfolio', 8th March 1989; Katharine Campbell, 'Liffe and the Matif bare their knuckles', 21st April 1989; Deborah Hargreaves, 'Appeal ruling fails to restore certainty', 9th March 1990; Jeffrey Brown, 'Bells and whistles count', 9th March 1990; Stephen Fidler, 'When family loyalties are placed under severe strain', 28th December 1990; Tracy Corrigan, 'Where innovation prevails', 13th March 1991; Barbara Durr, 'Plea for a level playing field', 13th June 1991; Tracy Corrigan, 'Ecu swaps market grows despite drawbacks', 24th October 1991; Simon London, 'Banks take expansive view', 19th March 1992; Tracy Corrigan, 'Techniques find new markets', 19th March 1992; Barbara Durr, 'Options exchanges worried by over-the-counter trading', 15th May 1992; Tracy Corrigan, 'End of rapid growth', 20th July 1992; Patrick Harverson and Tracy Corrigan, 'The threat of regulation stirs an unfettered giant', 11th August 1992; Tracy Corrigan and Patrick Harverson, 'Ever more complex', 8th December 1992; Patrick Harverson, 'It's time to know what's going on', 8th December 1992; Laurie Morse, 'New law lifts uncertainty', 8th December 1992; Tracy Corrigan, 'US pioneers lured to new frontier by rich packages', 8th December 1992; Richard Waters, 'Higher return, no extra risk', 8th December 1992.

114 Alexander Nicoll, 'Agreement among rivals', 19th March 1987.

115 David Lascelles and Stephen Fidler, 'Morgan Stanley sticks to equities', 29th February 1987; Alexander Nicoll, 'Agreement among rivals', 19th March 1987; Alexander Nicoll, 'Warning signs in global game', 21st April 1987; Stephen Fidler, 'More than a mere slogan', 7th May 1987; Alexander Nicoll, 'The rocky road to a global village', 27th May 1987; David Lascelles, 'Through the pain barrier', 21st September 1987; David Lascelles, 'New strengths and a ticket to the City's turf', 21st September 1987; David Lascelles, 'Thrive, merge or specialise', 21st September 1987; David Lascelles, 'Clearers look overseas', 21st September 1987; Alexander Nicoll, 'Liffe in search of greater liquidity', 30th September 1987; David Lascelles, 'Banking on an international status', 3rd November 1987; Deborah Hargreaves, 'Hybrids fight to escape regulation', 9th December 1987; Deborah Hargreaves, 'Regulators seek to protect retail customer in battle of look-alikes', 10th March 1988; Stephen Fidler, 'A force more respected than loved', 11th May 1988; John Paul Lee, 'Technology demonstrates its worth', 18th May 1988; Peter Montagnon, 'Securitisation can often be the key to the future', 18th May 1988; Steven Butler, 'Investment banks cash in on volatile oil prices', 1st July 1988; David Lascelles, 'Specialise if you're not a global player', 26th September 1988; Sean Heath, 'City's stability appreciated', 26th September 1988; Paul Taylor, 'Blow, not knockout', 28th September 1988; Janet Bush, 'Five banks with universal plans', 2nd May 1989; David Lascelles, 'Questions over the City's future', 22nd December 1989; David Lascelles, 'Cautious steps in the merchant bank forest', 2nd January 1990; Deborah Hargreaves, 'Chicago exchanges at variance', 9th March 1990; David Lascelles, 'The London cavern is the hub for Europe', 5th June 1990; Andrew Freeman, 'Tokyo institutions build up derivatives expertise', 25th July 1990; Martin Dickson, 'Now the Swiss call the shots', 17th December 1990; Tracy Corrigan, 'Where innovation prevails', 13th March 1991; Barbara Durr, 'Plea for a level playing field', 13th June 1991; Sara Webb, 'Poll names top three banks in swaps market', 17th September 1991; Juliet Sychrava, 'Electricity forward market is world first', 23rd October 1991; Tracy Corrigan, 'Europe takes a bigger share', 19th March 1992; Simon London, 'Banks take expansive view', 19th March 1992; Barbara Durr, 'Options exchanges worried by over-the-counter trading', 15th May 1992; Barbara Harrison, 'Exchanges defend their world title', 1st December 1992; Tracy Corrigan and Patrick Harverson, 'Ever more complex', 8th December 1992; Patrick Harverson, 'It's time to know what's going on', 8th December 1992; Laurie Morse, 'New law lifts uncertainty', 8th December 1992.

116 David Owen, 'Over the counter, round the law', 19th March 1987.

expertise to step beyond the bounds of their traditional data vending services.' She continued with the comment that 'Exchanges, information vendors and the OTC market are becoming linked in one large electronic market-place, with the boundaries between institutions ever more blurred.'[117] There was a competitive tension between the exchanges and the OTC market that drove both change and increased activity in both throughout the 1980s and into the 1990s.[118]

Conclusion

Competition created the need, technology provided the means, and the liberalization of markets domestically and internationally generated the opportunity for the revolution in derivatives markets that took place after 1970. By 1992 financial derivatives had established themselves as essential tools used by banks and large companies to protect themselves from the volatile conditions within which they now operated. At the same time others, especially the megabanks, saw futures, options, and swaps as a source of profit. By leveraging their capital and exploiting their global connections these banks could generate a growing revenue stream for themselves. Chicago was at the forefront of these developments, driven by the nature of the US financial system, especially the continuing restrictions placed on banks. Conversely these restrictions could also drive activity out of the USA with London being a major beneficiary, as it provided a convenient location from which to conduct operations without the rules and regulations that hampered them in the USA. Japanese banks and brokers, who suffered from similar restrictions, also turned to London while both Hong Kong and Singapore benefited in Asia. However, the pace of growth and change in derivatives that took place outside the USA was not just a spillover from the USA or even Japan. Instead, it reflected a genuine attempt to meet the need of local customers for products and markets dedicated to their needs. This need was initially met by existing US exchanges but from the mid-1980s there was an explosion in the number of specialist derivatives exchanges formed elsewhere in the world and a rapid growth in the OTC market through which banks traded with each other. These new exchanges experimented with electronic trading rather than copying existing practice with some ending in failures, as with Globex, while Germany's DTB was a success. At the same time the OTC derivatives market experienced exponential growth, being conducted between offices linked by telephones and computer screens.

[117] Deborah Hargreaves, 'International regulators slow to tame the machines', 22nd December 1989.

[118] David Waller, 'Reuters chases a forex scoop', 15th March 1989; Richard Waters, 'Towards Europe's super-league', 11th September 1989; Clive Cookson, '24-hour traders', 9th November 1989; Rachel Johnson, 'Reuters triumphs in the derivatives jungle', 21st December 1989; Deborah Hargreaves, 'International regulators slow to tame the machines', 22nd December 1989; Richard Waters, 'Rivals may yet collaborate', 2nd July 1990; Juliet Sychrava, 'Electricity forward market is world first', 23rd October 1991; Tracy Corrigan, 'Small markets stock up', 19th March 1992; Tracy Corrigan, 'Diversification is the spur', 19th March 1992; Barbara Durr, 'Options exchanges worried by over-the-counter trading', 15th May 1992; Barbara Harrison, 'Exchanges defend their world title', 1st December 1992; Laurie Morse, 'New law lifts uncertainty', 8th December 1992.

5
Equities and Exchanges, 1970–92

Introduction

It took much longer for a global equity market to develop after 1970 as compared to other financial instruments. Even after barriers to financial flows were removed equity investment was largely confined behind national boundaries because of political, currency, and liquidity risks. However, in the 1980s equities acquired global appeal and cross-border investment expanded rapidly, though remaining dwarfed by domestic holdings. By 1986 total cross-border equity holdings in the US, Europe, and Japan had reached $800bn and then grew to $1,300bn in 1991 despite the setback caused by the stock market crash of 1987. Nevertheless, the global equity market suffered from the lack of corporate stocks that could command a universal market. There was no equivalent among equities of those bonds that attracted all international investors, such as US government debt; a currency such as the US$ that underpinned global financial transactions; or highly liquid derivative contracts that could be used to hedge risk. There were important differences between equities and other financial instruments that reduced the extent of their appeal as financial instruments. This was not just in the enormous variety of equities in circulation, issued by widely divergent businesses in so many different currencies and denominations and with unique legal conditions. In the USA alone there were around 10,000 separate corporate stocks in the 1980s. That situation also applied to bonds but there the similarity ended. Unlike bonds, which paid a guaranteed rate of interest, there was no fixed return from equities, and so their value could fluctuate wildly depending on the performance of the management and the condition of the particular business they were engaged in. A sudden change in fortune could generate a huge capital gain or total loss, with an immediate impact on the share price. In contrast, bond prices were much more stable, being responsive to prevailing interest rates unless a default or devaluation was expected. Equities also differed from bonds because they gave their owners control over the businesses that had issued them. That element of control grew in importance in the second half of the twentieth century, as corporate reorganizations through mergers and acquisitions became a major feature of business life. Whereas the changing ownership of bonds left the issuers undisturbed, whether they were governments or businesses, that of stocks could have far-reaching consequences. The result was to give a value to equities separate from any predictable returns. It was these unique features attached to stocks that made the market in which they were traded much more complex than that of bonds.[1]

There were also major differences between the equity market and those for foreign exchange and swaps, which were inter-bank ones involving relatively few participants, being confined to those who were of sufficient scale and reputation to act as trusted

[1] Norma Cohen, 'A debate intensified by fear', 22nd May 1989; Richard Waters, 'A new deal for the survival of the Stock Exchange', 1st February 1990; Peter Marsh, 'They're breathing down London's neck', 26th May 1993; Andrew Fisher, 'Germany's stock answer', 22nd October 1996; Jeffrey Brown, 'From slow start to relentless build-up', 1st January 2000.

Banks, Exchanges, and Regulators: Global Financial Markets from the 1970s. Ranald Michie, Oxford University Press (2021).

DOI: 10.1093/oso/9780199553730.003.0005

counterparties. Banks were continually engaged in borrowing, lending, and swapping commitments between each other, as they balanced their assets and liabilities across time, space, and other variables, acting as their own guarantors for the deals they made. In contrast, the equity market involved a large number of more varied participants, ranging from large institutions to retail investors, most of whom were unknown to each other. This created counterparty risks as there was always the possibility of non-payment or non-delivery. It was for those reasons that stock exchanges evolved to provide not only a market where shares could be traded but also a way of minimizing or eliminating counterparty risk, price manipulation, and fraudulent behaviour through a set of rules and regulations. These rules and regulations covered all aspects of the market ranging from who could participate through the structure of the trading system to sanctions against misbehaviour. It was the combination of facilities for trading and these rules and regulations which attracted both companies and investors to the markets provided by stock exchanges as Martin Jacomb, an experienced investment banker, explained in 1988. A stock exchange was where 'members bring their business, and transact it with other members under clear market rules which ensure that bargains are properly and promptly settled. If members bring all their business to the central market, liquidity is improved; and it must be transparent enough to ensure that everyone can check that their deal was done at the right price.... Maximum liquidity is what market users need.'[2] The ultimate sanction used by stock exchanges to enforce rules and regulations, and persuade participants to pay the costs of providing and policing the market, was exclusion from the trading process. That sanction was effective when trading took place in a specific location and between individuals as entry could be barred and no alternative existed. It was much more difficult to apply when trading gravitated away from a physical space and was increasingly in the hands of a few large institutions, as was the case from 1970 onwards.[3]

The power possessed by stock exchanges could also be used to favour a few by limiting access and suppressing competition, allowing excessive charges to be levied while providing a poor service. The result was a creative tension between those with entry to the trading floor provided by exchanges and those prohibited, as the latter always had the possibility of making alternative trading arrangements if the restrictions and charges imposed became a major burden. The competitive advantage possessed by exchanges, which countered the charges they levied and the restrictions imposed, was that they were simultaneously the centre of liquidity and the source of reference prices. It was for these benefits that made members willing to pay fees and accept the rules and regulations imposed. In turn, these rules and regulations helped enforce the appeal of stock exchanges as centres of liquidity and reference prices because they led to the concentration of trading there. Anything that led trading to fragment jeopardized the appeal of stock exchanges, undermined their ability to charge fees for access, and the willingness of those who used them to pay the charges imposed. Once that happened the ability of stock exchanges to enforce their rules and regulations and impose their charges was weakened. What this meant was that stock

[2] Martin Jacomb, 'Fine-tuning the London market', 19th April 1988.

[3] Alexander Nicoll, 'International moves before Big Bang', 29th August 1985; John Moore, 'Goodison to outline foreign links plan', 31st October 1985; Alexander Nicoll, 'Swiss connection is prominent', 17th March 1986; Alexander Nicoll, 'Electronic Bridge boosts global equities trading', 23rd April 1986; John Plender, 'Capital loosens its bonds', 8th May 1986; Barry Riley, 'A unique global background', 3rd July 1986; Alexander Nicoll, 'The new market has an electronic heart', 27th October 1986; David Lascelles and Alexander Nicoll, 'An oddly quiet revolution', 4th February 1987; Norma Cohen, 'A debate intensified by fear', 22nd May 1989; Richard Waters, 'A new deal for the survival of the Stock Exchange', 1st February 1990.

exchanges had to tread a fine line between imposing rules and regulations, that assisted the functioning of the market they provided, against those that privileged the interests of the few who paid the fees they demanded for access. One prominent group in this wider community were banks, as they were often excluded by stock exchanges, or subjected to severe restrictions on their participation. Especially as banks grew in size and scale they had the ability to trade away from the market provided by a stock exchange, so avoiding the charges and restrictions imposed, though they based their transactions on the prices generated there. In turn that deprived the market of liquidity and undermined the quality of the prices generated, lessening the appeal of stock exchanges and so encouraging further fragmentation. Those familiar with the equity market and the role played by stock exchanges were conscious of the delicate balancing act they had to perform in order to retain the loyalty of the wider financial community and deliver the benefits of a regulated market.[4]

Users of stock exchanges wanted the regulatory features that contributed to liquidity and provided them with the confidence that they could trust the prices generated and counterparties to honour their bargains. They did not want to be forced to pay high charges for the privilege of accessing this market or obey rules and regulations that made it difficult for them to conduct an efficient business and meet the changing needs of their customers. What had happened after the Second World War was that government intervention tilted the balance of power in favour of those stock exchanges that remained in existence, allowing them to impose charges and enforce rules and regulations that favoured the few against the interests of the many. The surviving stock exchanges had become incorporated into the regulatory structure, either formally or informally, through which governments and central banks exercised control over national financial systems. In 1934 the US had established the Securities and Exchange Commission (SEC), and it provided the model for supervising the activities of exchanges in many countries. With their authority now backed by government, whether directly or indirectly, stock exchanges were better able to resist the forces of change, operate immune from competition, and impose their rules and regulations over national equity markets. Writing in 1989 David Lascelles reflected that 'Stock exchanges almost everywhere have proved to be highly conservative institutions, which cling to their privileges.'[5] It was only slowly that the power possessed by stock exchanges to impose their rules and regulations on the global equity market were removed from 1970 onwards. The process of doing so was both slow and piecemeal and involved government intervention to force the ending of restrictive practices and remove barriers to competition.[6]

Forces for Change

Though events such as May Day in New York in 1975 and Big Bang in London in 1986, when the New York Stock Exchange (NYSE) and the London Stock Exchange (LSE) respectively were forced through outside intervention to abandon a fixed scale of charges, were

[4] John Wyles, 'European financiers consider plans for joint stock exchange', 13th November 1980; Euromarkets Staff, 'Big reforms face bond dealers' association', 22nd May 1985; Quentin Peel, 'Financial integration makes slow progress', 4th June 1985; Rachel Davies, 'Invasion of the City increases', 15th July 1985; Alexander Nicoll, 'A banker rather than a regulator', 20th January 1987; Clare Pearson, 'Overcrowding inhibits new issues', 21st April 1987; John Plender, 'Cries of foul from the maze', 23rd September 1987; Alexander Nicoll, 'The heart of the world game', 21st October 1987.

[5] David Lascelles, 'Pitching for a share of London's work', 5th July 1989.

[6] Nigel Lawson, 'We must not take London's success for granted', 23rd October 2006.

hailed as landmark events, there were fundamental forces at work. It was the combination of regulatory intervention, the growing ability of banks to trade shares internally or between themselves, and the relocation of the market away from a physical trading floor that undermined the power of stock exchanges to dictate to the global equity market. In 1986 Alan Cane referred to these as 'The unholy trinity of increased competition, deregulation and technology',[7] while Stanislas Yassukovich, chairman of Merrill Lynch Europe, pointed out that, 'Many of the forces which led to the internationalisation of the debt market are now at work in the equity market.'[8] In the same year Alexander Nicoll reported that 'Everywhere, the equity market is leaping established boundaries…a globalisation of the equity market that is challenging assumptions about where and how to issue shares, and about who will own and trade them.…A round-the-clock trading market has begun to develop in the shares of the world's biggest companies, both outside domestic markets and time zones and away from stock exchange trading floors.'[9] He added in 1987 that 'Internationalisation, coupled with new technology, brings into question the very nature of a stock exchange.'[10] By 1992 Charles Batchelor concluded that 'Modern technology makes it irrelevant where an electronic market is based.'[11] Though many contemporaries were quick to forecast the end of stock exchanges, because of the possibilities offered by the new technology and what was taking place in other financial markets, they underestimated the unique features attached to equities. Those unique features meant that stock exchanges continued to play a central role in the global equity market. Nevertheless, their position was under threat from 1970 with the greatest challenge coming from the large banks as they sought to extent their dominance of other financial markets into equities.[12]

By the 1980s the combination of modern communications technology, the ending of exchange controls, and the increasingly international outlook of investors, was leading to the emergence of a global equity market. Institutional investors hunted for higher returns on their money while companies sought wider and deeper markets for their stock. Nevertheless, creating a global equity market that transcended national borders faced, in the words of Alexander Nicoll in 1986, 'great challenges for regulators, stock exchanges, investors and for companies'.[13] These difficulties included opposition from national governments facing an undermining of their authority.[14] Indicative of the strength of that opposition was the difficulty that the EU had in overcoming them, despite attempting to do so since 1960. There were fundamental differences between nation-states as reflected in language, culture, and legal systems and these made it very difficult to replicate internationally what the USA was able to do internally in terms of a single integrated stock market.[15] In 1985 Hans-Joeg Rudloff, deputy chairman of Credit Suisse First Boston, claimed that 'There

[7] Alan Cane, 'Systems tailored to market-makers', 16th October 1986.

[8] Alexander Nicoll, 'Round-the-clock trading brings a new challenge', 5th November 1985.

[9] Alexander Nicoll, 'Round-the-clock trading brings a new challenge', 5th November 1985.

[10] Alexander Nicoll, 'Everything to play for', 21st October 1987.

[11] Charles Batchelor, 'Enterprise looks for a way out', 22nd December 1992.

[12] William Dawkins, 'Expansion from a broader base', 12th March 1984; Charles Batchelor, 'Over-the-counter market set for expansion', 12th March 1984; Richard Lambert, 'The lessons Wall Street can teach London', 18th April 1984.

[13] Alexander Nicoll, 'Round-the-clock trading brings a new challenge', 5th November 1985.

[14] Barry Riley, 'Equities develop global market', 23rd November 1983.

[15] John Wyles, 'European financiers consider plans for joint stock exchange', 13th November 1980; Quentin Peel, 'Financial integration makes slow progress', 4th June 1985; Robert Rice, 'Legislative shortcomings in post-Big Bang era lead to calls for reform', 7th February 1990; Janet Bush, 'Enforcement of securities law remains politically popular', 7th February 1990; Alastair FitzSimons, 'EC Directives change securities markets', 15th February 1990; Richard Waters, 'Pipe brings dream of Euro-bourse closer to reality', 19th April 1990.

are no international equities. What we have are domestic shares distributed internationally. The real price of a stock is still set on its home stock exchange.'[16] In 1985 there were only an estimated 150 companies whose shares attracted international interest, and trading in these was concentrated on that exchange which provided the most liquid market.[17] As Fraser Jennings, joint managing director of Prudential Bache Capital Funding (Equities) in London pointed out in 1987, 'There are some stocks you can trade around the globe. There are others you can only trade when the home market is open.'[18] Most stocks were found in the latter category. In 1989 only seventy-one of the 5500 quoted by Nasdaq were also quoted in London. Even when shares were repackaged as American Depository Receipts (ADRs) or Global Depository Receipts (GDRs), so giving them international appeal, trading gravitated to a single centre.[19] In turn stock exchanges provided very domestically-focused stock markets, dominating trading in the stocks that they quoted, even when those included some of the world's largest multinational corporations. The NYSE, for example, had regained its market dominance after ending minimum commission rates in 1975, even though it persisted with numerous other restrictive practices, including discrimination against banks, a cap on the number of members and rules protecting trading on the floor from outside competition.[20] Nevertheless, what was becoming increasingly evident from the 1970s was the growing power of banks relative to stock exchanges as their size and scale allowed them to internalize trading, participate in inter-bank markets, and take positions in the market. In the USA the Glass–Steagall Act continued to restrict the freedom of banks to exercise this growing power domestically but internationally no such constraints applied if they chose to operate out of a London base, which many did. London was also a better location for the conduct of an international equity business, being conveniently placed in terms of the world's time zones and with access to complementary financial markets. The result was to make London the location for the emerging global equity market by the early 1980s, especially after the ending of UK exchange controls in 1979. Banks centralized their international equity trading operations in London, using it as hub from which to access other markets.[21]

[16] Alexander Nicoll, 'Round-the-clock trading brings a new challenge', 5th November 1985.

[17] Alexander Nicoll, 'International moves before Big Bang', 29th August 1985; Clive Wolman, 'Costs under scrutiny', 19th November 1986; David Goodhart, 'Hastening the revolution', 19th November 1986.

[18] Barry Riley, 'Seaq stretches the day', 21st October 1987.

[19] Barry Riley, 'Gower, after the City upheaval', 30th April 1984; Barry Riley, 'Why global traders are stepping up pressure', 21st February 1985; Alexander Nicoll, 'International moves before Big Bang', 29th August 1985; Alexander Nicoll, 'Round-the-clock trading brings a new challenge', 5th November 1985; Terry Byland, 'Wall Street dismayed at ADR levy', 25th March 1986; Richard Lambert, 'More products now need round-the-clock trading', 27th October 1986; Mark Nicholson, 'Venture still in its infancy', 27th September 1989; Gita Piramal, 'Indian stock market reform gathers pace', 5th March 1992; David Barchard, 'Investors go elsewhere', 21st May 1992; Anthony McDermott, 'More will own shares', 18th November 1992.

[20] Richard Lambert, 'The lessons Wall Street can teach London', 18th April 1984; John Moore and George Graham, 'The City digests a setback on the road to reform', 7th June 1985; Charles Batchelor, 'Concern expressed over electronic equity dealing', 18th November 1985; Alexander Nicoll, 'Dealers worry about fallout from Big Bang', 28th February 1986; Alexander Nicoll, 'Electronic Bridge boosts global equities trading', 23rd April 1986; Alan Cane, 'Systems tailored to market-makers', 16th October 1986; Clive Wolman, 'Small deals suffer', 21st October 1987; Boris Sedacca, 'Advanced system comes on stream', 10th November 1988; John Moore and George Graham, 'The City digests a setback on the road to reform', 7th June 1985; Desmond MacRae, 'How depositories raise efficiency', 3rd September 1990.

[21] John Makinson, 'London reflects scale of international flows', 23rd November 1983; John Moore, 'Uncertain time ahead for London houses', 28th November 1983; William Hall, 'Concentrating on the domestic market', 28th November 1983; John Moore, 'The fight to win back foreign business', 9th April 1984; Barry Riley, 'Increased emphasis placed on taking a global view', 7th December 1984; Barry Riley, 'Cross-border phenomenon', 7th December 1984; John Makinson, 'Prime area for diversification', 7th December 1984; Stephen Fidler, 'Don't throw out the baby', 29th June 1988; Stephen Fidler, 'A trickle of issues', 29th June 1988; Paul Taylor, 'Blow, not knockout',

Aiding the development of this global equity market was the transformation of international communications and the role played by information providers like Reuters and Telerate.[22] By 1986 Alexander Nicoll was able to report that the 'Global distribution of shares has been made possible by technology enabling share prices and data about companies to be flashed around the world instantaneously. Communications have enabled the largest securities houses, mainly American, to trade shares around the world, passing their books from New York to Tokyo to London and back to New York each day.'[23] Further boosting the cross-border trading in equities during the 1980s were the growing number of privatization issues as these produced the liquid stocks that were attractive to fund managers around the world. An estimate made for 1990 suggested that by then around 6 per cent of the equities that had been issued were held outside their home countries, though it was their domestic stock exchanges that remained the centre of liquidity in virtually all cases. Nevertheless, there was an expanding market where such stocks were traded between banks, especially when the relevant stock exchange was closed or a regime of high charges and restrictive practices remained in place.[24] One example of the growing mobility of

28th September 1988; David Lascelles, 'The barriers are falling', 2nd May 1989; David Lascelles, 'New services in UK high streets', 2nd May 1989; David Lascelles, 'Pitching for a share of London's work', 5th July 1989; David Lascelles and Richard Waters, 'New market disappointment for Citicorp', 17th January 1990; David Lascelles, 'The London cavern is the hub for Europe', 5th June 1990; Simon Thomas and Chris Collingwood, 'Clearers at the crossroads', 3rd September 1990; Richard Waters, 'In the shadow of Big Bang', 29th November 1990; Richard Waters, 'Revolution at a cosy British club', 21st October 1991; Richard Waters, 'Brokers learn the value of money', 4th November 1991; Richard Waters, 'Survival of the biggest', 11th December 1991; Haig Simonian, 'Battle looms over Italy's new securities law', 14th February 1992; Richard Waters, 'A tune-up for City trades', 9th April 1992; Maggie Urry, 'New structures that keep the stags at bay', 22nd June 1992.

[22] Barry Riley, 'Why global traders are stepping up pressure', 21st February 1985; Barry Riley, 'SEC urges controls on international securities trading', 22nd May 1985; Alexander Nicoll, 'International moves before Big Bang', 29th August 1985; Alexander Nicoll, 'Round-the-clock trading brings a new challenge', 5th November 1985; Charles Batchelor, 'Concern expressed over electronic equity dealing', 18th November 1985; Clive Wolman, 'Investor protection safety net remains', 16th December 1985; Terry Byland, 'Wall Street dismayed at ADR levy', 25th March 1986; Alexander Nicoll, 'Market wakes up early to competition', 17th April 1986; John Plender, 'Capital loosens its bonds', 8th May 1986; Alan Cane, 'Systems tailored to market-makers', 16th October 1986; Richard Lambert, 'More products now need round-the-clock trading', 27th October 1986; John Edwards, 'New rules will help private clients', 27th October 1986; Alexander Nicoll, 'Everything to play for', 21st October 1987; Alexander Nicoll, 'New class of seat may appeal to locals', 10th March 1988; Alexander Nicoll, 'Bittersweet birthday celebrations for options', 12th April 1988; David Lascelles, 'Less like a father-figure', 26th September 1988; Sean Heath, 'City's stability appreciated', 26th September 1988; Clive Wolman, 'Shearson bounces back after its Big Bang shake-out', 8th November 1988; Richard Waters, 'Revolution at a cosy British club', 21st October 1991; Charles Batchelor, 'Enterprise looks for a way out', 22nd December 1992.

[23] Alexander Nicoll, 'Global distribution should be good for share prices', 27th October 1986.

[24] Barry Riley, 'City regulator gets into gear', 20th July 1985; Barry Riley, 'A costly question for the futures markets', 19th August 1985; Barry Riley, 'Regulatory framework for City takes shape', 31st October 1985; Barry Riley, 'Selling self-regulation to the City', 2nd December 1985; Barry Riley, 'Regulatory framework for City takes shape', 31st October 1985; John Moore, 'SE firms urged to adapt in face of change', 21st November 1985; John Moore, 'Single main board envisaged to regulate services of 15,000 City concerns', 20th December 1985; Richard Lambert, 'More protection for investors', 21st December 1985; Alexander Nicoll, 'Big Board's ambitions reach towards London', 13th February 1986; Alexander Nicoll, 'Ticklish issue of share stabilisation', 11th July 1986; John Plender, 'An omelette yet to be tasted', 27th October 1986; Alexander Nicoll, 'The new market has an electronic heart', 27th October 1986; David Lascelles and Alexander Nicoll, 'An oddly quiet revolution', 4th February 1987; Alexander Nicoll, 'London's global ambitions signal aggressive mood', 5th February 1987; Haig Simonian, 'Thwarted by the tax', 17th February 1988; David Lascelles, 'Foundations laid, but plans still vague', 23rd June 1987; Guy de Jonquières, 'Trusting the market', 16th September 1987; Michael Blanden, 'A chance to move in on the stock market', 21st September 1987; Allison Maitland, 'Slow steps in the paper chase', 21st October 1987; Alexander Nicoll, 'The heart of the world game', 21st October 1987; Clive Wolman, 'Market hypothesis gains support', 21st October 1987; Christian Tyler, 'First shoots of huge growth', 21st October 1987; Deborah Hargreaves, 'Mixed response to black box trading', 23rd October 1987; David Lane, 'Curing a bad name', 20th February 1989; Barry Riley, 'A bridge between New York and Tokyo', 29th November 1990; Richard Waters, 'Level playing field may not be open to all-comers', 14th February 1991; Richard Waters, 'Farewell to the trading floor as markets plan

equity trading in the 1980s was the impact made by tax. The imposition of a turnover tax on Swedish shares in 1984 led to a rapid migration of trading to the London-based inter-bank market, for example.[25]

Contributing to the success of London's inter-bank equity market was the launch in 1985 of the LSE's Stock Exchange Automated Quotation (SEAQ) International service for the stock of non-UK companies. Through Seaq screens market-makers could exhibit prices at which they were prepared to buy and sell with deals taking place over the telephone. The result was a highly liquid market in which buyers and sellers could always deal as the market maker stood ready to act as the counterparty. With the introduction of Seaq International, trading in non-UK shares in London expanded rapidly, replacing the informal telephone market that already existed. By October 1986, thirty-six London-based firms, drawn from inside and outside the London Stock Exchange, made a market in 550 of the most actively traded international stocks.[26] What Seaq International provided was a global equivalent of Nasdaq in the USA, namely a network that connected the leading banks and brokers around the world into a highly-competitive and increasingly liquid market for stocks. Alan Nash, in charge of foreign equities trading for the US broker, Paine Webber, explained the implications in 1987 when he said, 'It won't take long for people interested in the German market to realise that they had better look at the prices in the London market before they deal.'[27] Seaq International was extensively used by global banks for trading international stocks as it gave them 'the ability to have instant liquidity any time of the day or night', according to John Tognito, in charge of global equity trading at Merrill Lynch.[28] Market makers using Seaq International were especially successful in capturing market share in the most actively traded European stocks. They could undercut the charges made by the incumbent exchanges while using the prices that their liquid markets were generating.[29] As national stock exchanges continued to provide either the only or most liquid market this London-based inter-bank market was most active during the European working day. There was reluctance among investors to trade at other times because of the risk that the price achieved would not reflect current market conditions. As Michael Newmarch, head of portfolio management at one of the UK's largest institutional investors, the Prudential Insurance Company, explained in 1985: 'We have taken the attitude that we

automation', 22nd July 1991; Richard Waters, 'Bourses build up defences', 24th September 1991; Norma Cohen, 'Clients move from global to local services', 24th September 1991; Antonia Sharpe, 'Monte Titoli's hidden vaults', 9th December 1991; Barbara Durr, 'Talent capsized by money wave', 19th March 1992; Eric Frey, 'Luring the local saver', 22nd May 1992; David Waller, 'Going for the lion's share', 1st July 1992; Barry Riley, 'The world as portfolio', 25th November 1992.

[25] Robert Taylor, 'Sweden to axe bond turnover tax', 26th January 1990; John Burton, 'The web spreads', 9th March 1990; John Burton, 'Eyeing EC systems', 3rd July 1990; Robert Taylor, 'Swedish investors' group applauds bourse tax move', 11th October 1991; John Burton, 'Sax, Sox, tax moves widen interest', 17th October 1991.

[26] John Moore, 'Goodison to outline foreign links plan', 31st October 1985; Alexander Nicoll, 'Market wakes up early to competition', 17th April 1986; Alexander Nicoll, 'The new market has an electronic heart', 27th October 1986; Richard Waters, 'Delays to Taurus keep costs high', 11th November 1991; Richard Waters, 'A tune-up for City trades', 9th April 1992.

[27] Alexander Nicoll, 'London's global ambitions signal aggressive mood', 5th February 1987.

[28] Barry Riley, 'Seaq stretches the day', 21st October 1987.

[29] Laura Raun, 'Loss of business stemmed', 21st April 1987; Stephen Fidler, 'Deregulate or risk being left behind', 21st October 1987; Katharine Campbell, 'OM seeks clearance to set up London subsidiary', 2nd June 1989; Haig Simonian, 'Playing a waiting game in Milan', 11th July 1990; Haig Simonian, 'Barrage of criticism for Italy's latest CGT', 6th February 1991; Richard Waters, 'Level playing field may not be open to all-comers', 14th February 1991; Ronald van de Krol, 'Confronting overseas competition', 4th October 1991; Ian Rodger, 'This difficult year', 17th December 1991; Richard Waters, 'International stock trading falls at the LSE', 12th February 1992.

will deal wherever we can get the best price.'[30] The 1987 crash exposed the shallow nature of the market for most corporate stocks, away from national stock exchanges.[31]

The London-based inter-bank equity market thrived when it provided a way of bypassing national taxes, charges, and restrictions but relied on the prices generated on individual exchanges. It also provided a means through which large investors could trade at negotiated prices directly with each other, through a bank or an interdealer broker, without disturbing the underlying market. That was especially important when they were making a large sale or purchase as that took time to complete, and secrecy was essential to prevent others taking advantage of them being forced buyers or sellers.[32] It was only the stock of those multinational companies based in the smaller countries that found their most liquid market in London. As Barry Riley reported in 1987 'An important feature of the Seaq International market is that it provides high liquidity in the heavily-traded stocks.'[33] Despite the initial success of Seaq International it was based on conditions that were both artificial and temporary.[34] The conditions were artificial because the centre of liquidity for most corporate stocks remained the domestic market. A detailed study of the global equities market undertaken by KPMG in 1989 found that it was made up of two distinct but unequal elements. Trading on behalf of foreign investors in domestic stocks in domestic markets was estimated to have a value of $1.6tn. This reflected the internationalization of investment as global banks provided fund managers with direct access to a growing range of markets around the world. Much smaller was trading in foreign stocks in markets other than their domestic one, such as Seaq international, as this amounted to only $0.6tn. Even then this trading often reflected the preferences of national investors for certain foreign stocks which was sufficient to generate a significant secondary market in a location such as London, with its high concentration of institutional fund managers. The role of Seaq International was also temporary because its attractions relied on other exchanges retaining the charges and restrictive practices that were losing them business. It was only a matter of time before the

[30] Barry Riley, 'Why global traders are stepping up pressure', 21st February 1985.

[31] Roderick Oram, 'Further transatlantic links on the way', 12th October 1987; Roderick Oram, 'Further transatlantic links on the way', 12th October 1987; Gordon Cramb, 'Aiming to be both liquid and transparent', 21st October 1987; Stephen Fidler, 'US stock exchanges wage listings war abroad', 20th April 1988; Barry Riley, 'Home looked safest', 14th October 1988; Simon Holberton, 'Mining a wider seam of shareholder loyalty and enhancing financial clout', 20th April 1990; Richard Waters, 'Rivals may yet collaborate', 2nd July 1990; Richard Waters, 'US, UK stock markets call off talks on link-up', 20th June 1991; Richard Waters, 'Farewell to the trading floor as markets plan automation', 22nd July 1991; Richard Waters, 'Man with a bull by the horns', 18th September 1991.

[32] William Dawkins, 'Expansion from a broader base', 12th March 1984; Charles Batchelor, 'Over-the-counter market set for expansion', 12th March 1984; Richard Lambert, 'The lessons Wall Street can teach London', 18th April 1984; Charles Batchelor, 'Stock Exchange launches its white paper on single-capacity trading', 20th July 1984; Alan Cane, 'A screen test for the City's dealers', 19th November 1984; William Dawkins, 'Boisterous youngster has come of age', 30th January 1985; William Dawkins, 'USM growth matched by that of its smaller rival', 30th January 1985; Stefan Wagstyl, 'Ultimate seal of approval', 30th January 1985; Richard Lambert, 'Capturing the market's mood', 1st July 1985; Terry Garrett, 'European markets are a step in right direction', 3rd December 1985; Lucy Kellaway, 'Rapid rise to maturity', 27th January 1986; Lucy Kellaway, 'The costs of entry', 27th January 1986; Richard Tomkins, 'Cost justification is deterrent', 27th January 1986; Lucy Kellaway, 'Attractions stretch to the US', 27th January 1986; Richard Tomkins, 'No rush to seize opportunity created', 27th January 1986; George Graham, 'The cost conscious competitor', 27th January 1986; Lucy Kellaway, 'Stock Exchange plans to bring in OTC as third tier', 1st April 1986; Barry Riley, 'The Stock Exchange extends its reach', 17th April 1986; Alice Rawsthorn, 'A liquidity test for the smaller exchanges', 27th October 1986; Alice Rawsthorn, 'Hazards of a new role', 20th January 1987; Alice Rawsthorn, 'Criteria for the young and small', 20th January 1987; John Plender, 'A rocky boat in the City', 22nd February 1990; Patrick Harverson, 'Brokers appeal against SEC ruling on small-order system', 24th October 1991; Richard Waters, 'Survival of the biggest', 11th December 1991; Patrick Harverson, 'The NYSE begins to show its age', 15th May 1992; Charles Batchelor, 'Enterprise looks for a way out', 22nd December 1992.

[33] Barry Riley, 'Seaq stretches the day', 21st October 1987.

[34] David Lascelles, 'Prospects look less certain', 29th November 1990.

rules and regulations that made these other exchanges uncompetitive, and the taxes and laws imposed by governments, were relaxed and then removed for, otherwise, these domestic markets would be relegated to trading only the less-liquid stocks. As it was, once the charges and restrictions that had driven trading to London were removed, domestic equity markets would recover their appeal, as they were the centres of liquidity. As Archibald Cox, head of Morgan Stanley's London office, explained as early as 1987, 'We realised you have got to be in the domestic market to some extent in order to be involved in cross-border flows.'[35] Trading in international stocks at the LSE peaked in 1990 and then declined.[36] By then it was becoming evident that Seaq International had no future in a world where the banks were gaining direct access to stock exchanges around the world, and the restrictive practices and high charges that had driven business away were coming to an end. At the same time stock exchanges were increasingly moving across to electronic trading systems, through which deals were matched automatically by computer, and this made external access much easier.[37] As early as 1987 Nigel Johnson-Hill, head of international equities trading at Shearson, Lehman Brothers' London subsidiary, had observed

[35] David Lascelles and Stephen Fidler, 'Morgan Stanley sticks to equities', 29th February 1987.

[36] Barry Riley, 'SEC urges controls on international securities trading', 22nd May 1985; John Moore and George Graham, 'The City digests a setback on the road to reform', 7th June 1985; Alexander Nicoll, 'International moves before Big Bang', 29th August 1985; John Moore, 'Goodison to outline foreign links plan', 31st October 1985; John Makinson, 'Advance of the Euroequity', 2nd November 1985; Alexander Nicoll, 'Swiss connection is prominent', 17th March 1986; John Plender, 'Capital loosens its bonds', 8th May 1986; Barry Riley, 'A unique global background', 3rd July 1986; David Lascelles and Alexander Nicoll, 'An oddly quiet revolution', 4th February 1987; Alexander Nicoll, 'London's global ambitions signal aggressive mood', 5th February 1987; David Lascelles and Stephen Fidler, 'Morgan Stanley sticks to equities', 29th February 1987; Alexander Nicoll, 'The big investors go global', 17th March 1987; Alexander Nicoll, 'Warning signs in global game', 21st April 1987; David Lascelles, 'Pressure mounts for global consistency', 21st April 1987; Christian Tyler, 'First shoots of huge growth', 21st October 1987; John Plender, 'A homing instinct', 14th November 1987; John Plender, 'A rocky boat in the City', 22nd February 1990; Simon Thomas and Chris Collingwood, 'Clearers at the crossroads', 3rd September 1990; Haig Simonian, 'Barrage of criticism for Italy's latest CGT', 6th February 1991; Richard Waters, 'Level playing field may not be open to all-comers', 14th February 1991; Richard Waters, 'Unbundling the City's top club', 5th March 1991; Richard Waters, 'Farewell to the trading floor as markets plan automation', 22nd July 1991; William Dawkins, 'Block trading review on the way', 9th September 1991; Norma Cohen, 'Clients move from global to local services', 24th September 1991; Richard Waters, 'Making sure SEAQ stays at the centre of cross-border share trading', 8th November 1991; Richard Waters, 'Delays to Taurus keep costs high', 11th November 1991; Richard Waters, 'Survival of the biggest', 11th December 1991; Richard Waters, 'An upheaval waiting to happen', 30th January 1992; Richard Waters, 'A tune-up for City trades', 9th April 1992.

[37] Alice Rawsthorn, 'Hazards of a new role', 20th January 1987; Alice Rawsthorn, 'Criteria for the young and small', 20th January 1987; Barry Riley, 'Seaq stretches the day', 21st October 1987; Clare Pearson, 'Leaping ahead on a nice greasy breakfast', 21st October 1987; Anatole Kaletsky, 'Passing their book round the world', 21st October 1987; Alan Cane, 'The electronic route to equity', 21st October 1987; John Edwards, 'London's rival', 30th April 1988; Clive Wolman, 'An empty space at the market's heart', 22nd November 1988; Barry Riley, 'Home looked safest', 14th October 1988; Vanessa Houlder, 'Market makers missed', 6th February 1989; Dominick Coyle, 'Europeans challenge the capital place for business', 17th June 1989; Richard Waters, 'Towards Europe's super-league', 11th September 1989; Alastair FitzSimons, 'EC Directives change securities markets', 15th February 1990; Richard Waters, 'Making the stock market relevant to its members', 19th February 1990; John Plender, 'A rocky boat in the City', 22nd February 1990; Richard Waters, 'A Grand Vision of the way to leave the maze', 27th February 1990; Richard Waters, 'Bourse battle for pride of place in Europe', 17th May 1990; David Lascelles, 'Banks seem set to move cautiously', 2nd July 1990; Richard Waters, 'Rivals may yet collaborate', 2nd July 1990; Deborah Hargreaves, 'Turbulence keeps global issues on the ground', 2nd July 1990; Richard Waters, 'In the shadow of Big Bang', 29th November 1990; Richard Waters, 'Unbundling the City's top club', 5th March 1991; Richard Waters, 'Farewell to the trading floor as markets plan automation', 22nd July 1991; William Dawkins, 'Block trading review on the way', 9th September 1991; Norma Cohen, 'Clients move from global to local services', 24th September 1991; Richard Waters, 'Making sure SEAQ stays at the centre of cross-border share trading', 8th November 1991; Richard Waters, 'Delays to Taurus keep costs high', 11th November 1991; Richard Waters, 'Survival of the biggest', 11th December 1991; Richard Waters, 'An upheaval waiting to happen', 30th January 1992; Haig Simonian, 'Battle looms over Italy's new securities law', 14th February 1992; Richard Waters, 'A tune-up for City trades', 9th April 1992.

'barriers breaking down all over the world, where before people were unable to invest outside their own borders'.[38]

As these barriers came down so the rationale behind Seaq International faded away. In 1991 Richard Waters dismissed Seaq International as 'a rudimentary price display mechanism'.[39] By then the LSE itself had admitted banks as members, abolished fixed charges, removed most of its restrictive practices, and ended floor trading in a process known as Big Bang which, according to Alexander Nicoll in 1987 had shaken up 'a sleepy and relatively inactive domestic market'.[40] The process had begun in 1983, under pressure from the UK government and was completed in 1986.[41] In addition, the LSE had agreed to merge with the International Securities Regulatory Organization (ISRO), which had been set up as a self-regulating agency for those involved in the global equity market.[42] To Clive Wolman in 1986, the merger with ISRO marked 'the takeover of the exchange by the large foreign, particularly US and Japanese financial conglomerates'[43] as most of LSE's largest members had been acquired by banks. His verdict was supported by Alexander Nicoll in 1987, when he claimed that, the 'international houses have essentially taken over the Stock Exchange'[44] with the intention of making London, 'the hub of the global stock market, at least for the European time zone'.[45] Barry Riley had reached a similar conclusion in 1986 when he wrote that 'The prize for London is the leading position in the European time zone in a seamless market that swings from Tokyo and other eastern centres in the morning through Europe and on to New York. This market is well established in US Treasury bonds and is becoming important for several hundred leading equities of international grade'.[46] The future envisaged was a global equity market in which trading gravitated from one pool of liquidity to the next.[47] Gordon Macklin, President of the National Association of Securities Dealers (NASD), was excited by this prospect and expected New York to be a central hub in this global equity market. He was keen that Nasdaq and the LSE would be key players. Writing in 1986 he considered that 'The prospect is bright that the forthcoming global equity market will draw on the experience of both London and Nasdaq and that the global equity market will, one day soon, consist of a series of London-compatible and Nasdaq-compatible automated quotations systems and competitive dealing systems'.[48] David Hunter, chairman of NASD, hailed this outcome as 'the beginning of the global

[38] Stephen Fidler, 'Minefields await the unprepared', 21st April 1987.

[39] Richard Waters, 'Making sure SEAQ stays at the centre of cross-border share trading', 8th November 1991.

[40] Alexander Nicoll, 'Warning signs in global game', 21st April 1987.

[41] Alan Cane, 'Sleepers awake to a Big Bang scramble', 13th February 1986.

[42] Barry Riley, 'City regulator gets into gear', 20th July 1985; Barry Riley, 'A costly question for the futures markets', 19th August 1985; Barry Riley, 'Regulatory framework for City takes shape', 31st October 1985; Barry Riley, 'Selling self-regulation to the City', 2nd December 1985; Barry Riley, 'Regulatory framework for City takes shape', 31st October 1985; John Moore, 'SE firms urged to adapt in face of change', 21st November 1985; John Moore, 'Single main board envisaged to regulate services of 15,000 City concerns', 20th December 1985; Richard Lambert, 'More protection for investors', 21st December 1985; Alexander Nicoll, 'Big Board's ambitions reach towards London', 13th February 1986; Alan Cane, 'Sleepers awake to a Big Bang scramble', 13th February 1986; Alexander Nicoll, 'Ticklish issue of share stabilisation', 11th July 1986; John Plender, 'An omelette yet to be tasted', 27th October 1986; Alexander Nicoll, 'The new market has an electronic heart', 27th October 1986; Richard Waters, 'Unbundling the City's top club', 5th March 1991.

[43] Clive Wolman, 'Gains in efficiency but monopoly risk', 27th October 1986. For a similar view see Alexander Nicoll, 'The heart of the world game', 21st October 1987

[44] Alexander Nicoll, 'Warning signs in global game', 21st April 1987.

[45] Alexander Nicoll, 'The heart of the world game', 21st October 1987.

[46] Barry Riley, 'The City Revolution', 27th October 1986.

[47] Alexander Nicoll, 'Global distribution should be good for share prices', 27th October 1986.

[48] Alan Cane, 'Market makers seek bells and whistles for competitive edge', 9th April 1986.

network for 24-hour equity trading... the start of a true world equity market.'[49] This emerging global equity market involved a struggle for control between the stock exchanges, where liquidity still resided, and the megabanks, that had built up an international network through which cross-border trading took place.

Rolling Revolution

This transformation of the global equities market in the 1980s involved a rolling revolution around the world. In 1987 Stephen Fidler observed that:

> The fear of remaining a backwater in the increasingly competitive financial marketplace is shaking off the cobwebs of stock exchanges around the world. Encouraged by the trend among western governments to lift barriers to international flows and advances in technology and communications, stock exchanges whose practices had hitherto often been unchanged for decades are in a state of flux. What has resulted is called *competitive deregulation*, and it is led by the fear of being left out of a huge and growing worldwide industry.[50]

There was a growing threat that trading would ebb away to the inter-bank market located in London, where Seaq gave it a strong competitive edge. Major Australian companies, for example, were a favourite among international investors, especially the mines, and were actively traded in London. This competition allied to government pressure to remove restrictive practices drove a major reorganization of the Australian stock market beginning in 1984, which included the ending of fixed commissions and admitting banks as members. In 1987 all six Australian stock exchanges merged into one, the Australian Stock Exchange, operating from a single trading floor. That floor was then replaced by fully automated trading through an electronic market called the Stock Exchange Automated Trading System (Seats).[51] For Canada the competition came from US exchanges as they increasingly listed the stock of the largest Canadian companies, for which they were able to provide a more liquid market. US investment banks were well established in Canada and they provided easy access to US exchanges. By 1990 44 per cent of the trading in the stock of major Canadian companies took place outside the country. In response the Canadian stock exchanges abandoned restrictive practices such as the exclusion of banks, which then bought up the largest brokers, and pressed ahead with the introduction of an electronic trading system. The Toronto Stock Exchange (ToSE) had been experimenting with computerized trading since the 1960s leading to the launch of the Computer Assisted Trading System (CATS) in 1977. In 1992 the decision was taken to end floor trading the following year, and switch entirely to automated trading.[52]

[49] Alexander Nicoll, 'Electronic Bridge boosts global equities trading', 23rd April 1986.

[50] Stephen Fidler, 'Deregulate or risk being left behind', 21st October 1987.

[51] Peter Wise, 'Depression after the comet', 30th April 1990; FT Staff, 'Australian SE to start automated trading system', 26th September 1990; Gwen Robinson, 'Another milestone nears', 24th March 1998; Russell Baker, 'ASX set to control its own destiny', 23rd September 1998.

[52] Peter Wise, 'Depression after the comet', 30th April 1990; Bernard Simon, 'Hard times hit Toronto brokers', 5th February 1991; Reuters, 'Toronto exchange to automate', 14th February 1992; Ian Rodger, 'The real time breakthrough', 6th December 1994.

However, it was in Europe that the rolling revolution in the equity market was most marked, driven forward by the inability of incumbent stock exchanges to resist the competition coming from London's inter-bank market. Writing in 1989 David Lascelles attributed the changes taking place in Europe as a reaction to London's Big Bang in 1986, which had 'set off a seemingly unstoppable chain reaction of smaller bangs throughout Europe'.[53] That is to credit Big Bang with an impact far greater than it had. Big Bang itself followed the rapid expansion of London's telephone-based inter-bank equity market, which had sucked in trading in the stocks of Europe's largest companies, especially after the introduction of the price display system provided by Seaq International. Stock exchanges located in Switzerland were caught up in the transformation taking place, even though banks had long dominated trading. As Richard Meier, director of the Zurich Exchange, claimed in 1990, 'We had our Big Bang almost 100 years ago',[54] despite that the loss of trading to London, in the stock of the largest Swiss companies, forced the abolition of fixed commission fees, the closure of a number of regional exchanges, and the development of an electronic trading system.[55] In Eastern and Central Europe change was being driven not by Big Bang in London but by the conversion of centrally-planned communist economies into market-based ones, involving the wholesale privatization of previously state-owned assets. In the wake of these developments stock exchanges were set up through which assets were traded. It was in 1991 that stock exchanges were established in Moscow and Warsaw while that in Budapest dated from 1988. Though some of these new exchanges included a physical trading floor they also adopted the latest computer-based trading technology and welcomed banks, and so integrating them into the global equity market.[56]

Within Europe the impact of what was happening in London was most marked in the EU, because of the removal of the protection that national boundaries had once provided national stock exchanges with. Committed to emulating the single integrated equity market that existed in the USA, and its perceived benefits in terms of the ability of business to raise finance and investors to access attractive investments, the European Commission pushed ahead in the 1980s with plans to remove government and institutional barriers to cross-border trading.[57] As these plans took shape it exposed national stock exchanges to

[53] David Lascelles, 'The barriers are falling', 2nd May 1989.

[54] Peter Martin, 'Bank feel the electronic impulse', 13th December 1990.

[55] William Dullforce, 'Soffex will eschew the ring's hurly burly', 10th March 1988; William Dullforce, 'Share registration rules under fire', 28th June 1988; William Dullforce, 'Prices ignore good forecasts', 19th December 1989; William Dullforce, 'How Geneva is still holding its ground', 9th October 1990; William Dullforce, 'Squalls in a safe haven', 13th December 1990; Peter Martin, 'Bank feel the electronic impulse', 13th December 1990; Ian Rodger, 'Overshadowed by Zurich', 21st November 1991; William Dullforce, 'Outlook fair but uncertain', 17th December 1991; Ian Rodger, 'This difficult year', 17th December 1991; Ian Rodger, 'Switzerland suffers setback over financial proposals', 29th January 1992; Ian Rodger, 'Worrying outflow of funds', 7th May 1992; Ian Rodger, 'London is now a banker bet for the Swiss', 2nd December 1992; Ian Rodger, 'Electronic trading approaches reality', 18th November 1993; Ian Rodger, 'Private banking provides fuel', 2nd December 1993.

[56] Christopher Bobinski and Anthony Robinson, 'Warsaw exchange opens with bubbly and braces', 17th April 1991; Nicholas Denton, 'Budapest's first year disappoints investors', 15th June 1991; Judy Dempsey, 'Legislative fillip sought', 30th March 1992; Judy Dempsey, 'Bulgaria enters the bourse business', 28th November 1991; Ariane Genillard, 'Prague plods on towards a regulated stock market', 15th May 1992; Michael Morgan, 'Investors dive in', 11th April 1997; Anatol Lieven, 'Past few months have been bumpy', 9th December 1997; Jan Cienski, 'Warsaw seeks partner to revamp bourse', 30th March 2010.

[57] David Lascelles, 'A potential financial capital for the EC', 25th September 1989; George Graham, 'Doubts about tax burden', 22nd October 1990; Richard Waters, 'Stalemate in the marketplace', 15th November 1990; Lucy Kellaway, 'Many moves on the way to market', 21st November 1990; Richard Waters and George Graham, 'Birth of a market needs burial of differences', 28th November 1990; David Lascelles, 'Prospects look less certain', 29th November 1990; Richard Waters, 'Warning on European capital market', 14th December 1990; Lucy Kellaway and Tim Dickson, 'Painful birth of single market', 19th December 1990; Richard Waters, 'Securities firms look across borders', 7th January 1991; Richard Waters, 'Level playing field may not be open to all-comers', 14th February 1991;

growing external competition, with trading in the stocks of Europe's leading companies gravitating to London.[58] In response European stock exchanges, both individually and collectively, were forced to devise strategies for their survival, which a number had already begun to do even before Big Bang in London. Those policy makers behind the single stock market initiative expected the outcome to be mergers between stock exchanges to create trans-national institutions as had already happened internally in many countries, like France and the UK. Though there were moves in this direction in the late 1980s and early 1990s it was not the direction of travel, as Richard Waters observed in 1990: 'Global warfare is breaking out among stock exchanges... The most obvious battleground is Europe.'[59] Tim Dickson added in 1991 that 'Europe's stock exchanges, far from integrating as some visionaries might have hoped, are competing more fiercely.'[60] The desire to remain independent was the overriding imperative in the member-owned stock exchanges of the 1980s.

Leading this European response was the Paris Bourse which was completely transformed by the end of the 1980s. Driven by fears that it was losing out not only to London but also Frankfurt, successive French governments of different political hues pushed through an agenda of reform. By 1992 the changes included the ending of fixed commission rates, the admission of banks as members, and the development of electronic trading and settlement systems. This did reclaim much of the business lost to London but the Paris Bourse lacked the overall liquidity found in the London market, which attracted institutional investors, while the costs attached to the new systems made it an expensive place to trade.[61] The Amsterdam Stock Exchange also responded to the competitive pressures it faced which its chairman, Baron Boudewijn van Ittersum, acknowledged in 1991, 'We are more vulnerable because we are a relatively small market and an open market, and we have large international

Angus Foster, 'Future of stock exchange comes to a head', 16th August 1991; William Dawkins, 'Block trading review on the way', 9th September 1991; Richard Waters, 'Bourses build up defences', 24th September 1991; William Dawkins, 'Small bang fall-out', 12th December 1991; Richard Waters, 'Vision of a grand strategy fades', 26th February 1992; Richard Waters, 'Markets start to multiply', 10th November 1992.

[58] Stephen Fidler, 'Deregulate or risk being left behind', 21st October 1987; Barry Riley, 'Bourses respond to London threat', 6th November 1987; John Plender, 'A homing instinct', 14th November 1987; Clive Wolman, 'The battle of the paper mountain', 3rd April 1989; Friso Endt, 'Takeover defences come under heavy fire', 30th June 1988; Friso Endt, 'The debate intensifies', 30th June 1988; David A Brown, 'Capital market in those of big changes', 30th June 1988; Nick Bunker, 'Electronic stock market takes a leap nearer', 13th February 1989; Karen Fossli, 'Liberalisation helps to fuel interest', 30th March 1989; John Wicks, 'A world leader must not be left behind', 25th April 1989; David Lascelles, 'The barriers are falling', 2nd May 1989; Judy Dempsey, 'The Börse finally wakes up', 16th May 1989; Dominick Coyle, 'Europeans challenge the capital place for business', 17th June 1989; Peter Bruce, 'The aim is to get it right on the night', 21st June 1989; Andrew Baxter, 'Liquidity poses the greatest problem', 21st June 1989; Peter Bruce, 'A patient approach to a near impossible job', 21st June 1989.

[59] Richard Waters, 'Rivals may yet collaborate', 2nd July 1990.

[60] Tim Dickson, 'Exposed by the market's transparency', 12th December 1991.

[61] George Graham, 'Faster growth than London's', 20th January 1987; George Graham, 'Paris adds to continuous market', 20th January 1987; Paul Betts, 'Banks rush to buy French brokers', 9th December 1987; George Graham, 'Major reforms under way', 29th September 1988; George Graham, 'Trading shows signs of renewed vitality', 3rd April 1989; George Graham, 'Year of quiet change', 2nd November 1989; George Graham, 'Change unsettles small investors', 3rd May 1989; George Graham, 'New weapons for the global fray', 5th June 1990; George Graham, 'Creating a modern system', 22nd October 1990; George Graham, 'Foreign investment doubles', 22nd October 1990; George Graham, 'In the front rank in Europe', 17th June 1991; William Dawkins, 'Bourse regulators back plan for reforms', 10th July 1991; William Dawkins, 'French brokers call for reforms', 18th July 1991; William Dawkins, 'French bourse heads for second wave of reforms', 9th September 1991; William Dawkins, 'Block trading review on the way', 9th September 1991; William Dawkins, 'France presses on with liberalisation', 26th September 1991; Tim Dickson, 'Exposed by the market's transparency', 12th December 1991; William Dawkins, 'Small bang fall-out', 12th December 1991; Tim Dickson, 'Exposed by the market's transparency', 12th December 1991; Alice Rawsthorn, 'French plan relaunch of second-tier market', 20th March 1992; Alice Rawsthorn, 'Re-engineering the Paris stock market', 24th March 1992; Alice Rawsthorn, 'Tomorrow will be better', 13th October 1992; Samer Iskandar, 'Technology overtakes tradition', 1st January 2000.

corporations for which we have to provide a home market.'[62] Despite the reforms the market provided by the Amsterdam Stock Exchange lacked the depth and breadth necessary to compete with London in trading the most liquid shares, including those of major Dutch companies.[63] This was the position found around Europe, especially in the smaller markets such as that provided by the Stockholm Stock Exchange. It attempted to broaden its market by developing an electronic trading system that linked the various Scandinavian exchanges into a single trading network, but that met strong resistance as all wanted to retain their independence. One step the Stockholm Bourse did take was to convert itself into a company in 1992 and float on its own market, so as to better position itself for a potential merger.[64]

In Spain the reforms of the 1980s led to the establishment of a nationwide electronic trading network that integrated trading, clearing, and settlement, overcoming strong regional opposition. In 1990 the past president of the Barcelona Bolsa, José Serna Masia, claimed that, 'After the installation of inter-connected screens and real time trading, the bolsa of Barcelona or that of Madrid no longer exists. What exists are the screens. There is no longer any reason for the physical existence of the bolsas.'[65] It was the threat of outside competition that drove through this radical transformation of the Spanish stock market,[66] and a similar process was happening across Europe, including Italy,[67] Portugal,[68] Belgium,[69] Denmark,[70] Greece,[71] and Luxembourg.[72] Typical of the outcome was the announcement made in 1990 by Attilio Ventura, the chairman of the Milan Stock Exchange: 'All [Italian]

[62] Ronald van de Krol, 'Confronting overseas competition', 4th October 1991.

[63] Laura Raun, 'Amsterdam bourse to test block trading', 13th March 1986; Laura Raun, 'Campaign to lead in Europe', 14th April 1986; Laura Raun, 'Loss of business stemmed', 21st April 1987; Laura Raun, 'Oldest bourse sets sights on full automation', 29th June 1988; Laura Raun, 'Dutch master plan', 28th March 1989; Laura Raun, 'Amsterdam SE set to cut fees', 15th December 1989; Laura Raun, 'Moves to recoup business', 12th June 1990; Laura Raun, 'A new mood of realism', 12th June 1990; Edi Cohen, 'Interest reappears', 4th September 1991; Ronald van de Krol, 'Merger pace accelerates', 4th September 1991; Ronald van de Krol, 'Confronting overseas competition', 4th October 1991; Ronald van de Krol, 'Action plan lifts Amsterdam's status', 12th September 1994; Ronald van de Krol, 'Poised for a shake-up', 12th September 1994.

[64] Sara Webb, 'Creating a true Nordic market', 30th March 1989; Katharine Campbell, 'OM seeks clearance to set up London subsidiary', 2nd June 1989; Robert Taylor, 'Sweden to axe bond turnover tax', 26th January 1990; John Burton, 'Stockholm bourse Sax opens on a sour note', 2nd August 1990; Robert Taylor, 'Swedish investors' group applauds bourse tax move', 11th October 1991; John Burton, 'Sax, Sox, tax moves widen interest', 17th October 1991; Robert Taylor, 'All change for Stockholm bourse', 25th February 1992; Simon Davies, 'Equity culture growing fast', 23rd January 1998.

[65] Gary Mead, 'Outpost that refuses to die', 16th November 1990.

[66] Tom Burns, 'Why bank beats Bolsa', 30th November 1989; Gary Mead, 'Outpost that refuses to die', 16th November 1990; David Owen, 'Regionals seek new role', 23rd May 1991; Peter Bruce, 'Downside emerges after fairy-tale beginning', 23rd October 1991; Tom Burns, 'Divided Meffsa looks both ways', 4th June 1992; Tom Burns, 'Domestic volumes dominate', 20th June 1994.

[67] Haig Simonian, 'Playing a waiting game in Milan', 11th July 1990; Haig Simonian, 'A new breed of institution in Milan', 14th December 1990; David Lane, 'Final curtain now in sight', 19th November 1990; Haig Simonian, 'Barrage of criticism for Italy's latest CGT', 6th February 1991; David Lane, 'Big Bang looms', 6th June 1991; Haig Simonian, 'Nerves on edge as the Milan bourse gears up for reform', 19th July 1991; Haig Simonian, 'Milan calculates costs of new technology', 26th July 1991; Haig Simonian, 'Counting the cost of technological change', 9th October 1991; Antonia Sharpe, 'Stocks clear first hurdle', 9th December 1991; Antonia Sharpe, 'Monte Titoli's hidden vaults', 9th December 1991; Antonia Sharpe, 'Floating the Sims', 9th December 1991; Haig Simonian, 'Battle looms over Italy's new securities law', 14th February 1992.

[68] David Waller, 'Fragile but promising', 23rd April 1991; Patrick Blum, 'Market in the doldrums', 4th March 1992; Tom Burns, 'Timing of launch was fortunate', 11th February 1997.

[69] Tim Dickson, 'Brussels braced for little bang reforms', 28th November 1990; Andrew Hill, 'Brussels Bourse takes stock of its finances', 16th August 1991; Andrew Hill, 'Little Bang a blow to small brokers', 25th October 1991; Andrew Hill, 'Impact of "little bang" is slightly muted', 3rd December 1992; Andrew Hill, 'Belfox thrives in the gentleman's club', 25th November 1993.

[70] Hilary Barnes, 'Drift of trade to London causes concern', 7th April 1994; FT Staff, 'Surviving in the free world', 21st March 1996.

[71] Kerin Hope, 'Soaring volumes strain the stock exchange system', 20th May 1994.

[72] Ronald van de Krol, 'Volumes need to rise', 4th November 1992.

stock exchanges will be unified in a single circuit, passing from ten physical locations to a single node for the whole country.'[73] In addition to the unification of national stock markets with electronic trading and processing systems restrictive practices were abandoned, fixed charges dropped, and banks admitted as members. One of the few exceptions to what was happening across Europe was the position in Austria. There the Vienna Stock Exchange continued to enjoy an official monopoly, which removed the competitive challenge that was driving change in other countries. As a consequence the Austrian stock market was unattractive to both local companies and investors, and lacked liquidity apart from during the occasional speculative booms as in 1985 and 1989.[74]

In contrast to Austria one of the greatest structural transformations in Europe took place in Germany, despite strong opposition from the numerous incumbent exchanges. There were eight stock exchanges in Germany and they clung to their independence in what was a federal country. Trading was migrating to Frankfurt, with around 70 per cent of turnover, but the market remained fragmented, undermining liquidity with large bid-offer spreads, high commission rates, and no facilities for borrowing stock. This led to the migration of trading to London in the 1980s. Even as late as 1992 David Waller considered that 'the German equity market is especially underdeveloped' and that 'Germany's fragmented stock market structure is a source of inefficiency and has helped to drive a significant proportion of turnover of the shares of Germany's largest companies to London.'[75] What he had not appreciated was how this was rapidly changing due to the enormous technological advances that had been made in the German stock market from the mid-1980s onwards, which gave it a strong competitive position in the 1990s. Driving the modernization of the German stock market were the large German banks. In the words of Haig Simonian in 1989, 'The arrival of a new generation of executives within some banks…combined with an ever stronger competition between financial markets and a heightened sense of the need for change, has made the banks bolder than ever before in forcing change.'[76] Leading this push for change was Rolf Breuer, the Deutsche Bank managing board member responsible for secondary market trading. He pressed for a shift away from auction-based floor trading to a computerized screen-based system in order to compete with London.[77] This transformation began with clearing and settlement as the banks already dominated the trading of stocks in Germany, which was increasingly concentrated in Frankfurt, with a 70 per cent share of turnover in 1989, followed by Düsseldorf. What emerged was a nationwide price reporting system, Inter-Banken Informations System (Ibis), the amalgamation of all Germany's share depositories into one, and the merger of the Frankfurt and Düsseldorf stock exchanges' data processing systems. Once completed with the introduction of a nationwide electronic market, the result was a system incorporating screen dealing with the automatic matching, clearing, and settlement of transactions. Many doubted that the existing technology would support such an ambitious plan. Richard Waters wrote in 1990 that 'It remains to be seen…whether these trading developments can create a system able to compete with SEAQI on international share deals.'[78] Though initial attempts to introduce such an integrated system failed, success came in 1991 with Ibis 2, but the migration from floor-based trading to the electronic system was slow. In 1992, Paul Berwein, a

[73] David Lane, 'Final curtain now in sight', 19th November 1990.
[74] Eric Frey, 'Luring the local saver', 22nd May 1992.
[75] David Waller, 'Going for the lion's share', 1st July 1992.
[76] Haig Simonian, 'Quiet revolution for German securities', 13th September 1989.
[77] David Waller, 'Bank chief's sights set on central role for Germany', 10th June 1992.
[78] Richard Waters, 'Banks compete for a share', 19th June 1990.

Bavarian stockbroker working for the German subsidiary of Warburgs, observed that 'Most of Germany's major stocks are quoted on all eight exchanges. There are different prices in Bremen, Stuttgart and Berlin. Arbitrageurs operate in between and what liquidity there is, is divided between all eight.' Nevertheless, he agreed that a transformation was taking place: 'Nothing has happened for thirty years, but now everything is in the process of change.'[79] By then Ibis 2 accounted for around 30 per cent of trading in the most liquid German stocks. As a result the Frankfurt Stock Exchange was increasingly recognized as the LSE's 'main competitor in the race to become the dominant European exchange.'[80] In 1992 a further stage was reached in the transformation of the German stock market when it was agreed to form a single stock exchange, Deutsche Börse, with Rolf Breuer as chairman. In turn the plan was to merge Deutsche Börse with the Deutsche Terminbörse, the German screen-based futures and options exchange, and the Deutsche Kassenverein, which handled the settlement of transactions. The result, according to David Waller in 1992, was that 'Germany now claims one of the more sophisticated stock market structures in Europe, providing one-stop shopping and settlement for investors wanting to buy equities and derivatives.'[81] In the course of a few years Germany had not only successfully integrated the trading and processing of equities into a single electronic market but was also proceeding to include derivatives.[82] This put it at the forefront of the revolution taking place in Europe.

The transformation of European stock markets from the mid-1980s onwards undermined what Barry Riley in 1987 called the LSE's 'head start.'[83] However, what left the LSE particularly vulnerable was its own failure to introduce an electronic trading system and its integration with clearing and settlement. In terms of trading there was an understandable reluctance to abandon a system that had proved such a success not only for the LSE with Seaq but also Nasdaq, in favour of an unproven electronic technology prone to breakdowns. As Alan Cane reported in 1986, 'Computer-based dealing rooms are expensive, subject to the whims of fashion and are often obsolete as soon as they are completed.' However, he added the critical point that 'They nevertheless hold the key to successful trading in today's geographically distributed markets.'[84] The dilemma for the LSE was that Seaq fitted the needs of the megabanks that were now in control of the LSE. What they wanted was a price display system that allowed them to see current prices and then negotiate large and complex deals over the telephone. Conversely, they also wanted to be provided with an electronic trading system through which sales and purchases could be made easily,

[79] Christopher Parkes and David Waller, 'Politics comes to the Finanzplatz', 24th January 1992.

[80] Charles Harrington, 'Global custodians are bullish about Taurus', 3rd September 1990.

[81] David Waller, 'Bonn has a change of heart', 26th October 1992.

[82] Haig Simonian, 'Quiet revolution for German securities', 13th September 1989; Stephen Fidler, 'W. Germany may suffer withholding tax legacy', 18th May 1990; Katharine Campbell, 'Anxious parents await DTB birth', 26th January 1990; Richard Waters, 'Banks compete for a share', 19th June 1990; Charles Harrington, 'Global custodians are bullish about Taurus', 3rd September 1990; Katharine Campbell, 'Risks and rewards of change in Frankfurt', 7th January 1991; Richard Waters, 'Level playing field may not be open to all-comers', 14th February 1991; Katharine Campbell, 'German bourses bid for technological heights', 12th June 1991; Katharine Campbell, 'German exchanges agree to Ibis system', 9th September 1991; Richard Waters, 'Bourses build up defences', 24th September 1991; Richard Waters, 'Frankfurt gains a foothold', 4th October 1991; Katharine Campbell, 'Plans to centralise provoke old squabbles', 11th October 1991; Katharine Campbell, 'Roles are reversed for city of bankers', 28th October 1991; Christopher Parkes and David Waller, 'Politics comes to the Finanzplatz', 24th January 1992; David Waller, 'Bank chief's sights set on central role for Germany', 10th June 1992; David Waller, 'Going for the lion's share', 1st July 1992; David Waller, 'German bourses combine to take on Europe', 8th October 1992; David Waller, 'Bonn has a change of heart', 26th October 1992; Andrew Fisher, 'Germany's stock answer', 22nd October 1996; Tony Barber, 'DBC strives for pivotal role', 9th July 1999.

[83] Barry Riley, 'Bourses respond to London threat', 6th November 1987.

[84] Alan Cane, 'Big need to integrate front and back offices', 16th October 1986.

cheaply, and quickly.[85] Delivering both proved very difficult but the LSE believed that it had plenty of time to do so. It underestimated the speed of change taking place on other European stock exchanges as they extended membership to banks, abandoned fixed charges and modernized their trading systems. Writing in 1986 Alan Cane was of the opinion that, 'While the pace of change means that no one can expect to hold the lead for long, there is no doubt that, at the moment, London is very much the front runner in electronic trading.'[86] As late as 1990 George Hayter, the LSE's Director of Services, stated that 'We don't believe in revolutions—we want to take the whole market forward gradually.'[87] It was not that the LSE failed to appreciate what needed to be done, but rather they miscalculated the time they had available. In 1986 George Hayter had explained what was required: 'We need one co-ordinated central market in order to achieve the best pricing mechanism, the best liquidity, and the most competitive marketplace. The different trading mechanisms need to be mutually supportive and inter-linked, and we will seek to achieve this through a combination of market rules and system facilities.'[88] In terms of processing the LSE's problem was that it was long committed to an electronic system that was so comprehensive that its complexity made it undeliverable. This system was called Taurus (Transfer and Automated Registration of Uncertified Stocks) and the planning behind it dated from 1981.[89] However, even by 1990 it had proved impossible to make it work, though efforts to do so continued.[90] Ultimately the LSE's delay in developing an electronic system that inte-

[85] For the development of the new trading system see Charles Batchelor, 'Stock Exchange launches its white paper on single-capacity trading', 20th July 1984; Alan Cane, 'A screen test for the City's dealers', 19th November 1984; Barry Riley, 'Where the Stock Exchange draws the line', 7th October 1985; Elizabeth Sawton, 'City unclear on Big Bang', 21st October 1985; Charles Batchelor, 'Concern expressed over electronic equity dealing', 18th November 1985; John Moore, 'SE firms urged to adapt in face of change', 21st November 1985; Alan Cane, 'Sleepers awake to a Big Bang scramble', 13th February 1986; Alan Cane, 'Market makers seek bells and whistles for competitive edge', 9th April 1986; Alan Cane, 'London Stock Exchange spells out its plans for automated trading', 10th April 1986; Alexander Nicoll, 'Electronic Bridge boosts global equities trading', 23rd April 1986; Alan Cane, 'Unsettled by Big Bang', 12th August 1986; Alan Cane, 'A Talisman for the future', 12th August 1986; Alan Cane, 'Big need to integrate front and back offices', 16th October 1986; Alan Cane, 'Systems tailored to market-makers', 16th October 1986; Jason Nisse, 'US projects are ahead by two years', 16th October 1986; Alan Cane, 'How they screened the biggest game', 27th October 1986; Nick Bunker, 'Watch Taurus toss out paper', 27th October 1986; Charles Batchelor, 'Smaller players carve out niches', 27th October 1986.

[86] Alan Cane, 'How they screened the biggest game', 27th October 1986.

[87] Richard Waters, 'A Grand Vision of the way to leave the maze', 27th February 1990.

[88] Alan Cane, 'London Stock Exchange spells out its plans for automated trading', 10th April 1986.

[89] Alan Cane, 'A screen test for the City's dealers', 19th November 1984; Barry Riley, 'Where the Stock Exchange draws the line', 7th October 1985; Elizabeth Sawton, 'City unclear on Big Bang', 21st October 1985; Charles Batchelor, 'Concern expressed over electronic equity dealing', 18th November 1985; John Moore, 'SE firms urged to adapt in face of change', 21st November 1985; Alan Cane, 'Sleepers awake to a Big Bang scramble', 13th February 1986; Alan Cane, 'London Stock Exchange spells out its plans for automated trading', 10th April 1986; Alan Cane, 'Unsettled by Big Bang', 12th August 1986; Alan Cane, 'A Talisman for the future', 12th August 1986; Nick Bunker, 'Watch Taurus toss out paper', 27th October 1986; Clive Wolman, 'Out of shape for the paper chase', 14th August 1987; Clive Wolman, 'Small deals suffer', 21st October 1987; Clive Wolman, 'The battle of the paper mountain', 3rd April 1989; Richard Waters, 'Man with a bull by the horns', 18th September 1991; Richard Waters, 'Fundamental questions', 12th November 1991.

[90] Jason Nisse, 'US projects are ahead by two years', 16th October 1986; Alexander Nicoll, 'Underpinning the market's liquidity', 19th March 1987; Clive Wolman, 'Out of shape for the paper chase', 14th August 1987; Clive Wolman, 'Small deals suffer', 21st October 1987; Alan Cane, 'Big-hearted visions of integrated trading', 28th October 1987; Alan Cane, 'From here to maturity', 30th October 1987; Elizabeth Sowton, 'Demand for a faster settlement process', 3rd December 1987; Clive Wolman, 'London's weakness', 14th October 1988; Andrew Freeman, 'London waits for Taurus', 20th February 1989; Clive Wolman, 'The battle of the paper mountain', 3rd April 1989; Alan Cane, 'Outlook bullish for the electronic market', 2nd May 1989; Richard Waters, 'Finding a role for the Exchange', 4th October 1989; Richard Waters, 'Taurus plan enters critical phase', 9th October 1989; Richard Waters, 'Paperless deals', 9th November 1989; Andrew Freeman, 'Bankers resolve to drive settlement back to the back office', 22nd December 1989; Richard Waters, 'A Grand Vision of the way to leave the maze', 27th February 1990; Katharine Campbell, 'No recipe for long-term success', 9th March 1990; Andrew Freeman, 'Many will struggle to meet the improvement timetable', 2nd July 1990; Andrew Freeman, 'Rethinking the package', 3rd

grated trading, clearing, and settlement lost it the lead it had established over other European stock exchanges with Big Bang. This was the verdict that Norma Cohen reached in 1991: 'The London Stock Exchange has been painfully slow off the mark. It is already years behind schedule in the development of its paperless settlements system, known as Taurus, and has not yet even begun to deal with trade confirmation. This compares with some other European financial centres, such as Germany, which already have linked electronic trading and settlement.'[91] By 1992 the initiative in Europe had passed from the LSE to Deutsche Börse and also the Paris Bourse.[92]

Despite the rapid pace of modernization among Europe's stock exchanges in the 1980s the European stock market remained a fragmented one, with only the LSE possessing the depth and breadth required to provide the level of liquidity that the megabanks and global investors looked for when buying and selling equities. In 1990 Regis Rouselle, chairman of the Paris Bourse, accepted it was simply too small to compete with London. The London market was around three times bigger in terms of the number of listed companies and market capitalization while its turnover was much greater because so many French shares were closely held and so little traded. Bengt Ryden, President of the Stockholm Bourse, reached a similar conclusion in 1990: 'The Nordic markets are too little on their own.' His plan was 'To create a common Nordic securities market.'[93] However, this required a degree of co-operation between stock exchanges and governments that was simply not forthcoming, even within the EU. At the most basic level of processing transactions the lack of common regulations and integration between national systems presented formidable barriers to establishing a single European stock market. According to Sean Heath in 1990, 'While international trades can be done in a few seconds with a simple telephone call, settlement of that transaction can take weeks, or months or never be done at all.'[94] He estimated that around 40 per cent of international trades failed at the settlement stage. Under these circumstances national stock exchanges continued to possess an immunity from competition despite the progress made towards a single market.[95] Efforts were made to foster co-operation between European stock exchanges to create a single stock market that would provide a pool of liquidity equivalent to that found on the NYSE, Nasdaq, or the Tokyo Stock Exchange. To Katharine Campbell in 1990 'the logic of a network of domestic exchanges,

September 1990; Desmond MacRae, 'How depositories raise efficiency', 3rd September 1990; Simon Thomas and Chris Collingwood, 'Clearers at the crossroads', 3rd September 1990; Charles Harrington, 'Global custodians are bullish about Taurus', 3rd September 1990; Sean Heath, 'Solution to settlement', 7th November 1990; Richard Waters, 'Unbundling the City's top club', 5th March 1991; Richard Waters, 'Liverpool Stock Exchange finally laid to rest', 23rd March 1991; Norma Cohen, 'Institutional investors flex their settlement muscles', 10th October 1991; Richard Waters, 'Fundamental questions', 12th November 1991; Richard Waters, 'Parliament approves Taurus changes', 12th February 1992; Richard Waters, 'A tune-up for City trades', 9th April 1992; Norma Cohen, 'Institutional investors flex their settlement muscles', 10th October 1991; Richard Waters, 'Fundamental questions', 12th November 1991; Richard Waters, 'Parliament approves Taurus changes', 12th February 1992; Richard Waters, 'A tune-up for City trades', 9th April 1992 Ian Hamilton Fazey, 'Capital keeps grip on HQs', 3rd August 1992; Barry Riley, 'Securities Institute sallies forth into the world', 16th September 1992; Richard Waters, 'Light at the end of the tunnel', 10th November 1992; Charles Batchelor, 'Enterprise looks for a way out', 22nd December 1992; Nuala Moran, 'Savings financed new system', 4th September 1996.

[91] Norma Cohen, 'Institutional investors flex their settlement muscles', 10th October 1991.

[92] David Lascelles, 'Pitching for a share of London's work', 5th July 1989; Richard Waters, 'Finding a role for the Exchange', 4th October 1989.

[93] John Burton, 'Eyeing EC systems', 3rd July 1990.

[94] Sean Heath, 'Solution to settlement', 7th November 1990.

[95] John Burton, 'Eyeing EC systems', 3rd July 1990; George Graham, 'Foreign investment doubles', 22nd October 1990; Sean Heath, 'Solution to settlement', 7th November 1990; Richard Waters, 'Vision of a grand strategy fades', 26th February 1992.

strong in their home products, but interlinked outside their borders through a joint clearing, if not trading, system, is compelling.'[96] Driving European co-operation was not only the desire to compete with stock exchanges located elsewhere in the world for international business but also an emerging threat from the inter-bank trading.[97] According to Deborah Hargreaves in 1990 the banks were working on 'a European-wide share trading network' for the stock of multinational companies which would operate through Reuters and Euroclear, and so bypass all the leading exchanges.[98] Having gained direct access to the stock exchanges, combined with the dropping of rules on fixed charges, there was now no impediment to banks cross-matching deals in-house, trading with each other or using the services of interdealer brokers. An estimate for 1991 suggested that as much as 43 per cent of equity trading in Europe did not take place on any of the exchanges but through the OTC market.[99]

The Limits to the Revolution

Though the pace and scale of change in the European equity market and a number of other countries was transformational from the mid-1980s onwards, that was not the case everywhere. Outside Europe stock exchanges were able to resist change as they were cocooned from competition, whether internal or external, behind barriers of both their own making and those maintained by national governments. This was even the case in the USA which had led the process of change in the 1970s. The USA had long possessed multiple stock exchanges competing for business with each other in a single market devoid of significant barriers. However, it is important not to exaggerate the degree of competition that existed. At the international level the USA remained detached from the developing global market. As Yoshihisa Tabuchi, President of Nomura, observed in 1988, 'Europe is a global market, whereas Americans are much less interested in global markets.'[100] Evidence of this lack of global orientation comes from the low proportion of foreign shares in the portfolios of US investors. Prior to the 1987 crash, when international investment was growing rapidly, US institutions had only 4 per cent of their portfolios in foreign stocks compared to 10 per cent for Japanese and 20 per cent for UK ones. When the stock of foreign companies did attract the interest of US investors it was often converted into American Depository Receipts (ADRs) denominated in US$s. ADRs in circulation in the USA rose from $24.1bn in 1985 to $123.2bn in 1992. ADRs were bearer documents issued by US banks that gave title to the underlying shares. Once a company registered with the SEC for an ADR programme, the products were created by a broker buying ordinary shares in the home market and delivering them to a depository bank in the US, which then held the shares and issued an ADR

[96] Katharine Campbell, 'No recipe for long-term success', 9th March 1990.

[97] James Andrews, 'Gearing up fast to meet Tokyo trading volume', 10th November 1988; Stephen Fidler, 'Europe falls behind in the securities race', 25th January 1989; Richard Waters, 'Towards Europe's super-league', 11th September 1989; George Graham, 'Year of quiet change', 2nd November 1989; Richard Waters, 'Bourse battle for pride of place in Europe', 17th May 1990.

[98] Deborah Hargreaves, 'CSFB to integrate European share trading', 8th February 1990.

[99] Richard Waters, 'Pipe brings dream of Euro-bourse closer to reality', 19th April 1990; Deborah Hargreaves, 'Race to create a Euro-share index', 21st June 1990; David Lascelles, 'Banks seem set to move cautiously', 2nd July 1990; Charles Harrington, 'Global custodians are bullish about Taurus', 3rd September 1990; Richard Waters, 'Farewell to the trading floor as markets plan automation', 22nd July 1991; Richard Waters, 'Bourses build up defences', 24th September 1991.

[100] Stefan Wagstyl, 'Risk of missing the global bus', 2nd December 1988.

certificate. This meant that there was a degree of separation between the trading of ADRs in the USA and the market in the underlying stocks abroad. The focus of the US investor remained the domestic market and that was served by US banks and US exchanges. Richard Waters concluded in 1992 that 'The US remains the world's biggest markets for corporate finance. Yet it remains virtually closed to foreign banks, which have never prospered in the fiercely competitive atmosphere of Wall Street.'[101]

Within the US domestic market the competition between stock exchanges was in attracting new issues. Joseph Hardiman, president, National Association of Securities Dealers, observed in 1988, 'Competition for listings gets keener and the competition to list existing companies gets keener.'[102] In contrast to the battle for new listings, competition between US exchanges at the level of trading in existing companies was relatively subdued. Once a stock was listed and a market established trading did not migrate from one exchange to another. Investors stuck to the venue which possessed the greatest liquidity and where the reference price was generated. Only if a company changed its listing did the market also move. For that reason both the NYSE and Nasdaq possessed a near monopoly of trading in the stocks of those companies each quoted, and so divided up the US stock market between them. Each exchange tried to gain control of a distinct segment of the US stock market whether it was large established companies for the NYSE or smaller more technologically-based companies in the case of Nasdaq. Squeezed between the NYSE and Nasdaq was the American Stock Exchange (Amex), the old curb market, and it focused, according to its president, Kenneth Leibler, in 1987 on 'looking for niches'.[103] This compartmentalization of the US stock market meant that neither the NYSE nor Nasdaq were under much pressure to change the way they operated, despite the SEC being mandated to promote competition. In 1975 the US Congress had proposed the creation of an integrated national market system for stocks that would link together all the trading floors in the USA. The intention of this Intermarket Trading System was to direct orders to whichever exchange could provide the best price at the lowest transaction cost. Even by 1988 this system was not yet in place because of the immense technical difficulties to be overcome. As both the NYSE and Nasdaq were relatively cheap trading venues, because of the economies of scale they enjoyed, their failure to change did not provoke either popular pressure for change or regulatory intervention. Under these circumstances the NYSE, for example, was able to maintain a physical trading floor and the privileged position of the specialists, despite both being products of a bygone era when trading was done on behalf of individual investors. Though there were an estimated 47 million individual investors in the US in the late 1980s it was financial institutions that increasingly dominated trading.

Rather than buying and selling individual stocks these institutions wanted to trade either large quantities of shares in individual companies or whole portfolios of stocks, and do so quickly as part of their fund management strategy. These institutional trades were overwhelming the ability of the trading floor and specialist system to cope because of their huge size and need for speed of execution. In contrast, the large brokers, especially those that were part of giant financial conglomerates, possessed the capacity to handle the block trades that the institutional investors were generating. The large investment banks were backed by substantial capital reserves and possessed a large network of clients through whom they could internally match buyers and sellers for big orders. However, the NYSE

[101] Richard Waters, 'Barings' transatlantic leap', 3rd July 1992.
[102] Stephen Fidler, 'US stock exchanges wage listings war abroad', 20th April 1988.
[103] Gordon Cramb, 'Aiming to be both liquid and transparent', 21st October 1987.

had a rule that transactions could not be executed off the floor of the exchange during trading hours. This was a way of concentrating business and so maintaining liquidity and narrow spreads. Trading outside normal working hours did bypass the specialists and one option for the NYSE was to allow even more of it to take place, but it was reluctant to concede that because it would further undermine the role played by the specialists and the use of the floor. This refusal to change the rule was justified on the grounds that it prevented market fragmentation which would undermine price.[104] In Martin Dickson's opinion in 1991, 'At the centre of the battle lies the question of whether New York's floor-based "continuous auction" trading system is in danger of becoming an expensive anachronism in an electronic age, or whether it is the best means of ensuring a fair and efficient market.'[105] By 1990 the Wall Street investment banks were frustrated by the NYSE's 'anachronistic, uncompetitive, exchange rules and high transaction costs', according to Janet Bush,[106] while Patrick Harverson in 1992 referred to the NYSE as 'an expensive anachronism'.[107] The result was that the NYSE did slowly lose market share, even in the stocks it quoted. In 1981 more than 75 per cent of the trading in all US stocks had been handled by the NYSE but that dropped to 50 per cent by 1991. The NYSE even struggled to hold on to trading of its own listed stocks. In 1981 it accounted for 82 per cent of all trades in NYSE stocks but only 67 per cent in 1991. Nevertheless, with volume rising the NYSE refused to change its trading system to meet the needs of the banks. Instead, it tried to attract international issues but this was made difficult, according to Patrick Harverson in 1992, by 'Strict US reporting regulations which dissuade many big foreign corporations from seeking a US listing.'[108] That was only part of the explanation because the attitude of the NYSE's own members was hostile to the changes internationalization required, as those could mean that the exchange would have to operate on a twenty-four hour basis. Even an attempt to extend trading hours by thirty minutes was strongly resisted by its members in 1992. As long as the NYSE could continue to dominate the market for the stocks it quoted the pressure for change remained subdued. This it was able to do as it remained the only market in which investors could be completely confident of buying and selling the stocks it quoted at close to current prices, while the regulatory regime favoured the flow of orders to the NYSE.

A similar situation existed at Nasdaq which had carved out for itself a successful niche in the US stock market. Not only did it control the market for the stock of small and emerging companies but it also held onto that of technology giants like Apple and Microsoft. Though Nasdaq had led the transformation of stock trading in the 1970s, with its screen-based price display system, it failed to progress in the 1980s to an electronic market. In 1992 the Arizona Stock Exchange was established with a computer-based market that automatically matched buyers and sellers of shares in US companies. In contrast, Nasdaq's automated screen-based system, Portal, was confined to less actively traded stocks. Like the NYSE Nasdaq also tried to develop an international presence, initially through a link with the LSE and then through Nasdaq International, so mirroring what the LSE had done with Seaq International. Nasdaq International was to have branches in Europe and the Far East so as to provide a single integrated global trading system. This led to questions over the rules to apply in each jurisdiction. The SEC wanted to apply US regulations to all Nasdaq trading whereas Nasdaq

[104] Janet Bush, 'Wall Street wants to deal wholesale', 30th August 1988.
[105] Martin Dickson, 'New York has a fresh champion', 2nd January 1991.
[106] Janet Bush, 'Referee tries to be fair to investors large and small', 16th August 1990.
[107] Patrick Harverson, 'The NYSE begins to show its age', 15th May 1992.
[108] Patrick Harverson, 'The competitive edge', 11th June 1992.

wanted to use local ones. Lyndon Jones, managing director of Nasdaq International in London, made clear in 1991 that, 'If Nasdaq International is going to have any chance of succeeding here, it has to operate under London rules.'[109] Nasdaq International eventually came into operation in 1992. What neither the NYSE nor Nasdaq could develop in the USA was an integrated trading, clearing, and settlement system to match what Deutsche Börse was doing. In 1972, because of concerns over the risks caused by an emerging settlement backlog a federal agency, the Depository Trust Company (DTC), was established through which accounts could be debited and credited automatically with cash or shares, and it served all stock exchanges.[110]

What the US experience reveals is that it was the presence or absence of competition that exerted a key influence on whether stock markets were transformed or not in the 1980s. That verdict also applied to Japan where the degree of change was slow and limited with the Tokyo Stock Exchange (TSE) occupying an increasingly dominant position. Rival stock exchanges such as Osaka and Nagoya were losing market share to Tokyo as it became the centre of liquidity for the leading Japanese corporate stocks, and so attracted institutional buying and selling from home and abroad. The Japanese securities and exchange law also banned off-market transactions that linked payments to market prices, which prevented the development of an active OTC market. Under these circumstances the TSE was able to maintain a regime of fixed commission rates, exercise tight control over the number

[109] Patrick Harverson, 'Unhappy new year greets NASD', 13th February 1991.

[110] John Plender, 'A homing instinct', 14th November 1987; Stephen Fidler, 'A trickle of issues', 29th June 1988; Stephen Fidler, 'In the eye of the storm', 18th November 1987; David Lascelles, 'After the rush, the shakeout', 8th May 1987; Clive Wolman, 'Out of shape for the paper chase', 14th August 1987; Roderick Oram, 'Further transatlantic links on the way', 12th October 1987; Gordon Cramb, 'Aiming to be both liquid and transparent', 21st October 1987; Clive Wolman, 'Small deals suffer', 21st October 1987; Stephen Fidler, 'US stock exchanges wage listings war abroad', 20th April 1988; Anatole Kaletsky, 'Big decisions ahead', 24th June 1988; Janet Bush, 'Wall Street wants to deal wholesale', 30th August 1988; Deborah Hargreaves, 'Brave new products', 14th October 1988; Boris Sedacca, 'Advanced system comes on stream', 10th November 1988; Janet Bush, 'Five banks with universal plans', 2nd May 1989; Stephen Fidler, 'Amex to launch options in fixed-income securities', 24th May 1989; Richard Waters, 'Stock Exchange may face US 24-hour trading', 10th June 1989; Janet Bush, 'Arguments intensify in the regulatory minefield', 26th June 1989; Deborah Hargreaves, 'Philly's fancy turns to thoughts of merger', 25th July 1989; Richard Waters, 'Towards Europe's super-league', 11th September 1989; Janet Bush, 'US gears up to meet the challenges of globalisation', 20th December 1989; Janet Bush, 'A pointer from New York', 9th March 1990; Deborah Hargreaves, 'Chicago exchanges at variance', 9th March 1990; Janet Bush, 'Magic ingredients for an outdated market', 23rd April 1990; Martin Dickson, 'NYSE seeks unified circuit breakers', 13th June 1990; Barbara Durr, 'Chicago lines up a link with Japan', 13th June 1990; Richard Waters, 'Rivals may yet collaborate', 2nd July 1990; Janet Bush, 'New rule will clear path', 2nd July 1990; Deborah Hargreaves, 'ADRs refuse to bow out gracefully', 20th July 1990; Janet Bush, 'Referee tries to be fair to investors large and small', 16th August 1990; Desmond MacRae, 'How depositories raise efficiency', 3rd September 1990; Martin Dickson, 'New York has a fresh champion', 2nd January 1991; Patrick Harverson, 'Unhappy new year greets NASD', 13th February 1991; Patrick Harverson, 'Big Board takes an after-hours gamble', 10th June 1991; Richard Waters, 'US, UK stock markets call off talks on link-up', 20th June 1991; Richard Waters, 'Farewell to the trading floor as markets plan automation', 22nd July 1991; Patrick Harverson, 'A welcome tonic', 22nd July 1991; Patrick Harverson, 'NYSE wakes up to the problem of early trading', 5th August 1991; Patrick Harverson, 'SEC decision on NASD trading system expected shortly', 9th October 1991; Patrick Harverson, 'NASD wins early-trading approval from SEC', 11th October 1991; Patrick Harverson, 'Brokers appeal against SEC ruling on small-order system', 24th October 1991; Barbara Durr, 'Exchange stakes out fresh index territory', 12th February 1992; Barbara Durr, 'Talent capsized by money wave', 19th March 1992; Patrick Harverson, 'The NYSE begins to show its age', 15th May 1992; Patrick Harverson, 'The competitive edge', 11th June 1992; Richard Waters, 'Barings' transatlantic leap', 3rd July 1992; Richard Waters, 'Markets start to multiply', 10th November 1992; Patrick Harverson, 'Daimler's arrival marks new spirit at US securities agency', 1st April 1993; Richard Waters, 'The price of a share of the cake', 31st January 1994; Edward Luce and Vincent Boland, 'Nasdaq goes global', 6th November 1999; John Labate and Andrew Hill, 'Ringing the exchanges', 6th March 2000; Don Cruickshank, 'Clearing away inefficiency', 16th May 2001; Alex Skorecki, 'NYSE rivals focus on costs', 21st April 2004; Anuj Gangahar, 'Nanoseconds matter as traders prepare for a shake-up', 14th September 2006; Deborah Brewster, 'US retail investors slump to record low', 2nd September 2008; FT Reporters, 'Solid capital has the upper hand', 23rd September 2008.

of members, and enforce many other restrictive practices aided by Japan's version of the Glass–Steagall Act that separated investment and commercial banking. Though there was a gradual embrace of electronic trading to cope with increasing turnover there was absence of structural and organizational change in Japan during the 1980s.[111] This resistance to change by the TSE meant that it was poorly positioned to capture a share of the growing international market in equities, creating opportunities for others in Asia to make the attempt. Following the temporary closure of the Hong Kong Stock Exchange (HKSE) in 1987, because of the stock market crash, there was a complete restructuring under government intervention. As Barry Riley reported in 1988, 'The Exchange was exposed as a club which was riddled with conflicts of interest, not only internally but also in respect of the disastrously unstable Futures Exchange'[112] At the heart of the restructuring was the move towards electronic trading and processing, the power given to the banks, and the decision to position the HKSE as an international market with a strong China focus.[113] Also aspiring to a pan-Asia role was the Singapore Stock Exchange (SSE), after the shock caused by Malaysian government ending the cross-listing arrangement it had with the Kuala Lumpur Stock Exchange (KLSE) in 1989. Singapore had provided the main market for the stock of numerous Malaysian companies but the split left the KLSE in control. Lacking a domestic market of its own the SSE focused on becoming an international centre for trading Asian corporate stocks. It supported that move with investment in electronic trading and processing technology and inviting the participation of foreign banks.[114]

Without the spur of adversity faced by both Hong Kong and Singapore, elsewhere in Asia the pace and degree of change was as slow as in Japan. In many countries there were no stock markets or those that existed were either moribund or closed to outsiders. Most stock exchanges operated under highly restrictive rules and regulations, and were supported by governments that protected them from competition. South Korea possessed one of Asia's most developed stock markets but foreign investors were denied access until 1991 and foreign firms were only permitted to become members of the Seoul Stock Exchange in 1992.[115] India was one of the slumbering giants of Asia's stock market with twenty-one

[111] Stephen Fidler, 'Deregulate or risk being left behind', 21st October 1987; John Plender, 'A homing instinct', 14th November 1987; Stephen Fidler, 'In the eye of the storm', 18th November 1987; James Andrews, 'Gearing up fast to meet Tokyo trading volume', 10th November 1988; Stefan Wagstyl, 'Risk of missing the global bus', 2nd December 1988; Stefan Wagstyl, 'Signposts to expansion', 8th March 1989; Stefan Wagstyl, 'Suffering from insecurity', 13th March 1989; Patti Waldmeir, 'Most continue to take long view', 13th March 1989; James Andrews, 'Reforms at hand', 13th March 1989; Patti Waldmeir, 'Big four still recruiting', 13th March 1989; David Lascelles, 'London is the springboard', 15th March 1990; Charles Harrington, 'London is now expected to re-emerge as the centre', 3rd September 1990; Richard Waters, 'The local traders fight back', 19th March 1991; Richard Waters, 'Life in the shadow of deregulation', 19th March 1991; Edward Balls, 'Tentative recovery stalls', 22nd July 1991; Emiko Terazono, 'Fears of new restrictions', 19th March 1992; Simon London, 'Profits are still flowing', 27th March 1992; Nigel Adam, 'New lending cut short', 27th March 1992; Simon London, 'Centre of European operations', 27th March 1992; Simon London, 'More call for change', 27th March 1992; Gwen Robinson, 'Backward in coming forward', 27th June 1997; Francesco Guerrera, 'Region weighs the need for a one-stop shop', 12th April 2006.

[112] Barry Riley, 'The exposure of a club', 26th October 1988.

[113] Barry Riley, 'New regulations, new faces', 14th October 1988; Barry Riley, 'The exposure of a club', 26th October 1988; Barry Riley, 'A question of survival', 26th October 1988; Barry Riley, 'The exposure of a club', 26th October 1988; Barry Riley, 'Regulators are balancing on a tightrope', 8th November 1989; Angus Foster, 'Future of stock exchange comes to a head', 16th August 1991; Philip Coggan, 'Some brokers remain uneasy about reform package', 20th November 1991; Simon Holberton, 'Shares and the Chinese', 27th April 1994.

[114] Joyce Quek, 'Singapore's Clob wins rapid acceptance', 18th January 1990; Peter Wise, 'Depression after the comet', 30th April 1990; Joyce Quek, 'A blessing in disguise', 9th August 1990; Philip Coggan, 'Nominee comes to the aid of the Clob', 8th February 1996.

[115] John Ridding, 'Prising an opening', 29th October 1991; Sara Webb, 'South Korean securities houses target City', 5th March 1992; Sara Webb, 'Analysts sceptical', 18th November 1992; Sara Webb, 'Going gets tough', 18th November 1992; Tracy Corrigan, 'Light at the end of the tunnel', 11th November 1993.

separate stock exchanges and a rapidly growing number of investors, which increased from 2m in 1982 to 15m in 1992. However, the stock market changed little in response. Each stock exchange monopolized its local market though the Bombay Stock Exchange, located in India's financial centre, dominated trading, with around two-thirds of the total. It operated as a closed community and continued to rely on a physical trading floor that was only open two hours a day, four days a week, while processing and settlement was both slow and subject to frequent breakdowns. The result was a stock market that lacked transparency and was inefficient, fragmented, and illiquid, generating prices that were unreliable and subject to manipulation. Change did not come until 1992, with the formation of the National Stock Exchange, as a rival to the Bombay Stock Exchange, and the partial opening up of the Indian stock market to foreign firms.[116] The situation in Pakistan was very similar. There were three stock exchanges in Karachi, Lahore, and Islamabad but 90 per cent of the trading took place in the first. Membership of the Karachi Stock Exchange was capped at 200 and the stock market was largely illiquid, prices lacked transparency, and trading was reliant on physical floors. Most sizeable transactions were negotiated privately.[117] In contrast, communist China was beginning to embrace change but under the strict control of the government. Government permission was required before a stock exchange could be opened with an unofficial one in Haikou closed down and other proposals rejected. Nevertheless, in 1990 two stock exchanges were established. One was in Shanghai, the old financial centre, while the other was in Shenzhen, located adjacent to Hong Kong. These grew out of informal markets that had been operating since the mid-1980s, reflecting growing popular enthusiasm for owning shares and the desire of state-owned enterprises to issue shares as a source of funding. These new exchanges incorporated both a trading floor and the latest electronic trading technology.[118]

What was happening in China epitomized an awakening interest in stock markets and stock exchanges across Asia. Until 1988 the Jakarta Stock Exchange in Indonesia was virtually moribund but was then sparked into activity through a package of deregulatory measures and the easing of restrictions on the access of foreigners to the market. The result was a dynamic but rather chaotic and under-regulated market.[119] The process taking place can be seen in the case of the Istanbul Stock Exchange (ISE). Though it could trace its origins to the nineteenth century its modern revival dated from the mid-1980s. In 1982 the government set up the Capital Market Board and this led to the establishment of a new ISE in 1984, though it did not open until 1985 and begin trading in 1986. The ISE received a boost in 1989 when the Turkish government allowed foreign investors access. This attracted the likes of Citibank as they saw the ISE as a way of integrating Turkey with the global stock market. As Maarten Hulshoff, general manager of Citibank in Istanbul, explained in 1990, 'Global markets are opening up, and I want to present Citibank as a gateway both for and to

[116] Alexander Nicoll, 'Regulation a tough task for the board', 16th September 1991; Gita Piramal, 'Indian stock market reform gathers pace', 5th March 1992; Naazneen Karmali, 'Early bird catches worm', 13th March 1995; Tony Tassell, 'Culture change on Dalal Street', 24th June 1997; Jeremy Grant, 'LSE aims to revive Delhi exchange', 9th November 2011.

[117] Simon Davies, 'When the bubble had to burst', 18th September 1992; Farhan Bokhari, 'Spurred on by foreign investors', 28th November 1994.

[118] John Elliot, 'Share dealing returns to Shanghai', 19th December 1990; John Elliot, 'Old tune is heard again', 24th April 1991; Angus Foster, 'Two bourses go on trial but development will be orderly', 20th November 1991; Simon Holberton, 'Foreigners join the queue for Shenzhen flotations', 3rd April 1992; Lynne Curry, 'Heavy demand for shares', 16th June 1992; Tony Walker, 'Big ideas on dance floor', 2nd June 1993; Simon Holberton, 'Regulators battle to catch up', 18th November 1993; Simon Davies, 'Vital role in restructuring', 8th December 1997.

[119] Paul Taylor, 'Consolidation worries the smaller firms', 22nd March 1991.

Turkish equity.'[120] The ISE incorporated both the latest computer technology and a physical trading floor but it was increasingly the former that became the preferred option for the exchanges being established across Asia.[121] In Thailand a computerized trading system was introduced in 1991. This automatically matched buyers and sellers.[122] Across the oil rich countries of the Middle East stock exchanges were established to capture the investments of wealthy locals. Kuwait's exchange dated from 1984 and in 1989 it moved to a fully automated dealing system. Bahrain and Oman both opened stock exchanges in 1989. However, elsewhere in the Middle East stock markets either did not exist or were inactive. That was the case in Egypt where the two stock exchanges, Cairo and Alexandria, imposed high commissions, limited membership to brokers, and relied on the call over system for trading. The problem for the Middle East was that no country possessed a large enough stock market to provide the liquidity sought by major institutional investors and so the leading companies of the region looked abroad for trading facilities, especially London.[123]

As in the Middle East the problem in Latin America was also the fragmented nature of the stock market because of the political divisions. Most Latin American countries lacked a share-owning culture and were too small to support a well-developed stock market, including the largest economies like Argentina and Brazil. Attempts were made to overcome fragmentation and generate liquidity in the early 1990s, with plans to link stock exchanges in Argentina, Brazil, Mexico, and Uruguay to create a Latin American market, but they made slow progress. Only with privatization were sufficient stocks issued to sufficient investors necessary to support an active market, as began to take place in Argentina in 1989. John Barham explained in 1991 the 'virtuous cycle' begun by Argentinian privatization, in which 'the narrow equity market will become more liquid as it expands, drawing in more investors, and creating a source of long-term finance for companies'.[124] The expectation was that this process would reverse years of stock market decline in which the number of companies listed on the Buenos Stock Exchange had fallen from 600 in 1960 to 200 in 1990. The Argentine government's climbing debt had left little scope for private borrowers while heavy corporate, wealth, and capital-gains taxes destroyed investor interest in stocks. Transaction taxes also reduced secondary market activity. In Brazil there was an infrastructure of nine stock exchanges but trading was dominated by São Paulo, with 60 per cent, and Rio de Janeiro at 35 per cent. Beginning in 1991, and the opening of the Brazilian market to foreign investors, followed by permission to Brazilian investors to invest abroad in 1992, this market was exposed to outside influence and competition. The result was a plan to both create an integrated national stock market and introduce the latest trading technology but these met with opposition as they would erode local monopolies. Even by 1992 most Latin American stock markets continued to lack liquidity with the partial exception of that located in Mexico City. As a result the larger listed companies in Mexico, Argentina, Chile, and Venezuela issued ADRs and GDRs which were traded in London and New York.[125] A similar situation prevailed in the Caribbean, leading stock exchanges there agreeing to

[120] Jim Bodgener, 'Immaturity exposed', 21st November 1990.

[121] Jim Bodgener, 'Immaturity exposed', 21st November 1990; Kerin Hope, 'Small investors desert bourse', 20th May 1991; Bob Vincent, 'Intent on expanding its services', 17th December 1991; David Barchard, 'Investors go elsewhere', 21st May 1992; Anthony McDermott, 'More will own shares', 18th November 1992.

[122] Victor Mallet, 'Curbs on a casino', 3rd December 1991.

[123] Mark Nicholson, 'Venture still in its infancy', 27th September 1989; Tony Walker, 'On the road to reform in Cairo's markets', 22nd October 1991.

[124] John Barham, 'Argentine dealers glimpse the future', 1st March 1991.

[125] John Barham, 'Argentine dealers glimpse the future', 1st March 1991; Christina Lamb, 'Brazil moves toward a single stock exchange', 17th September 1991; Canute James, 'Securities exchange set up in Santo Domingo', 16th

cross-list companies as the first step in the creation of a regional stock exchange. However, this still left major technical and organizational challenges to be overcome and progress was slow.[126]

For a variety of spatial or political reasons numerous stock markets around the world lacked the capacity to support the large liquid markets that businesses and investors increasingly required. That left them exposed to the fortunes of a few companies, leading to extremes of activity and inactivity. In 1989 the Stock Exchange of Mauritius was launched but only one stock, that of the Mauritius Commercial Bank, was liquid. This reduced their attractions to investors because of the risks involved, leaving most companies family controlled and banks the main source of external finance.[127] In all of Africa only the Johannesburg Stock Exchange (JSE) in South Africa, provided a market that was deep, broad, and stable, though progress was being made in the likes of Ghana and the Ivory Coast by the early 1990s, on the back of privatization programmes.[128] For political reasons the JSE was left in relative isolation while exchange controls limited its integration into the global stock market. With a monopoly of its domestic market the JSE was able to resist the tide of modernization including the ending of fixed commissions and the exclusion of banks. One effect was to deprive South Africa's largest companies of a liquid domestic market and so encourage them to explore alternative trading venues abroad given the extensive international interest in the country's leading mining stocks.[129] What the situation in Africa typified was that for all the progress made in Europe in the 1980s the power of entrenched monopolies, and the barriers to integration imposed by governments, continued to frustrate the development of a global equity market. Even in the USA the developments made by Nasdaq and the NYSE in the 1970s were not being built upon. Nevertheless, the emergence of London as the hub of a cross-border equity market did represent the beginnings of a global equity market while the emergence of Deutsche Börse indicated the institutional transformation that was taking place.

Conclusion

Though nothing on the scale and pace of what happened in European stock markets took place elsewhere in the world before 1992, the stirrings of change were evident in numerous different countries. There was a spread of stock markets around the globe and a willingness to embrace the latest technological advances. As national boundaries ceased to define market parameters stock exchanges lost their monopoly either to exchanges located in other countries or to OTC trading. This put pressure on those exchanges that relied upon restrictive practices to preserve their monopoly as they proved uncompetitive when the barriers were lowered. At the same time the use being made of stock markets, both by companies looking for finance and investors searching for assets that met their needs, was taking root

December 1991; Victoria Griffith, 'S. American trading agreement', 17th December 1991; Antonia Sharpe, 'New magnet for funds', 6th April 1992; Richard Lapper, 'New deal fuels price rises', 7th March 1996.

[126] Canute James, 'Taking stock of the Caribbean', 26th February 1991; Jane Croft, 'Brokers talk up the positive', 22nd November 2002; Canute James, 'Boost for Caribbean Exchange plan', 4th February 2003.

[127] Tony Hawkins, 'Buy-and-hold persists', 14th September 1992.

[128] Philip Gawith, 'Remarkable rehabilitation', 30th August 1991; Michael Holman, 'Reforms ease business climate', 4th August 1995; David Buchan, 'Investors take note', 2nd June 1997.

[129] Philip Gawith, 'New leader for a new era', 3rd June 1992.

in countries where they had long been absent or never before existed. What was emerging was a hierarchy of stock exchanges which favoured those that provided investors with a range and depth of liquid stocks, as these were ideal for the banks and other financial institutions that operated on a large scale. These exchanges were found in national financial centres resulting in the decline of those located elsewhere. Globally, it was in London, New York, and Tokyo that the deepest and broadest stock markets were to be found and so business gravitated to them because of the liquidity they could provide. Conversely, smaller and emerging markets were also attractive, despite their illiquidity, because of the opportunities they provided for investors to generate large returns by taking risks on potentially undervalued stocks, such as privatizations and new flotations. Privatization not only transferred ownership from the state but also created assets that were transferable, making them accessible to individual and institutional investors at home and abroad. It was this mix of liquidity and capital gains that was making stock markets into a dynamic force in global finance by the early 1990s, compared to their marginal role a decade or so ago.[130]

However, exchanges faced a number of serious challenges in capturing this rapidly growing stock market. The first was from banks whose growing scale and scope allowed them to internalize transactions. These banks were both major customers of exchanges and a threat to their very existence. The second was the transformation of the way trading was conducted as electronic networks replaced physical floors. The new technology of trading favoured the banks, as they could both afford and justify the investment. It left exchanges uncertain over whether to use the new technology to complement or replace physical floors, forcing them to invest in the former while maintaining the latter. It also created opportunities for new exchanges using electronic systems to challenge incumbents. Electronic markets offered large cost savings but they involved high expenditure on an unproven technology with an uncertain outcome. The third threat to exchanges was the role played by government-appointed regulators. These usurped the self-regulatory role traditionally played by stock exchanges and undermined their ability to force the centralization of trading and so create deep pools of liquidity. In turn that fragmentation of the stock market weakened the ability to regulate trading, whether by an exchange or government agency. Taken together these developments were capable of disrupting the near monopoly that established exchanges had long possessed though the actual challenge varied enormously around the world. In some countries, exchanges remained entrenched behind protective walls provided by governments and enshrined in legislation or through the inertia of trading because of the need to access the deepest pool of liquidity and the source of current prices. The result by 1992 was a situation in which stock exchanges were facing a very uncertain future, forcing them to formulate strategies that would ensure their survival. The forces unleashed in the 1980s had removed many of the barriers that had allowed them to resist the changes unleashed by the process of globalization, technological progress, and competition that was sweeping through financial markets.

The dilemma facing stock exchanges was how to position themselves in this changing global stock market. At one extreme were those investors who traded little for small amounts while at the other were institutional investors who traded frequently for large

[130] David Dodwell, 'Now for silver linings and tight rules', 10th March 1988; Chris Sherwell, 'Quality counts now', 14th October 1988; David Owen, 'Banks close the gap', 17th February 1988; Mark Nicholson, 'Venture still in its infancy', 27th September 1989; Barry Riley, 'Regulators are balancing on a tightrope', 8th November 1989; John Ridding, 'Investors pay high price for exposure', 27th November 1989; Bruce Jacques, 'Slimming programme', 10th December 1990; John Elliot, 'Share dealing returns to Shanghai', 19th December 1990.

amounts. At the same time stock exchanges had to meet the needs of both large companies, whose stock was widely held and highly liquid and was frequently turned over, and small quasi-private companies whose stock was closely held and little traded. It was very difficult for a single institution to cope with these very divergent requirements not only in terms of the trading system it used but also the rules that regulated behaviour. In the less competitive world that had existed before the 1980s stock exchanges could impose a structure on the market which users had to accept. By the beginning of the 1990s that was no longer possible. Any neglect of a particular segment of the market could be exploited by the banks or new entrants employing the latest technology. Attempts to co-ordinate a response among stock exchanges were also doomed to failure as each pursued their own self-interest rather than agree on a common front to be used against the banks on the one hand and government agencies on the other.

6
Regulation and Regulators, 1970–92

Introduction

Before 1970 regulators had relied on the principle of divide and rule as a way of keeping financial systems in order. What this meant in practice was that even in market-based economies authority was exercised behind national boundaries, aided by controls on international financial flows, and by insisting upon a degree of internal compartmentalization not only between banks and markets but also within the banking sector. These boundaries and divisions facilitated central control and direction while allowing a great deal of discretion to those running the banks and exchanges, so that they were able to regulate their own affairs within the confines of the parameters set for them. In some countries such as the USA and Japan, this compartmentalization was enshrined in law while in others it was a product of custom and practice, central bank influence, and long-standing institutional barriers. Over the 1950s and 1960s the ability of regulators to rely on a policy of divide and rule was slowly eroded. Faced with the growing liberalization of international trade and finance the need grew to put in place mechanisms that allowed payments and receipts to be made, and funds to flow from areas of surplus to those with shortages. As governments continued to impose controls on international financial flows, including investment beyond a country's borders, these arrangements encouraged the development of offshore financial centres, like Switzerland and Hong Kong, and the growth of alternative financial markets, such as that for Eurodollars and Eurobonds. By their very nature these offshore centres and markets were much less regulated. A similar erosion of regulatory control took place within those countries operating a market economy as governments gave up attempts to impose interest rates and direct investment. Governments and central banks tolerated these minor infringements because the main currents of financial activity remained under their control, though they did result in the slow erosion of the power of regulators.[1]

It was after 1970 that governments lost control over the global monetary system followed by control over domestic and international financial markets. Governments had contributed to what had happened not only through the removal of barriers to international financial flows but by also intervening to remove restrictive practices and stimulate competition. By 1987 Janet Bush could reflect on how 'The march of technology, the dismantling of capital controls, and other measures aimed at liberalizing world markets, has helped to develop integrated 24-hour global markets.'[2] Writing about the 1980s in 1991, Stephen Fidler concluded that, 'At the beginning of the decade the world could be split into a handful of

[1] Alexander Nicoll, 'Fast growth on back of market volatility', 11th December 1985; John Plender, 'Capital loosens its bonds', 8th May 1986; Helen Hague, 'Facing up to a cultural challenge', 9th January 1987; Stefan Wagstyl, 'Reforms on the way', 22nd June 1987; Kenneth Gooding, 'A boost for the market', 13th June 1988; Ralph Atkins, 'Zurich's precious tradition', 19th December 1988; Andrew Freeman, 'Spurred by the Americans', 20th February 1989; Kenneth Gooding, 'Havens of inertia', 22nd June 1992; Richard Mooney, 'At the tip of an iceberg', 22nd June 1992; John Plender, 'The limits of ingenuity', 17th May 2001; Daniel Dombey, 'Lack of growth signals need for reinvention', 7th June 2001.

[2] Janet Bush, 'Pressure grows for freer markets', 3rd June 1987.

Banks, Exchanges, and Regulators: Global Financial Markets from the 1970s. Ranald Michie, Oxford University Press (2021).

DOI: 10.1093/oso/9780199553730.003.0006

separate capital markets with little overlap among them.... But when government after government began to lift controls on the transfer of capital, the barriers between capital markets were removed and every financial intermediary, wherever based, became a potential competitor to every other.'[3] Even in those economies like Russia and China, where government control had been absolute, the breakdown of centrally-imposed pricing, and state-run distribution systems stimulated developments in banking and commodity and financial markets.[4] As the barriers to external financial flows and internal compartmentalization were removed regulators lost their ability to isolate national financial systems, and so force compliance. With porous borders it became an increasingly impossible task to prevent the flow of funds either out to offshore locations or in from alternative providers. At the same time a drive by governments to stimulate greater competition in the financial sector, in order to support the interests of users and promote economic growth, removed the protection that banks and exchanges had long enjoyed.[5] As Guy de Jonquières noted in 1988, 'After decades of operating along well-established lines, defined by the borders of their national markets and by traditional products and customer bases, commercial banks in almost every country are being forced to confront a confusing array of fresh challenges.'[6] Paul Cheeseright added in 1989 that 'Deregulation of the financial markets has changed that cosy, ordered world where each professional had a specified place in the scheme of things.'[7] By then the compartmentalized and controlled financial world of the 1950s and 1960s had given way to a much more competitive environment, in which the policy of regulation through divide and rule proved increasingly ineffective.[8]

Technological change contributed to this transformation by rendering boundaries between countries and activities increasingly meaningless. Physical space no longer dictated the location of a market because transactions took place over the telephone with prices displayed on screens. In the absence of exchange and other controls, payments and receipts flowed seamlessly through inter-bank networks that grew steadily in breadth and depth. In the face of these developments governments increasingly abandoned exchange controls and other attempts to contain or channel international financial flows. Making use of the new technology, financial innovation blurred distinctions between banks and financial markets, as well as between different types of banks, as new products were invented such as financial derivatives and money-market funds.[9] By the mid-1980s the consequences of these changes were challenging regulators the world over. Writing in 1986 John Plender reported that 'Huge structural changes in the capital and financial markets are the stuff of nightmares for bank supervisors and securities watchdogs.'[10] Alexander Nicoll observed in 1987 that 'Due both to deregulation and the globalisation of financial markets, barriers between the domestic and international sectors are breaking down.'[11] Norma Cohen noted in in 1989 that 'Global capital markets, while a bonanza for investors and institutions, have

[3] Stephen Fidler, 'When family loyalties are placed under severe strain', 28th December 1990; Simon London, 'Cedel's rise in turnover confirms trend', 5th February 1991.
[4] Leyla Boulton, 'Soviet oil and gas exchange opens this month', 11th June 1991; Lynne Curry, 'Heavy demand for shares', 16th June 1992.
[5] Simon London, 'Cedel's rise in turnover confirms trend', 5th February 1991.
[6] Guy de Jonquières, 'Risk, opportunities and arduous negotiations', 18th May 1988.
[7] Paul Cheeseright, 'The competition intensifies', 12th July 1989.
[8] Peter Marsh, 'They're breathing down London's neck', 26th May 1993.
[9] Alexander Nicoll, 'A banker rather than a regulator', 20th January 1987.
[10] John Plender, 'Watchdogs follow the sun', 27th October 1986.
[11] Alexander Nicoll, 'A banker rather than a regulator', 20th January 1987.

proved a headache for regulators.'[12] By 1990 Stephen Fidler concluded that 'The switch to screen-based trading...provide a continued and an ever-more complex challenge for the world's securities and banking regulators.'[13] This did not mean that regulators abandoned the attempt to supervise and police the financial system, as the need to do so remained as great as ever, especially after the risks of inter-connected banks and financial markets were exposed by the international debt crisis of 1982 and the global stock market crash of 1987.[14] In 1985 Alexandre Lamfalussy, director-general of the central bankers' central bank, the Bank for International Settlements (BIS), highlighted their fear that the world banking system had grown beyond the ability of national authorities to control it.[15] Barry Riley reflected in 1988 that, 'The fear, in the wake of last October's crash, is that, if the global market continues to develop faster than the regulators can adapt, the result could be a financial disaster which could set the international securities business back many years.'[16] Under these circumstances there was no desire to leave banks and financial markets unregulated. By 1991, at the time of another financial crisis, the Organization of Economic Co-operation and Development (OECD) was worried that recent developments in financial markets had left them vulnerable to a systemic failure caused by a liquidity freeze. They called for regulators to intervene.[17] The problem was that there was no obvious regulatory solution that could be quickly and easily put in place to cope with the emerging risks.

Complicating the regulatory response was the lack of unanimity among governments. Democratically elected governments were strongly influenced by public opinion, especially when backed by the media. That was rarely favourable to banks and financial markets. Governments introduced laws that responded to public pressure and reflected their own political priorities, and owed little to concerns about either the stability of the financial system or its efficient working. Regulators were then left with the task of implementing legislation that was inherently contradictory, drawing the financial system in different directions simultaneously and generating consequences that were both unpredictable and undesirable.[18] Barry Riley considered in 1991 that 'heavy-handed regulation' had restricted the development of financial markets in Germany.[19] The prominent British politician, Nigel Lawson, pointed out in 1992 the impossibility of predicting the results of regulatory intervention: 'Any radical reform, even if it achieves its objectives, is likely to bring about unforeseen side effects. This has proved particularly true of financial deregulation.'[20] Though the years after 1970 were associated with a process of financial deregulation that

[12] Norma Cohen, 'The bad apple in the other guy's barrel', 8th March 1989.

[13] Stephen Fidler, 'When family loyalties are placed under severe strain', 28th December 1990.

[14] Barry Riley, 'Reciprocity worries London', 29th June 1988; Stephen Fidler, 'A franchise under stress', 2nd July 1990.

[15] *Financial Times* Reporters, 'City well placed to benefit from banking trend', 10th July 1985.

[16] Barry Riley, 'Reciprocity worries London', 29th June 1988.

[17] Stephen Fidler, 'Covering risks of global volatility', 21st February 1991.

[18] Katharine Campbell, 'Risks and rewards of change in Frankfurt', 7th January 1991; William Dawkins, 'France presses on with liberalisation', 26th September 1991; Ronald van de Krol, 'Confronting overseas competition', 4th October 1991; Haig Simonian, 'Counting the cost of technological change', 9th October 1991; Robert Taylor, 'Swedish investors' group applauds bourse tax move', 11th October 1991; John Burton, 'Sax, Sox, tax moves widen interest', 17th October 1991; Tim Dickson, 'Exposed by the market's transparency', 12th December 1991; William Dawkins, 'Small bang fall-out', 12th December 1991; William Dullforce, 'Outlook fair but uncertain', 17th December 1991; Ian Rodger, 'This difficult year', 17th December 1991; Christopher Parkes and David Waller, 'Politics comes to the Finanzplatz', 24th January 1992; Robert Taylor, 'All change for Stockholm bourse', 25th February 1992; Ian Rodger, 'Worrying outflow of funds', 7th May 1992; David Waller, 'Going for the lion's share', 1st July 1992.

[19] Barry Riley, 'Big three join battle for supremacy', 4th July 1991.

[20] Nigel Lawson, 'Side effects of deregulation', 27th January 1992.

was not the case, as Nigel Lawson made clear: 'Financial deregulation in no way implies the absence of financial regulation for prudential purposes', giving as his reason that 'a financially deregulated economy, while more efficient and more dynamic, is less stable'.[21] Instead, what took place was a change in the regulatory regime, at both the national and international level, that reflected the need to respond to the fundamental changes taking place. The result was more not less regulation of the global financial system. What shrank was the degree and extent of direct control exercised by governments compared to the immediate post-war years. As governments moved away from central planning, state ownership, and direct control towards market-based structures, it was accompanied by regulatory regimes to supervise the new creations, whether they were banks or financial markets.[22] Gerald Corrigan, president of the Federal Reserve of New York, reflected in 1990, on the 'rapidly changing banking and financing environment', observing that it 'will provide a continued and an ever-more complex challenge for the world's securities and banking regulators'.[23]

Self Regulation

What was increasingly discarded in the search for new regulatory structures in the 1980s was the role played by self-regulation, even though continued progress was made in this direction, especially in financial markets. In the aftermath of the 1987 stock market crash Janet Bush had observed that 'The financial world has a way of conducting its own post-mortems and prescribing its own cures before the regulators and public opinion get in on the act.'[24] Those who participated directly in financial activities could not wait on the deliberations of regulators, and the long drawn out process of law making, driven by the poorly informed verdict of public opinion and the instant conclusions of the media. Instead, they devised their own remedies. As Deborah Hargreaves picked up from one veteran trader at the Chicago Board of Trade in 1988, 'You don't learn when you're winning. You only learn when you lose and have to question why.'[25] There was a growing recognition within finance that regulation was required as the volume of trading grew and participation became more varied. Accompanying that was a desire to make sure any new rules fitted the requirements of those engaged in the business, and that favoured self-regulation.[26] Supporting such a stance was the chairman of the London Metal Exchange (LME), Christopher Green, in 1988: 'We at the LME, while guardians of an orderly market, do not wish to be forced into interfering. In the meantime we have to recognise that exaggerated price movements can

[21] Nigel Lawson, 'Side effects of deregulation', 27th January 1992.

[22] Katharine Campbell, 'Risks and rewards of change in Frankfurt', 7th January 1991; Simon London, 'Captains of industry search for impeccable ratings', 9th January 1991; Stephen Fidler, 'Covering risks of global volatility', 21st February 1991; William Dawkins, 'France presses on with liberalisation', 26th September 1991; Ronald van de Krol, 'Confronting overseas competition', 4th October 1991; Haig Simonian, 'Counting the cost of technological change', 9th October 1991; Robert Taylor, 'Swedish investors' group applauds bourse tax move', 11th October 1991; John Burton, 'Sax, Sox, tax moves widen interest', 17th October 1991; Tim Dickson, 'Exposed by the market's transparency', 12th December 1991; William Dawkins, 'Small bang fall-out', 12th December 1991; William Dullforce, 'Outlook fair but uncertain', 17th December 1991; Ian Rodger, 'This difficult year', 17th December 1991; Christopher Parkes and David Waller, 'Politics comes to the Finanzplatz', 24th January 1992; Robert Taylor, 'All change for Stockholm bourse', 25th February 1992; Ian Rodger, 'Worrying outflow of funds', 7th May 1992; David Waller, 'Going for the lion's share', 1st July 1992.

[23] Stephen Fidler, 'A franchise under stress', 2nd July 1990.

[24] Janet Bush, 'Portfolio insurance loses its appeal', 10th March 1988.

[25] Deborah Hargreaves, 'Less risk and back to basics', 10th March 1988.

[26] Alexander Nicoll, 'A banker rather than a regulator', 20th January 1987; Clare Pearson, 'Overcrowding inhibits new issues', 21st April 1987.

exert undue harm on otherwise legitimate operators in the market and can damage the reputation of the exchange.'[27] He was well aware that while too light a regulatory regime could destabilize a market, leading to its near destruction, excessive regulations increased costs and reduced flexibility driving business away. Where trading was not already conducted through exchanges, such as in the foreign exchange and bond markets, those involved took steps to introduce a more regulated structure that attempted to balance the interests of all users.[28]

However, supporters of self-regulation faced opposition from the growing army of state-appointed officials whose responsibility was to oversee both banks and markets, and they followed a different agenda. Whereas those in finance regarded bank failures, speculative collapses, and scandals as regrettable but untypical it was precisely these events that the public focused upon, forcing regulators to respond. For those reasons state-appointed regulators focused on protecting the interests of buyers and sellers and savers and investors rather than monitoring the efficiency of the entire financial system. The question of stability only came to the fore in the wake of a major crisis, and these remained relatively uncommon. In contrast, those being regulated looked for measures that reduced the risks that they ran. These differences between the priorities of regulators and the regulated were also mirrored in the approach taken by separate regulators. Banking regulators were primarily concerned with the solvency and liquidity of both individual banks and the system as a whole. They were aware of how vulnerable a bank was not only to the consequences of poor judgement when making loans but also to a sudden collapse in trust, leading savers to withdraw their funds. In turn the failure of a single bank could have a contagious effect on the system as a whole unless the process was carefully managed. For those regulating financial markets the focus was on how to modify behaviour and minimize risk among those who participated in the buying and selling process, through the use of rules and regulations informed by changing practice. These differences between regulators created difficulties when individual business spanned both banking and financial market activity, and operated internationally, as was increasingly the case in the 1980s. Whereas central bankers and international organizations such as the BIS and the OECD prioritized the stability of the global financial system, national regulators operated at the local level and with mixed motives, with self-interest being among the most powerful.[29]

In this new world of regulation what was being eliminated was the role played by organizations that had traditionally policed their own affairs, such as the stock exchanges. In 1989 Laura Ram Raun described the Amsterdam Bourse as 'a self-regulated, private association with only vague legal obligations to anyone except its members, while the watchdog Dutch Securities Board has relatively limited powers'.[30] As other financial markets grew and matured they began to acquire these characteristics, as in the trading of Eurobonds, aware that if they did not act governments would intervene to remove abuses and impose discipline. Andrew Large was an expert on these Euromarkets, having been chief executive and deputy chairman of the Swiss Bank Corporation International, before becoming chair-

[27] Kenneth Gooding, 'Dangerous times at the metal exchange', 6th July 1988.

[28] Euromarkets Staff, 'Big reforms face bond dealers' association', 22nd May 1985; Rachel Davies, 'Invasion of the City increases', 15th July 1985.

[29] What reading the *Financial Times* reveals is how little reflection there was of the past especially the distant past. At most reference was made to the previous five years. I reached a similar conclusion when studying stock exchanges as the reasons for the introduction of major rule changes were largely forgotten when their repeal was being considered as they had developed a rationale of their own over the years.

[30] Laura Raun, 'Dutch master plan', 28th March 1989.

man of the UK's Securities Association, representing London-based brokers. In 1987 he stated that, 'There comes a time in the development of any market when its size and the nature and number of people that it embraces become such that governments simply cannot sit by.' For that reason the establishment of a regulatory regime for that Eurobond market was becoming inevitable, in his opinion. However, he warned that 'The one thing you can never forget in an international business is that it does not matter what rule is imposed by any government, if that rule does not meet the way that the market operates or the requirements of the investors and borrowers, then they will go and do it somewhere else.'[31] This was a plea for self-regulation whether in the form of exchanges or bodies such as the Association of International Bond Dealers (AIBD), dating from 1969. By the 1980s the AIBD was attempting to transform the unregulated Eurobond market from an informal club into a centralized body, with some of the rule-making and supervisory functions of a stock exchange. The AIBD was based in Zurich and operated under the laws of Switzerland. Its statutes, by-laws, rules, and recommendations were designed to provide self-regulation and co-operation between its members in all matters affecting transactions in international securities. By 1988 it had nearly 1000 members from forty-seven countries. These were mainly banks and financial institutions active in international capital markets in both the primary and secondary sectors. The focus of the AIBD was on tackling price manipulation, counterparty risk, and the operational features of the market whereas the concerns expressed by governments focused on investor protection.[32]

Both long-established exchanges and newer organizations like the AIBD were sandwiched between central banks, and the supervision they exercised over the banking system, and the growing number of national agencies with statutory powers, whose responsibility was financial markets. What stock exchanges had been able to do was devise a regulatory regime that provided a balance between permitting competition and exercising control. However, it was also used to stifle competition, stop change, and impose high charges on users, unless subjected to statutory oversight as in the case of Securities and Exchange Commission (SEC) in the USA. It was the replacement of unfettered self-regulation with SEC-style state regulation that most concerned market participants around the world in the 1980s. As João Rendeiro, the investment strategist with fund manager, Gestifundo, put it so succinctly in 1990, when expressing his concerns about the regulatory regime proposed for Portugal, 'If Portugal seeks to emulate the stringent rules of the US or similar stock exchanges, we run the risk of having a perfectly regulated market but no investors or quoted companies.'[33] He was one among many who were concerned about the implications of greater state involvement in markets. There was a fine line between rules that allowed abuses to flourish and risks to multiply, and those that drove business away. This was well understood by those familiar with the way markets operated but not by those who took a more legal stance.[34] However, by then the arguments in support of self-regulation had largely been lost, as responsibility for regulatory intervention was passed to statutory agencies. Country after country followed the model established by the USA when it created the Securities and Exchange Commission in 1934. A selection of the ones in operation by the

[31] Alexander Nicoll, 'A banker rather than a regulator', 20th January 1987.

[32] Alexander Nicoll, 'Markets to pay heavy price for regulation', 19th May 1987; Boris Sedacca, 'New trade-matching system launched', 10th November 1988.

[33] Peter Wise, 'Depression after the comet', 30th April 1990.

[34] Andrew Large, 'Save us from Section 62', 29th September 1987; John Plender, 'Cocktail of liberalisation', 17th November 1988; David Lascelles, 'Discreet charm of the Bank', 5th March 1990; Peter Martin, 'Debate centres on powers of supervision', 29th November 1990.

early 1990s included Bapepam (Indonesia), Capital Market Board (Turkey), Conseil des Bourse de Valeurs (France), Consob (Italy), Corporate Law Authority (Pakistan), Securities and Exchange Board of India (India), Securities and Futures Commission (Hong Kong), the Securities Supervisory Board (South Korea), and the China Securities Regulatory Commission (China). These were all given statutory powers to regulate the securities market, centralizing the powers originally exercised by stock exchanges, government departments, or central banks, with priority given to investor protection rather than stability or efficiency of operation. A few countries had yet to create such agencies, such as Germany, because of strong resistance to central authority but the trend had become unstoppable by then.[35] What was taking place in the 1980s was a simultaneous process of deregulation and re-regulation. Self-regulating bodies like exchanges were having their power reduced, but they were made answerable to statutory regulators, which were also given responsibility for overseeing markets in general, including those that had previously escaped any outside scrutiny. However, the degree of regulation that each market was subjected to varied both between and within countries, with important implications for those that flourished and those that did not.[36]

Regulatory Challenges

One of the greatest challenges facing regulators in the 1980s was in banking, with the steady disappearance of the distinctions between different types of banks. David Lascelles pointed this out in 1987 when he highlighted the blurring of 'the dividing line between banking and investment' and advocated new regulatory structures to cope with it.[37] The problem this posed regulators was especially acute in the USA, where the Glass–Steagall Act had imposed a legal separation between investment and deposit banking since the 1930s. Furthermore, in the USA legal barriers were also in place prohibiting interstate banking even though pressure was building up to permit nationwide banks as these could better respond to the changing demands of customers and intervene to prevent the mass failure of savings and loan institutions.[38] By 1988 Janet Bush was of the opinion that 'The force of the

[35] Paul Taylor, 'Consolidation worries the smaller firms', 22nd March 1991; David Waller, 'Fragile but promising', 23rd April 1991; David Lane, 'Big Bang looms', 6th June 1991; William Dawkins, 'Bourse regulators back plan for reforms', 10th July 1991; Alexander Nicoll, 'Regulation a tough task for the board', 16th September 1991; William Dawkins, 'France presses on with liberalisation', 26th September 1991; David Waller, 'Lack of regulator stalls DTB expansion', 12th February 1992; Gita Piramal, 'Indian stock market reform gathers pace', 5th March 1992; Simon Davies, 'When the bubble had to burst', 18th September 1992; David Waller, 'German bourses combine to take on Europe', 8th October 1992; Sara Webb, 'Analysts sceptical', 18th November 1992; Simon Holberton, 'Regulators battle to catch up', 18th November 1993; Mark Nicholson, 'Two busy years of regulatory power', 13th March 1995.

[36] Alexander Nicoll, 'A banker rather than a regulator', 20th January 1987; David Lascelles, 'Pressure mounts for global consistency', 21st April 1987; John Plender, 'Cries of foul from the maze', 23rd September 1987; Andrew Large, 'Save us from Section 62', 29th September 1987; David Lascelles, 'Grave doubts about the rule books', 21st October 1987; David Blackwell, 'Overlap must be cut', 10th March 1988; Katharine Campbell, 'US–UK deal on futures agreed', 24th April 1989; David Lascelles, 'Order in the marketplace', 25th September 1989; Janet Bush, 'US gears up to meet the challenges of globalisation', 20th December 1989; Martin Dickson, 'Helpless infant grows into mature part of the financial framework', 27th March 1998.

[37] David Lascelles, 'Regulator of the robust', 21st September 1987.

[38] Paul Taylor, 'Major banks spearhead era of massive re-organisation', 21st May 1984; Margaret Hughes, 'Quest for new sources of finance', 29th May 1984; Paul Taylor, 'Bankers Trust breaks ranks-again', 15th July 1985; David Lascelles, 'Global wrestling match hots up', 11th April 1986; John Plender, 'Deregulation gains that add up to zero', 29th August 1985; John Plender, 'Hard to pull off gracefully', 20th December 1985; David Lascelles, 'The stampede to become global players', 2nd April 1986; Bernard Simon, 'Obstacles yet to be surmounted', 28th

[Glass–Steagall] Act has, over the years, been eroded significantly and increasingly riven with loopholes.'[39] To Anatole Kaletsky, also writing in 1988, 'The days of the Glass–Steagall Act...are now clearly numbered.' He then added that, 'Meanwhile, the inter-state barriers which have hobbled the US banks' geographical development are disappearing even faster.'[40] What both Janet Bush and Anatole Kaletsky were picking up on in 1988 was the permission given to US commercial banks to underwrite commercial paper, mortgage-backed securities, and municipal revenue bonds. This brought them into direct competition with the investment banks. They were also aware of the emergence of both regional and super-regional banks that transcended state boundaries. This was all leading to the creation of universal banks providing the full range of banking facilities, such as Citibank or JP Morgan, and these posed a serious threat to the investment banks which had long monopolized the issue and distribution of bills, bonds, and stocks. Bracebridge Young, vice-president in charge of the commercial paper division of one of these, Goldman Sachs, admitted in 1988 that 'The commercial banks would be formidable competitors in the market. They are backed by a lot of capital, and they have good distribution networks.'[41] In 1989 the rule separating banking from the securities business was relaxed but still prevented the creation of US universal banks. In response to the blurring of the distinctions between banks the US investment banks sought direct access to the payments system and asked the Federal Reserve to offer them the emergency support it provided commercial banks in the event of a liquidity crisis. The large investment bank, Drexel Burnham Lambert, had been denied this support in 1990 and was allowed to fail, leaving unpaid financial obligations that required careful unwinding in order to avoid a banking crisis. However, there were divided opinions within those responsible for regulating US banking about any further relaxation of the Glass–Steagall Act. Someone like Gerald Corrigan, president of the NY Federal Reserve, was concerned that they did not sufficiently understand the business of investment banks, and so should not extend the lender-of-last-resort facility to them. In January 1992 he made his views clear: 'The growth and complexity of off-balance sheet activities and the nature of credit, price and settlement risk they entail should give us all cause for concern. I hope this sounds like a warning because it is.' Later in 1992 David Mullins, vice-chairman of the Federal Reserve, revealed a much more flexible attitude: 'I think president Corrigan was talking about the need for banks and regulators to understand the nature of these instruments better, and to develop the appropriate infrastructure to control and manage the risks.'[42] What his view reflected was confidence among banking regulators in the USA that they could cope with the growing complexity of banking and that the strict enforcement of the Glass–Steagall Act was no longer necessary.[43]

November 1986; David Lascelles, 'Shift is mixed blessing', 28th November 1986; Simon London, 'Captains of industry search for impeccable ratings', 9th January 1991.

[39] Janet Bush, 'A fragile monopoly', 17th February 1988.
[40] Anatole Kaletsky, 'Big decisions ahead', 24th June 1988.
[41] Janet Bush, 'A fragile monopoly', 17th February 1988.
[42] Patrick Harverson and Tracy Corrigan, 'The threat of regulation stirs an unfettered giant', 11th August 1992.
[43] Roderick Oram, 'Volatility spurs cross-trading', 3rd June 1987; Janet Bush, 'A fragile monopoly', 17th February 1988; John Paul Lee, 'Technology demonstrates its worth', 18th May 1988; Anatole Kaletsky, 'It's time to get to grips with the tough universal game', 18th May 1988; Anatole Kaletsky, 'Big decisions ahead', 24th June 1988; Stephen Fidler, 'Don't throw out the baby', 29th June 1988; Barry Riley, 'Reciprocity worries London', 29th June 1988; Janet Bush, 'Five banks with universal plans', 2nd May 1989; Janet Bush, 'Arguments intensify in the regulatory minefield', 26th June 1989; Janet Bush, 'US gears up to meet the challenges of globalisation', 20th December 1989; Richard Waters, 'Drexel's fall may spur the talking-shop', 2nd July 1990; Patrick Harverson, 'Stormy days for securities firms', 7th December 1990; Nigel Adam, 'Tough competition', 24th May 1991; Barbara Durr, 'Talent

Japan also applied the Glass–Steagall Act (Article 65) but somewhat differently, especially as it was modified over the years. In Japan banks were segregated not only between commercial and investment banking, as in the USA, but also between commercial and trust banking, preventing the former from managing investment funds. The effect of this compartmentalization, and the accompanying rules and regulations, was to stifle the development of Japanese financial markets. Restrictions imposed by the Japanese Ministry of Finance, for example, prevented the development of a commercial paper market in Japan until 1987, leaving banks with a monopoly over short-term financing. Conversely, the large securities houses were in a position to monopolize the equity market as potential competitors, especially banks, were excluded. It was only gradually that reforms took place in response to the lifting of interest-rate controls, as that intensified competition between banks for funds as well as contributing to the rapid growth of the inter-bank market. As in the USA this reluctance to reform the financial system was led by the regulators, fearful of any instability it might create, and the central bank, wary of losing the power it had to influence monetary conditions. Reinforcing this resistance to change was Japan's experience during the 1987 stock market crash. During that crash the Japanese financial system exhibited considerable stability due to its high level of liquidity and resilience. Nevertheless, the direction of travel, even in Japan, was towards liberalization because of the opportunities that it brought in terms of new financial products and new financial markets to meet the needs of customers, facing much greater volatility in terms of interest and exchange rates and looking for better investment or funding opportunities. The result was to slowly erode the divisions between different types of banks and between them and the giant brokerage houses.[44]

What banking regulators increasingly faced in the 1980s was the inability to enforce their rules domestically because of the opportunities to shift business to areas untouched by regulation, either at home or abroad. This was a complaint made by in 1986 by Gerald Corrigan, located as he was at the heart of New York's financial district: 'Events have undercut the effectiveness of many elements of the supervisory and regulatory apparatus historically surrounding banking and finance. If it can't be done onshore, it's done offshore; if it can't be done on the balance sheet, it's done off the balance sheet, and if it can't be done with a traditional instrument, it's done with a new one.'[45] His recommendation was that the degree of co-operation among regulators 'will have to intensify, both across borders and

capsized by money wave', 19th March 1992; Alan Friedman, 'Merger wave continues amid hopes for interstate reform', 20th May 1992; Richard Waters, 'Talk of mergers is in the air', 12th August 1996; Nikki Tait, 'Regulators reach over the counter', 20th September 1999; Gregory Meyer, 'Dilemma over limiting speculation', 4th August 2009.

[44] Barry Riley, 'Hedging lifts the five-date contract', 19th March 1987; David Lascelles, 'After the rush, the shakeout', 8th May 1987; Clare Pearson, 'Transfer of Euroyen bond centre to Tokyo suggested', 22nd May 1987; Janet Bush, 'Pressure grows for freer markets', 3rd June 1987; Lisa Martineau, 'Hedging helps the boom', 3rd June 1987; Lisa Martineau, 'The rules need to be eased', 17th February 1988; Stephen Fidler, 'Don't throw out the baby', 29th June 1988; James Andrews, 'Regulation on way out', 29th June 1988; Stefan Wagstyl, 'Firm rules bolster stability', 14th October 1988; Dominique Jackson, 'Futures scramble triggers global gold rush', 28th October 1988; James Andrews, 'The latecomer has potential', 20th February 1989; Stefan Wagstyl, 'Signposts to expansion', 8th March 1989; Stefan Wagstyl, 'Suffering from insecurity', 13th March 1989; Michiyo Nakamoto, 'Domestic market loses out', 13th March 1989; John Ridding, 'New set of much-needed hedging instruments', 13th March 1989; James Andrews, 'Sphere of influence', 13th March 1989; Patti Waldmeir, 'Big four still recruiting', 13th March 1989; Richard Lambert, 'Finance grows into a threat to the City', 1st June 1989; David Lascelles, 'Reforms progressing slowly', 9th July 1990; Edward Balls, 'Tentative recovery stalls', 22nd July 1991; Emiko Terazono, 'JGB futures stir bad memories', 20th October 1993; Gwen Robinson, 'Backward in coming forward', 27th June 1997.

[45] David Lascelles, 'The battle to keep tabs in the face of rapid change', 21st April 1986.

within countries.'[46] By then the main threat faced by banking regulators in both the USA and Japan was coming from the ability of their own banks to service their customers from a London base, and so evade the domestic restrictions imposed on them.[47] To Shijuro Ogata, Deputy Governor, Bank of Japan, the solution appeared obvious. All countries should take a common approach to financial regulation covering both banks and financial markets so that it would be impossible to escape regulation: 'The trend towards securitisation makes the old-fashioned type of supervision obsolete. We have to take a broad new look at supervision. There is more need to co-operate with other regulatory bodies.'[48] From the perspective of the USA and Japan the answer was a global Glass–Steagall Act, as that would close the loophole provided by the use of London from which to conduct a business that combined both investment and commercial banking, and the risks that presented.[49] The Bank for International Settlements (BIS) provided a basis of co-operation among banking regulators that was lacking for financial markets, which were flourishing in London.[50]

Prior to 1986 the UK lacked a regulatory authority covering the financial system. The one institution with real power was the Bank of England, which was under the control of the UK government and had a high degree of influence over banks and the London Stock Exchange. However, it confined its responsibilities to British banks and transactions involving the UK£. This left banks from outside the UK free to conduct whatever business they liked in London as long as it avoided the UK£. With international transactions largely based on the US$ this meant that most of which took place in London's financial markets escaped any regulatory oversight. This had made London a fertile ground for the growth of such products and markets as those involving the Eurodollar and the Eurobond from the late 1950s onwards and then the foreign exchange market in the 1970s. With the ending of UK exchange controls in 1979 London became an even more attractive base for foreign banks seeking to escape domestic regulations, as well as tap into the rapidly growing interbank markets. With Big Bang in 1986 the attractions of a London location for banks were further increased, as they were able to become members of the London Stock Exchange, so cementing their ability to conduct an international equities business from there.

In 1986 the UK did establish a comprehensive regulatory authority modelled on that of the USA.[51] What was created was a Securities and Investment Board (SIB), along the lines

[46] Stephen Fidler, 'A franchise under stress', 2nd July 1990.

[47] Barry Riley, 'London's the third leg of our stool', 27th October 1986.

[48] David Lascelles, 'The battle to keep tabs in the face of rapid change', 21st April 1986.

[49] John Plender, 'The risk of conglomerates slipping through the net', 25th September 1985; David Lascelles, William Hall and Peter Montagnon, 'The Fed weighs the risks', 22nd January 1986; Peter Montagnon, 'A need for banks to watch extent of commitment', 17th March 1986.

[50] This section on global banking owes much to the following articles: Peter Montagnon, 'Profound changes in culture', 19th March 1984; Mary Ann Sieghart, 'Increasing reliance on innovation as market declines', 19th March 1984; Mary Ann Sieghart, 'Rapid rise to prominence', 19th March 1984; David Lascelles, 'System more accessible to outsiders', 19th March 1984; John Makinson, 'Advance of the Euroequity', 2nd November 1985; Alexander Nicoll, 'Hesitant steps on road to success', 11th December 1985; Clive Wolman, 'Tax exemption for Euro and US bond dealers', 16th December 1985; Barry Riley, 'Foreign banks attracted by open policy', 8th January 1986; Alexander Nicoll, 'London hopes for sterling paper market', 14th March 1986; William Dullforce, 'Tax cuts urged to revive Swiss market', 14th March 1986; Alexander Nicoll, 'Trend towards globalisation', 17th March 1986; John Moore, 'Discount houses face up to radical change', 20th March 1986; Alan Cane, 'Rapid data: a vital commodity', 24th March 1986; Roy Garner, 'Larger companies lead the way', 24th March 1986; David Lascelles, 'When the walls come down', 23rd July 1986; Barry Riley, 'Strangers at the gilt-edged gate', 28th July 1986; Michael Blanden, 'Leading players take the plunge', 2nd October 1986; Peter Montagnon, 'Caution at the top end', 2nd October 1986; Alexander Nicoll, 'Global distribution should be good for share prices', 27th October 1986; Peter Montagnon, 'Pragmatic approach to City rules', 27th October 1986; Clive Wolman, 'Gains in efficiency but monopoly risk', 27th October 1986; Barry Riley, 'A big leap predicted', 27th October 1986; Maggie Urry, 'A subtle equation between risk and return', 28th November 1986; Haig Simonian, 'No early end to differences', 28th November 1986; Alexander Nicoll, 'The sour taste of success', 16th December 1986.

[51] David Lascelles, 'Regulator of the robust', 21st September 1987.

of the Securities and Investment Board (SEC) in the USA. At the same time the supervisory authority of the Bank of England was extended to cover a greater number and range of banks, as was already the case with the Federal Reserve. However, there was a fundamental difference between what the UK introduced in 1986 and which was already in place in the USA. The regulatory system introduced in the UK was driven by the belief that without adequate input and co-operation from those running the banks, and those active in financial markets, the regulator stood little chance of keeping pace with the changes that were transforming the business at that time. In periods of stability, when little was changing, a statutory regulator could effectively police banks and the market as it was dealing with a known situation and accepted modes of operation. In contrast, when rapid and extensive change was taking place, it was difficult for a statutory regulator to cope with what was happening or even understand it. At those times only self-regulation, with a degree of oversight, stood a chance of being effective as it was able to provide an immediate and targeted response that met current needs. The UK opted for a permissive regime that allowed banks and markets to develop in response to changing demands and opportunities. This was similar to the philosophy behind the Commodity Futures Trading Commission (CFTC) in the USA rather than the SEC. It could not have escaped the notice of those framing the legislation in the UK that the most dynamic component of the US financial system was the derivatives markets, under the supervision of the CFTC, rather than the stock market, under the authority of the SEC, which took a much more legalistic approach to its responsibilities.[52] As a result the balance of power within the UK's financial markets continued to reside with the self-regulating bodies rather than the SIB.[53]

The reform of the UK's regulatory system also gave greatly enhanced power to the Bank of England to supervise the British banking system. However, the Bank of England continued to focus on its domestic responsibilities rather than accept a role as supervisor of the foreign banks and international financial markets located in the City of London. The branches of foreign banks in London, for example, were left as the responsibility of foreign regulators not the Bank of England, and $-based markets remained outside its remit.[54] This

[52] John Edwards, 'Steps to improve competitiveness', 5th March 1985; John Edwards, 'Why the future may not work', 26th July 1985; Alexander Nicoll, 'A global defensive strategy', 11th December 1985; John Moore, 'Single main board envisaged to regulate services of 15,000 City concerns', 20th December 1985; Ian Hamilton Fazey, 'The manager still matters', 1st April 1986; Mark Meredith, 'Heed the southern giants', 2nd July 1986; James Buxton, 'Action south of the border', 2nd October 1986; David Lascelles, 'Now it's the Big Five', 2nd October 1986; David Lascelles, 'A Bill to launch a new regime', 2nd October 1986; Ian Hamilton Fazey, 'The message is getting across', 2nd October 1986; Edward Owen, 'Keeping the young at home', 2nd October 1986; John Plender, 'An omelette yet to be tasted', 27th October 1986; John Plender, 'Watchdogs follow the sun', 27th October 1986; Stefan Wagstyl, 'Glint of change in the gold market', 5th December 1986.

[53] Barry Riley, 'City regulator gets into gear', 20th July 1985; Barry Riley, 'A costly question for the futures markets', 19th August 1985; Barry Riley, 'Regulatory framework for City takes shape', 31st October 1985; Barry Riley, 'Selling self-regulation to the City', 2nd December 1985; Barry Riley, 'Regulatory framework for City takes shape', 31st October 1985; John Moore, 'SE firms urged to adapt in face of change', 21st November 1985; John Moore, 'Single main board envisaged to regulate services of 15,000 City concerns', 20th December 1985; Richard Lambert, 'More protection for investors', 21st December 1985; Alexander Nicoll, 'Big Board's ambitions reach towards London', 13th February 1986; Alexander Nicoll, 'Ticklish issue of share stabilisation', 11th July 1986; John Plender, 'An omelette yet to be tasted', 27th October 1986; Alexander Nicoll, 'The new market has an electronic heart', 27th October 1986; David Lascelles and Alexander Nicoll, 'An oddly quiet revolution', 4th February 1987; Alexander Nicoll, 'London's global ambitions signal aggressive mood', 5th February 1987; John Plender, 'Cries of foul from the maze', 23rd September 1987; Alexander Nicoll, 'The heart of the world game', 21st October 1987.

[54] Helen Hague, 'Facing up to a cultural challenge', 9th January 1987; David Lascelles, 'Why the transatlantic deal must be extended', 7th May 1987; David Lascelles, 'Regulator of the robust', 21st September 1987; David Lascelles, 'Midland storm-troopers fight to stem soaring losses', 27th January 1988; Clare Pearson, 'A healthy niche operation', 17th February 1988; John Paul Lee, 'Technology demonstrates its worth', 18th May 1988; Kenneth Gooding, 'A boost for the market', 13th June 1988; David Barchard, 'Good times are deceptive', 26th September 1988; David Lascelles, 'Less like a father-figure', 26th September 1988; David Barchard, 'Competing on all fronts',

national focus of the Bank of England was evident in the 1990–1 financial crisis when its focus was on supporting a core of systemically-important British banks whose activities lay at the heart of the £-Sterling-based payments system. In this it was no different from any other central bank.[55]

Nevertheless, the Bank of England was strongly influenced by the US Federal Reserve, which pushed it toward greater intervention in London's financial markets. In 1987, under pressure from the Federal Reserve, the Bank of England tried to force the SIB to follow the requirements imposed by SEC on US securities markets, in the interests of investor protection. This exposed the fundamental difference between the regulatory systems in place in each country. Whereas the SEC was a statutory body vested with the authority to keep the market in order and protect investors the SIB was a voluntary body that operated through Self Regulatory Organizations and it was with them that the real power lay in the UK. Under pressure from these SROs the SIB refused to follow SEC rules. This involved a battle between Andrew Large, a Swiss Bank executive who chaired the Securities Association, and Sir Kenneth Berrill, the SIB chairman, who took a civil service approach and wanted to take the SEC line.[56] Andrew Large won the battle, which was seen as a triumph for those who used the market over those who regulated it. He reflected in 1997 that 'We started from the word go with a determination to distinguish between the areas where investors require less or more protection. I think that's worked well. I'm quite often asked by regulators in other countries how we do it.'[57] As John Quinton, chairman of Barclays, stated in 1987, 'It must not be forgotten that regulation is the servant of the financial system.'[58] It also showed the limits to the power of US regulators to impose their standards and practices on other countries, even when accompanied with the threat that foreign firms would be excluded from doing business in the USA or acting for US customers. What this meant was that in a world of instant communications, freed from controls over international flows and without the agreement of the UK authorities, it was impossible for even the USA to impose its own regulations on banks or financial markets without risking the loss of business through borders that were becoming steadily more open. In turn, that affected the regulations they were able to apply domestically.[59]

This inability of national regulators to impose their will can be seen in the fast-expanding business of financial derivatives, where trading was shifting away from exchanges and onto the OTC market. When the derivatives market was located in exchanges they provided regulators with a means of exercising a degree of control and influencing behaviour. Members of exchanges obeyed the rules because it was in their self-interest to do so, for otherwise they could be excluded from participating in the market provided. Exchanges

11th February 1989; David Barchard, 'Supervisors' eye on the ball', 11th February 1989; David Barchard, 'A slack year', 12th July 1989; Richard Waters, 'Unbundling the City's top club', 5th March 1991; Sara Webb, 'Repo traders fight their corner', 24th July 1991; Barry Riley, 'Beginnings of a flight to safety', 24th July 1991.

[55] Barry Riley, 'Beginnings of a flight to safety', 24th July 1991; James Blitz, 'Banks gag on money market illiquidity', 15th October 1993; Robert Peston, 'Silent launch of the lifeboat', 19th October 1993.

[56] John Plender, 'Cries of foul from the maze', 23rd September 1987; Andrew Large, 'Save us from Section 62', 29th September 1987; David Lascelles, 'Grave doubts about the rule books', 21st October 1987; David Blackwell, 'Overlap must be cut', 10th March 1988; Norma Cohen, 'The bad apple in the other guy's barrel', 8th March 1989; David Lascelles, 'Order in the marketplace', 25th September 1989; Andrew Gowers, 'Planning blight in the City', 20th May 1997.

[57] Andrew Gowers, 'Planning blight in the City', 20th May 1997.

[58] David Lascelles, 'Grave doubts about the rule books', 21st October 1987.

[59] John Edwards, 'Steps to improve competitiveness', 5th March 1985; John Edwards, 'Why the future may not work', 26th July 1985; Alexander Nicoll, 'A global defensive strategy', 11th December 1985.

provided certainty that deals would be completed and that prices would not be manipulated. In the OTC market banks either traded directly with each other or through inter-dealer brokers, and there was neither an overall authority monitoring behaviour nor a formal market from which they could be excluded. Each participant was responsible for their own actions though counterparty risk was low because those involved were large banks. As long as OTC-traded derivatives were relatively simple and their use limited, regulators could largely ignore them. Increasingly that was not the case as the volume of trading expanded exponentially. This left regulators struggling to supervise an industry in flux and one that fell between the jurisdiction of banking and securities.[60] As Patrick Harverson observed in 1992, 'Hordes of government regulators across the globe are grappling with the question of how best to handle supervision of the over-the-counter financial derivatives market. Rarely can so many different agencies have taken up the same subject with so much enthusiasm.'[61]

The dilemma faced by regulators was how best to regulate this new market in financial derivatives without stunting its growth, as they recognized that their use both increased and diminished risks. Regulators welcomed financial derivatives as their use provided a mechanism through which banks and others could cover the risks they were running at times of currency, interest rate and stock and bond price volatility. Conversely, regulators were concerned about four types of risks posed by financial derivatives, the first two of which were common to all financial markets. Counterparty risk focused on the possibility of a party to a deal defaulting. The more that the large banks were involved, as in the OTC market, the less it was considered that a default was likely to take place. Settlement risk related to the breakdown of the clearing and settlement systems. This risk was confined to the market in financial derivatives provided by exchanges, as in the OTC market deals were often bespoke and conducted on a bilateral basis between large banks. More central to the derivatives market was the concern over operational risk. Here the issue was that those involved were unaware of their exposure to the risks that they were taking, because of the complex nature of the derivatives contracts and the off-balance sheet nature of the transactions. This was an emerging worry as more and more banks used derivatives both as a way to cover the risks they were taking and as a source of profit by acting as counterparties. Also a major issue in the derivatives market was the risk that a sudden move in the market price of the assets underlying the derivatives could have a major effect on the price of the derivatives themselves. Patrick Harverson and Tracy Corrigan in 1992 reported that, 'The greatest fear of regulators is that the default of a handful of big derivatives players could trigger a domino-like collapse among banks, securities houses and corporations linked by a grid of interconnected payment obligations.'[62] Hence the desire to regulate the market.

In the USA, where financial derivatives had originated and then developed rapidly, trading took place not only on exchanges but also on an active OTC market, while regulation was split between two separate agencies that followed different strategies and competed with each other. The Securities and Exchange Commission (SEC) was responsible for regulating stock exchanges, where options were traded, while the Commodity Futures Trading

[60] Deborah Hargreaves, 'Derivatives come of age', 13th March 1991; Barbara Durr, 'Options exchanges worried by over-the-counter trading', 15th May 1992; Patrick Harverson and Tracy Corrigan, 'The threat of regulation stirs an unfettered giant', 11th August 1992; Tracy Corrigan and Patrick Harverson, 'Ever more complex', 8th December 1992; Patrick Harverson, 'It's time to know what's going on', 8th December 1992; Tracy Corrigan, 'Volatility demands ingenuity', 8th December 1992; Laurie Morse, 'New law lifts uncertainty', 8th December 1992.

[61] Patrick Harverson, 'It's time to know what's going on', 8th December 1992.

[62] Patrick Harverson and Tracy Corrigan, 'The threat of regulation stirs an unfettered giant', 11th August 1992.

Commission (CFTC) covered the commodity exchanges, where futures were bought and sold. Both agencies had as their focus the protection of the retail investor rather than the operation of the market. The SEC took a very legalistic approach to its responsibilities and this restricted the ability of US stock exchanges to develop new products and practices. In contrast, the CFTC had responsibility for the commodity exchanges and followed a much less interventionist course than the SEC. The result was that it was the commodity exchanges that were given the freedom to develop financial derivatives. Despite pressure to combine the SEC and the CFTC into one regulatory agency this was resisted by many of those involved in derivatives because of a suspicion that the result would be to impose greater restrictions on the US market. The CFTC was, itself, under pressure, from both the commodity exchanges and politicians, to restrict the growth of derivatives trading in the OTC market. The banks were developing their own varieties of financial derivatives, which they then traded between themselves or with their customers, without the charges and restrictions incurred on exchanges. As David Owen observed in 1987, 'in apparent defiance of the letter of the law (in this case the Commodity Exchange Act) major Wall Street securities houses and banks are introducing a fast-expanding range of financial products which bear an uncanny resemblance to futures and options—but are traded over-the-counter'.[63] Under US law futures trading had to take place on a regulated exchange but this did not apply to forward contracts. Faced with the difficulty of separating a futures contract from a forward agreement the CFTC refused to force OTC trading onto the exchanges, despite intense lobbying as the volume of activity grew in the early 1990s. By then the CFTC was well aware of the consequences of such an action. In 1987, the CFTC had extended its regulatory regime to include swaps, which were tailor-made agreements that could run for an extended period without the need to continually adjust margins and positions. These were traded on the OTC market. As a result much of the business conducted in the USA migrated to London, which was beyond the jurisdiction of the CFTC. Though the CFTC had tried to prevent US customers accessing the London derivatives market in 1988 it decided in 1989 to halt its regulation of swaps in 1989, leading to a partial repatriation of the business back to the USA. By then the CFTC accepted that the exchange-traded and OTC markets complemented each other: a contract made in one was often matched by a reverse contract made in another so as to reduce the overall risk. This flexibility of the CFTC also extended internationally. The CFTC was willing to recognize the standards and practices of other regulators as equivalent to its own, and so facilitate the development of global markets in futures.[64] The result was that the OTC derivatives market was left largely unregulated.[65]

[63] David Owen, 'Over the counter, round the law', 19th March 1987.

[64] Terry Byland, 'Contracts take a fivefold leap', 19th March 1987; David Owen, 'Over the counter, round the law', 19th March 1987; David Lascelles, 'Grave doubts about the rule books', 21st October 1987; Deborah Hargreaves, 'Hybrids fight to escape regulation', 9th December 1987; Janet Bush, 'Portfolio insurance loses its appeal', 10th March 1988; Deborah Hargreaves, 'Regulators seek to protect retail customer in battle of look-alikes', 10th March 1988; Steven Butler, 'Investment banks cash in on volatile oil prices', 1st July 1988; Norma Cohen, 'The bad apple in the other guy's barrel', 8th March 1989; Katharine Campbell, 'US–UK deal on futures agreed', 24th April 1989; Janet Bush, 'US gears up to meet the challenges of globalisation', 20th December 1989; Deborah Hargreaves, 'SEC delays full opening of options competition', 11th January 1990; Peter Riddell and Deborah Hargreaves, 'Chicago protests over planned futures tax', 31st January 1990; Janet Bush, 'Enforcement of securities law remains politically popular', 7th February 1990; Deborah Hargreaves, 'Appeal ruling fails to restore certainty', 9th March 1990; Barbara Durr, 'US exchanges fight dual trading ban', 18th July 1990; Barbara Durr, 'Plea for a level playing field', 13th June 1991; Barbara Durr, 'Competition grows fiercer and spawns new alliances', 22nd July 1991; Barbara Durr, 'Options exchanges worried by over-the-counter trading', 15th May 1992; Tracy Corrigan, 'End of rapid growth', 20th July 1992; Patrick Harverson and Tracy Corrigan, 'The threat of regulation stirs an unfettered giant', 11th August 1992; Patrick Harverson, 'It's time to know what's going on', 8th December 1992.

[65] John Edwards, 'Steps to improve competitiveness', 5th March 1985; John Edwards, 'Why the future may not work', 26th July 1985; Alexander Nicoll, 'A global defensive strategy', 11th December 1985.

Regulatory Responses

Despite the failure of the US authorities to impose their regulations on other countries in the 1980s, it did not mean that its regulatory system was rejected. With the demise of the divide and rule structure of the 1950s and 1960s an alternative had to be found and that of the USA did provide one. Even though the regulations introduced in the USA over the course of the nineteenth and twentieth centuries had been fashioned in response to its domestic requirements they appeared to better resemble what was developing in the 1970s and 1980s than the command and control structures of the post-war years. It was also acknowledged that the USA possessed the largest and most advanced financial system in the world and thus one that other countries could aspire to. For that reason the regulations in place provided both a starting point and a template for others elsewhere in the world. The process that took place, and the complications involved, can be seen in what took place within the European Union (EU). In the 1980s the EU was at the forefront of the changes transforming the global financial system. It was attempting to create a single market in financial services, covering both banks and markets, through removing barriers and promoting the end to restrictive practices. This was all to be accomplished by 1 January 1993. The model being followed by the EU in framing this common market was the system already prevailing in the USA.[66] The problem was how to achieve that against the opposition from the individual nation-states as each attempted to use regulations to protect their national interest. Despite progress towards economic and political integration over the decades the EU in the 1980s remained a diverse collection of financial markets divided by different taxes, laws, and cultures. There were fundamental differences between member states in terms of the role played by banks and the way financial markets operated, for example. Writing in 1988 Guy de Jonquières observed that 'These differences cover a wide spectrum. At one end, Britain has a predominantly equity-based corporate finance system, an enthusiastic approach to most kinds of innovation and a commitment to international markets. At the other, West Germany's financial system is conservative, more inward-looking and built around the commercial banks, which are the main source of corporate finance.'[67] Retail banking, for example, was conducted along national lines, with David Lascelles commenting in 1990, that 'domestic banking markets are notoriously hard for outsiders to penetrate because of strong national cultures.'[68] In terms of regulations new differences were continually arising as national governments introduced new laws and agencies to cope with particular domestic issues as they arose. For these reasons there was considerable opposition throughout the

[66] Janet Bush, 'Portfolio insurance loses its appeal', 10th March 1988; Deborah Hargreaves, 'Less risk and back to basics', 10th March 1988; Stephen Fidler, 'Don't throw out the baby', 29th June 1988; Barry Riley, 'Reciprocity worries London', 29th June 1988; John Plender, 'Cocktail of liberalisation', 17th November 1988; Norma Cohen, 'The bad apple in the other guy's barrel', 8th March 1989; Karen Fossli, 'Liberalisation helps to fuel interest', 30th March 1989; David Barchard, 'A slack year', 12th July 1989; Paul Cheeseright, 'The competition intensifies', 12th July 1989; Stephen Fidler, 'Bank points to blurred boundaries', 8th February 1990; Peter Martin, 'Debate centres on powers of supervision', 29th November 1990; Richard Waters, 'Securities firms look across borders', 7th January 1991; James Buxton, 'Regional strategy for a second-tier alliance', 16th May 1991; Richard Waters, 'Europe extends the fuse leading to Big Bang', 29th May 1991; Barry Riley, 'Big three join battle for supremacy', 4th July 1991; Richard Waters, 'Bourses build up defences', 24th September 1991; David Barchard and Richard Lapper, 'Seeking a unified system', 18th December 1991; Christopher Parkes and David Waller, 'Politics comes to the Finanzplatz', 24th January 1992; Haig Simonian, 'Battle looms over Italy's new securities law', 14th February 1992; Richard Waters, 'Vision of a grand strategy fades', 26th February 1992; David Waller, 'Bank chief's sights set on central role for Germany', 10th June 1992; Simon London, 'Muted cheers for the single market', 11th June 1992; Robert Peston, 'Invisible threats sighted to City's international status', 8th July 1992.

[67] Guy de Jonquières, 'Risk, opportunities and arduous negotiations', 18th May 1988.

[68] David Lascelles, 'Banks seem set to move cautiously', 2nd July 1990.

member states of the EU to the proposal for a single market in financial services governed by a common set of regulations that applied across all countries.[69] Hisao Kobayashi, director and general manager of international co-ordination and planning at Japan's Dai Ichi Kangyo Bank, summed up the task facing the European Commission in 1988: 'The EC still consists of 12 countries each with its own history... Everyone agrees on the idea of integration but it will be hard to agree on the practical arrangements.'[70]

Even on the eve of this single market, at the end of 1992, it was accepted that much remained to be done. In theory any financial institution that had a licence in any of the twelve member countries of the EC, and the seven members of EFTA, could practice in any other. However, numerous barriers continued to exist that prevented the delivery of a pan-European market in financial services. National authorities continued to require compliance with national regulations and gave preference to nationally-based financial institutions. In 1992, according to Seiichi Takeda, senior vice-president of the Nomura Europe, 'There are still a lot of peculiarities in individual country markets, so penetration of the European market really means penetration into each country.'[71] The eventual approach taken by the European Union was to force national governments to end discrimination against non-nationals and encourage regulatory harmonization while accepting that important differences would remain. This outcome was only gradually achieved, being a modified version of what already existed in the USA. Financial regulation in the USA combined both nationwide, or federal, regulations with ones operating at a more local level, such as state regulations, along with an absence of barriers.[72] What was omitted in the EU, at this stage, was the creation of powerful regulatory agencies with a EU-wide mandate, as existed in the USA with the Securities and Exchange Commission (SEC) and the Commodity Futures Trading Commission (CFTC). Also omitted was an attempt to emulate the USA with a European equivalent of the Federal Reserve Board that took responsibility for banking supervision and acting as lender of last resort. Instead, under the 'single passport' provision, the central bank and regulatory authority of each member state was given the responsibility of supervising their own banks and markets, which could then compete for business throughout the EU.[73]

[69] Robert Peston, 'Invisible threats sighted to City's international status', 8th July 1992.

[70] Stefan Wagstyl, 'Japanese decide to hedge bets', 19th December 1988.

[71] Ian Rodger, 'A painful period', 13th November 1992.

[72] George Graham, 'Faster growth than London's', 20th January 1987; Janet Bush, 'Pressure grows for freer markets', 3rd June 1987; Haig Simonian, 'Banking growth bolsters demand', 3rd June 1987; Nancy Dunne, 'London scores sweet victory', 28th July 1987; Haig Simonian, 'Thwarted by the tax', 17th February 1988; Guy de Jonquières, 'Risk, opportunities and arduous negotiations', 18th May 1988; Haig Simonian, 'Liffe hijacks the Bund-wagon', 21st September 1988; Stefan Wagstyl, 'Japanese decide to hedge bets', 19th December 1988; David Lane, 'Curing a bad name', 20th February 1989; David Lascelles, 'Euromarkets face uncertain fate', 1st March 1989; Haig Simonian, 'A computer-based market', 8th March 1989; Sara Webb, 'Creating a true Nordic market', 30th March 1989; Karen Fossli, 'Liberalisation helps to fuel interest', 30th March 1989; Peter Bruce, 'A patient approach to a near impossible job', 21st June 1989; Richard Waters, 'Towards Europe's super-league', 11th September 1989; Lucy Kellaway, 'EC member states prepare law to protect against insider trading', 7th February 1990; Stephen Fidler, 'W. Germany may suffer withholding tax legacy', 18th May 1990; David Lascelles, 'Banks seem set to move cautiously', 2nd July 1990; Haig Simonian, 'A new breed of institution in Milan', 14th December 1990.

[73] Guy de Jonquières, 'Risk, opportunities and arduous negotiations', 18th May 1988; Stephen Fidler, 'Don't throw out the baby', 29th June 1988; George Graham, 'Major reforms under way', 29th September 1988; Eric Short, 'Unit trusts gear up for a European challenge', 12th November 1988; Stefan Wagstyl, 'Japanese decide to hedge bets', 19th December 1988; David Buchan, 'Brussels spreads the pain of tax on savers', 9th February 1989; Haig Simonian, 'European stock exchanges close ranks', 13th April 1989; David Lascelles, 'Single market faces further delay', 16th June 1989; David Lascelles, 'Pitching for a share of London's work', 5th July 1989; William Dullforce, 'Prices ignore good forecasts', 19th December 1989; Alastair FitzSimons, 'EC Directives change securities markets', 15th February 1990; Richard Nowinski and Robin Brooks, 'UK financial services face new and important EC Council directives', 12th April 1990; Stephen Fidler, 'W. Germany may suffer withholding tax

One example of the tensions underlying the eventual compromise can be seen from the remodelling of the European stock market. A number of different regulatory models were proposed, each backed by particular national governments and motivated by national interest, while the European Commission recommended the complete US model. In the French proposal, backed by Belgium, Italy, and Spain, each national stock exchange would be given regulatory authority over its national market, though subject to the supervision of a state-appointed national regulator. Banks would be prohibited from matching deals internally or trading between themselves, and so bypassing the authority of the stock exchange. Under the German proposal a central hub would be established to co-ordinate trading which would take place either on exchanges or through banks. Regulation would take place on a national basis and cover both exchanges and banks. With the British proposal, supported by the Netherlands, trading would take place through market-makers, who were largely under the control of banks. Again, each member country would take responsibility for regulating its own market. The European Commission wanted to establish a European equivalent of the SEC, which had regulatory control over stock exchanges and the investment banks that handled much of the trading. All that could be agreed on was the removal of barriers to the cross-border trading of equities within the EU, including that done by banks, with regulatory responsibility devolved to national authorities.[74]

Regulatory Solutions

With little or no prospect of re-erecting national boundaries or agreeing on the formation of a supra-national financial authority, there was a growing urgency to design and enforce rules and regulations in the 1980s that would apply to all, and so mitigate the risks inherent in any financial system,[75] though there was the possibility of devolving responsibility to self-regulating markets, such as those operated by exchanges, that ran counter to the prevailing belief that only when backed by the state could any authority be relied on to act in the public interest. There was a degree of suspicion attached to the self-interest of exchanges as they had a record of prioritizing the interests of their members at the expense

legacy', 18th May 1990; David Lascelles, 'Banks seem set to move cautiously', 2nd July 1990; George Graham, 'Doubts about tax burden', 22nd October 1990; Richard Waters, 'Warning on European capital market', 14th December 1990; Lucy Kellaway and Tim Dickson, 'Painful birth of single market', 19th December 1990.

[74] David Lascelles, 'A potential financial capital for the EC', 25th September 1989; George Graham, 'Doubts about tax burden', 22nd October 1990; Richard Waters, 'Stalemate in the marketplace', 15th November 1990; Lucy Kellaway, 'Many moves on the way to market', 21st November 1990; Richard Waters and George Graham, 'Birth of a market needs burial of differences', 28th November 1990; David Lascelles, 'Prospects look less certain', 29th November 1990; Richard Waters, 'Warning on European capital market', 14th December 1990; Lucy Kellaway and Tim Dickson, 'Painful birth of single market', 19th December 1990; Richard Waters, 'Securities firms look across borders', 7th January 1991; William Dawkins, 'Block trading review on the way', 9th September 1991; Richard Waters, 'Bourses build up defences', 24th September 1991; William Dawkins, 'Small bang fall-out', 12th December 1991; Richard Waters, 'Vision of a grand strategy fades', 26th February 1992.

[75] John Plender, 'Cocktail of liberalisation', 17th November 1988; Norma Cohen, 'The bad apple in the other guy's barrel', 8th March 1989; Martin Dickson, 'NYSE seeks unified circuit breakers', 13th June 1990; Richard Waters, 'Drexel's fall may spur the talking-shop', 2nd July 1990; Richard Waters and George Graham, 'Birth of a market needs burial of differences', 28th November 1990; Richard Waters, 'Heated dispute', 18th December 1991; Lynne Curry, 'Heavy demand for shares', 16th June 1992; Ian Rodger, 'Switzerland suffers setback over financial proposals', 29th January 1992; James Blitz, 'A top-hat tradition in the balance', 22nd June 1992; Robert Peston, 'Invisible threats sighted to City's international status', 8th July 1992; Richard Waters, 'Progress seen in world settlement systems says G30', 17th December 1992.

of customers.[76] However, some form of regulatory intervention was required to prevent future financial crises that could be more damaging than those of 1982 and 1987. What these crises had exposed was the way that banks were becoming complex, multiproduct, international businesses that were highly interconnected not only to each other but also to financial markets in general. The potential failure of any one of these megabanks posed a serious risk to the entire financial system. For banking regulators there was the vexed question of whether a central bank should intervene to prevent an individual bank from collapsing, because of fears that it would cause a liquidity crisis that would lead to a cascade of failures, with devastating consequences for the entire financial system. Conversely, the consequence of such intervention could be to encourage future risk-taking among banks in the belief that the central bank could always be relied upon to step in if the results pushed the bank to the point of collapse. This dilemma was known as Moral Hazard and was an issue central banks increasingly faced in the more turbulent years after 1970. As Robert Peston put it in 1993, 'If no bank were allowed to fail, depositors would not have to take into account the soundness of a bank before deciding where to place funds, and bank executives would feel under less pressure to manage their businesses prudently.'[77]

The underlying convention was that a central bank would only intervene to prevent a bank failure due to a liquidity crisis but not if the bank was insolvent. However, the larger and more complex banks became, and the more connected they were through the inter-bank financial markets, the less able were central banks to distinguish between a bank that was illiquid or insolvent as the question revolved around the values to be placed on its assets and liabilities. Only with hindsight was it possible to establish which loans a bank made would eventually be repaid in full and which investments could be sold at face value, but a decision of whether to intervene or not had to be made without that information being known. By 1990 banking and securities regulators were meeting regularly to grapple with the issues that the emerging megabanks posed.[78] Conversely, it was these megabanks that also provided a solution of how to regulate financial markets in the post divide and rule era. As banks grew in size they took on greater responsibilities for policing their own trading activity and accepting the counter-party risks that those generated. The large banks were already highly regulated, with central banks playing a major role in both supervising their activities and ensuring their stability. These megabanks could support an internal regulatory system covering much of the financial system, which made the task of regulators

[76] Barry Riley, 'Why global traders are stepping up pressure', 21st February 1985; Barry Riley, 'SEC urges controls on international securities trading', 22nd May 1985; Alexander Nicoll, 'International moves before Big Bang', 29th August 1985; Alexander Nicoll, 'Round-the-clock trading brings a new challenge', 5th November 1985; Charles Batchelor, 'Concern expressed over electronic equity dealing', 18th November 1985; Clive Wolman, 'Investor protection safety net remains', 16th December 1985; Terry Byland, 'Wall Street dismayed at ADR levy', 25th March 1986; Alexander Nicoll, 'Market wakes up early to competition', 17th April 1986; John Plender, 'Capital loosens its bonds', 8th May 1986; Alan Cane, 'Systems tailored to market-makers', 16th October 1986; Richard Lambert, 'More products now need round-the-clock trading', 27th October 1986; John Edwards, 'New rules will help private clients', 27th October 1986.

[77] Robert Peston, 'Silent launch of the lifeboat', 19th October 1993.

[78] David Lascelles, 'Calls to bring watchdogs into line', 14th August 1989; Lucy Kellaway and Richard Waters, 'Brittan pledges flexibility in EC financial services rules', 6th February 1990; Richard Lambert, 'Investment firms at mercy of single-passport talks', 9th October 1989; Richard Waters, 'Securities industry capital rules move closer', 30th January 1992; Stephen Fidler, 'Covering risks of global volatility', 21st February 1991; David Lascelles, 'Reforms fail to keep pace with changes in the markets', 24th May 1991; Richard Waters, 'Elusive international solution', 22nd July 1991; Simon London, 'Structures under stress', 22nd July 1991; Richard Waters, 'Brokers learn the value of money', 4th November 1991; Robert Peston, 'Enforcer rides into town', 3rd November 1992; Tracy Corrigan and Patrick Harverson, 'Ever more complex', 8th December 1992; Richard Waters, 'Progress seen in world settlement systems says G30', 17th December 1992.

much easier. As these megabanks were also becoming the major players in all the financial markets, and dominant in a number of them, they also provided regulators with a means of supervising those. The megabanks provided regulators with single points of entry into an increasingly large and varied financial sector. Finally, not only could these megabanks be subjected to close supervision but they were more likely to be resilient in a crisis, and so be in a position to warrant a central bank intervening to act as lender of last resort.[79]

It was over the course of the 1980s that a global regulatory regime for banking gradually took shape, with the BIS playing a key co-ordinating role. In contrast, progress towards the international regulation of financial markets was much more limited. An International Organization of Securities Commissions had been formed in 1983 for the Americas and it gradually evolved into a global network by 1989, with fifty members drawn from around the world. Its aim was to provide the same leadership for financial markets as the BIS did for banking but it lacked the experience, authority, and cohesion already established among bank supervisors. Despite focusing on securities it also had to deal with a much more disparate membership. In some countries securities trading was restricted to brokers, as continued to be the case in Japan, while in others it was in the hands of banks, as was the case across Continental Europe. This made it difficult to agree on a common strategy. Under these circumstances there was a tendency to rely on the internal mechanisms of an emerging elite of global brokers. These were considered to possess the resilience, connections, and experience to not only supervise their own staff and the business that they did but also cope with volatile conditions and even periodic crises. In the words of Richard Lambert in 1989, 'The giant securities firms can take care of themselves. They are already very international in their operations.'[80] Such a philosophy was very similar to that of the banking regulators who were putting their confidence in an emerging elite of global banks. The OECD was among a number of organizations that wanted brokers to emulate banks by agreeing to establish common regulatory standards and minimum capital reserves. However, such a course of action was unnecessary because the trend globally was the increasing convergence of financial activity under the control of the megabanks.[81]

The main focus among banking regulators, responding to an agenda set by central banks and co-ordinated by the BIS, was to make these megabanks more resilient, and so better able to cope with another financial crisis. This was done by requiring banks to allocate a given amount of capital to cover the risk attached to various types of business, calculated on the basis of how likely it was to leave the holder with losses. In referring to the capital-adequacy rules agreed in 1988 by the BIS's Basel Committee of bank supervisors, David Lascelles claimed that it meant that banking was 'the first industry ever to be regulated on a worldwide basis'.[82] These rules were to be phased in by 1993 and subjected all banks to the same capital disciplines. The intention was to ensure that all banks would be competing on equal terms, at least so far as the capital they held was concerned. The rules achieved this level playing field by applying a formula, based on the riskiness of assets, which measured

[79] Barbara Durr, 'Plea for a level playing field', 13th June 1991; Barbara Durr, 'Competition grows fiercer and spawns new alliances', 22nd July 1991; Emiko Terazono, 'Fears of new restrictions', 19th March 1992; Barbara Durr, 'Options exchanges worried by over-the-counter trading', 15th May 1992; Tracy Corrigan, 'End of rapid growth', 20th July 1992; Patrick Harverson and Tracy Corrigan, 'The threat of regulation stirs an unfettered giant', 11th August 1992; Patrick Harverson, 'It's time to know what's going on', 8th December 1992.

[80] Richard Lambert, 'Investment firms at mercy of single-passport talks', 9th October 1989.

[81] John Plender, 'Watchdogs follow the sun', 27th October 1986.

[82] David Lascelles, 'Rules permit local leeway', 2nd May 1989.

the adequacy of a bank's capital and then laid down minimum capital requirements. Under BIS rules, for example, loans secured on domestic property had only half the risk weighting assigned to most other types of lending. However, the formula only captured credit risk, which was a bank's exposure to a default by a borrower. It ignored trading risk, which was the exposure to a loss through the collapse in value of an investment, such as in securities or foreign exchange. In that way the formula reflected the compartmentalized world of the past, in which banks concentrated on using the money deposited by savers to provide short-term credit to borrowers, generating a return from the differential between the interest they paid and received.

What it did not reflect was the growing reality of the 1980s as commercial banks diversified into investment banking, which involved holding portfolios of assets that could rise or fall in value. Even foreign exchange had become an asset class rather than simply a service to customers and a way of reducing risk by matching of liabilities across currencies. In addition, these Basel rules were only applied piecemeal by countries and were subject to local interpretation, which greatly undermined the universality of the regulatory regime being imposed on banking. For these reasons, Huld Muller, the Dutch central banker who headed the Basel-based committee of supervisors when the rules were introduced, warned national bank supervisors that they needed to maintain a vigilant stance to ensure that banks did not manipulate the capital-adequacy rules to meet their own interests and so take on greater risks that they could cope with in a crisis. By 1991 it was already becoming apparent that this was exactly what banks were doing, according to Simon London: 'The different treatment of debt and equity in law and accountancy led to attempts to blur the distinctions. Regulation of the banking system, with the imposition of strict capital ratios which international banks must adhere to, has fuelled the search for new capital structures; the challenge is to design an instrument which looks like equity and is for the purposes of accounting, but qualifies as debt for the purposes of tax.'[83] The phasing in of the Basel requirements was forcing banks to restructure their business models. This included repackaging financial assets as securities, which bore a lower risk rating, and then selling them on, including to other banks. Feeding the risk assumptions implied by the BIS rules into their internal models encouraged banks to alter their behaviour in the confidence that it would generate higher returns at lower risks.[84] This mattered as it was through the megabanks that the global financial system was being regulated.

Conclusion

A perspective that focused on the EU and the USA would suggest that the years between 1970 and 1992 were ones of considerable change for the regulation of financial systems. What had happened after the Second World War was the replacement of the informal but fluid separation between money, credit, and capital with formal barriers through the intervention of governments and central banks. The economic, monetary, and financial crises of

[83] Simon London, 'Structures under stress', 22nd July 1991.

[84] David Lascelles, 'Rules permit local leeway', 2nd May 1989; Stephen Fidler, 'A franchise under stress', 2nd July 1990; Simon London, 'Secretive market set to enter the spotlight', 26th September 1990; Tracy Corrigan and Richard Waters, 'Japan turns to securitisation', 20th March 1991; David Lascelles, 'Reforms fail to keep pace with changes in the markets', 24th May 1991; Richard Waters, 'Salutary September', 8th December 1992; George Graham, 'BIS weighs expanded role', 9th June 1997.

the early 1970s exposed the inadequacies and consequences of these controls and led to the gradual dismantling of the barriers. In response to the dismantling of the barriers during the 1980s new financial structures began to emerge that blurred the distinctions both between different types of banks and different financial markets. This was certainly the case in the EU and the USA. However, in most of the rest of the world the process of change was more gradual. In those countries closely connected with either the USA or the EU such as Canada or Switzerland there was considerable change. The deregulation of Canadian financial services in 1988, for example, opened up the commercial paper market while banks were allowed to buy control of Canadian securities houses to create integrated operations. Even as far afield as Hong Kong, because of its strong international connections, new regulatory systems were introduced. In 1989 a Securities and Futures Commission was set up in Hong Kong in the wake of the 1987 financial crisis, the temporary closure of the stock exchange, and the arrest of its chairman, Ronald Li. However, those at Jardine Matheson, one of Hong Kong's leading financial and commercial businesses, were of the opinion that this agency would have little effect on addressing the fundamental problems that the crisis of 1987 exposed. In 1990 they were of the view that 'Regulators have been imported from every corner of the globe to impose detailed regulations on a financial community which broadly speaking divides into two halves—those who do not intend to obey the rules and those who do not understand them.'[85] The result was an immediate conflict between the Hong Kong Stock Exchange and the SFC on the rules and their implementation, illustrating the difficulties regulators faced in bringing order to financial markets.

In most of the rest of the world either nothing altered or only modest reforms were made. Many countries continued to impose exchange controls and either governments were in effective control of the financial system or banks and exchanges were allowed to operate as cartels and monopolies. Throughout the world regulators faced a dilemma between the benefits to be derived from control and the advantages to be derived from competition. Control brought stability but was achieved through allowing a few banks to monopolize the system as they had the resilience and self-interest to withstand a crisis. In markets liquidity required concentration of trading activity but competition came from market fragmentation with multiple platforms. The intervention of regulators tended to favour concentration over fragmentation as this provided them with an organization that had the power to police the market. However, it also put banks and exchanges in a position to exploit the power they were given. Even countries such as South Korea and Taiwan, whose economies were modernizing rapidly, continued to operate financial systems behind exchange controls which gave governments considerable power and rendered their banks and exchanges immune from competition.[86] Though much had taken place during the 1980s the pace of regulatory change was slow and hesitant. Nevertheless, what did emerge was the growing responsibilities being placed on a small number of megabanks as the key agents of regulation. Such was the size and diversity of these banks that they were increasingly trusted to police not only the business of banking itself but also the operation of financial markets where they were becoming the major players. Cast aside were self-regulating

[85] David Waller, 'Not all gloom and doom', 12th June 1990.

[86] David Owen, 'Banks close the gap', 17th February 1988; Barry Riley, 'A question of survival', 26th October 1988; David Housego, 'A bull market far from being tamed', 20th December 1988; R C Murthy, 'Economic fundamentals augur well', 11th September 1989; David Waller, 'Not all gloom and doom', 12th June 1990; Angus Foster, 'Future of stock exchange comes to a head', 16th August 1991; Angus Foster, 'Crusaders tighten their grip', 20th November 1991.

organizations such as exchanges as more and more trading took place in the OTC markets where the megabanks were the major players. In place of the compartmentalized and controlled world of the post-war years a new regulatory structure was being formed comprising national agencies like the SEC and the CFTC, international organizations such as the BIS, and the megabanks whose activities were beginning to straddle the globe and penetrate every element of the financial system.

7

Trends, Events, and Centres, 1993–2006

Introduction

At the beginning of the 1990s banks, exchanges, and regulators were all in a state of flux, facing a very uncertain future. The certainties of the past had been removed as internal and external barriers crumbled, destroying the world within which they had operated since the end of the Second World War. In its place the world was moving towards global 24-hour financial markets and an elite grouping of megabanks. These developments were driven by global economic integration, developments in technology, the retreat of government from policies favouring ownership and control, and the search by regulators for strategies that could cope with the end of compartmentalization. Though these trends continued in the 1990s and into the twenty-first century they faced numerous obstacles and experienced significant twists and turns that were instrumental in shaping the outcome. Even though barriers to international financial flows were reduced or removed the result was not a seamless global market, as major differences in language, cultures, laws, and taxes remained. These all contributed to the segregation of markets. Though many prophesied that the revolution in communications spelt the death of distance or the end of geography, when it came to the location of financial markets, that ignored the fact that time was not absolute but relative. Even when information travelled at the speed of light through fibre optic cables, those closest to the source had an advantage, which was vital in fast-moving markets. The effect was to generate a continued clustering of financial markets. Global markets had to have a core, which was where contact was instant and liquidity greatest. In addition, there continued to be a need for human interaction when complex deals were being negotiated. In turn, the more complex the deal the more it relied on a range and depth of services that only existed in those few locations that could support such a high degree of specialization. As Norma Cohen put it in 2001, 'Notwithstanding the electronic age, clustering is still important. The need to sit down and discuss strategy remains. You cannot do that by e-mail.'[1] Conversely, the ability to communicate at speed around the world, whether through voice or data, also permitted the diffusion of many financial activities to be closer to the customer, utilize cheaper staff and office costs or avoid high taxes and excessive regulations. In the years after 1992 the combination of increased mobility and the advantages of clustering continued to undermine established business models with major consequences for banks, exchanges, and regulators.

Banks had to respond to deregulation, changing habits among savers and borrowers, and a much more competitive environment as separation through distance and type disappeared. One result was to encourage a switch away from the lend-and-hold model of banking to the originate-and-distribute one. Faced with a more competitive and volatile environment the originate-and-distribute model provided banks with greater flexibility when balancing assets and liabilities, and so avoid being trapped by a liquidity crisis. The originate-and-distribute

[1] Norma Cohen, 'Square mile faces growing threat from the east', 8th September 2001.

Banks, Exchanges, and Regulators: Global Financial Markets from the 1970s. Ranald Michie, Oxford University Press (2021).

DOI: 10.1093/oso/9780199553730.003.0007

model relied on the existence of deep and broad markets where assets could be easily and quickly bought and sold. These markets were still in their infancy in the early 1990s, especially outside the USA, though they did grow in size and importance subsequently. Stepping into the gap were the emerging megabanks. With their size, scale, diversification, and global operations they could internalize the market, acting as counterparties to buyers and sellers from among their own customers, and trading with each other either directly, through interdealer networks, or by accessing the new generation of interactive electronic platforms. It was these megabanks that acted as the trusted counterparties in these global markets in which trading took place using the US$ as the common currency, even though the bulk of transactions took place outside the USA. The effect was to merge not only national and international markets but also those for different products, ranging from credit and currency to stocks and bonds. Epitomizing the transformation was the growth in the use of financial derivatives, especially those traded between banks. Financial derivatives entered the mainstream of global finance in the 1990s, becoming essential tools used by banks and large companies to protect themselves from the volatile conditions within which they now operated. Between 1990 and 2006 the outstanding value of interest-rate swaps, currency swaps, and interest-rate options rose from $3,450bn to $286,000bn. The megabanks created and traded these financial derivatives both as a means of minimizing risk and generating profits, by leveraging their capital and exploiting their global connections.[2]

In the face of all these changes it was stock exchanges that were experiencing the greatest challenges in the 1990s and into the twenty-first century. On the one hand there was a spread of stock markets around the globe as governments privatized state assets and investors turned to corporate stocks because of their combination of yield, capital gain, and liquidity. On the other hand national boundaries ceased to define the parameters within which a stock exchange operated, exposing them to both external competition and OTC markets. Stock exchanges faced a battle for survival, having lost support from the national governments they had once relied upon. Throughout the world government-appointed regulatory agencies were moving away from supporting restrictive practices practised by stock exchanges, justified in terms of the stability they brought and the contribution they made to creating liquid markets free from manipulation. Instead, regulatory agencies increasingly intervened to promote competition in the interests of both the consumer and the economy in general. These regulatory agencies also turned to the megabanks as a mechanism through which they could supervise the entire financial system, including both banking and financial markets. These megabanks were already closely monitored by central banks, because of the systemic risks they posed, and it was a simple step to channel regulation through them as their activities became universal and global. It was only the megabanks that possessed the size and scale required to support the staff necessary to maintain internal systems of supervision in which government-appointed regulators could have confidence. As national borders became meaningless, so the need for regulation to take place internationally grew, and it was the megabanks that provided a means of doing so, as they straddled the globe and penetrated every element of the financial system. The success of this approach was demonstrated as successive crises were surmounted, generating a belief that the global financial system that emerged in the 1990s was one that was not only capable of delivering continuous economic growth but was also resilient when faced

[2] Martin Wolf, 'The new capitalism', 19th June 2007; Jamie Chisholm, 'Record quota of shares are in foreign hands', 14th July 2007; Gillian Tett, 'Sub-prime in its context', 19th November 2007; Deborah Brewster, 'US retail investors slump to record low', 2nd September 2008.

with shocks. Unbeknown to those at the time this global financial system possessed the seeds of its own destruction, as became evident in 2007. In the same way as the faith placed in the power of government led to the crises of the 1970s, so the faith placed in the power of megabanks and unregulated markets after 1980 led to the Global Financial Crisis and its prolonged aftermath.

Technology

Trends in technology continued to act as a disruptive force in global financial markets between 1992 and 2007, transforming products, strategies, trading, and processing. As Edward Luce reported in 1999, 'The most important impetus for change comes from dramatic improvements in communications technology which allows huge volumes of data to circumnavigate the globe in real-time at near-zero cost.[3] Its effects were seen to pervade the operation of financial markets and banks, destroying the established order in its wake.[4] Andrew Large, chairman of the UK's Securities and Investment Board, had observed in 1995 that, 'In this era of global communications and state of the art technology, international investors, firms, investment exchanges and service providers can increasingly choose to do business wherever they like.'[5] The revolution in communications was a two-edged weapon. On the one hand it made it possible to manage a global bank from a central location, as it was possible to constantly supervise operations at a distance. On the other hand it enabled banks that had long enjoyed a local or national monopoly to be challenged.[6] The same applied to markets. No matter the degree of improvement made in the speed of communication, distance created delay. Latency was the delay in connecting to a market and it continued to encourage a clustering of trading activity.[7] Even minute difference mattered as Anuj Gangahar explained in 2006. Though the 'distance involved is a matter of a few metres and the impact it would have on speed is infinitesimal—shaving nanoseconds off transmission time through a shorter length of fibre-optic cable...those nanoseconds could make the difference between continuing to compete or falling by the wayside'.[8] Conversely, the instant access to financial information provided by the likes of Reuters (UK), Bloomberg (USA), and Thomson (Canada), and the electronic payments system supplied by the inter-bank agency, SWIFT, enabled all banks to participate in global markets wherever they were located. The use of electronic systems allowed more to be done at faster speeds and lower cost involving more complex trading strategies and numerous inter-connected transactions.[9]

The use made of advanced technology did vary between financial markets. The more competitive the market, the more standardized the product, and the greater the need for speed the more electronic trading was used. In the high-volume market for US Treasuries

[3] Edward Luce, 'New Technology is driving mating dances', 23rd March 1999.

[4] Jeremy Grant, 'Flat out: why regulators are rushing to keep up with mergers by exchanges', 13th July 2006.

[5] Norma Cohen, 'Competition comes to market', 23rd June 1995.

[6] Peter Martin, 'Multinationals come into their own', 6th December 1999; George Graham, 'Cottages consolidate', 6th December 1999.

[7] Sarah Underwood, 'IT evolution meeting demand for speed, efficiency and accuracy', 16th October 2006.

[8] Anuj Gangahar, 'Nanoseconds matter as traders prepare for a shake-up', 14th September 2006.

[9] Andrew Adonis, '6,000km under the seas', 17th August 1993; Andrew Adonis, 'Lines open for the global village', 17th September 1994; John Gapper, 'Uncertainty over expansion plans', 29th November 1994; Alan Cane, 'Why talk today is relatively cheap', 23rd December 1996; John Gapper, 'What price information', 20th July 1998; Tim Burt, 'A new vision of finance beckons as rivals prepare for court battle', 12th July 2003.

the proportion of total trading by volume executed electronically reached 35 per cent in 2006. In Europe 29 per cent of government bonds were traded on screen, by volume, in that year. In contrast, the less competitive the market, the more customized the products, and the less need for speed, the more voice trading continued in use. That was the case in the corporate bond market, for example.[10] The twin advances being made in communications and computing power in the 1990s made possible the prospect of fully integrated trading and processing systems. With Straight Through Processing (STP) all the stages involved in a financial transaction were linked, from collecting information and analysing data, through buying and selling, to final settlement. In 2002 an estimated 25 per cent of trades had failed due to breaks in the system caused by basic mistakes. Eliminating these with STP increased the certainty of completion, speeded up the process, and lowered costs. However, there was a reluctance to embrace STP because of its technological complexity as well as the costs involved in setting up such systems. Nevertheless, by the beginning of the twenty-first century developments in technology had revolutionized many financial markets.[11] By 2002 Philip Manchester could report that, 'For the past two decades, advances in computer and communications technology have combined with regulatory change to alter the global financial system completely. This has been most striking in securities trading and complex financial derivatives, where technology has expanded existing markets, created new ones and accelerated the processes that enable the markets to function.'[12]

The implications this had for established institutions like exchanges was considered immense. By 1995 Robert Rice claimed that 'national boundaries no longer exist as far as financial transactions and market forces are concerned....In an age of paperless trading where interests in securities are held through a multi-tiered system of banks and other financial intermediaries, transactions are effected by book-entry and domestic securities are traded internationally, existing laws have become obsolete.'[13] Some even predicted that the use of electronic communication networks would eliminate intermediation as buyers as sellers could trade directly.[14] The weakness of such a prediction was that it ignored the issue of counterparty risk, which was obvious to a broker such as Tom Sheridan of Barclays: 'Investors are highly unlikely to start dealing with each other and taking their chances as to whether the stock or the money ever appears.'[15] Where the new technology of trading was gaining traction throughout the 1990s and into the twenty-first century was in those markets dominated by megabanks and global fund managers, as they could be trusted to stand behind the deals made. Despite the high cost of electronic systems, and the rapid rate of obsolescence, those willing to make the investment had the opportunity of breaking into markets long regarded as monopolies.[16] As Aline van Duyn explained in 2000, 'The lines between stock exchanges, derivatives exchanges and other electronic systems are increasingly being blurred. Once a system is in dealing rooms, other products, be they derivatives

[10] Saskia Scholtes, 'Atlantic divide over e-trading', 5th December 2006.

[11] Philip Manchester, 'Powerful incentives for trading in real time', 3rd April 2002.

[12] Philip Manchester, 'Powerful incentives for trading in real time', 3rd April 2002.

[13] Robert Rice, 'No certainties about securities', 21st November 1995.

[14] James Mackintosh, 'Global computer network may be a recipe for disaster', 23rd March 1999; John Labate, 'Wall Street feels the tremors', 23rd March 1999; James Mackintosh, 'Bright lights, big City', 3rd July 1999; Edward Luce and John Labate, 'The trading bell tolls', 26th July 1999; Paul Solman, 'Trading in old methods', 3rd September 1999.

[15] James Mackintosh, 'Global computer network may be a recipe for disaster', 23rd March 1999.

[16] Tracy Corrigan, 'The tail still wags the dog', 26th May 1994; Richard Lapper, 'Revival of the floor show', 27th July 1995; John Gapper, 'Out with the old, in with the new', 28th February 1997; Edward Luce, 'New Technology is driving mating dances', 23rd March 1999; Alex Skorecki and Päivi Munter, 'Sea change for Eurozone bonds', 9th November 2004; Saskia Scholtes, 'Atlantic divide over e-trading', 5th December 2006.

or cash markets, can be added.'[17] The result was to throw down a challenge to exchanges in particular, as they had long enjoyed a relative immunity from competition. In 1999 Edward Luce was of the view that, 'Driven by new technology and the growing power of the world's largest institutional investors, exchanges are being confronted with the choice of sacrificing their autonomy or being sidelined in a shrinking domestic environment.'[18] For Andrew Fisher, also in 1999, 'The writing is on the wall for many of the world's stock exchanges and it is technology that will largely decide their fate.'[19] After a careful assessment of the challenges facing exchanges, carried out in 2000, Stephen Kingsley, of Arthur Andersen, concluded that 'Traditional exchanges are struggling to keep pace with this new reality. Screen trading has reduced the value created by the trading process, clearing and settlement remains fragmented and therefore costly in terms of the need for specialist staff, multiple relationships with depositaries and clearing houses, complex transfer arrangements and failed trades. In many markets the trading and clearing of cash and derivative products remain separate....the ability efficiently to manage cash, securities and margin is reduced as a consequence.'[20] Nevertheless, as long as exchanges continued to command unique pools of liquidity they were able to resist the forces of change unleashed by the rapid advances in technology.

Developments in the technology of communications and computing also influenced the products that were being bought and sold, the strategies being pursued, and the business models being adopted by banks. The development of ever more powerful computers in the 1990s made it easier for banks to design complex derivatives products that met specific customer requirements, for example. In 1995 Jerry Del Missier, head of interest rate and currency derivatives in Europe at Bankers Trust, claimed that 'protection can be structured to fit a specific risk profile'.[21] Faced with market risk, credit risk and operational risk banks turned to mathematical models and the processing power of computers to calculate their exposure and provide ways it could be managed. Philip Manchester claimed in 2002 that, 'The speed of movement in international capital markets demands fast responses and technology-based risk management is the only way investors can keep up.'[22] The volatile world of the 1990s required banks to constantly adjust their positions, whether to cover risks or make profits, and the technology of computing and communications provided them with the means of doing so, when in the hands of expert staff backed by resources of a megabank. There was also a requirement for markets through which they could do this.[23]

Government

No matter the degree and pace of change in the technology applied to finance its impact would have been limited unless accompanied by the actions of governments in removing barriers and pushing the deregulation of banks and exchanges. These actions were being prompted by the examples of what had taken place in the likes of the USA and the UK, and

[17] Aline van Duyn, 'Liffe battles with Eurex hots up', 11th September 2000.
[18] Edward Luce, 'New Technology is driving mating dances', 23rd March 1999.
[19] Andrew Fisher, 'Exchanges set for a global shake-out', 13th January 1999.
[20] Stephen Kingsley, 'A blueprint for the new exchange', 19th September 2000.
[21] Richard Lapper, 'New generation takes over', 16th November 1995.
[22] Philip Manchester, 'An aid to better investment decisions', 5th June 2002.
[23] Richard Lapper, 'New generation takes over', 16th November 1995; Philip Manchester, 'An aid to better investment decisions', 5th June 2002.

the success that they had achieved. In 1993 John Langton, the chief executive of the International Secondary Market Association (ISMA), claimed that 'Market forces cannot be resisted indefinitely. Markets smell unsustainable financial policies pretty quickly.'[24] Following on from inter-government agreements in 1993 and 1995 a major liberalization of the international trade in financial services, under the auspices of the World Trade Organization, was begun at the end of 1997. Building upon what had already taken place the object was to create, over a number of years, a competitive market in financial services operating within a multilateral framework of legally binding rules and regulations. Though many countries still remained wedded to the maintenance of internal and external barriers, both the USA and the EU agreed to open their financial markets fully to foreign competitors, while Japan made a partial commitment.[25] Citing the example of equity markets in 2000 Jeffrey Brown concluded that, 'Globalisation . . . looks unstoppable as trade and capital flows are increasingly liberalised and multinational companies continue to dominate the marketplace.'[26] It was not only by removing international barriers to financial flows that governments contributed to the expanding volume and reach of global financial markets, as domestic deregulation also made a major contribution. The UK's senior regulator, Andrew Large, linked the two in 1995: 'It is coming home to people that the international and domestic agendas are becoming very much the same.'[27] The result was to deepen and broaden international linkages. Globalization in the 1990s meant more markets trading more products on behalf of more banks in response to international supply and demand, relative interest rates, and global investment opportunities. Contributing to this was privatization, as governments sold off state assets, which often occupied a monopoly position in the supply of products and services. The result was to expose these activities to competitive forces, leading to a search for financial products that could provide stability, while stimulating financial markets directly through the trading of the stocks and bonds created.[28] Though the pace of change was not uniform across the world the direction of travel was. One country that only slowly faced up to the challenge posed by the removal of international barriers, and the greatly increased competition in financial services, was Japan. According to Gillian Tett it was only by 1999 that it became widely accepted in Japan that 'the cosy, protected financial system which rebuilt the country after the Second World War cannot cope with the demands of a modern, global economy'.[29]

Governments played a pivotal role in reshaping the global financial system through the removal of barriers and controls, the deregulation of markets and banks, and the privatization of state assets. Nevertheless, national differences remained strong, supported

[24] Brian Bollen, 'Nightmare for harmonisers', 28th October 1993.

[25] Peter Marsh, 'They're breathing down London's neck', 26th May 1993; Tracy Corrigan, 'On trial for dangerous dealing', 21st March 1994; John Plender, 'Through a market, darkly', 27th May 1994; Peter Norman, 'Payments and settlements', 8th August 1994; Henry Harington, 'Testing times for fund managers', 16th November 1995; Barry Riley, 'Free flow of finance', 27th September 1996; Guy de Jonquières, 'WTO risk to financial markets', 16th October 1997; Guy de Jonquières, 'Happy end to a cliff hanger', 15th December 1997; Frances Williams, 'New rules for a trillion-dollar game', 15th December 1997; John Plender, 'Out of sight, not out of mind', 20th September 1999; Jeffrey Brown, 'From slow start to relentless build-up', 1st January 2000.

[26] Jeffrey Brown, 'From slow start to relentless build-up', 1st January 2000.

[27] Richard Lapper, 'Regulators aim to gird the globe', 10th July 1995.

[28] Brian Bollen, 'Nightmare for harmonisers', 28th October 1993; Tracy Corrigan, 'Privatisation the driving force', 26th May 1994; Tracy Corrigan, 'Funds ready if the price is right', 14th September 1995; Richard Lapper, 'Pace of state sell-offs stepped up', 14th June 1996; William Dawkins, 'Last chance to catch up', 25th March 1997; James Kynge, 'China may form cotton exchange', 17th December 1998; Gillian Tett, 'Facing up to a wave of foreign competitors', 21st June 1999; Christopher Swann, 'Paris is Europe's top dog, but for how long', 11th November 1999.

[29] Gillian Tett, 'Facing up to a wave of foreign competitors', 21st June 1999.

by laws and taxes that reflected national priorities.[30] These differences even existed in a relatively homogenous region such as the EU, as well as between countries like the UK and USA with a shared heritage, let alone across the world. This can be seen from the detailed examination of the distribution of financial assets in different countries in 1999, carried out by David Hale, the global chief economist at Zurich Financial Services. What his study revealed was the huge divide between the market-orientated financial system of the USA and the continuing importance of banks elsewhere in the world. In the USA 84 per cent of financial assets were in the form of stocks and bonds with only 16 per cent in bank deposits. No major economy shared this structure. Even neighbouring Canada had 32 per cent in bank deposits compared to 68 per cent in stocks and bonds. Similar to Canada was the structure in Japan where 36 per cent of assets consisted of bank deposits compared to 64 per cent in stocks and bonds, which was despite its financial system sharing many of the characteristics of that of the USA, which had been imposed upon it after the Second World War. In marked contrast to the situation in the USA was that in Germany were only 35 per cent of financial assets was in stocks and bonds, leaving 65 per cent in bank deposits. The pattern in Germany was replicated in many other European countries including France. With close ties to both Europe and the USA the UK occupied a middle position. In the UK 52 per cent of financial assets were in bank deposits compared to 48 per cent in stocks and bonds. There were also further differences when stocks and bonds were separated out. Whereas in the UK 36 per cent of financial assets were in stocks and only 12 per cent in bonds the position in the USA was 43 per cent in stocks and 41 per cent in bonds. These differences were the product of centuries of financial development and continued to be influenced by governments passing laws and introducing taxes that reflected perceived national interest.[31]

As the policies of the past, involving government ownership, control and direction of economies, were abandoned in favour of a reliance on markets, that did not mean that the state had no role to play. Instead, it meant that those in power sought to shape their financial systems so as to deliver a particular agenda, informed by the advice they received from their favoured economists.[32] Much of this advice was based on US experience and prioritized the creation of competitive markets as the key route through which national financial systems would become more efficient, made more responsive to savers and borrowers, and better able to hold their own against rivals elsewhere in the world. This was the model that had worked for business in the USA and provided the rationale behind the process of privatization and market liberalization that was gathering pace around the world. In the 1990s this advice was increasingly applied to finance in the belief that a business such as banking was no different from any other, despite its exposure to liquidity crises.[33] The size and scale of the emerging megabanks, allied to the internal controls they used and the sophisticated risk-assessment models they employed, provided a reassurance that they were sufficiently robust to withstand any shock, including a liquidity crisis. Further reassurance was supplied by the willingness of these megabanks to comply with the rules laid down by the Bank for International Settlement (BIS), which were designed to make them more

[30] Guy de Jonquières, 'Single EU securities market at risk', 16th May 1995; Jonathan Wheatley, Ken Warn, and Mark Mulligan, 'Latin American brokers face home truths on local problems', 3rd March 2000.

[31] Andrew Fisher, 'Germany's stock answer', 22nd October 1996; Guy de Jonquières, 'WTO risk to financial markets', 16th October 1997; Christopher Swann, 'Dawning of the age of European equity', 15th December 1999; David Hale, 'Rebuilt by Wall Street', 25th January 2000.

[32] Edward Balls, 'No advantage in pseudo-scientific futurology', 21st February 1994.

[33] John Plender, 'Too close for comfort', 21st March 2000.

resilient.[34] With the threat of a liquidity crisis greatly diminished, and the resilience of the megabanks assured, governments could place the stability of the financial system in their hands. That left government-appointed regulators, like the Securities and Exchange Commission (SEC) in the USA to focus on the protection of the consumer. As William Donaldson, the chairman of the SEC, stated in 2005, 'our responsibility is to promote the interests of investors'.[35] Ignored in this attitude was the need to regulate behaviour in certain markets on a constant basis, as exchanges had traditionally done, so as to eliminate counterparty risk, ensure liquidity, and prevent manipulation.[36]

Also ignored was the continuing vulnerability of banks to mistakes by management and defaults by customers even when recent evidence of both was available for all to see. In 1995 John Plender commented, after the collapse of Barings Bank, that 'Throughout history banks have been wrecked by single individuals engaging in unauthorised transactions that have been concealed from top management.'[37] A few years later in 1998, after banks experienced losses on loans in Asia and Russia, George Graham posed the question of, 'How could the world's biggest international banks, with their sophisticated systems for assessing credit and advanced mathematical models for measuring risk, have made such a string of mistakes.'[38] He attached particular blame to an overdependence on advanced mathematical models, many of which were derived from the Black–Scholes options-pricing formula, used to measure and then price risk. It was this that had brought down the fund manager, Long-Term Capital Management. Leading banks had spent heavily on developing models to calculate their 'Value at Risk', which was a theoretical estimate of the maximum loss they would be likely to sustain from the effects of market swings on a particular investment portfolio over a specified period. These models had gained such credibility that they were recognized by the BIS's Basel Committee of banking supervisors for calculating market risk. One major weakness in the models was the absence of any allowance for liquidity. This omission was ignored because the freezing of markets was deemed highly unlikely. There were those at the time who cautioned banks against becoming dependent on such models when making investment decisions, such as Cees Mass, chief financial officer of the Dutch Bank, ING: 'The problem is that regular risk-management systems, particularly for market risk, take as their starting point that there are markets. In a financial crisis there is no liquidity and no market, and that turns market risk into event risk and credit risk.'[39] However, there remained a belief that the capital-adequacy rules set by the Basel Committee were sufficiently high so as to prevent a liquidity crisis bringing down a major bank, so that the only issue that needed to be covered was one of solvency.[40] William Plender remained unconvinced that the new financial system had discovered the magic formula that balanced high risk-taking with high returns in banking. In 1999 he stated that, 'If banking history has one consistent message, it is that large-scale changes in the structure and regulation of

[34] Richard Irving, 'Shock-absorbing models', 16th November 1995; George Graham, 'BIS weighs expanded role', 9th June 1997; George Graham, 'Weighing up the risks', 4th June 1999; David Hale, 'The world's banking superpower', 18th June 2003; Jane Croft, 'The danger of relying too much on only one tool', 22nd March 2011.

[35] William Donaldson, 'A simple new rule that gives investors priority', 8th April 2005.

[36] Edward Luce, 'Central trading cushion cleared for take-off', 9th February 1999; Norma Cohen, 'Club of bankers has come full circle', 16th November 2006.

[37] John Plender, 'The box that can never be shut', 28th February 1995.

[38] George Graham, 'Stark Staring Bankers', 5th October 1998.

[39] George Graham, 'Stark Staring Bankers', 5th October 1998.

[40] Richard Lapper, 'Regulators aim to gird the globe', 10th July 1995; Richard Irving, 'Shock-absorbing models', 16th November 1995; George Graham, 'BIS weighs expanded role', 9th June 1997; David Hale, 'The world's banking superpower', 18th June 2003; Charles Batchelor, 'Basel 2 favours high quality borrowers', 3rd November 2004.

this highly-leveraged industry are almost always followed by failures of banking supervision and financial crisis. In particular, liberalisation has an unremitting capacity for exposing flaws in the system.' He went on to warn that, 'It is impossible to predict the precise nature and timing of future banking crises. But the moral hazard that arises from some banks being too big to fail, combined with the dramatic changes in the structure of European banking, guarantees a crisis in the next decade.'[41]

The problem those expressing such views faced was the continuing absence of systemic banking crisis into the twenty-first century, leading governments to take a complacent view of global financial stability between 1992 and 2007. The new global financial system did experience a number of crises between but proved itself robust in each case.[42] These crises occurred in diverse countries ranging from the UK, USA and Japan to Mexico, Argentina, and Russia. These crises included both banks and markets with some caused by excessive lending on property and others by the bursting of a speculative bubble. In 2000, for example, the dot.com boom imploded in the USA, followed by similar collapses around the world. Between its peak in March 2000 and October 2002 the technology-heavy Nasdaq index fell 78 per cent, wiping out more than $6,500bn of the value of stocks. Other crises stemmed from corporate disasters as with Enron and Swissair while there were also classic government debt defaults as happened in the case of Argentina and Russia. Despite these differences there was one common feature to all these individual crises and that was the absence of a system-wide collapse involving banks that were central to the global payments system. Within four days of the September 11 2001 attack on Wall Street, trading in New York's financial markets had been restored while it had continued uninterrupted in London. The lack of bank failures was one feature that was much commented on, as with Charles Pretzlik in 2003: 'It is one of the most remarkable features of the recent economic and financial markets instability that there have been no serious casualties among the banks.'[43] According to Robert Pickel, chief executive of the International Swaps and Derivatives Association, the reason was because 'Financial institutions have become much more sophisticated at analysing their risk portfolios than they used to be; they have learnt the lessons of previous eras.'[44]

In the early twenty-first century it became generally accepted that banks had learnt the lessons of past crises and devised strategies that allowed them to cope with the increased risks posed by a more volatile global financial system. In 2005 Peter Thal Larsen noted that

[41] John Plender, 'Crisis in the making', 12th April 1999.

[42] Vanessa Houlder, 'Expensive vote of confidence', 3rd June 1993; Sara Webb, 'Tackling the ghost of Black Wednesday', 23rd December 1993; John Plender, 'The box that can never be shut', 28th February 1995; Norma Cohen, 'Industry joins the information age', 12th March 1999; Joshua Chaffin, 'Bankers emerging from cover after crisis', 12th November 1999; Gillian Tett, 'Crunch brings some benefits', 8th May 2000; John Labate, 'Decentralised exchange the hot topic of debate', 27th November 2001; Peter Thal Larsen, 'Heading for the trenches', 22nd February 2002; Vincent Boland, 'Banks find a way to spread their risk', 18th February 2003; David Hale, 'The world's banking superpower', 18th June 2003; Gary Silverman, Ed Crooks, and Vincent Boland, 'The hunt for yield hots up: investors and pension funds plunge deeper into illiquid and riskier assets', 22nd July 2003; Charles Pretzlik, 'Maintaining a resilience to risk—and shocks', 1st October 2003; Peter Thal Larsen, 'One shocking bank failure deposited a stern warning in the history books', 19th February 2005; Norma Cohen, Jeremy Grant and Andrei Postelnicu, 'Leading exchanges consider their moves in the race to consolidate', 11th March 2005; Jennifer Hughes, Richard Beales and Gillian Tett, 'The yield conundrum: as bond returns drift downwards, is risk soaring for investors', 17th June 2005; Peter Thal Larsen and James Drummond, 'Regulator's radar hunts for approach to hedge funds', 24th June 2005; Richard Waters, 'From Netscape to the Next Big Thing: how a dot.com decade change our lives', 5th August 2005; Christopher Brown-Humes, 'A grown-up Brady bunch? Why returns in emerging markets are vigorous—for now', 1st March 2006.

[43] Charles Pretzlik, 'Maintaining a resilience to risk—and shocks', 1st October 2003.

[44] Vincent Boland, 'Banks find a way to spread their risk', 18th February 2003.

'Investment banks have poured millions into developing sophisticated risk-management systems that measure the amount of capital they have at risk at any moment in time.'[45] The combination of internal risk controls within banks, and the ability to distribute the risks each was exposed to, appeared to have produced a financial system that was resilient in the face of successive crises. There remained a few who expressed concerns that it was not sufficiently resilient to cope with the credit bubble generated by central bank intervention in the wake of the collapse of the dot.com bubble. Fearing that this event represented a repeat of the Wall Street Crash, central banks lowered interest rates and pumped liquidity into the global financial system. As early as June 2005 Jennifer Hughes, Richard Beales, and Gillian Tett at the *FT* observed that, 'As investors gobble up riskier assets—such as mortgage-backed securities or risky leveraged buy-out loans-could they also be making themselves doubly vulnerable to any future shocks.' Whether this would lead to a systemic crisis was left open to debate, however, as they added the caveat that 'Optimists insist this remains unlikely.'[46] A year later in 2006 another *FT* columnist, Christopher Brown-Humes, expressed his concern that there was a 'current excess of global liquidity looking for a home' and that this could lead to a financial crisis. He added, though, that it would be confined to countries with less-developed financial systems.[47]

Under these conditions governments were sufficiently confident to press on with an agenda that promoted competition in financial services, confident that banks and regulators could cope with the increased volatility that accompanied reliance upon unregulated markets. One part of the world where this new ideology was fully embraced was the European Union. By emulating the single market for financial services found in the USA the European Commission was convinced that they would not only be promoting economic growth but also greater political integration. Conversely, the US government relaxed the prohibitions on both nationwide banking and the combination of commercial and investment banking. This allowed the establishment of universal banks along the Continental European model and branch banking along the British model. However, it was in the EU that the most radical changes were being forced through by governments rather than being a response to outside pressure, as was the case in the USA. Following on from the creation of the single market in financial services, implemented from 1993 onwards, was the Investment Services Directive, which was to be introduced by member states from 1 January 1996. This directive made it increasingly difficult for national governments to protect their domestic market from outside competition, though some were slow to put its provisions into practice.

This directive was followed by the plan to introduce a single currency for the European Union by 1999 though a number of member countries decided not to participate, including the UK, which hosted, in London, Europe's most important financial centre. Though a panoply of different accounting standards, tax regimes, and regulatory systems continued to hinder integration in Europe, the removal of the ability to discriminate along national lines, and the coming of a single currency, went far into making the EU a single market for financial services by 2000. Even by 1998 Simon Davies was of the opinion that 'The birth of the euro is leading to a wholesale restructuring of European financial markets.'[48] In response

[45] Peter Thal Larsen, 'One shocking bank failure deposited a stern warning in the history books', 19th February 2005.

[46] Jennifer Hughes, Richard Beales, and Gillian Tett, 'The yield conundrum: as bond returns drift downwards, is risk soaring for investors', 17th June 2005.

[47] Christopher Brown-Humes, 'A grown-up Brady bunch? Why returns in emerging markets are vigorous—for now', 1st March 2006.

[48] Simon Davies, 'Cost cuts fuel mergers', 17th July 1998.

to the Investment Services Directive, and in preparation for the disappearance of national currencies, banks and exchanges were repositioning themselves for a much more competitive environment. The expectation was that Europe's banks and financial markets would increasingly resemble those of the USA in terms of structure and the business model they used. This policy of the EU included following more recent US legislation such as that designed to foster competition between stock exchanges. As William Donaldson, chairman of the SEC, explained in 2005, 'The rule we (SEC) adopted, part of the regulation NMS reforms, is quite simple: when an investor sends an order to a market, the market can either execute the order at the best price then instantly available in the national market system or the market must send the order to the venue quoting the best price.'[49] The substance of Regulation NMS was then copied by the EU in its Markets in Financial Instruments Directive (Mifid) in 2006, because it was expected to deliver the competition between the region's fragmented stock exchanges, which was currently lacking, by breaking down barriers to cross-border trading in corporate stocks.[50]

What had happened was that through a mixture of ending barriers and controls, and then driving a market-based agenda, governments were altering the world within which banks, exchanges, and regulators operated. The result was to emphasize an international rather than national orientation, which benefited some and disadvantaged others. This change can be seen in the actions of fund managers. The prime movers of capital around the world were pension and investment funds with the quantity involved in a single transaction sometimes running to billions of dollars. In 2003 US pension funds had accumulated assets of \$7.5tn, which was more than the total for the next eight countries including Japan with \$2.9tn, \$1.4tn in the UK, and Canada at \$0.9tn. Though most continued to favour domestic assets some began selecting investments by sector rather than country. There were also a growing number of hedge funds that adopted a highly-leveraged strategy, and searched the world for liquid markets that would allow them to buy and sell quickly. It was only the largest banks that could handle transactions of the dimension and complexity generated by these institutional investors, leading to the concentration of the business in the hands of a decreasing number of leading commercial and investment banks.[51] As early as 1994 John Gapper and Tracy Corrigan reported on 'The battle for dominance of global financial services'[52] between European, Japanese, and US banks. As Peter Thal Larsen

[49] William Donaldson, 'A simple new rule that gives investors priority', 8th April 2005.

[50] John Gapper, 'New rules, new rivals, new order', 16th February 1996; George Graham and Gillian Tett, 'City fears profit loss by missing Target', 6th July 1996; Richard Waters, 'Talk of mergers is in the air', 12th August 1996; George Graham, 'Radical changes may lie ahead', 9th April 1997; Andrew Fisher, 'European bourses may get lift on back of Emu', 15th April 1997; Philip Coggan, 'Bourses fight for supremacy', 24th April 1997; Simon Davies and George Graham, 'Europe's Big Bang', 8th July 1998; Simon Davies, 'Cost cuts fuel mergers', 17th July 1998; Edward Luce, 'Emu to make Europe more like America', 18th December 1998; William Donaldson, 'A simple new rule that gives investors priority', 8th April 2005; Peter Thal Larsen, 'Many are miffed at the costly Mifid', 26th October 2006.

[51] James Blitz, 'New anxieties for the banks', 26th May 1993; John Gapper and Tracy Corrigan, 'Formidable rivals on a shifting battleground', 4th March 1994; John Gapper and Richard Lapper, 'Warburg breaks the bond', 11th January 1995; Richard Lapper, 'Alliances with a future', 7th September 1995; Laurie Morse, 'Futures shake-out tops conference agenda', 21st October 1996; John Gapper, 'A concentration of firepower', 31st January 1997; Simon Davies, 'Success masks market turmoil', 24th March 1998; Edward Luce, 'New Technology is driving mating dances', 23rd March 1999; Stephen Kingsley, 'Quest for a new role and a new strategy', 23rd March 1999; Torsten Stoermer, 'Sectors gain as country funds lose appeal', 27th July 1999; Joshua Chaffin, 'Bankers emerging from cover after crisis', 12th November 1999; Jeffrey Brown, 'From slow start to relentless build-up', 1st January 2000; Alex Skorecki, 'Pension moves may boost equity flows', 30th June 2000; Jacques de Larosière and Daniel Lebegue, 'Bringing harmony to Europe's markets', 14th September 2000; James Mackintosh, 'Venerable names will disappear', 26th January 2001; Peter Thal Larsen, 'Heading for the trenches', 22nd February 2002; Simon Targett, 'Pension gloom is lifting', 19th January 2004; Phil Davis, 'The search is now on for new ideas', 11th October 2004.

[52] John Gapper and Tracy Corrigan, 'Formidable rivals on a shifting battleground', 4th March 1994.

observed in 2002, 'Until only a few years ago, the conventional wisdom was that investment banks needed to build global scale, and needed to do so as quickly as possible. If they could not offer a full range of products in almost every country on earth, they would be condemned to play for ever in the second tier, if not even lower. Now even large banks are willing to concede they will not be able to dominate every business in every geographic region.'[53] Though that wisdom was upset by the bursting of the dot.com bubble it remained a major force directing business to the largest banks and the biggest financial centres. According to John Gapper by 1997, 'The large US investment banks have managed to persuade many issuers and investors around the world that they alone have the expertise and financial strength to carry off the biggest and most complex deals. They have won leading roles as advisers on the biggest privatisations and cross-border deals.'[54]

Such was the transformation taking place that government-appointed regulators around the world were at a loss at how to respond other than accept the situation as they found it. Jeremy Grant summed up their predicament in 2006 by posing the question, 'How do regulators oversee markets whose customers are in multiple time zones and whose trading platforms operate in cyberspace?' What he was picking up on was the views being expressed by the likes of Annette Nazareth, at the SEC in the USA: 'In all business the world is becoming small and flat and, with technology, geographical boundaries less relevant. You can keep having these separate rules in separate countries but the real challenge is to come up with a convergence of consistent rules so that the geographical boundaries themselves become less relevant to commerce, that's the trick. And that's what all the regulators are working hard to achieve.' The SEC chairman, Christopher Cox, saw the only solution in terms of common standards applied throughout the world: 'Harm to investors will be minimised if we agree to adhere to high-quality securities regulation and there is a strong degree of co-operation and co-ordination among regulators.' From the perspective of the SEC these standards would be those applied in the USA. Without common standards there would be no possibility of policing these global markets, unless the intention was to return to the controls of the past, as Reuben Jeffrey, the CFTC chairman, pointed out: 'One of the things we want to strive to do is not prevent globalisation of these markets or jeopardise the competitive position of US exchanges, which are core constituencies of ours.' Co-operation rather control was seen as the solution by the likes of Nick Weinreb, head of regulation, at Euronext 'It is not practical or realistic to expect that an exchange operating on a global basis can operate without co-operation between regulators.' A similar view was expressed by Peter Reits, executive board member, Eurex: 'We are operating in a global environment and we want to have, as an ideal, an identical regulatory regime.'[55] Regulation was no longer the prerogative of national governments in the globalized financial world that developed in the 1990s. However, governments continued to play a major role.

Competition between Financial Centres

By the 1990s financial services had emerged as a business to be valued, supported, and protected in its own right rather than simply an adjunct to the rest of an economy. In response governments around the world tried to protect what they already possessed while

[53] Peter Thal Larsen, 'Heading for the trenches', 22nd February 2002.
[54] John Gapper, 'A concentration of firepower', 31st January 1997.
[55] Jeremy Grant, 'Flat out: why regulators are rushing to keep up with mergers by exchanges', 13th July 2006.

others sought to attract more of the rapidly growing international business activity. Increasingly favoured were those financial centres that could provide global banks and fund managers with the markets and facilities they required. London and New York emerged as joint leaders among global financial centres, each possessing distinctive strengths and weaknesses. Chrystia Freeland explained in 2006 that 'While the City of London does dominate some types of international financial business, such as cross-border bank lending and foreign-exchange trading, New York retains its overall lead in important areas such as equity market turnover and investment banking revenue, thanks to its huge domestic market.'[56] This battle between financial centres took place at the wholesale level, involving the markets for foreign exchange, short-term money, derivative contracts, the stock of the world's largest companies, and the largest bond issues. Beyond this wholesale activity there existed much financial activity that took place at the local and national level, and this was done in national, or even local financial centres. In 1996 Robert Loewy, at HSBC, explained that 'You still have to service a number of core customers locally' while Julian Simmonds, at Citibank, observed that 'You don't have to have world class traders all over the world, but you do need to have world class sales people everywhere.'[57] What was important in retail financial services was maintaining close contact with customers and complying with the relevant regulations, taxes, and standards that varied from country to country. At the same time there was the constant issue of balancing the high costs involved in a global financial centre location with the benefits obtained from being there.[58]

As a location for financial activity the USA was unique in terms of its combination of depth, breadth, and homogeneity. Covered by a single currency and subject to a single regulatory regime it delivered a market unmatched anywhere else in the world. Elsewhere in the world markets were fractured along national boundaries, preventing the same scale being achieved domestically, with only Japan coming close. This superiority of the domestic market in the USA was recognized in 2006 by the likes of Peter Weinberg, chief executive officer of Goldman Sachs, who was in a position to make global comparisons: 'The US financial markets enjoy an enormous incumbency advantage as the largest, most liquid and most transparent in the world.'[59] This had major implications for New York as a financial centre as Chrystia Freeland made clear in 2006: 'New York retains its overall lead in important areas such as equity market turnover and investment banking revenue, thanks to its

[56] Chrystia Freeland, 'Capitalism's capital fears being caught out as London booms', 4th November 2006.

[57] Philip Gawith, 'Service central to Paribas forex move', 2nd February 1996.

[58] Tracy Corrigan, 'Exchanges fight for the future across Europe', 15th January 1993; Norma Cohen, 'Exploiting the differences', 30th April 1993; Ian Hamilton Fazey, 'Leeds to join network of Europe finance centres', 5th October 1993; Tracy Corrigan, 'Europe waits for floodgates to open', 20th October 1993; Ian Hamilton Fazey, 'Regional finance centres need a lift', 25th November 1993; Philip Gawith, 'Service central to Paribas forex move', 2nd February 1996; Philip Coggan, 'Obstacles to integration', 16th February 1996; Graham Bowley, 'Forex houses sanguine despite possibility of single currency', 6th December 1996; Justin Marozzi, 'Lure of the lion city', 18th February 1997; Guy de Jonquières, 'Happy end to a cliff hanger', 15th December 1997; Frances Williams, 'New rules for a trillion-dollar game', 15th December 1997; Vincent Boland, 'A place in the holy trinity', 26th March 1998; Gillian Tett, 'A bang or a whimper?', 1st April 1998; Simon Davies, 'Battle of the bourses', 14th May 1998; James Harding, 'First steps on the ladder', 19th May 1998; Peter Martin, 'Multinationals come into their own', 6th December 1999; Daniel Dombey, 'Lack of growth signals need for reinvention', 7th June 2001; Tony Barber, 'A tale of two complementary cities', 12th June 2002; Charles Pretzlik, 'Benefits to City would be only marginal at best, report concludes', 10th June 2003; Bertrand Benoit, 'Long-held dream has proved to be unrealistic', 10th June 2003; Andrew Hill, 'Financial inventors underpin success', 27th March 2006; Peter Weinberg, 'How London can close the gap on Wall Street', 30th March 2006; Chris Hughes and Norma Cohen, 'Thain is attracted by all the right things in London', 20th June 2006; Chrystia Freeland, 'Capitalism's capital fears being caught out as London booms', 4th November 2006.

[59] Peter Weinberg, 'How London can close the gap on Wall Street', 30th March 2006.

huge domestic market.'[60] New York did face domestic competition from low-cost locations elsewhere in the USA, including neighbouring areas in New Jersey and Connecticut. John Labate noted in 2001, that 'For two decades, brokerages and investment banks have steadily moved key operations out of downtown Manhattan, and increasingly out of New York City altogether.'[61] It was not only back office functions that had been relocated. A number of the largest US banks, for example, were run from cities in other states. Additionally the commodity exchanges in Chicago had developed a very successful business in financial derivatives whereas their New York counterparts had not. Nevertheless, New York remained the dominant financial centre in North America, being the centre of the money, stock, and bond markets and the key interface between the US financial system and that of the rest of the world.

The dominant position it occupied within the US financial system had a major influence on the way that New York developed as a financial centre between 1992 and 2007. With privileged access to the largest market for financial services in the world, New York was, inevitably, very domestically focused. The repeal of the Glass–Steagall Act, and the ending of the embargo on interstate banking, both of which took place in the 1990s, fostered a climate of rivalry within the US banking system. Similarly, in the early twenty-first century the government also legislated to destroy the monopoly enjoyed by the NYSE and Nasdaq in the market for the stocks they quoted, especially in the case of the former. This drove innovation across all financial activities ranging from new products to new markets, with these then being taken up elsewhere in the world. What New York lacked as a financial centre was the strong international orientation found in London, largely because it had no need to supplement its domestic business with an international one. Compounding this failure to vigorously pursue the international agenda were the taxes and regulations that encouraged foreign business to bypass New York in favour of other financial centres. In the years between 1992 and 2007 the most marked of these was the Sarbanes–Oxley Act of 2002, which discouraged foreign companies from having their stock listed on either the NYSE or Nasdaq, because of the strict regulatory conditions they would have to meet. This did not mean that individual US banks ignored the expanding international opportunities that came with globalization. In an era when governments and businesses turned to financial markets for solutions US banks, brokers, fund managers, and even exchanges provided them, whether it involved the securitization of assets or the provision of derivative contracts that reduced risks. In turn, that drove change elsewhere in the world.[62]

Apart from New York, the other big winner among financial centres, from the trend towards the globalization of finance, was London. In 2006 a trio of *FT* journalists, Fred Thal Larsen, Charles Pretzlik, and Chris Hughes, claimed that London was 'The dominant

[60] Chrystia Freeland, 'Capitalism's capital fears being caught out as London booms', 4th November 2006.

[61] John Labate, 'Decentralised exchange the hot topic of debate', 27th November 2001.

[62] Guy de Jonquières, 'WTO risk to financial markets', 16th October 1997; Gillian Tett, 'Big Bang or just a whimper?', 26th March 1998; Aline van Duyn, 'Bond markets extend to smaller firms', 19th May 2000; Joshua Chaffin, 'Banks scatter over Manhattan', 27th November 2001; John Labate, 'Decentralised exchange the hot topic of debate', 27th November 2001; Holly Yeager, 'Vulnerable industry learns lessons from the disaster', 22nd February 2002; Toby Shelley, 'Oil groups eye LSE's emerging market skill', 14th October 2003; Kevin Morrison, 'Private buyers fill bullion vaults', 16th April 2004; Andrew Hill, 'Financial inventors underpin success', 27th March 2006; Peter Weinberg, 'How London can close the gap on Wall Street', 30th March 2006; Chris Hughes and Norma Cohen, 'Thain is attracted by all the right things in London', 20th June 2006; Harvey Pitt, 'Sarbanes-Oxley is an unhealthy export', 21st June 2006; Neal Wolkoff, 'America's regulations are scaring the Sox off small caps', 1st August 2006; Clara Furse, 'Sox is not to blame-London is just better as a market', 18th September 2006; Chrystia Freeland, 'Capitalism's capital fears being caught out as London booms', 4th November 2006; Anuj Gangahar, 'Sox effect hits US exchanges', 28th November 2006.

financial centre of Europe, and a serious rival to New York on the global stage.'[63] It was located in the ideal time zone, used the language of international finance, and already possessed the legal, regulatory, and market infrastructure required. Within Europe London was the only financial centre that was of sufficient size to challenge New York and Tokyo and so business gravitated in its direction from across the Continent. As Joseph Cook, head of European capital at JP Morgan, put in 1996, 'There is a breadth of talent compared with other European centres.'[64] In turn, that European base allowed London to mount an increasingly successful challenge to New York for those activities that were truly international in character. To Martin Dickson in 2006, 'The more outstanding the international talent in the City, the more it increases London's competitive advantage, and the greater the advantage, the more it attracts fresh talent from around the world.' He added that 'There is a certain swagger about the City of London these days—a self-confidence born of success as it has strengthened its position as Europe's leading financial centre and a magnet for capital and talent from around the world.'[65] Important as talent was, the key to London's success as a financial centre was the liquidity of the international markets it hosted. This was recognized in 1994 by Christopher Taylor, at Barclays: 'There's a tendency for money dealing to gravitate towards London, to pool liquidity in one centre. The powerhouse is here.'[66] It was also the point emphasized in 2006 by Clara Furse, chief executive of the London Stock Exchange: 'London's competitive advantage is clear: it has the world's deepest pool of international liquidity; it has a wide range of institutional emerging market investors; it has broad analyst coverage; it offers an unrivalled choice of markets on which to list; it is the gateway to a budding Eurozone; and, critically, the City promotes world-class regulation and corporate governance standards.'[67] By shedding more peripheral financial activity to cheaper locations in the UK and abroad, and developing the Docklands as an adjunct financial centre, London was able to create the space for more internationally focused business in the 1990s.[68] Pen Kent, a director of the Bank of England, observed in 1996 that 'London has learned to make its living by using other people's money.'[69] By then John Gapper could claim that, 'The City of London is once more the world's leading international financial centre.'[70] Ten years after, in 2005, Scheherazade Daneshkhu reported that, 'No other advanced country has enjoyed Britain's success in deriving a large increase in export earnings from its financial sector.'[71] Echoing Pen Kent ten years before, Martin Wolf suggested in 2006 that 'The UK earns money from borrowing in safe assets and investing in riskier ones.'[72] Others referred to that outcome as 'Wimbledonization' of the City, in which London provided the stage upon which the world's bankers played. Gideon Rachman, writing in 2006, thought that 'There are few places that are as remorselessly global as the City of London. The City does business all over the world, is dominated by

[63] Peter Thal Larsen, Charles Pretzlik, and Chris Hughes, 'Big Bang celebrants find party has moved on', 28th October 2006.

[64] Richard Lapper, 'A tale of two cities', 12th June 1996.

[65] Martin Dickson, 'Capital Gain: how London is thriving and taking on the global competition', 27th March 2006.

[66] David Marsh, 'Powerhouse holds its ground', 4th March 1994.

[67] Clara Furse, 'Sox is not to blame—London is just better as a market', 18th September 2006.

[68] The Lex Column, 'Cracking the City Club', 6th February 1995; Richard Lapper, 'A tale of two cities', 12th June 1996.

[69] Richard Lapper, 'A tale of two cities', 12th June 1996.

[70] John Gapper, 'Painful struggle back to centre of world markets', 25th October 1996.

[71] Scheherazade Daneshkhu, 'Demand for professional expertise nets trade surplus', 12th September 2005.

[72] Martin Wolf, 'This stable isle: how Labour has steered an economy going global', 18th September 2006.

American banks and some 20–25% of its employees hail from the rest of Europe.'[73] Jeremy Isaacs, chief executive of Lehman Brothers in Europe and Asia wrote that 'London is an operating platform that connects to the rest of the world. That is its distinct advantage when compared to other financial centres.'[74] Though some in 2006 cautioned that London's position was vulnerable, most lauded the position it had achieved by then, and the evidence supported their verdict.[75]

The result by 2006 was that London was in a strong position to challenge New York as the leading financial centre of the world, on the basis of its international business, and was unmatched within the European time zone. The difficulty faced by all European financial centres, despite progress towards monetary and financial integration within the EU, was that fragmentation prevented any, other than London, achieving the scale required to compete with New York on the global stage. Each European financial centre could command its national market when the business was driven by domestic demand and protected by national laws and taxes. One of the motives behind a single European currency, introduced in 1999, was to overcome this fragmentation and, with the UK not participating, the expectation was that continental centres would benefit at the expense of London. Simon Davies reported in 1998, 'There is an intense European effort to prise business from London.'[76] The reverse turned out to be the case as London possessed the most liquid markets, even in the Euro, and so trading took place there rather than Frankfurt or Paris.[77] In contrast, those

[73] Gideon Rachman, 'How the Square Mile fell out of love with Brussels', 12th December 2006.

[74] Peter Thal Larsen, 'Action may be needed to maintain competitive advantage', 26th March 2006.

[75] Tracy Corrigan, 'Exchanges fight for the future across Europe', 15th January 1993; Ian Hamilton Fazey, 'Leeds to join network of Europe finance centres', 5th October 1993; Ian Hamilton Fazey, 'Regional finance centres need a lift', 25th November 1993; John Gapper and Tracy Corrigan, 'Formidable rivals on a shifting battleground', 4th March 1994; David Goodhart, 'Economy's world standing given a frank assessment', 25th May 1994; Norma Cohen, 'Competition comes to market', 23rd June 1995; John Plender, 'City plays growing role in drawing investors', 2nd October 1995; Richard Lapper, 'A tale of two cities', 12th June 1996; John Gapper, 'Painful struggle back to centre of world markets', 25th October 1996; Graham Bowley, 'Forex houses sanguine despite possibility of single currency', 6th December 1996; Guy de Jonquières, 'WTO risk to financial markets', 16th October 1997; Clay Harris, '"Trailblazer" with vision for London's future', 8th November 1997; Peter John, 'Foreign ownership drives expansion in the City', 19th March 1998; Simon Davies, 'Battle of the bourses', 14th May 1998; Norma Cohen, 'Square mile faces growing threat from the east', 8th September 2001; Ed Crooks, 'Capital keeps its prominence as European finance centre', 8th February 2002; Charles Pretzlik, 'Benefits to City would be only marginal at best, report concludes', 10th June 2003; Bertrand Benoit, 'Long-held dream has proved to be unrealistic', 10th June 2003; Toby Shelley, 'Oil groups eye LSE's emerging market skill', 14th October 2003; Rebecca Bream and Kevin Morrison, 'Miners move to London to tap a cash stream', 21st November 2003; Charles Batchelor, 'London leads in trading volumes', 23rd September 2004; Gillian Tett, 'The City struggles to escape from European Union red tape', 1st July 2005; Scheherazade Daneshkhu, 'Demand for professional expertise nets trade surplus', 12th September 2005; Joanna Chung, 'Middle Eastern businesses are looking towards the City for investors and to raise their profiles', 3rd February 2006; Kevin Morrison, 'Driven by a blistering rise in metal prices', 10th March 2006; Peter Thal Larsen, 'Action may be needed to maintain competitive advantage', 26th March 2006; Martin Dickson, 'Capital Gain: how London is thriving and taking on the global competition', 27th March 2006; Scheherazade Daneshkhu and Chris Giles, 'City becomes undeniable engine of growth', 27th March 2006; Andrew Hill, 'Financial inventors underpin success', 27th March 2006; Paul Myners, 'The Square Mile must fight to stay successful', 30th March 2006; Chris Hughes and Norma Cohen, 'Thain is attracted by all the right things in London', 20th June 2006; Martin Wolf, 'This stable isle: how Labour has steered an economy going global', 18th September 2006; Clara Furse, 'Sox is not to blame—London is just better as a market', 18th September 2006; Nigel Lawson, 'We must not take London's success for granted', 23rd October 2006; Peter Thal Larsen, 'Hats off: Big Bang still brings scale and innovation to finance in London', 26th October 2006; Peter Thal Larsen, Charles Pretzlik and Chris Hughes, 'Big Bang celebrants find party has moved on', 28th October 2006; Chrystia Freeland, 'Capitalism's capital fears being caught out as London booms', 4th November 2006; Gideon Rachman, 'How the Square Mile fell out of love with Brussels', 12th December 2006; Ben Smith, 'London sees rise in hedge funds', 17th April 2007.

[76] Simon Davies, 'Battle of the bourses', 14th May 1998.

[77] Tracy Corrigan, 'Exchanges fight for the future across Europe', 15th January 1993; Norma Cohen, 'Exploiting the differences', 30th April 1993; Ian Hamilton Fazey, 'Leeds to join network of Europe finance centres', 5th October 1993; Ian Hamilton Fazey, 'Regional finance centres need a lift', 25th November 1993; John Gapper and

European financial centres located in member countries that applied lower rates of taxation, like Luxembourg and Ireland, benefited from the introduction of the single currency as it removed an important barrier to the free flow of funds.[78] Such an option was not available to the larger European countries such as France and Germany and so their financial centres had to operate without the advantages delivered by a low tax and minimal regulations regime. The French government had long promoted Paris as a European financial centre and it did make headway in the 1990s. Gerd Hauser, a director of the Dresdner Bank, considered in 1997 that 'France has consistently developed its financial centre after the example of New York and created modern instruments.'[79] However, the failure to persuade the European Commission that euro-denominated transactions should be channelled through financial centres located within the Eurozone was a major blow to the ambitions of those promoting Paris as a financial centre. It also faced growing competition from Frankfurt, which had been chosen in 1993 as the location of the European Central Bank.[80] The growing ascendancy of Frankfurt over Paris reflected the success of the strategy of the German government, beginning with the Financial Markets Promotion Act (Finanzmarktförderungsgesetz) of 1994. That was followed by a further relaxing of taxes and regulations with the result that Frankfurt had overtaken Paris as the leading financial centre in continental Europe by 1998, though it remained a long way behind London as a global financial centre. Even German banks made London their base for international transactions.[81] Elsewhere in Europe financial centres struggled to retain a role other than serving the local market. Amsterdam, Brussels, and Stockholm all aspired to some kind of international status but with limited success.[82] Peter Eghardt, who chaired the Stockholm Chamber of Commerce, admitted in 2006 that 'We can't challenge London, which is clearly number one, but we can compete with European centres such as Frankfurt.'[83] Even Switzerland found it difficult to retain its position as an important financial centre in the 1990s, as it was forced to tighten regulations at a time when Luxembourg and Dublin were able to provide an attractive low tax/light

Tracy Corrigan, 'Formidable rivals on a shifting battleground', 4th March 1994; Philip Coggan, 'Obstacles to integration', 16th February 1996; Graham Bowley, 'Forex houses sanguine despite possibility of single currency', 6th December 1996; Guy de Jonquières, 'WTO risk to financial markets', 16th October 1997; Simon Davies, 'Battle of the bourses', 14th May 1998; Gillian Tett, 'The City struggles to escape from European Union red tape', 1st July 2005; Andrew Hill, 'Financial inventors underpin success', 27th March 2006; Gideon Rachman, 'How the Square Mile fell out of love with Brussels', 12th December 2006.

[78] Norma Cohen, 'Exploiting the differences', 30th April 1993; Andrew Hill, 'Belfox thrives in the gentleman's club', 25th November 1993; Daniel Dombey, 'Lack of growth signals need for reinvention', 7th June 2001; Daniel Dombey, 'Transatlantic invasion keeps industry thriving', 7th June 2001; Roxane McMeeken, 'Dublin closing the gap in race for hottest investments', 7th June 2001; Michael Mann, 'Watch out, the rivalry is beginning to hot up', 6th June 2002; Gillian Tett, 'The City struggles to escape from European Union red tape', 1st July 2005; Kate Burgess, 'Luxembourg edges, as London hedges', 19th November 2007.

[79] Andrew Fisher, 'Sights are set on overtaking Paris', 9th June 1997.

[80] David Buchan, 'Big Bang switch in 1999', 10th December 1996; Andrew Fisher, 'Sights are set on overtaking Paris', 9th June 1997; Andrew Jack, 'SBF, Matif join forces ahead of German link', 18th September 1997; George Graham, 'French banker hits at stock exchange alliance', 24th July 1998.

[81] David Waller, 'Frankfurt's role consolidated', 31st May 1994; David Waller, 'A tightening of the rules', 31st May 1994; David Waller, 'Resisting the bait of equity ownership', 14th July 1994; Andrew Fisher, 'Fewer bourses offer more for the investor', 10th May 1995; Judy Dempsey, 'Germany unveils plan to boost stock market competitiveness', 20th July 1996; Edward Luce, 'Liffe finds little comfort in tie-up with Frankfurt', 11th July 1998; Ed Crooks, 'Capital keeps its prominence as European finance centre', 8th February 2002; Tony Barber, 'A tale of two complementary cities', 12th June 2002.

[82] Ronald van de Krol, 'Action plan lifts Amsterdam's status', 12th September 1994; Andrew Hill, 'Belfox thrives in the gentleman's club', 25th November 1993; Michael Smith, 'Core of growing influence', 31st March 1998; David Ibison, 'Stockholm plots course as financial centre', 12th July 2006.

[83] David Ibison, 'Stockholm plots course as financial centre', 12th July 2006.

regulation environment within the Eurozone. The continuing imposition of transaction taxes and bi-polar nature of the Swiss financial markets, split between Zurich and Geneva, continued to restrict liquidity.[84]

Given the size of the Japanese economy, ranked as the second largest in the world between 1992 and 2007, and the developed state of Tokyo as a financial centre, it might have been expected that it would occupy a similar position in Asia as London did in Europe or New York in the Americas. However, rather than benefiting from the growing opportunities being generated internationally and, especially in Asia, Tokyo was in retreat as a financial centre in the 1990s. As a high cost location Tokyo was losing the foreign banks and brokers that had flocked there in the 1980s while even the Japanese themselves were using the markets and facilities available in Singapore and Hong Kong. The result was a downward cycle because the loss of business made Tokyo an even less attractive financial centre encouraging more to leave.[85] As early as 1994 Fumikage Nishi, of Nomura Securities, expressed a pessimistic view on the future of Tokyo as a financial centre: 'The only advantage it has is scale. But that will be insufficient, because without real deregulation, financial innovation in other Asian centres will rapidly outpace that in Japan.'[86] Lying at the heart of Tokyo's failure to develop as a global financial centre were the regulatory restraints under which it laboured, ranging from the continuing adherence to a version of the Glass–Steagall Act through the near monopoly of the Tokyo Stock Exchange that allowed it to resist reform, to the use of anti-gambling laws that stifled the development of derivatives. It was only slowly that these restrictions were relaxed. On 1 April 1998 Japan experienced its own Big Bang but, even then, many restrictions were retained as a way of protecting Japanese banks and financial markets from foreign competition.[87]

Of all other financial centres in Asia the one that gained most from Tokyo's lack of competitiveness was Singapore. Singapore was an island state with a very small domestic market and lacked access to its much larger neighbour, Malaysia, which even attempted to create a rival financial centre in Labuan, a small island of the coast of Borneo, in the 1990s. In the absence of a captive base Singapore had no alternative but to target the international market, and the activities neglected by Japan posed an easy target. As Philip Coggan reported in 1996, 'A successful financial services sector is an essential part of Singapore's long-term development plans. Financial services offer the kind of high value, high-tech businesses in which Singapore has a competitive advantage over its neighbours in the region.'[88] One area that Singapore specialized in as a financial centre was foreign exchange

[84] Ian Rodger, 'Brisk activity on most fronts', 18th November 1993; Ian Rodger, 'Private banking provides fuel', 2nd December 1993; Ian Rodger, 'The real time breakthrough', 6th December 1994; Frances Williams, 'The Savile Row of asset management', 31st October 1997; William Hall, 'Swiss exchange aims to lick stamp duty', 26th October 1998; Roxane McMeeken, 'Dublin closing the gap in race for hottest investments', 7th June 2001.

[85] Gerard Baker, 'Regional rivals hot on its heels', 19th October 1994; Emiko Terazono, 'Long road back to Tokyo', 28th March 1996; Nikki Tait, 'Sydney exchange sees future in commodities', 3rd January 1997; Vincent Boland, 'A place in the holy trinity', 26th March 1998; Gillian Tett, 'A bang or a whimper?', 1st April 1998.

[86] Gerard Baker, 'Regional rivals hot on its heels', 19th October 1994.

[87] Emiko Terazono, 'Known for know-how', 24th March 1993; Robert Thomson, 'High hopes demolished', 24th March 1993; Emiko Terazono, 'JGB futures stir bad memories', 20th October 1993; Emiko Terazono, 'Patience is running out', 26th May 1994; Gerard Baker, 'Regional rivals hot on its heels', 19th October 1994; William Dawkins, 'A big bang in slow motion', 10th December 1996; William Dawkins, 'Last chance to catch up', 25th March 1997; Gillian Tett, 'Big Bang or just a whimper?', 26th March 1998; Gillian Tett, 'Complex timetable for reforms package', 26th March 1998; Vincent Boland, 'Why Tokyo's bankers are definitely not for tennis', 26th March 1998; Vincent Boland, 'Stock exchange has taken steps to protect its position', 26th March 1998; Gillian Tett, 'A bang or a whimper?', 1st April 1998; Gillian Tett, 'Facing up to a wave of foreign competitors', 21st June 1999.

[88] Philip Coggan, 'It's just a small problem', 8th February 1996.

trading capitalizing on the number of international banks with offices there because of its commercial, transport and telecommunications infrastructure. Building on this forex market Singapore became a major centre for futures trading, with contracts based on Tokyo's Nikkei stock index, Euroyen interest rates, and Japanese Government bonds. Also contributing to Singapore's success as an Asian financial centre was the uncertainty hanging over Hong Kong, which came under Chinese control in 1997. The re-emerging strength of Hong Kong as a financial centre after 1997, and the recovery of Tokyo after the reforms of the late 1990s, curbed the ambitions of the authorities in Singapore by the beginning of the twenty-first century. By then the focus was increasingly on making Singapore the financial hub for South East Asia and the development of specialist areas such as private banking and wealth management to cater for the growing number of Asian millionaires.[89] In many ways Singapore and Hong Kong were very similar as Asian financial centres, both being small island states sharing a common British heritage in terms of laws and institutions. The difference between the two, and it was a very important one, was the close relationship between Hong Kong and China, which became much greater in 1997 when sovereignty passed from the UK to the People's Republic. This relationship gave Hong Kong privileged access to the vast and rapidly developing Chinese financial market. Conversely, it exposed Hong Kong to the emerging competition coming from Shanghai, which the Chinese government were intent on promoting as an international financial centre from 1992 onwards.[90] Fred Hu, a managing director at Goldman Sachs and a professor at Tsinghua University, Beijing, provided a comparison between Hong Kong and Shanghai as financial centres in 2006 which came down in favour if the former: 'While Shanghai has enormous potential, its ambition has been hobbled by mainland China's fragile institutions—the underdeveloped legal system, onerous and unpredictable regulations, a complex and punishing tax regime, the heavy and visible hand of government interference and rampant corruption. By contrast, rule of law, free press, open markets, transparency, unfettered capital mobility and a fully convertible currency are among Hong Kong's core assets.'[91] Under these conditions Hong Kong not only re-established its position as one of Asia's leading financial centres, after the uncertainties posed by political transition, but also enhanced it through closer links with the economy of mainland China. The result by 2006 was that Asia possessed three important financial centres each with particular strengths: that of Tokyo lay with its command of the Japanese financial system; Singapore concentrated on serving the international community through niche products and markets that avoided locally-imposed taxes and regulations; Hong Kong's position lay more in the middle as it acted as the interface between China and the world with a foot in each camp.[92]

[89] Andrew Gowers, 'Island of integrity', 29th March 1993; Emiko Terazono, 'JGB futures stir bad memories', 20th October 1993; Gerard Baker, 'Regional rivals hot on its heels', 19th October 1994; Kieran Cooke, 'Rising hub of global trading', 6th June 1995; Kieran Cooke, 'Offshore Labuan hits snags', 19th September 1995; Philip Coggan, 'It's just a small problem', 8th February 1996; Justin Marozzi, 'Lure of the lion city', 18th February 1997; James Kynge, 'Ingenious new ideas for futures', 9th May 1997; Gillian Tett, 'Big Bang or just a whimper?', 26th March 1998; Peter Montagnon, 'Reforms with a muted bang', 31st March 1998; Naoko Nakamae, 'Rivals agree to bury the hatchet', 31st March 2000; John Turnbull, 'On a quest to boost financial flows', 11th April 2001; John Burton, 'City-state may need more than stability to become leader', 12th April 2006.

[90] Tony Walker, 'Dragon with an eye on its futures', 2nd April 1994; James Harding, 'First steps on the ladder', 19th May 1998; Francesco Guerrera, 'Top dog at home but needs to appeal abroad', 12th April 2006; Fred Hu, 'Staying ahead of the game', 24th October 2006.

[91] Fred Hu, 'Staying ahead of the game', 24th October 2006.

[92] Gerard Baker, 'Regional rivals hot on its heels', 19th October 1994; James Kynge, 'Exotics reach the major league', 9th May 1997; Naoko Nakamae, 'Rivals agree to bury the hatchet', 31st March 2000; John Turnbull, 'On a quest to boost financial flows', 11th April 2001; John Burton, 'City-state may need more than stability to become

In turn these major financial centres had to compete with others that were coming to the fore as domestic financial systems were modernized and barriers restricting outside access were removed, as was the case in South Korea, where Seoul was developing as a financial centre.[93] The problem for most countries spread across Asia was that, individually, they lacked the scale that could support a major financial centre and lacked the impetus towards integration being exhibited by the European Union. This can be seen across the Middle East where no state was in a position to generate sufficient activity to support a large domestic financial centre while regional rivalry prevented the emergence of an international one, despite attempts by the likes of Dubai.[94] The sleeping giant in Asia throughout the years between 1992 and 2007 was India. Though change was taking place and Mumbai was an important domestic financial centre the inconvertibility of the rupee and a host of internal and external restrictions and barriers prevented India fully engaging with the international financial community.[95] What was true for Asia also remained true for much of the rest of the world. In both Latin America and Africa countries were either too small to support a major financial centre or placed restrictions that made it difficult for their own financial systems to integrate with those of other countries. Though compartmentalization was disappearing it still remained a potent force preventing global financial integration.[96]

Conclusion

What was taking place between 1992 and 2007 was a fundamental transformation of global financial markets but without any major event or crisis to mark what was taking place. There was nothing like May Day in New York in the 1970s or Big Bang in London to catch the media's attention nor something as dramatic as the Global Financial Crisis of 2008 to provoke a fundamental shift. Instead, there was a gradual and continuous process of change whose cumulative effects were far more profound compared to anything that had happened in the 1970s or 1980s. The result was to change the landscape of financial markets across North America, Europe, Asia, and Australasia and make inroads into Latin America and Africa. Driving this change was the intervention of governments and the disruptive effects of the technological revolution. The latter was a long-term trend dating back to the invention of the telegraph and the telephone in the nineteenth century but it took the twin process of deregulation and the removal of barriers to unleash its full potential. The effects were far reaching in the 1990s and into the twenty-first century. They encouraged the growth of megabanks that were simultaneously universal and global. Such banks extended themselves across the entire range of financial activities and operated across the entire globe. Their size, scale, and diversification gave them the capacity to not only internalize markets but to use their own resources to become trusted counterparties able to respond

leader', 12th April 2006; Francesco Guerrera, 'Top dog at home but needs to appeal abroad', 12th April 2006; Fred Hu, 'Staying ahead of the game', 24th October 2006.

[93] Anna Fifield, 'S. Korea steps up its efforts to become a hub', 12th April 2006.

[94] Kevin Morrison, 'Dubai to launch gold futures', 29th June 2005; Joanna Chung, 'Middle Eastern businesses are looking towards the City for investors and to raise their profiles', 3rd February 2006.

[95] Krishna Guha, 'India's NSE shrugs off satellite failure', 10th October 1997; John Burton, 'City-state may need more than stability to become leader', 12th April 2006; Khozem Merchant, 'Towering ambitions, masses of capital but let down by its poor infrastructure', 12th April 2006.

[96] Damian Fraser, 'Propelled into a new financial age', 20th October 1993.

to the sales or purchases of others. The effect was to transform the nature of markets, undermining the ability of exchanges to exercise control even in those areas where they had previously been dominant. Increasingly exchanges were being marginalized as trading became an inter-bank activity. Stock exchanges, in particular, found their very existence threatened while commodity exchanges had to re-invent themselves as markets for financial derivatives to survive. In this new world regulators were at a loss to know how to respond. The era of control and compartmentalization was over but what was to replace it remained unclear. It was becoming obvious that exchanges could not be relied upon to provide orderly markets, not least because they could not be trusted to act impartially, while most trading took place beyond their confines. The solution that emerged was to turn to the megabanks despite the risks that posed. The failure of such an institution had the capacity to destabilize the entire global financial system such was the level and extent of their interconnections. However, such an event was no longer contemplated as these megabanks devised models of business practice that appeared to eliminate the risks inherent in banking and could cope with the volatility of financial markets. At the international level central bankers introduced rules intended to make banking safer, avoiding the scourge of the liquidity crisis through the move from the lend-and-hold to the originate-and-distribute model. These rules were followed by the megabanks giving regulators the confidence that they could be relied on to deliver stability and resilience. Domestically, central banks already worked closely with the most systemically-important banks, as it was through them that they exercised monetary policy on behalf of national governments and intervened to maintain a degree of stability. As the megabanks exhibited their ability to prove resilient in several crises during the period from 1990 to 2007 it was not altogether surprising that governments, central banks, and regulators turned to them as a replacement for the control and compartmentalization strategy of the past that had failed in the 1970s.

8

Banks and Brokers, 1993–2006

Introduction

There was a banking crisis in the early 1990s centred on non-performing loans to third world countries, the property sector and leveraged buy-outs. This left many banks holding loans that could not be repaid, creating a natural reluctance to take risks. Where borrowers could maintain interest payments, or agree a plan for repaying the debt over time, banks rolled-over the loans. In other cases banks were left with either large losses or holding assets they could not sell. As David Lavarack, at Barclays Bank, admitted in 1993, 'We have been lending much too cheaply, because we have actually provided risk capital.'[1] Under these circumstances banks pulled back from lending where there was any risk of default, as with third world countries, or the possibility that the funds would become trapped in assets that could not be disposed of, such as commercial and industrial property. It was only slowly that banks returned to more generous lending policies, especially to businesses. In the meantime bank customers, especially large companies, made alternative arrangements. Rather than borrowing from a bank such companies turned to the issue of stocks and bonds, which were then sold to investors. Though all this was a standard response to any crisis, being reversed once banks built up reserves and confidence returned, this was not the case in the 1990s. By 1998 Simon Kuper reported that 'The banking sector is in flux.'[2] What was taking place was a permanent shift away from the lend-and-hold model of banking to the originate-and-distribute one, though the pace and scale was very unevenly spread around the world. As late as 2006 Chinese companies relied on banks for 90 per cent of their external finance, though they were beginning to turn to the bond market, which was a cheaper source of funds for large companies[3] Rather than raise finance through loans from banks, governments and companies issued bonds instead. Rather than accept the interest paid on bank deposits savers bought these bonds. Rather than hold loans until maturity, banks repackaged them as transferable securities and sold them on, releasing funds which could be used for further lending, and so repeat the cycle. Rather than act as intermediaries between savers and borrowers, banks moved into the realm of creators and retailers of financial assets. Helping drive this shift in the 1990s was the attitude of regulators. Increasingly those with authority over banking favoured the originate-and-distribute model over the lend-and-hold one. The former was believed to provide greater protection in the event of a liquidity crisis, and that was the event banking regulators most feared because of the threat of contagion it posed, as that could destabilize the entire financial system. Whereas a bank was tied to a borrower to whom it lent money, when that transaction took the form of a bond the resulting asset could be sold. In that way a bank could redistribute the risk it was exposed to while, if a liquidity crisis occurred, it could release the funds necessary to meet

[1] John Gapper, 'The equation that didn't add up', 2nd February 1993.
[2] Simon Kuper, 'Old divide is starting to crumble', 23rd January 1998.
[3] Jamil Anderlini, 'China's corporate bonds come of age', 15th June 2007.

Banks, Exchanges, and Regulators: Global Financial Markets from the 1970s. Ranald Michie, Oxford University Press (2021).

DOI: 10.1093/oso/9780199553730.003.0008

it by selling bonds, even at a loss, whereas that was difficult to achieve with loans, and certainly could not be achieved quickly.[4]

Reinvention of Banking

At the forefront of the changes taking place in global banking were developments in the USA. What was happening in the USA provided both a model to be followed and a disruptive force as US banks competed with banks located elsewhere in the world. US banks were being forced to reinvent themselves in the face of a rapidly altering world. The certainties of the past had been slowly crumbling since the 1970s but the pace of change was accelerating, as Richard Waters observed in 1993: 'The business of taking deposits and making loans—the traditional credit intermediation process of banks—has declined as large companies have turned to the securities and commercial paper markets to raise money from investors directly.'[5] Large companies were able to provide from internal sources the finance they required on a day-to-day basis rather than rely on banks for credit. Where they did look to banks for support was in raising large amounts of money for individual projects, including acquisitions at home and abroad. In response commercial banks like JP Morgan and trust companies such as Bankers Trust, led the way in moving into new financial products and markets, and they were followed by other commercial banks. It involved a new relationship between a bank and its business customers that merged the long-separated practices of commercial and investment banking. In turn the challenge posed by the commercial banks, using the leverage supplied by their depositor base, put pressure on the investment banks to match their scale. In 1997 one of the leading investment banks, Morgan Stanley, merged with one of the leading brokerage houses, Dean Witter, putting it in a position to offer institutional investors and corporate borrowers the expertise of the former and the retail distribution of the latter. In 2000 the investment banks went a step further by acquiring the dealers who made markets in the stocks they issued and traded. Merrill Lynch bought Herzog, Heine Geduld, who traded in Nasdaq stocks, while Goldman Sachs purchased Spear Leeds and Kellogg, a specialist at the NYSE. Taking these investment banks in another direction was the merger in 1997 between the brokers, Smith Barney, and the investment bank, Salomon Brothers, putting both under the control of the insurance company, Travelers. In turn Travelers merged with Citibank in 1998 creating a huge and highly-diversified financial group stretching from retail banking through investment banking and broking to insurance. This then prompted commercial bank mergers, such as that in 2000 between JP Morgan with Chase Manhattan Bank, creating a combined business that employed 102,000 people in 2001.

The result was the emergence of a group of US megabanks that engaged in both commercial and investment banking and increasingly diversified into every branch of financial activity. In 1999 Chase Manhattan had bought the San Francisco investment bank, Hambrecht and Quist as a way of moving into the financing of California's booming high-technology industry. Roger Taylor observed in 1999 how the 'The mainstream banks have taken over the industry.'[6] Also indicative of the changes was the conversion of the investment banks from partnerships into companies, with Goldman Sachs being one of the last

[4] Gillian Tett, 'Sub-prime in its context', 19th November 2007.
[5] Richard Waters, 'Easy option or unnecessary risk', 22nd July 1993.
[6] Roger Taylor, 'Shift in power accompanies a move westwards', 29th September 1999.

to do so in 1999. This gave them the scale and resources to compete with the commercial banks that were moving into their territory. By 2001 Citigroup employed 57,000 in corporate and investment banking division alone, placing it on a par with the leading Wall Street investment banks, where the top four (Goldman Sachs, Morgan Stanley, Merrill Lynch, and Bear Stearns) employed 170,000 in total. The repeal of the legislation that had prevented both nationwide and universal banking was little more than a belated recognition of the reality that was emerging in the 1990s. The passage of the Gramm–Leach–Bliley Act in 1999 finally swept away the divisions between commercial and investment banking. In 2002 the president of the securities arm of Bank of America, Carter McClelland, was able to claim as a consequence that 'We are able to have a conversation (with our corporate customers) that includes capital and investment banking services.'[7] Nevertheless, the legacy of barriers between different parts of the banking system acted as a restraint on integration, as it was difficult to bring together long-independent businesses. In addition, the bank deposit guarantee scheme, introduced in the 1930s, continued to distort the pattern of saving in the USA because investors took the view that, as long as their money was guaranteed, they should go for the best return regardless of the risks associated with individual institutions. Similarly, requirements regarding the assets that they held steered banks towards marketable securities rather than loans, stimulating the repackaging of mortgage debt as bonds and their subsequent resale. That then led to the general process of securitization through which banks turned illiquid financial assets such as loans, consumer instalment contracts, leases, and receivables into liquid securities that traded, to varying degrees, in the secondary debt capital market.[8]

It was the pattern of banking that developed in the USA in the 1990s that provided a model for the rest of the world, especially the UK. The outcome was a rapid convergence of banking activities in the UK that included the conversion of a number of the specialist mortgage providers, the building societies, into banks. The increasingly competitive environment that emerged encouraged either mergers between different institutions or

[7] Gary Silverman, 'Level playing field still elusive', 22nd February 2002.

[8] Richard Waters, 'Easy option or unnecessary risk', 22nd July 1993; Tracy Corrigan, 'Divisions hazy in OTC derivatives clearing battle debate', 13th September 1993; Laurie Morse, 'A two-pronged development', 20th October 1993; John Gapper, 'Transatlantic lesson on passing on risks', 22nd October 1993; John Gapper and Tracy Corrigan, 'Formidable rivals on a shifting battleground', 4th March 1994; John Gapper and Richard Lapper, 'Warburg breaks the bond', 11th January 1995; John Gapper, 'Big is beautiful once again', 6th October 1995; Barry Riley, 'Growth on a grand scale', 24th April 1997; Simon Kuper, 'Banks trade places as race for foreign exchange intensifies', 20th May 1997; Michael Dempsey, 'Trend-setters of the financial world', 2nd July 1997; Simon Kuper, 'Merrill makes up for lost time on forex', 14th July 1997; Tracy Corrigan and Clay Harris, 'Thundering herd comes storming in out of the blue', 20th November 1997; George Graham and Jane Martinson, 'Handful of firms set for a dominant role', 20th November 1997; Simon Kuper, 'Old divide is starting to crumble', 23rd January 1998; George Graham, 'Mixed fortunes in banking's second tier', 2nd March 1998; Edward Alden, 'Gains for US houses', 25th May 1999; Roger Taylor, 'Shift in power accompanies a move westwards', 29th September 1999; Vincent Boland, 'Market shows greater value and maturity', 28th June 2000; Gary Silverman, 'Grand vision of the future client', 28th January 2001; John Willman, 'Newly rich press for service', 26th January 2001; Gary Silverman, 'Bottom line is always in sight', 26th January 2001; John Labate, 'Fragmented trading boosts their worth', 26th January 2001; Charles Pretzlik and Gary Silverman, 'Investment bank job cuts reach 25,000', 13th August 2001; Charles Pretzlik and Gary Silverman, 'City partnerships that were forced to grow up', 8th January 2002; Gary Silverman and Charles Pretzlik, 'Bankers suffer an identity crisis as hard times hit', 22nd February 2002; Robert Clow, 'Dull but reliable business wins respect', 22nd February 2002; Gary Silverman, 'Level playing field still elusive', 22nd February 2002; Rebecca Bream, 'More debt and equity mergers on the cards', 9th September 2002; Vincent Boland, 'Banks find a way to spread their risk', 18th February 2003; Charles Batchelor, 'Taking the mystery out of securitisation', 28th September 2004; Charles Batchelor, 'Joining Europe's mainstream', 29th November 2004; Peter Thal Larsen and David Wighton, 'Record earning as sector recovers', 27th January 2005; Paul J. Davies, 'Concerns over rapid growth of CMBS deals among banks', 24th March 2006; David Wighton, 'Goldman buy-out lending soars', 17th July 2006; FT Reporters, 'Solid capital has the upper hand', 23rd September 2008; Peter Thal Larsen and Greg Farrell, 'Landscape shifts for investment banks', 23rd September 2008.

aggressive expansion to achieve the scale necessary to support a diversified business.[9] Reflecting on the mergers that had taken place John Willman concluded in 2000 that, 'Retail banking looks set to end up dominated by a few large groups, with smaller niche businesses serving particular markets.'[10] The verdict of Andrew Bolger in 2005 was that 'large banks were well placed to capitalise on market trends, because their size, strong profitability and business diversity helped them leverage growth opportunities and protected against predatory threats.'[11] In 2006, Jane Croft judged that, 'These days size does matter because expensive branches, technology and staff mean banks become more profitable if they can do more business with the same infrastructure.'[12] The competition between banks became intense, with John Wilman reporting in 2000 that 'Winning new business has been fiercely competitive for some years.'[13] Under these conditions British banks began copying US practice such as in the use of securitization, involving the repackaging of loans for sale to investors, including fellow banks. The issue of mortgage bonds by UK banks climbed from $25bn in 2002 to $200bn in 2006, for example.[14] UK commercial banks also attempted to enter investment banking, though with limited success as they could not compete with their US rivals, as these were well established in London. Accompanying this rapid change in the structure and practice of British banking after 1990 was a heavy investment in technology, so as to reduce the costs attached to servicing customers, and maximizing leverage when applied to both capital and deposits.[15]

Around the world banks in other countries followed the UK example and copied US banking practices, as their business customers looked to them to provide an equivalent range and depth of financial services. As businesses merged to create larger units they were better able to seek alternative sources of funding than that provided by banks. Evidence of the switch can be found in continental Europe which had traditionally been more dependent on bank finance than the USA. In 1995 European companies relied on banks for 75 per cent of their external long-term finance and bond markets for 25 per cent. By 2000 the ratio had fallen to around 66 per cent/34 per cent. European universal banks, such as Deutsche Bank, BNP Paribas, ABN Amro, and UBS, were well positioned to respond to this shift as they were equally at home in commercial and investment banking, but they faced competition from the US investment banks that had long experience in handling new issues and commanded a strong distribution network. That competition encouraged European banks to adopt some of the more recent US practices, such as the securitization

[9] John Gapper, 'The equation that didn't add up', 2nd February 1993; Richard Lapper, 'A rosy future for futures spells a charmed Liffe', 14th January 1995; John Plender, 'The box that can never be shut', 28th February 1995; Richard Lapper and Conner Middelmann, 'Risks of a concrete proposal', 21st August 1996; John Gapper, 'When the smile is wiped off', 8th March 1997; James Mackintosh, 'Balance of Power may be changing', 26th May 2000; John Willman, 'Banking on borrowed time', 6th November 2000; Andrew Bolger, 'Big players in the European game', 12th October 2005; Vanessa Houlder, 'Financial services' tax out of proportion', 7th November 2005; Peter Thal Larsen, 'How long can good times last?', 8th November 2005; Paul J. Davies, 'Securitisations set to keep on robust growth path', 3rd February 2006; Jane Croft, 'Profits in the billions underline the vital role of banking in the economy', 18th February 2006; Jane Croft, 'Bite-size former building societies turn heads of investors', 1st April 2006.

[10] John Willman, 'Banking on borrowed time', 6th November 2000.

[11] Andrew Bolger, 'Big players in the European game', 12th October 2005.

[12] John Willman, 'Banking on borrowed time', 6th November 2000.

[13] John Willman, 'Banking on borrowed time', 6th November 2000.

[14] Paul J. Davies, 'Raising the roof with covered bonds', 2nd November 2005; Jane Croft, 'Bite-size former building societies turn heads of investors', 1st April 2006; Paul J. Davies, 'Securitisation provides liquidity', 26th November 2008.

[15] John Willman, 'Banking on borrowed time', 6th November 2000; Emma Dunkley, 'Challenger banks branch out into business loans', 5th November 2015.

of debt and then sale to investors, as this would provide them with liquid funds and create scope to make fresh loans. In Japan the combination of commercial and investment banking continued to face legal obstacles because of Article 65 of the Securities Exchange Law, which was their version of the Glass–Steagall Act. Pressure to relax this law grew in the 1990s as companies turned to issuing bonds, rather than borrowing from banks, as a way of raising finance. The financial crisis experienced in Japan in 1997–8 revealed the lack of liquidity among its banks, and encouraged them to securitize loans and sell them on, while driving companies to switch to issuing bonds as a replacement of bank finance. As a result banks began putting pressure on the government to allow them to issue bonds. However, the Ministry of Finance exerted a tight control over financial deregulation and only permitted gradual and limited liberalization. Nevertheless, it had to relent as US banks began invading the Japanese market in the 1990s. Even then it was not be until 1999 that banks and brokers were allowed to compete with each other. There was an understandable fear in Japan that the relaxation of barriers between different types of banks would work in favour of the large US institutions that were already present in the country. By 1998 Citibank was building its own retail banking business in Japan while JP Morgan was forming an investment banking one. Merrill Lynch already possessed a strong presence after buying the network of thirty-three branches belonging the fourth largest Japanese broker, Yamaichi, after it had collapsed in 1997. The result was to drive Japanese banking towards the model developing in the USA, both in terms of structure and practice but nothing to the same extent in terms of exposure to illiquid property assets.[16]

Between 1992 and 2007 the compartmentalization of banking behind national boundaries and within distinct activities finally ended to be replaced by the growing power of the megabanks. This did not apply to all banking as the provision of retail services continued to take place on a largely national, or even local, basis because of the difficulty of managing such a business internationally in a world that remained divided by currencies, laws, taxes, regulations, languages, and even cultures. In retail banking what was important was direct contact with customers through an efficient distribution network, whether that involved branches or call centres, and the ability to develop trusted products that appealed to local demand. Even within the USA, and even more so across the EU, the removal of barriers to the spread of banking did not result in the immediate dominance of a few large banks managed from a single financial centre and providing the full range of financial services. Where the trend towards both globalization and universality did manifest itself was in wholesale banking, which involved providing a small number of corporate borrowers and institutional

[16] John Gapper and Tracy Corrigan, 'Formidable rivals on a shifting battleground', 4th March 1994; John Gapper and Norma Cohen, 'They've really got a hold on EU', 20th April 1994; Gerard Baker, 'Ripple effect of Tokyo's Big Bang', 24th November 1994; John Gapper and David Wighton, 'A squeeze too far in the City', 4th May 1995; Charles Smith, 'The pulse is weak', 28th March 1996; Gwen Robinson, 'Japanese go straight to markets to raise cash', 15th October 1996; Gillian Tett, 'Complex timetable for reforms package', 26th March 1998; Gillian Tett, 'Rivalry to replace cosy collaboration', 26th March 1998; Vincent Boland, 'Why Tokyo's bankers are definitely not for tennis', 26th March 1998; Gillian Tett, 'Wave of corporate flirting', 26th March 1998; Gillian Tett, 'Retail defences may start to fall', 21st June 1999; Charles Smith, 'Opportunities to ease the pain', 21st June 1999; Charles Smith, 'Banking parent provides strength', 21st June 1999; Louise Lucas, 'Esoteric products tap door', 17th December 1999; Paul Abrahams, 'State sales are likely to keep the ball rolling', 17th December 1999; Naoko Nakamae, 'Appetite for Samurais grows', 17th December 1999; Gillian Tett, 'Silence conceals significant tale', 8th May 2000; Gillian Tett, 'Crunch brings some benefits', 8th May 2000; Naoko Nakamae, 'Racing along the comeback trail', 8th May 2000; Charles Pretzlik, 'Euro gives a boost to bond markets', 26th May 2000; John Willman, 'US giants throw down gauntlet', 26th January 2001; Charles Batchelor and Alex Skorecki, 'German banks sign up for true sale', 10th July 2003; Stephen Fidler, 'Basel 2 boosts Europe's repo market', 29th November 2005; David Oakley and Gillian Tett, 'European bond market puts US in the shade', 15th January 2007; David Wighton, 'Prince shows his daring with move for Nikko', 7th March 2007.

investors with the full range of services they required. The demand for such services became a major influence on banks in the 1990s as the barriers between countries and different financial activities largely disappeared. Global fund managers required a bank to handle large and complex transactions while multinational companies looked to banks that could provide them with sophisticated ways of managing both their demands for credit and capital and employing temporarily idle funds. The result was the concentration of wholesale financial activity in the hands of a decreasing number of global banks. It was these banks that were regarded as the most trusted counterparties by fund managers when acquiring or disposing of assets, by corporate borrowers when seeking finance, and by each other when conducting deals in the money market and across different currencies and financial products. In 1994 over half the payments handled by Swift (Society for Worldwide Interbank Financial Telecommunication) was generated by only thirty-five banks out of the 4300 that used the service.[17]

Within wholesale banking there was an increasing pervasion of investment banking practices during the 1990s and into the twenty-first century. As early as 1993 Robert Peston had remarked:

> Investment banking habits have been having an even more profound effect on the relationship between banker and corporate client. Investment bankers regard all assets in their balance sheets as tradeable. Trading these assets is normally easy, because most of the assets are in the form of securities. However, only a relatively small proportion of the assets of most banks are securities. Most of their balance sheets consist of loans, either to companies or individuals, which have traditionally not been tradeable. In the past, when a bank made a loan to a company or individual, it was in effect contracting to maintain a relationship with the borrower till the loan was repaid. But not any longer. Many banks now want to be able to sell these loans. The reason for this change is that the worldwide recession has left banks with little spare capital. The ability to trade in loans allows a bank to rapidly adjust the size of its balance sheet to a level best suited to its capital resources.[18]

By 1995 John Gapper observed that 'Commercial banks are trying to offset a squeeze on margins from lending to large companies by moving into investment banking.'[19] Conversely, in 1997 George Graham and Jane Martinson noted that 'Investment banks are now hungry for the more stable fees they earn from asset management to offset their volatile and declining trading and underwriting profits.'[20] The convergence of commercial and investment banking practices in a single business did create tensions, which John Plender and Andrew Fisher reported on in 1995: 'Marrying the culture of commercial banking to investment banking is not easy.'[21] What was involved was the application of the financial engineering techniques developed by the investment banks to the wider banking market, involving the securitization of assets and much greater leverage through increasing the loan-to-deposit

[17] John Gapper, 'The equation that didn't add up', 2nd February 1993; Maggie Urry, 'A question of sink or swim on the main market', 4th March 1993; Vanessa Houlder, 'Weighed down with debts', 5th March 1993; Vanessa Houlder, 'Buildings take on new air of respectability', 25th May 1993; Vanessa Houlder, 'Expensive vote of confidence', 3rd June 1993; Richard Waters, 'New box of risk-management tricks', 20th October 1993; John Gapper, 'Lending climate tightens banking disciplines', 4th March 1994; Tracy Corrigan, 'Banks chase new business', 26th May 1994; Charles Pretzlik, 'Euro gives a boost to bond markets', 26th May 2000.

[18] Robert Peston, 'Loans that change their spots', 19th July 1993.

[19] John Gapper, 'Big is beautiful once again', 6th October 1995.

[20] George Graham and Jane Martinson, 'Handful of firms set for a dominant role', 20th November 1997.

[21] John Plender and Andrew Fisher, 'No end to the wave of buying', 16th June 1995.

ratio. This led to existing loans being repackaged as marketable securities as that met the needs of investors looking for higher yields and greater flexibility while releasing funds that banks could apply to further lending. By 2000 Aline van Duyn was reporting that, the 'Use of securitization, where debt repayments are backed by the future cash flows of a company's assets, is spreading around the world.'[22]

Megabanks

This switch to the originate-and-distribute model was associated with the growing power wielded by a small number of US investment banks, led by Goldman Sachs, Merrill Lynch, and Morgan Stanley; their rivals among US commercial banks, such as Citibank and JP Morgan; and a few European universal banks that were building up their international operations, like Deutsche Bank and Dresdner Bank from Germany, ABN Amro and ING from the Netherlands; and Credit Suisse and UBS from Switzerland. Initially, these European banks saw the acquisition of British investment banks as a quick route to international expansion and so a number followed Deutsche Bank, which had bought Morgan Grenfell in 1989. In 1995 alone Dresdner Bank bought Kleinwort Benson, Swiss Bank Corporation gained control of SG Warburg, and ING took ownership of Barings, after its spectacular collapse. Despite London's position as a global financial centre this strategy did not deliver the expected outcome. What it revealed was that, without a large Wall Street base these European banks, and also those from Japan, lacked the scale, expertise, connections, and capacity to match their US rivals. Credit Suisse was the only European bank to make a significant impact on the huge US market in the 1990s, and that was because of its control of the large US investment bank, First Boston. Recognizing this weakness the European banks sought to remedy it by buying their way in to Wall Street. In 1999 Credit Suisse bought Donaldson, Luftkin, and Jenrette; Deutsche Bank acquired Bankers Trust while Paine Webber fell to UBS. In numbers alone it meant these European universal banks could now match their US rivals. In 2001 employment numbers at Goldman Sachs were 23,000, Morgan Stanley on 64,500 and Merrill Lynch with 72,000 while Credit Suisse had 30,000, UBS 39,000, and Deutsche Bank 47,500. Through organic growth and acquisitions these European universal banks did pose an increasing challenge to their US rivals by the early twenty-first century, having had long experience of combining investment and commercial banking in a single business, and so being able to provide even the largest companies with loans, arrange issues of stocks and bonds, and handle the complex financial arrangements that mergers and acquisitions involved.[23] In 2002 Jorge Calderon, global head of debt capital markets at Deutsche Bank, considered that current trends in global business favoured universal banks like his: 'Increasingly, companies are looking for strategic partners and are looking for a mixture of bank borrowings and capital markets borrowing.'[24]

This merging of commercial and investment banking practices did cause some concern because of the greater risks it posed, especially in the UK, which was an early convert. As early as 1995 Antonia Sharpe expressed her fears that because 'A vigorous price war is gathering momentum in the increasingly cut-throat world of UK corporate banking' the

[22] Aline van Duyn, 'Bond markets extend to smaller firms', 19th May 2000.
[23] Peter Thal Larsen and Francesco Guerrera, 'Investment banks' future questioned', 16th September 2008.
[24] Rebecca Bream, 'Fixed-income business stays in the limelight', 22nd February 2002.

resulting competition 'had forced down lending margins to the point where banks might not be charging enough to compensate for the risks they are taking' and there was a 'danger that banks may engage in reckless lending, which could put the domestic banking system under pressure'.[25] A few years later Martin Wolf was of the opinion that the transformed nature of banks had increased the risks of failure with catastrophic consequences for the economy. He was of the opinion that 'Individually and, even more so, collectively, banks are a menace.' His solution was to split up banks into those that invested only in liquid assets and managed the payment system. That would leave the rest of the banking business to be handled by others. Though that was his preferred option he was aware of the impracticability of his suggestion at the time but concluded, nevertheless, that 'The days of banks that offered everything to everyone should end. The price they impose is not worth paying.'[26] What Wolff was contrasting at the time was the relatively trouble-free business of the banks that focused on domestic retail banking and mortgage lending compared to the losses experienced by those that engaged in lending to borrowers in Asia and Russia. The latter had become heavily influenced by mathematical models that provided precise measurements of potential gains and losses from holding a particular investment portfolio over a specified period. The flaw in these models, that underpinned the originate-and-distribute model, was the assumption of liquidity because a market always existed through which these bonds could be sold, even in a crisis. In contrast, in the lend-and-hold model there was no such assumption of liquidity, which acted as a restraint on the loans made, in terms of both amount and quality. Many bankers were fully aware of the difference between the two models, such as Cees Mass, chief financial officer of ING, the Dutch Bank that had bought Barings after its collapse in 1995. He commented in 1998 that, 'The problem is that regular risk-management systems, particularly for market risk, take as their starting point that there are markets. In a financial crisis there is no liquidity and no market, and that turns market risk into event risk and credit risk.'[27]

Nevertheless, the problem was believed to apply only in those countries with under-developed financial systems, which lacked deep markets, and not the likes of the USA, the UK, Continental Europe, and Japan. In any case the global banks based in these countries could rely on government support in the event of a crisis, being 'too big to fail' according to Peter Martin in 2002.[28] However, the possibility of failure was regarded as highly unlikely because their size and structure delivered a degree of resilience that no bank had ever possessed. Many expressed complete confidence in the resilience of those banks following the originate-and-distribute model. One was the US economist, Stephen Cecchetti in 2000: 'Instead of transforming deposits into loans, and retaining substantial risk on their balance sheets, banks are increasingly acting simply as brokers with a much closer match between the risk characteristics of their assets and liabilities. As a result, the US financial system is much less likely to suffer disruptions brought on by bank failures than it was even five years ago.'[29] By publicly praising the US model of banking prominent US economists encouraged its global adoption. Their views gained even more credibility in the wake of the collapse of the dot.com boom in 2000, as no bank failures followed that event. In 2003 Charles Pretzlik observed that 'It is one of the most remarkable features of the recent economic and

[25] Antonia Sharpe, 'A shift in the balance of power', 5th July 1995.
[26] Martin Wolf, 'Why banks are dangerous', 6th January 1998.
[27] George Graham, 'Stark Staring Bankers', 5th October 1998.
[28] Peter Martin, 'Trading on dangerous ground', 12th February 2002.
[29] Stephen Cecchetti, 'A legal challenge for Europe's markets', 17th August 2000.

financial markets instability that there have been no serious casualties among the banks.'[30] Under these conditions the risks exposed in the 1997–8 crisis faded from view and banks were encouraged to adopt the originate-and-distribute model because of its apparent success. As a result it was increasingly applied to all aspects of a bank's business including the routine activities of making short-term loans to customers and financing property purchases, management buy-outs, and take-over bids. These areas of domestic finance in developed countries had been the ones considered safe in the late 1990s compared to loans to emerging economies. Ignored by most were the risks being run by banks through an exposure to illiquid assets such as property of all kind and entire businesses, financed by short-term borrowing, as this was masked by the use of transferable securities and special purpose investment subsidiaries. This change in bank behaviour was supported by regulators, in the belief that the new ways of doing business reduced the risks being run through increased liquidity and greater diversification.

In the 1990s the structure and practice of global banking increasingly tilted in favour of those banks that could afford the overheads associated with a high-volume/low-margin business and could utilize the advantages provided by a strong balance sheet whether to supply funds to corporate borrowers or assets to institutional investors. The successful global banks were generating more and more of their profits from sophisticated trading systems which were expensive to develop and maintain and so also required a high volume of activity. It was only those banks with a strong capital base that could survive the fluctuations in the volume of business and the volatility in markets. The conclusion drawn by John Gapper in 1997 was that 'The large US investment banks have managed to persuade many issuers and investors around the world that they alone have the expertise and financial strength to carry off the biggest and most complex deals. They have won leading roles as advisers on the biggest privatisations and cross-border deals.'[31] The more that banking business flowed to these banks the more competitive they became because they were able to use the profits generated to invest in additional staff and advanced technology. An estimate made in 1997 indicated that a switch to flat screens could increase the density of trading desks in a bank's dealing room by 20 per cent, so expanding capacity without any additional cost for space. These global banks could also buy niche providers of those financial products that they did not already offer and expand their coverage into new markets. By 2001 in the view of James Mackintosh 'The sheer size of these banks makes it very difficult for others to compete head on, and has led several to start looking for alternative survival strategies.'[32] A group of largely US banks had achieved a position where they could treat the world as a single market for a wholesale banking services. They posed a threat to those that still focused on their national markets, forcing them to either retreat into niche areas or attempt to become global themselves. These global banks were pushing down the fees they could charge and narrowing the spread between buying and selling prices. Under these circumstances only the largest banks could prosper through leveraging their large balance sheets, investing in technology and expert staff, diversifying their activities, and opening offices around the world.[33]

[30] Charles Pretzlik, 'Maintaining a resilience to risk—and shocks', 1st October 2003.

[31] John Gapper, 'A concentration of firepower', 31st January 1997.

[32] James Mackintosh, 'Venerable names will disappear', 26th January 2001.

[33] James Blitz, 'New anxieties for the banks', 26th May 1993; Richard Waters, 'Easy option or unnecessary risk', 22nd July 1993; Tracy Corrigan, 'Divisions hazy in OTC derivatives clearing battle debate', 13th September 1993; Antonia Sharpe, 'Flexible friend for lenders', 28th October 1993; John Gapper and Tracy Corrigan, 'Formidable rivals on a shifting battleground', 4th March 1994; John Gapper and Norma Cohen, 'They've really got a hold on

The global ambitions of these megabanks were temporarily halted by the collapse of the speculative dot.com boom in 2001. In the wake of the bursting of that speculative bubble US banks not only cut their staff numbers, as business fell away and competition intensified, but also scaled back on the global expansion plans.[34] However, this was only a brief halt in their expansion plans. The likes of Goldman Sachs and Morgan Stanley, along with Deutsche Bank and UBS of Switzerland, remained committed to the universal model on a global scale, though there was now more caution over the precise strategy to be followed. Ken Moelis, head of investment banking in the USA for UBS Warburg made clear in 2002 that 'The underlying philosophy of globalisation—that investment banks need large distribution platforms to justify the costs of offering their products—has not changed.' He then added that, 'What is not clear, however, is what range of products they need to be able to offer to be competitive.'[35] Despite the setback posed by the collapse of the dot.com bubble the advance of global banking was not halted, and quickly resumed but in a new direction. Rather than having a strong stock market focus, from the promoting of high-technology companies to the trading in their shares, banks switched to money-market activity and securitization. The two were linked as the latter provided investors with the higher-yielding liquid assets in which short-term funds could be employed.[36] This led to an even greater embrace of the originate-and-distribute model of banking.

The resilience exhibited by the megabanks led those concerned about emerging risks in global finance to focus on the more peripheral parts of the financial system, especially hedge funds. This was the conclusion reached in 2006 by Nouriel Roubini, another US economist: 'Because of a greater regulation of banks, most financial intermediation in the past two decades has grown within this shadow system whose members are broker-dealers, hedge funds, private equity groups, structured investment vehicles and conduits, money-market funds and non-bank mortgage lenders.' It was this shadow banking system that was at risk in a crisis, not the banks themselves:

EU', 20th April 1994; George Black, 'Challenges for Swift', 15th November 1994; John Gapper, 'Uncertainty over expansion plans', 29th November 1994; John Gapper and Norma Cohen, 'Not yet the death knell', 10th December 1994; John Gapper and Richard Lapper, 'Warburg breaks the bond', 11th January 1995; John Gapper, 'Contest to guard the nest-egg', 7th February 1995; John Gapper and David Wighton, 'A squeeze too far in the City', 4th May 1995; Richard Lapper, 'Strategic global electronic connections', 16th November 1995; Philip Coggan, 'Obstacles to integration', 16th February 1996; John Kingman, 'Doors thrown open to the world', 28th March 1996; Graham Bowley, 'UK pushes for equal access to Target', 17th December 1996; John Gapper, 'A concentration of firepower', 31st January 1997; Barry Riley, 'Growth on a grand scale', 24th April 1997; Michael Dempsey, 'Trend-setters of the financial world', 2nd July 1997; George Graham and Jane Martinson, 'Handful of firms set for a dominant role', 20th November 1997; Samer Iskandar and Edward Luce, 'Big issue for Europe', 4th February 1998; George Graham, 'Mixed fortunes in banking's second tier', 2nd March 1998; Andrew Fisher, 'Exchanges set for a global shake-out', 13th January 1999; Richard Adams, 'Brokers alter shape of things to come', 25th June 1999; James Mackintosh, 'Venerable names will disappear', 26th January 2001; John Willman, 'US giants throw down gauntlet', 26th January 2001; Charles Pretzlik, 'Benefits to City would be only marginal at best, report concludes', 10th June 2003; Alex Skorecki, 'Web power helps smaller customers', 27th May 2004; Päivi Munter and Charles Batchelor, 'Citigroup coup stirs up emotions', 11th August 2004; Kate Burgess, 'Discord stirs in a polite world', 18th January 2005; Philip Stafford, 'Selling without making waves', 23rd November 2005; Chris Hughes, 'Lehman sets record on LSE', 14th August 2006; Sundeep Tucker, 'Deal flows spur change of tactic', 10th October 2006; Joanna Chung and Gillian Tett, 'Trading suspension raises eyebrows', 24th January 2007.

[34] Peter Thal Larsen, 'Heading for the trenches', 22nd February 2002.

[35] Peter Thal Larsen, 'Heading for the trenches', 22nd February 2002.

[36] Charles Pretzlik and Gary Silverman, 'Investment bank job cuts reach 25,000', 13th August 2001; Bayan Rahman and Charles Pretzlik, 'Merrill set to cut 20 brokerages', 28th December 2001; Peter Thal Larsen, 'Heading for the trenches', 22nd February 2002.

> Like banks, most members of this system borrow very short-term and in liquid ways, are more highly leveraged than banks (the exception being money-market funds) and lend and invest into more illiquid and long-term instruments. Like banks, they carry the risk that an otherwise solvent but liquid institution may be subject to a self-fulfilling and destructive run on its liquid liabilities. But unlike banks, which are sheltered from the risk of a run—via deposit insurance and central banks' lender-of-last-resort liquidity—most members of the shadow system did not have access to these firewalls that prevent runs.[37]

Ever since the collapse of Long-Term Capital Management in 1998 it was those newer institutions that used short-term funds to invest in long-term assets that caused greatest concern to those whose responsibility it was to maintain financial stability. Banks that had adopted the originate-and-distribute model were assumed to have shifted the risks that they ran in making loans onto others, while achieving a scale of operations that made them highly resilient through lessening their exposure to any specific loss.

In their place had appeared a new species of fund manager, the hedge fund, and it was these that were viewed with suspicion by the authorities regulating banks. Unlike the fund managers of the past, who adopted a buy and hold strategy, hedge funds used a buy and sell strategy or even a sell and buy strategy, and this required active trading and an appetite for risk-taking. By 2005 there were 8000 hedge funds managing assets valued $1,200bn, of which more than half ($700bn) was in the USA and the rest largely in Europe ($300bn). This was only 1.5 per cent of all assets managed by institutions but indicative of the active trading policy of the hedge-fund managers was that their buying and selling generated between 25 per cent and 50 per cent of commissions paid to brokers. Hedge funds aimed to make money irrespective of market conditions and did so by taking a contrary position to the general trend, dipping in and out of markets on a short-term basis. For this purpose they not only used banks as brokers but also borrowed either money or stocks on an extensive basis, depending on the position they took. This allowed them to tap into the inter-bank money market, where banks borrowed and lent amongst each other, and access the holdings of passive fund managers, like pension funds and insurance companies, who were willing to supply stocks and bonds on a temporary basis. These actions by hedge funds involved risks that banks and fund managers were reluctant to take themselves, because losses could expose them to a crisis of confidence among depositors and investors. Any crisis of confidence could be very serious for a bank as it could lead to a liquidity crisis leading to massive outflows of funds. In contrast, if a hedge fund collapsed the bank that had lent it money and carried out trading was not immediately implicated, and so could avoid a liquidity crisis, while those who had lent it stocks and bonds could expect to recover their assets over time. In the meantime substantial profits could be made through the business generated by the hedge funds.[38]

[37] Nouriel Roubini, 'The shadow banking system is unravelling', 22nd September 2006.

[38] Robert Peston, 'Loans that change their spots', 19th July 1993; John Plender and Andrew Fisher, 'No end to the wave of buying', 16th June 1995; John Gapper, 'Big is beautiful once again', 6th October 1995; Richard Lapper, 'An important new frontier is opening', 22nd November 1996; John Gapper, 'When the smile is wiped off', 8th March 1997; Simon Kuper, 'Banks trade places as race for foreign exchange intensifies', 20th May 1997; George Graham and Jane Martinson, 'Handful of firms set for a dominant role', 20th November 1997; Antonia Sharpe, 'A shift in the balance of power', 5th July 1995; Martin Wolf, 'Why banks are dangerous', 6th January 1998; Samer Iskandar and Edward Luce, 'Big issue for Europe', 4th February 1998; George Graham, 'Mixed fortunes in banking's second tier', 2nd March 1998; George Graham, 'Stark Staring Bankers', 5th October 1998; John Plender, 'Crisis in the making', 12th April 1999; Vincent Boland, 'Market shows greater value and maturity', 28th June 2000; Stephen Cecchetti, 'A legal challenge for Europe's markets', 17th August 2000; John Willman, 'US giants

Interdealer Brokers

The conventional view of a bank is that of a financial institution that accepts deposits from savers and then uses them to lend to borrowers. While fundamentally correct such a view is simplistic because the task of balancing the interests of both parties while generating a profit required banks to constantly lend to and borrow from each other. A bank's best customer was other banks not only to complete the circle of payments and receipts generated by customers but also as they matched assets against liabilities over time, space, and type. For these reasons the most active of financial markets were those that handled transactions between banks whether they were lending otherwise idle funds or accessing finance to cover a temporary shortage. A banking system was much more than a collection of individual banks for it involved the continuous interaction between all its separate components at many different levels in order to deliver the seamless web of contact and communication that underpinned a complex global economy. As Christine Moir said in 1996, 'the money market is a truly global one'.[39] This was a market without an institutional form for it connected all banks to each other either directly or indirectly. Illustrative of the web of connections was the fact that a financial information provider such as Reuters in 2004 supplied a network of 327,000 terminals worldwide while its rival, Bloomberg, had 180,000. Though the inter-bank market lacked a physical location, especially at a time when technology was eliminating delays in communication, it contained major hubs where bank offices clustered such as London and New York. It was in those centres that banks maintained the staff and equipment necessary to trade across the entire range of financial instruments that comprised the lifeblood of a modern money market, and where the speed of communication was fastest. In the face of the huge volume of transactions taking place in this inter-bank market governments left both surveillance and policing to the banks themselves rather than empowering any regulatory authority whether self or statutory. Stephen Pritchard observed in 2002 that 'banks are responsible for their own checks, both to filter out customers who might have links to crime and to detect transaction patterns that suggest

throw down gauntlet', 26th January 2001; Charles Pretzlik and Gary Silverman, 'Investment bank job cuts reach 25,000', 13th August 2001; Norma Cohen, 'Square mile faces growing threat from the east', 8th September 2001; Charles Pretzlik and Gary Silverman, 'City partnerships that were forced to grow up', 8th January 2002; Peter Martin, 'Trading on dangerous ground', 12th February 2002; Gary Silverman and Charles Pretzlik, 'Bankers suffer an identity crisis as hard times hit', 22nd February 2002; Rebecca Bream, 'Fixed-income business stays in the limelight', 22nd February 2002; Rebecca Bream, 'More debt and equity mergers on the cards', 9th September 2002; Pauline Skypala, 'Pressure on banks raising risk to buyers', 26th September 2003; Charles Pretzlik, 'Maintaining a resilience to risk—and shocks', 1st October 2003; Elizabeth Rigby, 'FSA examines a burgeoning industry', 22nd May 2004; Elizabeth Rigby, 'The bankers' new best friends', 22nd July 2004; Charles Batchelor, 'Long pedigree of the clearing house for short-term funds', 23rd July 2004; Charles Batchelor, 'Taking the mystery out of securitisation', 28th September 2004; Charles Batchelor, 'Joining Europe's mainstream', 29th November 2004; Kate Burgess, 'Discord stirs in a polite world', 18th January 2005; Peter Thal Larsen and David Wighton, 'Record earning as sector recovers', 27th January 2005; James Drummond, 'The attraction is still there', 27th January 2005; Peter Thal Larsen, 'One shocking bank failure deposited a stern warning in the history books', 19th February 2005; Philip Coggan, 'If they all rush for the exit at the same time', 28th May 2005; Charles Batchelor, 'Don't get carried away by the lure of cheap borrowing', 28th May 2005; Philip Stafford, 'Selling without making waves', 23rd November 2005; Jim Pickard, 'CMBS demand set to increase', 13th January 2006; Paul J. Davies, 'Securitisations set to keep on robust growth path', 3rd February 2006; Paul J. Davies, 'Concerns over rapid growth of CMBS deals among banks', 24th March 2006; David Wighton, 'Goldman buy-out lending soars', 17th July 2006; Chris Hughes, 'Lehman sets record on LSE', 14th August 2006; Nouriel Roubini, 'The shadow banking system is unravelling', 22nd September 2006; Iain Morse, 'Market jostling sees ownership rise', 9th October 2006; Paul J. Davies, 'Failure of LBOs a risk to debt markets', 1st December 2006; Gillian Tett, 'Regulators weigh up supra-national intervention', 19th November 2007.

[39] Christine Moir, 'Consolidation on the cards', 1st March 1996.

criminal behaviour'.[40] Though dominated by banks this inter-bank market increasingly involved the participation of large multinational companies in the 1990s. These businesses also experienced periods when they faced temporary shortage or excesses of funds and also made and received payments on a global basis. Rather than acting through their bankers such companies sought direct involvement in the global money market and it was impossible to deny them access. Governments also had a stake in this money market as they used it as a way of influencing the supply of the money and determining interest rates though this had become much more difficult as national barriers had crumbled. To a large degree the constant ebb and flow of the global money market went unrecognized unless any serious problems emerged and that was not the case between 1992 and 2007.

Central to the operation of these inter-bank markets were the interdealer brokers. It might have been expected that the emergence of the megabanks would have eliminated the need for interdealer brokers as they acted as intermediaries between banks. They conducted deals over the telephone through networks that connected them to the largest banks, with prices and other information displayed on screens provided by the likes of Reuters, Bloomberg, and Thomson. As the megabanks grew into global institutions whose trading spanned all products they possessed the ability to either internalize transactions or deal directly with each other, so cutting out the need for intermediation. The development of interactive electronic platforms, that both displayed prices and matched sales and purchases, also threatened the interdealer brokers. What ensured the survival of the interdealer brokers was their response as they not only embraced the electronic technology themselves but also grew in scale and reach so as to provide banks with greatly improved intermediation services. As Charles Gregson, the deputy managing director of one interdealer broker, explained in 1994, 'In a niche business, it is possible to set up in a garret with a few telephones and deal successfully, but to broaden the business requires a substantial investment in information technology and people.'[41] Though there remained a need for an interdealer broker to conduct negotiations over the telephone with multiple parties when complex products were involved, what ensured their survival was their success in retaining a stake in the high-volume trading that took place between banks. They did that by continuing to provide banks with a service that they either could not replicate or could only do at greater cost. This they did by expanding themselves so that they could match the banks in terms of coverage, whether it was in products or places, as well as investing in the technology and staff required, while keeping costs low. As the volume and variety of trading in the OTC markets expanded exponentially so the interdealer brokers were able to support a global network of offices, the use of sophisticated and expensive computing and communications equipment, and the employment of highly-trained staff who were highly remunerated.

Driving this transformation was the level of competition between interdealer brokers as their clients, the world's largest banks, limited the number of connections they maintained, and confined their trading to a small number of trusted intermediaries. As Garry Jones, chief executive of ICAP Electronic Broking Europe, put it bluntly in 2004, 'If you are not number one or number two in your space, it is going to be very hard to break in.'[42] The 1990s was a decade when interdealer brokers either expanded aggressively or abandoned the business. There was a spate of mergers and acquisitions that left a small number of dominant firms by the beginning of the twenty-first century. The merger of Prebon Yamane

[40] Stephen Pritchard, 'A race to stay ahead of fraudsters', 5th June 2002.
[41] Simon Davies, 'Taking a position in the market', 28th June 1994.
[42] Alex Skorecki, 'Icap says phone broking rules market', 4th June 2004.

and M. W. Marshall in 1999 resulted in a business with more than 2000 staff located in offices around the world. A subsequent merger, with Tullett and Tokyo in 2004, pushed the numbers employed to more than 3000. The resulting business, Tullet Prebon, was run out of London by Terry Smith. Even larger was another firm, ICAP, also run out of London. ICAP was the creation of Michael Spencer, about whom Terry Smith said in 2003, 'He'll take big risks.'[43] In 1998 ICAP took over one of its main rivals, Exco, followed by another, Garban, in 1999, to create the world's largest interdealer broker. By then the interdealer brokers were developing their own electronic platforms, though they continued to regard the combination of voice broking and price display as superior. According to Aline van Duyn in 2001, 'For some traders and investors, it remains important to have someone to talk to who can tell you why a market is moving, as well as what the latest price is.'[44] By the end of the 1990s it was becoming evident that both systems were in demand from banks, forcing the interdealer brokers to respond. For that reason the leading brokers began to offer both options as well a hybrid model that combined traditional voice-based dealing over the phone with electronic support tools to cut costs and improve efficiency. In 2002 Doug Cameron reported that 'ICAP is confident that the future will include a role for traditional brokers, as human judgement remains fundamental for difficult trading calls.'[45]

The interdealer broker that had made the boldest move into electronic broking was the New York firm of Cantor Fitzgerald, run by Howard Lutnick. Cantor Fitzgerald began as a traditional voice broker in the US Treasury market. From 1996 they began to develop an electronic bond-trading platform, eSpeed, which became operational in 1999, and quickly established a leading position in the Treasury market. Such was its success that after its New York offices were destroyed in the attack on the World Trade Center in 2001, Cantor Fitzgerald abandoned voice broking and rebuilt its US Treasury operations around its electronic platform, eSpeed. What it had identified was that electronic systems not only allowed the same transaction to take place more quickly and at a lower cost but they also supported both a much greater volume of dealing and ones that were much more complicated. Such was the threat to trading in US Treasuries posed by eSpeed that the banks, which had previously dominated the market, formed a rival electronic platform, BrokerTec, in 1999. By 2002 these two platforms dominated trading in US Treasuries. Cantor Fitzgerald's e-Speed was in the lead with 53 per cent compared to BrokerTec's 47 per cent. In a highly liquid market such as that for US government debt, trading quickly migrated to electronic platforms, as it was relatively easy to match sales and purchases at current prices. Recognizing the triumph of electronic trading in US Treasuries ICAP took the opportunity to acquire BrokerTec in 2003, when the fourteen banks that owned it were forced to sell on anti-trust grounds. That was quickly followed with a link to MarketAccess as ICAP sought to cover both US government and corporate bonds and serve wholesale and retail customers, so enhancing its position as the leading interdealer broker in the world. It continued to operate both voice broking and electronic platform, but its chief executive, Michael Spencer, was already convinced the future was electronic, being quoted in 2004 saying, 'I envisage a day not too far distant when the majority of ICAP's services, apart from a few very illiquid or structured products, are available electronically.... The ramifications of a big multi-product platform, with liquidity in all cash bonds and repo as well as derivatives in many

[43] Robert Orr, 'Founder of Icap is new chairman of Numis', 30th April 2003.
[44] Aline van Duyn, 'Only the best will survive', 28th March 2001.
[45] Doug Cameron, 'Ways to enhance voice-broking services', 3rd April 2002.

currencies, are huge. The ability to cross trade spreads and products would be massively enhanced. Market efficiency would be taken to a new level.'[46]

By 2006 the world of interdealer brokers had been reduced to a small group of global businesses dominated by ICAP, Cantor Fitzgerald, and Tullet Prebon. Even though the threat remained from the megabanks and alternative electronic markets, the interdealer brokers continued to play a vital role. Operating from hubs in London, New York, and a number of Asian financial centres including Tokyo, Singapore, and Hong Kong, and directly connected to the dealing floors of the megabanks and other financial institutions, they were especially good at matching sales and purchases across a wide range of financial instruments. They held especially strong positions in the debt of emerging economies as well as those of smaller developed countries, such as Denmark, as these lacked liquid domestic markets and were also extensively held internationally. The segment of the market that interdealer brokers were most secure in was that which required negotiation. As Mike Beale, Chairman of the London Wholesale Market Brokers' Association, said in 1998, 'The broker can always make you a price and also has the advantage of offering the client anonymity.'[47] Interdealer brokers were ideally placed to provide a dealing service when the level of turnover was too low for any single bank to maintain a trading team to handle transactions. In contrast, an interdealer broker could justify the time and expertise involved as they came to constitute the entire market. In addition, interdealer brokers were in the position of being able to provide their customers, whether banks or fund managers, with the confidentiality they required when undertaking large and complex deals or when they wanted to conceal a temporary vulnerability. What the survival of the interdealer brokers reveals is the way that the rise of the megabanks was both a threat to other components of the global financial system and a source of profitable opportunities for others. What was clear was that survival meant change.[48]

[46] Alex Skorecki, 'Bold vision demands a response', 14th December 2004.

[47] Jonathan Guthrie, 'Sighs of relief as Exco takeover get nod of approval', 27th October 1998.

[48] Barry Riley, 'A new asset class created', 7th February 1994; Hilary Barnes, 'Drift of trade to London causes concern', 7th April 1994; Sara Webb, 'Dutch win back state debt trade', 16th May 1994; Antonia Sharpe, 'Amsterdam prepares to fight back', 16th June 1994; Simon Davies, 'Taking a position in the market', 28th June 1994; Philip Gawith, 'Brokers lose their voices on the small screen', 15th December 1995; Nicholas Denton, 'Banks plan clearing house for trade in emerging market debt', 10th June 1996; Richard Adams, 'An artificial and antiquated straightjacket', 5th December 1996; Graham Bowley, 'Historic day for way Bank goes to work', 3rd March 1997; James Mackintosh, 'Brokers reach merger agreement', 12th October 1997; Jonathan Guthrie, 'Sighs of relief as Exco takeover get nod of approval', 27th October 1998; Clay Harris, 'Brokers agree merger terms', 16th February 1999; Clay Harris, 'Bid to set up biggest wholesale money broker', 10th June 1999; Clay Harris, 'Garban and Intercapital in £300m merger', 3rd July 1999; Alan Beattie, 'Tullett and Bloomberg plan new broking system', 5th July 1999; Andrea Mandel-Campbell, 'Not just a traditional market for shares', 19th March 2001; Aline van Duyn, 'Only the best will survive', 28th March 2001; Martin Dickson, 'The market is another country for City's go-between', 7th April 2001; Doug Cameron, 'Ways to enhance voice-broking services', 3rd April 2002; Doug Cameron and Jennifer Hughes, 'Citigroup to join online currency platform', 8th April 2002; Alex Skorecki, 'Voice-broked bond trading holds its own', 19th March 2003; Robert Orr, 'Founder of Icap is new chairman of Numis', 30th April 2003; Alex Skorecki, 'Icap forms bond trading alliance with MarketAxess', 22nd March 2004; Elizabeth Rigby, 'Collins Stewart eyes Prebon', 27th May 2004; Alex Skorecki, 'Icap says phone broking rules market', 4th June 2004; Alex Skorecki, 'Cantor split off bucks the trend', 18th August 2004; Alex Skorecki, 'Bold vision demands a response', 14th December 2004; Alex Skorecki, 'Cantor wrestles to stay Treasury heavyweight', 8th February 2005; Sarah Spikes, 'Icap chief caps a 20-year rise to the stars', 22nd April 2006; Sarah Spikes, 'Icap snaps up EBS for £464m', 22nd April 2006; Saskia Scholtes, 'Electronic battle heats up', 28th July 2006; Tobias Buck and Gillian Tett, 'Battle heats up over Europe's bond markets', 30th November 2006; Sarah Spikes and Peter Thal Larsen, 'Interdealer broking behind rapid growth', 19th December 2006.

Conclusion

While the dot.com boom did not halt the rise of the megabanks or the switch to the originate-and-distribute model of banking, the environment within which banks operated was changed. Driven by fears that the bursting of the dot.com speculative bubble was a repeat of the Wall Street Crash of 1929, and could have similar damaging consequences for global financial and economic stability, governments and central banks intervened by lowering interest rates. This policy was followed in the USA, the UK, Japan, and across the Eurozone. The effect was to pump liquidity into the global financial system, which had the desired effect of preventing a crisis. The result was to instil a belief that concerted central bank intervention could prevent the liquidity and solvency crisis that had destabilized banking in the past. Accompanying this was an almost universal belief that a new way of banking had been discovered that was simultaneously safer and more profitable than anything that had existed before. This new model of banking was associated with the rise of the megabanks as they had the capacity to absorb shocks through portfolio diversification and sophisticated risk-management techniques.[49] In 2005 Peter Thal Larsen reported that 'Investment banks have poured millions into developing sophisticated risk-management systems that measure the amount of capital they have at risk at any moment in time' and these 'allow them to step in quickly whenever they see losses appearing'.[50] Charles Batchelor endorsed that verdict, claiming that, 'The banks are stronger financially and are adept at hedging their risks so they are in a stronger position.'[51] However, the short-term medicine of low interest rates used to prevent a global financial crisis had damaging longer-term consequences for the banking system. A climate of cheap and abundant liquidity encouraged banks to borrow short-term funds at low rates of interest, and invest in long-term assets generating a higher yield. Their profits came from the differential between the interest paid and received. The result was the build-up of a huge international carry trade in which money was borrowed cheaply in dollars, euros, and yen to invest in countries with higher interest rates such as Iceland, New Zealand, Hungary, Turkey, Australia, and South Africa, relying on the stability of both interest rates and exchange rates to remove the risks that banks were running. By 2006 there were growing concerns that this stability could not be relied upon indefinitely but until something emerged to undermine confidence the global carry trade continued to drive the securitization bubble, drawing in banks in its wake. The willingness of banks to lend ever more money to fund private equity takeovers, for example, showed no sign of abating at the very end of 2006, with leverage ratios continuing to rise as they competed with each other for the business.[52]

Complicit in this state of affairs were those regulating banking around the world. Since the introduction of the Basel rules in 1988 by the Bank for International Settlement, banks had been encouraged to provide long-term finance more by way of the issue of bonds than

[49] John Gapper and Tracy Corrigan, 'Formidable rivals on a shifting battleground', 4th March 1994; Jane Croft, 'The danger of relying too much on only one tool', 22nd March 2011.

[50] Peter Thal Larsen, 'One shocking bank failure deposited a stern warning in the history books', 19th February 2005.

[51] Charles Batchelor, 'Don't get carried away by the lure of cheap borrowing', 28th May 2005.

[52] Charles Pretzlik, 'Maintaining a resilience to risk—and shocks', 1st October 2003; Peter Thal Larsen, 'One shocking bank failure deposited a stern warning in the history books', 19th February 2005; Philip Coggan, 'If they all rush for the exit at the same time', 28th May 2005; Charles Batchelor, 'Don't get carried away by the lure of cheap borrowing', 28th May 2005; Jane Croft, 'Profits in the billions underline the vital role of banking in the economy', 18th February 2006; Ivar Simensen and Sundeep Tucker, 'Iceland raises key interest rate as vulnerable currencies are hit', 31st March 2006; Paul J. Davies, 'Failure of LBOs a risk to debt markets', 1st December 2006.

through loans. The rationale behind such a recommendation was that bonds could be sold to relieve a liquidity crisis whereas loans could not. This undermining of the lend-and-hold model of banking had been encouraged in 1994 when the mark to market requirement was introduced in the USA, being later followed by other countries. The aim of the mark to market requirement was to make banks aware of the risks that they are running when purchasing and holding bonds, which was masked if they remained valued at their purchase price but had declined in price. Regulators assumed that a mark to market policy would force banks to be more cautious. Instead, it encouraged banks to expand lending if assets rose in value, as that increased the cover they had available in case of a default. Conversely, if assets fell in value a bank would have to cut back lending to maintain the leverage ratio, giving rise to a liquidity crisis because of the signals being transmitted. Bankers tried to convince regulators that a mark-to-market policy could be destabilizing but failed at a time of rising asset prices. The Basel Rules themselves also encouraged banks to take greater risks. As early as 1999 George Graham had reported that the capital-adequacy requirements had 'started to destabilise the global financial system by giving banks perverse incentives to make riskier loans'.[53] Operating within the Basel rules banks had tended to migrate towards riskier loans in each band, as these generated higher rates of return from the same level of capital provision. In response new rules were introduced which relied less on a fixed formula, under which capital requirements were set for particular categories of loans, and allowed banks more discretion when assessing the risks involved. Under the new rules use was to be made of external credit-rating agencies so that each loan could be scored as well as given an internal credit rating by the banks. In addition, instead of banks lending and borrowing from each other on an unsecured basis, collateral would have to be provided. To make this requirement more acceptable to the banks the range of collateral was widened, being less restricted to government debt. It was expanded to include those bonds being created by securitization. The effect of forcing banks to hold collateral against the loans they made encouraged them to repackage and sell on debt rather than retain it until maturity. By repackaging loans and selling them on a bank could not only release funds for further lending, and do so repeatedly, but it could also provide itself with the collateral to match its borrowing in the inter-bank money market, instead of relying on unsecured short-term loans.

By 2006 the incoming Basel 2 rules had become the main driver in the switch from the buy-and-hold model of banking to the originate-and-distribute one. The flaw in the way the originate-and-distribute model was being used was that the banks either held onto the bonds created or bought those generated by other banks rather than selling them to investors. That left the banks liable in the event of a default rather than placing the risk with long-term investors who were not dependent upon short-term borrowing to finance their holdings. The problem with many of the new securities being created was they lacked the established markets that had developed for both government debt and the stocks and bonds issued by the largest companies. The market for these new securities was dependent upon the very banks that had issued them. As long as it was one or two banks that needed to access liquidity by selling such bonds then there was not a problem with this. The problem would occur when there was a collective liquidity crisis for then none would be able to sell the bonds they held as there would be no buyers, even at greatly reduced prices. In pressing banks to hold more liquid assets, those who had framed the new rules under Basel

[53] George Graham, 'Weighing up the risks', 4th June 1999.

2 had forgotten that a market structure also needed to be put in place, and none was. The result was to produce a false confidence in the ability of banks to cope with a liquidity and then solvency crisis, as that depended on the ability to sell securities for which no public market existed.

The new Basel rules were a product of the Bank for International Settlement (BIS), which had taken increased responsibility for the international effort to reduce or remove the financial risks that were inherent in a global banking system operating in a competitive environment. The BIS acted as the co-ordinating body for the world's central bankers, dictating the rules that systemically-important banks were expected to follow. Though the stability of the banking system had long been a core responsibility of national central banks after the Second World War, governments increasingly prioritized their other roles. In particular, central banks had become the agency through which national governments implemented their monetary policies in a world of fluctuating interest rates, volatile exchange rates, and free financial flows. When the European Central Bank was established in 1999 to act for those countries belonging to the Eurozone, John Plender observed that it 'has been given a mandate to focus almost exclusively on monetary policy, with only a limited peripheral role in banking supervision and no responsibility for providing liquidity support to individual banks. There is no central provider or co-ordinator of emergency liquidity in the event of a crisis.'[54] Though this was an extreme example of the position that national central banks now occupied it was typical of the situation prevailing around the world. Instead of banking stability being the product of active intervention by central banks, responsibility had been devolved to the BIS and the rules and regulations it framed regarding capital adequacy. Central to the implementation of these rules were the megabanks as they were considered to have reached a size and scale that allowed them to absorb huge losses and support sophisticated internal controls that monitored the behaviour of staff. As long as they followed the Basel rules then the risk of a liquidity or solvency crisis was regarded as minimal. However, these banks interpreted the Basel rules in such a way as to allow them to satisfy the demands of their customers and generate the profits expected by their owners. This was an inevitable outcome of the highly-competitive environment they found themselves in prior to the global financial crisis. As competition intensified between banks the margins at which they operated shrank, making them increasingly vulnerable to shocks.[55]

[54] John Plender, 'Crisis in the making', 12th April 1999.

[55] Laurie Morse, 'A two-pronged development', 20th October 1993; Richard Irving, 'Shock-absorbing models', 16th November 1995; George Graham, 'BIS weighs expanded role', 9th June 1997; John Plender, 'Crisis in the making', 12th April 1999; George Graham, 'Weighing up the risks', 4th June 1999; John Willman, 'Bank backs changes in accounting', 26th June 2000; Charles Batchelor, 'Joining Europe's mainstream', 29th November 2004; Peter Thal Larsen, 'One shocking bank failure deposited a stern warning in the history books', 19th February 2005; Paul J. Davies, 'Raising the roof with covered bonds', 2nd November 2005; Stephen Fidler, 'Basel 2 boosts Europe's repo market', 29th November 2005; Jim Pickard, 'CMBS demand set to increase', 13th January 2006; Paul J. Davies, 'Securitisations set to keep on robust growth path', 3rd February 2006; Paul J. Davies, 'Markit to launch trade finance and index service', 30th November 2006.

9

Bonds and Currencies, 1993–2006

Introduction

There was a spectrum of funding sources open to any borrower in a modern market economy, ranging from self-finance through bank loans and mortgages to the issue of bills, bonds, and stocks. The same applied to savers with the options being available including bank deposits, negotiable securities, and direct holdings of property. The diversity of financial assets in existence can be seen through examining bonds alone. At one extreme were the numerous bonds that were issued in relatively small amounts by businesses and held until maturity by investors familiar with their particular characteristics, such as duration and currency, as well as their terms and conditions. Though ownership of these could be transferred it was rarely done so. What was important was that such bonds could be sold, if required, unlike loans, which could not. At the other extreme were those bonds issued in vast amounts by stable governments and in currencies such as the US$, as these commanded universal appeal because of their security and liquidity. For such bonds the existence of a market generating constantly-updated prices, and where they could be easily, quickly, and cheaply bought and sold, was of critical importance. However, bonds were but one type of financial instrument in circulation. The switch from the lend-and-hold model of banking to the originate-and-distribute one generated a growing variety of financial assets, as existing loans were converted into transferable debts that were then sold to investors and traded in secondary markets. A calculation made for 2006 estimated that whereas the total value of bank deposits stood at \$38,500 there was far more outstanding, at \$58,300, in the form of bonds, loans, and asset-backed securities.[1]

The securitization of assets had long been widely practised. Since the eighteenth century mortgage banks in Germany and Denmark had raised funds by issuing bonds backed by their assets. However, the whole process of securitization reached a new level of sophistication in the USA between 1992 and 2007, and was increasingly taken up in other countries. In 2000 Aline van Duyn observed that the 'Use of securitization, where debt repayments are backed by the future cash flows of a company's assets, is spreading around the world.'[2] The growing popularity of the originate-and-distribute model encouraged the conversion of loans into assets capable of being sold to an investor, whether it involved short-term credit card expenditure and automobile finance or long-term funding of home ownership and commercial property development. Securitization, for example, was used to fund mega-takeover bids. Bonds were sold to investors with their value dependent on the anticipated income stream of the acquired company. As long as two key criteria were met, which was the predictability of cash flows and the level of diversification of the assets in backing the bonds, then securitization could be applied. In 1998 Simon Davies believed that 'The

[1] Gillian Tett, 'Sub-prime in its context', 19th November 2007.
[2] Aline van Duyn, 'Bond markets extend to smaller firms', 19th May 2000.

Banks, Exchanges, and Regulators: Global Financial Markets from the 1970s. Ranald Michie, Oxford University Press (2021).

DOI: 10.1093/oso/9780199553730.003.0009

possibilities are almost endless',[3] while Adrienne Roberts in 2003 concluded that, 'In theory, almost anything can be securitized if it generates predictable cash-flows.'[4] The attraction of securitization to banks was that by repackaging loans as bonds, which could then be sold to a third party, they could shift much of the risk of a borrower defaulting to investors, including other banks, while releasing funds for new loans, and so repeat the process. Securitization allowed a bank to simultaneously expand its volume of lending and so meet customer demand; grow its business and so increase its profits for the benefit of shareholders and employees; reduce its exposure to risk by swapping part of its loan portfolio for those of other banks; and meet regulatory guidelines without having to maintain a large capital reserve. There appeared no downside to such a strategy and so securitization quickly gained traction among banks. Some saw it as a way of expanding in highly-competitive banking markets, as in the USA and UK. Others saw securitization as a means of holding onto existing customers, as in Japan where banks were already pulling back from making loans to companies before the 1997 crisis because of perceived risks, while yield-hungry savers were searching for higher returns than those available from deposit accounts. Crucial to the originate-and-distribute model of banking, and the securitization that accompanied it, was the development of markets in which the resulting products could be bought and sold. Without the liquidity that the existence of such markets provided, the bonds, bills, obligations, notes, and other securities in circulation were little different from the loans made by banks to their customers or to each other, under the lend-and-hold model of banking.

Despite the rapid expansion in the circulation of fixed-income instruments the financial markets that generated the highest volume of trading were those involving the constant lending, borrowing, and trading that took place between banks in the domestic and international money markets. Banks had to continuously adjust to fluctuations in the supply of and demand for the funds they had at their disposal as some customers deposited money while others made withdrawals. They had always to be in a position to accept these deposits and meet withdrawals while responding to requests for loans, as otherwise they would lose business to rival banks. All around the world, from Russia to Lebanon, local money markets operated through which banks continuously adjusted their position by buying and selling bills, for example. Towering above these local money markets was the trading in Treasury bills in the USA because of its immense size and depth. This was where any bank could access and employ funds to any amount, confident that its actions would not disturb prices and that deals made would be honoured. Important as these inter-bank markets were, the greatly increased scale of banks, and their nationwide operations did facilitate the internalization of credit flows. Where the development of such banks was impeded, as in the USA, a domestic inter-bank money market continued to thrive, as indicated by the continued use of commercial paper, or short-dated financial instruments of less than a year's duration. In 1994 the value of commercial bills outstanding in the USA stood at $570bn while in Europe it was only $112bn.

The other change that came from the emergence of large banks was the reduction in the fear of default when banks borrowed and lent amongst each other. Such was the degree of confidence they had in each other that German banks dispensed with the need for collateral when making loans to each other. The same situation applied to the megabanks operating in London's international money market. In addition banks were in constant need to

[3] Simon Davies, 'Myriad possibilities', 1st May 1998.
[4] Adrienne Roberts, 'ABS debt thrives on innovation', 22nd October 2003.

balance assets and liabilities over time and space, as well as other variables such as currency, whether to reduce the risks they were running or to generate profits in order to meet their costs, pay their staff, and remunerate their owners. At a time of global economic integration and currency volatility it was, therefore, not surprising that the largest financial market of all in the world at the end of the twentieth century and the beginning of the twenty-first was that where foreign exchange was traded. Spanning all the world's currencies and time zones, banks traded foreign exchange with each other so as to match their commitments with their holdings. As the volume and variety of financial flows around the world grew, generated by payments and receipts for all manner of transactions, banks faced a continuous struggle to adjust their positions so as not to face a catastrophic loss due to any sudden changes. The simplest way of doing that was to swap assets and liabilities among themselves as for every debit there was a credit. In the foreign exchange spot market current commitments across currencies were matched while in the forward market it was future commitments, with a constant interplay between the two as banks either sought to cover their exposure or profit from it.[5]

Foreign Exchange Market

In 2004 Jennifer Hughes referred to the foreign exchange market as 'The largest, most dynamic market in the world....Centred in Tokyo, London, and New York, traders deal smoothly across borders and time-zones, often in multiples of $1bn, in transactions that take less than a second.'[6] Writing with Krishna Guha she claimed that its turnover was 'far greater that equity or bond markets.'[7] In 1992 the daily turnover in the foreign exchange market stood at $880bn, which was a 42 per cent increase over the figure for 1989. By 1995 the total had reached $1,230bn, so maintaining the previous explosive rate of growth. By way of comparison this daily amount was five times greater than the annual turnover achieved in global equity markets. It was also far greater than the total value of international trade in goods and services. The foreign exchange market traded in four days what it took the world to achieve in a year. This exponential rate of growth was not sustained in the later 1990s, with daily foreign exchange trading being estimated at $1,500bn a day by 1998 and then dropping to $1,200bn by 2001. Activity in the foreign exchange market was driven by the volatility and variety of currencies, and that dipped in 1999 with European monetary union. That eliminated trading between individual currencies such as the mark, franc, peseta, guilder, and lira, as they were replaced with a single unit, the Euro, covering

[5] Leyla Boulton, 'Birth of a hundred markets', 23rd February 1993; Antonia Sharpe, 'Cash haven lures investors', 26th May 1994; Philip Gawith and Richard Lapper, 'A step away from City tradition', 2nd January 1996; Conner Middelmann, 'Domestic market is struggling', 1st March 1996; Roula Khalaf, 'Private sector is quick to adjust', 8th November 1996; Khozem Merchant, 'Market for ECP opens up via Trax', 7th September 1999; Joshua Chaffin, 'Recovery from rare default is taking time', 21st June 2001; Elizabeth Wine, 'Sidelined cash may stay out of stocks', 4th January 2002; Stephen Pritchard, 'A race to stay ahead of fraudsters', 5th June 2002; Charles Batchelor, 'EuroMTS launches European T-bill platform', 16th March 2004; Charles Batchelor, 'Long pedigree of the clearing house for short-term funds', 23rd July 2004; Charles Batchelor, 'London leads in trading volumes', 23rd September 2004; Alex Skorecki, 'Bank of England lights a fuse', 30th November 2004; Jennifer Hughes, 'Bankers divided on need for backstop', 4th May 2006; Scheherazade Daneshkhu and Chris Giles, 'City becomes undeniable engine of growth', 27th March 2006; Michael Mackenzie and Saskia Scholtes, 'Regulators issue a warning at bond trading's wild frontier', 13th November 2006.

[6] Jennifer Hughes, 'Where money talks very loudly', 27th May 2004.

[7] Jennifer Hughes and Krishna Guha, 'World foreign exchange trading soars to a peak of $1,900bn a day', 29th September 2004.

most of Western Europe. However, growth then picked up, reaching $1,900bn a day by 2004. This was a reflection of the changing use to which currency trading was being put. In the past the prime reason behind foreign exchange trading was for banks to cover the risks they were exposed to through the transactions they handled on behalf of customers. Initially these were producers and consumers who were buying and selling internationally, and so had to make or receive payments in different currencies. Added to that from the 1970s were the activities of borrowers who tapped international markets for funds or investment institutions with huge portfolios of stocks and bonds spread around the world. These international activities exposed banks to foreign exchange risks, as there were inevitable delays between payments and receipts. Banks covered these risks by trading in the foreign exchange market, as it was there that each could match its assets and liabilities denominated in different currencies with the reverse position taken by others. However, certain banks recognized that they were in a position to not only provide a service to customers, and reduce their risks through the foreign exchange market, but also to generate substantial profits by acting as counterparties whether in the spot market or through forward transactions. Multinational companies and hedge-fund managers also spotted opportunities for gain in the foreign exchange market and so they also participated, driving up turnover and so compensating for the loss of business because of greater monetary stability and fewer currency pairs to be traded.[8]

This expansion in the size of the global foreign exchange market was not accompanied by a parallel trend in the number of those handling the trading of currencies or locations in which it took place, with the reverse being the case. Instead of ever more banks being drawn into the foreign exchange market, as a product of global financial integration, the business of trading currencies became concentrated in the hands of a small number of global banks. Foreign exchange had never been much traded on exchanges and this continued to be the case in the 1990s. It was 'barely traded on stock exchanges',[9] according to Tracy Corrigan in 1993. Instead, foreign exchange trading was an inter-bank market, because there was little need for the regulations dealing with default and price manipulation that exchanges provided. Foreign exchange transactions were of very short duration being conducted between banks that could be relied upon to honour their commitments. Though occasional defaults did take place they were rare and largely concerned settlement risk, which was a bank's overnight exposure in an open transaction. Indicative of the low priority given to addressing counterparty risk in the foreign exchange market was the lack of immediate response to those defaults that did occur, beginning with collapse of Bankhaus Herstatt, a small Cologne bank, in 1974. This was followed by subsequent failures as with Drexel Burnham Lambert in 1990, the Bank of Credit and Commerce International in 1991 and Barings Bank in 1995. All these involved minor players and each encouraged the further concentration of foreign exchange activity in the hands of a few global banks.

[8] Tracy Corrigan, 'Traditional split in derivatives is less clear-cut', 25th January 1993; James Blitz, 'All change in foreign exchanges', 2nd April 1993; James Blitz, 'New anxieties for the banks', 26th May 1993; Philip Gawith, 'Forex surge masks maturing market', 24th October 1995; Philip Gawith, 'Exotic but not for faint hearts', 15th May 1996; Richard Lapper and Philip Gawith, 'Forex market growth slowing, says BIS', 31st May 1996; George Graham, 'Forex trading system planned', 15th September 1999; Christopher Swann and Doug Cameron, 'FXall set to intensify battle in online currency trading', 10th May 2001; Doug Cameron, 'Currenex to form exchange', 26th November 2001; Alex Skorecki, 'Forex system that takes the waiting out of wanting', 4th January 2002; Jennifer Hughes, 'Where money talks very loudly', 27th May 2004; Jennifer Hughes and Krishna Guha, 'World foreign exchange trading soars to a peak of $1,900bn a day', 29th September 2004; Jennifer Hughes, 'FX firebrand dream of revolution', 9th May 2006; Steve Johnson, 'London rules new wave of FX deals', 18th July 2006.

[9] Tracy Corrigan, 'Traditional split in derivatives is less clear-cut', 25th January 1993.

Only the biggest banks could convince each other and their customers that they had the financial resources to provide the service required, and carry the liquidity and credit risk involved in large-scale trading. By 1998 there was a core of thirteen banks that dominated the global foreign exchange market, trading with each other and a few large corporations, and acting on behalf of a host of smaller client banks. The banks that dominated the global foreign exchange market by then were led by a group from the USA—Citibank, Chase Manhattan, JP Morgan, Goldman Sachs, Merrill Lynch, Bank of America—and from Europe—HSBC, Deutsche, UBS, Credit Suisse, ABN-Amro, NatWest, and Barclays. Mergers between these and smaller banks had the effect of both eliminating the number of core players and concentrating activity in those that remained. These global banks provided a liquid 24-hour market in the world's main currencies, which was used by smaller or regional banks, both for themselves and their customers, as they possessed neither the capacity, expertise, nor connections to compete. The foreign exchange market also provided the megabanks with a means through which they could lend and borrow among themselves in complete confidence that loans would be repaid in full and on time. Any failure to not do so would destroy the mutual confidence that existed and end the participation of the offending bank, with disastrous consequences for the business that it could do.

Mirroring the dominance of the foreign exchange market by a handful of global banks was the increasing concentration of trading in a few locations around the world, as it was only there that the required depth of liquidity could be found. Here London continued to exert its pull resulting from its convenient time-zone location combined with the presence there of so many offices belonging to the world's banks. In 1992 daily turnover in the foreign exchange market in London was $300bn compared to New York on $192bn and Tokyo on $126bn, and that lead was either maintained or grew in subsequent years. In 1994 David Marsh referred to London as the 'hub of the world-wide foreign exchange market'.[10] In 2002, Alex Skorecki credited London with 'the lion's share of forex trade'.[11] An estimate for 2006 placed foreign exchange turnover in London at twice the New York level, being $1,029bn per day compared to $577bn. Banks were choosing to centralize foreign exchange trading in those locations where they could simultaneously access liquidity and diversity. By 1996 Deutsche Bank was conducting its foreign exchange trading from only four financial centres compared to thirty-seven in 1990. As Guy Whitaker observed in 1997, 'Business is gravitating to where the markets are most liquid.'[12] He was head of foreign exchange trading at Citibank, the leading bank in the business at that time. Whereas London and New York retained or increased their positions in the global foreign exchange market, that of Tokyo faded, despite the importance of its economy and the use of the Yen as an international currency. Though Tokyo was the leading centre for foreign exchange trading in Asia in 1992 its volume ($126bn) was less than the combined total for Singapore ($76bn) and Hong Kong Kong ($61bn). In contrast, London's total ($300bn) for the same year was almost twice the combined total of its three nearest European rivals, namely Zurich ($68bn), Frankfurt ($57bn), and Paris ($36bn), each of which had the advantage of hosting trading in their domestic currencies, which were used internationally. The regulatory restrictions placed on the operation of markets and the activities of banks continued to hamper Tokyo when it came to the foreign exchange market. Seizing this opportunity was Singapore as it emerged as a serious rival to Tokyo as the Asian centre for the global foreign

[10] David Marsh, 'Powerhouse holds its ground', 4th March 1994.
[11] Alex Skorecki, 'Forex system that takes the waiting out of wanting', 4th January 2002.
[12] Simon Kuper, 'Dealers on the spot as margins narrow', 18th April 1997.

exchange market, especially with the uncertainty over Hong Kong caused by its transfer from British to Chinese rule. As trading in Asian currencies other than the yen grew Singapore emerged as an even more serious rival to Tokyo. By 2004 Tokyo's share of foreign exchange trading was down to 8 per cent, which was half the level it had been ten years before.[13]

Bond Markets

The market in fixed-income financial products also expanded enormously in the years between 1992 and 2007 as banks embraced the originate-and-distribute model. A requirement of the originate-and-distribute model was a market in which they could be traded and, again, it was the megabanks that were at the centre of the developments that took place. The variety of fixed-income products in circulation required an equivalent mix of market mechanisms through which they could be traded. These ranged from direct negotiation between buyer and seller, as with any property transaction, to the rapid transfer and payment of standardized assets as found in the trading of government debt. The better the market the lower the interest that had to be promised. Investors made their choice from a spectrum that extended from low liquidity and high yield at one end to high liquidity and low yield at the other. Even within the most actively traded government bonds there was a huge difference between US Treasuries, where turnover averaged $400bn a day in 2003 compared to around $15bn for the UK equivalent. Most trading in fixed-income products took place directly between banks, or through interdealer brokers, as they bought and sold either on their own behalf or for and with their customers. Though an estimated 800 banks from fifty countries participated in the global bond market in the 1990s most of the trading was in the hands of around ninety from ten countries. Within that there was a small inner grouping that dominated the market. As competition intensified the profit that could be generated from trading bonds shrank to very low levels, squeezing out those that could not reduce costs through economies of scale or the resources to act as counterparties. In 2004 the top ten were Citigroup, Deutsche Bank, Credit Suisse, JP Morgan, Morgan Stanley, Lehman Brothers, UBS, Merrill Lynch, Goldman Sachs, and Bank of America. These banks could leverage their huge holdings of bonds and large liquid reserves by buying and selling on their own account until a favourable opportunity to reverse the deal arose.

Overall the bond market was vast in terms of the number of issues, with national and local governments, large and small companies, and numerous different agencies all being involved. It was even possible to subdivide, or strip, bonds into the interest paid and the underlying asset, trading each separately. Throughout the world there were local bond

[13] Andrew Gowers, 'Island of integrity', 29th March 1993; James Blitz, 'All change in foreign exchanges', 2nd April 1993; David Marsh, 'Powerhouse holds its ground', 4th March 1994; Kieran Cooke, 'Rising hub of global trading', 6th June 1995; Philip Gawith, 'Forex market growth startles exchanges', 20th September 1995; Philip Gawith, 'Forex surge masks maturing market', 24th October 1995; Philip Gawith, 'Service central to Paribas forex move', 2nd February 1996; Philip Coggan, 'It's just a small problem', 8th February 1996; Richard Lapper and Philip Gawith, 'Forex market growth slowing, says BIS', 31st May 1996; Graham Bowley, 'Forex houses sanguine despite possibility of single currency', 6th December 1996; Simon Kuper, 'Dealers on the spot as margins narrow', 18th April 1997; James Kynge, 'Exotics reach the major league', 9th May 1997; Alan Beattie, 'Fighting spirit seeps into dried-up markets', 25th June 1999; Alex Skorecki, 'Forex system that takes the waiting out of wanting', 4th January 2002; David Ibison, 'Banks lose hope sun will rise on Japan's Big Bang', 14th February 2003; Charles Pretzlik, 'Benefits to City would be only marginal at best, report concludes', 10th June 2003; Bertrand Benoit, 'Long-held dream has proved to be unrealistic', 10th June 2003; Scheherazade Daneshkhu and Chris Giles, 'City becomes undeniable engine of growth', 27th March 2006; Andrew Hill, 'Financial inventors underpin success', 27th March 2006; Steve Johnson, 'London rules new wave of FX deals', 18th July 2006.

markets, catering for small issues that appealed to local investors and were little traded. Many investors looked for high yields and took a buy-and-hold approach to bonds, being prepared to sacrifice liquidity for higher returns. In contrast, other investors favoured liquidity over yield and so looked to those issued in large amounts in currencies such as the US$. More generally, the USA dominated the global bond market, not only with the US$ being the most favoured currency of issue but also as that country was responsible for 45 per cent of the $34.4tn outstanding in 1999. The Eurozone generated a further 21 per cent and Japan 16 per cent, leaving the rest of the world with the remaining 18 per cent. The fragmented nature of the US banking system had long encouraged the use of bonds as they provided a means through which banks could employ spare funds, access additional finance, and diversify exposure in terms of both assets and liabilities. Elsewhere in the world much of this could be accomplished within banks through their ability to spread themselves geographically and across different sectors of an economy. The US reliance on bonds was most apparent when those issued domestically were separated from international issues. In 1999 $29.4tn (85 per cent) of the global total were classed as domestic compared to only $5.0tn (15 per cent) that were international. Of the domestic bonds issued 50 per cent were in the USA. In contrast, the USA was much less dominant among international issues accounting for only 23 per cent compared to Eurozone countries on 32 per cent. The international bond market was used extensively by countries around the world for a variety of different reasons, and this supported the London-centred Eurobond market. One of the commonest reasons for favouring an international bond was when the domestic market was too shallow to support issues made by the central government or to finance large infrastructure projects, as that applied to numerous small countries around the world. Even in larger countries international bond issues were attractive to corporate borrowers where government issues monopolized the domestic market, which was the case in many Latin American countries. In addition, international issues were also used as a way of circumventing either restrictions or taxes imposed on domestic issues, as was the case in Japan and across the European Union. Whether a domestic or an international issue was made the global and international bond market grew strongly between 1992 and 2007, driven by the rising tide of government debt, the privatization of state assets, and the switch away from bank loans as a source of corporate finance. Beginning with the Latin American debt crisis, and then that experienced in Asia and Russia in the late 1990s, investors including banks moved away from syndicated loans to bond issues as the latter were easier to dispose of if the priority was to maintain or restore liquidity.[14]

[14] Leyla Boulton, 'Birth of a hundred markets', 23rd February 1993; Barry Riley, 'A new asset class created', 7th February 1994; Hilary Barnes, 'Drift of trade to London causes concern', 7th April 1994; Sara Webb, 'Dutch win back state debt trade', 16th May 1994; Tracy Corrigan, 'Mood is sombre as bears spoil the fun', 26th May 1994; John Gapper, 'Cold logic wins out at Warburg', 10th January 1995; John Gapper and Richard Lapper, 'Warburg breaks the bond', 11th January 1995; Barry Riley, 'The honeymoon is over', 4th December 1995; Nicholas Denton, 'Banks plan clearing house for trade in emerging market debt', 10th June 1996; Samer Iskandar, 'Electronic trading system for Eurobonds', 23rd January 1998; Simon Davies, 'Junk bonds are back in fashion', 1st May 1998; Simon Davies, 'Myriad possibilities', 1st May 1998; Charles Smith, 'Banking parent provides strength', 21st June 1999; Edward Luce, 'Bonding together', 6th August 1999; Khozem Merchant, 'Avalanche of change hits Alpine retreat', 14th September 1999; Vincent Boland, 'A revolution just waiting to happen', 31st March 2000; Aline van Duyn, 'Trading costs reach unacceptable levels', 8th September 2000; Aline van Duyn, 'Only the best will survive', 28th March 2001; Martin Dickson, 'The market is another country for City's go-between', 7th April 2001; Vincent Boland, 'RepoClear to include UK gilts service', 22nd August 2001; Vincent Boland, 'Cash conduit that secures London's reputation', 12th September 2001; Alex Skorecki, 'London Clearing House mulls link with Clearnet', 15th February 2002; Doug Cameron and Jennifer Hughes, 'Citigroup to join online currency platform', 8th April 2002; Stephen Pritchard, 'A race to stay ahead of fraudsters', 5th June 2002; Alex Skorecki and James Politi, 'LCH offers new cash and repo gilts service', 5th August 2002; Jenny Wiggins, 'Electronic bond trading still has a future', 6th

As the volume and variety of fixed-interest securities in circulation rose rapidly, investors looked for some form of reassurance that borrowers were creditworthy. In 1997 Paul McCarthy, chief executive of Duff and Phelps, a ratings agency, observed that 'You cannot expect investors or fund managers to have the resources or expertise to rate these securities on their own.'[15] Stepping into this gap were credit-rating agencies such as his along with Moody, Standard and Poor, and Fitch. These charged companies and governments a fee for awarding them a credit rating, without which investors could not be persuaded to buy, especially in the USA. The result was to make these rating agencies the 'gatekeepers' of the global capital market rather than the banks as they switched from the lend-and-hold to the originate-and-distribute model. The agencies were of critical importance in rating more specialized issues. Those bonds coming from major sovereign governments and large multinational corporations could command a market in their own right without the need to obtain the seal of approval from a ratings agency. As investors were presented with greater varieties of bonds, ratings agencies were placed in an increasingly powerful position, leading some to question their impartiality as they competed with each other for the business of issuers. In 1997 Karl Bergqwist, head of credit research at HSBC Markets in London, warned that, 'What we don't want to see happening is a situation where the agencies get into a ratings competition war to win business. Rating inflation is always a danger.'[16] What was prompting his scepticism of the ratings being awarded to many bonds was their failure to identify and price the risks attached to emerging market debt in the late 1990s. This weakness in the role performed by the credit-ratings agencies continued to be a concern. Vincent Boland and Aline van Duyn noted in 2001 that, 'Since the bond markets are effectively unregulated, the role of the credit-ratings agencies is becoming crucial; they have become the markets' *de facto* regulators.'[17]

However, as investors sought alternatives to corporate stock in the wake of the collapse of the dot.com speculative bubble, such concerns were ignored because of the attractive returns promised by many of the new bond issues, especially those attached to the securitization of assets such as home loans and automobile purchases in mature economies like the USA and the UK. These bonds were backed by property or a definite income stream and so appeared far safer than the promises made by governments and companies, which had proved illusory, or the even more elusive prospects of high-technology enterprises. The guaranteed returns made securitized assets especially attractive in the low inflation environment that existed in the early twenty-first century. Nevertheless, there were those who continued to warn investors that too much reliance should not be placed on the ratings such bonds had been awarded. In 2004 Alex Skorecki noted that collateralized debt obligations were 'popular with institutional investors because they improve returns' but

September 2002; Alex Skorecki, 'Voice-broked bond trading holds its own', 19th March 2003; Alex Skorecki, 'Electronic trading "cuts costs"', 4th June 2003; Alex Skorecki, 'Gilts still stuck in 17th century', 29th January 2004; Alex Skorecki, 'Icap says phone broking rules market', 4th June 2004; Alex Skorecki and Päivi Munter, 'Sea change for Eurozone bonds', 9th November 2004; Saskia Scholtes, 'Electronic battle heats up', 28th July 2006; Michael Mackenzie and Saskia Scholtes, 'Regulators issue a warning at bond trading's wild frontier', 13th November 2006; David Oakley and Gillian Tett, 'European bond market puts US in the shade', 15th January 2007; Joanna Chung and Gillian Tett, 'Trading suspension raises eyebrows', 24th January 2007; Jamil Anderlini, 'China's corporate bonds come of age', 15th June 2007.

[15] Edward Luce, 'Split in ratings', 25th August 1997.
[16] Edward Luce, 'Split in ratings', 25th August 1997.
[17] Vincent Boland and Aline van Duyn, 'Investor moods prove difficult to interpret', 21st June 2001.

noted that they were also 'complex, opaque and often risky'.[18] By 2005 there were concerns that another speculative bubble was building up but this time centred on property rather than corporate stocks. In that year Philip Coggan suggested that 'The value of all financial assets, including equities and bonds, may be inflated by the recent low levels of real short-term interest rates, which have encouraged investors to chase yield and take greater risks.'[19] Such warnings appeared to have had no effect as bond sales backed by property assets continued in 2006.[20]

By 2004 the issue of asset-backed securities overtook those for corporate debt in the USA, peaking at $773.1bn in 2006. A similar trend was observable in US mortgage-backed securities, which reached $1,253.1bn in 2006. Banks saw securitization as a simple way of complying with their regulatory requirements while increasing their profitability, as the funds released could be lent to others. As Simon Davies reported in 1998, 'Securitisation is an easy way of increasing returns by taking regulatory capital that is tied up in low-yielding assets off the balance sheet.'[21] Further regulatory requirements then pushed banks even

18 Alex Skorecki, 'Complex, opaque and risky—yet popular', 29th November 2004.

19 Philip Coggan, 'Arguments persist over assessing valuations', 10th October 2005.

20 Barry Riley, 'A new asset class created', 7th February 1994; Tracy Corrigan, 'Mood is sombre as bears spoil the fun', 26th May 1994; Tracy Corrigan, 'Privatisation the driving force', 26th May 1994; Tracy Corrigan, 'Banks chase new business', 26th May 1994; Tracy Corrigan, 'Securitisation: a viable financing option', 22nd August 1994; John Gapper, 'Uncertainty over expansion plans', 29th November 1994; John Gapper and Richard Lapper, 'Warburg breaks the bond', 11th January 1995; Conner Middelmann, 'Shift to a higher gear', 19th September 1995; Barry Riley, 'The honeymoon is over', 4th December 1995; John Kingman, 'Painful jolt ends bull run', 28th March 1996; Andrew Fisher, 'European bourses may get lift on back of Emu', 15th April 1997; Jonathan Wheatley, 'Warmer international reception for paper', 10th June 1997; Edward Luce, 'Split in ratings', 25th August 1997; Samer Iskandar, 'Definitions of a new financial instrument', 5th December 1997; Samer Iskandar, 'Electronic trading system for Eurobonds', 23rd January 1998; Samer Iskandar and Edward Luce, 'Big issue for Europe', 4th February 1998; Christine Moir, 'New rules in changed world', 24th March 1998; Simon Davies, 'Myriad possibilities', 1st May 1998; John Ridding, 'A way out of the crisis', 1st May 1998; Norma Cohen, 'Industry joins the information age', 12th March 1999; Arkady Ostrovsky, 'Back-office emerges from shadows', 23rd March 1999; George Graham, 'Weighing up the risks', 4th June 1999; David Hale, 'Rebuilt by Wall Street', 25th January 2000; Vincent Boland, 'Debt on the net', 28th January 2000; Aline van Duyn, 'Coredeal signs up two new backers', 5th March 2000; Vincent Boland, 'A revolution just waiting to happen', 31st March 2000; Judy Dempsey, 'Tel Aviv mulls tax reforms', 8th May 2000; Aline van Duyn, 'Bond markets extend to smaller firms', 19th May 2000; Rebecca Bream, 'Surge in M&A comes to the rescue', 19th May 2000; Rebecca Bream, 'Healthy pipeline of deals is emerging', 19th May 2000; Aline van Duyn, 'Only the best will survive', 28th March 2001; Richard Lapper and Mark Mulligan, 'Picture continues to darken', 28th March 2001; Vincent Boland and Aline van Duyn, 'Investor moods prove difficult to interpret', 21st June 2001; Rebecca Bream, 'Signs of progress in a volatile market', 21st June 2001; Aline van Duyn, 'UK companies embrace cashflow securitisation', 12th July 2001; Vincent Boland, 'RepoClear to include UK gilts service', 22nd August 2001; Vincent Boland, 'Cash conduit that secures London's reputation', 12th September 2001; Aline van Duyn, 'Investors in bonds ask companies for a little respect', 13th May 2002; Alex Skorecki and James Politi, 'LCH offers new cash and repo gilts service', 5th August 2002; Jenny Wiggins, 'Electronic bond trading still has a future', 6th September 2002; Jenny Wiggins, 'History catches up with deals', 7th October 2002; Arkady Ostrovsky, 'From chaos to capitalist triumph', 9th October 2003; Alex Skorecki, 'Global future forecast for covered bonds', 13th November 2003; Alex Skorecki, 'Icap forms bond trading alliance with MarketAxess', 22nd March 2004; Charles Batchelor, 'Future income protecting the present', 23rd March 2004; Alex Skorecki, 'Complex, opaque and risky—yet popular', 29th November 2004; Jennifer Hughes, 'Securitisation gets security conscious', 2nd March 2005; Jennifer Hughes, Richard Beales, and Gillian Tett, 'The yield conundrum: as bond returns drift downwards, is risk soaring for investors', 17th June 2005; Gillian Tett and Tony Tassell, 'A swing into bonds: why equities are losing their allure for global investors', 10th October 2005; Philip Coggan, 'Arguments persist over assessing valuations', 10th October 2005; Ivar Simensen, 'UK regulator warned over transparency', 6th December 2005; Jim Pickard, 'CMBS demand set to increase', 13th January 2006; Paul J. Davies, 'Securitisations set to keep on robust growth path', 3rd February 2006; Paul J. Davies, 'Concerns over rapid growth of CMBS deals among banks', 24th March 2006; Scheherazade Daneshkhu and Chris Giles, 'City becomes undeniable engine of growth', 27th March 2006; Andrew Hill, 'Financial inventors underpin success', 27th March 2006; Paul J. Davies, 'Securitisation enters a fresh phase of life', 25th April 2006; Saskia Scholtes, 'Fitch unveils new agency', 19th October 2006; Chris Giles, 'Into the storm', 14th November 2008; Paul J. Davies, 'Securitisation provides liquidity', 26th November 2008.

21 Simon Davies, 'Myriad possibilities', 1st May 1998.

further towards securitization in the judgement of Charles Batchelor: 'The imminent arrival of Basel 2, which will tighten rules governing the collateral that banks must hold against different classes of loan, is expected to give a further boost to securitisation.'[22] Securitization allowed a bank to remove assets from its balance sheet and so make new loans off the same capital base. Jennifer Hughes, Richard Beales, and Gillian Tett did point out in 2005 that the assets that banks were disposing of involved higher levels of risk: 'As investors gobble up riskier assets—such as mortgage-backed securities or risky leveraged buy-out loans—could they also be making themselves doubly vulnerable to any future shocks?' However, they added the caveat that 'Optimists insist this remains unlikely.'[23] Most did remain optimistic until the crisis began to break in 2007. What Hughes, Beales, and Tett did not spot was that the risks were not confined to investors but also extended to banks, despite the switch from the lend-and-hold to the originate-and-distribute model. Like most others at the time their focus was on solvency, whether it was that of those who were borrowing through the issue of bonds and their equivalents or the banks and fund managers that held these securitized assets. What they, like the ratings agencies, ignored was the question of liquidity. They had not appreciated the significance of the lack of a deep and broad market for most bonds in general and securitized assets in particular, and the effects a crisis of confidence could have on that.[24] By then the practice of securitization had taken hold not only in the USA but across the world.[25]

[22] Charles Batchelor, 'Future income protecting the present', 23rd March 2004.

[23] Jennifer Hughes, Richard Beales, and Gillian Tett, 'The yield conundrum: as bond returns drift downwards, is risk soaring for investors', 17th June 2005.

[24] John Gapper, 'Transatlantic lesson on passing on risks', 22nd October 1993; Antonia Sharpe, 'Flexible friend for lenders', 28th October 1993; Tracy Corrigan, 'Banks chase new business', 26th May 1994; Patrick Harverson and Antonia Sharpe, 'Market stopped in its tracks', 26th May 1994; John Gapper, 'Uncertainty over expansion plans', 29th November 1994; Antonia Sharpe, 'Opportunities to make money in Europe', 10th June 1996; Gwen Robinson, 'Japanese go straight to markets to raise cash', 15th October 1996; Samer Iskandar and Edward Luce, 'Big issue for Europe', 4th February 1998; Simon Davies, 'Myriad possibilities', 1st May 1998; Charles Smith, 'Banking parent provides strength', 21st June 1999; Louise Lucas, 'Esoteric products tap door', 17th December 1999; Paul Abrahams, 'State sales are likely to keep the ball rolling', 17th December 1999; Naoko Nakamae, 'Appetite for Samurais grows', 17th December 1999; David Hale, 'Rebuilt by Wall Street', 25th January 2000; Bayan Rahman, 'Global players enjoy feast', 8th May 2000; Gillian Tett, 'Crunch brings some benefits', 8th May 2000; Aline van Duyn, 'Bond markets extend to smaller firms', 19th May 2000; Rebecca Bream, 'Surge in M&A comes to the rescue', 19th May 2000; Rahul Jacob and Naoko Nakamae, 'Prospects promising in year of the deal', 19th May 2000; Aline van Duyn, 'UK companies embrace cashflow securitisation', 12th July 2001; Stephen Pritchard, 'A race to stay ahead of fraudsters', 5th June 2002; Adrienne Roberts, 'ABS debt thrives on innovation', 22nd October 2003; Charles Batchelor, 'Future income protecting the present', 23rd March 2004; Adrian Michaels and Jenny Wiggins, 'Regulators plan overhaul', 31st March 2004; Alex Skorecki, 'Icap says phone broking rules market', 4th June 2004; Charles Batchelor, 'Long pedigree of the clearing house for short-term funds', 23rd July 2004; Charles Batchelor, 'London leads in trading volumes', 23rd September 2004; Charles Batchelor, 'Taking the mystery out of securitisation', 28th September 2004; Alex Skorecki and Päivi Munter, 'Sea change for Eurozone bonds', 9th November 2004; Alex Skorecki, 'Reuters takes battle to Bloomberg', 23rd November 2004; Charles Batchelor, 'Joining Europe's mainstream', 29th November 2004; Ivar Simensen, 'A roller-coaster ride at Welcome Break', 29th November 2004; Jennifer Hughes, 'Investor appetite for paper shows few signs of abating', 29th November 2004; Alex Skorecki, 'Bank of England lights a fuse', 30th November 2004; Charles Batchelor and Jane Fuller, 'Inland revenue in talks on securitisation', 22nd December 2004; Jennifer Hughes, 'Securitisation gets security conscious', 2nd March 2005; Jennifer Hughes, Richard Beales, and Gillian Tett, 'The yield conundrum: as bond returns drift downwards, is risk soaring for investors', 17th June 2005; Stephen Fidler, 'How the Square Mile defeated the prophets of doom', 10th December 2005; Scheherazade Daneshkhu and Chris Giles, 'City becomes undeniable engine of growth', 27th March 2006; Andrew Hill, 'Financial inventors underpin success', 27th March 2006; Paul J. Davies, 'Securitisation enters a fresh phase of life', 25th April 2006.

[25] John Gapper, 'Transatlantic lesson on passing on risks', 22nd October 1993; Antonia Sharpe, 'Flexible friend for lenders', 28th October 1993; Antonia Sharpe, 'Opportunities to make money in Europe', 10th June 1996; *Financial Times*, 'Investing in bonds: now back in favour', 9th November 1998; Norma Cohen, 'Industry joins the information age', 12th March 1999; Aline van Duyn, 'Bond markets extend to smaller firms', 19th May 2000; Alex Skorecki, 'Icap forms bond trading alliance with MarketAxess', 22nd March 2004; Adrian Michaels and Jenny Wiggins, 'Regulators plan overhaul', 31st March 2004; Jennifer Hughes, 'Investor appetite for paper shows few

One of the first locations outside the USA to embrace securitization was the UK where the issue of mortgage bonds by UK banks climbed from $25bn in 2002 to $200bn in 2006. Continental Europe followed closely as both issuers and investors were familiar with bonds as there was a large government bond market in existence. European investors were also significant purchasers of the mortgage bonds and other asset-backed securities being generated in the USA. From that position it was only a short step to the practice of securitization. Beginning in 1999 the Italian government began raising funds by securitizing cash flows from specific state assets and then selling bonds to investors whose income came from these revenue streams. This was picked up on by other heavily-indebted European governments, namely Greece and Portugal, as the bonds were not classified as national debt and so were outside what was permitted under their commitments to the single currency. The problem in Europe, even more than in the USA, was the fragmented nature of the bond market. The introduction of the euro in 1999 did help to deepen and broaden the European bond market, allowing individual governments and companies to borrow much larger amounts than in the past when they were confined to investors located in their home country. However, differing regulations and legal requirements across Europe continued to prevent the creation of a seamless market, in the judgement of Vincent Boland in 2001: 'Regulators in all European Union countries have differing standards and requirements and issuers have no choice to meet them. This is costly and time-consuming.'[26] By 2004 there was $4.6tn of Eurozone debt outstanding versus $10.4tn from the US Treasury but in Europe each country using the single currency was responsible for its own fiscal policy, including the size and nature of its borrowing. This meant that bonds issued by the German and Austrian governments, for example, commanded a different price in 2004 though both were denominated in Euros and were triple-A rated. The reason was the lower liquidity of Austria's bonds compared to those of Germany.

Despite Switzerland being the world's largest centre for private wealth management it also lacked a liquid market for Swiss franc bonds, discouraging investors from buying them because they had to wait until they matured. Mike Neumann, head of debt capital markets at Deutsche Bank's Swiss office, explained the problem in 1998: 'To come in and go out (of the market), you need a degree of liquidity and a degree of transparency. Compared with euro and dollar markets, Switzerland is just very small.'[27] Under these conditions there was a tendency for the European bond markets to concentrate in London, other than those that were closely held by local investors, as was the case with many of the more specialized issues such as the mortgage bonds, or Pfandbriefe, in Germany. The UK was not in the single currency but London was already a well-established location for the global bond market. London catered for large international issues, especially Eurobonds, which had become a routine, high-volume, low-margin business by the 1990s. What London possessed was a dense cluster of banks that both issued new bonds for government and corporate borrowers worldwide and bought and sold existing bonds on behalf of institutional investors from around the globe. This facility was extensively used by emerging economies, such as Turkey, that lacked the ability to issue and then trade their own bonds, as well as smaller developed economies, like Denmark, whose domestic market could not support

signs of abating', 29th November 2004; Charles Batchelor and Jane Fuller, 'Inland revenue in talks on securitisation', 22nd December 2004; Michael Mackenzie and Saskia Scholtes, 'Regulators issue a warning at bond trading's wild frontier', 13th November 2006.

[26] Vincent Boland, 'Euro gives spur for updating', 21st June 2001.

[27] Alice Ratcliffe, 'Banking on an outsider status', 13th October 1998.

the deep and broad market required for the largest issues. London could then bring this expertise, infrastructure, and connections to Eurozone issues as rival centres in Europe lost the advantage that had come from handling national issues in national currencies which were sold to local investors.[28]

After Europe another obvious location for the revival of the bond market was Asia. Though developments did take place across Asia the pace of progress in Japan was both slow and limited because of tight regulation imposed by the Ministry of Finance and the reluctance of financial authorities to cede control. Nevertheless, by 2000 the Japanese government bond market was vying with the US Treasury market as the biggest government debt market in the world. However, it attracted little international interest as Japanese institutions dominated the market holding more than 90 per cent of the total outstanding. The Japanese corporate bond market also grew in importance as companies switched from a reliance on bank finance, especially after the crisis of 1997–8 led to a drying up of cheap and abundant loans. Despite this growth in the domestic bond market it continued to suffer problems relating to efficiency, settlement, and liquidity, which encouraged the use of an alternative Euroyen bond market in London. The problems of the Japanese bond market in the 1990s also encouraged the authorities in Hong Kong and Singapore to offer an alternative

[28] Tracy Corrigan, 'Dull can be dynamic', 27th May 1993; Barry Riley, 'A new asset class created', 7th February 1994; Hilary Barnes, 'Drift of trade to London causes concern', 7th April 1994; Sara Webb, 'Dutch win back state debt trade', 16th May 1994; Tracy Corrigan, 'Mood is sombre as bears spoil the fun', 26th May 1994; Patrick Harverson and Antonia Sharpe, 'Market stopped in its tracks', 26th May 1994; Antonia Sharpe, 'Amsterdam prepares to fight back', 16th June 1994; Barry Riley, 'The honeymoon is over', 4th December 1995; FT Staff, 'Surviving in the free world', 21st March 1996; Antonia Sharpe, 'Opportunities to make money in Europe', 10th June 1996; Graham Bowley, 'Bankers ponder whether to seize the day', 19th November 1996; John Barham, 'Designs on neighbours', 6th December 1996; George Graham, 'Radical changes may lie ahead', 9th April 1997; Richard Adams, 'Market developed out of a disaster', 9th April 1997; Jonathan Wheatley, 'Warmer international reception for paper', 10th June 1997; Samer Iskandar, 'Electronic trading system for Eurobonds', 23rd January 1998; Stanislas Yassukovich, 'Single market for equities', 26th January 1998; Christine Moir, 'New rules in changed world', 24th March 1998; Simon Davies, 'Powerful forces for change', 30th April 1998; Simon Davies, 'Myriad possibilities', 1st May 1998; Edward Luce, 'A cloud over Frankfurt's ambitions', 24th June 1998; Alice Ratcliffe, 'Banking on an outsider status', 13th October 1998; William Hall, 'Swiss exchange aims to lick stamp duty', 26th October 1998; Edward Luce, 'Bankers and Brussels at odds over impact on London', 9th December 1998; Edward Luce, 'Agencies to target Europe's burgeoning bond market', 17th December 1998; Norma Cohen, 'Industry joins the information age', 12th March 1999; Arkady Ostrovsky, 'Back-office emerges from shadows', 23rd March 1999; Edward Luce, 'Hub and spokes proposal for root and branch reform', 14th May 1999; Vincent Boland and Edward Luce, 'Electronic bond trading system to expand range', 26th July 1999; Edward Luce, 'Bonding together', 6th August 1999; Arkady Ostrovsky, 'Clearers jostle for dominance', 20th September 1999; Arkady Ostrovsky, 'JP Morgan targets e-trading', 25th October 1999; Edward Luce, 'LCH introduces real-time settlement on Euro-MTS', 14th December 1999; Aline van Duyn, 'Euro helps prompt a shift to equities', 19th May 2000; Aline van Duyn, 'Why closer links with Europe could lead to US costs', 1st September 2000; Patrick Jenkins, 'Commissions on German share deals to decline', 2nd September 2000; Aline van Duyn, 'Trading costs reach unacceptable levels', 8th September 2000; Aline van Duyn, 'Bond market has operators on the line', 21st June 2001; Vincent Boland, 'Euro gives spur for updating', 21st June 2001; Aline van Duyn, 'UK companies embrace cashflow securitisation', 12th July 2001; Vincent Boland, 'RepoClear to include UK gilts service', 22nd August 2001; Vincent Boland, 'Cash conduit that secures London's reputation', 12th September 2001; Alex Skorecki and James Politi, 'LCH offers new cash and repo gilts service', 5th August 2002; Alex Skorecki, 'Global future forecast for covered bonds', 13th November 2003; Ivar Simensen, 'Inaugural issuer back after 40 years', 27th May 2004; Alex Skorecki, 'Euro bond traders get back on phone', 27th August 2004; Aline van Duyn and Päivi Munter, 'How Citigroup shook Europe's bond markets with two minutes of trading', 10th September 2004; Ivar Simensen, 'Branching out from their German roots', 29th November 2004; Päivi Munter, 'Flair keeps deficit in check', 29th November 2004; Charles Batchelor, 'A brief jargon buster', 29th November 2004; Alex Skorecki, 'Citi trades broke gentleman's deal', 3rd February 2005; Ivar Simensen, 'UK regulator warned over transparency', 6th December 2005; Joanna Chung, 'EU securitisation may have passed peak', 7th December 2005; Stephen Fidler, 'How the Square Mile defeated the prophets of doom', 10th December 2005; Jim Pickard, 'CMBS demand set to increase', 13th January 2006; Paul J. Davies, 'Securitisations set to keep on robust growth path', 3rd February 2006; Scheherazade Daneshkhu and Chris Giles, 'City becomes undeniable engine of growth', 27th March 2006; Andrew Hill, 'Financial inventors underpin success', 27th March 2006.

venue to cater not only to countries throughout Asia but to the Japanese themselves. That competition forced the Japanese government to drive through further reforms of the domestic bond market though it stopped short of an embrace of securitization.[29]

It was not only securitization that the world was copying from the USA in the 1990s. Another US practice, related to the bond market, that was spreading from the US was the use of the repo facility. By 2006 the value of trading in the European repo market had overtaken that in the USA fuelled by changes in the capital-adequacy ratios banks had to abide by under new Basel rules. A repo was an agreement to simultaneously sell and then repurchase a bond at a fixed price and date. The bond provided collateral for the loan and the repurchase agreement guaranteed repayment. The use of repos was an established feature of the US money market, being an alternative to unsecured lending among banks. By 2006 the repo market had become the engine of liquidity for the US Treasury market, which had a daily turnover of $1,900bn. Outside the USA the growth of the repo market faced obstacles from central banks, as it diminished their ability to exercise control and created counterparty risks. In Europe, for example, the repo market became established first in Paris rather than London because the French government was more supportive than the Bank of England. Similarly in Japan the growth of the Tokyo repo market was stunted by the restrictions imposed. Nevertheless, as the barriers were removed repo markets began to flourish around the world from the mid-1990s onwards. Repo markets were especially popular among investment banks, as they did not have access to the inter-bank markets where commercial banks borrowed and lent among each other without the use of collateral. They were also popular with corporate treasurers, who had traditionally placed excess cash with banks, but could now directly access repo markets and benefit from higher returns and greater security. The repo market was used extensively as a way of either employing spare funds remuneratively or accessing additional funds cheaply, while maintaining control over either liquidity or a portfolio of assets. The risk attached to the repo market was that the counterparty would fail to repurchase leaving the lender holding bonds that they were either unable to sell or only at a loss compared to the value of the loan. Hence the preference in repo transactions for US Treasury bonds, which were highly liquid, subject to little change in price, were denominated in US$s, and had the security of the US government behind them. The downside was the low returns they generated, which encouraged their substitution with higher-yielding bonds, such as securitized assets. The problem there was the lower quality of these alternative bonds and, more importantly, their lack of liquidity compared to US Treasuries.[30]

[29] Barry Riley, 'A new asset class created', 7th February 1994; Emiko Terazono, 'Patience is running out', 26th May 1994; Gerard Baker, 'Regional rivals hot on its heels', 19th October 1994; Conner Middelmann, 'Shift to a higher gear', 19th September 1995; Emiko Terazono, 'The worst may be over', 28th March 1996; Nicholas Denton, 'Banks plan clearing house for trade in emerging market debt', 10th June 1996; Gwen Robinson, 'Japanese go straight to markets to raise cash', 15th October 1996; John Barham, 'Designs on neighbours', 6th December 1996; John Ridding, 'A way out of the crisis', 1st May 1998; Gillian Tett, 'No longer a Cinderella', 1st May 1998; Charles Smith, 'Banking parent provides strength', 21st June 1999; Naoko Nakamae, 'Steady progress with JGBs', 21st June 1999; Louise Lucas, 'Esoteric products tap door', 17th December 1999; Paul Abrahams, 'State sales are likely to keep the ball rolling', 17th December 1999; Naoko Nakamae, 'Appetite for Samurais grows', 17th December 1999; Naoko Nakamae, 'Prices still resilient despite jitters', 8th May 2000; Gillian Tett, 'Crunch brings some benefits', 8th May 2000; Rahul Jacob and Naoko Nakamae, 'Prospects promising in year of the deal', 19th May 2000; Alexandra Schmertz, 'JGB market in scramble to introduce electronic trading', 25th October 2000.

[30] Richard Lapper and Philip Gawith, 'London braces itself for a repo revolution', 2nd January 1996; Philip Gawith and Richard Lapper, 'The new kid in the City', 1st March 1996; Richard Lapper, 'Clarifying a complicated subject', 1st March 1996; Graham Bowley, 'Troubled road to reform', 1st March 1996; Richard Lapper, 'Traders starting to catch on', 1st March 1996; Norma Cohen, 'Learning lessons from the US', 1st March 1996; Emiko Terazono, 'Move to create a new market', 1st March 1996; Brian Bollen, 'Europe takes to tri-party', 1st March 1996;

Electronic Revolution

Throughout the years between 1992 and 2007 global financial markets experienced an electronic revolution that totally transformed the way trading was conducted. Prior to then trading was dependent upon the telephone, and took place through direct voice communication. This was either between banks or through the intermediation of interdealer brokers. For the foreign exchange market the electronic revolution began to change in 1992 when Reuters 2000 was launched as this transformed the price display service it already provided into an interactive trading network. Rival systems followed in 1993 such as Minex, aimed at the Asian market, and Electronic Broking Services (EBS) for the US market. In these automated systems a foreign exchange dealer posted buy and sell prices on the screen to which another dealer responded by typing instructions on to the terminal. Only when the deal was done were the identities of both parties revealed. That exposed dealers to counterparty risk unlike the use of either a trusted broker or trading directly with another bank. For that reason there was some hesitation in switching to automated dealing, which deprived the new systems of liquidity. Liquidity was essential in what was a high-risk, high-volume, low-margin business as it allowed deals to be made quickly at current prices. In a bid to improve liquidity and build up a global network EBS and Minex merged in 1995. Nevertheless, as the great advantage of these automated systems was that they were both faster and cheaper than voice brokers, they succeeded in gaining traction among banks.

Reuters and EBS served different segments of the foreign exchange market. EBS was used extensively in the wholesale or interbank market, which was dominated by the megabanks. The wholesale market was where a small number of global banks traded with each other either for profit or to offset the risks they were taking through exposure to currency volatility. These banks also conducted a retail trade, dealing with their own customers and often acting as counterparties when providing them with their currency requirements. For this purpose they developed internal networks linking customers with the bank. These customers included smaller banks, who could not afford a dedicated team of foreign exchange staff and provide them with the space and technology they required. In contrast, Reuters serviced the needs of the smaller banks, providing them with access to current prices and the ability to have their buy and sell orders automatically matched, so reducing their dependence upon the global banks. By 2003 EBS had 2000 terminals in dealing rooms around the world and had captured the high volume end of the foreign exchange market conducted by the global banks, handling trading in the most liquid currencies such as the

Brian Bollen, 'Baby with a big future', 1st March 1996; Christine Moir, 'Consolidation on the cards', 1st March 1996; Andrew Jack, 'More liquid than London', 1st March 1996; Conner Middelmann, 'Domestic market is struggling', 1st March 1996; Antonia Sharpe, 'The haves and the have-nots', 1st March 1996; Philip Gawith, 'Gilt repo may hasten change', 1st March 1996; Graham Bowley and Richard Lapper, 'Gilt-edged opportunities', 19th June 1996; Graham Bowley, 'Repos may keep City on top', 6th November 1996; Richard Adams, 'An artificial and antiquated straightjacket', 5th December 1996; Graham Bowley, 'Historic day for way Bank goes to work', 3rd March 1997; Samer Iskandar, 'Safer lending of securities', 5th December 1997; Edward Luce, 'Discount market follows the top hat into history', 23rd December 1998; Arkady Ostrovsky, 'Back-office emerges from shadows', 23rd March 1999; Arkady Ostrovsky, 'Clearers jostle for dominance', 20th September 1999; Nikki Tait, 'LCH seeks twin in the US', 11th November 1999; Vincent Boland, 'RepoClear to include UK gilts service', 22nd August 2001; Vincent Boland, 'Cash conduit that secures London's reputation', 12th September 2001; Alex Skorecki and James Politi, 'LCH offers new cash and repo gilts service', 5th August 2002; Jenny Wiggins, 'Electronic bond trading still has a future', 6th September 2002; Jennifer Hughes, 'Guide to make fails safer', 28th March 2006; Jennifer Hughes, 'Bankers divided on need for backstop', 4th May 2006; Michael Mackenzie and Saskia Scholtes, 'Regulators issue a warning at bond trading's wild frontier', 13th November 2006; David Oakley, 'European repo trading grows Euro 500bn in year', 2nd March 2007.

Euro, Yen, and the $. Reuters controlled a much larger network, with 24,000 connections in 1998, but these included many who traded in smaller amounts and in less-liquid currencies. Bloomberg attempted to break the duopoly established by EBS and Reuters. In 1996 it began offering a similar service but it was difficult to dislodge Reuters and EBS. Each had established control over key sections of the market, becoming centres of liquidity.

The success of Reuters and EBS did not mean that electronic trading systems displaced the voice brokers totally. In 1999 Alan Beattie reported that 'The currency markets have a reputation as one of the last outposts of barrow-boy raucousness, where deals are shouted down phones and prices relayed by the constant burble of the "squawk box"—the two-way loudspeakers that sit on top of every trader's screen, providing perpetual communication with the voice brokers who traditionally bring buyers and sellers together.'[31] For many companies, fund managers and smaller banks foreign exchange was a by-product of another transaction, whether it was a financial one or a sale or purchase of goods and services. They were content to give the business to a global bank or place it in the hands of an interdealer broker, and pass the cost on to their client or absorb it within the business. There were also numerous currency pairings or transactions for small amounts that took time to arrange and involved negotiation and here the interdealer brokers remained essential. Even the global banks made use of their services as none could justify the expense of maintaining a team sufficient to cover all currencies and deals. Despite the continued role played by these voice brokers the foreign exchange market moved inexorably towards an electronic future. The whole process of dealing in foreign exchange, from initial inquiry through to trade and settlement, increasingly took place without a single human involvement, whether it involved internal bank networks, those provided by EBS and Reuters, or the growing proliferation of alternative systems. One was FXall that catered for the foreign exchange requirements of institutional investors, such as hedge funds, who were trading foreign exchange not as an adjunct to an existing business but as an asset which offered the prospect of substantial gain through frequent buying and selling. What they wanted was a dealing service that was both cheap and fast and could handle the volume of buying and selling that they produced. By 2005 high-volume standardized transactions in the foreign exchange market were largely automated, whether wholesale or retail. One outcome was the merger in 2006 of the largest interdealer broker, ICAP, with the biggest interdealer platform, EBS, so combining telephone and electronic trading.[32]

[31] Alan Beattie, '"Barrow boys" at risk as the currency markets switch on', 6th July 1999.

[32] James Blitz, 'Foreign exchange dealers enter the 21st century', 13th September 1993; Philip Gawith, 'Technology on the march', 2nd June 1994; Patrick Harverson, 'Exco staff suffer as world markets slow', 24th November 1995; Philip Gawith, 'Brokers lose their voices on the small screen', 15th December 1995; Philip Gawith, 'Exotic but not for faint hearts', 15th May 1996; Simon Kuper, 'Bleak days ahead for forex traders', 24th December 1996; Richard Adams, 'Voice-brokers are lapsing into silence', 18th April 1997; Simon Kuper, 'Reuters falls behind EBS in electronic broking', 30th June 1997; Simon Kuper, 'Old order gives way to the new', 5th June 1998; Simon Kuper, 'Information on the button', 5th June 1998; John Gapper, 'What price information', 20th July 1998; Alan Beattie, 'Floor presence thins out', 25th June 1999; Richard Adams, 'Brokers alter shape of things to come', 25th June 1999; Alan Beattie, 'Tullett and Bloomberg plan new broking system', 5th July 1999; Alan Beattie, '"Barrow boys" at risk as the currency markets switch on', 6th July 1999; Christopher Swann and Doug Cameron, 'FXall set to intensify battle in online currency trading', 10th May 2001; Doug Cameron, 'Currenex to form exchange', 26th November 2001; Geoffrey Nairn, 'Internet fails to transform the foreign exchange world', 5th June 2002; Tim Burt, 'Bloomberg in forex challenge to Reuters', 21st May 2003; Jennifer Hughes, 'Traders set to take the forex challenge', 22nd May 2003; Tim Burt, 'A new vision of finance beckons as rivals prepare for court battle', 12th July 2003; Jennifer Hughes, 'Where money talks very loudly', 27th May 2004; Jennifer Hughes, 'History goes full circle as volume is king', 27th May 2004; Jennifer Hughes, 'The mouse takes over the floor', 27th May 2004; Jennifer Hughes, 'A veteran with a proud record of service', 27th May 2004; Jennifer Hughes, 'Interbank online action set to soar', 25th February 2005; Jennifer Hughes, 'Eurex issues a challenge to CME', 17th June 2005; Jennifer Hughes,

It was not only in the foreign exchange market that trading was transformed by the electronic revolution for the same was happening in the bond market. Again, it was data providers that sensed an opportunity to extend their business beyond the provision of information to operating trading systems. These data providers already maintained a global network of terminals that provided traders and investors with current bond prices. It was a short step to making the links interactive so that buying and selling could take place, as had already been done successfully in the foreign exchange market. The bond market existed on two main levels. The first level was the one at which a small core of banks traded either directly with each other or through interdealer brokers. This was the wholesale market and involved huge volumes being bought and sold at margins as banks adjusted their assets and liabilities, employed spare funds, and topped-up shortages by trading with each other. This was a closed market to which only the most trusted counterparties were admitted and operated with its own code of conduct. At the other level was the retail market where banks traded with their own customers by selling bonds to them or buying bonds from them. Reuters and Bloomberg had long supplied banks with the technology and connections that supported their retail bond-trading operations, as they had the infrastructure to do so. What they now sought to do was become active participants in actual trading. This had already been done by TradeWeb, which was strong in sovereign debt, having provided a trading platform for US Treasuries in 1998, and MarketAxess, which was strong in corporate debt, where it began operating in 2000. These platforms took trading away from the conventional order-driven market, where the bank put up prices and then responded to customers, to one where customers put in a request for quotes and the banks responded. This altered the balance of power away from the bank to the customer as it provided the latter with choice.

What these information providers initially failed to grasp was that whereas the foreign exchange market was a global one, operating on a 24/7 basis, the bond market was not. Instead, it consisted of pools of liquidity found at particular levels and in particular locations, and it was to these that trading gravitated. New York was the centre of trading in US Treasuries, Tokyo for Japan Government bonds, and London for Eurobonds. There were then much smaller pools of liquidity for less-actively-traded bonds, usually in each country's financial centre and these were able to resist the gravitational pull of the likes of London and New York. Under these circumstances the advantages of an international trading network were limited. Instead, it was the real time prices that information providers supplied that were useful as they were a major influence on market behaviour around the world. In addition, the extensive nature of the connections provided by the information providers worked to their disadvantage. In 2004 Bloomberg had terminals on the desktops of more than 250,000 professional investors and brokers around the world. However, active trading in bonds was, in every case, confined to a small group of trusted counterparties who accepted the terms and conditions applied in each market and had the power to police behaviour through the ability to exclude those who did not comply. Liquid markets required far more than the passive connections that the information providers could supply, no matter how extensive these were. To make a market liquid required the active participation of banks and brokers either willing to take a position in the market for the prospect of profit or generate buying and selling because of the fees they earned. Recognizing this reality Thomson in 2004 took over TradeWeb, which was a

'Lava Platform to challenge duopoly', 25th April 2006; Jennifer Hughes, 'FX firebrand dream of revolution', 9th May 2006; Steve Johnson, 'London rules new wave of FX deals', 18th July 2006.

dedicated bond-trading platform serving 1500 institutional customers spread across the USA and Europe.[33]

In those countries where such markets were appearing for the first time the electronic option was often the first choice, as in Moscow in 1993. It was also used extensively for trading the debt of emerging economies in the 1990s. Even in well-established markets it was being chosen as a way of recapturing lost trading. As Lee Olesky, chief executive of BrokerTec, observed in 1999, 'The technology now exists to concentrate a multitude of different markets on the same screen.'[34] By 2001 Stanley Shelton, executive vice-president of the giant US fund manager, State Street, claimed that 'There are more than 300 bond-trading systems if all the various banking and financial websites are included, and all of them cannot remain operational because most of the business models will not generate enough revenues even if they are able to attract trading volumes.'[35] In corporate bonds the number of electronic platforms peaked at eighty in 2000 but fell to forty in 2003 as many failed to achieve the necessary level of liquidity to attract users. One electronic platform that did catch on was EuroMTS. This was owned by a consortium of banks and catered for trading in euro-denominated government bonds, taking advantage of the introduction of a single currency for most members of the European Union in 1999. EuroMTS had begun in 1988 as Mercato dei Titolo di Stato (MTS), to provide a market for Italian government bonds. In 1998 it was privatized, coming under the ownership of fifty-five banks. The following year it was adopted by EU governments as the platform of choice for trading Eurozone debt. By 2005 it handled over 50 per cent of Eurozone government bond trading and, in that year it was acquired by the pan-European stock exchange, Euronext, and the Borsa Italiana as they expanded their trading into fixed interest and away from a reliance on stocks. Another bond-trading platform that caught on was BrokerTec, which was also owned by a consortium of banks and focused on the market for US government debt. It captured a growing share of the market in US Treasuries, reaching 40 per cent in 2003, when it was acquired by ICAP, the interdealer broker.

The size and diversity of the global bond market meant that several trading systems could co-exist. Some systems were designed for cross-border trading while others met national requirements. Some catered for the high-volume wholesale market while others met a retail need. Some provided a market for the small number of government and corporate bond issues that were highly liquid while others provided a means through which the much less liquid but much more numerous ones could be bought and sold. No single platform could meet all needs and not all trading was suited to electronic platforms of any kind, especially those involving complex deals. In Europe in 2003 70 per cent of government debt was traded electronically while such platforms had hardly made an impact on corporate bonds, reflecting the relative size and the liquidity of the different issues. In 1999 Lee Amaitis, chief executive in Europe for the interdealer broker, Cantor Fitzgerald, observed, 'The higher the volume and turnover in a market, the easier it is to trade it electronically. We will see high-volume and low-margin bonds migrate very quickly to the

[33] Philip Gawith, 'Brokers lose their voices on the small screen', 15th December 1995; Alan Beattie, 'Tullett and Bloomberg plan new broking system', 5th July 1999; Alan Beattie, '"Barrow boys" at risk as the currency markets switch on', 6th July 1999; Alex Skorecki, 'Gilts still stuck in 17th century', 29th January 2004; Alex Skorecki and Päivi Munter, 'Sea change for Eurozone bonds', 9th November 2004; Alex Skorecki, 'Reuters takes battle to Bloomberg', 23rd November 2004; Tim Burt, 'Reuters loses market share', 28th April 2005; Andrew Edgecliffe-Johnson, 'Glocer needs to be clearer to get growth message across on Reuters', 24th February 2006.

[34] Edward Luce, 'Bonding together', 6th August 1999.

[35] Aline van Duyn, 'Only the best will survive', 28th March 2001.

screen, while the trickier, less-liquid instruments will probably continue to be traded over the telephone.'[36] There were also national differences reflecting the attitude of central banks and the degree of competition permitted by the authorities. While there was a relatively rapid migration to electronic systems for trading for US government debt the process was very slow in Japan where regulatory barriers prevented the creation of the large liquid markets that would support investment in electronic trading systems. Across Europe the roll-out of electronic trading was patchy. By 2003 trading in the bonds issued by continental governments was70 per cent electronic while the figure for UK government debt was only7 per cent. Despite the variations the period between 1992 and 2007 witnessed the triumph of electronic markets across a growing range of financial products.[37]

Conclusion

In the wake of the emergence of megabanks, and the adoption of the originate-and-distribute model of banking, global financial markets were transformed between 1992 and 2007.

[36] Edward Luce, 'Bonding together', 6th August 1999.

[37] Leyla Boulton, 'Birth of a hundred markets', 23rd February 1993; Antonia Sharpe, 'Amsterdam prepares to fight back', 16th June 1994; Philip Gawith, 'Brokers lose their voices on the small screen', 15th December 1995; Nicholas Denton, 'Banks plan clearing house for trade in emerging market debt', 10th June 1996; Samer Iskandar, 'Electronic trading system for Eurobonds', 23rd January 1998; Edward Luce and Khozem Merchant, 'Cantor launches electronic trading for bonds', 2nd July 1999; Alan Beattie, 'Tullett and Bloomberg plan new broking system', 5th July 1999; Alan Beattie, '"Barrow boys" at risk as the currency markets switch on', 6th July 1999; Vincent Boland and Edward Luce, 'Electronic bond trading system to expand range', 26th July 1999; Edward Luce, 'Bonding together', 6th August 1999; Khozem Merchant, 'Avalanche of change hits Alpine retreat', 14th September 1999; Arkady Ostrovsky, 'JP Morgan targets e-trading', 25th October 1999; Edward Luce, 'LCH introduces real-time settlement on Euro-MTS', 14th December 1999; Vincent Boland, 'A revolution just waiting to happen', 31st March 2000; Aline van Duyn, 'Coredeal signs up two new backers', 5th March 2000; Aline van Duyn, 'Why closer links with Europe could lead to US costs', 1st September 2000; Patrick Jenkins, 'Commissions on German share deals to decline', 2nd September 2000; Aline van Duyn, 'Trading costs reach unacceptable levels', 8th September 2000; Alexandra Schmertz, 'JGB market in scramble to introduce electronic trading', 25th October 2000; Florian Gimbel, 'Electronic swap systems set to go live', 20th December 2000; Aline van Duyn, 'Only the best will survive', 28th March 2001; Martin Dickson, 'The market is another country for City's go-between', 7th April 2001; Vincent Boland, 'RepoClear to include UK gilts service', 22nd August 2001; Vincent Boland, 'Cash conduit that secures London's reputation', 12th September 2001; Peter John, 'Fat Finger syndrome can be bad for financial health', 9th December 2001; Alex Skorecki, 'London Clearing House mulls link with Clearnet', 15th February 2002; Doug Cameron, 'Ways to enhance voice-broking services', 3rd April 2002; Doug Cameron and Jennifer Hughes, 'Citigroup to join online currency platform', 8th April 2002; Alex Skorecki and James Politi, 'LCH offers new cash and repo gilts service', 5th August 2002; Jenny Wiggins, 'Electronic bond trading still has a future', 6th September 2002; Alex Skorecki, 'Voice-broked bond trading holds its own', 19th March 2003; Alex Skorecki, 'Electronic trading "cuts costs"', 4th June 2003; Arkady Ostrovsky, 'From chaos to capitalist triumph', 9th October 2003; Alex Skorecki, 'Gilts still stuck in 17th century', 29th January 2004; Charles Batchelor, 'EuroMTS launches European T-bill platform', 16th March 2004; Alex Skorecki, 'Icap forms bond trading alliance with MarketAxess', 22nd March 2004; Alex Skorecki, 'Icap says phone broking rules market', 4th June 2004; Päivi Munter and Charles Batchelor, 'Citigroup coup stirs up emotions', 11th August 2004; Alex Skorecki, 'Cantor split off bucks the trend', 18th August 2004; Alex Skorecki, 'Euro bond traders get back on phone', 27th August 2004; Aline van Duyn and Päivi Munter, 'How Citigroup shook Europe's bond markets with two minutes of trading', 10th September 2004; Alex Skorecki, 'Electronic trading of CDSs expands', 3rd November 2004; Alex Skorecki and Päivi Munter, 'Sea change for Eurozone bonds', 9th November 2004; Alex Skorecki, 'Reuters takes battle to Bloomberg', 23rd November 2004; Alex Skorecki, 'Bold vision demands a response', 14th December 2004; Alex Skorecki and Martin Arnold, 'Euronext in talks to buy MTS trading platform', 5th January 2005; Alex Skorecki, 'Citi trades broke gentleman's deal', 3rd February 2005; Alex Skorecki, 'Cantor wrestles to stay Treasury heavyweight', 8th February 2005; Päivi Munter, 'Bonds trading needs clarity', 29th April 2005; Päivi Munter, 'ESpeed leads bidding for MTS', 4th May 2005; Päivi Munter, 'ESpeed increases its offer for MTS', 16th June 2005; Päivi Munter, 'European group wins bid for MTS', 2nd July 2005; Sarah Spikes, 'Icap chief caps a 20-year rise to the stars', 22nd April 2006; Saskia Scholtes, 'Electronic battle heats up', 28th July 2006; Joanna Chung and Gillian Tett, 'MTS chief hedges bets on global expansion', 19th October 2006; Tobias Buck and Gillian Tett, 'Battle heats up over Europe's bond markets', 30th November 2006; Gillian Tett, 'Dominant role of MTS could be undermined', 2nd November 2007; Gillian Tett, 'MTS grip under threat', 19th November 2007.

This transformation extended all the way from the products being traded to the adoption of electronic platforms to handle the volume and variety of trading taking place. Such was the success of these financial markets that the question of liquidity appeared to have been banished. Whether it was in the foreign exchange market or that for securitized assets the underlying assumption was that all financial products could be bought and sold at prices that were known to all. The danger in such an assumption was that those investing in such financial products, or accepting them as collateral, did so in the belief that, regardless of circumstances, they could be sold to others. This was the case in the repo market, for example, where the securities used in transactions widened beyond US Treasury bonds and their equivalent, to include securitized assets that were much less liquid. In 2001 the UK's Debt Management Office recognized this trend and introduced a system that allowed those in the repo market to borrow any security from the government if they were suddenly in very short supply. This was copied by Australia and New Zealand, but not in the USA. By 2006 the US Treasury was considering plans to provide a lender-of-last-resort facility to the Treasury Bond market, where there was a total of $4,000bn in circulation. The difficulty was that these comprised numerous different issues, which posed a challenge if a shortage of any particular one developed. What did exist in the USA were tri-party arrangements in which a custodian bank was included in the arrangement made between the two counterparties. However, this was only a partial solution to the risk of default. As long as those involved in the global financial markets were the world's largest banks, then the question of counterparty default and subsequent lack of liquidity was little considered. Such was the size and scale of these banks that they could act as trusted counterparties when trading either with each other or through interdealer brokers.

Nevertheless, in the wake of financial crises in Asia and Russia in the late 1990s, banks became more aware of the risks they were running and looked for remedies. The question of counterparty risk had long been faced in the foreign exchange market, and it had taken many years before a solution was devised and then accepted. Such was the confidence that counterparties had in each other when trading currencies that George Graham considered in 1996 that 'banks reckon the probability one of their main foreign exchange trading partners will default is small'. However, banks were under pressure from central banks to address the issue, because the 'sums involved are so huge that if a default were to occur, the entire banking system could be shaken'.[38] What worried central banks was the risk that a miscalculation by one bank in the foreign exchange market could lead to its failure and, because of the size of the losses, this would have major consequences for the global financial system. Such was the size of the foreign exchange market, and the way it was conducted, that central banks lacked any meaningful control. As Jennifer Hughes explained in 2004, 'The trading of currencies across borders with no centralised exchanges, and the lack of any regulatory body with a global reach, means the foreign exchange market falls under several national jurisdictions, no one of which can claim overall control.'[39] What regulation of the foreign exchange market there was took place through the national agencies responsible for banking supervision. In the absence of a global regulator for a global market, reliance was placed on self-regulation, and this was considered to be effective. One example was the eventual solution to the issue of settlement risk in the foreign exchange market. Various plans were put forward and the eventual outcome was the creation by twenty of the world's largest banks of Continuous Linked Settlement Services (CLS) in 1998. This operated

[38] George Graham, 'Foreign exchange groups plan merger', 9th December 1996.
[39] Jennifer Hughes, 'Taking their law into their own hands', 27th May 2004.

as a bank, accepting and making payments, but only completing transactions when they matched, so eliminating settlement risk for those who used the service. The formation of CLS met the concerns of central banks, leaving a core of global banks to handle the normal routine of trading and willing to accept the risks that involved. Larry Rechnagel, chief executive of CLS services, explained its position in 1998: 'We haven't taken all risk out of the system. There is still replacement risk, forward risk, liquidity risk. What we have protected against is catastrophic failure, and that is what the central banks are concerned about.'[40] It took until 2000 for the CLS Bank to be fully operational, and 2002 before all technical and administrative hurdles had been overcome. By then what was in place was a payment netting system that virtually eliminated settlement risk by, in effect, the CLS Bank acting as a trusted third party between the two counterparties to a trade. To reflect the use of the US$ as the key currency used in the foreign exchange market and the central role played by US banks, it was decided that CLS be domiciled in New York and regulated by the Federal Reserve, even though most trading took place in London.[41]

Whereas the foreign exchange market devised its own solution to the risks it faced by the formation of the CLS Bank most other markets turned to the use of clearing houses as a remedy, including the repo market. A clearing house stood between the two parties to an agreement, guaranteeing payment or delivery in return for a fee, and being provided with collateral in an amount related to the risk of default. Clearing houses acted as central counterparties in bilateral trades and, by doing so, they removed counterparty risk, introduced anonymity, allowed banks to reduce the amount of capital tied up in the operation through netting, and cut back office expenses. The result was to encourage more trading by lowering both costs and risks. In 1999 the London Clearing House set up RepoClear to cater specifically for the repo market, and it rapidly attracted a growing volume of business. This use of clearing houses in the repo market followed what had already been put in place elsewhere. When combined with settlement the use of clearing houses delivered a system that handled payments and deliveries between counterparties and did so on a net basis, minimizing the need for huge transfers of money and bonds between banks as the volume of trading grew exponentially. Centralized clearing and settlement had the added advantage of greatly reducing the amount of collateral a bank had to maintain until a transaction was completed as well as covering the possibility of a counterparty default. In both the USA and Europe clearing houses developed to provide this service for the bond market, with Euroclear in Brussels, Cedel in Luxembourg, the London Commodity House in London, and the Depository Trust and Clearing Corporation in the USA. In addition there were a

[40] George Graham, 'Banks settle down to action', 5th June 1998.

[41] Tracy Corrigan, 'Traditional split in derivatives is less clear-cut', 25th January 1993; James Blitz, 'All change in foreign exchanges', 2nd April 1993; James Blitz, 'New anxieties for the banks', 26th May 1993; Tracy Corrigan, 'Divisions hazy in OTC derivatives clearing battle debate', 13th September 1993; James Blitz, 'ERM crisis quicken activity', 20th October 1993; George Graham, 'BIS outlines forex settlement risk strategy', 28th March 1996; George Graham, 'Foreign exchange groups plan merger', 9th December 1996; George Graham, 'Chase plans new forex derivative', 29th April 1997; George Graham, 'New forex bank to cut risk', 9th June 1997; Simon Kuper, 'Merrill makes up for lost time on forex', 14th July 1997; George Graham, 'Global payments bodies to merge', 1st October 1997; Simon Kuper, 'Old order gives way to the new', 5th June 1998; George Graham, 'Banks settle down to action', 5th June 1998; Alan Beattie, 'Fighting spirit seeps into dried-up markets', 25th June 1999; Christopher Swann, 'Big banks play game of brinkmanship', 25th June 1999; Alan Beattie, 'Floor presence thins out', 25th June 1999; George Graham, 'Forex trading system planned', 15th September 1999; Alex Skorecki, 'Forex system that takes the waiting out of wanting', 4th January 2002; Alex Skorecki, 'Web power helps smaller customers', 27th May 2004; Jennifer Hughes, 'Taking their law into their own hands', 27th May 2004; Jeremy Grant and Peter Garnham, 'LCH.Clearnet looks at forex markets', 16th October 2008; Jennifer Hughes, 'A lesson in how to run a smooth global settlement system', 21st August 2009; Chris Flood, 'Regulators stalk secretive financial giants', 24th February 2014.

variety of other clearing houses specializing in meeting the needs of various markets. Anticipating an electronic future Simon Ellen, chairman of the International Securities Market Association (ISMA)'s Council of Reporting Dealers (CRD) looked forward in 1998 to a time when 'One single click of a mouse makes it all happen: trade, confirmation and settlement.'[42] Such a system would cover 35,000 different fixed-income securities and pointed the way forward.[43] However, on the eve of the global financial crisis such a system was not yet in place. Instead, what existed was a vast number of bills, bonds, notes, and obligations in circulation whose liquidity was dependent upon the willingness of banks to act as counterparties to every sale, whether that meant using their own funds to make purchases or acting as intermediaries.

[42] Samer Iskandar, 'Electronic trading system for Eurobonds', 23rd January 1998.

[43] Leyla Boulton, 'Birth of a hundred markets', 23rd February 1993; Barry Riley, 'A new asset class created', 7th February 1994; Hilary Barnes, 'Drift of trade to London causes concern', 7th April 1994; Sara Webb, 'Dutch win back state debt trade', 16th May 1994; Tracy Corrigan, 'Mood is sombre as bears spoil the fun', 26th May 1994; John Gapper, 'Cold logic wins out at Warburg', 10th January 1995; John Gapper and Richard Lapper, 'Warburg breaks the bond', 11th January 1995; Barry Riley, 'The honeymoon is over', 4th December 1995; Nicholas Denton, 'Banks plan clearing house for trade in emerging market debt', 10th June 1996; Samer Iskandar, 'Electronic trading system for Eurobonds', 23rd January 1998; Simon Davies, 'Junk bonds are back in fashion', 1st May 1998; Charles Smith, 'Banking parent provides strength', 21st June 1999; Edward Luce, 'Bonding together', 6th August 1999; Khozem Merchant, 'Avalanche of change hits Alpine retreat', 14th September 1999; Vincent Boland, 'A revolution just waiting to happen', 31st March 2000; Aline van Duyn, 'Trading costs reach unacceptable levels', 8th September 2000; Aline van Duyn, 'Only the best will survive', 28th March 2001; Martin Dickson, 'The market is another country for City's go-between', 7th April 2001; Vincent Boland, 'RepoClear to include UK gilts service', 22nd August 2001; Vincent Boland, 'Cash conduit that secures London's reputation', 12th September 2001; Alex Skorecki, 'London Clearing House mulls link with Clearnet', 15th February 2002; Doug Cameron and Jennifer Hughes, 'Citigroup to join online currency platform', 8th April 2002; Stephen Pritchard, 'A race to stay ahead of fraudsters', 5th June 2002; Alex Skorecki and James Politi, 'LCH offers new cash and repo gilts service', 5th August 2002; Jenny Wiggins, 'Electronic bond trading still has a future', 6th September 2002; Alex Skorecki, 'Voice-broked bond trading holds its own', 19th March 2003; Alex Skorecki, 'Electronic trading "cuts costs"', 4th June 2003; Alex Skorecki, 'Gilts still stuck in 17th century', 29th January 2004; Alex Skorecki, 'Icap says phone broking rules market', 4th June 2004; Alex Skorecki and Päivi Munter, 'Sea change for Eurozone bonds', 9th November 2004; Saskia Scholtes, 'Electronic battle heats up', 28th July 2006; Michael Mackenzie and Saskia Scholtes, 'Regulators issue a warning at bond trading's wild frontier', 13th November 2006; Jeremy Grant, 'Party mood might elude LCH.Clearnet', 29th April 2008.

10
Commodities and Derivatives, 1993–2006

Introduction

If any financial product or market could be taken as representative of the changes that took place in the years leading up to the Global Financial Crisis of 2008 then derivatives would be the one most likely to be chosen. Derivatives blossomed in volume and variety during the 1990s, leading some to claim it had become the largest financial market in the world. The outstanding value of interest-rate swaps, currency swaps, and interest-rate options rose from $3,450bn in 1990 to $286,000bn in 2006. Derivatives were increasingly viewed as the solution to the volatility that followed the ending of government controls. They provided a means of insuring against fluctuations in prices, exchange rates, and interest rates, the default of borrowers, the collapse of issuers of securities, and the miscalculation of investors. In a world of uncertainty a derivatives contract could be used to guarantee a particular outcome regardless of the turn of events. Those guarantees underpinned countless decisions as they generated confidence that the risks being taken were predictable and manageable. The certainty that derivatives provided required willing counterparties and there was a ready supply of these, attracted by the potential profits to be made while accepting the possibility of loss. Commodity markets had long offered the ability to reduce exposure to risks in a narrow range of products through forward contracts that locked in future prices, regardless of the state of the harvest, production problems, or interruptions to the supply chain. These had morphed into futures and options and it was but a short step to design contracts that covered the new risks emerging in a world when prices could not be fixed by the intervention of governments and the operation of cartels. Through the use of derivatives, buyers and sellers, borrowers and investors, savers and lenders, could experience the flexibility derived from liquid markets, combined with the returns generated by a long-term commitment, without the rigidity imposed by government controls, corporate collusion, and the suppression of competition produced by division and compartmentalization. Derivatives offered a means of coping with the risks and volatility produced by open and competitive markets, where prices, exchange rates and interest rates experienced wild fluctuations and counterparties defaulted on deals. As Jos Schmitt, general manager of the Brussels-based derivatives exchange, Belfox, put it in 1993: 'Turmoil is very good for us, not so much for the volume itself, but because these periods make people try to use our contracts.'[1]

For that reason derivatives were embraced by all ranging from regulators to speculators. In 1993 Tracy Corrigan was of the view that 'Futures exchanges have now positioned themselves at the heart of the world's financial markets.'[2] A few did point out that derivatives could magnify rather than reduce risks, which could have major destabilizing consequences. These warnings emerged in the aftermath of the 1992 financial crisis when some

[1] Andrew Hill, 'Belfox thrives in the gentleman's club', 25th November 1993.
[2] Tracy Corrigan, 'Quirky offshoots gain respect', 20th October 1993.

Banks, Exchanges, and Regulators: Global Financial Markets from the 1970s. Ranald Michie, Oxford University Press (2021).

DOI: 10.1093/oso/9780199553730.003.0010

futures and options markets 'proved more volatile and less liquid than derivatives traders had assumed',[3] according to Richard Waters in 1993. Prior to the crisis banks had increasingly used derivatives to cover the risks being taken, and there was concern that these would not provide adequate protection against loss. James Blitz reported in 1993 that 'governments and central bankers are increasingly concerned about the possibilities of a credit default in the derivatives sector that would destabilize markets'.[4] As years passed in which derivatives coped with the consequences of crisis they gained in popularity, while the uses to which they were put became many and varied. That was the position by the late 1990s. Peter Hancock, head of JP Morgan's risk management and capital committees, explained in 1999 that, 'What derivatives made possible was the unbundling of a wide spectrum of risks that previously were inseparable, so they could be measured, monitored, and managed.'[5] Trevor Price, managing director at Credit Suisse First Boston, went further that year when he claimed that 'derivatives are the electricity of the capital markets connecting its different parts'.[6] In 2000 Jerry del Missier, global head of interest-rate derivatives at Barclays Capital, extolled the virtues of derivatives: 'The ability to remove or spread risk is beneficial for the financial system and gives investors new opportunities to buy new assets. This puts investors in a position to judge whether a derivative or cash instrument is the best way to go. Derivatives allow access to a product that would otherwise not be available.'[7]

By the beginning of the twenty-first century derivatives had been integrated into mainstream financial activities, used by banks, investors, and companies to hedge or take on risks. As Rajeev Misra, head of credit trading at Deutsche Bank, explained in 2002, 'The derivatives business is not just driven by trading, but by using your sales force and applying derivatives to different parts of the markets. You need good structures and salesmen to provide client solutions. You make money by solving problems for clients, and this requires continuous innovation.'[8] In 2003 Robert Pickel, chief executive of the International Swaps and Derivatives Association, spoke for all those involved with derivatives when he stated that 'Derivatives today are an integral part of corporate risk management among the world's leading companies. Across geographic regions and industry sectors, the vast majority of these corporations rely on derivatives to hedge a range of risks to which they are exposed in the normal course of business.'[9] Virtually all of the world's largest companies used derivatives to help manage their risks, especially those involving fluctuations in exchange and interest rates. Derivatives had contributed to a revolution in financial markets by making them more connected, efficient, and transparent. Through the use of derivatives banks could economize on the amount of capital that needed to be set aside to cover the loans they made, so releasing additional funds for borrowers ranging from businesses through property developers to homeowners around the world. The currency risk involved in the geographical diversification of portfolios had been reduced or eliminated by the development of foreign exchange derivatives. This stimulated a huge expansion in international investment, to the benefit of investors through higher returns while providing borrowers

[3] Richard Waters, 'Easy option or unnecessary risk', 22nd July 1993.
[4] James Blitz, 'ERM crisis quicken activity', 20th October 1993.
[5] Arkady Ostrovsky, 'The odds are good on future growth', 20th September 1999.
[6] Arkady Ostrovsky, 'The odds are good on future growth', 20th September 1999.
[7] Vincent Boland, 'Market shows greater value and maturity', 28th June 2000.
[8] Rebecca Bream, 'Unified approach increases efficiency', 22nd February 2002.
[9] Aline van Duyn, 'Uncertainty hits derivatives use', 10th April 2003.

with access to more plentiful finance at lower cost. As banks faced an increasingly competitive environment, to the advantage of savers and borrowers, derivatives helped them to counter the increased volatility that came with deregulation. Credit derivatives provided a way of covering the risk that counterparties could go bankrupt, delay repayment or default, providing reassurance to lenders. The effect was to make them more willing to lend both to their customers and to each other. Credit default swaps provided investors with a means of protecting themselves against business failure when buying corporate bonds, encouraging them to purchase securitized assets. One consequence of this use of derivatives was to separate lenders and investors from borrowers as the risks attached to a particular loan or bond could be transferred to others. To some this was a major benefit as it reduced exposure to a loss while for others it increased risk-taking because it was no longer necessary for the lender or investor to assess the ability of the borrower or issuer of a bond to service their debt and repay the loan when it matured. There was even a derivatives contract that tracked volatility itself. In 1992 Robert Whaley devised the Volatility Index, or Vix, that provided a measure of market volatility based on the S&P 500. A derivatives contracts based on this was introduced in 2004 followed by another in 2006.

The overall result was to propel the exponential growth of the financial derivatives market. There are different measures for the size of this market ranging from the value outstanding on a gross or net basis to the amount traded. With so much of the market being conducted on an OTC basis it was not always easy to capture its true dimension. The notional value of outstanding derivatives in the OTC market was initially estimated at $4,500bn in 1992 but that was later revised to produce a figure of $7,000bn. The indicator that best captures the growth of the financial derivatives market in all its aspects and over time is the notional value of outstanding contracts. The derivatives market was divided into two distinct parts. On the one hand there was an exchange-based market which was highly liquid and involved trading in homogenous futures and options contracts. On the other hand there was the OTC market in swaps and options, which consisted of specially tailored, but often illiquid, instruments created by banks and sold directly to companies and other financial institutions. It was only from 1998 onwards that the Bank for International Settlement (BIS) began collecting comprehensive and comparable data for both the exchange-traded and OTC markets. Prior to that many categories of derivatives traded in the OTC market were omitted from the data collected, making comparisons difficult both over time and between the exchange-traded and OTC market. Nevertheless, using what data is available for the 1993–8 period suggests that the notional value of derivatives outstanding rose from $16,245bn to $64,536bn. Driving this growth was the OTC market where the amount outstanding grew six-fold, from $8,474bn to $50,987bn. In contrast, the figure for the exchange-traded market only doubled from $7,771bn to $13,549bn. Whereas in 1993 the exchange-traded and OTC derivatives market were roughly equal in size, by 1998 the split was 80/20 in favour of the latter. This pattern of rapid growth, driven by the OTC market, was then repeated for the 1998–2006 period. The BIS data indicated that the total for the notional amount outstanding grew from $88,359bn in 1998 to $442,892bn in 2006. This increase consisted of a rise from $8,072bn to $24,760bn for exchange-traded products, or a tripling in nine years, but a fivefold rise for those found on the OTC market, from $80,277bn to $418,132bn. Whereas the OTC market was already responsible for 90 per cent of the total outstanding in 1993, by 1998 its share had reached 94 per cent. It was in the OTC market that banks swapped assets and liabilities across diverse currencies, interest rates, and exposures as they sought either to reduce risk by sacrificing potential gains or generate profits by taking on additional risk. Derivatives allowed banks to do both and they made increasing use of the facilities provided between 1993 and 2006.[10]

Commodity Derivatives

The exponential growth of financial derivatives in the twenty years before the Global Financial Crisis overshadowed their use in commodity markets, with major implications for commodity exchanges as trade-related contracts were replaced with financial ones. This further blurred the distinctions between commodity and stock exchanges, encouraging the development of multiproduct platforms. Nevertheless, the demand for commodity derivatives also grew rapidly as governments abandoned efforts to control prices and suppress fluctuations, recognizing the ultimate futility of such policies in the face of an increasingly open-world economy. Under the 1995 General Agreement on Trade and Tariffs governments agreed to limit intervention in agriculture, with prices being left more to market forces. Accompanying the ending of price controls in most countries was a quickening pace of internal deregulation, which ended the power of monopoly suppliers of commodities including energy in the form of electricity. However, many of these commodities did not lend themselves to being traded on open markets. Creating a market in electricity, and devising suitable derivative products, faced serious obstacles, for example. The lack of a robust and reliable pricing mechanism on which forward prices could be based made it difficult to design a futures contract that was simultaneously attractive to producers, users, lenders, and investors. There were also few participants in the electricity market depriving it of the liquidity required to support a successful futures contract. Nevertheless, there were continued attempts to develop markets and derivative products for electricity during the 1990s and into the twenty-first century, indicating their attractions, not least for banks. Without derivatives banks were reluctant to become involved in a market because of the risks posed by price volatility, as that could expose them to large losses. In turn, that cut out an important source of credit.

[10] Tracy Corrigan, 'Traditional split in derivatives is less clear-cut', 25th January 1993; John Gapper, 'IMF study warns in $8,000bn derivatives market', 24th September 1993; Tracy Corrigan, 'Volume rises to record levels', 24th September 1993; Tracy Corrigan, 'Moving on to centre stage', 20th October 1993; Laurie Morse, 'Swaps trade dodges issue', 20th October 1993; Tracy Corrigan, 'Swaps market may be bigger than estimated', 16th November 1993; Tracy Corrigan, 'The tail still wags the dog', 26th May 1994; Laurie Morse, 'London could become global swaps centre', 27th March 1997; George Graham, 'Bank bows to outcry on derivatives', 7th June 1997; Nikki Tait, 'Uncertain futures ahead', 23rd March 1998; Samer Iskandar, 'The search for growth', 1st May 1998; Samer Iskandar, 'Market explodes into life', 17th July 1998; Khozem Merchant, 'Maverick market gains credibility', 20th September 1999; Arkady Ostrovsky, 'The odds are good on future growth', 20th September 1999; John Plender, 'Out of sight, not out of mind', 20th September 1999; Vincent Boland, 'Market shows greater value and maturity', 28th June 2000; Sarah Laitner, 'Demand for debt puts swaps at the cutting edge', 25th September 2001; Rebecca Bream, 'A form of protection for the rising risk of defaults', 25th September 2001; Aline van Duyn and Vincent Boland, 'Industry flourishes in bear market turmoil', 7th October 2002; James Politi, 'Changing hopes boost volumes', 7th October 2002; Aline van Duyn, 'Credit derivatives unmasked', 21st March 2003; Charles Batchelor, 'Essential, controversial, popular and profitable', 5th November 2003; Charles Batchelor and Alex Skorecki, 'Banks look to create one index', 30th January 2004; Jeremy Grant, 'A single-product boutique is not the way: is one-stop shopping coming to US exchanges?', 14th September 2004; John Plender, 'Shock of the new: a changed financial landscape may be eroding resistance to systemic risk', 16th February 2005; Richard Beales, 'Fed receives commitments on CDS', 6th October 2005; John Authers, 'Spread of derivatives reshapes the markets', 25th January 2006; Richard Beales, 'Boom time for derivatives markets', 16th March 2006; Saskia Scholtes, 'Electronic battle heats up', 28th July 2006; Gillian Tett, 'Déjà vu as markets face new challenge', 16th November 2006; Gillian Tett, 'Driven faster by low rates, more users and technology', 18th November 2006; Martin Wolf, 'The new capitalism', 19th June 2007; Robin Wigglesworth, 'The fearless market', 19th April 2017. (The data for 1998 to 2006 is that produced on financial derivative instruments by the Bank for International Settlement.)

Where it was possible to design suitable contracts and generate liquid markets this was the solution turned to, as the ending of controls and monopolies led to much greater price volatility. Commodity exchanges were continually experimenting with new contracts. Some of these were successful but most were not, failing to appeal to producers or banks. Beginning in the mid-1990s there were successive attempts to introduce futures and options contracts on widely traded commodities subject to volatile prices, such as wood pulp, coal, steel, and plastics. However, it often proved impossible to agree on a contract that attracted widespread support. In the absence of dedicated contracts to be used as a way of hedging exposure to volatile prices proxies were used among those derivative contracts that were widely traded and so possessed a liquid market.

Increasingly the function of a commodity exchange was to provide key reference prices and a liquid market for derivative contracts, which could be used to offset risks. The movement of physical commodities was in the hands of multinational corporations, who could internalize flows, or global traders who matched buyers and sellers internationally. Exemplifying the relationship that now existed between the actual trading of commodities and the markets where they were priced was the position of the London Metal Exchange (LME). The LME continued to offer buyers and sellers the possibility of physical delivery for deals arranged on its trading floor. However, most trading took place away from the exchange and did not involve physical delivery. Instead, the trading that did take place at the LME set indicative world prices and provided users with a means of covering their exposure to volatile prices. Steve Johnson reported in 2004 that 'Almost all bigger companies regularly use hedging to protect themselves from unexpected and potentially costly swings in interest rates, fuel costs and foreign exchange rates.'[11] This was especially the case with large producers like oil and mining companies or large consumers such as airlines, food manufacturers, and coffee blenders. Derivative contracts provided the certainty that underpinned long-term decisions by business and the willingness of banks and institutional investors to provide the finance required.

The effect was to boost activity in existing established exchanges, such as the Chicago Board of Trade (CBOT), where wheat contracts were traded, the New York Mercantile Exchange (Nymex) with its oil derivatives, and LME with its key metals contracts. In addition new exchanges were established to cater for particular products in specific locations, with a proliferation across Asia. By 2004 the verdict of Craig Donohue, the chief executive of the Chicago Mercantile Exchange (CME), was that 'Asia is broadly in the same place that Europe was 15 years ago and the same place North America was thirty years ago with respect to derivatives markets, hedging and risk management. But things are moving very rapidly.'[12] By then China had three commodity exchanges. Regulatory restrictions and political rivalries fragmented Asian commodity markets despite attempts by centres such Singapore and Dubai to become international hubs. The position was clearly put in 1997 by Les Hosking, chief executive of the Sydney Futures Exchange, who sensed an opportunity for his own institution: 'You have well-established trading centres for the northern hemisphere in Chicago and New York, and for Europe in London. The question is, is there going to be a similar centre in this part of the world?'[13] To some the need for such a centre no longer existed because of the advances made in the technology of communication and trading in the 1990s. Nikki Tait wrote in 1997 that 'The growth of screen-based trading and

[11] Steve Johnson, 'Fears rise on change to regime', 27th May 2004.
[12] Jeremy Grant, 'Chicago exchanges look to Asia', 15th June 2004.
[13] Nikki Tait, 'Sydney exchange sees future in commodities', 3rd January 1997.

telecommunications links...mitigate against physical concentration.'[14] Though premature in reaching such a judgement the technological revolution was transforming commodity markets, removing the protection that distance and governments had delivered in the past.

Among commodity exchanges there was a two-way pull in the 1990s. US commodity exchanges were losing out to exchanges located elsewhere in the world that could offer contracts more attuned to local conditions and time zones. Conversely, there was a reverse drive towards concentration as trading fell under the control of the largest producers and consumers, or the financial institutions that provided the short-term credit required, as these preferred to buy and sell in those markets offering the deepest pools of liquidity. Such markets could cope with large sales and purchases without disturbing the underlying price to any significant degree. One effect was to generate competition between the commodity exchanges located in such centres as Chicago, London, and New York. According to Kevin Morrison in 2004, 'Futures exchanges have become far more aggressive in recent years, expanding internationally into new markets and providing new competition to incumbents.'[15] In 2005 he went on to reflect that, 'Commodity exchanges were seen not too long ago as members-only clubs, secretive and closed to the outside world. They were perceived as overseeing trading, such as that in futures contracts, that few in the investment world understood or knew anything about. That has changed in the past five years.'[16] What commodity exchanges were experiencing was a huge shift in the composition of those who used them with growing interest from banks. Banks needed to constantly monitor the risks they ran when providing credit or holding stocks of commodities in the expectation of gain. They were much less interested in guaranteeing sales and purchases at fixed prices in specific commodities, as was the case with the merchants and brokers who had once dominated activity on exchanges. The effect was to emphasize those aspects of a contract that were of most use in covering the financial risks being run by banks. This brought commodity exchanges closer to the possibility of mergers to create multiproduct markets. Encouraging this were developments in the technology of trading. By switching to the use of computers trades could be processed faster, prices displayed quicker, and greater trading capacity provided while delivering more certainty that transactions would be completed. All this could be achieved electronically at a lower cost because it required fewer staff and less space. This allowed those exchanges that made the shift to electronic trading to reduce their charges and improve their service to users, so enabling them to challenge long-established incumbents that had not. However, installing and constantly updating the electronic technology involved a high level of capital expenditure, which could only be justified through an increased volume of business passing through the electronic platforms created. As Richard Reinert, chairman of the International Petroleum Exchange, explained in 1997, 'There's enormous pressure to bring systems, companies and markets together. What you're seeing in financial markets in terms of consolidation you're beginning to see in exchanges.'[17] The issues faced by commodity exchanges revolved around staying independent or merging with another exchange, and switching wholly or partially from open-outcry-floor-based trading to the use of electronic screens and computer matching of deals. These potential mergers were not confined to neighbouring exchanges doing a similar business, as was the case of Nymex/Comex in 1994, but also extended to different types of exchanges in

[14] Nikki Tait, 'Sydney exchange sees future in commodities', 3rd January 1997.
[15] Kevin Morrison, 'Energy exchanges turn up the heat', 1st November 2004.
[16] Kevin Morrison, 'Changing their old image', 22nd November 2005.
[17] Gary Mead, 'IPE in outcry over options for reform', 3rd December 1997.

different countries. However, achieving such mergers was difficult as it had to overcome the opposition of the members of exchanges, as they not only used the institution but also owned it. They were not enthusiasts for change when it could threaten their livelihood, as with the switch to electronic trading, or a merger with another exchange, as that meant a loss of control over future decision making.

In 1995 Laurie Morse referred to the 'Remarkably competitive world of derivatives trading.'[18] In this competition between commodity exchanges those based in the USA benefited from two major advantages over their peers. The first was that all their contracts were denominated in US$s, the dominant international currency. The second was the liquidity that they could already provide, which was superior to any found elsewhere in the world. This provided commodity exchanges like CBOT in Chicago and Nymex in New York with a strong competitive position at a time when globalization broke down national barriers and produced a gravitational drift towards the most international and most liquid of markets. Conversely, US commodity exchanges also suffered from two major disadvantages. The first was related to the contracts that they traded which were geared to meet US domestic needs rather than those of the global economy. The main oil contract traded on Nymex, for example, was based on West Texas Intermediate, which was not sold internationally and so did not reflect the changing balance between supply and demand in the global market. The second was the time zone in which the US markets were located. This was inconvenient for most users outside the Americas, including those in Asia and Europe. Though efforts were made by US exchanges to extend trading hours to cater for international demand these left long periods in which the level of liquidity was low, so removing one of their key competitive advantages. These weaknesses left the US commodity exchanges vulnerable to external competition especially from London, which was located in the European time zone bridging Asia and the Americas, if suitable contracts could be devised. Despite this vulnerability US commodity exchanges fought hard in the 1990s to retain the dominance they had achieved. Their response included mergers to reduce costs, new contracts designed to appeal internationally, and the use of electronic technology to extend trading times and improve delivery. The response also extended to alliances and even proposed mergers with exchanges located elsewhere in the world, so as to offer customers access to a continuous, liquid, global market. Delaying the response was strong opposition from the members of each commodity exchange, especially the numerous individuals who lacked the scale and resources of the banks.[19]

Though US commodity markets were closely associated with Chicago, where both the CBOT and CME were located, it was New York that was the largest centre for commodities trading in the world in the 1990s. Whereas Chicago's leading commodity contracts were in wheat, those of New York were for oil, and it was that product that increasingly dominated international trade rather than those of agriculture. For that reason the most important commodity exchange in the world in the 1990s was Nymex, as it was home to the dominant oil contract. What happened to Nymex between 1992 and 2007 indicates that decisions not inevitability determined the fate of individual exchanges. Nymex clung too long to an open

[18] Laurie Morse, 'Rappaport takes long view after NY exchange merger', 12th April 1995.

[19] Laurie Morse, 'Consolidating for the futures', 27th January 1993; Deborah Hargreaves, 'Future looks brighter for EU farm futures', 18th November 1996; Christine Moir, 'Mirror on a domestic scene', 27th June 1997; Paul Solman, 'Online trading set to grow at metal exchange', 20th June 2000; Kevin Morrison, 'Nymex disadvantaged by futures rules', 15th April 2006; Kevin Morrison, 'LME steps on to a long and winding road', 18th May 2006; Kevin Morrison, 'Nymex within days of Comex deal', 12th June 2006; Chris Flood, 'LME sees sharp rise in turnover', 18th July 2006; Jeremy Grant, 'Market revived to instil a dose of competition', 28th November 2006.

outcry trading floor and failed to expand its international presence. In contrast, the success of the InterContinental Exchange (ICE), an upstart from Atlanta, Georgia, provides the reverse story as it prospered by combining the OTC and exchange-traded derivatives market for commodities, and pursuing a policy of international expansion, using London as its base for global operations. As it was Nymex began the 1990s with a coup as it took over its New York rival, the New York Commodity Exchange (Comex), which had been in merger discussions with CBOT from Chicago. This merger was completed in 1994 and extended the range of commodities traded by Nymex into gold and silver futures contracts, though the compromise agreed left Comex with considerable autonomy, making full integration difficult. Nevertheless, it made Nymex the largest commodity exchange in the world, overtaking the CBOT in the process. At the same time Nymex launched an after-hours electronic trading system for energy options and futures, with the intention of meeting the growing international competition coming from the International Petroleum Exchange in London. In 1995 that led to a tie up with the Sydney Futures Exchange to extend live trading into the Asia-Pacific time zone. That was followed with links to other exchanges in an attempt to establish a worldwide network. Nymex also moved into futures contracts on other energy products such as electricity in 1996 and coal in 2001, building on the position it had established for itself in oil and gas. Finally, it had already reduced the expenses involved in maintaining a trading floor, as well as establishing close links with other New York commodity exchanges, by sharing facilities with not only Comex but also the Coffee, Sugar, and Cocoa Exchange (CSCE), and the New York Cotton Exchange (NYCE).

Nevertheless, there were warning signs that Nymex was losing its grip on the commodity derivatives market. Though the volume of trading in Nymex's oil and gas contracts regularly dwarfed those of London's International Petroleum Exchange (IPE) they mainly catered for US demand. By 1995 the IPE's Brent contract was used as the pricing benchmark for 65 per cent of the world's crude oils. In 1999 Nymex did approach the IPE with a merger plan but failed to carry it off, losing out to ICE in 2001. Similarly, though the Comex contracts in precious metals were a great success, with global appeal, it failed to dent the prime position in the world market for the likes of copper and aluminium held by the LME in London. Comex even failed to capitalize on the crisis that hit the LME in 1995, when the senior copper trader of Sumitomo, Yasuo Hamanaka, lost $2.6bn on unauthorized deals. Another example of Nymex failure to adapt to change was in the technology of trading. Nymex stuck to open-outcry trading long after other commodity exchanges had moved to electronic platforms. This commitment reflected a common view at the time, according to Adrienne Roberts: 'Many people believe that a trader with good instincts can put transactions together faster than an electronic system.'[20] Fred Schoenhut, chairman of the New York Board of Trade (Nybot) stated as such in 2004: 'We are firmly convinced that open outcry in our core markets, executed by the experts that we have on the trading floor, offer the liquidity and order flow that our customers need.'[21] It was not until 2006 that Nymex was forced to face the inevitable and introduce electronic trading side by side with pit trading, and then it had to rely on the CME's Globex trading system for that purpose.[22] By then

[20] Adrienne Roberts, 'IPE split over digital future', 23rd March 2001.

[21] Jeremy Grant, 'Board looks beyond frozen orange juice', 30th November 2004.

[22] Laurie Morse, 'Chicago and New York exchanges plan merger', 26th January 1993; Kenneth Gooding, 'London traders sceptical about US merger', 27th January 1993; Laurie Morse, 'New York exchange makes time for night shift', 18th June 1993; Laurie Morse, 'Rappaport takes long view after NY exchange merger', 12th April 1995; Laurie Morse and Robert Corzine, 'London oil market reaches out to Asia', 9th June 1995; James Harding and Laurie Morse, 'New York tests the water in global village', 10th July 1995; James Harding, 'Mating season

Nymex was being upstaged by its Atlanta rival, ICE, which had only come into existence in 2000.

ICE was set up in Atlanta by Jeff Sprecher, and grew by servicing the thriving OTC market in commodity derivatives. It was an early convert to electronic trading, hosting a range of energy and precious-metal contracts. Where the counterparties involved were large multinational companies or well-known investment banks the risk of default was considered small but that limited the clientele. In order to expand ICE needed to offer greater certainty that transactions would be completed. In 1995 Shamus Martin of GNI in London, who was active in energy futures, was of the opinion that 'major companies are pushing their people to use exchanges instead of over-the-counter trading. At least they can see what's going on when the trading is based on an exchange.'[23] As Nymex was not interested in a link with ICE it turned to IPE in London as an alternative. By acquiring IPE in 2001 ICE gained access to a clearing house, the LCH in London, and that removed much of the risk element from ICE trades as well as reducing errors through automating paperwork while saving on the amount of capital to be set aside in case of default. For its part ICE brought to the IPE its expertise in designing and running an electronic exchange. Richard Ward, the IPE chief executive, made clear in 2001 that the ICE takeover meant radical change: 'We don't intend to engage Nymex in a war. We have started to move our company in a strategic direction, from open outcry to electronic, and we'll continue on this path and not divert ourselves.'[24]

arrives for futures markets', 11th July 1995; Laurie Morse, 'New York exchange merger proposal expected today', 13th July 1995; Richard Lapper, 'Alliances with a future', 7th September 1995; Richard Lapper, 'Strategic global electronic connections', 16th November 1995; Kenneth Gooding and Stefan Wagstyl, 'SIB calls for big changes at metal exchange', 20th December 1996; Laurie Morse, 'Nymex switches on to an electric future', 24th December 1996; Simon Davies, 'IPE may switch to electronic trading', 25th September 1997; Stefan Wagstyl and Kenneth Gooding, 'Not such a shining example', 6th October 1997; Kenneth Gooding, 'LME changes rules to halt short-sell manipulations', 28th October 1998; Paul Solman, 'IPE and Nymex to step up talks', 22nd January 1999; Robert Corzine, 'Energy Groups set to tender for IPE stake after merger talks fail', 10th May 1999; Nikki Tait, 'Nymex feels the draught', 27th October 1999; Paul Solman and Nikki Tait, 'Last shout for open outcry', 9th March 2000; Paul Solman, 'LME to consult on mutual status', 11th May 2000; Gerard McCloskey, 'Coal trading settles in UK', 23rd August 2000; Adrienne Roberts, 'IPE searching for technology partner', 11th January 2001; Adrienne Roberts, 'IPE split over digital future', 23rd March 2001; Adrienne Roberts, 'Dotcom deals expected', 28th March 2001; Mary Chung, 'IPE stays calm over New York challenge on Brent contracts', 22nd August 2001; Nikki Tait, 'ICE to offer facility via London Clearing House', 30th August 2001; Adrienne Roberts, 'Exchanges trading on an uncertain future', 25th September 2001; Jeremy Grant, 'LME considers steel futures', 21st March 2003; Kevin Morrison, 'Nymex eyes future in Europe', 15th October 2004; Kevin Morrison, 'Energy exchanges turn up the heat', 1st November 2004; Kevin Morrison, 'Dublin debut for Nymex gets muted reception', 2nd November 2004; Jeremy Grant, 'Board looks beyond frozen orange juice', 30th November 2004; Kevin Morrison, 'Open outcry as futures exchange opens in London', 13th September 2005; Kevin Morrison, 'Nymex feels an unwelcome pinch', 11th October 2005; Kevin Morrison, 'ICE to make waves with flotation', 18th October 2005; Jennifer Hughes, 'NYBOT to offer electronic trading', 26th January 2006; Kevin Morrison, 'ICE goes online with West Texas', 3rd February 2006; Jeremy Grant, 'Nymex's long road to the electronic age', 17th February 2006; Jennifer Hughes and John Authers, 'Taking the floor: how a screen role will challenge New York's market debutant', 7th March 2006; Kevin Morrison, 'Nymex restricts voting rights', 17th March 2006; Kevin Morrison, 'An exodus from floor to screen', 7th April 2006; Kevin Morrison, 'Nymex disadvantaged by futures rules', 15th April 2006; Kevin Morrison, 'LME steps on to a long and winding road', 18th May 2006; Doug Cameron, 'ICE announces plans for first coal futures', 1st June 2006; Kevin Morrison, 'Nymex relents and allows electronic trade', 12th June 2006; Kevin Morrison, 'LME reacts to Nymex challenge', 3rd July 2006; Kevin Morrison, 'Nymex clears path to IPO', 4th August 2006; Kevin Morrison, 'Nybot set to accept $1bn offer from ICE', 14th September 2006; Kevin Morrison and Doug Cameron, 'CME grapples with possible metals conflict', 19th October 2006; Walt Lukken, 'Exchange regulation in a world without borders', 1st November 2006; Kevin Morrison, 'Pits stop proves a winning formula', 9th November 2006; Kevin Morrison, 'ICE keen on forming LCH.Clearnet partnership', 20th November 2006; John Authers and Norma Cohen, 'An end to the old order', 28th November 2006; Kevin Morrison, 'Realignment of Futures', 28th November 2006; Kevin Morrison, 'Nymex and LME go head to head', 1st December 2006.

[23] Laurie Morse and Robert Corzine, 'London oil market reaches out to Asia', 9th June 1995.

[24] Mary Chung, 'IPE stays calm over New York challenge on Brent contracts', 22nd August 2001.

To an observer at the time, such as Mary Chung, this involved an enormous risk: 'The IPE is pinning its hopes on customers embracing the new technology and not defecting to Nymex. This is a huge gamble.'[25] That gamble paid off and ICE decided to float as a company in 2005, ignoring attempts by Nymex to buy it. The following year ICE took on Nymex directly with an electronic WTI contract run from London. ICE then moved onto Nymex's own territory by acquiring the New York Board of Trade in 2006, which gave it control of a US clearing house, the New York Clearing Corporation. By then ICE Futures had become a serious rival to Nymex in its key energy derivatives. What ICE had done successfully was marry the OTC and exchange-traded markets and the twin locations of New York and London into a vertical silo operation that offered customers not only an electronic trading platform but also straight through processing involving clearing and settlement.[26]

[25] Mary Chung, 'IPE stays calm over New York challenge on Brent contracts', 22nd August 2001.

[26] Charles Batchelor, 'A trading headache revealed by a bomb', 5th April 1993; Deborah Hargreaves, 'Cutting raw material risks', 20th October 1993; Antonia Sharpe, 'Unsung hero is unique', 20th October 1993; Kenneth Gooding, 'Metals business booms', 5th May 1994; Laurie Morse and Robert Corzine, 'London oil market reaches out to Asia', 9th June 1995; Robert Corzine, 'Prospect of UK competition sparks gas trading plans', 9th June 1995; James Harding and Laurie Morse, 'New York tests the water in global village', 10th July 1995; James Harding, 'Mating season arrives for futures markets', 11th July 1995; Laurie Morse, 'New York exchange merger proposal expected today', 13th July 1995; Laurie Morse, 'LCE in talks on Chicago futures link', 20th July 1995; Richard Lapper, 'Alliances with a future', 7th September 1995; Richard Lapper, 'Strategic global electronic connections', 16th November 1995; Richard Lapper, 'Liffe to take trading space at stock exchange', 12th December 1995; Kenneth Gooding, 'Former LME chairman defends clearing system', 19th July 1996; Peter John, 'LCH provides crisis cover for derivatives', 6th August 1996; Kenneth Gooding, 'LME prepares to celebrate after a difficult year', 4th October 1996; Deborah Hargreaves, 'Liffe may take on olive oil futures', 29th October 1996; Deborah Hargreaves, 'Future looks brighter for EU farm futures', 18th November 1996; Kenneth Gooding and Stefan Wagstyl, 'SIB calls for big changes at metal exchange', 20th December 1996; Graham Bowley, 'MG to move metal trading to London', 1st May 1997; Kenneth Gooding, 'The LME bites the bullet of change', 13th June 1997; Simon Davies, 'IPE may switch to electronic trading', 25th September 1997; Stefan Wagstyl and Kenneth Gooding, 'Not such a shining example', 6th October 1997; Gary Mead, 'Exchange of copper bottomed guarantees', 6th October 1997; Kenneth Gooding, 'LME may act on ring membership', 7th October 1997; Gary Mead, 'IPE in outcry over options for reform', 3rd December 1997; Gary Mead, 'Foundations upon which bullion trading is built', 22nd June 1998; Gary Mead, 'IPE forms link with Norwegian exchange', 2nd July 1998; Kenneth Gooding, 'LME changes rules to halt short-sell manipulations', 28th October 1998; Paul Solman, 'IPE and Nymex to step up talks', 22nd January 1999; Edward Luce, 'Central trading cushion cleared for take-off', 9th February 1999; Robert Corzine, 'Energy Groups set to tender for IPE stake after merger talks fail', 10th May 1999; Nikki Tait, 'Nymex feels the draught', 27th October 1999; Paul Solman, 'Liffe to end open outcry dealing', 9th March 2000; Paul Solman and Nikki Tait, 'Last shout for open outcry', 9th March 2000; Paul Solman, 'LME to consult on mutual status', 11th May 2000; Paul Solman, 'Online trading set to grow at metal exchange', 20th June 2000; Paul Solman, 'Gold delivers a hard lesson', 28th June 2000; Gerard McCloskey, 'Coal trading settles in UK', 23rd August 2000; Ruth Sullivan, 'Metal exchange loses reforming chief executive', 6th January 2001; Adrienne Roberts, 'IPE searching for technology partner', 11th January 2001; Ruth Sullivan, 'Metal exchange takes jump into electronic trading', 22nd January 2001; Adrienne Roberts, 'IPE split over digital future', 23rd March 2001; Adrienne Roberts, 'Dotcom deals expected', 28th March 2001; Adrienne Roberts, 'Soft commodity traders find the going hard', 3rd July 2001; Mary Chung, 'IPE stays calm over New York challenge on Brent contracts', 22nd August 2001; Nikki Tait, 'ICE to offer facility via London Clearing House', 30th August 2001; Adrienne Roberts, 'Exchanges trading on an uncertain future', 25th September 2001; Toby Shelley, 'Baltic Exchange seeks to fill a gap', 5th July 2002; Jeremy Grant, 'LME considers steel futures', 21st March 2003; Kevin Morrison, 'IPE set to move towards ending open outcry trade', 6th October 2003; Kevin Morrison, 'LME steeled to broaden its base', 13th November 2003; Kevin Morrison, 'Mixed response to LME upgrade', 2nd December 2003; Kevin Morrison, 'IPE might delay electronic move', 19th December 2003; Kevin Morrison and Charles Pretzlik, 'Standard changes as Rothschild leaves gold business', 15th April 2004; Kevin Morrison, 'Private buyers fill bullion vaults', 16th April 2004; Alex Skorecki, 'IPE sees future in electricity', 2nd June 2004; Kevin Morrison and Tom Braithwaite, 'Nymex aims to take on IPE with London trading floor', 15th February 2005; Kevin Morrison, 'Open outcry moves closer to silence', 8th March 2005; Kevin Morrison, 'Changing their old image', 22nd November 2005; Kevin Morrison, 'ICE goes online with West Texas', 3rd February 2006; Kevin Morrison, 'OFT refuses to lift trading ban on LME', 3rd March 2006; Kevin Morrison, 'An exodus from floor to screen', 7th April 2006; Kevin Morrison, 'Nymex disadvantaged by futures rules', 15th April 2006; Kevin Morrison, 'LME eyes profit-making option', 17th May 2006; Kevin Morrison, 'LME steps on to a long and winding road', 18th May 2006; Chris Flood, 'LME clears the way for consolidation', 31st May 2006; Doug Cameron, 'ICE announces plans for first coal futures', 1st June 2006; Kevin Morrison, 'Nymex relents and allows electronic trade', 12th June 2006; Kevin Morrison, 'LME reacts to Nymex challenge',

As the takeover of IPE by ICE in 2001 revealed, there were three key elements to success among commodity exchanges by the twenty-first century. The first was a US base. The second was an electronic platform. The third was the use of London as a trading location. A number of London's commodity exchanges continued to generate globally-accepted reference prices and provide contracts, which offset the risks run by major producers and consumers. One was the London Metal Exchange (LME). In 1996 Kenneth Gooding claimed that the LME was 'the world's biggest, most liquid and most globally representative base metal market.'[27] However, it was an exception among London's commodity exchanges, squeezed between the greater liquidity of those in the USA and better connections in those located in producer countries. During the 1990s all commodity exchanges were facing major decisions and the choices made determined their future. One was the question of open–outcry versus electronic trading. In 1994 the LME considered the issue but decided to stick to open outcry because that fitted the nature of the contracts traded and the needs of its users. LME's chairman, Raj Bagri, stated that 'We don't know what lies ahead when technology is changing so fast. But we believe we will continue to trade the way we are trading today for at least another 10 years.'[28] At the time this was the right call as the LME retained the loyalty of its global clientele. In contrast, by 2000 the LME was taking electronic trading very seriously as its chief executive, David King, admitted: 'In order to retain our position as the world's number one metals exchange, we also need to embrace technology.'[29] The problem all commodity exchanges faced in making the transition from open outcry to an electronic platform was that it did not suit all, as another chairman of the LME, Simon Heale, explained in 2003, 'With electronic systems you tend to go to more vanilla products because they are easy to trade, but the complexity of the LME lends itself more naturally to open-outcry than it does to an electronic system.'[30] Among commodity exchanges there was also the dilemma of whether to retain the mutual structure or convert into a business and issue shares to investors. As Lynton Jones, the chief executive of the IPE, concluded in 1999, 'Mutuality is fine in a closed regional market or country, but not in a global market. It means you move at the pace of the slowest member.'[31] Ultimately decisions had to be taken and the consequences accepted because commodity trading took place in a competitive environment in which rival exchanges competed with each other. The London Commodity Exchange was increasingly marginalized in the face of competition from New York and those located in producer countries, and eventually succumbed to a merger with London's financial derivatives exchange, Liffe, in 1996. The IPE delayed the switch to electronic trading and was acquired by ICE in 2001. The LME got the balance right and continued to thrive.

By then commodity exchanges were facing a growing threat from the rapid expansion of the OTC market. Instead of using the facilities of exchanges multinational companies and banks were trading either directly with each other or using interdealer brokers to act as intermediaries. Whether buying or selling on screen or over the telephone it was this

3rd July 2006; Chris Flood, 'LME sees sharp rise in turnover', 18th July 2006; Chris Flood, 'LME sees sharp rise in turnover', 18th July 2006; Kevin Morrison, 'Pits stop proves a winning formula', 9th November 2006; Kevin Morrison, 'Realignment of Futures', 28th November 2006; Kevin Morrison, 'Nymex and LME go head to head', 1st December 2006.

27 Kenneth Gooding, 'LME prepares to celebrate after a difficult year', 4th October 1996.
28 Kenneth Gooding, 'Metals business booms', 5th May 1994.
29 Paul Solman, 'LME to consult on mutual status', 11th May 2000.
30 Kevin Morrison, 'Mixed response to LME upgrade', 2nd December 2003.
31 Robert Corzine, 'Energy Groups set to tender for IPE stake after merger talks fail', 10th May 1999.

method of arranging deals that was growing rapidly in popularity. What this OTC market lacked was the guarantees that came from exchange trading and here the London Commodity House (LCH) spotted an opportunity to remedy that weakness. In 1999 LCH decided to launch a clearing service for non-exchange-traded derivatives. Through the use of a clearing house the OTC market became an exchange-like market.[32] The OTC market provided a variety of specially tailored derivative contracts that allowed those using them to hedge their exposure to increasingly volatile conditions. These contracts both competed with and supplemented those traded on commodity exchanges. There was constant flux between the exchange-traded and OTC market as each copied the other in the design and introduction of new contracts. As the OTC market lacked the regulatory structure of the exchanges it could always offer the cheaper and more flexible option, but without the guarantees that regulated markets could provide. This forced exchanges to explore ways of improving the service that they provided, contemplate radical changes in the way trading was conducted, and even merge with arch rivals as a way of achieving the economies of scale that would lower costs. However, commodity exchanges faced an uphill task in meeting the challenge of the OTC market because of the changing nature of the users of derivatives and their requirements. Given the size and reputation of the main users of commodity futures and options, numbering among the largest companies and banks in the world, they could provide counterparties with the security that payments and deliveries would be completed according to the terms of the contract, and did not require either an exchange or a clearing house to stand behind them. In a wide range of commodities and products, producers and consumers could make bilateral arrangements involving not only physical delivery at fixed prices but also purchase bespoke contracts that covered the risks they ran from sudden changes in prices, with banks acting as counterparties. In turn those banks could cover their exposure through exchange-traded standardized contracts. In this way the OTC and exchange-traded commodity markets both competed with and complemented each other, with the global banks and largest producers active in both. What was common to both was the move away from contracts geared to the needs of merchants and brokers and towards financial derivatives of all descriptions.[33]

[32] Adrienne Roberts, 'IPE searching for technology partner', 11th January 2001; Adrienne Roberts, 'Dotcom deals expected', 28th March 2001; Mary Chung, 'IPE stays calm over New York challenge on Brent contracts', 22nd August 2001; Nikki Tait, 'ICE to offer facility via London Clearing House', 30th August 2001; Kevin Morrison, 'Energy exchanges turn up the heat', 1st November 2004; Kevin Morrison, 'Nymex feels an unwelcome pinch', 11th October 2005; Kevin Morrison, 'ICE to make waves with flotation', 18th October 2005; Kevin Morrison, 'ICE goes online with West Texas', 3rd February 2006; Jeremy Grant, 'Nymex's long road to the electronic age', 17th February 2006; Kevin Morrison, 'Nymex disadvantaged by futures rules', 15th April 2006; Kevin Morrison, 'Nymex relents and allows electronic trade', 12th June 2006; Kevin Morrison, 'Nybot set to accept $1bn offer from ICE', 14th September 2006; Kevin Morrison, 'Pits stop proves a winning formula', 9th November 2006; Kevin Morrison, 'ICE keen on forming LCH.Clearnet partnership', 20th November 2006; Kevin Morrison, 'Realignment of Futures', 28th November 2006.

[33] Sara Webb, 'Limited scope for development', 20th October 1993; Tony Walker, 'Dragon with an eye on its futures', 2nd April 1994; Laurie Morse, 'CBOT to assist Poland with new futures exchange', 10th November 1994; Andrew Jack, 'The Matif success story', 14th November 1994; Laurie Morse and Robert Corzine, 'London oil market reaches out to Asia', 9th June 1995; James Harding and Laurie Morse, 'New York tests the water in global village', 10th July 1995; James Harding, 'Mating season arrives for futures markets', 11th July 1995; Laurie Morse, 'New York exchange merger proposal expected today', 13th July 1995; Laurie Morse, 'LCE in talks on Chicago futures link', 20th July 1995; Richard Lapper, 'Alliances with a future', 7th September 1995; James Harding, 'Farmers face challenge of futures', 16th November 1995; Andrew Jack, 'Paris market opens doors to wheat futures trading', 5th July 1996; Greg McIvor, 'Finnish bourse aims to feed off pulp volatility', 16th August 1996; Greg McIvor, 'Swedish group to launch London pulp futures', 30th August 1996; Tony Tassell, 'Pepper futures exchange for India', 16th October 1996; Deborah Hargreaves, 'Price rises put spotlight on hedging', 6th November 1996; Deborah Hargreaves, 'Future looks brighter for EU farm futures', 18th November 1996; Andrew Jack, 'Miracle helps birthday celebrations', 10th December 1996; Laurie Morse, 'Nymex switches on to an electric future', 24th

Financial Derivatives

Regardless of the growth and changes experienced by commodity derivatives the main development from 1992 to 2007 was the exponential expansion of financial derivatives.

The use of currency derivatives, for example, offered a way of covering the risks that came from exposure to foreign exchange volatility as well as opportunities for making profits. At a time of currency volatility these derivatives were used by pension funds and insurance companies to hedge against changes in exchange rates as these could affect their holdings of bonds and equities. Multinationals also made extensive use of foreign exchange derivatives because of the nature of their business, involving as it did payments and receipts in multiple currencies.[34] Underpinning the continued growth in the financial derivatives market was not only an increased use of existing products, such as those to cover fluctuations in exchange rates and interest rates but also other risks such as counterparty default, lack of liquidity, business failures, and transactional complications. As Vincent Boland observed in 2001, regarding derivatives, 'By their nature they are creatures of risk, volatility and uncertainty.'[35] No matter the precise nature of the risk there appeared to be a derivative that could be used to cover it, whether provided by exchanges, the OTC market, or both. Competition between exchanges and the OTC market continually generated variations of

December 1996; Nikki Tait, 'Sydney exchange sees future in commodities', 3rd January 1997; Greg McIvor, 'Helsinki offers hedge against pulp volatility', 4th February 1997; Graham Bowley, 'MG to move metal trading to London', 1st May 1997; Gary Mead, 'OMLX prepares pulp contract', 7th May 1997; Christine Moir, 'Mirror on a domestic scene', 27th June 1997; Stefan Wagstyl and Kenneth Gooding, 'Not such a shining example', 6th October 1997; Gary Mead, 'IPE in outcry over options for reform', 3rd December 1997; Greg McIvor, 'Smoothing out the peaks and troughs', 8th December 1997; Gary Mead, 'Foundations upon which bullion trading is built', 22nd June 1998; Gary Mead, 'IPE forms link with Norwegian exchange', 2nd July 1998; Kenneth Gooding, 'LME changes rules to halt short-sell manipulations', 28th October 1998; Paul Solman, 'IPE and Nymex to step up talks', 22nd January 1999; Robert Corzine, 'Energy Groups set to tender for IPE stake after merger talks fail', 10th May 1999; Paul Solman, 'Liffe to end open outcry dealing', 9th March 2000; Paul Solman and Nikki Tait, 'Last shout for open outcry', 9th March 2000; Paul Solman, 'Online trading set to grow at metal exchange', 20th June 2000; Paul Solman, 'Gold delivers a hard lesson', 28th June 2000; Gerard McCloskey, 'Coal trading settles in UK', 23rd August 2000; Matthew Jones and Bettina Wassener, 'March date set for EEX derivatives', 31st January 2001; Alex Skorecki, 'Markets braced for ISD changes', 22nd May 2003; Kevin Morrison, 'LME steeled to broaden its base', 13th November 2003; Steve Johnson, 'Fears rise on change to regime', 27th May 2004; Alex Skorecki, 'IPE sees future in electricity', 2nd June 2004; Jeremy Grant, 'Chicago exchanges look to Asia', 15th June 2004; Richard McGregor, 'Dalian overtakes CBOT on soya', 18th June 2004; Kevin Morrison, 'Energy exchanges turn up the heat', 1st November 2004; James Boxell, 'Oil in the workings of high finance', 20th December 2004; Kevin Morrison, 'Nybot sees future in pulp trading', 22nd December 2004; Alex Skorecki, 'Carbon emissions trading fires up', 14th January 2005; Kevin Morrison, 'APX wants slice of gas trading pie', 3rd February 2005; Kevin Morrison, 'LME bets on future in plastics', 26th May 2005; Kevin Morrison, 'Steel Futures next on LME list', 27th May 2005; Kevin Morrison, 'Dubai to launch gold futures', 29th June 2005; Kevin Morrison, 'Nymex feels an unwelcome pinch', 11th October 2005; Kevin Morrison, 'LME nears a decision on steel futures', 28th October 2005; Kevin Morrison, 'Dubai moves into gold futures', 18th November 2005; Kevin Morrison, 'Changing their old image', 22nd November 2005; Kevin Morrison, 'Emissions and ethanol join the newcomers', 22nd November 2005; Khozem Merchant, 'Mumbai exchange could fetch $650m', 17th March 2006; Jennifer Hughes and Anuj Gangahar, 'CBOT soon to go electronic on agri-trades', 27th April 2006; Kevin Morrison, 'LME steps on to a long and winding road', 18th May 2006; Doug Cameron, 'ICE announces plans for first coal futures', 1st June 2006; Chris Flood, 'LME sees sharp rise in turnover', 18th July 2006; Doug Cameron, 'Introspection succeeded by internationalism', 26th September 2006; Kevin Morrison, 'Nymex and LME go head to head', 1st December 2006; Barney Jopson, 'Delicate art of tea pricing in Mombasa', 2nd September 2009; Jack Farchy, 'Metdist owners poised to reap benefits of LME bidding tussle', 3rd October 2011.

[34] James Blitz, 'ERM crisis quicken activity', 20th October 1993; Richard Lapper and Philip Gawith, 'Forex market growth slowing, says BIS', 31st May 1996; Laurie Morse, 'US exchanges seek to stem fall in volumes', 2nd July 1996; Alan Beattie, 'Knocking spots into the background', 25th June 1999; Jennifer Hughes, 'FX firebrand dream of revolution', 9th May 2006.

[35] Vincent Boland, 'All bets on hold as market waits out crisis', 25th September 2001.

existing contracts, tailored to meet specific requirements, or new ones to cover additional risks. Laurie Morse picked up on the creative energy displayed in the derivatives industry in 1993 when she observed that, 'Ideas for managing credit exposure while at the same time allowing reasonable market access and a healthy measure of innovation range from a centralised derivatives clearing house to a more sophisticated generation of standardised bilateral swaps contracts.'[36] Banks were both the major users of derivatives and their principal providers. As businesses grew in size, the bank providing them with short-term credit and long-term loans was exposed to potentially destabilizing losses in the event of a default, and so looked to derivatives as a way of limiting the risk they ran. A simple solution was to swap part of that exposure with another bank in a similar position but to a different customer. In this way the bank maintained its relationship with its customer while diversifying the risk it was running if that customer should default. A derivatives contract was a means of doing so and these became increasingly popular during the 1990s. Richard Waters was of the opinion in 1993 that 'Thriving markets have developed in swaps and other new financial products, in the process creating one of the most profitable activities for the handful of large banks which dominate the business.'[37] This was to the advantage of a small group of megabanks that were able to provide these derivative products not only for use within the banking sector but also for those businesses and fund managers of sufficient size to purchase such cover independently. Having invested in the expertise required to design customized derivative contracts, and possessed of the capital necessary to withstand large losses caused by their exposure, a small elite of banks acted as counterparties to the deals being made. As Richard Waters went on to explain:

> Sophisticated computer systems and highly-qualified staff are needed to price derivatives correctly and to enable the banks which sell derivatives to manage their own risks. This has limited the number of institutions able to trade, and added a premium to their efforts. Companies and investors have been prepared to pay the banks' big profit margins on such products for the benefits they convey—a clear case of technological leap forward that has benefited those financial institutions which made the investment early enough.[38]

Financial derivatives became an essential feature of banking in the 1990s as competition forced them to offer more flexible terms to both savers and borrowers, which exposed them to greater risks at a time of interest-rate volatility. Banks had to cope with having to finance fixed-rate loans with variable rate deposits or variable rate lending with fixed-rate borrowing. To cover these risks they increasingly looked to derivatives. The invention of credit derivatives in the 1990s made credit a tradeable asset class. By mid-2006 a notional \$26,000bn in credit derivatives was outstanding. Prior to credit derivatives there was a division between banks that made loans and institutional investors that bought bonds. After credit derivatives it was easier for banks to repackage loans into bonds and sell these to investors with hedge funds being particularly active purchasers. As the nature of banking changed the effect was to increase demand for derivatives. Instead of a bank acting as an intermediary between savers and borrowers, as in the lend-and-hold model, accepting the liquidity and solvency risks involved, the originate-and-distribute model was adopted. The use of financial derivatives became an integral part of this originate-and-distribute

[36] Laurie Morse, 'Derivatives industry scrambles to find some kind of infrastructure', 12th July 1993.
[37] Richard Waters, 'Easy option or unnecessary risk', 22nd July 1993.
[38] Richard Waters, 'Easy option or unnecessary risk', 22nd July 1993.

model as it provided investors with a guarantee that the securitized assets they bought would retain their value, regardless of the ability of the issuer to maintain interest payments and redeem the principal on maturity. Credit Default Swaps provided insurance against the risk that a bond would go into default and the amount outstanding grew from $631bn in 2001 to $34,500bn in 2006. Without the ability to withdraw money at notice from a bank or the liquidity of a public market, investors looked to a derivatives contract to provide them with the reassurance that their investment was safe and could be realized on demand. Another use of derivatives was by fund managers seeking to either reduce or increase exposure to particular stock markets without having to incur the cost of holding a balanced portfolio of the shares traded on each. In this way they could achieve the gains from selective investment while avoiding the losses. As institutional investors switched from bonds to equities the use of equity derivatives allowed them to hedge the greater risk of price volatility in stocks compared to bonds. The likes of hedge funds, for example, took large positions in currency, bond, and equity markets and used derivatives to either cover their risks or enhance their returns, depending on the strategy being followed. George Graham reported in 1997 that 'Some banks see an opportunity to develop a new and active market in credit derivatives.'[39] The credit-derivatives market, which had only begun in 1992, reached a total of $900bn outstanding in 2000. Growth was stimulated by financial crises and bank collapses as those generated considerable interest in a contract that covered the risk of default, especially from pension funds and insurance companies seeking to protect the value of their portfolio. However, these new types of derivatives remained dwarfed by the more traditional varieties. In 2005 outstanding credit derivatives stood at $17,300bn and equity derivatives at $5,600bn, but the figure for interest-rate derivatives was $213,200bn. What this indicated was that the principal use of financial derivatives continued to be banks swapping exposure so as to reduce the risk they were running. When netted out the total outstanding for OTC derivatives contracts shrank to $9,400bn in 2005, revealing that 96 per cent of contracts were matching bilateral deals. This meant that only 4 per cent of the total involved the use of derivatives contracts as speculative counters through which banks and fund managers expected to generate profits through predicting the future.[40]

[39] George Graham, 'Bank bows to outcry on derivatives', 7th June 1997.

[40] James Blitz, 'An insurance or a threat to stability?', 26th May 1993; Laurie Morse, 'Derivatives industry scrambles to find some kind of infrastructure', 12th July 1993; Richard Waters, 'Easy option or unnecessary risk', 22nd July 1993; Antonia Sharpe, 'Hedge against stock swings', 20th October 1993; John Plender, 'Through a market, darkly', 27th May 1994; Richard Lapper, 'A rosy future for futures spells a charmed Liffe', 14th January 1995; Henry Harington, 'Vanilla the flavour of the times', 16th November 1995; Antonia Sharpe, 'Latest tool to manage risks', 16th November 1995; Graham Bowley, 'New breed of exotics thrives', 16th November 1995; Laurie Morse, 'Flow of capital slows down', 16th November 1995; Graham Bowley, 'At the heart of everyday life', 16th November 1995; Christine Moir, 'A drift towards experience', 16th November 1995; Richard Lapper, 'An important new frontier is opening', 22nd November 1996; Samer Iskandar, 'Management by mathematics', 31st March 1997; Laurie Morse, 'Traders turn credit risks into profits', 23rd May 1997; George Graham, 'Bank bows to outcry on derivatives', 7th June 1997; Samer Iskandar, 'Fierce battle rages for market share', 27th June 1997; Samer Iskandar, 'Great expectations of a promising future', 27th June 1997; Samer Iskandar, 'The search for growth', 1st May 1998; Vincent Boland, 'Chastened but resurgent', 17th July 1998; Samer Iskandar, 'Market explodes into life', 17th July 1998; Khozem Merchant, 'Maverick market gains credibility', 20th September 1999; Arkady Ostrovsky, 'The odds are good on future growth', 20th September 1999; John Plender, 'Out of sight, not out of mind', 20th September 1999; Rebecca Bream, 'Corporate sector embraces credit swaps', 9th March 2000; Claire Smith, 'Fastest-growing risk protector', 19th May 2000; John Plender, 'The limits of ingenuity', 17th May 2001; Vincent Boland, 'All bets on hold as market waits out crisis', 25th September 2001; Sarah Laitner, 'Demand for debt puts swaps at the cutting edge', 25th September 2001; Rebecca Bream, 'A form of protection for the rising risk of defaults', 25th September 2001; Rebecca Bream, 'Unified approach increases efficiency', 22nd February 2002; Aline van Duyn and Vincent Boland, 'Industry flourishes in bear market turmoil', 7th October 2002; Rebecca Bream, 'Plenty of bad news for a market to thrive on', 7th October 2002; Arkady Ostrovsky and Aline van Duyn, 'Volumes rise as investors seek security amid turmoil', 7th October 2002; Nic Cicutti, 'Derivatives' terms made easy', 26th October 2002; Aline

Without the technological revolution taking place in the 1990s the exponential expansion that took place in the derivatives market would not have been possible. In 2003 Philip Manchester captured the contribution of technology to the revolution in the derivatives market: 'Technology lies at the heart of modern derivatives trading. Without high-speed communications and powerful computing engines to cope with complex financial instruments, the derivatives market would not exist. Indeed the information-rich nature of derivatives contracts makes them an ideal application for information technology. It follows that advances in technology drive the market.' He then added that 'The most obvious technology-driven change is the ongoing disappearance of the traditional open-outcry exchanges.'[41] It was not only in the trading of derivatives that a revolution was taking place. Beginning in the early 1990s an increase in accessible and affordable computer power allowed banks to design more sophisticated derivative contracts and also monitor their own exposures quickly and accurately. Jeremy Grant and Alex Skorecki captured the interaction between product design and trading technology in 2004, when they observed that 'As fast as new trading engines can be invented, traders have to update or die.'[42] Hedge funds, for example, thrived on the opportunities generated by new derivative products, computer-driven numerical analysis, and the speed and capacity provided by electronic trading systems. They competed to generate profits by arbitraging between different assets through rapid buying and selling. Though the overwhelming bulk of the derivatives business became located in the OTC market the fate of the CME's Globex trading system and the battle between Liffe and the DTB for the Bund contract epitomize the technological revolution taking place, and the winners and losers it produced.[43]

Derivative Exchanges

The Chicago commodity exchanges were pioneers of financial futures and this dominated their trading activity in the 1990s. Though there was a degree of co-operation between the Chicago Board of Trade (CBOT) and Chicago Mercantile Exchange (CME) in such areas as

van Duyn, 'Credit derivatives unmasked', 21st March 2003; Aline van Duyn, 'Uncertainty hits derivatives use', 10th April 2003; Aline van Duyn, 'Banks could adopt derivatives code', 30th May 2003; Jeremy Wiggins, 'US commercial banks' holding of derivatives climb by 9%', 9th June 2003; Charles Batchelor, 'Essential, controversial, popular and profitable', 5th November 2003; Päivi Munter, 'Protection becomes more desirable', 5th November 2003; Charles Batchelor, 'Restructuring at risk from CDSs', 19th October 2004; Peter Thal Larsen and Charles Batchelor, 'Credit derivatives go through "pain process"', 24th February 2005; Richard Beales, 'Fed receives commitments on CDS', 6th October 2005; Jennifer Hughes, 'Customising risk in Chicago', 28th October 2005; John Authers, 'Spread of derivatives reshapes the markets', 25th January 2006; Richard Beales, 'Boom time for derivatives markets', 16th March 2006; Saskia Scholtes, 'A spectacular parting of the ways', 23rd August 2006; Richard Beales, 'New instruments call the tune', 20th October 2006; Jeremy Grant and Doug Cameron, 'Lords of the Windy City', 21st October 2006; Gillian Tett, 'Driven faster by low rates, more users and technology', 18th November 2006; Paul J. Davies and Richard Beales, 'New players join the credit game', 14th March 2007; Gillian Tett, 'Swaps soar as investors pile in', 28th May 2007.

41 Philip Manchester, 'Driving change in ways of trading in markets', 5th November 2003.

42 Jeremy Grant and Alex Skorecki, 'Software vendors globalise pit', 3rd March 2004.

43 Richard Waters, 'Easy option or unnecessary risk', 22nd July 1993; Patrick Harverson, 'Integration top of the agenda', 20th October 1993; Richard Lapper, 'New generation takes over', 16th November 1995; Richard Irving, 'Shock-absorbing models', 16th November 1995; Richard Lapper, 'An important new frontier is opening', 22nd November 1996; Samer Iskandar, 'Management by mathematics', 31st March 1997; Laurie Morse, 'Traders turn credit risks into profits', 23rd May 1997; Nikki Tait, 'Technology spawns new range of rivals', 28th March 2001; Philip Manchester, 'Driving change in ways of trading in markets', 5th November 2003; Jeremy Grant and Alex Skorecki, 'Software vendors globalise pit', 3rd March 2004; Jeremy Grant, 'A single-product boutique is not the way: is one-stop shopping coming to US exchanges?', 14th September 2004.

trading technology the two remained fierce rivals and this spurred change, such as a willingness to contemplate the end of open-outcry trading and conversion from mutual to corporate status. By 2005 both the CBOT and CME had become listed companies, allowing them to overcome the opposition to change among members. Internationally, the CME had flirted with international mergers in the 1990s, in a bid to create a trading network that spanned the globe, but none materialized. Nevertheless, the CME appeared well placed to provide such a network on its own with its Globex trading system. The central idea of Globex was to provide an electronic trading platform that linked the CME with exchanges around the world, so as to provide a continuous global market. During normal working hours the trading of derivatives on each exchange would be through open outcry, making it the centre of liquidity for the contracts it hosted. That would then be followed by after-hours trading using Globex's electronic platform. The aim was to remedy the geographical disadvantage of Chicago as a centre of derivatives trading, as it was located at one end of the time spectrum that began in Asia and had Europe at the centre. Though Chicago had the most liquid derivatives contracts that was the case only during normal working hours, greatly reducing their appeal and encouraging competition from alternative derivative exchanges located elsewhere in the world, such as Liffe in London and Simex in Singapore. A critical mass of experienced traders was required to support a high level of liquidity and that was only available during working hours. The solution was to pass trading from one floor to another, using the Globex system as the link. In this way trading in derivative products with a global appeal would pass seamlessly around the world, providing banks with a market that was continuously liquid. This would give those exchanges that signed up as members of Globex an advantage over all others, so attracting business from around the world, further enhancing their appeal. The CME would be at the centre of this network but each exchange would retain its independence. Along with the CME the other backer of Globex was Reuters, which had largely borne the development costs, in the expectation of replicating its success in the foreign exchange market. After years of delay Globex was finally launched in 1992 with both the CME's rival Chicago derivatives exchange, CBOT, and the French derivatives exchange, the Matif in Paris, agreeing to participate. With the CME's existing connection to Simex in Singapore, this provided Globex with its global network.[44]

Initial results proved disappointing for Globex, as it failed to generate the turnover expected. What had been underestimated was the degree to which trading in derivatives was tied to specific markets and was not transferable around the world. Once the Chicago exchanges closed for the day trading was too thin in their products to generate the level of liquidity that would attract additional buyers and sellers. By October 1993 Tracy Corrigan reported that Globex had yet to establish itself because 'The battle for a critical mass of

[44] Laurie Morse, 'Chicago and New York exchanges plan merger', 26th January 1993; Kenneth Gooding, 'London traders sceptical about US merger', 27th January 1993; Laurie Morse, 'CME seeks strength through harmonisation', 23rd August 1994; Laurie Morse, 'LCE in talks on Chicago futures link', 20th July 1995; Paul Solman and Nikki Tait, 'Last shout for open outcry', 9th March 2000; Paul Solman, 'LME to consult on mutual status', 11th May 2000; Paul Solman, 'Gold delivers a hard lesson', 28th June 2000; Jeremy Grant, 'CCX takes Chicago by storm', 16th November 2004; Jeremy Grant, 'Board looks beyond frozen orange juice', 30th November 2004; Kevin Morrison, 'Changing their old image', 22nd November 2005; Kevin Morrison, 'Emissions and ethanol join the newcomers', 22nd November 2005; Jennifer Hughes, 'NYBOT to offer electronic trading', 26th January 2006; Jennifer Hughes and Anuj Gangahar, 'CBOT soon to go electronic on agri-trades', 27th April 2006; Kevin Morrison, 'LME steps on to a long and winding road', 18th May 2006; Kevin Morrison, 'Nymex within days of Comex deal', 12th June 2006; Kevin Morrison, 'Nymex clears path to IPO', 4th August 2006; Doug Cameron, 'Introspection succeeded by internationalism', 26th September 2006; Kevin Morrison and Doug Cameron, 'CME grapples with possible metals conflict', 19th October 2006.

volume on the system has yet to be won.'[45] Without that there was a reluctance to buy or sell these products because of uncertainty over the prices at which deals could be done. With these disappointing results Liffe decided not to join the network while CBOT abandoned Globex in 1994. Each exchange wanted to remain the centre of a unique pool of liquidity, tied to the particular derivative products it traded, and was unwilling to share that position with another. It was not only in concept that Globex was flawed. The technology that it used, and developed at considerable cost, was quickly superseded by that developed for other exchanges as they introduced electronic platforms for all their trading. Recognizing this the CME itself made the decision in 1997 to adopt the French NSC electronic trading system to replace the Reuters' platform used by Globex. This was followed in 1999 by the relaunch of Globex as an alliance of derivatives exchanges rather than an attempt to create an integrated global market. This new version of Globex recognized the existence of separate pools of liquidity, accessible in turn around the world, rather than a single one that was integrated and indivisible. However, the global banks that were the main users of derivatives had little to gain from this alliance as they could already access the markets provided by these exchanges, having become members. Instead, the CME itself began using the Globex electronic platform for trading a growing range of products during the working day, abandoning its original concept though proclaiming it a success as a pioneer of electronic trading.[46]

Credit for pioneering the electronic trading of derivatives credit needs to be given to developments in Europe in the 1990s. The Swiss Options and Financial Futures Exchange (Soffex) had become the world's first electronic derivatives market when it was launched in 1988, but it took time to perfect its trading system and attract users. Ten year later it merged with Germany's Deutsche Terminbörse (DTB) to form Eurex. It was the success of DTB that led to the breakthrough for the electronic trading of futures and options, culminating in its triumph over Liffe, which had continued to rely on open outcry. From the outset the DTB was designed as a fully-electronic market, with no physical trading floor. Its trading system was based on the technology used by Soffex but benefited from the technical difficulties they overcame. The DTB was launched in 1992 as direct competitor to Liffe, the leading derivative exchange in Europe at the time. Liffe traded derivatives contracts open outcry in London, with one of its most successful being based on ten-year German government bonds. German banks were major users of this Bund contract to hedge their operations in the underlying cash market for German government debt, making it an obvious target for the Frankfurt-based DTB. By 1994 David Waller observed that, 'Competition is

[45] Tracy Corrigan, 'Quirky offshoots gain respect', 20th October 1993.

[46] Tracy Corrigan, 'DTB and Matif in co-operation agreement', 14th January 1993; Tracy Corrigan, 'Exchanges fight for the future across Europe', 15th January 1993; Tracy Corrigan and Laurie Morse, 'Trouble after hours', 3rd June 1993; Laurie Morse, 'New York exchange makes time for night shift', 18th June 1993; Tracy Corrigan, 'Moving on to centre stage', 20th October 1993; Tracy Corrigan, 'Quirky offshoots gain respect', 20th October 1993; Laurie Morse, 'CME seeks strength through harmonisation', 23rd August 1994; Laurie Morse, 'Both sides benefit from London–Chicago link', 16th March 1995; Richard Lapper, 'Revival of the floor show', 27th July 1995; Samer Iskandar, 'Fierce battle rages for market share', 27th June 1997; Edward Luce, 'New Technology is driving mating dances', 23rd March 1999; Nikki Tait, 'Electronic threat prompts action', 23rd March 1999; Edward Luce, 'New Technology is driving mating dances', 23rd March 1999; Edward Luce, 'Future is uncertain after frantic year', 23rd March 1999; Jeremy Grant and Alex Skorecki, 'Electronic trading is dealt a double blow', 12th July 2002; Jeremy Grant, 'CME gambles on electronic success', 17th June 2002; Jeremy Grant and Vincent Boland, 'Chicago is their kinda town: but how long can the city's futures traders keep Eurex's electronic exchange at bay?', 16th October 2003; Jeremy Grant, 'CME reduces fees for European customers', 11th November 2003; Jeremy Grant, 'A single-product boutique is not the way: is one-stop shopping coming to US exchanges?', 14th September 2004; Kevin Morrison and Doug Cameron, 'CME grapples with possible metals conflict', 19th October 2006; Doug Cameron, 'The price was right', 28th November 2006.

nakedly evident in the battle between the London International Financial Futures Exchange (Liffe), London's futures and options exchange, and the Deutsche Terminbörse, Germany's screen-based equivalent.'[47] In this battle over the Bund contract Liffe continued to rely on open-outcry trading, convinced that it delivered advantages that no electronic platform could match. In 1997 Edward Luce and Samer Iskandar compared the two ways of trading: 'On a London trading floor the size of a football pitch, young men in red, orange and green jackets leap up and down, yelling and gesticulating. In Frankfurt, meanwhile, a computer in a cupboard whirs quietly, and traders around the world connected to it sit clicking at their screens.'[48] Using the competitive edge that came from the lower costs attached to electronic trading, the DTB succeeded in attracting users but long trailed behind Liffe as it could not match the latter's liquidity. Daniel Hotson, the chief executive of Liffe, expressed his confidence in 1997 that its open-outcry system and the presence of traders, known as locals, who were always ready to buy and sell, provided a competitive edge that the DTB could never match: 'There is an element of liquidity provided by local traders which is impossible to simulate in an electronic environment. The savings generated by this liquidity more than make up for the cheaper costs of trading on an electronic system.'[49] This liquidity allowed traders and investors to buy or sell the equivalent of billions of dollars in seconds, as traders used their own money to act as counterparties, in the expectation of reversing the deal at a profit.

In automated trading buyers and sellers fed quotes into a centralized computer system, which automatically matched trades according to time and price priority rules. Liquidity was reliant on reaching a volume of transactions that was sufficient to match sales and purchases on a continuous basis. Until that level was achieved Liffe's open outcry delivered superior liquidity, which meant that it continued to attract custom, despite the higher costs. This prevented the DTB's electronic platform reaching the level of trading required to provide it with liquidity equal to or better than of Liffe. Open outcry had other advantages as well. The greater transparency of electronic systems, which was regarded as a benefit by many, was detrimental by those who expected to reverse a deal in the near future. Their large buy or sell orders were immediately visible on screens across the market, allowing others to profit by taking a reverse position. In the more personalized world of the trading floor, dealers could conceal their positions and move large orders more quickly, frequently breaking orders into small portions in order to find buyers or sellers. For that reason trading in the Bund contract continued to favour Liffe rather than the DTB, with a 70/30 split in 1994. It was not that those at Liffe were unaware of the threat posed by the DTB and blind to the possibilities of electronic trading. In 1995 the current chairman, Jack Wigglesworth, stated that 'Liffe's vision of the future is to have a fully integrated order-driven automated market in which users are able to trade both cash and equity derivatives through a single screen.'[50] However, the technology was not yet available to provide the liquidity such a market required, and so the best policy was to stick with open outcry. However, by 1997 the DTB was beginning to erode Liffe's superiority as it tailored its system to meet the needs of users while its lower charges attracted a growing volume of business. Once that point was reached trading quickly switched from Liffe to the DTB in the key ten-year Bund contract. In 1998 DTB was responsible for 60 per cent of trading in the

[47] David Waller, 'Frankfurt's role consolidated', 31st May 1994.
[48] Edward Luce and Samer Iskandar, 'Liffe or death struggle', 19th September 1997.
[49] Edward Luce and Samer Iskandar, 'Liffe or death struggle', 19th September 1997.
[50] Richard Lapper and Norma Cohen, 'Liffe to extend automated trading', 13th September 1995.

ten-year German government bond futures contract. This shattered the implicit belief that once an exchange had established itself as the centre of liquidity for a particular derivatives contract it could not lose that trading to another.[51]

The year 1998 represented a seismic shift in the competition between open outcry and electronic trading in the trading of derivatives. What had happened to Liffe's Bund contract showed all derivative exchanges how vulnerable the open outcry trading system had become to those employing an electronic platform. As Edward Luce observed in 1998, 'The success of the DTB's electronic system called into question the viability of Liffe's more expensive floor-based trading system.'[52] Later the same year he concluded that 'Trading floors are losing out to electronic trading systems.'[53] It was in that year that electronic trading systems gained acceptance because they were not only cheaper and quicker than open outcry but were also able to match or surpass the level of liquidity in many high-volume contracts. Vincent Boland concluded that 'technological advances have led to the virtual eclipsing by electronic markets of traditional open outcry trading floors'.[54] Recognizing what had happened Liffe introduce its own electronic trading system, allowing it to retain other contracts but it never regained that linked to the Bund.[55] What the battle over the Bund had revealed was the need for derivatives exchanges to remain competitive if they

[51] Alex Skorecki, 'How London lost the battle of the Bund', 16th October 2003.

[52] Edward Luce, 'Liffe's limited reform plan fails to impress critics', 23rd April 1998.

[53] Edward Luce, 'The future of futures', 30th June 1998.

[54] Vincent Boland, 'Logical development in a fast-changing world', 13th October 1998.

[55] Tracy Corrigan, 'DTB and Matif in co-operation agreement', 14th January 1993; Tracy Corrigan, 'Exchanges fight for the future across Europe', 15th January 1993; David Waller, 'Technology is the weapon against London', 1st July 1993; Tracy Corrigan, 'Quirky offshoots gain respect', 20th October 1993; David Waller, 'Frankfurt's role consolidated', 31st May 1994; Conner Middelmann, 'Merits of open-outcry challenged', 14th July 1994; Richard Lapper, 'A rosy future for futures spells a charmed Liffe', 14th January 1995; Laurie Morse, 'Both sides benefit from London-Chicago link', 16th March 1995; Richard Lapper, 'Liffe may list Matif products switched from open outcry', 17th May 1995; Andrew Fisher, 'New rules benefit Frankfurt', 17th May 1995; Richard Lapper, 'Strong growth in volume', 17th May 1995; Richard Lapper, 'Revival of the floor show', 27th July 1995; Richard Lapper and Norma Cohen, 'Liffe to extend automated trading', 13th September 1995; Richard Lapper, 'Liffe to take trading space at stock exchange', 12th December 1995; Edward Luce and Samer Iskandar, 'Exchanges walk the thin line that separates rivalry and war', 14th July 1997; Vincent Boland, 'Liffe and DTB vie for supremacy', 5th August 1997; Edward Luce and Nikki Tait, 'Exchanges struggle with costs', 5th September 1997; Edward Luce and Samer Iskandar, 'Liffe or death struggle', 19th September 1997; Samer Iskandar, 'Survey sees Liffe dominant in Europe', 7th October 1997; Edward Luce, 'Liffe blow as German contract is dropped', 5th March 1998; Samer Iskandar and Edward Luce, 'Liffe grasps the nettle of electronic trading', 10th March 1998; Samer Iskandar and Edward Luce, 'Move to a life less ordinary', 11th March 1998; Nikki Tait, 'Uncertain futures ahead', 23rd March 1998; Edward Luce, 'Liffe's limited reform plan fails to impress critics', 23rd April 1998; Edward Luce, 'A cloud over Frankfurt's ambitions', 24th June 1998; Edward Luce, 'The future of futures', 30th June 1998; Simon Davies, 'Futures trade in the balance', 8th July 1998; Edward Luce, 'Liffe finds little comfort in tie-up with Frankfurt', 11th July 1998; Paul Solman, 'No time to be complacent', 17th July 1998; Vincent Boland, 'Logical development in a fast-changing world', 13th October 1998; Edward Luce, 'Liffe to focus on forging new alliances and changing rules', 3rd November 1998; Edward Luce, 'Eurex set to address complaints', 20th November 1998; Edward Luce, 'Liffe will open share ownership to non-members', 18th December 1998; Nikki Tait, 'Older birds can still fly', 13th January 1999; Nikki Tait, 'Exchanges look to their electronic futures', 22nd March 1999; Edward Luce, 'New Technology is driving mating dances', 23rd March 1999; Nikki Tait, 'Marriage proposals dominate the sector', 23rd March 1999; Tony Barber, 'Börse's innovative chief strikes the right note', 23rd March 1999; Samer Iskandar, 'E-advantage has yet to make mark', 14th May 1999; Edward Luce, 'Breathing a second lease of life into Liffe', 27th July 1999; Edward Luce, 'Exchanges in world flux', 20th September 1999; Edward Luce, 'Hard global pressure on Liffe', 20th September 1999; Paul Solman, 'Liffe to end open outcry dealing', 9th March 2000; Paul Solman and Nikki Tait, 'Last shout for open outcry', 9th March 2000; Vincent Boland, 'Dotcom venture to aid recovery', 31st March 2000; Nikki Tait, 'The floor is going electronic', 28th June 2000; Aline van Duyn, 'Liffe plans a push into equity markets', 7th September 2000; Aline van Duyn and Nikki Tait, 'Liffe plans futures on single stocks', 8th September 2000; Aline van Duyn, 'A future of opportunity', 4th October 2000; Vincent Boland, 'Liffe back in the black after reinventing itself', 22nd March 2001; Nikki Tait, 'Technology spawns new range of rivals', 28th March 2001; Alex Skorecki, 'A returning hero with eyes set on the west', 16th January 2003; Alex Skorecki, 'How London lost the battle of the Bund', 16th October 2003.

were to hold onto the business that they did. This meant a heavy and continuous investment in electronic technology, leading to the rapid demise of physical trading floors for futures and options across the world. A consequence of that was mergers between exchanges, especially on a national basis, in order to generate the volume of trading that would justify the costs involved. In 1999 Edward Luce concluded that, 'Driven by technology and the seemingly inexorable drive to concentrate liquidity, exchanges have been demutualising, merging and switching to electronic trading.'[56]

This process had already happened in Germany in 1995 when the DTB became part of Deutsche Börse. What followed in 1997 was a merger between DTB and Soffex to create Eurex, hailed by Antionette Hunziker-Ebneter, the chief executive of the Swiss Exchange, as 'the world's first common technical platform with standardised rules and regulations and a joint clearing house. This is likely to become standard practice within just a few years, but in Switzerland it is already a reality.'[57] Across Europe there were mergers between derivative and stock exchanges to form multiproduct electronic platforms. In 1997 the French derivatives market, the Matif, followed the route already taken by the DTB and merged with the Paris Bourse. In 1998 the Stockholm Stock Exchange and the Swedish derivatives exchange, OMX merged. The founder of OMX, Olof Stenhammar, had the grander ambition of creating a Europe-wide electronic market covering both equities and derivatives, beginning with the Scandinavian countries.[58] However, that initiative was driven forward by the French. In 1999 Pascal Samaran, the chief executive officer of Matif, accepted that 'The distinction between cash and derivatives products is disappearing and so are the differences between OTC trading and traditional forms of trading,... In order to survive you have to provide service on the Europe-base level.'[59] Later the same year he expressed the view that, 'It is our firm belief that derivatives and their underlying market should be run jointly, and that they should be electronic.'[60] By then he had become deputy chief executive of the Paris Bourse, in charge of markets and products. That year the trading floor was closed and business transferred to an electronic platform. In 2001 the Matif and Liffe ended up under common ownership, when the latter was acquired by Euronext. Euronext had been formed the previous year by the merger between the Paris Bourse, owner of the Matif, and the exchanges in Amsterdam and Brussels. This brought together the derivative markets these exchanges controlled.[61]

[56] Edward Luce, 'Future is uncertain after frantic year', 23rd March 1999.

[57] Vincent Boland, 'Logical development in a fast-changing world', 13th October 1998.

[58] Andrew Jack, 'SBF, Matif join forces ahead of German link', 18th September 1997.

[59] Arkady Ostrovsky, 'Back-office emerges from shadows', 23rd March 1999.

[60] Samer Iskandar, 'Shaped for a common platform', 20th September 1999.

[61] Tracy Corrigan, 'DTB and Matif in co-operation agreement', 14th January 1993; Tracy Corrigan, 'Exchanges fight for the future across Europe', 15th January 1993; Ian Rodger, 'Brisk activity on most fronts', 18th November 1993; Andrew Hill, 'Belfox thrives in the gentleman's club', 25th November 1993; Ian Rodger, 'Private banking provides fuel', 2nd December 1993; Laurie Morse and Tracy Corrigan, 'European futures trade comes of age', 31st December 1993; Conner Middelmann, 'Merits of open-outcry challenged', 14th July 1994; Ronald van de Krol, 'The EOE will be humming in 1996', 12th September 1994; Andrew Jack, 'The Matif success story', 14th November 1994; Ian Rodger, 'The real time breakthrough', 6th December 1994; Richard Lapper, 'Liffe may list Matif products switched from open outcry', 17th May 1995; Richard Lapper, 'Strong growth in volume', 17th May 1995; Richard Lapper, 'Innovation in swaps and oranges', 23rd May 1995; Andrew Jack and Richard Lapper, 'Volumes drop by 31 per cent', 16th November 1995; Richard Lapper, 'Strategic global electronic connections', 16th November 1995; Richard Lapper and Andrew Jack, 'Aiming for a meeting of markets', 24th November 1995; Andrew Jack, 'Matif celebrates 10 speculative years', 22nd February 1996; David Brown, 'Strategy for a single entity', 29th October 1996; Samer Iskandar, 'Exchanges go into battle', 22nd November 1996; Laurie Morse, 'Liffe sets its sights on the No 1 spot', 22nd November 1996; Andrew Jack, 'Miracle helps birthday celebrations', 10th December 1996; Samer Iskandar, 'Exchanges square up for a fight', 17th December 1996; Tom Burns, 'Timing of launch was fortunate', 11th February 1997; William Hall, 'EBS doubters shaken off', 28th February 1997; Samer Iskandar, 'Euro set to

It was not only in Europe that the triumph of the DTB, renamed Eurex, had consequences because it reverberated around the world, as Edward Luce picked up on in 1999:

> The most important impetus for change comes from dramatic improvements in communications technology which allows huge volumes of data to circumnavigate the globe in real-time at near-zero cost. This advantage enabled Eurex, the Frankfurt-based electronic futures exchange, to poach the vital future on the 10-year German government bond from floor-based Liffe last year even though most of the demand was coming from London and US screens.[62]

Nevertheless, the Chicago derivatives exchanges remained the last bastion of open outcry trading in derivatives, claiming its superiority over all others. Edward Luce warned in 1999 that, 'If the CBOT continues to resist change, it is only a matter of time before competitors seek to undercut the exchange by launching a fully-electronic version of the CBOT's leading contracts.'[63] Though the CME was regarded as a pioneer of electronic trading, with its Globex system, it continued to restrict its use to after-hours trading, and was no readier than CBOT to abandon open outcry. Jack Sandner, the CME chairman, accepted in 2000 that, 'It's going to be an electronic world' but he added that 'The question is how it's going to get there—and how long it's going to take.'[64] By then one of the Chicago exchanges, the Cboe, which traded options, was facing serious competition from an entirely new electronic exchange. In 1997 David Krell and Gary Katz, who both worked in the options division of the NYSE, started planning an electronic exchange. In 2000 they formed the International Securities Exchange, the first all-electronic US options exchange. This was a fully-electronic exchange that traded options on the 600 leading US stocks. In 2003 David Krell, the chief executive of the ISE, explained their aim: 'When we arrived, we tightened

shrink volumes', 28th February 1997; Richard Adams and Andrew Jack, 'Matif invites bets on EMU', 22nd March 1997; Edward Luce, 'Euro fever starts scramble', 27th June 1997; Edward Luce and Krishna Guha, 'DTB plans challenge to Liffe', 10th July 1997; Edward Luce and Samer Iskandar, 'Exchanges walk the thin line that separates rivalry and war', 14th July 1997; Vincent Boland, 'Liffe and DTB vie for supremacy', 5th August 1997; Andrew Jack, 'SBF, Matif join forces ahead of German link', 18th September 1997; Simon Davies, 'Equity culture growing fast', 23rd January 1998; Samer Iskandar and Edward Luce, 'Liffe grasps the nettle of electronic trading', 10th March 1998; Samer Iskandar and Edward Luce, 'Move to a life less ordinary', 11th March 1998; Nikki Tait, 'Uncertain futures ahead', 23rd March 1998; Tim Burt, 'Alliances are just the beginning', 24th March 1998; Tim Burt, 'Special partners sought', 14th April 1998; Edward Luce, 'A cloud over Frankfurt's ambitions', 24th June 1998; Simon Davies, 'Futures trade in the balance', 8th July 1998; Paul Solman, 'No time to be complacent', 17th July 1998; Vincent Boland, 'Logical development in a fast-changing world', 13th October 1998; Greg McIvor, 'Choice between merging or being marginalised', 27th October 1998; Edward Luce, 'Eurex set to address complaints', 20th November 1998; Arkady Ostrovsky, 'Back-office emerges from shadows', 23rd March 1999; Tony Barber, 'Börse's innovative chief strikes the right note', 23rd March 1999; Samer Iskandar, 'Turning point for SBF's chairman', 23rd March 1999; Edward Luce, 'Future is uncertain after frantic year', 23rd March 1999; Samer Iskandar, 'E-advantage has yet to make mark', 14th May 1999; Edward Luce, 'Hard global pressure on Liffe', 20th September 1999; Samer Iskandar, 'Shaped for a common platform', 20th September 1999; Christopher Brown-Humes, 'Cocky OM decides to play David and Goliath', 28th August 2000; Nicholas George, 'Stockholm legend has tough battle ahead', 31st August 2000; Aline van Duyn, 'Looking to an electronic future', 23rd February 2001; Nikki Tait, 'Technology spawns new range of rivals', 28th March 2001; Vincent Boland, 'Failure to achieve victory puts LSE in the line of fire', 31st October 2001; Sarah Laitner, 'Euronext set for Liffe', 28th December 2001; Jeremy Grant, 'CBOT starts battle for market share', 13th January 2003; Alex Skorecki, 'Will Williamson fly even higher now he has finished with Liffe?', 15th April 2003; Joshua Levitt, 'Taking stock of futures market', 21st October 2003; Norma Cohen, 'Club of bankers has come full circle', 16th November 2006.

[62] Edward Luce, 'New Technology is driving mating dances', 23rd March 1999.
[63] Edward Luce, 'New Technology is driving mating dances', 23rd March 1999.
[64] Nikki Tait, 'The floor is going electronic', 28th June 2000.

bid-ask spreads, brought in fresh capital to provide liquidity and increased the size of contracts—with automation. We tried to reform a marketplace where customers were begging for reformation.'[65] By the end of 2003 the ISE had become the largest US options exchange with the Cboe's floor trading increasingly relegated, according to Bill Brodsky, its chairman, to handling 'orders that are either too complex or too large for the (electronic) systems that exist'.[66] The competition faced by these Chicago derivatives exchanges intensified after the collapse of the dot.com speculative bubble. Suffering from a loss of the profits made from floating new technology companies the US investment banks, who were major users of derivatives, sought to reduce expenditure, and one obvious saving was on the fees they paid exchanges.

The catalyst that drove the US derivatives exchanges to finally embrace electronic trading were the actions of Eurex. Following on from its triumph over Liffe in the Bund contract, and its merger with Soffex, Eurex spotted an opening in the USA. Rudolf Ferscha, the chief executive of Eurex, explained in 2004 that 'We are an exchange with a global vision and we need to be in the US.'[67] Eurex took the bold decision to establish its own US exchange, which would begin by trading CBOT financial futures contracts electronically. The CBOT responded by turning to Euronext/Liffe for an alternative, and superior, electronic technology, realizing that it could not rely on open outcry alone. In the words of Jeremy Grant, writing in 2003, the result was to be a war between the two European derivative exchanges conducted on US soil: 'The move (by Eurex) sets the stage for a bitter battle between Eurex and arch-rival Euronext-Liffe for a share of the US derivatives market.'[68] It was not clear who the victor would be. The judgement of Jeremy Grant was that 'Ultimately the victor will be the one that commands the greatest liquidity.' He cautioned that, 'It has historically been hard for one exchange to prise liquidity in a product from an exchange that has dominated trading in that product.'[69] The chairman of the CBOT, Nick Neubauer, was confident of winning this war for his exchange, regardless of the ambitions of either Eurex or Euronext. His conclusion at the time was that, 'I think it's more difficult for an exchange that's not local to compete in another country.'[70] His assessment turned out to be correct but only after forcing the CBOT to turn to electronic trading, slash fees, and forge a common clearing link with the CME. Even before Eurex launched its US exchange in 2004 both CBOT and CME were preparing themselves for the expected competition by investing in their own electronic platforms, tailoring their charges to retain customer loyalty and launching products that matched those of the European derivative exchanges. As early as 2004 over half the trading on both the CBOT and CME had switched to their electronic platforms and the share of open outcry was in rapid decline. Jeremy Grant was of the opinion in 2004 that he was witnessing 'the gradual death in the US of the open outcry system'.[71] By 2006 Eurex recognized the futility of its challenge and so abandoned it. Seeing off that challenge had brought the Chicago rivals, CBOT and CME, together to a degree that had appeared impossible in the past. The outcome was an agreed merger announced in 2006,

[65] Jeremy Grant, 'Trading volumes buoyed by rise in markets', 5th November 2003.
[66] Jeremy Grant, 'Trading volumes buoyed by rise in markets', 5th November 2003.
[67] Elizabeth Rigby, 'Windy City rivals may feel fresh blast of competition', 2nd April 2004.
[68] Jeremy Grant, 'Euronext-Liffe and CBOT mull further links', 11th January 2003.
[69] Jeremy Grant, 'Landscape altered by earthquake', 5th November 2003.
[70] Jeremy Grant, 'Euronext-Liffe and CBOT mull further links', 11th January 2003.
[71] Jeremy Grant, 'A single-product boutique is not the way: is one-stop shopping coming to US exchanges?', 14th September 2004.

which would support further investment in electronic trading and processing.[72] That was a course of action that was already well established around the world.[73]

[72] Tracy Corrigan, 'Traditional split in derivatives is less clear-cut', 25th January 1993; Laurie Morse, 'Consolidating for the futures', 27th January 1993; Tracy Corrigan and Laurie Morse, 'Trouble after hours', 3rd June 1993; Laurie Morse, 'CBOT aims to boost its international appeal', 18th June 1993; Laurie Morse, 'European futures links encounter local opposition', 21st July 1993; Laurie Morse and Tracy Corrigan, 'European futures trade comes of age', 31st December 1993; Tracy Corrigan, 'The tail still wags the dog', 26th May 1994; Laurie Morse, 'CME seeks strength through harmonisation', 23rd August 1994; Richard Lapper, 'A rosy future for futures spells a charmed Liffe', 14th January 1995; Laurie Morse, 'Both sides benefit from London–Chicago link', 16th March 1995; Laurie Morse and Robert Corzine, 'London oil market reaches out to Asia', 9th June 1995; Richard Lapper, 'Revival of the floor show', 27th July 1995; Richard Lapper, 'Alliances with a future', 7th September 1995; Richard Lapper, 'Strategic global electronic connections', 16th November 1995; Laurie Morse, 'CME seen to get something for nothing', 22nd November 1996; Laurie Morse, 'Liffe sets its sights on the No 1 spot', 22nd November 1996; William Hall, 'EBS doubters shaken off', 28th February 1997; Laurie Morse, 'CBOT warming to the computer', 6th March 1997; Laurie Morse and Samer Iskandar, 'Rivals unite in a marriage of convenience', 6th May 1997; Samer Iskandar, 'Fierce battle rages for market share', 27th June 1997; Edward Luce and Nikki Tait, 'Exchanges struggle with costs', 5th September 1997; Nikki Tait, 'Uncertain futures ahead', 23rd March 1998; Paul Solman, 'No time to be complacent', 17th July 1998; Nikki Tait, 'Older birds can still fly', 13th January 1999; Nikki Tait, 'Exchanges look to their electronic futures', 22nd March 1999; Nikki Tait, 'Marriage proposals dominate the sector', 23rd March 1999; Nikki Tait, 'Electronic threat prompts action', 23rd March 1999; Edward Luce, 'Hard global pressure on Liffe', 20th September 1999; Nikki Tait, 'Exchange President keeps his options open', 28th February 2000; Nikki Tait, 'There's life in the old bourses yet', 31st March 2000; Nikki Tait, 'ISE takes another step closer to launch', 25th May 2000; Nikki Tait, 'Fierce battle to take lead', 28th June 2000; Aline van Duyn, 'In search of efficiency', 28th June 2000; Nikki Tait, 'The floor is going electronic', 28th June 2000; Aline van Duyn, 'Cash bond trading explored', 8th September 2000; Nikki Tait, 'Technology spawns new range of rivals', 28th March 2001; Nikki Tait, 'Catalogue of woes starts to take a toll', 28th March 2001; Nikki Tait, 'Americans poised to be offered contracts', 21st June 2001; Nikki Tait, 'Chicago traders stay entrenched in the bull-pit', 25th September 2001; Andrei Postelnicu, 'Easy trades thrive on a complex platform', 25th September 2001; Vincent Boland, 'US markets face up to technology gap', 6th June 2002; Christopher Bowen, 'Upstarts upset the applecart', 6th June 2002; Jeremy Grant, 'CME gambles on electronic success', 17th June 2002; Jeremy Grant and Alex Skorecki, 'Electronic trading is dealt a double blow', 12th July 2002; Jeremy Grant, 'Euronext-Liffe and CBOT mull further links', 11th January 2003; Jeremy Grant, 'CBOT starts battle for market share', 13th January 2003; Alex Skorecki, 'A returning hero with eyes set on the west', 16th January 2003; Alex Skorecki, 'Will Williamson fly even higher now he has finished with Liffe?', 15th April 2003; Jeremy Grant and Alex Skorecki, 'Eurex makes inroads into US', 28th May 2003; Alex Skorecki, 'Derivatives sector faces up to Eurex's assault on the US', 9th June 2003; Alex Skorecki, 'ISE takes battle to Chicago', 18th June 2003; Jeremy Grant and Alex Skorecki, 'Chicago plans for Eurex attack', 19th September 2003; Jeremy Grant and Vincent Boland, 'Chicago is their kinda town: but how long can the city's futures traders keep Eurex's electronic exchange at bay?', 16th October 2003; Alex Skorecki, 'How London lost the battle of the Bund', 16th October 2003; Jeremy Grant, 'Eurex faces vote on clearing house', 20th October 2003; Jeremy Grant, 'Battle looms between CBOT and Eurex', 31st October 2003; Jeremy Grant, 'Landscape altered by earthquake', 5th November 2003; Alex Skorecki, 'Latecomer presses its advantage', 5th November 2003; Philip Manchester, 'Driving change in ways of trading in markets', 5th November 2003; Jeremy Grant, 'Trading volumes buoyed by rise in markets', 5th November 2003; Jeremy Grant, 'From strangle to straddle in a few seconds', 5th November 2003; Jeremy Grant, 'CME reduces fees for European customers', 11th November 2003; Alex Skorecki, 'Chicago meets electronic challenge', 4th December 2003; Jeremy Grant, 'CBOT retaliates in Eurex battle', 4th February 2004; Jeremy Grant, 'New exchange shakes up pricing', 4th February 2004; Jeremy Grant and Alex Skorecki, 'Software vendors globalise pit', 3rd March 2004; Alex Skorecki, 'From the scream to the screen', 10th March 2004; Alex Skorecki, 'Liffe goes to war with CME', 16th March 2004; Elizabeth Rigby, 'Windy City rivals may feel fresh blast of competition', 2nd April 2004; Alex Skorecki, 'CBOT in move to hit back at Eurex', 16th April 2004; Jeremy Grant, 'Traders consider their options', 27th April 2004; Jeremy Grant, 'CME seeks to broaden its business', 10th June 2004; Jeremy Grant, 'Chicago enters electronic future', 10th August 2004; Jeremy Grant, 'A single-product boutique is not the way: is one-stop shopping coming to US exchanges?', 14th September 2004; Alex Skorecki, 'Liffe tops SGX in Eurodollar contracts', 6th October 2004; Jeremy Grant, 'NQLX listing of Eurodollar future on hold', 2nd November 2004; Norma Cohen, 'Deutsche Börse chief's overture to the world', 8th November 2004; Jennifer Hughes, 'Eurex issues a challenge to CME', 17th June 2005; Jennifer Hughes, 'Eurex issues a challenge to CME', 17th June 2005; Jennifer Hughes, 'Currency futures trading record', 25th August 2005; Patrick Jenkins and Doug Cameron, 'D Börse sticks with plan for Eurex in US', 10th January 2006; Jennifer Hughes, 'NYBOT to offer electronic trading', 26th January 2006; Jennifer Hughes and John Authers, 'Taking the floor: how a screen role will challenge New York's market debutant', 7th March 2006; Doug Cameron, 'Chicago rises to the European challenge', 15th March 2006; John Authers, 'Revenues rise at CBOT', 20th April 2006; Doug Cameron, 'CME lifts profile in Europe via acquisition', 6th July 2006; Jeremy Grant, 'Man Group nabs 70% of Eurex US', 28th July 2006; Jeremy Grant, 'Man injects life into dying Börse arm', 31st July 2006; Doug Cameron, 'Introspection succeeded by internationalism', 26th September 2006; John Authers and Norma Cohen, 'Clearing the floor: how a regulatory overhaul is helping rivals to close in on the Big Board', 14th September 2006; Doug Cameron, 'Chicago takes the top spot in derivatives', 18th October 2006; Norma Cohen, 'A clash of titans: why big banks are wading into the stock exchange fray', 24th November 2006; Anuj Gangahar, 'Krell swansong fulfils global ambitions', 1st May 2007; Gregory Meyer, 'Trading', 7th July 2016.

[73] Nikki Tait, 'The floor is going electronic', 28th June 2000; Jeremy Grant, 'From strangle to straddle in a few seconds', 5th November 2003.

What had long delayed the conversion from open outcry to electronic trading among US derivatives exchanges, like many others around the world, was mutual ownership as it threatened the livelihood of many individual members. The victory of the DTB over Liffe in 1998, followed by the attempted invasion of the US market by Eurex, forced those running member-owned derivatives exchanges to recognise that electronic trading was the way forward. Unless it was embraced they would face a loss of business with their future existence threatened. As early as 2000 those running the CBOT and CME were preparing for the eventual triumph of electronic trading by investing in new technology and taking steps towards demutualization, but at different rates. The CME did demutualize in 2000 but it took until 2003 before it became a publicly-listed company. Freed from constraints imposed by mutuality the CME soon began to explore different options. Craig Donohue, the chief executive, expressed the CME's vision of the future in 2004 'I think we will become a more broadly diversified financial services firm, given the convergence that's happening across products and platforms.'[74] The response of the CBOT was slower but in the same direction, also involving demutualization, and then listing as a public company in 2005. The Cboe was also under pressure from the ISE, which had floated on the NYSE in 2005. In response the Cboe also demutualized. By 2006 the whole world of US derivative exchanges was in the process of transformation with ideas of multi-asset electronic platforms operating on a global basis gaining ground. One outcome was the agreed merger between the CME and the CBOT in 2006. Once mutuality ended it changed the landscape within which derivative exchanges operated, opening up the possibility of mergers between rivals, at home and abroad, and the creation of multiproduct platforms combining derivatives with equities as was taking place elsewhere in the world. The difficulty such moves faced in the USA was the regulatory divide between futures on the one hand and equities and options on the other. This had the effect of preventing the development of multiproduct platforms though this was the direction of travel around the world. A single electronic platform could serve many users and the higher the volume of business that passed through it the lower the cost of each transaction. This provided a huge competitive advantage to those exchanges that could achieve economies of scale whether through continuous global trading or by providing a platform for a multitude of financial products.[75]

[74] Jeremy Grant, 'A single-product boutique is not the way: is one-stop shopping coming to US exchanges?', 14th September 2004.

[75] Laurie Morse, 'CBOT warming to the computer', 6th March 1997; Nikki Tait, 'Uncertain futures ahead', 23rd March 1998; Gwen Robinson, 'SFE in push to go fully electronic', 6th April 1998; Edward Luce, 'Liffe's limited reform plan fails to impress critics', 23rd April 1998; Edward Luce, 'Liffe will open share ownership to non-members', 18th December 1998; Edward Luce, 'New Technology is driving mating dances', 23rd March 1999; Edward Luce, 'Breathing a second lease of life into Liffe', 27th July 1999; Nikki Tait, 'Pit in the dumps', 20th September 1999; Nikki Tait, 'Exchange President keeps his options open', 28th February 2000; Nikki Tait, 'There's life in the old bourses yet', 31st March 2000; Virginia Marsh, 'Markets taking stock of the future', 4th July 2000; Nikki Tait, 'Catalogue of woes starts to take a toll', 28th March 2001; Jeremy Grant, 'CME gambles on electronic success', 17th June 2002; Jeremy Grant, 'Battle looms between CBOT and Eurex', 31st October 2003; Jeremy Grant, 'A single-product boutique is not the way: is one-stop shopping coming to US exchanges?', 14th September 2004; Doug Cameron, 'Chicago rises to the European challenge', 15th March 2006; Doug Cameron, 'CME damps speculation of LSE bid', 17th March 2006; Anuj Gangahar, 'ISE to launch stock exchange', 20th April 2006; Norma Cohen and Doug Cameron, 'Participants get ready for realignment', 22nd May 2006; Doug Cameron, 'NYSE pulls rug from under Chicago Mercantile's feet', 30th May 2006; Doug Cameron, 'Rivals' rude health spells out merger potential', 28th June 2006; Doug Cameron, 'Chicago Board Options Exchange sets ball rolling for market listing', 28th June 2006; John Authers and Norma Cohen, 'Clearing the floor: how a regulatory overhaul is helping rivals to close in on the Big Board', 14th September 2006; Doug Cameron, 'Introspection succeeded by internationalism', 26th September 2006; Doug Cameron, 'Chicago takes the top spot in derivatives', 18th October 2006; Anuj Gangahar and Norma Cohen, 'Traders fear fee increase in wake of $8bn link-up', 19th October 2006; Joanna Chung and Martin Arnold, 'European worries do not make sense', 19th October 2006; Jeremy Grant and Doug Cameron, 'Lords of the Windy City', 21st October 2006; Doug Cameron, 'CME's over-the-counter drive to continue', 25th

Despite the slow switch to electronic trading Chicago remained the centre of the exchange-traded derivatives business. The liquidity of the contracts traded on the CME, CBOT, and Cboe, whether by open outcry or on electronic platforms, continued to attract global interest while no foreign challenger could dislodge their control of the vast US market. Though an increased amount of derivatives trading was taking place locally it still generated a rising volume of activity for Chicago's exchanges, whether conducted electronically or open outcry. In 2006 John Thain, the chief executive at the NYSE, observed that for the CME, 'Gradually, a bigger percentage of their products have traded electronically. It's now 85%. But the less-liquid contracts and the options-type products continue to trade in the pit. There is more trading in the pit than there was five years ago.'[76] In contrast, the new derivative exchanges that appeared around the world quickly adopted electronic trading, or did so from the outset. Typical of these was the Kuala Lumpur Options and Financial Futures Exchange (Kloffe), founded in 1995. John Duggan, its chief operating officer, explained the motivation behind the launch: 'Malaysia has seen the growth in the derivatives markets in other parts of the world and the substantial development of its own capital markets, and decided it needed a derivatives industry to be a well-rounded market.'[77] Kloffe was expected to add liquidity to the cash equities market, trading a contract based on the Kuala Lumpur Stock Exchange's composite index, as well as allowing local investors to better manage their risks. Kloffe was to be a screen-based exchange, using the technology used by DTB and Soffex. Most of these new derivative exchanges developed contracts using the local currency and based on locally-traded stocks and bonds, as was the case in Latin America and South Africa where the volume of trading grew rapidly in the 1990s. Nevertheless, many foreign banks and fund managers continued to use US exchanges because of access to dollar-denominated contracts.[78]

The failure of Tokyo to emerge as a centre for derivatives trading in Asia created opportunities for a number of exchanges located elsewhere in that continent. Within Japan the Osaka Securities Exchange had benefited from the lack of support for derivatives by the Tokyo Stock Exchange, and the high charges it imposed. In 1998 Osaka was responsible for 77 per cent of trading in futures and virtually all options in Japan. However, the entire Japanese derivatives business had been seeping overseas due to the high cost of operating in that country and the numerous regulatory barriers imposed on the business. It was as late as 1999 that Naoko Nakamae noted that, 'The process of deregulation is slowly getting rid of the regulatory irritants that prevented Japan from being a leading contender in the derivatives world.'[79] Until that process was completed the Japanese derivatives market

October 2006; Doug Cameron, 'CME-CBOT deal set to come under increased scrutiny', 22nd November 2006; Doug Cameron, 'The price was right', 28th November 2006; Anuj Gangahar, 'Volumes increase by the month', 28th November 2006.

[76] John Authers and Norma Cohen, 'Clearing the floor: how a regulatory overhaul is helping rivals to close in on the Big Board', 14th September 2006.

[77] Conner Middelmann, 'Step closer to becoming a well-rounded market', 16th November 1995.

[78] Damian Fraser, 'Propelled into a new financial age', 20th October 1993; Conner Middelmann, 'Step closer to becoming a well-rounded market', 16th November 1995; Nikki Tait, 'Sydney exchange sees future in commodities', 3rd January 1997; James Kynge, 'Ingenious new ideas for futures', 9th May 1997; Jonathan Wheatley, 'Small victory for exchange', 10th June 1997; Jonathan Wheatley, 'Ready for foreign flows', 27th June 1997; Christine Moir, 'Mirror on a domestic scene', 27th June 1997; Edward Luce, 'Hard global pressure on Liffe', 20th September 1999; Victor Mallet, 'Rainbow colours of the future', 20th September 1999; Joshua Levitt, 'Taking stock of futures market', 21st October 2003; Jeremy Grant, 'Chicago exchanges look to Asia', 15th June 2004; Alex Skorecki, 'Liffe tops SGX in Eurodollar contracts', 6th October 2004; John Authers and Norma Cohen, 'Clearing the floor: how a regulatory overhaul is helping rivals to close in on the Big Board', 14th September 2006.

[79] Naoko Nakamae, 'Deregulation opens doors slowly to investors', 23rd March 1999.

remained underdeveloped considering the size and sophistication of its financial system. Exploiting this position Singapore, in particular, became an alternative market to Osaka and Tokyo, with a third of trading in the Nikkei 225 futures contract in 1998. Through developing Japanese rather than domestic futures contracts the Singapore International Monetary Exchange (Simex) had capitalized on the inability of the Japanese derivatives market to meet domestic and international demand. Though not located in Asia those running the Sydney Futures Exchange (SFE) also spotted that Japanese weakness, and attempted to take Tokyo's place in the Asia-Pacific time zone. By 1998 30 per cent of trading on the SFE was generated outside Australia. What was happening was a mixture of competition and co-operation between derivatives exchanges as each tried to support its position in an increasingly global industry. Liffe and the Tokyo International Financial Futures Exchange (Tiffe), for example, reached an agreement to trade Tiffe's Euroyen contract in London but only when trading closed in Tokyo. The nature of this agreement reflected the problem with such alliances as no exchange was willing to compromise the control it had over trading in particular contracts. Each was happy to share after-hours trading as that did not affect liquidity but none were willing to countenance competition during the times their exchange was open. This made the pursuit of 24-hour liquidity through a series of exchange alliances impossible, even though this was the desire of the global banks and fund managers that generated most of the trading.[80] Instead, it was this facility that the OTC market was increasingly able to provide.

OTC Derivatives

Challenging the position of all derivatives exchanges, whether established or new, large or small, was the rapidly expanding OTC market. In the OTC market trading took place on a bilateral basis, either directly between banks or through interdealer brokers. Such arrangements did not require a trading system provided by an exchange, whether located in an open outcry pit or an electronic network. Instead it was based on trust between the counterparties, aided by proximity as that cut down the delay between contact and completion. That favoured a location where the banks were already clustered, especially as each deal was frequently linked to an overall strategy aimed at matching assets and liabilities across a range of variables, preserving liquidity, employing funds to best advantage, and operating within defined risk and return parameters. There were only a few centres in the world that possessed the dense clustering of bank offices from which such varied transactions were conducted, along with the interdealer brokers who serviced their every need. Chicago was not one of them, despite the presence of the CBOT, CME, and Cboe. Nor were Frankfurt, Paris, Sydney, or Singapore, though they also hosted major derivative exchanges, such as

[80] Andrew Gowers, 'Island of integrity', 29th March 1993; Emiko Terazono, 'JGB futures stir bad memories', 20th October 1993; Gerard Baker, 'Regional rivals hot on its heels', 19th October 1994; Richard Lapper, 'Alliances with a future', 7th September 1995; Richard Lapper, 'Strategic global electronic connections', 16th November 1995; Conner Middelmann, 'Step closer to becoming a well-rounded market', 16th November 1995; Nikki Tait, 'Sydney exchange sees future in commodities', 3rd January 1997; James Kynge, 'Ingenious new ideas for futures', 9th May 1997; Gillian Tett, 'Traders gamble on an anomaly', 17th July 1998; Gwen Robinson, 'Screen test looms', 17th July 1998; Nikki Tait, 'US leaves foreigners out in the cold', 30th October 1998; Gwen Robinson, 'Record trading as merger talks go on', 23rd March 1999; Naoko Nakamae, 'Deregulation opens doors slowly to investors', 23rd March 1999; Virginia Marsh, 'Australian futures market calls it a day', 29th March 2001; David Turner, 'Japan needs derivatives to compete', 10th August 2006; Delphine Strauss, 'ISE faces test from Turkey's trading past', 22nd September 2009; Lindsay Whipp, 'Ambitions to recapture its glory days', 8th February 2010.

DTB, Matif, SFE, and Simex. Instead, dense bank clusters were found in London, Tokyo, and New York, but it was only the first of these that was in a position to provide what the OTC derivatives market required. Tokyo had failed to develop as a centre for derivatives trading because of the restrictions imposed by the Japanese government. Until 1999 OTC derivatives had been banned and the exchange-traded market stunted by controls and regulations. Of the $13,291bn in OTC derivatives outstanding in the world in 1999, only $12.6bn was Japanese, or less than 0.1 per cent. Another potential location for the global OTC derivatives market was New York, but it failed to capitalize on the opportunities it had, losing out to Chicago within the USA.

In contrast London played host to the development of Liffe, which was a deliberate attempt to replicate what had already been achieved in Chicago. The success of Liffe then nurtured the growth of derivatives trading in London, and this remained despite the loss of the Bund contract to Frankfurt in 1998. The rapid switch to electronic trading by Liffe, followed by its acquisition by Euronext, maintained London as a major European centre for exchange-traded derivatives, especially those at the shorter-end of the interest-rate spectrum. Added to its time-zone advantages and its position as the leading centre in the world for bank offices, London was the natural location for the emerging OTC derivatives market. It was in London that the inter-bank swaps market experienced explosive growth.[81] It would be a mistake to regard the exchange-traded and OTC derivatives markets as being in direct competition. Banks were major users of both exchange-traded and OTC derivatives as they complemented each other. Through the active buying and selling of exchange-traded derivatives banks could offset some of the risks they ran with the OTC derivative contracts they provided to their customers. In 1993 Joseph Bauman, responsible for developing global derivatives at Citibank, explained that, 'Risks we take from our clients often flow back to the exchanges.'[82] Both the exchange-traded and OTC derivatives markets were also exposed to competition from the growing ability of banks to use their internal networks to lay off risks, rather than rely on the wholesale markets, as that saved on the commission paid and the margin required. By 1997 Laurie Morse concluded that, 'OTC swaps dealing has become so standardised in sectors such as dollar-denominated interest-rate transactions, that banks are finding they can net their risks within their own books, reducing their need to use futures exchanges to lay off interest-rate exposure.'[83] The exchange-traded and OTC markets served different functions and there was constant flux between the two. Exchanges copied successful OTC instruments and the OTC market emulated the products and practices of the exchanges. The OTC derivatives market was a constant source of innovation driven by the interaction of supply and demand. 'As is always the case in the financial industry...the really innovative and interesting business in derivatives is to be found in the over-the-counter market' was the conclusion reached by Vincent Boland in 2000.[84] Suppliers of derivatives responded to the needs of users for products that covered an expanding range of the risks that they were exposed to. These included currency and interest-rate volatility through fluctuations in stock prices to the default of those issuing bonds or to whom loans had been made. In turn, some of these tailor-made products generated a general appeal, becoming standardized and widely traded after the fashion of those provided by exchanges, with interdealer brokers providing the market intermediation. In

[81] The data is taken from the Bank for International Settlement, Financial Derivative Instruments, 1993–2017.
[82] Tracy Corrigan, 'Moving on to centre stage', 20th October 1993.
[83] Laurie Morse, 'Traders turn credit risks into profits', 23rd May 1997.
[84] Vincent Boland, 'Market shows greater value and maturity', 28th June 2000.

turn, these contracts were adapted and adopted by exchanges, which could offer a number of advantages over the OTC market. As Edward Condon, head of European-listed derivatives at Credit Suisse First Boston (CSFB), put it in 2003, 'On a listed market you have transparency, uniformity and price competitiveness. And derivatives that are cleared through an exchange do not require the banks to carry the transaction on their balance sheets.'[85]

By their very nature OTC transactions were opaque, being conducted by private negotiation between two parties, with or without an interdealer broker acting as an intermediary. In contrast, trading on an exchange was conducted in the open, whether in a pit or an electronic network, with the price and terms being seen by all. Exchange-traded contracts were also much more liquid as they consisted of standard products that were bought and sold in volume by brokers and dealers, who continuously adjusted their position in the light of constantly changing prices. OTC derivatives were little traded once negotiated being retained to cover a particular risk, though the amount of secondary trading did grow steadily. In addition to transparency and liquidity the other advantage of the exchange-traded market over the OTC one was the reduced risk of counterparty default. The exchanges took responsibility for ensuring that deals were completed by passing transactions either through their in-house clearing facility or used a specialist provider such as the London Clearing House. John Damgard, president of the Washington-based Futures Industry Association, highlighted this element in 2004 when he noted that, 'The CME has a very viable clearing house that stands between counterparties as a financial guarantee and that's a huge benefit to the exchange-traded markets.'[86] The use of clearing made a vital contribution to the reduction of systemic risk in the derivatives markets. By taking a small margin for each trade, and a lump sum from each participant in the scheme, a clearing house assembled sufficient funds to pay creditors if the transaction was not completed or one of its members failed. By acting as counterparty to each trade a clearing house reduced the potential of a big failure causing a domino effect throughout the markets. In contrast, in the OTC market the security of the deal depended on the counterparty meeting its obligations. Among the global banks and international fund managers there was, usually, complete confidence that neither side would default while acknowledging the degree of exposure if one should occur. However, this level of trust did not apply outside a close group of global banks. Smaller or more local banks struggled to generate a high level of trust upon their peers, as did those upon whom suspicion fell during a financial crisis. Banks that could not command the trust of others, either permanently or temporarily, found it difficult to engage with the OTC derivatives market, so leaving the business to the few that could.

As a result OTC trading was largely in the hands of a small group of global banks with unimpeachable reputations because of their size and scale. They could choose to place their business either through exchanges, the OTC market, or match transactions internally. Key to expanding the number of participants in the OTC market, and reducing counterparty risk, was the introduction of clearing facilities. By transferring the risk of a default to a clearing house, which would guarantee completing, the number able to participate in the OTC market could be expanded. In turn that would make the OTC more competitive, and better able to challenge the exchanges in terms of charges and liquidity. Laurie Morse was reporting on the initiatives aimed at opening up the OTC market as early as 1993: 'Ideas for

[85] Charles Batchelor, 'Essential, controversial, popular and profitable', 5th November 2003.
[86] Jeremy Grant, 'CME seeks to broaden its business', 10th June 2004.

managing credit exposure while at the same time allowing reasonable market access and a healthy measure of innovation range from a centralised derivatives clearing house to a more sophisticated generation of standardised bilateral swaps contracts.'[87] With central clearing the credit quality of counterparties would be less of an issue. Spotting this weakness in the OTC derivatives market, those exchanges with their own clearing facilities, and independent clearing houses, moved in to offer their services. Complicating the ability of clearing houses to cater for the OTC derivatives market was the unique nature of many swap contracts as this made them difficult to value and match with alternatives. One clearing house that persevered with the attempt was the London Commodity House (LCH), but it took three years before it was able to provide it. After its reorganization in 1996, when the investment banks took control, the London Commodity House (LCH) began exploring the possibility of providing clearing facilities for the global swaps market, which was largely located in London. In 1997 David Harding, the LCH chief executive, indicated that, 'Our aim is to be the best exchange clearing house in the world, but LCH can also deliver other significant benefits for its members through the provision of central services.' It was not until 1999 that LCH was ready to launch SwapClear, a clearing system for the OTC interest-rate swaps market. In the USA the Chicago-based Options Clearing House served as a central clearer for the US options market. In France the settlement organization, Sicovam, offered its services to the OTC derivatives market while established exchanges like CME and CBOT planned a role for themselves through their in-house clearing facilities. Patrick Arbor, chairman of CBOT, observed in 1998 that, 'In today's technology-driven global markets, over-the-counter derivatives and exchange-traded derivatives are intertwined and converging.'[88]

The result of the developments taking place in the 1990s was to blur the distinction between the exchange-traded and OTC market in the case of derivatives. There was a two-way pull between exchange-traded and OTC derivatives. As derivatives markets developed and contracts became commoditized there tended to be a shift from OTC to exchanges, especially if counterparty risk became an issue. Conversely, the flexibility of OTC contracts, customized to match specific needs, and not dictated by the requirements of either exchanges or regulators, exerted a major appeal, especially as clearing facilities became available and liquidity improved. By the late 1990s the OTC market was on the winning side. An estimated 90 per cent of all derivatives turnover was conducted on the OTC market compared to 70 per cent in 1996. This prompted Edward Luce to note in 1999 that, 'While London, Paris and Frankfurt battle it out for supremacy in the market for conventional exchange-traded products, the private "over-the-counter" market for derivatives is taking off. The banks, in other words, are doing it for themselves without the help of the exchanges.'[89] The conclusion he reached later in 1999 was that 'Few... doubt that power is shifting from the owners of the exchanges to their largest customers or that the main action is now taking place outside the exchanges altogether.'[90] Nevertheless, in any financial crisis, such as that associated with the bursting of the dot.com bubble in 2000, there was a switch back to the exchanges because of concerns over counterparty risk, but as these faded the ascendancy of the OTC market resumed.

87 Laurie Morse, 'Derivatives industry scrambles to find some kind of infrastructure', 12th July 1993.
88 Nikki Tait, 'Changes create new risks', 17th July 1998.
89 Edward Luce, 'Breathing a second lease of life into Liffe', 27th July 1999.
90 Edward Luce, 'Exchanges in world flux', 20th September 1999.

Where the OTC market continued to be weak in the 1990s was in the application of electronic technology. The technology was taken up rapidly in the area of processing transactions but only slowly when it came to trading. As with clearing the difficulty lay in the unique nature of many of the contracts as these were handled through negotiation, later confirmed in writing, and did not lend themselves to matching by computer. Philippe Khuong-Huu, head of LabMorgan, JP Morgan's e-finance unit, referred in 2000 to a swap agreement as 'a three-page long contract between two parties'. The problem to be overcome, in his view, was 'to find a way of transcribing those contracts electronically'.[91] The solution was to use a common coding system as this allowed the information contained in a derivatives contract to be electronically transferred. Once this was done it became possible to trade OTC derivatives, such as interest-rate swaps, on electronic platforms rather than through voice brokers. These platforms were provided either by investment banks for the use of their clients, such as Orbit from JP Morgan, or by start-up companies, such as Creditex, which launched in 2000 an electronic trading system for credit default swaps. Others then followed. By 2004 the switch from voice-broking to electronic platforms in the OTC market began to take hold, having begun with short-dated interest-rate swaps as these were easier to standardize. In 2006, Creditex, which had a strong position trading credit derivatives in the European market merged with CreditTrade, to help it expand in the USA and Asia. The combined business handled $2,000bn worth of trades a year, making it able to provide its banking customers with the global liquidity they sought when buying and selling derivatives in the OTC market. The success of the likes of Creditex put pressure on the interdealer brokers. They had handled around half of all OTC derivatives transactions through their teams of voice brokers located in the major financial centres, with the rest taking place directly between the banks. In response, the interdealer brokers launched their own electronic platforms as OTC derivatives increasingly resembled the standardized, liquid products found on exchanges. These were traded at low margins and high volume forcing the interdealer brokers to find ways of reducing costs and increasing capacity, and so they turned to electronic platforms. As with derivative exchanges the pace of change was more rapid in Europe than in the USA. In 2005 50 per cent of credit derivatives were traded electronically in Europe compared to only 7 per cent in the USA. Despite the increasing triumph of electronic trading in OTC derivatives voice broking was still required to cope with the more complex bespoke instruments. The attractions of OTC derivatives remained the ability to design a contract to fit the precise needs of each party to a bilateral deal, and, often, this could only be done through negotiation. The drawback was such contracts tended to be illiquid whether traded on electronic platforms or by voice brokers. With such derivatives there was no public market, as provided by an exchange, leaving prices to be generated by complex computer valuations based on calculations focused on probabilities, volatility, and future costs. These tended to ignore the question of liquidity, making the assumption that the underlying assets could always be sold.[92]

[91] Arkady Ostrovsky, 'Working towards a seamless link', 28th June 2000.

[92] Tracy Corrigan, 'DTB and Matif in co-operation agreement', 14th January 1993; Tracy Corrigan, 'Exchanges fight for the future across Europe', 15th January 1993; Tracy Corrigan, 'Traditional split in derivatives is less clear-cut', 25th January 1993; James Blitz, 'An insurance or a threat to stability?', 26th May 1993; Laurie Morse, 'Derivatives industry scrambles to find some kind of infrastructure', 12th July 1993; Tracy Corrigan, 'Divisions hazy in OTC derivatives clearing battle debate', 13th September 1993; John Gapper, 'IMF study warns in $8,000bn derivatives market', 24th September 1993; Tracy Corrigan, 'Volume rises to record levels', 24th September 1993; Tracy Corrigan, 'Moving on to centre stage', 20th October 1993; Antonia Sharpe, 'Hedge against stock swings', 20th October 1993; Tracy Corrigan, 'Quirky offshoots gain respect', 20th October 1993; Laurie Morse, 'Swaps trade dodges issue', 20th October 1993; Tracy Corrigan, 'Swaps market may be bigger than estimated', 16th November

Conclusion

There were highly polarized attitudes towards derivatives before the Global Financial Crisis. Reflecting these were the views of Warren Buffett and Alan Greenspan in 2003. Warren Buffett was one of the world's most successful investors, who, as chairman of Berkshire Hathaway, took large stakes in established companies and held them over the long-term. He warned that 'Large amounts of risk, particularly credit risk, have become concentrated in the hands of relatively few derivatives dealers. Derivatives are financial weapons of mass destruction that, while now latent, are potentially lethal.'[93] As a long-term investor with a portfolio of carefully selected assets liquidity was not a priority to him and nor was the need for diversification. To him derivatives were dangerous because they separated the investor from the investment and encouraged a short-term mentality. In contrast, Alan Greenspan was the world's most influential banker, as chairman of the Federal Reserve Board. To him 'The benefits of derivatives, in my judgement, have far exceeded their costs.'[94] As a banker he could appreciate the contribution that derivatives made to liquidity and the ability to reduce risk through diversification. Rebecca Bream had picked up on this division of opinion regarding derivatives in 2002 when she wrote, 'Promoters of credit derivatives argue that this spreads risk throughout the financial system, avoiding concentrations that can lead to systemic crises. Critics say, however, that it is now hard to see who are the ultimate risk takers when a company collapses.'[95] In the absence of systemic crises, especially after the bursting of the dot.com bubble in 2000, those who emphasized the benefits delivered by derivatives continued to triumph over those warning of the

1993; Tracy Corrigan, 'The tail still wags the dog', 26th May 1994; John Plender, 'Through a market, darkly', 27th May 1994; Emma Davey, 'Slow but steady convergence', 16th November 1995; Graham Bowley, 'New breed of exotics thrives', 16th November 1995; Henry Harington, 'Testing times for fund managers', 16th November 1995; Richard Lapper, 'New generation takes over', 16th November 1995; Richard Metcalfe, 'Forex options in the long term', 22nd November 1996; Laurie Morse, 'Regulators to voice fears for US futures', 10th March 1997; Laurie Morse, 'London could become global swaps centre', 27th March 1997; Laurie Morse, 'Futures trading slackens', 31st March 1997; Samer Iskandar, 'Management by mathematics', 31st March 1997; Laurie Morse, 'Traders turn credit risks into profits', 23rd May 1997; Katy Massey, 'New house rules for exchanges', 27th June 1997; Edward Luce, 'The future of futures', 30th June 1998; Nikki Tait, 'Changes create new risks', 17th July 1998; Gillian Tett, 'Traders gamble on an anomaly', 17th July 1998; Edward Luce, 'Liffe to focus on forging new alliances and changing rules', 3rd November 1998; Edward Luce, 'Central trading cushion cleared for take-off', 9th February 1999; Nikki Tait, 'LCH expects go-ahead for swaps clearing', 22nd March 1999; Edward Luce, 'Future is uncertain after frantic year', 23rd March 1999; Naoko Nakamae, 'Deregulation opens doors slowly to investors', 23rd March 1999; Edward Luce, 'Breathing a second lease of life into Liffe', 27th July 1999; Edward Luce, 'Exchanges in world flux', 20th September 1999; John Plender, 'Out of sight, not out of mind', 20th September 1999; Rebecca Bream, 'Corporate sector embraces credit swaps', 9th March 2000; Claire Smith, 'Fastest-growing risk protector', 19th May 2000; Vincent Boland, 'Market shows greater value and maturity', 28th June 2000; Rebecca Bream, 'Profusion of platforms looking for a niche', 28th June 2000; Arkady Ostrovsky, 'Working towards a seamless link', 28th June 2000; Florian Gimbel, 'Electronic swap systems set to go live', 20th December 2000; Alex Skorecki, 'Bigger share of derivatives for exchanges', 2nd October 2002; Aline van Duyn and Vincent Boland, 'Industry flourishes in bear market turmoil', 7th October 2002; Jeremy Grant, 'Battle looms between CBOT and Eurex', 31st October 2003; Charles Batchelor, 'Essential, controversial, popular and profitable', 5th November 2003; Päivi Munter, 'Protection becomes more desirable', 5th November 2003; Alex Skorecki, 'How to make a banker's heart race', 5th November 2003; Jeremy Grant, 'CME seeks to broaden its business', 10th June 2004; Jeremy Grant, 'A single-product boutique is not the way: is one-stop shopping coming to US exchanges?', 14th September 2004; Alex Skorecki, 'Market is making switch to electronic', 8th October 2004; Richard Beales, 'New CD electronic broker goes live', 6th December 2005; Saskia Scholtes, 'Electronic battle heats up', 28th July 2006; Gillian Tett, 'Déjà vu as markets face new challenge', 16th November 2006; Gillian Tett, 'Driven faster by low rates, more users and technology', 18th November 2006; Hal Weitzman, 'Humble OTC emerges from shadows', 2nd February 2009.

[93] Charles Batchelor, 'Essential, controversial, popular and profitable', 5th November 2003.
[94] Charles Batchelor, 'Essential, controversial, popular and profitable', 5th November 2003.
[95] Rebecca Bream, 'Plenty of bad news for a market to thrive on', 7th October 2002.

potential dangers. This was evident to Päivi Munter in 2003 when he reported that, 'Interest-rate swaps, the world's biggest financial market, have continued to grow as violent swings in government bond yields and exchange rates prompted investors to seek protection against interest rate and currency risk. But the market is also attracting investors who trade swaps for the arbitrage opportunities.'[96]

What derivatives offered was a means of insuring against loss while enjoying the higher returns that a willingness to take risks produced. For that reason derivatives were welcomed by regulators, in the belief that they would make banks more resilient in a crisis, and by bankers themselves as they reduced the risks associated with long-term investment where the returns were higher.[97] In the wake of the collapse in the 1970s of the controlled and compartmentalized world that had emerged after the Second World War, financial derivatives appeared to offer security against the volatility that now existed. For that reason they were generally welcomed, despite the misgivings of a few. Financial derivatives had also proved themselves in the years between 1992 and 2007 as a series of financial crises, banking collapses, and speculative bubbles had been surmounted without bringing down the global financial system or causing the shocks that had taken place in 1982 or 1987. In financial derivatives the world did, indeed, appear to have discovered a means of combining the best of all worlds.

[96] Päivi Munter, 'Protection becomes more desirable', 5th November 2003.

[97] James Blitz, 'An insurance or a threat to stability?', 26th May 1993; Laurie Morse, 'Derivatives industry scrambles to find some kind of infrastructure', 12th July 1993; Richard Waters, 'Easy option or unnecessary risk', 22nd July 1993; John Gapper, 'IMF study warns in $8,000bn derivatives market', 24th September 1993; Tracy Corrigan, 'Volume rises to record levels', 24th September 1993; Tracy Corrigan, 'Moving on to centre stage', 20th October 1993; James Blitz, 'ERM crisis quicken activity', 20th October 1993; Tracy Corrigan, 'Quirky offshoots gain respect', 20th October 1993; Tracy Corrigan, 'The tail still wags the dog', 26th May 1994; John Plender, 'Through a market, darkly', 27th May 1994; Antonia Sharpe, 'Latest tool to manage risks', 16th November 1995; Laurie Morse, 'Flow of capital slows down', 16th November 1995; Graham Bowley, 'At the heart of everyday life', 16th November 1995; Henry Harington, 'Testing times for fund managers', 16th November 1995; Richard Lapper, 'An important new frontier is opening', 22nd November 1996; Samer Iskandar, 'Euro set to shrink volumes', 28th February 1997; Laurie Morse, 'Traders turn credit risks into profits', 23rd May 1997; George Graham, 'Bank bows to outcry on derivatives', 7th June 1997; Michael Prest, 'Fear of "cats" results in new products', 27th June 1997; Samer Iskandar, 'Great expectations of a promising future', 27th June 1997; Edward Luce and Samer Iskandar, 'Liffe or death struggle', 19th September 1997; Samer Iskandar, 'The search for growth', 1st May 1998; Samer Iskandar, 'Market explodes into life', 17th July 1998; Khozem Merchant, 'Maverick market gains credibility', 20th September 1999; Arkady Ostrovsky, 'The odds are good on future growth', 20th September 1999; John Plender, 'Out of sight, not out of mind', 20th September 1999; Rebecca Bream, 'Corporate sector embraces credit swaps', 9th March 2000; Claire Smith, 'Fastest-growing risk protector', 19th May 2000; Vincent Boland, 'Market shows greater value and maturity', 28th June 2000; John Plender, 'The limits of ingenuity', 17th May 2001; Rebecca Bream, 'Market participants react to regulatory straitjacket', 25th September 2001; Claire Smith, 'Synthetic deals take on natural growth curve', 25th September 2001; Rebecca Bream, 'A form of protection for the rising risk of defaults', 25th September 2001; Aline van Duyn and Vincent Boland, 'Industry flourishes in bear market turmoil', 7th October 2002; Rebecca Bream, 'Plenty of bad news for a market to thrive on', 7th October 2002; Arkady Ostrovsky and Aline van Duyn, 'Volumes rise as investors seek security amid turmoil', 7th October 2002; Nic Cicutti, 'Derivatives' terms made easy', 26th October 2002; Aline van Duyn, 'Credit derivatives unmasked', 21st March 2003; Aline van Duyn, 'Uncertainty hits derivatives use', 10th April 2003; Aline van Duyn, 'Banks could adopt derivatives code', 30th May 2003; Jeremy Wiggins, 'US commercial banks' holding of derivatives climb by 9%', 9th June 2003; Charles Batchelor, 'Essential, controversial, popular and profitable', 5th November 2003; Päivi Munter, 'Protection becomes more desirable', 5th November 2003; Charles Batchelor and Alex Skorecki, 'Banks look to create one index', 30th January 2004; Alex Skorecki, 'Liffe goes to war with CME', 16th March 2004; Alex Skorecki, 'CBOT in move to hit back at Eurex', 16th April 2004; Charles Batchelor, 'Restructuring at risk from CDSs', 19th October 2004; Alex Skorecki, 'Electronic trading of CDSs expands', 3rd November 2004; John Plender, 'Shock of the new: a changed financial landscape may be eroding resistance to systemic risk', 16th February 2005; Peter Thal Larsen and Charles Batchelor, 'Credit derivatives go through "pain process"', 24th February 2005; Richard Beales, 'Fed receives commitments on CDS', 6th October 2005; Jennifer Hughes, 'Customising risk in Chicago', 28th October 2005; Richard Beales, 'New CD electronic broker goes live', 6th December 2005; John Authers, 'Spread of derivatives reshapes the markets', 25th January 2006; Richard Beales, 'New instruments call the tune', 20th October 2006; Jeremy Grant and Doug Cameron, 'Lords of the Windy City', 21st October 2006; Gillian Tett, 'Driven faster by low rates, more users and technology', 18th November 2006.

11
Equities and Exchanges, 1993–2006

Introduction

In the 1990s the pressures on traditional stock exchanges were so intense that inertia was no longer an option. Writing at the end of the decade Stephen Kingsley, head of the European Financial Services Industry practice at Arthur Andersen, concluded that, 'The last few years have seen enormous changes in the way in which exchanges operate. There is no reason to think that the pace of change is about to slow.'[1] These pressures included the globalization of investment, deregulation, dismantling of capital controls, cheap and rapid communication, and powerful computing. The effect was to undermine the grip that exchanges had once exerted over national stock markets. No longer were the members of exchanges the filter through which buying and selling passed because of the control they exercised over access to both information and the market. Current prices were available to all who had access to a computer terminal and were willing to pay for information. Reuters vice president for America, David Gaynes, reflected in 1998 on what his company and others had achieved: 'The big change is how much information the public is getting from organisations such as Reuters that traditionally only served the financial community with very specific financial information that we today bring to everybody.'[2] Alternative means of trading stocks were also proliferating, undermining and then destroying the exclusive privileges long enjoyed by those belonging to stock exchanges. This was evident to John Gapper in 1996: 'The forces of technology, regulation and competition are combining to break down barriers among exchanges and liberalise national markets.'[3] Leading this attack on the power of stock exchanges were the banks. As banks grew in scale and scope they were either able to internalize many transactions or trade between themselves, cutting out the exchanges, and charges and restrictions they imposed. There had long been an ambiguous relationship between banks and exchanges, as they were both rivals and heavy users. The technological changes taking place in the 1990s steered them towards the use of alternative trading mechanisms forcing stock exchanges to respond.

It mattered less and less to the global banks whether they traded through a stock exchange, an Electronic Communication Network, or matched transactions internally, as all became available to them. By 2006 a number of the largest banks had formed internal trading platforms, called internal crossing networks or dark pools, that anonymously matched the buy and sell orders they were either receiving from customers or generating themselves. Bill Neuberger, head of electronic trading at Morgan Stanley, explained what this meant: 'Orders coming into the system will have the ability to interact with Morgan Stanley order flow before being routed externally to exchanges.'[4] This possibility of internalizing transactions had long existed. What had changed was that technology made it much

[1] Stephen Kingsley, 'Quest for a new role and a new strategy', 23rd March 1999.
[2] Geoff Nairn, 'IT is still changing the face of trading', 24th March 1998.
[3] John Gapper, 'New rules, new rivals, new order', 16th February 1996.
[4] Anuj Gangahar, 'Banks begin to dip into "dark pools"', 19th October 2006.

Banks, Exchanges, and Regulators: Global Financial Markets from the 1970s. Ranald Michie, Oxford University Press (2021).

DOI: 10.1093/oso/9780199553730.003.0011

easier to accomplish, while the scale and scope of the business done by the largest banks, meant that they received a large share of the total volume of buying and selling. Bill Cline, head of the capital markets practice at Accenture, was one who highlighted the implications this had for all stock exchanges in 2006: 'This is a threat to the exchange as the traditional hub of liquidity. These dark pools are an alternative mechanism to the traditional exchange, absent many of the fees and costs of an exchange.'[5] The result was the fragmentation of the stock market. Stock exchanges no longer had the means to force the centralization of trading through their members. In turn, this had consequences for the liquidity of the market, the reliability of prices, the cost of trading, and the ability to regulate behaviour. This put increasing pressure on stock exchanges to alter fundamentally their pattern of ownership, the composition of their membership, the way they were organized, and the structure of the market they provided.

What was also changing rapidly in the 1990s was the internationalization of investment. As fund managers grew in size, confidence, and knowledge they were more willing to expand their portfolio choices beyond the domestic equity market, aided by the removal of restrictions on international financial flows. Again, this put pressure upon stock exchanges as they were exposed to a two-way pull of trading drifting abroad and growing external interest in the market they provided. No longer was each stock exchange providing a compartmentalized market comprising the equity issued by national companies and held by national investors. By 1995 the cross-border dealing in securities had reached $35,000bn. Much was driven by privatization. The stock issued by privatized utilities could not be immediately absorbed in their domestic market, because they were too small to cope with the amount. Conversely, the stock of such companies appealed to institutional investors from around the world precisely because the amount generated liquidity while the guaranteed earnings meant security. As these privatized utilities also offered the potential of high returns the combination was irresistible to global fund managers. For the same reasons these fund managers were also increasingly interested in the corporate stock already traded on stock markets around the world, but faced barriers in the form of locally-imposed regulations and taxes.

The solution was the increased use made of American Depository Receipts (ADRs) and Global Depository Receipts (GDRs) in the 1990s. Depository receipts represented underlying securities but could be bought and sold in their own right. They were created when the shares of a company were bought on its home stock market and deposited with a custodian, usually a bank located in a global financial centre such as New York or London. These ADRs and GDRs were attractive to international investors because they were usually issued in US$s, rather than the currency of the country in which the company was based, and were often easier to trade than the underlying shares. Conversely, depository receipts were attractive to large companies located in small countries, or those without an established equity tradition, because of the access they provided to sources of capital beyond their domestic boundaries. Nevertheless, important as internationally held stocks were becoming they remained dwarfed by domestically held issues, meaning that the centre of liquidity was, almost always, located in the national stock exchange. Here there were considerable differences between countries though the importance of stock markets was growing both absolutely and relatively around the world. In 1995 the ratio of stock market capitalization to GDP ranged, among the world's most developed economies, from highs of 127 per cent

[5] Anuj Gangahar, 'Banks begin to dip into "dark pools"', 19th October 2006.

in Switzerland, 122 per cent in the UK, 90 per cent in the USA, and 87 per cent in Japan to lows of 32 per cent in France, 24 per cent in Germany, and 18 per cent in Italy.[6]

Profound as this process of change was it went largely unnoticed, as no single event marked it out. Though owing much to what had happened in the past, including the establishment of Nasdaq in 1971, May Day in 1975, and Big Bang in 1986, these later developments possessed their own momentum. This can be seen in how the trading system created by Nasdaq, revolutionary in its day, was surpassed by others. What Nasdaq showed was how a communications network could replace a physical space in providing a market for corporate stock, but it was not an electronic stock market. What Nasdaq provided was an electronic network that displayed the prices at which dealers were willing to buy and sell. Actual trading took place by voice communication over the telephone, which replaced face-to-face contact on the floor of a stock exchange. It was this system that the LSE copied in 1986. Only much later did Nasdaq and the LSE adopt a market structure comprising a network of interactive screens and a powerful computer that automatically matched buying and selling orders. By then other exchanges, such as Deutsche Börse, had already made the move to fully-electronic trading, completing the revolution that others had begun but failed to take forward. These other exchanges had also made the jump to a vertical-silo model, which placed the entire trading process, beginning with the initial order to final payment or delivery, within a self-contained electronic network. As early as 1995 the vertical silo was regarded as the ultimate goal for the stock market, with Alan Cane writing that, 'Paperless trading, where trade details are transmitted automatically and electronically between counterparties at every stage of the investment process, is one of the grand concepts promised by the advent of the information society.'[7]

Here the stock market was following what had already happened elsewhere in the financial system. The achievements of the Society for Worldwide Interbank Financial Telecommunication (Swift), in introducing an electronic inter-bank messaging system, had proved what was possible for the global payment system, and the ambition was to replicate it for stocks. With Straight-Through-Processing (STP) an entire transaction would be completely automated, eliminating the delays and mistakes that contributed to counterparty risk. It was estimated in 2000 that 20 per cent of all trades were not completed on time while 20 per cent of cross-border trades failed completely, because of the basic inputting errors that occurred as sales and purchases moved through the system. Simple as the concept of STP was it did require a number of major technical and financial hurdles to be overcome. One was the need to agree on common standards for the key components of trading and processing, without which it would be impossible to computerise all the stages and links. Another was the huge cost involved in developing and rolling out the technology required. All that had to be done despite the possibility that any new system might be

[6] Peter Marsh, 'They're breathing down London's neck', 26th May 1993; Tracy Corrigan, 'Funds ready if the price is right', 14th September 1995; Martin Brice, 'Mexican crisis makes its mark', 14th September 1995; Barry Riley, 'Caught off balance by Wall Street', 4th December 1995; Maggie Urry, 'Success could bring extinction', 1st February 1996; George Graham, 'Emerging markets lift global securities trade', 16th February 1996; John Gapper, 'New rules, new rivals, new order', 16th February 1996; Andrew Fisher, 'Germany's stock answer', 22nd October 1996; John Plender, 'Stock market splits', 16th August 1997; Geoff Nairn, 'IT is still changing the face of trading', 24th March 1998; John Labate and Khozem Merchant, 'Mixed results for ADRs as issuance slows down', 23rd March 1999; Christopher Swann, 'Dawning of the age of European equity', 15th December 1999; Aline van Duyn, Bertrand Benoit and Tony Major, 'Members likely to welcome merger', 4th May 2000; Alex Skorecki, 'Pension moves may boost equity flows', 30th June 2000; Astrid Wendlandt, 'Urgent need for consolidation', 14th July 2000; John Plender, 'Exchange values', 3rd September 2000; Aline van Duyn, 'Trading costs reach unacceptable levels', 8th September 2000; Saskia Scholtes, 'Atlantic divide over e-trading', 5th December 2006.

[7] Alan Cane, 'Rivalry delays progress', 6th November 1995.

unable to handle the variety and volume of trading that took place in corporate stocks, compared to the simpler money transfers handled by banks.

Nevertheless, it was those that gambled on the eventual success of the new technology that were rewarded by taking a growing share of the stock market, because of the superior service at lower cost that they could provide. This had a very disruptive influence on stock exchanges. Once an exchange had established itself as the centre of liquidity for a particular stock it rarely lost that position. Buyers and sellers were reluctant to trade anywhere else for fear of receiving an inferior price and experiencing delays in completing a transaction because of a lack of depth. As Vincent Boland observed in 2001, 'The biggest strength of established exchanges is their ability, so far at least, to keep the liquidity pools they own.'[8] That was the case as long as each exchange provided the same level of service and imposed similar charges, as this removed the incentive to direct orders to an alternative market. The effect of electronic trading and processing was simultaneously to introduce an incentive to switch and make it easy to do.

The more competitive the market, the more standardized the product, and the greater the need for speed the more pressure was placed on stock exchanges to use the new technology to maintain the loyalty of the banks and fund managers that generated most of the business being done. Even in the less competitive markets, that operated at lower speeds and catered for more individual products, the need for a trading floor disappeared as transactions were negotiated over the telephone by the likes of the interdealer brokers. Electronic trading systems co-existed with these voice-based transactions, as the huge variety of stocks and investors continued to provide scope for both, but in all cases the physical floor was becoming redundant. This was visible to all as Alex Skorecki reported in 2004:

> Helsinki, like many, stands forlorn, its elegant trading chamber with desks and parquet floors has been yawningly empty since the 1990s. Dublin, equally ravishing and equally empty, hosts the occasional business dinner....Some exchanges are completely gone. The citizens of Chicago fought in vain to save theirs in the early 1970s. A few are holding out, albeit with their trading floors silent....as electronic trading has done away with the need for trading floors, the owners of the prestigious buildings have been faced with the choice of selling, finding new uses, continuing to inhabit in a shrunken state, or bulldozing....For a Greek temple in fully functioning exchange mode the nostalgic financial tourist must go to New York, where they hold out against the electronic revolution.[9]

This did not mean that the trading that these floors once epitomized had morphed into a single global pool ready to be placed under the authority of a single institution though many believed that to be the case.[10]

[8] Vincent Boland, 'World's bourses look to find a new role', 28th March 2001.

[9] Alex Skorecki, 'Old stock exchange buildings never die, they're just rented out to hair salons', 28th July 2004.

[10] Alan Cane, 'Rivalry delays progress', 6th November 1995; Simon Davies, 'Success masks market turmoil', 24th March 1998; Michael Prest, 'Time for a new exchange', 24th March 1998; Geoffrey Nairn, 'Braced for big upheavals', 1st July 1998; Peter Martin, 'Trading places', 2nd July 1998; Edward Luce, 'New Technology is driving mating dances', 23rd March 1999; Astrid Wendlandt, 'Winner gets to rule the world', 31st March 2000; Carlos Grande, 'Heavy dealing stretches systems to limit', 6th April 2000; Vincent Boland, 'System breakdown a boost for alternative trading', 7th April 2000; Philip Coggan, 'City of London no newcomer to upheaval', 4th May 2000; Vincent Boland, 'The next big market force', 10th November 2000; John Labate and Vincent Boland, 'Nasdaq attempts to lure London exchange', 17th December 2000; Bettina Wassener, 'Fed rate cut boosts call for extended trading', 17th January 2001; Vincent Boland, 'World's bourses look to find a new role', 28th March 2001; Aline van Duyn and Bettina Wassener, 'Deutsche Börse in deal to boost US trading', 1st June 2001; Dominic Hobson, 'Goal: trades that never touch the sides', 6th July 2001; Martin Dickson, 'Entering the endgame with a badly weakened

Stock Exchanges and the Equity Market

The disappearance of the physical floor involved much more than a switch to a new way of trading for stock exchanges. Stock exchanges provided a bundle of services covering the production, collection, and dissemination of accurate prices; the supervision of trading; the settlement of transactions; the authorization of market participants; and the administration and regulation of company listings. A stock exchange was a solution to a complex set of problems only one of which was a space where trading took place. By concentrating trading into the hands of a few, meeting at particular times in a specific place, a liquid market was created that delivered accurate and reliable real time pricing. Conversely, this placed those who had access to this market in a privileged position, making them willing to pay for membership, and so generate the income necessary to support the regulation and infrastructure required. Rules covered the likes of counterparty risk and market manipulation, generating confidence in both trading practices and current prices for members and the wider public. Central to the enforcement of these rules by stock exchanges was the ultimate sanction of exclusion from the trading floor, as this deprived a member from access to the market and knowledge of current prices. Once access to the closed trading system became irrelevant, whether it involved a physical floor or the network of market-makers, then the power of stock exchanges to exercise discipline disappeared. The result was to expose the contradictions that had always existed at the heart of stock exchanges. Philip Coggan, writing in 2002, picked up on some of these:

> The ideal stock exchange would combine three, not necessarily compatible, functions. Investors want liquidity because a more liquid market means keen prices and the ability to make larger trades. Regulators, clients and investors want transparency so that they can be sure that deals are done at the best possible prices and the market is not rigged in favour of insiders. But investors also want anonymity so that other market participants cannot use knowledge of their position to push prices against them.[11]

Once stock exchanges lost the power to make their rules effective the force of mutual self-interest quickly waned. The new structure of trading that electronic platforms delivered, benefited some members while penalizing others. The large banks and brokers, handling a high-volume business and able to internalize transactions, gained. Those providing individual investors with a bespoke service lost, as they no longer gained privileged access to prices and the market. It was the former who pressed for change while the latter resisted it. As stock exchanges were member-owned organizations, with each member having an equal vote regardless of the business that they did, that opposition was often sufficiently

position', 3rd November 2001; Francesco Guerrera, 'Clearing the air after integration', 6th June 2002; Vincent Boland, 'US markets face up to technology gap', 6th June 2002; Joseph Leahy, 'Thirst grows for capital pools', 6th June 2002; Alex Skorecki, 'T+1 pipedream is close to reality', 6th June 2002; Philip Coggan, 'Market slide provokes a new deal for shares', 28th September 2002; Alex Skorecki, 'Old stock exchange buildings never die, they're just rented out to hair salons', 28th July 2004; Jeremy Grant, 'A single-product boutique is not the way: is one-stop shopping coming to US exchanges?', 14th September 2004; Adrian Michaels and Norma Cohen, 'Borsa Italiana to study public offering', 19th January 2006; Norma Cohen, 'Special relationship on the horizon', 30th January 2006; Sarah Underwood, 'IT evolution meeting demand for speed, efficiency and accuracy', 16th October 2006; Norma Cohen, 'Headlong scramble for speed', 28th November 2006; Saskia Scholtes, 'Atlantic divide over e-trading', 5th December 2006; Georges Ugeux, 'Exchange battles mask Europe's silence', 3rd January 2007.

[11] Philip Coggan, 'Market slide provokes a new deal for shares', 28th September 2002.

numerous to block any development that might endanger the survival of a particular group. For that reason the initial step pursued by those seeking change within an exchange was demutualization followed by conversion into a company and then a move to quoted status. This switch had three benefits. Firstly, it allowed a stock exchange to raise the finance required to develop and install an electronic trading and processing platform by either issuing new shares or borrowing guaranteed by the prospects of increased income. Secondly, it removed the ability of a group of members to block change in order to protect their position, even though, collectively, they handled only a small proportion of the trading. Thirdly, it created opportunities to merge with other exchanges that had followed a similar path and become businesses run for profit rather than clubs organized for the benefit of members. By 2000 Vincent Boland reported that, 'One issue now dominates market thinking: separating the ownership of trading platforms from that of trading processors and central counterparties as the best way of making massive cost savings.'[12]

A major effect of demutualization was to make stock exchanges much more outward focused, as the power of members to influence strategy was weakened. As mutual organizations stock exchanges were tools to be used to further the business interests of the members rather than meet the needs of the wider financial community or operate as independent businesses able to respond to changing challenges and opportunities. Once restructured as quoted companies, stock exchanges could pursue a strategy that included merging with other exchanges trading different products or the same products but in different countries. This horizontal-silo model was particularly attractive to US stock exchanges, because the vertical-silo model was closed to them. In the USA in the 1990s around 90 per cent of trading in corporate stocks was processed by a single organization, the Depository Trust and Clearing Corporation (DTCC). The huge size of the DTCC's operations generated significant economies of scale, so that it was able to provide an efficient low-cost service, making it popular with its customers. The near monopoly the DTCC possessed over processing stock transactions provided another feature, which banks and brokers also welcomed. This was the ability to conduct business on a net basis, so saving the need to hold collateral against all transactions until completion. The DTCC also acted as a central counterparty so removing the risk of default. With their experience of the DTCC US investment banks pressed for the horizontal-silo to be adopted in those countries where clearing and settlement was often provided by the national stock exchange, as was the case across much of the rest of the world.

The advantage of integrating trading and processing was that a deal was reduced to a single transaction. Though the cost of the transaction could be higher than in the USA, where the different parts of the process were undertaken separately, the overall charges could be less, through a reduction in the administrative time and expense involved in having to deal with separate institutions. It was also easier to introduce STP when restricted to a subset of stocks traded on a single exchange under the control of one institution, compared to what was required when applied to the entire global market. This gave those stock exchanges that combined electronic trading with electronic clearing and settlement a very powerful incumbent position. The drawback of the integration of trading and processing was that it tied buyers and sellers to a particular exchange because of the convenience provided by a single point of contact. The vertical model made it difficult to generate competition between stock exchanges, contributing to the monopoly they enjoyed over trading the

[12] Vincent Boland, 'The next big market force', 10th November 2000.

stocks that they quoted. It also made it difficult for new electronic trading platforms to take trading away from exchanges, as they faced the difficult task of finding an alternative provider of clearing and settlement services. For those reasons regulators with a remit to increase competition favoured the horizontal rather than the vertical model, as did the global banks whose business led them to use multiple stock exchanges. Pushing all their trading through a single clearing house would allow them to gain the benefits from netting on a global scale.

What the horizontal silo also offered to exchanges was the possibility of expanding either the range of financial instruments traded on an exchange or its geographical coverage through mergers. Meyer Frucher, the chief executive of the Philadelphia Stock Exchange, was one who emphasized the multiproduct future that beckoned, reflecting the strides his institution had made in combining trading in equities and options. As he said in 2004, 'Exchanges are going to have to change. They understand that a single-product "boutique" is not the way forward. I think you'll see a trend towards a multiple-product entity: equities, options, futures, traded side-by-side.'[13] Neither the multiproduct nor the multicountry model proved easy to achieve, despite their obvious attractions. Pushing more trading through an expensively constructed and maintained electronic platform was an obvious way to share costs, reduce charges, and so attract more business, with immediate gains to liquidity and profitability. As always it was difficult to prise a market away from its established centre of liquidity. 'This suggests that ambitious exchanges that want to acquire more can do so only through acquisition', was the verdict of Vincent Boland in 2001.[14]

This had already taken place in the mutual era but was confined to exchanges located in the same country and doing a similar business, leading to the emergence of a single institution controlling the entire national market for corporate stocks. Doing the same for exchanges trading different products, such as stocks and derivatives, or operating in different countries, proved a near impossible task. Especially when controlled by members each exchange fought for its independence while national governments long remained committed to preserving the sovereignty of stock exchanges as national institutions. This was despite the growing predicament they faced, as Edward Luce spelled out in 1999: 'Driven by new technology and the growing power of the world's largest institutional investors, exchanges are being confronted with the choice of sacrificing their autonomy or being sidelined in a shrinking domestic environment.'[15] Though many mergers were proposed, and even attempted, few were consummated. One that was completed was the 2006 merger between the NYSE and the transnational European exchange, Euronext. This prompted Georges Ugeux, a former executive vice president at the NYSE, to exclaim that, 'The past year has redefined the landscape of exchanges around the world.'[16] Euronext itself was a triumph for the Paris Bourse as it had successfully combined the French stock and futures exchanges into one, following that by merging with the national exchanges of Belgium, Portugal, and the Netherlands, before finally acquiring the UK's derivatives market, London Financial Futures Exchange (Liffe). What the NYSE/Euronext merger represented was the triumph of the horizontal model, propelling the combination to a prime position within the global stock market.

[13] Jeremy Grant, 'A single-product boutique is not the way: is one-stop shopping coming to US exchanges?', 14th September 2004.

[14] Vincent Boland, 'World's bourses look to find a new role', 28th March 2001.

[15] Edward Luce, 'New Technology is driving mating dances', 23rd March 1999.

[16] Georges Ugeux, 'Exchange battles mask Europe's silence', 3rd January 2007.

NYSE/Euronext was a proactive response to a situation in which all national stock exchanges lost the immunity from competition they had once enjoyed, as Michael Prest noted in 1998: 'Technology, particularly screen trading, allied to order-driven systems, has largely demolished national boundaries.'[17] Simon Davies was of a similar opinion: 'Competition has convulsed a world of hitherto protected markets as technological advances have made a stock exchange's location increasingly irrelevant to investors.'[18] National boundaries no longer defined national stock markets as global banks and fund managers controlled the flow of funds, picking and choosing where to buy and sell, according to where they could achieve the best deal. By 2006 Mamoun Tazi, of Man Securities, judged that 'the end-game in securities exchanges is a single, 24-hour, global market.'[19] Philip Coggan had speculated in 2000 that 'The logical end of this process is, of course, one global stock exchange.'[20] In place of numerous individual exchanges there would emerge a single institution, commanding a common pool of liquidity, with a number of the largest exchanges embracing this ambition. 'The race is on to become the global stock exchange' was Astrid Wendlandt's observation in 2000. What she, and others at the time, based this judgement upon was the global nature of the speculative boom taking place in high-technology companies. In her view 'Cross-border investment accounts for the bulk of turnover in equities and investors want a one-stop shop that will be cheaper to use and easier to access than any stock exchange now.'[21]

Sensing the opportunity Frank Zarb, chairman and CEO of Nasdaq, which was the US exchange chosen by many of these technology companies, followed a strategy from 1998 that included building up a global network for trading stocks. The weakness of this strategy was that its justification died along with the collapse of the bubble in 2000, as the result was a retreat of the global stock market to behind national boundaries. What these predictions did not take into account was the fundamental structure of the global stock market, which remained fragmented and localized, reflecting the nature of stock ownership across the world. Most trading continued to take place on a national basis being between investors from the same country holding the stock of companies doing a largely national business. In the place of an integrated global stock market there existed national pools of liquidity, still largely under the control of national stock exchanges. There was a lack of liquidity for virtually all stocks outside the normal trading hours in their home market. In 2002, after the speculative mania had burst, Joseph Leahy reported that 'Twenty-four hour trading is not yet enough of a reality globally to ensure adequate liquidity.'[22]

What was undoubtedly the case was that stock exchanges could no longer rely on national boundaries for protection from competition under all circumstances. As early as 1997, John Langton, chief executive and secretary-general of the International Securities Market Association, was of the opinion that, 'With new technology, geographical advantage don't count for much.'[23] What was happening was that trading was moving away from those exchanges lacking depth and breadth as it was increasingly in the hands of global banks and international fund managers. Their priority was liquidity followed by speed and cost, as Andrew Fisher made clear in 1997: 'Ultimately...it will be the big institutional

[17] Michael Prest, 'Time for a new exchange', 24th March 1998.
[18] Simon Davies, 'Success masks market turmoil', 24th March 1998.
[19] Adrian Michaels and Norma Cohen, 'Borsa Italiana to study public offering', 19th January 2006.
[20] Philip Coggan, 'City of London no newcomer to upheaval', 4th May 2000.
[21] Astrid Wendlandt, 'Winner gets to rule the world', 31st March 2000.
[22] Joseph Leahy, 'Thirst grows for capital pools', 6th June 2002.
[23] Philip Coggan, 'Bourses fight for supremacy', 24th April 1997.

investors which will decide where they want to trade. They will go where the market is most liquid, the product range is most diverse, and the back-office facilities are cheapest and most efficient.'[24] They favoured exchanges that could provide the first and second and put pressure on all exchanges to improve the others, including the speed of execution and processing, and to lower their charges. Banks had long employed idle funds in holding corporate stocks or lending to those that did, and that grew in importance before the Global Financial Crisis. The risk from such a strategy was that a bank would not be able to extricate itself when required but that was reduced if only those stocks that could be quickly sold at current market prices were used. Hence the desire for liquidity above all other considerations, whether it was found on the floor of the NYSE or the electronic platform operated by Deutsche Börse. Though long-term investors, such as pension funds and insurance companies, had much less need for liquidity it was becoming a more important consideration for them because of stock lending. By lending stock held in their portfolios long-term investors could both retain ownership and generate extra returns, and this is what they increasingly did in the 1990s and into the twenty-first century. By 2000 the value of securities that were currently lent out stood at an estimated $473bn, with around 75 per cent of the business being done in the USA.

One explanation for the growth in stock lending was the proliferation of Exchange Traded Funds (ETFs). These had been devised in the early 1990s and rapidly gained in popularity, especially in the USA. An ETF was an investment created by a bank or fund manager through depositing stocks into a portfolio and then issuing depository receipts to investors. What attracted investors to ETFs was the combination of transparency, flexibility, security, and returns. These depository receipts were quoted and traded on stock exchanges, and reflected the value of a diversified portfolio of stocks. Portfolio managers focused on liquid stocks, as these could be easily bought and sold as that allowed the size and composition of the ETF to be quickly adjusted. Stocks were often borrowed until a particular transaction was completed, as ETFs were used for both hedging and speculation. The increased use made of ETFs added to the established practice of short-sellers borrowing stock for delivery, while they waited a favourable turn in the market. The result was to encourage a preference for liquidity by both banks and fund managers, and that led them to choose those markets that could deliver it. In turn, their constant buying and selling led the stocks they selected to become more liquid, so making the exchanges in which this was done even more attractive, as Candice Adams, from Deutsche Börse, explained in 2002: 'The more liquid the market, the tighter the spreads and the more cost-efficient it is to trade—which, in turn, attracts more investors.'[25]

This preference for liquidity made smaller exchanges highly vulnerable to competition, as it was the larger ones that could provide the desired depth and breadth. Bayan Rahman noted this in 2003 in the case of Japan: 'In an age of high-speed communication and advanced technology, the need for local bourses is in doubt.'[26] Regardless of size no stock exchange was immune. Though better able than most to resist the pressure for change, because of its entrenched position in the huge US stock market, even the NYSE was forced to recognize that it had to respond. Prior to the collapse of the dot.com boom in 2000 the need for change was masked by the general increase in stock market activity driven by the speculative bubble in technology, media, and telecommunications (TMT) stocks. As Niall

[24] Andrew Fisher, 'Bigger is better in bourses' brave euro world', 15th July 1997.
[25] Florian Gimbel, 'Exchange tries to stay ahead of the pack', 28th October 2002.
[26] Bayan Rahman, 'Japan's bourses face an uncertain future', 12th December 2003.

Macleod, from the Wall Street brokers, Salomon Smith Barney, put it, 'Encouraged by the prospect of startling returns for TMT stocks, the flows became self-fulfilling. More money chased stocks higher, attracting yet more money.'[27] This mania then spread worldwide, as Vincent Boland reported in 2000: 'The internet stock surge has spread from the US, with retail investors driving many initial public offerings to dizzy heights despite the fact that many of the companies being floated are unlikely to make profits for years—if ever.'[28] When that bubble burst later in 2000 all stock exchanges were forced to face up to the need for change as the volume of business fell away, competition intensified, and customers demanded a reduction in charges. Some went as far as to suggest that stock exchanges no longer performed a unique role, as all the functions they performed could be done by others, more efficiently and more cheaply, in the new electronic age. Beginning in the USA Electronic Communication Networks (ECNs) operated as mini-exchanges, matching buy and sell orders for a minimal fee on their own networks. James Mackintosh, writing in 1999, predicted that, 'In the brave new electronic future investors wanting to buy or sell will simply search the internet for like-minded investors ready to deal with them, according to some futurologists.'[29]

However, other factors were at work. Along with concerns about counterparty risk there were others related to liquidity, speed, certainty, and other variables that influenced the choice of which market to use. In 2000 Ehrlich and Mann observed that 'Some traders may be willing to sacrifice some price increment to be able to trade large lots, others may demand speed of execution that allows them to get the prices they first see, some might want the assurance of various regulatory or cultural features, some incremental price improvement, some diversification.'[30] A stock exchange delivered certainty. That certainty covered the ability to complete a sale and purchase quickly as that meant that stocks could always be converted from money, producing no return, into assets that did, and then reverse the process when the need arose. This difference between an exchange and a market was something John Thain recognized, and used in 2006 to justify the role played by the NYSE at a time when it faced increasing competition. Reflecting on the proliferation of rival electronic markets in the USA he suggested that, 'It's not very hard to create new exchanges and new marketplaces.' He then added, the rider, that 'It's hard to create the liquidity pool but it's not very hard to create the marketplace.'[31] What he meant was that though mathematical programming and electronic computers could match sales and purchases, at the market price, as long as the order flow of each was in equilibrium, it could not do so if the balance was in one direction or the other. In the stock market, with such a variety of different securities, the ebb and flow of trading meant that buying and selling pressure was often unbalanced, making it difficult to complete transactions unless a market-maker intervened to act as a temporary counterparty. To do so on a consistent basis market-makers had to have an incentive, which is what stock exchanges provided them with through exclusive access to the trading floor and attaching privileges to the status of market-maker. With the advent of ECNs those privileges vanished and with them also disappeared a major source of liquidity for quoted stocks. To a degree this loss of this liquidity was of limited concern to the global banks and fund managers as they possessed the

[27] Arkady Ostrovsky, 'Technology drives the markets', 19th May 2000.

[28] Vincent Boland, 'Time for the faint-hearted to beware', 19th May 2000.

[29] James Mackintosh, 'Bright lights, big City', 3rd July 1999.

[30] Everett Ehrlich and Michael Mann, 'One size does not fit all', 16th October 2000.

[31] Jennifer Hughes and John Authers, 'Taking the floor: how a screen role will challenge New York's market debutant', 7th March 2006.

capacity to provide it for themselves. They could absorb selling by using their own funds to purchase stock, which they held until an opportunity arose to sell at a profit, either quickly or over time. Conversely, they could supply a demand for stocks either from their own portfolio or by borrowing, until covering the deficit by a later purchase. Their ability to act as buyers and sellers of last resort reduced the importance that exchanges possessed as sources of liquidity.[32]

The introduction of electronic-trading technology allowed the established exchanges to be challenged despite their dominant hold over liquidity because of the ability to offer a cheaper and faster service accessible to all including those who were not members. The triumph of electronic trading was a product of the power of the megabanks as they could invest in the technology and staff required to use these markets. In the past, intervention by governments would have protected the exchanges from competition but that was no longer the case. Rather than government intervention creating a more competitive environment it was the rising power of the megabanks that achieved that outcome. What government intervention did was undermine those markets where self-regulation was important, not least in concentrating trading so as to provide both liquidity and transparency, namely the stock exchanges. These required a different rationale compared to the markets for bonds, currencies, money, and derivatives. The result was to remove the self-regulating element from the equity markets, encouraging not only fragmentation but the explosive growth of new securities. These securities were solely dependent on the megabanks for their market but lacked the scrutiny, depth, and breadth provided by the regulated market and the lender of last resort in the case of financial instruments tied to the money market. As Stephen Kingsley concluded in 1999 from his survey:

> Traditional exchanges are struggling to keep pace with this new reality. Screen trading has reduced the value created by the trading process, clearing and settlement remains fragmented and therefore costly in terms of the need for specialist staff, multiple relationships with depositaries and clearing houses, complex transfer arrangements and failed

[32] Philip Coggan, 'Bourses fight for supremacy', 24th April 1997; Andrew Fisher, 'Bigger is better in bourses' brave euro world', 15th July 1997; John Labate, 'Wall Street feels the tremors', 23rd March 1999; Stephen Kingsley, 'Quest for a new role and a new strategy', 23rd March 1999; James Mackintosh, 'Bright lights, big City', 3rd July 1999; Edward Luce, 'Hoist by their own petard', 20th September 1999; Caroline Daniel, 'As mania grows, prices are leaping ahead', 10th March 2000; Alan Beattie, Rahul Jacob and Gerard Baker, 'Regulators alarmed over high-tech mania', 16th March 2000; Vincent Boland, 'World's bourses jostle for position as upstarts elbow in', 31st March 2000; Patrick Jenkins, 'How to find the best price', 8th April 2000; Vincent Boland, 'Time for the faint-hearted to beware', 19th May 2000; Arkady Ostrovsky, 'Technology drives the markets', 19th May 2000; Stephen Kingsley, 'A blueprint for the new exchange', 19th September 2000; Everett Ehrlich and Michael Mann, 'One size does not fit all', 16th October 2000; Alex Skorecki, 'Banks form platform for short-sellers', 22nd March 2001; Simon Targett, 'It's the liquidity that matters', 28th March 2001; Alex Skorecki, 'The line becomes blurred', 18th July 2001; Philip Coggan, 'Competition intensifies among rival exchanges', 31st October 2001; Vincent Boland, 'Trading Up', 27th May 2002; Andrei Postelnicu, 'Invisible trades come under scrutiny', 6th June 2002; John Labate, 'High-tech systems jolt old markets into action', 6th June 2002; Alex Skorecki, 'Securities lending joins the internet age', 22nd October 2002; Alex Skorecki, 'Investors track down a hybrid source of income', 28th October 2002; Florian Gimbel, 'Exchange tries to stay ahead of the pack', 28th October 2002; Stephen Phillips, 'System suppliers in a state of high flux', 3rd April 2002; Bayan Rahman, 'Japan's bourses face an uncertain future', 12th December 2003; Andrei Postelnicu, Lionel Barber and David Wighton, 'A great part of America: John Thain sets out to restore trust in the New York Stock Exchange', 2nd April 2004; Jennifer Hughes and John Authers, 'Taking the floor: how a screen role will challenge New York's market debutant', 7th March 2006; Sarah Underwood, 'IT evolution meeting demand for speed, efficiency and accuracy', 16th October 2006; Anuj Gangahar, 'Banks begin to dip into "dark pools"', 19th October 2006; Norma Cohen, 'Club of bankers has come full circle', 16th November 2006; Christopher Brown-Humes, 'Consolidation is fevered but all bets are still on', 28th November 2006; Norma Cohen, 'Level playing fields', 28th November 2006; Saskia Scholtes, 'Atlantic divide over e-trading', 5th December 2006.

> trades. In many markets the trading and clearing of cash and derivative products remain separate.... the ability efficiently to manage cash, securities and margin is reduced as a consequence.[33]

Some exchanges sought to guarantee their survival through vertical integration as that gave them much greater control of the market in the stocks they quoted through offering buyers and sellers a complete package. Other exchanges pursued horizontal integration in the expectation that the sacrifice of independence it required would be accompanied by a much stronger position within the global stock market. In both the vertical and horizontal model the extension of the product range was also pursued as it offered the prospect of survival through diversification. Though these opportunities were open to all exchanges the outcomes were different, being dependent upon the choices made and the extent to which the different strategies were successfully managed. The decisions taken between 1992 and 2007 determined the fate of many stock exchanges.

Varieties of Response

The years between 1990 and 2007 were the era of the stock exchange. Throughout the world stock exchanges were being formed, revitalized, or restructured in the face of the enormous changes taking place. In terms of the technology of trading, for example, few individual exchanges were large enough to finance the technology needed to run a fully-electronic market. At the same time the inexorable march of globalization exposed stock exchanges to competition while opening up possibilities of alliances and mergers. It was stock exchanges that provided a market for the stocks that were generated by the privatization programmes, the conversion of existing businesses into public companies and the new ventures seeking to engage with the technology underpinning the dot.com boom. Borrowers turned to stock exchanges as a source of finance where they engaged with investors seeking either reliable returns or speculative gains. The result was a remarkable transformation of the role played by stock exchanges within financial systems. From being either marginal or non-existent in most countries stock exchanges regained the position of importance in the 1990s that they had once occupied prior to the First World War. This transformation of exchanges covered ownership, membership, trading, and the processing of transactions. However, the response was not uniform. Some exchanges embraced change while others resisted it.

Some existing exchanges were exposed to a growing intensity of competition that made response essential. This was the case in Canada, as the alternative of using a US stock exchange was readily available. In the mid-1990s around 250 Canadian companies were listed on both the Toronto Stock Exchange (TrSE) and a US exchange, and 25 per cent of the trading in their shares took place there. A number of Canadian companies had grown so large that their size exceeded the demand from retail shareholders in Canada, leading them to list on a bigger US exchange such as the NYSE. Nasdaq also attracted Canadian high-technology companies. In addition Canadian institutional investors, who owned 80 per cent of Canadian equities, increasingly traded away from the exchanges. In 1999 as much as 60 per cent of all trading on the TrSE was done internally by the large bank-owned Canadian brokerages, as that allowed them to capture both ends of the commission as well

[33] Stephen Kingsley, 'A blueprint for the new exchange', 19th September 2000.

as profit from the spread between bid and ask prices. The result damaged the reliability of the prices displayed by exchanges and eroded the liquidity they could provided, so making them less attractive trading venues compared to either the NYSE and Nasdaq or the internal markets operated by the banks and their fund managers. As mutual organizations it was difficult for Canadian exchanges to respond to these challenges, as doing so required radical change. Eventually in 1998 the TrSE took the decision to transform itself from a non-profit organization into a private, for-profit company. That took place in 2000. Another proposal was to end long-standing rivalries and link Canada's four exchanges into a single unit. By 2006 the TrSE had emerged as the dominant equity market in Canada, with a global speciality in mining companies.[34]

Another stock exchange that fully engaged with globalization was the Australian Stock Exchange (ASX). According to Virginia Marsh in 2000, the ASX was 'at the forefront of the consolidation and technological changes sweeping world markets. It demutualized and listed two years ago, already has trading arrangements with Nasdaq and Singapore, and is one of the ten exchanges, including New York, Paris and Tokyo, that plan to link trading systems and develop common rules to create the Global Equity Market.'[35] The problem that the ASX faced was the small size of the domestic market leading Australian institutional investors to turn to foreign stocks because of their liquidity while local companies outgrew their investor base and so listed abroad to satisfy international demand. In order to retain the loyalty of both issuers and investors in an increasingly open economy the ASX had to respond to the challenges it faced. As early as 1996 its members voted to demutualize and convert itself into a shareholder-owned company listed on its own exchange. This was a bold attempt to bypass the barriers to reform, which members had successively blocked, and took place in 1998, making it the first stock exchange to obtain a direct listing. In the words of Richard Humphry, the ASX's managing director, in 1999, 'A handful of other exchanges took the first step of demutualising, but none was listed. I don't count the case of Stockholm, which demutualised and later became a subsidiary of a company that was already listed.'[36] The ASX had ambitions to become a multiplatform exchange serving Australia, New Zealand, and the wider Asia-Pacific region. In pursuance of this ambition it proposed a merger with the Sydney Futures Exchange (SFE) in 1999. This would allow the costs associated with computerized trading and processing to be shared, but it was blocked by the Australian regulatory authorities, because of concerns that it would reduce competition. That decision was not reversed until 2006 and only then because of fears that the ASX had become vulnerable to a foreign takeover. By then it was evident that other stock exchanges were combining with derivative exchanges to produce strong national units, as in Hong Kong, Singapore, and South Korea. The ASX's own attempt to expand internationally, by acquiring the New Zealand Stock Exchange (NKSE) was rebuffed by that organization. Nevertheless, the ASX was the dominant exchange in the region, with, like the Toronto Stock Exchange, an international role as a centre for mining stocks.[37]

[34] Ian Rodger, 'The real time breakthrough', 6th December 1994; Edward Alden, 'Canadian exchanges act to stem listings losses', 6th November 1998; Edward Alden, 'An unsettling performance', 25th May 1999; Edward Alden, 'TSE members set to vote for restructuring', 10th June 1999; Graham Bowley, 'Montreal exchange given reprieve', 12th November 1999; Edward Alden, 'Fierce struggle with the giant next door', 31st March 2000.

[35] Virginia Marsh, 'Australia, NZ consider stock exchange deal', 15th August 2000.

[36] Gwen Robinson, 'Record trading as merger talks go on', 23rd March 1999.

[37] Nikki Tait, 'ASX members consider future of their club', 17th October 1996; Nikki Tait, 'ASX members vote to demutualise exchange', 19th October 1996; Nikki Tait and Nicholas Denton, 'ASX to offer fund raising on internet', 12th June 1997; Gwen Robinson, 'Another milestone nears', 24th March 1998; Vincent Boland, 'ASX set to demutualise next month', 22nd September 1998; Russell Baker, 'ASX set to control its own destiny', 23rd

In contrast to the stock exchanges in Australia and Canada the Tokyo Stock Exchange (TSE) failed to fully engage with the changes taking place. The result was that foreign companies delisted from the TSE and the proportion of Japanese shares traded abroad grew. The pressure for change at the TSE was subdued as it was legally protected from both a foreign takeover and competition from an OTC market. It was not until 2004 that the OTC market was allowed to compete with the established exchanges. The TSE was the dominant stock exchange in Japan being the centre of liquidity for the country's leading corporate stocks. In 1998 the TSE handled 80 per cent of trading in the Japanese stock market. Under the circumstances the members of the TSE were long able to resist demutualization, the ending of fixed commission rates, and the admission of banks as members.[38] Under the circumstances the TSE failed to act as a disruptive force in Asia through acting as a magnet for those companies outgrowing their domestic base or those fund managers searching for a deep and broad market in international stocks. Without such a disruptive force it was difficult to overcome the divisions that existed in Asia because of different currencies and rules and regulations.[39]

September 1998; Gwen Robinson, 'Record trading as merger talks go on', 23rd March 1999; Gwen Robinson, 'Cry goes out for screen trading', 16th April 1999; Gwen Robinson, 'A revolutionary in a changing world', 26th July 1999; Virginia Marsh and William Dawkins, 'ASX seeks to extend links with London', 10th March 2000; Virginia Marsh, 'Cultural barriers impede progress', 28th April 2000; Virginia Marsh, 'NZ Stock exchange in talks on merger', 8th May 2000; Virginia Marsh, 'Markets taking stock of the future', 4th July 2000; Virginia Marsh, 'Australia, NZ consider stock exchange deal', 15th August 2000; Virginia Marsh, 'ASX, NZ exchange spell out objectives', 20th December 2000; Virginia Marsh, 'NZSE accuses ASX for failure of merger talks', 23rd February 2001; Anna Fifield, 'Swimmer breathes new life into NZSE', 6th May 2003; Virginia Marsh and Doug Cameron, 'Australian exchanges team up to regain lost ground', 29th March 2006; Louise Lucas, 'Exchange expands at home so it can make its mark abroad', 6th September 2006.

[38] Gerard Baker, 'Regional rivals hot on its heels', 19th October 1994; Charles Smith, 'The pulse is weak', 28th March 1996; Emiko Terazono, 'Long road back to Tokyo', 28th March 1996; Richard Lapper, 'Brokers need volumes', 25th March 1997; William Dawkins, 'Last chance to catch up', 25th March 1997; Louise Lucas, 'Doors are swinging open', 9th May 1997; Gwen Robinson, 'Backward in coming forward', 27th June 1997; Richard Lambert, 'Wider horizons beckon New York Exchange', 24th September 1997; Gillian Tett, 'Big Bang calls for some swift reforms', 24th March 1998; Gillian Tett, 'Big Bang or just a whimper?', 26th March 1998; Gillian Tett, 'Complex timetable for reforms package', 26th March 1998; Gillian Tett, 'Rivalry to replace cosy collaboration', 26th March 1998; Vincent Boland, 'Why Tokyo's bankers are definitely not for tennis', 26th March 1998; Vincent Boland, 'Stock exchange has taken steps to protect its position', 26th March 1998; Gillian Tett, 'Visitors grab some juicy prizes', 21st June 1999; Charles Smith, 'Opportunities to ease the pain', 21st June 1999; Louise Lucas, 'Softer requirements attract start-ups', 17th December 1999; Alexandra Nusbaum, 'Mothers planning to be nimble', 17th December 1999; Bayan Rahman, 'Disclosure and liquidity will be key', 31st March 2000; Bayan Rahman, 'Global players enjoy feast', 8th May 2000; Bayan Rahman, 'Troubled times for Mothers', 8th May 2000; Bayan Rahman, 'TSE members vote for privatisation', 27th September 2001; Vincent Boland, 'Nasdaq falls foul of bear market', 9th August 2002; Vincent Boland and Alex Skorecki, 'Time called on 24-hour marketplace', 27th June 2003; Bayan Rahman, 'Japan's bourses face an uncertain future', 12th December 2003; David Turner, Joanna Chung and Andrei Postelnicu, 'Tokyo exchange undone by lack of investment', 23rd January 2006; David Turner, 'Tokyo exchange chief seeks tie-up with foreign bourse', 8th April 2006; Francesco Guerrera, 'Region weighs the need for a one-stop shop', 12th April 2006; David Turner, 'International dimension is missing link', 12th April 2006; Anna Fifield, 'S. Korea steps up its efforts to become a hub', 12th April 2006; David Turner, 'Tokyo exchange ready for Chinese listings', 26th April 2006; David Turner, Virginia Marsh and Justine Lau, 'TSE keeps close eye on battle for bourse', 24th May 2006; David Turner, 'Tokyo exchange sets timetable for 2009 listing', 27th June 2006; Song Jung-a and Mariko Sanchanta, 'TSE and Korea exchange move towards link-up', 7th July 2006; Norma Cohen, 'TSE chief promises to strengthen infrastructure', 17th July 2006; David Turner, 'Japan needs derivatives to compete', 10th August 2006; Anuj Gangahar, 'Nasdaq's man of action', 16th October 2006; David Turner, 'TSE and NYSE in talks over alliance', 28th October 2006; David Turner and Norma Cohen, 'Nomura to buy broker Instinet', 3rd November 2006; David Turner, 'TSE would like to meet suitors with view to friendship but not marriage', 7th November 2006; Ivar Simensen, 'Exchange looks east for new partnerships', 16th November 2006; David Turner, 'Still a cosy and cosseted world', 28th November 2006; David Turner and Kaori Suzuki, 'TSE considers anti-takeover measures', 29th November 2006.

[39] Joseph Leahy, 'Thirst grows for capital pools', 6th June 2002; Francesco Guerrera, 'Region weighs the need for a one-stop shop', 12th April 2006; Geoff Dyer, 'Cosmopolis dreams large', 12th April 2006; Francesco Guerrera,

The failure of the TSE to step up to the challenges of the 1990s meant that Asia lacked a stock market that was sufficiently deep and broad so as to generate the liquidity required. In 2000 by stock market capitalization the share of Japan was 76 per cent compared to Hong Kong on 9 per cent and then a long tail comprising Taiwan (5 per cent), South Korea (4 per cent), Singapore (2 per cent), Malaysia (2 per cent) and China (1 per cent). Apart from Japan most countries lacked the scale required to support a liquid stock market on their own, regardless of the advances made in membership, regulations, and trading systems. Under these circumstances there was little temptation for owners of businesses to convert them into public companies and so expose their shares to uncertain and volatile stock markets. Even the shares of those businesses that had converted into companies remained closely-held by family owners, and so were little traded. Even merging all stock exchanges into one within a single country, let alone on a transnational basis, was difficult because of institutional and governmental barriers, though this would create a more liquid market, and one capable of supporting investment in the latest trading technology. Reflecting the deep rivalry between national stock exchanges in Asia was that between Kuala Lumpur (KLSE) and Singapore (SSE). Despite the proximity of a highly-developed stock exchange in Singapore, the Malaysian government actively promoted the interests of the KLSE by placing restrictions on the ability of the SSE to provide a market for Malaysian stocks.[40] One of the few countries to develop a deep and broad equity market in Asia, other than Japan, was South Korea. In 2005 the Korean Stock Exchange (KSE) merged with Kosdaq, a specialist technology exchange, and the Korean Futures Exchange. That was followed by its listing as a public company in 2006 in order to raise funds to upgrade its trading system and to enhance its ability to compete with other Asian exchanges.[41]

The route chosen by the stock exchanges in Singapore and Hong Kong was to become the transnational centre for equity trading in Asia, as both lacked a domestic base but had a strong international orientation. The Singapore Stock Exchange (SSE) invested heavily in a computerized order-driven trading system, admitted foreign banks as members, relaxed its listing requirements, demutualized, converted itself into a listed company, and merged with the local derivatives exchange. By 2006 it was operating using the vertical-silo model. Nevertheless, the SSE had failed to emerge as a major market for corporate stocks as these continued to be traded on national exchanges. Though the ownership of corporate stocks

'Outsiders are eager to take the spoils', 12th April 2006; Anna Fifield, 'S. Korea steps up its efforts to become a hub', 12th April 2006.

[40] Conner Middelmann, 'Shift to a higher gear', 19th September 1995; Philip Coggan, 'Nominee comes to the aid of the Clob', 8th February 1996; James Kynge, 'Sime Darby delists from London exchange', 15th October 1996; James Kynge, 'Singapore to ease SE listing requirements', 10th March 1997; James Kynge, 'Battle is on for the hub role', 19th May 1997; Naoko Nakamae, 'Rivals agree to bury the hatchet', 31st March 2000; John Burton, 'Malaysia relaxes short-selling ban', 24th March 2006.

[41] Victor Mallet, 'Manipulators targeted', 7th February 1994; Alexander Nicoll, 'Learning from misfortune', 7th February 1994; Jose Galang, 'Watchdog vigilant', 7th February 1994; John Burton, 'Protectionist policy', 7th February 1994; Nikki Tait, 'Tested to the limit', 12th September 1994; James Whittington, 'New system will multiply deals', 9th June 1995; Conner Middelmann, 'Shift to a higher gear', 19th September 1995; Philip Coggan, 'Nominee comes to the aid of the Clob', 8th February 1996; Jonathan Birchall, 'Caution the watchword in the birth of Vietnamese securities', 26th June 1998; Edward Luce, 'Philippine SE moves toward self-regulation', 29th October 1996; Justin Marozzi, 'Lure of the lion city', 18th February 1997; Justin Marozzi, 'Philippine derivatives planned', 10th March 1997; Louise Lucas, 'Capital raisers fly high', 9th May 1997; Louise Lucas, 'Doors are swinging open', 9th May 1997; Naoko Nakamae, 'Rivals agree to bury the hatchet', 31st March 2000; Barry Riley, 'Free float presented with a bumpy ride', 5th April 2000; Peter Montagnon, 'Nanny state loosens its grip', 28th April 2000; Joe Leahy, 'Regional alliance is long overdue', 28th March 2001; Douglas Wong, 'Former Morgan Grenfell man heads SGX', 20th January 2003; Anna Fifield, 'Korea Exchange seeks foreign capital', 18th March 2005; Song Jung-a and David Turner, 'Tokyo may take stake as Korea Exchange plans IPO', 18th November 2006.

was becoming more dispersed the greatest concentration continued to lie in the countries where they were based, making those the centres of liquidity.[42] The other contender for the role of Asia's leading internationally-orientated stock exchange was the Hong Kong stock exchange (HKSE.). Like the SSE the HKSE also faced the limitations of a small domestic market. However, Hong Kong had close links with China, which became closer in 1997 after the ending of British colonial rule. By offering greater liquidity and applying higher regulatory standards Chinese companies listed on the HKSE enhanced their appeal to international investors. At the same time the HKSE proceeded with a programme of modernization involving the admission of foreign firms as members and the introduction of a computerized trading in 1993, followed by electronic clearing and settlement in 1994 and an order matching system in 1995. The costs associated with these electronic systems also drove the HKSE to merge with the local derivatives exchange, demutualize, and become a listed company by 2000. The result was a new exchange, Hong Kong Exchanges and Clearing (HKEx).[43]

One of the greatest transformations in Asia was in China. By 2001 there were an estimated 58m retail investors in China and 1050 companies were listed on the Shanghai and Shenzhen stock exchanges. However, these exchanges struggled to impose internationally accepted standards of accounting, disclosure, corporate governance, and transparency, making international investors wary of using them Instead, they turned to the HKSE, where a number of large Chinese companies were also listed, because it was better regulated, had the capacity to handle extremely large and complex equity offerings, and possessed the stability that came from the presence of international fund managers and a pool of experienced investors. A number of Chinese companies in the high-technology sector also listed on Nasdaq. As Francesco Guerrera reported in 2006, 'By and large, non-technology Chinese companies have opted for Hong Kong, with only tech companies opting for Nasdaq because of the higher valuations and specialist investor base.'[44] Though China, and its trio of stock exchanges, was the emerging giant of the Asian stock market by 2006, it was held back by its regulatory difficulties.[45]

The other emerging Asian giant among stock markets was India. Unlike China India had a long and continuous equity tradition dating back to the mid-nineteenth century. In 1992

[42] Conner Middelmann, 'Shift to a higher gear', 19th September 1995; Philip Coggan, 'Nominee comes to the aid of the Clob', 8th February 1996; Justin Marozzi, 'Lure of the lion city', 18th February 1997; Louise Lucas, 'Doors are swinging open', 9th May 1997; Naoko Nakamae, 'Rivals agree to bury the hatchet', 31st March 2000; Peter Montagnon, 'Nanny state loosens its grip', 28th April 2000; Joe Leahy, 'Regional alliance is long overdue', 28th March 2001; Douglas Wong, 'Former Morgan Grenfell man heads SGX', 20th January 2003.

[43] Simon Davies, 'Focus on a dynamic present', 20th October 1993; Simon Holberton, 'Shares and the Chinese', 27th April 1994; Louise Lucas, 'Growth plan may not be so smooth', 27th April 1994; Louise Lucas, 'Small brokers on the rack in HK', 1st August 1996; Louise Lucas, 'Capital raisers fly high', 9th May 1997; Louise Lucas, 'Doors are swinging open', 9th May 1997; Louise Lucas, 'Lessons from the crash', 24th March 1998; Geoffrey Nairn, 'Braced for big upheavals', 1st July 1998; Louise Lucas, 'Exchange prepare for wedding bells', 11th August 1999; Naoko Nakamae, 'Rivals agree to bury the hatchet', 31st March 2000; Rahul Jacob, 'Modernisation plan sparks recovery', 28th April 2000; Joe Leahy, 'Regional alliance is long overdue', 28th March 2001; Joseph Leahy, 'Thirst grows for capital pools', 6th June 2002.

[44] Francesco Guerrera, 'Outsiders are eager to take the spoils', 12th April 2006

[45] Tony Walker, 'Big ideas on dance floor', 2nd June 1993; Tony Walker, 'Dragon with an eye on its futures', 2nd April 1994; Simon Holberton, 'Shares and the Chinese', 27th April 1994; James Harding, 'Mammon comes to Shanghai', 18th March 1997; Louise Lucas, 'Capital raisers fly high', 9th May 1997; Simon Davies, 'Vital role in restructuring', 8th December 1997; Simon Davies, 'Success masks market turmoil', 24th March 1998; James Harding, 'First steps on the ladder', 19th May 1998; James Harding, 'Contradiction in markets', 23rd March 1999; Richard McGregor, 'China sets its sights on stock market efficiency', 26th January 2001; Richard McGregor, 'Seriously out of step with the economy', 16th December 2003; Geoff Dyer, 'Cosmopolis dreams large', 12th April 2006; Francesco Guerrera, 'Outsiders are eager to take the spoils', 12th April 2006; Sundeep Tucker, 'A battle for hearts and wallets', 24th October 2006; Fred Hu, 'Staying ahead of the game', 24th October 2006.

India had twenty-two separate stock exchanges, with the most important being that of Bombay. As each stock exchange monopolized a particular segment of the market there was little pressure for change. This was especially true of the Bombay Stock Exchange (BSE), which dominated trading, being located in the country's financial centre. The BSE accounted for two-thirds of Indian stock market turnover in 1994. In response the banks, who were excluded from stock exchange membership, developed an alternative inter-bank market. The unwillingness of the BSE to embrace change led the Ministry of Finance to encourage competition by opening up the domestic market to foreign firms from 1992 onwards, and to back the formation of a Bombay-based rival, the National Stock Exchange (NSE), which opened in 1995. Unlike the BSE, which relied on a physical trading floor, trading on the NSE was screen-based with terminals located across India. In 1996 computerized trading was introduced. The NSE also extended membership to banks. By 1997 trading volume at the NSE had overtaken the BSE, forcing it to respond with the introduction of a new trading system. This allowed it to reclaim its position within the Indian stock market, as it remained the most liquid market. By 2000 the BSE accounted for 55 per cent of all equity trading in India followed by the NSE on 35 per cent. By 2006 the Indian stock market had moved from a position of relative backwardness to become one of the most modern in the space of ten years.[46]

The fundamental problem with Asia was that almost every country had its own stock exchange and most were too small to support the liquid markets that would attract trading from across the entire continent or even serve the largest companies and institutional investors. This was not helped by the official support each received from national governments and the restrictions placed on access for non-domestic investors. The result was to prevent the emergence of a dominant stock exchange in the region or successful transnational alliances. A similar position existed in Latin America, which also suffered from the absence of an equity culture. As Jonathan Wheatley noted in 1997, 'Many Brazilian companies remain culturally disinclined to share control.'[47] This left most stock exchanges with little trading activity and no incentive to change. John Barham was of the view in 1999 that 'Local and international investors still view Latin American equity markets as little more than gambling dens of varying degrees of sophistication.'[48] It was only with privatization, the conversion of businesses into companies, and the relaxation of restrictions on foreign investors that pressure was placed on stock exchanges to reform their membership and organization and switch to electronic trading. This did produce some change in Mexico

[46] Stefan Wagstyl, 'Rival market gives Bombay impetus to reform', 23rd November 1993; Stefan Wagstyl, 'Avalanche of paper threatens investment in India', 1st February 1994; Farhan Bokhari and Mervyn de Silva, 'Foreign buyers cast a spell', 7th February 1994; Martin Brice, 'Four years of explosive growth for GDR's', 10th November 1994; Naazneen Karmali, 'Early bird catches worm', 13th March 1995; Conner Middelmann, 'Comet burns out', 13th March 1995; Mark Nicholson, 'Two busy years of regulatory power', 13th March 1995; Mark Nicholson and Alexander Nicoll, 'First take an aspirin', 13th March 1995; Peter Montagnon and R C Murthy, 'Bombay regulators again in the dock', 21st March 1995; Martin Brice, 'Mexican crisis makes its mark', 14th September 1995; Antonia Sharpe, 'New issues end dry spell', 12th April 1996; Special Correspondent, 'Poised for a comeback after 27 years', 12th April 1996; Mark Nicholson, 'India poised to begin electronic share trading', 6th September 1996; Tony Tassell, 'Domestic debt shapes up', 10th March 1997; Kunal Bose, 'Regional exchanges fail screen test', 10th March 1997; Tony Tassell, 'Risk business lures entrepreneurs', 10th March 1997; Tony Tassell, 'End of the paper chase in sight', 10th March 1997; Tony Tassell, 'Culture change on Dalal Street', 24th June 1997; Krishna Guha, 'India's NSE shrugs off satellite failure', 10th October 1997; Khozem Merchant, 'Straight on for global market', 5th May 2000; David Ibison, 'Market feels effects of uncertainty', 5th May 2000; Khozem Merchant and David Ibison, 'Slowly, the net begins to close in', 5th May 2000; Joe Leahy, 'Farewell to the old family brokers' club', 10th October 2006; Jeremy Grant, 'LSE aims to revive Delhi exchange', 9th November 2011.

[47] Jonathan Wheatley, 'Warmer international reception for paper', 10th June 1997.

[48] John Barham, 'Crisis causes investors to turn their eyes away', 23rd March 1999.

and Peru. Even Latin America's biggest and most developed equity market, the São Paulo in Brazil, lacked a deep and broad equity market because so many companies were tightly controlled by family groups or owned by foreign multinationals. A major reform did take eventually take place in Brazil in 2000 when all nine exchanges merged into one, which improved liquidity and supported investment in electronic trading and processing. Though such mergers could be achieved within individual Latin American states, barriers imposed by governments made it impossible to create a regional exchange for Latin America.

The result was to leave most Latin American markets lacking depth and breadth, encouraging both investors and companies to look abroad. In 2006 an estimated 52 per cent of trading in Latin American equities took place through ADRs listed in New York.[49] A similar situation also existed in Africa, where there were over thirty different stock exchanges by the end of the 1990s. All were far too small to support a liquid market in local stocks, with exception of the Johannesburg Stock Exchange (JSE) in South Africa. However, it failed to attract either investors or companies from outside South Africa, apart from Namibia. Conversely, safe in the monopoly it enjoyed over its domestic market, and being a member-owned institution, it delayed accepting banks as members, ending fixed commissions, or switching to electronic trading. Along with government-imposed restrictions and taxes this kept the local stock market relatively illiquid, encouraging the largest companies with the greatest international following to list their stocks in London.[50] A similar fragmented equity market existed in the Middle East, though the reasons there were bitter local rivalries. This made any attempt to create an integrated stock market impossible to achieve, with no stock exchange being able to reach the size or scale necessary to support a deep and broad stock market, even after banks had been admitted as members, restrictive practices and excessive charges ended, and electronic trading and processing introduced. Potential candidates did exist such as the Tel Aviv Stock Exchange in Israel and the Istanbul Stock Exchange in Turkey but neither were able to broaden their appeal beyond their own boundaries.[51] For some parts of the world geography precluded the creation of deep and

[49] David Pilling, 'Big Bang for Chile capital markets', 27th January 1994; Angus Foster, 'Stock market soars to dizzy heights', 7th February 1994; John Barham, 'Lenient but lopsided', 7th February 1994; David Pilling, 'New sparkle to market image', 7th February 1994; Damian Fraser, 'Edging closer to US standards', 7th February 1994; Richard Lapper, 'New deal fuels price rises', 7th March 1996; Jonathan Wheatley, 'The time has come, the analysts say', 10th June 1997; Geoff Dyer, 'Family-run companies in search of finance', 10th June 1997; Jonathan Wheatley, 'Warmer international reception for paper', 10th June 1997; John Barham, 'Crisis causes investors to turn their eyes away', 23rd March 1999; Ken Warn, 'Rival plan for Argentine stocks', 22nd February 2000; Jonathan Wheatley, Ken Warn, and Mark Mulligan, 'Latin American brokers face home truths on local problems', 3rd March 2000; Ken Warn, 'Buenos Aires exchange links with the LSE', 14th April 2000; Geoff Dyer, 'Drive for liquidity continues', 19th March 2001; Andrea Mandel-Campbell, 'Mexican stock exchange at loggerheads with brokers', 20th March 2001; Richard Lapper and Mark Mulligan, 'Picture continues to darken', 28th March 2001; Tony Tassell, 'Smaller centres offer a more exotic allure', 1st March 2006; Jonathan Wheatley, 'Brazil backwater hits top rank', 19th November 2007.

[50] Gordon Cramb, 'Unthinkable achieved', 18th November 1993; Michael Holman, 'Continent of hazard and opportunity', 7th February 1994; Leslie Crawford, 'Kenyans go on equity buying spree', 31st December 1994; Michael Holman, 'Reforms ease business climate', 4th August 1995; John Kingman, 'Doors thrown open to the world', 28th March 1996; Joel Kibazo, 'A step back to yesterday', 5th November 1996; Mark Ashurst, 'Foreigners spark feeling of euphoria', 25th March 1997; David Buchan, 'Investors take note', 2nd June 1997; Michelle Joubert, 'South African companies head for the open door', 22nd March 1999; Victor Mallet, 'On the move to electronic settlement', 23rd March 1999; Gillian O'Connor, 'Credit given for change to London listing', 15th December 1999; William MacNamara, 'Johannesburg listing boom could spawn an African version of Aim', 18th October 2007; Jeremy Grant, 'Exchange: Aiming to build on success', 4th November 2011.

[51] Emma Tucker, 'Not the bustling place it used to be', 22nd April 1993; Mark Nicholson, 'Law stifles more than it enables', 22nd April 1993; Sheila Jones, 'The market moves ahead', 25th November 1993; Mark Nicholson and James Whittington, 'Magic carpet not ready for take-off', 7th February 1994; Michael Holman, 'Continent of hazard and opportunity', 7th February 1994; FT Staff, 'A superficial culture', 3rd November 1994; James Whittington, 'The market wakes up', 15th May 1995; Julian Ozanne, 'Symptom of change', 6th June 1995; Roula

broad equity markets as was the case across the island states of the Caribbean. Attempts were made in the 1990s to address the problem of market fragmentation but no country was willing to accept the disappearance of its own stock exchange despite the obvious benefits. Roy Johnson, chairman of Jamaica's stock exchange, expressed his frustration in 2003:

> The most efficient model would be a single electronic stock exchange to service all the markets involved. The model we have pursued over the past five years is grossly inefficient and extremely expensive. Markets in Barbados, Trinidad and Tobago, the Bahamas, the Eastern Caribbean and Jamaica have spent substantial sums acquiring hardware and software, when one platform could easily have handled all the trading and settlement requirements for the region.[52]

Even if these rivalries could be overcome there remained the problem that the level of trading was low, because most businesses were family owned and even those that were listed had a small free float.[53]

Despite the existence of numerous nation-states and long-standing political rivalries in Europe it was that continent that led the way in responding to the transformation of stock markets between 1992 and 2007. In Europe there was a proliferation of stock exchanges, ranging from recently established ones in the countries of Eastern Europe, emerging from decades of state ownership and control, through some of the oldest in the world in the countries of Western Europe. These exchanges were highly diverse including those of global importance such as Frankfurt, London, and Paris and others that were so small as to be largely unknown.[54] Regardless of this diversity all went through a process of transformation. The Athens Stock Exchange, for example, introduced an electronic trading system, reformed its regulations, altered its ownership structure, and positioned itself to cater for global fund managers.[55] What made Europe different from other continents and regions were the actions of the European Union involving the introduction of a single market in

Khalaf, 'Bourse starts to modernise', 28th November 1995; Sean Evers, 'Cairo sets a busy timetable for privatisation', 4th October 1996; Roula Khalaf, 'Appetite survives political turmoil', 8th November 1996; Avi Machlis, 'All eyes are on Netanyahu', 8th November 1996; Roula Khalaf, 'Private sector is quick to adjust', 8th November 1996; Sean Evers, 'Cairo becomes a hot favourite', 8th November 1996; Roula Khalaf, 'Casablanca hopes for index funds', 8th November 1996; Robert Allen, 'Control held behind closed doors', 8th November 1996; Samer Iskandar, 'Unrelenting flow of funds boost region', 8th November 1996; John Barham, 'Designs on neighbours', 6th December 1996; Mark Huband, 'Egyptian groups take the public road', 27th March 1997; John Barham, 'Chaotic yet successful', 24th March 1998; Mark Huband, 'Firing industry's engine', 12th May 1998; Charles Clover, 'Kazakh bourse awaits helping hand from privatisations', 26th June 1998; Leyla Boulton, 'Going from one extreme to the other', 23rd March 1999; Mark Huband, 'Spread the message to the masses', 31st March 2000; Mark Huband, 'Expansion is just weeks away', 11th April 2000; Robin Allen, 'Private sector hopes rise', 11th April 2000; Richard Cowper, 'Struggling to spread its wings', 10th May 2000; Roula Khalaf, 'Keeping the foreigners happy', 10th May 2000; Robin Allen, 'New Floor sets scene for growth', 9th April 2001; Alex Skorecki, 'Dubai pins hope on shares', 23rd September 2003; Neil Macdonald, 'Iraq exchange set to spur recovery', 5th December 2005; Fiona Symon, 'How to maintain momentum', 7th December 2005; Tobias Buck, 'Push to raise Palestinian bourse's profile', 17th March 2010.

52 Canute James, 'Boost for Caribbean Exchange plan', 4th February 2003.

53 Richard Lapper, 'A slice of NY's pie', 7th June 1996; Andrew Bolger, 'Still open after Wall Street shuts', 25th May 2001; Canute James, 'Boost for Caribbean Exchange plan', 4th February 2003.

54 Kerin Hope, 'Progress is slow but steady', 6th April 1998; Alex Skorecki, 'Unfortunate few caught in steps of giants', 17th February 2000; Jan Cienski, 'Warsaw seeks partner to revamp bourse', 30th March 2010.

55 Kerin Hope, 'Soaring volumes strain the stock exchange system', 20th May 1994; Kerin Hope, 'Regulations become stricter', 20th May 1994; Kerin Hope, 'Scandal prompts tighter rules', 28th February 1997; Vincent Boland, 'ASX set to demutualise next month', 22nd September 1998; Mark Huband, 'Spread the message to the masses', 31st March 2000.

financial services in 1997 and the creation of a single currency for the Eurozone in 1999. These actions transformed the landscape within which Europe's stock exchanges operated, despite differing corporate laws, accountancy rules, and stock exchange regulations that long continued to support divisions along national boundaries. Simon Davies reported in 1998 that, 'It is a time of unprecedented change for Europe's stock exchanges.'[56] Some even predicted the emergence of a single European stock exchange, as did Andrew Fisher in 1997: 'Eventually, a single European stock exchange will develop in the euro zone...'[57] That common currency did not arrive until 1999 but long before then European stock exchanges were positioning them in what Greg McIvor described in 1998 as an 'intensifying battle for market share among European bourses...'[58]

Examples of the pace and degree of change was the transformation of Frankfurt Stock Exchange from a European backwater into a powerhouse under the title of Deutsche Börse, incorporating the vertical-silo model and covering both equities and derivatives. Another was the conversion of the Paris Bourse into a pan-European exchange operator, Euronext, covering both multiple countries and multiple products. Finally there was the emergence of OMX which grouped the Scandinavian and Baltic equity and derivative exchanges into a single organization.[59] Though lying outside the EU the Zurich Stock Exchange was caught up in what was happening and also took a pro-active stance, centralizing trading, embracing the latest technology, adopting the vertical-silo model, and even relocating certain of its activities to London, so as to better appeal to users.[60] Missing from this catalogue was the London Stock Exchange (LSE), which had begun the whole process of change in Europe with its global trading system, SEAQ International in 1985, and Big Bang reforms of 1986. In 1993 Richard Waters reported that the LSE 'supports a successful international share market in London that has left every other stock exchange in Europe searching for a way to compete.'[61] However, the LSE failed to respond to the challenges that its own actions had unleashed, as European stock exchanges ended restrictive practices, embraced the new technology, reduced charges, and admitted banks as members. Rather than use the LSE and

[56] Simon Davies, 'Equity culture growing fast', 23rd January 1998.

[57] Andrew Fisher, 'Euro likely to start equities ball rolling', 18th November 1997.

[58] Greg McIvor, 'Choice between merging or being marginalised', 27th October 1998.

[59] Andrew Fisher, 'Euro likely to start equities ball rolling', 18th November 1997; Greg McIvor, 'Choice between merging or being marginalised', 27th October 1998; Simon Davies, 'Equity culture growing fast', 23rd January 1998; Joia Shillingford, 'The number of exchanges can only become smaller', 5th November 1998; Alex Skorecki, 'Pension moves may boost equity flows', 30th June 2000; Norma Cohen and John Authers, 'LSE investors are holding out for another bidder to emerge', 21st February 2006.

[60] Ian Rodger, 'Electronic trading approaches reality', 18th November 1993; Ian Rodger, 'Private banking provides fuel', 2nd December 1993; Ian Rodger, 'The real time breakthrough', 6th December 1994; Ian Rodger, 'Bugs balk Switzerland's big bang', 22nd June 1995; Ian Rodger, 'December date set for start-up', 26th October 1995; William Hall, 'Delays have plagued electronic bourse', 28th October 1996; William Hall, 'EBS doubters shaken off', 28th February 1997; William Hall, 'New chief executive injects a fresh sense of purpose', 13th October 1998; Vincent Boland, 'Swiss exchange set to move blue chip trading to London base', 11th July 2000; Vincent Boland, 'Tradepoint and SWX seal Virt-x merger', 24th October 2000; Vincent Boland, 'Anglo-Swiss merger yields a new market', 14th November 2000; Vincent Boland and Bettina Wassener, 'Deutsche Börse takes the cautious approach', 11th May 2001; Vincent Boland, 'D-Day for a stock market migrant', 25th June 2001; Alex Skorecki, 'Virt-x off to brisk start with UK trades', 26th June 2001; Alex Skorecki, 'Seamless market opens up', 16th November 2001; Alex Skorecki, 'Virt-X might merge to survive', 28th December 2001; Vincent Boland, 'US markets face up to technology gap', 6th June 2002; Alex Skorecki, 'Virt-X fails to meet European market share target', 26th June 2002; William Hall and Alex Skorecki, 'Swiss exchange in move to control blue chips', 20th December 2002; Philip Coggan, 'Swiss caught out as the 1990s bubble burst', 10th December 2003; Haig Simonian, 'Swiss look outside their borders', 25th May 2006; Haig Simonian, 'SWX to plot its strategic options', 4th July 2006; Norma Cohen, 'Swiss exchange to cut its tariffs', 4th September 2006; Norma Cohen, 'SWX reduces its Virt-x trading fees', 5th September 2006.

[61] Richard Waters, 'Survival through a part-exchange', 22nd April 1993.

Seaq International, banks based in London could trade directly on those exchanges offering the greatest pool of liquidity and these were the national stock exchanges, as the largest concentration of ownership in any single company continued to be located in the country in which was based. According to Aline van Duyn and John Labate in 2000, 'Of the many thousands of stocks listed on exchanges around the world, few have a following in overseas markets.'[62] The global stock market comprised a series of separate but linked pools rather than a single homogenous one.[63] That did not mean that the LSE was not well positioned to capture a leading position within this global stock market, as Clara Furse, when chief executive of the LSE, understood in 2006:

> It has the world's deepest pool of international liquidity; it has a wide range of institutional emerging market investors; it has broad analyst coverage; it offers an unrivalled choice of markets on which to list; it is the gateway to a budding Eurozone; and, critically, the City promotes world-class regulation and corporate governance standards.[64]

Given these advantages, and the early start it had with Big Bang in 1986, it was realistic to expect that the LSE would have emerged as a leader among European stock exchanges.[65] That is not what happened and the explanation lies in the decisions taken by those leading the LSE.[66] A vocal critic was Martin Dickson. Writing in 2000 his analysis was that:

> Although it is now owned by shareholders they still act as if it is a member-owned mutual, since this is in their individual business interests... The exchange has never really wanted strong leadership because its members are fractious and fractional. The interests of the large international firms... are quite different from those of the retail houses that hold many of the votes...'[67]

[62] Aline van Duyn and John Labate, 'GEM and iX choose different paths', 8th June 2000.

[63] Richard Waters, 'Survival through a part-exchange', 22nd April 1993; Ian Hamilton Fazey, 'Regional finance centres need a lift', 25th November 1993; John Gapper, 'Crisis at liquidity leader', 16th February 1996; Henry Harington, 'Behind the remote reality', 16th February 1996; Alex Skorecki, 'Unfortunate few caught in steps of giants', 17th February 2000; Aline van Duyn and John Labate, 'GEM and iX choose different paths', 8th June 2000; Vincent Boland, 'Securing a future', 5th March 2001; Norma Cohen, 'The race to buy the LSE has become an endurance contest', 12th February 2005; Ruben Lee, 'Get the stock exchange sale right', 14th December 2005.

[64] Clara Furse, 'Sox is not to blame—London is just better as a market', 18th September 2006.

[65] Clara Furse, 'Sox is not to blame—London is just better as a market', 18th September 2006; Nigel Lawson, 'We must not take London's success for granted', 23rd October 2006; Peter Thal Larsen, 'Hats off: Big Bang still brings scale and innovation to finance in London', 26th October 2006; Peter Thal Larsen, Charles Pretzlik, and Chris Hughes, 'Big Bang celebrants find party has moved on', 28th October 2006.

[66] John Thornhill, 'Helping to oil the market's wheels', 27th April 1994; Martin Brice, 'Receipts valued at $10bn', 8th November 1994; Norma Cohen, 'Competition comes to market', 23rd June 1995; Norma Cohen, 'A City flea waits to draw blood', 4th September 1995; Christine Moir, 'Matchbook trading matures', 6th November 1995; Robert Peston, 'Nasdaq plans European exchange', 5th November 1999; Vincent Boland, 'Swiss exchange set to move blue chip trading to London base', 11th July 2000; Vincent Boland, 'D-Day for a stock market migrant', 25th June 2001; Alex Skorecki, 'Virt-x off to brisk start with UK trades', 26th June 2001; Patrick Jenkins and Norma Cohen, 'Seifert's downfall: how a shareholder revolt sent his plans for Deutsche Börse up in smoke', 25th May 2005; John Authers, 'Merging Nasdaq with the LSE makes real strategic sense and creates deep liquidity', 11th March 2006; Chris Hughes and Norma Cohen, 'Thain is attracted by all the right things in London', 20th June 2006; Andrew Hill, 'Financial inventors underpin success', 27th March 2006; John Authers and Jeremy Grant, 'NYSE says it could set up London exchange', 27th June 2006; Norma Cohen, 'Nasdaq goes back on the offensive', 13th December 2006.

[67] Martin Dickson, 'Don Cruickshank's problems are only just beginning', 16th September 2000.

These internal divisions continued to hamper decision-making at the LSE right up to 2007. In 2001 Vincent Boland considered that the LSE was 'hamstrung by vested interests and poor management'.[68] As early as 1995 the anonymous Lex Column in the *FT* was used as a vehicle to articulate general discontent that the successes of Big Bang were being lost through opposition to further reform as the 'The job was only partly done'.[69] This was a theme taken up by others. George Graham in 1997 referred to Big Bang as 'half-completed'[70] while Philip Coggan in 2000 referred to it as 'only a first step'.[71] What had happened was that the LSE failed to keep pace with the rapid pace of change that was taking place elsewhere. Vincent Boland concluded in 1999 that the LSE 'appeared to be floundering',[72] accusing it in 2000 of being the 'one European exchange yet to set out a coherent European vision',[73] and 'struggling to define its role in an increasingly pan-European trading environment'.[74] The same conclusion was reached by Alex Skorecki in 2003 when he reported that the LSE was struggling 'to redefine its role in a globalizing industry'.[75]

One early example of the failure of leadership was the inability to develop and then introduce an electronic system for processing transactions, called Taurus. After years of development this was abandoned in 1993.[76] What made that decision so significant was that it meant the LSE was not able to move towards the vertical-silo model of integrating trading and processing, as was happening elsewhere in Europe.[77] Combined with the

[68] Vincent Boland, 'A healthy appetite for Liffe', 29th September 2001.

[69] The Lex Column, 'Cracking the City Club', 6th February 1995.

[70] George Graham, 'All change at the exchange', 20th October 1997.

[71] Philip Coggan, 'City of London no newcomer to upheaval', 4th May 2000.

[72] Vincent Boland, 'A pan-European enthusiast', 23rd March 1999.

[73] Vincent Boland, 'Euronext puts pressure on European markets', 22nd March 2000.

[74] Vincent Boland, 'Shadow over new talks on potential Frankfurt merger', 6th April 2000.

[75] Alex Skorecki, 'Unexpected choice could prove ideal fit for LSE's missing piece', 9th April 2003.

[76] Michael Prest, 'Time for a new exchange', 24th March 1998; Edward Luce, 'Liffe finds little comfort in tie-up with Frankfurt', 11th July 1998; Aline van Duyn, 'Liffe plans a push into equity markets', 7th September 2000; Vincent Boland, 'Exchange chairman rejects link with Liffe', 4th October 2000; Vincent Boland, 'A buying opportunity for the LSE', 24th May 2001; Vincent Boland, 'Bid for Liffe would be icing on the cake for LSE', 15th August 2001; Vincent Boland, 'Liffe chairman denies LSE bid talks', 23rd August 2001; Vincent Boland, 'A healthy appetite for Liffe', 29th September 2001; Charles Pretzlik, 'LSE set to face competition in move for Liffe', 13th October 2001; Peter Martin, 'The end of Liffe as we know it', 30th October 2001; Lina Saigol, 'LSE left exposed by bid failure', 30th October 2001; Vincent Boland, 'Failure to achieve victory puts LSE in the line of fire', 31st October 2001; Philip Coggan, 'Competition intensifies among rival exchanges', 31st October 2001; Vincent Boland and Charles Pretzlik, 'How the LSE managed to miss an open goal', 3rd November 2001; Charles Pretzlik, 'LSE talking to four potential partners', 7th November 2001; Alex Skorecki, 'Exchange glory in their listed status', 23rd February 2002; Alex Skorecki, 'London exchange goes into derivatives', 30th July 2003; Charles Pretzlik, Patrick Jenkins and Alex Skorecki, 'New LSE chairman ready for action', 18th September 2003; Norma Cohen, 'Concerns over competition and governance', 14th December 2004; Joanna Chung, 'Derivatives spotlight on Russian companies', 29th November 2006.

[77] Richard Waters, 'The plan that fell to earth', 12th March 1993; Andrew Jack, Norma Cohen, John Gapper, Maggie Urry, and Ian Hamilton Fazey, 'Angry City takes stock of lost money and time', 12th March 1993; Richard Waters and Alan Cane, 'Sudden death of a runaway bull', 19th March 1993; Richard Waters, 'Survival through a part-exchange', 22nd April 1993; Peter Martin, 'Exchange to look at US option for trading system', 23rd April 1993; David Waller, 'Technology is the weapon against London', 1st July 1993; Barry Riley, 'On the way to speedier settlements', 9th December 1993; Christopher Price, 'Braced for radical changes', 9th December 1993; Robert Peston and Norma Cohen, 'Country gent in exchange of fire', 15th January 1994; Barry Riley, 'Empty vaults will bring new opportunities', 29th November 1994; Norma Cohen, 'Cash-generating practice', 29th November 1994; Sheila Jones, 'SE edges towards full automation', 2nd June 1995; George Graham, 'Blood on the road to the promised land', 5th March 1996; Nuala Moran, 'Not a moment too soon', 3rd July 1996; Nuala Moran, 'Strategic IT development by the securities industry', 3rd July 1996; Nuala Moran, 'Savings financed new system', 4th September 1996; Christopher Brown-Humes, 'CrestCo unveils pan-European network for share settlement', 14th September 1998; George Graham, 'CrestCo wins gilt and money market settlement', 19th September 1998; Christopher Brown-Humes, 'CrestCo to pay maiden dividend, give rebates', 23rd September 1998; Jean Eaglesham, 'Tight timetable turned to rare working success', 9th July 1999; Vincent Boland, 'A share in the future', 18th January 2000; Vincent Boland, 'LSE to phase in central counterparty service', 9th March 2000; Norma

Taurus debacle was the delay in moving towards a fully-electronic market. The LSE long relied on the quote-driven system in which market-makers posted on screen the prices at which they would trade, with deals completed using the telephone. The alternative was an order-driven system in which a computer automatically matched buyers and sellers, which was cheaper and faster. It was not until 1997 that LSE introduced its own order-driven electronic trading system, by which time other stock exchanges had made rapid advances in integrating electronic trading and processing, taking business away from the LSE as a result.[78] Another example of the failure of leadership was the failure to merge with Liffe, which dominated the trading of financial derivatives in London, even though this was the direction of travel across Europe.[79] As Michael Prest noted in 1998, 'London is now the only important European financial centre where the cash and derivatives markets are independently owned and run.'[80] Liffe was eventually acquired by Euronext in 2001.[81] The result was that despite the opportunities open to it the LSE lost out to other European stock exchanges, notably Frankfurt and Paris.

By the beginning of the 1990s the competition coming from London posed a serious challenge to all Europe's stock exchanges, which took time to respond being member-owned organizations. In 1993 Henri Servais, president of the Brussels Bourse, expressed the frustration of those trying to force through reforms upon a reluctant stock exchange membership: 'It's very difficult to get them to accept changes and challenges.' He was quite clear on what was required if they were to survive: 'We need to be able to offer an excellent service, at a low price, or we will disappear in favour of other regulated markets.'[82] There were

Cohen, 'Merger of bourses prompts Crest to cut fees', 24th April 2000; Aline van Duyn, 'European clearers urged to merge', 20th June 2000; Alex Skorecki, 'Europe's bourse masters play game with no rules', 30th May 2002; Alex Skorecki and Daniel Dombey, 'Crest is to merge with Euroclear', 5th July 2002; Alex Skorecki, 'Stock exchanges play for a winning position', 8th July 2002; Alex Skorecki, 'Happy end nears for a tale of two cities', 4th September 2002; Charles Pretzlik, Patrick Jenkins, and Alex Skorecki, 'New LSE chairman ready for action', 18th September 2003; Norma Cohen, 'Big banks and listed companies welcome referral of LSE bids', 30th March 2005.

[78] Norma Cohen, 'Competition comes to market', 23rd June 1995; Norma Cohen, 'A City flea waits to draw blood', 4th September 1995; John Gapper, 'Crisis at liquidity leader', 16th February 1996; George Graham, 'Stockbrokers to urge end of stamp duty on deals', 21st February 1996; George Graham and Norma Cohen, 'Investment experts spurn reforms', 22nd February 1996; George Graham, 'Blood on the road to the promised land', 5th March 1996; George Graham, 'New chief sent to the Tower', 15th June 1996; John Gapper, 'Tradepoint loss rises to £5.7m', 15th August 1996; John Gapper, 'Harmony after a turbulent period', 28th February 1997; Philip Coggan, 'Bourses fight for supremacy', 24th April 1997; Jane Martinson, 'Slow burn before Big Bang 2', 6th October 1997; George Graham, 'Much more a small fizz than a Big Bang', 17th October 1997; Jean Eaglesham, 'Important long-term effects for the small investor', 17th October 1997; George Graham, 'Order-driven system will bring London into line', 17th October 1997; George Graham, 'All change at the exchange', 20th October 1997; George Graham, 'Electronic book settling down', 24th March 1998; Geoff Nairn, 'IT is still changing the face of trading', 24th March 1998; George Graham, 'Stock Exchange poised to fine tune the trading system that went electric', 30th March 1998; Norma Cohen, 'Exchange set to announce deals changes', 25th May 1998; George Graham, 'Exchange lobbied on behalf of small investors', 11th July 1998; Jane Martinson, 'No Sets please, we're large institutions', 8th August 1998; Clay Harris, George Graham, and John Labate, 'Small deal backs big plans for Tradepoint', 7th May 1999; Vincent Boland, 'Sets wins over investors', 18th August 1999; Vincent Boland, 'A share in the future', 18th January 2000; Arkady Ostrovsky and Astrid Wendlandt, 'Tradepoint wins backing of clearing houses', 11th February 2000; Vincent Boland, 'LSE to phase in central counterparty service', 9th March 2000; Patrick Jenkins, 'How to find the best price', 8th April 2000; Aline van Duyn, 'Sets may be scrapped early next year', 4th May 2000; Alex Skorecki, 'Turnover on bourses hits record levels', 3rd January 2001; Vincent Boland, 'LSE revamps trading structure', 26th February 2001; Vincent Boland, 'Securing a future', 5th March 2001; Alex Skorecki, 'LSE milestone for Sets trade', 9th July 2002; Alex Skorecki, 'LSE buying time while it searches for a new chief', 26th November 2002; Kate Burgess and Norma Cohen, 'Controversial LSE plan raises fears of a Balkanised market', 13th November 2004; Chris Hughes, 'Lehman sets record on LSE', 14th August 2006.

[79] Vincent Boland, 'Exchange chairman rejects link with Liffe', 4th October 2000.

[80] Michael Prest, 'Time for a new exchange', 24th March 1998.

[81] Edward Luce, 'Liffe finds little comfort in tie-up with Frankfurt', 11th July 1998.

[82] Andrew Hill, 'Belfox thrives in the gentleman's club', 25th November 1993.

thirty-two separate stock exchanges in the EU in 1996 and only in the face of a serious loss of business, either actual or potential, was it possible to persuade the membership to take action. It was often necessary to break the power of the members through demutualization before substantial progress be made, which John Gapper picked up on in 1997: 'The exponents of such moves argue that exchanges can only react to a changing competitive environment properly if they are freed from the partial interests of brokers.'[83] Europe's smaller stock exchanges were especially exposed to the growing competition as trading gravitated to those that could provide the liquidity demanded by the global banks and fund managers. As that competition intensified the momentum behind change grew, overcoming the obstacles that members put in its way. John Gapper observed in 1996 that, 'Europe's stock exchanges no longer have the option of simply staying the same.'[84] He followed that up in 1997 by expressing the view that 'Only the largest European exchanges may stand a chance in a global marketplace.'[85] One result was to force mergers between stock exchanges in those countries where many separate ones existed. In the mid-1990s Italy completed the transition from ten stock exchanges to one, dominated by Milan, while also introducing a computerized trading system and accepting banks as members. The resulting institution, the Milan Borsa, was then privatized in 1997, coming under the control of the banks.[86] These mergers also went further to include both stock and derivative exchanges, which could support the heavy investment required in electronic trading and processing systems. In 2006 Norma Cohen and John Authers considered that, 'The ability of exchanges, particularly those operating within the Eurozone, to operate a single platform for the trading of a wide variety of instruments, including cash equities, derivatives and bonds, opens the door for the slashing of costs and increasing profit margins.'[87] One example of where this took place was Spain, where the process was backed by the Spanish banks, concerned about losing control over their domestic market in an increasingly competitive environment.[88] In 2003 the Bolsas y Mercados Espanoles (BME) was formed by merging Spain's stock and derivative exchanges. The case for of multi-assets exchanges was becoming compelling because of the convergence of both financial instruments and those that traded them, with the barriers between different financial intermediaries disappearing.[89]

[83] John Gapper, 'Out with the old, in with the new', 28th February 1997.

[84] John Gapper, 'New rules, new rivals, new order', 16th February 1996.

[85] John Gapper, 'Out with the old, in with the new', 28th February 1997.

[86] Andrew Hill, 'Borsa link may usher new era for Milan', 18th October 1996.

[87] Norma Cohen and John Authers, 'LSE investors are holding out for another bidder to emerge', 21st February 2006.

[88] George Graham, 'Beyond the storm, small will be beautiful', 19th October 1998.

[89] Richard Waters, 'Survival through a part-exchange', 22nd April 1993; Ian Hamilton Fazey, 'Regional finance centres need a lift', 25th November 1993; Andrew Hill, 'Belfox thrives in the gentleman's club', 25th November 1993; Anthony Robinson, 'Creating capitalism without capital', 7th February 1994; Peter Wise, 'Lisbon shapes up for change', 7th February 1994; Peter Wise, 'Outlook for growth remains bright', 22nd February 1994; Hilary Barnes, 'Drift of trade to London causes concern', 7th April 1994; Tom Burns, 'Domestic volumes dominate', 20th June 1994; Andrew Hill, 'More sell-offs expected next year', 24th November 1994; Vincent Boland, 'Floor needed to keep prices in Czech', 13th March 1995; Vincent Boland, 'Greater transparency on the way', 2nd June 1995; Norma Cohen, 'Competition comes to market', 23rd June 1995; John Gapper and Richard Lapper, 'Europe unlocked for dealers', 2nd January 1996; John Pitt, 'Storm gathers from the east', 16th February 1996; John Gapper, 'New rules, new rivals, new order', 16th February 1996; Christine Moir, 'Once more unto a breach?', 16th February 1996; Henry Harington, 'Behind the remote reality', 16th February 1996; FT Staff, 'Surviving in the free world', 21st March 1996; John Thornhill, 'Reining in wild expansion', 11th April 1996; Kevin Done, 'Concern over corporate disclosure', 26th April 1996; Vincent Boland, 'Consolidation process under way', 26th April 1996; Andrew Hill, 'Borsa link may usher new era for Milan', 18th October 1996; Christopher Bobinski, 'Warsaw exchange proves to be a robust youngster', 30th October 1996; Tom Burns, 'Timing of launch was fortunate', 11th February 1997; Paul Betts, 'Year of reckoning for the ugly caterpillar', 28th February 1997; Anthony Robinson, 'An enviable reputation', 28th February 1997; Christine Moir, 'Barriers go up in Europe', 28th February 1997; John Thornhill, 'Strange beast

The problem for smaller European countries was that nationally-based mergers, even extending to all exchanges, was still insufficient to produce the scale required to support a sophisticated electronic trading and processing platform or generate the level of liquidity sought by banks and fund managers. One region of Europe most exposed to this happening was Scandinavia and around the Baltic because of the number of small countries located there, all with their own exchanges. These were either long-established exchanges as in Denmark, Norway, and Sweden or those recently formed in Estonia, Latvia, and Lithuania after the break-up of the Soviet Union. Though it meant a loss of independence the quest for survival drove exchanges in these countries to amalgamate into a single cross-border unit, as this would produce a market with the resources to support an electronic platform and the liquidity to attract banks and fund managers.[90] As Paul Erik Skaanning-Jorgensen, the deputy director of the Copenhagen Exchange, made clear in 1997: 'The time seems right now, when you have had concentrations nationally, to look at what we could do on a regional scale.' He also noted the benefits of sharing costs in developing electronic trading systems: 'Trading systems are extremely expensive and exchanges have spent colossal sums on them.'[91] The Stockholm Stock Exchange demutualized in 1992 and became publicly listed in 1993, being the first to do so. It was then acquired in 1998 by the OM group, operator of the Swedish derivatives market. The resulting company, OMX, became the nucleus of a group of exchanges spanning Scandinavia and the Baltic.[92] Leading the

is eye-catching', 28th February 1997; Michael Morgan, 'Investors dive in', 11th April 1997; Andrew Fisher, 'European bourses may get lift on back of Emu', 15th April 1997; Philip Coggan, 'Bourses fight for supremacy', 24th April 1997; Guy Dinmore, 'Slow progress made in Zagreb', 28th May 1997; Andrew Fisher, 'Bigger is better in bourses' brave euro world', 15th July 1997; Andrew Fisher, 'Euro likely to start equities ball rolling', 18th November 1997; Paul Betts, 'Market half the size it should be', 10th December 1997; Paul Betts, 'Stemming the Gucci Trail', 10th December 1997; Simon Davies, 'Equity culture growing fast', 23rd January 1998; John Gapper, 'Out with the old, in with the new', 28th February 1997; Michael Prest, 'Time for a new exchange', 24th March 1998; Simon Davies, 'Cost cuts fuel mergers', 17th July 1998; Vincent Boland, 'ASX set to demutualise next month', 22nd September 1998; George Graham, 'Beyond the storm, small will be beautiful', 19th October 1998; Greg McIvor, 'Choice between merging or being marginalised', 27th October 1998; Joia Shillingford, 'The number of exchanges can only become smaller', 5th November 1998; Aline van Duyn, 'Sets may be scrapped early next year', 4th May 2000; Tom Burns, 'Foreign funds in a fever', 28th March 2001; Alex Skorecki, 'Waiting to play kingmaker', 31st October 2002; Leslie Crawford and Norma Cohen, 'BME unveils plan to seek a public listing', 28th April 2005; Norma Cohen and John Authers, 'LSE investors are holding out for another bidder to emerge', 21st February 2006.

90 Hugh Carnegy, 'Two dynamic exchanges', 20th June 1996.

91 George Graham, 'Radical changes may lie ahead', 9th April 1997.

92 Hugh Carnegy, 'Two dynamic exchanges', 20th June 1996; Hugh Carnegy, 'Speculation about mergers', 28th February 1997; Greg McIvor, 'Old perceptions are swept aside', 11th March 1997; George Graham, 'Radical changes may lie ahead', 9th April 1997; Philip Coggan, 'Bourses fight for supremacy', 24th April 1997; Greg McIvor, 'Sweden and Denmark to link bourses', 12th June 1997; Simon Davies, 'Equity culture growing fast', 23rd January 1998; Tim Burt, 'Alliances are just the beginning', 24th March 1998; Tim Burt, 'Special partners sought', 14th April 1998; Peter Martin, 'Trading places', 2nd July 1998; Greg McIvor, 'Choice between merging or being marginalised', 27th October 1998; Valeria Skold and Tim Burt, 'Oslo set to join Nordic bourse tie-up', 11th December 1998; Peter John, Nicholas George and Vincent Boland, 'Stock Exchanges start talks on synchronising hours in Europe', 1st March 1999; Nicholas George, 'Consolidation will be a reality in May', 23rd March 1999; Nicholas George, 'Northern lights lead way for neighbours', 26th July 1999; Edward Luce and John Labate, 'The trading bell tolls', 26th July 1999; Nicholas George, 'Baltic exchanges battle for dominance', 7th September 1999; Vincent Boland, 'Jiway sets fee of 7 euros per contract', 31st May 2000; Vijai Maheshwari, 'Baltic states prepare to join Nordic alliance', 15th June 2000; Christopher Brown-Humes, 'Cocky OM decides to play David and Goliath', 28th August 2000; Nicholas George, 'Niche player relishes a new role on world stage', 29th August 2000; *FT* Reporters, 'Sweden's platform must prove itself on the global stage', 31st August 2000; Claire MacCarthy, 'Team spirit brings gains all round', 31st October 2000; Rafael Behr, 'Beefing up for the battle of the Baltics', 8th March 2001; Christopher Brown-Humes, 'Glory days have faded since OM's audacious LSE bid', 24th August 2001; Alex Skorecki, 'Lithuania joins Baltic collection', 1st April 2004; Nicholas George, 'OMX in talks with Danish stock exchange', 4th October 2004; Rupini Bergstrom, 'OMX goal of integrated marketplace a step nearer', 16th November 2004; Rupini Bergstrom, 'Icelandic exchange considers merger', 28th July 2005; David Ibison,

process of consolidation in Central and Eastern Europe was the Vienna Stock Exchange, which introduced a computer-driven trading system in 1996. However, it faced strong rivalry from the Warsaw Stock Exchange in Poland, which not only valued its independence but saw opportunities for itself to become the hub of a regional grouping.[93]

One European stock exchange with continent-wide ambitions was the Paris Bourse. By the mid-1990s the French stock market had been both centralized and modernized. These reforms had succeeded in repatriating trading in French shares from London. The next step was the amalgamation of the cash and futures markets into one. This took place in 1997 with the French derivatives exchange, the Matif, being acquired by the operator of the Paris Bourse, the Société des Bourses Françaises (SBF). In the words of Jean-François Théodore, the chairman of the SBF, the aim was 'to create critical mass on the eve of the new era of the euro'. He explained that, 'At a time when most major markets are organized under a single roof, it's about being able to talk with one voice for the cash and derivatives exchanges in the world of tomorrow.'[94] However, that domestic integration was only a step on the path to a bigger plan involving international co-operation. Increasingly those running the Paris Bourse concluded that only a strategy of internationalization could preserve its position as one of the leading exchanges in Europe, and that unless action was taken it could end up being submerged in a pan-European institution led from either Frankfurt or London. In 2000 the Paris, Amsterdam, and Brussels exchanges merged, forming Euronext. Euronext was a single market covering equities, derivatives, and commodities with Euroclear providing settlement and Clearnet acting as a central counterparty. Despite the involvement of both Euroclear and Clearnet this was not the vertical-silo model as neither was integrated into Euronext. Euroclear was an independent Brussels-based settlement agency, which acquired Sicovam, the French settlement agency, in 2000. Clearnet was the French clearing house but it merged with the British clearing house, LCH, in 2003, reducing Euronext's stake from 80 to 40 per cent. This separation of trading and processing reflected current thinking, according to Vincent Boland in 2000: 'One issue now dominates market thinking: separating the ownership of trading platforms from that of trading processors and central counterparties as the best way of making massive cost savings.'[95]

'Stockholm plots course as financial centre', 12th July 2006; David Ibison, 'OMX open to transatlantic deal', 20th July 2006; Norma Cohen, Lina Saigol, and Neil Hume, 'Nasdaq in early talks to acquire OMX', 11th September 2006; Norma Cohen and Anuj Gangahar, 'Nasdaq looks at Europe growth via Sweden', 14th September 2006; Lars Ottersgard, 'Global ambitions can be achieved through a single voice', 14th November 2012.

[93] Michael Morgan, 'Reforms boost Vienna', 28th February 1997; Vincent Boland, 'Reforms promised', 14th May 1997; Guy Dinmore, 'Slow progress made in Zagreb', 28th May 1997; Graham Bowley, 'German, Austrian exchanges in talks', 25th September 1997; Anatol Lieven, 'Past few months have been bumpy', 9th December 1997; Andrew Fisher and Eric Frey, 'Frankfurt and Vienna SEs to co-operate', 6th April 1998; Stefan Wagstyl, 'Wrong perception and harsh reality', 27th October 1998; Rebecca Bream, 'Neighbours get too close for comfort', 31st March 2000; John Reed, Robert Anderson, and Kester Eddy, 'Unified trading faces battle to justify worth', 2nd November 2000; Arkady Ostrovsky, 'From chaos to capitalist triumph', 9th October 2003; Jan Cienski, 'Warsaw says farewell to the lean years', 21st October 2003; Eric Frey, 'Vienna Bourse looks to the east', 15th July 2004; Christian Holler, 'Bourses agree alliance', 16th August 2004; Jan Cienski and Alex Skorecki, 'Warsaw exchange at crossroads', 3rd September 2004; Haig Simonian, 'Seeking a starring role in the new EU', 25th October 2004; Mark Andress, 'Sleepy laggard shows signs of life', 1st November 2004; Mark Andress, 'Prague SE sees future in IPOs', 2nd November 2004; Robert Anderson and Mark Andress, 'Slovakia bourse to go private', 10th June 2005; Mark Andress, Robert Anderson, and Jan Cienski, 'Vienna plans local consolidation', 16th June 2005; Haig Simonian, 'Vienna exchange's quiet expansion', 14th June 2006; Kester Eddy, 'Bourse sees privatisation as big opportunity', 31st October 2013.

[94] Andrew Jack, 'SBF, Matif join forces ahead of German link', 18th September 1997.

[95] Vincent Boland, 'The next big market force', 10th November 2000.

In 2002 the Lisbon Stock Exchange joined Euronext but there the process stopped. No other exchange agreed to participate, with the acquisition of Liffe in 2002 done through an expensive takeover bid, after Euronext had been converted into a company in 2001. Other exchanges toyed with the idea of joining Euronext but none did. Euronext tried hard to persuade the LSE to become a participant and held merger discussions with Deutsche Börse, but all came to nothing. Though Euronext adopted a federal structure the result was that the separate pools of liquidity were combined into one, with the loss of trading in Amsterdam and Brussels to Paris, as it could provide the greatest depth and breadth. This acted as a warning to other European exchanges and so made them reluctant to join Euronext. Such was the case with the Borsa Italiana, for example.[96] Fearing a takeover by Deutsche Börse Euronext chose to merge with the NYSE in 2006, becoming the European base for the world's first global equities and derivatives exchange. It spanned seven exchanges and six time zones with the expectation that its size and diversity would make it into the dominant force within global financial markets. This merger frustrated the attempts to create a single exchange covering the Eurozone as Georges Ugeux, a former executive vice president at the NYSE, noted in 2007 that, 'It is extraordinary that neither the European Commission nor Ecofin, the committee of European finance ministers, have encouraged the European exchanges to get together.' In his opinion 'The Eurozone badly needs deeper and more fungible pools of liquidity if it wants to compete effectively with the US.'[97] Despite the emergence of the Eurozone and the progress made towards economic and financial integration in the EU, in 2006 it still remained a collection of individual states where individual self-interest triumphed over collective objectives.[98]

[96] Antonia Sharpe, 'Amsterdam prepares to fight back', 16th June 1994; Ronald van de Krol, 'Action plan lifts Amsterdam's status', 12th September 1994; Ronald van de Krol, 'Poised for a shake-up', 12th September 1994; Ronald van de Krol, 'Dutch challenge London', 16th February 1996; David Brown, 'Strategy for a single entity', 29th October 1996; Gordon Cramb, 'Two pioneers are extending the frontiers', 28th February 1997; Simon Davies, 'Equity culture growing fast', 23rd January 1998; Simon Davies, 'Success masks market turmoil', 24th March 1998; Michael Smith, 'Core of growing influence', 31st March 1998; James Blitz, Tom Burns, Gordon Cramb and Greg McIvor, 'New axis stirs mixed feelings across Europe', 8th July 1998; Vincent Boland and Simon Davies, 'Amsterdam SE chief seeks to join alliance', 30th July 1998; Clay Harris, 'The network solution', 5th November 1998; Gordon Cramb, 'Benelux markets form trading link', 25th November 1998; Peter Wise, 'Rescued from a life of obscurity', 4th May 2001; Ian Bickerton, 'Dutch bourse in survival struggle', 28th March 2006.

[97] Georges Ugeux, 'Exchange battles mask Europe's silence', 3rd January 2007.

[98] Andrew Jack, 'Local bourse shuts as Paris calls the tune', 8th November 1995; Andrew Jack, 'The French revolution', 16th February 1996; Andrew Jack, 'French Bourse seeking European collaboration', 13th February 1997; Andrew Jack, 'Dreaming of an alliance', 28th February 1997; Andrew Fisher and Andrew Jack, 'German, French bourses in link-up talks', 21st June 1997; Andrew Jack, 'SBF plans equities exchanges link', 10th July 1997; Andrew Fisher, 'Bigger is better in bourses' brave euro world', 15th July 1997; Andrew Jack, 'SBF, Matif join forces ahead of German link', 18th September 1997; Simon Davies, 'Equity culture growing fast', 23rd January 1998; Andrew Jack, 'News takes Paris exchange by surprise', 8th July 1998; Edward Luce and Vincent Boland, 'Paris seethes at offer of second class berth', 18th July 1998; George Graham, 'French banker hits at stock exchange alliance', 24th July 1998; Vincent Boland and Samer Iskandar, 'Nine into one will just not go', 20th November 1998; Vincent Boland and Samer Iskandar, 'Paris deal sets up pact on continental trading', 20th November 1998; Vincent Boland, 'Milan joins bourses alliance', 12th March 1999; Samer Iskandar, 'Turning point for SBF's chairman', 23rd March 1999; Samer Iskandar, 'Paris Bourse enjoys a long hot summer', 7th September 1999; Samer Iskandar, 'Technology overtakes tradition', 1st January 2000; Samer Iskandar and Vincent Boland, 'French move to harmonise settlements', 28th February 2000; Vincent Boland and Neil Buckley, 'Europe exchanges to merge', 16th March 2000; Vincent Boland, 'Merged European bourse plans to expand into London and US', 21st March 2000; Vincent Boland, 'Merger reshapes the financial landscape', 31st March 2000; Astrid Wendlandt, 'Winner gets to rule the world', 31st March 2000; Astrid Wendlandt, 'Urgent need for consolidation', 14th July 2000; Astrid Wendlandt, 'Settlement books set to double', 14th July 2000; Tim Steele, 'Markets bent on shortening the cycle', 14th July 2000; Samer Iskandar, 'Paris bids for Europe's crown', 10th November 2000; Vincent Boland, 'The next big market force', 10th November 2000; Peter Wise, 'Rescued from a life of obscurity', 4th May 2001; Raphael Minder, 'Flotation by Euronext to raise Euro700m', 5th July 2001; Sarah Laitner, 'Euronext set for Liffe', 28th December 2001; Alex Skorecki, 'London Clearing House mulls link with Clearnet', 15th February 2002; Alex Skorecki, 'Time for London to pull off a deal', 6th June 2002; Alex Skorecki, 'T+1 pipedream is close to reality', 6th

Throughout the 1990s and into the twenty-first century the elephant in the room when it came to stock exchange consolidation in Europe was Deutsche Börse. In 2000 Vincent Boland referred to Werner Seifert, chief executive of Deutsche Börse, as 'the prime mover in the rush to integrate Europe's equity markets'.[99] Deutsche Börse was the perennial partner but always emerged as the jilted suitor. Despite the constant rejections it experienced Deutsche Börse emerged as the most successful European exchange by 2006 through its vertical-silo and the combination of equity and derivatives trading. Deutsche Börse was formed in 1993. Rolf Breuer was chairman and Werner Seifert, a Swiss national with a background in finance and technology, appointed chief executive. From the inception of Deutsche Börse the model it chose to follow was the vertical-silo, as Rolf Breuer made clear in 1993: 'We now have one organisation to handle the entire range of stock-exchange business. Right from the beginning of the process of placing an order, to the end where the order is wound up, the client need only deal with one organisation. The whole process has been brought under one roof—for derivatives as well as for securities—something you don't find in London, Paris or New York.'[100] Deutsche Börse was a combination of the Frankfurt Börse, the DTB (the German derivatives exchange), and the Kassenverein (the German agency for settling transactions). In 1994 Rolf Breuer claimed that, 'Everything connected with securities dealing is now under one roof, from dealing and settlement to software development and clearing. To have it all together like this gives us a tremendous competitive advantage. We can streamline investments, pool our resources and develop technology much more effectively than our rivals.'[101] This concentration of activity made the domestic market for German stocks more liquid, attracting trading that had previously taken place in London. This was a principle aim behind the formation of Deutsche Börse, according to Rolf Breuer in 1994, as it was designed to ensure 'that anyone who wants to do business in D-Mark denominated securities does it via the German market and not in London'.[102]

June 2002; Alex Skorecki, 'Stock exchanges play for a winning position', 8th July 2002; Alex Skorecki, 'Deutsche Börse offers deal to Dutch', 10th September 2003; Charles Pretzlik, Patrick Jenkins, and Alex Skorecki, 'New LSE chairman ready for action', 18th September 2003; Alex Skorecki, 'European exchanges slash fees', 1st October 2003; Alex Skorecki, 'All eyes are on Euronext', 8th December 2003; Norma Cohen, 'Euronext plan for UK trades', 22nd March 2004; Norma Cohen, 'Eurosets Dutch Trading Service captures 30% of equity trading', 25th May 2004; Norma Cohen, 'Merger talks stall over Euronext, D Börse HQ', 12th January 2006; Ian Bickerton, 'Dutch bourse in survival struggle', 28th March 2006; Norma Cohen and John Authers, 'NYSE stock offering lifts exchanges', 6th May 2006; Norma Cohen, 'Deutsche Börse woos Euronext', 12th May 2006; Norma Cohen, 'Worried Italian banks to discuss Borsa offering', 17th May 2006; Norma Cohen, 'Euronext in state of flux over future', 17th May 2006; Norma Cohen, 'Rivals race to finalise bids for Euronext', 22nd May 2006; Ian Bickerton, 'Euronext takes its time to reflect on merger options', 24th May 2006; Gerrit Wiesmann, Richard Milne, and Andrew Wallmeyer, 'Deutsche Börse hints at sweeter Euronext offer', 25th May 2006; Norma Cohen, 'LSE shrugs off threat to listings', 5th June 2006; Jeremy Grant, 'Regulators face uncharted waters if deal goes ahead', 9th June 2006; Chris Hughes and Norma Cohen, 'Loss of light touch poses threat to LSE', 14th June 2006; Jeremy Grant, 'Hurdles appear in the race for exchange consolidation', 15th June 2006; John Authers and Norma Cohen, 'Exchange merger poses question of liquidity', 19th June 2006; Norma Cohen and John Authers, 'New Deutsche Börse bid to lure Euronext from NYSE', 20th June 2006; Norma Cohen and John Authers, 'New Deutsche Börse bid to lure Euronext from NYSE', 20th June 2006; *FT* Reporters, 'Euronext snubs latest D Börse offer', 21st June 2006; Norma Cohen, 'NYSE pressed to beat D Börse', 30th August 2006; Norma Cohen, 'Borsa Italiana aims for pan-European exchange', 13th October 2006; Norma Cohen, 'Hopes recede for merger of European exchanges', 16th October 2006; Christopher Brown-Humes, 'Consolidation is fevered but all bets are still on', 28th November 2006; Georges Ugeux, 'Exchange battles mask Europe's silence', 3rd January 2007.

[99] Vincent Boland, 'Heat is on to create pan-regional market', 31st March 2000.
[100] David Waller, 'Germany takes stock', 7th May 1993.
[101] David Waller, 'Resisting the bait of equity ownership', 14th July 1994.
[102] David Waller, 'Resisting the bait of equity ownership', 14th July 1994.

The outcome of this strategy, and the investment it required, was the launch of a fully-electronic trading system, Xetra, in 1997. By 2004 94 per cent of all transactions in Germany took place via the electronic trading system, Xetra. Following on from that success Deutsche Börse positioned itself to become the hub of a pan-European equity and derivatives market. Rolf Bruer stated in 1997 that 'In the Europe of the euro, there's no place and no need in the long term for 32 stock exchanges and 23 futures and options exchanges.'[103] That plan then took a new turn in 1998 as it became clear that the UK would not join the Euro, and that the LSE was willing to engage in some form of co-operation. By then those running the LSE had begun to accept that relying on Seaq and the presence of so many global banks in London would not deliver it control of the European equity market. From this stemmed the proposed link between the LSE and Deutsche Börse, both of which were using electronic trading systems designed by Andersen Consulting. That would not only deliver a prime position in the Eurozone to Deutsche Börse but also a way into the global stock market, via the LSE. Attractive as this concept was it proved impossible to implement in practice as disputes arose about the participation of other European exchanges and agreeing on such issues as ownership, trading technology, and common rules and regulations.

Though Deutsche Börse was pursuing the vertical-silo model, that was not to the exclusion of the horizontal-silo strategy, involving mergers with other exchanges. The expectation in 1999 was that the horizontal-silo model would triumph, as that was the preferred option of both EU regulators and the banks. The regulators regarded the vertical-silo as anti-competitive, because it made it difficult to generate competition between exchanges, while the banks relished the prospect of netting transactions through the use of a single counterparty, and so reducing the capital required to support trading. The vertical-silo model flew in the face of what banks, fund managers, and regulators wanted, as exemplified by the views of the European Securities Forum, which represented twenty-four of the world's biggest banks. In 2001 the chairman, Pen Kent, and the senior manager, Darren Fox, of the European Securities Forum, which represented twenty-four of the world's biggest banks, complained that the vertical-silo created 'local monopolies' that were 'used to capture transaction flow and keep costs high at the expense of users' and so stood in the way of a genuine pan-European capital market that could be at least as deep and liquid as the capital market in North America.'[104]

Sensing the direction of travel Deutsche Börse agreed in 1999 to merge its in-house clearing house with that operated by Cedel, the Luxembourg-based clearer of cross-border securities transactions owned by a consortium of over ninety banks and securities houses. The outcome was Clearstream. According to Vincent Boland in 2001, 'Despite its fifty per cent stake, Deutsche Börse appears to have little control over Clearstream.'[105] At that stage the expectation was that a European copy of the US's Depository Trust and Clearing Corporation (DTCC) would be created. As it became clear that it would not, Deutsche Börse reversed its position. Other European stock exchanges also embraced the vertical-silo model, such as those in Italy and Spain. The Borsa Italiana took over Monte Titoli, the agency responsible for settling transactions and, in 2001, its chief executive, Massimo Capuana, lauded the advantages of the vertical model: 'We have built up the technical

[103] Andrew Fisher, 'Bigger is better in bourses' brave euro world', 15th July 1997.
[104] Pen Kent and Darren Fox, 'Why providers should merge', 28th March 2001.
[105] Vincent Boland, 'Deutsche Börse puts sentiment on new issues market to the test', 2nd February 2001.

platforms to be able to offer virtually any kind of product investors want. We have our own clearing house, so our time to market can be rapid and our costs low.'[106]

With the conversion of Deutsche Börse into a publicly-listed company in 2001 it was in a position to purchase the 50 per cent of Clearstream it did not already own, which it did in 2002. By taking full control of Clearstream, and also Eurex, Deutsche Börse was able to offer users an integrated electronic platform for not only trading equities and derivatives but also processing the transactions. This was an attractive proposition to those financial institutions conducting a large and diversified business as it provided them with a single institution with which to deal rather than keeping track of multiple agencies. Using the vertical-silo model Werner Seifert was convinced that Deutsche Börse could become a global powerhouse in both equities and derivatives. However, he was also aware that there were limits to what could be achieved internationally from a Frankfurt base compared to London and so he made several attempts to acquire the LSE, but none were successful, leading to his eventual resignation, along with of Rolf Bruer. Despite the failure to acquire the LSE their legacy was to have made Deutsche Börse into the most successful exchange in Europe. Bettina Wassener wrote in 2002 that 'Under the leadership of Werner Seiffert, the (Deutsche) Börse has turned the Frankfurt Stock Exchange from a medium-sized operator into a highly-profitable international competitor that boasts state-of-the-art trading technology, such as the Xetra trading system.'[107] In 2003 Alex Skorecki referred to Deutsche Börse as 'arguably the most forward-looking aggressive and opportunistic exchange in the world'.[108] The following year Patrick Jenkins and Norma Cohen reported that it was Werner Seifert, who should be 'credited with the vision that has transformed what was once a sleepy regional stock exchange into an international securities trading platform'.[109] Norma Cohen explained in 2005 that 'He has transformed a provincial bourse into an international trading powerhouse. He foresaw technology's ability to cut costs, won back trading in key futures contracts and, through competition, forced the London International Financial Futures Exchange to join the modern world.'[110] Deutsche Börse combined equities and derivatives in an operation that fully integrated trading, clearing, and settlement. This made it very competitive in those products for which it provided a market.[111]

[106] Fred Kapner, 'Borsa to adopt a contrarian stance', 28th March 2001.

[107] Bettina Wassener, 'High hopes come down to earth', 25th November 2002.

[108] Alex Skorecki, 'Deutsche Börse mystery tests loyalty', 11th November 2003.

[109] Patrick Jenkins and Norma Cohen, 'A determined player', 18th December 2004.

[110] Norma Cohen, 'A chance to reform capital markets', 7th March 2005.

[111] David Waller, 'Germany takes stock', 7th May 1993; David Waller, 'Technology is the weapon against London', 1st July 1993; David Waller, 'Frankfurt's role consolidated', 31st May 1994; David Waller, 'Resisting the bait of equity ownership', 14th July 1994; David Waller, 'Resisting the bait of equity ownership', 14th July 1994; Andrew Fisher, 'Fewer bourses offer more for the investor', 10th May 1995; Andrew Fisher, 'New rules benefit Frankfurt', 17th May 1995; Andrew Fisher, 'German stock market seeks ambitious revamp', 1st June 1995; Andrew Fisher, 'The market that comes to you', 16th February 1996; Andrew Fisher, 'New era dawns in Germany', 28th February 1997; Andrew Fisher, 'Sights are set on overtaking Paris', 9th June 1997; Andrew Fisher and Andrew Jack, 'German, French bourses in link-up talks', 21st June 1997; Andrew Fisher, 'Bigger is better in bourses' brave euro world', 15th July 1997; Andrew Fisher, 'Frankfurt exchange adds new dimension', 28th November 1997; Andrew Fisher, 'Looking over borders', 24th March 1998; Michael Prest, 'Time for a new exchange', 24th March 1998; Andrew Fisher and Eric Frey, 'Frankfurt and Vienna SEs to co-operate', 6th April 1998; Simon Davies, 'Battle of the bourses', 14th May 1998; Barry Riley, 'Aim for bourse without borders', 18th May 1998; Simon Davies and George Graham, 'Europe's Big Bang', 8th July 1998; Andrew Fisher, 'London link offers way into top tier', 8th July 1998; Christopher Adams, 'Promise of greater liquidity welcomed', 8th July 1998; George Graham, 'Partnership must aim for common rules and systems', 8th July 1998; Simon Davies, 'Stock exchanges get down to details of European alliance', 9th July 1998; Simon Davies, 'Cost cuts fuel mergers', 17th July 1998; Edward Luce and Vincent Boland, 'Paris seethes at offer of second class berth', 18th July 1998; Vincent Boland and Simon Davies, 'Amsterdam SE chief seeks to join alliance', 30th July 1998; Joia Shillingford, 'The number of exchanges can only become smaller', 5th November 1998; Vincent Boland, 'Europe's exchanges meet to bolster alliance', 18th

December 1998; Uta Harnischfeger and Vincent Boland, 'Dispute hits London–Frankfurt link', 24th February 1999; Vincent Boland, 'Frankfurt and London put on a brave face', 1st March 1999; Vincent Boland, 'Milan joins bourses alliance', 12th March 1999; Vincent Boland, 'Super bourse takes place slowly', 23rd March 1999; Tony Barber, 'Börse's innovative chief strikes the right note', 23rd March 1999; Vincent Boland, 'Pan-European exchange moves closer', 5th May 1999; Vincent Boland, 'Race to save the superbourse speeds up', 7th June 1999; Edward Luce, 'Clearers settle on continent', 9th July 1999; Tony Barber, 'DBC strives for pivotal role', 9th July 1999; Edward Luce, 'LSE moves towards anonymous trading', 25th August 1999; Vincent Boland, 'Bourse alliance squabbles may delay trading harmonisation', 31st August 1999; Vincent Boland, 'Italian clearer seeks links', 14th September 1999; Vincent Boland, 'European exchanges divided on technology platform', 21st September 1999; Vincent Boland, 'Plan for single Europe bourse shelved', 24th September 1999; Geoffrey Nairn, 'Bourse rivalries overshadowed by single currency's arrival', 6th October 1999; Vincent Boland, 'London SE to change share trading', 6th October 1999; William Hall, 'Bold Vienna tries to shed its coy image', 27th October 1999; Edward Luce, 'Deutsche Börse may demutualise', 3rd December 1999; Tony Major, 'When good things come in small investors', 9th February 2000; Vincent Boland, 'Frankfurt pushes exchange link nearer break-up', 1st March 2000; Vincent Boland, 'Heat is on to create pan-regional market', 31st March 2000; Astrid Wendlandt, 'Fragments in need of piecing together', 31st March 2000; Tony Barber, 'Young guns take slice of the action', 31st March 2000; Vincent Boland and Tony Barber, 'Seifert draws close to the summit', 18th April 2000; Vincent Boland, 'Proposed exchange merger looks set for a rocky ride', 20th April 2000; Vincent Boland, 'LSE and Deutsche Börse clear merger obstacle', 22nd April 2000; Aline van Duyn, 'European clearers urged to merge', 20th June 2000; Astrid Wendlandt, 'Urgent need for consolidation', 14th July 2000; Tim Steele, 'Markets bent on shortening the cycle', 14th July 2000; Vincent Boland, 'Alliances heighten need for clearing unity', 20th July 2000; Aline van Duyn, 'Why closer links with Europe could lead to US costs', 1st September 2000; Patrick Jenkins, 'Commissions on German share deals to decline', 2nd September 2000; Aline van Duyn, 'Trading costs reach unacceptable levels', 8th September 2000; Vincent Boland, 'Collapse of exchange merger must not derail cost-cutting', 19th September 2000; Vincent Boland, 'Waiting time for groups with an eye on the LSE', 17th October 2000; Vincent Boland, 'LSE to go-it-alone for trading shares in Europe', 20th October 2000; John Reed, Robert Anderson and Kester Eddy, 'Unified trading faces battle to justify worth', 2nd November 2000; Alex Skorecki, 'Turnover on bourses hits record levels', 3rd January 2001; Bettina Wassener and Vincent Boland, 'Deutsche Börse chief awaits chance to test the market', 18th January 2001; Bettina Wassener, 'Driving ambition for a listed Deutsche Börse', 22nd January 2001; Vincent Boland and Bettina Wassener, 'LSE to select chief amid fears on rivals' IPOs', 23rd January 2001; Vincent Boland, 'Deutsche Börse puts sentiment on new issues market to the test', 2nd February 2001; Vincent Boland, 'European settlement systems under fire', 22nd March 2001; Vincent Boland, 'World's bourses look to find a new role', 28th March 2001; Vincent Boland, 'Progress of alliances is slow', 28th March 2001; Fred Kapner, 'Borsa to adopt a contrarian stance', 28th March 2001; Aline van Duyn, 'Hopes for unity are diminished', 28th March 2001; Pen Kent and Darren Fox, 'Why providers should merge', 28th March 2001; Vincent Boland, 'Progress of alliances is slow', 28th March 2001; Vincent Boland and Bettina Wassener, 'Deutsche Börse takes the cautious approach', 11th May 2001; Andrew Bolger, 'LSE poised to confirm float plans', 21st May 2001; Aline van Duyn and Bettina Wassener, 'Deutsche Börse in deal to boost US trading', 1st June 2001; Rick Butler, 'Where the rubber meets a regulatory road', 6th July 2001; Vincent Boland, 'Clearstream set for takeover battle', 31st October 2001; Daniel Dombey and Alex Skorecki, 'LSE reaches deal on Euroclear', 13th December 2001; Vincent Boland and Daniel Dombey, 'The changing face of Europe's markets', 2nd January 2002; Alex Skorecki, 'London Clearing House mulls link with Clearnet', 15th February 2002; Charles Pretzlik and Vincent Boland, 'LSE in new talks on merger', 26th April 2002; Vincent Boland, 'Trading Up', 27th May 2002; Alex Skorecki, 'Europe's bourse masters play game with no rules', 30th May 2002; Francesco Guerrera, 'Clearing the air after integration', 6th June 2002; Alex Skorecki, 'T+1 pipedream is close to reality', 6th June 2002; Alex Skorecki, 'Stock exchanges play for a winning position', 8th July 2002; Alex Skorecki, 'Happy end nears for a tale of two cities', 4th September 2002; Alex Skorecki, 'Waiting to play kingmaker', 31st October 2002; Bettina Wassener, 'High hopes come down to earth', 25th November 2002; Bertrand Benoit and Alex Skorecki, 'The market has been burnt badly... retail investing has been wiped out for a whole generation', 27th November 2002; Alex Skorecki, 'Deutsche Börse rejects calls for clearing reform', 28th May 2003; Bettina Wassener, 'Doing well in troubled times', 10th June 2003; Alex Skorecki and Paul J Davies, 'Clearing houses set for £800m marriage', 26th June 2003; Alex Skorecki, 'London explores alternatives', 26th June 2003; Alex Skorecki, 'European exchanges slash fees', 1st October 2003; Alex Skorecki, 'Deutsche Börse mystery tests loyalty', 11th November 2003; Alex Skorecki, 'Rivals vie for Amsterdam blue chips', 12th November 2003; Alex Skorecki, 'Vertical Expansion under fire', 20th January 2004; Alex Skorecki, 'Deutsche Börse softens its stance', 3rd March 2004; Alex Skorecki, 'Euronext plans to hit back at rival LSE', 20th March 2004; Alex Skorecki, 'Steps taken to tackle share trade barriers', 14th April 2004; Patrick Jenkins, 'Germany's exchanges fight for survival', 14th July 2004; Norma Cohen, 'Seeking an all-share formula to merge Europe's stock exchanges', 26th October 2004; Norma Cohen, 'Deutsche Börse chief's overture to the world', 8th November 2004; Norma Cohen, 'A compelling case for joining forces', 13th December 2004; Patrick Jenkins and Norma Cohen, 'Deutsche Börse courts LSE for European exchange union', 14th December 2004; Norma Cohen, 'Concerns over competition and governance', 14th December 2004; Patrick Jenkins, 'Another shot at his London prize', 14th December 2004; Norma Cohen, 'LSE a target for bid battle as it spurns Deutsche Börse', 14th December 2004; Norma Cohen, 'Exchange in competition spotlight', 15th December 2004; Patrick Jenkins and Norma Cohen, 'A determined player', 18th December 2004; Norma Cohen, 'LSE the key to European

Though the actions of the EU, in driving forward a single market and a single currency, did transform the European equities market between 1992 and 2007, it was a half-completed revolution. By failing to tackle underlying differences in regulations and taxes, or impose an integrated clearing and settlement system, the European equity market remained a fragmented one, comprising a series of separate national pools. In 2000 the judgement of Stephen Kingsley, from Arthur Andersen Consultants, was that, 'Whoever comes up with the pan-European trading platform with an integrated clearing and settlement system will be the winner in Europe.'[112] Such an institution never materialized even though Norma Cohen reported in 2004 that 'It is perhaps no exaggeration to conclude that inefficiencies in clearing and settlement represent the most important barrier to integrated financial markets in Europe.'[113] Under these circumstances, and despite its failure to grasp the opportunities open to it, it was only the LSE that operated on a global scale, competing with the NYSE and Nasdaq for international listings, whether on its main market or on AIM, which appealed to smaller and more speculative ventures. After the collapse of the dot.com bubble it was only AIM that survived among the specialist markets that European stock exchanges had created to service high-technology companies.[114]

domination', 10th January 2005; Norma Cohen, 'Frankfurt body faces post-trade services hurdle', 28th January 2005; Norma Cohen, 'A chance to reform capital markets', 7th March 2005; Deborah Hargreaves, 'Consolidation remains top of the agenda', 8th March 2005; Norma Cohen, 'Börse left rudderless at crucial moment', 10th May 2005; Patrick Jenkins, 'Visionary who fell foul of investors', 10th May 2005; Patrick Jenkins and Bettina Wassener, 'Wake-up call to corporate Germany', 10th May 2005; Patrick Jenkins and Norma Cohen, 'Seifert's downfall: how a shareholder revolt sent his plans for Deutsche Börse up in smoke', 25th May 2005; Norma Cohen and Patrick Jenkins, 'LSE suitors face bid constraints', 30th July 2005; Norma Cohen, 'Commission calls for end to European vertical silo model', 30th July 2005; Norma Cohen, 'Börse still in the running to buy LSE', 4th August 2005; Benn Steil, 'Europe's security markets need new plumbing', 11th August 2005; Tobias Buck, 'Dealing costs must be cut, says Brussels', 13th September 2005; Norma Cohen, 'Merger talks stall over Euronext, D Börse HQ', 12th January 2006; Tobias Buck and Norma Cohen, 'Call to break up exchanges', 20th February 2006; Patrick Jenkins and Norma Cohen, 'Bourses attack bank moves to upset trading structures', 21st February 2006; Patrick Jenkins and Norma Cohen, 'Bourses attack bank moves to upset trading structures', 21st February 2006; George Parker, Christine Mai, and Norma Cohen, 'EU issues deadline to exchanges on charges', 7th March 2006; Kurt Viermetz, 'No need to tinker with the integrated clearing model', 13th April 2006; Norma Cohen, 'Deutsche Börse woos Euronext', 12th May 2006; Norma Cohen, 'Euronext in state of flux over future', 17th May 2006; Norma Cohen, 'Rivals race to finalise bids for Euronext', 22nd May 2006; Ian Bickerton, 'Euronext takes its time to reflect on merger options', 24th May 2006; Gerrit Wiesmann, Richard Milne, and Andrew Wallmeyer, 'Deutsche Börse hints at sweeter Euronext offer', 25th May 2006; Tobias Buck, 'Competition absent in clearing: EU', 25th May 2006; Haig Simonian, 'Swiss look outside their borders', 25th May 2006; Richard Milne, Doug Cameron, and Anuj Gangahar, 'D Börse might be in danger of losing again', 3rd June 2006; Norma Cohen and John Authers, 'New Deutsche Börse bid to lure Euronext from NYSE', 20th June 2006; *FT* Reporters, 'Euronext snubs latest D Börse offer', 21st June 2006; Haig Simonian, 'SWX to plot its strategic options', 4th July 2006; Norma Cohen, 'EU securities code receives mixed review', 12th July 2006; Norma Cohen, 'NYSE pressed to beat D Börse', 30th August 2006; Norma Cohen, 'Swiss exchange to cut its tariffs', 4th September 2006; Norma Cohen, 'D Börse facing fresh calls to expose Eurex to competition', 15th September 2006; Norma Cohen, 'Borsa Italiana aims for pan-European exchange', 13th October 2006; Norma Cohen, 'Hopes recede for merger of European exchanges', 16th October 2006; Christopher Brown-Humes, 'Consolidation is fevered but all bets are still on', 28th November 2006; Mark Mulligan, 'Enviable BME prepares for next challenge', 21st June 2007.

[112] Vincent Boland, 'Heat is on to create pan-regional market', 31st March 2000.

[113] Norma Cohen, 'Exchange in competition spotlight', 15th December 2004.

[114] Richard Gourlay, 'Pan-Europe stock market planned', 16th November 1994; Andrew Hill, 'More sell-offs expected next year', 24th November 1994; Richard Gourlay and Christopher Price, 'Capital idea for the small investor', 17th June 1995; Andrew Jack, 'The French revolution', 16th February 1996; Christopher Price, 'LSE sets the pace', 17th May 1996; Christopher Price, 'Cool reception for new exchanges', 28th February 1997; Michael Morgan, 'Reforms boost Vienna', 28th February 1997; Andrew Fisher, 'Börse bonus', 4th March 1997; Peter Temple, 'Easdaq set for listings surge', 19th April 1997; Philip Coggan, 'Bourses fight for supremacy', 24th April 1997; Vincent Boland, 'Reforms promised', 14th May 1997; Christopher Price, 'Juniors gather strength', 30th May 1997; Simon Davies, 'Equity culture growing fast', 23rd January 1998; Vincent Boland, 'Easdaq's aim is to break down the barriers', 24th March 1998; Michael Smith, 'Core of growing influence', 31st March 1998; Andrew Fisher and Eric Frey, 'Frankfurt and Vienna SEs to co-operate', 6th April 1998; Paul Betts, 'Italian bourse plans new

In the wake of the dot.com bubble a new force was beginning to emerge that was also proving disruptive for all Europe's stock exchanges. This was trading located outside the traditional exchanges using the latest electronic technology to connect buyers and sellers and automatically match sales and purchases. Collectively these new systems were referred to as Electronic Communication Networks (ECNs) and had been developed from the late 1990s onwards in the USA. By 1999 they were attracting the interest of European-based banks and fund managers, according to Geoffrey Nairn, as they were 'increasingly frustrated at the failure to create a pan-European market in equities trading'.[115] Though these ECNs made little headway in Europe by 2006, compared to the USA, the threat they posed was forcing exchanges to respond. These alternative trading systems were cheap to set up and cheap to use, allowing them both to enter the industry and then undercut the exchanges. They could also offer large investors the anonymity they wanted as that meant they could complete their buying and selling without alerting competitors to their strategies and so secure better liquidity and lower bid-to-offer spreads. The threat was that these ECNs, either singly or collectively, would succeed in creating a pan-European equity market and so take trading away from the established exchanges, beginning with their most liquid stocks, as these were held internationally. The base of operation chosen by these ECNs was London which was a repeat of what had happened in the 1980s with the appearance of Seaq International. This time the ability of national stock exchanges to resist the advances made by these new electronic trading platforms were far weaker because of the removal of barriers driven forward by the European Commission. The one protection that remained was with those exchanges operating the vertical-silo model, especially if they had also diversified away from a dependence on the equity market by adding derivatives to their portfolio. This is what Deutsche Börse had done but not the LSE.[116]

segment', 26th June 1998; Katharine Campbell, 'Easdaq seeks new chief as rival threatens', 11th December 1998; Edward Luce, 'Emu to make Europe more like America', 18th December 1998; Vincent Boland, 'Euro.NM seeks London presence, but is uncertain about AIM', 8th January 1999; Sharmila Devi, 'Battle is on to acquire listings', 23rd March 1999; Vincent Boland, 'Exchanges broaden their global appeal', 11th June 1999; Arkady Ostrovsky, 'Securities leaders lift Easdaq', 30th July 1999; Robert Peston, 'Nasdaq plans European exchange', 5th November 1999; Vincent Boland, 'Nasdaq concentrates European minds', 8th November 1999; Tony Barber, 'Celebrations turn to sober reflection', 2nd December 1999; Edward Luce, 'Deutsche Börse may demutualise', 3rd December 1999; Sheila Jones, 'Manchester seeks virtual stock market for Europe', 26th January 2000; Philip Coggan, 'High-tech stock slide hits Europe', 16th March 2000; Alex Skorecki, 'Newcomers face reality as euphoria fades', 23rd March 2000; Bertrand Benoit, 'Steely nerves are an asset for investors', 22nd May 2000; Tim Bartz and Ina Bauer, 'Neuer Markt prepares for foreign influx', 31st July 2000; Bertrand Benoit, 'Tough lessons for the Neuer Markt', 4th October 2000; Alex Skorecki, 'Euro.NM alliance to cease by year-end', 5th October 2000; Bertrand Benoit, 'Testing times for a once solid market', 23rd October 2000; Samer Iskandar, 'Paris bids for Europe's crown', 10th November 2000; Florian Gimbel and Raphael Minder, 'Bleak outlook for high-growth sectors', 11th January 2001; Juliana Ratner, 'Nasdaq looks to strike deal with Easdaq', 31st January 2001; Rafael Behr, 'Beefing up for the battle of the Baltics', 8th March 2001; Bertrand Benoit, 'Frankfurt has muscle to upstage Brussels', 2nd April 2001; Vincent Boland, 'Nasdaq's lacklustre European launch leaves executives talking of long term', 16th July 2001; Joe Nagel, 'The Neuer Markt meltdown', 18th July 2001; Vincent Boland and John Labate, 'Sell, sell, sell as exchanges eye consolidation', 30th January 2002; Alex Skorecki, 'Italian market most liquid', 26th February 2002; Bertrand Benoit, 'Gloomy fifth birthday for ailing Neuer Markt', 8th March 2002; Vincent Boland, 'Trading Up', 27th May 2002; Bertrand Benoit and Alex Skorecki, 'The market has been burnt badly...retail investing has been wiped out for a whole generation', 27th November 2002; Fred Kapner, 'Nuovo Mercato enters blue-chip era', 14th October 2003; Rupini Bergstrom, 'OMX planning a rival to AIM', 6th October 2005; Patrick Jenkins and Norma Cohen, 'Timely decision to resurrect Deutsche Börse small-cap index', 18th October 2005; Patrick Jenkins, 'Germany's innovative streak', 28th March 2006; Mark Odell, 'Aim fatigue emerges on oil and gas', 4th January 2007.

115 Geoffrey Nairn, 'Bourse rivalries overshadowed by single currency's arrival', 6th October 1999.

116 Vincent Boland, 'Dealers opt for the alternative', 23rd March 1999; John Labate and Clay Harris, 'Fighting for a share', 26th May 1999; Vincent Boland, 'Race to save the superbourse speeds up', 7th June 1999; Edward Luce, 'Too many cooks', 30th July 1999; James Mackintosh, 'Electronic network planned to bypass stock

It was in the USA that the threat posed by these ECNs had first materialized, as they were a response to the conditions prevailing there. Though stock exchanges around the world were increasingly subject to global forces, developments in the USA largely responded to internal pressures. In 2001 the US stock market was almost half the world total, measured by market capitalization. In addition to the huge holdings of fund managers, around 85 million Americans owned stocks. With this vast domestic constituency to serve, US stock exchanges and their members naturally made it their focus, and they faced little competition from abroad. In the interests of investor protection the Securities and Exchange Commission made it difficult for foreign stock exchanges to enter the US market. In 2002 Vincent Boland wrote, 'For years the Securities and Exchange Commission has wrapped the US markets in a cocoon of regulatory protection to keep them safe from foreign competition.'[117] Secure in their command of the market in the stocks that they quoted, and experiencing a rising volume of trading, both the NYSE and Nasdaq resisted pressure for change, both in terms of the technology employed and their ownership structure. The NYSE dominated the market in the stocks of the largest companies while Nasdaq occupied a similar position for those in the high-technology sector, which was growing rapidly. Collectively, both Nasdaq and the NYSE were dominant within the US stock market, for trading gravitated to those exchanges that could offer the greatest depth and breadth, as that was what the increasingly dominant institutional investors wanted. By 2004 institutional investors accounted for around half of trading volume.

One aspect of the business done for institutional investors was programme trading in which multiple stocks were bought and sold collectively. By 2005 such trading accounted for 46 per cent of all transactions, by value, and was done at very low rates of commission. In addition, 28 per cent of all US equity trading in 2005 was a product of mathematical models that automatically generated the timing and size of orders, with the transactions completed at high speed in order to profit from small and temporary price fluctuations. This algorithmic trading favoured the liquid markets that the NYSE and Nasdaq could provide. As a consequence large regional exchanges, like the Chicago Stock Exchange, were losing the market in local stocks that had long sustained them. Even the New York-based stock exchange, Amex, was under pressure but it found salvation by providing a market for Exchange Traded Funds (ETFs) from 1993. ETFs were collective funds whose individual units were tradeable like shares. ETFs were popular among investors as they combined the

exchanges', 30th July 1999; Vincent Boland, '"Superbourse" faces competition', 23rd August 1999; Edward Luce, 'LSE moves towards anonymous trading', 25th August 1999; Vincent Boland, 'Bourse alliance squabbles may delay trading harmonisation', 31st August 1999; Vincent Boland, 'Bourses may face rival single system', 14th September 1999; Vincent Boland, 'European exchanges divided on technology platform', 21st September 1999; Vincent Boland, 'Deutsche and ABN in Tradepoint move', 24th September 1999; Edward Luce, 'A step towards a leaner forum for liquidity', 4th October 1999; Geoffrey Nairn, 'Bourse rivalries overshadowed by single currency's arrival', 6th October 1999; Vincent Boland, 'Frankfurt to seek global investor base', 7th December 1999; Vincent Boland, 'Heavyweights attracted by promise of anonymity', 31st March 2000; Tony Barber, 'Young guns take slice of the action', 31st March 2000; Alex Skorecki, 'London holds back from opening all hours', 20th April 2000; James Mackintosh, 'Watchdogs draft rules for new stock markets', 26th September 2000; Alex Skorecki, 'Stock exchanges play for a winning position', 8th July 2002; Francesco Guerrera, 'Brussels plans share trading shake-up', 27th September 2002; Francesco Guerrera and Vincent Boland, 'Pitfalls lurk in drawing up new trading rules', 28th September 2002; Bettina Wassener, 'Doing well in troubled times', 10th June 2003; Doris Grass, 'Stock exchanges attack proposed EU rule changes', 29th August 2003; Roger Blitz, 'City launches Brussels office to boost EU clout', 19th January 2004; Norma Cohen, Jeremy Grant and Andrei Postelnicu, 'Leading exchanges consider their moves in the race to consolidate', 11th March 2005; Päivi Munter, 'Italian Exchange aims to partner up', 10th August 2005.

117 Vincent Boland, 'Next step for Nasdaq marked by challenges', 19th December 2002.

higher returns of a long-term investment with the flexibility of holding a highly liquid asset. By 2001 $80bn had been invested in ETFs, and they accounted for around two-thirds of trading on Amex. Such was their success that they began to be quoted by the other US exchanges, including the NYSE.

Despite their dominance both Nasdaq and the NYSE faced increasing competition within the USA, reflecting their failure to keep pace with the technological change that was transforming trading. Market-makers continued to lie at the centre of Nasdaq's telephone-based trading system while the NYSE remained committed to its physical floor and the central role played by specialists. Aggregating transactions, through forcing them to go through market-makers or specialists, meant that the entirety of supply and demand was captured, producing transparent and reliable prices and a depth of liquidity that permitted large sales and purchases to be made. Maurice Greenberg, the chairman and chief executive of the insurance group AIG, a major trader in stocks, recognized in 2003 the importance of the role played by the specialist: 'The specialist's job is to buy shares when investors are selling and sell shares when investors are buying. By making a ready market he reduces unnecessary violent swings in prices that are detrimental to the interests of both buyers and sellers and undermine the confidence of the investing public.'[118] However, in his view the specialists were no longer able to perform this job because they lacked the capital required, even after mergers between them. Institutional investors the size of AIG possessed both the resources and the network to accomplish all that specialists could offer, and so resented having to use them when they bought and sold corporate stocks.

Greenberg was not alone in regarding the floor-based trading system of the NYSE, and the central role of specialists, as no longer fitted for the twenty-first century. In 2004 Alex Skorecki pointed out that, 'The NYSE, with its auction system in which specialists match buyers and sellers, looks anomalous in an increasingly electronic world.'[119] Reflecting the pressure on specialists by 2003 their numbers had dropped to seven compared to fifty in 1990. Of those that remained only one, Labranche, was independent, as the others had been acquired by the likes of Goldman Sachs and Bear Stearns. That merging of brokers and specialists caused conflicts of interest as it combined those acting for buyers and sellers, with a dealer performing the role of market intermediary. A similar situation was emerging with Nasdaq market-makers as they had to grow in size in order to act as secure counterparties. One that did was Knight Capital. By 2000 it accounted for around 9 per cent of the volume of trading in Nasdaq stocks. However, this also meant that these large market-makers were in a position to match bargains internally, especially when they became integrated into the large banking and broking businesses, as was increasingly the case. As a result both the NYSE and Nasdaq were losing market share to OTC trading, which also benefited from being subject to far fewer federal regulations and so operated with lower costs and greater flexibility. In 1993 around one-third of all turnover in NYSE-listed stocks already took place away from the floor. Several large brokerage houses, including members of the NYSE, operated an internal market in NYSE listed stocks, passing the business through regional stock exchanges to meet regulatory requirements.

Facilitating this competition with the NYSE was the nationwide clearing and settlement system in place in the USA, as this was available to all. This system became even more comprehensive in 1999 when the Depositary Trust Corporation merged with the National Securities Clearing Corporation to form the Depository Trust and Clearing Corporation

[118] Maurice Greenberg, 'Shake up the NYSE specialist system or drop it', 10th October 2003.
[119] Alex Skorecki, 'NYSE rivals focus on costs', 21st April 2004.

(DTCC). In 2004 Jill Considine, the chairman and chief executive of DTCC, explained the background to the centralization of the clearing and settling stock transactions in the USA, while leaving trading in the hands of individual exchanges:

> Over the years, as trading volumes grew and regional firms became national companies, traders began complaining about the need to maintain separate collateral accounts at each clearing and settlement organisation. Broker/dealer customers became tired of the costs resulting from the need to reconcile end-of-day balances with multiple clearing houses, each with different and often incompatible rules. There was a growing realisation that there was little opportunity to take advantage of the efficiencies and risk reduction that would result from multilateral netting.... It took three decades but in the end the broker/dealers and the banks got what they wanted—a highly-efficient clearing and settlement system to satisfy their needs, one that they themselves own and continue to oversee. Today, DTCC subsidiaries clear and settle nearly all US market transactions in equities and bonds, as well as clear trades in government and mortgage-backed securities. To clear and settle an equity trade in the US market now costs about 9 cents. Through multilateral netting, DTCC reduces by 97 per cent the total value of equity trade obligations that require financial settlement.[120]

What this meant was absence of vertical-silos in the US equity market, which had the potential to block the growth of alternative trading platforms.

Over the course of the 1990s a serious threat to Nasdaq and then the NYSE emerged from the development of Electronic Communication Networks (ECNs). Douglas Atkins, the chief executive of one of these, Instinet, explained in 1999 that 'ECNs are exploiting inefficiencies in the US market. Their success is a sign of how much catching up those exchanges have to do.'[121] ECNs operated as mini-exchanges, matching buy and sell orders for a minimal fee on their own networks. They developed in the 1990s first to handle small orders in which investors specified the upper and lower price limits between which they would deal. This was a business that broker/dealers or market-makers were not interested in. From that the ECNs moved on to marrying buyers with sellers in a split second for liquid stocks and less than a minute for less-actively traded stocks. One of the first ECNs was Instinet. By 1995 Instinet accounted for 13 per cent of trading in Nasdaq stocks. Other ECNs included Island and Archipelago. These ECNs had a major breakthrough in 1997, after a ruling by the SEC opened up the market in Nasdaq-listed stocks. This followed evidence that Nasdaq market-makers were colluding to maintain artificially-wide trading spreads. By 2003 ECNs accounted for 55 per cent of trading in Nasdaq listed stocks.

ECNs were blocked from providing a market in stocks listed by the NYSE prior to 1979, reflecting the protection extended by the SEC to established exchanges but not to Nasdaq. In 2001 Vincent Boland wrote that the SEC 'has a reputation for protecting the interests of established US exchanges.'[122] Matthew Andersen, the chief executive of Island, had gone further in 1999, stating that 'The NYSE is a monopoly.'[123] The success of these ECNs in Nasdaq-listed stocks, and the threat that they would do the same for NYSE-listed ones,

[120] Jill Considine, 'Let the customers decide on European clearing', 21st January 2004.
[121] Edward Luce and John Labate, 'The trading bell tolls', 26th July 1999.
[122] Vincent Boland, 'Securing a future', 5th March 2001.
[123] John Labate and Clay Harris, 'Fighting for a share', 26th May 1999.

forced both of these exchanges to consider embracing electronic trading technology. By 1999 Edward Luce and John Labate were of the opinion that:

> The New York Stock Exchange must do something radical to meet the competitive threat posed by new technology. With the rapid growth of electronic quasi-exchanges—or Electronic Communication Networks the NYSE has appeared increasingly antiquated over the past two years. From the ringing of the exchange floor bell at the start of trading every morning to the fact that the NYSE still quotes prices in fractions rather than decimals, it is hard to escape a sense of an institution from a bygone age.[124]

The rapid advance of a multiplicity of ECNs, numbering nine by 2000, drained liquidity from Nasdaq and the NYSE rendering them less competitive. In the face of this competition the NYSE and Nasdaq even discussed a merger in 2000 but that failed to materialize.

The degree of competition then intensified in 2002 when Archipelago, the Chicago-based ECN, founded by Jerry Putnam, and the San Francisco-based Pacific Stock Exchange, teamed up to create an electronic stock exchange. Stephen Phillips hailed it as 'the world's first fully automated exchange',[125] ignoring the advances made elsewhere in the world. Another ECN, Island, took a similar path to Archipelago, and linked up with the Cincinnati Stock Exchange. Through these links to established stock exchanges the ECNs gained access to the market in NYSE-listed stocks. Nevertheless, both Nasdaq and the NYSE continued to attract custom because each provided the largest pool of liquidity in the stocks that they quoted. As John Labate observed in 2002, 'Liquidity tends to follow liquidity' but he added that 'what traders want is faster and less expensive access to buyers and sellers on the other side'.[126] Nasdaq's market-makers and the NYSE's trading floor continued to offer a service that met the needs of most users. In 2002, for example, the NYSE floor continued to handle 80 per cent of the volume of trading in NYSE-listed stocks. As John Labate explained:

> Traditionally, the floor of the NYSE has been the place to have these large orders handled. Working for their trading clients, brokers on the floor are able to shop an order around the crowd of other floor-based brokers there, without revealing so many details about it that it sways the market. Many still prefer this method because of the high level of trust among the brokers. Supporters argue that such a system cannot be replicated by electronic means.[127]

However, as more trading flowed into the hands of the ECNs or was internalized within banks the threat to both Nasdaq and the NYSE, as centres of liquidity for the stocks that they listed, grew. Nasdaq was then hit by a downturn in trading volume in the wake of the collapse dot.com bubble, as that had focused on the high-technology stocks in which it specialized. Vincent Boland even raised the question in 2002 of whether, 'Does anybody in this post-bubble, post-technology investing climate need the Nasdaq any more, at least in its present form?'[128] In contrast, trading at the NYSE was more stable as investors bought

124 Edward Luce and John Labate, 'The trading bell tolls', 26th July 1999.
125 Stephen Phillips, 'System suppliers in a state of high flux', 3rd April 2002.
126 John Labate, 'High-tech systems jolt old markets into action', 6th June 2002.
127 John Labate, 'Terrorist threats a constant concern', 6th June 2002.
128 Vincent Boland, 'Next step for Nasdaq marked by challenges', 19th December 2002.

the stocks of the companies listed there for the income generated. Nevertheless, the failure of the NYSE to embrace the new electronic trading systems left it increasingly out of touch with market developments, as Jerry Putnam, the chairman and chief executive of Archipelago, observed in 2003: 'As technology has improved, the NYSE has distanced itself from change.'[129] There were even those who doubted whether there was still a role for the NYSE in the face of the market provided by the ECNs. One of these in 2003 was Edward Nicoll, the chief executive of Instinet: 'The New York Stock Exchange is such a powerful brand that people don't ask themselves if this model works. We have technology that allows people to trade directly with each other, so we can now have a completely open and transparent marketplace where everyone can have access. There is no reason in the world to have this marketplace any more.'[130]

Nevertheless, the NYSE continued to remain largely unchallenged in trading the stocks it quoted. John Reed, the interim chairman of the NYSE in 2003 attributed this success to the fact that it 'the world's largest, most liquid stock market and home to the biggest global companies.'[131] The NYSE also benefited from the ability of the specialists to post the best buying or selling prices most of the time, as that meant that business had to be directed to it, even though it could not match other venues in terms of timing, depth of market, certainty of execution, speed and cost. Under the rules of the SEC a sale or purchase had to be executed where the best price was quoted and that was usually the NYSE because it was the central marketplace. These prices could change after an order was placed with the result that the customer did not always end up with the best available price. In contrast, the price quoted by a bank or on an electronic communication network that matched orders automatically was firm. Despite this continued dominance of the market in NYSE-quoted stocks by 2004 it was becoming clear that major changes were required, as it could not rely on regulations to maintain its position. With the proposed introduction of the New Market System (RegNMS) regulations by the SEC in 2005 the NYSE was to lose its near monopoly of trading in the stocks it quoted. As William Donaldson, the chairman of the SEC, explained: 'The rule we (SEC) adopted, part of the regulation NMS reforms, is quite simple: when an investor sends an order to a market, the market can either execute the order at the best price then instantly available in the national market system or the market must send the order to the venue quoting the best price.'[132]

This new rule replaced the Intermarket Trading System (ITS) one, which had directed orders to the NYSE as specialists quoted the best prices in NYSE stocks. Anticipating the threat this change posed the NYSE's new chief executive, John Thain, who had a technology background and experience with Goldman Sachs, admitted in 2004 that 'I need to come up with what the role of the NYSE will be and where the industry is going because it can't stay the way it is.'[133] He was instrumental in pushing through a series of changes that repositioned the NYSE for a more competitive environment. In 2005 the NYSE took a quick step towards electronic trading by deciding to take over Archipelago, the largest of the ECNs. Nasdaq quickly followed the same track under the guidance of Robert Greifeld,

[129] Vincent Boland, 'Could a probe of trading practices trigger reform of the New York Stock Exchange?', 12th May 2003.

[130] Vincent Boland, 'Could a probe of trading practices trigger reform of the New York Stock Exchange?', 12th May 2003.

[131] Vincent Boland, Andrei Postelnicu, and Lionel Barber, 'I am a revolutionary. But we need a careful, deliberative process. There is only one New York Stock Exchange', 13th November 2003.

[132] William Donaldson, 'A simple new rule that gives investors priority', 8th April 2005.

[133] Andrei Postelnicu, Lionel Barber, and David Wighton, 'A great part of America: John Thain sets out to restore trust in the New York Stock Exchange', 2nd April 2004.

who also had a technology background, by buying Instinet, the second largest ECN. Accompanying this rapid embrace of electronic technology both Nasdaq and the NYSE also took the decision to become publicly-listed companies. In acquiring Archipelago the NYSE switched from a mutual organization controlled by the owners of its 1366 seats into a publicly-listed company. Such a move had been proposed back in 1999 but came to nothing at the time, before resurfacing in 2003. At the same time Nasdaq shed its ownership by the National Association of Securities Dealers (NASD), from which it had originated, and also became a company. However, the acquisition of Archipelago and Instinet did not remove the threat from ECNs as others took their place. Investment banks were rapidly developing 'dark pools' in which trading took place away from the 'light', and thus escaped public disclosure and other regulatory requirements. Traders were becoming acutely aware that even advertising an interest in buying or selling a particular share could move the market against them and raise the cost of trading. As a result, speed and anonymity in dealing rose in importance encouraging the diversion of trading into these 'dark pools' where bargains could be matched internally by the megabanks in a manner designed to limit both dealing costs and market impact costs. These dark pools were a threat to both NYSE and Nasdaq as the traditional hub of liquidity, as they provided an alternative mechanism to the trading floor minus many of the fees and costs. New electronic trading systems were set up. One was the Better Alternative Trading System (Bats) located in Kansas City and employing only twenty-one staff. In 2006 Larry Tabb, a financial technology consultant and head of the Tabb Group, summed up the position when he observed that, 'The biggest threat to the NYSE is that brokers are internalising more, and both external and internal crossing networks are gaining greater share.'[134]

The NYSE and Nasdaq had long enjoyed the network effects of an incumbent. The more who used the network the more useful it became to all users and so more joined creating a virtuous circle of high volume, wide choice, tighter spreads, and competitive prices. By removing transactions from the regulated exchanges these dark pools and electronic networks damaged the price discovery process as a smaller proportion of the buying and selling passed through the market provided by an exchange. No longer was being the centre of liquidity sufficient to make Nasdaq and the NYSE immune from competition as alternatives now existed. What advances in technology were doing was cutting out human intervention in the trading process. Trades were made automatically with algorithmic engines co-located within the exchange, so avoiding the time it took for pricing information to flow between the market and the investor. This reduced latency, or the delay between the receipt of the order and its completion. It was this world that both the NYSE and Nasdaq had to adapt to by 2006 if they were to survive.[135]

[134] John Authers and Anuj Gangahar, 'In-house clearing threat to NYSE', 9th August 2006.

[135] Laurie Morse, 'Chicago returns to its 19th century origins', 15th May 1993; Patrick Harverson, 'SEC study could bring equities trading shake-up', 15th June 1993; Richard Waters, 'The price of a share of the cake', 31st January 1994; Ronald Cohen, 'Special care for young companies', 8th March 1994; Maggie Urry, 'Nasdaq operator unveils proposals to calm critics', 22nd March 1995; Maggie Urry, 'SEC clears the final T+3 hurdle', 17th May 1995; Norma Cohen, 'NYSE reviews non-US share trading', 15th June 1995; Maggie Urry, 'Questions over youth's behaviour', 23rd August 1995; Maggie Urry, 'Trio battle for foreign issuers' favour', 1st February 1996; Maggie Urry, 'Success could bring extinction', 1st February 1996; Tracy Corrigan, 'Nasdaq's new regime', 13th January 1997; Tracy Corrigan, 'Daunting price but high rewards', 1st May 1997; John Plender, 'Stock market splits', 16th August 1997; Richard Lambert, 'Wider horizons beckon New York Exchange', 24th September 1997; Richard Waters, 'A share in Nasdaq's future', 22nd January 1998; Richard Waters, 'A tale of two trade cultures', 24th March 1998; Geoff Nairn, 'IT is still changing the face of trading', 24th March 1998; Geoffrey Nairn, 'Braced for big upheavals', 1st July 1998; Richard Waters, 'The view from Wall Street', 8th July 1998; Andrew Fisher, 'Exchanges set for a global shake-out', 13th January 1999; James Mackintosh, 'Global computer network may be a recipe for

disaster', 23rd March 1999; John Labate, 'Wall Street feels the tremors', 23rd March 1999; John Labate and Clay Harris, 'Fighting for a share', 26th May 1999; James Mackintosh, 'Bright lights, big City', 3rd July 1999; Edward Luce and John Labate, 'The trading bell tolls', 26th July 1999; Edward Luce, 'Hoist by their own petard', 20th September 1999; Christopher Price, 'Wider market's sideshow', 29th September 1999; Edward Luce and Vincent Boland, 'Nasdaq goes global', 6th November 1999; Vincent Boland, 'A share in the future', 18th January 2000; David Hale, 'Rebuilt by Wall Street', 25th January 2000; Sheila Jones, 'Manchester seeks virtual stock market for Europe', 26th January 2000; Simon Targett, 'Preparing for invasion by the Spider men', 3rd March 2000; John Labate, 'Wall Street takes a long, hard look at its (e-) future', 3rd March 2000; John Labate and Andrew Hill, 'Ringing the exchanges', 6th March 2000; John Labate, 'US plan for electronic exchange', 15th March 2000; Philip Coggan, 'High-tech stock slide hits Europe', 16th March 2000; Vincent Boland, 'World's bourses jostle for position as upstarts elbow in', 31st March 2000; Astrid Wendlandt, 'Fragments in need of piecing together', 31st March 2000; Astrid Wendlandt, 'Winner gets to rule the world', 31st March 2000; James Mackintosh, 'Old timers start to play catch-up', 31st March 2000; John Labate, 'Wall starts to crack as pressure intensifies', 31st March 2000; John Labate, 'Hoping to leapfrog the regulators', 31st March 2000; John Labate, 'Market visionary and architect of change', 31st March 2000; Simon Targett, 'Low-cost track for all indices', 5th May 2000; Elizabeth Wine, 'Mutual funds can breathe again as new threat recedes', 31st May 2000; Tim Steele, 'Markets bent on shortening the cycle', 14th July 2000; John Labate, 'NYSE costs lower than Nasdaq', 9th January 2001; John Labate, 'Nasdaq receives platform approval', 11th January 2001; Adrienne Roberts, 'IPE searching for technology partner', 11th January 2001; Bettina Wassener, 'Fed rate cut boosts call for extended trading', 17th January 2001; John Labate, 'Fragmented trading boosts their worth', 26th January 2001; Ian Orton, 'A small world may be a riskier home', 24th February 2001; Vincent Boland, 'Nasdaq-Easdaq negotiations to take weeks longer', 1st March 2001; Vincent Boland, 'Securing a future', 5th March 2001; Alex Skorecki, 'Banks form platform for short-sellers', 22nd March 2001; Vincent Boland, 'World's bourses look to find a new role', 28th March 2001; Vincent Boland, 'Progress of alliances is slow', 28th March 2001; John Labate, 'Master of the cautious, careful approach', 28th March 2001; John Labate, 'Seamless, smooth and secure', 28th March 2001; John Labate, 'NYSE poised for concerted push on ETFs', 12th July 2001; John Labate, 'Nasdaq falls in second quarter', 22nd August 2001; John Labate, 'Nasdaq faces challenge from smaller exchanges', 7th November 2001; Vincent Boland and John Labate, 'Sell, sell, sell as exchanges eye consolidation', 30th January 2002; John Labate, 'Instinet plan could deal a blow to Nasdaq', 13th February 2002; Stephen Phillips, 'System suppliers in a state of high flux', 3rd April 2002; John Labate, 'Selling Nasdaq's strengths to the market', 10th April 2002; Vincent Boland, 'Trading Up', 27th May 2002; Vincent Boland, 'US markets face up to technology gap', 6th June 2002; John Labate, 'Failure is not an option', 6th June 2002; John Labate, 'Terrorist threats a constant concern', 6th June 2002; Andrei Postelnicu, 'Invisible trades come under scrutiny', 6th June 2002; Andrei Postelnicu, 'Sprightly operator defies the market's gloom', 6th June 2002; John Labate, 'High-tech systems jolt old markets into action', 6th June 2002; Alex Skorecki, 'T+1 pipedream is close to reality', 6th June 2002; Alex Skorecki, 'Securities lending joins the internet age', 22nd October 2002; Alex Skorecki, 'Investors track down a hybrid source of income', 28th October 2002; Vincent Boland, 'Next step for Nasdaq marked by challenges', 19th December 2002; Andrei Postelnicu, 'A once endangered species still roams the floor', 17th April 2003; Charles Pretzlik, 'The financial revolution that never was', 9th May 2003; Vincent Boland, 'Could a probe of trading practices trigger reform of the New York Stock Exchange?', 12th May 2003; Andrei Postelnicu, 'A card game in which one player sees all the hands', 12th May 2003; Vincent Boland, 'Nasdaq halts IPO and pulls out of Europe', 27th June 2003; Vincent Boland and Alex Skorecki, 'Time called on 24-hour marketplace', 27th June 2003; Gary Silverman, 'NYSE chief's $139m deal rubs salt into the wounds', 29th August 2003; Vincent Boland and Andrei Postelnicu, 'Specialist firms hit by fall-out at NYSE', 26th September 2003; Maurice Greenberg, 'Shake up the NYSE specialist system or drop it', 10th October 2003; Elizabeth Wine, 'NYSE competitors step up reform calls', 20th October 2003; Alex Skorecki, 'Exchanges divided by more than time zones', 6th November 2003; John Gapper, 'The Big Board must end its costly costume drama', 11th November 2003; Vincent Boland, Andrei Postelnicu, and Lionel Barber, 'I am a revolutionary. But we need a careful, deliberative process. There is only one New York Stock Exchange', 13th November 2003; Vincent Boland and Jeremy Grant, 'Mergers likely amid exchange turmoil', 1st December 2003; David Wells, 'New NYSE chief seeks to restore a ring of confidence', 15th January 2004; Jill Considine, 'Let the customers decide on European clearing', 21st January 2004; Andrei Postelnicu, 'Fast market proposals might spell danger for NYSE traders', 24th February 2004; Andrei Postelnicu and David Wighton, 'NYSE members keep listing question afloat', 8th March 2004; Andrei Postelnicu, Lionel Barber, and David Wighton, 'A great part of America: John Thain sets out to restore trust in the New York Stock Exchange', 2nd April 2004; Alex Skorecki, 'NYSE rivals focus on costs', 21st April 2004; Jeremy Grant, 'CHX considers a partnership to boost volume', 19th May 2004; Alex Skorecki, 'LSE tries the smart order route', 25th May 2004; Jeremy Grant, 'Hedging with options in vogue as bourses decline', 27th May 2003; Jeremy Grant, 'Chicago enters electronic future', 10th August 2004; Andrei Postelnicu, 'Listing chief sets sights abroad', 23rd August 2004; Jeremy Grant, 'A single-product boutique is not the way: is one-stop shopping coming to US exchanges?', 14th September 2004; David Wighton and Andrei Postelnicu, 'UBS bets on exchange listing', 18th October 2004; Jeremy Grant, 'Archipelago ahead in race for early trades', 18th January 2005; Norma Cohen, Jeremy Grant, and Andrei Postelnicu, 'Leading exchanges consider their moves in the race to consolidate', 11th March 2005; William Donaldson, 'A simple new rule that gives investors priority', 8th April 2005; David Wells, David Wighton, and Andrei Postelnicu, 'Archipelago shares gain 60% on NYSE deal', 22nd April 2005; Norma Cohen, 'Europe to contend with stronger rival', 22nd April 2005; Jeremy Grant, 'Merger will bring mutual benefits', 22nd April 2005; David Wighton and Jeremy Grant, 'Thain forces pace of change to maintain market share', 22nd April 2005; David Wighton and David Wells, 'NYSE clients demand independent units', 28th April 2005;

Faced with an increasingly competitive domestic market both the NYSE and Nasdaq looked outward as a way of generating extra business. The NYSE had long attracted the largest multinationals through its ability to provide them with a highly liquid market for their stock. Nasdaq was also turning itself into the global market for high-technology stocks. What Nasdaq and the NYSE were playing on was the access to US investors that a foreign company acquired when it obtained a listing on a US stock exchange, because of the rigorous requirements they had met. As Dick Grasso, NYSE chairman, explained in 1995, 'US investors want to own the share in the currency but with the transparency, cost, liquidity and depth of the US market.'[136] From this developed an attempt by both Nasdaq and the NYSE to develop global stock markets under their own control, in the belief that investors wanted to be able to trade stocks on a 24-hour basis. Initially this took the form of alliances as Frank Zarb, the chairman of Nasdaq, explained in 2000: 'With hubs in the US, Japan and Europe, investors would have unlimited access to nearly every kind of stock in every kind of market.'[137] In response the NYSE developed a global alliance of ten exchanges, aimed at creating a single trading platform, one set of trading rules, and clearing through one central counterparty. Richard Grasso, the chairman of the NYSE, explained the plan in 2000: 'These partners are going to work to create a platform to allow equities trading to

John Gapper, 'Stock exchanges go peer-to-peer', 28th April 2005; Kate Burgess and Andrei Postelnicu, 'Why Aim is foreign target of choice', 3rd September 2005; John Authers and Andrei Postelnicu, 'NYSE members vote for merger', 7th December 2005; Norma Cohen, 'LSE's secret software weapon meets traders' need for speed', 24th February 2006; John Authers, 'NYSE plans to diversify after Archipelago merger finalised', 6th March 2006; Jennifer Hughes and John Authers, 'Taking the floor: how a screen role will challenge New York's market debutant', 7th March 2006; John Authers, 'Merging Nasdaq with the LSE makes real strategic sense and creates deep liquidity', 11th March 2006; Jennifer Hughes, 'Jury out on NYSE trade plan', 24th March 2006; Peter Weinberg, 'How London can close the gap on Wall Street', 30th March 2006; Anuj Gangahar, 'Seismic shift looms for trading', 21st April 2006; Anuj Gangahar, 'Exchanges wait on new rules', 5th May 2006; Norma Cohen and John Authers, 'NYSE stock offering lifts exchanges', 6th May 2006; John Authers and Anuj Gangahar, 'Euronext integration no bar to success', 23rd May 2006; John Authers, 'Wall Street's mergermeister', 27th May 2006; Doug Cameron, 'NYSE pulls rug from under Chicago Mercantile's feet', 30th May 2006; Anuj Gangahar, 'Fund managers do their maths', 31st May 2006; Doug Cameron and Anuj Gangahar, 'Banks plan to take CHX minority stake', 22nd June 2006; Anuj Gangahar, 'Chairman of the Amex gains focus', 6th July 2006; Paul J. Davies, 'A brouhaha over best execution', 18th July 2006; John Authers and Anuj Gangahar, 'In-house clearing threat to NYSE', 9th August 2006; Norma Cohen, 'Nasdaq's market share of NYSE stocks soars', 16th August 2006; Norma Cohen and John Authers, 'Nasdaq prepares for price war if NYSE cuts tariffs', 21st August 2006; Norma Cohen, 'NYSE pressed to beat D Börse', 30th August 2006; Norma Cohen, 'SWX reduces its Virt-x trading fees', 5th September 2006; John Authers and Norma Cohen, 'Clearing the floor: how a regulatory overhaul is helping rivals to close in on the Big Board', 14th September 2006; Anuj Gangahar, 'Nanoseconds matter as traders prepare for a shake-up', 14th September 2006; Anuj Gangahar, 'Nasdaq's man of action', 16th October 2006; Jeremy Grant, 'SEC set to relax margin rules in move to cut trading costs', 16th October 2006; Sarah Underwood, 'IT evolution meeting demand for speed, efficiency and accuracy', 16th October 2006; Anuj Gangahar, 'Banks begin to dip into "dark pools"', 19th October 2006; David Turner and Norma Cohen, 'Nomura to buy broker Instinet', 3rd November 2006; Jeremy Grant, 'Self-regulation to oversee US broker-dealers', 11th November 2006; Norma Cohen, 'Goldman to begin off-exchange trades', 13th November 2006; Gillian Tett, 'Déjà vu as markets face new challenge', 16th November 2006; Anuj Gangahar, 'Europe banks mirror US trading strategy', 17th November 2006; Norma Cohen, 'Nasdaq's hunter sees an end to the chase', 21st November 2006; Norma Cohen, 'A clash of titans: why big banks are wading into the stock exchange fray', 24th November 2006; David Wighton, 'Nasdaq's marathon man', 25th November 2006; Anuj Gangahar, 'Threat of duopoly increases pools of dark liquidity', 28th November 2006; Anuj Gangahar, 'Volumes increase by the month', 28th November 2006; Norma Cohen, 'Level playing fields', 28th November 2006; Norma Cohen, 'Headlong scramble for speed', 28th November 2006; James Blitz, 'Stamp Duty on non-resident exchange traded funds to go', 30th November 2006; Saskia Scholtes, 'Atlantic divide over e-trading', 5th December 2006; Norma Cohen, 'Shareholders sceptical about LSE proposals', 20th December 2006; Steve Johnson, 'eBay for portfolio trades debuts', 4th June 2007; Deborah Brewster, 'US retail investors slump to record low', 2nd September 2008; John Authers and Michael Mackenzie, 'Technology endures in spite of Nasdaq fall', 10th March 2010.

[136] Norma Cohen, 'NYSE reviews non-US share trading', 15th June 1995.

[137] John Labate and Vincent Boland, 'Nasdaq attempts to lure London exchange', 17th December 2000.

follow the sun. The idea is that each of the partners will retain their brands and lists [of stocks] and then plug into the global partnership.'[138] As each stock exchange continued to protect its domestic market from competition, the NYSE's global alliance failed to deliver an integrated global equity market. For Nasdaq it was the bursting of the dot.com bubble that destroyed the global ambitions as investor interest in high-technology stocks evaporated around the world. Nasdaq closed down its Japanese hub in 2002 and its European one in 2003. Instead, both returned to a reliance on the pulling power of their US operations to attract multinational companies and global fund managers

However, that pulling power was badly dented by the passage of the Sarbanes–Oxley Act in 2002, in response to the Enron scandal. This had the effect of making the USA an increasingly difficult place for foreign companies to obtain and then maintain a listing because of the regulatory burden, despite the attractions of the depth and breadth of the US equity market. Chris Hughes and Norma Cohen noted in 2006 that 'the rising tide of shareholder lawsuits against directors of US-listed companies has deterred international companies from seeking New York listings. Sarbanes–Oxley regulation has added further cost and hassle to listing in the US.'[139] With the prospect of attracting new listings from abroad greatly reduced because of the regulatory burden now in place, and increasing domestic competition coming from ECNs, especially after the introduction of RegNMS, both Nasdaq and the NYSE looked to acquire foreign stock exchanges. Such acquisitions had the potential to generate higher profits in less competitive markets while also providing a base to be used to attract foreign listings, beyond the reach of US regulators. The prime target for both the NYSE and Nasdaq was the LSE but it proved to be an increasingly expensive catch as it was also the target of both Deutsche Börse and Euronext. Desperate to complete an international deal so as to compete with each other internationally, and not to overpay for the LSE when its future value was uncertain because of the threat of ECNs, in 2006 the NYSE bought the Paris-based Euronext and Nasdaq acquired the Stockholm-based OMX. With these acquisitions both were better positioned to compete for international listings especially as the legal risks and costs involved in a US listing could be avoided through a European one.

The Euronext acquisition also gave the NYSE control over a derivatives exchange in the shape of the London-based Liffe. What it did not do was produce an integrated global market for equities, as Larry Tabb noted 'The consolidation of the NYSE and Euronext will not directly either increase or reduce liquidity.'[140] The markets controlled by each exchange remained separate, divided by legal and currency barriers. Instead, both acquisitions were a product of the regulatory climate in the USA as Harvey Pitt, who had been chairman of the SEC from 2001 to 2003, reflected in 2006. In his opinion Sarbanes–Oxley's 'one-size-fits-all approach to regulation stifles innovation, creativity, risk-taking and competitiveness'. The outcome was that, 'Confronted with the prospect of declining relevance in a global economy, US exchanges have sought to acquire foreign exchanges.'[141] As with developments within the USA itself, the international strategy being pursued by both Nasdaq and the NYSE were driven by domestic considerations, whether it was to be better able to compete with each other or the evade the regulatory straightjacket imposed upon them.[142]

[138] Aline van Duyn, Bayan Rahman, and John Labate, 'Ten exchanges plan global market', 8th June 2000.

[139] Chris Hughes and Norma Cohen, 'Loss of light touch poses threat to LSE', 14th June 2006.

[140] John Authers and Norma Cohen, 'Exchange merger poses question of liquidity', 19th June 2006.

[141] Harvey Pitt, 'Sarbanes–Oxley is an unhealthy export', 21st June 2006.

[142] Norma Cohen, 'NYSE reviews non-US share trading', 15th June 1995; Richard Lambert, 'Wider horizons beckon New York Exchange', 24th September 1997; Jonathan Wheatley, Ken Warn and Mark Mulligan, 'Latin

Conclusion

The years between 1992 and 2007 witnessed a transformation of the global equity market. Borne along by a wave of privatizations and the activities of megabanks and global fund

American brokers face home truths on local problems', 3rd March 2000; Astrid Wendlandt, 'Winner gets to rule the world', 31st March 2000; Edward Alden, 'Fierce struggle with the giant next door', 31st March 2000; Bayan Rahman, 'Disclosure and liquidity will be key', 31st March 2000; Vincent Boland and John Labate, 'UK and Germany consider Nasdaq deal', 28th April 2000; Khozem Merchant, 'Straight on for global market', 5th May 2000; David Ibison, 'Market feels effects of uncertainty', 5th May 2000; William Hall, 'Global shares face a long uphill battle', 31st May 2000; Aline van Duyn and John Labate, 'GEM and iX choose different paths', 8th June 2000; Aline van Duyn, Bayan Rahman and John Labate, 'Ten exchanges plan global market', 8th June 2000; Virginia Marsh, 'Australia, NZ consider stock exchange deal', 15th August 2000; Aline van Duyn and Charles Pretzlik, 'Deutsche Börse ready to defend merger with LSE', 28th August 2000; Aline van Duyn, John Labate and Virginia Marsh, 'Bid may reignite interest from other bourses', 28th August 2000; John Plender, 'Exchange values', 3rd September 2000; Vincent Boland, 'Selling the appliance of alliance', 11th November 2000; John Labate and Vincent Boland, 'Nasdaq attempts to lure London exchange', 17th December 2000; Vincent Boland, 'Nasdaq-Easdaq negotiations to take weeks longer', 1st March 2001; Geoff Dyer, 'Drive for liquidity continues', 19th March 2001; Vincent Boland, 'World's bourses look to find a new role', 28th March 2001; John Labate, 'Master of the cautious, careful approach', 28th March 2001; Richard Lapper and Mark Mulligan, 'Picture continues to darken', 28th March 2001; John Labate and Aline van Duyn, 'Nasdaq dispels any doubts over its European ambitions', 31st March 2001; Aline van Duyn and Bettina Wassener, 'Deutsche Börse in deal to boost US trading', 1st June 2001; John Labate and Joseph Leahy, 'Trading system is set to start pilot scheme', 8th June 2001; Charles Pretzlik and Vincent Boland, 'LSE in new talks on merger', 26th April 2002; Charles Pretzlik and Alex Skorecki, 'LSE plays down US merger talk', 24th May 2002; Vincent Boland, 'Trading Up', 27th May 2002; Vincent Boland, 'US markets face up to technology gap', 6th June 2002; Joseph Leahy, 'Thirst grows for capital pools', 6th June 2002; Vincent Boland, 'Nasdaq falls foul of bear market', 9th August 2002; Jane Croft, 'Brokers talk up the positive', 22nd November 2002; Vincent Boland, 'Nasdaq halts IPO and pulls out of Europe', 27th June 2003; Vincent Boland and Alex Skorecki, 'Time called on 24-hour marketplace', 27th June 2003; Andrei Postelnicu, 'A little breathing space', 7th July 2003; Andrei Postelnicu, 'Listing chief sets sights abroad', 23rd August 2004; Kate Burgess and Andrei Postelnicu, 'Why Aim is foreign target of choice', 3rd September 2005; Francesco Guerrera and Andrei Postelnicu, 'A not so foreign exchange: China shuns the west as a location for its big corporate share offers', 18th November 2005; Stephen Fidler, 'How the Square Mile defeated the prophets of doom', 10th December 2005; Tony Tassell, 'Smaller centres offer a more exotic allure', 1st March 2006; Norma Cohen, 'Nasdaq bids £2.4bn for LSE', 11th March 2006; John Authers, 'Merging Nasdaq with the LSE makes real strategic sense and creates deep liquidity', 11th March 2006; Peter Weinberg, 'How London can close the gap on Wall Street', 30th March 2006; David Blackwell, 'Scattering of seedlings turns into a forest', 30th March 2006; Norma Cohen and Ben White, 'LSE remains a bid target for stateside suitors', 31st March 2006; Norma Cohen, 'LSE awaits new suitor as Nasdaq pulls bid', 31st March 2006; Norma Cohen, 'Euronext risks investor wrath', 4th April 2006; David Turner, 'Tokyo exchange chief seeks tie-up with foreign bourse', 8th April 2006; Francesco Guerrera, 'Outsiders are eager to take the spoils', 12th April 2006; Kate Burgess, John Authers, Norma Cohen, and Patrick Jenkins, 'End of the phoney war as global consolidation nears', 13th April 2006; Norma Cohen and John Authers, 'Nasdaq increases LSE stake to 18.7%', 4th May 2006; Norma Cohen, 'UK stockbrokers seek clarification from Nasdaq', 12th May 2006; David Wighton, 'Selling the attractions of Euronext', 22nd May 2006; Norma Cohen and Doug Cameron, 'Participants get ready for realignment', 22nd May 2006; Ian Bickerton, 'Euronext takes its time to reflect on merger options', 24th May 2006; John Authers, 'Wall Street's mergermeister', 27th May 2006; Richard Milne, Doug Cameron and Anuj Gangahar, 'D Börse might be in danger of losing again', 3rd June 2006; Norma Cohen, 'LSE shrugs off threat to listings', 5th June 2006; Jeremy Grant, 'Regulators face uncharted waters if deal goes ahead', 9th June 2006; Chris Hughes and Norma Cohen, 'Loss of light touch poses threat to LSE', 14th June 2006; Jeremy Grant, 'Hurdles appear in the race for exchange consolidation', 15th June 2006; Norma Cohen, John Authers and Jeremy Grant, 'NYSE says it could set up London exchange', 19th June 2006; John Authers and Norma Cohen, 'Exchange merger poses question of liquidity', 19th June 2006; Chris Hughes and Norma Cohen, 'Thain is attracted by all the right things in London', 20th June 2006; Harvey Pitt, 'Sarbanes–Oxley is an unhealthy export', 21st June 2006; Norma Cohen, 'NYSE pressed to beat D Börse', 30th August 2006; Norma Cohen, 'SWX reduces its Virt-x trading fees', 5th September 2006; Norma Cohen, Lina Saigol and Neil Hume, 'Nasdaq in early talks to acquire OMX', 11th September 2006; John Authers and Norma Cohen, 'Clearing the floor: how a regulatory overhaul is helping rivals to close in on the Big Board', 14th September 2006; David Blackwell, 'Junior market must learn to play by the new rules', 2nd October 2006; Malini Guha and Anuj Gangahar, 'Accelerating flow from US', 10th October 2006; Norma Cohen, 'Funds hint at price for LSE deal', 11th October 2006; Norma Cohen, 'LSE scorns final Nasdaq bid', 21st November 2006; Christopher Brown-Humes, 'Consolidation is fevered but all bets are still on', 28th November 2006; Anuj Gangahar, 'Sox effect hits US exchanges', 28th November 2006; Norma Cohen, 'Nasdaq goes back on the offensive', 13th December 2006; Norma Cohen, 'Shareholders sceptical about LSE proposals', 20th December 2006; Francesco Guerrera and John Authers, 'Institutions increase equity stakes', 22nd January 2007; Gillian Tett and Anuj Gangahar, 'Deals on dark pools set to surge', 31st January 2007.

managers international investment in equities boomed. Though the collapse of the dot.com boom around 2000 did provide a setback it was only a brief one and the expansion of the 1990s then resumed. What did not result from this transformation of the global equity market was the emergence of a single pool of liquidity. This had proved an elusive goal in the 1980s and remained so in 2006. Instead, what existed were unique pools of liquidity confined to specific corporate stocks, and this continued to fragment the global equity market. Liquidity was a chicken-and-egg problem. Investors did not want to buy shares in a company that traded infrequently while companies did not want to list on an illiquid market. This hindered the development of stock markets where liquidity was absent and benefited those where it was plentiful. Despite the emergence of national stock markets all around the world few possessed the depth and breadth to provide the liquidity that attracted investors to corporate stocks or persuaded those running businesses to issue shares. In contrast, there were a few stock markets located in a small number of global financial centres that were liquid and it was these that attracted those companies aspiring to become multinational enterprises.

Though the development of the global equity market made an impact everywhere the pace and extent of change was not uniform as can be seen in what happened to stock exchanges. Though the technology of trading was being revolutionized, destroying the immunity from competition that had once existed, some stock exchanges were in a position to resist its consequences, sheltering behind institutional walls and national barriers. That was the case in most countries of the world including both Japan and the USA. Where the ability to resist change was weakest was in Europe, especially within the European Union. There the drive towards a single market in financial services, the removal of barriers between national states, and the introduction of a single currency for most nation-states made it impossible for stock exchanges to protect themselves against competition. A number embraced the challenge, converting themselves into either multiproduct or multicountry exchanges far removed from the national institutions they had been in the past. The ultimate achievement was the emergence of a number of global exchanges by 2006, in the race to create the first global, 24-hour a day trading platform. Demutualization had made such a prospect possible as exchanges were now in a position to either merge or mount takeover bids. The need to finance the technology required for sophisticated trading systems, including constant updates, was also encouraging exchanges to contemplate mergers across borders as that would provide the scale required to support the investment. However, considerable doubt existed over whether they delivered anything above being the sum of their parts. By then the whole question of what contribution exchanges made to the operation of the equity market was open to question. With megabanks able to internalize transactions or trade between themselves, and electronic communication networks replicating the facilities of an exchange but without the costs and restrictions, there appeared to be little justification for the institutions that had once dominated stock markets around the world. Even their role as regulatory bodies was usurped by state-appointed agencies that were better able to cope with a world populated by megabanks, global fund managers, and multiproduct, multicountry institutions.

12

Regulation and Regulators, 1993–2006

Introduction

By the 1990s the combination of internal deregulation and globalization led to a spectacular growth in the value of financial transactions both inside countries and across borders. There was a commensurate increase in pressure on payment and settlement systems to cope with the huge volume and variety of transactions. All this was of concern to those who regulated financial systems around the world. As Richard Lapper pointed out in 1995, 'The international integration of financial markets, prompted by deregulation and liberalisation, has increased the danger of systemic breakdown: the risk that the failure of one bank or securities house will trigger the collapse of others.'[1] To Laurie Morse in 1996 the task facing those attempting to regulate the rapidly-growing use of derivatives was immense. In her words, 'Trying to put a regulatory safety net around the global derivatives market is akin to trying to catch rain water in a sieve.'[2] The speed and extent of the changes taking place, assisted by the advances made in the technology of communication and data handling, forced regulators to search for new ways of coping with the consequences, as the methods of the past were becoming inadequate. Globalization meant that national boundaries could no longer define the parameters within which financial systems operated, as all became integrated into international flows of short-term money and long-term finance. In 2000 one financial regulator, David Clementi at the Bank of England, posed the dilemma faced by all by then: 'In a world where a German trader can trade on an exchange in London with a counterparty in the US who uses a French technology provider and a Belgian settlement agent, the question of how to ensure that all parts of the process are regulated effectively is a tough one.'[3] Jeremy Grant made a virtually identical point in 2006: 'How do regulators oversee markets whose customers are in multiple time zones and whose trading platforms operate in cyberspace?'[4]

The complexities arose not only from the process of globalization and technological change but also from the disappearance of the barriers that had long separated different components within national financial systems. Rather than serving separate communities banks and financial markets increasingly competed with each other. Within banking itself the distinctive role of particular types of banks was disappearing as all competed to attract savers and borrowers. This blurring of distinctions was recognized by regulators but they found it difficult to produce a response, and certainly one that met the wishes of all the different parties involved. There was a general acceptance among regulators that the forces of globalization and convergence had to be met with new solutions. All understood the risks inherent in both banks and markets and the destabilizing effects of a crisis of

[1] Richard Lapper, 'Regulators aim to gird the globe', 10th July 1995.
[2] Laurie Morse, 'Crisis control proves difficult', 22nd November 1996.
[3] Vincent Boland, 'Tentative steps towards greater accountability', 28th June 2000.
[4] Jeremy Grant, 'Flat out: why regulators are rushing to keep up with mergers by exchanges', 13th July 2006.

Banks, Exchanges, and Regulators: Global Financial Markets from the 1970s. Ranald Michie, Oxford University Press (2021).

DOI: 10.1093/oso/9780199553730.003.0012

confidence. Attractive as calls were to force a return to a simpler era of finance they ignored the fundamental forces at work, which had destroyed the effectiveness of previous regulatory systems. Instead, it was recognized that new ways of regulating the financial systems had to be found that matched the changes that were taking place. This was the expectation from those engaged in financial services. In 1993 Dirk Hazell, secretary-general of one trade association, the International Primary Market Association (IPMA), explained their thinking: 'Regulators' objectives, one of which must be to permit the markets to work efficiently, are more likely to be achieved if regulators work with the grain of the market and having consulted leading practitioners, than if rules are suddenly imposed from an ivory tower, in this case their practical application may well prove uncertain.'[5] Similarly, Nick Weinreb, head of regulation at the pan-European exchange operator, Euronext, stated that, 'It is not practical or realistic to expect that an exchange operating on a global basis can operate without co-operation between regulators.'[6] Similarly, Peter Reits, an executive board member at the derivatives exchange, Eurex, took the view that 'We are operating in a global environment and we want to have, as an ideal, an identical regulatory regime.'[7]

One regulator who recognized the reality of the new situation, and the need to work with those in the industry in devising solutions, was the vastly experienced economist and banker, Alexandre Lamfalussy. He was tasked by the European Union to make recommendations for reforming securities market regulation. His verdict in 2000 was that such reforms were beyond him and other regulators without the active participation of those engaged in finance: 'Things are changing so fast that if you do not have the appropriate and continuous input from the market practitioners you will not get anywhere.'[8] To him effective regulation could only emerge through regulators engaging with the financial system not imposing rules from outside. There was also a response to the changing situation within the financial sector itself, which had a long tradition of successful self-regulation. The International Secondary Market Association (ISMA) introduced in the 1990s a Global Master Repurchase Agreement. This was adopted in thirty-five separate jurisdictions and brought a degree of standardization to the repo market, where banks lent and borrowed from each other on the basis of agreed terms and collateral. The rapidly growing derivatives market also devised a means through which banks could protect themselves against the risks they were now running, such as the default of a major borrower. US banks increasingly used a form of insurance called Credit Default Swaps (CDS). CDSs allowed a bank to cover its exposure to a particular customer by swapping some of it with another bank, accepting in return part of their exposure to different customers. Between 2001 and 2006 the total notional volume of credit default swaps outstanding rose from $631bn to $34,500bn in 2006, driven by the increasing use of credit derivatives by banks to remove risk from their balance sheets and so comply with the new Basel 2 capital-adequacy rules.

Complicating the task of regulators were the policies followed by national governments, as they intervened in both the structure and operation of banks and financial markets. As John Langton, chief executive of the International Secondary Market Association (ISMA) noted in 1993, 'Market forces cannot be resisted indefinitely. Markets smell unsustainable financial policies pretty quickly.'[9] National governments imposed limits upon what

[5] Brian Bollen, 'Nightmare for harmonisers', 28th October 1993.

[6] Jeremy Grant, 'Flat out: why regulators are rushing to keep up with mergers by exchanges', 13th July 2006.

[7] Jeremy Grant, 'Flat out: why regulators are rushing to keep up with mergers by exchanges', 13th July 2006.

[8] Peter Norman and Deborah Hargreaves, 'Long haul for Lamfalussy on securities markets' regulation', 28th December 2000.

[9] Brian Bollen, 'Nightmare for harmonisers', 28th October 1993.

regulators could achieve or set unrealistic goals that could never be met. To Francesco Guerrera in 2006 'Cack-handed regulations' helped explain the failure of Shanghai to emerge as an international financial centre.[10] The resulting rules and regulations national governments imposed influenced financial activity around the world. 'Too much regulation could drive activity offshore. Too little could open up scope for abuse' was how Peter Thal Larsen put it in 2006.[11] The differences between the attitude of the Financial Services Authority (FSA) in the UK and the Securities and Exchange Commission (SEC) in USA were considered to have played a major part in the drift of business away from New York and towards London, especially after the Sarbanes–Oxley Act in the USA in 2002. Chris Hughes and Norma Cohen judged that by 2006, 'The FSA's light-touch regulatory regime is widely regarded as a source of competitive advantage for the LSE in persuading overseas companies to list in London. By contrast, the rising tide of shareholder lawsuits against directors of US-listed companies has deterred international companies from seeking New York listings. Sarbanes–Oxley regulation has added further cost and hassle to listing in the US.'[12] One who supported this assessment was Alan Yarrow, vice-chairman of the German investment bank, Dresdner Kleinwort Wasserstein. In 2006 he claimed that the FSA, compared to the SEC 'has a completely different philosophical approach to regulation. It is moving towards a principles-based regime, while the US relies heavily on compliance with specific detailed rules. The FSA tells you what you can't do and, as long as you operate within certain principles, you can do what you want and innovate.'[13] In contrast, the SEC told businesses what they could do and expected compliance.

The difficulty faced by regulators was how to balance the demands created by globalization with domestic considerations, especially calls for intervention in the aftermath of a crisis or scandal. Reuben Jeffrey, the chairman of the Commodity Futures Trading Commission (CFTC) in the USA, spoke about this dilemma in 2006: 'One of the things we want to strive to do is not prevent globalisation of these markets or jeopardise the competitive position of US exchanges, which are core constituencies of ours.'[14] The solution the CFTC adopted was to hold back on intervention. In contrast, Christopher Cox, the chairman of the SEC, wanted to impose uniform regulations on the world: 'Harm to investors will be minimised if we agree to adhere to high-quality securities regulation and there is a strong degree of co-operation and co-ordination among regulators.'[15] The divergent approaches from the SEC and the CFTC in the USA reflected the lack of unanimity among regulators around the world on how to respond to the challenges they faced. National regulators had also to cope with the contradictory policies of their own governments. Governments wanted a financial system that was simultaneously competitive and stable. A more competitive financial system delivered efficiency gains and better served its users, which contributed to economic growth. However, the greater the degree of competition the more participants were tempted to evade regulations that hampered their ability to do business, and so gain an advantage over rivals. As Annette Nazareth, the director of the US's Securities and Exchange Commission's (SEC) market regulation division stated in 2004, 'One of the problems is that competition is so fierce that it creates an environment where people look the

[10] Francesco Guerrera, 'Top dog at home but needs to appeal abroad', 12th April 2006.
[11] Peter Thal Larsen, 'Action may be needed to maintain competitive advantage', 26th March 2006.
[12] Chris Hughes and Norma Cohen, 'Loss of light touch poses threat to LSE', 14th June 2006.
[13] Chris Hughes and Norma Cohen, 'Loss of light touch poses threat to LSE', 14th June 2006.
[14] Jeremy Grant, 'Flat out: why regulators are rushing to keep up with mergers by exchanges', 13th July 2006.
[15] Jeremy Grant, 'Flat out: why regulators are rushing to keep up with mergers by exchanges', 13th July 2006.

other way on regulatory issues.'[16] Under these circumstances the level of risk-taking grew, with consequences for the stability of the financial system. Conversely, if the priority among regulators was delivering stability then constraints were placed on competition so as to dampen down risk-oriented behaviour. However, a less competitive financial system was likely to deliver lower returns to savers, force borrowers to pay more for loans, and limit the supply of funds. As John Plender reflected in 2000, 'The privileges granted to banks in an allegedly over-cosy relationship with government and regulators go far beyond what is needed for systemic soundness.'[17]

The ideal was a balance between competition and stability but that was always difficult to achieve and then maintain. Tracy Corrigan noted in 1994 that 'The risk regulators face is that the rapid evolution of the world's financial markets may have created a potentially dangerous cocktail of aggressive traders, speculative investors, and highly-complex financial instruments which users might not fully understand.'[18] Pauline Skypala made a similar judgement in 2003: 'The risks of mis-selling are increasing as banks and other financial companies battle for market share.'[19] In the years before the Global Financial Crisis of 2008 regulators were aware of the risks emerging from a financial system in flux and were looking for solutions within the parameters set by national governments. They were also conscious that whatever they came up with would contain flaws. Speaking philosophically in 1997, after a long career as a lawyer, a regulator and a banker, Lord Alexander observed that 'to seek perfection in a regulatory system is illusory'.[20] Nevertheless, various approaches to achieving regulatory perfection were made through the 1990s and in the years before the beginnings of the crisis in 2007.[21]

An obvious way forward, and one recommended by many, was greater co-operation between national regulators as this would both cope with the effects of globalization and spread best practice. The problem faced by regulators as expressed in 2005 by Sir Callum McCarthy, chairman of the UK's financial regulator, the Financial Services Authority (FSA), was that 'Most regulation is rooted in national legislation. But the business of large firms is increasingly complex and global.'[22] International co-operation was the preferred option of both the SEC and CFTC, concerned that their unilateral actions would place US financial markets at a disadvantage. Desirable as international co-operation was it was difficult to achieve. Each country's financial system was the product of long-established national characteristics and shaped by a unique set of circumstances. Vincent Boland recognized this reality in 2003 when he observed that 'Capital markets have a veneer of seamlessness

[16] Jeremy Grant, 'Traders consider their options', 27th April 2004.
[17] John Plender, 'Too close for comfort', 21st March 2000.
[18] Tracy Corrigan, 'On trial for dangerous dealing', 21st March 1994.
[19] Pauline Skypala, 'Pressure on banks raising risk to buyers', 26th September 2003.
[20] Lord Alexander, 'Bring it all under one roof', 28th February 1997.
[21] Brian Bollen, 'Nightmare for harmonisers', 28th October 1993; Tracy Corrigan, 'On trial for dangerous dealing', 21st March 1994; Richard Lapper, 'Regulators aim to gird the globe', 10th July 1995; Laurie Morse, 'Crisis control proves difficult', 22nd November 1996; Lord Alexander, 'Bring it all under one roof', 28th February 1997; John Plender, 'Too close for comfort', 21st March 2000; Peter Norman and Deborah Hargreaves, 'Long haul for Lamfalussy on securities markets' regulation', 28th December 2000; Pauline Skypala, 'Pressure on banks raising risk to buyers', 26th September 2003; Jeremy Grant, 'Traders consider their options', 27th April 2004; Peter Thal Larsen, 'Action may be needed to maintain competitive advantage', 26th March 2006; Francesco Guerrera, 'Top dog at home but needs to appeal abroad', 12th April 2006; Chris Hughes and Norma Cohen, 'Loss of light touch poses threat to LSE', 14th June 2006; Vincent Boland, 'Tentative steps towards greater accountability', 28th June 2000; Jeremy Grant, 'Flat out: why regulators are rushing to keep up with mergers by exchanges', 13th July 2006; Gillian Tett, 'Swaps soar as investors pile in', 28th May 2007.
[22] Sir Callum McCarthy, 'Europe's financial regulators must exploit existing ties', 22nd August 2005.

that masks different methods of operation, regulatory frameworks and legal norms.'[23] These differences made it impossible to agree a common regulatory framework for the global financial system, or even specific parts of it, let alone the establishment of anything akin to a global super-regulator. Even establishing the jurisdiction of national supervisors was no easy matter at a time when transnational businesses were developing rapidly. Jurisdiction could be allocated according to where a financial institution's head office was located, be delegated to the national authority of the host country, or be vested with an international agency.

For banks the question of jurisdiction threw up the issue of who was the ultimate liquidity provider in the case of a crisis. As banks were the most vulnerable to both liquidity and solvency crises, and posed the highest systemic risk, it was there that the focus of regulators was greatest. The furthest the world got towards the global regulation of financial activity were the actions agreed among national banking regulators, as co-ordinated by the Basel-based Bank for International Settlement (BIS) and its committee of bank supervisors. The outcome was agreed rules and regulations covering different aspects of a bank's operations. Banks were already heavily regulated at the national level and were subjected to stringent capital requirements under these Basel rules. Philip Manchester, writing in 2002, observed that 'banks and financial institutions are obliged to prove they are financially fit enough to meet their liabilities'.[24] However, the supervision of banks, even at the national level, had become increasingly complicated as they adopted a more diversified structure during the 1990s. In 1998, Christine Mandell, at Bank of America in New York, posed the question of 'who's an investment bank these days? It can be very difficult to distinguish.'[25] The changing nature of banking, with the boundaries between different types proving increasingly fluid, posed a serious challenge to banking regulators. Their response then made a significant contribution to the structure and operation of banks, including their relationship to financial markets. Wrapped up in this was the shift from the lend-and-hold model of banking to the originate-and-distribute one.

Banking and Regulation

Even before the 1990s international co-ordination had already attempted to impose a degree of uniformity on banks, under the set of Basel Rules dating from 1988. These were designed to reduce the exposure of banks to a liquidity crisis. The rules set banks target requirements for the capital they had to set aside for particular categories of loans. They were rolled out during the 1990s. Over time the increasing reliance placed upon the Basel Rules had the effect of increasing not decreasing the level of risk that a bank was exposed to. George Graham picked up on this in 1999 when he reported that there were signs that the Basel Rules had 'started to destabilise the global financial system by giving banks perverse incentives to make riskier loans'.[26] In 2003 Avinash Persaud, an expert on international finance, stated that a complete overhaul of the Basel Rules was required: 'We need regulation that focuses more on avoiding market failures; that is simpler, and so easier to

[23] Vincent Boland, 'Enthusiasm is growing for direct access in US and European securities markets', 24th May 2003.
[24] Philip Manchester, 'An aid to better investment decisions', 5th June 2002.
[25] Simon Kuper, 'Old divide is starting to crumble', 23rd January 1998.
[26] George Graham, 'Weighing up the risks', 4th June 1999.

enforce; and that serves the global economy better.'[27] The rules were revised leading to new guidelines, called Basel 2, which took effect from December 2006 onwards. These gave banks more discretion when assessing the risks involved when making each loan rather than applying a formula-driven approach. The need for such a revision exposed the weakness of any rule-based system that attempted to apply a uniform model to the business of making loans, regardless of timing and circumstances, especially when banking was in state of flux. The imposition of these rules encouraged banks to take the attitude that, as long as they were complied with, regulators were satisfied, and so banks could continue with an existing strategy in the belief that the risks they were taking were acceptable. This formula-driven approach replaced the discretionary behaviour of bankers using their knowledge, training, and experience to assess each situation based on its individual merits. However, faith in the Basel Rules had been reinforced as they had come through one test unscathed. No major banks had failed after the collapse of the speculative dot.com boom. However, by 2004 warning signs were emerging which were picked up on by Sir Andrew Large, who was at the time responsible for financial stability at the Bank of England: 'In the present benign environment, there is a possibility that lenders, borrowers and investors may be inclined to underestimate long-run vulnerabilities and take on too much risk.'[28] Despite these warning signs banks around the world continued to expand their lending based on following the Basel rules.

The way that banks did business changed in response to the Basel Rules. This was the switch from the lend-and-hold model of banking to the originate-and-distribute one. Instead of a bank making a loan, which it retained until maturity, loans were repackaged as securities, which were sold to investors, so releasing funds that could be re-lent and so the cycle could be repeated. Under the Basel Rules lower risk was attached to assets that were transferable unlike long-term loans that were not. This encouraged banks to offload the most risky loans by repackaging them as securities, which were then sold to investors, attracted by the combination of yield and transferability. Another response by banks was to make better use of the funds that they had to retain to meet withdrawals and redemptions. These could be channelled to investment vehicles that promised to pay high rates of interest for short-term funds as they used them to purchase the securitized assets. In this way banks shifted some of their own risks onto others, so satisfying the requirements of the Basel Rules. One group of investment vehicles that blossomed as result of the strategy being pursued by banks were hedge funds. These were active traders who used short-term funds obtained from banks to move aggressively and rapidly in and out of markets, generating high returns in the process. Between 1992 and 2005 the assets controlled by hedge funds rose from $100bn to $1,000bn. By 2004 the size and operations of hedge funds, and their connections to banks, were beginning to alarm bank regulators such as Timothy Geithner, President of the Federal Reserve of New York: 'It is the combination of the capacity for leverage, the complexity in assessing the risks they present, together with their apparent importance in many markets, that makes hedge funds an important focus of attention from a systemic perspective.'[29]

Though there were emerging concerns that the exposure of banks to hedge funds could cause problems, there was also increasing confidence that banks themselves were more resilient than they had ever been because of the switch to the originate-and-distribute

[27] Avinash Persaud, 'The Basel plan must get back to market basics', 3rd September 2003.
[28] Jane Croft and Scheherazade Daneshkhu, 'Bank warns on risks of property lending', 13th December 2004.
[29] Kate Burgess, 'Regulators test hedge funds' formula', 11th March 2005.

model. Writing in 2000 the US economist, Stephen Cecchetti, was one of those who took this view: 'Instead of transforming deposits into loans, and retaining substantial risk on their balance sheets, banks are increasingly acting simply as brokers with a much closer match between the risk characteristics of their assets and liabilities. As a result, the US financial system is much less likely to suffer disruptions brought on by bank failures than it was even five years ago.'[30] Though pioneered in the USA this originate-and-distribute model of banking was spreading worldwide, under the influence of the Basel Rules. European banks, for example, were turning to the repo market for inter-bank lending and borrowing, in which transactions took place on a secured basis.

Banks used the repo market to lend out bonds in exchange for cash to balance their books at the end of each day. The volume of trading in the European repo market tripled between 2001 and 2006, overtaking that of the US repo market. This sharp rise in trading had been fuelled by changes in the capital-adequacy ratios that banks had to abide by under Basel 2. Those meant that European banks had to carry more capital to cover unsecured loans than for secured loans, such as repo finance, as that used securities as collateral. In turn, that encouraged the conversion of loans into securitized assets as these could be used for collateral.

It was the promise that the assets provided as collateral could be easily and quickly transferred that made the repo market a safer way to conduct inter-bank lending and borrowing compared to unsecured loans between banks. However, risks remained if this promise of transferability evaporated, as was always a possibility in any market. In the case of many bonds and securitized assets the market lacked both depth and breadth making it likely that in a crisis sales would become impossible. The markets in which these securitized assets traded were largely unregulated, suffered from a lack of price transparency, and often depended upon a single counterparty. The most liquid of these markets was that for US Treasury bonds where $1,900bn was traded daily in 2006. However, even here the US Treasury was sufficiently concerned that it could break down that it discussed with market participants in 2006 what could be done to prevent that happening. One solution suggested was that a lender-of-last-resort facility would be provided. What this reflected was the degree to which the risks once largely associated with banks had spread out into the wider financial system. This then posed a threat to banks that relied on these markets to balance their assets and liabilities and cover their exposure to sudden defaults, withdrawals, and redemptions.

For these reasons there remained some who were not convinced that the changes that had taken place had made banks safer. One of these was Martin Wolf, the influential columnist at *FT*. In a 1998 article entitled 'Why banks are dangerous' he stated that 'The days of banks that offered everything to everyone should end. The price they impose is not worth paying.'[31] However, his solution was a return to the compartmentalized world of the past, which flew in the face of all that happened since the 1970s. He recommended that universal banks should be split up, being replaced by two types of bank. One would accept deposits from savers, manage the payment system, restrict its lending to short-term loans and invest only in safe liquid assets. That would leave the rest of the banking business to be handled by others. In many ways this was an attempt to replicate the structure of banking that had emerged in Britain in the late nineteenth century and been imposed in the USA with the Glass–Steagall Act. However, both the UK and US banking systems had been

30 Stephen Cecchetti, 'A legal challenge for Europe's markets', 17th August 2000.

31 Martin Wolf, 'Why banks are dangerous', 6th January 1998.

forced to adapt to the radically-changed circumstances experienced in the late twentieth century. In 1986 the compartmentalization of the British financial system was brought to an end while in 1999 the Glass–Steagall Act was repealed in the USA under the Gramm–Leach–Bliley Act. This Act swept away the remaining divisions between commercial and investment banking dating from the inter-war years. Reflecting the convergence of financial activity within financial institutions in the USA in 2006, the Bond Market Association and the Securities Industry Association merged to form the Securities Industry and Financial Markets Association. As Micah Green, president of the Bond Market Association, commented at the time, 'Even just three years ago the markets hadn't converged as much as they have now, and geographical boundaries were higher. The differences between types of firms was more distinct and now they are almost identical.' What did not follow was a single regulator in the USA. The Federal Reserve regulated the commercial banks, as they were regarded as systemically important being deposit-taking institutions, but did not cover the Wall Street investment banks, which were left with the SEC. This was despite the fact that each was moving into the others' territory.

Outside the USA an alternative approach to regulation was to merge individual regulators into a single national agency. By 2005 the number of countries with unified national regulators for financial services had risen to thirty-eight, or almost double the twenty in 2000. These included Japan, Singapore, Taiwan, Ireland, Hungary, Bulgaria, and several Scandinavian countries. In 2002 Germany created a new unified regulatory authority because, there, as in other countries, the growth of financial conglomerates had reached a stage where separate regulatory authorities could no longer cope. Among the first of the countries to adopt this approach was the UK. In 1997 the chairman of the NatWest Bank, Lord Alexander, had advocated the advantages of bringing all financial regulation under the control of a single body covering both wholesale and retail activities, seeing it as an improvement over the fragmented system under the control of the Securities and Investment Board (SIB), dating from 1986:

> The system created by the Financial Services Act ten years ago was designed to achieve statutory backing for regulation but to ensure that practitioners continued to be fully involved.... This separation of responsibilities creates inefficiencies...More fundamentally, the body setting the standards cannot drive through the implementation...that is why what is needed is for SIB to become the single regulatory body—but one with the capacity to deal differently in regulating wholesale and retail activities. Wholesale activities need a comparatively light regulatory touch because they are dealings between professionals. Retail activities need much more demanding supervision, and should carry a much greater obligation of disclosure and explanation.[32]

In 1997 the UK established the Financial Services Authority (FSA). The FSA was given responsibility for regulating Britain's entire financial sector, including the banking system, which had previously been left with the Bank of England.

It was this inclusion of deposit-taking banks within the coverage of the FSA that led to the strong opposition in the UK to a unified regulator, and explains why many countries, including the USA, chose not to go down this route. In developing regulatory agencies in the 1990s the Chinese authorities introduced one for financial markets, the China Securities

[32] Lord Alexander, 'Bring it all under one roof', 28th February 1997.

Regulation Commission, and one for banks, the China Banking Regulatory Commission. This recognized the distinctions between the two central components of the financial system. In the UK as early as 1993, when the possibility of a unified regulator was no more than a plan, Robin Leigh-Pemberton, who had been Governor of the Bank of England, between 1983 and 1993, having previously chaired one of Britain's largest banks, the NatWest, expressed his opposition, 'I understand the arguments for hiving off. And there have been moments when I've been sorely tempted to say the Bank would be better off to be relieved of this very difficult function. But my opinion still remains that on balance it is best that supervision is carried out in the central bank.' He believed that the Bank of England needed to 'remain very close to the banking industry, partly in order to better work its market operations but chiefly also to have its finger on the pulse for lender-of-last-resort functions'.[33] Expressing the views of the trade body, the British Bankers' Association, in 1995 Sir Nicholas Goodison, an ex-chairman of the London Stock Exchange but now a banker, warned that 'there was a very close nexus' between preserving the stability of the financial system and supervising banks, and that 'There is a colossal value in those two parts being in one institution.'[34] What bankers focused on was the link between the supervision of the banking system and the role played by the Bank of England as lender of last resort. It was its role as supervisor that gave the Bank of England the insight required to both anticipate an emerging liquidity crisis and intervene to prevent it destabilizing the entire system. However, those concerns were ignored. The supervision of banks was placed in the hands of the FSA, with responsibility to act as lender of last resort being shared by the Bank of England, the FSA, and the UK Treasury.

This division of responsibility remained a concern to those connected with British banking but was alleviated during the time that Eddie George was governor. On his appointment in 1993 it was reported by Peter Norman and Richard Lambert that 'Achieving stability is Mr George's prime policy goal.'[35] On his retirement in 2003 he was described by Ed Crooks as, 'One of the most successful governors in the Bank's history... a pillar of composure in crises such as Black Wednesday or the collapse of Barings.'[36] Sir Brian Williamson, chairman of Liffe, added that Eddie George had a 'genuine feel for how markets worked and what they could deliver',[37] but believed this was not widely shared at the Bank of England by the time he was replaced as governor by Mervyn King. Mervyn King's background was not banking but academia, being a monetary economist. With his appointment the Bank of England switched its focus from financial to monetary stability. In 2005 Scheherazade Daneshkhu and Chris Giles reported that Mervyn King 'is adamant that the most important thing the bank does is monetary policy'. They considered that 'Mr King, who has served most of his time on the monetary policy side, has found defining the job of financial stability most difficult.'[38] That year the Bank of England replaced the experienced banker, Sir Andrew Large, with the ex-civil servant, Sir John Gieve, as the person with responsibility for financial stability, while cutting back the resources it devoted to monitoring and assessing the risks being run by banks. The Bank of England did try to reassure the banks that it was well prepared to act as lender of last resort in the event of a crisis. Chris Giles reported this reassurance in 2005, 'If the country is ever engulfed in a crisis, such as

[33] Peter Norman, 'Highs and lows of a dizzy decade', 23rd June 1993.
[34] John Gapper, 'Bankers support role of Old Lady', 25th July 1995.
[35] Peter Norman and Richard Lambert, 'A steady hand at the tiller', 1st July 1993.
[36] Ed Crooks, 'Bank owes much to the loyalty of "Steady Eddie"', 28th June 2003.
[37] Ed Crooks, 'Bank owes much to the loyalty of "Steady Eddie"', 28th June 2003.
[38] Scheherazade Daneshkhu and Chris Giles, 'King acts to avoid nightmare scenario', 17th January 2005.

the collapse of an important financial institution... the Bank's role will be to respond quickly, in partnership with the Treasury and the Financial Services Authority'. Nevertheless, he remained sceptical: 'Tests earlier this year produced some worrying results. People were not sure who to talk to or where to go. After repeated tests, Sir Andrew Large, the Deputy Governor being replaced by Sir John Gieve, was more confident that the authorities could cope.'[39] Sir Andrew Large provided further reassurance in his resignation letter to the chancellor, when he stated that 'We have put in place operational arrangements between the tripartite authorities and with the private sector to deal with crises if they were to occur.'[40]

However, these doubts lingered into 2006 as many felt that the FSA neglected banking supervision, and lacked the resources to carry it out. According to one British banker interviewed by James Mackintosh, the FSA regarded banking supervision as no more than 'filling in forms and ticking boxes'.[41] Overwhelmed with the increasing volume and variety of supervision it was expected to carry out the FSA focused on retail financial services, prioritizing the protection of individual savers and investors, while leaving the wholesale business to the large banks confident that they could police themselves. When created in 1997 the FSA was a ten-way merger of agencies overseeing banks, insurers, building societies, independent financial advisers, and the stock exchange. That alone gave it 12,000 separate businesses to cover, which was extended to 50,000 in 2004. The effect was to leave the British banking system largely free of supervision, and the potential lender of last resort, the Bank of England, largely disconnected from the banks to which it would have to provide with support in a crisis. This was a serious weakness given the role played by the City of London at the heart of the global inter-bank money markets.

This policy shift by the Bank of England to focus on monetary policy rather than financial stability was not an isolated one but reflected a change in emphasis around the world. John Plender pointed out in 1999 that the newly-established European Central Bank (ECB) 'has been given a mandate to focus almost exclusively on monetary policy, with only a limited peripheral role in banking supervision and no responsibility for providing liquidity support to individual banks. There is no central provider or co-ordinator of emergency liquidity in the event of a crisis.'[42] Increasingly, the need for any central bank to act as lender of last resort was being questioned, leaving them free to abandon a direct role in banking supervision and so concentrate on implementing the government's monetary policy. In 1993 Robert Peston was still of the view that 'no central bank can afford to be completely divorced from supervision. As the lender of last resort, it needs to be kept abreast of the health of commercial banks. Its monetary policy role also requires it to be confident that the payment system is sound.'[43] By 2000 John Plender was speaking in the past tense when he reflected that 'All debate on regulation in banking is coloured by the notion that banks are "special". Their vulnerability to contagious runs on deposits means no one dares contemplate a number of banks being forced to close for fear of disruption to the wider economic and financial system.'[44] He was one, among many, who doubted whether banks continued to occupy a special position within the financial system. In 1996, Peter Cooke, an international expert on banking supervision, had even suggested that 'Bigger banks than

[39] Chris Giles, 'Old Lady forced to adapt as world has grown more complex and risky', 18th October 2005.
[40] Chris Giles, 'Old Lady forced to adapt as world has grown more complex and risky', 18th October 2005.
[41] James Mackintosh, 'Financial police prepare for a firmer hand', 6th July 2001.
[42] John Plender, 'Crisis in the making', 12th April 1999.
[43] Robert Peston, 'The risks of regulating', 25th January 1993.
[44] John Plender, 'Too close for comfort', 21st March 2000.

before can probably be allowed to fail than in earlier days', though he warned that 'it is quite another matter to say that the international financial marketplace can tolerate a major meltdown'.[45] As banks replaced the lend-and-hold model of operation with the originate-and-distribute one they lost their apparent vulnerability to liquidity crises, caused by the mismatch between assets and liabilities. It was this situation that had justified the need to combine the close supervision of the banking system with the role of a lender of last resort, as the central bank was required to intervene to prevent a bank failing if it faced a liquidity crisis. If banks were no longer exposed to a liquidity crisis then they could be regulated along with all other components of a financial system.

Acting as lender of last resort had always posed a dilemma for central bankers because it raised the issue of moral hazard. Moral hazard arose when the actions taken to save a bank from failure encouraged behaviour that increased the probability of future failures. In 1993 Robert Peston provided an extreme example: 'If no bank were allowed to fail, depositors would not have to take into account the soundness of a bank before deciding where to place funds, and bank executives would feel under less pressure to manage their businesses prudently'.[46] The problem a central bank faced was distinguishing between a liquidity crisis, when intervention was justified, and a solvency one, when it was not. In a classic liquidity crisis a bank held assets that exceeded its liabilities but was short of the cash to meet withdrawals. If it was allowed to collapse those holding deposits in all banks could take fright and all rush to withdraw their funds, leading to a systemic crisis as the banking system operated on the basis of a mismatch between the liquidity of assets compared to liabilities. By acting as lender of last resort the central bank supplied the cash required to cover the temporary shortfall and so not only saved the particular bank from collapse but also avoided a systemic crisis. Conversely, a bank facing a solvency crisis was one in which liabilities exceeded assets, making it insolvent, which could be the result of excessive risk-taking in the pursuit of profit resulting in losses when borrowers subsequently defaulted. Under these circumstances intervention to save a bank from failure was not justified as it would encourage excessive risk-taking in the future and so increase the likelihood of failure. The problem arose in distinguishing between a liquidity and a solvency crisis as only with hindsight did it emerge what the true situation was, because of the difficulty in placing a value on outstanding loans by estimating the probability of repayment. Making such a distinction was a matter of judgement and had to be done quickly so as to prevent a rush of withdrawals from all banks.

As the network of connections grew and the volume of transactions expanded central banks were increasingly aware that the failure of a major bank could result in multiple subsequent failures leading to a global systemic liquidity crisis. The solution devised in the 1990s was the introduction of real time gross settlement systems, which would eliminate the risks generated from the constant borrowing and lending that took place between banks. This had worked well in the foreign exchange market and was applied more generally to inter-bank transactions. It meant that there was little need for central banks to act as lenders of last resort because banks were no longer exposed to a liquidity crisis caused by the build-up of exposure when transactions took place on a net basis. The international money market, through which banks borrowed from and lent to each other on an unsecured basis, already operated without recourse to a lender of last resort, despite the risks that a default could dry up liquidity and so cause a cascade of collapses. These

[45] George Graham, 'Forex dealers move to limit settlement risk', 5th June 1996.
[46] Robert Peston, 'Silent launch of the lifeboat', 19th October 1993.

inter-bank flows were centred on London but used the US$ as its vehicle currency. The UK's central bank, the Bank of England, could not lend US$s on its own account, as only the US Federal Reserve Bank was in a position to do that. This meant that there was no overall lender of last resort to this inter-bank market. In the event of a liquidity crisis each participating bank would have to look to the central bank of its own country for support, but no such eventuality either occurred or was expected prior to the Global Financial Crisis.

In a world dominated by the activities of a few megabanks the function performed by a lender of last resort was no longer considered necessary. These banks used the originate-and-distribute model, diversified their assets and liabilities both sectorally and internationally, employed the most talented staff using the latest technology to calculate the risks they ran, and operated on such a scale that they were considered immune from either a liquidity or solvency crisis. In searching for a regulatory response to the changing world of finance in the 1990s these global universal banks appeared to offer the best solution. The risk of any of these megabanks failing was regarded as close to negligible. They had the ability to supervise staff, monitor the performance of loans, and shift funds to where and when required both quietly and quickly. These banks commanded the confidence of their peers and the trust of their users. They were of sufficient size to internalize financial transactions that once passed through open markets, including those provided by exchanges. Furthermore, these banks were already subjected to strict supervision by national regulators as well as close monitoring from central banks. They also had to adhere to internationally-agreed standards through the Basel Rules. These banks could be left to compete with each other to the benefit of both savers and borrowers, and the efficiency of the entire financial system. What these global universal banks appeared to offer regulators in the 1990s was the ideal combination of stability and competition with no further intervention required.

That was a view shared by the megabanks themselves, judging from the comment made in 2000 by Bill Winters, the global head of markets at JP Morgan, when discussing the regulation of markets: 'I don't see what they could achieve beyond what they achieve by regulating the participants. It is not clear what regulation would achieve.'[47] To him the financial activities he was engaged in straddled the entire field of banking and financial markets, and as his bank was already closely monitored and highly-regulated there was no need for further intervention. The regulatory response to globalization and the end of compartmentalization was to recognize the new world of finance that was emerging in the 1990s, and work with it. That world gave a prime position to the megabanks and, by regulating these, the entire financial system could be monitored and supervised. The outcome by 2006 was a global financial system believed to be both stable and competitive. Its performance prior to the Global Financial Crisis, which first began to reveal itself in 2007, fully supported that verdict, and regulators and central bankers could all claim to have made an important contribution in achieving it.[48]

[47] Vincent Boland, 'Tentative steps towards greater accountability', 28th June 2000.

[48] Peter Martin, 'As independent as they feel', 25th January 1993; Robert Peston, 'The risks of regulating', 25th January 1993; Peter Norman, 'Highs and lows of a dizzy decade', 23rd June 1993; Peter Norman and Richard Lambert, 'A steady hand at the tiller', 1st July 1993; Laurie Morse, 'Quest for definitive answers', 20th October 1993; Patrick Harverson, 'Temperature has cooled markedly', 20th October 1993; Brian Bollen, 'Nightmare for harmonisers', 28th October 1993; Tracy Corrigan, 'On trial for dangerous dealing', 21st March 1994; John Gapper, 'More alert and questioning', 27th July 1994; Peter Norman, 'Payments and settlements', 8th August 1994; John Plender, 'The box that can never be shut', 28th February 1995; Norma Cohen, 'Competition comes to market', 23rd June 1995; Richard Lapper, 'Regulators aim to gird the globe', 10th July 1995; John Gapper, 'Bankers support role of Old Lady', 25th July 1995; Richard Irving, 'Shock-absorbing models', 16th November 1995; John Gapper, 'World banking and securities watchdogs aim to co-operate', 21st May 1996; George Graham, 'Forex dealers move to limit

Devolving regulatory responsibility to the megabanks was also a way of coping with those national jurisdictions that took advantage of any rules by providing a more liberal environment, usually combined with tax concessions. Offshore financial centres operated regulatory systems that were sufficiently permissive to attract those escaping restrictions in the likes of New York, London, and Tokyo but with enough safeguards to reassure potential users. Achieving this balance was both elusive and transitory and took place in a competitive environment. In Asia Singapore vied with Hong Kong while in Europe Dublin challenged Luxembourg. In most cases only relatively small countries were successful in becoming offshore centres as it was difficult to design a regulatory regime that assured national

settlement risk', 5th June 1996; Laurie Morse, 'Crisis control proves difficult', 22nd November 1996; Stephanie Flanders, 'Market bears revive Tobin's ratio', 13th January 1997; Lord Alexander, 'Bring it all under one roof', 28th February 1997; Andrew Gowers, 'Planning blight in the City', 20th May 1997; George Graham, 'BIS weighs expanded role', 9th June 1997; Samer Iskandar, 'Fierce battle rages for market share', 27th June 1997; Michael Prest, 'Pressure on rule-makers', 27th June 1997; Jim Kelly, 'Auditors face up to the future', 27th June 1997; Guy de Jonquières, 'Happy end to a cliff hanger', 15th December 1997; Frances Williams, 'New rules for a trillion-dollar game', 15th December 1997; Martin Wolf, 'Why banks are dangerous', 6th January 1998; Christine Moir, 'New rules in changed world', 24th March 1998; John Ridding, 'Rival markets battle for the top spot', 27th April 1998; George Graham, 'Weighing up the risks', 4th June 1999; John Plender, 'Out of sight, not out of mind', 20th September 1999; Jeffrey Brown, 'From slow start to relentless build-up', 1st January 2000; John Plender, 'Too close for comfort', 21st March 2000; James Mackintosh, 'Balance of Power may be changing', 26th May 2000; Vincent Boland, 'Tentative steps towards greater accountability', 28th June 2000; Stephen Cecchetti, 'A legal challenge for Europe's markets', 17th August 2000; Peter Norman and Deborah Hargreaves, 'Long haul for Lamfalussy on securities markets' regulation', 28th December 2000; James Mackintosh, 'Financial police prepare for a firmer hand', 6th July 2001; Gary Silverman, 'Level playing field still elusive', 22nd February 2002; Philip Manchester, 'Why collaboration will be crucial', 3rd April 2002; Stephen Pritchard, 'A race to stay ahead of fraudsters', 5th June 2002; Philip Manchester, 'An aid to better investment decisions', 5th June 2002; Hugh Williamson, 'New regime takes root', 12th June 2002; Vincent Boland, 'Enthusiasm is growing for direct access in US and European securities markets', 24th May 2003; David Hale, 'The world's banking superpower', 18th June 2003; Ed Crooks, 'Bank owes much to the loyalty of "Steady Eddie"', 28th June 2003; Avinash Persaud, 'The Basel plan must get back to market basics', 3rd September 2003; Charles Pretzlik, Jane Croft, and Kate Burgess, 'The Financial Services Authority has been reactive, not aggressive. It must go out and make the market work', 20th September 2003; Pauline Skypala, 'Pressure on banks raising risk to buyers', 26th September 2003; Jeremy Grant, 'Traders consider their options', 27th April 2004; David Dombey, 'Call for lead EU financial supervisor', 16th June 2004; Charles Batchelor, 'Basel 2 favours high quality borrowers', 3rd November 2004; Charles Batchelor, 'Joining Europe's mainstream', 29th November 2004; Jane Croft and Scheherazade Daneshkhu, 'Bank warns on risks of property lending', 13th December 2004; Scheherazade Daneshkhu and Chris Giles, 'King acts to avoid nightmare scenario', 17th January 2005; Kate Burgess, 'Regulators test hedge funds' formula', 11th March 2005; Barney Jopson, 'Financial watchdog eager to show its cuddly side after years of growling', 11th August 2005; Sir Callum McCarthy, 'Europe's financial regulators must exploit existing ties', 22nd August 2005; Chris Giles, 'Old Lady forced to adapt as world has grown more complex and risky', 18th October 2005; Tom Braithwaite, 'Financial chiefs pay tribute to City-minded practitioner', 18th October 2005; Paul J Davies, 'Raising the roof with covered bonds', 2nd November 2005; Stephen Fidler, 'Basel 2 boosts Europe's repo market', 29th November 2005; Ivar Simensen, 'UK regulator warned over transparency', 6th December 2005; Barney Jopson, 'Regulatory reform not going by the book', 16th January 2006; Scheherazade Daneshkhu and Chris Giles, 'Warning of risks in over-valued markets', 18th January 2006; John Authers, 'Spread of derivatives reshapes the markets', 25th January 2006; Richard Beales, 'Regulator warns on trading backlogs', 26th January 2006; Barney Jopson, 'Countries follow UK in merging regulators', 7th February 2006; Peter Thal Larsen, 'Action may be needed to maintain competitive advantage', 26th March 2006; Peter Thal Larsen and Barney Jopson, 'Good behaviour key to regulator's remit', 28th March 2006; Francesco Guerrera, 'Top dog at home but needs to appeal abroad', 12th April 2006; Jennifer Hughes, 'Bankers divided on need for backstop', 4th May 2006; Jeremy Grant, 'Regulators face uncharted waters if deal goes ahead', 9th June 2006; Chris Hughes and Norma Cohen, 'Loss of light touch poses threat to LSE', 14th June 2006; Jeremy Grant, 'Regulators' boundaries may soon start to blur', 19th June 2006; Jennifer Hughes, 'Securities bodies prepare to merge', 29th June 2006; Jeremy Grant, 'Flat out: why regulators are rushing to keep up with mergers by exchanges', 13th July 2006; Jeremy Grant and Chrystia Freeland, 'Brokering change: how Cox is building a consensus as regulation goes global', 4th August 2006; Barney Jopson, 'City institutions perform double act in risk alerts', 21st August 2006; Jeremy Grant, 'Capital, traders and fraudsters are all completely mobile', 28th November 2006; Jeremy Grant, Stephanie Kirchgaessner and Francesco Guerrera, 'Panel calls for regulatory loosening', 1st December 2006; David Oakley, 'European repo trading grows Euro 500bn in year', 2nd March 2007; Jamil Anderlini, 'China's corporate bonds come of age', 15th June 2007; Jennifer Hughes and Peter Thal Larsen, '"Twin peaks" watching duties', 23rd June 2007.

governments that domestic banks were properly supervised and domestic investors protected while also proving attractive to foreign companies and investors seeking the freedom to operate without restrictions. Certain locations had found and then maintained this balance led by Switzerland. In 1995 an estimated 35 per cent of the money placed into tax havens by the individually wealthy went to Switzerland. Similarly, it was calculated in 2004 that of the $580,000bn held offshore a total of $130,000bn was in Switzerland, or 22 per cent. Among the numerous offshore centres spread around the world only Switzerland was of a size that could support a liquid financial market as opposed to a location with regulatory and tax advantages. Those who wanted a higher rate of return on their money or the ability to liquidate assets quickly had to forgo the tax and regulatory advantages of offshore centres and turn to the likes of London and New York. Not only could money earn a better rate of interest in these financial centres but they also possessed the financial markets with the depth and breadth that made it easy to buy and sell stocks, bonds, and other assets. The problem that offshore centres faced was that a lax regulatory regime had insufficient appeal to attract those activities where liquidity was of paramount importance and even acted as a disincentive in those where strong regulation was an attraction, as among many investors. For that reason regulation was less of a powerful force driving trading to offshore financial centres than it was for the placing of cash and assets where it would receive the highest return and remain liquid.[49]

Exchanges and Regulation

Exchanges had long been responsible for regulating specific financial markets, notably those for stocks and derivatives. What exchanges brought to these markets, other than a permanent mechanism that facilitated trading, were rules of conduct that assured all users that prices reflected the balance of supply and demand, that sales and purchases would be completed according to agreed terms and conditions, and that any transgressions would be detected and punished. By providing these guarantees exchanges not only served the interests of their members but also gave the public confidence in the financial instruments being bought and sold. In many countries institutional investors were prohibited from investing in securities that were not listed on a recognized or regulated stock exchange in order to protect their customers. What exchanges needed to achieve was a balance between the level of regulation that was sufficiently flexible to attract those issuing securities or introducing new financial products, and sufficiently rigid to satisfy those who bought and sold stocks and derivatives and required to be reassured regarding their value and transferability. Maintaining this balance did mean that exchanges lost the business of those who refused to comply with the standards they set or were willing to accept a higher degree of risk than they provided. There was always a market outside the exchanges unless prohibited by law.

[49] John Gapper, 'Contest to guard the nest-egg', 7th February 1995; John Turnbull, 'On a quest to boost financial flows', 11th April 2001; Daniel Dombey, 'Lack of growth signals need for reinvention', 7th June 2001; Daniel Dombey, 'Transatlantic invasion keeps industry thriving', 7th June 2001; Roxane McMeeken, 'Dublin closing the gap in race for hottest investments', 7th June 2001; Michael Mann, 'Watch out, the rivalry is beginning to hot up', 6th June 2002; Tony Barber, 'A tale of two complementary cities', 12th June 2002; Simon Targett, 'Time to open up Europe's money centre', 26th May 2003; John Murray Brown, 'The Irish stock exchange's special role', 8th November 2004; Lucy Warwick-Ching, 'Offshore industry faces gathering storm', 27th November 2004; Peter Thal Larsen, 'Action may be needed to maintain competitive advantage', 26th March 2006; Kate Burgess, 'Luxembourg edges, as London hedges', 19th November 2007.

Also, with the ending of barriers to the free flow of funds certain exchanges stepped in to offer a less-regulated trading environment while complying with investment mandates to have stocks or bonds quoted. In the 1990s the stock exchanges located in Luxembourg, Dublin, Bahamas, and Bermuda were among those hoping to attract international investors through a less restrictive regulatory regime for those issuing securities. A listing there made these securities eligible for inclusion in the portfolios of those investment and hedge funds whose mandates restricted them to stocks traded on exchanges, even though the level of trading was minimal or non-existent. In general, though, investors placed their confidence in the stocks that were listed on the exchanges that had a reputation for maintaining high standards. The Hong Kong Stock Exchange was preferred over that of Shanghai by foreign investors in Chinese stocks for that reason. In Russia the inability of the emerging stock exchange to impose regulatory discipline on the domestic market hampered its development in the 1990s and drove companies to list abroad. Conversely, the increase of regulatory oversight in India helped attract foreign investors to Indian shares. In the USA the high burden of the regulatory requirements imposed by the Sarbanes–Oxley Act of 2002, following the Enron and WorldCom scandals, discouraged foreign companies from listing in the USA, and encouraged US companies to list abroad. One response was for US exchanges to acquire foreign exchanges as an alternative base for their operations.

However, it was only in certain financial markets that the services of an exchange, and the regulated environment it introduced, were required. Other financial markets developed without formal rules, as in the case of inter-bank borrowing and lending as well as trading in currencies and the use of swaps. These could dispense with the regulatory authority of an exchange because trading took place between a few counterparties who trusted each other and took responsibility for their own actions. The market for some financial instruments, like bonds, had long straddled both the regulated exchanges and unregulated OTC trading. Even though these markets dispensed with exchanges they still required a degree of self-regulation that governed the way trading was conducted and what could be expected from counterparties. The strength of self-regulation, whether involving an exchange or not, was that it was very responsive to the changing interests and priorities of participants while imposing a degree of discipline that reduced or eliminated counterparty risk and the manipulation of the market. Its weakness lay in the power it gave to a small group, such as the members of an exchange, to control the market and operate it in such a way that benefited themselves. This could involve the exclusion of potential competitors with many exchanges refusing to allow banks to become members.

Self-regulation was always open to criticism because of issues relating to conflicts of interest, inadequate investor protection, insider trading, and charges imposed on users. As Bill Brodsky, chairman of the Chicago Board Options Exchange, said in 2004, 'Self-regulation is a privilege and not a right. If we don't handle it right, we'll lose it.'[50] To many members of exchanges self-regulation provided them with a means of maintaining their privileges. Such institutions were resistant to change as their members clung to rules and regulations that either excluded banks or forced them to comply with a code of behaviour that restricted their ability to compete. What had become increasingly common by the 1990s was the establishment of a government-appointed body that supervised exchanges, to prevent such behaviour among member-owned institutions. This followed practice in the USA where exchanges retained their independence but were subjected to the authority

[50] Jeremy Grant, 'Traders consider their options', 27th April 2004.

of the Securities and Exchange Commission (SEC), in the case of stocks and options, and the Commodity Futures Trading Commission (CFTC), in the case of commodities and futures. It was this pattern that was increasingly copied around the world. The Securities and Exchange Board of India (SEBI) was established in 1992, for example, combining the powers originally exercised by the stock exchanges, the finance ministry, the department of company affairs, and the controller of capital issues. In the 1994 the Financial Markets Promotion Act in Germany led to the Bundesaufsichtsamt für den Wertpapierhandel, which was a version of the SEC. In some countries these statutory agencies covered different markets while in others they included all among their responsibilities. The Comision Nacional del Mercado de Valores regulated all Spain's markets. With the exception of Canada, which used only provincial agencies, all this regulation took place on a national basis.

These statutory regulators worked closely with exchanges as this gave them greater control over the market. In 2006 Ben Steil reported that 'Regulators have generally welcomed the entry of exchanges into the OTC derivatives space.'[51] Government-appointed regulatory agencies lacked the staff and the expertise, including the likes of the SEC and the CFTC, to exercise day-to-day supervision of active markets. For that reason OTC markets were either banned, as was the case in Japan, or left largely unregulated, which happened in the USA. When left unregulated OTC markets relied on the ability of the participants to police themselves. The close relationship between regulatory agencies and exchanges meant that national monopolies were preserved even after barriers to cross-border trading had been removed and the electronic revolution had made global markets a possibility. In much of the world, such as Latin America and the Middle East, the regulatory structures in place meant that individual exchanges were unable to extend their trading beyond their own boundaries, and so these regions lacked the scale required to provide the deep and broad markets that users increasingly looked for. This drove those in search of liquidity to use those exchanges that could provide it, as was the case with Chicago for derivatives and New York for stocks. Unlike banking with its Basel Rules there was very limited agreement on common standards among those who regulated exchanges. The Madrid-based International Organization of Securities Commissions was largely ineffective, as it proved very difficult to agree on the harmonization of rules across different nation states. The alternative approach taken was for national regulators to formally recognize each other's markets as having equivalent regulations, controls, and supervision and so permit external access. Even this was difficult to achieve as it clashed with the priority given to investor protection, which often involved insulating exchanges with high standards from competition, as that could force them to lower these standards.

By the 1990s the relationship between national regulators and national exchanges was being steadily undermined because of the effects of globalization, deregulation, and technological change. Annette Nazareth, an SEC commissioner, was of the view in 2006 that, 'In all business the world is becoming small and flat and, with technology, geographical boundaries less relevant. You can keep having these separate rules in separate countries but the real challenge is to come up with a convergence of consistent rules so that the geographical boundaries themselves become less relevant to commerce, that's the trick. And that's what all the regulators are working hard to achieve.'[52] As barriers to international financial flows were lowered and investment horizons widened trading on exchanges was no longer a domestic affair, while the growing multinational nature of business diffused the

[51] Benn Steil, 'Derivatives exchanges owe much to wise regulation', 28th November 2006.

[52] Jeremy Grant, 'Flat out: why regulators are rushing to keep up with mergers by exchanges', 13th July 2006.

ownership of many equities around the world. Writing about corporate stocks in 1995 Norma Cohen had concluded that, 'The needs of investors have become so diverse that it is no longer possible to rely on a single centralised market regulated by a single set of rules.'[53] Under these circumstances it became difficult for exchanges to impose regulations and charges unilaterally if these had the effect of rendering the markets they provided unattractive. Though exchanges retained the power to dominate a market because of the liquidity they provided, that was not always sufficient to overcome disadvantages associated with controls on access, high charges, and restrictive trading practices. As more trading relocated from exchanges the less they could rely on liquidity to attract custom. A small number of global companies had their shares listed on multiple exchanges presenting investors with the opportunity to buy and sell through the one with the lowest charges and the best service, aided by the electronic links now in place. However, this became less common as banks gained membership of exchanges around the world and so directed their buying and selling to a single pool of liquidity.

With more trading seeping away into OTC markets, conducted internally within banks, or directed abroad, it was becoming clear that a reliance upon the self-regulation of exchanges, with or without the oversight of a body such as the SEC, did not meet the needs of fast-expanding financial markets where trading was dominated by global banks and covered diverse but closely-linked products. No longer could the regulation of these markets be left to member-controlled institutions, each specializing in particular products, such as stock, options, and futures, and operated within national boundaries. Instead of making a valuable contribution to regulation, exchanges were increasingly viewed in the 1990s as over-protected institutions that had abused their position by imposing conditions and charges that benefited their members at the expense of users. By the beginning of the twenty-first century a number of exchanges had been converted into profit-maximizing companies answerable to shareholders and employing a business model that searched out opportunities irrespective of product or jurisdiction. Others were in the process of following the same route. As exchanges were floated and became aggressive profit-seeking companies they could no longer be relied upon to fulfil regulatory functions for the whole market. As Ben Steil said in 2006, 'Demutualisation has transformed the CME from a staid broker-dealer utility into a fierce and creative competitor to banks and exchanges alike.'[54] Despite the preference of regulators to operate through exchanges because of the control they could exercise over their members this switch to a corporate form made them unsuitable as the means through which markets were regulated. By 2006 the LSE, for example, had become nothing more than a trading platform as it had lost its wider regulatory powers. Nevertheless, some, such as the Tokyo Stock Exchange continued to occupy a privileged position as both a market and a regulator.

The question that increasingly arose was whether exchanges were needed at all, given the high level of regulation imposed on the banks that increasingly dominated trading activity. Many financial transactions were already handled by banks, through the operation of an internal market, direct dealing between each other, or through an intermediary such as an interdealer broker. At the same time a growing volume of financial instruments in circulation were not traded on regulated exchanges such as the products of the boom in securitization and the swaps arranged between banks. The effect was to greatly increase the trading activity that bypassed exchanges. As the regulators found it difficult to monitor these transactions,

[53] Norma Cohen, 'Competition comes to market', 23rd June 1995.
[54] Benn Steil, 'Derivatives exchanges owe much to wise regulation', 28th November 2006.

because they took place privately and in huge volumes, both surveillance and policing were left in the hands of banks themselves rather than any regulatory authority. This was the case in currency trading, which was the world's largest financial market. As banks were already left with responsibility for a variety of important financial markets it appeared to be a logical step in the 1990s to extend that to those where exchanges still exercised a degree of regulatory control. From the perspective of the regulator the priority was investor protection and the detection and prevention of criminal activity not the maintenance of a market. That latter task could be left to the banks especially as exchanges became profit-maximizing companies. When operating as companies, exchanges were no different from banks, and thus there was no requirement for them to be given special regulatory powers as they had in the past.

Regulators switched from being protective of the interests of exchanges to demanding that they drop those restrictive practices that had been used to concentrate the market under their control. What was emerging in the 1990s was a regulatory model that split responsibility between the statutory agencies on the one hand and the megabanks on the other. In this model there was no place for exchanges, especially as these were considered a barrier to the competitive markets that regulators sought to achieve as the best way of generating efficiency of delivery and fairness to users. In the judgement of one legal expert, Tim Plews, co-head of the financial services practice at Clifford Chance, the international law firm, by 2006 'Multilateral trading facilities play the same role as exchanges yet are not subject to the same regime.'[55] This was a position he regretted from observing what the combination of self-regulation and statutory regulation had delivered in the UK: 'Innovation by UK exchanges has been essential to bridge the gap between privately negotiated over-the-counter transactions and publicly available price formation in a wide range of asset classes. Rule changes to facilitate innovation have been part of the daily interchange between the FSA and exchanges. This has been noiseless and effective.'[56] However, around the world the justification for extending privileges to exchanges, in order to support the regulatory role they performed was rapidly waning during the 1990s and into the twenty-first century.[57]

55 Tim Plews, 'The "Balls clauses" are a mixed blessing for the City', 29th November 2006.

56 Tim Plews, 'The "Balls clauses" are a mixed blessing for the City', 29th November 2006.

57 Tracy Corrigan, 'Europe waits for floodgates to open', 20th October 1993; Louise Lucas, 'Watchdogs do their best', 27th April 1994; Richard Lapper, 'A slice of NY's pie', 7th June 1996; David Waller, 'Resisting the bait of equity ownership', 14th July 1994; Mark Nicholson, 'Two busy years of regulatory power', 13th March 1995; Peter Montagnon and R. C. Murthy, 'Bombay regulators again in the dock', 21st March 1995; Richard Lapper, 'Innovation in swaps and oranges', 23rd May 1995; Norma Cohen, 'Competition comes to market', 23rd June 1995; Norma Cohen and Alison Smith, 'Heat turned on self-regulation', 28th July 1995; Roula Khalaf, 'Bourse starts to modernise', 28th November 1995; John Thornhill, 'Reining in wild expansion', 11th April 1996; Edward Luce, 'Philippine SE moves toward self-regulation', 29th October 1996; Ruben Lee, 'In good faith', 17th December 1996; Christine Moir, 'New rules in changed world', 24th March 1998; Edward Alden and Scott Morrison, 'Canada's stock dealing reputation takes a knock', 25th May 1998; James Harding, 'Contradiction in markets', 23rd March 1999; John Labate and Clay Harris, 'Fighting for a share', 26th May 1999; Jeffrey Brown, 'From slow start to relentless build-up', 1st January 2000; James Mackintosh, 'Share trade tax revenue doomed, says regulator', 10th January 2000; Vincent Boland, 'FSA to commence alternative exchanges inquiry', 24th January 2000; Jonathan Wheatley, Ken Warn, and Mark Mulligan, 'Latin American brokers face home truths on local problems', 3rd March 2000; Alan Beattie, Rahul Jacob and Gerard Baker, 'Regulators alarmed over high-tech mania', 16th March 2000; Philip Coggan, 'High-tech stock slide hits Europe', 16th March 2000; John Labate, 'Market visionary and architect of change', 31st March 2000; Khozem Merchant, 'Straight on for global market', 5th May 2000; Vincent Boland, 'Tentative steps towards greater accountability', 28th June 2000; Richard Lapper and Mark Mulligan, 'Picture continues to darken', 28th March 2001; Andrew Bolger, 'Still open after Wall Street shuts', 25th May 2001; Vincent Boland and John Labate, 'Sell, sell, sell as exchanges eye consolidation', 30th January 2002; Stephen Pritchard, 'A race to stay ahead of fraudsters', 5th June 2002; Philip Coggan, 'Market slide provokes a new deal for shares', 28th September 2002; Vincent Boland, 'Enthusiasm is growing for direct access in US and European securities markets', 24th May 2003; Doris Grass, 'Stock exchanges attack proposed EU rule changes', 29th August 2003; Alex

This can be seen in the case of derivatives where there was a 'love/hate' relationship between regulators and the market. Legal definitions of derivatives did not adequately capture what they were, who was allowed to trade them, and how to enforce agreements. The opaqueness of derivatives was compounded by their capacity to simultaneously magnify or reduce risk. Auditors, for example, struggled with how to measure the risks contained in derivative contracts. Financial derivatives were used by speculators betting on the expectation of a price rise or fall in the value of the underlying stocks, bonds, or currencies. The leverage a future or option contract provided allowed speculators to magnify the potential returns if the prediction proved correct but also increased exposure to large losses. Conversely, derivatives were used extensively by those who wanted to insure against a loss, such as a bank exposed to currency fluctuations or a fund manager to volatile stock prices. Some regulators took a relaxed attitude towards the speculative element attached to derivatives, as was the case in Malaysia. In 1995 Khairil Annuar, a director at Malaysia's Securities Commission, expressed the opinion that, 'Speculation per se isn't bad—it adds liquidity... A few bubbles of speculation in a stream of enterprise is to be expected, but not the other way round.'[58] Conversely, in Japan even after the controls on derivatives were relaxed in 1998 the regulatory environment continued to restrict their use. Generally, though the 'love' relationship was in the ascendancy between 1992 and the Global Financial Crisis of 2008. In the 1992 financial crisis regulators were alerted to the risks posed by

Skorecki, 'Exchanges divided by more than time zones', 6th November 2003; Jeremy Grant, 'Traders consider their options', 27th April 2004; Alex Skorecki, 'Tax advantage drives CFD growth', 23rd September 2004; Peter Norman, 'Securities watchdog sharpens its teeth', 25th October 2004; John Murray Brown, 'The Irish stock exchange's special role', 8th November 2004; Alex Skorecki, 'Trading without stamp duty', 13th November 2004; Charles Batchelor and Jane Fuller, 'Inland revenue in talks on securitisation', 22nd December 2004; Deborah Hargreaves, Norma Cohen, and Barney Jopson, 'Europe looks to new law on securities', 26th January 2005; Norma Cohen, Jeremy Grant, and Andrei Postelnicu, 'Leading exchanges consider their moves in the race to consolidate', 11th March 2005; Arkady Ostrovsky, 'Russia's IPO rush: companies touch down in London seeking growth and status', 20th July 2005; Tobias Buck, 'Dealing costs must be cut, says Brussels', 13th September 2005; Barney Jopson, 'European regulators learn to sing in harmony', 17th November 2005; Francesco Guerrera and Andrei Postelnicu, 'A not so foreign exchange: China shuns the west as a location for its big corporate share offers', 18th November 2005; Ivar Simensen, 'UK regulator warned over transparency', 6th December 2005; Stephen Fidler, 'How the Square Mile defeated the prophets of doom', 10th December 2005; John Authers, 'Spread of derivatives reshapes the markets', 25th January 2006; George Parker, Christine Mai, and Norma Cohen, 'EU issues deadline to exchanges on charges', 7th March 2006; John Burton, 'Malaysia relaxes short-selling ban', 24th March 2006; Peter Weinberg, 'How London can close the gap on Wall Street', 30th March 2006; David Turner, 'International dimension is missing link', 12th April 2006; Francesco Guerrera, 'Top dog at home but needs to appeal abroad', 12th April 2006; David Wighton, 'Selling the attractions of Euronext', 22nd May 2006; David Turner, Virginia Marsh, and Justine Lau, 'TSE keeps close eye on battle for bourse', 24th May 2006; Jeremy Grant, 'Regulators face uncharted waters if deal goes ahead', 9th June 2006; Chris Hughes and Norma Cohen, 'Loss of light touch poses threat to LSE', 14th June 2006; Gillian Tett, 'FOA worried by US regulatory aspirations', 14th June 2006; Jeremy Grant, 'Hurdles appear in the race for exchange consolidation', 15th June 2006; John Authers and Norma Cohen, 'Exchange merger poses question of liquidity', 19th June 2006; Harvey Pitt, 'Sarbanes–Oxley is an unhealthy export', 21st June 2006; Jennifer Hughes, 'Securities bodies prepare to merge', 29th June 2006; Anuj Gangahar, 'Chairman of the Amex gains focus', 6th July 2006; Paul J. Davies, 'FSA backing for UK bond markets', 6th July 2006; Jeremy Grant, 'Flat out: why regulators are rushing to keep up with mergers by exchanges', 13th July 2006; Neal Wolkoff, 'America's regulations are scaring the Sox off small caps', 1st August 2006; Jeremy Grant and Chrystia Freeland, 'Brokering change: how Cox is building a consensus as regulation goes global', 4th August 2006; Chris Hughes, 'A controversial investment choice', 5th September 2006; Benn Steil, 'Derivatives exchanges owe much to wise regulation', 28th November 2006; Norma Cohen, 'Level playing fields', 28th November 2006; Jeremy Grant, 'Capital, traders and fraudsters are all completely mobile', 28th November 2006; Tim Plews, 'The "Balls clauses" are a mixed blessing for the City', 29th November 2006; James Blitz, 'Stamp Duty on non-resident exchange traded funds to go', 30th November 2006; Jeremy Grant, Stephanie Kirchgaessner, and Francesco Guerrera, 'Panel calls for regulatory loosening', 1st December 2006; Chris Hughes, 'Concerns grow for rules as global deals loom', 1st December 2006; Robert Cookson, 'Doubts on Hong Kong secondary listings', 18th May 2011.

[58] Conner Middelmann, 'Step closer to becoming a well-rounded market', 16th November 1995.

derivatives to bank stability. As James Blitz reported, in 1993, 'Governments and central bankers are increasingly concerned about the possibilities of a credit default in the derivatives sector that would destabilise markets.'[59] However, as time passed and derivatives moved from being speculative counters to becoming hedging tools used in mainstream finance the attitude of regulators towards them became more positive.

When used for speculation derivatives attracted the attention of regulators acting to protect retail investors from losses because of unwise bets on the rise or fall of prices or the manipulation of the market by professional traders. This responsibility was shared with exchanges, who acted to police trading activity. In many countries regulated exchanges were charged with supervising and regulating all derivatives activity. For the USA the Securities and Exchange Commission (SEC) had responsibility for options, as these were traded on stock exchanges, while the Commodity Futures Trading Commission (CFTC) monitored futures, which were bought and sold on commodity exchanges. Elsewhere in the world it was usually one regulatory authority that oversaw both, especially as futures contracts took on an increasingly financial nature. The changing use of futures did lead to pressure in the USA to merge the responsibilities of the SEC and the CFTC but these came to nothing. Each organization fought for its independence, backed by those who feared the power of a single authority, especially one that took the more legalistic approach of the SEC. In addition to the complication for regulators, caused by the changing nature and use of futures and options contracts, there was the exponential growth in those that were traded away from exchanges. In particular, the growing practice through which banks swapped exposure to particular risks left regulators at a loss to know what action to take. In one way the swap market reduced the risk an individual bank ran because it was either diluted by being shared with others or eliminated through matching it with an opposite risk. Conversely, swap arrangements exposed the entire banking sector to these risks, which, if they were of sufficient magnitude, could overwhelm it. However, the increasing view among regulators was that activity in the derivatives market contributed to stability and that the involvement of the largest banks, especially those with diverse activities spread around the world, meant that responsibility could be devolved to participants rather than placed in the hands of statutory agencies. As these banks were already tightly regulated at the national level, and the Bank for International settlements (BIS) provided global oversight there was no need for a further layer of supervision.

What was taking place in the derivatives market was a split between the retail and the wholesale at the level of supervision and regulation. This can be seen in the case of the USA. In 1992 the OTC derivatives market, for example, was exempted from CFTC regulation because of its wholesale nature, as it involved professionals dealing with each other. Conversely, derivative exchanges were subjected to increased monitoring, as they catered more for the retail end of the market. Derivative exchanges attracted those looking for safeguards against market manipulation and counterparty default, and they were willing to accept the limited range of products, the highly-regulated trading environment, and the charges levied. In contrast, the OTC market attracted those who were little concerned by counterparty risk, relished the variety of contracts on offer, and looked for the cheapest deals. The rapidly developing OTC market in credit default swaps, for example, was almost entirely used by professionals. In 2003 banks, securities houses, hedge funds, and insurance companies, collectively, bought and sold 90 per cent of all credit default swaps. While

[59] James Blitz, 'ERM crisis quicken activity', 20th October 1993.

leaving the wholesale market to finance professionals and focusing on investor protection at the retail end regulators neglected the question of liquidity. The assumption made for those futures and options traded on exchanges was that there would always be a market. As that was the case between 1992 and the Global Financial Crisis of 2008 there was little to counter this assumption and so it was increasingly ingrained in the thinking of regulators. That assumption of liquidity was then transferred to the rapidly expanding OTC derivatives market, despite the knowledge that a large number of swap agreements were specifically worded and so not easily transferrable. In these cases another assumption was made which was that liquidity was not required. The megabanks and other financial institutions involved in the OTC derivatives market were simply too big to fail and so could be relied upon to act as counterparties to any deal, regardless of the circumstances. The only apparent weakness among them was to be found in the hedge funds, as they were relatively new, highly specialized, and lacked the depth and breadth of the banks, securities houses, and insurance companies. However, they played a relatively minor role in the derivatives market. In 2003 they were responsible for only 15 per cent of the credit default swaps bought and sold. To a large degree regulators devolved responsibility to the megabanks as they could be relied upon to safeguard their positions and possessed the expertise and capital required to either avoid or cover any losses. The risks involved with derivatives was recognized but discounted under the conditions that prevailed between 1992 and 2007.[60]

Varieties of Regulation

Though the general trend throughout the period between 1992 and 2007 was towards deregulation of financial activity, though retaining an important role for statutory bodies, Japan proved something of an exception. There the pace of change remained slow and its extent limited. The Tokyo Stock Exchange (TSE), for example, long continued its dual role of provider and regulator of the stock market. Even in the 1990s there was a reluctance in Japan to permit the post-war structure of the financial system to unravel, including the compartmentalization of specific activities. This meant continuing regulatory restraints on all types of financial innovation, and resistance to the acceptance of foreign banks and securities houses into the financial system. Gerard Baker in 1994 reported that, 'Tokyo's markets are still hidebound by restrictions that deter domestic and foreign investors and

[60] Richard Waters, 'Easy option or unnecessary risk', 22nd July 1993; Laurie Morse and Tracy Corrigan, 'Derivatives no threat to banking system, say experts', 22nd July 1993; Laurie Morse, 'Quest for definitive answers', 20th October 1993; James Blitz, 'ERM crisis quicken activity', 20th October 1993; Sara Webb, 'Limited scope for development', 20th October 1993; Conner Middelmann, 'Step closer to becoming a well-rounded market', 16th November 1995; Richard Irving, 'Shock-absorbing models', 16th November 1995; Laurie Morse, 'Regulators to voice fears for US futures', 10th March 1997; Samer Iskandar, 'Fierce battle rages for market share', 27th June 1997; Michael Prest, 'Pressure on rule-makers', 27th June 1997; Jim Kelly, 'Auditors face up to the future', 27th June 1997; Samer Iskandar, 'The search for growth', 1st May 1998; Jim Kelly, 'Standard procedures', 17th July 1998; Nikki Tait, 'Changes create new risks', 17th July 1998; Edward Luce, 'Exchanges in world flux', 20th September 1999; Nikki Tait, 'Regulators reach over the counter', 20th September 1999; John Plender, 'Out of sight, not out of mind', 20th September 1999; Nikki Tait, 'There's life in the old bourses yet', 31st March 2000; John Plender, 'The limits of ingenuity', 17th May 2001; Aline van Duyn, 'Credit derivatives unmasked', 21st March 2003; Aline van Duyn, 'Banks could adopt derivatives code', 30th May 2003; Charles Batchelor, 'Essential, controversial, popular and profitable', 5th November 2003; Charles Batchelor, 'Restructuring at risk from CDSs', 19th October 2004; John Authers, 'Spread of derivatives reshapes the markets', 25th January 2006; Richard Beales, 'Regulator warns on trading backlogs', 26th January 2006; David Turner, 'Japan needs derivatives to compete', 10th August 2006; Richard Beales, 'New instruments call the tune', 20th October 2006; Jeremy Grant and Doug Cameron, 'Lords of the Windy City', 21st October 2006.

limit the scope for raising capital.'[61] Though it was increasingly acknowledged that the restrictions in place prevented Tokyo from competing internationally, and the Japanese financial system from becoming more efficient, it proved difficult to carry out anything other than the most limited reforms with the result that restrictions remained in place. In 1995 Guy de Jonquières judged that the interventions of the Japanese authorities had prevented the liberalization of the financial system and protected national institutions from competition: 'The result had been to stifle essential innovation, distort the allocation of capital, increase risks in the banking sector and drive profitable business offshore.'[62]

The tight regulation exercised by the Ministry of Finance was only gradually and slowly relaxed because the financial authorities wanted to retain control. The effect of the burden of regulation was to prevent the development of the derivatives market, discourage foreign companies from listing on the TSE, and encourage trading to migrate to Singapore and Hong Kong. According to Fumikage Nishi, of Nomura Securities, in 1994, 'The only advantage it (Tokyo) has is scale. But that will be insufficient, because without real deregulation, financial innovation in other Asian centres will rapidly outpace that in Japan.'[63] Within Japan the rigidity of the financial system was increasingly clashing with the changing ways that businesses financed themselves. The Japanese equivalent of the US Glass–Steagall Act (Article 65 of the Securities Exchange Law) prevented banks from undertaking brokerage activity, which meant they could not issue stocks and bonds. However, as companies moved towards issuing stocks and bonds, rather than borrowing from banks, the banks began to demand to be allowed to issue bonds, which they were granted in the mid-1990s. Following that the banks wanted to be allowed to trade equities as savers were looking to stocks for a higher return than bank deposits.

In response to the relaxation of the controls imposed on banks entering the broking business, so the brokers wanted the freedom to move into banking. In 1994 Kaname Seki, managing director of the Japan Securities Dealers Association, wanted 'wider deregulation quickly to enlarge the market and create genuinely open competition.'[64] The pressure the brokers exerted did bring them concessions, further blurring the distinctions enshrined in post-war legislation. By 1994 the Ministry of Finance was facing an increasing momentum for change as one relaxation led to pressure for more because of the forces unleashed amounted to, in the words of Gerard Baker, 'a self-propelling organising machine.'[65] However, the speed of progress was slow with proposals taking years to pass into law, and then more time was taken before being fully implemented. This was despite the recognition that urgent and radical reform was required as business was lost to both London and Singapore because of Japanese restrictions. In a number of cases, such as the trading in corporate stocks, it was only the liquidity of the Japanese market that compelled financial activity to continue taking place there. In the case of derivatives the verdict of Naoko Nakamae, in 1999, was that 'The process of deregulation is slowly getting rid of the regulatory irritants that prevented Japan from being a leading contender in the derivatives world.'[66] By the end of the 1990s considerable progress had been made in breaking down the cartels, which had traditionally segregated and protected different financial sectors, and removing obstacles to the participation of foreign banks and brokers in the financial

[61] Gerard Baker, 'Ripple effect of Tokyo's Big Bang', 24th November 1994.
[62] Guy de Jonquières, 'Single EU securities market at risk', 16th May 1995.
[63] Gerard Baker, 'Regional rivals hot on its heels', 19th October 1994.
[64] Gerard Baker, 'Ripple effect of Tokyo's Big Bang', 24th November 1994.
[65] Gerard Baker, 'Ripple effect of Tokyo's Big Bang', 24th November 1994.
[66] Naoko Nakamae, 'Deregulation opens doors slowly to investors', 23rd March 1999.

system. The result had been to drive up the level of competition and encourage innovation. However, it was accepted that much remained to be done. Even by 2006, for example, legal restrictions on derivatives continued to restrict the growth of the Japanese derivatives market while encouraging the TSE to remain an inward focused institution secure in its ability to dominate the large domestic market.[67]

The regulatory authorities in the USA could also pursue an agenda that not only ignored what was happening elsewhere in the world but also the consequences it had for the international competitiveness of US markets. This was due to the vast size of the domestic market. Long before the Sarbanes–Oxley Act of 2002 the Securities and Exchange Commission's (SEC) requirement that foreign companies had to comply with US accounting standards discouraged them from applying for a listing on a US stock exchange. The authority of the SEC was further enhanced in 1996 when it was given sole jurisdiction over companies going public on the national market, over-riding state legislation. The SEC was widely regarded as the most powerful regulatory agency in the world, being the one that many countries chose to emulate in terms of rulings and operations. Edward Luce in 1998 considered 'The Securities and Exchange Commission in the US is considered to be one of the most interfering regulators in the world.'[68] However, within the USA the SEC did not possess undisputed authority. It shared responsibility with the Commodity Futures Trading Commission (CFTC), which covered those exchanges where futures contracts were traded. Though attempts were made to merge the SEC and the CFTC, under the control of the former, this did not happen, despite the blurring of distinctions between once separate financial markets. When the CFTC was set up in 1974 to regulate futures contracts these were based on the trading of commodities on commodity exchanges. That left the SEC to regulate the trading of stocks in stock exchanges. By the 1990s the CFTC largely regulated financial futures, which brought it closer to the stocks and options that were overseen by the SEC. What neither the SEC nor the CFTC did was regulate trading that took place outside the exchanges, whether in stocks or futures, even though this grew to major proportions in the 1990s and into the twenty-first century. An estimate for 2006 suggested that most buying and selling of derivatives in the USA took place on the Over-The-Counter (OTC) market while the likes of the New York Stock Exchange (NYSE) was steadily losing control of trading even in those stocks that it listed, let alone those that it did not.

It was this steady drift of trading away from exchanges during the 1990s that led US regulators to change their attitude towards these institutions. The conventional wisdom in the USA was that the regulated exchanges could be relied upon to police financial markets, under the supervision of the SEC and the CFTC, while the concentration of trading activity

[67] Emiko Terazono, 'Known for know-how', 24th March 1993; Robert Thomson, 'High hopes demolished', 24th March 1993; Emiko Terazono, 'Patience is running out', 26th May 1994; Gerard Baker, 'Regional rivals hot on its heels', 19th October 1994; Gerard Baker, 'Ripple effect of Tokyo's Big Bang', 24th November 1994; Guy de Jonquières, 'Single EU securities market at risk', 16th May 1995; William Dawkins, 'A big bang in slow motion', 10th December 1996; William Dawkins, 'Last chance to catch up', 25th March 1997; Richard Lapper, 'Restrictions set to ease', 25th March 1997; Gwen Robinson, 'Backward in coming forward', 27th June 1997; Gillian Tett, 'Big Bang calls for some swift reforms', 24th March 1998; Gillian Tett, 'Big Bang or just a whimper?', 26th March 1998; Gillian Tett, 'Complex timetable for reforms package', 26th March 1998; Naoko Nakamae, 'Deregulation opens doors slowly to investors', 23rd March 1999; Gillian Tett, 'Facing up to a wave of foreign competitors', 21st June 1999; Gillian Tett, 'Fresh education heralds a shift', 21st June 1999; David Turner, 'International dimension is missing link', 12th April 2006; David Turner, Virginia Marsh and Justine Lau, 'TSE keeps close eye on battle for bourse', 24th May 2006; Song Jung-a and Mariko Sanchanta, 'TSE and Korea exchange move towards link-up', 7th July 2006; David Turner, 'Japan needs derivatives to compete', 10th August 2006; David Turner, 'TSE and NYSE in talks over alliance', 28th October 2006; Chris Hughes, 'Concerns grow for rules as global deals loom', 1st December 2006.

[68] Edward Luce, 'Bankers and Brussels at odds over impact on London', 9th December 1998.

in one location improved liquidity and produced more accurate pricing. The regulated nature of trading on exchanges attracted customers because of the safeguards in place, as it generated confidence in both the product and the price. The role of the SEC and the CFTC was to both supervise and support the exchanges, especially the largest of these, as they could support a comprehensive regulatory structure and house the deepest and broadest markets. Under these circumstances it was difficult to challenge incumbent exchanges, especially the likes of the NYSE and the CBOT. It was during the 1990s that this support for exchanges from the SEC and CFTC began to wane as their ability to control the market for stocks and derivatives declined. In futures attempts were made in the 1990s to force all trading through the exchanges, in order to impose regulatory control, but this failed. That failure encouraged an alternative stance, which was to impose a much lighter regulatory regime on the derivatives exchanges, as that would allow them to meet the challenge coming from the OTC market. What followed was a growing belief that the derivatives market as a whole could be left to police itself. Trading was increasingly in the hands of the big banks and brokers, operating for themselves or major investment institutions, and they did not require the protection of the regulators.

In the case of the SEC and the stock exchanges the role of the regulator was complicated by the mass participation of individual investors in the market, and they expected to receive a degree of protection. As the chairman of the SEC said in 2005, 'our responsibility is to promote the interests of investors'.[69] The issue was how best to provide that protection. For most of the SEC's existence this was achieved through directing trading to the NYSE as it could be relied upon to deliver a regulated environment under their supervision. In turn the SEC condoned such restrictive practices as a fixed fee structure, restrictions on the type and number of members, and controls on access to current prices. By the 1990s the fee structure had been abandoned and the criteria for membership widened but the controls over price dissemination remained. In addition, the SEC's own Intermarket Trading System (ITS) rule directed that all orders had to be sent to the exchange posting the best price. In the case of NYSE-quoted stocks that was almost always the NYSE because of the role played by the specialists in generating the reference prices even though it was not necessarily the best market in terms of the costs incurred, the time taken for a transaction or even the eventual price achieved. However, without a change in that rule, and the forced dissemination of prices, it was difficult for any other trading platform to challenge the NYSE as the market for NYSE-listed stocks. The same applied to Nasdaq with Nasdaq-listed stocks because of the role played by its market-makers. The verdict of Vincent Boland in 2001 was that 'The SEC balances its undoubted success in protecting investors from scams with an unashamedly protectionist stance towards existing US market structures.'[70]

Conversely, an alternative view was emerging which suggested that exchanges like the NYSE were failing to respond to the new developments taking place, especially in electronic trading, and because of their continuing restrictive practices they no longer served the interests of investors. The slow but steady loss of market share to Electronic Communication Networks (ECNs) was making regulators aware that they were failing to supervise the whole market. In 2000 the SEC decided to invite ECNs to apply to become regulated exchanges, so giving them the same status as the NYSE. By then there were also doubts about the regulatory effectiveness of the NYSE, which had failed to deal with the build-up of the speculative dot.com bubble. In contrast, the absence of any significant failures among

[69] William Donaldson, 'A simple new rule that gives investors priority', 8th April 2005.

[70] Vincent Boland, 'Euro gives spur for updating', 21st June 2001.

US investment banks in the wake of the bursting of the bubble suggested that they could be relied upon to police themselves. In terms of investor protection the strategy changed from one favouring the regulated exchanges to fostering competition among exchanges. In that way investors would obtain the best deal as exchanges competed for their business. The result was the replacement of the ITS rule in 2005 with the New Market System (NMS) rule. As William Donaldson explained, 'The rule we (SEC) adopted, part of the regulation NMS reforms, is quite simple: when an investor sends an order to a market, the market can either execute the order at the best price then instantly available in the national market system or the market must send the order to the venue quoting the best price.'[71] Combined with the forced disclosure by the NYSE of current prices this new policy allowed alternative markets to operate on the current prices generated by the exchanges but to undercut them in terms of charges and service. Under the NMS system the exchanges were expected to lose their dominance, being replaced by a nationwide electronic market in which the banks were the major players and exchanges like the NYSE had lost their key regulatory role. It was in 2006 that Nasdaq was finally recognized as a stock exchange by the SEC.

This shift also reflected the changing international environment within which exchanges operated. Both the SEC and the CFTC had imposed restrictions on the operation of electronic exchanges located overseas, but wanting to operate in the USA, on the grounds of investor protection. The effect was to provide US exchanges with a degree of protection from foreign competition. In the opinion of Edward Luce in 1999, 'If it were not for the fact that the US regulator, the Commodities Futures Trading Commission, is still running what is effectively a protectionist show (with foreign exchanges limited to a certain number of screens and requiring lengthy approval from the regulator before launching new products), the Europeans would probably be in competition rather than alliance with their Chicago counterparts.'[72] The CFTC, for example, took a long time to approve the use of Liffe's electronic trading system, Connect, in the USA. However, by 2003, when the CBOT and CME sought to use regulations to protect themselves from attempts by Eurex to break into the US derivatives market, it was not forthcoming. Until then the lack of competition from those exchanges using electronic platforms removed the stimulus driving the switch away from open outcry. For that reason the imminent arrival of Eurex on US soil in 2004 acted as a catalyst for change in the US derivatives industry.[73]

Ignoring what was happening internationally was increasingly not an option for US regulators, as US exchanges themselves extended their activities abroad through alliances and mergers. As Mark Lackritz, President, Securities Industry Association, observed in 2005, 'Three years ago you didn't have the NYSE bidding for Euronext and you didn't have the scale of cross-border flows you have today.'[74] The Atlanta-based InterContinental Exchange (ICE) had taken over the London-based International Petroleum Exchange (IPE) in 2001, converting it into ICE Futures. In 2006 the New York-based NYSE merged with the Paris-based Euronext while the New York-based Nasdaq merged with the Stockholm-based OMX. The result was a series of multiproduct, multijurisdiction exchanges, which no single regulator could hope to supervise. Even the SEC would have difficulty as it lacked the

[71] William Donaldson, 'A simple new rule that gives investors priority', 8th April 2005.

[72] Edward Luce, 'Hard global pressure on Liffe', 20th September 1999.

[73] Nikki Tait, 'US leaves foreigners out in the cold', 30th October 1998; Edward Luce, 'Hard global pressure on Liffe', 20th September 1999; Vincent Boland, 'Dotcom venture to aid recovery', 31st March 2000; Alex Skorecki, 'A returning hero with eyes set on the west', 16th January 2003; Alex Skorecki, 'Derivatives sector faces up to Eurex's assault on the US', 9th June 2003; Jeremy Grant, 'Eurex faces vote on clearing house', 20th October 2003.

[74] Jennifer Hughes, 'Securities bodies prepare to merge', 29th June 2006.

experience of derivatives, for that continued to be covered by the CFTC in the USA. There was also a strong resistance around the world to devolving stock market supervision to the SEC, because of its reputation for both intervention and the protection of US interests. The spectre of the US regulations introduced under the Sarbanes–Oxley Act being imposed throughout the world was not welcomed by other regulatory agencies. A much simpler solution was for exchanges to abandon any regulatory functions, especially as they were already replacing a mutual structure with a corporate form. In their place national regulatory agencies would take responsibility for national financial markets with banks, as the main users of the markets, being entrusted with day-to-day supervision of buying and selling whether it took place on an exchange or the rapidly expanding OTC market, domestically or internationally.[75]

Unlike regulation in Japan, which was used to preserve the status quo, or in the USA, where it was driven by a desire to improve internal competition and external protection, in Europe regulation was a weapon employed to achieve the goal of greater unity within the EU. Those forging ahead with the plan for an integrated European economy saw in regulation

[75] Norma Cohen, 'NYSE reviews non-US share trading', 15th June 1995; Ruben Lee, 'Why regulators must let markets decide', 20th June 1995; Richard Waters, 'Talk of mergers is in the air', 12th August 1996; Laurie Morse, 'Regulators to voice fears for US futures', 10th March 1997; Jim Kelly, 'World accounting wins more converts', 9th June 1997; Richard Waters, 'A share in Nasdaq's future', 22nd January 1998; Simon Kuper, 'Old divide is starting to crumble', 23rd January 1998; Stanislas Yassukovich, 'Single market for equities', 26th January 1998; Christine Moir, 'New rules in changed world', 24th March 1998; Nikki Tait, 'Changes create new risks', 17th July 1998; Nikki Tait, 'US proposes stiff tests for foreign futures exchanges', 20th July 1998; Edward Luce, 'Bankers and Brussels at odds over impact on London', 9th December 1998; Edward Luce and John Labate, 'The trading bell tolls', 26th July 1999; Nikki Tait, 'Regulators reach over the counter', 20th September 1999; John Labate, 'Market visionary and architect of change', 31st March 2000; Vincent Boland, 'Euro gives spur for updating', 21st June 2001; Vincent Boland and John Labate, 'Sell, sell, sell as exchanges eye consolidation', 30th January 2002; Gary Silverman, 'Level playing field still elusive', 22nd February 2002; Alex Skorecki, 'Derivatives sector faces up to Eurex's assault on the US', 9th June 2003; David Hale, 'The world's banking superpower', 18th June 2003; Andrei Postelnicu, 'A little breathing space', 7th July 2003; Andrei Postelnicu, 'Fast market proposals might spell danger for NYSE traders', 24th February 2004; Jeremy Grant, 'Traders consider their options', 27th April 2004; David Wighton, 'NYSE fights to retain its dominance', 12th June 2004; Charles Batchelor and Jane Fuller, 'Inland revenue in talks on securitisation', 22nd December 2004; Deborah Hargreaves, Norma Cohen, and Barney Jopson, 'Europe looks to new law on securities', 26th January 2005; Norma Cohen, Jeremy Grant, and Andrei Postelnicu, 'Leading exchanges consider their moves in the race to consolidate', 11th March 2005; Francesco Guerrera and Andrei Postelnicu, 'A not so foreign exchange: China shuns the west as a location for its big corporate share offers', 18th November 2005; Stephen Fidler, 'How the Square Mile defeated the prophets of doom', 10th December 2005; Peter Weinberg, 'How London can close the gap on Wall Street', 30th March 2006; Anuj Gangahar, 'Seismic shift looms for trading', 21st April 2006; David Wighton, 'Selling the attractions of Euronext', 22nd May 2006; Doug Cameron, 'Futures exchanges' role under review', 30th May 2006; Jeremy Grant, 'Regulators face uncharted waters if deal goes ahead', 9th June 2006; Chris Hughes and Norma Cohen, 'Loss of light touch poses threat to LSE', 14th June 2006; Gillian Tett, 'FOA worried by US regulatory aspirations', 14th June 2006; Jeremy Grant, 'Hurdles appear in the race for exchange consolidation', 15th June 2006; John Authers and Norma Cohen, 'Exchange merger poses question of liquidity', 19th June 2006; Harvey Pitt, 'Sarbanes–Oxley is an unhealthy export', 21st June 2006; Jennifer Hughes, 'Securities bodies prepare to merge', 29th June 2006; Anuj Gangahar, 'Chairman of the Amex gains focus', 6th July 2006; Gillian Tett and Anuj Gangahar, 'Surge in equity derivatives trade', 11th July 2006; Jeremy Grant, 'Flat out: why regulators are rushing to keep up with mergers by exchanges', 13th July 2006; Paul J. Davies, 'A brouhaha over best execution', 18th July 2006; Neal Wolkoff, 'America's regulations are scaring the Sox off small caps', 1st August 2006; Jeremy Grant and Chrystia Freeland, 'Brokering change: how Cox is building a consensus as regulation goes global', 4th August 2006; Norma Cohen, 'SWX reduces its Virt-x trading fees', 5th September 2006; John Authers and Norma Cohen, 'Clearing the floor: how a regulatory overhaul is helping rivals to close in on the Big Board', 14th September 2006; Anuj Gangahar, 'Nanoseconds matter as traders prepare for a shake-up', 14th September 2006; Jeremy Grant, 'SEC set to relax margin rules in move to cut trading costs', 16th October 2006; Jeremy Grant, 'US looks to regain edge by relaxing margin rules', 20th October 2006; Benn Steil, 'Derivatives exchanges owe much to wise regulation', 28th November 2006; Norma Cohen, 'Level playing fields', 28th November 2006; Jeremy Grant, 'Capital, traders and fraudsters are all completely mobile', 28th November 2006; Tim Plews, 'The "Balls clauses" are a mixed blessing for the City', 29th November 2006; James Blitz, 'Stamp Duty on non-resident exchange traded funds to go', 30th November 2006; Jeremy Grant, Stephanie Kirchgaessner and Francesco Guerrera, 'Panel calls for regulatory loosening', 1st December 2006; Chris Hughes, 'Concerns grow for rules as global deals loom', 1st December 2006; Gregory Meyer, 'Dilemma over limiting speculation', 4th August 2009.

a way of merging an EU-wide financial market, fractured by different tax and regulatory regimes, into a single unit. In 2005 Oliver Lodge referred to the 'Europeanisation of regulation'[76] as directives from Brussels were incorporated into national laws. An estimated two-thirds of new financial regulations in the EU were being generated centrally by then. Though this created the impression of an EU-wide regulatory system having been put in place by then, this was not the case. Reflecting the inability to harmonize taxes and regulations across the EU was the continued success enjoyed by Luxembourg and Dublin in attracting a diverse range of financial activities. They did this by providing a more liberal regulatory environment and a lower tax regime than other countries within the EU, especially Germany and the UK, where the main financial markets were located. The EU was unwilling to tackle these anomalies because of concerns that any action would drive the business to non-member states, such as Switzerland, where the rules would not apply.

Fundamental to the creation of a single market for financial services in the EU were taxes and regulations that applied to all. Only that would create the conditions under which financial services became based in those locations possessing the greatest competitive advantage, but that position was never reached. In pursuing regulatory harmonization the European Commission faced strong, and often successful opposition from national governments committed to protecting their markets from external competition. Alexandre Lamfalussy observed in 2000 that, even after the introduction of the Euro, the EU's financial markets were 'not integrating fast enough and there is not a genuine single market'.[77] The model that the European Commission was trying to follow was that of the USA, where certain powers were delegated to the individual states, and a degree of diversity permitted, but strong central control rested with such bodies as the Federal Reserve, the SEC, and the CFTC. In 2002 Francesco Guerrera and Vincent Boland concluded that if Frits Bolkestein, the EU commissioner for financial services, had his way, the result would be to 'bring Europe closer to the US'.[78] The problem he faced was that the EU was not the USA but a collection of national states that retained a high degree of independence and lacked the homogeneity produced by centuries of unity.

The opposition of national governments made it impossible to harmonize taxes and regulations across the EU or even establish a single regulatory agency with enforcement powers. Attempts were made in 2000 to create a Securities and Exchange Commission for the EU but they failed. A Paris-based Committee of European Securities Regulators (CESR) was set up but it was relegated to co-ordinating the actions of national agencies, not enforcing commonly agreed standards and rules. As Vincent Boland reported in 2001 'Regulators in all European Union countries have differing standards and requirements and issuers have no choice to meet them. This is costly and time-consuming.'[79] In that year fifteen separate barriers to cross-border share trading in the EU were identified. The European Commission worked hard to remove or reduce these but progress was both slow and partial, being frustrated not only by national governments but also established institutions. One example of this was the failure of the European Commission to break up the vertical silos operated by a number of exchanges, even though they were considered a major barrier to market integration. Deborah Hargreaves, Norma Cohen, and Barney Jopson reported in

[76] Oliver Lodge, 'Not waving but drowning in regulation', 7th March 2005.

[77] Peter Norman and Deborah Hargreaves, 'Long haul for Lamfalussy on securities markets' regulation', 28th December 2000.

[78] Francesco Guerrera and Vincent Boland, 'Pitfalls lurk in drawing up new trading rules', 28th September 2002.

[79] Vincent Boland, 'Euro gives spur for updating', 21st June 2001.

2005 that 'Officials are keen to avoid an entity that encompasses a stock exchange and clearing and settlement arm, becoming too complacent and not keeping ahead of market developments.'[80] The remedy was to split such combinations but this was not achieved. A persistent fear throughout the EU was that regulatory harmonization would favour London to the disadvantage of their financial centres, and this concern grew in the wake of the introduction of the Euro, even though the UK did not adopt the single currency. According to Patrick Jenkins in 2005 'Single-market standardisation and technological advance across the European Union have made the British capital the continent's hub in areas such as sales and trading in equities and bonds—to the detriment of continental centres such as Frankfurt, Paris and Milan.'[81] The introduction of the Euro had led to a marked consolidation of Europe's wholesale financial markets and this benefited London, as it was already the largest single location for such activity. In response national governments turned to regulation as a way of blunting the City of London's competitive advantage in financial services.

Frustrated by their inability to drive through EU-wide regulations supervised by a European SEC the European Commission chose the next best option, which was to force the removal of discriminatory barriers and use competition to push through uniformity of practice. This led to the EU's Investment Services Directive (ISD) of 1996. The ISD was designed to open up competition between the EU's thirty-two stock exchanges and twenty-four derivatives exchanges, as they would no longer be protected by national boundaries. At the heart of the new regime in Europe was the idea that all firms trading in securities would be equally qualified to do so. In the words of John Gapper in 1996, investment firms regulated in one country could gain a passport 'permitting them to operate in all others as banks and securities houses.'[82] This included the right to participate in other countries' stock markets. The ISD was accompanied by the Capital Adequacy Directive (CAD), which required banks to allocate capital to cover risks of losses through adverse movements in the markets for shares, bonds, and currencies, so creating a level playing field across the member states. The combination of the ISD and the CAD simultaneously removed barriers to cross-border competition within the EU while imposing common capital requirements so that all those participating in the common market had to operate under the same conditions.

Though they removed barriers and set minimum standards these directives did not harmonize regulations across the EU. They left considerable scope for national governments to interpret the rules in different ways, which worked to prevent the emergence of a uniform regulatory structure across the EU, while many governments simply delayed implementing the directives. The ISD came into force in January 1996 but a year later six countries still had to implement it, including Germany. Nevertheless, the effect of the directives was to force the member states of the EU to end the national monopolies of national stock exchanges. The law protecting the members of the Italian exchanges from external competition was ruled illegal by the European Court of Justice, for example. Membership of exchanges had to be opened up to banks and brokers located anywhere in the EU, regardless of whether they had a physical presence in the country in which it was located. However, in a number of European countries there remained a legal requirement for all trading in certain financial instruments to be conducted through exchanges, which prevented the growth of alternative OTC markets. This acted to prevent the development of pan-European electronic markets accessible from throughout the EU, which could challenge exchanges.

[80] Deborah Hargreaves, Norma Cohen, and Barney Jopson, 'Europe looks to new law on securities', 26th January 2005.

[81] Patrick Jenkins, 'Faltering financial centre sees bright lights amid gloom', 6th December 2005.

[82] John Gapper, 'New rules, new rivals, new order', 16th February 1996.

The expectation of the European Commission was that the directives would force exchanges to become more competitive by lowering their charges, ending restrictive practices, opening up membership and standardizing their rules and regulations. Though this did happen to a degree national exchanges continued to occupy a dominant position in the market for stocks and derivatives. They remained the centre of liquidity for the products they provided a market for, as well as being the location where current prices were produced. This made it difficult to generate competition. However, it was those national exchanges that operated the vertical-silo model that were regarded as the greatest barriers to competition by the European Commission. By bundling trading, clearing, and settlement into a single package they made it difficult for other exchanges, or the independent Electronic Communication Networks (ECNs), to provide an alternative trading system on its own, though they could be cheaper. Without unbundling it was impossible to break down the power of the vertical silos and the European Commission failed to achieve that. With exchanges increasingly viewed by the European Commission as barriers to integration, EU regulators turned to promoting the interests of the banks. By then it was becoming apparent that an increasing share of trading in financial markets bypassed the exchanges. An estimate made in 2003 suggested that around 25 per cent of all trading handled by the largest investment banks was undertaken internally rather than through exchanges.

In 2002, under a new Investment Services Directive, the European Commission proposed to enshrine in law the right of all investors to trade shares directly with each other and with banks, rather than be required to use exchanges as was still the case in France, Italy, and Spain. Also the distinctions traditionally drawn between exchange-regulated markets, banks internalizing transactions between buyers and sellers, and electronic trading platforms all disappeared. All could provide markets providing they abided by broadly similar rules. The intention was to undermine the ability of national exchanges to dominate national markets and so stimulate trade across borders, leading to the creation of a single market, which was the overriding aim of the European Commission. There was a risk of market fragmentation but that was expected to be only temporary. The regulators appeared to be siding with the banks against the exchanges, which, in any case, were becoming profit-orientated companies. As banks were already large and highly regulated there was no need to directly regulate financial markets. Instead, basic rules could be laid down relating to transparency and operation, focusing especially on the perspective of the investor, and the banks would then be monitored to ensure compliance. Banks would be left free to trade on exchanges, match deals in-house, use electronic markets, or through any OTC facility. The outcome was the Markets in Financial Instruments Directive (Mifid) introduced in 2006. Its stated aim was to create a single and seamless market for capital and financial services within the EU. This was to be achieved by breaking down the national monopolies enjoyed by national stock exchanges. What the final shape of the securities market would be was unknown as it would be the product of the competitive environment unleashed. What Mifid represented was the demise of exchanges as market regulators in the EU. In their place power rested with agencies under the control of national governments as these would have responsibility for supervising the banks and framing the rules under which markets operated. In taking this route the EU was following the USA in placing regulation in the hands of national authorities, who then devolved day-to-day management of the market to the banks.[83]

[83] Norma Cohen, 'Exploiting the differences', 30th April 1993; Guy de Jonquières, 'Single EU securities market at risk', 16th May 1995; John Gapper and Richard Lapper, 'Europe unlocked for dealers', 2nd January 1996; John Simkins, 'Milan bourse ready for EU reforms', 2nd February 1996; John Gapper, 'New rules, new rivals, new

Conclusion

Throughout the world in the years before the Global Financial Crisis, the regulation of financial activity became the responsibility of government-appointed agencies. These agencies framed the rules under which markets operated and supervised the general activity that took place. However, these agencies lacked the staff and practical expertise required to supervise the constant trading that took place, which grew rapidly in volume, variety and complexity. In the past, day-to-day market supervision had been left to the exchanges in such products as stocks and derivatives or left unregulated being the responsibility of those involved. However, as the nature of exchanges changed, and more and more trading took place on the unregulated markets, exchanges could no longer be relied upon to provide market supervision. In their place the regulatory agencies assumed more responsibility for themselves, while recognizing banks, especially the largest, as the vehicles through which day-to-day supervision of the markets was conducted. The once important self-regulatory role of exchanges was abandoned in this new world. New products, such as securitized assets, that would once have been listed and then traded on exchanges were not. Instead,

order', 16th February 1996; Christine Moir, 'Once more unto a breach?', 16th February 1996; John Gapper, 'Out with the old, in with the new', 28th February 1997; *FT* Staff, 'Surviving in the free world', 21st March 1996; Andrew Hill, 'Time to solve problems', 26th November 1996; Christine Moir, 'Barriers go up in Europe', 28th February 1997; George Graham, 'Radical changes may lie ahead', 9th April 1997; Andrew Fisher, 'European bourses may get lift on back of Emu', 15th April 1997; Andrew Fisher, 'Bigger is better in bourses' brave euro world', 15th July 1997; Stanislas Yassukovich, 'Single market for equities', 26th January 1998; Christine Moir, 'New rules in changed world', 24th March 1998; Simon Davies and George Graham, 'Europe's Big Bang', 8th July 1998; Edward Luce, 'Bankers and Brussels at odds over impact on London', 9th December 1998; James Mackintosh, 'Share trade tax revenue doomed, says regulator', 10th January 2000; Aline van Duyn, 'Trading costs reach unacceptable levels', 8th September 2000; Peter Norman, 'European SEC plan spurned', 16th September 2000; James Mackintosh, 'Watchdogs draft rules for new stock markets', 26th September 2000; Peter Norman and Deborah Hargreaves, 'Long haul for Lamfalussy on securities markets' regulation', 28th December 2000; Peter Norman and Vincent Boland, 'Caution over pace of market regulation', 16th February 2001; Tom Burns, 'Foreign funds in a fever', 28th March 2001; Vincent Boland, 'LSE chairman calls for a split in exchange activities', 26th April 2001; Vincent Boland, 'Rift opens between LSE and Europe', 27th April 2001; Vincent Boland, 'Euro gives spur for updating', 21st June 2001; Francesco Guerrera, 'Brussels plans share trading shake-up', 27th September 2002; Francesco Guerrera and Vincent Boland, 'Pitfalls lurk in drawing up new trading rules', 28th September 2002; Charles Pretzlik, 'The financial revolution that never was', 9th May 2003; Alex Skorecki, 'Markets braced for ISD changes', 22nd May 2003; Simon Targett, 'Time to open up Europe's money centre', 26th May 2003; Doris Grass, 'Stock exchanges attack proposed EU rule changes', 29th August 2003; Roger Blitz, 'City launches Brussels office to boost EU clout', 19th January 2004; Mark Andress, 'Prague SE sees future in IPOs', 2nd November 2004; Alex Skorecki, 'Europe's paperless trail', 25th January 2005; Deborah Hargreaves, Norma Cohen and Barney Jopson, 'Europe looks to new law on securities', 26th January 2005; Oliver Lodge, 'Not waving but drowning in regulation', 7th March 2005; Tobias Buck, 'Dealing costs must be cut, says Brussels', 13th September 2005; Barney Jopson, 'European regulators learn to sing in harmony', 17th November 2005; Stephen Fidler, 'Basel 2 boosts Europe's repo market', 29th November 2005; Patrick Jenkins, 'Faltering financial centre sees bright lights amid gloom', 6th December 2005; Stephen Fidler, 'How the Square Mile defeated the prophets of doom', 10th December 2005; Barney Jopson, 'Regulatory overhaul brings rising hope', 16th February 2006; Tobias Buck and Norma Cohen, 'Call to break up exchanges', 20th February 2006; Patrick Jenkins and Norma Cohen, 'Bourses attack bank moves to upset trading structures', 21st February 2006; George Parker, Christine Mai, and Norma Cohen, 'EU issues deadline to exchanges on charges', 7th March 2006; Peter Thal Larsen, and Barney Jopson, 'Good behaviour key to regulator's remit', 28th March 2006; Kurt Viermetz, 'No need to tinker with the integrated clearing model', 13th April 2006; Tobias Buck, 'Competition absent in clearing: EU', 25th May 2006; Paul J Davies, 'FSA backing for UK bond markets', 6th July 2006; Norma Cohen, 'Brussels to act on securities', 10th July 2006; Norma Cohen, 'EU securities code receives mixed review', 12th July 2006; Norma Cohen, 'SWX reduces its Virt-x trading fees', 5th September 2006; Peter Thal Larsen, 'Many are miffed at the costly Mifid', 26th October 2006; Peter Thal Larsen, 'Banks switch view of Mifid', 16th November 2006; Peter Thal Larsen and Barney Jopson, 'Cost analysis of Mifid rules confirms FSA chief's doubts', 25th November 2006; Tim Plews, 'The "Balls clauses" are a mixed blessing for the City', 29th November 2006; James Blitz, 'Stamp Duty on non-resident exchange traded funds to go', 30th November 2006; Martin Wolf, 'The new capitalism', 19th June 2007.

they were approved by rating agencies. Banks then provided the market through which they were bought and sold, while the government-appointed agencies looked on.

However, there was an inherent contradiction in this support for banks among regulators. The regulators wanted banks to take responsibility for market regulation, but that was best achieved by the megabanks as they had the scale and resources to recruit, train, pay, and police the appropriate staff unlike small banks. At the same time regulators wanted the banking system to become more competitive, which was interpreted as having numerous individual banks engaged in a struggle for business, but that meant less attention to regulatory activity. As banks grew larger, and the volume and complexity of financial transactions expanded, so more and more responsibility was devolved to them and away from gatekeepers whether they were exchanges or accountants. The megabanks became the trusted gatekeepers of the financial system under the overall supervision of statutory regulatory authorities. In this new regulatory system there was no place for self-regulation as practised by exchanges. Self-regulation had imposed a financial burden on exchanges, which would only be borne if privileges were obtained in return. When exchanges were reduced to the same level as OTC markets or ECNs then these privileges disappeared. Furthermore, the expense attached to regulation forced exchanges to levy higher charges on their users than was the case with OTC markets or ECNs.

In a world where exchanges competed against each other for business, and with alternative markets, the cost of regulation could not be passed onto the customer through higher fees, as that would drive business away. However, exchanges did possess two major competitive advantages as they were the centre of liquidity and where the current market price was determined. If the balance of trading shifted away from exchanges then so would their command of liquidity. Similarly, if access to current prices became freely available then trading could take place outside an exchange in full confidence that it reflected current market conditions. Intervention by regulators, at the beginning of the twentieth century, was aimed at making prices freely available, in the interests of the investor, which encouraged trading to migrate away from exchanges. In turn, that undermined the position of exchanges as centres of liquidity. Though exchanges continued to be treated as semi-official organizations their regulatory authority was being rapidly eroded by the role played by statutory agencies, who intervened to undermine their monopoly power by forcing the instant dissemination of prices, greater transparency, and increased competition. In turn, regulators then attempted to extend the reach of their authority by recognizing these new trading platforms as exchanges. The problems faced by regulators then became even more difficult with cross-border mergers.

13

Trends, Events, and Centres, 2007–20

Introduction

To many the Global Financial Crisis that engulfed the world in 2008 was an event that could not happen because of the trends that had preceded it. The emergence of the megabanks, the switch to the originate-and-distribute model, the introduction of the Basel Rules, and the use of derivative contracts were all meant to make the global financial system much more resilient. Proof that this was the case came with the absence of a crisis following the collapse of the dot.com speculative bubble. Under the collective guidance of central banks the world appeared to have discovered the secret of how to deliver a financial system that met the needs of all users and was also both competitive and stable. This system balanced the desire of governments to pursue independent economic, monetary, and financial policies with the free movement of funds around the world and relatively stable exchange rates. Not all were convinced that the impossible had been achieved. They saw the Global Financial Crisis as the inevitable consequence of the trends that had been gathering pace since the 1970s. The removal of barriers to international financial flows, combined with the national deregulation of banks and markets, had resulted in an unstable cocktail that threatened to explode at any moment. The various financial crises that had occurred during the 1980s and 1990s provided ample warnings of this instability but they went unheeded. Governments had lost the ability to control markets as the volume of transactions expanded exponentially and took place without any regulatory supervision or even human involvement. The products being traded had become so complex that they were little understood even though increasing reliance was being placed on them to cover risks. Banks had become so big and complex that they had outgrown national financial systems, becoming the conduits through which an integrated global economy operated on a 24/7 basis. As leverage and volatility rose increased faith was placed in business models and mathematical formulas to deliver the stability that had once been associated with the pre-1970s era of control and compartmentalization.

Though the Global Financial Crisis was preceded by a transformation in the composition, structure, and operation of financial markets that did not mean that the former was the inevitable product of the latter. The problem with predicting the outcome of trends is that they generate conflicting results, which are then interpreted with the benefit of hindsight. The changes that had taken place since the 1970s produced both stability and instability. The trends that preceded the crisis contributed to what happened but so did the responses. Before, during, and after the crisis decisions were taken that influenced the outcome. Trends laid the groundwork for what took place but what made it happen were the individual responses of profit-maximizing bankers and fund managers, myopic regulators and central bankers, greedy savers and investors, self-interested politicians and administrators, and over-confident experts and advisors. The Global Financial Crisis was neither the inevitable results of trends nor the responsibility of a few. Instead, it was caused by the interaction of underlying forces and individual responses, shaped by the decisions taken by

Banks, Exchanges, and Regulators: Global Financial Markets from the 1970s. Ranald Michie, Oxford University Press (2021).

DOI: 10.1093/oso/9780199553730.003.0013

those seeking to gain the maximum advantage from the situation they found themselves in. It was those decisions that dictated the direction of travel but they were not the only ones that could have been taken.

In terms of trends the big winners in the years before the crisis were the megabanks as these met the needs of an integrated world economy and the operations of giant multinational corporations. In a world where the barriers to market integration had been removed, both nationally and internationally, megabanks were able to thrive. These megabanks were the trusted counterparties to all transactions so that payments and receipts could move seamlessly around the world; assets and liabilities continuously matched across all variables; and savers and investors linked to borrowers for the benefit of all. These banks had become too big to fail not because of any implied support from a national government but because of their depth and breadth, their internal controls and supervision, and the way they structured their business. Their existence reassured governments, regulators, and central banks that the stability of the global financial system could be safely left in their hands, absolving them of responsibility. The other big winner before the Global Financial Crisis were those financial products that contributed to the flexibility and the stability of the global financial system, removing the need for governments to intervene or central banks to act as lenders of last resort. These products included securitized assets as these lessened the reliance upon the lend-and-hold model and the threat of a liquidity crisis that accompanied it. In its place banks could operate the originate-and-distribute model in which loans were converted into disposable assets which could be sold to meet withdrawals and redemptions. There was also a wide range of derivative products that covered the risks associated with the volatility of stock and bond prices, exchange rates and interest rates, and the risk of counterparty default whether of customers to whom loans had been made or fellow banks.

The main losers in this process were the regulated markets. As the balance between the megabanks and the markets they used tilted in favour of the former the need to regulate the process of buying and selling or borrowing and lending was no longer considered necessary. All that could be left to the megabanks, especially as they were already regulated. Self-regulating exchanges were not only unnecessary but their existence distorted the operation of competitive marketplaces because of the power they gave to their members. Instead of exchanges the megabanks could be left to deal with each other and their customers, in full confidence that the supervision they were already subjected to, along with their own self-interest, would result in markets that were simultaneously liquid and transparent. What requirement there was for regulation was placed in the hands of government-appointed agencies whose mission was to protect savers and investors from their own folly and the actions of the corrupt and fraudulent. The mission of the regulators was no longer to ensure that the market functioned and was stable by reducing counterparty risk and exposure to manipulation. Stock and commodity exchanges were relics of a bygone age in an era when the inter-bank and Over-The-Counter Markets were dominant. Even central banks lost one of their prime functions in this remodelled financial system, which was to act as lenders of last resort in a liquidity crisis, distinguishing between those banks that were solvent and those that were not. The size and diversification of the megabanks, adherence to the Basel Rules, the operation of the originate model of banking, and the use of derivatives meant that a liquidity crisis was highly unlikely, especially in a developed economy. What that meant was that central banks could confine themselves to ensuring that the environment within which banks operated was stable in terms of prices, interest rates, and exchange rates. Money not banking became the focus of central banks. A new hierarchy had emerged within the global financial system in which governments had stepped back from direct intervention, central banks restricted themselves to acting as guardians of monetary stability, and regulators focused on protecting the interests of the innocent and the vulnerable. That left the megabanks with responsibility for the functioning of not only the banking system but also financial markets as the distinctions between the two, as well as within banking itself, became so blurred as to become meaningless. Such were the most marked features of the trends preceding the Global Financial Crisis.

Technology

Underlying these trends was the revolution that took place in the technology of finance. Writing in 2008 Ross Tieman suggested that 'For a decade, investment banks, traders and exchanges have been engaged in a technology race, in which the fastest computers net the biggest profits.' The result was 'a global switch to electronic trading'.[1] By then computer-driven trading based on algorithmic models accounted for 40 per cent of transactions in US markets and was rising worldwide. The ability to process and transmit vast amounts of information, and to buy and sell at the speed of light, transformed the way markets functioned and the actions of banks and fund managers. Bill Cline, an expert on the operation of financial markets, claimed in 2007 that 'everyone can trade directly with everyone else. The hub-and-spoke network does not really stand up any longer.'[2] The result was to make financial markets cheaper to use, more accessible, and more transparent. As Norma Cohen observed in 2007, 'nothing communicates aggregate demand more immediately and accurately than the actual price a buyer or seller paid a split-second earlier'.[3] These advances in the technology of communication and trading allowed global banks to provide savers, investors, and borrowers with access to deep pools of liquidity, including ones for the assets generated by securitization. Banks were also able to continuously adjust and match their positions with regard to assets and liabilities over time, type, currency, and all other variables, and so reduce the risks they were exposed to. Before the crisis it was the positive aspects of the technological revolution that were emphasized.

In the wake of the crisis it was the destabilizing effects of this technological revolution that were emphasized. The connectivity that technology had provided, and the ability to trade in volume and at speed, was blamed for increased volatility as it removed the barriers that had contained the transmission of buying and selling pressure. Technology was also blamed for the increased reliance on computer-based trading strategies that destabilized markets. These negative comments led to calls for curbs on the electronic revolution that was sweeping financial markets but little changed, despite the crisis. By then the revolution in computing and communications had become so embedded in the way that trading took place that there was no willingness to reverse what had happened. Writing in 2010 Jeremy Grant and Michael Mackenzie reported that 'Advances in technology have been so great in the past five years that markets are now overwhelmingly driven by machines rather than humans punching orders into a keyboard.'[4] It was as if the Global Financial Crisis had never happened for all the impact it had. The reason was because the new technology had

[1] Ross Tieman, 'Algo trading: the dog that bit its master', 19th March 2008.
[2] Anuj Gangahar, 'Chicago's program for change', 20th March 2007.
[3] Norma Cohen, 'Reuters to join scramble for real-time data', 11th July 2007.
[4] Jeremy Grant and Michael Mackenzie, 'Ghost in the machine', 18th February 2010.

become a vital ingredient in the way financial markets operated. By 2017 the inter-bank communications system, Swift, was handling 7bn messages a year, connecting more than 11,000 banks into a single network spanning the world.

Within this network international transactions flowed seamlessly whether they involved the continuous making and receiving of payments; matching assets and liabilities over time, place, amount, and currency; or providing the credit and capital without which economic activity would cease. Michael Mackenzie himself observed that 'Today, equities are transacted in microseconds or 1,000 times faster than the human eye can blink, while sophisticated electronic systems underpin trading across global bond and foreign exchange markets.'[5] Frits Vogel, head of swaps at the interdealer broker, ICAP, considered that 'Any market that is highly liquid, offers continuous trading and has tight bid-ask spreads suits electronic trading.'[6] By 2016 Robin Wigglesworth reported that 'Trading has never been easier and costs never lower thanks to human intermediaries being rendered obsolete.'[7] Serving this electronic marketplace was an embedded infrastructure of computers and communication networks that continued to expand and improve, with investments in new underwater fibre optic cables and microwave transmitters that provided connections at the speed of light. In 2012 a 7,800km high-speed fibre-optic cable was in place linking Tokyo, Hong Kong, and Singapore.[8]

[5] Michael Mackenzie, 'Regulators push technology to track trades in real time', 29th September 2010.

[6] Izabella Kaminska, 'Man and machinery in perfect harmony', 28th September 2010.

[7] Robin Wigglesworth, 'Algorithms bring benefits but fears of accidents grow', 1st June 2016.

[8] Gillian Tett, 'Dark Liquidity system to launch', 5th February 2007; Norma Cohen, 'Kansas City undercuts NYC', 9th February 2007; Anuj Gangahar, 'Chicago's program for change', 20th March 2007; Norma Cohen, 'Doors open as industry removes barriers', 30th March 2007; Norma Cohen, 'Competitive age dawns in Europe', 3rd April 2007; Michael Mackenzie, 'Global trade facilitators behind a 24-hour market', 20th April 2007; Norma Cohen, 'Reuters to join scramble for real-time data', 11th July 2007; Anuj Gangahar, 'Nasdaq chief says sector will fragment', 8th January 2008; Ross Tieman, 'Algo trading: the dog that bit its master', 19th March 2008; Ross Tieman, 'When microseconds really count', 19th March 2008; Jeremy Grant, 'Geeks grow into the kingmakers', 21st October 2008; Jeremy Grant, 'Bourses in data arms race', 15th September 2009; Peter Garnham, 'Net brings power to the people', 29th September 2009; Michael Mackenzie and Jeremy Grant, 'Trading co-locate takes root in Essex hangar', 30th September 2009; Jeremy Grant, 'Screens replacing screams in the dealing room', 2nd October 2009; Jeremy Grant and Michael Mackenzie, 'Ghost in the machine', 18th February 2010; Michael Mackenzie and Jeremy Grant, 'Liffe proves its worth to NYSE', 4th March 2010; Jeremy Grant, 'Plunge places focus on safety of the share markets', 11th May 2010; Michael Mackenzie, '"Flash glitch" fears force SEC hand', 13th May 2010; Aline van Duyn, Michael Mackenzie and Jeremy Grant, 'That sinking feeling', 2nd June 2010; Jeremy Grant, 'Emerging markets dump old trading habits', 9th September 2010; Jeremy Grant, 'Light speed ahead', 27th September 2010; Jennifer Hughes, 'Innovation drives trading surge', 28th September 2010; Izabella Kaminska, 'Man and machinery in perfect harmony', 28th September 2010; Michael Mackenzie, 'Regulators push technology to track trades in real time', 29th September 2010; Aline van Duyn and Telis Demos, 'Flash Crash: market reforms to be examined', 5th October 2010; Philip Stafford, 'Regulators show united front', 20th October 2010; Hal Weitzman, 'Co-location set to reap up to $40 million for CME', 29th October 2010; Jeremy Grant, 'Market structures face test of trust', 3rd November 2010; Telis Demos and Aline van Duyn, 'Debate reopens over equity trades', 21st December 2010; Gregory Meyer, 'High-speed commodities traders under crash scrutiny', 10th March 2011; Jennifer Hughes, 'Focus on speed blurs big picture', 29th March 2011; Hal Weitzman and Telis Demos, 'Ultra-fast trading firms hit headwinds in race to be first', 14th July 2011; Janina Conboye, 'Computers create demand for a different set of skills', 14th July 2011; Jeremy Grant, 'Barriers higher for Asian dominance in algo trading', 24th August 2012; Kara Scannell, 'Rise of machines prompts SEC to join the tech war', 6th March 2013; Elaine Moore, 'Humans or machines: who's running the markets?', 16–17th March 2013; Gill Plimmer and Philip Stafford, 'Cable hub gives City edge on Frankfurt', 7th May 2013; Philip Stafford, 'Deutsche Börse unfurls plan for European champion', 27–28th February 2016; Robin Wigglesworth, 'Algorithms bring benefits but fears of accidents grow', 1st June 2016; Gregory Meyer and Nicole Bullock, 'Algo traders look beyond need for speed in quest to gain competitive edge', 31st March 2017; Robin Wigglesworth, 'Hedge funds seek to park quantum revolution', 2nd November 2017; Philip Stafford, 'Selling time to traders: the physicist who measures deals in microseconds', 5th February 2018; Robin Wigglesworth and Stefania Palma, 'Quant funds take creative tack to gain recruitment edge over Silicon Valley', 29th September 2018.

It was not only the revolution in communications that continued unabated, for the same was true of the investment in the computer-driven processing and analysing of data by banks, and the employment of sophisticated trading strategies based upon the results. In 2013 Erozan Kurtas, the SEC's Head of the Quantitative Analysis Unit, judged that 'The use of quantitative techniques and computer-driven algorithms has changed the market structure and financial world drastically in the past decade.'[9] Through the combination of sophisticated mathematical models, automated trading programs, and communication at the speed of light it was possible to spot momentary price discrepancies and either generate large profits through high-frequency trading or cover an exposure to risk by buying or selling assets. These strategies had been developing before the crisis and continued unabated afterwards. Critics continued to claim that these high-frequency trading strategies led to wild swings in individual stocks, and even entire markets, with damaging consequences for all participants. One example citied was the flash crash that occurred in the USA on 6th May 2010, when the stock market dropped suddenly due to a wave of selling. Jeremy Grant, writing that month, commented that 'A technological revolution that has allowed trading at almost the speed of light, combined with fragmentation of trading across multiple kinds of venues, produced a sequence of events that turned the US equity markets into a dangerous quagmire last week.'[10] In contrast, others claimed that high-frequency trading reduced volatility, because the greater volume of transactions increased the depth of the market. What became evident was that all the high-frequency traders were doing was exploiting market fragmentation by buying and selling for the profits to be made from minute price differences. Arbitrageurs had long conducted this type of trading within and between markets, and it contributed to both stability, by equalizing prices, and instability through sudden spikes in buying and selling. Technology facilitated a great increase in the speed and volume of financial transactions but the strategies and objectives remain unaltered, and so there was little attempt to reverse what was taking place.[11]

[9] Kara Scannell, 'Rise of machines prompts SEC to join the tech war', 6th March 2013.

[10] Jeremy Grant, 'Plunge places focus on safety of the share markets', 11th May 2010.

[11] Gillian Tett, 'Dark Liquidity system to launch', 5th February 2007; Norma Cohen, 'Kansas City undercuts NYC', 9th February 2007; Anuj Gangahar, 'Chicago's program for change', 20th March 2007; Norma Cohen, 'Doors open as industry removes barriers', 30th March 2007; Norma Cohen, 'Competitive age dawns in Europe', 3rd April 2007; Michael Mackenzie, 'Global trade facilitators behind a 24-hour market', 20th April 2007; Norma Cohen, 'Reuters to join scramble for real-time data', 11th July 2007; Anuj Gangahar, 'Nasdaq chief says sector will fragment', 8th January 2008; Ross Tieman, 'Algo trading: the dog that bit its master', 19th March 2008; Ross Tieman, 'When microseconds really count', 19th March 2008; Jeremy Grant, 'Geeks grow into the kingmakers', 21st October 2008; Jeremy Grant, 'Bourses in data arms race', 15th September 2009; Peter Garnham, 'Net brings power to the people', 29th September 2009; Michael Mackenzie and Jeremy Grant, 'Trading co-locate takes root in Essex hangar', 30th September 2009; Jeremy Grant, 'Screens replacing screams in the dealing room', 2nd October 2009; Jeremy Grant and Michael Mackenzie, 'Ghost in the machine', 18th February 2010; Michael Mackenzie and Jeremy Grant, 'Liffe proves its worth to NYSE', 4th March 2010; Jeremy Grant, 'Plunge places focus on safety of the share markets', 11th May 2010; Michael Mackenzie, '"Flash glitch" fears force SEC hand', 13th May 2010; Aline van Duyn, Michael Mackenzie and Jeremy Grant, 'That sinking feeling', 2nd June 2010; Jeremy Grant, 'Emerging markets dump old trading habits', 9th September 2010; Jeremy Grant, 'Light speed ahead', 27th September 2010; Jennifer Hughes, 'Innovation drives trading surge', 28th September 2010; Izabella Kaminska, 'Man and machinery in perfect harmony', 28th September 2010; Michael Mackenzie, 'Regulators push technology to track trades in real time', 29th September 2010; Aline van Duyn and Telis Demos, 'Flash Crash: market reforms to be examined', 5th October 2010; Philip Stafford, 'Regulators show united front', 20th October 2010; Hal Weitzman, 'Co-location set to reap up to $40 million for CME', 29th October 2010; Jeremy Grant, 'Market structures face test of trust', 3rd November 2010; Telis Demos and Aline van Duyn, 'Debate reopens over equity trades', 21st December 2010; Gregory Meyer, 'High-speed commodities traders under crash scrutiny', 10th March 2011; Jennifer Hughes, 'Focus on speed blurs big picture', 29th March 2011; Hal Weitzman and Telis Demos, 'Ultra-fast trading firms hit headwinds in race to be first', 14th July 2011; Janina Conboye, 'Computers create demand for a different set of skills', 14th July 2011; Jeremy Grant, 'Barriers higher for Asian dominance in algo trading', 24th August 2012; Kara Scannell, 'Rise of machines prompts SEC to join the tech war', 6th March

Trends versus Events

The trends in technology were unchanged by the Global Financial Crisis. Nor was there a return to the pre-1970s world with a reimposition of international barriers or highly-compartmentalized financial structures. Nevertheless there was every indication that other pre-crisis trends would not be allowed to continue. Megabanks had been at the epicentre of the Global Financial Crisis, with the failure of Lehman Brothers in September 2008, and intervention to save others from a similar fate, being the most visible of all that happened. The conclusion drawn by many was that trends in banking over the preceding decades had rendered the system increasingly unstable with the crisis being the inevitable result. As Patrick Jenkins, Brooke Masters, and Tom Braithwaite reflected in 2011:

> With hindsight, it is clear the structure of the (banking) sector was an accident waiting to happen. Institutions had grown distorted in the pursuit of bumper profits. They held little equity capital to protect themselves—and what they did have was in many cases amplified by as much as fifty times with debt instruments. Vast profits were made from borrowing cheaply, often short-term, and assuming that the risks inherent in products from domestic mortgages to complex derivatives were negligible.[12]

In the eyes of many the repeal on 12th November 1999 of the Glass–Steagall Act, originally passed in the USA on 16th June 1933, was believed to have led directly to the crisis. As late as 2018 Jeff Merkley, a US senator, stated that, 'When that law was repealed in 1999, some predicted disaster. They were right.'[13] The deregulation of banking was not confined to the USA but took place across the world, and was widely used as an explanation of the financial crisis. In 2009 the German finance minister, Peer Steinbruck, pointed to the 'combination of cheap money, deregulation and a race for returns by executives undeterred by the risks'.[14] In Britain Howard Davies, who had chaired the industry regulator, the Financial Services Authority, highlighted in 2009 the situation that had developed by the eve of the crisis: 'In the light of new instruments, the huge increase in trading volumes and greater volatility in some markets, the total capital in the world's banking system was small. It is also clear that the quality of capital was allowed to deteriorate, with the growth of hybrid instruments which failed to act as cushions when the market went south.'[15]

As the Glass–Steagall Act was believed to have delivered sixty-six years of banking stability for the USA the solution was its reimposition there and adoption around the world. This was the policy urged on governments by respected experts.[16] However, such a conclusion ignored the underlying reality that the deregulation of banking was driven by underlying

2013; Elaine Moore, 'Humans or machines: who's running the markets?', 16–17th March 2013; Gill Plimmer and Philip Stafford, 'Cable hub gives City edge on Frankfurt', 7th May 2013; Philip Stafford, 'Deutsche Börse unfurls plan for European champion', 27–28th February 2016; Robin Wigglesworth, 'Algorithms bring benefits but fears of accidents grow', 1st June 2016; Gregory Meyer and Nicole Bullock, 'Algo traders look beyond need for speed in quest to gain competitive edge', 31st March 2017; Robin Wigglesworth, 'Hedge funds seek to park quantum revolution', 2nd November 2017; Philip Stafford, 'Selling time to traders: the physicist who measures deals in micro-seconds', 5th February 2018; Robin Wigglesworth and Stefania Palma, 'Quant funds take creative tack to gain recruitment edge over Silicon Valley', 29th September 2018.

12 Patrick Jenkins, Brooke Masters, and Tom Braithwaite, 'Hunt for a common front', 8th September 2011.
13 Jeff Merkley, 'Avoid past mistakes and preserve key bank safety law', 26th June 2018.
14 Peer Steinbruck, 'A tax on trading to share the costs of the crisis', 25th September 2009
15 Howard Davies, 'We need urgently to rationalise the rules on capital', 25th September 2009.
16 Martin Arnold, 'How US banks took over the financial world', 17th September 2018.

forces. At the time of its repeal the Glass–Steagall Act was considered neither effective nor enforceable because of the fundamental changes that had taken place, which blurred and even removed the distinctions between different types of banks. As that reality became clear there was a retreat by those backing a new version of the Glass–Steagall Act and enforced dismemberment of the megabanks. Nevertheless, that did not mean that there was not a desire to reverse many of the developments that had taken place in the decades prior to the crisis. The Global Financial Crisis shattered confidence in the resilience of the megabanks and the reliance placed on the use of the originate-and-distribute model. In the wake of the crisis the regulatory environment faced by the megabanks became hostile while securitization was regarded as a prime contributor to the preceding credit bubble. Securitization fell out of favour while regulations such as Dodd Frank in the USA, and those enacted internationally under the new Basel 2 rules, forced the megabanks to withdraw from certain activities, either through direct prohibitions or by introducing much higher capital requirements. This hampered their competitiveness. Writing in 2016 Harriet Agnew and Patrick Jenkins considered that 'Banks themselves are now in decline, cowed by a regulatory clampdown following the 2008 crash.'[17] In their place arose a shadow banking system that could escape the regulations because they were either too small or not classified as systemically important. Robin Wigglesworth and Ben McLannahan reflected in 2018 that 'Since the financial crisis, regulatory changes have aimed to purge leverage, primarily by curtailing the role banks have traditionally played in providing it.'[18]

Nevertheless, underlying trends continued to favour the megabanks. They possessed depth and breadth across a wide range of financial activities, and that was what global fund managers and multinational corporations wanted. It was the megabanks that could afford the costs associated with the latest advances in the technology of communication and computing as well as pay the high salaries commanded by the staff with the required expertise, as these could be spread over a huge organization. It was also the megabanks that were in the best position to cope with the much greater level of regulation introduced after the crisis as, again, the costs of compliance could be distributed over their entire business. As Oliver Ralph observed in 2019, 'A decade after the peak of the financial crisis, there is little sign that politicians and regulators around the world are taking their foot off the pedal when it comes to pursuing the financial services industry.'[19] Banks had either to be big enough to cope with the regulatory consequences of that pursuit or small enough to operate in the shadows and so escape detection. The result was to provide megabanks with competitive advantages over most other banks, despite the greater regulatory scrutiny and capital requirements they were subjected to. They possessed inherent economies of scale and these resurfaced as the aftershock of the Global Financial Crisis faded away. Nevertheless, it did leave the megabanks exposed to the competition of rival financial institutions like fund managers as the liquidity risks they ran were ignored, and so they were subjected to a much lighter regulatory regime.[20]

[17] Harriet Agnew and Patrick Jenkins, 'What's next for the City', 3rd September 2016.

[18] Robin Wigglesworth and Ben McLannahan, 'Liquidity outs leverage as the big worry for investors', 4th May 2018.

[19] Oliver Ralph, 'Conduct replaces capital as focus', 25th March 2019.

[20] David Oakley and Gillian Tett, 'European bond market puts US in the shade', 15th January 2007; Paul J Davies and Richard Beales, 'New players join the credit game', 14th March 2007; *FT* Reporters, 'Solid capital has the upper hand', 23rd September 2008; Peter Thal Larsen and Greg Farrell, 'Landscape shifts for investment banks', 23rd September 2008; Javier Blas, 'Commodities players bid to close the gap on big two', 28th November 2008; John Plender, 'Originative sin', 5th January 2009; Adrian Cox, 'Multiple threats still loom for the investment banking model', 1st April 2009; Gillian Tett and Aline van Duyn, 'On the march', 9th June 2009; Howard

Before the crisis the rise of megabanks appeared unstoppable. In the immediate aftermath of the crisis they appeared doomed, facing dismemberment and controls because governments had been forced to intervene to prevent their collapse, as they were too big to fail. As Martin Arnold wrote in 2014 'These institutions are too big, complex and systemically important to fail. This is why governments have recently been forced to bail them out.'[21] However, the megabanks were not broken up and they rebuilt their position at the centre of the global financial system. They regained their position as trusted counterparties, both to each other and their customers. They also regained the trust of regulators who could see no other way of exercising supervision of the most complex components of the global financial system. Similarly, central banks had no alternative but to put their trust in the megabanks as they not only provided the essential plumbing and architecture of that global financial system but also the means of stabilizing it in the face of potential liquidity crises. Changes were forced on the megabanks but not the reversal of trends forecast by many at the time of the crisis and its immediate aftermath.[22]

Davies, 'We need urgently to rationalise the rules on capital', 25th September 2009; Anousha Sakoui and Brooke Masters, 'UK businesses' finance options undergo rethink', 21st January 2010; Francesco Guerrera and Justin Baer, 'Doubts beset mission to trim giants' girth', 23rd January 2010; *FT* Reporters, 'Proposals fail to forge consensus in Europe', 23rd January 2010; Jennifer Hughes, 'S&P warns on UK mortgage securities', 10th September 2010; Justin Baer, 'From recession to regulation', 27th September 2010; Brooke Masters and Francesco Guerrera, 'Threat to small business', 27th September 2010; Patrick Jenkins, 'New regulatory standards are the next big unknown', 8th October 2010; Jeremy Grant, 'Back office in leading role', 20th October 2010; Brooke Masters, 'Trade finance may become a casualty', 20th October 2010; Aline van Duyn, 'Sector resized and reshaped', 28th October 2010; Brooke Masters and Jeremy Grant, 'Shadow boxes', 3rd February 2011; Jane Croft, 'The danger of relying too much on only one tool', 22nd March 2011; Brooke Masters, 'A real problem for regulators', 22nd March 2011; Brooke Masters, 'League battle over bank risk will end in tiers', 21st June 2011; Patrick Jenkins, Brooke Masters and Tom Braithwaite, 'Hunt for a common front', 8th September 2011; Megan Murphy, 'Search for new approaches has begun', 9th September 2011; Brooke Masters, Henny Sender and Dan McCrum, '"Shadow banks" move in amid regulatory push', 9th September 2011; Brooke Masters and Tom Braithwaite, 'Bankers versus Basel', 3rd October 2011; Paul J. Davies, 'Lack of experience restrains investment in liquidity swaps', 3rd October 2011; Tracy Alloway, 'Counterparty risk makes an anxious return', 27th October 2011; Tracy Alloway, 'Financial system creaks as loan lubricant dries up', 29th November 2011; Patrick Jenkins and Richard Milne, 'Caught in the grip', 2nd December 2011; Tracy Alloway, 'Higher capital demands and dearer funding bring a dual burden', 2nd December 2011; Brooke Masters, 'Reveal leverage ratio ahead of rivals banks told', 2nd December 2011; Tracy Alloway, 'Traditional lenders shiver as shadow banking grows', 29th December 2011; Brooke Masters, 'Banks learn the liquidity lessons from tough rules', 30th December 2011; Patrick Jenkins, Tom Braithwaite and Brooke Masters, 'New force emerges from the shadows', 10th April 2012; Paul J. Davies, 'Banks look to insurers for lessons', 16th April 2012; Sharlene Goff, 'Policymakers recognise SMEs need more funding options', 16th April 2012; Anousha Sakoui, 'Restructuring could lift M&A market', 30th May 2012; Daniel Schäfer, 'A small slice of the action', 30th May 2012; Barbara Ridpath, 'Crisis—and regulation—can breed opportunity', 30th May 2012; Brooke Masters, 'Safety net plans raise industry ire', 19th March 2013; Philip Stafford, 'Industry strives to find its form', 5th November 2014; Martin Arnold, 'Carney's too big to fail buffer represents clear progress despite doubt', 9th December 2014; Philip Stafford, 'Exchange chiefs eye deals to tap new markets', 31st December 2015; Harriet Agnew and Patrick Jenkins, 'What's next for the City', 3rd September 2016; Caroline Binham, 'Shadow banking grows beyond $45tn', 6th March 2018; Robin Wigglesworth and Ben McLannahan, 'Liquidity outs leverage as the big worry for investors', 4th May 2018; Laura Noonan, 'Financials', 12th June 2018; Gillian Tett, 'When the world held its breath', 1st September 2018; John Gapper, 'My naïve part in the downfall of Lehman', 13th September 2018; Martin Arnold, 'How US banks took over the financial world', 17th September 2018; Chris Flood, 'Bond liquidity issues prompt investors to turn to ETFs', 17th September 2018; Mark Vandevelde, 'Financial Crisis', 20th September 2018; Colby Smith, 'Borrowers want dollars—some more than others', 20th September 2018; Robin Wigglesworth and Joe Rennison, 'New credit ecosystem blossoms as portfolio trades surge', 11th October 2018; Claire Jones, Caroline Binham, and Sam Fleming, 'Fed governor to head global finance police', 21st November 2018; Oliver Ralph, 'Conduct replaces capital as focus', 25th March 2019.

[21] Martin Arnold, 'Carney's too big to fail buffer represents clear progress despite doubt', 9th December 2014.

[22] Francesco Guerrera and John Authers, 'Institutions increase equity stakes', 22nd January 2007; Gillian Tett, 'Funds are ousting the banks', 27th April 2007; Norma Cohen, 'Mifid ushers in a new era of trading', 23rd May 2007; Gillian Tett, 'Sub-prime in its context', 19th November 2007; Jennifer Hughes, 'US stands out on worldwide language', 19th November 2007; Ross Tieman, 'Algo trading: the dog that bit its master', 19th March 2008;

Another target for reversal that emerged at the time of the crisis was derivatives. The invention and widespread use of derivative contracts had masked the risks being taken by lenders and investors, encouraging them to increase their exposure because of the attractive returns on offer. Under these circumstances there were calls after the crisis for derivatives to be banned, especially those that were traded on the OTC market. The problem with an outright ban was that regulators wanted to preserve the benefits they delivered, in terms of insuring against losses, while curbing their use by speculators seeking to increase their exposure to gains. The one could not be separated from the other but achieving a balance between the two proved very difficult. As a result the value of derivative contracts outstanding continued to grow until 2013 before beginning to fall back, with the 2017 level being much the same as that in 2007. Nevertheless, action was taken to limit the risks posed by these derivative contracts. Of particular concern was action to prevent a repeat of the 2008 crisis, when the failure of Lehman Brothers had produced a collapse of confidence as it was counterparty to so many of these contracts. The solution adopted was to encourage the use of clearing houses, as these were committed to completing the terms of a contract if one of the counterparties defaulted. By 2019, according to Jim Brunsden, 'Regulators see clearing houses as a critical part of the financial infrastructure, since they act as central counterparties between sellers and buyers of shares and derivatives.'[23] Philip Stafford observed that 'Clearers are pillars of global stability, standing between parties in a deal and managing the risk of contagion if one side defaults.'[24] Clearing houses provided this service before the crisis, but they became central to the process in its aftermath. Philip Stafford further commented in 2019, 'Clearing houses stand between the counterparties to a trade and, given their role in helping to manage the wider risk if one side defaults, have grown in systemic importance sine the financial crisis.'[25] Regulators had seized on clearing houses as a way of retaining the flexibility of the OTC markets, where banks traded with each other or through interdealer brokers and electronic platforms, while limiting the risks being run. What had not happened was any attempt to force the trading of derivatives through

Deborah Brewster, 'US retail investors slump to record low', 2nd September 2008; Lindsay Whipp, 'Domestic investors remain wary', 14th October 2008; Gillian Tett and Aline van Duyn, 'On the march', 9th June 2009; John Authers, 'Model of sophistication offers brighter future', 1st October 2009; Michael Mackenzie, Francesco Guerrera and Gillian Tett, 'A course to chart', 4th January 2010; Anousha Sakoui and Brooke Masters, 'UK businesses' finance options undergo rethink', 21st January 2010; Peggy Hollinger, 'Pensions Tensions', 27th May 2010; Brooke Masters and Jeremy Grant, 'Shadow boxes', 3rd February 2011; Brooke Masters, 'A real problem for regulators', 22nd March 2011; Tracy Alloway, 'Financial system creaks as loan lubricant dries up', 29th November 2011; Tracy Alloway, 'Traditional lenders shiver as shadow banking grows', 29th December 2011; Paul J. Davies, 'Banks look to insurers for lessons', 16th April 2012; Shawn Donnan, 'Ebbs and capital flows', 22nd August 2017; Caroline Binham, 'Shadow banking grows beyond $45tn', 6th March 2018; Gillian Tett, 'When the world held its breath', 1st September 2018; Chris Flood, 'Bond liquidity issues prompt investors to turn to ETFs', 17th September 2018; Mark Vandevelde, 'Financial Crisis', 20th September 2018; Colby Smith, 'Borrowers want dollars—some more than others', 20th September 2018; Robin Wigglesworth and Joe Rennison, 'New credit ecosystem blossoms as portfolio trades surge', 11th October 2018; Robin Wigglesworth, 'Asset managers seek an entrée to the trillion-dollar club', 26th October 2018; Gregory Davis, 'Index funds are not to blame for market volatility', 31st October 2018; Chris Flood, 'Global debt pile creates new chances in nascent market', 5th November 2018; Claire Jones, Caroline Binham, and Sam Fleming, 'Fed governor to head global finance police', 21st November 2018.

[23] Jim Brunsden and Philip Stafford, 'UK clearing houses face threat of pressure to move to EU', 14th March 2019.

[24] Philip Stafford, 'LSE shrugs off Brexit worries to gain boost from clearing', 2nd May 2019.

[25] Philip Stafford, 'European customers handed clearing house access to contain Brexit fallout', 19th February 2019.

regulated exchanges rather than be negotiated directly between banks or through interdealer brokers, which had been one of the options proposed.[26]

This failure to restore exchanges to a central position in the derivatives market was replicated across all financial instruments, though regulators had briefly flirted with such an idea at the time of the crisis. What had impressed regulators was the resilience of the markets provided by exchanges compared to the freezing of a number of the OTC variety. In particular, many securitized assets became unsaleable or even impossible to value with catastrophic consequences for those banks that were holding them as liquid securities. However, even after the crisis regulators continued to be wary of restoring power to exchanges, as they had exploited the monopoly position they had possessed in the past. In particular, those exchanges operating the vertical-silo model, which combined trading and processing, were able to force users to pay the charges they levied, as there was little alternative available. Though regulators ceased to press for the break-up of these vertical silos, they remained unhappy with their anti-competitive nature and so reluctant to grant greater powers to those exchanges operating them. Also, it was recognized that those inter-bank markets that possessed both depth and breadth, such as that for foreign exchange, had functioned normally throughout the crisis and continued to do so thereafter. This meant that there was no urgent pressure to return exchanges to primacy within financial markets. The result was that inter-bank markets were either left undisturbed by the crisis or quickly revived as they provided essential elements in the global financial system through which payments were made and received and banks balanced assets and liabilities across time, space, and currencies. That left exchanges to provide niche markets, especially for corporate stocks, while most trading remained of the OTC variety.[27]

[26] David Oakley and Jim Pickard, 'Banks move in on property derivatives', 5th March 2007; Paul J. Davies and Richard Beales, 'New players join the credit game', 14th March 2007; Gillian Tett, 'Funds are ousting the banks', 27th April 2007; Gillian Tett, 'Swaps soar as investors pile in', 28th May 2007; Gillian Tett, 'Growth brings loss of oversight', 28th May 2007; Arturo Cifuentes, 'Credit of the big three rating agencies under fire', 12th September 2007; Gillian Tett, 'OTC derivatives hold their own', 19th November 2007; Ross Tieman, 'Algo trading: the dog that bit its master', 19th March 2008; Jeremy Grant, 'LCH.Clearnet faces derivatives battle', 28th September 2010; Philip Stafford, 'Regulators show united front', 20th October 2010; Jeremy Grant and Nikki Tait, 'NYSE link-up faces hurdles', 11th February 2011; Jeremy Grant, 'Conduits of contention', 16th June 2011; Anuj Gangahar, 'Finding a mechanism to save the trades', 1st August 2011; Robin Wigglesworth and Joe Rennison, 'New credit ecosystem blossoms as portfolio trades surge', 11th October 2018.

[27] David Oakley and Gillian Tett, 'European bond market puts US in the shade', 15th January 2007; Gillian Tett and Anuj Gangahar, 'Deals on dark pools set to surge', 31st January 2007; David Oakley, 'European repo trading grows Euro 500bn in year', 2nd March 2007; Norma Cohen, 'Competitive age dawns in Europe', 3rd April 2007; Michael Mackenzie, 'Global trade facilitators behind a 24-hour market', 20th April 2007; Anuj Gangahar, 'Weight behind LiquidityHub grows', 9th May 2007; Norma Cohen, 'Mifid ushers in a new era of trading', 23rd May 2007; Martin Wolf, 'The new capitalism', 19th June 2007; Arturo Cifuentes, 'Credit of the big three rating agencies under fire', 12th September 2007; Paul J. Davies, 'Bond markets likely to escape strict transparency', 2nd November 2007; Gillian Tett, 'Sub-prime in its context', 19th November 2007; Gillian Tett, 'OTC derivatives hold their own', 19th November 2007; Anuj Gangahar, 'Nasdaq chief says sector will fragment', 8th January 2008; Gillian Tett and Aline van Duyn, 'On the march', 9th June 2009; Michael Mackenzie, 'Push to reduce risks in short-term funding', 22nd June 2009; David Oakley, 'Europe's ravaged landscape begins to stabilise', 11th September 2009; Jennifer Hughes, 'Currency derivatives caught in US clearing net', 20th November 2009; Michael Mackenzie, Francesco Guerrera and Gillian Tett, 'A course to chart', 4th January 2010; Anousha Sakoui and Brooke Masters, 'UK businesses' finance options undergo rethink', 21st January 2010; Michael Mackenzie, 'Regulators push technology to track trades in real time', 29th September 2010; Jennifer Hughes, 'Currency markets ready for the next big thing', 20th October 2010; Jeremy Grant, 'Market structures face test of trust', 3rd November 2010; Tracy Alloway, 'Counterparty risk makes an anxious return', 27th October 2011; Tracy Alloway, 'The debt penalty', 11th September 2013; Chris Flood, 'Bond liquidity issues prompt investors to turn to ETFs', 17th September 2018; Philip Stafford, 'European customers handed clearing house access to contain Brexit fallout', 19th February 2019; Jim Brunsden and Philip Stafford, 'UK clearing houses face threat of pressure to move to EU', 14th March 2019; Eva Szalay and Philip Stafford, 'Citigroup calls for burden of managing risky trades to be shared more widely', 17th April 2019; Philip Stafford, 'LSE shrugs off Brexit worries to gain boost from clearing', 2nd May 2019.

Finally, the crisis led to criticism of regulators for failing to prevent the build-up of risk-taking and of central banks for not stepping in as lenders of last resort earlier, and calls for both to be more interventionist. The global financial system that developed prior to the financial crisis had been forged by deregulation underpinned by a belief in free markets. That process of deregulation was then halted, and even put in reverse. Instead, there was a wave of legislation designed to mitigate risk and protect the financial system from shocks. This transformed the relationship between regulators and regulated. Nevertheless, without a reimposition of international barriers to financial flows, and strict divisions between particular components of national financial systems, regulators faced major obstacles in imposing much stricter control over both banks and markets. Though there was general agreement that intervention was required to make the global financial system safer after what had happened, there was no unified approach over how this was to be done while preserving an open, liberal world economic order. All that central banks and statutory regulators could agree upon were restrictions on the level of leverage and degree of risk-taking that had fuelled the credit bubble that had preceded the crisis. Beyond these general principles there was an unwillingness of any central bank or national regulator to introduce and then enforce regulations that would disadvantage their own banks and markets. Regulators were well aware of the mobility of financial activity through the steps taken by banks and companies to minimize the taxes they paid or avoid the regulations they were subjected to, and how this had benefited offshore centres and led to the displacement of activities into the shadow banking sector. What could be agreed were a new set of Basel rules designed to prevent excessive risk-taking by banks but these were then left to national authorities to interpret and enforce. The rules themselves created problems for regulators as they had difficulty distinguishing sufficiently between risk-averse and risk-taking activities, leading to the suppression of the former and the encouragement of the latter, which was the opposite of what was intended. As the immediacy of the crisis faded there was, therefore, a rolling back of regulation in recognition that the initial response had been too draconian. What had never been attempted was a return to the controlled and compartmentalized world that had existed before the 1970s.[28]

[28] David Oakley, 'European repo trading grows Euro 500bn in year', 2nd March 2007; Peter Thal Larsen, 'Regulators face global challenge', 23rd March 2007; Norma Cohen, 'Doors open as industry removes barriers', 30th March 2007; Norma Cohen, 'Competitive age dawns in Europe', 3rd April 2007; Paul J. Davies, 'Bond markets likely to escape strict transparency', 2nd November 2007; Gillian Tett, 'OTC derivatives hold their own', 19th November 2007; Hannah Glover, 'Spotlight turns to the mechanics of securities lending', 8th September 2008; Peter Thal Larsen, 'A lot to be straightened out', 31st March 2009; Adrian Cox, 'Multiple threats still loom for the investment banking model', 1st April 2009; John Plender, 'Re-spinning the web', 22nd June 2009; Jeremy Grant, 'Innovative ideas fail to lighten European mood over dark pools', 25th September 2009; Aline van Duyn and Jeremy Grant, 'Use of clearers to rein in OTC derivatives poses fresh dilemma', 15th January 2010; Samantha Pearson, 'US plans threaten LatAm FX', 20th January 2010; Masa Serdarevic, 'Sungard offers access to exchanges', 22nd January 2010; Francesco Guerrera and Justin Baer, 'Doubts beset mission to trim giants' girth', 23rd January 2010; *FT* Reporters, 'Proposals fail to forge consensus in Europe', 23rd January 2010; Francesco Guerrera and Megan Murphy, 'Tripped up', 25th January 2010; Martha Tirinmanzi and Mike Hemphill, 'Management of risk remains an issue for the buyside user', 2nd August 2010; Patrick Jenkins and Brooke Masters, 'The money moves on', 15th September 2010; Justin Baer, 'From recession to regulation', 27th September 2010; Brooke Masters and Francesco Guerrera, 'Threat to small business', 27th September 2010; Jeremy Grant, 'LCH.Clearnet faces derivatives battle', 28th September 2010; Michael Mackenzie, 'Regulators push technology to track trades in real time', 29th September 2010; Aline van Duyn and Telis Demos, 'Flash Crash: market reforms to be examined', 5th October 2010; Patrick Jenkins, 'New regulatory standards are the next big unknown', 8th October 2010; Brooke Masters, 'Trade finance may become a casualty', 20th October 2010; Jennifer Hughes, 'Currency markets ready for the next big thing', 20th October 2010; Philip Stafford, 'Competitive market requires deep pockets', 20th October 2010; Jeremy Grant, 'Market structures face test of trust', 3rd November 2010; Aline van Duyn, 'Regulator set to rule on Wall Street's swaps power', 13th January 2011; Brooke Masters and Jeremy Grant, 'Shadow boxes', 3rd February 2011; Jeremy Grant and Nikki Tait, 'NYSE link-up faces hurdles', 11th February 2011; Brooke Masters, 'A

Philip Stafford, writing in 2018, reflected on what had happened since the crisis, and whether it had produced any substantial change compared to the underlying forces at work:

> Ten years on from the height of the financial crisis it is tempting to look back at the havoc precipitated by the collapse of Lehman Brothers and think we have come a long way. Waves of overlapping reforms, such as the Dodd–Frank Act, Basel 3 and Mifid 2, have been passed to make financial institutions and markets safer. Banks have to set aside more capital for trading, and clearing houses—which sit between parties in a deal to manage credit risk—have become the biggest crash barriers. Banks now cannot leverage their own balance sheets and hold inventory and positions in the market on behalf of clients quite as aggressively as they once did. However, the last decade has also seen rapid technological changes. Trading is increasingly performed by machines using automated systems that fire off trades in fractions of a second without human intervention. Artificial intelligence is also beginning to creep into markets, as some participants explore whether computers can 'learn' from huge amounts of markets data. Regulators now view these twin trends with some trepidation.[29]

What he did not mention was that the megabanks were still a key part of the global financial system, led by a quintet from the USA. It was only they that possessed the size, spread, and scale required by a world economy in which the process of financial integration had intensified rather been reversed since the crisis. This was a process which had begun in the 1970s and proved unstoppable despite the Global Financial Crisis of 2008. However, this did not mean that the character and composition of the global financial system was unaltered by the crisis. Much changed as a result of the crisis, especially as a result of the intervention that followed from both those regulating financial systems and the actions of central banks attempting to make it more resilient. The crisis made an impact but its lasting legacy had more to do with the reaction that followed rather than the event itself.[30]

real problem for regulators', 22nd March 2011; Tom Braithwaite, Brooke Masters and Jeremy Grant, 'A Shield Asunder', 20th May 2011; Jeremy Grant, 'Conduits of contention', 16th June 2011; Brooke Masters, 'League battle over bank risk will end in tiers', 21st June 2011; Anuj Gangahar, 'Finding a mechanism to save the trades', 1st August 2011; Megan Murphy, 'Search for new approaches has begun', 9th September 2011; Brooke Masters, Henny Sender and Dan McCrum, '"Shadow banks" move in amid regulatory push', 9th September 2011; Brooke Masters and Tom Braithwaite, 'Bankers versus Basel', 3rd October 2011; Tracy Alloway, 'Counterparty risk makes an anxious return', 27th October 2011; Paul Taylor, 'How to make ready for regulation', 9th November 2011; Brooke Masters, 'Reveal leverage ratio ahead of rivals banks told', 2nd December 2011; Tracy Alloway, 'Traditional lenders shiver as shadow banking grows', 29th December 2011; Robin Wigglesworth, 'Taming the traders', 20th March 2012; Patrick Jenkins, Tom Braithwaite and Brooke Masters, 'New force emerges from the shadows', 10th April 2012; Anousha Sakoui, 'Restructuring could lift M&A market', 30th May 2012; Barbara Ridpath, 'Crisis—and regulation—can breed opportunity', 30th May 2012; Brooke Masters, 'Safety net plans raise industry ire', 19th March 2013; Philip Stafford, 'Q and A : Algorithms', 23rd August 2013; Chris Giles, 'Carney tears up rule book on help for struggling banks', 25th October 2013; Martin Arnold, 'Carney's too big to fail buffer represents clear progress despite doubt', 9th December 2014; Philip Stafford, 'Exchange chiefs eye deals to tap new markets', 31st December 2015; Philip Stafford, 'Deutsche Börse unfurls plan for European champion', 27–28th February 2016; Philip Stafford, 'Europe's regulatory crackdown set to ease', 25th May 2016; Harriet Agnew and Patrick Jenkins, 'What's next for the City', 3rd September 2016; Philip Stafford, 'Brexit brings headache to industry weary of regulation', 11th October 2016; Hans Hoogervorst, 'Do not blame accounting rules for the financial crisis', 4th October 2018; Philip Stafford, Nicole Bullock, and Kadhim Shubber, 'Shares in US exchanges hit after rebuke from regulator over high data charges', 18th October 2018; Claire Jones, Caroline Binham and Sam Fleming, 'Fed governor to head global finance police', 21st November 2018.

[29] Philip Stafford, 'Fresh risks emerge from the depth', 1st October 2018.

[30] Ian Fleming, Philip Stafford, and Jim Brunsden, 'Iran sanctions pose dilemma for Swift', 18th May 2018; Emiko Terazono, 'Banks and energy traders back blockchain launches', 20th September 2018; Philip Stafford,

Financial Centres

Financial centres provide a means of assessing the impact made by the Global Financial Crisis in reversing pre-crisis trends, and also measure its significance compared to later shocks. High among these later shocks was the regulatory response to the revelations regarding market manipulation by the megabanks and the consequences of Britain's decision to leave the European Union. Each of these had an impact on the relative standing of financial centres that lessened the consequences of the Global Financial Crisis. Prior to the crisis there had been predictions that the effect of the trends in the technology of communications would be to concentrate financial activity in a few global financial centres. Conversely, others speculated that the consequence would be a diffusion of financial activity among many. Those who favoured the former emphasized the need for speed when trading in fast-moving markets, the networking opportunities derived from co-location, and the economies of scale that came from clustering. Those suggesting the latter pointed to the virtual elimination of the delay in connecting buyers and sellers, the importance of being close to the customer, and the lower costs attached to locations away from global financial centres. Both sets of forces were at play leading to a constant flux of activity between financial centres. Prior to the crisis the outcome was an increasing gravitational pull towards the global financial centres of London and New York. These were the locations of the main financial markets and the densest concentrations of bank offices. In the wake of the crisis there was a growing expectation that both London and New York would lose out as financial centres. Nouriel Roubini predicted as such in 2009:

> The roles of New York and London as major financial centres are being reduced as the financial crisis reveals the weakness of the Anglo-Saxon model of lightly-regulated finance. Over time, alternative financial centres, both traditional (Tokyo, Singapore, Hong Kong) and new (Dubai, Shanghai, Mumbai, São Paulo, Moscow) will emerge as the Bric countries (Brazil, Russia, India and China) and other emerging markets (especially in the oil-exporting Gulf) increase their share of global GDP).[31]

Conversely, in the same year James Pickford was of the opinion that the status of London and New York as financial centres remained unchallenged. Focusing particularly on London he judged that its 'status as one of the world's leading financial centres appears assured. The financial hub of Europe has escaped relatively unscathed from the worst effects of the financial crisis. It remains the biggest player in a number of markets, such as foreign exchange.... Is it time to treat London's worries over its competitive position as nothing more than the natural paranoia of a market leader?'[32] Ten years later Caroline Binham and Patrick Jenkins judged London and New York to still be the leading financial centres.[33] The available evidence from London and New York's share of global financial

'Fresh risks emerge from the depth', 1st October 2018; Don Weinland, 'Banks race to launch blockchain trade platforms', 9th November 2018.

[31] Nouriel Roubini, 'Nouriel Roubini calls for radical reforms for the broken financial system', 2nd November 2009.

[32] James Pickford, James Wilson, Haig Simonian, 'Big hubs keep the wheels of industry turning', 10th May 2012.

[33] Caroline Binham and Patrick Jenkins, 'Bailey signals need for Brexit talks focus on financial services', 8th May 2019.

markets pointed to a rise in their dominant position not a decline.[34] In 2007 the combined share of London and New York in global foreign exchange trading was 52 per cent whereas in 2016 it was 57 per cent and 60 per cent in 2019. Their continuing dominance was even more marked in another measure of importance, which was the trading of OTC interest-rate derivatives. The combined share of New York and London rose from 68 per cent to 80 per cent over the same period.[35] What this illustrates is how problematic it is to use trends to predict particular outcomes given the complexity of the forces at work.

The reason for this continuing inertia of financial activity lay in the nature of the business that took place in financial markets and the continuing importance played by the speed of connection. The co-location of trading platforms and servers, for example, shaved only microseconds off the time lag, or latency, in which computerized trading programs reacted to market opportunities. However, eliminating that delay was sufficiently important for banks to make them pay a premium for the privilege of co-hosting their computer with that which provided the market network. Since data travelled at the speed of light the difference in speed between a co-located server and one 200 miles away was about a millisecond. That difference was sufficient to either take advantage of a market opportunity or complete a transaction before the market reacted. On the fringes of both London and New York there were huge data centres accommodating the computers of traders and those that matched buy and sell orders. Each of those cities was a global hub for a dense network of communication links that connected them both to each other and to other financial centres. Britain's westerly location and New York's easterly one meant that they comprised the key locations in a transatlantic trading system that connected the likes of Frankfurt and Paris with Chicago and Toronto. Alone that was not sufficient to give them a vital edge but combined with the clusters of financial businesses based there, and the embedded trading infrastructure, it made it difficult, if not impossible, to replicate the advantages they possessed.

The power of this embedded infrastructure, ranging from networks of fibre optic cables through a dense pool of skilled labour to access to specialist support services, gave London and New York a continuing competitive edge in attracting and retaining financial business. This was borne out by the research carried out into the potential impact of Brexit on London as a European financial centre. As a report in 2017 by the corporate law firm, Freshfields Bruckhaus Deringer, concluded, 'If firms transfer business out of the UK...it is unlikely that all business will be moved to a single EU member state. Any such transfer is instead likely to occur on a fragmented basis across multiple jurisdictions as firms seek to be closer to their customers.'[36] In their analysis there was no alternative to London as a financial centre in the European time zone. This was the same conclusion reached by Omar Ali, UK financial services leader at the professional services firm, Ernst and Young, in the same year: 'The variety of locations firms are selecting only confirms the fact that the UK's financial ecosystem is unique and very hard to replicate in other European jurisdictions.'[37] The only alternative to London was New York as it could match it in terms of the depth and breadth of financial services it could provide, though it was poorly located to serve global markets because of its time zone. Whereas London could straddle the Asian and American

[34] Philip Stafford and Eva Szalay, 'London pulls away from New York in forex and swaps as it shrugs off Brexit', 17th September 2019.

[35] BIS, Triennial Central Bank survey. Each of these cities was the hub for national foreign-exchange trading.

[36] Omar Ali, 'Dublin is top destination for financial groups post-Brexit', 9th May 2017.

[37] Omar Ali, 'Dublin is top destination for financial groups post-Brexit', 9th May 2017.

trading day New York was on the fringes. Eva Szalay emphasized this point in 2019 when she observed that 'London's location, straddling time zones between Asia and the US, gave it a key advantage.'[38]

Nevertheless, barriers continued to exist to the gravitational pull of London and New York as financial centres, allowing others not only to exist but also thrive. One was cost as both those cities were very expensive locations, and that continually drove business away to cheaper locations. Another was the difference between countries thrown up by culture, language, and regulation as these made it important to remain close to the customer. As Peter Norman pointed out in 2008, 'The EU cannot reproduce the single language, currency, legal system and more or less uniform tax laws of the US.'[39] For these reasons even in the EU, which hosted London, a number of major financial centres co-existed, serving particular constituencies. Similarly, in Asia, despite the improvement in communications there were at least fifteen significant financial centres, reflecting the importance of national identities, laws, regulations, and taxes. Even in the case of the USA two important financial centres continued to co-exist, namely New York and Chicago. This was the product of the liquidity provided by the specialist markets that each hosted. For these reasons the distribution and hierarchy of financial centres remained relatively unchanged by the global financial crisis. There was no haemorrhaging of financial activity from London and New York as a result.[40]

Nevertheless, that did not mean that the crisis had no effect on the hierarchy of financial centres, even though the underlying trends remained. However, the competition faced by London and New York as financial centres was blunted by the continued fragmentation of the global market along national lines. This made it difficult for any single centre to emerge with the depth and breadth to challenge them. That fragmentation left London and New York well placed to provide cross-border financial services for distant regions of the world, as they possessed the necessary depth and breadth. As an international financial centre London had a time zone advantage over New York as it straddled the trading day in both Asia and the Americas while occupying the European one. Humphrey Percy, head of the Bank of London and the Middle East, explained in 2008 that London had 'The right time zone for dealing with Asia and the Middle East, a huge talent pool, and a concentration of diverse markets.'[41] Similarly, Phil Cutts, chief executive of private banking at Credit Suisse in the UK, emphasized in 2014 that 'London has a strategic advantage because of its central time-zone. You can talk to every client around the world within a working day.'[42] That advantage lay with any European financial centre but London occupied the prime position among them all. In 2007 Chris Brown-Humes referred to London as 'The undisputed

[38] Eva Szalay, 'Jump in London rupee trades rings alarms', 18th September 2019.

[39] Peter Norman, 'Call to improve plumbing of fund processing', 31st March 2008.

[40] Ross Tieman, 'When microseconds really count', 19th March 2008; Peter Norman, 'Call to improve plumbing of fund processing', 31st March 2008; James Pickford, James Wilson, Haig Simonian, 'Big hubs keep the wheels of industry turning', 10th May 2012; Nouriel Roubini, 'Nouriel Roubini calls for radical reforms for the broken financial system', 2nd November 2009; Samantha Pearson, 'US plans threaten LatAm FX', 20th January 2010; Jeremy Grant and Michael Mackenzie, 'Ghost in the machine', 18th February 2010; Hal Weitzman, 'Co-location set to reap up to $40 million for CME', 29th October 2010; Jeremy Grant, 'Market structures face test of trust', 3rd November 2010; Jeremy Grant, 'Barriers higher for Asian dominance in algo trading', 24th August 2012; Gill Plimmer and Philip Stafford, 'Cable hub gives City edge on Frankfurt', 7th May 2013; Philip Stafford, 'Bourse tie-ups put clearing risk in spotlight', 5–6th March 2016; Omar Ali, 'Dublin is top destination for financial groups post-Brexit', 9th May 2017; Philip Stafford, 'Selling time to traders: the physicist who measures deals in microseconds', 5th February 2018; BIS, Triennial Central Bank survey, 2016.

[41] Shyamantha Asokan, 'UK leads in sowing seeds for a sector', 19th July 2008.

[42] Daniel Schäfer, 'Capital gains from foreign money and time zone', 10th June 2014.

capital of European finance—even though it is not part of the Eurozone—and it is eclipsing New York as the leading world centre in certain financial markets.'[43] In Europe the likes of Frankfurt, Amsterdam, and London were all important telecommunications hubs but London's had a much stronger gravitational pull, driven by the presence of so many dealing desks and fund managers and the ability to absorb fixed costs through higher turnover. London did face competition from Zurich and Geneva in banking, Dublin and Luxembourg in fund management, and Frankfurt and Paris in derivatives and bonds but none could match its universal appeal, especially in terms of the liquidity of its markets. Nevertheless, both London and New York lost back-office functions to cheaper locations. However, there was a relative shift between London and New York in favour of the former. The Sarbanes–Oxley Act, passed in the USA in the wake of the Enron scandal, undermined New York as a financial centre because of the conditions and restrictions imposed, leading to foreign businesses turning to London and US banks conducting more of their international activities from there. Between 2002 and 2006, for example, London's share of hedge-fund assets rose from 10 per cent to 21 per cent whereas New York's fell from 45 per cent to 36 per cent. Each could provide the nexus of fund managers, investment banks, prime brokers, and financial markets that hedge funds required but London could offer a more relaxed regulatory environment.

Compared to both London and New York, Tokyo was losing ground as an international financial centre before the crisis. The long delays in the deregulation of Tokyo's financial markets had undermined their international competitiveness in terms of the products traded, the systems used, and the charges made. This was reflected in the departure of many of the foreign financial institutions that had attempted to base their Asian operations there. Even in 2007 Japan still had highly-restrictive rules governing the separation of banking and securities, which made it difficult to develop and market new financial products which involved a cross-over between banking and broking. The separation also increased costs and caused delays in bringing new products to fruition, and this discouraged foreign financial institutions from making Tokyo their Asian hub. The weakness of Tokyo left openings for other Asian financial centres. Alternatives to Tokyo in Asia existed in the form of Mumbai in India and Shanghai in China but, like Tokyo, they did little more than dominate their vast domestic markets and had a limited international appeal because of the restrictions in place. In contrast Hong Kong and Singapore had very limited domestic markets and so were forced to expand internationally. Singapore had become the main financial hub for south-east Asia and was a leading centre for currency and oil trading. Hong Kong had positioned itself as the gateway to China, exploiting the strict capital controls that continued to prevent the integration of Chinese and global markets, and was Asia's leading centre for international banking.

Spotting the opportunities created by the failure of Tokyo to command the Asian market the South Korean authorities did promote Seoul as an international financial centre through a rapid pace of deregulation. In 2007 Yoon Jeung-hyun, Chairman of South Korea's Financial Supervisory Commission, explained the motivation for the removal of the regulations that had held back the development of financial markets in South Korea: 'In order for Korea to leap forward and become a great market, a big bang in the financial industry will be necessary.'[44] However, regulatory change was not enough by itself to make a financial centre internationally competitive, as Rhee Nam-uh, head of equity research at

[43] Chris Brown-Humes, 'Fear of business going elsewhere', 19th November 2007.
[44] Anna Fifield, 'Seoul looks to echo London big bang', 26th June 2007.

Merrill Lynch in Seoul, made clear. Seoul 'needs the legal framework, regulatory support, transparency, infrastructure, a supply of quality people and a market friendly environment'.[45] As those other elements were lacking, international business in Asia continued to gravitate to Hong Kong and Singapore because they possessed these. In the Middle East Dubai was also intent on exploiting the lack of a dominant financial centre in the region by positioning itself as the cross-roads of international transactions in currencies, commodities, and stocks, hoping to benefit from being located between Tokyo and London in the world's time zones. Dubai was not alone in this ambition as it was shared by Doha in Qatar and Manama in Bahrain. However, no financial centre in the Middle East had made a breakthrough before the crisis with even the largest, Istanbul, lacking the depth and breadth required to become a serious contender as a regional financial centre let alone an international one.[46]

Post Crisis

The Global Financial Crisis then changed the financial world within which London and New York had become the dominant players. In the wake of the financial crisis, which many blamed on the activities of the global banks and trading in OTC markets, governments began to consider ways of curbing both of these. Any intervention to do so would be detrimental to London and New York as they were the locations from which these banks conducted an international business, and where OTC markets thrived because of the dense cluster of bank offices. In their place other centres were expected to prosper benefiting from being closer to savers and borrowers or producers and consumers. In mining finance, where London was a global leader, Sydney in Australia and Toronto in Canada were expected to gain as they contained pools of investors ready to finance mining exploration. Similarly, Hong Kong was expected to grow as a centre for trading metals as it was close to

[45] Anna Fifield, 'Seoul looks to echo London big bang', 26th June 2007.

[46] Ben Smith, 'London sees rise in hedge funds', 17th April 2007; Michiyo Nakamoto, 'Market failure', 8th May 2007; Anna Fifield, 'Seoul looks to echo London big bang', 26th June 2007; Sundeep Tucker, 'Asia seeks its centre', 6th July 2007; James Drummond, 'Raft of bourses crowds market', 24th July 2007; David Ibison, 'Borse Dubai bid for OMX faces test over respectability', 18th August 2007; Michiyo Nakamoto, 'Call to pull down barriers', 14th September 2007; Simeon Kerr, 'Qatar's 10-year financial plan', 21st September 2007; Peter Garnham, 'London's dominance of global forex grows', 27th September 2007; Tom Mitchell, 'Integration of bourses is not black and white', 23rd October 2007; Chris Hughes, 'London poised to cement leading position', 3rd November 2007; Simeon Kerr, 'Dubai dazzles but Riyadh is the big prize', 19th November 2007; Chris Brown-Humes, 'Fear of business going elsewhere', 19th November 2007; Ivar Simensen, 'Frankfurt fights back', 19th November 2007; Simeon Kerr, 'Bourses at war for business', 20th November 2007; Bernard Simon and Anuj Gangahar, 'TSX joins consolidation race with Montreal deal', 11th December 2007; Ross Tieman, 'When microseconds really count', 19th March 2008; Simeon Kerr and Jeremy Grant, 'Qatar's ambition revealed in plans for exchange', 25th June 2008; Haig Simonian, 'Zurich hopes revamp will help it climb global ranks', 15th July 2008; Shyamantha Asokan, 'UK leads in sowing seeds for a sector', 19th July 2008; Vanessa Houlder and Michael Peel, 'Harbours of resentment', 1st December 2008; Brooke Masters, 'Banks move to Belfast and Bournemouth', 19th March 2009; Haig Simonian, 'A vault unlocked', 24th March 2009; Delphine Strauss, 'ISE faces test from Turkey's trading past', 22nd September 2009; Simeon Kerr, 'Nasdaq Dubai blow as DP World looks to London', 7th January 2010; Lindsay Whipp, 'Ambitions to recapture its glory days', 8th February 2010; Andrew Bounds, 'Liverpool takes title as second city of wealth management', 29th March 2010; Jeremy Grant, 'NYSE plans to launch interest rate futures', 7th April 2010; Kevin Brown and Sundeep Tucker, 'A high-flying rivalry', 26th April 2010; Kevin Brown, 'SGX to offer OTC derivatives clearing', 21st September 2010; Chris Bryant, 'Welcome to the plumbing capital of the world wide web', 17th April 2014; Nicholas Megaw, 'High-speed trading masts face slowdown', 28th March 2016; Caroline Binham and Patrick Jenkins, 'Bailey signals need for Brexit talks focus on financial services', 8th May 2019; Philip Stafford, 'Singapore exchange plans to tighten grip as Asia's largest forex trading hub', 11th June 2019; Patrick Jenkins and Philip Stafford, 'Exchanges', 14th September 2019.

China, the main market for the world's mineral production, with London, again, expected to lose out. The main casualty was predicted to be London as its strength lay in the unregulated inter-bank markets it hosted and these were the ones most threatened by government intervention. In contrast New York could rely upon the position it occupied within the vast US market and its relative immunity to international competition.

Despite these predictions the Global Financial Crisis made little impact on London and New York due to the fundamentals attached to the co-location of financial activity. Despite its far greater exposure to international competition London soon recovered as a global financial centre. One effect of the regulatory response to the Global Financial Crisis in the USA was to encourage US asset managers, hedge funds, and investment banks to switch business to London in order to avoid the new US rules. As Philip Stafford observed in 2013, 'A difference in regulatory regime can mean a difference in millions of dollars of collateral that investors have to put up to back their derivatives trades.'[47] However, London also faced its own regulatory restrictions, especially in the wake of the exposure of various financial scandals and market manipulation. Much of this regulatory intervention was domestic but others came from the European Commission. By 2012 Brooke Masters reported that the European Commission was 'generating reams of financial rules, many aimed at reining in short selling, high-frequency trading, shadow banking and other specific activities.'[48] These rules were being interpreted differently by national governments with consequences for pan-European operations, fuelling suspicion that they were motivated by a desire to shift financial activity away from London and towards other financial centres in Europe. Phil Davis claimed in 2011 that 'Much of the post-crisis rule-making emanating from the European Union has a political element to it.'[49] One example was the drive within the Eurozone to force transactions involving that currency to take place within it, justified by the need to improve monitoring and supervision. In 2012 Christian Noyer, the Governor of the Bank of France, stated that, 'We're not against some business being done in London but the bulk of the business should be under our control.'[50] By 2013 John Gapper reflected growing concerns in London about the consequences of such actions when he wrote that, 'One does not need to be paranoid to imagine the City being slowly dismembered, with its euro listing and trading businesses switching to Frankfurt while its international and emerging markets operations move to New York or Hong Kong to evade EU-wide regulations.'[51]

Attempts by regulators to enforce standardized financial regulations across the EU risked undermining London's unique financial ecosystem. Regulations were designed to fit the universal banking model not the diversity of markets and intermediaries that populated the City of London. However, most of these measures were either dropped or modified, lessening their impact, while increased uniformity did make it easier for London-based banks to service the entire EU market. Increasingly the main threat to London's standing as a global financial centre after the crisis came from within the UK itself, fed by the regulatory response to the revelations relating to the mis-selling of financial products and the manipulation of markets that had emerged subsequently. By 2013 the experienced banker, Evelyn de Rothschild, was warning that, 'To maintain its global stature, it is vital that

[47] Philip Stafford, 'US funds transfer trades to London', 18th October 2013.
[48] Brooke Masters, 'Wariness over EU's level playing field', 10th May 2012.
[49] Phil Davis, 'London feels the force of regulation', 16th May 2011.
[50] John Thornhill and Patrick Jenkins, 'Ties that bind', 2nd April 2013.
[51] John Gapper, 'Europe finally takes its bite from the City of London', 21st February 2013.

Britain's financial sector be understood to have rules and regulations that are effective detriments of bad behaviour, but that also promote the dynamism our economy needs.'[52] As it was, government intervention to restrict financial activity in the wake of the crisis was not confined to the EU and the USA but was applied generally after the financial crisis. This affected those financial centres hoping to benefit from the relocation of both bank offices and trading. Actions by the German government undermined the attractions of Frankfurt as a financial centre; the imposition of a transaction tax in South Korea reduced the attractions of Seoul; discrimination against foreign investors by Chile restricted the appeal of Santiago.

More generally, potential rivals to London and New York continued to lack their depth and breadth and so were only able to compete in niche areas such as asset management and commodity trading or play a regional role. Giles Wilkes, a former special adviser to the Department of Business, Innovation, and Skills, judged in 2015 that when it came to London as a centre of global finance, 'There are few cities that can match its depth of professional services, its pool of business talent or the sheer creative buzz.'[53] A similar verdict could be passed on New York but on no other financial centre. That left the position of both London and New York as global financial centres relatively unchanged five years after the crisis. Governments elsewhere in the world had tried to take advantage of the opportunities the crisis presented, especially the restrictions that followed, such as the Russian government's promotion of Moscow as a financial centre in 2011 and the Chinese government's support for Shanghai in 2012. Dubai even offered a zero tax rate to attract banks and fund managers. The problems with these attempts was that a centre had to be able offer more than low taxes and light regulation if it was to attract international business. A financial centre had to possess a strong financial ecosystem to support those doing business, and a regulatory regime that incorporated internationally accepted standards with user-friendly rules. This was what Singapore had successfully managed to do. It was a relatively low-cost location situated close to Asia's emerging markets, offered attractive tax and regulatory incentives, used the English legal system, provided access to a skilled labour force, and could provide an abundance of financial and other services ranging from insurance, arbitration, and logistics. Another country with a strong financial ecosystem was Switzerland and so it continued to attract business to Zurich and Geneva, especially that conducted on wafer-thin margins where even small differences in the tax paid could make a major difference to profitability. However, the success of neither Singapore nor Switzerland undermined London and New York as financial centres. Rather, they fed off the success of these financial centres by offering tax efficient solutions in niche areas.[54]

[52] John Thornhill and Patrick Jenkins, 'Ties that bind', 2nd April 2013.

[53] Giles Wilkes, 'Wanted: bankers to electrify the British economy', 7th March 2015.

[54] Jeremy Grant and Brooke Masters, 'Brokers set out to fight backlash against OTC trade', 28th April 2009; Ben Hall and Scheherazade Daneshkhu, 'Overarching ambition', 24th July 2009; Nouriel Roubini, 'Nouriel Roubini calls for radical reforms for the broken financial system', 2nd November 2009; William MacNamara, Miles Johnson, and Matthew Kennard, 'Hong Kong vies with London for IPO supremacy', 27th January 2010; Paul J. Davies, 'NY insurance market on horizon', 5th March 2010; Brooke Masters, 'New York vies with City for finance crown', 12th March 2010; Sam Jones, 'Dublin entices funds with softer regulation', 6th September 2010; Javier Blas and Nikki Tait, 'France leads the charge on commodities rules reform', 9th September 2010; Daniel Thomas, 'London tops Europe property list', 11th October 2010; Jeremy Grant, 'Market structures face test of trust', 3rd November 2010; Brian Groom, 'Lenders confident of riding out crisis thanks to low risk appetite', 18th November 2010; Javier Blas, 'Geneva set to trump London in oil trading', 23rd November 2010; Javier Blas, 'Switzerland sees inflow of Russian oil traders at expense of London', 8th February 2011; Phil Davis, 'London feels the force of regulation', 16th May 2011; Jeremy Grant, 'Drive for consolidation leaves clock ticking for LCH. Clearnet', 13th June 2011; Jeremy Woolfe, 'London's sway weakens as EU authorities gain power', 15th August 2011; Rachel Morarjee, 'Merger creates market less prone to squabbling', 4th October 2011; Brooke Masters, Jeremy

Continuing Challenges, 2014–20

The role played by financial centres, especially those with a large international business, was being affected by the continuing actions taken by regulators around the world to better insulate their countries from imported banking crises. Banks were being forced to convert branches into subsidiaries which could then be supervised by the host central bank rather than the central bank of the country in which the bank had its head office. The result was to limit the ability of megabanks to operate as an integrated business with a single head office and a branch network spread throughout the world. Prior to the crisis these megabanks had been expanding their retail operations worldwide but they now drew back from that strategy in the face of both the risks that the crisis exposed and then the actions taken by regulators. Instead, the focus was on wholesale activities and there London and New York continued to act as magnets, pulling in banks from around the world because of the depth and breadth of the services and markets they could provide. In turn the presence of these banks spawned new services and markets. Harriet Agnew commented in 2015 that 'The cluster of banks in London has drawn in hedge funds, asset managers, private equity and professional services firms.' She continued by claiming that 'London is a gateway to Europe, home to 250 foreign banks employing 160,000 people... financial services account for a fifth of the UKs annual economic output. The driving force behind this is the European single market, which offers easy access to 500m people across 28 EU member states.'[55] Recognizing the uniqueness of London as a financial centre, and what would be lost if it was undermined, the European Central Bank, which had been pressing since 2011 for Euro clearing to be located in the Eurozone, agreed in 2015 that it could continue to take place in

Grant, and Chris Bryant, 'Warning of unintended outcomes with Tobin tax plans', 6th October 2011; Simon Rabinovitch and Robert Cookson, 'China unlikely to impose big bang reforms', 24th February 2012; Brooke Masters, 'Cities hold firm amid Eurozone upheaval', 10th May 2012; James Pickford, James Wilson, Haig Simonian, 'Big hubs keep the wheels of industry turning', 10th May 2012; Ross Tieman, 'Second tier focuses on specialised approach', 10th May 2012; Brooke Masters, 'Wariness over EU's level playing field', 10th May 2012; Haig Simonian and Eric Frey, 'Regional ambitions thwarted', 16th May 2012; Jeremy Grant and Javier Blas, 'Singapore fights for commodities trade supremacy', 23rd May 2012; Alex Barker and Daniel Schäfer, 'Scandal-wracked City braced for closer scrutiny', 30th June 2012; David Oakley, Jim Pickard, and Kate Burgess, 'No silver bullet to end City short-termism', 24th July 2012; Patrick Jenkins and Brooke Masters, 'London's precarious position', 30th July 2012; Simon Mundy, 'S. Korea to tax derivatives will hit volumes, bankers warn', 9th August 2012; Jennifer Thompson, Patrick Jenkins, and Daniel Schäfer, 'MPs to probe London job losses', 9th November 2012; Jude Webber, 'Santiago aims to be hub for global investment', 14th November 2012; Patrick Jenkins and Alex Barber, 'City bankers fret over being on the margins', 5th December 2012; *FT* Reporters, 'Regions boosted by bank plans to move 3,000 jobs out of City', 10th December 2012; John Murray Brown, 'Cardiff seeks to rebrand itself as a centre for financial services', 31st December 2012; Ralph Atkins, 'With the volume turned down', 12th February 2013; John Gapper, 'Europe finally takes its bite from the City of London', 21st February 2013; Daniel Schäfer and Tom Braithwaite, 'Lawyers comb details for way round the rules', 1st March 2013; Emiko Terazono and Javier Blas, 'Swiss question role of commodities traders in economy', 27th March 2013; John Thornhill and Patrick Jenkins, 'Ties that bind', 2nd April 2013; Javier Blas, 'Tougher times for the trading titans', 15th April 2013; Gill Plimmer and Philip Stafford, 'Cable hub gives City edge on Frankfurt', 7th May 2013; Lina Saigol, 'New money put City's reputation at risk', 18th May 2013; Alex Barber and Kara Scannell, 'Plans to shift Libor heart to Europe', 7th June 2013; James Pickford, 'The global city with a gift for reinvention', 11th June 2013; Ed Hammond, 'Change of inhabitants transforms City', 10th June 2013; Evelyn de Rothschild, 'Banking must pursue the holy grail of confidence', 25th June 2013; Kate Allen, 'Canary Wharf set to double workforce', 19th August 2013; Vanessa Houlder, 'Trouble abroad for the City?', 10th September 2013; Josh Noble, 'UK's share of renminbi trade leaps', 9th October 2013; Philip Stafford, 'US funds transfer trades to London', 18th October 2013; Edwin Heathcote, 'Creative tension: City absorbs the new and adapts the old', 4th December 2013; James Pickford, 'The capital's unique selling point', 4th December 2013; Brian Groom, 'London powers ahead of regions as north–south divide grows wider', 12th December 2013; Giles Wilkes, 'Wanted: bankers to electrify the British economy', 7th March 2015.

[55] Harriet Agnew, 'City fears loss of access and influence in event of Brexit', 9th February 2015.

London. The threat of new EU rules on the use of derivatives was already beginning to drive business away from London and towards New York and Singapore.

In contrast, London was of growing importance as a location for international wealth management. As more wealthy people from around the world relocated to London so bankers catering to the wealthy opened offices there, further enhancing London's appeal as a base for the world's wealthy. The newly-arrived wealthy individuals were coming from Russia, the Middle East, South Africa, and India as well as other European countries like Italy and France. By 2014 London had more billionaires than any other city in the world and it was replacing New York as second after Switzerland for private wealth management. Jurg Zeltner, chief executive of UBS's wealth management arm in London, claimed by then that it 'is clearly becoming the hub for ultra-high net worth people'.[56] Though Switzerland dominated the business of safeguarding and investing the wealth of the world's richest people, with $6.8tn under management in 2016, it was in relative decline as the relaxing of its strict secrecy laws made tax evasion more difficult. Faced with increased regulation by the EU a number of London-based fund managers had shifted their operations to Geneva, only to discover that they faced tough new oversight from Finma, the Swiss national markets regulator, which reduced the advantages they had hoped to gain, especially as staffing costs were higher there than in London.

What was evident was that no cities in the world could match London and New York in terms of their depth, breadth, and international appeal when it came to financial services. Though London possessed strengths in such areas as inter-bank money and currency markets, and international wealth management, there remained no doubt that New York retained its position as the most important financial centre in the world. An estimate for 2014 indicated that 502,400 worked in financial services in New York compared to 367,300 in London, leading Christian Meissner, global head of corporate and investment banking at Bank of America Merrill Lynch, to exclaim that, 'As much as London might think it's the financial centre, I think New York is still ultimately the centre of the financial system. It's the dollar, it's the Fed—it's because US capital markets and the US economy are the deepest, it has the largest number of big companies.'[57] A calculation made in 2016, based on a more like-for-like basis, suggested that the financial centres were more comparable in size, as the numbers were 331,000 in New York compared to 358,000 in London. Deeper analysis indicated that New York was a much more a domestic- and retail-orientated financial centre than London, as it relied on the size of the US economy for its continuing prominence. In contrast, London served the international financial community. However, there were no sign that either was in danger of being eclipsed though each was losing less location-critical activities, such as fund management, because of lower costs and easier recruitment. In the USA New York was facing competition from the likes of Denver, Atlanta, Charlotte, and Nashville while tax advantages and lighter regulation favoured Dublin and Luxembourg over London, though all were within the EU. In contrast, Tokyo continued in relative decline, as both Singapore and Hong Kong became serious rivals in Asia. By 2014 Singapore had become Asia's largest centre for both commodity and foreign exchange trading. Hong Kong's strength lay in equities trading and banking with developing links to the Chinese market. Both competed with Switzerland in wealth management, reflecting the rapid growth in the numbers of Asia's rich. Though Singapore and Hong Kong had benefited from the damage caused to London and New York by the crisis, followed by the forced

[56] Daniel Schäfer, 'Capital gains from foreign money and time zone', 10th June 2014.
[57] Michael Pooler, 'New York and London vie for financial crown', 2nd October 2014.

deleveraging and increased regulation, their rise was more due to the growth of China's economy and the inability of Tokyo to project itself as an Asian financial centre and the limited competition coming from Shanghai.[58]

Added to the legacy of the crisis and the impact of regulation a new element was added to the mix of influences on the location of financial centres by Britain's decision to leave the EU in 2016. Over the years of the UK's membership of the EU, and especially since the emergence of a single market in financial services, London had consolidated its position as the financial centre of an increasingly integrated European economy. Through the right of passporting, a bank or other financial institution could serve the entire EU market from a single location, and many had chosen to do this from a base in London, especially those from the USA. That had made London into not only the wholesale centre for European finance but also, increasingly, a retail one as well, serving customers directly wherever they were located. London-based fund managers, for example, had thrived under these conditions. That was now under threat because they would lose access to the European market, and a number of European cities, ranging from Frankfurt and Paris to Dublin and Warsaw, stepped in to host those banks and other financial institutions being displaced from London.

Also under threat were certain wholesale activities that had long been concentrated in London. Philip Stafford concluded in 2016 that 'Scores of banks, exchanges and trading venues have based their operations in the UK in recent years, attracted by a mix of the favourable time zone, language, expertise and regulatory approach. Whether they stay will now depend on political decisions.'[59] The European Commission, for example, driven by the demands of the Eurozone members, revived its plans to centralize financial activity within the Eurocurrency area. Ever since the creation of the Euro there had been a desire among Eurozone governments to locate trading and clearing of Euro-denominated activity within the Eurozone. Conversely, banks wanted to locate their trading where the market was deepest and broadest and that was London, whether for Euro-denominated or dollar-denominated interbank activity, and that included clearing. For users clearing was expensive but banks and brokers clawed back some outlay by posting margin to back their derivatives trades at the same clearing house. This would be lost if the EU forced clearing to take place in the Eurozone. With trading taking place using multiple currencies, among which the $ not the Euro was dominant, there remained a strong case for a single trading venue and a single clearing house, and London was the obvious location. In 2016 London processed $1.2tn a day of deals denominated in a variety of currencies of which Euro-denominated swaps were around half. That business was now threatened by political decisions. London's legal framework and time zone made it an ideal offshore location from which to manage default risks by off-setting dollar–euro swap deals while US markets were

[58] Sam Fleming, 'Foreign banks meet BoE over branch rules', 27th February 2014; Patrick Jenkins and Claire Jones, 'Eurozone bank rules menace City prosperity, warns lobby', 19th March 2014; Alice Ross, 'Business coups help raise profile', 17th April 2014; Michael Pooler, 'New York and London vie for financial crown', 2nd October 2014; Jeremy Grant, 'Singapore eyes Hong Kong's financial crown', 17th October 2014; Henry Sanderson, 'Global metals trading challenges regulators', 25th November 2014; Harriet Agnew, 'City fears loss of access and influence in event of Brexit', 9th February 2015; Giles Wilkes, 'Wanted: bankers to electrify the British economy', 7th March 2015; Martin Arnold, 'Birmingham banks on appeal as financial centre', 26th March 2015; Alex Barker and Claire Jones, 'ECB agrees UK clearing houses can work outside currency area', 30th March 2015; Miles Johnson, 'Geneva's bright lights lose their allure', 1st August 2015; David Sheppard and Neil Hume, 'Traders fear new derivatives rules', 26th October 2015; Laura Noonan, 'Relocation threat for thousands of London investment bank staff', 7th January 2016; Oliver Ralph, 'Future Risks', 26th May 2016; Martin Arnold and Laura Noonan, 'Finance capitals face low-cost challengers', 10th June 2016; Jim Brunsden and Alex Barker, 'City to be sidelined by capital markets plan', 30th June 2016; Owen Walker, 'Small is beautiful for big fund groups', 4th March 2019.

[59] Philip Stafford, 'Brexit brings headache to industry weary of regulation', 11th October 2016.

closed. The US authorities were happy for London to continue to play its current role as it complemented rather than competed with New York. It was the EU authorities that wanted a change.

In 2016 Gregory Meyer observed that 'Markets have become increasingly placeless' and 'open in any time zone'. However, he added that they were 'regulated by national laws'.[60] The reality was that the location of financial markets was heavily influenced by having an appropriate legal and fiscal structure. This was the case with insurance-linked securities, such as catastrophe bonds. Bermuda was the centre of the insurance-linked securities industry because of its concentration of reinsurance companies and a supportive regulatory regime. Another example was the location of aviation finance. Dublin was where around half the world's leased aircraft were managed from and that was due to the regulatory and tax advantages it provided. These had led to the build up of expertise in Dublin that linked finance, debt issuance, and accounting in the field of aircraft leasing. Once established it was then difficult for other financial centres to compete for the business. However, regulatory intervention could also be used to prise activities away from established financial centres, and this is what the EU attempted to do from 2016 onwards in the case of London. Resisting this attempt was the depth and diversity of, in the words of Harriet Agnew in 2016, 'London's financial ecosystem' which 'relies on businesses being able to access the people and skills that they need when they need them'.[61] With 360,000 employed in financial services in London, of whom 80,000 had been sourced from elsewhere in the world, it was in a strong position to deliver what those operating in international markets required. However, specialist activities, such as global fund management, could be lured from London through regulatory intervention as locations such as Dublin and Luxembourg already possessed their own financial services ecosystems devoted to that branch of finance.

The conclusion drawn by Omar Ali, the leader of a team studying UK financial services at Ernst and Young, was that in 2017, 'The variety of locations firms are selecting only confirms the fact that the UK's financial ecosystem is unique and very hard to replicate in other European jurisdictions.'[62] In his view 'no one European centre is emerging as a compelling alternative to London'.[63] This was also the conclusion drawn by an equivalent group at the City law firm, Freshfields Bruckhaus Deringer: 'If firms transfer business out of the UK...after Brexit, it is unlikely that all business will be moved to a single EU member state. Any such transfer is instead likely to occur on a fragmented basis across multiple jurisdictions as firms seek to be closer to their customers.'[64] In 2017 Reza Moghadam, a vice-chairman at Morgan Stanley, explained the complications involved in relocating that bank's business, currently undertaken in London, to another European location. Establishing

> a subsidiary, as a legally separate entity, is expensive, duplicating not only fixed costs such as management and information systems, but also capital costs. A subsidiary needs more capital since it cannot diversify risk in the small continental market as effectively as in London. The parent needs more capital as loans to the subsidiary from London count as outside exposures. The result: lower bank profitability and return on equity, and so pressure to scale back services or raise prices.

[60] Gregory Meyer, 'Trading', 7th July 2016.
[61] Harriet Agnew, 'City urges open philosophy on immigration', 5th October 2016.
[62] Martin Arnold, 'Brexit relocation threats surge in City', 9th May 2017.
[63] Laura Noonan, 'Dublin emerges as top choice for post-Brexit bases in EU', 11th July 2017.
[64] Martin Arnold, 'Brexit relocation threats surge in City', 9th May 2017.

In contrast, 'The investment banking arms of EU banks are based in London, where they access a high-volume, low-cost global market as branches. As such, they are overseen by EU supervisors and capitalised as consolidated entities, without the duplication of fixed costs or capital needs that subsidiaries endure.' The conclusion drawn was that 'the required ecosystem of bankers, traders, lawyers and technology is simply missing in Europe. For now, London is the only town in the game.'[65] A similar verdict was delivered in 2017 by David Noonan, non-executive chairman of Nomura Europe: 'London is our hub—our European headquarters. We intend that to continue.'[66]

Taking a general view Philip Stafford in 2017 was confident that 'despite the uncertainty over what Brexit will mean for London's status as a global financial centre, its physical location remains a huge draw for firms needing to transmit trades at high speed around the world'.[67] The City did have an inbuilt advantage as a trading hub because it lay at the centre of a dense network of submarine fibre-optic cables, laid in the 1980s, as it was through these that trading was conducted. In a thirty-mile radius from the City were a cluster of technology sites that powered the highly-computerized trading of shares, currencies, bonds, commodities, and derivatives contracts that connected markets in the Americas, Europe, Asia, Africa, and the Middle East. Around that cluster was a wider one of data providers, markets, and traders. It was in London that the computers of over 200 banks, brokers, traders, and hedge funds gathered data from different venues for inputting into their own trading systems, benefiting from the city's strategic location midway between financial centres in Asia and North America. As Philip Stafford and Roger Blitz stated in 2017, 'The majority of Europe's critical infrastructure for trading forex, as well as shares and derivatives, is clustered in a 30-mile radius around the City.'[68] Later in the year he referred to London as 'pre-eminent in foreign exchange and over-the-counter derivatives, used by investors to hedge their portfolios against swings in currencies, interest rates and commodity prices'.[69] To be the fastest to a deal, traders placed their own equipment as close as possible to an exchange's own servers which housed the electronic order book, and this required them to be in London. This provided an inertia which Brexit was unlikely to affect as only a small number of traders had invested in the technology required to maintain the advantages that speed provided when buying and selling financial products.

The regulations aimed at shifting Euro-denominated business away from London were not the only new obstacle that it faced after 2016 because it was also subjected to the tightening of regulations within the EU, which continued to apply to it. The implementation of Mifid 2 took place in January 2018, when the UK had not yet left the EU. However, though the regulations being imposed by the EU had the power to undermine London as a financial centre there was no guarantee that they would provide a major benefit to other European financial centres. The obvious alternative was not Frankfurt or Paris but the only other financial centre that could provide an equivalent ecosystem to London, and that was New York. In the case of derivatives Chicago was also a viable alternative. With 45,000 working in derivatives and related activities in Chicago in 2016 it benefited from a dense web of infrastructure, expertise, and capital devoted to the derivatives industry. The largest US banks used London as the hub for their global business and their easiest course of

[65] Reza Moghadam, 'Branch out to avoid a Brexit capital markets crunch', 20th July 2017.
[66] Laura Noonan, 'Banks scale back on plans for City jobs exodus', 14th December 2017.
[67] Philip Stafford, 'Data centres help London retain cachet', 24th February 2017.
[68] Philip Stafford and Roger Blitz, 'Undersea cables boost euro trading', 6th July 2017.
[69] Philip Stafford, 'Brexit poses threat to London's role as global hub', 10th October 2017.

action was to transfer that to their existing offices in their home country rather than develop new facilities elsewhere in Europe. As so much of the world's financial transactions took place in US$s, including those involving the euro, it would be impossible to insist that they took place within the Eurozone rather than the USA. What was happening in the EU was also reflected elsewhere in the world where pressure from regulators was also continuing to drive banks to favour regional financial centres. According to Philip Stafford, Laura Noonan, and Hannah Murphy in 2017 'Some of the biggest investment banks route their Asian trading through London',[70] but this was under threat from local regulators who favoured international centres like Singapore and Hong Kong or national centres such as Tokyo, Shanghai, Seoul, and Mumbai. However, none of these were yet in a position to challenge London and New York ten years after the Global Financial Crisis. Alice Han wrote in 2018 that a successful financial centre requires 'a strong national economy, the rule of law and robust institutions that give investors confidence that their assets are secure'.[71] Shanghai, like most financial centres around the world, was not yet in a position to mount a challenge to London and New York as international financial centres ten years after the Global Financial Crisis had taken place, inflicting serious damage on the banking systems of both the USA and the UK.[72]

Results

Driven by fears over the disruptive consequences of complex, opaque, and fast-moving global markets and banks that were considered too big to be allowed to fail, after the Global Financial Crisis regulators continually looked for ways of controlling both. This did have

[70] Philip Stafford, Laura Noonan and Hannah Murphy, 'Banks seek reprieve on key part of Mifid 2 rules', 14th December 2017.

[71] Alice Han, 'Shanghai needs resilience if it is to challenge London', 8th May 2018.

[72] Jim Brunsden and Alex Barker, 'City to be sidelined by capital markets plan', 30th June 2016; *FT* Reporters, 'Europe plots a bank heist', 1st July 2016; Philip Stafford and Roger Blitz, 'Battle intensifies over London's euro clearing role', 5th July 2016; Gregory Meyer, 'Trading', 7th July 2016; Jennifer Hughes, 'Singapore-Hong Kong battle heats up', 29th July 2016; Harriet Agnew and Patrick Jenkins, 'What's next for the City', 3rd September 2016; Harriet Agnew, 'City urges open philosophy on immigration', 5th October 2016; Philip Stafford, 'Brexit brings headache to industry weary of regulation', 11th October 2016; Philip Stafford, 'US eyes prize if swaps shift from London', 20th October 2016; Leo Lewis and Kama Inagaki, 'Tokyo renews push as financial hub', 22nd November 2016; Gregory Meyer, 'City retains role as capital of the derivatives industry', 16th December 2016; Vincent Boland, 'Capital's ecosystem offers fertile ground for growth', 24th January 2017; Philip Stafford, 'Data centres help London retain cachet', 24th February 2017; Philip Stafford, 'City confident of keeping infrastructure edge', 23rd March 2017; Gregory Meyer and Nicole Bullock, 'Algo traders look beyond need for speed in quest to gain competitive edge', 31st March 2017; Martin Arnold, 'Brexit relocation threats surge in City', 9th May 2017; Oliver Ralph, 'Slip in market share knocks London role in reinsurance', 9th May 2017; Philip Stafford, 'Debate over post-Brexit clearing of euro swaps focuses on margin costs', 13th June 2017; Martin Arnold and Laura Noonan, 'US banks warn of fund fragmentation if hard Brexit throws up high barriers', 21st June 2017; Philip Stafford and Roger Blitz, 'Undersea cables boost euro trading', 6th July 2017; Laura Noonan, 'Dublin emerges as top choice for post-Brexit bases in EU', 11th July 2017; Reza Moghadam, 'Branch out to avoid a Brexit capital markets crunch', 20th July 2017; Philip Stafford, Emma Dunkley, and Jim Brunsden, 'Financial services groups go Dutch to ensure EU access', 5th August 2017; Philip Stafford, 'Mifid vies with Brexit as City traders' top concern', 11th August 2017; Philip Stafford, 'Brexit poses threat to London's role as global hub', 10th October 2017; Laura Noonan, 'Banks look to route business via HK', 23rd October 2017; Philip Stafford, 'Brexit unleashes a three-way battle over clearing', 25th October 2017; Oliver Ralph, 'Singapore moves in on catastrophe bonds', 2nd November 2017; Arthur Beesley, 'Dublin on a high as China aviation sector surges', 6th November 2017; Sarah Gordon, 'Edinburgh more upbeat on Brexit than London', 20th November 2017; Barney Thompson, 'Brexit puts legal hub at risk, City warns', 23rd November 2017; Chris Flood, 'European regulators move to mitigate Brexit threat', 11th December 2017; Ralph Atkins, 'The decline of the Swiss private bank', 12th December 2017; Laura Noonan, 'Banks scale back on plans for City jobs exodus', 14th December 2017; Philip Stafford, Laura Noonan, and Hannah Murphy, 'Banks seek reprieve on key part of Mifid 2 rules', 14th December 2017.

consequences for London and New York as global financial centres. However, ten years after the collapse of Lehman Brothers their attempts had done little to dislodge London and New York from the prime positions they had long occupied, as no other centres possessed their unique advantages. Also, these actions by regulators were increasingly supplemented and then supplanted by other considerations that had little to do with the crisis itself. One of the most powerful were protectionist measures designed to enhance the standing of particular national financial centres of which the most obvious was the intervention of the European Commission acting on behalf of the member countries that had joined the single currency, the euro. The UK had remained outside this currency zone but London had become the dominant centre in which the trading and clearing of the euro, and euro-denominated products, took place, much to the annoyance of the governments of those countries that had joined. However, as long as the UK remained a member of the EU, and the euro was not the official currency of all member states, it was impossible to implement policies that would undermine London's role. That position ended in 2016 with the UK's decision to leave the EU. This created the opportunity for action to be taken, cutting out the role played by London traders and clearers in any transaction related to the euro and, more generally, London-based banks and fund managers in serving EU customers. The intention was to favour financial centres located within the EU, such as Amsterdam, Copenhagen, Dublin, Frankfurt, Luxembourg, Malta, Milan, and Paris over not only London but also Geneva and Zurich in Switzerland. As financial services was, in the words of Alex Barber in 2018, 'a highly-regulated sector',[73] this gave those framing laws within the EU considerable power to influence the location of activity, and this was directed at securing an advantage over London and the Swiss centres.

EU-wide moves in this direction were bolstered by the actions of regulators within individual member countries. French regulators, for example, tried in 2018 to force asset managers serving EU customers to set up branches inside the EU and to place restrictions on EU investors accessing services provided externally, such as in London. According to Christian Noyer, the former Governor of the Bank of France, 'Banks and asset managers will try to concentrate trading operations in one EU location. That doesn't mean London won't remain the largest financial centre. Paris could become the big trading hub in continental Europe.'[74] These moves were beginning to make some headway in 2019 but still had little to show. In order to attract banks and others from London regulators elsewhere had to offer concessions relating to regulations and taxes that could have far reaching consequences within their own country. This was the challenge facing the various European governments that housed financial centres hoping to profit from the effects on London of the UK leaving the EU. One of the few continental European financial centres that could provide international banks with facilities that matched London was Amsterdam. It could offer a regulatory structure friendly to trading, a stable legal system, a central location with good connections, and a financial ecosystem. Philip Stafford noted in 2018 that 'Amsterdam has emerged as the biggest beneficiary as London-based trading venues make alternative arrangements for Brexit, which threatens to disrupt the pass-porting system that firms have used to access markets in Europe from the UK'.[75] However, it lacked the depth and breadth of even Frankfurt or Paris let alone London, which meant its appeal was a limited one. The

[73] Alex Barber, 'Brexit talks near deal on financial services', 6th November 2018.

[74] Patrick Jenkins and Stephen Morris, 'Paris set to be post-Brexit trading hub as UK defends City's global credentials', 1st October 2018.

[75] Philip Stafford, 'Amsterdam is biggest winner as trading groups set up plans for Europe bases', 4th July 2018.

European cities with greater appeal were those with a more established position such as those that had grown as centres of the fund management industry, like Luxembourg and Dublin, through the tax and regulatory advantages they offered. By 2019 Dublin had become one of the world's biggest fund management centres leading Carin Bryans, head of JP Morgan's office in that city to report that 'We have found huge benefits co-locating technology, operations and the business...it speeds up the innovation process so much. It also ensures that you get over obstacles quickly.'[76] It was those locations with an existing financial ecosystem and a huge cluster of skills that were best placed to benefit from any displacement of activity from London.

However, there were none that could match London as a trading centre in such areas as the inter-bank money, currency, and derivatives market. Writing in 2019 Christopher Giancarlo, the chairman of the US's Commodity Futures Trading commission (CFTC) stated categorically that 'London is, and will remain, a global centre for derivatives trading and clearing.'[77] Jim Brunsden and Philip Stafford added that 'London dominates the market for clearing euro-denominated trades, handling the vast majority of interest rate, commodity and credit contracts.'[78] Nevertheless, certain activities were being transferred out of London by 2019 in response to EU requirements that they had to take place within member countries, even though it meant splitting up integrated operations. The risk was if those banks with integrated operations were required to move them from London, it would not benefit another centre within Europe. The most likely beneficiary was New York. Colm Kelleher, the president of Morgan Stanley, warned in 2019 that this was the most likely outcome, observing that 'Finance is global, not regional.' What he had concluded was that Europe's basic problem was that continental financial markets were too small and fragmented to justify an extensive ecosystem of asset managers, lawyers, and accountants that London and New York possessed. Forcing global banks to relocate away from London would lead them towards New York, rather than rival financial centres in continental Europe, certainly in the short-run and perhaps permanently: 'Because of the paramount importance of scale, liquidity and risk diversification, capital markets are intrinsically global.'[79] Mark Wiedman, the senior managing director, of the global fund manager, BlackRock, reached the same conclusion: 'Our European operations are centred around a single hub, we have a single operational model, a single set of funds. Post Brexit, that is going to be fractured.'[80]

To a large degree London and the other European financial centres complemented each other rather than competed and so any loss for the former was not a gain for the latter. Unlike the USA the European market for financial services was so fragmented that it could not support a global financial centre on its own. London was in a position to be a global financial centre because of its longstanding and extensive international business, especially its links to the USA and Asia. As Oliver Robinson, a director of Aima, the hedge-fund association, wrote in 2018, it was London that provided global capital markets with 'a central time zone, a respected legislative and political system, and a deep global talent pool.'[81]

[76] Laura Noonan, 'City has power to lure business without Brexit', 13th February 2019.

[77] Philip Stafford, 'US and UK strike eleventh-hour accord to minimise no-deal Brexit disruption', 26th February 2019.

[78] Jim Brunsden and Philip Stafford, 'UK clearing houses face threat of pressure to move to EU', 14th March 2019.

[79] Colm Kelleher, 'The EU misses the point on finance after Brexit', 24th April 2019.

[80] Owen Walker, 'BlackRock warns of Brexit break', 23rd September 2019.

[81] Philip Stafford and Hannah Murphy, 'City of London agonises over jumping on crypto bandwagon', 26th May 2018.

Similarly, in derivatives, London was the main global hub for originating, executing, and booking deals in derivatives and managing the daily price fluctuations on the contracts. Under these circumstances the actions of the EU would result in marginal gains for a diversity of continental cities, the undermining of London as a financial centre, the fragmentation of the European market for financial products, and the enhancing of the position of New York despite its time-zone disadvantages. In many ways this reflected the fundamentals underpinning the hierarchy of financial centres around the world and why the shock of the Global Financial Crisis failed to generate any fundamental change, even though it was widely expected to do so, and why, at least in the short-run, an event such as Brexit had the same limited consequences. Philip Stafford and Eva Szalay concluded in 2019 that 'Many banks, brokers and asset managers have opened EU offices and begun shifting some assets to the bloc in preparation for Brexit, but have largely kept their daily activities in the UK.'[82] Trends reflecting underlying forces were a major influence on the location of financial centres and it took events such as world wars and political revolutions to alter these.[83]

[82] Philip Stafford and Eva Szalay, 'London pulls away from New York in forex and swaps as it shrugs off Brexit', 17th September 2019.

[83] Philip Stafford, 'Selling time to traders: the physicist who measures deals in microseconds', 5th February 2018; Owen Walker, 'Spooked fund managers look at rivals to London', 19th February 2018; Olaf Storbeck, 'Germany eyes looser labour laws to woo banks', 21st February 2018; Philip Stafford, 'Brexit anxieties grow over London's vital market infrastructure', 22nd February 2018; Nathan Brooker, 'How the crash created one global city', 17th March 2018; Alice Han, 'Shanghai needs resilience if it is to challenge London', 8th May 2018; Philip Stafford, 'Bloomberg picks Amsterdam for EU trade base', 9th May 2018; Philip Stafford, 'Thomson to move forex derivatives out of London', 16th May 2018; Philip Stafford and Hannah Murphy, 'City of London agonises over jumping on crypto bandwagon', 26th May 2018; Philip Stafford, 'Frankfurt narrows gap with London as incentive scheme boosts euro clearing', 13th June 2018; Chris Flood, 'Forget passports! Trade must go on', 18th June 2018; Philip Stafford and Ralph Atkins, 'London worries it will be the EU's next target after Swiss stand-off', 29th June 2018; Philip Stafford, 'Amsterdam is biggest winner as trading groups set up plans for Europe bases', 4th July 2018; Patrick Jenkins and Caroline Binham, 'City financiers struggle to unite on post-Brexit regulation', 5th July 2018; Ralph Atkins and Philip Stafford, 'Switzerland's crypto ambitions get boost from digital platform launch by exchange', 7th July 2018; Martin Arnold, Owen Walker, and David Keohane, 'BlackRock and Citi succumb to allure of Paris after Macron vows less red tape', 9th July 2018; Martin Arnold, 'JP Morgan head warns of tough Brexit effect', 11th July 2018; Philip Stafford, 'European regulators to rewrite share trading rules after fears of Brexit hit', 14th July 2018; Emma Dunkley, 'Mainland's curbs spell downside for HK bourse in contest for listings', 21st July 2018; Patrick Jenkins, George Parker, and Alex Barker, 'UK refuses to give up on post-Brexit plan for City', 24th July 2018; Philip Stafford, 'Deutsche Bank's Frankfurt move revives City concerns', 31st July 2018; Hannah Murphy, 'TP Icap names Paris as its EU base after Brexit', 8th August 2018; Katie Martin, 'City secures hold on offshore renminbi trade as daily volume soars to £69bn', 27th September 2018; Philip Stafford, Stephen Morris, and Jim Brunsden, 'Banks look at exit from UK derivatives', 1st October 2018; Patrick Jenkins and Stephen Morris, 'Paris set to be post-Brexit trading hub as UK defends City's global credentials', 1st October 2018; Philip Stafford, 'Key London markets in the lurch under a no-deal Brexit', 1st October 2018; Alex Barber, 'Brexit talks near deal on financial services', 6th November 2018; Philip Stafford, 'ABN Amro's clearing business seeks London licences to prepare for Brexit', 22nd November 2018; Philip Stafford and Jim Brunsden, 'Concerns mount for European banks over positions in UK clearing houses', 11th December 2018; Jim Brunsden and Philip Stafford, 'Brussels set to extend access to Swiss exchanges for another six months', 18th December 2018; Kate Allen and Philip Stafford, 'EU sovereign debt costs at risk if access to City banks ends with no-deal Brexit', 4th January 2019; Jim Brunsden and Mehreen Khan, 'Brussels to drag UK into court over tax breaks for commodities traders', 24th January 2019; Eva Szalay, 'London gains ground in renminbi trading drive', 30th January 2019; Eva Szalay, 'London charm offensive pays off in race for renminbi', 9th February 2019; Owen Walker, 'EU27 nations change laws to help UK fund groups survive no deal', 11th February 2019; Philip Stafford, 'Traders face anxious wait for Brexit guidance', 12th February 2019; Arthur Beesley, 'Cautious Dublin reaps benefits of Brexit exodus', 13th February 2019; Laura Noonan, 'City has power to lure business without Brexit', 13th February 2019; Laura Noonan and Claire Jones, 'Central bank has bigger stick to win respect at home and abroad', 13th February 2019; Philip Stafford, 'BoE official warns EU on pitfalls of UK clearing house regulation post-Brexit', 15th February 2019; Philip Stafford, 'European customers handed clearing house access to contain Brexit fallout', 19th February 2019; Jo Johnson, 'Politicians must stand up for the City after EU exit', 21st February 2019; Siobhan Riding, 'Supermancos, the fund businesses that are winning big from Brexit', 25th February 2019; Philip Stafford, 'US and UK strike eleventh-hour accord to minimise no-deal Brexit disruption', 26th February 2019; Eva Szalay, 'Offshore currency trade poses challenge for India's central bank', 6th March 2019; Stephen Morris, 'London easily tops league of best-paid European financiers', 12th March 2019; Jim Brunsden and Philip Stafford, 'UK clearing houses

Conclusion

The trends that drove change in global financial markets before the crisis were very powerful and so could neither be easily stopped nor reversed. Megabanks, for example, were not dismembered but recovered from the calamity of the crisis and continued to play a central role in global finance. The banks themselves and those who regulated them recognized that they were exposed to risks despite their size, diversity, and the business model that they followed. The liquidity issues that all banks faced had not disappeared and so greater care had to be taken when financing long-term loans with short-term borrowing, whether this was done following a lend-and-hold or originate-and-distribute model. Though there was some displacement of financial activity into the shadow banking system this did not represent a reversal of past trends but more a rebalancing between different components. Even for the megabanks the crisis did not lead to a reversal of previous trends but more a modification of behaviour and a scaling back of ambition. The crisis had made apparent the dangers of both universal and international banking but the response was not to voluntarily abandon it or introduce laws to prevent it. Instead, it was recognized that the megabanks served the modern financial system and so ways had to be found to deliver its benefits while minimizing the risks it created. This is what banks themselves, along with regulators, sought to achieve after the crisis.

Despite the role played by derivatives in the Global Financial Crisis they remained essential tools in the way that both volatility and risks were covered Nevertheless, they did experience change as those using them were forced to have their transactions processed through clearing houses as way of containing the consequences of counterparty default. What had not happened was any revival of the importance of exchanges in either the derivative or stock market even though this had once appeared likely. Instead, trading in financial instruments continued to take place primarily through inter-bank or Over-The-Counter markets with ever greater reliance on computers to both generate trades, match buying and selling and process transactions. In contrast, the inertia of financial centres remained with the duo of London and New York continuing to dominate though their demise had been predicted as one of the consequences of the Global Financial Crisis. Finally, the Global Financial Crisis did not witness a revival in the role of government because it had never been removed. Though the new world of finance was one of freedom,

face threat of pressure to move to EU', 14th March 2019; Jim Brunsden and Claire Jones, 'ECB attacks EU proposals for boosting clearing house oversight', 18th March 2019; Philip Stafford, 'No-deal Brexit share trade ruling sparks accusations of EU land Grab', 21st March 2019; Laura Noonan, Stephen Norris, and David Crow, 'City's top lenders hold fire on Brexit exodus', 2nd April 2019; Colm Kelleher, 'The EU misses the point on finance after Brexit', 24th April 2019; Philip Stafford, 'LSE shrugs off Brexit worries to gain boost from clearing', 2nd May 2019; Caroline Binham and Patrick Jenkins, 'Bailey signals need for Brexit talks focus on financial services', 8th May 2019; Philip Stafford and Philip Georgiadis, 'EU markets regulator abandons no-deal block on big UK stocks', 30th May 2019; Philip Stafford and Mehreen Khan, 'London venues poised to delist Swiss stocks as Bern's EU dispute drags on', 26th June 2019; Philip Stafford, 'Swiss stock trading shifts away from the EU exchanges after Brussels-Bern dispute', 2nd July 2019; Jennifer Thompson, 'French fail to capitalise on Brexit as number of Paris funds falls', 8th July 2019; Attracta Mooney, 'Could London be Berned like the Swiss?', 8th July 2019; Philip Stafford, 'Brussels eyes payment plan for exchanges' trading data', 12th July 2019; Siobhan Riding, 'Europe bickers over passporting future', 5th August 2019; Philip Stafford, 'Cboe to open Dutch hub for trading shares of EU groups amid Brexit uncertainty', 4th September 2019; Philip Stafford and Eva Szalay, 'London pulls away from New York in forex and swaps as it shrugs off Brexit', 17th September 2019; Eva Szalay, 'Jump in London rupee trades rings alarms', 18th September 2019; Owen Walker, 'BlackRock warns of Brexit break', 23rd September 2019; Philip Stafford, 'Swiss trading volumes rise but so do costs after EU ends equivalence rules', 25th September 2019; Tommy Stubbington, 'Eurozone bailout fund ditches English law for bonds in fresh Brexit hit to UK', 27th September 2019.

integration, and instability it was not without a major role for governments, central banks, and regulators. There had existed before the crisis a vast array and depth of legislation, direction, supervision, and regulation that governed the environment within which financial activity took place and dictated what could and could not be done. That continued after the crisis but it experienced change. The certainties of the control and compartmentalization era had disappeared and a new regulatory structure had been formed to take its place. What the crisis represented was one step on the way to refashioning the global financial system.

14

Global Financial Crisis

Causes, Course, and Consequences, 2007–20

Introduction

The Global Financial Crisis was a rolling affair. Some date its beginning to 9th August 2007 when the French bank, BNP Paribas, suspended redemptions from three investment funds. This triggered a massive withdrawal of liquidity from the market for asset-backed securities. The following day the Federal Reserve, the European Central Bank, and the Bank of Japan pumped liquidity into the market. Their collective action was followed, belatedly, on 14th September 2007, when the Bank of England bailed out the small British bank, Northern Rock. Those moves appeared to signal the end of the crisis, but that was not the case. On 17th February 2008 the Northern Rock Bank was taken into state ownership by the British government after attempts to find a buyer had failed. In the USA on 16th March 2008 JP Morgan Chase bought the investment bank, Bear Stearns, which was in financial difficulty. Those acquisitions appeared to signal another end to the crisis but again that was not the case. On 14th September 2008 the Bank of America bought the US investment bank, Merrill Lynch, having first attempted to acquire Lehman Brothers, but failed to gain Federal Reserve guarantees against the risks that involved. That was immediately followed on 15th September 2008 by Lehman Brothers filing for bankruptcy, which led to another crisis that was far greater than any of the preceding ones. That crisis led to massive government intervention in the USA and Western Europe, to prevent a wave of bank failures that could have led to the collapse of the global financial system.

Many have suggested that the Global Financial Crisis was an accident waiting to happen, being the result of trends dating from the 1970s. However, these same trends had provided the global financial system with a resilience that appeared to make a Global Financial Crisis impossible. The lack of one following the collapse of the dot.com bubble suggested that the underlying trends had delivered the resilience that all sought. The depth and breadth of global financial markets provided a level of liquidity by guaranteeing that sales and purchases could always be made. The size and scale reached by the megabanks gave individual financial institutions the capacity to cope with whatever adverse conditions they had to face. This ability to cope was further strengthened by the use of derivatives as these provided insurance against the risks of both defaults by borrowers and the volatility of interest rates and exchange rates. Risks could be redistributed to such a degree that no event could be sufficiently catastrophic to cause the failure of a major bank as the entire system could be drawn in to absorb a loss. Finally, the central banks of the world, acting collectively, had perfected rules of behaviour that were applied to systemically-important banks and so reduced the level of risk that they were exposed to. The scourge of a liquidity crisis leading to a bank run had been removed by the simple device of converting loans into transferable assets and providing a market through which they could be sold at a moment's notice.

Banks, Exchanges, and Regulators: Global Financial Markets from the 1970s. Ranald Michie, Oxford University Press (2021).

DOI: 10.1093/oso/9780199553730.003.0014

Regulatory agencies were also in place that supervised financial systems, including both banks and financial markets, and so were in a position to identify and deal with any signs of impending difficulty. This removed the threat of a solvency crisis for any systemically-important institution. Under these circumstances a crisis of the magnitude of the one that took place in 2008 was considered impossible. But the impossible happened.

One the major reasons the impossible happened was the consequences of the central bank and regulatory intervention in the global financial system that had preceded the crisis. In the wake of the bursting of the dot.com bubble central banks pumped liquidity into the global financial system, fearing a repetition of the aftermath of the Wall Street Crash of 1929, which was a banking crisis followed by a worldwide economic depression of the 1930s. This created a lax monetary environment, which encouraged further risk-taking, particularly in the USA. In the case of the USA regulatory intervention dating back to the mid-nineteenth century, had left a legacy of financial instability. This was most evident in the banking system, where it had undermined the development of resilient banks and encouraged an excessive reliance upon financial markets among both savers and borrowers. Beginning in the nineteenth century legislation had placed barriers in the way of interstate banking. The result was to halt the development of banks that were sufficiently large and spatially diversified, so that they could successfully operate the lend-and-hold model of banking. Through the ability to move funds internally, maintain ample reserves, and match assets and liabilities such banks were highly resilient in a liquidity crisis, as examples elsewhere in the world proved such as Canada and the UK. Those restrictions placed on the growth of nationwide banks were then compounded in the 1930s by the legislative response to the Wall Street Crash of 1929. With the Glass–Steagall Act barriers were erected preventing the development of banks that combined the whole range of financial activities. The result was to halt progress towards banks that were large and sectorally diversified. By possessing a large capital base and choosing their investments carefully, including holding liquid assets and operating the originate-and-distribute model, these universal banks were also resilient in the face of a liquidity crisis though vulnerable in an economic catastrophe, as had happened in Germany and Austria between the wars. It was only in the 1990s that these legislative barriers to both nationwide and universal banking were removed in the USA, leaving little opportunity for the banks that then emerged to devise methods of operation that provided resilience in the face of a crisis. The Global Financial Crisis of 2008 was the first test that these new banking structures faced.

These were not the only examples of the impact made by legislation on the US banking system, which left it vulnerable when faced with a major financial crisis. In the 1930s the US government had also introduced a cap on the interest paid by banks on deposits. This was to discourage banks from taking excessive risks in order to pay depositors the returns they promised when competing for their savings. By the 1970s this cap penalized depositors as the rise in inflation resulted in real rates of interest that were negative. In response financial products were devised that evaded the cap and so paid a higher rate of interest but offered the flexibility of deposit accounts. Out of this emerged the negotiable instrument of deposit, which then became the basis of the Eurodollar market in London. Another response was Merrill Lynch's cash management account that allowed it to compete for deposits with the established banks. A major change then came in 1993 when the Securities and Exchange Commission (SEC), which was the regulator responsible for these money-market funds, allowed them to fix their net asset values at $1 a share by dropping mark-to-market accounting. This meant money-market funds could guarantee depositors that their cash would be repaid in full, while receiving a rate of interest above that paid by banks on deposits. As a result these money-market funds were able to attract the savings that would, otherwise, have flowed to banks, providing them with that stable retail base upon which to operate the lend-and-hold model. By 2008 the total placed in money-market funds had reached $3.8tn. Both savers and corporate treasurers used these funds to park their short-term cash, confident that their deposits could not lose value while the yield was higher than anything a bank could provide. Defaults and downgrades of assets had threatened to undermine the guarantee that the value of a holding could not decline but it was not until the Global Financial Crisis itself that these were taken so seriously that there were panic redemptions. Faced with the equivalent of a bank run the US Treasury was forced to intervene to guarantee the net asset values of these money-market funds. As John Gapper explained in 2012, 'The old-fashioned bank run, with depositors lining up outside banks to withdraw cash, has been updated to corporate treasurers wiring money from money-market funds at any hint of trouble.'[1] What this exemplified was how a series of decisions, each taken for sensible reasons, could fundamentally distort the working of the US financial system.

However, rather than viewing what had taken place in the USA as the product of a unique set of circumstances prior to the Global Financial Crisis the US financial system became regarded as the ideal which all should emulate. The suppression of both nationwide and universal banking, and the competition for savings coming from money-market funds, had prevented the development of banks that were committed to the lend-and-hold model using either retail deposits or a large capital as sources of finance. In its place there was a high reliance upon the originate-and-distribute model, where banks acted as intermediaries between savers and borrowers rather than accepting responsibility for the loans that they made using the funds supplied by savers making deposits. Instead of holding assets in the form of loans, they were converted into liquid securities and sold, so releasing new funds, which were lent to others, so repeating the process. Unlike in the lend-and-hold model, in the originate-and-distribute model banks had little incentive to monitor the creditworthiness of those to whom they lent, as the loans were repackaged and sold on. Also, within the originate-and-distribute model the differential tax treatment applied to stocks over bonds favoured the issue of fixed-interest securities. Interest payments on debt were tax deductible while dividend payments were not. This encouraged loans to be refinanced not through a stock issue but one of bonds. The result was heavily-indebted businesses faced with the necessity of making interest payments and repaying maturing loans even in an economic downturn, which could lead to bankruptcy. This situation even applied to banks themselves as they had become over-reliant on debt rather than equity. If the repackaged loans were retained they were now liquid securities, which, if required, could be sold, so quickly and easily releasing funds, which was not the case with loans. This allowed a bank to increase its leverage as it was no longer required to possess either a large capital or liquid reserves to cover defaults, redemptions, and withdrawals. Problems would only occur if the market for such securities froze but that was considered increasingly unlikely before the crisis.

What made US practice universal was that the originate-and-distribute model was also recommended to all banks prior to the crisis. To regulators the originate-and-distribute model appeared a safer mode of operation than the lend-and-hold one because it freed banks from holding illiquid assets, in the shape of loans to customers, as these had been converted into liquid securities which could be sold if required. The various crises that took

[1] John Gapper, 'Don't leave the financial system resting on quicksand', 30th August 2012.

place in the 1980s, and the collapse of Long-Term Capital Management in 1998, had alerted regulators to the risks of financing long-term investments with short-term funds without an adequate cushion of liquid assets. That was a lesson that hedge funds learnt for themselves, and so they adjusted their strategies, while regulators encouraged banks to switch from unsecured lending to the provision of funds against collateral. Under the Basel 2 rules a bank could operate on less capital if its lending was secured against collateral. The originate-and-distribute model fitted this strategy perfectly as a bank could repackage its loans as securities and sell them to another bank. The bank selling the loans could then lend more and so repeat the process while the purchasing bank could increase its leverage as it could hold less capital against these securitized assets. However, the assumption of regulators was that banks held highly-marketable government debt, like US Treasuries, not corporate and mortgage bonds and securities assets, which was much less liquid. Regulators also made the assumption that all such securities could always be sold regardless of circumstances.

However, a process of market fragmentation was taking place that replaced deep pools of liquidity, as in the case of US Treasury bonds and the stock issued by large companies, with multiple shallow pools where securitized loans were traded. In the crisis triggered by the collapse of Lehman Brothers these shallow markets froze and the value of securitized assets plunged, leaving banks with huge losses, casting doubt on their solvency let alone their liquidity. This made them untrustworthy counterparties and so other markets froze. In response banks cut back on lending both to each other and to their customers, aggravating the problems each faced. In that sense the Global Financial Crisis was an accident waiting to happen in the USA and a number of other countries, including the UK. In turn, through the web of connections that had developed through the inter-bank markets, that crisis quickly became a global affair. That suggests that the crisis was the inevitable consequence of certain trends that had emerged in the 1990s led by developments in the USA. However, the Global Financial Crisis was neither an overnight sensation nor without warning signs, but a long drawn out process dating from early 2007. This meant that alternative decisions taken at the time, especially by central banks and regulators, could have produced different outcomes. Whereas it could be argued that a crisis of some kind was inevitable, and a number had taken place over the years since 1970, the results were not necessarily of the magnitude and duration of what did take place. It is only by tracing the actual course of the crisis, and identifying its chief characteristics that it becomes possible to establish whether different decisions would have produced different consequences.

That approach then needs to be followed when assessing the central bank response to the crisis and the regulatory consequences, as those transformed the environment within which financial activity took place. While the immediate impact of the crisis faded as time passed, as was the case with all such events, the legacy it created, in terms of the actions of central banks and regulators, was much more permanent, setting off further changes and developments. However, the effect of both the crisis and its legacy varied between banks, exchanges and the regulators. For some, such as the megabanks, the implications were profound and of longer duration because they were seen as being both too big to fail and exposed to a potential liquidity crisis if action was not taken. Conversely, the effects of the crisis on exchanges were simultaneously shallow and brief as the existing trends soon resurrected themselves. There was to be no return to primacy among markets for exchanges despite the resilience they had exhibited during the crisis. Instead, the trading of stocks, bonds, currencies, and derivatives continued to be dominated by intra- and inter-bank arrangements and electronic platforms. What became more centre stage as a result of the crisis was the role played by central banks and national regulators and the relationship between them. No longer could central banks stand idly by while a liquidity crisis built up. Even megabanks could be overwhelmed by a liquidity crisis and central banks, acting singly and collectively, had to be ready to pre-empt such an event or deal with one if it did occur. Similarly, regulators had to take greater responsibility for the functioning and stability of markets rather than concentrating solely on protecting the interests of the user. The result was to change the freedom that banks and markets had enjoyed before the crisis. Whereas the environment within which banks and markets operated before the crisis had been shaped by the actions of central banks and regulators, emanating from the 1970s and even much longer before, those afterwards owed much to their response, which was both deep and enduring.

Crisis, 2007

By February 2007 concerns were being expressed over the mounting risks to which lenders in the US mortgage market were exposed to. That month there was the latest failure among the specialist mortgage lenders. In this case it was the California-based, ResMAE Mortgage Corporation. A housing downturn had begun in the USA in 2006 as demand weakened, leading to a growing number of borrowers defaulting on their loans. Jane Croft referred in February 2007 to 'A raft of profit warnings from subprime lenders following falling house prices and rising consumer defaults.'[2] By March 2007 more than twenty-five subprime mortgage companies in the USA had closed since late 2006, while other lenders had written down losses on subprime loans in the face of late payments and defaults. This was beginning to affect the bigger specialist lenders such as New Century Financial and Countrywide, and even a number of the large diversified banks such as HSBC and Citigroup. New Century Financial itself collapsed in April 2007. At this stage the response from the megabanks was to buy up distressed loans at a discount, seeing the downturn as an opportunity to acquire assets that could be used for their 'lucrative securitisation business', according to Richard Beales and David Wighton in February 2007.[3]

US investment banks such as Merrill Lynch, Lehman Brothers, and Morgan Stanley, as well as international banks like Credit Suisse, Deutsche Bank, and Barclays, had developed a lucrative business of granting credit lines to US mortgage lenders, buying up the loans they made, and then repackaging them to sell on to investors worldwide. However, by March 2007 they were having difficulty placing new securities with investors, which would deprive them of the funds required to sustain this business. Early that month Michael Mackenzie and Saskia Scholtes expressed their concern that, 'The danger for Wall Street is banks will be left holding billions of dollars of subprime mortgage loans they hoped to sell to investors.'[4] Nevertheless, the large banks appeared confident that they could cope with any downturn in the US mortgage market, and were taking steps to cut their exposure. Bear Stearns, the biggest Wall Street underwriter of mortgage-backed securities, had started to wind down its securitization business in 2006, as borrowers began to fall behind with payments or even defaulted. By May 2007 Saskia Scholtes was reporting that, 'In the past few months there has been a sharp increase in late payments and defaults on subprime

[2] Jane Croft, 'Lucrative market may yet prove house of cards', 20th February 2007.
[3] Richard Beales and David Wighton, 'Concerns mount over risky lending in US market', 14th February 2007.
[4] Michael Mackenzie and Saskia Scholtes, 'Subprime securitisation threat', 7th March 2007.

mortgages, or home loans made to borrowers with patchy credit histories. The problems have forced dozens of lenders to shut their doors and resulted in a spate of lawsuits as Wall Street banks try to recover losses on soured loans.'[5] These concerns over the performance of subprime mortgages were not confined to the USA but extended to Europe. In the UK the Kensington Group, a specialist subprime mortgage lender, was also in difficulty. The UK had been experiencing a buy-to-let fuelled housing bubble, with the number of investment mortgages rising from 28,700 in 1998 to 849,000 in 2006. Despite these concerns the European issuance of bonds backed by mortgages and other debt continued to grow rapidly in response to strong demand from investors. This drove up leverage levels and pushed down safeguards and interest rates, as was already the case in the USA. What was different was that there was less awareness of the emerging risks in Europe. As late as May 2007 Jane Croft praised the UK's Northern Rock Bank, impressed by its 'strong profit growth' and 'the lowest cost base in Europe'.[6] Northern Rock was to feature at the centre of Britain's banking crisis a few months later.

Though regulators and central banks were aware of the rising leverage levels among the megabanks they remained confident that they possessed the resilience to cover any losses. Instead, their focus was on the risks posed by peripheral financial institutions, especially hedge funds, and the connections these had to the megabanks. This focus stemmed from the collapse of the fund manager, Long-Term Capital Management (LTCM), in 1998. It had an equity capital of $4.8bn but had leveraged this by a factor of over twenty-five times to create assets of $125bn. Its strategy was to use short-term funds borrowed from banks and others to hold high-yielding government debt, and so generate a profit from the interest-rate differential. This strategy collapsed with the devaluation of the Russian rouble followed by Russia's declaration of a debt moratorium in August 1998. Faced with the potential collapse of LTCM the New York Federal Reserve had been forced to intervene to prevent wider contagion through LTCM's 60,000 trading positions. The fear was that this would be repeated in the case of the growing number and size of the hedge funds, as they also operated on the basis of borrowed funds and taking speculative positions in different asset classes. As Paul J. Davies reported in March 2007, 'Leverage levels are part of a complicated pattern of risk that includes uncertain correlations between asset classes—in part created by the operations of wide-ranging, diversified hedge funds—and the speed at which losses can be transmitted between funds, banks and other parts of the financial system.'[7] Regulators and central bankers long remained focused on the emerging threat to stability posed by hedge funds operating at the margins of the financial system rather than the activities of the mainstream banks. In particular there was a strong belief the switch from the lend-and-hold to the originate-and-distribute model, presided over by central banks, removed the threat of a systemic crisis.

Nevertheless, the risks posed by connections between the different parts of the financial system was beginning to exercise the minds of central bankers early in 2007. In April of that year Roger Cole, director of banking supervision at US Federal Reserve, expressed his worries: 'The concern is that in the event of a major financial shock, the complex web of exposures among highly-leveraged hedge funds and dealer institutions may increase the risk that problems at one financial institution would spread to others.'[8] By May 2007 it was

[5] Saskia Scholtes, 'Deutsche files subprime writs', 1st May 2007.
[6] Jane Croft, 'Bid spotlight once again falls on A&L', 28th May 2007.
[7] Paul J. Davies, 'The dangers inherent in imprudent lending', 5th March 2007.
[8] James Mackintosh, 'Investors still pile in', 27th April 2007.

becoming evident that investor resistance to securitization issues was growing while liquidity was drying up in the secondary market. In response hedge funds were selling equities as a way of increasing their liquidity while banks were turning to derivatives to cover themselves against potential losses. The use of credit default swaps reduced the risks being run by banks and investors as they provided insurance against a default. These tactics gave the required reassurance, leading many to believe the current difficulties were both minor and temporary, and so provided a buying opportunity rather than a signal to sell. Regulators were also reassured that the financial system could absorb small-scale shocks, as nothing greater was expected. As long as those conditions prevailed neither banks nor fund managers could afford to ignore the opportunities that presented themselves because of the profits to be made. Whether it was the sale and purchase of securitized assets or the use of highly-leveraged finance for mergers, acquisitions, buy-outs, or buy-ins, no one could refuse to participate, whatever the risks, as the alternative was to be left out of subsequent deals and then be overtaken by more aggressive rivals. This meant that banks, in particular, were committing themselves to purchase assets that lacked the liquidity of corporate stocks listed on exchanges or readily saleable government bonds, such as those issued by the US Treasury. Instead, they held the likes of Collateralized Debt Obligations (CDOs), which were rarely traded.

Many of the new securities in circulation were designed to be held until maturity but were treated as liquid because a bank made a market in them, using a complex mathematical model to generate a price at which they could be bought and sold. By June 2007 the risks posed by these supposedly liquid assets had become evident. Saskia Scholtes and Gillian Tett reported that 'The big risk now is that if thousands of banks and investment groups suddenly have to slash the value of the securities they hold, the wave of accounting losses might at best leave investors wary of purchasing all manner of complex financial instruments. At worst, it could trigger more distressed sales and a broader repricing of financial assets, not just in the subprime sector but in other illiquid markets too.'[9] Banks had tried to distance themselves from the risks posed when financing long-term loans from short-term borrowings by establishing separate structured investment vehicles (SIVs). These SIVs acted as conduits through which the banks channelled funds into securitized assets. However, these SIVs were often provided with guarantees that the bank would buy back the assets they held. Even if that was not the case the bank owning the SIV was exposed to reputational damage if it got into financial difficulty.

What crystalized the issues surrounding these securitized assets, and the risks they posed to banks, were the emerging difficulties of some of the specialist mortgage lenders, as their lack of diversification made them especially vulnerable. However, as long as the difficulties remained confined to the more peripheral financial institutions the risks to the financial system as a whole appeared limited. Megabanks, in particular, had sufficient depth and breadth to cover losses, which were expected to be small. The collateral backing these securitized assets remained sound, as it was mainly residential and commercial property or the earning streams of profitable businesses and employed individuals. That confidence was shattered in August 2007 when rumours began circulating that a number of British banks were in financial difficulty. This was confirmed when the Bank of England revealed that it had made an emergency loan to at least one UK bank on the twentieth of that month following an advance of £4bn on June 29th. The seriousness of this action was played down

[9] Saskia Scholtes and Gillian Tett, 'Does it all add up?', 28th June 2007.

at the time with those banks believed to have been in receipt of the loans publicly denying it. Chris Giles reported that, 'Some of the banks thought to be most vulnerable to shortages of finance, including Northern Rock, denied they had made use of the borrowing facility. Most refused to comment.'[10] As the Bank of England had been steadfast among central banks in publicly refusing to provide emergency liquidity its actions suggested that the crisis was far more serious than many had previously believed.

Bob Diamond, president of one of Britain's biggest banks, Barclays, tried to deflect attention from his institution by suggesting that it was 'Those people that applied a fair amount of leverage to subprime portfolios without permanent funding are the people right now that are having the most difficult time in the market. This is not a credit crisis. This is a liquidity and a confidence crisis.'[11] This was an open invitation for central banks to step in as lenders of last resort and provide the liquidity that the financial system required. Though there was a hint, and no more, from some at the time that there might be, according to Gillian Tett, 'a banking crunch', what was considered more likely was a global stock market crash because 'credit risk has been distributed to a much wider pool of investors than before'.[12] At that stage concerns over liquidity were confined to the smaller and more specialized mortgage lenders, and was not expected to lead to a solvency crisis for the UK banking system. What was being ignored was the exposure of some of Britain's largest banks to a collapse in property prices, especially in the commercial sector. British banks had been lending extensively for property development, especially RBS and HBOS, with the total debt secured on commercial property in the UK rising from £49bn in 1999 to £187bn in 2006. What was now looming was a repeat of the 1992 banking crisis, which had centred on bank lending to finance property development and led to Bank of England intervention to prevent a systemic crisis.

Nevertheless, the immediate cause of the crisis was not a collapse of the property market but a lack of liquidity in the inter-bank markets caused by a collapse of confidence. Prior to the crisis banks had been repackaging subprime loans into asset-backed securities. Immediately before the crisis an estimated $700bn of securitized assets were in circulation in the world's financial system, along with another $600bn of similar securities, and $390bn in Collateralized Debt Obligations. These asset-backed securities were not traded on public markets and there were no current prices making it impossible to value them. The result was to make it difficult to calculate whether a bank holding these securities was illiquid or insolvent or both. If illiquid a bank could expect central bank support, in its role as lender of last resort, but not if it was insolvent, as that would raise the issue of moral hazard. Moral hazard was when the central bank intervened to save a bank that had become insolvent, because of excessive risk-taking in the search for profits, as that could lead others to follow the same course. By saving such a bank from collapse the central bank not only condoned risk-taking but encouraged it. As it was the European Central Bank provided liquidity support to the European money market after the German lender IKB was forced to seek a bailout in July because of subprime losses.

In contrast, the Bank of England refused to do the same for the UK money market, citing the issue of moral hazard, despite repeated urging from the UK's Financial Services Authority and senior bank executives. Chris Giles and Peter Thal Larsen reported that 'Since the crisis first broke in early August, bank executives had been urging regulators to

[10] Chris Giles, 'Bank stresses actions are not unusual', 22nd August 2007.

[11] Gillian Tett, Peter Thal Larsen, and Neil Hume, 'Barclays Capital banker quits', 24th August 2007.

[12] Gillian Tett, 'Doomed to repeat it?', 27th August 2007.

address the shortage of liquidity in the money markets by broadening the range of collateral against which the Bank of England would be willing to lend. The European Central Bank and the Federal Reserve had already taken this step.'[13] It was not until the crisis broke out that the Bank of England was forced to act, as that made it accept the seriousness of what was happening. Following the sequence of events reveals the missed opportunities the Bank of England had to take pre-emptive action. On Friday 14th September. Adam Applegarth, the chief executive of Northern Rock, commenting on the news that the Bank of England would provide emergency funding, had said 'These facilities are only provided to companies with a sound future.'[14] On Saturday 15th September there was a run on Northern Rock branches after news of the Bank of England bailout was publicized in the media. On Sunday 16th September that run continued online, overwhelming the Northern Rock website and forcing its closure. Intervention by the government then followed on Monday 17th September through a guarantee to depositors that their money was safe. The run died away on Tuesday 18th September. It was only on Wednesday 19th September that the Bank of England provided £10bn in liquidity support to the UK money market. Writing on 22nd September 2007 Chris Giles and Peter Thal Larsen produced their own assessment on what had happened:

> On Monday evening Mervyn King believed the first real crisis of his Bank of England stewardship had—as he put it to friends—been sorted. Beset by images of customers rushing to withdraw their money from Northern Rock, Alastair Darling, the Chancellor of the Exchequer, had offered depositors a blanket assurance that their cash was safe. But within five days, Mr King's optimism had been proved comprehensively and humiliatingly unfounded. In one of the most extraordinary weeks in British banking history—one which saw the global credit squeeze spill on to the nation's streets—the Bank had on Wednesday performed an abrupt volte face. It had decided to extend emergency lending against mortgage collateral to all banks—a step that just 24 hours earlier the governor had privately ruled out.[15]

Many believed that this action, 'if it had only come a few weeks earlier, would probably have saved Northern Rock, and its depositors, from the crisis they had just suffered.'[16] In turn that intervention might have saved the British banking system from suffering its first liquidity crisis since 1866, and the destabilizing consequences it had through a collapse of confidence.

As it was, the Northern Rock Crisis in the UK had focused international attention on the importance of liquidity to the stability of the banking system, and forced central bankers to take account of it. In December 2007 Peter Thal Larsen reflected upon what had been learnt: 'Ever since it was bailed out by the government in September, Northern Rock has served as a stark reminder of the crucial importance of liquidity in the banking system. The notion that a large, solvent and well-capitalised bank could run out of money was not a possibility that bankers or regulators had spent much time discussing. Ever since, they have

[13] Chris Giles and Peter Thal Larsen, 'Week that shook the banking world', 22nd September 2007.
[14] Chris Giles and Peter Thal Larsen, 'Week that shook the banking world', 22nd September 2007.
[15] Chris Giles and Peter Thal Larsen, 'Week that shook the banking world', 22nd September 2007.
[16] Chris Giles and Peter Thal Larsen, 'Week that shook the banking world', 22nd September 2007.

talked about little else.'[17] He then added this warning to central bankers and financial regulators that a focus on solvency was not sufficient:

> Liquidity has always been a central issue to the banking system. At their core, banks use short-term funding from retail depositors and the money markets to finance longer-term loans. As a result, there is always a possibility that a bank will not be able to raise enough cash to meet its obligations. Until this summer, however, the assumption was that a bank with sufficient capital would always be able to raise cash if needed.[18]

Despite the Northern Rock debacle in the UK by November 2007 the worst of the financial crisis appeared to be over. Central banks had injected liquidity into the global financial system and those banks that were at risk of failure, and most likely to destabilize the entire banking system, had been saved. By then, according to Jonathan Wheatley, 'The world is awash with liquidity.'[19] Though all subprime loans were now suspect, and asset-backed securities remained difficult to value, there was a return of confidence. Jonathan Wheatley claimed that 'Emerging market assets are offering both high returns and a safe haven.'[20] As Gillian Tett pointed out, 'On sheer size, subprime securities are dwarfed by other asset classes, such as equities.'[21] No global bank had required support from its central bank, with failures confined to marginal institutions. Since the collapse of Long-Term Capital Management in 1998 reforms had been introduced to improve the resilience of the global banks including the use of derivatives that allowed counterparty risk to be redistributed to others.

By the end of 2007 the financial crisis appeared to have been surmounted. The crisis had been confined to the periphery of the financial system in the USA and Western Europe and those banks that had failed were marginal players. The megabanks had proved that they were sufficiently resilient to surmount a crisis of this kind, proving to central bankers and regulators that their strategy of relying upon them for the stability and orderly functioning of the global financial system had been the correct one. The Bank of England had been forced to compromise on the hard line it had taken over the question of moral hazard, and follow the more pragmatic stance of the Federal Reserve and the ECB in terms of providing liquidity. The scare was over and the financial world could return to normal. There had been no Global Financial Crisis. However, new risks had grown up around banks, especially the risks posed by off-balance-sheet entities such as structured investment vehicles. There was also evidence that the sub-prime crisis in the USA was spreading into other sectors of finance as banks cut back on lending and the scale of default rose. As bank capital was squeezed and the perception of risk rose, investment backs had begun to pull back from trading, for example. The saga was not over though many thought it was. What the crisis of 2007 had also revealed was the lack of co-ordination and speed among central banks and regulators when faced with a situation that required urgent intervention. As Gillian Tett reflected in November 2007, 'It is one thing for the different national regulators to co-operate in creating long-term policy reforms; it is quite another for them to act quickly, in a unified manner, when turmoil hits.'[22] However, these were all issues for the

[17] Peter Thal Larsen, 'FSA concedes that rules only go so far', 20th December 2007.
[18] Peter Thal Larsen, 'FSA concedes that rules only go so far', 20th December 2007.
[19] Jonathan Wheatley, 'Bovespa float inspires other exchanges', 19th November 2007.
[20] Jonathan Wheatley, 'Bovespa float inspires other exchanges', 19th November 2007.
[21] Gillian Tett, 'Sub-prime in its context', 19th November 2007.
[22] Gillian Tett, 'Regulators weigh up supra-national intervention', 19th November 2007.

future as the immediate crisis had passed through successful intervention and structural resilience, as had been the case with previous episodes such as the collapse of LTCM and the bursting of the dot.com bubble.[23]

Crisis, January to June 2008

Despite this confidence in the stability of the global financial system, by the beginning of January 2008 there were mixed views on what the future held. At this stage the banking collapses that had occurred were still regarded as isolated incidents among the smaller players, who had over-extended themselves and so became vulnerable when denied access to short-term funding. In contrast, the larger and more resilient banks had responded to the changed situation by drawing back from riskier lending and adjusting their balance sheets to reflect the new reality. 'Some observers hope the worst is almost past as banks face up to their losses' was the conclusion reached by Gillian Tett in January 2008.[24] There was little fear that a systemic crisis was likely, as the worst of the liquidity squeeze in the inter-bank market had passed. Banks had been hoarding cash and refusing to lend to each other due to concerns over potential losses related to complex debt products and the vehicles that funded them. Those liquidity issues had been addressed in mid-December 2007 by the world's leading central banks, led by the Federal Reserve, pumping billions into the banking system. Bank rescues were also a regular feature of the US banking system and there were procedures for handling them, and so the occasional failure was only to be expected. What was required was for other countries to adopt these as such events would occur in the future and needed to be anticipated and contained. That was now happening.

Nevertheless, some observers were not convinced that all was well with the global financial system. They pointed to fundamental problems that could not be solved through central banks providing liquidity. When Northern Rock had been provided with public funding in September 2007 the assumption was that this was an emergency measure of a temporary nature, similar to those that had been conducted in 1984 and 1991. Northern

[23] Richard Beales and David Wighton, 'Concerns mount over risky lending in US market', 14th February 2007; Jim Pickard, 'Number of buy-to-let mortgages rises 30-fold in past decade', 15th February 2007; Jane Croft, 'Lucrative market may yet prove house of cards', 20th February 2007; Paul J. Davies, 'The dangers inherent in imprudent lending', 5th March 2007; Michael Mackenzie and Saskia Scholtes, 'Subprime securitisation threat', 7th March 2007; Ben White, 'Buoyant Bear Stearns shrugs off subprime woes', 16th March 2007; Paul J. Davies, 'RMBS register hot first quarter', 3rd April 2007; David Oakley and Saskia Scholtes, 'Flurry of activity in banks for CDSs', 3rd April 2007; James Mackintosh, 'Investors still pile in', 27th April 2007; David Oakley and Anuj Gangahar, 'Volatility fears fuel equity derivative surge', 23rd May 2007; John Authers and Gillian Tett, 'Snapping Point', 23rd May 2007; Jane Croft, 'Bid spotlight once again falls on A&L', 28th May 2007; Paul J. Davies, 'Europe's hottest trades', 28th May 2007; Gillian Tett, 'Swaps soar as investors pile in', 28th May 2007; Gillian Tett, 'Growth brings loss of oversight', 28th May 2007; Peter Thal Larsen, 'Number behind the M&A boom', 30th May 2007; Saskia Scholtes and Gillian Tett, 'Does it all add up?', 28th June 2007; Chris Giles, 'Bank stresses actions are not unusual', 22nd August 2007; Gillian Tett, Peter Thal Larsen and Neil Hume, 'Barclays Capital banker quits', 24th August 2007; Gillian Tett, 'Doomed to repeat it?', 27th August 2007; David Oakley, 'Record repurchase volumes for Europe', 29th August 2007; Peter Thal Larsen, George Parker, Chris Giles, and Lina Saigol, 'Recriminations fly at handling of Rock Crisis', 19th September 2007; Chris Giles and Peter Thal Larsen, 'Week that shook the banking world', 22nd September 2007; Jim Pickard, 'Ominous signs for students of history', 28th September 2007; Gillian Tett and Paul J. Davies, 'What's the damage', 5th November 2007; Gillian Tett, 'Sub-prime in its context', 19th November 2007; Gillian Tett, 'OTC derivatives hold their own', 19th November 2007; Gillian Tett, 'Regulators weigh up supra-national intervention', 19th November 2007; Jonathan Wheatley, 'Bovespa float inspires other exchanges', 19th November 2007; Stacy-Marie Ishmael, 'Fall-out from subprime crisis spreads', 27th November 2007; Peter Thal Larsen, 'FSA concedes that rules only go so far', 20th December 2007; Chris Hughes, 'Triple blow sends cost of trading soaring', 24th December 2007.

[24] Gillian Tett, 'Pressures for a rethink are on the rise', 23rd January 2008.

Rock was regarded as both viable and solvent and so was expected to attract a buyer, and there were a number who were interested. However, by February 2008 that had not happened as Jane Croft and Chris Giles reported, 'The government has been trying since then to find a buyer for the bank that would enable the £25bn in Bank of England loans to be repaid.'[25] What was slowly becoming apparent was that the originate-and-distribute model of banking involved major risks as it relied upon the continuous availability of short-term funds and the willingness of investors to purchase repackaged loans in ever greater quantities. That environment no longer existed and this had implications for the health of the global financial system. Towards the end of January 2008 Gillian Tett expressed the doubts that many were raising when she questioned whether '21st century financial innovation' had 'made the banking system more efficient and robust or is it time to return to a simpler model of global finance?'[26]

One who concluded that the risks now outweighed the benefits was Peter Thal Larsen, who emphasized the vulnerability of banks to a combination of a liquidity and a solvency crisis. Whereas before the crisis 'the banks' apparent ability to pass on much of their risk meant the scope for creating new credit was almost limitless,'[27] its legacy was a collapse of trust in the new financial instruments and the markets they were traded in. This undermined the value of securitization issues and with it the originate-and-distribute model. Issues of asset-backed securities, for example, had risen from $102.1bn in 2000 to a peak of $773.1bn in 2006 but fell away during 2007 and did not recover in 2008. This undermined the model upon which securitization was based, especially the survival of the Special Purpose Vehicles (SIVs) that used low-cost short-term debt to fund investments in the longer-term and higher-yielding securities that securitization generated. This process had been encouraged by the Basel capital-adequacy rules, as it was believed to make the financial system safer through the ability of banks to shift risk to others. However, banks had often provided guarantees to those buying bonds, as that made them more saleable, and this left them liable in the case of a default. This model of financing was now under threat as it became more difficult to access short-term funding and to sell on loans as repackaged debt. The result was to force SIVs to sell assets to meet funding requirements, halt operations, wind down completely, or rely on emergency funding from their parent bank. Some SIVs were even absorbed by their parent bank because of the commitments it had made to them. Stacy-Marie Ishmael warned in early January that, 'The surviving vehicles are expected to face intensifying liquidity problems in the coming weeks, as their medium-term debt starts to come due for repayment. Two-thirds of all medium-term funding for SIVs comes due for repayment by October, with almost $40bn due within the next three months.'[28] What she was commenting on was not an end to a crisis but the beginning of a new one that was escalating out of control. It was becoming apparent that the difficulties being experienced within the financial sector in both the USA and Western Europe were not confined to specialist mortgage lenders and hedge funds, as was initially believed, but extended to the megabanks, notably those that had been taking huge risks, leaving them with massive subprime losses.

What took place during 2008 was a gradual evaporation of confidence in the entire global financial system. Financial products such as collateralized debt obligations were

[25] Jane Croft and Chris Giles, 'Fury over Rock Nationalisation', 18th February 2008.
[26] Gillian Tett, 'Pressures for a rethink are on the rise', 23rd January 2008.
[27] Peter Thal Larsen, 'Payback Time', 7th January 2008.
[28] Stacy-Marie Ishmael, 'Victoria woes rock SIV sector', 9th January 2008.

little traded, making valuation reliant on prices generated by complex computer models. Once the accuracy of the calculations underpinning these models was questioned investors became increasingly unwilling to buy them, and banks to accept them as collateral when making loans. One response among banks was to turn more and more to derivatives as a way of hedging their exposure to the greater volatility they were experiencing and the increased risk of defaults among borrowers. In turn this exposed them to other risks as Robert Cookson, Sarah O'Connor and Paul J. Davies had already warned in January 2008 'As the disruption in credit markets continues and the prospects of a slowing economy and rising defaults increases, banks would do well to triple-check the financial strength of all their counterparties.'[29] Their view was that the largest banks were not fully aware of the counterparty risk they were exposed to when buying insurance against defaults. These were in the form of Credit Default Swaps (CDSs), of which there were $45,000bn outstanding by the end of 2007. CDSs provided banks with insurance against corporate default. The seller of a CDS agreed, in return for a premium, to pay the face value of the policy to the buyer in the event of a default. This had helped maintain confidence in the likes of CDOs and so sustain the originate-and-distribute model. As doubts emerged that those selling CDSs would be in a position to honour their commitments, if faced with major defaults, so the willingness of investors to purchase CDOs fell. Bill Gross, manager of Pimco, the world's largest bond fund, pointed out in January 2008 that 'The conduits that hold CDS contracts are, in effect, non-regulated banks' and had 'no requirements to hold reserves'.[30]

As the security offered by CDS contracts evaporated banks took measures to safeguard themselves against the consequences of a potential liquidity crisis that could easily turn into a solvency one because of the problem of valuation. These measures included cutting back on lending and building up reserves. As one banker, Andrea Cicione, the credit strategist at BNP Paribas, explained, 'We know that in times of distress things typically get much worse than one would rationally anticipate—markets take advantage of forced sellers, banks tighten their lending standards, credit availability evaporates...'[31] Such a response made the likelihood of a liquidity crisis more likely as it exposed the weakness of those banks most dependent upon short-term borrowing to finance long-term lending. As that happened these banks found it more difficult to access short-term funds, bringing them to the brink of collapse as they found it difficult to repay maturing loans or meet depositor withdrawals. Once that was known a bank run would begin, spreading throughout the banking system, endangering the liquid and solvent as well as the illiquid and insolvent. Though regulators and central banks were aware of the seriousness of the emerging liquidity and potential solvency issues that plagued the shadow banking sector they did not fully recognise the implications it had for the regulated banks, especially the megabanks. There remained the assumption among regulators and central banks that different parts of the financial system operated independently and so the megabanks were isolated from the problems of their smaller peers and the unregulated. Also, there was widespread confidence that the megabanks were sufficiently diversified to cope with the losses they might experience. The reality was that all components of the financial system, especially those that operated out of the twin financial centres of London and New York, were closely

[29] Robert Cookson, Sarah O'Connor, and Paul J. Davies, 'Painful lessons to be learnt for CDSs', 11th January 2008.

[30] Saskia Scholtes and Gillian Tett, 'Shipwrecks and casualties warning for credit markets', 11th January 2008.

[31] Robert Cookson, Sarah O'Connor, and Paul J. Davies, 'Painful lessons to be learnt for CDSs', 11th January 2008.

intertwined and the cumulative effect of what was happening in the unregulated periphery was having a destabilizing impact on the regulated core.

Nevertheless, secure in the belief that they had dealt with the crisis through their intervention in late 2007, and in the resilience of the megabanks, regulators and central bankers took almost no action until faced with the potential collapse of the major US investment bank, Bear Stearns, in March 2008. It had fully embraced the originate-and-distribute model and so was most exposed when that business faded away, suffering an inevitable liquidity crisis as a consequence. However, it was an attractive takeover target for a US commercial bank wanting to diversify into investment banking, if it could be bought at a low price. JP Morgan Chase stepped in and bought it in a deal backed by Federal Reserve with $29bn of public money. Bear Stearns was regarded as facing a liquidity not a solvency crisis and so eligible for Federal Reserve assistance. What had made the Federal Reserve provide that support was the threat posed to the financial system if Bear Stearns had collapsed because of the role it played in the credit-derivatives market. That role made it a counterparty to numerous transactions. As Stacy-Marie Ishmael, Saskia Scholtes, and Aline Van Duyn reflected in April 2008, 'If Bear had defaulted, the market would have had to unravel the complex web of trades in which the broker was involved and to determine the settlement of contracts to be paid.'[32] This was a stark warning of the risks to the global financial system that would result from the collapse of a systemically-important bank, which Bear Stearns had become, even though it was neither a deposit taker nor a key component of the payments system. Like the other US investment banks Bear Stearns was regulated by the SEC, not by the Federal Reserve, but the former had no capacity to provide the liquidity support it now required when it got into difficulties. The way US banking had been evolving both before the abolition of the Glass–Steagall Act, and after its repeal, led to a fusion of the different types of bank and the removal of the artificial distinction that had long existed. Hence the desire of JP Morgan Chase to acquire Bear Stearns as it provided it with the opportunity of becoming a universal bank and so compete with those already in that position. The willingness of JP Morgan Chase to rescue Bear Stearns had confirmed to the Federal Reserve that megabanks were too big to fail either because individually they were large and diversified or collectively they would intervene to prevent such an event as it would destabilize them all.

The troubles that had pushed Bear Stearns close to failure did not disappear on its rescue, because conditions remained unsettled. There was some recovery in confidence because another liquidity crisis had been averted but conditions in the global money market remained tight. US money-market funds, for example, were the second-largest funding source for US banks after customer deposits, with assets totalling $4tn. This was usually lent to banks through the purchase of short-term securities but continuing concerns about bank stability made them reluctant to buy bank-issued debt. This left banks short of liquidity, and so unwilling to lend to the inter-bank market. As Dominic Konstam, head of interest-rate strategy at Credit Suisse, noted in April 2008, 'Banks are hoarding cash because funding from the asset-backed commercial paper market has fallen sharply while money-market funds are lending on a short-term basis and are restricting their supply.'[33] As Jim Reid, the credit strategist at Deutsche Bank, explained in May 2008, 'In the new financial climate, banks are slowly changing their mode of operations. They are moving from a world where

[32] Stacy-Marie Ishmael, Saskia Scholtes, and Aline van Duyn, 'Time to address counterparty risk', 8th April 2008.

[33] Gillian Tett and Michael Mackenzie, 'Debate over Libor breeds a crisis of confidence', 22nd April 2008.

they would be happy to lend to anybody to one where they are much more careful.'[34] Banks were losing liquidity as those to whom they had made commitments drew out the funds which they were unable to replace by new borrowing, as investors were not buying their equity and bond issues because of concerns about bank liquidity. Once doubts emerged about the ability of banks to repay borrowings then it became difficult for them to raise additional funds, which had the effect of worsening their liquidity position, and so made it even more difficult to raise new funds. Any sign that a bank was having difficulty raising funds in the inter-bank market could lead to doubts about its suitability as a counterparty, creating an immediate liquidity crisis. That encouraged banks to return false London Interbank Offered Rates (Libor) 'so as not to fan fears they have funding problems',[35] according to Michael Mackenzie and Gillian Tett in June 2008. Libor was the reference rate of interest at which banks lent to and borrowed from each other. The fear was that if a bank revealed that it had to pay a high rate for any money it was borrowing this would send a signal that it lacked the confidence of its peers. In turn that could lead to a bank run as depositors rushed to withdraw funds while maturing loans were cashed in rather than rolled over. At all costs a bank had to maintain public confidence, for any suspicion that it might be in difficulty would precipitate a liquidity crisis in the conditions that prevailed by mid-2008.

By June 2008 conditions were emerging that suggested that another financial crisis was imminent. This had the potential to be much greater than any of those that had occurred in the recent past as it was unlikely to stop with the marginal components of the financial system, such as the specialist mortgage lenders or hedge funds, but could engulf a number of the major banks. Whether this crisis was likely to be halted with injections of liquidity from central banks was also in doubt, as it was becoming more a question of bank solvency because of the difficulty of valuing assets. Most securitization issues lacked a public market, being reliant on prices generated by complex mathematical models run on high-powered computers. As these were no longer trusted it was becoming impossible to value assets which made them impossible to sell and difficult to use as collateral. With central banks focused on domestic considerations, little attention was paid to the drying up of liquidity in the global interbank market, though this could affect every bank as all were connected to it, directly or indirectly. Central to this global inter-bank market were a small group of US megabanks as it largely operated on the basis of the US$. Only US banks had exclusive access to the Federal Reserve, being able to draw on it for funds, and so they had become the key conduit through which liquidity was injected into the global financial system. However, the worsening credit squeeze in the USA, along with growing concerns about bank solvency, meant that US banks were hoarding their $s, which had serious consequences for all other banks. There were alternative sources of liquidity in the shape of other central banks but none of these had direct access to $s, as that was the US currency, and only the Federal Reserve had the power to create more. One central bank that could have done more, because the global interbank market was centred in London, was the Bank of England. Writing in June 2008 David Lascelles, an expert in international finance, judged that 'The Bank is uniquely placed to understand banks and markets, and to provide guidance to both of these.'[36] However, it had withdrawn from direct engagement with the money market located on its doorstep, replacing it with a focus on domestic monetary policy,

[34] David Oakley, 'Banks' reluctance to part with cash keeps the heat on Libor', 23rd May 2008.
[35] Michael Mackenzie and Gillian Tett, 'Libor remarks fail to put unease to rest', 2nd June 2008.
[36] David Lascelles, 'The Bank needs a stronger role in the City', 16th June 2008.

where it acted on behalf of the UK Treasury. That left the global money market dependent upon its own resources.[37]

Crisis, July to December 2008

Over the course of July 2008 the signs of a new financial crisis emerged. Whereas in the past the rating agencies had been able to reassure investors that assets had a definite and reliable value, by August 2008 that confidence had evaporated. Paul J. Davies reported that investors believed that banks involved in securitizing assets had 'been finding ways to get the highest level of return for the safest ratings'.[38] As trust was undermined so investors refused to buy assets whose value depended on the judgements made by a rating agency. Existing assets also proved either unsaleable or at a price generated by the bank's own computer model. With such securities impossible to value and unsaleable rumours spread that those banks that were large holders were no longer safe. In July Michael Mackenzie reported that the 'whispering campaign', which many believed had brought down Bear Stearns, was happening again.[39] The SEC regarded the situation as so serious that it took action against the short sellers, who were blamed for depressing the share price of the banks considered most at risk. That was the limit of its powers as it could not act as lender of last resort. What the collapse of Bear Stearns had revealed was the degree to which the investment banks were embedded in the financial system through the use of credit derivatives. These linked deposit banks, investment banks, hedge funds, mutual funds, and financial institutions, such as the giant insurance company, AIG, into a complex network which was meant to deliver stability and resilience but also exposed them to huge losses if a shock to the system was sufficiently big to knock out one component. As Michael Mackenzie and Nicole Bullock reported in July 2008, 'Major banks and brokerages have become tightly bound by a chain of credit-derivatives trades.'[40] The value of Credit Default Swaps outstanding, for example, rose from $1,563bn in 2002 to $54,511bn in 2008. As awareness of that exposure grew so did the reluctance to lend to those banks most engaged in providing

[37] Paul J. Davies and Saskia Scholtes, 'Interbank rate easing drives liquidity hopes', 3rd January 2008; Peter Thal Larsen, 'Payback Time', 7th January 2008; Stacy-Marie Ishmael, 'Victoria woes rock SIV sector', 9th January 2008; Robert Cookson, Sarah O'Connor, and Paul J. Davies, 'Painful lessons to be learnt for CDSs', 11th January 2008; Saskia Scholtes and Gillian Tett, 'Shipwrecks and casualties warning for credit markets', 11th January 2008; Sam Jones and Stacy-Marie Ishmael, 'No relief in sight for CDO investors', 11th January 2008; Chris Giles and Krishna Guha, 'Liquidity shortages appear to ease', 16th January 2008; Chris Hughes and Jeremy Grant, 'City Limits', 21st January 2008; Gillian Tett, 'Pressures for a rethink are on the rise', 23rd January 2008; Jane Croft and Chris Giles, 'Fury over Rock Nationalisation', 18th February 2008; George Parker and Jimmy Burns, 'Modern precedents for public ownership', 18th February 2008; James Mackintosh, 'Hedge funds pose dilemma for regulators', 5th March 2008; Ross Tieman, 'Algo trading: the dog that bit its master', 19th March 2008; Stacy-Marie Ishmael, Saskia Scholtes, and Aline van Duyn, 'Time to address counterparty risk', 8th April 2008; Gillian Tett and Michael Mackenzie, 'Debate over Libor breeds a crisis of confidence', 22nd April 2008; Anuj Gangahar, 'Boomtime for derivatives as investors bet on volatility', 25th April 2008; Paul J. Davies, 'Moody's reviews six SIVs for downgrade', 25th April 2008; Gillian Tett and Paul J. Davies, 'Battle-scarred bankers lapse into a hoarding habit', 8th May 2008; Michael Mackenzie, 'Equities rally as optimists discount credit crunch', 20th May 2008; David Oakley, 'Banks' reluctance to part with cash keeps the heat on Libor', 23rd May 2008; Michael Mackenzie and Gillian Tett, 'Libor remarks fail to put unease to rest', 2nd June 2008; Gillian Tett and Daniel Oakley, 'European banks in chase for dollars', 10th June 2008; David Lascelles, 'The Bank needs a stronger role in the City', 16th June 2008; Gillian Tett, Aline van Duyn, and Paul J. Davies, 'A re-emerging market? Bankers are seeking simpler ways to sell on debt', 1st July 2008; Anousha Sakoui, 'Stability possible for leveraged loan pricing as backlog declines', 9th July 2008; Gillian Tett, 'A year that shook faith in finance', 4th August 2008.

[38] Paul J. Davies, 'Effort to bring credit ratings into clearer focus gathers pace', 5th August 2008.

[39] Michael Mackenzie, 'Mixed response to SEC selected protectionism', 17th July 2008.

[40] Michael Mackenzie and Nicole Bullock, 'Deadline is looming for derivatives clean-up', 22nd July 2008.

credit derivatives. In early September Jay Hooley, the president and chief operating officer at the fund managers, State Street in Boston, had made clear the position of institutions such as his: 'There has been a flight to quality as investment managers and hedge funds look to the safety and soundness of their counterparties. We have seen increased demand from hedge funds to act as custodian for their assets, as concerns grow about their prime brokers.'[41] Prime brokers were owned by the investment banks and acted as counterparties to those involved in buying and selling assets, lending and borrowing money or trading in derivatives.

One of the largest prime brokers was Lehman Brothers, whose worsening financial position was attracting growing attention by August 2008. Lehman had been a leading underwriter of mortgage-backed securities and this had left it with large holdings after the subprime crisis curtailed investor appetite for these fixed-income products. As it wrote down the value of these assets, and could not raise fresh capital, fears surfaced that it was in serious financial difficulty. As a result it found it increasingly difficult to borrow in the interbank money market because of concerns that it would be unable to repay. Under these circumstances Lehman Brothers could no longer repay maturing debts which holders were unwilling to roll over. Unlike the earlier crisis surrounding Bear Stearns the worsening outlook for the value of securitized assets meant that serious solvency issues now surrounded a bank in difficulties such as Lehman Brothers. Nevertheless Lehman Brothers remained an attractive takeover target for a commercial bank seeking to expand into investment banking. One of those interested in such a merger was Bank of America but it would not proceed without government guarantees, because of the risks that were now apparent to all. As these guarantees were not forthcoming the Bank of America turned its attention to another investment bank, Merrill Lynch, and acquired it instead. The British bank, Barclays, also considered buying Lehman Brothers but it also required government guarantees, which were also refused. That left Lehman Brothers stranded, facing an immediate liquidity crisis and a possible solvency one. It had no option but to file for bankruptcy, as it could not meet its repayment commitments when they became due.

Those guarantees had not been forthcoming because the Federal Reserve judged that Lehman Brothers was insolvent because of the weight of overvalued mortgage-backed securities it carried. Rescuing an insolvent bank raised the spectre of moral hazard, which had not applied in the case of Bear Stearns, as it was considered only to be suffering from illiquidity. Also, as Lehman Brothers was an investment bank the Federal Reserve did not regard it as systemically important, unlike a large commercial bank holding deposits from members of the public, playing a central role in the payments system, and providing the credit that business and the public relied upon. As rumours about the survival of Lehman Brothers had been flying around for months the Federal Reserve did not anticipate that its ultimate demise would cause a shock of sufficient dimensions to destabilize the entire US financial system. Based on those assumptions the Federal Reserve calculated that Lehman Brothers could be allowed to fail with only limited consequences. Its failure would also act as a warning to other banks that they could not rely on government support if they indulged in excessive risk-taking for the sake of high profits. In taking this stance the Federal Reserve was doing no more than following expert international opinion as that advised central banks against supporting insolvent financial institutions. On 16th September 2008 the highly-respected financial advisor, Avinash Persaud, wrote that 'Lehman had to fall to save the

[41] Brian Bollen, 'The sector stays aloft in a risky climate', 8th September 2008.

financial system.'[42] The *FT*'s own US correspondent, John Gapper, subsequently admitted that he was one among many who held the same view, but admitted ten years later that it was an error of judgement: 'It was soon evident that the Fed and the US government had little choice but to salvage the system by propping up other banks, no matter how unpalatable it was. Letting them all go the way of Lehman would have punished the financial elite for its recklessness and avoided moral hazard, but the economic cost was too high.'[43] As subsequent events quickly revealed, the refusal of the Federal Reserve to provide either guarantees or direct support was a disastrous miscalculation based on a failure to appreciate the risks that had built up in the financial system. Regulatory intervention had encouraged banks to offload risky assets and use derivatives to insure against losses. This lulled central banks into a false sense of security that a bank failure could be contained, even one the size of Lehman Brothers, because the risks they were exposed to were limited. As the US economist, Gary Gorton, reflected in 2012, 'We did not believe a bank run could happen in a developed economy.'[44] In 2018 Nick Bailey, who had been head of regulation at the LSE at the time of the Lehman crisis, expressed the same view: 'Lehman was a global titan. The idea that it would collapse was unthinkable.'[45]

The confidence that the Federal Reserve had, that any crisis stemming from the collapse of Lehman Brothers could be easily contained, quickly evaporated as the sequence of events demonstrated. On 11th September Lehman's had faced an immediate downgrade of its credit ratings, meaning that it was no longer a trusted counterparty in financial transactions. As the support expected from the Federal Reserve was not forthcoming, and no other bank stepped in to buy it as a going operation, Lehman Brothers filed for bankruptcy on 15th September. The signal this sent was that no bank was safe. Mark Kiesel, a portfolio manager at Pimco, remarked that 'The Lehman bankruptcy set a precedent that nothing is too big to fail.'[46] Neil McLeish, an analyst at Morgan Stanley, expressed the same view: 'Prior to Lehman, there was an almost unshakable faith that the senior creditors and counterparties of large, systemically-important financial institutions would not face the risk of outright default.'[47] Lehman Brothers had been the fourth largest US investment bank and the scale of its operations meant that it reached into the very fabric of not only the US financial system but that of the world. Lehman Brothers was a party to hundreds of billions of dollars' worth of bilateral OTC derivatives contracts covering credit, interest rates, equities, and commodities, all of which were now of questionable value because it no longer stood behind them. In the words of Peter Thal Larsen, on 1st October, Lehman Brothers had 'served as a counterparty to billions of hedges and other derivative contracts.'[48] Michael Mackenzie, who had been following the unfolding crisis closely, reported that in the immediate aftermath of the Lehman Brothers collapse 'Banks scrambled for cash yesterday in the repurchase or repo market as they sought to fund assets and the Federal Reserve eased restrictions on types of securities that could be used in its liquidity programmes.'[49] The result was a freeze in short-term lending among banks and financial institutions as trust evaporated, even though there was no evidence that contracts made had not been

[42] Avinash Persaud, 'Lehman had to fall to save the financial system', 16th September 2008.
[43] John Gapper, 'My naïve part in the downfall of Lehman', 13th September 2018.
[44] Gary Gorton, 'Banking must not be left to lurk in the shadows', 21st November 2012.
[45] Nick Bailey, 'We live in a bubble in financial services', 15th September 2018.
[46] Michael Mackenzie and Rachel Morarjee, 'Fear reigns as spectre of a global recession looms large', 9th October 2008.
[47] Aline van Duyn, Deborah Brewster and Gillian Tett, 'The Lehman Legacy', 13th October 2008.
[48] Peter Thal Larsen, 'Never become too dependent on your bank', 1st October 2008.
[49] Michael Mackenzie, 'Repo sector scramble', 16th September 2008.

honoured. On 14th October, Michael Mackenzie reflected that 'Lehman Brothers' bankruptcy sparked a breakdown in trust between financial institutions, which act as counterparties to each other in short-term lending.'[50] On 21st October Jeremy Grant noted that 'The collapse left banks and other institutions with huge trading positions in which Lehman was the counterparty.'[51]

Faced with an immediate collapse in confidence the US government had been forced to take control of the insurance company, AIG, on 16th September. AIG was a major counterparty to those contracts that guaranteed to pay out if a borrower defaulted. The government injected $85bn into AIG so as to reassure those holding such contracts that they would be honoured. That did not prevent the panic spreading. In the face of an unremitting demand for cash, and the interbank market at a standstill, the Federal Reserve had no alternative but to inject massive amounts of liquidity into the system or accept a complete meltdown with unimaginable consequences. On 18th September 2008 the Federal Reserve, in concert with other leading central banks, pumped $180bn into global money markets. The following day the US government was forced to guarantee the solvency of money-market mutual funds as they were facing a bank-like run with savers rushing to close their accounts. These funds had boomed because of the cap placed on the interest paid to depositors by US banks and had become major players in the interbank money market. The interbank market lay at the foundation of the banking system as it was where banks borrowed from and lent to each other to cover the temporary shortages that continuously occurred through the mismatch of assets and liabilities. However, those actions were insufficient to stop the panic spreading. On 25th September the Washington Mutual, a leading retail bank was on the verge of collapse because of a bank run. By 28th September the crisis reached European banks, with the UK government forced to take over the mortgage provider, the Bradford and Bingley Bank. On 7th October the UK government launched a £400bn bank rescue plan, as it recognized that the crisis was not confined to a few small banks specializing in mortgage finance. Chris Giles wrote on 10th October 2008, that 'The world's financial regulators are in full panic mode. That is to be expected. Banks have failed; wholesale markets have frozen; financial systems have flirted with collapse.... The crisis exposed an enormous failure in risk management in the private sector and an equally large regulatory failure across swathes of the financial system.'[52] Lehman's collapse had a chain effect, which grew in magnitude as it rippled out, not just in the USA but across the world. Lehman Brothers had been the leading equity trader in both London and Tokyo prior to its collapse, for example.

Though Paul J. Davies, writing on 10th October 2008, was correct in stating that 'First and foremost, the credit crisis has been a liquidity crisis',[53] the problem was that it did not stop there. If it had that could have been met with a strong injection of liquidity from the Federal Reserve. What had not been appreciated was the fragility of the banking system because of the use of the originate-and-distribute model linked to the reliance on short-term funds and the guarantees provided through credit derivatives. The collapse of Lehman Brothers on liquidity was two-fold. The first was to make it difficult to value many of the securities used as collateral for secured borrowing. That meant they were either unsuitable for that purpose or only at a substantial discount. The second was that fear of further bank

[50] Michael Mackenzie, 'London interbank lending rates ease', 14th October 2008.
[51] Jeremy Grant, 'Clearers step into limelight', 21st October 2008.
[52] Chris Giles, 'Conceptual issues at heart of reform', 10th October 2008.
[53] Paul J. Davies, 'High noon chimes for collateral with no name', 10th October 2008.

collapses led all banks to hoard liquidity in the event of another crisis. Even when central banks provided liquidity they only did so early in the morning whereas a bank would not know its net position until the end of the day, encouraging it to remain more liquid that it need have been. Faced with the necessity of restoring the liquidity that had previously come from the inter-bank market, banks unloaded those assets that could still be sold, which drove the prices down. That turned a liquidity crisis into a solvency one as the value of assets fell while that of liabilities remained the same. The lack of liquidity also restricted the ability of banks to lend to their business customers, so impairing their ability to finance their day-to-day business, making it difficult for them to repay maturing loans or even survive. With the future of business borrowers in doubt so was the value of the loans that banks had made to them, which again turned a liquidity crisis into a solvency one. Once these doubts were raised, whether based on reality or not, depositors withdrew funds and lenders to banks refused to roll-over loans when they matured. This spread the crisis to banks previously untouched as fears were raised of mass defaults among their borrowers, and mass withdrawals among their depositors, as access to cash became the overriding priority. Equity markets were not immune as prices fell dramatically, affecting those who were financing speculative positions using borrowed funds. The most vulnerable were the smaller markets as they lacked the depth and breadth necessary to absorb losses. Both the Jakarta Stock Exchange in Indonesia and the Nigerian Stock Exchange faced a crisis in October 2008, indicating the global ramifications rippling out of New York and London.

One major effect of the crisis was a collapse in trust among banks. Bilateral deals that would have been done as a matter of routine in the past were either avoided or put through exchanges and clearing houses as way of reducing counterparty risk. This was all driven by fear of what might happen rather than actual reality. David Rutter, the deputy chief executive of electronic broking at ICAP, the world's largest interdealer broker, presented an optimistic verdict on the actual state of the market on 15th October: 'The OTC financial markets are functioning very well and OTC market participants—banks, brokers, prime brokerage clients and post-trade providers—have worked together to respond to the increased volatility.'[54] The problem was that the bankruptcy of Lehman Brothers made all market participants aware of counterparty risk and the consequences of default. The result was to freeze activity across all markets ranging from money to commodities. This led banks to hoard cash, which deepened and spread the liquidity crisis. With the bankruptcy of Lehman Brothers neither banks nor money-market funds would lend to a bank that was rumoured to be in trouble. As this could, potentially, apply to all, the whole inter-bank market froze, with banks around the world being unwilling to lend to each other because of the perceived risks. Prior to the crisis many banks had borrowed in the wholesale markets to lend more than they held in retail deposits. Since the crisis they had been unable to do that and faced having to close, as they were unable to meet withdrawals of deposits or repay money they had borrowed. As late as December 2008 Richard Gorelick, a fund manager running his own business, RGM Advisers in Austin, Texas, observed that, 'There really aren't a lot of people out there willing to take risk right now.'[55] Investors were wary of buying the securities issued by banks preferring US Treasury bills and bonds because of their combination of safety and liquidity, despite the low yields. Banks remained wary of lending to each other for fear that unsecured loans might not be repaid and the collateral provided for secured ones was of dubious value.

[54] Peter Garnham, 'Forex market soars with little sign of change in trading system', 15th October 2008.
[55] Jeremy Grant, 'New breed of trader heads for Europe', 4th December 2008.

As late as December 2008 Peter Thal Larsen was reporting that, 'Ever since the crisis started in August 2007, banks have struggled to access funding from institutional investors and the money markets. Initially investors shunned bonds backed by mortgages. But after Lehman Brothers collapsed in mid-September, the market for bank debt dried up almost completely.'[56] Banks stopped taking on new commitments because of the increased risks attached to lending to businesses, especially small- and medium-sized companies, while falling property values made buildings less secure collateral than in the past. Peter Thal Larsen explained the situation in December 2008: 'As the recession bites, default rates are increasing, while falling property prices mean likely losses are also rising. So banks have to set aside more capital against the same loans, prompting them to rein in new lending.'[57] Central banks did ease the situation by providing facilities that allowed banks to swap illiquid loans for liquid government bonds but these were used to refinance existing debt rather than make new loans. Conversely, regulations were imposed that forced banks to hold more capital as a means of ensuring that they were better able to meet withdrawals and redemptions as well as cover losses. This had the effect of further reducing what they were able to lend, whether to their own customers or to the inter-bank market. The immediate reaction to the crisis from the financial authorities was thus a contradictory one as it combined massive injections of liquidity with an insistence that banks hold bigger capital cushions for even relatively low-risk activities. As banks were now perceived as being at risk of collapse this made it both difficult and expensive for them to raise additional capital.

Governments also intervened in other ways at the time of the crisis. There was particular focus on curbing the activities of hedge funds as they were blamed for destabilizing the global financial system by a practice known as short-selling. In short-selling a hedge fund sold bank shares they did not own in the expectation of buying them back, and delivering to those to whom they had been sold, after the price had fallen due to the pressure of selling that they had engineered. By November, seventeen countries had banned or restricted short-selling, including the USA, UK, Germany, France, Switzerland, Australia, Taiwan, and Japan. Those who carried out this practice were the butt of criticizm by politicians, regulators, and the media even though most sales came from investors with genuine concerns about the stability of banks, and there was little evidence that the actions of short-sellers had much effect. This attack on hedge funds and short-sellers was all part of a search for scapegoats to blame for the crisis. These ranged from individual bankers and hedge-fund managers through credit-ratings agencies to a financial system which appeared to operate beyond the bounds of human control, reliant as it was on models and products designed by physicists and mathematicians and traded at high speed on super-computers. In October 2008 Paul J. Davies criticized 'A system that simply trusts in collateral without regard to its particulars' because it 'is one that fosters the creation of ever more hideously complex credit products, whose cash flows are ever harder to analyse.'[58]

The complexity and opaqueness of the global financial system left central banks, regulators, and governments floundering to identify what had gone wrong and how to respond to it both at the time and subsequently. Given the intervention by governments around the world to save banks from collapse there was a widespread belief at the time that the cause of the crisis was the emergence of banks that were too big to fail. The argument was that these banks took greater and greater risks in the search for collective profits and individual

[56] Peter Thal Larsen, 'Withdrawal unavailable', 6th December 2008.
[57] Peter Thal Larsen, 'Withdrawal unavailable', 6th December 2008.
[58] Paul J. Davies, 'High noon chimes for collateral with no name', 10th October 2008.

bonuses, safe in the knowledge that, in the event of the crisis, governments would intervene to save them. As this was what did happen it provided evidence that this had been the case. Forgotten in such a conclusion was the important fact that Lehman Brothers had been allowed to slip into bankruptcy on September 2008. It had not been considered too big to fail by the Federal Reserve even though it turned out to be. The banking model followed by Lehman Brothers was one shaped by regulatory intervention which favoured the originate-and-distribute model over lend-and-hold and encouraged the use of derivatives as a means of insuring against risk. Also, as an investment bank Lehman Brothers was not supervised by the Federal Reserve but the SEC, and so did not have direct access to its lender-of-last resort facility, as was the case with banks that accepted deposits from the public. It was what happened to Lehman Brothers that led to the acceptance that certain banks were too big to fail because of the scale of their operations and the degree to which they were embedded in the financial system. No longer were the banks in this category confined to those central to the payments system and exposed to a liquidity crisis for it now extended to a range of others.

Nevertheless, many were quick to suggest that the universal banking model pursued by the likes of Lehman Brothers was deeply flawed and government intervention was required to break them up. John Gapper wrote as early as September 2008 that, 'The full-service investment bank, buying and selling shares and bonds for customers as well as advising companies and trading with its own capital, is doomed. In order to generate the revenues needed to match larger institutions, banks such as Lehman scurried into risk-taking that eventually sunk them.'[59] With Lehman Brothers gone and both Bear Stearns and Merrill Lynch acquired by US commercial banks, namely JP Morgan Chase and Bank of America respectively, only Morgan Stanley and Goldman Sachs were left as investment banks. After the collapse of Lehman Brothers, buying and selling shifted away from them because of the perceived risk of failure. Even if they were saved those using them faced the temporary immobilization of their funds and assets. The beneficiaries were major diversified banks such as JP Morgan, Citigroup, and Bank of America. Facing a loss of business Morgan Stanley and Goldman Sachs quickly converted their status to that of commercial banks. Instead of being regulated by the SEC they fell under the responsibility of the Federal Reserve so ending the distinction between the different types of banks that had existed under Glass–Steagall. It took the collapse of Lehman Brothers for the Federal Reserve to accept that there were banks other than those accepting deposits that had become too big to fail, and to which it had to extend lender-of-last-resort facilities when a liquidity crisis arose.[60]

[59] John Gapper, 'The last gasp of the broker-dealer', 16th September 2008.

[60] Ellen Kelleher and Alice Ross, 'Run unlikely', 9th July 2008; Michael Mackenzie, 'Mixed response to SEC selected protectionism', 17th July 2008; Michael Mackenzie and Nicole Bullock, 'Deadline is looming for derivatives clean-up', 22nd July 2008; Gillian Tett, 'A year that shook faith in finance', 4th August 2008; Paul J. Davies, 'Effort to bring credit ratings into clearer focus gathers pace', 5th August 2008; Ben White, 'Lehman shares slide on fears over results', 20th August 2008; Michael Mackenzie, 'Money markets hope for autumn thaw', 1st September 2008; David Blackwell and Philip Stafford, 'Party over as investors walk away from Aim', 3rd September 2008; Anousha Sakoui, 'More UK companies turn to asset-based borrowing', 8th September 2008; Brian Bollen, 'The sector stays aloft in a risky climate', 8th September 2008; Krishna Guha, 'Poser for Paulson', 13th September 2008; Krishna Guha and Henny Sender, 'No bail-out this time around', 13th September 2008; Peter Thal Larsen and Francesco Guerrera, 'Investment banks' future questioned', 16th September 2008; Michael Mackenzie, 'Repo sector scramble', 16th September 2008; David Oakley and Michael Mackenzie, 'Interbank credit lines dry up', 16th September 2008; Paul J. Davies and Aline van Duyn, 'Collapse of bank shakes foundations of the CDS industry', 16th September 2008; Avinash Persaud, 'Lehman had to fall to save the financial system', 16th September 2008; John Gapper, 'The last gasp of the broker-dealer', 16th September 2008; Chris Hughes and Francesco Guerrera, 'A week that shook the system to its core', 20th September 2008; Joanna Chung, Henry

The question does arise, however, of why it took the collapse of Lehman Brothers for the Federal Reserve to recognize its lender-of-last-resort obligation and that early intervention was required so as to pre-empt a crisis. The near collapse of Bear Stearns provided ample warning of what the consequences of a major investment bank failure could be but they went unheeded. That was unlike the situation in the UK where the Bank of England intervened to save systemically-important banks before an unstoppable panic took place. This was a complete reversal of the Bank of England's position from a year before, when it had failed to intervene in time to prevent the imminent collapse of the Northern Rock Bank, sparking a crisis in the British banking system. According to Chris Giles, writing in February 2009, this failure to intervene reflected the hardline stance of Mervyn King, the governor of the Bank of England. He had changed the Bank of England's focus away from banking stability to one on monetary policy: 'Mervyn King, first as chief economist, then as deputy governor and, since 2003, as governor, has placed monetary economics at the heart of everything the Bank does.'[61] He continued this criticism of Mervyn King in 2012:

> Already shorn of banking supervision and government debt management in the post-1997 changes, Sir Mervyn wanted to create a modern monetary authority concentrating on monthly decisions on interest rates. Although one of the BoE's two core purposes was 'to ensure financial stability' it seems he neither enjoyed nor fully understood the influence the BoE still had in calming financial excess by use of its powerful voice....

Sender, and James Mackintosh, 'Short-selling ban catches funds out', 20th September 2008; James Mackintosh and Deborah Brewster, 'Evidence falls short of talk in assault on speculation', 20th September 2008; Anuj Gangahar and Deborah Brewster, 'Hedging industry resents taking blame for turmoil', 20th September 2008; *FT* Reporters, 'Solid capital has the upper hand', 23rd September 2008; Peter Thal Larsen and Greg Farrell, 'Landscape shifts for investment banks', 23rd September 2008; Peter Thal Larsen, 'Never become too dependent on your bank', 1st October 2008; Gillian Tett, Paul J. Davies, and Aline van Duyn, 'A new formula? Complex finance contemplates a more fettered future', 1st October 2008; Gillian Tett, 'Complex system built on flimsy foundations', 2nd October 2008; John Aglionby, 'Jakarta exchange closed indefinitely', 9th October 2008; Michael Mackenzie and Rachel Morarjee, 'Fear reigns as spectre of a global recession looms large', 9th October 2008; Paul J. Davies, 'High noon chimes for collateral with no name', 10th October 2008; Chris Giles, 'Conceptual issues at heart of reform', 10th October 2008; Aline van Duyn, Deborah Brewster, and Gillian Tett, 'The Lehman Legacy', 13th October 2008; Javier Blas and Jeremy Grant, 'Rush to put private commodities contracts on public exchanges', 13th October 2008; Javier Blas, 'Worldwide credit squeeze triggers changes in commodities trading', 14th October 2008; Michael Mackenzie, 'London interbank lending rates ease', 14th October 2008; Jeremy Grant, Gillian Tett, and Aline van Duyn, 'Calls for derivatives clearing intensify', 15th October 2008; Peter Garnham, 'Forex market soars with little sign of change in trading system', 15th October 2008; Paul J. Davies, 'Armageddon fears ease, but lending needs to begin again', 16th October 2008; James Mackintosh and Jennifer Hughes, 'New York steals UK hedge funds business', 17th October 2008; Nicole Bullock, 'Credit easing but cost of debt remains expensive', 21st October 2008; David Oakley, 'Search for safety sparks record flows into money market funds', 21st October 2008; Jeremy Grant, 'Time of crisis also gives opportunities', 21st October 2008; Hal Weitzman, 'Exchanges have their eyes on the next opportunity', 21st October 2008; Jeremy Grant, 'Clearers step into limelight', 21st October 2008; Jeremy Grant, 'Baikal strategy remains unclear', 30th October 2008; Jeremy Grant and Anuj Gangahar, 'Spotlight on role of electronic trading in recent volatility', 30th October 2008; Joe Leahy and Sundeep Tucker, 'Exchanges urged to work together', 5th November 2008; Chris Hughes, 'No more easy money', 11th November 2008; Chris Giles, 'Into the storm', 14th November 2008; Jeremy Grant, 'New breed of trader heads for Europe', 4th December 2008; Peter Thal Larsen, 'Withdrawal unavailable', 6th December 2008; Aline van Duyn, 'Securitisation sector braced for a long, painful haul', 5th December 2008; Anuj Gangahar, 'Algorithmic trades produce snowball effect on volatility', 5th December 2008; Aline van Duyn, 'SecondMarket enters new territory', 11th December 2008; Tom Burgis, 'Regulator intends to shake up the bourse', 30th September 2010; Michiyo Nakamoto and Patrick Jenkins, 'Bowed by over-ambition', 2nd August 2012; Gary Gorton, 'Banking must not be left to lurk in the shadows', 21st November 2012; John Gapper, 'My naïve part in the downfall of Lehman', 13th September 2018; Nick Bailey, 'We live in a bubble in financial services', 15th September 2018; Christian Thwaites, 'I have become extremely suspicious about an industry I have worked in since 1981', 15th September 2018.

[61] Chris Giles, 'King's faded realm', 16th February 2009.

> Staff found presenting financial stability issues in front of the new governor frightening because of his apparent disdain for their work.... he preferred to assume markets were likely to be efficient and crises would not occur.[62]

Prior to the Northern Rock crisis the Bank of England had expressed concern about financial stability but took no action. This was despite emerging signs of a credit bubble fuelled by the ready availability of funds through remortgaging homes. This was apparent to the likes of Norma Cohen and Cynthia O'Murchu writing in 2011: 'Homeowners in some of the nation's poorest areas put themselves at increased risk of mortgage arrears or repossession as a result of the dramatic rate at which they withdrew equity from their homes in the run up to the credit crunch in 2007.'[63] At the peak of the pre-crisis credit boom in the UK, interest-only loans represented a third of all mortgage sales and up to 75 per cent of borrowers had not put in place a means of repaying the money borrowed. The assumption was that rising asset prices would allow the loan to be repaid leaving a large profit. By allowing one of the major mortgage lenders, the Northern Rock Bank, to collapse, the Bank of England calculated that a message would be sent to other banks that they needed to restrain lending, and so defuse the credit bubble. That calculation turned out to be a major error of judgement, which was followed by a delayed reaction to the consequences for the British banking system. The deputy governor, Sir John Gieve, later admitted that, 'The Bank reacted very slowly and reluctantly in summer and autumn 2007 and we were lucky the outcome wasn't worse.'[64] In the end the Bank of England was forced to intervene to prevent the Northern Rock collapse destabilizing the entire British banking system. The assessment of Tom Braithwaite and Francesco Guerrera in 2010 was that the 2007 crisis in the UK had centred around a specialist 'mortgage lender that expanded its business aggressively on the back of short-term wholesale market funding' and had to be 'rescued by the UK government when the market dried up in 2007'.[65]

Though the Bank of England's focus on monetary policy remained as long as Mervyn King was Governor, the events surrounding the Northern Rock collapse did make the institution as a whole much more aware of its banking responsibilities. No longer could it ignore banks and stand aside when they faced a crisis. Unlike the Federal Reserve the Bank of England had learnt that preventing a bank failing was as important as avoiding moral hazard, if the risk was a systemic crisis, and that could apply equally to a specialist mortgage lender as well as diversified deposit bank. Each case was unique and the response had to be carefully judged so as to avoid the risks of a systemic crisis on the one hand against the question of moral hazard on the other. The expectation in August 2007 was that Northern Rock could be allowed to fail because it was a relatively small and specialized lender lacking systemic importance. However, in the British context what happened proved an enormous shock as Anousha Sakoui recalled in the wake of the Lehman Brothers collapse a year later: 'The sight of people queuing outside the Northern Rock bank was a seminal moment.... It was the first run on an English bank since 1866.'[66] Reinforcing this verdict that the Northern Rock collapse was a tipping point in British banking history were the comments made in December 2010 by Patrick Jenkins and Jennifer Hughes, when they

62 Chris Giles, 'Mervyn King', 5th May 2012.
63 Norma Cohen and Cynthia O'Murchu, 'Owners risked homes as crash neared', 19th December 2011.
64 Chris Giles, 'Mervyn King', 5th May 2012.
65 Tom Braithwaite and Francesco Guerrera, 'A Garden to Tame', 15th November 2010.
66 Anousha Sakoui, 'New Powers create legal uncertainty', 15th September 2008.

reflected that the scenes of queues outside branches on Friday September 14th 2007, as anxious depositors at Northern Rock tried to retrieve their cash, 'are by now firmly embedded in British banking history as one of the industry's most shameful episodes. A run on a bank was not seemly in a modern European economy.'[67] The lesson that emerged was that a bank failure in Britain, even a relatively small one, could have very serious consequences for the entire banking system. It shattered the trust in banks that had grown up over years, as they had remained stable despite successive wars and economic turmoil. With that trust lost another failure could spark a liquidity crisis that would bring down other banks, including solvent ones. At all costs future failures had to be avoided, especially as, prior to the Lehman Brothers collapse, 'UK bank balance sheets were so large, debt-laden and short of liquidity that the financial system remained sensitive to any setback in economic recovery or market movements...UK banks entered the crisis heavily dependent on volatile inflows of wholesale deposits that can—and have—been quickly withdrawn in comparison with deposits from retail customers that are much more stable.'[68] This was the judgement of Norma Cohen in June 2009.

For those reasons the Bank of England had no alternative but to intervene to save UK banks in 2008 when the spillover from the Lehman Brothers collapse threatened the entire banking system. This was the lesson that had been learnt from the Northern Rock debacle. In contrast to the USA, where bank failures were regular occurrences, because of the fragmented nature of its banking system, that was not the case in the UK. Legislation in the USA had prevented the creation of large and resilient banks along UK lines. Interstate branch banking was banned for over a century while the Glass–Steagall Act prevented the emergence of universal banks for over fifty years. Faced with regular bank collapses in the USA mechanisms existed to provide reassurance to savers in the form of deposit insurance, and to arrange the orderly closure of failing institutions. For that reason the Federal Reserve took a much more relaxed attitude to bank failures than did the Bank of England or most other central banks. The Federal Reserve was willing to contemplate the collapse of Bear Stearns but did not have to face that dilemma because JP Morgan Chase saw its acquisition as a fast route into investment banking. Without such a willing purchaser for Lehman Brothers, because of the altered circumstances by August 2008, the Federal Reserve was forced to decide between letting it fail or intervening to save it at considerable cost and risk to itself. It chose to let it fail in the belief that the consequences would be both limited and manageable. In contrast, the Bank of England, like other central banks, took the alternative view when faced with the same situation. While the criticism made by Chris Giles in 2014 that the Bank of England 'did nothing, not because it failed to spot the growth of credit but because it genuinely believed it to be benign and necessary to keep inflation on target'[69] was correct in describing the lead up to the 2007 crisis, it was not when applied to the 2008 crisis. Though Mervyn King may not have moved on from prioritizing monetary policy over financial stability, that did not apply to many of the staff at the Bank of England who had been empowered by the events of 2007. Thus they were ready to intervene in 2008 and did so before a systemic crisis erupted. In contrast, as Bear Stearns did not fail, the Federal Reserve remained convinced that Lehman Brothers could be allowed to collapse without severe consequences for the financial system, which was a reversal of the decision taken in 1998 to save Long-Term Capital Management.

[67] Patrick Jenkins and Jennifer Hughes, 'Big Gaps to fill in', 9th December 2010.
[68] Norma Cohen, 'System remains vulnerable to shocks', 26th June 2009.
[69] Chris Giles, 'The Old Lady is right that prudential policy is not everything', 19th June 2014.

In the British case Jane Croft explained the situation at length in September 2008:

> Northern Rock was the first big victim of a crisis that has slashed banks' profits, wreaked havoc in the mortgage market and raised the spectre of bad debt causing a further painful twist in the spiral. Until last summer, banks were generating vast profits thanks to cheap debt from the capital markets, which they in turn used to fund new loans to consumers and for corporate deal-making. But once the markets froze on August 9 2007, some UK banks found they lacked the liquid finance to support their lending commitments. Northern Rock—with a relatively small pool of deposits from savers and dependence on capital markets for 75 per cent of its funding—was the first to hit the buffers. News that it had approached the Bank of England for an emergency loan triggered the first run on a bank since Victorian times. Northern Rock may have been the first high-profile casualty, but the closure of securitisation markets has seen all the UK's banks scrambling to access funding for their mortgage loans. Some lenders that relied on securitisation have withdrawn from the mortgage market. The total number of mortgage deals available to customers has slumped from 30,000 products last August to just over 6,000. The Bank of England launched a £50bn special liquidity scheme in April aimed at restoring confidence to the markets. The scheme, which has been widely used by all the banks, allows high-grade assets to be pledged to the Bank in return for more liquid Treasury bills. This has helped liquidity a little, although mortgage finance remains constrained.....However, although liquidity is less of an issue, banks are now having to contend with repairing their capital bases, which have been battered through huge write-downs and bad debts. Regulators require all banks to hold a certain amount of capital to absorb future losses. But in recent months this capital cushion has been eroded by huge write-downs on the value of banks' complex assets such as collateraliszed debt obligations, which are rooted in US subprime mortgages. As a result, banks have been forced to seek fresh capital infusions from overseas sovereign wealth funds and through rights issues. Between them Royal Bank of Scotland, Bradford and Bingley, HBOS and Barclays have raised £21bn from investors. The huge write-downs have taken their toll on banks' profitability with RBS and Bradford and Bingley reporting losses in the first half of 2008 and others such as HBOS, Lloyds and Barclays reporting sharp profit falls. A second problem is looming for the banks that could force them to raise even more capital. As the financial turmoil hits the real economy, they are facing a steady rise in bad debts from consumers and corporate customers. The plummeting housing market is also leading to higher losses and arrears.[70]

Initially the solution was to persuade Lloyds Bank to buy HBOS but that did not stop the unfolding crisis in the British banking system. The next step was for the government to provide financial assistance to both Lloyds/HBOS and RBS/NatWest. At the height of the 2008 financial crisis the Bank of England extended loans up to an intraday peak of £61.5bn to RBS and HBOS. The specialized mortgage bank, Bradford and Bingley, was also placed under state control. All were experiencing the beginnings of a bank run due to rumours that they were in serious financial difficulties. Banks were also allowed to swop mortgage bonds, which they were unable to sell, for more liquid assets with the Bank of England. This degree of intervention, and the lead provided by the Bank of England, reflected an

[70] Jane Croft, 'A long and winding road to recovery: the banks', 13th September 2008.

acceptance that the system of financial regulation introduced in Britain in 1997 had failed both to fully mitigate the crisis and then deal with it once it happened.[71]

Reaction to the Crisis Part One: 2009

What had not been appreciated was that the failure of Lehman Brothers would destabilize the entire financial system of the USA and then spread outwards to the rest of the world. The impact was magnified in scale and duration because of the way that Lehman Brothers had conducted its business. Not being a deposit-taking bank it had relied heavily on repo funding, where it borrowed money for short periods pledging securities as collateral. Bankruptcy meant this money would not be repaid while casting doubt on the value of the collateral, making it impossible to sell. What followed was a catastrophic chain reaction, which was only halted by massive government bailouts and liquidity injections. The longer-term legacy was a very weakened global banking system. Peter Thal Larsen reported in January 2009, that 'As losses mount...bankers are concerned they will be forced to hold ever increasing amounts of capital to support existing assets. Until they have a clear idea of how much capital they need for old loans banks are understandably reluctant to commit to new lending.'[72] This included those banks that had proved themselves to be sufficiently resilient to not require capital injections from governments. Typical of those were Canada's five largest banks. They had received liquidity support but had to write-down the value of billions of dollars of assets and troubled loans. The effect was to greatly reduce the supply of credit, depriving borrowers of the finance they required for their everyday business and so endangering their ability to service existing debt and repay loans. That further destabilized the banking system as it compounded a lack of liquidity with serious concerns over solvency, as banks were forced to mark down the value of assets even further. Such was the situation around the world, even among those banks that had not pursued the originate-and-distribute agenda or indulged in excessive lending funded by short-term borrowing. The climate of fear infected all.

[71] Jane Croft, 'A long and winding road to recovery: the banks', 13th September 2008; Anousha Sakoui, 'New Powers create legal uncertainty', 15th September 2008; Jane Croft, 'B&B poised for state ownership', 29th September 2008; Kate Burgess, 'Credit crunch: a final twist in rocky road for ex-mutual', 29th September 2008; Paul J. Davies, 'Securitisation provides liquidity', 26th November 2008; Chris Giles, 'King's faded realm', 16th February 2009; James Sassoon, 'Britain deserves a better system of financial regulation', 9th March 2009; George Parker and Chris Giles, 'Turner goes in to bat for "whipping boy" FSA', 24th June 2009; Norma Cohen, 'System remains vulnerable to shocks', 26th June 2009; Daniel Pimlott, 'Retreat on idea that big lenders need to be split', 18th December 2009; Jennifer Hughes, 'Doubt for safety of bundling up loans', 18th December 2009; Tom Braithwaite and Francesco Guerrera, 'A Garden to Tame', 15th November 2010; Patrick Jenkins and Jennifer Hughes, 'Big Gaps to fill in', 9th December 2010; Norma Cohen and Cynthia O'Murchu, 'Owners risked homes as crash neared', 19th December 2011; Tanya Powley, 'FSA sees "common sense" on mortgage overhaul', 19th December 2011; Peter Sands, 'The perils of 1970s-style regulation', 29th March 2012; Chris Giles, 'Ill-prepared Treasury did not see dangers brewing', 30th March 2012; Chris Giles, 'King admits he should have shouted about risk', 3rd May 2012; Chris Giles, 'Mervyn King', 5th May 2012; Chris Giles, 'BoE bows to pressure for probes into crisis', 22nd May 2012; Chris Giles, 'The bank that roared', 14th July 2012; Sharlene Goff, 'Taxpayers left in queue as old brand shuts up shop', 13th September 2012; Chris Giles, 'Carney tears up rule book on help for struggling banks', 25th October 2013; Alex Barker, 'Brussels forces BoE to rethink banks lifeline', 11th April 2014; Chris Giles, 'The Old Lady is right that prudential policy is not everything', 19th June 2014. For more on this and the differences between banking in the UK and the USA see R. C. Michie, 'Nature or Nurture: The British financial system since 1688', in Matthew Hollow, Folarin Akinbami, and Ranald Michie (eds), *Complexity and Crisis: Critical perspectives on the evolution of American and British Banking*, Cheltenham: Edward Elgar, 2016, pp. 60–84.

[72] Peter Thal Larsen, 'Reviving flow of credit will take greater intervention', 17th January 2009.

One casualty of the crisis, for example, was the financing of commercial property development. The collapse in the market for mortgage-backed securities made it impossible to sell them, depriving property developers of the finance needed to complete existing projects, let alone embark on new ones. It also proved difficult to sell completed buildings because of the uncertain economic outlook as doubts emerged over the ability of tenants to pay the rent, with some defaulting. In January 2009 Daniel Thomas, Rachel Minder, Daniel Pimlott, Alan Rappeport, and Michiyo Nakamoto reported that 'The global commercial property market boom came to a crashing halt last year, with some countries reporting among the worst capital declines on record.'[73] These were countries like the USA and across the EU where property developers had used highly-leveraged loans to fund speculative building rather than owner occupiers raising long-term finance, as in Asia. There had been a huge increase in bank lending for commercial property development around the world between 2001 and 2007 and that continued to hang over them after the collapse of Lehman Brothers. An estimated $5tn of commercial property debt was still outstanding by December 2009 in the USA and Europe alone. Faced with the inability of borrowers to repay these loans on maturity, because of a lack of investor interest, and an unwillingness to call in the loans and bankrupt the borrowers because property valuations would collapse with forced sales, banks had no alternative but to roll them over as long as borrowers continued to pay interest. Otherwise they would have to take ownership of the property, as collateral for the unpaid loan, and accept a loss when the property was valued for sale, exposing them to concerns over their solvency.

The legacy of the crisis was to greatly impair the ability of banks to lend as they could not extricate themselves from their existing commitments or raise additional capital. The severity of the crisis had even affected markets as deep and broad as that for foreign exchange because of the lack of trust between banks. It was estimated in August 2009 that currency trading had dropped 20 per cent since the crisis as hedge funds, who had been the biggest drivers of growth in global foreign exchange markets, withdrew because of the inability to access finance to fund their operations. In the days after the collapse of Lehman Brothers not one bank was willing to lend. The money markets had broken down, overwhelmed by fear. It was only gradually, in response to the vast amount of liquidity pumped into the markets by central banks, and record low interest rates, that the banks begun to lend to each other. Though some recovery had taken place a year after the collapse of Lehman Brothers, banks were continuing to restrict their lending as they sought to repair their balance sheets and deleverage. In addition, counterparty risk remained a big factor with banks choosing very carefully those to whom they would lend and for how long. Don Smith, an economist at the interdealer broker ICAP, observed in August 2009, that 'Lending is much more name-specific than it was before Lehman collapsed. Banks will lend to the strong institutions, but they are more reluctant to offer money to the smaller or riskier institutions, or they want a premium to do so.'[74] Despite the severity of the crisis observers were beginning to detect signs of recovery in the inter-bank market by the end of 2009 though there remained a long way to go.

However, that recovery now faced new obstacles in the form of regulatory intervention that was aimed at making the financial system safer. In August 2009 John Plender expressed the view that, 'In a financial world where trust is lacking, the only way to prevent bad

[73] Daniel Thomas, Rachel Minder, Daniel Pimlott, Alan Rappeport, and Michiyo Nakamoto, 'Market is shaken to its foundations', 22nd January 2009.

[74] David Oakley, 'Lenders are slow to regain lost confidence', 10th September 2009.

behaviour is tough regulation. The scale of the financial debacle is such that it would be natural to expect a hefty regulatory response on these behavioural issues as well as systemic risk.'[75] What was quickly forgotten was the contribution that regulatory intervention had made to creating the conditions that had led to the crisis in the first case. John Plender himself, was one of those pointing the finger at regulators as a prime cause of the crisis shortly after it took place. In January 2009, he wrote, 'In the credit bubble, much of the impetus for driving loans off balance sheets into securitised form came from the risk-weighted capital regime introduced by the Basel committee of international bank regulators. By encouraging off-balance sheet activity, the regime turned banking into a shorter-term, more transactional business.'[76] Nevertheless, it was to regulators that governments turned when looking for ways of remedying the flaws in the global financial system that the crisis had exposed. Their response was to propose draconian measures designed to prevent a repetition of the credit bubble that preceded the crisis and to make banks much more resilient. According to Brooke Masters in October 2009, 'Roundly criticised for their failure to prevent the financial crisis, regulators have become more proactive and intrusive.'[77]

The problem regulators faced was how to balance contradictory objectives. There was no obvious answer to the question of how to combine dynamism with conservatism in a single set of regulations so as to deliver a financial system that preserved the innovation and flexibility that had fuelled global economic growth with the stability and resilience that had been absent at the time of the crisis. Prior to the crisis the balance of opinion was towards leaving markets largely unregulated as any intervention would blunt competition and undermine flexibility and efficiency. Hence the willingness to condone the expansion of OTC markets. This reluctance to intervene also extended to banks as they were relied upon to police themselves within a framework of general supervision and adherence to common rules, such as those of the Basel Committee of the Bank for International Settlement. The issue of counterparty risk was recognized and the solution put in place was the greater use of collateral as a restraint on risk-taking and a guarantee in case of default. The total value of cash, bonds, and equities held as collateral rose from $200bn in 2000 to $2,100bn in 2008. As Kirit Bhatia, global head of collateral management at JP Morgan Worldwide Securities Services, explained in 2009: 'Counterparty risk is a critical concern and collateral management has always been a very effective tool for addressing counterparty risk.'[78] What the collapse of Lehman Brothers had exposed was the limits of that collateral. About 30 per cent of the collateral Lehman had pledged to cover its borrowings turned out to be illiquid as it was hard to trade and therefore hard to value. Prior to the crisis institutional investors had regularly lent liquid but low-yielding securities from their portfolio to other market participants, in return for others that generated a higher rate of return but were less liquid. The liquid securities were then sold as a quick way of raising cash to meet a temporary shortfall, being repurchased when the original investor wanted them back. After the crisis investors were no longer willing to do that because of concerns that the collateral would fall in value or prove unsaleable, while the original securities would be lost because of a default by the borrower. Deprived of this source of funding banks were forced to cut back their lending.

[75] John Plender, 'Shame gene has disappeared from the financial system', 17th August 2009.
[76] John Plender, 'Originative sin', 5th January 2009.
[77] Brooke Masters, 'Long road to regulation', 26th October 2009.
[78] Steve Johnson, 'Concerns over risks sharpens the focus', 6th April 2009.

This tightening of credit was made worse by new banking regulations that curtailed the freedom to operate that banks had enjoyed before the crisis, especially the use of derivatives and the combination of deposit and investment banking. In early 2009 Peter Thal Larsen observed that 'Regulators are set to restrict the amount of risk that banks take on. They may also be tempted to restrict their overall size.'[79] An over-riding priority among central banks and regulators was a desire to tackle the issue of banks that were too big to fail, and so prevent the repeat of a situation where governments had to provide huge amounts of public money in order to save failing financial institutions. For regulators this meant intervening to prevent the financial engineering, high leverage, and excessive risk-taking that had fuelled the credit bubble. Initially that was seen as forcing a return to the lend-and-hold model rather than the originate-and-distribute one. Attractive as such a solution appeared it became quickly apparent that it was not possible to achieve. The lend-and-hold model had thrived in a world of borders and boundaries that included controls over the free movement of funds around the world and the strict compartmentalization of financial activity within countries. Without recreating that world it was not possible to undo all the developments in finance that had taken place since the 1970s as that would also mean losing the benefits they had brought.

Instead, the attempt had to be made to refashion the financial system in such a way that it retained the benefits while eliminating the risks. Both the emergence of megabanks and the use of derivatives, widely blamed for causing the crisis, were a response to the challenges and opportunities that had emerged from the 1970s onwards. It was exposure to the increased volatility of interest rates and exchange rates, and the risk of default among major borrowers, that led banks to make increasing use of derivative contracts. In that way losses could be shouldered collectively and so prevent the collapse of an individual bank that could then spread the fear of failure throughout the system. Similarly, the larger and more diversified the bank the more resilient it was, making it too big to fail. Finally, the switch to the originate-and-distribute model meant that a bank could unload assets when the need arose and so meet the pressure coming from a liquidity crisis from its own resources. For those reasons the new developments had not only been endorsed by regulators but also recommended. What was required after the crisis was a different philosophy of banking but this only a gradually took shape.

By June 2009 the message had sunk home that a new way of conducting business was required. In the words of Ross Tieman:

> The world's financiers are doing their homework. After an era of buying and selling assets they did not fully understand, and taking risks they did not comprehend, financial wizards are learning to wise-up. The era of rising markets and easy profits, in which everything increased in value, is over. Now, traders, investors and even bank managers need real knowledge and better ways of assessing risk, to identify under-valued assets that might just perform better than the two per cent return on a Treasury bill.[80]

However, this was an issue for the longer term. The short-term priority was to restore counterparty trust and so encourage banks to begin lending again. Prior to the crisis regulators had believed that the combination of powerful regulatory agencies and the supervision of banks that were too big to fail made the financial system resilient, with little

[79] Peter Thal Larsen, 'Too early to declare death of "universal banking"', 15th January 2009.

[80] Ross Tieman, 'Knowledge and old-fashioned skill are back in favour', 22nd June 2009.

consideration given to systemic risk. After the crisis the combination of regulated exchanges and clearing houses was seen as having the capacity to achieve that resilience, along with the requirement for all banks to be better capitalized, hold greater reserves and use less leverage. What the crisis had done was make regulators recognize that banks were not the same as other financial institutions and so had to be treated differently, because of their exposure to liquidity issues. The problem was that the increased capital requirements placed on banks, combined with the lack of trust among counterparties, continued to have a devastating effect on the level of lending and the willingness to take risks.

A short-term fix was required and this was found in the use of clearing houses, influenced by the resilience they had exhibited during the crisis. By matching counterparties and settling transactions the Depository Trust and Clearing Corporation (DTCC) in the USA had played a crucial role in stabilizing markets after the Lehman Brothers collapse. It was now eager to be given an enhanced role. In July 2009 Donald Donahue, chairman and chief executive of the DTCC claimed that 'DTCC is a firewall to stop contagions, in the event of a firm failure, across each of the financial asset classes we support.'[81] A clearing house provided the certainty that if a participant in a market failed all others would know immediately what their exposure was. A clearing house also required participants to deposit money or assets to be used in the event of a default and was available to cover defaults. However, the OTC market had operated largely without the use of a clearing house, leaving multiple counterparties exposed when Lehman Brothers failed. An estimated 80 per cent of derivative trades, for example, had taken place as private bilateral arrangements. The solution devised by regulators was to convert these into standardized contracts traded on exchanges and processed by clearing houses. This was a reversal of the pre-crisis policy of regulators, which was to break-up those exchanges that combined clearing and settlement with a trading platform. An exchange like Deutsche Börse was quick to publicize the contribution its integration of trading and clearing could make to diffusing a crisis. In June 2009 Reto Francioni, the Swiss-born chief executive of Deutsche Börse, claimed that, 'Having trading and risk management under one roof meant we could act quickly and efficiently. The liquidity pools were always there, helping build trust in price discovery.... We delivered our services at a very high level of quality during the crisis. If you are a service provider and no one is talking about you, you are doing a good job.'[82]

The risks of empowering institutions such as his was that it favoured entrenched monopolies, which could undermine competition, increase charges, and curb innovation with longer term consequences for liquidity. For that reason the policy was opposed by the large banks, as they had developed their own internal trading systems or dealt directly with each other and used interdealer brokers as intermediaries. However, these large banks had been discredited because of the government support they had received during the crisis while exchanges had continued to operate normally. As a result the US government, followed by the EU, moved to require the clearing of all standardized OTC derivatives contracts through regulated central counterparties, whether owned by exchanges or independent bodies. This recommendation was backed by the Bank for International Settlement (BIS), responsible for the Basel Rules. The use of clearing houses did raise the spectre of an even greater crisis in the future if they collapsed, especially as no agreement could be reached to provide them with a lender of last resort. Those operating in the foreign exchange market warned regulators that central clearing was unnecessary and possibly dangerous as it would

[81] Michael Mackenzie, 'DTCC paves way for all roads to lead to its warehouse', 1st July 2009.
[82] James Wilson, 'More than just a historic trading floor', 30th June 2009.

concentrate risk in a single institution rather than being spread across a small number of the world's largest and most resilient banks.

Market participants, keen to reduce the risks of trading with parties whose creditworthiness they could not reliably assess, were already driving more products into clearing houses. However, the actions of regulators went too far as they attempted to force all derivative contracts onto exchanges or through clearing houses, even though a significant proportion were entirely unsuited to either. Most OTC swaps contracts were of a bespoke nature designed for a specific purpose and so could not be converted into standard products traded on an exchange. Also, if they were forced through clearing houses collateral would be demanded that could make them too expensive for either side. In February 2009, the Wholesale Market Brokers Association, whose members often acted as intermediaries in the arranging of swaps between banks, warned that 'there is a danger that policy decisions are being considered that may attempt to force OTC products on to exchanges, resulting in a dramatic reduction in liquidity and product flexibility in markets essential for trading and hedging'.[83] They followed this up in October 2009 when their chief executive, Alexander McDonald, pointed out that, 'We would hope that policymakers are aware of the wide range of OTC products across the financial, energy and commodity markets that are unlikely ever to be considered as eligible for central clearing.'[84]

By forcing through central clearing, regulators limited the use of derivative contracts with damaging consequences for those companies that used them to manage their exposure to the volatility of currencies, fluctuations in the cost of commodities, and to safeguard future liabilities. The effect was to either leave them exposed to these risks or discourage them from engaging in such activities to the disadvantage of those reliant upon the services they provided. Even the exchanges, that expected to benefit from the shift of derivative contracts away from the OTC market, were opposed to such a move if driven by legislation. Adam Kinsley, head of regulation at the LSE, said in 2009, 'I don't think it's the right way for regulators to force inappropriate products on-exchange.'[85] Similarly, Mark Ibbotson, chief operating officer at the futures division of NYSE Euronext, said 'It could damage the security of a clearing house to force products on to a clearing house that shouldn't be there.'[86] The independent clearing houses also warned that there were limitations to what they could achieve, as Roger Liddell, chief executive of LCH.Clearnet, made clear in 2009: 'Clearing houses manage risk; they don't work miracles. In this headlong rush to clearing, we must take care that clearing does not become an end in itself. If it does, there is a danger that we simply transfer, rather than reduce, systemic risk.'[87] In November 2009 Chris Willcox, global head of rates trading at JP Morgan, expressed his view that, 'Even the clearing houses themselves agree on the need to ensure only products with sufficient liquidity and price transparency in the market are deemed suitable for clearing.'[88] Nevertheless, the regulators remained determined to force as much as possible of the trading through clearing houses regardless of whether they were suitable or not. By May 2009 large amounts of swaps contracts had been moved to centralized clearing.[89]

[83] Jeremy Grant, 'Exchanges and brokers at odds over crisis blame', 20th February 2009.

[84] Jeremy Grant, 'The humdrum has fresh significance', 21st October 2009.

[85] Jeremy Grant, 'Exchanges warn on OTC clearing', 4th June 2009.

[86] Jeremy Grant, 'Exchanges warn on OTC clearing', 4th June 2009.

[87] Jeremy Grant, 'NYSE Euronext joint venture to capitalise on rising demand for clearing', 19th June 2009.

[88] Jeremy Grant, 'Clearing up the system', 2nd November 2009.

[89] John Plender, 'Originative sin', 5th January 2009; Jeremy Grant, 'European data service poses threat to LSE', 12th January 2009; Peter Thal Larsen, 'Too early to declare death of "universal banking"', 15th January 2009; Peter Thal Larsen, 'Reviving flow of credit will take greater intervention', 17th January 2009; Daniel Thomas, Rachel

Reaction to the Crisis Part Two: 2010

By 2010 a degree of stability had returned to global financial markets after the events associated with the collapse of Lehman Brothers. However, the level of liquidity remained low because of the restrictions imposed by regulators and central banks and the continuing lack of trust between counterparties. Asset managers, for example, held massive portfolios of low yielding but liquid government bonds, which they could have lent to banks in return for higher-yielding asset-backed securities like corporate and mortgage bonds. In turn the banks could then have used the government bonds as collateral for inter-bank loans so providing them with the liquidity they needed. This was not happening as asset managers

Minder, Daniel Pimlott, Alan Rappeport, and Michiyo Nakamoto, 'Market is shaken to its foundations', 22nd January 2009; Jeremy Grant, 'Post-trade services come into their own', 2nd February 2009; Paul J. Davies, 'Credit derivatives drive hits a wall', 2nd February 2009; Nikki Tait and Jeremy Grant, 'Agreement reached over European CDS clearance', 20th February 2009; Christopher Mason and Bernard Simon, 'Canada bank prove envy of the world', 20th February 2009; Jeremy Grant, 'Exchanges and brokers at odds over crisis blame', 20th February 2009; Jeremy Grant, 'Why the future for clearer is anything but clear', 5th March 2009; James Sassoon, 'Britain deserves a better system of financial regulation', 9th March 2009; Aline van Duyn, 'Worries remain even after CDS clean-up', 11th March 2009; Michael Mackenzie, 'Changes welcomed for crucial area of finance', 13th March 2009; Peter Thal Larsen, 'A lot to be straightened out', 31st March 2009; Adrian Cox, 'Multiple threats still loom for the investment banking model', 1st April 2009; Steve Johnson, 'Concerns over risks sharpens the focus', 6th April 2009; Pauline Skypala, 'Rethink under way as some securities lending suspended', 6th April 2009; Michael Mackenzie, Nicole Bullock, and Gillian Tett, 'Big Bang arrives for credit default swaps industry', 8th April 2009; John Plender, 'Homeward Bound', 30th April 2009; Aline van Duyn and Anuj Gangahar, 'Exchanges big winners in OTC overhaul', 15th May 2009; Nikki Tait, 'Europe on the same wavelength as US, but moving more slowly', 15th May 2009; Gillian Tett, Aline van Duyn, and Jeremy Grant, 'Let battle commence', 20th May 2009; Jeremy Grant, 'OTC derivatives plan lifts shares', 2nd June 2009; Jeremy Grant, 'Exchanges warn on OTC clearing', 4th June 2009; Gillian Tett and Aline van Duyn, 'On the march', 9th June 2009; Michael Mackenzie, 'OTC markets to get stronger oversight', 18th June 2009; Krishna Guha, 'US seeks safety allied to dynamism', 18th June 2009; Jeremy Grant, 'NYSE Euronext joint venture to capitalise on rising demand for clearing', 19th June 2009; Michael Mackenzie and Aline van Duyn, 'Costs set to rise amid shake-up in derivatives trading', 19th June 2009; Michael Mackenzie, 'Push to reduce risks in short-term funding', 22nd June 2009; Henny Sender, 'Lehman creditors in fight to recover disputed collateral', 22nd June 2009; Ross Tieman, 'Knowledge and old-fashioned skill are back in favour', 22nd June 2009; John Plender, 'Re-spinning the web', 22nd June 2009; George Parker and Chris Giles, 'Turner goes in to bat for "whipping boy" FSA', 24th June 2009; Jeremy Grant, 'Clearing not the cure-all for financial system woes', 26th June 2009; James Wilson, 'More than just a historic trading floor', 30th June 2009; Chris Giles, 'BIS calls for wide global financial reforms', 30th June 2009; Michael Mackenzie, 'DTCC paves way for all roads to lead to its warehouse', 1st July 2009; Hal Weitzman and Jeremy Grant, 'Futures brokers fear new capital rules', 6th July 2009; Jeremy Grant and Nikki Tait, 'Eurex and ICE lead clearing race after Liffe setback', 6th July 2009; Gillian Tett and Aline van Duyn, 'Under restraint', 7th July 2009; Steve Johnson, 'How to breathe life back into bonds', 20th July 2009; Jeremy Grant, 'Tullett predicts rebound for OTC derivatives', 5th August 2009; John Plender, 'Shame gene has disappeared from the financial system', 17th August 2009; Jennifer Hughes, 'FX faces prospect of two-tier pricing', 21st August 2009; Jane Croft and Patrick Jenkins, 'Mutual suspicion', 3rd September 2009; David Oakley, 'Lenders are slow to regain lost confidence', 10th September 2009; Michael Mackenzie, 'Run on banks left repo sector highly-exposed', 11th September 2009; David Oakley, 'Europe's ravaged landscape begins to stabilise', 11th September 2009; Patrick Jenkins, 'Investment banks enjoy companies' bond boom', 14th September 2009; Jeremy Grant, 'Exchanges body issues dark pools warning', 23rd September 2009; John Authers, 'A risky revival', 26th September 2009; Peter Garnham, 'Keeping its head as others lost theirs', 29th September 2009; Jennifer Hughes, 'Concern over scope of initiatives', 29th September 2009; Henry Smith, 'Reverberations from volatility in the real economy', 6th October 2009; Sophia Grene, 'Taking the sting out of fluctuation', 6th October 2009; Jeremy Grant, Richard Milne, and Aline van Duyn, 'Collateral damage', 7th October 2009; Jennifer Hughes, 'Bankers seek to detoxify the alphabet soup', 13th October 2009; Bernard Simon, 'Making capital from strong financial base', 13th October 2009; Jeremy Grant, 'Sweeping changes are on the way', 21st October 2009; Jeremy Grant, 'The humdrum has fresh significance', 21st October 2009; Jeremy Grant, 'US clearing proposal fuels tension', 23rd October 2009; Brooke Masters, 'Long road to regulation', 26th October 2009; Aline van Duyn, 'Numbers game', 2nd November 2009; Jeremy Grant, 'Clearing up the system', 2nd November 2009; Jennifer Hughes, 'Currency derivatives caught in US clearing net', 20th November 2009; Daniel Thomas, 'Vacant Possessions', 7th December 2009; David Blackwell, 'Signs of recovery seen after years of famine', 16th December 2009; Norma Cohen, 'Bank lists obstacles on path to stability', 18th December 2009; Norma Cohen, 'Crisis thrusts debt-financing theorem back under the spotlight', 5th April 2010; John Gapper, 'Don't leave the financial system resting on quicksand', 30th August 2012.

were no longer confident that their liquid assets would be returned, and they would be left holding ones that were difficult to sell and impossible to value. Particularly vulnerable were the valuation of securities dependent upon a single bank rather than a public market. By 2010 the estimated default rate on Collateralized Debt Obligations (CDOs) issued in the USA in 2007 was 90 per cent leaving holders, spread across the world, with astronomical losses. What the crisis exposed was the wildly optimistic assumptions that had been made about default rates with the figure of 3 per cent, which had prevailed in 2001, being used. When forced to sell these securities banks had to accept whatever price they could obtain, converting a liquidity crisis into a solvency one. As a consequence banks continued to concentrate upon survival by building up reserves to cover existing and future losses, especially as this was the course directed by central banks and regulators. That left banks unwilling to provide the finance that their customers had previously relied upon, encouraging businesses and governments to turn to the bond markets as an alternative.

Further undermining trust within the banking community was the exposure of the way that Lehman Brothers had masked its financial difficulties before the crisis, as this could apply to all banks. Prior to the crisis banks had used repurchase agreements (repos) extensively for short-term borrowing. In a repo transaction a lender of funds received collateral as security for a short-term loan, which the borrower guaranteed to repurchase, so repaying the money. Following accounting conventions rules, a bank classified the amount lent as an asset while entering the amount that had to be repaid as a liability, with the two matching. Lehman Brothers did not adhere to these conventions. It classed the securities it provided as collateral as a sale and so did not enter a matching liability, even though it was committed to repurchasing them. The cash it received was used to purchase securities, which were also classed as assets. This gave misleading signals to counterparties. Those who had lent Lehman Brothers money in a repo transaction assumed that the collateral they held would be repurchased, and so they treated it as highly liquid, whereas Lehman Brothers treated the same assets as a disposal, and so made no provision for their redemption payment when the maturity date arrived. When their actions were exposed it undermined the entire repo market, which took a long time to recover. Nevertheless, over the course of 2010 there were signs of a return of confidence with even securitization finding favour again. Rob Joliffe, joint global head of debt capital markets at UBS, claimed in February 2010 that, 'securitisation has been and will again be an important funding tool for banks—although new issue volumes will take some time to recover to pre-crisis levels. It is coming back, but now more as a funding tool and will offer less opportunities for capital relief.'[90] However, the degree of recovery was slow.

Contributing to the continued delay in the recovery of the global money market was the increased role played by central banks as they pumped in liquidity as a way of preventing the financial crisis becoming an economic depression. Even before the crisis the actions of central banks had distorted money-market activity. The response to the bursting of the dot.com bubble in 2000 was a period of low interest rates as the Federal Reserve cut interest rates aggressively. The result was to make it much easier to borrow money helping to fuel the asset bubble that led up to the crises of 2007 and 2008. In March 2010 John Authers and Michael Mackenzie connected that intervention of the Federal Reserve to the conditions which led ultimately to the collapse of Lehman Brothers in 2008: 'Arguably, the dot.com

[90] Jennifer Hughes, 'Greek drama darkens mood', 25th February 2010.

boom ushered in the historically low interest rates from the Federal Reserve that are now widely blamed for allowing the housing and credit bubbles. It also paved the way for lightly-regulated hedge funds to succeed mainstream mutual funds as the critical drivers of the market.'[91] One element of that credit boom was the global carry trade that involved borrowing in Yen in Japan at low rates of interest and then relending in other countries and currencies at higher rates of interest. After the crisis the global carry trade centred on borrowing $s in the USA, because of the ultra-low interest rates maintained there by the Federal Reserve, and relending the proceeds elsewhere in the world. What this did achieve was to overcome the sharp credit contraction and $ shortage that had followed the Lehman Brothers crisis. However, it hampered the restoration of normal inter-bank borrowing and lending, especially as this continued to be regarded with suspicion because of the role it had played in deepening and spreading the crisis. Lord Adair Turner, chair of the UK's Financial Services Authority, pointed out at the end of 2010, that 'Interconnectedness between different categories of financial institution increases the potential impact of a shock in any one sector and increases the danger of feedback loops.'[92]

Again, regulators turned to clearing as the solution. In the wake of the collapse of Lehman Brothers it became apparent that it was not only the break-down of the inter-bank money market that could paralyse the financial system because the same result would come from the default of one bank at the centre of a tangled web of contracts. Deals ranging from interest-rate swaps to currency forwards would be worthless if the bank writing the contracts went under. Rather than being used as a mechanism for diffusing risk the financial crisis revealed that these contracts also spread risks from one counterparty to another. Hence the attraction of a clearing house as it could eliminate these counterparty risks by standing in the middle of the trade. A clearing house had a pool of capital, collected upfront payments, and required collateral as a margin against potential losses. However, the introduction of central clearing was increasingly complicated by an unwillingness to agree uniform regulations. Countries within the EU refused to accept the creation of a single authority while in the USA there were differences between those supervising banks and exchanges. Also, as time passed there was growing resistance to mandatory clearing because of the costs and restrictions it involved. With the recovery of trust between counterparties the need for clearing of any kind disappeared. Before the crisis the share of oil trades routed via clearing houses was only 10 per cent but it rose to 80 per cent in the wake of the Lehman bankruptcy, but it had fallen back to 50 per cent by 2010. To many market participants clearing was a temporary measure only required in the midst of the crisis, and then dispensed with as normal conditions returned. Clearing houses imposed conditions, levied charges, and demanded collateral to cover potential losses, whereas counterparties relied on each other to honour their contracts and designed them to fit precise requirements. Those involved also had their own way of lowering risks by identifying and tracking their exposure and reducing the delay between a trade and its completion. Particularly resistant to the mandatory use of a central clearing house was the foreign exchange market as it had operated trouble free during the crisis, having solved its own issues of counterparty risk back in 2002 when the CLS Bank was set up. In September 2009 Jas Singh, global head of Treasury at Thomson Reuters, had referred to the foreign exchange market as the 'poster child for how over-the-counter financial markets should work.'[93]

[91] John Authers and Michael Mackenzie, 'Technology endures in spite of Nasdaq fall', 10th March 2010.
[92] Paul J. Davies and Izabella Kaminska, 'Banks seek help from new set of institutions', 22nd December 2010.
[93] Peter Garnham, 'Keeping its head as others lost theirs', 29th September 2009.

However, to regulators clearing was seen as a permanent and universal solution to the issue of how to limit the degree of risk within the financial system, and so they tried to force it upon markets. In March 2010 Jennifer Hughes reported that, 'Since the financial crisis, regulators and officials have clamped down on OTC markets, preferring to move trading to more transparent electronic platforms and to force trades to be officially recorded in so-called repositories.'[94] By then regulators across Asia were copying the mandatory use of clearing houses for certain categories of OTC derivatives, as had already been introduced in the USA and EU, where it was now being extended to other financial markets. However, it was recognized that clearing, in solving one problem, also created another. A clearing house was the ultimate too-big-to-fail or too-interconnected-to-fail financial institution, but no government would stand guarantor given the scale and international nature of their business. This meant that clearing houses had to be robust enough to withstand a default by any of their members both through their own funds and those posted as margin. That was best achieved by giving them a monopoly but that clashed with another objective of regulators, which was to encourage competition. Of particular concern to regulators were those exchanges that combined trading with post-trade services. This gave users little option but to place all their business through them, and so put them in a position to exploit their position through high charges and restrictive practices.

Another area where regulators faced a dilemma over whether to prioritize stability or competition was the situation in many financial markets. Concentration created markets that were deep and broad which made them more liquid and transparent, and this contributed to stability. Conversely, such markets could be more expensive to use and often involved restrictive practices because they handed a monopoly to an institution such as an exchange, which favoured its members and owners. In contrast, competition fragmented markets but they were also cheaper and more flexible as they responded better to the needs of users. Such markets were also shallow and narrow, with opaque pricing and a tendency to freeze in a crisis, because they were dependent upon a small number of intermediaries and counterparties. The problem with outside intervention in markets was that it upset the balance between concentration and competition rather than allow the needs of the users to dictate the balance. Prior to the crisis regulators in both the USA and the EU focused on creating increased competition in the market whereas after the crisis the focus was on mitigating risk. The result were contradictory policies as exchanges were favoured because they often combined trading with clearing, and so reduced counterparty risk, but OTC markets were also favoured because of their lower charges and greater flexibility.

Allied to the regulatory intervention in markets was that involving banks. Whereas before the crisis megabanks were favoured by regulators, because they were considered too big to fail, that policy was reversed with the collapse of Lehman Brothers. In the immediate wake of the financial crisis regulators in the USA considered splitting up these banks, with a return to the division between deposit banking and investment banking mandated by the Glass–Steagall Act. In 2010 the then president of the United States, Barack Obama, told the American people that 'Never again will the American taxpayer be held hostage by a bank that is too big to fail.'[95] That policy did not gain traction outside the USA, where universal banking was long entrenched, such as Continental Europe. The authorities in the USA also pulled back from splitting up the big banks because it was recognized that it was not the banks that combined deposit-taking with investment banking that were at the heart of the

[94] Jennifer Hughes, 'Revolution in the cosy world of bonds', 1st March 2010.

[95] David Crow, 'Banks strain to effect a post-crisis funding fix', 25th March 2019.

crisis. That was understood by 2010 as Tom Braithwaite and Francesco Guerrera picked up on. To them it was specialized financial institutions like Long-Term Capital Management in 1998 and Lehman Brothers in 2008 that were the principal cause: 'All built risky positions that paid handsome profits before they turned bad. Each operated beyond the glare of banking regulators and without limits on their use of debt as they made big bets on assets ranging from Russian government bonds to US residential property.'[96] Such was the variety of financial institutions that existed, the complex mix of activities that each was engaged in, and the web of connections radiating from derivative contracts as well as lending and borrowing, that it was impossible to split up them up. Equally difficult was designing regulations that applied to all. There was the real danger that in attempting to frame comprehensive regulations additional risks would be created. Conversely if only the largest banks were targeted then those omitted could expand their business exploiting the restrictions placed on others, which, again, could result in increased risks.

Nevertheless, long after the crisis regulators in the USA remained determined to tackle the issue of too-big-to-fail banks, especially the issue of proprietary trading where they used their own money to finance positions in the market. This was despite evidence emerging that the main cause of the crisis was not proprietary trading. An assessment made in 2010 of the losses made by banks operating in London during the crisis, including those of foreign origin, revealed that only 13 per cent came from proprietary trading compared to 70 per cent from structured credit, and that this was likely to be the position for banks operating out of other financial centres. What this suggests is that banks, in their normal course of business, had simply taken excessive risks in their lending, and had retained insufficient liquidity to cover themselves when a crisis arose. Even the Bank of England, which had initially favoured dismembering banks that were too big to fail, was pulling back from that policy by 2010. Nevertheless, so entrenched was the view that the crisis was a product of banks placing large bets on dubious financial products that legislation was framed to prevent it happening again, rather than addressing the issue of the financial climate within which they had operated and the risk-taking that had encouraged. This was especially the case in the USA with its legacy of the Glass–Steagall Act.

The Dodd–Frank Act, passed in the USA in 2010, tried to control the degree of risk that banks and other financial institutions could accept. One consequence of the way it did this, according to Aline van Duyn and Francesco Guerrera, was that, 'Large financial groups whose failure would put the whole system at risk will have to cut back on risk and set aside more capital than before the crisis.'[97] A particular target was the bilateral contracts struck directly between banks, such as swaps, and the trading that took place outside the regulated markets. This was beyond the oversight of regulators and so it was to be either prohibited, restricted, or forced to go through exchanges and clearing houses. By the end of 2010 tough new rules, coupled with tightened regulatory scrutiny, and the continuing lack of trust between counterparties, forced the megabanks to scale back operations. This was the situation not only in the USA, with the Dodd–Frank legislation, but also around the world as new Basel rules forced banks to hold more capital. By undermining the internal markets that the megabanks had built up, which had made them highly competitive, opportunities were created for more specialist financial institutions as well as altering the balance of power between the investment banks that issued and traded securities and the fund managers who bought and held them. Nevertheless, by the end of 2010 the biggest US banks

[96] Tom Braithwaite and Francesco Guerrera, 'A Garden to Tame', 15th November 2010.

[97] Aline van Duyn and Francesco Guerrera, 'Dodd–Frank bill is no Glass–Steagall', 28th June 2010.

that had survived the crisis had also weathered the post-crisis storm and were now re-established at the heart of the global financial system.[98]

Reaction to the Crisis Part Three: 2011–20

Though the collapse of Lehman Brothers had taken place in September 2008 its consequences were still working their way through the global financial system more than ten years later. That was partly due to the size, duration, and nature of the credit boom that preceded the crisis as it took time to unwind the commitments made. In 2012 banks in the USA and the EU were still coping with an overhang of illiquid assets, which they could only dispose of at deeply discounted prices, making it difficult for them to expand their lending capacity until they did. It was estimated that in 2009 the stock of illiquid assets held by banks amounted to $360bn and this still stood at $50bn in 2014. It took until 2014 before the total funding that banks provided to business globally overtook the pre-crisis level. In terms of loans alone, excluding stock and bond issues, the pre-crisis position was not reached until 2015. By then most US and European banks had largely dealt with their overhanging debt problems and were ready to resume normal business. However, what the crisis had done was shatter the confidence that sophisticated mathematical models could be relied upon to generate investment strategies producing high returns without high risks. These models had been dependent upon assumptions that made no allowance for exceptional and unforeseen circumstances. The crisis then made all aware that such circumstances could take place. Also included in those assumptions was a low rate of default, the

[98] Michael Mackenzie, Francesco Guerrera, and Gillian Tett, 'A course to chart', 4th January 2010; Aline van Duyn and Jeremy Grant, 'Use of clearers to rein in OTC derivatives poses fresh dilemma', 15th January 2010; Samantha Pearson, 'US plans threaten LatAm FX', 20th January 2010; Anousha Sakoui and Brooke Masters, 'UK businesses' finance options undergo rethink', 21st January 2010; Masa Serdarevic, 'Sungard offers access to exchanges', 22nd January 2010; Francesco Guerrera and Justin Baer, 'Doubts beset mission to trim giants' girth', 23rd January 2010; *FT* Reporters, 'Proposals fail to forge consensus in Europe', 23rd January 2010; Francesco Guerrera and Megan Murphy, 'Tripped up', 25th January 2010; Aline van Duyn and Nicole Bullock, 'Ruling on Lehman creates new CDO doubts', 9th February 2010; Sam Jones, 'Alert over short-selling disclosure rules', 9th February 2010; Jennifer Hughes, 'Post-crisis wrangle over the best way to measure value', 11th February 2010; Jeremy Grant, 'Icap and Nasdaq in OTC expansion', 18th February 2010; Peter Garnham, 'Fears rise for future of dollar carry trade', 24th February 2010; Robert Cookson, 'Asian regulators launch reforms for OTC derivatives', 25th February 2010; Aline van Duyn, 'SEC backs new trade disclosure rules', 25th February 2010; Jennifer Hughes, 'Greek drama darkens mood', 25th February 2010; Jennifer Hughes, 'Revolution in the cosy world of bonds', 1st March 2010; Jennifer Hughes, 'FSA plays down prop trading impact', 2nd March 2010; John Authers and Michael Mackenzie, 'Technology endures in spite of Nasdaq fall', 10th March 2010; Gregory Meyer, 'Push for clearing houses fails to move leading oil traders', 12th March 2010; Jennifer Hughes, 'Fooled again', 19th March 2010; Nicole Bullock, Michael Mackenzie, and Aline van Duyn, 'Fed exit looms over US mortgages', 26th March 2010; Jeremy Grant, 'Fresh questions raised over regulation of clearing houses', 1st April 2010; Geraldine Lambe, 'Settlement model aids FX market success', 12th April 2010; Michael Mackenzie, 'Repo market faces struggle to pull back from slump', 15th April 2010; Aline van Duyn, 'Derivatives traders search for ways to appease regulators', 23rd April 2010; Aline van Duyn and Francesco Guerrera, 'Dodd–Frank bill is no Glass–Steagall', 28th June 2010; Henny Sender, 'Short measures', 9th July 2010; Aline van Duyn, Michael Mackenzie and Hal Weitzman, 'Derivatives dealers brace for clearing shake-up', 14th July 2010; Ruth Sullivan, 'Anxiety grows over new powers for ESMA', 19th July 2010; Jeremy Grant, 'Buyside wakes up to impact of legislation', 2nd August 2010; Megan Murphy and Francesco Guerrera, 'Prop-hostile climate throws up some tough calls for banks', 4th August 2010; Aline van Duyn, 'Derivative Dilemmas', 12th August 2010; Justin Baer, 'From recession to regulation', 27th September 2010; Jennifer Hughes, 'Currency markets ready for the next big thing', 20th October 2010; Philip Stafford, 'Competitive market requires deep pockets', 20th October 2010; Aline van Duyn, 'Pressure mounts over derivatives clearing', 3rd November 2010; Francesco Guerrera, Justin Baer, and Patrick Jenkins, 'A sparser future', 20th December 2010; *FT* Reporters, 'Before and after: how the investment banks had to change shape post-crisis', 21st December 2010; Paul J. Davies and Izabella Kaminska, 'Banks seek help from new set of institutions', 22nd December 2010.

liquidity of assets, and the reliability of the results generated by credit-ratings agencies. In contrast, the crisis produced high default rates while assets became impossible to sell or even price, undermining the models upon which banks had based their strategies and the trust they had placed in counterparties. What the crisis also revealed was that the rating provided by an agency was much less reliable than the scrutiny and market testing provided by an exchange. More fundamentally the crisis destroyed the trust that was the bedrock upon which any financial system was based, especially banking. Writing in 2018 John Authers made this clear, ten years after the collapse of Lehman Brothers, which he had witnessed first hand: 'Finance is all about trust...without trust, finance collapses...Trust then died with the credit crisis of 2008 and its aftermath.... Once lost, trust is very hard to retrieve.' Among all financial institutions he highlighted banks as being most vulnerable to a collapse of trust: 'Banks are fragile constructs. By design they have more money lent out than they keep to cover deposits. A self-fulfilling loss of confidence can force a bank out of business, even if it is perfectly well run.' He then went on to warn that, 'Without trust in financial institutions themselves, or those who work in them, or the media who cover them, the next crisis could be far more deadly than the last.'[99]

What was required was a replacement for the reliance placed on models and mathematics and that took time to develop, especially at a time when trust in counterparties was lacking. The repo, or repurchase market, for example, had been heavily used by broker-dealers such as Lehman Brothers, to obtain short-term wholesale funding. The abrupt withdrawal of repo funding in 2008 constituted a run on these banks and alerted regulators to the general vulnerability of all financial institutions that used short-term loans to finance long-term lending, while relying on the liquidity of the assets created to cover the risks such a strategy involved. With the risks exposed by the collapse of a key counterparty, the repo market was discredited and took a long time to recover. It was not only the repo market that was damaged by the crisis because the collapse of confidence infected the whole securitization process in which repackaged loans were sold to investors, on the understanding that their liquidity was maintained not by the existence of an active public market but by the guarantees provided by the issuer. The value of those guarantees had evaporated in 2008 and it proved very difficult to restore the level of trust required to attract potential investors. The value of Credit Default Swaps outstanding, which provided a form of insurance against counterparty risk, peaked at $60tn in 2007 and then fell from $40tn outstanding in 2008 before reaching a mere $8tn in 2018. With counterparty risk remaining a major feature of financial markets their revival was long delayed. As late as 2018 Chris Flood observed that 'Traditional bond markets in the US and Europe are less liquid than before the financial crisis, which has made trading of individual fixed-income securities more difficult, particularly for portfolio managers who want to conduct large transactions.' The principal explanation he gave for this continuing state of affairs was not the breakdown in trust at the time of the crisis but the consequences of the regulations introduced after the collapse of Lehman Brother: 'Regulatory changes have made it more expensive for banks to hold large inventories of bonds, which has hindered their role as liquidity providers in fixed-income markets.'[100]

In response to the crisis there was a wave of legislation designed to mitigate risk and protect the financial system from shocks. The first response had been to ensure survival of both individual institutions and the system as a whole, once the consequences of a collapse

[99] John Authers, 'Trust', 6th October 2018.
[100] Chris Flood, 'Bond liquidity issues prompt investors to turn to ETFs', 17th September 2018.

of an institution the size of Lehman Brothers was recognized. That justified massive government support to halt a cascade of collapses by restoring trust and unblocking frozen markets. Once the situation had been stabilized the next step was to rebuild both businesses and the system so that they could perform the functions required of them. That was accompanied by intervention to ensure that the outcome was a more resilient financial system, both in terms of its constituents and overall. That had largely been accomplished by 2010, when full consideration could be given to the future shape of the financial system. The global panic sparked by the collapse of Lehman Brothers had shown regulators that they needed co-ordinated, cross-border plans to deal with a Global Financial Crisis, and this needed to be led by a single institution if the speed of decision-making was to match the severity of the crisis. However, implementing such a plan proved impossible. The obvious candidate to lead any response was the Federal Reserve, and it had been forced to act as lender of last resort to the global banking system in the crisis. Prior to the crisis banks from outside the USA borrowed from wholesale markets to obtain the US$s they required, as that was the currency in which international banking was conducted. That also allowed them to compete with US banks.

During the crisis those sources of funds dried up forcing the Federal Reserve to step in and provide emergency liquidity as only it could manufacture additional US$s. The US Federal Reserve made $s available to central banks in Japan, UK, Switzerland, Canada, and the Eurozone. However, continuing in that role would constrain the freedom of the Federal Reserve to act in the support of the domestic policies pursued by the US government. For similar reasons no other central bank, including the Bank of England or the European Central Bank, would undertake such a role, or even possess the resources to do so in a world where the US$ was the supreme international currency. Conversely, there was an unwillingness to cede authority to either an international agency or one amongst them. In 2019 the banking consultant Simon Samuels, concluded that 'Today, as in 2008, it will be down to taxpayers in the home country to rescue their own banks.'[101] It was even difficult to agree on common requirements for the reserves that banks needed to provide if faced, again, with a liquidity crisis. In 2019 Caroline Binham, David Crow, and Patrick Jenkins were of the view that, 'There is no universal policy for banks' liquidity requirements.'[102] In a piece with Siobhan Riding, Caroline Binham highlighted the divisions between different regulators even over an issue as central as liquidity, noting the 'Divergent positions of central bankers and securities regulators over the direction of fund liquidity rules.'[103] The International Organization of Securities Commissions (Iosco) supported a diversity of recommendations among countries and institutions whereas the BIS's Financial Stability Board wanted a universal approach. Though both organizations co-operated in devising new rules to strengthen standards it was difficult to agree on a common approach that would cover both banks and markets and all countries.

What was put in place as a result of the crisis was a global network of currency swap arrangements between central banks, which could be quickly deployed in the face of a threat to international stability. However, this was only available for emergency use and not to provide a constant stabilizing influence on the global money market. The BIS's Basel Committee on Banking Supervision (BCBS) did set global standards under which banks

[101] Simon Samuels, 'The ECB should resist the lure of bigger banks', 31st January 2019.
[102] Caroline Binham, David Crow, and Patrick Jenkins, 'Lenders told to triple liquid assets as Brexit protection', 11th March 2019.
[103] Caroline Binham and Siobhan Riding, 'Iosco fires back at BoE in spat over fund rules', 22nd July 2019.

operated while its Financial Stability Board (FSB) did try to identify future risks that could destabilize the global banking system, and recommend the action that central banks and national regulators should take. However, in a world fragmented by national interest and regulatory barriers their power was limited. Without either a global regulator or a global lender of last resort there was little alternative but to continue to rely on the megabanks to provide the resilience that the global financial system would require in the face of any future crisis. The largest of these banks had assets in excess of $2tn and controlled over 1000 subsidiaries, which placed them beyond the capacity of any single national regulator to supervise or a national central bank to support in the event of failure, other than the Federal Reserve in the USA. Faced with this situation the solution was to operate a monetary policy that injected liquidity into the system in the face of any potential problem and ensure that the megabanks were in a position to withstand any shock, regardless of its severity, including a depositor run, a freeze in the credit markets, or an unexpectedly high demand for credit from existing clients. For the banks this translated into a demand for them to hold more capital and reserves so as to be better able to absorb losses and so not require government support. What the collapse of Lehman Brothers had revealed was that high levels of leverage were not unique to marginal players in the financial system such as hedge funds but extended to the megabanks.

Faced with the requirements placed on the megabanks to hold a large buffer of cash, sovereign bonds, and top-quality corporate bonds that could be quickly liquidified, it was only slowly that they were able to resume lending at pre-crisis levels. Compounding their lending constraints was the falling use of Credit Default Swaps (CDS) as a way of obtaining protection against the default of Collateralized Debt Obligations (CDOs). Without a CDS there was increased risk attached to a CDO and so investors were reluctant to purchase them, which made it harder for banks to sell them. In turn that made banks unwilling to make loans, which, in the past, would have been repackaged and sold on as CDOs. Generally, banks retreated from products that demanded more capital because of the high leverage ratio imposed on them. Currency instability also hampered the movement of funds around the world because of the increased risks. There was a sharp decline of short-term financial flows since the financial crisis with a switch towards long-term investment. The fall between 2007 and 2017 was estimated at 65 per cent, with the main cause being a collapse of cross-border bank lending as the megabanks retreated from international business. Driven by the need to rebuild their capital base, focus on their most profitable activities, and the barriers and requirements imposed by regulation the megabanks became more specialized. Megabanks were also put under pressure from governments to compartmentalize their operations along national lines so as to both insulate them from external difficulties and simplify intervention and support in the event of a crisis.

As megabanks retreated it left only a small number in the USA with the scale to undertake a business that was both universal and global, because they had control of their domestic market, which was, by far, the largest in the world. In 2019 the five largest US banks held 45 per cent of total US banking assets compared to 40 per cent in 2007. As Martin Arnold explained in 2018, US banks 'benefit from a dominant position in a homogenous domestic market that boasts the world's largest investment banking fee pool.' He contrasted that with the fragmented nature of the European market which could not support global banks, and led to their withdrawal from many operations in Asia, Europe, and the USA: 'Europe has no truly pan-European banks' was his verdict.[104] The result was that

[104] Martin Arnold, 'How US banks took over the financial world', 17th September 2018.

US banks were in an even stronger position globally ten years after the crisis than they had been before, aided by the domestic amalgamations that had taken place, such as that between JP Morgan Chase/Bear Stearns and Bank of America/Merrill Lynch. These banks, along with Goldman Sachs and Morgan Stanley, could look to the Federal Reserve for direct support in a crisis. In contrast, their European rivals were in full retreat apart from Barclays, which had acquired the US operations of Lehman Brothers at the time of the crisis. Without monetary integration in Europe these banks also lacked a single lender of last resort. Tim Throsby, the head of corporate and investment banking at Barclays, having previously been with JP Morgan, claimed in 2018 that 'We're the only European bank that's deadly serious... about having a serious transatlantic corporate and investment bank. The US is the largest capital market in the world and the most lucrative.'[105] The assessment of Laura Noonan in 2018 was that, 'Crisis-era mergers, such as Barclays' assimilation of the US arm of Lehman Brothers, JP Morgan's purchase of Washington Mutual and the Bank of America-Merrill Lynch deal, have left the surviving banks with greater economies of scale. A succession of cost-cutting plans has made them leaner and an M&A boom has boosted fee income.'[106] By then all the leading megabanks were from the USA led by JP Morgan, Citibank, Goldman Sachs, Bank of America, and Morgan Stanley whereas their European competitors had slipped back, including Deutsche Bank, Credit Suisse, and UBS. With its large pan-Asian network HSBC continued to see a future for itself as a megabank, and was investing accordingly as its head of global banking and markets, Amir Assaf emphasized in 2019: 'The ease with which clients can access, monitor and manage their assets will improve as we and the industry continue to invest in innovative technology and services.'[107]

Nevertheless, it was the US megabanks that were now dominant. In 2006 the leading three banks trading fixed-income products, currencies, and commodities (collectively known as FICC) were Goldman Sachs, Citibank, and Deutsche Bank. They had a 35 per cent share of the business done by the top twelve megabanks. By 2018 the leading three were Goldman Sachs, Citibank, and JP Morgan and their share had increased to 45 per cent. As Laura Noonan explained in 2019 'There will always be demand for FICC activities such as hedging foreign exchange rates and offering derivatives that give companies and institutions certainty that they can meet their long-term obligations.'[108] It was a small group of US megabanks that were willing to undertake the heavy investment in technology and expertise required to conduct such trading on the scale required, and so it was they that were in a dominant position ten years after the crisis that witnessed the collapse of one of their number and the disappearance of two others by merger. In contrast, Stephen Morris and David Crow referred in 2019 to the European megabanks 'dwindling ability to compete with a resurgent Wall Street'.[109]

Compounding the difficulties faced by European megabanks in competing with their US peers were the regulations introduced in 2019 under the new version of the Mifid (Market in Financial Instruments Directive) The aim of Mifid 2 was to push through a division between fund managers, the buy side of a transaction, and the megabanks, acting on the sell side, so as to generate more competition. However, its effect was, according Simon Bound, global head of research at Morgan Stanley in 2019, to 'further concentrate the

[105] Laura Noonan, 'Financials', 12th June 2018.
[106] Laura Noonan, 'Financials', 12th June 2018.
[107] Laura Noonan, 'Transaction work is fastest growth area for big banks', 8th March 2019.
[108] Laura Noonan, 'Goldman to wield axe on bond unit as peers sit tight', 8th February 2019.
[109] Stephen Morris and David Crow, 'Axe swings at European banks after lamentable fourth quarter', 22nd February 2019.

equities business among bulge bracket banks.'[110] That was because only they could cover the increased costs involved by spreading it over the large volume of trading they conducted. Kevin Cronin, at the fund managers, Invesco, took a similar view: 'No single asset manager could possibly give themselves the depth of coverage that sell-side research provides—it's impossible to replicate. It's an entire ecosystem that benefits from broker research. It's not just asset managers, but retail investors and smaller companies in the capital markets.'[111] The US megabanks were highly competitive because they enjoyed huge economies of scale courtesy of their domestic market and the global importance of the US$. Their European peers could only compete by bundling buy-side and sell-side activities together, and so spreading the costs involved, but Mifid 2 outlawed that. Andrea Vismara, the chief executive an Italian investment bank, Equita, complained in 2019 that 'European regulators have spent a lot of time analysing and promoting regulatory changes aimed at increasing transparency and investor protection, but they have overlooked the impact on the industry and, most importantly, on companies' access to capital markets.' He continued by saying that 'The current environment is stifling competition and is unduly favouring global banks, investors and companies... Regulators have failed so far to understand the intricacies of the European investment banking landscape and the need for active support for this important sector.'[112] It was in 2019 that Deutsche Bank finally closed down its global equities business with the loss of 18,000 jobs. That had implications for its other activities because without a presence in equity sales and trading, corporate clients and asset managers would migrate to those banks providing the full range of services.

Nevertheless, even these US megabanks had to refocus their activities after the crisis in the wake of the new regulations they were subjected to. The persistence of the too-big-to-fail problem in the eyes of the regulators had led to the introduction of measures that forced the largest to increase their reserves and pull back from risk-taking. Laura Noonan wrote in 2018 that:

> Investment banks have spent much of the decade under a shadow since the meltdown of the US mortgage market. They have watched private equity firms and hedge funds take their place at the top of the finance food chain. Executives have complained loudly that the regulations in place after the crisis have hampered their ability to compete... Regulations have in effect banned them from once lucrative activities such as trading stocks on their own behalf and co-investing in funds with clients. Areas including trading structured products have all but dried up as clients balked at the collapse in value of some instruments and revelations of widespread manipulation of others, especially mortgage-backed bonds.[113]

The megabanks not only closed down particular operations but also abandoned particular countries, so reversing the advances they had made before the crisis. James Forese, head of investment banking at Citibank, reflected in 2018 that 'We became a much more focused and much simpler business.'[114] One measure of Citibank's retreat was that the number of clients they serviced fell from 32,000 in 2007 to 12,000 in 2018. Robin Wigglesworth and

[110] Richard Henderson, 'US fund managers mimic Brussels rules on research', 10th May 2019.
[111] Richard Henderson, 'US fund managers mimic Brussels rules on research', 10th May 2019.
[112] Andrea Vismara, 'Mifid 2 drags down an ecosystem along with Europe's banks', 15th May 2019.
[113] Laura Noonan, 'Financials', 12th June 2018.
[114] Laura Noonan, 'Financials', 12th June 2018.

Ben McLannahan reported in 2018 that 'Since the financial crisis, investment banks have beat a retreat from their historic role in the buying and selling of equities and bonds.' They highlighted the role played in this retreat by regulatory intervention: 'Since the financial crisis, regulatory changes have aimed to purge leverage, primarily by curtailing the role banks have traditionally played in providing it.'[115] In 2019 Robin Wigglesworth himself observed that 'Since the financial crisis, stricter regulations and commercial pressures have forced many banks to pare back or close their once-vast proprietary and market-making desks.'[116] Instead, these banks were now acting as intermediaries rather than employing their own capital.

This made some financial markets riskier as the megabanks no longer acted as shock absorbers, using their own capital and holdings of stocks and bonds. The level of liquidity in a market could vary during the day and over the year, creating a need for counter cyclical buyers and sellers to act as shock absorbers, driven by the potential gains they could make whether selling in anticipation of a fall or buying in the expectation of a rise. The megabanks had occupied this role before the crisis but the combination of the collapse in trust and then the regulatory intervention afterwards led to them scaling back these activities, with serious consequences for market volatility. In 2018 Joe Rennison and Philip Stafford reported that:

> Tough regulations introduced after 2009 with the intention of stabilising markets are fuelling far more volatile swings in asset prices... as banks have retreated from their traditional roles of providing two-way prices for investors in listed futures and over-the-counter arenas for equities, bonds and foreign exchange. These markets have also become increasingly electronic with market-making activity gravitating towards high-speed trading firms, which by their nature do not extend support for prices once volatility heats up.[117]

In 2019 Eva Szalay reported that 'Some also blame reforms brought in after the 2009 financial crisis, which have made banks reluctant to take on risk and act as shock absorbers for markets.'[118] In the place of the megabanks appeared the High-frequency Traders (HFTs). These HFTs bought and sold at speed in response to market signals. They lacked both the capital and the holdings of the megabanks and so could not act as shock absorbers, though they did contribute to maintaining equilibrium over different assets and markets. Conversely the automated responses of the HFTs to volatility could also accentuate a rise or fall as Andrei Kirilenko, the former chief economist at the CFTC, warned in 2019: 'We just have to accept that financial markets are nearly fully automated and try to make sure that things don't get so technologically complex and inter-connected that it's dangerous to the financial system.'[119] One example of these was the Chicago-based firm, DRW, which had taken over Lehman Brothers" trading in foreign exchange, interest rate, and agriculture futures. By 2018 it was one of a number of mainly privately-owned proprietary trading firms that bet their own capital on the world's exchanges using ultrafast computers to

[115] Robin Wigglesworth and Ben McLannahan, 'Liquidity outs leverage as the big worry for investors', 4th May 2018.

[116] Robin Wigglesworth, 'IMF warns of "tip of the iceberg" threat over volatility', 12th April 2019.

[117] Joe Rennison and Philip Stafford, 'Traders find receptive ear among regulators to relax capital rules', 10th July 2018.

[118] Eva Szalay, 'Fears over forex trading going bump in the night', 6th March 2019.

[119] Robin Wigglesworth, 'Markets: Volatile Times', 10th January 2019.

execute deals in fractions of a second. Despite their presence, markets were left shallower after the withdrawal of the megabanks, exposing them to greater volatility and to bouts of illiquidity.

It was not only in trading activities that megabanks were replaced by alternatives. Patrick Jenkins observed in 2015 that 'While banks have been forced to accept tougher regulatory capital requirements, making much of their core lending more expensive, challengers from outside banking are only lightly regulated.'[120] This was most evident in the USA. In 2013 non-banks provided 30 per cent of the federally guaranteed mortgage loans but 60 per cent in 2018. This reflected the recovery of the originate-and-distribute model with the mortgage lenders active in the business focusing on borrowers with poor credit ratings. As Sam Fleming, Joe Rennison, and Robert Armstrong observed in 2019, 'While post-crisis regulation forced traditional banks to have larger amounts of capital and more resilient liquidity backstops, the non-banking sector is much more loosely supervised.'[121] Private equity firms like Blackstone also stepped into the gap vacated by the megabanks. By 2018 there was a total of $12tn outstanding in the global non-financial corporate bond market, and around one-fifth was from providers other than banks. Since the financial crisis banks had lost their position as the primary suppliers of international credit. Borrowers switched to debt issuance where a greater proportion was taken up by megafund managers rather than absorbed by megabanks. By 2018 debt securities made up 57 per cent of international credit compared to 48 per cent in 2008. One of these fund managers, Jim Switzer, head of credit rating at the investment group, Alliance Bernstein, explained his position in 2018, 'We're not playing the role of banks. But when we are also liquidity providers in a dislocated market, we get better execution'[122] That same year Mark Vandevelde wrote about what had been happening: 'By setting up huge lending arms, they have been transformed from heavyweight dealmakers that took stakes in companies into the principal bankers for a large tract of corporate America.'[123] He continued by referring to 'lightly-regulated asset managers that have filled the void as banks are forced to retreat from risky deals. Unlike banks, which are dependent on deposits and other short-term funding, these funds raise money from long-term investors such as insurance companies and pension funds.'[124] Regulators were content to condone the shift because they considered megafunds to be less exposed to the liquidity issues of the megabanks, because they financed long-term investments with long-term borrowing from institutions looking for higher rates of return. Nevertheless, they did face risks if those who had borrowed from them defaulted and they could not repay the insurance companies and pension funds who supplied them with funds.

Generally, the consequence of the new rules introduced since the crisis was to restrict the operation of the megabanks and the relationship they had to OTC. This had implications for the entire financial system. New regulations required banks to hold more capital, reduce leverage rates, and pass more business through clearing houses where collateral was required. Taking their lead from the USA other regulators followed in the adoption of these rules. In 2011 Tanya Powley reported that in Britain 'The FSA wants to bring in tougher affordability tests to make sure banks lend money only to people who can afford to pay it

[120] Patrick Jenkins, 'Start-up threat to creaking banks', 14th October 2015.

[121] Sam Fleming, Joe Rennison, and Robert Armstrong, 'Non-bank lenders under scrutiny after taking big share in US mortgage market', 10th April 2019.

[122] Robin Wigglesworth and Joe Rennison, 'New credit ecosystem blossoms as portfolio trades surge', 11th October 2018.

[123] Mark Vandevelde, 'Financial Crisis', 20th September 2018.

[124] Mark Vandevelde, 'Financial Crisis', 20th September 2018.

back.'[125] The effect was to magnify and prolong the actions banks took at the time of the crisis to safeguard themselves by increasing their capital, pull back from risk-taking, and reinforce liquidity buffers. As the awareness of risk had been heightened by the crisis, banks altered the mix of assets required to match their liabilities, with a much greater focus on quality and liquidity. Tracy Alloway picked up on this in 2011, when it emerged that the use of collateral in the financial system had fallen from $10,000bn in 2007 to $6,000bn in 2010: 'One reason collateral use has fallen is that market participants are more vigilant about the creditworthiness of counterparties and how business partners might use collateral sent to them.'[126] The actions of regulators made the shortage of credit even greater while extending its duration. As banks responded to the requirements of regulators by increasing their reserves the easiest route was not to lend to each other. This cut the supply of credit across the system. Banks had used the inter-bank market to tap into the excess liquidity present in the banking system to supplement temporary shortages, allowing each to operate with a lower margin. With banks restricting the amount they placed in the inter-bank market, and the counterparties they would deal with, this supply of funds dried up forcing each bank to operate with a higher level of liquidity. This cut the amount each bank could lend to its customers.

That led those borrowers unable to obtain finance to seek alternatives, which they found from those financial institutions that were less constrained by the regulations. Shadow banks flourished as they were sufficiently small or marginal to operate beyond the gaze of the regulators. Investors also turned to the products and services that these shadow banks could offer, attracted by the higher returns obtained from direct lending to businesses. In 2019 there were 4000 different groups of fund managers around the world running 95,000 separate funds. Curbs on the ability of the megabanks to hold vast inventories of bonds, under the Basel 3 rules, and restrictions placed on the trading that banks did on their own account, under the Volcker rules, made financial markets much less liquid. In turn that made it more difficult to raise funds through the issue of bonds, as investors were reluctant to buy them because of their lack of liquidity. Inventories of corporate bonds held by banks, for example, fell from $200bn in 2008 to $45bn in 2012. This left investors searching for alternatives which megafunds like BlackRock and Vanguard provided in the shape of Exchange Traded Funds (ETFs), as they could offer higher returns at a time of low interest rates generated by central bank intervention. After the financial crisis central banks launched aggressive monetary easing, which pushed up bond and share prices and drove down yields. By 2012 government bonds yielded 2 per cent and investment-grade corporate bonds managed 4 per cent. Conversely, a real estate loan could offer returns of up to 11 per cent, but was much less liquid. In searching for an improved combination of yield and liquidity investors opted for strategies that favoured funds that tracked broad market trends, like ETFs. These combined low-cost and tax advantages with the flexibility and transparency of shares as they were traded on exchanges. In 2019 Attracta Mooney and Peter Smith reflected that 'As markets soared on the back of quantitative easing, passive funds delivered strong returns and investors piled in, while many active managers have struggled to outperform.'[127]

[125] Tanya Powley, 'FSA sees "common sense" on mortgage overhaul', 19th December 2011.
[126] Tracy Alloway, 'Financial system creaks as loan lubricant dries up', 29th November 2011.
[127] Attracta Mooney and Peter Smith, 'Deal of the decade: how BlackRock buying BGI changed the industry', 6th May 2019.

In an era of ultra-low interest rates it was difficult for active fund managers to generate returns higher than the market average but their costs remained the same, encouraging investors to turn to a cheaper alternative in the form of ETFs. What investors sought was the perfect combination of complete safety, high returns, and high liquidity, adjusted according to their own preferences, and the one financial product that promised this was an Exchange Traded Fund. Equity ETFs dominated but Bond ETFs were growing in popularity. By 2018 the passive investment industry had accumulated $5.6tn under management, and this was mainly in the form of ETFs. An increasing number of these ETFs were using leverage to increase returns and take greater risks with the derivative contracts to which they were linked. The number following that course had risen steadily from only 110 in 2007 to 886 in 2017, when they were handling funds valued at $80bn. By 2017 ETFs amounted to 13 per cent of global investment assets while index funds were around 10 per cent of the value of global equity and bond market capitalization. In 2018 Gregory Davis, chief investment officer at Vanguard, explained that an index fund was a ready-made diversified portfolio with low-cost fees and it was ideal for buy and hold investors: 'With one trade, individuals can own a portfolio that is broadly diversified and low cost.'[128] However, there were risks attached to ETFs. Investors assumed that ETF shares were liquid because they could always buy and sell them, but that liquidity depended on the ability to acquire or dispose of the underlying assets. That had been the case when banks were able to use their capital to hold a portfolio of underlying securities allowing them to act as counterparties to investors. In the wake of the financial crisis and the subsequent regulations the banks were not in a position to do this, exposing the underlying illiquidity of the assets included in ETFs.

Another development in the ten years after the Global Financial Crisis was the growth of the leveraged loan market, where credit was extended to lowly rated but highly-indebted companies. This more than doubled in size to $1.4tn between 2008 and 2018. Again it was a response to central banks forcing down interest rates and buying up debt that led investors to look elsewhere for higher returns. Their search was met by companies wanting to borrow, and finding existing avenues closed, because of the restrictions placed on banks. They both turned to leveraged loans, despite the greater risk, because of the likelihood of defaults. Leveraged loans had performed relatively well throughout the financial crisis, and investors were attracted by the fact that the debt was backed by specific assets, and ranked higher than bonds in terms of repaying investors in the event of a default by the borrower. In the search for yield in the years that followed the Global Financial Crisis investors became more willing to swap both the quality of assets supplied as collateral, and the liquidity of the financial instruments they held, for the higher returns being promised by borrowers. This extended beyond leveraged loans into the private debt market which was even less liquid. Robin Wigglesworth observed in 2019 that, 'Unlike leveraged loans, private debt is typically not widely traded, and unlike bonds, the market is largely unregulated and opaque.'[129] Nevertheless, the size of the US private debt market rose from $300bn in 2010 to $700bn in 2018. Since the crisis companies had taken advantage of low interest rates and strong demand for higher-yielding bonds to issue ever increasing quantities of them.

Private debt, property assets, and trade finance were all areas where banks employed the lend-and-hold model, but regulations requiring them to maintain more capital to cover the risk of default either led them not participate in the business or sell on the debt to others.

[128] Gregory Davis, 'Index funds are not to blame for market volatility', 31st October 2018.
[129] Robin Wigglesworth, 'Non-bank lending surge stirs painful subprime memories', 5th February 2019.

This created opportunities for specialist banks and other financial businesses such as asset managers. Regulatory intervention since the crisis was reshaping the financial system. As banks remained reluctant to lend, initially because their balance sheets were too fragile but later due to regulatory constraints, shadow banks stepped in to fill the void. These were financial institutions less affected by the new regulations. The result was a mixture of competition between banks for business and co-operation in particular activities. Banks lent hedge funds money, for example, that was then put into equities, derivatives, and other assets where values could fluctuate wildly, exposing them to potential losses. This shadow banking system had been emerging prior to the crisis as banks had ramped up their ability to lend by packaging up existing loans, through securitization, and selling them on. When Lehman Brothers collapsed uncertainty over the creditworthiness of these complex securities led to the abandonment of securitization. However, by 2015 securitization was recovering, especially among those banks lacking access to retail deposits, and this was underpinning the development of an even larger shadow banking sector because of the controls and restrictions placed on the megabanks. One example of the retreat of the megabanks was found in the repo market. By 2014 the combination of hedge funds, mutual funds, and real estate trusts had become the biggest users of the repo market as the megabanks withdrew. They were using the market to raise short-term funds to finance long-term investments such as mortgage assets, corporate bonds, and municipal debt.

However, it took time for these alternatives to banks to develop leading to pressure to relax some of the most stringent requirements imposed in the immediate aftermath of the crisis. As early as 2012 Sharlene Goff highlighted the contradictions in government policy, which simultaneously wanted banks 'to hold larger capital buffers and remove risky loans from their balance sheets' and 'increase lending'.[130] In response governments were forced to pull back from more extreme levels of intervention, such as dismembering megabanks, banning derivatives, and outlawing OTC markets. It was increasingly recognized that all of these were integral components of a financial system that served the needs of an integrated global economy. Helping to fuel the backtracking of governments over the dismemberment of megabanks, for example, were emerging doubts that they had been the central cause of the crisis, and whether any measures aimed at curbing their activities would be effective. The French central banker, Jacques de Larosière, reflected in 2012, that, 'The crisis has shown that bank failures are not related to specific structures, but to excessive risk-taking. The institutions that were the hardest hit by the crisis were those that pursued risky operations either in trading or in more traditional activities, be they specialised or not.'[131] Increasingly regulators recognized that the risks in banking were not confined to megabanks but were a generic feature applying to all institutions that financed long-term investment with short-term borrowing, whether operating on a retail or wholesale basis. Regulators faced the dilemma that by encouraging competition in banking they would better serve both savers and borrowers but the cost would be paid in terms of increased instability and even another crisis because newer entrants were willing to take greater risks as they had less to lose and more to gain than the incumbents. This was the perennial problem of framing regulations that tried to achieve incompatible goals and so pulled in opposite directions.[132]

130 Sharlene Goff, 'Policymakers recognise SMEs need more funding options', 16th April 2012.

131 Jacques de Larosière, 'Do not be seduced by the simplicity of ringfencing', 27th September 2012.

132 Sam Jones, 'Customers cast a more critical eye on the field', 21st March 2011; Elaine Moore, 'Uncertainty in an evolving landscape', 21st March 2011; Jane Croft, 'The danger of relying too much on only one tool', 22nd

March 2011; Sharlene Goff, 'Near-death experience has left deep scars', 22nd March 2011; Jeremy Grant, 'Central counterparties eye wave of opportunities', 22nd March 2011; Jeremy Grant, 'Chill wind blows over plans for market mergers', 17th May 2011; Tom Braithwaite, Brooke Masters, and Jeremy Grant, 'A Shield Asunder', 20th May 2011; Aline van Duyn and Richard Milne, 'Arbiters under fire', 25th July 2011; Sharlene Goff, 'Risk is the new "sexy" job at the bank', 14th July 2011; Patrick Jenkins, Brooke Masters, and Tom Braithwaite, 'Hunt for a common front', 8th September 2011; Phillip Stephens, 'Vickers hands victory to the bankers' shop steward', 13th September 2011; Jo Johnson, 'Ringfence and regulate in haste, repent at leisure', 13th September 2011; Paul J. Davies, 'Lack of experience restrains investment in liquidity swaps', 3rd October 2011; Tracy Alloway, 'Counterparty risk makes an anxious return', 27th October 2011; Paul Taylor, 'How to make ready for regulation', 9th November 2011; Tracy Alloway, 'Financial system creaks as loan lubricant dries up', 29th November 2011; Tracy Alloway, 'Higher capital demands and dearer funding bring a dual burden', 2nd December 2011; Tanya Powley, 'FSA sees "common sense" on mortgage overhaul', 19th December 2011; Ed Hammond, 'Pressure on banks' real estate loans', 6th January 2012; Robin Wigglesworth, 'Taming the traders', 20th March 2012; Paul J. Davies, 'Banks look to insurers for lessons', 16th April 2012; Sharlene Goff, 'Policymakers recognise SMEs need more funding options', 16th April 2012; Michael Mackenzie, Nicole Bullock, and Telis Demos, 'JP Morgan loss exposes dangers of derivatives', 16th May 2012; Barbara Ridpath, 'Crisis—and regulation—can breed opportunity', 30th May 2012; Patrick Jenkins and Brooke Masters, 'London's precarious position', 30th July 2012; Gill Plimmer, 'Financial sector rescues off-set sell-offs', 13th August 2012; John Gapper, 'Don't leave the financial system resting on quicksand', 30th August 2012; Jacques de Larosière, 'Do not be seduced by the simplicity of ringfencing', 27th September 2012; Tracy Alloway, 'BlackRock moves in as banks retreat', 2nd October 2012; Shahien Nasiripour and Brooke Masters, 'Regulators edge towards "every country for itself"', 10th December 2012; Brooke Masters and Shahien Nasiripour, 'Basel move aims to stoke recovery', 8th January 2013; Kate Burgess and Caroline Binham, 'BBA sets out plans to monitor standards', 16th January 2013; Ed Hammond and Brooke Masters, 'FSA clampdown on mortgage-backed loans sparks friction', 17th January 2013; Alice Ross, 'Reversal of euro carry trade inflicts global pain', 30th January 2013; Tracy Alloway and Nicole Bullock, 'Banks offer debt product to help skirt new liquidity rules', 30th January 2013; Ralph Atkins, 'With the volume turned down', 12th February 2013; David Oakley, 'Asset managers fill the gap as banks retreat', 4th March 2013; Ralph Atkins and Mary Watkins, 'Eurozone crisis forces funding rethink for banks', 15th March 2013; Tracy Alloway and Arash Massoudi, 'ETFs under scrutiny in market turbulence', 28th June 2013; Tom Braithwaite, Michael Mackenzie, Tracy Alloway, and Gina Chon, 'Dust starts to settle on the derivatives revolution', 12th September 2013; Tracy Alloway and Michael Mackenzie, 'Default swaps face risk of extinction', 16th October 2013; Philip Stafford, 'Fears grow over rules on derivatives trading', 19th December 2013; Chris Flood, 'Regulators stalk secretive financial giants', 24th February 2014; Tracy Alloway and Arash Massoudi, 'Non-bank lending steps out of the shadows', 26th February 2014; Sam Fleming, 'Foreign banks meet BoE over branch rules', 27th February 2014; Patrick Jenkins, 'Humbled financiers reassess their culture', 17th March 2014; Chris Flood, 'Side pockets: a curiosity shop of esoteric assets', 21st April 2014; Tracy Alloway, 'Big investors replace banks in $4th repo market', 30th May 2014; Sophia Grene, 'Non-banks colonise former bank territory', 2nd June 2014; Tom Braithwaite, Martin Arnold, and Tracy Alloway, 'Tough choices confront traditional lenders', 18th June 2014; Tracy Alloway, 'Call for reforms to broker-dealing', 14th August 2014; Martin Arnold and Camilla Hall, 'Big banks are giving up on global ambitions', 19th October 2014; Gina Chon, 'Regulators wrestle with cross-border strategy', 24th October 2014; John Kenchington, 'Investors are being urged to stress test fixed income funds', 3rd November 2014; Martin Arnold, 'Carney's too big to fail buffer represents clear progress despite doubt', 9th December 2014; Andrew Bolger, 'Corporate loans rise above pre-crisis levels', 11th February 2015; Joel Lewin, 'Exchange traded fund assets top $3tn', 6th May 2015; Thomas Hale, 'Riskier RMBS sales to double last year's total', 9th October 2015; Patrick Jenkins, 'Start-up threat to creaking banks', 14th October 2015; Philip Stafford, 'Europe's regulatory crackdown set to ease', 25th May 2016; Joe Rennison and Philip Stafford, 'Fears grow that global reforms to derivatives will fragment into a patchwork of local standards', 23rd September 2016; Philip Stafford, 'Brexit brings headache to industry weary of regulation', 11th October 2016; Nicole Bullock, 'High-frequency traders adjust to overcapacity and leaner times', 10th March 2017; Henny Sender, 'US retreat from global system lets China in', 5th April 2017; Thomas Hale, 'Shadow banks step into the spotlight', 5th April 2017; Eric Platt and Robert Smith, 'Efforts to harmonise risky-loans rules in doubt', 6th June 2017; Shawn Donnan, 'Ebbs and capital flows', 22nd August 2017; Philip Stafford, 'Brexit unleashes a three-way battle over clearing', 25th October 2017; Gregory Meyer, 'DRW unit joins top rank of traders with nearly $1bn revenues over two years', 16th January 2018; Robin Wigglesworth, 'Exchange traded products face scrutiny as worries deepen', 15th February 2018; Nathan Brooker, 'How the crash created one global city', 17th March 2018; Robin Wigglesworth and Ben McLannahan, 'Liquidity outs leverage as the big worry for investors', 4th May 2018; Philip Stafford, 'Frankfurt narrows gap with London as incentive scheme boosts euro clearing', 13th June 2018; Joe Rennison and Philip Stafford, 'Traders find receptive ear among regulators to relax capital rules', 10th July 2018; Gillian Tett, 'When the world held its breath', 1st September 2018; John Authers, 'Time to confess that I hushed up Wall St's scariest day', 8th September 2018; Laura Noonan and Patrick Jenkins, 'Financial Crisis', 13th September 2018; Martin Arnold, 'How US banks took over the financial world', 17th September 2018; Chris Flood, 'Bond liquidity issues prompt investors to turn to ETFs', 17th September 2018; Mark Vandevelde, 'Financial Crisis', 20th September 2018; Colby Smith, 'Borrowers want dollars—some more than others', 20th September 2018; Philip Stafford, 'Fresh risks emerge from the depth', 1st October 2018; Hans Hoogervorst, 'Do not blame accounting rules for the financial crisis', 4th October 2018; John Dizard, 'Brexit could be a toy train crash for derivatives', 8th

Impending Crisis?

Ten years after the Global Financial Crisis most global financial markets had recovered their previous vitality and appeared to be operating as they had before that event took place. One example was the foreign exchange market where trading in 2019 reached another peak, being estimated at $6.6tn a day. However, in the ten years since the collapse of Lehman Brothers government intervention had forced through a fundamental redesign of the global banking and trading environment. Writing in 2019 Gillian Tett concluded that, 'A decade of extraordinary monetary experiments has left the system badly distorted. In particular the injection of huge amounts of liquidity into the global financial system

October 2018; Robin Wigglesworth and Joe Rennison, 'New credit ecosystem blossoms as portfolio trades surge', 11th October 2018; Gregory Davis, 'Index funds are not to blame for market volatility', 31st October 2018; Laura Noonan, 'Financials', 12th June 2018; John Authers, 'Trust', 6th October 2018; Caroline Binham, 'Ringfence rules come into effect for UK banks', 2nd January 2019; Robin Wigglesworth, 'Markets: Volatile Times', 10th January 2019; Lindsay Fortado and Laura Noonan, 'Banks bet on hedge fund prime broking fees', 10th January 2019; Nicholas Megaw, 'Challenger banks struggle to smash glass ceiling', 14th January 2019; Laura Noonan and Robert Armstrong, 'Earnings reveal true picture of hard-hit banks', 14th January 2019; David Crow and Stephen Morris, 'The battle for Barclays', 21st January 2019; Joe Rennison and Colby Smith, 'Debt machine risks running out of control', 22nd January 2019; Gavin Jackson, 'Bank of England plays down surge in risky corporate loans', 24th January 2019; Joe Rennison, 'Investors flock to CLOs with ghost of previous loan vehicles left in the past', 29th January 2019; Simon Samuels, 'The ECB should resist the lure of bigger banks', 31st January 2019; Robin Wigglesworth, 'Non-bank lending surge stirs painful subprime memories', 5th February 2019; Claire Jones and Stephen Morris, 'ECB to test how long banks can last without fresh funds', 7th February 2019; Laura Noonan, 'Goldman to wield axe on bond unit as peers sit tight', 8th February 2019; Megan Greene and Dwight Scott, 'Do leveraged loans pose a threat to the US economy?', 12th February 2019; Laura Noonan, 'Weak margins drag on safe banks' ambitions', 13th February 2019; Chris Flood, 'BlackRock and Vanguard pull in 57% of global fund flows', 18th February 2018; Philip Stafford, 'European customers handed clearing house access to contain Brexit fallout', 19th February 2019; Oliver Ralph, 'Insurers warned over vulnerability to risky debt after stretch for yield', 22nd February 2019; Stephen Morris and David Crow, 'Axe swings at European banks after lamentable fourth quarter', 22nd February 2019; Philip Stafford, 'EU licence boost for investors in Irish assets', 2nd March 2019; John Dizard, 'Grandma will lose in a clearing house crisis, too', 4th March 2019; Eva Szalay, 'Fears over forex trading going bump in the night', 6th March 2019; Joe Rennison, 'BIS sounds alarm on risk of corporate debt fire sale', 6th March 2019; Delphine Strauss, Philip Stafford, and Claire Jones, 'BoE and ECB launch swap line to buffer banks in event of post-Brexit turmoil', 6th March 2019; Sam Fleming, 'Global regulator starts leveraged loans scrutiny', 8th March 2019; Laura Noonan, 'Transaction work is fastest growth area for big banks', 8th March 2019; Caroline Binham, David Crow, and Patrick Jenkins, 'Lenders told to triple liquid assets as Brexit protection', 11th March 2019; Jim Brunsden and Philip Stafford, 'UK clearing houses face threat of pressure to move to EU', 14th March 2019; Joe Rennison and Sujeet Indap, 'Wall Street strives to clean up credit default swaps industry', 14th March 2019; Madison Darbyshire, 'Basel watchdog adopts tougher line after urging banks to be wary of risks', 14th March 2019; Philip Stafford, 'Vix volatility spike prompts shake-up at leading equity options clearing house', 20th March 2019; Oliver Ralph, 'Conduct replaces capital as focus', 25th March 2019; David Crow, 'Banks strain to effect a post-crisis funding fix', 25th March 2019; Siobhan Riding, 'Watchdogs probe systemic risks of passive fund growth', 1st April 2019; Andrew Whiffin, 'BoJ's dominance raises concern on distorting influence', 1st April 2019; Chris Flood, 'Bond funds head for $1tn landmark', 1st April 2019; Sam Fleming, Joe Rennison, and Robert Armstrong, 'Non-bank lenders under scrutiny after taking big share in US mortgage market', 10th April 2019; Robin Wigglesworth, 'IMF warns of "tip of the iceberg" threat over volatility', 12th April 2019; Richard Henderson, 'Landmark for exchange traded bond funds as assets crash through $1tn', 24th April 2019; Philip Stafford, 'LSE shrugs off Brexit worries to gain boost from clearing', 2nd May 2019; Attracta Mooney and Peter Smith, 'Deal of the decade: how BlackRock buying BGI changed the industry', 6th May 2019; Richard Henderson, 'US fund managers mimic Brussels rules on research', 10th May 2019; Andrea Vismara, 'Mifid 2 drags down an ecosystem along with Europe's banks', 15th May 2019; Philip Stafford, 'Futures exchanges put faith in "Flash Boys" speed bumps', 30th May 2019; Judith Evans, 'Building a real estate bubble', 19th June 2019; Philip Stafford, 'Mifid 2 rules tighten Wall Street's grip on Europe', 27th June 2019; Stephen Morris and Olaf Storbeck, 'Humbled giant struggles to silence doubters', 9th July 2019; John Dizard, 'H20 is an omen: a liquidity crisis lurks', 15th July 2019; Caroline Binham and Siobhan Riding, 'Iosco fires back at BoE in spat over fund rules', 22nd July 2019; Philip Stafford, 'Global regulators delay big bang rules by a year to stop last minute scramble', 24th July 2019; Philip Stafford, 'BGC signs trio of high-frequency trading firms to boost European equity options', 25th July 2019; Caroline Binham, 'BoE presses banks for living wills to limit bailout damage', 31st July 2019; Sheila Blair, 'Congress should stay out of new bank rules for loan losses', 5th August 2006; David Crow, 'The last man in European investment banking', 23rd August 2019; *FT* Reporters, 'Fed analyses regulation's role in sudden rates jump', 2nd October 2019.

under the programme of quantitative easing.'[133] What had been a quick fix by central banks, to prevent the global economy sliding into a world depression after the crisis, had become a permanent feature, influencing the behaviour of banks and financial markets. Accompanying this intervention at the level of quantitative easing (QE) was another involving regulatory changes. The most influential of these was the Volcker Rule in the USA, which banned the US megabanks from making short-term investments with their own money, known as proprietary trading. Added to that were the more stringent Basel rules. These had the effect of making many trading activities less profitable for the megabanks leading to their withdrawal from the business or to change the way they conducted their trading. The megabanks had turned to electronic trading platforms as these allowed them to dip in and out of positions more quickly and so operate with much leaner trading inventories and therefore keep capital requirements at a minimum. As a consequence, 'Financial markets have changed pretty dramatically since the crisis' according to Charles Himmelberg, a Goldman Sachs strategist, in 2018.[134] In 2019 Philip Stafford took a similar view noting that 'Global capital markets are changing, with more automation but also complicated investment strategies that connect different asset classes. Decision-making relies more on machines and new sources of information.' He warned that, 'To keep up, regulators also require more accurate information.'[135]

Using currency trading as an example, Olaf Storbeck and Philip Stafford pointed out in 2019 that 'The foreign exchange market is changing rapidly as the banks that have long dominated the market pare back their operations in response to tougher regulations and competitive pressures.'[136] From the perspective of the stock market, which had suffered little at the time of the crisis, the longer-term consequences of intervention were also profound. The extended period of low interest rates, and the easy availability of funding, had discouraged private companies from converting into public ones and existing ones from making new issues, while encouraging established public companies to de-list their shares and go private. As Robert Buckland, an analyst at Citibank, pointed out in 2019, 'Stock markets are not competitive places to raise capital or sell companies right now. Public equity markets are shrinking because companies can find cheaper capital elsewhere.'[137] Similarly, investors could find better returns in private equity compared to stocks and bonds. More generally, as regulators tightened capital requirements, banks had withdrawn from trading, depriving the markets of liquidity, whether for stocks, bonds, derivatives, and other financial instruments. In the pursuit of quantitative easing central banks across the world had bought up government debt depriving these markets of liquidity and exposing them to both manipulation and increased volatility. By 2018 the Bank of Japan, for example, owned around 43 per cent of outstanding sovereign bonds. The shortage of the highly-rated government debt also deprived the global money market of the collateral used to support inter-bank lending and borrowing. These changes had been led by the USA. However, as the memory of the crisis faded so US authorities changed direction as they recognized the damage that regulatory intervention was doing to the efficient

[133] Gillian Tett, 'Repo markets mystery reminds us we are flying blind', 20th September 2019.

[134] Robin Wigglesworth and Ben McLannahan, 'Liquidity outs leverage as the big worry for investors', 4th May 2018.

[135] Philip Stafford, 'LSE has to beat Bloomberg at its own game', 19th August 2019.

[136] Olaf Storbeck and Philip Stafford, 'Deutsche Börse in talks to acquire Refinitiv foreign exchange assets', 12th April 2019.

[137] Richard Henderson, 'Shrinking share listings show radical shift to private sphere', 27th June 2019.

functioning of the financial system and the international competitiveness of US banks and markets. Eric Platt and Robert Smith reported as early as 2017 that, 'Just as the European Central Bank has finalised the framework of its regulation on leveraged lending, to mirror existing US guidelines, Washington is looking for reverse gear.'[138] These guidelines had been introduced in 2013 to prevent banks from financing riskier transactions in case markets seized up, and demand for the bonds and loans they were underwriting dried up. There were now doubts about the value of these guidelines and the consequences they had. However, any retrenchment by either central banks or regulators from the policies introduced to cope with the crisis was difficult to achieve because of fears that it would destabilize the global financial system and lead to a repeat of what had happened in 2008.

The consequences of regulatory intervention had been to prevent the global financial system evolving in ways that would make it structurally more resilient, without relying on central bank support and regulatory intervention. Activity had been displaced from the megabanks, as they were regarded as the prime source of instability, but fundamental issues had not been addressed. The problem with external intervention was that it was not driven by the goal of improving the resilience and efficiency of the global financial system but in responding to the changing moods of public opinion and the policy imperatives of governments around the world. Power rested with national agencies and meeting a domestic agenda was paramount for them. As the consequences of the crisis faded so other issues rose up the agenda, and came to dictate the actions of central banks and regulators. These ranged from the necessity of responding to the crisis over the Euro within the EU or the recognition by the Chinese government that it faced an emerging financial crisis, having successfully insulated itself from the first impact of the crisis, but only at the cost of stimulating a domestic asset bubble. That agenda was also strongly influenced by public anger over a number of financial practices that were exposed, such as the selling of risky or inappropriate financial products and the manipulation of financial markets. The revelations regarding these scandals underpinned public pressure in the USA and Europe for even greater intervention in financial systems. In 2014 Patrick Jenkins reported that 'Misjudgement of human factors, the failure of technology and rogue traders have caused huge reputational damage' to the entire banking sector.[139] With an estimated $1.7tn having been invested by then by national governments to prevent financial institutions from collapsing, these popular demands could not be easily resisted by politicians. As late as 2019 Oliver Ralph observed that 'There is little sign that politicians and regulators around the world are taking their foot off the pedal when it comes to pursuing the financial services industry.'[140] The experienced banker Vikram Pandit complained in 2019 that while 'Politicians still worry about banks that are too big to fail, regulators struggle to supervise such big institutions.'[141]

Taking a reflective view of the financial sector Sarah Gordon confessed in 2019, that:

> the lesson I learnt from the financial crisis, and the years since, is that ignorance of financial affairs is widespread—and dangerous. Yes, the banks were responsible for egregious behaviour. Yes, policymakers from central bankers to regulators to finance ministers

[138] Eric Platt and Robert Smith, 'Efforts to harmonise risky-loans rules in doubt', 6th June 2017.
[139] Patrick Jenkins, 'Humbled financiers reassess their culture', 17th March 2014.
[140] Oliver Ralph, 'Conduct replaces capital as focus', 25th March 2019.
[141] Vikram Pandit, 'Outdated rules are holding back financial innovation', 19th September 2019.

> failed to address distortions in the market that, in retrospect, look glaringly obvious. But the 'ordinary' people who feel so robbed by those in charge also bear a responsibility.

There she was referring to those who 'took out a mortgage on a house with practically no equity', borrowed 'several times their monthly income on credit cards', or deposited their savings 'in a little-known bank offering incredible rates'.[142] Whereas in the aftermath of the crisis intervention had been driven by the instability it caused, later it was a product of the perception of how those in finance conducted themselves in their dealings with their customers and each other. There were a few who recommended that banks and financial markets should be allowed to evolve. One was Niki Beattie, founder of Market Structure Research, who said in 2019 that 'You have to let markets evolve and let it decide.'[143] That was a strategy that found favour among some regulators, like Brian Quintenz, a commissioner at the Commodity Futures Trading Commission (CFTC) in the USA: 'The goal of financial markets is not to protect or shelter the less informed. Market efficiencies are earned—they are created through research, investment and intellectual property'[144] However, that was not advice that found universal favour among the media and politicians. As a result the global financial system appeared no more stable ten years after the collapse of Lehman Brothers than it had been before.

There were even growing concerns that one of the stabilizing devices promoted since the crisis, namely clearing houses, had the potential of concentrating and accentuating risk rather than diffusing and deflating it. Building on the action taken in both 2009 and 2010 regulators promoted clearing houses as the solution to counterparty risk. Writing in 2019 Philip Stafford referred to clearing houses as 'pillars of global stability, standing between parties in a deal and managing the risk of contagion if one side defaults'.[145] In the aftermath of the crisis regulators had taken steps to not only become much better informed about activity in the various financial markets, so as to spot any build-up of leverage that could be potentially destabilizing, but also to reduce the risks that could create through the use of clearing houses. Derivatives, for example, had been widely blamed for exacerbating the crisis because banks often only demanded minimal collateral to backstop trades. As a result regulators demanded that more of these bilateral OTC trades passed through clearing houses. For those that could not, because of their non-standard nature, traders were required to post far more collateral, or margin, to cover losses both from fluctuating market prices and from any defaults. This increased costs for banks, which was why they were reluctant to use clearing houses. The issue was how best to achieve this objective. Clearing worked best when vast amounts of trades were pooled together, with losses and gains across the market for equities, swaps, and repo cancelling each other out. In times of market stress, a stable clearing house lessened the threat of contagion spreading the type of crisis seen after the demise of Lehman Brothers in 2008. For that reason regulators pressed for financial transactions to go through clearing houses. In 2019, Jim Brunsden and Philip Stafford observed that 'Regulators see clearing houses as a critical part of the financial infrastructure, since they act as central counterparties between sellers and buyers of shares and derivatives.'[146] However, national interest also came into play with governments reluc-

[142] Sarah Gordon, 'Making sense of the City', 9th March 2019.
[143] Philip Stafford, 'Futures exchanges put faith in "Flash Boys" speed bumps', 30th May 2019.
[144] Philip Stafford, 'Futures exchanges put faith in "Flash Boys" speed bumps', 30th May 2019.
[145] Philip Stafford, 'LSE shrugs off Brexit worries to gain boost from clearing', 2nd May 2019.
[146] Jim Brunsden and Philip Stafford, 'UK clearing houses face threat of pressure to move to EU', 14th March 2019.

tant to force all transactions through clearing houses, especially when they were located in a separate jurisdiction over which they had no control.

What did not accompany this drive by regulators to push business through clearing houses was any meaningful attempt to make such institutions more resilient. Attempts to introduce global standards for clearing houses had failed before the crisis, in 2001 and 2004. They continued to be resisted even after the crisis, foiled by a desire to promote competition and prevent the creation of all-powerful monopolies. There was also no agreement on providing clearing houses with a lender of last resort, even though regulators were driving business in their direction. Philip Stafford wrote in 2018 that 'The financial crisis made the clearing industry a priority for regulators keen to contain the threat of contagion in the derivatives market. Entities from companies to banks use derivatives to manage their exposure to interest-rate risks, and clearing houses sit between the two counterparties to a trade.'[147] He added in 2019 that 'Clearing houses stand between the counterparties to a trade and, given their role in helping to manage the wider risk if one side defaults, have grown in systemic importance since the financial crisis.'[148] However, the implications of a failure of a clearing house was ignored despite it being pointed out by John Dizard in 2018, that 'a favourite post-crisis fix, mandatory clearing of derivatives contracts, has concentrated rather than dissipated financial risk.'[149] By 2019 there was increased concern among regulators that their commitment to clearing houses may have created increased risk, because of their lack of resilience in the face of increased volatility let alone a crisis. Philip Stafford reported in 2019 that 'Global regulators are growing concerned that their push to mandate more clearing of assets in markets is creating more linkages between banks and clearing houses... such linkages could destabilise markets under certain circumstances.'[150]

Clearing houses only addressed one of the risks that had come to the fore during the crisis, namely counterparty default. There were others and they were reappearing a decade after the crisis, caused by the displacement of activity away from the megabanks and into the shadow banking sector. Writing in 2018 Gillian Tett reported that 'Non-bank investors have been taking dangerous risks, partly because super-loose monetary policy has made borrowing so cheap.'[151] John Authers noted that 'Now, risks lie in bloated asset prices, levered investments, and in pension funds that hold them. The next crisis will not be about banking.'[152] What they were picking up on were the emerging concerns being expressed by those within the global finance industry. Gregory Davis, the chief investment officer at the global fund managers, Vanguard, considered that 'Markets are jittery. Volatility is increasing.'[153] Hans Hoogervorst, chair of the International Accounting Standards Board, observed 'Markets swimming in debt and overpriced assets.'[154] Nevertheless, there was a strong reluctance among regulators to relax the rules they had put in place because of fears that it would unleash another credit bubble and they would be forced to intervene once again. In 2018 Martin Gruenberg, chair of the Federal Deposit Insurance Corporation

[147] Philip Stafford, 'Frankfurt narrows gap with London as incentive scheme boosts euro clearing', 13th June 2018.

[148] Philip Stafford, 'European customers handed clearing house access to contain Brexit fallout', 19th February 2019.

[149] John Dizard, 'Brexit could be a toy train crash for derivatives', 8th October 2018.

[150] Philip Stafford, 'Vix volatility spike prompts shake-up at leading equity options clearing house', 20th March 2019.

[151] Gillian Tett, 'When the world held its breath', 1st September 2018.

[152] John Authers, 'Time to confess that I hushed up Wall St's scariest day', 8th September 2018.

[153] Gregory Davis, 'Index funds are not to blame for market volatility', 31st October 2018.

[154] Hans Hoogervorst, 'Do not blame accounting rules for the financial crisis', 4th October 2018.

(FDIC), in the USA, held firm to the rules introduced after the crisis when he stated that, 'This simple approach has served well in addressing the excessive leverage that helped deepen the financial crisis.'[155]

However, there were signs that another credit bubble was building up, with the potential to have the same damaging consequences as the Global Financial Crisis. Though the market for residential mortgage-backed securities and asset-backed securities had not fully recovered from its pre-crisis peak, that for commercial mortgage-backed securities and collateralized debt obligations (CLOs) had. Writing in 2019 Judith Evans concluded that 'The global real estate boom is drawing to a close after a decade of cheap money that followed the financial crisis.'[156] There had been a huge influx of institutional capital into property, driven there by the low interest rates and falling bond yields caused by quantitative easing. The result, according to Sam Zell, an experienced Chicago-based property developer, was that 'There is too much capital chasing too few opportunities.'[157] Instead of banks, as before the crisis, funding had come from the shadow banking sector. As Judith Evans explained, 'Lightly-regulated and opaque debt funds have partially filled a vacuum left by the banks' post-crisis retreat from real estate lending.'[158] The expectation was that the risks involved were not at the same level as in 2007–8 because debt levels were lower, mortgage regulation tighter, and speculative building more modest. Nevertheless, real estate prices had been forced up, especially in the major cities of the world, as sovereign wealth funds, pension funds, and insurance companies chased such investments. As Josh Zegen, co-founder of the US real-estate private-equity firm, Madison Realty Capital, pointed out, 'There may be a bubble in credit, and it's not with the banks but with the debt funds...We are already seeing cracks in the system with loans not hitting their business plans.'[159] Matt Borstein, global head of commercial real estate at Deutsche Bank, was also worried as 'Loan-to-value ratios have been really disciplined but there has been an aggressiveness in loan pricing which seems to know no bounds right now.'[160]

For Gavin Jackson in 2019 it was the whole leveraged loan market that was a concern to regulators: 'Regulators across the world have flagged leveraged loans as an area of concern, pointing to declining lending standards and falling protections for investors as a possible indicator of financial risk.'[161] As the popularity of leveraged loans had grown so the quality of the assets provided as collateral had fallen, leaving lenders vulnerable if there was an economic downturn. However, reassurance was provided by the likes of Dwight Scott, the president of GSO Capital Partners, which was a division of the fund managers Blackstone: 'Fears that a liquidity mismatch as occurred in 2008 will recur in the leveraged loan market are misplaced.' Whereas in 2008 the problem arose because it was banks holding such products, and they relied on short term borrowing, by 2019 it was institutional investors that were most exposed and they financed their holdings of Collateralized Loan Obligations (CLOs) with long-term funds. The point he made was that 'Unlike banks, which often hold

[155] Joe Rennison and Philip Stafford, 'Traders find receptive ear among regulators to relax capital rules', 10th July 2018.
[156] Judith Evans, 'Building a real estate bubble', 19th June 2019.
[157] Judith Evans, 'Building a real estate bubble', 19th June 2019.
[158] Judith Evans, 'Building a real estate bubble', 19th June 2019.
[159] Judith Evans, 'Building a real estate bubble', 19th June 2019.
[160] Judith Evans, 'Building a real estate bubble', 19th June 2019.
[161] Gavin Jackson, 'Bank of England plays down surge in risky corporate loans', 24th January 2019.

loans until repaid, today's investor base actively buys and sells loans... If a loan's risk profile changes, investors can sell.'[162]

It was not only in a possible collapse of property prices that regulators identified growing risks to the global financial system after a decade of quantitative easing and regulatory intervention. Some pointed to the lack of liquidity in the assets underlying many ETFs, if investors rushed to sell and banks did not step in as purchasers. ETFs traded throughout the day but the underlying assets could be illiquid, creating a potential stock market collapse. Writing in 2019 Claire Jones and Stephen Morris observed that 'Supervisors remain concerned that a liquidity drought caused by a market shock could still lead to difficulties in some lenders.'[163] Those concerns extended beyond banks to open-ended funds that promised investors instant withdrawals of their money but had invested heavily in stocks that were little traded. One of the most vocal critics of the promises made by these was Amin Rajan, the chief executive of the consultancy, Create-Research: 'If investors want high returns, they have to accept lower liquidity. They can't have something for nothing.'[164] What he had identified was a fundamental flaw in the design of open-ended funds that promised instant repayment but held assets that lacked a market and so were difficult to sell. He wrote in 2019 that 'Liquidity is the most overlooked risk in asset allocation. It provides oxygen to markets but unlike other risks it cannot be diversified away.' As a result of the regulations designed to enhance the resilience of the global financial system banks no longer held large portfolios of assets, and so were not in a position to provide liquidity by buying when others were selling. This was dangerous because he added that, 'In this prolonged era of low rates, quantitative easing by the central banks has led investors to climb higher up the risk curve in search of yield.'[165] These conditions had fostered a belief that central banks could be relied on to provide liquidity when required. In making banks more resilient, the actions of governments, regulators, and central banks had exposed fund managers to a potential liquidity crisis.

The predicament faced by open-ended funds was becoming increasingly critical in 2019 when no less a person than Mark Carney, governor of the Bank of England, considered that they were 'built on a lie'.[166] By then both the BIS's Financial Stability Board, which Mark Carney had previously chaired, and the International Organization of Securities Commissions (Iosc), were beginning to respond to the concerns being expressed by those involved in the fund management industry. Steven Maijoor, the chairman of the European Securities and Market Authority (Esma) commented that 'The resilience of the fund sector is of growing importance, as it accounts for an increasing part of the EU's financial system. Therefore, it is crucial to ensure that the fund industry is resilient and is able to absorb economic shocks.'[167] Within the fund industry Megan Greene, the global chief economist at Manulife Asset Management, highlighted the fact that falling standards of investment had increased the probability of defaults leading to a liquidity crisis as investors attempted to sell their holdings.[168] It was becoming evident by 2019 that fund managers and insurance

[162] Megan Greene and Dwight Scott, 'Do leveraged loans pose a threat to the US economy?', 12th February 2019.

[163] Claire Jones and Stephen Morris, 'ECB to test how long banks can last without fresh funds', 7th February 2019.

[164] Jennifer Thompson, 'Liquidity risk moves centre stage', 1st July 2019.

[165] Amin Rajan, 'Illiquidity will amplify the magnitude of a bear market', 5th August 2019.

[166] Chris Giles and Owen Walker, 'BoE head urges stricter rules for funds', 27th June 2019.

[167] Chris Flood, 'Esma warns on bond fund liquidity risk', 9th September 2019.

[168] Megan Greene and Dwight Scott, 'Do leveraged loans pose a threat to the US economy?', 12th February 2019.

companies had moved into riskier assets in the search for higher yields on their investments as yields in safer categories fell in response to the aggressive easing policies being followed by the world's central banks since the crisis. This did leave them vulnerable in a downturn, because of the illiquid nature of the assets they held, though, given the depth and diversification of their holdings, few were of the opinion that the largest were in any risk of collapse. Mark Rouck, the group credit officer for insurance at the ratings agency, Fitch, judged in 2019 that 'Insurers have a very strong liquidity position overall so there is not a significant risk.' He considered a bank-type run unlikely because, 'Life insurance typically has very significant constraints and there are penalties involved if customers redeem and put their contracts back to the insurance company.'[169]

Though the risk of an insurance company collapsing appeared remote that was not the case with the more specialized funds, as a number in the industry admitted. Those who ran these funds were worried that if the climate within which they operated changed they would find themselves facing a sudden liquidity crisis. One who raised this issue in 2019 was Pascal Blanque, the chief investment officer at Amundi Asset Management:

> The main risk I see is liquidity mismatches at the fund level. That is why regulation is needed, the sooner the better and it is in the interest of the asset managers not to deny the problem. There has been some denial but it is a systemic problem. The truth is that liquidity is poorly defined as policy and has not historically been an area of focus for the buy-side. But we are already seeing a shrinkage in dollar-based liquidity and we are seeing capital controls being imposed in various forms across the world.

He added that:

> A missing element in modern portfolio theory has been liquidity. All assets are liquid at any moment—this is simply wrong. People took liquidity for granted, which has been a serious failure in how portfolios have been built. We have to expand risk factors into liquidity and shape liquidity when building a portfolio. Ten or twelve years after the crisis you still have the industry operate with the most simplistic and, to an extent, crude, measure of historical volatility. I have tried to bring liquidity as an extension of the risk concept, but there is a lot of work left to do.[170]

His judgement was backed by Yves Perrier, the chief executive of Amundi, who considered that 'Liquidity is a fundamental question when we manage investment funds.'[171] What Pascal Blanque was at pains to stress was that, due to central banks buying up and holding bonds since the crisis, and the long period of low interest rates, fund managers such as him had been forced to take greater risks to obtain yield by buying less-liquid assets 'Banks are less risky since the crisis but the risk has been shifted elsewhere in the system.'[172] Iain Stealey, a fund manager at JP Morgan Asset Management, admitted that, 'You look around the world and wonder what you can buy with yield these days. It's a very challenging

[169] Oliver Ralph, 'Insurers warned over vulnerability to risky debt after stretch for yield', 22nd February 2019.
[170] John Dizard, 'Eyes front, fund bosses, it's Carney's army now', 1st July 2019.
[171] Owen Walker and Chris Flood, 'Amundi will backstop funds in a crunch', 5th August 2019.
[172] Katie Martin, 'Funds face trade-off between liquidity and performance, warns Amundi chief', 6th August 2019.

environment.'[173] Kristina Hopper, chief global market strategist at Invesco, said the same: 'There is definitively yield scarcity in markets.'[174]

Echoing the growing chorus of those warning of a potential liquidity crisis in the fund management industry in 2019 was Chris Turner, an analyst at the private bank, Berenberg: 'Investment funds have grown significantly larger since the financial crisis but liquidity across many financial instruments has deteriorated which is a challenge for many portfolio managers.'[175] Another was Paul Myners, the experienced fund manager, currently chairman of the UK operations of the Stockholm-based Cevian Capital, Europe's biggest activist investor: 'What we've seen in the last ten years is a big movement of risk into fund management, away from banks. Fund managers run leverage and liquidity risks that are way beyond those that banks are now allowed to run.... the maturity mismatch is high.' He blamed regulators for what had taken place: 'The regulators have been very, very slow to see some of these risks. They've been very, very slow to look at the governance of funds.' His view was that regulators were 'inherently poor at anticipating the future'.[176] Edward Park, the deputy chief investment officer at the fund manager, Brooks Macdonald, pointed out in 2019, 'Open-ended collective funds which hold illiquid assets have a fundamental mismatch as their daily dealing structure doesn't match the reality of trading the underlying investments.'[177] Darius McDermott, the managing director at the fund manager, Chelsea Financial Services, drew a contrast between open-ended funds and the closed-end variety in the form of investment trusts: 'The closed-end structure is particularly suitable for specialist trusts holding assets that cannot be easily or swiftly bought and sold, such as property, private equity or very small companies. This is because managers don't have to sell holdings to release money back to investors to liquidate their investments.'[178]

These concerns about open-ended funds coming from regulators and within the industry were taken up by outside observers. Attracta Mooney reported in 2019 that 'As investors rushed into less-liquid corners of the investment universe in the hunt for yield, fears have built up of heightened structural risks.'[179] Caroline Binham and Siobhan Riding drew attention to those funds that 'let investors withdraw cash daily, yet the assets they hold can sometimes take weeks or months to realise a fair price'.[180] Chris Flood reflected that 'QE programmes and a decade of ultra-low interest rates have inflated stock markets worldwide.'[181] In the wake of the Global Financial Crisis the central bank policy of QE had stoked up liquidity while regulatory intervention had driven the megabanks away from asset markets with the objective of avoiding a repeat of the 2008 Global Financial Crisis. The expanded role played by fund managers was one consequence of this, and they responded to the QE programmes by taking greater risks when choosing the assets they purchased and held. Where this was done in a closed fund, which did not allow investors to withdraw their money, then the risk lay in the value of the holding, which could fall as well as rise. However, when the fund was of an open-ended type, which allowed holders to redeem on demand, then a liquidity risk was created especially if the assets that had been

[173] Robin Wigglesworth, 'Negative yields force investors to snap up riskier debt', 16th August 2019.
[174] Robin Wigglesworth, 'Negative yields force investors to snap up riskier debt', 16th August 2019.
[175] Owen Walker and Chris Flood, 'Amundi will backstop funds in a crunch', 5th August 2019.
[176] Owen Walker, 'Regulators have been slow to see liquidity risk', 5th August 2019.
[177] Kate Beioley, 'Woodford lifts the lid on open-ended funds', 22nd June 2019.
[178] Kate Beioley, 'Woodford lifts the lid on open-ended funds', 22nd June 2019.
[179] Attracta Mooney, 'Liquidity crunches heat up debate over capital buffers', 16th September 2019.
[180] Caroline Binham and Siobhan Riding, 'Iosco fires back at BoE in spat over fund rules', 22nd July 2019.
[181] Chris Flood, 'The $14tn debt challenge', 5th August 2019.

purchased were not easy to sell. In 2019 Chris Flood reported that 'Fund liquidity'[182] had become a high priority for regulators having been identified first in the USA and then picked up on in the EU. The preferred response among central banks and regulators was to subject funds to the same conditions applied to banks as had happened after the financial crisis. Attracta Mooney wrote in 2019 that 'In the wake of the financial crisis, regulators took a close look at the balance sheets of banks, forcing them to lift cash reserves.'[183] By 2019 it was evident that the focus could no longer be confined to banks if another liquidity crisis was to be avoided but Vikram Pandit considered in 2019 that they were not up to the task: 'We are trying to regulate a digital world with twentieth century architecture that was designed for physical assets.'[184] One key problem was that while banks could look to central banks as lenders of last resort, fund managers could not, and their liquidity risks were now of major concern. As John Dizard pointed out, 'Asset managers' portfolio liquidations are not bank runs. The industry does not have systemic oversight by bank regulators and central banks.'[185]

As a consequence of this situation attention was once again on the lack of a lender of last resort to the global money market. The only bank with the resources to fill this role was the Federal Reserve Bank of New York (NY Fed). It could supply the global money market with the US$s it required, as this was the currency in use when banks borrowed and lent between each other, even though this mainly took place in London. The problem was that the US Federal Reserve's first priority was to act as an arm of the US government in its implementation of US monetary policy. Its second priority was to safeguard the stability of the US financial system. Only after these had been attended to did it consider its international role, which was to act as lender of last resort to the repo market which was where all turned to when they needed to cover a temporary shortfall that could not be otherwise met from the internal redistribution of funds or the inter-bank market. 'Repurchase agreements are a crucial market where banks and investors borrow money in exchange for Treasuries and other high-quality collateral to cover short-term funding needs'[186] was how Joe Rennison described it in 2019. He added in a piece with Laura Noonan that it was a 'vital but unexciting'[187] means of covering short-term funding needs by exchanging US treasuries and other safe assets for money. It was through the repo market that individual banks and fund managers could access a common pool of liquidity to cover a temporary shortfall, and so minimize the level of funds that had to be kept idle in case of emergency. The NY Fed acted as lender of last resort to this market and when it was slow to respond the outcome was a liquidity crisis. In the past quantitative easing had caused an explosion in the level of reserves that banks place on deposit with the NY Fed, hitting a peak of $2.9tn in 2014. That provided them with ample reserves which they could call upon to meet their individual liquidity requirements or lend out to the wider market. Liquid reserves were highly concentrated in the megabanks. Since the financial crisis they had been obliged to meet a high-liquidity coverage ratio (LCR) by holding cash and high-quality assets such as US Treasuries, as these could be sold quickly in a crisis. In 2019 the four largest US banks, namely JP Morgan Chase, Bank of America, Citigroup, and Wells Fargo held $377bn in cash reserves, which was more than the combined total for the next twenty-one. However,

[182] Chris Flood, 'EU regulator rejects FCA's criticism', 16th September 2019.
[183] Attracta Mooney, 'Liquidity crunches heat up debate over capital buffers', 16th September 2019.
[184] Vikram Pandit, 'Outdated rules are holding back financial innovation', 19th September 2019.
[185] John Dizard, 'H20 is an omen: a liquidity crisis lurks', 15th July 2019.
[186] Joe Rennison, 'Repo pressure eases despite fears over bank lending at end of quarter', 1st October 2019.
[187] Joe Rennison and Laura Noonan, 'Week of repo turbulence rattles Wall Street traders', 21st September 2019

as the NY Fed drew back from QE these reserves shrank to $1.3tn in 2019, which was insufficient to maintain constant liquidity. Regulations required the megabanks to track intraday liquidity but this was difficult to estimate. No bank had exactly the same profile when trying to match assets and liabilities. Depending on the judgement the megabanks made they could withhold funds to preserve their own liquidity position, causing a shortfall in the market, putting pressure on the NY Fed to intervene as lender of last resort.

Any failure by the NY Fed to respond could cause a liquidity crisis. Making it difficult for the NY Fed to respond was its lack of understanding of the global money market, which now extended beyond the confines of the megabanks. As Simon Potter, a senior official at the NY Fed, observed in 2019 'Money markets have been and are now changing quickly in response to regulatory, technology and business model incentives.'[188] Most activity in the repo market took place by 9 am New York time, as that was the afternoon in London, the centre of the global money market. It was then that liquidity pressure was greatest and the NY Fed was called to act if there was any shortfall in the market. The problem was that the NY Fed was focused on domestic conditions and was insufficiently responsive to the use being made of the repo market internationally. As Gillian Tett explained in 2019 'Neither the Fed nor investors completely understand how the cogs of the modern financial machine mesh.'[189] What had happened since the Global Financial Crisis was that governments, central banks, and regulators had reacted to the problems they faced without either a co-ordinated or long-term strategy. The problems were global but the response was national despite the efforts of institutions like the Bank for International Settlement. What had been accomplished was to prevent a Global Financial Crisis becoming a global economic depression akin to that of the 1930s. What had not taken place was any attempt to restructure the global financial system in such a way that it became more resilient that it had been before. Action had been taken to remove risks from the banking system but all that had done was shift it to elsewhere in the financial system that was less able to cope if a crisis did occur. There was no mechanism to provide a lender of last resort to act when a liquidity crisis occurred especially if it did not involve one or more of the megabanks. The shadow banking sector, including the megafunds, and the clearing houses had no central bank standing behind them to intervene if they faced a liquidity crisis. Even the megabanks were left dependent upon the NY Fed which took a very narrow and nationalistic approach to its responsibilities and was not fully aware of the position it had come to occupy.[190]

[188] Gillian Tett, 'Repo markets mystery reminds us we are flying blind', 20th September 2019.

[189] Gillian Tett, 'Repo markets mystery reminds us we are flying blind', 20th September 2019.

[190] Eric Platt and Robert Smith, 'Efforts to harmonise risky-loans rules in doubt', 6th June 2017; Robin Wigglesworth and Ben McLannahan, 'Liquidity outs leverage as the big worry for investors', 4th May 2018; Sarah Gordon, 'Making sense of the City', 9th March 2019; Oliver Ralph, 'Conduct replaces capital as focus', 25th March 2019; Gabriel Wildau, 'China struggling to quit debt addiction', 25th March 2019; Hudson Lockett and Leo Lewis, 'Japanese watchdog calls for Citigroup to be fined for spoofing bond orders', 27th March 2019; Olaf Storbeck and Philip Stafford, 'Deutsche Börse in talks to acquire Refinitiv foreign exchange assets', 12th April 2019; Philip Stafford, 'Futures exchanges put faith in "Flash Boys" speed bumps', 30th May 2019; Judith Evans, 'Building a real estate bubble', 19th June 2019; Kate Beioley, 'Woodford lifts the lid on open-ended funds', 22nd June 2019; Chris Giles and Owen Walker, 'BoE head urges stricter rules for funds', 27th June 2019; Richard Henderson, 'Shrinking share listings show radical shift to private sphere', 27th June 2019; Jennifer Thompson, 'Liquidity risk moves centre stage', 1st July 2019; Tommy Stubbington, 'Investor alarm sounded over amazing disappearing Bunds', 12th July 2019; John Dizard, 'H20 is an omen: a liquidity crisis lurks', 15th July 2019; Caroline Binham and Siobhan Riding, 'Iosco fires back at BoE in spat over fund rules', 22nd July 2019; Philip Stafford, 'BGC signs trio of high-frequency trading firms to boost European equity options', 25th July 2019; Caroline Binham, 'BoE presses banks for living wills to limit bailout damage', 31st July 2019; Owen Walker and Chris Flood, 'Amundi will backstop funds in a crunch', 5th August 2019; Owen Walker, 'Regulators have been slow to see liquidity risk', 5th August 2019; Chris Flood, 'The $14tn debt challenge', 5th August 2019; Amin Rajan, 'Illiquidity will amplify the magnitude of a bear market', 5th August 2019; Katie Martin, 'Funds face trade-off between liquidity and performance,

Conclusion

The Global Financial Crisis of 2008 was a major event in world history. What it represented was a stage on the way the global financial system was refashioning itself as it moved from an era of control and compartmentalization to freedom and fusion. That stage appeared to have been achieved prior to the crisis but what had been left undone was the need to build in the degree of resilience required to withstand the shocks that every market-based financial system was exposed to periodically. Many believed that stage had been reached only to be proved wrong in 2008. As a result they blamed the Global Financial Crisis on the trends that had begun with the unravelling of the era of control and compartmentalization that had begun in the 1970s. However, many of those trends that contributed to instability had a much longer ancestry, especially in the USA, where they can be traced to the actions of government in both the mid nineteenth century and, again, in the 1930s. Conversely, there were more recent trends that did contribute to stability such as the development of megabanks, the invention of financial derivatives and the growth of markets that were both deep and broad. The problem was the inability to distinguish between those trends contributing to instability and those making for instability at a time when the Global Financial Crisis seemed to overwhelm the whole system. However, to attribute the Crisis to negative trends outweighing positive ones fails to accept that what took place extended over a two-year period. During the years 2007 and 2008 there was ample opportunity for intervention to minimize what was taking place and then mitigate its consequences. Some actions were taken but signals were ignored and opportunities missed by both central banks and regulators. What took place in 2008 was not the inevitable product of decisions taken earlier in the 1970s, 1980s, or 1990s. Instead, it was decisions taken in 2007 and 2008 that made a critical contribution to what took place becoming a financial crisis of global importance.

A similar verdict can be passed on the response to the crisis. Important as that response was in averting a world economic depression, where it failed was allowing the global financial system to evolve in ways that combined the dynamism and flexibility that had emerged from the 1970s onwards with the resilience it so lacked when faced with a major crisis. Instead, central bank and regulatory intervention undermined the process of evolutionary change and distorted both the world of banking and that of global financial markets. Quantitative easing injected vast amounts of liquidity into the global financial system as it was used not only to prevent a world economic collapse but to massage every fluctuation in

warns Amundi chief', 6th August 2019; Mohamed El-Erian, 'Relying on liquidity runs risk of leaving investors in hot water', 6th August 2019; Robin Wigglesworth, 'Negative yields force investors to snap up riskier debt', 16th August 2019; Philip Stafford, 'LSE has to beat Bloomberg at its own game', 19th August 2019; Robert Armstrong, 'Warnings sounded over watered-down Volcker', 23rd August 2019; Joe Rennison and Philip Stafford, 'Rise of MarketAxess mirrors demise of traders on Wall Street', 30th August 2019; Chris Flood, 'Esma warns on bond fund liquidity risk', 9th September 2019; Siobhan Riding, 'Luxembourg watchdog eyes tougher liquidity rule', 9th September 2019; Attracta Mooney, 'Liquidity crunches heat up debate over capital buffers', 16th September 2019; Chris Flood, 'EU regulator rejects FCA's criticism', 16th September 2019; Laurence Fletcher, 'Tumbling yields see debt securitisation hit pre-crisis levels', 17th September 2019; Philip Stafford and Eva Szalay, 'London pulls away from New York in forex and swaps as it shrugs off Brexit', 17th September 2019; Joe Rennison and Brendan Greeley, 'Soaring repo rate puts spotlight on Fed policy', 19th September 2019; Joe Rennison and Brendan Greeley, 'Soaring repo rate puts spotlight on Fed policy', 19th September 2019; Vikram Pandit, 'Outdated rules are holding back financial innovation', 19th September 2019; Gillian Tett, 'Repo markets mystery reminds us we are flying blind', 20th September 2019; Joe Rennison and Laura Noonan, 'Week of repo turbulence rattles Wall Street traders', 21st September 2019; Joe Rennison and Brendan Greeley, 'New York Fed defends response to turmoil', 25th September 2019; John Dizard, 'Fed standing repo facility comes into view', 30th September 2019; Joe Rennison, 'Repo pressure eases despite fears over bank lending at end of quarter', 1st October 2019; *FT* Reporters, 'Fed analyses regulation's role in sudden rates jump', 2nd October 2019.

economic activity. It raised the spectre of moral hazard as it encouraged the expectation that injections of liquidity would always take place, so covering up the consequences of highly-risky investment decisions. Another product of intervention was the displacement of financial activity away from the megabanks, that were highly resilient because of their diversified operations, into a shadow banking sector that was less robust. There was also an even greater concentration of risk in the global financial system because of the use of clearing houses. One dilemma that was never addressed was how to balance the stability and resilience of the financial system so as to prevent another crisis with sufficient competition to keep markets liquid and functioning smoothly. All could agree that greater co-operation was required but not the direction and pace that should take. Another dilemma that was never addressed was the role of lender of last resort to the global financial system, covering not only megabanks but also all systemically-important institutions including megafunds and clearing houses. With the continuing dominance of the US$ the only candidate for that role was the NY Fed but the US government was reluctant to place it in this position while others were unwilling to cede the loss of national authority involved. As a consequence, the global financial system continued to lack the resilience it required making the likelihood of another financial crisis greater and greater as time passed.

15

Banks and Brokers, 2007–20

Introduction

For banking the Global Financial Crisis of 2008 appeared to mark a major change in direction. Before the crisis a small number of banks had established themselves at the centre of the world's financial system. These banks transcended national boundaries and time zones as they extended their operations around the globe. Located in all the leading financial centres, but with London and New York playing a key role, these banks managed global empires through an ever-expanding international network that was never at rest. These banks also spread themselves over a growing diversity of activities that destroyed the compartmentalized structures of the past. They were neither commercial banks, savings banks, investment banks nor brokers, dealers, traders or asset managers but universal banks because they carried out all these functions to a lesser or greater degree. They engaged in both short-term borrowing and long-term infrastructure investment and the trading in stocks, bonds, bills, obligations, options, futures and swaps. These banks blossomed under the originate-and-distribute model, as they made and repackaged loans before selling them on so as to resupply themselves with new funds, repeating the process time after time. Such was their size, scale and spread, and the structure of the business they conducted, that these banks were regarded as too big to fail not only by those who worked for them, used them and traded with them but also by the regulators responsible for supervising financial systems and the central banks tasked with preserving financial and monetary stability.

The existence of these megabanks was a living symbol that the scourge of liquidity and solvency crises had been eradicated, at least from the financial systems of the developed economies. If evidence was required to prove that this was now the case then the ease with which these banks had coped with speculative dot.com boom and bust in 2000–1 provided it. Confidence in these banks was then enhanced rather than diminished by the mini-crisis of 2007, as they appeared to possess the resilience required to withstand its consequences. It was for that reason that the financial crisis of 2008 was such a shock as it involved the collapse of one of these megabanks, Lehman Brothers, along with government intervention across the world to prevent others sharing its fate. With the illusion shattered that these megabanks were unsinkable, attention turned to what could be done to reduce the risks they posed to financial stability because of their size and connections. Portrayed as the new robber barons there were strident calls for these megabanks to be broken up or, at least, reduced in size and their power curbed. They were held responsible for the Global Financial Crisis and so it was they that were expected to pay the ultimate penalty. Accompanied by a reaction against globalization, which had provided the stage upon which they could flourish, and universality, as that had exposed them to high risk activities, the days of the megabanks acting as masters of the universe appeared over in the wake of the Global Financial Crisis.

With the failure of one of these megabanks, Lehman Brothers, being a key feature of the Global Financial Crisis the conclusion drawn by many at the time, and subsequently, was

Banks, Exchanges, and Regulators: Global Financial Markets from the 1970s. Ranald Michie, Oxford University Press (2021).

DOI: 10.1093/oso/9780199553730.003.0015

that they posed too great risk and that intervention was required. As Patrick Jenkins, Brooke Masters, and Tom Braithwaite reflected in 2011:

> With hindsight, it is clear the structure of the (banking) sector was an accident waiting to happen. Institutions had grown distorted in the pursuit of bumper profits. They held little equity capital to protect themselves—and what they did have was in many cases amplified by as much as fifty times with debt instruments. Vast profits were made from borrowing cheaply, often short-term. And assuming that the risks inherent in products from domestic mortgages to complex derivatives were negligible.[1]

To many economists, such as Sir John Vickers, these megabanks were engaged in 'a lot of activities which I believe were completely unproductive'.[2] In the light of the risks exposed during the Global Financial Crisis, and with the support of eminent economists, the reluctance of governments to intervene in the way the megabanks operated was removed, with many recommending a return to the compartmentalization of banking as practised in the USA under the Glass–Steagall Act.[3] However, the conditions that had underpinned the Glass–Steagall Act no longer existed, which was why it had been repealed in the end. Nevertheless, that did not mean that there was not a desire to reverse many of the developments in global banking that had taken place in the decades prior to the crisis, especially the role played by the megabanks. While recognizing that vital role in the functioning of the global financial system, the legacy of the Global Financial Crisis was a desire to make them more resilient in the face of periodic crises. It was this desire that underpinned the intervention that followed the crisis and the legislation it produced. As Philip Stafford observed in 2018, 'Banks now cannot leverage their own balance sheets and hold inventory and positions in the market on behalf of clients quite as aggressively as they once did.'[4] Nevertheless, a group of megabanks remained systemically important causing continuing concerns to both central banks and regulators[5]

Pre-Crisis 2007

Prior to the Global Financial Crisis banks were subjected to growing challenges as savers looked beyond them as a home for spare funds and businesses relied less on bank loans for finance. Both savers and borrowers turned to financial markets instead. Those banks that best met these challenges were those that positioned themselves to attract savers with specialist products, cater to the needs of business borrowers by arranging issues of stocks and bonds, and employed their own capital for trading purposes rather than act only on behalf of clients. The effect was to blur the distinction between the different types of banks as the

1 Patrick Jenkins, Brooke Masters, and Tom Braithwaite, 'Hunt for a common front', 8th September 2011.

2 Martin Arnold, 'How US banks took over the financial world', 17th September 2018.

3 Peer Steinbruck, 'A tax on trading to share the costs of the crisis', 25th September 2009; Howard Davies, 'We need urgently to rationalise the rules on capital', 25th September 2009; Jeff Merkley, 'Avoid past mistakes and preserve key bank safety law', 26th June 2018; Martin Arnold, 'How US banks took over the financial world', 17th September 2018.

4 Philip Stafford, 'Fresh risks emerge from the depth', 1st October 2018.

5 Ian Fleming, Philip Stafford and Jim Brunsden, 'Iran sanctions pose dilemma for Swift', 18th May 2018; Emiko Terazono, 'Banks and energy traders back blockchain launches', 20th September 2018; Philip Stafford, 'Fresh risks emerge from the depth', 1st October 2018; Don Weinland, 'Banks race to launch blockchain trade platforms', 9th November 2018.

lend-and-hold model gave way to the originate-and-distribute one. Banks that collected deposits from savers were under pressure because of the low rate of interest they paid. They could only raise that rate by charging borrowers more, but that was difficult because of competition between banks. The result was to squeeze the margin between the rates banks paid for the money they borrowed and that which they received on loans. In response to the low rates paid on deposits savers turned to alternative products delivering higher yields, such as money-market funds or bonds paying a fixed rate of return. Meanwhile borrowers also turned to bonds as a means of obtaining funds more cheaply than through a bank loan. In response to the changing demands of their customers banks had little alternative but to alter the way they operated if they wished to stay in business. This change was most marked in the USA where the Glass–Steagall Act had long given a legal base to the compartmentalization of banking and so helped preserve it in the face of the forces undermining it. That act was finally abolished in 1999, acknowledging the gradual erosion that had been taking place as commercial banks moved into the securities market and investment banks adopted money-market funds. Internationally, there emerged a group of megabanks. Their international spread of branches and offices made them global while their wide range of activities made them universal. These included a strong showing from the USA including Bank of America, Bear Stearns, Citigroup, Goldman Sachs, Lehman Brothers, Merrill Lynch, JP Morgan Chase, and Morgan Stanley. They did not have the field to themselves as they faced competition from Europe in the form of ABN Amro, Barclays, BNP Paribas, Credit Suisse, Deutsche Bank, HSBC, RBS, Société Generale, and UBS while Nomura from Japan was developing a global footprint.

Universal banking had long existed on a national basis, most notably in countries such as Germany and Switzerland, and to a lesser degree in France and Italy, but was being rapidly adopted around the world prior to the Global Financial Crisis. The repeal of the Glass–Steagall Act in the USA was followed by a partial relaxation of a similar law in Japan, which had long underpinned compartmentalization, and similar moves in countries such as South Korea. Where there was no legal division between different types of banking, but more a separation based on custom and practice, the process was more evolutionary, as in the UK. By 2007 Peter Thal Larsen considered that 'the UK's biggest banks are now increasingly dependent on their investment banking arms for profits—and growth'.[6] Running counter to the growing adoption of universal banking was the development of more specialized financial institutions, such as hedge funds. By 2007 hedge funds controlled 1.5 per cent of global assets and accounted for over half of US bond trading and 40 per cent of equity trading. What these counter trends reflected was the continuous flux that existed in financial markets and the complex relationships that it generated. Hedge funds and banks both competed for business and relied on each other. The liquidity injected into the financial system by hedge funds helped banks reduce the risks they took in holding stocks and bonds by providing them with a ready market. Conversely, hedge funds relied on banks to execute sales and purchases, and to supply them with the short-term funds and the borrowed securities they used to maintain the positions they took in the market. What were being squeezed in the years before the Global Financial Crisis were those banks that stuck to the traditional lend-and-hold model of business and confined their activities to a single country. Pressure from all sides, including the regulators, was forcing them to change the business that they did and the way it was conducted.

[6] Peter Thal Larsen, 'Investment banking has fresh attraction', 14th March 2007.

What was most marked in banking before the crisis was the increasing replacement of the lend-and-hold model by the originate-and-distribute one. In the lend-and-hold model banks made loans which were retained until maturity, relying on the stability of the depositor base to avoid the possibility of a liquidity crisis. In the originate-and-distribute model banks continued to make loans but these were subsequently repackaged as bonds and sold to investors, which simultaneously released new funds for lending and removed the risk of a liquidity crisis. The use of the originate-and-distribute model increased the use made of the inter-bank money market as a way of raising funds, as the expectation was that money borrowed there would be easily repaid when the loans were securitized and sold on. Borrowing in the inter-bank market also created the opportunity for specialist institutions like hedge funds and money-market funds to finance holdings of bills and bonds, as these could be quickly sold if the borrowed funds had to be repaid. The inter-bank market was where banks collectively either employed their liquid reserves or tapped when covering a temporary shortage. Money could be obtained at very low interest rates in the inter-bank market on the understanding that it would be repaid on demand or at the end of the short period for which it was lent. This made the inter-bank market unsuitable for the finance of long-term loans, though that attraction was always there because these paid a higher rate of interest compared to the cost at which short-term money could be borrowed.

However, with the switch to the originate-and-distribute model, banks expected to repackage and sell on long-term loans allowing them to repay the money borrowed in the inter-bank market. Short-term money could also be used to hold these repackaged loans as they were now in a form that made them easily saleable if the bank was required to repay the money it had borrowed to finance their purchase. There were two weaknesses in such operations. The first weakness was that it relied upon the continuing availability of short-term money in the inter-bank market, though its huge depth and spread, and the presence of central banks as lenders of last resort, provided the reassurance that these conditions would always prevail. The second weakness was that it relied upon the ability to sell the repackaged loans throughout their life, not only when created but also subsequently as holders using borrowed funds relied on their liquidity. This required the existence of both a primary and a secondary market. In both, reassurance was provided by those banks that repackaged and sold loans, as they also guaranteed redemption on maturity and provided the market in which they were subsequently bought and sold. Such was the size and scale of the megabanks that they were able to operate their own internal markets, as well as trading with each other to match sales and purchases either directly or through interdealer brokers. In that way they could provide investors with liquid markets without the need to have stocks and bonds listed on regulated exchanges. The megabanks could be relied on to either arrange sales and purchases or use their own capital and portfolio holdings to act as counterparties.

Such was the confidence in these megabanks that when problems in the originate-and-distribute model began to appear early in 2007 they were considered immune. In early 2007 one of the largest of the megabanks, HSBC, was forced to write down losses on US subprime loans in the face of late payments and defaults, but there were no doubts about either its liquidity or solvency. In March 2007 Michael Mackenzie and Saskia Scholtes cautioned that 'The danger for Wall Street is banks will be left holding billions of dollars of subprime mortgage loans they hoped to sell to investors.'[7] However, they did not suggest

[7] Michael Mackenzie and Saskia Scholtes, 'Subprime securitisation threat', 7th March 2007.

that this would lead to the collapse on any of them. In 2008 Neil McLeish, an analyst at Morgan Stanley, expressed the common view that, 'Prior to Lehman, there was an almost unshakable faith that the senior creditors and counterparties of large, systemically-important financial institutions would not face the risk of outright default.'[8] Such was this 'unshakable faith' that banks like Merrill Lynch, Lehman Brothers, and Morgan Stanley, as well as their international competitors such as Credit Suisse, Deutsche Bank, and Barclays, took the opportunity to buy up the loan books of the specialist lenders in trouble, confident that they could be repackaged and sold on at a profit. In doing so they received official approval as regulators favoured banks holding bonds as assets rather than loans, because it was presumed that the former were more liquid than the latter. The result was an increase in the leverage ratios of these banks as they continued to invest short-term funds in long-term bonds confident in the continuing supply of the former and the continuing liquidity of the latter.[9]

Pre-Crisis 2008

The world in which the megabanks had thrived changed in 2008. In May, after the near collapse of Bear Stearns, Jim Reid, a credit strategist at Deutsche Bank, observed that, 'In the new financial climate, banks are slowly changing their mode of operations. They are moving from a world where they would be happy to lend to anybody to one where they are much more careful.'[10] By then the megabanks faced tightening access to short-term money in the inter-bank market, difficulties in raising additional capital, increasing redemptions of funds as loans they had taken out matured, and the growing inability to sell stocks and bonds, including the products of repackaged loans. These raised concern over their liquidity, which led to questions of solvency once doubts were raised over the ability of those who

[8] Aline van Duyn, Deborah Brewster, and Gillian Tett, 'The Lehman Legacy', 13th October 2008.

[9] David Oakley and Gillian Tett, 'European bond market puts US in the shade', 15th January 2007; Joanna Chung and Gillian Tett, 'Trading suspension raises eyebrows', 24th January 2007; Geoff Dyer, 'Concerns at market bubble float over China', 31st January 2007; Gillian Tett and Anuj Gangahar, 'Deals on dark pools set to surge', 31st January 2007; Richard Beales and David Wighton, 'Concerns mount over risky lending in US market', 14th February 2007; Jane Croft, 'Lucrative market may yet prove house of cards', 20th February 2007; Anuj Gangahar, 'Banks back move for block trading', 1st March 2007; David Oakley, 'European repo trading grows Euro 500bn in year', 2nd March 2007; Paul J. Davies, 'The dangers inherent in imprudent lending', 5th March 2007; Brian Bollen, 'They created the game—so they invent the rules', 5th March 2007; Michael Mackenzie and Saskia Scholtes, 'Subprime securitisation threat', 7th March 2007; Michiyo Nakamoto, 'Bid reflects a shifting climate', 7th March 2007; Richard Beales and Gillian Tett, 'Hedge funds rival banks for share of US Treasury market', 9th March 2007; Peter Thal Larsen, 'Investment banking has fresh attraction', 14th March 2007; Sundeep Tucker, 'Merrill evolves a strategy for survival in the Asian climate', 15th March 2007; Ben White, 'Buoyant Bear Stearns shrugs off subprime woes', 16th March 2007; Peter Thal Larsen, 'Global, universal, unmanageable? Why many are wary of bank mega-mergers', 29th March 2007; David Oakley and Saskia Scholtes, 'Flurry of activity in banks for CDSs', 3rd April 2007; James Mackintosh, 'Investors still pile in', 27th April 2007; Michiyo Nakamoto, 'Citigroup deal could broker new shake-up', 30th April 2007; Ben White, 'London's rise concentrates minds in US', 26th May 2007; Peter Thal Larsen, 'Number behind the M&A boom', 30th May 2007; Anna Fifield, 'Seoul looks to echo London big bang', 26th June 2007; Song Jung-a, 'Brokerage sector looks set for consolidation', 26th June 2007; Gillian Tett and Paul J. Davies, 'What's the damage', 5th November 2007; Peter Thal Larsen and Francesco Guerrera, 'Investment banks' future questioned', 16th September 2008; Peter Thal Larsen and Greg Farrell, 'Landscape shifts for investment banks', 23rd September 2008; Javier Blas, 'Commodities players bid to close the gap on big two', 28th November 2008; Aline van Duyn, Deborah Brewster and Gillian Tett, 'The Lehman Legacy', 13th October 2008; Gillian Tett and Aline van Duyn, 'Under restraint', 7th July 2009; Anousha Sakoui and Brooke Masters, 'UK businesses' finance options undergo rethink', 21st January 2010.

[10] David Oakley, 'Banks' reluctance to part with cash keeps the heat on Libor', 23rd May 2008.

had borrowed funds to repay on maturity. Confidence finally evaporated with the collapse of Lehman Brothers, as Michael Mackenzie explained at the time:

> Ever since fragile money markets started freezing up in the middle of September, the crisis in the global financial system has deepened.... Since the bankruptcy of Lehman Brothers, money-market funds and other lenders have ceased providing funds to a banking system they believe is in deep trouble. In turn that has impaired the commercial paper market in the US and Europe, where companies rely on short-term funds, threatening the broader economy. It has also rippled up the chain and effectively stalled trading across global fixed-income markets.[11]

William O'Donnell, a strategist at UBS, was more succinct: 'People can't fund, can't leverage and can't trade.'[12] It was problems such as these that generated the growing belief that the concept of the megabank was dead. In September 2008 John Gapper made the comment that, 'The full-service investment bank, buying and selling shares and bonds for customers as well as advising companies and trading with its own capital, is doomed. In order to generate the revenues needed to match larger institutions, banks such as Lehman scurried into risk-taking that eventually sunk them.'[13] Before the crisis there was widespread confidence in megabanks because of the supposed resilience generated from the diversity of operations and global spread. With the crisis this diversity and spread was seen to expose these megabanks to risks of sufficient magnitude to bring them down. Megabanks were regarded not only as too big to fail, having forced governments to bail them out in a crisis, but also too big to manage, as the revelations emerged about the misbehaviour of staff motivated solely by the large bonuses they could expect from success and the absence of any penalty attached to losses. The collective pay-out of banker's bonuses in New York had reached $33.2bn in 2007.[14]

Post Crisis, 2009–11

The global financial crisis shattered confidence in both the megabanks and in the originate-and-distribute model. Rather than contribute to a shrinking and sharing of risk it had magnified and spread it. By selling on packaged loans banks had been able to increase their lending from the money they received, and by continuously repeating the process any constraint on their ability to lend was removed. The result was a credit bubble, drawing in ever more borrowers with poor repayment histories or more speculative business propositions as the risk of a default was, ultimately, to be borne by others. The lend-and-hold model

[11] Michael Mackenzie, 'Money markets hope for autumn thaw', 1st September 2008.

[12] Michael Mackenzie, 'Money markets hope for autumn thaw', 1st September 2008.

[13] John Gapper, 'The last gasp of the broker-dealer', 16th September 2008.

[14] David Oakley, 'Banks' reluctance to part with cash keeps the heat on Libor', 23rd May 2008; Ben White, 'Lehman shares slide on fears over results', 20th August 2008; Michael Mackenzie, 'Money markets hope for autumn thaw', 1st September 2008; Anousha Sakoui, 'More UK companies turn to asset-based borrowing', 8th September 2008; John Gapper, 'The last gasp of the broker-dealer', 16th September 2008; Peter Thal Larsen and Francesco Guerrera, 'Investment banks' future questioned', 16th September 2008; Aline van Duyn, Deborah Brewster, and Gillian Tett, 'The Lehman Legacy', 13th October 2008; James Mackintosh and Jennifer Hughes, 'New York steals UK hedge funds business', 17th October 2008; Nicole Bullock, 'Credit easing but cost of debt remains expensive', 21st October 2008; Hal Weitzman, 'Hunt is stepped up for the rogue traders', 21st October 2008; Brooke Masters, Lina Saigol, and Greg Farrell, 'Closing door: bankers' bonuses', 30th October 2008; Peter Thal Larsen, 'Withdrawal unavailable', 6th December 2008.

meant a long-term relationship between the bank and those to whom it made loans as these were held until maturity. In contrast, the originate-and-distribute model was a transaction-based one as the bank passed on the loan to another once it had been repackaged. One immediate effect of the crisis was thus to kill the securitization process and force banks back to the lend-and-hold model, which restricted their ability to lend. There was also a reaction against the megabanks because, rather than their business model delivering resilience it exposed them to a multitude of risks, whether coming from particular countries or activities. Once the implications of the Lehman Brothers collapse were recognized, governments and central banks were forced to intervene to prevent further failures, at enormous cost to taxpayers. Under these circumstances there were calls for the megabanks to be broken up or, at least, subjected to tight control over what they were allowed to do, the amount of capital they had to hold and the degree of leverage they could apply when making loans using the funds supplied by depositors. At the time it appeared that a complete reversal of pre-crisis banking trends was going to take place. Some of these banks had assets in excess of $2tn and controlled over 1000 subsidiaries. This was beyond the capacity of any single national regulator to supervise or to support in the event of failure, certainly outside the USA.[15]

Even without any government intervention the crisis produced a reversal in the importance of banking within the financial system as they cut back lending in order to protect their position. Between 2000 and 2008 bank loans as a share of global GDP had doubled to 20 per cent. That was then followed by a sharp contraction after the crisis. Though the Global Financial Crisis had peaked in 2008 bank lending long remained subdued, whether to governments, companies, individuals, and to each other. The crisis left banks in a fragile state with any adverse circumstances leading to a tightening of credit as they cut back on lending because they could not obtain the funds from depositors, the capital market, or other banks. After 2007 market uncertainty was generally met with a swift withdrawal of short-term funding which, in turn, made default more likely. Banks hoarded cash in case another liquidity crisis occurred. There was also a need for increased capital and reserves to meet such an eventuality. The financial crisis made banks more risk averse and so led them to cut back on funding, especially to small- and medium-sized enterprises as they were the most likely to default on loans. In addition, the actions of regulators put pressure on banks to rebuild capital and reserves and to take fewer risks, which led them to reduce lending. In response to complaints from borrowers, governments did put pressure on banks to increase their lending, placing them in an impossible dilemma according to Sharlene Goff in 2012: 'Regulators want them to hold larger capital buffers and remove risk loans from their balance sheets but at the same time they are under pressure from the government to increase lending to SMEs.'[16] Faced with a shortage of lending from banks borrowers switched to alternative means as a way of raising finance. Whereas in 2008 debt securities made up 48 per cent of international credit by 2018 the figure was 57 per cent.

Despite the chorus of calls during and after the crisis, for action to be taken to break up the megabanks and curtail their risky activities, there were those who cautioned against any precipitate action. In January 2009 Peter Thal Larsen, an informed observer of trends in banking, declared that it was 'Too early to declare death of universal banking.'[17] He had available to him the example of the five banks that dominated Canadian banking and had

[15] Martin Arnold, 'Carney's too big to fail buffer represents clear progress despite doubt', 9th December 2014.
[16] Sharlene Goff, 'Policymakers recognise SMEs need more funding options', 16th April 2012.
[17] Peter Thal Larsen, 'Too early to declare death of "universal banking"', 15th January 2009.

proved resilient in the crisis, even though they had embraced the universal model. Rather than a flawed model of banking it was increasingly recognized that the origins of the crisis lay with a general expansion of long-term lending financed by short-term borrowing with inadequate levels of capital and reserves. This degree of risk-taking was not confined to the megabanks but had been adopted by all manner of financial institutions. All got drawn into the repackaging of loans and their resale as bonds whether the proceeds were used to finance the mortgages taken out by eager homebuyers or the highly-leveraged buy-outs and take-over bids pursued by corporate raiders. Neither of these actions was unique to the megabanks but were taken up by a wide variety of financial institutions including, for example, mutually-owned building societies in the UK. In 2010 Patrick Jenkins observed that 'In Britain, theoretically safe, simple building societies from Derbyshire to Dunfermline have collapsed after straying into racy lending and investments.'[18] Those banks, of whatever type or size, that had continued to rely on retail deposits to finance loans and maintained adequate reserves to meet contingencies, largely weathered the financial crisis without the need for government support. They included a number of megabanks but all suffered collective reputational damage. That undermined their status as trusted counterparties able to borrow unlimited quantities in the global money markets and use these funds to conduct a massive programme of lending, repackaging of loans, and sale of bonds.

As the various practices that had underpinned the pre-crisis credit boom were exposed the level of trust in banks of all kinds was slow to recover. There remained the possibility that not only would loans to them not be repaid while the collateral they provided was of unknown value. Deprived of easy access to the global money market and unable to securitize and resell loans the megabanks were deprived of the tools that had provided them with such a competitive advantage before the crisis. When confidence did slowly return, permitting a revival of both the money market and securitization, the ability of the megabanks to resume their activities remained constrained. The principal reason for this situation was the actions taken by regulators determined to prevent any repeat of what had taken place during the crisis. This intervention by regulators was widely supported around the world. There was an underlying public animosity towards banks that generated support for policies designed to curb their power, even in countries that had escaped the crisis. Canadian banks, for example, had proved to be both resilient and well managed but this did not mean that they were well regarded by the public. Writing in 2009 Bernard Simon observed that 'Canadians have long had a love–hate relationship with the banks, valuing their stability but complaining incessantly about high fees, surly service and towering profits.'[19] What the crisis did was give power to the numerous and perennial critics of banking and so provide popular support for draconian measures to prevent any repeat of what had taken place.[20] The megabanks were the most visible points of attack.

[18] Patrick Jenkins, 'Mutuals seek means to adapt and survive', 6th September 2010.

[19] Bernard Simon, 'Making capital from strong financial base', 13th October 2009.

[20] Peter Thal Larsen, 'Too early to declare death of "universal banking"', 15th January 2009; Peter Thal Larsen, 'Reviving flow of credit will take greater intervention', 17th January 2009; Christopher Mason and Bernard Simon, 'Canada bank prove envy of the world', 20th February 2009; John Plender, 'Homeward Bound', 30th April 2009; Hal Weitzman and Jeremy Grant, 'Futures brokers fear new capital rules', 6th July 2009; Gillian Tett and Aline van Duyn, 'Under restraint', 7th July 2009; David Oakley, 'Lenders are slow to regain lost confidence', 10th September 2009; Michael Mackenzie, 'Run on banks left repo sector highly-exposed', 11th September 2009; David Oakley, 'Europe's ravaged landscape begins to stabilise', 11th September 2009; Patrick Jenkins, 'Investment banks enjoy companies' bond boom', 14th September 2009; Jennifer Hughes, 'Bankers seek to detoxify the alphabet soup', 13th October 2009; Bernard Simon, 'Making capital from strong financial base', 13th October 2009; Daniel Thomas, 'Vacant Possessions', 7th December 2009; Norma Cohen, 'Bank lists obstacles on path to stability', 18th December 2009; Jennifer Hughes, 'Doubt for safety of bundling up loans', 18th December 2009; Nicole Bullock,

Even without the intervention of regulators megabanks faced a check to their business model due to the Global Financial Crisis. Those running these banks were now much more aware of the risks they were taking while their customers were also conscious of how dependent they were on a single institution and so took steps to diversify. The crisis led the megabanks to reduce the leverage they applied to their capital and assets by lending money and securities to their clients on a temporary basis. Funds kept in reserve had been lent to clients secure in the knowledge they would be immediately repaid when required, so preserving liquidity. Similarly, securities being kept as the next line of reserve were also lent out temporarily, secure in the knowledge that they would also be quickly replaced when called for, again preserving liquidity. All that changed with the crisis. After the collapse of Lehman Brothers lenders reduced the amount they were willing to lend and demanded more and better collateral as security for the loans that they made. That situation then endured for years afterwards such was the magnitude of the crisis, and the fragile state in which many banks were left. Continuing fears over the strength of the economic recovery, government defaults, corporate failures, and further bank collapses all combined to prevent megabanks pursuing the aggressive lending policies that had characterized the pre-crisis years. Instead, they conserved liquidity and preferred to deposit money with central banks rather than lend it to customers or each other. Under these circumstances central banks became a major source of liquidity as they injected money into the system in an attempt to prevent a renewed bout of bank failures.[21]

However, increasingly it was not the legacy of the crisis that stopped megabanks reviving pre-crisis practices. More pervasive and prolonged were the new regulations, such as those under the Basel 3 rules, which they were subjected to. These were designed to make banks more resilient and prevent a repeat of the financial crisis. These new rules prioritized holdings of high-quality capital and easy to sell assets, which undermined the competitiveness of the megabanks both when conducting low risk and routine lending and high-risk bespoke transactions. What these new rules lacked was the flexibility that went with the exercise of judgement as that meant a willingness to trust bank managements over the

Michael Mackenzie, and Aline van Duyn, 'Fed exit looms over US mortgages', 26th March 2010; Norma Cohen, 'Crisis thrusts debt-financing theorem back under the spotlight', 5th April 2010; Aline van Duyn, 'Derivative Dilemmas', 12th August 2010; Patrick Jenkins, 'Mutuals seek means to adapt and survive', 6th September 2010; Sharlene Goff, 'Building Societies refuse to roll over', 6th September 2010; Tom Braithwaite and Francesco Guerrera, 'A Garden to Tame', 15th November 2010.

[21] Francesco Guerrera and Justin Baer, 'Doubts beset mission to trim giants' girth', 23rd January 2010; *FT* Reporters, 'Proposals fail to forge consensus in Europe', 23rd January 2010; Patrick Jenkins, 'Poll finds solid support for tougher action', 25th January 2010; Pauline Skypala, 'Advance of the index trackers', 1st February 2010; Jennifer Hughes, 'Greek drama darkens mood', 25th February 2010; Jennifer Hughes, 'FSA plays down prop trading impact', 2nd March 2010; Jennifer Hughes, 'Fooled again', 19th March 2010; Philip Augar and John McFall, 'Is it time to strip the banks of their clutter?', 18th June 2010; Aline van Duyn and Francesco Guerrera, 'Dodd–Frank bill is no Glass–Steagall', 28th June 2010; Megan Murphy and Francesco Guerrera, 'Prop-hostile climate throws up some tough calls for banks', 4th August 2010; Sharlene Goff, Jennifer Hughes, and Patrick Jenkins, 'Mortgage-backed securities market gathering steam', 16th September 2010; Brooke Masters, '"Too big to fail" debate still muddled', 17th September 2010; Justin Baer, 'From recession to regulation', 27th September 2010; Brooke Masters and Francesco Guerrera, 'Threat to small business', 27th September 2010; Emma Saunders, 'Finance chiefs aim to raise debt', 11th October 2010; Jeremy Grant, 'Back office in leading role', 20th October 2010; Brooke Masters, 'Trade finance may become a casualty', 20th October 2010; Justin Baer, 'Proprietary traders weigh up new options', 25th October 2010; Aline van Duyn, 'Sector resized and reshaped', 28th October 2010; Tom Braithwaite and Francesco Guerrera, 'A Garden to Tame', 15th November 2010; Vincent Bevins, 'Caution and tough regulation are all-weather assets', 15th November 2010; Francesco Guerrera, Justin Baer, and Patrick Jenkins, 'A sparser future', 20th December 2010; *FT* Reporters, 'Before and after: how the investment banks had to change shape post-crisis', 21st December 2010; Paul J. Davies and Izabella Kaminska, 'Banks seek help from new set of institutions', 22nd December 2010.

quality and quantity of the assets they held. In some cases, for example, the equity of large corporations was both more liquid and more stable than the debt of some sovereign states, but regulators forced banks to hold the latter not the former. That absence of trust dated not only from what had happened in the crisis but also the subsequent revelations regarding bank behaviour such as the mis-selling of financial products, the manipulation of markets, and the rogue behaviour of a few employees. Fuelled by public anger and the pressure from politicians, regulators had little alternative but to demand dramatically higher capital requirements. These forced megabanks to scale back capital-intensive activities even though their structure made them able to operate with low levels of capital and a high level of leverage while providing strong resilience in the face of both liquidity and solvency crises.

As the megabanks reviewed the cost of doing business, the changed perception of the risks they were exposed to, and the regulations under which they had to operate in terms of capital and leverage, they cut back or abandoned certain types of business. One example of the consequences these regulations had for the universal banks was its effects on the finance of international trade. Trade finance was a low-margin business that involved extensive inter-bank lending and borrowing, supported by the provision of collateral. It was a relatively risk-free business and was ideal for the megabanks, because of their extensive branch and correspondent networks spread around the world. However, despite being relatively risk-free it was not treated as such under the new regulations. New leverage rules, risk-weighting requirements, and liquidity ratios all drove up trade finance costs, leading smaller banks to abandon the business and larger backs to reduce the amount of lending they provided, to the disadvantage of underlying economic conditions. Another example of the consequences of the new Basel rules, requiring banks to hold additional capital against risky assets, was in corporate lending. Not only was the ratio of reserves to assets forced up from 2 per cent to 7 per cent but there was also a higher weighting given to the risk classification of such assets. The impact was most pronounced on lending to smaller businesses as that carried more risk than providing large companies with loans because they were more dependent upon bank finance. Emma Saunders explained why in 2010, 'Companies with higher leverage—a higher ratio of debt to equity capital—are typically considered riskier, as cash flow is committed in advance to pay creditors. The more leveraged a company is, the greater the risk that it will struggle to repay or refinance its debt.'[22] Under these circumstances these were the businesses that banks were more likely to refuse loans to when forced to ration the supply of credit.

With banks constrained in the lending they could do after the crisis the larger companies turned directly to the capital markets, which they were able to do because of their high credit ratings. There they could negotiate better terms than those available from their bankers. Big companies could raise capital by issuing stocks and bonds and so could finance themselves without the assistance of banks. However, such a course was not open to small- and medium-sized enterprises as the costs of bond issues on their behalf made them unattractive to most investors because of the relatively small amounts they wanted to raise. This left these businesses with a prolonged shortage of finance that spread far beyond those countries that had been at the epicentre of the crisis. It was reported in 2010 that whereas large companies in Brazil had no difficulty in raising finance, small- and medium-sized ones struggled to do so. Such was the connectivity in an integrated global economy

22 Emma Saunders, 'Finance chiefs aim to raise debt', 11th October 2010.

that the rules framed by regulators to make banking safer had consequences for all. Routine and low-margin activities such as trade finance and lending to regular customers were rendered prohibitively expensive in an attempt to curb those activities considered unusual and high risk.

The megabanks were further threatened by the moves forcing them to reduce or even divest certain activities either because they were no longer permitted to pursue them or they had been made unprofitable. No government went so far as to force the splitting up of megabanks, despite enduring popular and political demands. In 2011 Phillip Stephens wanted 'the complete institutional separation of high-street banking from the socially useless casino operations of the investment banks'.[23] Nevertheless, conditions were imposed on them such as a degree of compartmentalization by sector and country or the forced withdrawal from certain types of trading activity. These conditions increased costs and reduced the advantages of the integrated model that lay at the heart of the megabanks, and had made them so successful before the crisis. In 2011 Sharlene Goff traced the implications:

> By separating the retail and investment banking arms of universal institutions...intricate, efficient funding links developed over decades will be severed. Banks will no longer be able to prop up one part of the group with another; nor, crucially, to tap wholesale markets as diversified businesses—a status that has entitled them to cheaper funding. Tougher capital requirements are likely to mean riskier activities, from loans to lower earners to the most sophisticated fixed-income and derivative-trading products, become more expensive.[24]

Despite her warnings action was taken by regulators to force megabanks to change the way they did business while recognizing the contribution they made to the operation of an efficient and resilient financial system. Regulators wanted to appease governments, driven by popular and media pressure demanding a break up or compartmentalization of the megabanks. Central banks were aware of the continuing risks that megabanks posed if one got into difficulties.

One of the first governments to propose intervention aimed at the megabanks was that of the USA. Their intention was to limit the size of banks and restrict the range of activities they were engaged in, so making them less of a risk if they got into difficulties. To Francesco Guerrera and Justin Baer in 2010, this 'proposed policy reverses decades of deregulation and consolidation that created a pyramid-like US financial system with thousands of smaller banks at the bottom and a handful of giant international groups at the top'.[25] Though there were still over 8000 banks in the USA the top four controlled 35 per cent of all deposits in 2009 compared to only 5 per cent in 1998. They were even more dominant in investment banking. The level of concentration had been increased during the crisis by mergers encouraged by the government as a way of saving failing banks and creating stronger groups. Bear Stearns and Washington Mutual had fallen to JP Morgan Chase, allowing it to expand simultaneously in investment and retail banking. Bank of America had expanded its investment banking operations by acquiring Merrill Lynch, while Wells Fargo had doubled up in retail banking by taking over Wachovia. There were calls to reverse this consolidation, including adopting a new version of the Glass–Steagall Act, prohibiting

[23] Phillip Stephens, 'Vickers hands victory to the bankers' shop steward', 13th September 2011.
[24] Sharlene Goff, 'The price of protection', 12th September 2011.
[25] Francesco Guerrera and Justin Baer, 'Doubts beset mission to trim giants' girth', 23rd January 2010.

the combination of commercial and investment banking, but legislators contented themselves with placing restrictions on what US megabanks could do. These focused on preventing the megabanks from trading on their own account as this was widely blamed for exposing them to a high level of risk. Initially other countries appeared to follow the US authorities in this direction but most pulled back from going this far. What was increasingly recognized was that proprietary trading had played a very small role in the lead up to the crisis. Instead, what emerged was the need to tighten up on auditing procedures because of the way certain banks had massaged their balance sheets before and during the crisis. Lehman Brothers had classed the securities it provided as collateral as a sale but did not enter a matching liability even though it was committed to repurchasing them. As it also classified the cash it received as an asset it was able to suggest to those from whom it borrowed that it was in a much stronger position financially than it actually was. That issue was tackled by new accounting procedures and this reflected the response to the crisis at the industry level. Though largely unnoticed it was these small incremental changes that addressed the issues that emerged after the crisis, and contributed to the banking system becoming more resilient.

Despite these incremental changes the US authorities pressed ahead with a ban on proprietary trading in 2010 under the Dodd–Frank Act. The effect of the US legislation was to force banks to hold more capital and restrict the range of activities they could pursue, which eroded the megabank model. The conclusion reached by Aline van Duyn and Francesco Guerrera in 2010 was that 'large financial groups whose failure would put the whole system at risk will have to cut back on risk and set aside more capital than before the crisis'.[26] As a result much of the trading in securities shifted from Goldman Sachs, Morgan Stanley, JP Morgan, Citigroup, and Bank of America. Their place was taken by hedge funds, as they were not considered systemically important, and so escaped the restrictions placed on the universal banks. More generally, tough new rules coupled with tightened regulatory scrutiny forced universal banks in both the USA and Europe to become more focused, leading them to dispose of selected activities and even locations. This also created opportunities for specialist banks to gain business, as these escaped the restrictions placed on the universal banks. These smaller banks often hired the staff being made redundant, as these possessed the requisite skills and contacts, and so quickly took up those activities being off-loaded, including providing megabanks with the services they had previously undertaken themselves. Also, in the wake of the financial crisis regulators had taken steps to protect national financial systems from contagion, spread through branches of foreign banks operating in their country. The effect was to undermine the business models of the megabanks as that relied on treating the world as a single integrated unit, and not having to set up separately capitalized subsidiaries in every country and comply with local regulations.

However, underlying forces continued to favour the megabanks. They possessed depth and breadth across a wide range of financial activities, and that was what global fund managers and multinational corporations continued to demand. It was the megabanks that could afford to invest in the latest advances in the technology of communication and computing as well as pay the salaries commanded by the staff with the required expertise. It was also these banks that were in the best position to cope with the post-crisis world dictated by governments as that involved a much greater level of regulation. They could spread the

[26] Aline van Duyn and Francesco Guerrera, 'Dodd–Frank bill is no Glass–Steagall', 28th June 2010.

costs of compliance over their entire business and devise modes of operation that sidestepped the most onerous of the controls imposed. They remained the counterparties of choice in all financial transactions because of their perceived resilience. What had changed as a result of the financial crisis was that all were much more aware of risk and looked for ways of reducing it. This hit smaller and newer banks most, because they took the greater risks and so were considered the least secure counterparty. As Sir Robert Wainwright, senior partner at the accountancy firm, Deloitte's, stated in 2019, 'By definition, the start-up banks have a higher risk appetite. There's often a conflict of interest. You want to move quickly, but you have to build resistance quickly as well. It's a matter of how you balance that. It's a wide challenge for the sector.'[27] Also, under Basel 3 rules, designed to make banks more resilient and prevent a repeat of the financial crisis, new leverage rules, risk-weighting requirements, and liquidity ratios drove up costs most for the smaller banks, leading them to abandon certain types of business, which were picked up by the larger banks, as they were better able to spread the extra costs.[28] The assessment of Justin Baer in 2010 was that:

> One consequence of the crisis is that it has left the survivors bigger and more powerful than they were before. Institutions such as JP Morgan Chase, Goldman Sachs and Bank of America are almost ubiquitous: from commodities trading and retail brokerage to credit cards and cash management, there are few financial services markets that they do not dominate. The massive scale these banks now enjoy will make it harder than ever for smaller institutions to compete.[29]

Short-term Consequences

By 2012 governments were becoming increasingly aware of the wider consequences of the regulatory reaction that had followed the crisis, especially its adverse impact on the finance available to small- and medium-sized enterprises (SMEs). As a result they began to press banks to increase lending as the lack of funds was seen as a major reason for the slow pace of economic recovery. Sharlene Goff reported in 2012 on the contradictory messages that governments were sending to the banks: 'Regulators want them to hold larger capital buffers and remove risky loans from their balance sheets but at the same time they are under pressure from the government to increase lending to SMEs.'[30] Writing in 2013 Anne-Sylvaine Chassany and Henny Sender identified the post-crisis regulation as the main cause for the shortage of finance: 'To make the banks safer, regulators in the US and Europe

[27] Paul Murphy, 'Cyber-attacks target banks' easy pickings', 25th March 2019.

[28] Elaine Moore, 'Post Office moves to expand banking', 18th January 2014; Sharlene Goff, 'Challenger leaders square up to the big four', 25th January 2014; John Gapper, 'There is no such thing as the banking profession', 13th February 2014; Sharlene Goff, 'Scrutiny puts free banking in question', 19–20th July 2014; Emma Dunkley, 'Challengers fail to loosen big four's grip', 5th January 2015; Laura Noonan, Caroline Binham, and Martin Arnold, 'Investment banks face baptism of fire after City watchdog's opening salvo', 20th February 2015; Barney Thompson, 'Banks seen as better run than newspapers', 26th March 2015; Patrick Jenkins, 'Banker bashing is back as public resentment returns', 8th May 2015; Caroline Binham and Patrick Jenkins, 'Regulators plan to internationalise UK regime', 12th June 2015; Emma Dunkley, 'Challenger banks branch out into business loans', 5th November 2015; Paul Murphy, 'Cyber-attacks target banks' easy pickings', 25th March 2019.

[29] Justin Baer, 'From recession to regulation', 27th September 2010.

[30] Sharlene Goff, 'Policymakers recognise SMEs need more funding options', 16th April 2012.

require banks to hold more capital. This has made them more reluctant to lend to smaller companies, and they charge more for the money when they do.'[31] Though many continued to blame the shortage of finance on a lack of competition between providers, by 2016 the informed consensus was that regulations were primarily responsible. However, there was strong resistance to any relaxation of these regulations. Continuing worries that the megabanks remained a threat to financial stability prevented any major change in policy. Even if one had been considered, public animosity towards banking in general, and megabanks in particular, made a reversal impossible. In the media the megabanks continued to be held responsible for the crisis, while the subsequent revelations regarding the behaviour of individual banks and bankers in mis-selling financial products and manipulating markets, prevented any rehabilitation of their reputation. Writing in 2015 Patrick Jenkins observed that, 'For many, the words scandal and banking have become almost synonymous because of a succession of misdeeds—interest-rate and foreign exchange price fixing, mis-selling insurance and investment, laundering drug money, breaching sanctions, the list goes on.'[32]

Nevertheless, the banks themselves were already returning to some of the strategies that had been popular before the crisis. As early as 2010 securitization was being used because, according to Rob Joliffe, joint global head of debt capital markets at UBS, it was 'an important funding tool for banks'. What he accepted was that 'new issue volumes will take some time to recover to pre-crisis levels'.[33] It remained difficult to sell repackaged loans because of the loss of trust in credit ratings, while the absence of a credit default swaps increased the risk that investors were exposed to. There was also a question over liquidity as that was dependent upon the market provided by the banks. Using their status as reliable counterparties in the past banks had borrowed low-yielding government bonds from asset managers, providing, in return, higher-yielding corporate and mortgage bonds that were the product of securitization. The banks then used the government bonds as collateral for inter-bank loans so providing them with the funds needed to finance their securitization programmes. Since the crisis asset managers were reluctant to swap government bonds for securitized debt even though it would boost their returns at a time of very low interest rates. This deprived banks of an easy route through which to increase their lending, forcing them to cut back on the finance they could provide to their customers. In response alternative sources of finance developed. Multinational companies, for example, stepped in to provide the finance previously supplied by the megabanks, such the credit required in commodity trading or infrastructure development. An even more noticeable effect of the new regulations was the expansion of the shadow banking sector. This sector comprised smaller and more specialized financial institutions that largely escaped the regulatory requirements placed on the megabanks. By imposing tougher capital and liquidity requirements on megabanks, simultaneously increasing their costs and lowering the amount of lending they could do, regulators encouraged the growth of financial companies replicating the business done by banks but without the compliance burden. This was evident in India. Faced with the inability of India's state-owned banks to provide them with finance, because of the overhang of bad debts, both corporate and retail borrowers turned to the shadow banking system. In China a large and unregulated shadow banking sector had also grown up since the crisis.

[31] Anne-Sylvaine Chassany and Henny Sender, 'Forced into the shadows', 7th June 2013.
[32] Patrick Jenkins, 'Banker bashing is back as public resentment returns', 8th May 2015.
[33] Jennifer Hughes, 'Greek drama darkens mood', 25th February 2010.

This displacement was most evident in the USA where, in compliance with the new rules introduced under the Dodd–Frank Act, US megabanks had also to dismantle their proprietary trading operations. The requirement extended to the investment banks as Goldman Sachs and Morgan Stanley had reregistered as commercial banks while Bear Stearns and Merrill Lynch had been acquired by commercial banks. Taking their place were the likes of Jefferies and Co. This bank had been launched in 2007 with 200 clients but had 350 by 2009. Many of these had migrated from Merrill Lynch. When Bank of America acquired Merrill Lynch it sold the latter's prime brokerage unit to the French bank, BNP Paribas, but that led many clients to look for an alternative. By 2011 the size of the shadow banking system in the USA was estimated at $16,000bn, which made it larger than the regulated banking system, which had assets of $13,000bn. As Brooke Masters commented in 2011, 'These shadow banks have taken on part or all of the maturity transformation role of banks—matching short-term depositor funds with long-term lending—and much of the attendant risk, but they do not have the same requirements to hold capital and liquid assets against losses or a rash of customer withdrawals or failures.'[34] Vikram Pandit, the chief executive of Citigroup, made clear in 2011 that the growth of shadow banks would not lead to a safer financial system: 'Shifting risk into unregulated or differently regulated sectors won't make the banking system safer. On the contrary, overall risk in the system could actually rise.'[35] Despite the emerging risks evident in the size and growth of the shadow banking sector regulators were reluctant to change their attitude towards the megabanks.[36] The result was a shift of financial activity away from the megabanks and into the hands of the shadow banking sector. One of the early beneficiaries were the hedge funds as they moved into the

[34] Brooke Masters, 'A real problem for regulators', 22nd March 2011.

[35] Brooke Masters and Jeremy Grant, 'Shadow boxes', 3rd February 2011.

[36] Brooke Masters and Jeremy Grant, 'Shadow boxes', 3rd February 2011; Sam Jones, 'Customers cast a more critical eye on the field', 21st March 2011; Elaine Moore, 'Uncertainty in an evolving landscape', 21st March 2011; Brooke Masters, 'A real problem for regulators', 22nd March 2011; Sharlene Goff, 'Report dismisses merger U-turn', 2nd–3rd April 2011; Richard Milne, 'Money for nothing-and the debt is (almost) for free', 25th May 2011; Brooke Masters, 'League battle over bank risk will end in tiers', 21st June 2011; Sharlene Goff, 'Risk is the new "sexy" job at the bank', 14th July 2011; Patrick Jenkins and Megan Murphy, 'Again on the edge', 15th August 2011; Patrick Jenkins, Brooke Masters and Tom Braithwaite, 'Hunt for a common front', 8th September 2011; Megan Murphy, 'Search for new approaches has begun', 9th September 2011; Brooke Masters, Henny Sender, and Dan McCrum, '"Shadow banks" move in amid regulatory push', 9th September 2011; Sharlene Goff, 'The price of protection', 12th September 2011; Phillip Stephens, 'Vickers hands victory to the bankers' shop steward', 13th September 2011; Jo Johnson, 'Ringfence and regulate in haste, repent at leisure', 13th September 2011; Sharlene Goff, 'Vickers Report', 13th September 2011; Brooke Masters, 'Industry worries about the impact of new rules', 20th September 2011; Brooke Masters and Tom Braithwaite, 'Bankers versus Basel', 3rd October 2011; Paul J. Davies, 'Lack of experience restrains investment in liquidity swaps', 3rd October 2011; Patrick Jenkins, Rachel Sanderson, and Miles Johnson, 'Banks Contemplate shrunken future', 14th October 2011; Paul Taylor, 'How to make ready for regulation', 9th November 2011; Tracy Alloway, 'Financial system creaks as loan lubricant dries up', 29th November 2011; Patrick Jenkins and Richard Milne, 'Caught in the grip', 2nd December 2011; Tracy Alloway, 'Higher capital demands and dearer funding bring a dual burden', 2nd December 2011; Brooke Masters, 'Reveal leverage ratio ahead of rivals banks told', 2nd December 2011; Norma Cohen, 'Lenders warned over profit and bonus pay-outs', 2nd December 2011; Jack Farchy, 'Potential credit crunch risks hobbling raw materials trade', 6th December 2011; Javier Blas, 'Unfashionable actor takes centre stage', 21st December 2011; Tracy Alloway, 'Traditional lenders shiver as shadow banking grows', 29th December 2011; Brooke Masters, 'Banks learn the liquidity lessons from tough rules', 30th December 2011; Patrick Jenkins and Brooke Masters, 'Banks test CDO-style finance for trade', 9th April 2012; Sharlene Goff, 'Policymakers recognise SMEs need more funding options', 16th April 2012; Javier Blas and Jack Farchy, 'Trafigura plans trade funding drive', 2nd May 2012; Robin Wigglesworth, Jim Pickard and George Parker, 'Big project finance hit by squeeze on banks', 3rd May 2012; Javier Blas and Ajay Makan, 'Commodities credit crunch eases', 6th February 2013; Anne-Sylvaine Chassany and Henny Sender, 'Forced into the shadows', 7th June 2013; Andrew Bolger, 'Corporate loans rise above pre-crisis levels', 11th February 2015; Patrick Jenkins, 'Banker bashing is back as public resentment returns', 8th May 2015; Philip Stafford, 'Europe's regulatory crackdown set to ease', 25th May 2016; Simon Mundy, 'Investors in India spooked by the shadow financiers', 22nd February 2019; Gabriel Wildau, 'China struggling to quit debt addiction', 25th March 2019; Benjamin Parkin, 'Mutual funds in India seek to restore faith of skittish investor', 2nd July 2019.

territory once dominated by the universal banks. Sam Jones wrote in 2012 that 'Hedge funds are no longer regarded as high-risk, frontier traders, gambling with the wealth of billionaires. Instead they are increasingly seen as an integral part of the modern asset management business.'[37] The megabanks lent extensively to hedge funds, which exposed them to the risks that they took. A similar situation existed with money-market funds. These mimicked the behaviour of banks by promising that money placed with them could be easily withdrawn and could not fall in value, exposing them to the same liquidity risks. By 2012 US money-market funds had assets of $3tn with another $1tn in those operating in Europe. Banks increasingly relied on them as an alternative to inter-bank borrowing, and so were indirectly exposed to their liquidity risks. In response regulators attempted, under the new Basel rules, to rein in the behaviour of hedge funds and money-market funds because of the liquidity risks they were exposed to and their connections to mainstream banking. This was welcomed by the megabanks with Marc Gilly, global head of prime brokerage at Goldman Sachs, saying in 2012 that, 'Basel and other regulation is forcing recognition of the true cost of financing. This is something we are welcoming and ready for.'[38]

Generally, the regulatory focus on large and systemically-important banks since the financial crisis had created openings for all manner of shadow banks. By 2011 the total assets of the regulated banking sector were estimated at $130tn but there was another $67tn in the unregulated or shadow banking sector, covering a huge variety of different institutions. The US had the largest shadow banking sector with $23tn in assets, or a third of the global total, and these were an important source of short-term lending not only to companies but also banks. In turn that caused problems for regulators, as they had to cope with the risks posed by new and unmonitored shadow banks as well as the established banks. Michel Barnier, the EU commissioner overseeing financial services, estimated that by 2012 shadow banking represented over a quarter of the world's financial sector. For that reason it was not surprising that Vikram Pandit, the chief executive of Citigroup, complained that 'You cannot address systemic risk unless you tackle things other than banks. We've gravitated from a hub-and-spoke world, where everything used to go through large financial institutions, to a network of millions of points of contact with each other.'[39] The response was a partial reappraisal of the role played by global universal banks, including their responsibility for the crisis. As the experienced banker and regulator, Jacques de Larosière, reflected in 2012, 'Bank failures are not related to specific structures, but to excessive risk-taking. The institutions that were the hardest hit by the crisis were those that pursued risky operations either in trading or in more traditional activities, be they specialised or not.'[40] Following on from that analysis Paul Volker, the former chairman of the Federal Reserve, cautioned that the attempt to ring fence particular segments of a banking system would prove largely ineffective, even though this was the proposal being made in both the UK and the EU.[41]

By then it was evident that the curbs placed on the megabanks had encouraged the growth of rival financial institutions that could operate on the same scale, and they were all US-based. One was the fund manager, BlackRock, which held an estimated 5 per cent of all

[37] Sam Jones, 'Big spending clients keep providers on their toes', 26th March 2012.

[38] Sam Jones, 'The mood music is about to change', 26th March 2012,

[39] Patrick Jenkins, Tom Braithwaite, and Brooke Masters, 'New force emerges from the shadows', 10th April 2012,

[40] Jacques de Larosière, 'Do not be seduced by the simplicity of ringfencing', 27th September 2012,

[41] Andrew Haldane, 'We should go further still in unbundling banks', 3rd October 2012; Patrick Jenkins, 'Volker attacks Vickers reforms', 18th October 2012,

the investable assets in the world in 2012. This allowed it to match buying and selling internally, providing liquidity from its own resources whether in terms of sales or purchases. It could circumvent the dealer network controlled by the banks. Fund managers such as BlackRock had come to occupy a strong position by 2012 because the demand for collateral in the form of safe assets had escalated since the crisis. Fund managers held huge portfolios of government and corporate bonds. By 2011 it was estimated that $38.2tn in government securities was in circulation along with corporate and other bonds at $11.5tn. In addition there were securitization assets of $12.9tn that were considered safe as well as $8.4tn in gold. It was these high-quality assets that were in demand as collateral to support inter-bank lending, borrowing, and trading and not those that had come to the fore prior to the crisis. The growth of a large shadow banking sector was particularly acute in the USA because of the more interventionist stance taken by that country's regulators. They were followed along this path by regulators in the EU. In contrast, authorities in Australia, Canada, China, Japan, and Singapore took a more relaxed attitude, recognizing that it was better to operate through the regulated banks. This created opportunities for banks located in these countries to step into the international activities being relinquished by US and European banks, such as trade finance. Here the Japanese banks were the biggest winners followed by those operating from Singapore.

However, megabanks based outside the USA faced a serious obstacle in taking business away from their US rivals, which was access to $ denominated funds, as that was the principal currency used in international trade and finance. Lack of access to $s, for example, forced French universal banks to pull back from trade finance. Prior to the crisis $ funds had been in plentiful supply as the US banks were active participants in the inter-bank markets. That ended with the freeze in the inter-bank market during the crisis. What then followed were regulations that encouraged US banks to prioritize liquidity over profits, and so they pulled back from the inter-bank markets, depriving banks located outside the USA from accessing cheap supplies of $s. Despite the domestic restrictions imposed on them this left US banks in a powerful position as they had a huge and captive domestic market and direct access to the currency upon which international trade and finance operated, namely the US$. The Japanese investment bank, Nomura, could not match the power of these global US banks, even though it had acquired the non-US operations of Lehman Brothers in 2008. Michiyo Nakamoto and Patrick Jenkins identified its weakness when they wrote in 2012, that 'Even with the Lehman acquisition, Nomura is still tiny compared with leading US and European banks.'[42] Deprived of Lehman's US base, as that was bought by Barclays, Nomura discovered that without the business that it had generated globally there was insufficient activity to maintain the viability of the branches located elsewhere in the world. Access to dollar funding was crucial for all banks attempting to develop and maintain an international business and US banks were best placed to obtain that. In 2012 all the leading megabanks were from the USA, comprising Bank of America, CitiGroup, Goldman Sachs, JP Morgan, and Morgan Stanley. They were distancing themselves from the chasing pack of Barclays, Deutsche Bank, Credit Suisse, HSBC, Société Generale, Royal Bank of Canada, and UBS. In the world there were only a small number of banks that could process transactions reaching into the trillions a day, ranging from credit-card payments to stock purchases, as that required an extensive scale of operations, a global network, a reputation that generated trust, a large capital, and a heavy investment in

[42] Michiyo Nakamoto and Patrick Jenkins, 'Bowed by over-ambition', 2nd August 2012,

IT. Of these, those from the USA were best placed because their control of the US market generated the required capacity and gave them access to unlimited supplies of $s, which was the international currency.[43]

Long-term Consequences 1

Though there was some reconsideration of the most stringent requirements placed on the largest banks in the wake of the crisis, once introduced they proved somewhat unmoveable. With the likes of David Crow pointing out in 2019 that, 'A decade later, the largest US banks have only become bigger',[44] the too-big-to-fail problem continued to influence regulators around the world as they sought to avoid taxpayer bailouts by forcing systemically-important banks to increase their ability to absorb losses by either raising additional funds or pulling back from risk-taking. As a consequence the regulations in place by 2012 took on a permanent form, and were instrumental in the reshaping of the global banking system as it evolved during the rest of the decade. The restrictions placed on banks regarding the assets they had to hold, and the level of liquidity they had to maintain, made it difficult for them to compete with an emerging shadow banking sector, which grew strongly as a consequence. Though the implications of their actions were recognized by regulators, including its consequences for the supervision and stability of the global financial system, there remained a strong reluctance to make any significant alterations because of the lingering lack of trust in banks, reinforced by continuing revelations of past mistakes and misconduct. By 2019 the total fines levied on banks for defrauding customers and manipulating markets, had

[43] Ed Hammond, 'Pressure on banks' real estate loans', 6th January 2012; Jeremy Grant, 'New rules are struggle for industry and regulators', 23rd January 2012; Patrick Jenkins, 'Banks face a perfect storm that is getting worse', 25th January 2012; Brooke Masters, 'Shadow banking poses threat to broader stability, FSA head warns', 15th March 2012; Robin Wigglesworth, 'Taming the traders', 20th March 2012; Jeremy Grant, 'LSE seeks holy grail of clearing from LCH.Clearnet deal', 20th March 2012; Steve Johnson, 'EU shadow banking plan rapped', 26th March 2012; Sam Jones, 'Big spending clients keep providers on their toes', 26th March 2012; Sam Jones, 'The mood music is about to change', 26th March 2012; Patrick Jenkins and Brooke Masters, 'Banks test CDO-style finance for trade', 9th April 2012; Patrick Jenkins, Tom Braithwaite, and Brooke Masters, 'New force emerges from the shadows', 10th April 2012; Dan McCrum, 'Hybrid model eyed for money market funds', 10th April 2012; Sam Jones, 'Volker Rule', 10th April 2012; Sarah Mishkin, 'Asian lenders step up their push into trade finance', 12th April 2012; James Wilson and Daniel Schäfer, 'Double entry at Deutsche', 13th April 2012; Robin Wigglesworth, 'Bonds find favour over syndicated lending', 13th April 2012; Paul J. Davies, 'Banks look to insurers for lessons', 16th April 2012; Sharlene Goff, 'Policymakers recognise SMEs need more funding options', 16th April 2012; Sam Jones, 'Hedge funds feel pinch from new banking rules', 18th April 2012; Anousha Sakoui, 'Restructuring could lift M&A market', 30th May 2012; Daniel Schäfer, 'A small slice of the action', 30th May 2012; Barbara Ridpath, 'Crisis—and regulation—can breed opportunity', 30th May 2012; Brian Groom, 'Access denied', 31st May 2012; Michael Kavanagh, 'Beyond the bean counters', 31st May 2012; Jonathan Guthrie, 'A doomed golden age for UK plc', 31st May 2012; Brooke Masters, 'UK banks lead world on liquidity rules', 22nd June 2012; Sharlene Goff, 'The middle is still the safest bet', 25th June 2012; Robin Wigglesworth, 'Rising Expectations', 25th June 2012; Chris Giles, 'BoE loosens regulations on liquid asset holdings', 30th June 2012; Michiyo Nakamoto and Patrick Jenkins, 'Bowed by over-ambition', 2nd August 2012; John Gapper, 'Don't leave the financial system resting on quicksand', 30th August 2012; Philip Stafford, 'Battle for derivatives clearing heats up', 11th September 2012; Jacques de Larosière, 'Do not be seduced by the simplicity of ringfencing', 27th September 2012; Tracy Alloway, 'BlackRock moves in as banks retreat', 2nd October 2012; Andrew Haldane, 'We should go further still in unbundling banks', 3rd October 2012; Patrick Jenkins and Daniel Schäfer, 'New York is a tall order for Europeans', 4th October 2012; Patrick Jenkins, 'Volker attacks Vickers reforms', 18th October 2012; Ralph Atkins, Philip Stafford, and Brooke Masters, 'Collateral Damage', 25th October 2012; Daniel Schäfer, 'Once-neglected segment is now banking's belle of the ball', 30th October 2012; Brooke Masters, 'Regulators peer into financial shadows', 19th November 2012; Shahien Nasiripour and Brooke Masters, 'Regulators edge towards "every country for itself"', 10th December 2012; Shahien Nasiripour, Dan McCrum, and Mary Watkins, 'Regulators want end of money fund fixed price', 21st February 2013; Laura Noonan, 'Weak margins drag on safe banks' ambitions', 13th February 2019.

[44] David Crow, 'Banks strain to effect a post-crisis funding fix', 25th March 2019.

reached $276.8bn. There was also the underlying fear that any relaxation of liquidity requirements would lead banks to return to excessive lending, especially on property, because of the much higher returns that would produce. Under these circumstances the Basel Committee of Banking Supervisors continued to recommend that banks held a portfolio of liquid assets against short-term credit commitments so as to be better able to absorb losses and avoid calling on governments for support. Megabanks were also discouraged from making complex and risky loans and lending without collateral and encouraged to compartmentalize their operations along national lines to both insulate them from external difficulties and simplify intervention and support if they got into difficulties. The cumulative effect was to reduce their willingness to fund large projects such as office building, housing estates, and infrastructure development even as demand for them picked up. The inevitable result was other financial institutions stepped in to fill the void left by the banks, and this was the case across the entire range of financial activities once dominated by the megabanks.

This process of substitution was both gradual and partial. Asset managers and private equity funds, for example, lacked the skills, experience, and contacts that the megabanks had built up over many years, especially when it came to dealing with smaller and more obscure borrowers. Nevertheless, these alternative providers did establish themselves, especially in the USA. There real estate investment trusts (REITs) grew quickly in popularity with their assets doubling between 2007 and 2013, reaching $443bn. A REIT used short-term borrowing to buy long-term mortgage bonds profiting from the interest-rate differential. Another group of US financial institutions that operated in a similar way were Business Development Companies (BDCs). Though regarded as alternatives to banks these asset managers often worked closely with them. They provided banks with a way of continuing to engage in those activities that regulations were pushing them out of. Regulations forced systemically-important banks to hold more liquid assets, so safeguarding their position in the event of another liquidity crisis. Such assets generated low returns meaning the bank was less profitable. By channelling funds through shadow banks the regulated banks could invest in higher-yielding assets while maintaining the liquidity requirements imposed on them. Jonathan Bock, an analyst at Wells Fargo, acknowledged this in 2014: 'As regulators restructure the banking system they are moving illiquid products that were once on bank balance sheets into more public investment vehicles and that creates an investment opportunity.'[45] Banks faced a choice of either withdrawing from particular businesses or engaging with others who did not have to comply with the stringent regulations under which they had to operate. One way, for example, was to continue lending but to sell the loans to others, so releasing the capital they had committed to the business. Asset managers were keen to invest in the potentially higher-yielding assets that banks were shedding, such as bundles of mortgages and leveraged loans, as a way of boosting returns amid low interest rates. Pension funds looked for secure, long-term income streams that infrastructure debt could provide. At the other end of the spectrum banks lent short-term money to hedge funds which was then used to finance the trading activities that banks were either barred from or had been made unprofitable because of the capital requirements placed upon them. The banks gained from the interest paid by the hedge funds while satisfying the regulators over the matter of liquidity.

[45] Tracy Alloway and Arash Massoudi, 'Non-bank lending steps out of the shadows', 26th February 2014.

The shadow banking sector had been growing before the crisis but received an enormous boost from the regulations subsequently imposed on the megabanks, and then maintained long after the crisis was over. Assets in the shadow banking sector were estimated to have grown from $26.1tn in 2002 to $71.2tn in 2012. The USA stood out as the country in which the shadow banking system made greatest progress. Whereas by 2012 the regulated banking sector was seven times the size of the shadow banking one, by assets, in Japan, followed by France and Germany at four times and the UK at twice, in the USA the position was reversed. There the shadow banking system was almost twice the size of the regulated one. However, the shadow banking sector was not a perfect substitute for the regulated banks, especially of the megabank variety. This can be seen in terms of the trading activity that these banks had previously carried out. Megabanks had played a central role in financial markets before the crisis because they were able to supply demand for stocks and bonds from their extensive inventories or make purchases by leveraging the capital, reserves, and other funds at their disposal. In the face of stricter regulations following the crisis it became much less profitable to hold large portfolios, while the level of leverage they were allowed to employ was cut back. Trading on their own account was also either restricted or banned. One measure of the effect was the size of the bond inventories held by banks. This had reached a peak of $235bn in 2007 but fell to only $54bn in 2013. Banks no longer acted as shock absorbers when faced by increases in buying or selling using their own capital and holdings of stocks and bonds. Though banks did rebuild stocks of assets, depleted in the wake of the crisis and the regulations introduced, they remained far from the position they occupied before the crisis. In 2018 Joe Rennison and Philip Stafford placed responsibility for the change on the 'tough regulations introduced after 2009 with the intention of stabilising markets' as these were 'fuelling far more volatile swings in asset prices... as banks have retreated from their traditional roles of providing two-way prices for investors... These markets have also become increasingly electronic with market-making activity gravitating towards high-speed trading firms, which by their nature do not extend support for prices once volatility heats up.'[46] The leverage rule, agreed in 2014 under Basel 3, reduced trading and so made markets less liquid. Though the Basel 3 rules were modified once their consequences became apparent this only happened gradually as regulatory authorities were unwilling to reverse the regulations they applied.

The regulations also affected the repo market. Since the crisis regulators had sought to reduce banks' reliance on short-term funding via repurchase agreements, where banks borrowed money, providing bonds as collateral accompanied by the promise to repurchase them at a later date. The new regulations were designed to restrict the use of this inter-bank market as a source of long-term funds, which was considered a major contributor to the build-up of risk. Through borrowing in the inter-bank market the leverage ratio of US investment banks had risen from 10.4 in June 2007 to a peak of 40.7 in February 2009, forcing the US Treasury to intervene to provide support or face another crisis. The new rules introduced under Basel 3 meant banks had to retain higher levels of capital leaving them with less to lend in the repo market. This left banks without ready access to short-term funding, forcing central banks to provide liquidity to avoid a renewed credit crunch. In the place of banks other financial institutions became major users of the inter-bank market, as Christopher Thompson observed by 2014: 'As banks wind down their repo trading much repo business is set to migrate to the less-regulated "shadow" banking sector, such as hedge

[46] Joe Rennison and Philip Stafford, 'Traders find receptive ear among regulators to relax capital rules', 10th July 2018.

funds.'[47] Unlike banks, however, these shadow banks lacked access to the lender-of-last-resort facilities provided by central banks such as the Federal Reserve, creating the risk that liquidity could quickly dry up. For banks the ability to borrow cash from investors such as money-market funds by pledging bonds as collateral was integral to their daily funding needs. It was an important conduit for collateral to move around the financial system and helped settle trades and meet derivatives margin requirements. However, the combination of central bank intervention in global money markets and the tougher capital standards imposed on banks meant that the repo market shrank, making it a much less effective mechanism for redistributing liquidity around the financial system. This forced banks to maintain much higher levels of individual liquidity, and so less willing to lend to their customers. It also meant that banks were much more dependent upon central banks as a source of liquidity.[48]

[47] Christopher Thompson, 'Basel 3 rules to hit repo trading', 7th February 2014.

[48] Brooke Masters and Shahien Nasiripour, 'Basel move aims to stoke recovery', 8th January 2013; Kate Burgess and Caroline Binham, 'BBA sets out plans to monitor standards', 16th January 2013; Ed Hammond and Brooke Masters, 'FSA clampdown on mortgage-backed loans sparks friction', 17th January 2013; Tracy Alloway and Nicole Bullock, 'Banks offer debt product to help skirt new liquidity rules', 30th January 2013; David Oakley, 'Shadow banks fill infrastructure debt void', 1st February 2013; Brooke Masters and Jennifer Thompson, 'Smaller banks face "glass ceiling"', 11th February 2013; David Oakley, 'Asset managers fill the gap as banks retreat', 4th March 2013; Ralph Atkins and Mary Watkins, 'Eurozone crisis forces funding rethink for banks', 15th March 2013; Brooke Masters, 'Safety net plans raise industry ire', 19th March 2013; Tracy Alloway, 'Banks debate liquidity trade-off', 19th March 2013; Daniel Schäfer, 'Regulation threat to global banks', 12th April 2013; Brooke Masters, Philip Stafford, and Michael Mackenzie, 'Libor heads for history in hunt for new bank rate', 24th April 2013; Shahien Nasiripour and Tom Braithwaite, 'Out to break the banks', 1st May 2013; Philip Stafford, 'MTS prepares US push to tap into institutional demand', 2nd May 2013; Daniel Schäfer, 'Fragmented business offers huge potential for mergers', 7th May 2013; Anne-Sylvaine Chassany and Henny Sender, 'Forced into the shadows', 7th June 2013; Tracy Alloway and Arash Massoudi, 'ETFs under scrutiny in market turbulence', 28th June 2013; Ralph Atkins and Michael Stothard, 'A change of gear', 1st July 2013; Philip Stafford and Brooke Masters, 'Libor deal commences rehabilitation of benchmark', 10th July 2013; Gregory Meyer and Jack Farchy, 'Wall Street falls out of love with commodities trading business', 5th August 2013; Tom Braithwaite and Patrick Jenkins, 'Balance sheet battles', 15th August 2013; Tracy Alloway, 'Goldman promotes its bond platform', 23rd August 2013; Tracy Alloway, 'The debt penalty', 11th September 2013; Andrew Bounds, 'Alternative financials fill gap left by banks', 12th September 2013; Patrick Jenkins and Daniel Schäfer, 'Banks suffer as derivatives trade shifts to the "shadows"', 12th September 2013; Tracy Alloway and Michael Mackenzie, 'Goldman restructures electronic bond trading platform', 23rd September 2013; Ellen Kelleher, 'Obscure property vehicle could carry Armageddon-style risk', 18th November 2013; Tracy Alloway, 'Buyers struggle to find a safe landing', 21st November 2013; Tracy Alloway and Michael Mackenzie, 'Big banks back digital venue for bond traders', 25th November 2013; Christopher Thompson, 'Basel 3 rules to hit repo trading', 7th February 2014; Chris Flood, 'Regulators stalk secretive financial giants', 24th February 2014; Tracy Alloway and Arash Massoudi, 'Non-bank lending steps out of the shadows', 26th February 2014; Chris Flood, 'Hedge funds transmit most risk', 28th April 2014; Tracy Alloway, 'Big investors replace banks in $4th repo market', 30th May 2014; Sophia Grene, 'Non-banks colonise former bank territory', 2nd June 2014; Patrick Jenkins and Sam Fleming, 'Alternative finance steps out of the shadow', 16th June 2014; Patrick Jenkins and Sam Fleming, 'Taking another path', 17th June 2014; Tom Braithwaite, Martin Arnold, and Tracy Alloway, 'Tough choices confront traditional lenders', 18th June 2014; Sam Fleming and Gina Chon, 'Push begins to put lenders' house in order', 19th June 2014; Sam Fleming and Gina Chon, 'Boutique banks flourish as larger institutions rethink business models', 12th August 2014; Tracy Alloway, 'Call for reforms to broker-dealing', 14th August 2014; Tom Braithwaite and Vivianne Rodrigues, 'Wall Street's biggest lenders blame bond volatility on tight regulation', 17th October 2014; Martin Arnold and Camilla Hall, 'Big banks are giving up on global ambitions', 19th October 2014; John Kenchington, 'Investors are being urged to stress test fixed income funds', 3rd November 2014; Philip Stafford, 'Industry strives to find its form', 5th November 2014; Daniel Schäfer, 'Shrinking margins and higher costs drive down returns', 5th November 2014; Gregory Meyer, 'Oil price swings come too late for banks who made desk cutbacks', 5th November 2014; Michael Mackenzie, 'Search for liquidity tests firms' talent for innovation', 5th November 2014; Philip Stafford, 'Fall in value of LCH.Clearnet interest rate swaps', 28th November 2014; Martin Arnold, 'Carney's too big to fail buffer represents clear progress despite doubt', 9th December 2014; Joe Rennison, 'Fitch warns of growing repo threat', 18th June 2015; Joe Rennison and Philip Stafford, 'Complexity clouds the case for repo clearing', 19th June 2015; Thomas Hale, 'Riskier RMBS sales to double last year's total', 9th October 2015; Thomas Hale, 'Non-banks rebuild UK home loan landscape', 4th February 2016; Philip Stafford, 'Voice brokers answer call for liquidity', 12th August 2016; Harriet Agnew and Patrick Jenkins, 'What's next for the City', 3rd September 2016; Philip Stafford, 'ICAP's new direction reflects changing future of derivatives', 6th October 2016; Philip Stafford, 'Brexit brings headache to industry weary of

Long-term Consequences 2

The regulations introduced after the Global Financial Crisis were not just directed at banks in general. They took specific aim at megabanks as they were considered to be beyond the ability of national authorities and national central banks to regulate and control. Only by forcing them to become smaller, more national and more specialized was it possible to reduce them to a state where national governments could regain their influence. This ambition was further reinforced though the scandals surrounding the mis-selling of products and the rigging of key benchmarks. These had confirmed the view that the megabanks were a law unto themselves and that action had to be taken to make them more accountable. These moves continued even as it became apparent that the megabanks played an essential role in providing the financial infrastructure required in an integrated global economy populated by multinational companies, though it was not pursued with the same determination by all countries, leading to an uneven playing field. Nevertheless, the intervention had its consequences. The sharp decline of international financial flows since the financial crisis, with an estimated 65 per cent fall between 2007 and 2017, was associated with curbs placed on the activities of the megabanks. In response banking became more regional and more specialized. The Global Financial Crisis stopped the march of the megabanks as the dominant players in global financial markets. They pulled back from many key areas such as commodities and fixed-income trading, leaving a gap in the market to be filled by others that were more lightly regulated. As Daniel Schafer reported in 2014 investment banks, in particular, were:

> being forced to rethink, redesign, and shrink their trading operations in the face of much tougher regulatory requirements and against a backdrop of revenue declines and cost pressures. Investment banks have not only had to comply with stricter capital rules, and deal with much higher compliance and information technology costs, they have also seen high-margin complex products make way for simpler less profitable instruments.[49]

By then a number of the megabanks were in the process of disposing of those activities considered non-core while expanding others, making them much more focused financial institutions. Writing in 2015 Oliver Ralph considered that 'The universal banking model is broken...' They were placed at a competitive disadvantage because of the regulations that were applied to them and not to their smaller competitors. He also considered that they were unmanageable because of their size, scale, and diversity: 'Complexity was a big problem in the crisis, when banks struggled to understand what was on their own balance sheets

regulation', 11th October 2016; Philip Stafford, 'Central banks warned on repo volatility', 13th April 2017; Chris Flood, 'Liquidity enables big ticket trades', 18th June 2018; Joe Rennison and Philip Stafford, 'Traders find receptive ear among regulators to relax capital rules', 10th July 2018; Chris Flood, 'Bond liquidity issues prompt investors to turn to ETFs', 17th September 2018; Philip Stafford, 'Bloc must find its own path, shorn of British expertise', 17th November 2018; David Crow, 'Banks strain to effect a post-crisis funding fix', 25th March 2019; Eva Szalay and Jane Croft, 'Five banks face forex-rigging lawsuits in London', 30th July 2019; Caroline Binham, 'BoE presses banks for living wills to limit bailout damage', 31st July 2019; Sheila Blair, 'Congress should stay out of new bank rules for loan losses', 5th August 2006; Nicholas Megaw, 'Sting in the tail for banks caught in PPI scandal', 10th September 2019; Attracta Mooney, 'Liquidity crunches heat up debate over capital buffers', 16th September 2019; Nicholas Megaw, 'Challenger banks struggle against big four', 30th September 2019; *FT* Reporters, 'Fed analyses regulation's role in sudden rates jump', 2nd October 2019.

[49] Daniel Schäfer, 'Shrinking margins and higher costs drive down returns', 5th November 2014.

let alone everybody else's.'[50] Faced with an increasingly hostile regulatory environment the megabanks responded by becoming less universal and less global. Credit Suisse chose to concentrate on wealth management lured by its established position and the combination of stable and high returns it offered. In contrast, Morgan Stanley decided to move away from wealth management outside the USA, selling its European and Middle Eastern wealth management division to Credit Suisse. In its place Morgan Stanley decided to increase its commitment to investment banking in the USA, buying the Smith Barney retail brokerage division from Citigroup. In commodities trading Goldman Sachs, Citigroup, and BNP Paribas took the decision to remain committed while Morgan Stanley, JP Morgan, Deutsche Bank, Credit Suisse, and Barclays (having acquired the US operations of Lehman Brothers), all pulled back. The effect of these contrary moves was to slowly erode the megabank model as each bank reassessed its position in the light of the national and international regulations that they were increasingly subjected to and the effect these had on their overall profitability. The result was to create opportunities for smaller and more specialist financial institutions ranging from international commodity brokers to global wealth managers. These shadow banks attracted talented individuals from the megabanks as they could offer them high rewards unconstrained by any bonus caps imposed either to appease political pressure or to cross-subsidize less profitable operations.

As the world's financial system gradually stabilized, megabanks faced attack from three separate directions. The first was from regulators in the form of the controls that either prevented them engaging in certain types of activity or introduced additional costs that made these activities less profitable. The second was from smaller banks that moved into those areas that the large banks were moving out of either voluntarily because of low profitability or new regulations. The third was from ex-employees who operated in those areas that remained highly profitable but believed they could capture those rewards for themselves rather than share them with others either through a combined bonus pool or with the shareholders in the form of dividends. The combination of these attacks was to shrink the business done by the megabanks while leaving them intact. However, the effect was not the same for all universal banks because those based in the USA became increasingly more powerful than before. The crisis had removed the last vestiges of the Glass–Steagall Act as it led to the mergers between two of the largest investment banks and two of the largest commercial banks, in the case of Bear Stearns/JP Morgan and Merrill Lynch/Bank of America, while the two other leading investment banks, namely Goldman Sachs and Morgan Stanley, converted into commercial banks while retaining their investment banking operations. Along with Citigroup, which had already moved in the direction of combining commercial and investment banking, this gave the USA five megabanks. Even though regulations forced them to shed particular activities they were in a position to dominate world markets as they already controlled the vast US market, operated on the basis of the US$ and could look to the Federal Reserve as lender of last resort. As James Forese, head of investment banking, Citibank, reflected in 2018, 'We became a much more focused and much simpler business.'[51]

This gave them a strong competitive advantage over foreign competitors with even the UK bank, Barclays, which had acquired the US base of Lehman Brothers, struggling to compete. The continental European challenge of Deutsche Bank, BNP Paribas, Société Generale, UBS, and Credit Suisse faded away. Stephen Morris, David Crow, and Olaf

[50] Oliver Ralph, 'Universal banks', 30th March 2015.
[51] Laura Noonan, 'Financials', 12th June 2018.

Storbeck concluded in 2018, that only Barclays and Deutsche Bank could compete with their US rivals but they 'remain dwarfed by their Wall Street peers after a painful decade of restructuring that has left them smaller and less profitable in almost every business line'.[52] In particular, by 2018 Deutsche Bank was regarded by the hedge-fund manager, Davide Serra, as 'subscale everywhere with a weak US franchise'.[53] The British bank, RBS, which had briefly aspired to become a megabank, was dismembered under government ownership while even HSBC, with a strong Asian base and an international network, found it difficult to compete. In addition there were other megabanks that chose to focus on commercial and retail banking, especially in their domestic market, as with Wells Fargo from the USA, Santander from Spain, Commerzbank from Germany, and the Chinese and Japanese banks. Nomura from Japan gave up its attempt to become a global bank, despite acquiring Lehman Brothers' non-US network in 2008. In 2018 Commerzbank sold its trading business to the French bank, Société Generale. The reason, according to David Keohane, was that trading activities were 'too capital-intensive and because it was so complex'.[54] Tim Throsby, head of corporate and investment banking at Barclays, claimed in 2018 that his bank was the only challenger to the US megabanks left standing: 'We're the only European bank that's deadly serious... about having a serious transatlantic corporate and investment bank. The US is the largest capital market in the world and the most lucrative.'[55] Since the Global Financial Crisis megabanks had been forced to make difficult decisions about where they wanted to position themselves. Some retreated to the safety of their domestic market while others built upon niche positions by acquiring the business of others. As Laura Noonan observed in 2018, 'Regulations have in effect banned them from once lucrative activities such as trading stocks on their own behalf and co-investing in funds with clients. Areas including trading structured products have all but dried up as clients balked at the collapse in value of some instruments and revelations of widespread manipulation of others, especially mortgage-backed bonds.'[56]

What remained was a small group of five US megabanks. In 2009 those five US banks accounted for 48 per cent of global wholesale market activity. By 2014 this had grown to 59 per cent. In contrast, the share of the top five European megabanks fell from 35 per cent to 31 per cent over the same period. That US dominance continued to grow in subsequent years as no country or region could provide a base to match that found in the USA, even the Eurozone. Martin Arnold pointed out in 2018 that US banks benefited 'from a dominant position in a homogenous domestic market that boasts the world's largest investment banking fee pool' while 'Europe has no truly pan-European banks'.[57] There were no pan-European banks equivalent to their pan-American rivals, and so they lacked the scale to be globally competitive. Scale was vital according to Bernhard Hodler, chief executive of Swiss private bank Julius Baer. Writing in 2018 he concluded that, 'In the mass-market business, size really matters.'[58] The USA remained, by far, the largest single financial market in the world. One measure was assets under management. This was estimated at $80tn in 2017 and had almost doubled since 2007, when it stood at $48tn. Of that 2017 figure almost half,

52 Stephen Morris, David Crow, and Olaf Storbeck, 'Deutsche is all downside while Barclays blooms', 25th October 2018,

53 Stephen Morris, David Crow, and Olaf Storbeck, 'Deutsche is all downside while Barclays blooms', 25th October 2018,

54 David Keohane, 'SocGen buys Commerzbank's EMC business', 4th July 2018,

55 Laura Noonan, 'Financials', 12th June 2018,

56 Laura Noonan, 'Financials', 12th June 2018,

57 Martin Arnold, 'How US banks took over the financial world', 17th September 2018,

58 Martin Arnold, Patrick Jenkins and Laura Noonan, 'Banking', 12th July 2018,

or $37tn, was located in the USA, providing a huge competitive advantage to US-based financial institutions as the home-country bias meant that they dominated that market. JP Morgan was the largest retail lender in the USA and, in the words of Jamie Dimon, its CEO, they benefited from 'a lot of capital, liquidity and hardly any unsecured short-term funding'.[59] Another US bank, Morgan Stanley, had the resources to complete a trade involving a $1bn bond portfolio in three hours. With the US$ being the currency of choice in international finance that meant that US-based banks and fund managers were also in a position to dominate the global market, especially after the financial crisis. That crisis had frozen global money markets, through which US$s had been freely available to all, and it had never fully recovered because of the subsequent actions of central banks and regulators. Deprived of supplies of US$s, and largely shut out of the US market, non-US banks and fund managers struggled to compete with their US peers in the ten years following the financial crisis.[60]

However, this did not mean that US megabanks went unchallenged. Laura Noonan's assessment in 2018 was that 'Investment banks have spent much of the decade under a shadow since the meltdown of the US mortgage market. They have watched private equity firms and hedge funds take their place at the top of the finance food chain. Executives have complained loudly that the regulations in place after the crisis have hampered their ability to compete.'[61] Despite their advantages the regulations under which they were forced to operate led them to reduce their lending, and withdraw from a number of activities that they had previously dominated. Writing in 2018 Robin Wigglesworth and Ben McLannahan reflected that, 'Since the financial crisis, regulatory changes have aimed to purge leverage, primarily by curtailing the role banks have traditionally played in providing it,'[62] In contrast, Sam Fleming, Joe Rennison, and Robert Armstrong pointed out that 'While

[59] Laura Noonan and Patrick Jenkins, 'Financial Crisis', 13th September 2018,

[60] Daniel Schäfer, 'Shrinking margins and higher costs drive down returns', 5th November 2014; Oliver Ralph, 'Universal banks', 30th March 2015; James Shotter, Laura Noonan and Martin Arnold, 'Top brass set to advise against full exit from retail operations', 24th April 2015; Henry Sanderson, 'Exchange pushes the pedal to the metal', 10th June 2015; Joe Rennison, 'Fitch warns of growing repo threat', 18th June 2015; Frederic Oudea, 'Europe needs home grown bulge bracket banks', 12th October 2015; Martin Arnold, 'SocGen to merge Kleinwort with Hambros', 16th March 2016; Laura Noonan, Joe Rennison, and Thomas Hale, 'Lenders trim budgets for maths and models', 24th May 2016; John Authers and Mary Childs, 'Overpriced, underperforming', 25th May 2016; Laura Noonan, 'Wall Street deal fees eclipse European rivals', 10th June 2016; Henny Sender, 'US retreat from global system lets China in', 5th April 2017; Thomas Hale, 'Shadow banks step into the spotlight', 5th April 2017; Shawn Donnan, 'Ebbs and capital flows', 22nd August 2017; Sam Fleming and Alistair Gray, 'Fed research points to risk from non-banks', 9th March 2018; Laura Noonan, 'Financials', 12th June 2018; David Keohane, 'SocGen buys Commerzbank's EMC business', 4th July 2018; Martin Arnold, Patrick Jenkins and Laura Noonan, 'Banking', 12th July 2018; Jennifer Thompson, 'China and Latin America help send assets towards $80tn', 23rd July 2018; Owen Walker, 'New rules will shine a light on securities lending', 30th July 2018; Laura Noonan and Patrick Jenkins, 'Financial Crisis', 13th September 2018; Martin Arnold, 'How US banks took over the financial world', 17th September 2018; Robin Wigglesworth and Joe Rennison, 'New credit ecosystem blossoms as portfolio trades surge', 11th October 2018; Stephen Morris, David Crow, and Olaf Storbeck, 'Deutsche is all downside while Barclays blooms', 25th October 2018; Caroline Binham, 'Ringfence rules come into effect for UK banks', 2nd January 2019; Lindsay Fortado and Laura Noonan, 'Banks bet on hedge fund prime broking fees', 10th January 2019; Nicholas Megaw, 'Challenger banks struggle to smash glass ceiling', 14th January 2019; David Crow and Stephen Morris, 'The battle for Barclays', 21st January 2019.

[61] Laura Noonan, 'Financials', 12th June 2018; Simon Samuels, 'The ECB should resist the lure of bigger banks', 31st January 2019; Laura Noonan, 'Goldman to wield axe on bond unit as peers sit tight', 8th February 2019; Stephen Morris and David Crow, 'Axe swings at European banks after lamentable fourth quarter', 22nd February 2019; Laura Noonan, 'Transaction work is fastest growth area for big banks', 8th March 2019; Philip Stafford, 'Mifid 2 rules tighten Wall Street's grip on Europe', 27th June 2019; Stephen Morris and Olaf Storbeck, 'Humbled giant struggles to silence doubters', 9th July 2019; David Crow, 'The last man in European investment banking', 23rd August 2019; Robert Armstrong, 'Warnings sounded over watered-down Volcker', 23rd August 2019.

[62] Robin Wigglesworth and Ben McLannahan, 'Liquidity outs leverage as the big worry for investors', 4th May 2018.

post-crisis regulation forced traditional banks to have larger amounts of capital and more resilient liquidity backstops, the non-banking sector is much more loosely supervised.'[63] The role previously played by the megabanks was increasingly taken by a rampant shadow-banking sector.

Though there were problems of defining shadow banks by 2016 the sector was estimated to account for 13 per cent of total global financial assets, or $45tn. This compared to $180tn, or 53 per cent held by banks. By 2016 there were, for example, 8474 hedge funds managing $2.9tn. Though dominated by activity in the USA, shadow banking had become a world-wide force by then, controlling, for example, $7tn in Chinese assets, or 15.5 per cent of the total. In the USA non-bank lenders were responsible for half of the mortgages granted to US residential home owners in 2016 and 30 per cent of loans to mid-sized US companies in 2018. Globally, companies had turned to the bond market as a direct source of funds rather than borrowing from banks. By 2018 the value of the corporate bonds in circulation in the world stood at $12tn and accounted for one-fifth of borrowing by companies. As the business of non-banks grew they increasingly resembled banks by borrowing short and lending long, exposing it to a potential liquidity crisis. In 2016 one calculation suggested that 72 per cent of the assets held by shadow banks was susceptible to runs like banks. Growing in popularity were Commercial Mortgage-Backed Securities (CMBS) that were sold directly to investors. These bundled pools of mortgages on offices and shopping centres into a single bond, with the interest paid out of the repayments of borrowers. The debt was then sliced into tranches with different risk and return profiles so as to appeal to a wide range of investors from risk-taking individuals to risk-averse pension funds. Colby Smith concluded in 2018 that, 'To satisfy their voracious appetites for higher-yielding loans, investors have grown increasingly willing to stomach fewer protections for the same price and leverage.'[64] One category of debt that was growing strongly by then was leveraged loans, with $1.3tn in circulation. These were loans made to highly-indebted companies that were attractive to investors because of the high rates of interest paid. In many cases these loans were repackaged and sold on through collateralized loan obligations.

Beginning in the USA private equity firms like Blackstone were quick to move into the financing gap vacated by banks. Mark Vandevelde wrote in 2018, that:

> lightly-regulated asset managers have filled the void as banks are forced to retreat from risky deals. Unlike banks, which are dependent on deposits and other short-term funding, these funds raise money from long-term investors such as insurance companies and pension funds. By setting up huge lending arms, they have been transformed from heavy-weight dealmakers that took stakes in companies into the principal bankers for a large tract of corporate America.[65]

This was most easily done in the case of large and established companies in need of substantial loans, and it was only later that fund managers extended their lending to small- and medium-sized enterprises. Fund managers were less able than banks to estimate the likelihood of a default among small- and medium-sized businesses because they lacked both experience in this field, and the relationship that came from handling other aspects of a

[63] Sam Fleming, Joe Rennison and Robert Armstrong, 'Non-bank lenders under scrutiny after taking big share in US mortgage market', 10th April 2019.

[64] Colby Smith, 'Systemic risk fears intensify over leveraged loan boom', 30th October 2018.

[65] Mark Vandevelde, 'Financial Crisis', 20th September 2018.

company's financial affairs. Fund managers in the USA were less at a disadvantage in this respect as they had long absorbed bond issues. However, with low yields elsewhere in the financial markets, such as from fixed-income instruments and equities, along with increased volatility of stock and bond prices, fund managers around the world turned to direct lending to business as a means of generating higher returns. As competition between them intensified, as was the situation by 2016, they were willing to accept lower returns and accept greater risks. What this reflected was the way that the financial system responded to the restrictions placed on the megabanks and it was of increasing concern to regulators. Regulators became aware that the risks to the stability of the financial system they were attempting to control by restricting bank lending, and especially high levels of leverage, had shifted to the shadow banking system. The reaction from regulators was not to reduce the restrictions placed on banks, so that they could resume lending to the customers they knew and understood best and in ways that they were long familiar with in terms of risks and rewards. Instead, regulators sought to extend their restrictions to those elements of the shadow banking system they could easily identify and police. The dilemma facing regulators was how to regulate the banking system in such a way and to such a degree that it could continue to meet the demands of borrowers, and so remove the need for alternative providers who, potentially, also posed a risk to financial stability.

It was not just borrowers who turned to fund managers in the wake of the Global Financial Crisis and the much stricter regulatory regime that followed it. Investors also turned away from the megabanks as they could no longer guarantee the liquidity and the stability that was sought. An important consequence was the growth of passive funds that mimicked an index. By 2018 an estimated $10tn in assets was managed in this way. Among these Exchange Traded Funds (ETFs) were increasingly popular as they promised diversification, liquidity, and simplicity at a low cost. Gregory Davis, the chief investment officer at the fund managers, Vanguard, explained the merits of an ETF in 2018, 'With one trade, individuals can own a portfolio that is broadly diversified and low cost.'[66] Between 2007 and 2017 the assets held in ETFs grew from $800bn to $4.2tn. Of that $3tn was in the USA, $700bn in Europe, and $200bn in Japan. By 2016 nearly 40 per cent of the US equity assets under management were in the hands of ETFs, and other index-tracking funds, while their share in the bond market was 20 per cent. Globally, 13 per cent of global investment assets were in ETFs by 2017. These investments were largely in the hands of a small number of global fund managers led by BlackRock, Vanguard, State Street, BNY Mellon, Fidelity, Invesco, and Pimco, each of whom controlled assets in excess of $1tn.

BlackRock, run by Larry Fink, had made an astute move in 2009 when it bought the San Francisco fund managers, BGI (Barclays Global Investors), when Barclays was desperately looking for funds to avoid having to seek support from the British government in the aftermath of the crisis. This made BlackRock into the world's largest fund manager with $2.8tn assets, having bought Merrill Lynch Investment Management (MLIM) in 2006. By 2019 BlackRock was managing $6.5tn, having become the leader in passive investing, which had boomed in the aftermath of the crisis and central bank intervention. As Attracta Mooney and Peter Smith wrote in 2019, 'As markets soared on the back of quantitative easing, passive funds delivered strong returns and investors piled in, while many active managers have struggled to outperform.'[67] Scale is important in passive fund management and that was

[66] Gregory Davis, 'Index funds are not to blame for market volatility', 31st October 2018.

[67] Attracta Mooney and Peter Smith, 'Deal of the decade: how BlackRock buying BGI changed the industry', 6th May 2019.

what BlackRock had gained with the BGI acquisition, and what other fund managers tried to match subsequently. In 2018 Invesco bought Oppenheimer Funds from Massachusetts Mutual, for example. As these fund managers grew in size they were able to challenge the megabanks in a variety of different ways. The megafunds could also spread the costs of regulation, and invest in the technology required to keep up with rivals. In his review of fund managers in 2018 Alexander Blostein, at Goldman Sachs, concluded that 'Fees matter, and if you have scale, you can probably be more competitive on pricing.'[68] Size not only gave the largest fund managers a competitive advantage for it also allowed them to internalize transactions, so cutting out the services they had previously relied upon the megabanks to provide. As Marty Flanagan, the chief executive of Invesco, put it in 2018, by being so big 'You end up being more relevant for clients, and that really matters.'[69]

Unlike the megabanks the megafunds were not constrained in their ability to use their own capital to make purchases or supply a demand from their own vast holdings of stocks and bonds. Jim Switzer, head of credit rating at the investment group, Alliance Bernstein, indicated the role they were playing by 2018: 'We're not playing the role of banks. But when we are also liquidity providers in a dislocated market, we get better execution.'[70] This meant that those managing ETFs could continually adjust the portfolio through internal sales and purchases as they controlled such a large share of the market. As many of the bonds in circulation lacked liquidity, the ability of a global fund manager to provide it greatly increased the appeal that they had to investors, especially in ETFs. As Michael John Lytle, chief executive of Tabula Investment Management, explained in 2018, 'Fixed income is not a single asset class when you think about the differences between government bonds, investment-grade, high-yield, emerging market debt, mortgage-backed securities and the US municipal bond market.'[71] That made many of the issues illiquid which was the situation that Chris Flood reported on in 2018, 'Most bond trades are still conducted via private over-the-counter transactions, unlike equities where the majority of trading occurs on regulated exchanges.'[72] Prior to the crisis the megabanks were able to overcome the problem of illiquidity by leveraging both the huge funds and vast portfolios under their control. It was this ability that they lost as a result of the 2008 crisis and the regulatory intervention that followed. Their place then taken by the megafunds.[73]

[68] Robin Wigglesworth, 'Asset managers seek an entrée to the trillion-dollar club', 26th October 2018.

[69] Robin Wigglesworth, 'Asset managers seek an entrée to the trillion-dollar club', 26th October 2018.

[70] Robin Wigglesworth and Joe Rennison, 'New credit ecosystem blossoms as portfolio trades surge', 11th October 2018.

[71] Chris Flood, 'Global debt pile creates new chances in nascent market', 5th November 2018.

[72] Chris Flood, 'Global debt pile creates new chances in nascent market', 5th November 2018

[73] Philip Stafford, 'Voice brokers answer call for liquidity', 12th August 2016; Harriet Agnew and Patrick Jenkins, 'What's next for the City', 3rd September 2016; Attracta Mooney, 'Fund houses take on banks over lending', 5th September 2016; Chris Flood, 'Market leaders face pressure from upstarts', 12th December 2016; Robin Wigglesworth, 'Brutal culls ensure the ETF graveyard is full', 15th December 2016; Thomas Hale, 'Bypassing the banks', 28th December 2016; Charles D. Ellis, 'Technology and low returns: the end for active investing?', 21st January 2017; Robin Wigglesworth, 'ETFs and index-trackers coin it in with 20% share of US bond market', 6th February 2017; Thomas Hale, 'Shadow banks step into the spotlight', 5th April 2017; Shawn Donnan, 'Ebbs and capital flows', 22nd August 2017; Jennifer Thompson, 'Regulators descend on booming market', 11th September 2017; Philip Stafford, 'Voice brokers fight to survive Europe's shake-up', 10th October 2017; Ian Smith, 'Could ETFs survive a sudden downturn in the market?', 14th October 2017; Chris Flood, 'Global assets to sell to $145tn by 2015', 30th October 2017; Ian Smith, 'Could ETFs survive a sudden downturn in the market?', 14th October 2017; Robin Wigglesworth, 'Exchange traded products face scrutiny as worries deepen', 15th February 2018; Sam Fleming and Alistair Gray, 'Fed research points to risk from non-banks', 9th March 2018; Laura Noonan, 'Financials', 12th June 2018; David Keohane, 'SocGen buys Commerzbank's EMC business', 4th July 2018; Martin Arnold, Patrick Jenkins, and Laura Noonan, 'Banking', 12th July 2018; Jennifer Thompson, 'China and Latin America help send assets towards $80tn', 23rd July 2018; Owen Walker, 'New rules will shine a light on securities lending', 30th July 2018; Attracta Mooney, 'Passive funds hit new highs on wave of investor approval', 10th

Long-term Consequences 3

The curbing of the megabanks also had implications for the interdealer brokers who had grown to prominence from the 1970s onwards by servicing the inter-bank and OTC markets that they spawned. They had become essential players in the global markets for a wide variety of financial instruments. In 2007 Michael Mackenzie claimed that 'The interdealer market is the bulwark of the global financial system, as it allows banks and other financial institutions to trade bonds, currencies and derivatives across all time zones and from every major financial centre.'[74] During the 1980s the interdealer brokers had become central to the market in interest-rate futures while growth in the 1990s was fuelled by credit derivatives and related products. To Philip Stafford in 2016 an interdealer broker remained 'a cog that helps grease the wheels of global trading across a range of markets from interest rates, commodities, and currencies to numerous types of derivatives for global banks'.[75] Interdealer brokers were integral parts of a global financial community, simultaneously competing against and cooperating with each other. Hannah Murphy in 2018 observed that 'The world of brokers is a close network of long friendships and intense rivalries.'[76]

Interdealer brokers acted as intermediaries between banks and their dealings with each other and with other financial institutions, facilitating trading in bills, bonds, currencies, commodities, and derivatives either on the telephone or electronically on screens. Initially the service they provided relied on communication over the telephone but voice brokers were increasingly displaced by electronic trading networks. Electronic broking was extensively used for simpler financial instruments while the telephone was still required when brokers had to negotiate large deals involving complex products between their customers. New and unfamiliar financial instruments needed to be explained, while the most liquid and standardized did not. The latter quickly migrated to electronic platforms while the former remained in the hands of the voice brokers. Interdealer brokers also provided anonymity to both parties in a transaction, which was of value to those banks and fund managers seeking to hide their identity when conducting large sales and purchases. Interdealer brokers were experts in making markets in illiquid assets and large blocks of shares. It took time to construct deals in these and this had to be done in secrecy. If not, others could take advantage of the situation, using their knowledge to force prices up or down. As Terry

September 2018; Laura Noonan and Patrick Jenkins, 'Financial Crisis', 13th September 2018; Chris Flood, 'Bond liquidity issues prompt investors to turn to ETFs', 17th September 2018; Martin Arnold, 'How US banks took over the financial world', 17th September 2018; Mark Vandevelde, 'Financial Crisis', 20th September 2018; Robin Wigglesworth and Joe Rennison, 'New credit ecosystem blossoms as portfolio trades surge', 11th October 2018; Stephen Morris, David Crow, and Olaf Storbeck, 'Deutsche is all downside while Barclays blooms', 25th October 2018; Robin Wigglesworth, 'Passive Attack: The story of a Wall Street revolution', 22nd December 2018; Lindsay Fortado and Laura Noonan, 'Banks bet on hedge fund prime broking fees', 10th January 2019; Chris Flood, 'BlackRock and Vanguard pull in 57% of global fund flows', 18th February 2018; Chris Flood, 'Bond funds head for $1tn landmark', 1st April 2019; Joe Rennison, 'MarketAxess muscles into ETFs with Virtu tie-up', 8th April 2019; Sam Fleming, Joe Rennison and Robert Armstrong, 'Non-bank lenders under scrutiny after taking big share in US mortgage market', 10th April 2019; Attracta Mooney and Peter Smith, 'Deal of the decade: how BlackRock buying BGI changed the industry', 6th May 2019; John Dizard, 'Eyes front, fund bosses, it's Carney's army now', 1st July 2019; Owen Walker and Chris Flood, 'Amundi will backstop funds in a crunch', 5th August 2019.

[74] Michael Mackenzie, 'Global trade facilitators behind a 24-hour market', 20th April 2007.
[75] Philip Stafford, 'ICAP's new direction reflects changing future of derivatives', 6th October 2016.
[76] Hannah Murphy, 'Mifid spoils the mood at junior market party', 13th October 2018.

Smith, chief executive of Tullett-Prebon, said in 2009, 'It's a mistake to believe that everything is made better by instant transparency.'[77]

As both exchanges and interdealer brokers embraced electronic trading they increasingly became rivals for the same business. Among the interdealer brokers ICAP was one of the most aggressive in moving in this direction. In 2003 ICAP had bought a US electronic bond-trading platform, BrokerTec, and that was followed in 2006 with a US-based foreign exchange electronic broker, EBS. In 2004 it had tried to buy the European-based electronic bond platform MTS, and then made another attempt in 2007. However, it was thwarted in that later attempt when the LSE took full control of MTS after acquiring Borsa Italiana. To Michael Spencer, the chief executive, of ICAP, the future lay with global electronic trading, stating in 2007 that, 'If we acquired MTS we would bring about the globalisation of the Eurozone government bond market for the first time.'[78] Faced with the failure to acquire MTS, ICAP then used its US electronic broker, BrokerTec, as a way of challenging MTS as the market for Eurozone government bonds. To Spencer there was a battle for global dominance between interdealer brokers and the regulated exchanges. By 2007 the London-based ICAP was the largest of the interdealer brokers, handling transactions of $1,500bn a day across currencies, bonds, energy products, and derivatives and operating from a network of offices stretching from Sydney through Tokyo and London to New York. It faced strong competition from another London-based firm, Tullet Prebon, managed by Terry Smith; the New York-based Cantor Fitzgerald, where Howard Lutnick was in charge; another US firm, GFI, founded by Michael Gooch; and the Swiss-based Compagnie Financière Tradition. In 2007 the estimated market share of each placed ICAP in the lead on 31 per cent, followed by Tullett Prebon (18 per cent), Tradition (14 per cent), Cantor (12 per cent), and GFI (11 per cent).

That meant that the five top firms were responsible for 86 per cent of all transactions handled by interdealer brokers. Each had particular specialities but they increasingly operated globally and made markets across the entire range of financial instruments. In that way they could best serve their principal customers, which were the megabanks. What the concentration reflected was the economies of scale that the largest firms enjoyed. By investing heavily in expert staff and advanced technology, developing extensive international networks, and covering an ever-expanding range of financial instruments, these interdealer brokers could provide the megabanks with a trading service that matched their requirements. They acted as middlemen for banks trading financial instruments on a continuous basis through all time zones, operating in offices located across the world, but with London, New York, Tokyo, and Singapore being key hubs. The megabanks relied on them to conduct the high-volume inter-bank trading that was essential if they were to manage risk by offsetting the liabilities they had with clients such as hedge funds, money managers, and corporations. Interdealer brokers fed traders at banks with a constant stream of information via telephones and 'squawk boxes' and through screens. An interdealer broker saw what and where a bank wanted to buy and sell, and at what price, and then tried to match that with a counterparty, earning a commission for their trouble. They did not take positions, as that was the responsibility of the banks. This made them central players in the pre-crisis global financial markets.

The Global Financial Crisis threatened the business of the interdealer brokers. The megabanks retreated from the riskier assets traded on the OTC market, where interdealer

[77] Jeremy Grant and Brooke Masters, 'Brokers set out to fight backlash against OTC trade', 28th April 2009.
[78] Norma Cohen and Gillian Tett, 'Icap sets sights on MTS platform', 25th June 2007.

brokers had thrived. In addition, regulators intervened to curb OTC trading, blaming their lack of transparency for the build up of risk that had led to the crisis. The remedy was to force trading through exchanges and clearing houses, as that would provide better supervision and regulation as well as guarantees that deals would be completed. Robin Wigglesworth observed in 2019 that 'Since the financial crisis, stricter regulations and commercial pressures have forced many banks to pare back or close their once-vast proprietary and market-making desks.'[79] All this ran counter to the role played by interdealer brokers as these acted as intermediaries between and for the megabanks, arranging sales and purchases but accepting no counterparty responsibility, which lay with the sellers and purchasers. If trading was conducted on exchanges, or passed through clearing houses, the role of the interdealer brokers would be greatly diminished. The exchange would provide the platform through which trading would be conducted while clearing houses would ensure completion. Also if counterparties to every deal had to be made known then the anonymity provided by interdealer brokers was not required, encouraging direct contact between buyers and sellers. The more regulators forced trading through exchanges and clearing houses, and the greater the demand for the immediate reporting of every transaction, the less was the need to employ interdealer brokers to handle transactions. The effect was to force interdealer brokers to change their business model and embrace electronic trading even more quickly. This led to a greater convergence between exchanges and interdealer brokers, as both operated electronic platforms as did the banks themselves.

Philip Stafford summarized in 2016 the radically changed world in which the interdealers brokers now operated, contrasting it with the conditions that had underpinned their rise to prominence:

> Deregulation ended fixed commissions, ushering in electronic trading. It also kicked off a boom in risk management. Big companies going global needed complex tools to hedge their risk to adverse interest-rate or currency moves. For that they needed big investment banks and with it was born the modern global derivatives market. Banks transacted interest rates, corporate bonds, currencies, and credit deals and hedged their own risks in futures markets. Then the financial crisis struck, spurring a regulatory crackdown from policy makers. New rules on leverage have made it more expensive for banks to use their balance sheets to hold inventory or trade and finance positions in OTC derivatives markets. Not helping banks navigate a more costly world of doing business has been the suppression of bond yields and market volatility due to central bank policy, reducing the need among companies and portfolio managers to use derivatives for hedging risk.[80]

Tougher capital standards weighed on the ability of banks to warehouse corporate bonds and facilitate transactions for investors such as asset managers, hedge funds, and insurers. This forced them to withdraw from market making and so they generated much less trading for the interdealer brokers. Furthermore, both to reduce costs, and in response to regulatory pressure to prevent market manipulation, banks increasingly turned away from the use of interdealer brokers and towards electronic platforms. By 2013 electronic trading accounted for 74 per cent of the market in fixed-income products, currencies, and commodities, for example, with much more being conducted by high-frequency traders than the

[79] Robin Wigglesworth, 'IMF warns of "tip of the iceberg" threat over volatility', 12th April 2019.
[80] Philip Stafford, 'ICAP's new direction reflects changing future of derivatives', 6th October 2016.

megabanks. Trading took place without intermediation being fully automated and conducted through links between computers.

Nevertheless, there remained a role for interdealer brokers in voice trading, where large or complex deals were negotiated away from regulated markets. OTC trading was split between dealers trading with their clients and dealers trading with each other in order to offset their clients' business. This was done using both voice trading and electronic markets. Interdealer brokers acted as gatekeepers filtering out those counterparties over which there were doubts regarding reliability. For that reason interdealer brokers continued to be preferred by those conducting large trades where a counterparty default could endanger a complex series of deals if one part of the chain broke. Institutional investors had long been wary of flagging their intentions for fear of having the price move against them. For that reason, even after the introduction of electronic trading platforms, interdealer brokers continued to handle much of the trading. However, their market share was being steadily eroded as banks retreated from trading because of tougher capital regulations. As banks withdrew, their place was taken by electronic market-makers, unconstrained by the capital rules that were driving banks out. These included Citadel Securities in interest-rate swaps, Virtu Financial in US Treasuries, and XTX in foreign exchange. These firms did not have the same relationship with the interdealer brokers as had the banks. At the same time there was a proliferation of electronic trading platforms such as MarketAxess and Tradeweb in bonds. In 2016 Rick McVey, the chief executive of MarketAxess, admitted that 'The regulatory changes have been very positive for us.'[81] MarketAxess had been established in 2000 and became the largest electronic bond-trading platform in the USA. The US corporate bond market grew from $5tn in 2008 to $8tn in 2016 on the back of ultra-low interest rates. Banks remained responsible for the primary market but regulatory changes in the wake of the financial crisis were forcing them out of secondary trading. This created an opening for the likes of MarketAxess. Its share of the trading in US corporate bonds grew from 4.5 per cent in 2010 to 13 per cent in 2016. In association with BlackRock, the largest asset manager in the world, it then launched OpenTrading, which was an anonymous trading venue allowing investors to trade directly with each other, without the need for intermediation. By 2018 MarketAxess handled 86 per cent of the electronic trading in US corporate bonds.

In 2014 the same five interdealer brokers still remained dominant, namely ICAP and Tullet Prebon of the UK, GFI and BGC (the renamed Cantor) of the USA, and Tradition of Switzerland. However, the challenge they faced was growing in intensity putting pressure on these firms. Since the financial crisis regulators had been trying to turn the trading in financial products away from a bilateral telephone-based market into an anonymous electronic-based one, with the aim of reducing the risks posed to the global financial system. This favoured electronic platforms, known as Swap Execution Facilities (SEFs), over voice brokers, for example, undermining the role played by the interdealer brokers. These electronic platforms were owned by a variety of providers, including information companies like Bloomberg and Thomson Reuters; leading US investment banks; or exchanges like Nasdaq and the LSE. Interdealer brokers did respond to the challenge they posed by developing their own electronic platforms. In 2015 the Swiss interdealer broker, Tradition, set up an electronic trading venue, DBV-X, in London to cater for the repo market. Even more ambitious was ICAP. Its chief executive, Michael Spencer, stated in 2016 that 'My dream is to create the world-leading, multi-product global electronic network for over-the-counter

[81] Joe Rennison, 'Bond trading platform muscles in as banks retreat', 29th September 2016.

products.'[82] By then he considered that voice broking had no future, and so ICAP sold that division and concentrated, instead, on developing electronic trading platforms. His assessment was that 'The declining risk appetite of banks means that the OTC markets will have to be opened up to a whole new group of market participants. Initially, it will be electronic firms like Citadel, Virtu, DRW...Lots of people are leaving banks to set up independent trading outfits. This trend is not going to stop.'[83]

However, other interdealer brokers continued to see a future for voice brokers, while accepting that electronic markets posed a serious threat. One who believed in voice broking was Shaun Lynn, president of BGC, which sold its electronic bond platform, eSpeed, to Nasdaq in 2013: 'The market is going electronic but it's going with the brokers. The exchange itself is electronic, but the broker executes for you on a range of other related products, from asset swaps to basic trades, that come of it.'[84] Adopting a similar view was John Phizackerley, the chief executive of Tullett Prebon. He continued to maintain that OTC markets 'depend upon the intervention and support of voice brokers for their liquidity and effective operation.'[85] That did not mean these interdealer brokers that remained committed to voice broking did not have to change in order to survive. Facing a growing squeeze on their business, as the megabanks retreated from trading the remaining voice brokers merged to achieve economies of scale. Over the 2015–16 period BGC acquired GFI, creating one dominant New York-based business, while ICAP sold its voice broking services to Tullet Prebon, leading to one dominant London-based operation. With their enhanced depth and breadth these merged units could provide the megabanks, as well as hedge funds and institutional investors, with the liquidity and variety they demanded from voice brokers. Writing in 2018 Philip Stafford judged that Tullet Prebon's acquisition of ICAP's voice broking business, to form TP ICAP, gave it 'the scale to compete in swaps and fixed-income trading as the market was being transformed by the advance of electronic trading, and tougher regulations that squeezed the investment banks that are its main customers and piled on the broker's own compliance costs.'[86] By then TP ICAP employed 3300 brokers globally, being the world's largest interdealer broker with a 45 per cent share of the business. The combined BGC/GFI had a 34 per cent market share leaving Tradition a distant third with 21 per cent. Five had become three to save on costs, increase depth and spread, and reduce expenses by cutting down the number of brokers they dealt with. Conversely, as megabanks offloaded trading activities they turned to brokers to complete deals once done by an in-house team. This generated trading for the remaining voice brokers, as there remained large and complex deals to be negotiated in secret. The megabanks continued to buy and sell financial products with their own clients, and then offset those transactions by dealing between themselves, both over the phone and on electronic venues, though the latter was gaining over the former in terms of volume.

In contrast to TP ICAP, BGC, and Tradition, ICAP, shorn of its voice brokers, renamed itself NEX and focused on the provision of electronic markets, where it proved very successful. In 2017 NEX's BrokerTec, for example, had 80 per cent of the US Treasury bond market, dwarfing Nasdaq's eSpeed, which had languished since being sold by Cantor Fitzgerald. In 2013 eSpeed (later renamed Nasdaq Fixed Income) had 40 per cent of the

[82] Philip Stafford, 'ICAP chief prepares for radical change of direction', 26th February 2016.
[83] Philip Stafford, 'ICAP's new direction reflects changing future of derivatives', 6th October 2016.
[84] Philip Stafford, 'Voice brokers answer call for liquidity', 12th August 2016.
[85] Philip Stafford, 'ICAP's new direction reflects changing future of derivatives', 6th October 2016.
[86] Philip Stafford, 'Departure of TP ICAP chief eposes tensions at top', 11th July 2018.

market but this had shrunk to 15 per cent in 2017, with another electronic platform, Dealerweb, having 5 per cent. However, reflecting the increasing convergence of OTC and Exchange-based trading in the electronic age, and under greater regulatory scrutiny, NEX was bought by the CME in 2018. The strategy of the CME was to create a common platform for trading US Treasuries, and the interest-rate futures contracts that were based on US government debt. This would allow banks to economize on the capital they were required to set aside to back their bond and futures trading activity. With control over both the cash and the futures market in US Treasuries, where turnover was \$500bn a day in 2018, the CME could push the entire trading through its own clearing house. The acquisition of NEX also gave the CME entry into the European government bond market. NEX's electronic platform was responsible for a large share of trading in the European repo market. What the fate of NEX reflected was what had happened to the interdealer brokers. They retained a niche role as voice brokers, where they conducted complex negotiations between banks. However, the trading in financial products had largely gravitated to the electronic platforms and they were under the control of exchanges, information providers, and banks while much of the actual dealing was in the hands of high-frequency traders. The fifty years between 1970 and 2020 had witnessed the rise and fall of the interdealer brokers as a major force in global financial markets.[87]

[87] Michael Mackenzie, 'Global trade facilitators behind a 24-hour market', 20th April 2007; Sarah Spikes and Norma Cohen, 'It's still good to talk on the cutting edge', 10th May 2007; Norma Cohen and Gillian Tett, 'Icap sets sights on MTS platform', 25th June 2007; David Oakley, 'Austria gives nod to MTS Eurozone rival', 1st July 2008; Brooke Masters, 'Set apart by Englishness', 14th August 2008; Jeremy Grant, 'Planned merger comes at crucial time for industry', 14th August 2008; Jeremy Grant, 'Interdealer brokers join forces on OTC issues', 9th March 2009; Jeremy Grant and Brooke Masters, 'Brokers set out to fight backlash against OTC trade', 28th April 2009; Jeremy Grant, 'Tullett predicts rebound for OTC derivatives', 5th August 2009; Jonathan Wheatley, 'São Paulo adopts a more international approach', 21st October 2009; Alistair Gray, 'Tullett hangs on to phone trading', 9th March 2010; Philip Stafford, 'High-speed electronic trading leaves regulator far behind', 3rd November 2010; Jeremy Grant, 'D Börse–NYSE merger "bad for markets"', 5th July 2011; Jeremy Grant, 'Industry in the midst of a maelstrom', 10th October 2011; Michael Mackenzie, 'Libor probe shines light on voice brokers', 17th February 2012; Philip Stafford and Simon Mundy, 'Icap nets exchange licence in deal for Plus unit', 19th May 2012; Philip Stafford and Michael Mackenzie, 'Interdealer brokers braced for shake-up', 22nd November 2012; *FT* Reporters, 'Daily fix that spiralled out of control', 20th December 2012; Philip Stafford, Arash Massoudi and Michael Mackenzie, 'Nasdaq sets stage for HFT in Treasuries', 5th April 2013; Philip Stafford, 'Settlement a blow to Spencer', 26th September 2013; Daniel Schäfer and Delphine Strauss, 'Moves into forex etrading speed up', 4th March 2014; Philip Stafford, 'Colourful world of interdealers faces deep structural changes', 3rd June 2014; Philip Stafford, 'Sense of urgency underpins fresh scrutiny of markets', 16th September 2014; Michael Mackenzie, 'Swap traders resist moves to increase use of platforms', 16th September 2014; Michael Mackenzie, 'Search for liquidity tests firms' talent for innovation', 5th November 2014; Jeremy Grant, 'SGX in talks on Asian trading platform for corporate bonds', 17th November 2014; Philip Stafford, 'Swiss broker to set up London repo venue', 19th May 2015; Philip Stafford, 'ICAP chief prepares for radical change of direction', 26th February 2016; Philip Stafford, 'Voice brokers answer call for liquidity', 12th August 2016; Joe Rennison, 'Bond trading platform muscles in as banks retreat', 29th September 2016; Philip Stafford, 'ICAP's new direction reflects changing future of derivatives', 6th October 2016; Joe Rennison, 'Lutnick makes Treasury trading comeback', 16th May 2017; Philip Stafford, 'Personal touch critical as banks trim brokers', 29th June 2017; Philip Stafford, 'Amsterdam chosen as Tradeweb's EU base', 4th August 2017; Philip Stafford, 'Voice brokers fight to survive Europe's shake-up', 10th October 2017; Gregory Meyer, 'From ranchers to fund managers, algos cause a stir', 10th October 2017; Joe Rennison and Alexandra Scaggs, 'US Treasury dealers accused of collusion', 17th November 2017; Philip Stafford, 'Spencer considers a financial future without Nex', 17th March 2018; Philip Stafford, 'CME eyes pole position in Treasury trades with audacious bid for Nex', 28th March 2018; Philip Stafford, 'CME clinches Spencer's Nex in deal set to shake up \$500bn Treasuries market', 29th March 2018; Philip Stafford, 'Fintech alley cat gets the cream with £670bn CME deal', 31st March 2018; Philip Stafford, 'CME expects no asset sales after Nex purchase', 3rd April 2018; Philip Stafford, 'Electronic trading pioneer throws down gauntlet to BrokerTec on Treasuries', 8th June 2018; Robin Wigglesworth and Joe Rennison, 'Algos blaze trail in odd lots segment of US corporate bonds', 15th June 2018; Philip Stafford, 'Departure of TP ICAP chief eposes tensions at top', 11th July 2018; Joe Rennison, 'Bloomberg snatches corporate bond trade data partner from rival Thomson Reuters', 26th July 2018; Hannah Murphy, 'TP Icap names Paris as its EU base after Brexit', 8th August 2018; Robin Wigglesworth and Joe Rennison, 'New credit ecosystem blossoms as portfolio trades surge', 11th October 2018; Robin Wigglesworth,

Conclusion

In the years between 2007 and 2020 the major influence on the way banks developed was not the crisis of 2008 but the regulatory backlash that followed. Regulators faced a perennial problem of balancing priorities ranging from the protection of savers and investors through the need to make the financial system more resilient and punish criminal behaviour to promoting greater competition and encouraging increased efficiency These priorities were not given the same weight by all national regulators, as well as generating different responses. Underlying it all was the question of how to balance the freedom given to market-based financial institutions to provide the finance required in a dynamic economy with the risks posed by unregulated or lightly-regulated institutions and markets lacking safeguards that protected against risks that could undermine the whole system. What happened was that the pendulum swung back and forth between these two aims with equilibrium being an impossible goal because the global financial system was in a constant state of flux. Prior to the crisis the emphasis had swung in the direction of prioritizing competition by removing controls whereas afterwards it swung towards achieving stability at all costs by imposing draconian rules on the main players. The inevitable consequence of the former was to destabilize the financial system by removing self-correcting mechanisms while the latter drove activity into the shadows where it could escape regulatory control. The problem was that once introduced regulations became a permanent feature of the financial landscape and had a profound impact on the shape of the global banking system.

Initially, the collapse of Lehman Brothers had led to a switch away from the megabanks with their survival in doubt. There was a desire among bank customers to diversify away from dependence upon a single provider because of fears that loans would not be repaid, collateral would not be returned, and credit lines would be frozen. The megabanks themselves responded to the crisis by increasing their capital reserves, overhauling their risk management, reinforcing their liquidity buffers, vetting borrowers more carefully, assessing loans and investments for liquidity as well as solvency, and closing down those activities suffering from a lack of business and poor profitability. This left many of their customers to seek alternative providers of the services the megabanks had, previously, been keen to supply. That was then compounded by regulatory intervention that further restricted the ability of the megabanks to do business in the way they had before the crisis, leaving even more of their customers unprovided for. As the demand for credit, capital, and financial services slowly picked up the inability of the megabanks to respond encouraged others to take their place. The more regulators restricted the activities of the megabanks the greater was the displacement of activity into financial institutions that replicated the role that they played, whether it was the use of short-term funds for long-term investment, the securitization of loans, or trading on their own account.

Nevertheless, this regulatory intervention did not spell the demise of the megabanks because only they were in a position to supply an increasingly integrated world economy with the infrastructure it required to operate. However, within this continuing need for the services of megabanks it was only those based in the USA that were in a position to fully

'Markets: Volatile Times', 10th January 2019; Robin Wigglesworth, 'IMF warns of "tip of the iceberg" threat over volatility', 12th April 2019; Philip Stafford, 'Mifid 2 rules tighten Wall Street's grip on Europe', 27th June 2019; Philip Stafford, 'BGC signs trio of high-frequency trading firms to boost European equity options', 25th July 2019; Joe Rennison and Philip Stafford, 'Rise of MarketAxess mirrors demise of traders on Wall Street', 30th August 2019.

benefit. They had almost exclusive access to the giant US market, which dominated the global demand for financial services. This gave them a scale in terms of depth, which no others could match. As the currency of international finance remained the US$ the drying up of global liquidity during the crisis, followed by continuing constraints, privileged those banks that had access to unlimited quantities of $s: that was those based in the USA. They could borrow and lend internationally in their own currency, which made it easier and cheaper to balance assets and liabilities across currencies. Damaging as the crisis and subsequent regulatory intervention was for US-based megabanks they emerged stronger as a result because their rivals suffered even more of a setback. In contrast, the Global Financial Crisis, and the regulatory intervention it provoked, spelled the end of the interdealer brokers as the key intermediaries between the megabanks. They were already under severe pressure as electronic markets replaced voice trading. They then had to cope with the decline in trading by their main customers, the megabanks, and the intensification of the switch to electronic platforms. This left the interdealer brokers with a niche role while exchanges and others provided the electronic markets that users of all kinds turned to.

16
Bonds and Currencies, 2007–20

Introduction

Though markets are normally associated with regulated institutions such as exchanges, of far greater importance was that trading which took place without them. Ranked among the largest and most active financial markets in the world were those involving fixed-income financial instruments and currencies, and these took place through direct contact between buyers and sellers, the intermediation of interdealer brokers and, increasingly, the use of electronic platforms that matched sales and purchases. These markets were essential tools used by banks in their constant adjustment of assets and liabilities across time and space, as well as type, or the lending and borrowing they did between each other so as to profitably employ the resources at their command. Money was simultaneously a unit of account, a store of value, and a means of payment and the transactions that banks made in these financial markets reflected activity across all three, whether undertaken individually or collectively. Much of this activity could be handled by direct dealing between banks, operating from strategically placed trading floors around the world, where expert staff and advanced technology was employed for the purpose. This was an electronic world in flux that was pushing traditional exchanges and the voice brokers towards oblivion, though leaving a role for those who negotiated bespoke deals or handled complex products. That, at least, was how it appeared on the eve of the Global Financial Crisis, but that event was to change the environment within which these markets operated. The power of the megabanks was undermined, and with it the trust that had allowed them to become the counterparties in any transaction. In their place new arrangements were made that altered the balance of power in the market, though the advance of the electronic trading platforms was unstoppable.

Bonds

Prior to the Global Financial Crisis bond markets were growing rapidly as corporate and other borrowers moved away from a reliance on banks for funds. Even in China, where companies relied on banks for 90 per cent of their external finance, a corporate bond market was developing despite regulatory resistance. Large Chinese companies had discovered that it was much cheaper to borrow in the bond market than directly from banks. This had long been the case in the USA where the issue of bonds was an established alternative to a bank loan. That practice spread around the world as capital markets broadened and deepened in response to the twin forces of globalization and liberalization. Deeper and broader markets made it possible for companies to borrow, through the issue of bonds, at lower rates of interest than using a bank, while the enhanced liquidity of bonds made them an increasingly attractive investment compared to the low rates paid on bank deposits. A lack of liquidity had long been a major impediment to investment in those bonds offering attractive yields. Investors faced a choice between the liquid but low-yielding bonds issued

Banks, Exchanges, and Regulators: Global Financial Markets from the 1970s. Ranald Michie, Oxford University Press (2021).

DOI: 10.1093/oso/9780199553730.003.0016

by the national governments of major economies and large multinational corporations, and the illiquid but high-yielding ones issued by smaller countries and companies. The improvements in the bond market made higher-yielding bonds more liquid and that meant they attracted a growing pool of investors.

Nevertheless, there remained an enormous gulf in liquidity between the likes of US Treasury bonds and those of smaller states and most companies, reflected in the rate of interest that had to be paid in order to entice investors. This can be seen in the disparity of yields within the EU. The EU had tried to create a single bond market that possessed greater depth and breadth and thus liquidity, and so emulate the situation within the USA. However, individual governments within the EU continued to issue their own bonds. This meant that those from smaller states such as the Czech Republic, Hungary, and Poland lacked the liquidity of those issued by France, Germany, and Italy. Even after the launch of the single European currency, the Euro, in 1999, which did not cover all member states, individual countries continued to issue separate debt, though now in the same currency. The result was that the euro-denominated government bond market remained compartmentalized compared with that for US Treasuries, especially when doubts emerged over the survival of the currency union. This was despite trading being concentrated on EuroMTS, a pan-European electronic trading system for euro-denominated government bonds. What this was testimony to was the unwillingness among governmental and corporate borrowers to sacrifice the individual nature of their bond issues in return for lower borrowing costs, and the inability of market mechanisms to compensate for the underlying lack of liquidity that caused.

Crisis, 2007–8

By the end of 2007 an estimated $52.2tn in fixed-income debt was in circulation in the world. Of this 50 per cent ($26.5tn) was in central government debt with close to another 10 per cent ($4tn) having been issued by lower tier public authorities. Around 20 per cent ($11tn) represented the debt of corporations but this was now matched by another 20 per cent ($10.7tn) in the form of asset-backed securities of all types. This fixed-interest debt was marginally greater than both the total value of equity outstanding ($50.6tn) and significantly higher than the amount outstanding in bank deposits ($38.5tn). By itself the corporate debt outstanding, at $11tn, was almost twice corporate loans ($6.1tn), reflecting the rapid growth in the use of bonds to finance business rather than borrowing from banks. The preference for bonds over equities was partly driven by the more favourable treatment of the latter over the former in the tax system of many countries. As bonds were classed as loans the interest paid was tax deductible while dividend payments were not. This encouraged leveraged buyouts in which publicly traded companies were taken private by debt-financed private equity investors. This exposed businesses to the threat of bankruptcy if the interest paid on bonds could not be maintained, which was not the case with a missed dividend payment.

Also contributing to the rapid expansion of the global bond market before the crisis was the service provided by interdealer brokers and electronic trading platforms. These reduced the costs of trading and improved liquidity, helping to widen participation in the bond market beyond a small number of banks and other specialists. Electronic trading, in particular, was reshaping the bond market at both the wholesale and retail end. Electronic platforms such as BrokerTec, controlled by ICAP, and eSpeed, developed by Cantor Fitzgerald, catered for the trading between banks, brokers, and hedge funds. In contrast,

Tradeweb, an online bond-trading platform owned by the data providers, Thomson, linked dealers with their customers. It had begun in the USA in 1998, and then expanded into Europe followed by Asia, so allowing it to provide a 24-hour market. By 2007 the average daily trading volume on Tradeweb was in excess of $200bn while BrokerTec and eSpeed averaged $300bn. The facility to trade bonds cheaply and quickly attracted the likes of hedge funds, especially in in the most liquid market, such as that for US Treasury bills and bonds. The hedge funds employed sophisticated computer-driven models to trade very frequently, whenever a buying and selling opportunity arose through tiny differences in prices. By 2007 they accounted for over half of US bond trading. Most of this was driven by the possibility of speculative gains but their actions made a major contribution to the liquidity of the bond market, which enhanced its appeal to investors generally.

However, it was the role played by the megabanks that was central to the expansion of the global bond market before the crisis. Banks such as Goldman Sachs, with investment banking origins, had spotted that the issue of bonds not only played to their established strengths as brokers and traders, but also allowed them to compete with the commercial banks in attracting savers and meeting the financial needs of borrowers. By embracing the originate-and-distribute model of banking, investment banks could compete with their commercial rivals who had the ability to leverage their huge depositor base and employ the lend-and-hold model. In the originate-and-distribute model a bank repackaged loans, which they had either made or bought from another bank, and then sold them to investors as a bond, generating new funds which could also be lent. In the lend-and-hold model a bank held onto the loans that it made until maturity, tying up the funds received from depositors, which prevented it from making new loans. Investment banks had long employed the originate-and-distribute model as they issued stocks and bonds on behalf of clients such as companies and governments. These stocks and bonds appealed to investors searching for either variable income streams, as came from stocks, or fixed ones generated by bonds. By listing these securities on stock exchanges they could be bought and sold at close to the current market price, so providing them with the liquidity that investors desired. In the case of major government bond issues, such as US Treasuries, an established inter-bank market delivered the same result. What had grown rapidly before 2007 was the application of that procedure to the conversion of existing loans into bonds, such as those used to finance house and other property purchases, followed by their resale to investors. These bonds were neither listed nor possessed an inter-bank market, but were accompanied by the expectation or even promise that the issuer would maintain their liquidity. That promise rested on the reputation and actions of the bank handling the issue. As the banks following this practice were numbered among the largest in the world, those promises were deemed credible. Such was the popularity of this originate-and-distribute model among both borrowers and investors that the commercial banks had little option but to embrace it as well, or risk losing their customers to those that did.

Banks were further encouraged to adopt the originate-and-distribute model because of the greater flexibility it provided them with. Unlike loans, bonds could be subsequently bought and sold, allowing banks to constantly balance their assets and liabilities and manage their cash flow. One product of this switch was the rapid growth of the repo market, where banks either lent out bonds in exchange for cash or bought bonds using cash. Between 2002 and 2007 the repo market doubled in USA and Europe. In the tri-party repo market a custodian bank acted as an intermediary, matching cash lenders with those seeking to finance their assets, such as those holding portfolios of fixed-income securities. Those doing the borrowing pledged assets, which they promised to repurchase. Under this procedure the liquidity of the asset was guaranteed by the borrower of the funds. As bonds provided collateral for loans, and could be sold in the event of a default, banks could borrow at a lower rate of interest than standard overnight rates. The repo market was well established in the USA but was being rapidly adopted elsewhere in the world before the crisis. This growth was encouraged by the capital-adequacy ratios banks had to abide by under Basel 2. Banks had to carry more capital to cover unsecured loans than they did for secured loans, such as repo finance, as that used bonds as collateral. The assumption made by regulators was that bonds possessed a liquid market. By treating all bonds as liquid the regulators created the illusion that banking had become safer, but that rested on the ability to resell. In turn that depended upon interdealer brokers and electronic markets matching sales and purchases and banks being willing to use their own capital to buy while selling from their own holdings. This worked well when liquid assets such as US Treasury bills and bonds were used, as this type of collateral could easily be sold. As long as these conditions prevailed then the growth of the bond market could be sustained.

However, prior to the crisis corporate and mortgage bonds were increasingly substituted for more liquid government debt, such as US Treasuries. This reflected the drive by investment banks and investors to boost their leverage and generate higher profits. In 2008 Paul J. Davies pointed out the dangers this posed: 'A system that simply trusts in collateral without regard to its particulars is one that fosters the creation of ever more hideously complex credit products, whose cash flows are ever harder to analyse.'[1] Those who understood the nature of the bond market were aware of risks at the time, such as John Holman, head of fixed-income markets at NYSE Euronext. In April 2007 he observed that 'The corporate bond market is very fragmented and lacks transparency, so small investors are really beholden to the dealers.'[2] Though investors increasingly regarded the new fixed-income instruments being generated by securitization as liquid they were rarely traded. Instead, they were designed to be held until maturity, and priced according to complex mathematical models rather than current transactions in the market. The underlying lack of liquidity in the bond market rose to the surface during 2007. In the middle of that year Saskia Scholtes and Gillian Tett pointed out the implications of what had arisen:

> The big risk now is that if thousands of banks and investment groups suddenly have to slash the value of the securities they hold, the wave of accounting losses might at best leave investors wary of purchasing all manner of complex financial instruments. At worst, it could trigger more distressed sales and a broader repricing of financial assets, not just in the subprime sector but in other illiquid markets too.[3]

This lack of liquidity increasingly spread to all the markets in which these securitized products were traded, stoking up fears among banks and investors. This led them to both redeem bonds on maturity and refuse to purchase further issues. By July 2007 it was being widely reported that the market in many of the fixed-interest products had seized up. These included ABSs (asset-backed securities), RMBSs (residential mortgage-backed securities), CMBSs (commercial mortgage-backed securities), CDOs (collateralized debt obligations), and CLOs (collateralized loan obligations). An estimated $10.7tn of these securities were in circulation by the end of 2007, though only $1.8tn was considered in danger of default.

[1] Paul J. Davies, 'High noon chimes for collateral with no name', 10th October 2008.
[2] Saskia Scholtes, 'NYSE Euronext unveils bond platform', 23rd April 2007.
[3] Saskia Scholtes and Gillian Tett, 'Does it all add up?', 28th June 2007.

As with any financial crisis it was fear that defaults would spread that made the situation far worse, as this meant all bonds were suspect. As a result it became increasingly difficult to sell any of the securitized debt in existence, and even government and corporate debt was regarded with suspicion. Canada's asset-backed commercial paper market, for example, froze in August 2007 when twenty highly-leveraged trusts, or conduits, were unable to roll over maturing paper as a result of turmoil in the US subprime market. Increasingly investors shunned assets perceived to be risky and so liquidity dried up. Only investment-grade corporate bonds and the issues of major governments continued to be tradeable.[4]

By the beginning of 2008 a degree of confidence appeared to be returning to the bond market after government and central bank intervention. Nevertheless, there remained continuing concerns over the value of complex debt products, which made them difficult or even impossible to trade. Under these circumstances banks confined their lending to overnight loans unless backed by collateral of undoubted security, such as US Treasuries. Rather than fading away, these concerns intensified during 2008, as further questions emerged over the price and liquidity of securitized assets and the stability of those banks most reliant on the originate-and-distribute model. Regulators contributed to the spreading fear over the value and liquidity of bonds by reversing their support for the originate-and-distribute model over the lend-and-hold one. This further undermined confidence in the bond market. Writing in April 2008 Dominic Konstam, head of interest-rate strategy at Credit Suisse, stated that, 'Banks are hoarding cash because funding from the asset-backed commercial paper market has fallen sharply while money-market funds are lending on a short-term basis and are restricting their supply.'[5] This had serious consequences for the bond market as the two had become closely linked. US money-market funds, with assets totalling $4tn, pulled back from purchasing the short-term debt issued by banks, for example. Prior to the crisis banks had anticipated refinancing their lending by selling bonds but they were now unable to do so, while facing the need to redeem those that were maturing. This situation contributed to the collapse of Lehman Brothers but its aftermath made it much worse.

[4] David Oakley and Gillian Tett, 'European bond market puts US in the shade', 15th January 2007; Joanna Chung and Gillian Tett, 'Trading suspension raises eyebrows', 24th January 2007; David Oakley, 'European repo trading grows Euro 500bn in year', 2nd March 2007; Joanna Chung, 'Tradeweb expands into Asian trade hours', 7th March 2007; Richard Beales and Gillian Tett, 'Hedge funds rival banks for share of US Treasury market', 9th March 2007; Gillian Tett and Joanna Chung, 'Hedge funds are at the gates of the eurozone's cosy bond club', 13th March 2007; Gillian Tett and Tobias Buck, 'Trade body seeks talks on future of MTS', 14th March 2007; David Oakley and Saskia Scholtes, 'Flurry of activity in banks for CDSs', 3rd April 2007; Gillian Tett and Joanna Chung, 'MTS to decide on hedge fund access', 20th April 2007; Michael Mackenzie, 'Activists focus on battle for eSpeed', 20th April 2007; Saskia Scholtes, 'NYSE Euronext unveils bond platform', 23rd April 2007; James Mackintosh, 'Investors still pile in', 27th April 2007; Gillian Tett, 'Funds are ousting the banks', 27th April 2007; Anuj Gangahar, 'Weight behind LiquidityHub grows', 9th May 2007; Peter Thal Larsen, 'Number behind the M&A boom', 30th May 2007; Jamil Anderlini, 'China's corporate bonds come of age', 15th June 2007; Saskia Scholtes and Gillian Tett, 'Does it all add up?', 28th June 2007; David Oakley, 'Record repurchase volumes for Europe', 29th August 2007; Joanna Chung and Gillian Tett, 'MTS plans to broaden trading beyond banks', 27th September 2007; David Oakley, 'Square Mile fears losing its edge', 1st October 2007; Joanna Chung, 'MTS goes for investor order driven trading', 3rd October 2007; Paul J. Davies, 'LiquidityHub launches swaps product', 23rd October 2007; John Murray Brown, 'Desmond surprises with ISTC bond deal', 3rd November 2007; Gillian Tett and Paul J. Davies, 'What's the damage', 5th November 2007; Gillian Tett, 'Sub-prime in its context', 19th November 2007; Gillian Tett, 'MTS grip under threat', 19th November 2007; Bernard Simon and Gillian Tett, 'Restructuring for ABCP market', 27th December 2007; Gillian Tett, Aline van Duyn, and Paul J. Davies, 'A re-emerging market? Bankers are seeking simpler ways to sell on debt', 1st July 2008; John Plender, 'Originative sin', 5th January 2009; Michael Mackenzie, 'Push to reduce risks in short-term funding', 22nd June 2009; Michael Mackenzie, 'DTCC paves way for all roads to lead to its warehouse', 1st July 2009; Gillian Tett and Aline van Duyn, 'Under restraint', 7th July 2009; Nicole Bullock, Michael Mackenzie and Aline van Duyn, 'Fed exit looms over US mortgages', 26th March 2010; Norma Cohen, 'Crisis thrusts debt-financing theorem back under the spotlight', 5th April 2010; Michael Mackenzie, 'Repo market faces struggle to pull back from slump', 15th April 2010.

[5] Gillian Tett and Michael Mackenzie, 'Debate over Libor breeds a crisis of confidence', 22nd April 2008.

What emerged after the Lehman Brothers' collapse was that about 30 per cent of the collateral it had pledged as security for loans turned out to be hard to trade or even to value. According to Michael Mackenzie in September 2008 the consequences of its failure 'rippled up the chain and effectively stalled trading across global fixed-income markets'.[6] Though centred in the USA this was a global crisis. With US banks hoarding $s the global financial system was deprived of the currency through which inter-bank borrowing and lending largely took place. In the face of the escalating crisis central banks were forced to widen the categories of bonds they would accept in return for loans, as the supply of the most marketable, such as US Treasuries, dried up. Many of the securities created prior to financial crisis were simply unsaleable once banks stopped acting as counterparties, and the values assigned by rating agencies and complex mathematical formulas were discredited.[7]

Post Crisis, 2009–12

In the immediate wake of the 2008 crisis both the primary and secondary bond markets, other than that for US Treasuries, remained depressed. With $9tn in US Treasury bonds in circulation by 2011 they remained the core of global reserve assets, with nearly half held by foreign investors and central banks. They served a crucial function by being the most liquid of assets and a safe haven in times of market stress. In contrast, the crisis had shattered trust in many other bonds, including both new issues and those already in circulation, as they lacked a public market and were impossible to value. In the crisis these bonds became either unsaleable or only at deeply discounted prices, leaving investors wary of accepting them as collateral for a loan, temporarily swapping them for lower-yield bonds such as US Treasuries, or buying them outright. What the crisis had done was to bring to the surface the uncomfortable truth that in normal circumstances bonds were often illiquid. Though collectively vast the bond market was highly fragmented, as they were issued in a variety of forms and with different yields and conditions so as to appeal to a wide spectrum of investors. This variety made the market for individual bonds very shallow, which was why they were little traded on exchanges, as these catered for standardized products and large

6 Michael Mackenzie, 'Money markets hope for autumn thaw', 1st September 2008.

7 Paul J. Davies and Saskia Scholtes, 'Interbank rate easing drives liquidity hopes', 3rd January 2008; David Rule, 'Time is nigh to rethink basis of floating rate debt', 10th April 2008; Gillian Tett and Michael Mackenzie, 'Debate over Libor breeds a crisis of confidence', 22nd April 2008; Gillian Tett and Paul J. Davies, 'Battle-scarred bankers lapse into a hoarding habit', 8th May 2008; Gillian Tett and Daniel Oakley, 'European banks in chase for dollars', 10th June 2008; Gillian Tett, Aline van Duyn, and Paul J. Davies, 'A re-emerging market? Bankers are seeking simpler ways to sell on debt', 1st July 2008; Anousha Sakoui, 'Stability possible for leveraged loan pricing as backlog declines', 9th July 2008; Paul J. Davies, 'Effort to bring credit ratings into clearer focus gathers pace', 5th August 2008; Ben White, 'Lehman shares slide on fears over results', 20th August 2008; Michael Mackenzie, 'Money markets hope for autumn thaw', 1st September 2008; Anousha Sakoui, 'More UK companies turn to asset-based borrowing', 8th September 2008; Hannah Glover, 'Spotlight turns to the mechanics of securities lending', 8th September 2008; Michael Mackenzie, 'Repo sector scramble', 16th September 2008; Paul J. Davies, 'High noon chimes for collateral with no name', 10th October 2008; Michael Mackenzie, 'London interbank lending rates ease', 14th October 2008; Chris Hughes, 'No more easy money', 11th November 2008; Anuj Gangahar, 'Liquidnet and NYSE Arca link up as exchange dip into dark pools', 25th November 2008; Paul J. Davies, 'Securitisation provides liquidity', 26th November 2008; Peter Thal Larsen, 'Withdrawal unavailable', 6th December 2008; Aline van Duyn, 'Securitisation sector braced for a long, painful haul', 5th December 2008; John Plender, 'Originative sin', 5th January 2009; Michael Mackenzie and Aline van Duyn, 'Costs set to rise amid shake-up in derivatives trading', 19th June 2009; Henny Sender, 'Lehman creditors in fight to recover disputed collateral', 22nd June 2009; Norma Cohen, 'System remains vulnerable to shocks', 26th June 2009; Michael Mackenzie, 'Run on banks left repo sector highly-exposed', 11th September 2009; Henny Sender, 'Short measures', 9th July 2010; Jennifer Hughes, 'SP warns on UK mortgage securities', 10th September 2010.

quantities, while the electronic platforms struggled to find a format that would meet the needs of bonds. In 2010 Jennifer Hughes reported that 'The corporate bond market stands in sharp contrast to other asset classes such as foreign exchange and equities, where electronic dealing has revolutionised the marketplace, broadening the range of participants and sending trading volumes soaring. But participants have struggled to take the corporate bond market electronic because of the sheer range of issues outstanding, most of which trade only occasionally.'[8]

Hence the importance of the role played by the megabanks acting either as counterparties or facilitating transactions by operating their own bond-trading systems. These systems connected the banks and their customers into a network through which new issues could be made and subsequent sales and purchases handled. That had relied on the banks acting as counterparties so as to even up the fluctuations in supply and demand that bedevilled rarely-traded bonds. This meant that banks, with their ready access to funds and their ability to hold a large inventory of illiquid paper, were at the centre of the bond market. However, in the crisis, and then the restrictions that followed, banks were in no position to support the bond market, depriving it of liquidity. As Jennifer Hughes, Michael Mackenzie, and Scheherazade Daneshkhu explained in 2010:

> Bond dealing has historically been far less liquid than stock trading because of the sheer variety of outstanding bonds. This has meant the market has been dominated by banks which, until the crisis, used their vast inventories to act as central market bankers. However, post-crisis balance sheet constraints have shrunk their desire to hold so many bonds with consequences for investors, who claim they have struggled to find prices, and for issuers who fear borrowing could become more expensive.[9]

The bond inventories of banks peaked at $235bn in 2007 and then fell to $62bn in 2013. As a result the banks lacked both the ability to supply bonds in demand by investors or the willingness to buy those being sold. Banks no longer acted as the 'warehouse' for bonds, meeting demand from their holdings and then replenishing that stock by purchasing those being offered to them by investors. The intervention of regulators, including the Basel 3 regulatory capital standards, and the Volcker rule, which banned proprietary trading by banks, had made holding big inventories of bonds a more expensive and riskier operation for banks. In the absence of the active role played by banks investors were forced to either hold onto bonds that had become unsaleable or accept huge losses from a disposal at greatly reduced prices. In addition to the intra-bank market there was an OTC bond market maintained by interdealer brokers, with sales and purchases handled on an individual basis through matching buyers and sellers. Most corporate bond trading, for example, took place over the telephone on a bilateral basis. However, it could involve significant delays with prices only arrived at after negotiation.

Despite the structural problems of the bond market and the legacy of the crisis, it staged a recovery from 2009 onwards. That took much longer in the element comprising securitized assets such as mortgage-backed bonds, as they remained shunned by investors. In contrast, governments turned to the bond market for finance because the economic downturn shrank tax receipts while expenditure rose as they struggled to avoid a recession.

[8] Jennifer Hughes, 'Revolution in the cosy world of bonds', 1st March 2010.

[9] Jennifer Hughes, Michael Mackenzie, and Scheherazade Daneshkhu, 'Paris Project recommends central clearing for bonds', 27th April 2010.

Government bonds were eagerly purchased by investors seeking a safe haven in the troubled environment that followed the crisis. In the repo market, for example, where $1.8bn was outstanding as collateral in 2012, virtually all was now in the form of short-dated government debt. Companies also turned to the bond market for funding in the face of the withdrawal of banks from lending. The value of private placements, where companies tapped investors directly for funds rather than borrowing from a bank, rose sharply in 2010, for example. Banks handled these placements but did not provide the money themselves. It was not only the lack of bank loans that drove companies towards bonds but also the relative cost. With cheap inter-bank funding constrained, banks charged more for the finance they did provide. In contrast, bonds were priced relative to the low central bank base rates, making them a highly-competitive alternative to bank borrowing. However, bond-based finance was only available to the larger and more established companies, as they could justify the size of issue that covered the expenses involved and provide the security demanded by risk-averse investors. In turn these corporate bond issues were attractive to investors because the yield they offered was higher than those of banks at a time of historically low interest rates.

In the face of the revival of the bond market there was a growing need to provide the trading facilities required to generate liquidity. Those handling bond issues were aware that the price attached to an issue was directly related to liquidity delivered by an active secondary market. Due to the lack of liquidity in Latin America's domestic bond markets, for example, the largest companies from the region used New York when making bond issues. There they could borrow at a lower rate of interest because the secondary market generated greater liquidity, making their bonds attractive to a large pool of international investors and lowering the rate of interest that had to be paid. In the past the megabanks would have provided that liquidity but that was no longer the case as Jennifer Hughes and Philip Stafford observed in 2010:

> Corporate bond trading has historically been far less liquid than stock trading because of the sheer variety of outstanding bonds. That had left banks with a central market-maker role because of their ability to hold large inventories. After the financial crisis the banks' desire to maintain such inventory has weakened in the face of regulatory changes, notably the higher level of capital they will have to hold.[10]

The megabanks were increasingly unable or unwilling to act as a direct counterparty to their clients' trades as they lacked the confidence that they could find a third-party buyer to take on the position afterwards. In contrast, bond issues were becoming a major important source of corporate funding and investors were attracted to them because of the returns on offer.

What was missing was an active secondary market as that restricted the liquidity of bonds and the solution was seen to be the electronic matching of buyers and sellers. Patrick Humphries, speaking on behalf of the London Stock Exchange (LSE,) observed in 2010 that 'The overwhelming direction of travel internationally is for people to look at bringing products onto electronic order books. The advantages of an open, transparent system are being debated across all asset classes.'[11] One group that stepped into the void left by the banks were the global fund managers, as they had the size and the resources to create an

[10] Jennifer Hughes and Philip Stafford, 'MTS to expand into corporate debt', 16th November 2010.
[11] Steve Johnson, 'UK plan to open up bond trade', 1st February 2010.

internal market. In 2010 BlackRock, the world's biggest fund manager with $3.5tn of assets under management, or 5 per cent of the global total, decided to launch a trading platform, the Aladdin Trading Network, which was in operation by 2012. Exchanges also sensed that the growth of the bond market combined with the withdrawal of the banks presented them with an opportunity. The Eurozone government bond-trading platform, MTS, operated out of London by the LSE, took the decision in 2010 to expand its coverage to corporate bonds. Similar developments took place in Paris, reflecting rivalry between the two financial centres. All were hoping to emulate what was already happening in New York. In the USA the likes of Liquidnet, BrokerTec, and MarketAccess had established successful bond-trading platforms. Liquidnet provided a model to follow. It had been formed in 2001 by Seth Merrin, as an electronic market for institutional investors. In his role as chief executive officer he made large claims for his market as early as November 2008: 'Liquidnet is now a global institutional marketplace, which offers large, buy-side investors the ability to source block liquidity from a worldwide community of institutional investment firms, streaming liquidity from the world's largest exchanges and leading broker-dealers, and strategic access to the open-market.'[12] There was no lack of emerging contenders for the bond-trading crown being vacated by the global universal banks in the wake of the crisis and the restrictions that followed.[13]

[12] Anuj Gangahar, 'Liquidnet and NYSE Arca link up as exchange dip into dark pools', 25th November 2008.

[13] Ross Tieman, 'Knowledge and old-fashioned skill are back in favour', 22nd June 2009; Gillian Tett and Aline van Duyn, 'Under restraint', 7th July 2009; Michael Mackenzie, 'Network of companies designed to help central bank manage liquidity', 16th July 2009; Michael Mackenzie, 'Ranks of US primary dealers growing once more', 16th July 2009; Steve Johnson, 'How to breathe life back into bonds', 20th July 2009; Steve Johnson, 'Fear for corporate bonds trade', 20th July 2009; Michael Mackenzie, 'Run on banks left repo sector highly-exposed', 11th September 2009; David Oakley, 'Europe's ravaged landscape begins to stabilise', 11th September 2009; Patrick Jenkins, 'Investment banks enjoy companies' bond boom', 14th September 2009; Jennifer Hughes, 'Bankers seek to detoxify the alphabet soup', 13th October 2009; Steve Johnson, 'New bond market faces fight', 30th November 2009; Michael Mackenzie, Francesco Guerrera, and Gillian Tett, 'A course to chart', 4th January 2010; Jennifer Hughes, 'Paris targets a French revolution in bond trading', 26th January 2010; Steve Johnson, 'UK plan to open up bond trade', 1st February 2010; Aline van Duyn and Nicole Bullock, 'Ruling on Lehman creates new CDO doubts', 9th February 2010; Jennifer Hughes, 'Post-crisis wrangle over the best way to measure value', 11th February 2010; Jennifer Hughes, 'Greek drama darkens mood', 25th February 2010; Jennifer Hughes, 'Revolution in the cosy world of bonds', 1st March 2010; Michael Mackenzie, 'Repo market faces struggle to pull back from slump', 15th April 2010; Jennifer Hughes, Michael Mackenzie, and Scheherazade Daneshkhu, 'Paris Project recommends central clearing for bonds', 27th April 2010; Jennifer Hughes, 'Private Placement deals find favour in search for funding', 24th August 2010; David Oakley, 'European repo trading bounces back', 16th September 2010; Sharlene Goff, Jennifer Hughes, and Patrick Jenkins, 'Mortgage-backed securities market gathering steam', 16th September 2010; Michael Mackenzie, 'Regulators push technology to track trades in real time', 29th September 2010; Emma Saunders, 'Finance chiefs aim to raise debt', 11th October 2010; Jennifer Hughes and Philip Stafford, 'MTS to expand into corporate debt', 16th November 2010; Patrick Jenkins and Jennifer Hughes, 'Big Gaps to fill in', 9th December 2010; Paul J. Davies and Izabella Kaminska, 'Banks seek help from new set of institutions', 22nd December 2010; Dan McCrum, 'BlackRock trading platform plan set to hit Wall St profit centres', 29th December 2010; Steve Johnson, 'Securities owners keen to lend again but income falls', 21st March 2011; Michael Mackenzie, Dan McCrum, and Richard Milne, 'Investors warn on the impact of S&P's US move', 20th April 2011; Richard Milne, 'Money for nothing-and the debt is (almost) for free', 25th May 2011; Tracy Alloway, 'Collateral Rush spells challenges for Europe's banks', 20th October 2011; Tracy Alloway, 'Financial system creaks as loan lubricant dries up', 29th November 2011; Patrick Jenkins and Richard Milne, 'Caught in the grip', 2nd December 2011; Nicole Bullock and Ajay Makan, 'Reform debate swirls in the CLO sector', 23rd December 2011; Robin Wigglesworth, 'Bonds find favour over syndicated lending', 13th April 2012; Brooke Masters and David Oakley, 'Financial regulators take aim at repo trading markets', 27th April 2012; Philip Stafford, 'Nasdaq OMX to launch derivatives in UK', 22nd June 2012; Brooke Masters, 'UK banks lead world on liquidity rules', 22nd June 2012; Robin Wigglesworth, 'Rising Expectations', 25th June 2012; Tracy Alloway, 'BlackRock moves in as banks retreat', 2nd October 2012; Ralph Atkins, Philip Stafford, and Brooke Masters, 'Collateral Damage', 25th October 2012; Vivianne Rodrigues, 'Groups prepare to play catch-up', 14th November 2012; Samantha Pearson, 'Change is in the air for stocks', 14th November 2012; David Oakley, 'Switch to bonds signals end for cult of equity', 20th November 2012; Tracy Alloway and Arash Massoudi, 'ETFs under scrutiny in market turbulence', 28th June 2013; Tracy

Creating a New Market, 2013–20

By 2018 world debt outstanding was estimated at $164tn or 225 per cent of global GDP, which was higher in absolute and relative terms than before the financial crisis. This increase had been driven by a combination of the restrictions placed on banks and the ultra-low interest rates and the quantitative-easing programmes introduced by the central banks in the wake of the crisis. Companies took advantage of low interest rates to issue bonds paying a fixed rate of interest and investors bought these for the guaranteed income rather than the variable one generated from equities. In the US the value of outstanding corporate bonds quickly rose from $5tn in 2008 to $8tn in 2015. This made the bond market even more important than it had been before the crisis. However, in the aftermath of the crisis regulators imposed tight controls on banks, which restricted the range of bonds they could hold. This was because many bonds had become impossible to sell, leaving those banks holding them facing a liquidity crisis, and forcing governments and central banks to provide support. By the first quarter of 2009 the total illiquid assets held by banks was estimated to have reached $360bn. This then shrunk to $50bn in 2013 as buyers gradually appeared who were willing to take the risk of buying these assets at a large discount, in the expectation that they could either be sold at a profit or be redeemed at face value on maturity. This allowed regulators to relax the conditions imposed on banks, allowing them to widen the range of bonds they could hold. Nevertheless, banks remained under pressure to hold only the most liquid of bonds in the shape of government debt, while the other restrictions imposed, along with heightened perceptions of risk, continued to prevent them playing the active role in the bond market that they had done before the crisis. The tougher capital regulations made banks less willing to hold inventories of bonds and less able to act as both intermediaries and shock absorbers. Banks' holdings of high-grade debt, including treasuries, mortgage-backed securities, and corporate bonds, fell from $524bn at the end of 2007 to $170bn in July 2015.

This continuing withdrawal of banks mattered because of the nature of the bonds in circulation, which lacked uniformity and standardization, making high levels of liquidity difficult to achieve. Michael John Lytle, chief executive of Tabula Investment Management, summed up the position in 2018 when he stated that 'Fixed income is not a single asset class when you think about the differences between government bonds, investment-grade, high-yield, emerging market debt, mortgage-backed securities and the US municipal bond market.'[14] The US corporate bond market, despite its size with $9tn in circulation in 2013, did not provide a single pool of liquidity because of the number, variety, and size of the issues in circulation. Around 40 per cent of bond issues were smaller than $1bn and came with a variety of redemption dates, existed in multiple forms with different characteristics, and were often held until maturity. Of the 30,000 investment-grade corporate bonds circulating in the USA in 2013 only twenty traded more than ten times a day. In 2013 trading volume in the US corporate bond market was $18.2bn compared to the $9.2tn in circulation. That can be contrasted with the trading volume in the US Treasury market, which was $655bn compared to its size of $11.3tn. This made the latter a highly-liquid market while the former was not. The same lack of liquidity applied to the bonds issued by US municipal,

Alloway, 'Goldman promotes its bond platform', 23rd August 2013; Tracy Alloway, 'Buyers struggle to find a safe landing', 21st November 2013.

[14] Chris Flood, 'Global debt pile creates new chances in nascent market', 5th November 2018.

state, and regional governments. In 2018 Robin Wigglesworth and Joe Rennison referred to the bond market as a 'vast but old-fashioned corner of the financial system, with little transparency and trading often conducted by telephone.'[15] Chris Flood, also writing in 2018, reported that 'Most bond trades are still conducted via private over-the-counter transactions, unlike equities where the majority of trading occurs on regulated exchanges.'[16] That meant there was a major role to be played by the megabanks acting as counterparties to buyers and sellers. A block trade, for example, involved a bank buying and holding a portfolio of bonds and then gradually selling them when profitable opportunities arose. It was only the megabanks that were in a position to do this with deals often being over $15m.

The difficulty the megabanks faced in conducting this type of business was due to the regulatory intervention that followed the crisis of 2008 and then remained in place. In 2018 Chris Flood reported that 'Regulatory reforms enacted after the financial crisis have led to significant reductions in the inventories of bonds held by broker-dealers and banks. At the same time, corporate bond issuance has increased significantly as companies moved to take advantage of low interest rates to improve their funding positions.'[17] He was picking up on the complaints made by those working for these banks. One was Eric Wiegand, head of ETF strategy at DES, the asset management arm of Deutsche Bank. In his opinion 'The role of banks and brokers as a facilitator of trades has shrunk. So it is more difficult for institutional investors to trade large portfolios of bonds.'[18] In 2018 Joe Rennison and Philip Stafford attributed the increased volatility, being regularly experienced in the bond market, to this regulatory intervention:

> Tough regulations introduced after 2009 with the intention of stabilising markets are fuelling far more volatile swings in asset prices... as banks have retreated from their traditional roles of providing two-way prices for investors in listed futures and over-the-counter arenas for equities, bonds and foreign exchange. These markets have also become increasingly electronic with market-making activity gravitating towards high-speed trading firms, which by their nature do not extend support for prices once volatility heats up.[19]

They were following others who had been expressing similar views since 2013.

One measure of the change was the collateral used by the megabanks when they borrowed and lent among each other and with investors such as hedge funds, insurers, or pension funds. The financial crisis made all involved much more aware of the risk of default, and so they were reluctant to swap low-yielding but highly-liquid bonds for high-yielding but less-liquid ones, despite the return to be generated because of the interest-rate differential. In 2007 the collateral being reused in the financial system had reached $10,000bn whereas by 2010 it had shrunk to $6,000bn or by 40 per cent. As Tracy Alloway explained in 2011, 'One reason collateral use has fallen is that market participants are more vigilant about the creditworthiness of counterparties and how business partners might use collateral sent to them.'[20] The consequence of this can be seen in the changed relationship

[15] Robin Wigglesworth and Joe Rennison, 'The Future of Trading', 10th May 2018.
[16] Chris Flood, 'Global debt pile creates new chances in nascent market', 5th November 2018.
[17] Chris Flood, 'Liquidity enables big ticket trades', 18th June 2018.
[18] Chris Flood, 'Liquidity enables big ticket trades', 18th June 2018.
[19] Joe Rennison and Philip Stafford, 'Traders find receptive ear among regulators to relax capital rules', 10th July 2018.
[20] Tracy Alloway, 'Financial system creaks as loan lubricant dries up', 29th November 2011.

between insurance companies and banks. Insurers mostly avoided the worst of the financial crisis. As Paul J. Davies explained in 2012:

> It is almost impossible for an insurer to suffer a run on its funding base. In the panic that swept through markets from 2007 to 2009, it did not have that worry about the liability side of its balance sheet. Banks have deposits that can be withdrawn at any time and large amounts of short-term funding from the commercial paper, interbank and bond markets, which dried up very quickly as the crisis grew. In most cases, it was short-term money from markets that disappeared and caused the biggest problems for banks, rather than old-fashioned runs perpetrated by retail customers. Insurers, on the other hand, are funded by the premiums paid for insurance policies—crucially these payments cannot be stopped at the whim of the policy holder. Instead, the policies only pay out when specific events happen.[21]

Policy holders could not demand their money back in the way that bank depositors could. Also, insurers had not invested heavily in mortgage-backed bonds, collateralized debt obligations, and other novel financial instruments and so avoided the problems attached to these. Attracted by the discounts on offer in the wake of the financial crisis, insurers then acquired these financial products from banks through swap arrangements through which banks obtained more liquid assets from the insurance companies. Insurance companies usually held far more liquid assets, like government bonds, than they needed to meet emergency payments and so they were willing to swap these low-yielding assets with banks, for higher-yielding but less-liquid assets. Conversely, banks now needed liquid assets, which they could turn into cash, to meet withdrawals and redemptions as well as meeting the increased liquidity requirements imposed by regulators. In this way banks acquired easy to sell but low-yielding government debt from the insurance companies, on a temporary basis, while insurance companies acquired higher-yielding but less-liquid assets from the banks. However, this arrangement exposed insurance companies to the liquidity risks of the banks if they were not in a position to return the assets when required to do so. As a result long-term investors, ranging from insurance companies to independent fund managers became much more wary of holding illiquid bonds in the wake of the crisis. Michael John Lytle, the chief executive of Tabula Investment Management, observed in 2018 that 'Fixed income is not a single asset class when you think about the differences between government bonds, investment-grade, high-yield, emerging market debt, mortgage-backed securities and the US municipal bond market.'[22] Without the role played by the megabanks in making a market in many of these bonds they lacked the liquidity that made investors willing to purchase and hold them, and that was the position long after the crisis.[23]

[21] Paul J. Davies, 'Banks look to insurers for lessons', 16th April 2012.

[22] Chris Flood, 'Global debt pile creates new chances in nascent market', 5th November 2018.

[23] Francesco Guerrera and John Authers, 'Institutions increase equity stakes', 22nd January 2007; Gillian Tett, 'Funds are ousting the banks', 27th April 2007; Norma Cohen, 'Mifid ushers in a new era of trading', 23rd May 2007; Gillian Tett, 'Sub-prime in its context', 19th November 2007; Jennifer Hughes, 'US stands out on worldwide language', 19th November 2007; Ross Tieman, 'Algo trading: the dog that bit its master', 19th March 2008; Deborah Brewster, 'US retail investors slump to record low', 2nd September 2008; Lindsay Whipp, 'Domestic investors remain wary', 14th October 2008; Gillian Tett and Aline van Duyn, 'On the march', 9th June 2009; John Authers, 'Model of sophistication offers brighter future', 1st October 2009; Michael Mackenzie, Francesco Guerrera and Gillian Tett, 'A course to chart', 4th January 2010; Anousha Sakoui and Brooke Masters, 'UK businesses' finance options undergo rethink', 21st January 2010; Peggy Hollinger, 'Pensions Tensions', 27th May 2010; Brooke Masters and Jeremy Grant, 'Shadow boxes', 3rd February 2011; Brooke Masters, 'A real problem for regulators', 22nd March 2011; Tracy Alloway, 'Financial system creaks as loan lubricant dries up', 29th November 2011;

The effects of the withdrawal of the banks was even felt in the most liquid bond market of all, which was that for US Treasuries, with greater volatility being reported in 2014. US Treasury Bonds were regarded as the world's safest and most liquid asset, being regarded as a better alternative to holding cash, which generated no return. That status relied on it retaining its liquidity but central bank quantitative-easing programmes had pulled Treasury bonds out of the market. By 2018 the world's leading central banks such as the Federal Reserve, ECB, and Bank of Japan held $15.3tn of assets, of which about two-thirds was made up of government bonds. Outstanding government debt by then was $49tn of which 20 per cent was held by central banks. At the same time regulatory measures increased the need for banks to hold more of these bonds. The Liquidity Coverage Ratio forced US banks to hold a large reserve of US Treasuries, for example, which were not traded so immobilizing them. The effect was to reduce overall liquidity in the US Treasury market, causing increasing volatility because of a lack of depth. Banks had difficulty acquiring highly-liquid bonds to use as collateral in the repo market. They turned to corporate bonds as a substitute but this created the risk that the bonds could not be sold in the event of a default. In 2015 70 per cent of corporate bond repo transactions had a maturity of five days or less because of the risk that they were illiquid. This undermined the operation of the inter-bank market, which played a vital role in redistributing liquidity around the global banking system.

Prior to the crisis banks had acted as the 'warehouse' for bonds, meeting demand from their holdings, which they replenished by purchasing those offered to them by investors. Bryan Pascoe, global head of debt capital markets at HSBC, reflected in 2013 that, 'Banks' trading desks historically had an important role as warehouses and providers of liquidity in the credit markets.' He then added that 'While still relevant this has certainly been impacted by the tougher regulatory environment.'[24] New regulations and tougher risk-management standards forced banks to hold smaller inventories of bonds and to pull back from making a market in them. By 2016 banks had turned to agency trading rather than taking positions using their own capital. The contribution of trading to banking profits fell from $84bn in 2012 to $60bn in 2015. In 2012 20 per cent of bank trading profits came from the primary market and 80 per cent from the secondary market. By 2015 37 per cent came from the primary market and 63 per cent from secondary trading. This reflected the retreat of banks from the secondary market. Though others took the place of the megabanks, so restoring a degree of liquidity, they possessed neither the portfolios nor the capital and so were less able to act as shock absorbers or make markets. As a result markets became more volatile, which was not the aim of the new rules introduced by regulators. These rules were designed to prevent a build-up of risk by preventing the megabanks holding large portfolios of high-yielding bonds, which then proved illiquid in a crisis. Under the Volcker rule in the USA banks were prohibited from proprietary trading and restricted in their ability to hold

Tracy Alloway, 'Traditional lenders shiver as shadow banking grows', 29th December 2011; Paul J. Davies, 'Banks look to insurers for lessons', 16th April 2012; Shawn Donnan, 'Ebbs and capital flows', 22nd August 2017; Caroline Binham, 'Shadow banking grows beyond $45tn', 6th March 2018; Gillian Tett, 'When the world held its breath', 1st September 2018; Chris Flood, 'Bond liquidity issues prompt investors to turn to ETFs', 17th September 2018; Mark Vandevelde, 'Financial Crisis', 20th September 2018; Colby Smith, 'Borrowers want dollars—some more than others', 20th September 2018; Robin Wigglesworth and Joe Rennison, 'New credit ecosystem blossoms as portfolio trades surge', 11th October 2018; Robin Wigglesworth, 'Asset managers seek an entrée to the trillion-dollar club', 26th October 2018; Gregory Davis, 'Index funds are not to blame for market volatility', 31st October 2018; Chris Flood, 'Global debt pile creates new chances in nascent market', 5th November 2018; Claire Jones, Caroline Binham, and Sam Fleming, 'Fed governor to head global finance police', 21st November 2018.

[24] Ralph Atkins and Michael Stothard, 'A change of gear', 1st July 2013.

securities. At the same time the Basel 3 capital rules made it less profitable for banks to hold assets while the increased liquidity-coverage ratio required them to hold more cash and easily saleable securities. In 2018 Chris Flood commented on the consequences: 'Regulatory reforms enacted after the financial crisis have led to significant reductions in the inventories of bonds held by broker-dealers and banks.' He then added that 'At the same time, corporate bond issuance has increased significantly as companies moved to take advantage of low interest rates to improve their funding positions.'[25]

In the US the value of outstanding corporate bonds rose from $6tn in 2009 to $9.3tn in 2019, with a further $16tn in US government debt. Globally, an estimated $55tn had been invested in bonds by 2019. The problem faced by purchasers of these bonds was that they were difficult to re-sell as banks were no longer willing to make a market in them by acting as counterparties. Those who replaced the megabanks in these financial markets were the high-frequency traders, who focused on a rapid turnover, with sales and purchases driven by computer-driven programs. Writing in 2018 Philip Stafford reported that high-frequency traders had 'stepped in to support two-way pricing in markets in the past decade as investment banks have retreated'.[26] However, these high-frequency traders lacked the shock-absorbing capacity of the banks and so their sudden sales and purchases could accentuate rather than dampen price fluctuations, as they moved quickly to take and reverse positions in the market. The verdict of Chris Flood in 2018 was that 'Traditional bond markets in the US and Europe are less liquid than before the financial crisis, which has made trading of individual fixed-income securities more difficult, particularly for portfolio managers who want to conduct large transactions.' He was clear as to where the cause was: 'Regulatory changes have made it more expensive for banks to hold large inventories of bonds, which has hindered their role as liquidity providers in fixed-income markets.'[27]

Regulators had limited ideas of how to react to these changes in the way the bond market operated, and the sudden spikes in prices that took place. In 2015 Joe Rennison observed that 'High-frequency trading has arrived but regulators are still figuring out what to do about it.'[28] The only response appeared one of urging participants to act responsibly, judging from the views of Greg Medcraft in 2015. He was chairman of the International Organization of Securities Commissions, which represented regulators from 120 jurisdictions around the world. In his words, 'There's been a lack of market discipline in the past by banks in taking bonds on to their books. That doesn't build sustainable liquidity. The way to do it is to be an agent, matching buyers and sellers.... If a market is going to work effectively, it's important that participants have trust and confidence in it.'[29] There was no recognition here of the role played in the past by banks acting as shock absorbers through trading on their account. Instead, there were complaints about the lack of transparency, whether it involved trades between big banks and other large operators, those conducted electronically on ICAP's BrokerTec and Nasdaq's eSpeed, or those between banks and investors executed over the phone or via closed trading systems by Bloomberg and Tradeweb. In the interests of fairness the regulators wanted transparency even though this opened up the market to the high-frequency traders, and limited the ability of the megabanks to close deals without alerting others to their intentions and taking positions

[25] Chris Flood, 'Liquidity enables big ticket trades', 18th June 2018.
[26] Philip Stafford, 'Bloc must find its own path, shorn of British expertise', 17th November 2018.
[27] Chris Flood, 'Bond liquidity issues prompt investors to turn to ETFs', 17th September 2018.
[28] Joe Rennison, 'HFT's role in Treasuries give regulators pause', 2nd September 2015.
[29] Philip Stafford, 'Confidence shaken by violent swings', 13th October 2015.

against them. The more that details of trades were made public the more that banks and fund managers either pulled back from the market because of the volatility or used alternatives to conceal what they were doing to stop the market moving against them.

In the absence of banks, fund managers did move in to fill the gap they left by absorbing issues of bonds. Fidelity, for example, had $1.9tn under management and so was in a position to both internalize sales and purchases as well as engage in block trades with large banks. However, the fund managers were not perfect substitutes for the banks as they operated a buy and hold model rather than a buy and sell one. Whereas banks had been willing to trade bonds on their own account and accept the risks involved, supplying liquidity to the market as a result, these institutional investors were much more reluctant to do so. Hedge funds and high-frequency traders were willing to operate buy and sell strategies but they lacked the resources to hold onto portfolios of bonds while awaiting a favourable exit. This meant that neither was in a position to replace the banks, depriving the bond market of the liquidity it had previously enjoyed. As a result it was very difficult to accurately price most bonds in the secondary market, making it impossible for investors to know what they would receive if they sold; what they had to pay if they wanted to buy; and what value they had as collateral. Recognizing this difficulty the global banks introduced 'dark pools' through which their own customers could trade. However, these customers were reluctant to trust platforms owned and operated by a single bank, scarred by the experience of the crisis. Attempts were made to broaden the appeal of 'dark pools' by merging in-house platforms but it proved difficult to persuade rival banks to co-operate.

Independent electronic platforms did try and fill the gap vacated by the banks. By 2014 in the USA MarketAxess, Bloomberg, and MTS Bonds were all competing for a slice of the bond market. Rick McVey, chief executive MarketAxess, acknowledged in 2016 that 'The regulatory changes have been very positive for us.'[30] By May 2015 MarketAccess was handling 5000 trades a day, worth an average of $2.4bn, in US investment-grade corporate bonds, which was 16 per cent of the total. By 2019 its market share had risen to 20 per cent of investment-grade bonds. In 2019 MarketAxess agreed to buy LiquidityEdge, where US Treasuries were traded. Other electronic trading platforms also grew, such as Tradeweb, which had been founded in 1996. It launched a platform for US dollar-denominated investment-grade corporate bonds while another was Posit FI from the International Technology Group (ITG). This was a fixed-income dark pool which, according to Frank DiMarco, head of fixed-income trading at ITG, would 'allow clients to place larger orders without adversely affecting the bond's price. Benefits are found in the containment of information leakage, trading anonymously, and the potential to trade at a more advantageous price.'[31] By 2013 the likes of ICE and Nasdaq from the USA and MTS from Europe were also expanding their bond market operations. By 2018 Market Access operated the world's largest bond-trading platform with a turnover of around $150bn a month. It had an 86 per cent share of the electronic trading of US corporate bonds but that was restricted to institutional clients. However, the bond market proved highly resistant to full automation because of the vast number of bespoke securities that were in circulation. It remained difficult to match buyers and sellers despite the increasing sophistication of electronic trading systems. In the USA, investment-grade corporate bonds were increasingly traded electronically, rising from 10 per cent in 2008 to 20 per cent in 2018, but this meant that 80 per cent were not.

[30] Joe Rennison, 'Bond trading platform muscles in as banks retreat', 29th September 2016.

[31] Attracta Mooney, 'Managers turn to dark pools to carry out trades', 2nd March 2015.

The situation was much worse in many other bond markets despite the penetration of US bond-trading platforms.

The underlying problem in the bond market was a fundamental lack of liquidity for most issues, because of the diversity in circulation. This could not be solved through improvements of market mechanisms. Attempts to match buyers and sellers of individual bonds anonymously, using algorithmic programs, were often defeated by the variety of issues and the lack of turnover. The multiplicity of trading venues also fragmented the market, undermining the ability to generate sufficient volume in one platform, from which could emerge reliable prices and the certainty that sales and purchases could be made. This multiplicity was encouraged by regulators, as they promoted competition not concentration, regarding the latter as a means through which investors could be exploited. In the years after the crisis the ability of investors to trade bonds deteriorated, as banks were forced to cut back their trading arms as a result of commercial pressures and more onerous capital regulations. This lack of liquidity had serious consequences, as investors were attracted to bonds through promises that they could be readily sold. Though fund managers had stepped in to replace the banks as purchasers of the bonds being issued in the primary market they did not play such an active role in the secondary market. This deprived the secondary market of liquidity and so increased the level of volatility when buyers or sellers wanted to either acquire or unload large holdings. In turn that posed the risk of a new liquidity crisis if these fund managers were ever in a position of needing to liquidate bonds to meet large-scale withdrawals or redemptions. Fund managers were also increasingly involved in securities lending, with around $2.3tn of assets being lent out globally by 2018, as this generated additional profits from the differential between bond yields, but this was usually a product of both the degree of liquidity and the risk of default. Regulatory intervention had helped to make banks more resilient but it had spread risk to other parts of the financial system, including fund managers. In turn that liquidity risk could become a solvency one if their bond holdings became not only unsaleable but also impossible to value.[32]

[32] Brooke Masters and Shahien Nasiripour, 'Basel move aims to stoke recovery', 8th January 2013; Tracy Alloway and Nicole Bullock, 'Banks offer debt product to help skirt new liquidity rules', 30th January 2013; David Oakley, 'Shadow banks fill infrastructure debt void', 1st February 2013; David Oakley, 'Asset managers fill the gap as banks retreat', 4th March 2013; Michael Mackenzie, Dan McCrum, and Tracy Alloway, 'Electronic trading set to muscle in on corporate debt', 4th April 2013; Stephen Foley, 'Battle is on to make bonds more transparent', 2nd May 2013; Philip Stafford, 'MTS prepares US push to tap into institutional demand', 2nd May 2013; Tracy Alloway and Arash Massoudi, 'ETFs under scrutiny in market turbulence', 28th June 2013; Ralph Atkins and Michael Stothard, 'A change of gear', 1st July 2013; Tracy Alloway, 'Goldman promotes its bond platform', 23rd August 2013; Tracy Alloway, 'The debt penalty', 11th September 2013; Andrew Bounds, 'Alternative financials fill gap left by banks', 12th September 2013; Tracy Alloway and Michael Mackenzie, 'Goldman restructures electronic bond trading platform', 23rd September 2013; Tracy Alloway, 'Buyers struggle to find a safe landing', 21st November 2013; Tracy Alloway and Michael Mackenzie, 'Big banks back digital venue for bond traders', 25th November 2013; Chris Flood, 'Side pockets: a curiosity shop of esoteric assets', 21st April 2014; Camilla Hall, 'Citi unveils pricing tool for block trades', 24th April 2014; Tracy Alloway, 'Big investors replace banks in $4th repo market', 30th May 2014; Sophia Grene, 'Non-banks colonise former bank territory', 2nd June 2014; Tracy Alloway, 'Call for reforms to broker-dealing', 14th August 2014; Tracy Alloway and Michael Mackenzie, 'Bond Traders dealt a new hand', 24th September 2014; Tom Braithwaite and Vivianne Rodrigues, 'Wall Street's biggest lenders blame bond volatility on tight regulation', 17th October 2014; Michael Mackenzie, 'Search for liquidity tests firms' talent for innovation', 5th November 2014; Jeremy Grant, 'SGX in talks on Asian trading platform for corporate bonds', 17th November 2014; Tracy Alloway and Philip Stafford, 'Protocol plan to boost bond liquidity', 25th November 2014; Andrew Bolger, 'Corporate loans rise above pre-crisis levels', 11th February 2015; Attracta Mooney, 'Managers turn to dark pools to carry out trades', 2nd March 2015; Joe Rennison, 'Fitch warns of growing repo threat', 18th June 2015; Robin Wigglesworth, 'Maturity mismatch sparks fears of financial drought', 19th June 2015; Robin Wigglesworth, 'Asset manager calls for more regulation', 19th June 2015; Joe Rennison and Philip Stafford, 'Complexity clouds the case for repo clearing', 19th June 2015; Joe Rennison, 'Bond traders grow nervous over

Currencies

Like the bond market, that for foreign exchange was also one dominated by inter-bank trading and an absence of formal structures. The foreign exchange market was where banks constantly matched their assets and liabilities not only across the diverse currencies of the world but also current and future payments and receipts. Operating at the very centre of the world's financial infrastructure, where money in all its forms was in constant circulation, banks adjusted their positions on a continuous basis to avoid being left exposed to a sudden liquidity crisis in one department or another. In 2007 Peter Garnham observed that 'The foreign exchange market is the world's most liquid and widely traded financial market. Open 24 hours a day, seven days a week.'[33] Operating out of key locations around the world, ranging from Singapore and Tokyo in Asia, through London in Europe and New York in the Americas, the foreign exchange market was always active, creating the opportunity for

glitch potential', 2nd July 2015; Joe Rennison, 'Treasury trading swept up in rapid change', 10th July 2015; Joe Rennison, 'US Treasuries hit by liquidity concerns', 30th July 2015; Joe Rennison, 'HFT's role in Treasuries give regulators pause', 2nd September 2015; Philip Stafford, 'Confidence shaken by violent swings', 13th October 2015; Joe Rennison, 'Transparency beckons for US Treasury trade', 18th February 2016; Joe Rennison and Robin Wigglesworth, 'Outsiders struggle to shake up Treasury trade', 31st August 2016; Joe Rennison, 'Bond trading platform muscles in as banks retreat', 29th September 2016; Joe Rennison, 'BGC set for Treasuries trading push', 1st December 2016; Thomas Hale, 'Shadow banks step into the spotlight', 5th April 2017; Philip Stafford, 'Central banks warned on repo volatility', 13th April 2017; Eric Platt and Gregory Meyer, 'Exchanges jump on index data as banks beat a retreat', 3rd June 2017; Philip Stafford, 'City traders put Brexit back-up plans into action', 2nd August 2017; Philip Stafford, 'Amsterdam chosen as Tradeweb's EU base', 4th August 2017; Robin Wigglesworth and Joe Rennison, 'Goldman expands algo bond trading programme as investors look to cut costs', 17th August 2017; Joe Rennison, 'Pace of reform in bond market slows to a crawl under Trump', 10th October 2017; Philip Stafford, 'LSE admits case for tougher EU oversight', 1st November 2017; Joe Rennison and Alexandra Scaggs, 'US Treasury dealers accused of collusion', 17th November 2017; Joe Rennison, 'Senators press regulators to clarify position over Treasury market reform', 2nd November 2017; Caroline Binham, 'Shadow banking grows beyond $45tn', 6th March 2018; Joe Rennison, 'High-speed traders have their say on Treasury data', 2nd April 2018; Robin Wigglesworth and Joe Rennison, 'The Future of Trading', 10th May 2018; Philip Stafford, 'Electronic trading pioneer throws down gauntlet to BrokerTec on Treasuries', 8th June 2018; Robin Wigglesworth and Joe Rennison, 'Algos blaze trail in odd lots segment of US corporate bonds', 15th June 2018; Eric Platt, 'Wall St banks join forces to form debt platform', 18th June 2018; Chris Flood, 'Liquidity enables big ticket trades', 18th June 2018; Robert Smith, 'Big buyers pull back from US debt', 18th June 2018; Joe Rennison and Philip Stafford, 'Traders find receptive ear among regulators to relax capital rules', 10th July 2018; Alexandra Scaggs and Joe Rennison, 'Investors seek cover against fire sales as headwinds approach', 26th July 2018; Joe Rennison, 'Bloomberg snatches corporate bond trade data partner from rival Thomson Reuters', 26th July 2018; Owen Walker, 'New rules will shine a light on securities lending', 30th July 2018; Kate Allen and Keith Fray, 'Central banks' balance sheets start to shrink', 28th August 2018; Joe Rennison, 'Hunt for yield drives stronger demand for riskier slices of US mortgage securities', 31st August 2018; Chris Flood, 'Bond liquidity issues prompt investors to turn to ETFs', 17th September 2018; Mark Vandevelde, 'Financial Crisis', 20th September 2018; Robin Wigglesworth and Joe Rennison, 'New credit ecosystem blossoms as portfolio trades surge', 11th October 2018; Caroline Binham, 'BoE warns over rapid growth of high-risk corporate lending', 18th October 2018; Robin Wigglesworth, 'Asset managers seek an entrée to the trillion-dollar club', 26th October 2018; Colby Smith, 'Systemic risk fears intensify over leveraged loan boom', 30th October 2018; Chris Flood, 'Global debt pile creates new chances in nascent market', 5th November 2018; Owen Walker, 'Fintech targets fund managers with securities lending platform', 5th November 2018; Philip Stafford, 'Corners of Wall Street remain undeterred by crypto crash', 28th November 2018; Joe Rennison and Colby Smith, 'Debt machine risks running out of control', 22nd January 2019; Joe Rennison, 'BIS sounds alarm on risk of corporate debt fire sale', 6th March 2019; Philip Stafford and Nicole Bullock, 'Bond platform Tradeweb joins IPO rush in windfall for investment banks', 8th March 2019; Hudson Lockett and Leo Lewis, 'Japanese watchdog calls for Citigroup to be fined for spoofing bond orders', 27th March 2019; Joe Rennison, 'MarketAxess muscles into ETFs with Virtu tie-up', 8th April 2019; Don Weinland, 'Beijing set to open up bond futures trading to local banks', 23rd May 2019; John Dizard, 'H20 is an omen: a liquidity crisis lurks', 15th July 2019; Robin Wigglesworth, 'Negative yields force investors to snap up riskier debt', 16th August 2019; Joe Rennison and Philip Stafford, 'Rise of MarketAxess mirrors demise of traders on Wall Street', 30th August 2019; Laurence Fletcher, 'Tumbling yields see debt securitisation hit pre-crisis levels', 17th September 2019.

[33] Peter Garnham, 'Currencies establish themselves as asset class', 5th March 2007.

banks to make and unwind their positions as circumstances changed. Peter Garnham, writing later in 2007, claimed that the 'Foreign exchange is the market that never sleeps—but it really springs to life when London's traders reach their desks. London dominates the world's largest financial market, accounting for more than a third of the daily volumes in foreign exchange. Unlike other financial markets, there is no centrally-cleared market for foreign exchange. Instead, the market stays open 24 hours a day.'[34] He continued that eulogy to the foreign exchange market in 2009 when he reported that 'From Monday morning in New Zealand, currency prices are changing 24 hours a day, moving continuously across the globe for five days until trading shuts down on Friday after the US close.'[35] This activity created openings for others, like hedge funds, to profit from tiny and momentary price differences that appeared, while their trading contributed to overall liquidity. Before the crisis hedge funds were the biggest drivers of growth in global foreign exchange markets as they discovered its possibilities as an asset class. During that period hedge-fund trading reached 20 per cent of global FX volume.

To support their trading in the foreign exchange market banks, brokers and hedge funds invested heavily in the staff, accommodation, and technology required to handle the huge volume of transactions that took place. Turnover was estimated at around $3.3tn a day by 2007, with most trading place through the use of automated, complex trading strategies using dedicated online platforms. By then much of the risk of counterparty default had been eliminated through the establishment of the CLS (Continuous Linked Settlement) Bank by a consortium of leading global financial institutions. It operated a payment netting system that virtually eliminated settlement risk by acting as a trusted third party between the two counterparties to a deal. The success of this CLS system proved itself during the Global Financial Crisis when foreign exchange transactions were unaffected by the turbulence and illiquidity that temporarily destroyed other markets. More banks turned to the CLS system as a result of the crisis because of the guarantees it provided. As it was foreign exchange trading continued as normal during the crisis, especially that which took place between banks. The overall level did drop to $3tn in 2009 but this was due to a severe contraction in hedge-fund activity. Trading then recovered to $4tn a day in 2010. This resilience of the foreign exchange market during the crisis led Jas Singh, global head of Treasury at Thomson Reuters, to claim in 2009 that it was 'a poster child for how over-the-counter financial markets should work.'[36] The foreign exchange market's resilience even led to its increasing use by fund managers as a way of hedging valuation and liquidity risk.[37]

[34] Peter Garnham, 'Quant techniques drive volumes ever higher', 19th November 2007.

[35] Peter Garnham, 'Net brings power to the people', 29th September 2009.

[36] Peter Garnham, 'Keeping its head as others lost theirs', 29th September 2009.

[37] Peter Garnham, 'Currencies establish themselves as asset class', 5th March 2007; John Authers, 'London blows its trumpet too loudly', 19th November 2007; Sundeep Tucker, 'Rivals to HK and Singapore emerge', 19th November 2007; Peter Garnham, 'Quant techniques drive volumes ever higher', 19th November 2007; Peter Garnham, 'Forex market soars with little sign of change in trading system', 15th October 2008; Steve Johnson, 'A little oasis of calm for currencies', 2nd February 2009; Jennifer Hughes, 'A lesson in how to run a smooth global settlement system', 21st August 2009; Jennifer Hughes, 'FX faces prospect of two-tier pricing', 21st August 2009; Peter Garnham, 'Keeping its head as others lost theirs', 29th September 2009; Jennifer Hughes, 'Concern over scope of initiatives', 29th September 2009; Jennifer Hughes, 'Concern over scope of initiatives', 29th September 2009; Henry Smith, 'Reverberations from volatility in the real economy', 6th October 2009; Sophia Grene, 'Taking the sting out of fluctuation', 6th October 2009; Kevin Brown, 'SGX to offer OTC derivatives clearing', 21st September 2010; Geraldine Lambe, 'FX markets ride wave of widening appeal', 4th October 2010; Josh Noble, 'UK's share of renminbi trade leaps', 9th October 2013; Katie Martin and Philip Stafford, 'Banter banned as forex traders clean up act', 23rd May 2015.

Post-Crisis

Though the foreign exchange market had functioned normally during the crisis it was threatened with disruption afterwards by the actions taken by regulators. In the wake of the crisis regulators, especially in the USA, attempted to push all trading either through exchanges or make the use of clearing houses compulsory. This was to include currency transactions that were largely traded in bespoke bilateral deals between banks, central banks, institutional investors, hedge funds, and companies. The intention was to reverse the position of the foreign exchange market as the 'mostly unregulated, largest financial market in the world',[38] according to Daniel Schafer and Delphine Strauss in 2014. Trading took place in an OTC market and did not require the structure of an exchange to either facilitate transactions or regulate behaviour. There was also no need for a clearing house as counterparty risk had been largely eliminated by the establishment of the CLS Bank. In a joint venture in 2006 CME and Reuters had attempted to create a foreign exchange trading platform, FXMarketSpace, which would include an integral clearing house. It was abandoned in 2008 due to a lack of demand. Nevertheless, the collapse of Lehman Brothers, by triggering a series of defaults with multiple counterparties, had made policy makers, regulators, and central banks committed to avoid a repetition of such an event. They identified the commitments made between banks in the foreign exchange market as a threat to the stability of the global financial system, even though observers such as Jennifer Hughes in 2010 referred to it as 'the world's biggest trading operation, operating smoothly across borders around the clock'.[39] The crisis had destroyed trust in self-regulated markets, including those that had functioned trouble-free. In response public oversight and legally-enforceable safeguards were demanded. The most draconian of these was the Dodd–Frank Wall Street Reform and Consumer Protection Act, passed in the USA in 2010. This introduced mandatory clearing for all OTC swap contracts, and these included currency transactions. Lying behind this was also national self-interest as currency trading was dominated by US$ transactions, but took place largely in London. Greater regulation could be used to force a shift to New York or Chicago. However, this attempt by the US authorities to force foreign exchange trading to take place either on exchanges or through clearing houses was strongly resisted by all the major participants, including the largest US banks. They were able to point out that no such action was required in the case of the foreign exchange market, which had a history of addressing and solving its own difficulties, and were answerable not to national regulators but to central banks, both singly and collectively.

When currencies began floating freely in the 1970s their role in the global payments system meant that the nascent market came under the watchful eye of central banks. As the market grew central banks formalized their role but maintained oversight through pressure and consensus not regulation. They also began working together through the Bank for International Settlement (BIS), most notably in pushing the banks in the 1990s to create a global settlement system. The way the foreign exchange market had evolved, and proved resilient during the crisis, was now threatened by the intervention of national financial regulators. Central clearing would mean that banks would have to post collateral to support their trades, which would increase costs and deprive them of funds that could be profitably employed elsewhere. It would also increase the charges they made for the service provided. Foreign exchange contracts were used daily by companies and investors to

[38] Daniel Schäfer and Delphine Strauss, 'Moves into forex etrading speed up', 4th March 2014.
[39] Jennifer Hughes, 'Worries over threat of "heavy touch"', 30th March 2010.

protect themselves from the risks of adverse currency movements. They had provided global businesses and fund managers with the confidence to engage in international trade and investment at a time of currency volatility as the risks posed by such volatility could now be hedged. The actions being taken by regulators threatened access to such arrangements by either forcing banks to increase their charges or scale back their participation. This would either leave businesses and fund managers running the risk of currency volatility or reluctant to engage in international transactions, at the same time forcing foreign exchange trading through a few clearing houses meant creating a new danger for the financial system if one of them should collapse.

As it was, the risks that concerned the regulators had already been addressed either through the internal mechanisms put in place by the global banks or the establishment of the CLS Bank. In 2010 30 per cent of the daily value of foreign exchange trades were transacted directly between client and bank meaning that the risks were internally monitored and managed. The remaining 70 per cent were largely inter-bank transactions and CLS settled 70 per cent of these, using a combination of payment-versus-payment in central bank funds and multilateral payment netting. This eliminated settlement risk. With these procedures already in place, and backing from the world's central banks, the foreign exchange market was able to withstand the post-crisis challenge from the regulators. Nevertheless, the increased regulatory requirements placed on the megabanks, because of their systemic importance, did force them to retreat from some of the riskier aspects of the foreign exchange trading. However, as Eva Szalay explained in 2019, 'For banks, currency trading costs are often part of a complex equation.'[40] To some, such as the megabanks, it was a major source of profits while to others, especially the smaller banks, it was a service that they provided to their customers.

At the heart of the foreign exchange market were ten banks accounting for 70 per cent of the turnover in 2007, and this rose to 77 per cent in 2010. The crisis contributed to their dominance, as they were considered the most trusted counterparties. These banks provided foreign exchange services to the global banking system. They also enjoyed economies of scale and network advantages, which continued to grow through heavy investment in human expertise, electronic technology, and modern trading floors. In 2018 the delay between a bank receiving a request to trade and accepting the order was down to 37 milliseconds. By 2014 most trading was conducted electronically, though voice trading remained important where traders took risks as market-makers. Such was the size of the turnover conducted by each of the leading banks in the foreign exchange market that they could internalize trades and so capture the profit from the bid-ask spread themselves, without incurring much risk as they could instantly offset buy and sell deals. As they constituted a small group of trusted counterparties they also traded with each other without the need for collateral. As Eva Szalay reported in 2019, 'The world's foreign exchange markets do not open or close through the working days of the week. Instead, they operate continuously from Monday to Friday.'[41] Liquidity was normally plentiful in the currency market apart from the period between the New York market closing and the Asian markets opening, creating opportunities for greater volatility, and so little trading took place over the period. Richard Anthony, head of European cash currency trading at HSBC, explained in 2019 that 'During the transition from New York to Asia, there are many fewer human traders at their desks and the ratio of electronic participation to voice is higher than at other times of

[40] Eva Szalay, 'Banks resist demand to shed more daylight on forex charges', 16th May 2019.
[41] Eva Szalay, 'Fears over forex trading going bump in the night', 6th March 2019.

the day.'[42] In contrast, the greatest liquidity was found during the London trading hours and so this attracted the bulk of trading. In 2019 Eva Szalay explained that London's success in attracting trading in both the Chinese renminbi and Indian rupee was that 'London's location, straddling time zones between Asia and the US, gave it a key advantage.'[43]

Despite the depth and efficiency of the global foreign exchange market it was not immune from the actions taken by regulators to restrict the activities of the megabanks, especially through the imposition of higher capital requirements to support their trading activities, which exposed them to the actions of high-frequency traders. Olaf Storbeck and Philip Stafford wrote in 2019 that 'The foreign exchange market is changing rapidly as the banks that have long dominated the market pare back their operations in response to tougher regulations and competitive pressures.'[44] By then regulators were introducing tougher rules for those deals privately negotiated between banks and did not pass through a clearing houses, leading the megabanks to either pull back from the business, demand collateral, or charge more for the service that they provided customers with. What had changed by then was the renewed attention of regulators in response to the revelations of market manipulation. The dominance of the foreign exchange market by a small number of banks, engaged in direct trading between each other or operating through interdealer brokers, made collusion relatively easy, despite the vast volume of transactions. This market manipulation was exposed in 2014 leading to a number of the regulatory authorities imposing large fines. By 2019 the fines paid by fifteen banks over currency manipulation had reached $12bn. The banks had also agreed in 2017 to a Global Code of Conduct for the foreign exchange market, and accept the supervision of the Bank for International Settlement. Exchanges had also tried to move into the foreign exchange market. In 2015 both the US-based exchange operator, Bats, and Deutsche Börse in Europe, had attempted to establish a presence in the foreign exchange market.

However, trading remained dominated by the megabanks, with Citibank the leading player. Of the total turnover of $5.3tn a day in 2015 only $200bn went through exchanges like the CME or local currency venues in Moscow, Mumbai, and São Paulo. Another $1.1tn a day was traded on electronic platforms operated by the likes of Bloomberg, Thomson Reuters, and ICAP. This left the banks handling a turnover of $4tn a day or 80 per cent of the total. The banks moved quickly to address the weaknesses in the foreign exchange market that the manipulation scandal had exposed. A Global Foreign Exchange Committee (GFXC) was established comprising the world's central banks and the biggest currency trading banks. This committee introduced and then supervised a code of conduct for the market and was, itself, answerable to the Bank for International Settlements. Though turnover had slipped to $5.1bn a day by 2017 it thus remained firmly in the hands of the banks. According to Philip Stafford, 'Most currency trading is conducted between banks, away from exchanges, creating a fragmented market that regulators have found difficult to police.'[45] The only way that exchanges could gain a foothold in the foreign exchange market was by buying the existing electronic trading platforms, which the CME did in 2018 when it acquired NEX. It was the electronic markets spin-out from ICAP, the leading interdealer

[42] Eva Szalay, 'Fears over forex trading going bump in the night', 6th March 2019.

[43] Eva Szalay, 'Jump in London rupee trades rings alarms', 18th September 2019.

[44] Olaf Storbeck and Philip Stafford, 'Deutsche Börse in talks to acquire Refinitiv foreign exchange assets', 12th April 2019.

[45] Philip Stafford, 'Fears over "last look" spur tighter FX code', 20th December 2017.

broker. Even then the banks remained in control as it was they that largely generated the trading that took place.[46]

Conclusion

Though damaged by the Global Financial Crisis bond markets quickly recovered benefiting from the needs of governments and companies to borrow and the inability of banks to lend. However, in the ten years after the crisis the bond market emerged in a new form. The restrictions placed on the megabanks forced them to reduce the role they had played as they were no longer able to leverage their funds by buying and holding bonds to the same degree, while their trading activities were drastically curbed. Though others emerged to replace the role previously played by the megabanks, such as the global fund managers, hedge funds, and high-velocity traders, even collectively they did not provide a substitute for what had been lost. The global fund managers followed a predominantly passive policy and so tended to hold the bonds that they bought until maturity. In contrast, the hedge funds did adopt active trading strategies but lacked the resources to hold bonds for any significant period. Even more extreme was the position of the high-velocity traders as they bought and sold very quickly in large quantities and for minute gains, which could either accentuate or counter price fluctuations. What was missing were the ability and willingness of the megabanks to absorb sales using their own funds and meet demand from their own holdings. This had contributed to making the bond market both more liquid and more stable. However, such actions were tainted by what had happened at the time of the crisis and so regulators intervened to prevent it, without recognizing the contribution it had

[46] Jennifer Hughes, 'Concern over scope of initiatives', 29th September 2009; Jeremy Grant, 'First steps towards clearing for FX', 6th October 2009; Jeremy Grant, Richard Milne, and Aline van Duyn, 'Collateral damage', 7th October 2009; Jennifer Hughes, 'Worries over threat of "heavy touch"', 30th March 2010; Geraldine Lambe, 'Settlement model aids FX market success', 12th April 2010; Geraldine Lambe, 'FX markets ride wave of widening appeal', 4th October 2010; Jeremy Grant, 'Industry pleads its case against rules forged in heat of crisis', 29th March 2011; Jennifer Hughes, 'So where do they make their money?', 29th March 2011; Daniel Schäfer and Delphine Strauss, 'Moves into forex etrading speed up', 4th March 2014; Daniel Schäfer and Sam Fleming, 'Scandal puts city's reputation on the line', 6th March 2014; Daniel Schäfer and Sam Fleming, 'Forex probe poised to eclipse Libor cases', 10th March 2014; Delphine Strauss, 'Five big banks extend their domination of forex trading', 9th May 2014; Daniel Schäfer, 'Shrinking margins and higher costs drive down returns', 5th November 2014; Roger Blitz and Philip Stafford, 'BATS plans to open UK forex platform', 25th March 2015; Martin Arnold, 'Barclays admits rigging the market', 21st May 2015; Katie Martin and Philip Stafford, 'Banter banned as forex traders clean up act', 23rd May 2015; Philip Stafford, 'Exchanges seek slice of $5tn forex pie', 7th August 2015; Philip Stafford, 'US eyes prize if swaps shift from London', 20th October 2016; Jane Wild, 'Central banks eye digital money', 2nd November 2016; Madison Marriage, 'Scandalous past still haunts forex industry', 12th December 2016; Philip Stafford, 'Brexit poses threat to London's role as global hub', 10th October 2017; Philip Stafford, 'Fears over "last look" spur tighter FX code', 20th December 2017; Katie Martin, 'Trading data show tougher rule book improves banks' forex behaviour', 4th September 2018; Eva Szalay, 'Yen traders wrongfooted as flash crash strikes during Asia's witching hour', 4th January 2019; Eva Szalay, 'London charm offensive pays off in race for renminbi', 9th February 2019; Katie Martin, 'Swiss franc hit by mini-flash crash during Asian session', 12th February 2019; Eva Szalay, 'Fears over forex trading going bump in the night', 6th March 2019; Eva Szalay, 'Offshore currency trade poses challenge for India's central bank', 6th March 2019; Olaf Storbeck and Philip Stafford, 'Deutsche Börse in talks to acquire Refinitiv foreign exchange assets', 12th April 2019; Eva Szalay and Philip Stafford, 'Citigroup calls for burden of managing risky trades to be shared more widely', 17th April 2019; Eva Szalay, 'Asset managers scramble to cut banks out of forex dealing', 18th April 2019; Eva Szalay and Rochelle Toplensky, 'Banks look for closure in EU benchmark probe', 11th May 2019; Eva Szalay, 'Banks resist demand to shed more daylight on forex charges', 16th May 2019; Philip Stafford, 'Singapore exchange plans to tighten grip as Asia's largest forex trading hub', 11th June 2019; Eva Szalay, 'UK watchdog lends teeth to currency trading code', 28th June 2019; Eva Szalay and Jane Croft, 'Five banks face forex-rigging lawsuits in London', 30th July 2019; Philip Stafford and Eva Szalay, 'London pulls away from New York in forex and swaps as it shrugs off Brexit', 17th September 2019; Eva Szalay, 'Jump in London rupee trades rings alarms', 18th September 2019.

made to the functioning of the bond market. As a result a new source of instability arose among those financial institutions that financed holdings of illiquid bonds but were exposed to sudden withdrawals from investors. These financial institutions lacked the access to the lender-of-last-resort facilities available to banks, once the central banks recognized that intervention was required.

The foreign exchange market emerged largely unchanged from the Global Financial Crisis, the regulatory intervention that followed, and even the later revelations over collusion and manipulation. It remained the preserve of the megabanks despite attempts to move trading away from them. Though estimates vary depending upon whether net or gross trading is measured, the triennial calculations made by the Bank for International Settlement indicate that the foreign exchange market went from strength to strength over the years. Using the gross data suggest that trading in the foreign exchange market had grown before the crisis from \$1.7tn a day in 2001 to \$4.3tn in 2007 and then reached \$5tn in 2010 and \$6.7tn in 2013. It then fell back marginally, dropping to \$6.5tn in 2016, before expanding rapidly to \$8.9tn a day in 2019.[47] What the foreign exchange market delivered throughout was a mechanism through which banks could receive and make payments across all the different currencies of the world. It also allowed banks to continually adjust their present and future exposure to risks posed by currency volatility. In turn the foreign exchange market created opportunities for banks and others to generate profits both on their own account and through the services they provided to others such as multinational companies, global fund managers, and any who were exposed to currency risks. Central banks, both individually and collectively, were aware of the vital role played by the foreign exchange market in both facilitating international financial flows and maintaining equilibrium. For that reason those banks that dominated the foreign exchange market were acknowledged as the most systemically important in the world, and so able to look to central banks for support in a crisis and also subjected to careful monitoring. In contrast, regulators were more aware of the risks being run by those banks and so were keen to limit their exposure and subject the foreign exchange market to greater control. As it was, the central banks won the day and the foreign exchange market was not subjected to the regulations imposed on the other activities of the global banks or the operation of other financial markets.

Generally, global financial markets, whether for bonds or currencies, proved highly resilient during and after the Global Financial Crisis, being either unaffected throughout or quickly recovering thereafter. That did not mean that they were not unaffected and that they did not have to change. Both the bond and currency markets suffered consequences from the actions taken to curb the power and influence of the megabanks and had to make adjustments as a consequence, though these were relatively minor. They were also subjected to the intervention of regulators determined to remove any potential risks as a way of preventing the repeat of another financial crisis. In the case of the foreign exchange market this intervention was extended to them even though they had been untroubled in the crisis and had posed no systemic risk. Fuelling the actions of regulators in the foreign exchange market was the public outcry over market manipulation that came to light after the crisis. In the case of the bond market the combined actions of the central banks, with quantitative easing, and regulators, with curbs on the megabanks, generated new areas of volatility and instability. The longer these policies remained in place the greater the likelihood that a future crisis would occur, but one that would centre not on the banks but other components of the financial system.

[47] BIS, Triennial Bank Survey, 2019.

17

Commodities and Derivatives, 2007–20

Introduction

By the twenty-first century the physical buying and selling of commodities was increasingly internalized within multinational companies or conducted through bilateral negotiations between either monopoly producers or monopsony consumers. In the cocoa market, for example, though there were numerous producers in West Africa, which dominated international supplies, demand was concentrated in the hands of the three largest chocolate manufacturers, namely Mars, Mondelez, and Nestle. In the market for gold, trading was conducted directly between a small group of buyers and sellers in London, where 7500 tonnes, or 596,000 bars, worth $300bn, were stored in bank vaults in 2017. What trading did not take place in this way was largely handled by a small number of transnational companies, who matched supply and demand on a global basis, whether it was fuels such as oil and coal; metals ranging from aluminium, zinc, and copper to lead, nickel, and cobalt; or agricultural products like sugar, wheat, corn, barley, rice, and cotton. These companies operated out of locations that offered a combination of light-touch regulation and low taxation, such as Geneva in Switzerland and Singapore. Even small differences in taxation and compliance costs made a huge difference to their profitability because they operated on wafer-thin margins. By 2012 the numbers employed in commodity trading in Switzerland totalled 10,000 while there were an estimated 12,000 working in Singapore. Nevertheless, the balance of trading still tended to favour Geneva. In oil in 2012 35 per cent of trading took place in Geneva compared to 15 per cent in Singapore; in agricultural commodities it was Geneva on 20 per cent and Singapore on 15 per cent.

However, Singapore was expanding rapidly as a commodity trading centre, being the base for three large international traders, namely Olam, Noble, and Wilmar, and the location of offices for many more, especially from Japan. In 2012 Jennifer Ilkiw, head of Asia–Pacific operations at Intercontinental Exchange, noted that, 'We are seeing the Japanese move their trading desks to Singapore. Partly it is the need to be close to other traders, so they are coming here rather than anywhere.'[1] Singapore was a key location for those commodity trading firms servicing the Chinese market, and the specialist brokers that provided connections between them, such as Tullett Prebon, ICAP, and Tradition. Regardless of the location of their head offices the companies handling the trade in commodities conducted a global operation, as Paul Kinney, director of Cargill Cotton in Liverpool, explained: 'Due to time zone differences, it is almost impossible to manage a truly global cotton trading company from one head office. It is essential to have two management and trading centres.'[2] With one of these offices being in the United States, because of its importance as a commodity producer and consumer, the other was often in either Geneva or Singapore, though other centres were also important such as Liverpool for cotton. Examples of these

[1] Jeremy Grant and Javier Blas, 'Singapore fights for commodities trade supremacy', 23rd May 2012.
[2] Andrew Bounds, 'Liverpool's legacy strengthens the fabric of global cotton trading', 9th April 2012.

Banks, Exchanges, and Regulators: Global Financial Markets from the 1970s. Ranald Michie, Oxford University Press (2021).

DOI: 10.1093/oso/9780199553730.003.0017

companies included the Swiss-based Glencore, which dominated that trading in metals, other than that which took place outside long-term agreements between suppliers and consumers. In 2010 it handled 60 per cent of the trading in zinc, 50 per cent in copper, 45 per cent in lead, and 22 per cent in aluminium. In contrast, it had only a 3 per cent share of the oil market, as that was dominated by another group of Swiss-based companies, namely Vitol, Trafigura, Gunvor, and Mercuria. Similarly, Glencore's share of grain trading was only 9 per cent as that was in the hands of another group of traders, namely Archer Daniels Midland, Bunge, Cargill, and Louis Dreyfus.

It might have been expected that as international trade became internalized within multinational companies, or conducted by global trading companies, the need for organized commodity markets would disappear. That had already happened in national markets as products moved from producers to consumers through managed supply chains. It was now taking place globally with a large proportion of international trade comprising movement between the subsidiaries of the same company, whether it was oil or motor vehicles. However, there remained a dual role for organized commodity markets. The first was to deliver reliable pricing. As the world moved from fixed prices to one of much greater volatility the demand for constantly updated reference prices grew. Fluctuations in iron ore prices encouraged the mining companies and steel makers to demand benchmark prices at which they could buy and sell. The Canadian Wheat Board, for example, had long dictated the price of Canadian wheat as it was the monopoly buyer, but that ended in 2013. As Brad Vantan, president of ICE Futures Canada, said in 2012, 'The marketplace has gone 69 years without an open market and price discovery.'[3] In its place a mechanism had to be put in place through which prices could be established that reflected the changing currents of global supply and demand, and that created opportunities for markets through which this could be done. That could be done easily in a commodity such as wheat, which was relatively homogenous and produced and traded in bulk. In contrast tea lacked homogeneity and there were numerous producers in different countries making it difficult to price, leading to market volatility. The global benchmark price for tea was set by auctions in Mombasa as Kenya was the largest exporter of black tea, though only the third largest producer. Conversely, the international price of coffee was largely driven by the trading of coffee futures in New York even though supply came mainly from Brazil, which accounted for 25 per cent of the total in 2019.

The volume and variety of commodity transactions meant it was no simple matter achieving prices that were both widely accepted and responsive to changing market conditions. Pricing was often the product of a series of fine judgements, with small differences in timing, quality, source, shipping, and destination influencing the final outcome. In 2013 David Wech, analyst at oil consultancy, JBC Energy in Vienna, observed that, 'In the physical market every deal is unique.'[4] In that year \$2.5tn in transactions in the global commodity markets were dependent upon prices collected by reporters working for a variety of agencies and trade journals. The market in cobalt, for example, which generated a turnover of \$2bn per annum, used prices taken from the assessments made by journalists employed by the publication, *Metal Bulletin*. The Baltic Dry Index, which charted the cost of transporting commodities, such as iron ore and grain in bulk, was compiled by canvassing a panel of shipbrokers. Nevertheless, the ability of commodity markets to generate prices, by whatever means this was achieved, played a vital role in underpinning international trade.

[3] Bernard Simon, 'Open wheat market takes root in Canada', 2nd February 2012.
[4] Ajay Makan and Javier Blas, 'Price probe ripples across oil world', 18–19th May 2013.

It provided producers, consumers, and all others involved in the process, such as the banks that financed the movement of commodities, with a degree of confidence that the decisions they took would generate profits, either in the short, medium, or long term, and not leave them exposed to large losses.

The second function that commodity markets fulfilled was to design and make available contracts that could neutralize or magnify risk. All those involved in the production, purchase, movement, and financing of international trade were potential purchasers of contracts that would cover, or hedge, the risks that they were taking. Conversely, there were others who saw in such contracts a way of employing funds profitably by shouldering those risks, either wholly or in part: deregulated electricity markets led major generators and users to purchase contracts that fixed prices. Highly-volatile commodity prices experienced in the likes of cocoa or cotton led both producers and large consumers to hedge their exposure through futures contracts. The lack of such contracts for tea made it difficult for those involved to cover price volatility. There were also contracts that allowed the costs associated with shipping freight to be hedged. The same contracts could be used by large consumers to hedge the cost of future purchases of raw materials and fuels; by large producers to cover a sudden fall in what they received for their output; by speculators betting on the future direction of prices; by banks to minimize the risks they were running when financing stocks of commodities; and by fund managers investing in companies exposed to future fluctuations in commodity prices. All those looked for ways to reduce the risks that they were running. Conversely, others saw that by acting as counterparties to those seeking to hedge their risks they could generate profits, while accepting the possibility of losses. Chinese commodity markets, for example, attracted individual investors who used futures contracts, such as those for steel and iron ore, to bet on the rise and fall of prices. In major financial centres such as London and New York, there were few retail investors willing to take these risks, and so they were undertaken by global banks and fund managers. In either case their action added liquidity to the market, which benefited those using the contracts to safeguard themselves against unexpected price volatility. In that way the contracts traded on either commodity exchanges or arranged bilaterally on the OTC market provided a means of reducing risks, whether it involved palm oil contracts at Bursa Malaysia, copper contracts at the LME, or wheat contracts at the CBOT, and that all contributed to the growth of international trade.

Even before the crisis there was a battle between the exchanges and the OTC market as each tried to gain an advantage over the other. The exchanges could provide heavily-traded standardized contracts that were highly liquid, but charged for the service they provided and imposed strict rules and regulations. In contrast, direct trading between buyers and sellers was conducted free of charge, while those arranged by brokers were customized to suit the interests of particular buyers and sellers. There were numerous commodities in which the level of trading or the specialized nature of the product could not sustain an organized market, and these were traded bilaterally. With most trading in gold and silver confined to fourteen banks it was largely conducted through direct telephone contact between them or even negotiations within a single bank. Exchanges continually experimented with different contracts in the hope that they would catch on and so capture the trading taking place. Conversely, those operating in the OTC market tried to emulate the contracts being traded on the exchanges. Many new commodity contracts were introduced but most failed. Jonathan Parman, co-head of agriculture at commodity brokers, Marex Spectron, suggested in 2015 that 'There's no such thing as a perfect contract.'[5] Writing in

[5] Emiko Terazono, 'Rival exchanges whip up a cocoa war', 24th March 2015.

2018 Emiko Terazono and Gregory Meyer claimed, 'There have been plenty of failed new agricultural contracts.'[6] There was continuous innovation in derivative contracts with most ending in failure as they failed to generate sufficient interest to reach a level of liquidity that made them viable. As Gregory Meyer observed in 2019, 'The history of futures markets is littered with innovative contracts that fail to catch on.'[7]

As the difference between commodity and financial futures and options became increasingly blurred exchanges faced difficult decisions in deciding which users to serve. Producers, consumers, and traders wanted contracts that met the needs of those involved in the physical delivery of commodities in terms of grades, quantities, and delivery times. In contrast, those who financed the global commodity trade, and speculated on the rise and fall of prices, wanted standard contracts that were simple and cheap to buy and sell. Increasingly the contracts traded on the exchanges favoured the latter as these generated a large turnover and thus justified the costs they had to meet. In contrast, the OTC market favoured the former, as these were bilateral deals negotiated to meet a specific set of circumstances. One of the few exchanges to persevere in serving both the physical and the financial users was the LME, and it found it an increasingly difficult task to satisfy the interests of both sets of users. Making the task of the exchanges more difficult was the switch to electronic markets as these were less flexible when attempting to match the interests of both sides to a deal. This use of electronic trading systems was an integral part of a process that was underway, in which digital technology was transforming international trade all the way from accessing information through monitoring the movement of commodities to final delivery and payment. By digitizing contracts, letters of credit, invoices, and other paperwork, and using electronic information systems, it was becoming faster, cheaper, and more secure to complete a trade and settle a commodity transaction compared to the exchange of physical documents which led to delays and mistakes.

This increased use of digital information provided a huge boost to those pushing forward with the creation of electronic platforms for commodity trading. As Etienne Amic, chairman of Vortexa, a company making cargo tracking software, explained in 2018: 'In agriculture, metals or energy, the traders are looking to gather data on a large scale and run machine-learning algorithms to find patterns linking fundamentals with price movements.'[8] In the same year Philipp Bussenschutt, the chief commercial officer at EDF trading (EDFT), the London-based trading arm of the French electricity group, explained their approach: 'We want to be able to extract data and put it into algorithms. We then plan to move to machine learning in order to improve decision-making in trading and, as a result, our profitability... It's another tool that traders have to understand.' He added the warning that increased information flow, and the use of computers using mathematical programs to make decisions and execute trades, could increase volatility: 'We notice that the fundamentals and prices get out of balance in the market with the increased volumes executed by algos.'[9] To his data scientist colleague at EDFT, Peter Leoni, this was all part of a learning process associated with the introduction of a new way of trading: 'It is really a combination of knowing what to look for and using the right mathematical tools for it.'[10] Others were less certain that electronic trading would sweep away all human involvement, though that

[6] Emiko Terazono and Gregory Meyer, 'CME's Black Sea wheat futures contract stirs interest of traders and hedge funds', 4th April 2018.

[7] Gregory Meyer, 'Nodal Exchange to start trading futures in the cost of hiring freight trucks', 28th March 2019.

[8] Emiko Terazono, 'Resources traders seek data wizards to combat squeeze on margins', 11th July 2018.

[9] Emiko Terazono, 'Resources traders seek data wizards to combat squeeze on margins', 11th July 2018.

[10] Emiko Terazono, 'Resources traders seek data wizards to combat squeeze on margins', 11th July 2018.

was the direction of travel. In 2018, according to Gert-Jan van den Akker, the president of Cargill's agricultural supply chain division, 'Humans have always played a vital role in trading and understanding futures markets but we're no longer relying on human brain-power alone.'[11] Gerard Delsad, the chief information officer at the commodity trader, Vitol, remained confident in 2018, that there remained a role for humans: 'You still need the trader to give some ideas, some hints, where to look, and then you can find some interesting stuff.'[12] However, this role was becoming more a residual one as trading shifted onto electronic platforms.

Such was the ability of electronic trading systems to cope with increased capacity and global usage at lower costs, that they replaced physical trading floors all over the world. By 2007 70 per cent of trading done on Nymex, by volume, took place electronically. On the LME in 2016 only 10 per cent of trading took place on the floor, or Ring, with the rest conducted either electronically or over the telephone. Both JP Morgan and Goldman Sachs ran their own trading platforms for LME metals, with contracts better suited to financial purposes than those traded on the LME which were orientated to actual users of the metals. On the CME by 2017 54 per cent of trading in precious metals futures was fully automated, 49 per cent for soya beans and wheat, and 65 per cent of crude oil. This meant the trade was conducted without any human intervention. The problem in the commodity market was the diversity of the parties involved, and the bespoke nature of their requirements, did not lend themselves to the use of a common platform and the standardization of contracts in all cases. Energy markets such as those for gas, coal, power, and emissions took on a hybrid nature as a result, with individual deals negotiated over the phone by brokers while block trades were conducted electronically on exchanges.[13]

[11] Emiko Terazono, 'Resources traders seek data wizards to combat squeeze on margins', 11th July 2018.

[12] Emiko Terazono, 'Resources traders seek data wizards to combat squeeze on margins', 11th July 2018.

[13] Will McSheedy and Jennifer Hughes, 'Dubai sticks to electronic trading', 18th January 2007; Jeremy Grant, 'McGraw-Hill forced to reveal energy trading data', 1st May 2007; Sundeep Tucker, 'Asia seeks its centre', 6th July 2007; James Drummond, 'Raft of bourses crowds market', 24th July 2007; Kerin Hope, 'Greek ship owners likely to set course back to Athens', 12th February 2008; Kerin Hope, 'Greek shipping chiefs prepare to abandon UK after tax crackdown', 12th February 2008; Jeremy Grant, 'Energy platforms in final tussle for clearer advantage', 19th May 2008; Jeremy Grant, 'Imarex to launch shipping contract', 12th June 2008; Javier Blas and Lindsay Whipp, 'Asia accepts the need for commodities exchange hub', 22nd October 2008; Ed Crooks and Jeremy Grant, 'Nasdaq to launch UK power market', 27th November 2008; Javier Blas, 'BHP shocks sector on iron ore spot prices', 30th July 2009; Javier Blas, 'Wall Street and miners to gain as benchmark system is left behind', 30th July 2009; Javier Blas, 'Price critical to global inflation', 30th July 2009; Gregory Meyer, 'Banks back strict energy-trading limits', 30th July 2009; Javier Blas, '"Beginning of the end" for gold miner hedging', 14th September 2009; Javier Blas, 'Sweet taste of success for Cargill as sugar market soars higher', 22nd October 2009; Lindsay Whipp, 'Co-location to get Tokyo up to speed', 2nd November 2009; Gregory Meyer, 'Regulators aim to curb the massive passives', 25th November 2009; Javier Blas, 'Annual contract system collapses', 31st March 2010; David Oakley and Javier Blas, 'Explosive rise in iron ore derivatives trading forecast over next 10 years', 31st March 2010; Javier Blas and Gregory Meyer, 'All you can eat', 19th May 2010; Javier Blas, 'Into the spotlight', 9th July 2010; Leslie Hook, 'Beijing seeks to widen gold trading', 4th August 2010; Joe Leahy, 'Ambani makes a play for stake in ICEX', 19th August 2010; Joe Leahy, 'Aspirant Indian bourse fights regulator', 1st October 2010; Leslie Hook, 'Ambition to build China's futures', 29th October 2010; Javier Blas, 'Geneva set to trump London in oil trading', 23rd November 2010; Leslie Hook, 'Rapid growth but influence stunted by restrictions', 30th November 2010; Gregory Meyer, 'Bunge rides on volatility of food markets', 29th December 2010; Javier Blas, 'Glencore trading empire unveiled', 15th April 2011; Javier Blas, 'Veil slowly lifts on a secretive profession', 24th May 2011; Jan Cienski, 'Capitalism has taken root, capital markets not yet', 21st June 2011; Javier Blas, 'Battle for cereals derivatives heats up', 20th October 2011; Bernard Simon, 'Open wheat market takes root in Canada', 2nd February 2012; Andrew Bounds, 'Liverpool's legacy strengthens the fabric of global cotton trading', 9th April 2012; Jeremy Grant and Javier Blas, 'Singapore fights for commodities trade supremacy', 23rd May 2012; Gregory Meyer, 'Grain trade feels need for speed in longer day', 12th June 2012; Jeremy Grant, 'To take on Shanghai and Hong Kong: specialise', 27th July 2012; Jeremy Grant, 'Singapore OTC trades hit by turmoil', 2nd November 2012; Javier Blas and Ajay Makan, 'Commodities credit crunch eases', 6th February 2013; Emiko Terazono and Javier Blas, 'Swiss question role of commodities traders in economy', 27th March 2013; Javier Blas, 'Tougher times for the trading titans', 15th April 2013; Ajay

Commodity Derivatives and the Crisis

Commodity derivatives were a tiny component of the global derivatives market, comprising only $2.6tn of the $633tn traded in the OTC market in 2012, for example. Also they neither contributed to the Global Financial Crisis nor were directly affected by it. Nevertheless, they were caught up in the regulatory backlash that followed the crisis. They were then targeted by regulators after the scandals involving the manipulation of exchange and interest rates. The intention of regulators in the wake of the Global Financial Crisis was to force the trading of all derivatives to take place either on exchanges or to be processed through a clearing house. Even without the intervention of regulators both these were standard responses among those trading commodity derivatives to any increase in counterparty risk, having been evident after the collapse of the oil trader, Enron, in 2001. As concerns faded so the OTC market revived and the use of a clearing house fell. What happened after 2008 was that regulatory intervention kept up the pressure to route business either to exchanges or through clearing houses. There had long been criticism of OTC commodity markets by regulators every time there were sudden price spikes. These were attributed to the ability to manipulate trading in the less-regulated environment of the OTC market. The 2008 crisis justified intervention to prevent not just perennial abuses but also to provide greater stability and certainty to the trading process.

Despite the regulatory push to force the trading of commodity futures contracts onto exchanges and through clearing houses, by 2010 the OTC market revived as the risk of counterparty default faded. Major producers and consumers of commodities looked to derivative contracts to lock in forward prices and so protect themselves against being caught off-guard by sudden fluctuations in prices. They wanted to obtain this cover as cheaply as possible and the OTC market was where this was available. The companies, banks, and hedge funds involved preferred to trade in the OTC market because costs were low, bespoke deals could be arranged, and collateral was not required. In the OTC market traders accepted counterparty risk rather than post collateral, and were little concerned about exposure to abuse because of confidence in each other. The Israeli Diamond Exchange, for example, was completely reliant on trust between members as that greatly

Makan and Javier Blas, 'Price probe ripples across oil world', 18–19th May 2013; Gregory Meyer, 'BP joins banks as US Swaps dealer', 12th July 2013; Gregory Meyer, 'Trading houses sow the seeds of change', 19th September 2013; Jack Farchy, 'Cobalt shift on pricing sets post-Libor trend', 19th November 2013; Gregory Meyer and Neil Hume, 'Goldman thrives in commodities as rivals melt away', 16th July 2014; Philip Stafford, 'Industry strives to find its form', 5th November 2014; Henry Sanderson, 'Global metals trading challenges regulators', 25th November 2014; Henry Sanderson and Neil Hume, 'LME chief to meld metals with electronic age', 4th February 2015; Gregory Meyer, 'Global cotton futures contract clears hurdle', 18th June 2015; Henry Sanderson, 'LME vows to keep open outcry trading floor', 19th February 2016; Yang Yuan, Christian Shepherd, Wan Li, Lucy Hornby, Neil Hume, 'China's speculators rattle raw materials traders', 7th May 2016; John Reed, 'Under the magnifying glass', 13th May 2016; Gregory Meyer, 'Trading', 7th July 2016; Philip Stafford, 'Watchdog raises ICE-Trayport worries', 17th August 2016; Henry Sanderson, 'Ex-LME chief plans to launch rival platform', 2nd March 2017; John Aglionby, 'Purple tea tipped for place at Kenya auction', 2nd June 2017; Neil Hume and David Sheppard, 'London sitting on $300bn worth of bullion', 2nd August 2017; Neil Hume, 'Grain traders reap few rewards from record crops due to intense competition', 9th August 2017; Emiko Terazono, 'Russia's rise shakes up global grain landscape', 17th November 2017; Anjli Raval, 'China launch aims to create first Asian benchmark for oil deals', 10th February 2018; Tom Hancock, 'Shanghai unveils renminbi oil futures to rival WTI and Brent benchmarks', 27th March 2018; Emiko Terazono and Gregory Meyer, 'CME's Black Sea wheat futures contract stirs interest of traders and hedge funds', 4th April 2018; Emiko Terazono, 'Resources traders seek data wizards to combat squeeze on margins', 11th July 2018; Emiko Terazono, 'Banks and energy traders back blockchain launches', 20th September 2018; Don Weinland, 'Banks race to launch blockchain trade platforms', 9th November 2018; Gregory Meyer, 'Nodal Exchange to start trading futures in the cost of hiring freight trucks', 28th March 2019; Emiko Terazono, 'Traders wake up to cost of coffee volatility as farmers down tools', 17th April 2019.

reduced administrative and regulatory expenses. Evidence of the gradual revival of trust in commodity markets comes from the use of clearing houses for oil futures. This had risen from 10 per cent to 80 per cent of all contracts in the wake of the Lehman bankruptcy but then fell back to 50 per cent by 2010. More permanent were the effects of the restrictions placed on the megabanks by regulators and central banks. Commodity traders like Glencore, Trafigura, Louis Dreyfus, and Noble, relied on the megabanks, such as Goldman Sachs, Morgan Stanley, BNP Paribas, and Barclays, to meet the costs of financing stocks and providing the collateral demanded by exchanges and clearing houses. Post-crisis those sources were constrained because of regulations forcing banks to hold more capital in reserve and cut back on lending. In 2010 JP Morgan had expanded its commodities business by buying that being sold by RBS. By 2013 it was being forced to reduce its commitment to commodities because of the new rules and regulations being introduced, as was the case with other megabanks. Those from the USA were also affected by the ban on proprietary trading. Morgan Stanley sold out to Mercuria, a Swiss commodities trading group, as a consequence. In 2016 Garry Jones, the chief executive of the London Metal Exchange (LME) blamed regulators for the withdrawal of the megabanks: 'What is causing banks to leave commodities is the amount of capital they need to put up.'[14]

The withdrawal of the banks drained liquidity from commodity markets. Their loss was partly filled by others that were less heavily regulated. The large trading houses benefited, for example, as they were well capitalized and could tap the money market directly. Goldman Sachs did remain committed to the commodities business while banks such as Citigroup, Macquarie, and BNP Paribas took the decision to expand in this area because of the withdrawal of others. Chinese banks also moved into the finance of commodity trade and followed this up with increased participation in commodity markets generally. Having a physical commodities business gave them a greater insight into the market, allowing them to better manage the risks involved. China's largest bank, the Industrial and Commercial Bank of China, linked up with the South African bank, Standard Bank, so that it could offer a full range of commodity services to its Chinese customers. However, as a number of megabanks actively involved in commodities trading shrank, so did the ability to smooth out price fluctuations, as they had acted as counterparties to so many deals. This created opportunities for high-frequency traders to generate profits from greater price volatility. A renewed drive for regulatory intervention in the commodity markets then came in the wake of the market manipulation scandals. Commodity pricing was often the product of expert valuation based on privately gathered information rather than trading on the open market. These prices were then used in derivative contracts but, beginning with the Libor scandal, doubts emerged on their reliability. Conversely, those who had supplied prices, such as the interdealer brokers, were either unwilling to continue doing so, in case they were drawn into a price-fixing scandal leading to reputational damage and even criminal prosecution, or realized that they were in possession of valuable information which they could charge for or retain for their own benefit. One market affected in this way was that for precious metals, particularly gold and silver. Though there was no evidence that manipulation had ever taken place, the prices generated were discredited, and alternatives sought from information provided by the exchanges and companies such as Thompson Reuters, with the whole process overseen by the London Bullion Market Association. This

[14] Henry Sanderson and Neil Hume, 'Bullion banks seek alternative to gold exchange', 13th August 2016.

intervention, combined with the restrictions and increased capital requirements placed on banks, undermined the advantages of the OTC market.[15]

In contrast to the OTC market, the crisis and subsequent scandals relating to manipulation boosted the importance of commodity exchanges, as they were considered more reliable in terms of both pricing and the completion of deals. However, these exchanges were also experiencing enormous change. The shifting balance of international trade, especially the growth of Asian markets, was encouraging exchange formation in such locations as China and the Middle East, leading to growing competition for those long established in the USA and Western Europe. Not only were these new exchanges closer to end-users but they also introduced contracts tailored to meet the needs of producers and consumers outside North America and Western Europe. However, many of these new commodity exchanges failed to attract an international following, as they were restricted to domestic users. It was not until 2018 that commodity futures traded in Shanghai were made accessible to foreigners, beginning with crude oil. Also, with the products traded on commodity exchanges becoming increasingly financial in nature the differences between them and stock exchanges disappeared. This led to mergers between exchanges, regardless of products and location, especially as they were forced to invest heavily in electronic platforms. Users switched to automated trading systems because of their advantages in terms of lower costs, greater speed, and increased capacity when matching sales and purchases. These platforms were at their most efficient when employed to their maximum capacity. Also, when combined with integrated clearing and settlement, these exchanges provided users with a single package covering all the stages from initiating a trade through its matching and process to final payment or delivery. Regardless of the consequences of either the

[15] Gregory Meyer, 'Push for clearing houses fails to move leading oil traders', 12th March 2010; Hal Weitzman, 'CME to launch cheese futures', 6th May 2010; Javier Blas and Gregory Meyer, 'All you can eat', 19th May 2010; Gregory Meyer, 'US bans insider trading on official commodities data', 23rd July 2010; Jack Farchy, 'Tide turns against annual contracts for raw materials', 10th August 2010; Javier Blas and Greg Farrell, 'Food producers hedge their way through wheat turmoil', 13th August 2010; Gregory Meyer and Jack Farchy, 'Farmers left short-changed by a margin call squeeze', 23rd November 2010; Javier Blas, 'UBS prioritises agriculture in new division', 1st December 2010; Gregory Meyer, 'An example for regulators to study', 4th November 2011; Patrick Jenkins and Brooke Masters, 'Banks test CDO-style finance for trade', 9th April 2012; Javier Blas and Jack Farchy, 'Trafigura plans trade funding drive', 2nd May 2012; Hal Weitzman, 'ICE shifts OTC energy swaps to futures', 1st August 2012; Vivianne Rodrigues, 'Sophisticated market drives liquidity', 3rd October 2012; Jeremy Grant, 'Singapore OTC trades hit by turmoil', 2nd November 2012; Ajay Makan, 'Search is on for a new gas pricing benchmark', 10th May 2013; Ajay Makan and Javier Blas, 'Price probe ripples across oil world', 18–19th May 2013; Gregory Meyer, 'BP joins banks as US Swaps dealer', 12th July 2013; Gregory Meyer and Jack Farchy, 'Wall Street falls out of love with commodities trading business', 5th August 2013; Xan Rice, 'In search of a new standard', 15th April 2014; Neil Hume, Xan Rice and Daniel Schäfer, 'Gold fix on the spot after Barclays fine', 24th May 2014; Xan Rice, 'Thomson Reuters and CME win bid to set silver price', 12th July 2014; Gregory Meyer and Neil Hume, 'Goldman thrives in commodities as rivals melt away', 16th July 2014; Xan Rice, 'New Solver price strips away cloak of secrecy', 17th July 2014; Sam Fleming and Neil Hume, 'City regulators to police more benchmarks', 26th September 2014; Gregory Meyer, 'Oil price swings come too late for banks who made desk cutbacks', 5th November 2014; Henry Sanderson, 'ICE to run electronic gold benchmark', 8th November 2014; Henry Sanderson, 'Regulators prize open London gold market', 13th November 2014; Gregory Meyer, 'Sun sets for trading pioneer Phibro as prices tumble', 3rd February 2015; Henry Sanderson, 'Chinese banks stake their claim on the LME', 11th February 2015; Henry Sanderson, 'Traders warn on gold liquidity as banks stay away', 19th May 2015; Henry Sanderson, 'Exchange pushes the pedal to the metal', 10th June 2015; Henry Sanderson, 'London gold trade wrestles with modernity', 5th February 2016; John Reed, 'Under the magnifying glass', 13th May 2016; Neil Hume, 'London unveils bullion futures platform', 9th August 2016; Henry Sanderson and Neil Hume, 'Bullion banks seek alternative to gold exchange', 13th August 2016; Henry Sanderson, 'Regulator says banks back plan for more transparency in London's gold trade', 19th August 2016; Henry Sanderson, 'Gold market ready to reveal how much bullion is deposited in London's vaults', 6th February 2017; David Sheppard and Anjli Raval, 'Plans to upgrade Brent trigger calls for caution', 27th February 2017; Gregory Meyer, 'DRW unit joins top rank of traders with nearly $1bn revenues over two years', 16th January 2018.

Global Financial Crisis or the market manipulation scandals, commodity exchanges were in the midst of a period of major change at this time.

What users of a commodity exchange wanted was a market with as near 24-hour trading as possible, as that allowed them to continuously monitor their exposure to price fluctuations and adjust their positions accordingly. This adjustment reflected conditions not only in the underlying physical market but also other variables that had a major influence. These variables included interest rates, as these affected the cost of financing stocks in transit or in warehouses; exchange rates against the US$ as that was the currency in which most commodities were priced; and the performance of financial markets as that influenced the attractions of commodities as an asset class. It was the need to continually adjust to changes in all these variables that drove turnover in the commodity exchanges. In 2013 the size of the physical market in oil, for example, was $2.4tn but the value of oil contracts traded on exchanges was $22.8tn; the size of the physical gold market was $104bn while the value of contracts traded on exchanges was $6.3tn; the size of the physical copper market is $143bn but the value of the exchange-traded contracts was $10.9tn. Increasingly driving this turnover were not producers, consumers or traders, though they relied on the results, but those with a financial interest in the commodity trade, such as the banks and fund managers. As they were already the dominant users of the stock exchanges the result was a steady convergence between the market being served by both. In Japan in 2007 the Tokyo Stock Exchange considered moving into commodities, for example.

However, the most common pattern were mergers between commodity and stock exchanges. This was facilitated by the conversion of exchanges from mutual organizations serving the particular interests of their members, such as commodity traders, into public companies being run for profit by their owners. Writing in 2007 Anuj Gangahar and Norma Cohen reflected that 'Exchanges, which only a few years ago were largely owned by their users, have been snapped up by investors convinced that they must be big and global in scope to deliver economies of scale.'[16] Michael Henry, a senior executive in Accenture's global Capital Markets practice, referred in 2008 to 'An ongoing battle for market share between virtually all of the world's largest exchanges.'[17] By 2011 Jack Farchy and Jeremy Grant observed that there was a 'Wave of consolidation as exchanges seek to capitalise on booming interest in commodities.'[18] Those mergers took place both within countries and internationally. Examples of national mergers included, in 2011, that between the Moscow Interbank Currency Exchange (Micex) and the Russian Trading Systems (RTS), to create a single electronic platform for equities, derivatives, and commodities. That year the Mercado a Termino de Rosario (Rofex) and Mercado de Valores de Rosario (MervaRos) in Argentina also merged to create a single market combining commodity futures and equities. However, it was in the USA that the most important mergers took place revolving around the Chicago-based CME. In 2007 the CME acquired its Chicago rival, the CBOT, and then moved to take over the New York-based Nymex.

As early as 2007 Nymex was regarded as being vulnerable to a takeover bid because it had failed to move into financial derivatives and was slow to adopt electronic trading. That year Anuj Gangahar and Norma Cohen reported that Nymex was 'seen by many as being too limited in its product and geographic reach to remain an island in the ongoing global

[16] Anuj Gangahar and Norma Cohen, 'Three named as Nymex merger talks starts', 16th June 2007.
[17] Anuj Gangahar and Hal Weitzman, 'CME-Nymex tie-up sets scene for showdown', 26th August 2008.
[18] Jack Farchy and Jeremy Grant, 'LME has already seen a "raft of interest"', 29th September 2011.

consolidation of exchanges'.[19] To counter its lack of diversification Nymex launched a futures contract for uranium in 2007 followed in 2008 with one for steel. Neither of these was able to emulate the success it had enjoyed with its oil and gas contracts of the past, encouraging other exchanges to consider acquiring it, including the NYSE and Deutsche Börse as well as the CME. It was the CME that was willing to pay the highest price and so it gained control of Nymex in 2008. This gave it a dominant position within the USA, as it combined the two leading derivatives exchanges in Chicago and New York and was home to the leading energy, metals, and agricultural contracts as well as those in financial contracts. What it lacked was a strategy for international expansion, which Michael Henry immediately spotted, remarking in 2008 after the Nymex acquisition, that 'If the CME wants to be a global player, it will have to attempt more challenging strategic moves in the future, such as acquiring a cash market or overseas exchange.'[20] Larry Tabb, an expert on financial markets, similarly questioned the wisdom of CME confining itself to the USA: 'Will the tightly and vertically integrated CME strategy of being the largest global player in an increasingly global market play out?'[21]

However, what the CME had was its own electronic trading platform and integrated clearing house. Those provided it with the ability to bring new products to the market quickly while giving it protection from rivals, as it allowed it to offer users a single package combining trading and processing and the ability to cross-subsidize whichever component faced competition. Once under the control of the CME, Nymex was rapidly integrated into its electronic platforms, including the more complex option contracts. In 2016 Nymex's trading floor was closed with trading shifted to computer screens. By then half the trading in US crude oil futures took place on automated systems using mathematical programs. Nymex's trading computer was located in a data centre in Aurora, Illinois. Building on its commanding position as the dominant US commodity exchange the CME also introduced new contracts to cater for different segments of the market. In 2010, for example, it launched a futures contract for cheese. In the USA cheddar cheese had, since 1997, been priced at a daily ten-minute auction on the floor of the CME. That was then used as a reference price for all other cheese. This market involved a physically-delivered spot contract chiefly traded by large food companies. In contrast, the new cheese futures contract was electronically traded and accessible for virtually twenty-four hours a day during the week. In the absence of such a contract, cheese manufacturers had been forced to rely on CME's milk and dry whey contracts as a reference point. The new contract was designed to give them a more direct hedge against their exposure to fluctuations in cheese prices. The CME also orientated itself to serve an increasingly global clientele but from a US base. By 2016 a quarter of the total volume of trading taking place on the CME originated outside the USA. In response in 2012 and again in 2017 the CME launched contracts based on wheat exports from Russia and the Ukraine as that region emerged as a major exporter. The CME also denominated contracts in currencies other than the US$ such as the Chinese renminbi, Russian rouble, and the Brazilian real in order to retain and even expand its pool of international users. Once a commodity futures contract achieved a certain level of liquidity, it was difficult for a competing contract to attract trading away even though it offered a better fit in terms of time zone or physical specification. Nevertheless, those contracts traded on

[19] Anuj Gangahar and Norma Cohen, 'Three named as Nymex merger talks starts', 16th June 2007.

[20] Anuj Gangahar and Hal Weitzman, 'CME–Nymex tie-up sets scene for showdown', 26th August 2008.

[21] Anuj Gangahar and Hal Weitzman, 'CME–Nymex tie-up sets scene for showdown', 26th August 2008.

the CME, whether for wheat or oil, that were based on US supply and demand conditions, did face growing competition from foreign rivals by 2017.

In contrast, those exchanges lacking the advantages that its US base gave the CME regarded foreign acquisitions as a means of international expansion. This made the London Metal Exchange an attractive target because, in the words of Jack Farchy and Jeremy Grant in 2011, it 'hosts the futures contracts used as global industry benchmarks for base metals from copper to nickel'.[22] The LME's contracts were used as the pricing benchmark for 80 per cent of the global trade in non-ferrous metals. Though both the CME and ICE tried to acquire the LME they were outbid by Hong Kong Exchanges and Clearing (HKEx) in 2012. Control over the LME provided the HKEx with trading and hedging facilities in the global metal market. Through the acquisition of the LME the HKEx attempted to establish itself as a bridge between the international and the Chinese markets, spanning cash equities to commodity derivatives. After the acquisition of the LME HKEx took steps to develop a commodities business with renminbi-denominated futures contracts in zinc, copper, and nickel and US$ contracts in thermal coal, all of which were important for Chinese consumers. This left the LME competing in the international metal market with the CME, which owned the US metal exchange, Comex through its acquisition of Nymex, and Asia's rising star in the shape of the Shanghai Futures Exchange in metal trading. This competition extended over a growing range of minerals as the LME took on Comex's highly-liquid gold futures contract. The dilemma that the LME faced was how to balance the interests of the global metal trade with those of the banks and the fund managers. As Michael Overlander, head of the commodity broker Sucden, pointed out in 2017, 'There's nobody out there who can guarantee with a cast-iron certificate that if you change the model it's definitely going to work.'[23] The LME used both an electronic trading system and an open outcry ring, though 90 per cent of transactions went through the former by 2018.

The fundamental problem the LME faced was trying to satisfy the demands of mining companies and industrial users of metals, who wanted physical delivery and customized contracts, while appealing more to hedge funds, asset managers, and algorithmic traders, who did not want physical delivery and preferred standard contracts. The core of the LME's difficulty was that it used individual daily delivery dates, which were designed for physical metal users who wanted to hedge the date of a shipment or sale. However, this was unattractive to hedge funds and other investors due to the difficulty of finding a willing buyer for a contract with such a specific delivery date. They wanted contracts with a fixed monthly delivery date. In order to meet that demand banks such as JP Morgan created their own platforms for trading standard contracts using the volume of business they handled to internally match buying and selling. This included acting as the counterparty themselves, thus cutting out the brokers trading open outcry. Despite this dilemma, and the competition it faced, the LME remained the world's leading metals exchange setting the global reference price for the likes of aluminium, copper, and zinc. In 2018 Henry Sanderson and Neil Hume referred to the LME as 'The world's leading metals exchange, setting the global reference prices for industrial metals such as aluminium and copper. Among its main customers are miners, manufacturers and merchants who use the exchange to lock in or hedge prices. It is also used by investment banks to wager on the direction of prices.'[24]

[22] Jack Farchy and Jeremy Grant, 'LME has already seen a "raft of interest"', 29th September 2011.
[23] Henry Sanderson and Neil Hume, 'Crunch time for increasingly brittle LME', 9th February 2017.
[24] Henry Sanderson and Neil Hume, 'LME trading volumes soar on price swings and trade war', 8th October 2018.

Despite the complications of its contracts they retained their appeal. In contrast, the LME had difficulty in devising a gold contract that would compete with that offered by Comex, despite London being a centre of the physical market for precious metals. In 2017 Kare Eged, head of precious metals at LME, claimed its new gold contract would bridge the division between the physical and financial users of the LME: 'It brings together the daily structure of the OTC market with the monthly futures approach of existing international exchange offerings, while also providing a solution to pressing challenges such as ongoing regulatory change, increased transparency requirements and the threat of market fragmentation.'[25] However, the gold futures contract traded at Comex in New York was widely used by hedge funds, banks, and gold buyers to hedge their exposure to price fluctuations, and remained popular.

The commodity exchange with the greatest ambition both to conquer the US market and to establish itself internationally was the US-based Intercontinental Exchange (ICE). It had acquired the London-based International Petroleum Exchange, and used its Brent crude contract to challenge the West Texas Intermediate (WTI) crude one traded on Nymex. In this it was successful as the WTI contract reflected domestic trading conditions in the USA while the Brent one was a proxy for the global market, especially Middle East crude being shipped to China and Japan. With that success ICE then built up a transatlantic portfolio of commodity exchanges before buying NYSE Euronext in 2012. This gave it control not only of the NYSE but also London's leading derivatives exchange, Liffe, and so provided it with a base to compete with the CME's near monopoly in the USA. That competition broke out in such commodities as cocoa and cotton as ICE used its international network to challenge the CME, which fought back using its dominant position in the US market. What the battle between ICE and the CME epitomized was the position of global commodity markets by the second decade of the twenty-first century, which was that they transcended national boundaries. As Gregory Meyer, writing in 2016, observed, 'Markets have become increasingly placeless, regulated by national laws but open in any time zone.'[26] Though both US-based ICE and the CME were engaged in a global struggle for international supremacy that allowed them to play one jurisdiction off against another. In 2019 Gregory Meyer reported that 'Unlike most futures markets where a single exchange dominates, ICE and CME compete fiercely for volume in oil and natural gas and have recently had to fend off a Nasdaq futures exchange.'[27]

In this the CME had the advantage of embedded liquidity, as it was very difficult to challenge an established contract. On the other hand ICE could leverage its time zone advantages, especially its considerable presence in London, which straddled the Asian and North American markets and dominated those in Europe. One arena in which this competition was played out was in the global oil market. The main benchmark in oil was the ICE Brent futures contract traded on the ICE Futures Europe exchange. As a proxy for oil exported from the Middle East the Brent crude contract was used as the reference price in two-thirds of global oil deals, and underpinned billions of dollars of related trading in energy futures, options, and swaps. The rival contract was provided by the CME being based on WTI, which had been developed by Nymex. The disadvantage of WTI was that it was a product

[25] Henry Sanderson, 'Lacklustre launch for LME gold contract as big bullion banks back rival venture', 11th July 2017.

[26] Gregory Meyer, 'Trading', 7th July 2016.

[27] Gregory Meyer, 'Intercontinental Exchange muscles into New York harbour heating oil futures', 26th June 2019.

of the domestic market for oil in the USA rather than global supply and demand conditions. However, by 2017 it was emerging as a global contender as the US became a global oil exporter on the back of the expansion of shale production. In order to meet this competition, in 2018 ICE transferred its North American oil and natural gas futures contracts from the jurisdiction of European regulators to that of the CFTC in the USA, as that allowed it to operate under less onerous rules. ICE also acquired NGX, a North American natural gas, electricity, and oil marketplace, which strengthened its US base, whereas the CME had abandoned its London operation in 2017.[28] No longer were commodity exchanges national

[28] Chris Flood and Christopher Brown-Humes, 'LME plans to see off challenges with dual expansion moves', 5th January 2007; Saskia Scholtes, 'Nymex to launch first uranium contract', 17th April 2007; Richard Beales, 'ICE plans to set up clearing unit', 1st May 2007; David Turner, 'TSE to launch exotic products to view with other bourses', 2nd June 2007; Anuj Gangahar and Norma Cohen, 'Three named as Nymex merger talks starts', 16th June 2007; Javier Blas, 'Nymex to offer steel futures contract', 5th August 2008; Anuj Gangahar and Hal Weitzman, 'CME–Nymex tie-up sets scene for showdown', 26th August 2008; Ed Crooks and Jeremy Grant, 'Nasdaq to launch UK power market', 27th November 2008; Hal Weitzman, 'Regulation threat to CME dominance', 27th January 2010; Gregory Meyer, 'Nymex floor loses its voice to electronics', 1st June 2011; Philip Stafford, 'CME steps up Asian push with revamp of renminbi futures', 12th July 2011; Jeremy Grant and Jack Farchy, 'LME receives offers of interest', 24th September 2011; Jack Farchy and Jeremy Grant, 'LME has already seen a "raft of interest"', 29th September 2011; Jack Farchy, 'Metdist owners poised to reap benefits of LME bidding tussle', 3rd October 2011; Rachel Morarjee, 'Merger creates market less prone to squabbling', 4th October 2011; Javier Blas, 'Battle for cereals derivatives heats up', 20th October 2011; Jack Farchy, 'Sticklers for tradition rule roost when it comes to sale of LME', 16th December 2011; Jeremy Grant, 'Two Argentine exchanges agree to combine forces', 17th December 2011; Jack Farchy and Jeremy Grant, 'Prospect of LME's sale puts clearing in focus', 23rd February 2012; Gregory Meyer, 'Backlash brews over longer trading day for grain futures', 16th May 2012; Gregory Meyer, 'Grain trade feels need for speed in longer day', 12th June 2012; Jack Farchy and Robert Cookson, 'LME chief set for £10m after agreeing £1.4bn sale to HKEx', 16th June 2012; Jack Farchy, 'Deal would aid path to China growth', 18th June 2012; Josh Noble, 'HKEx unveils plan to be "gateway for China"', 16th January 2013; Alex Barber and Kara Scannell, 'Plans to shift Libor heart to Europe', 7th June 2013; Jack Farchy, 'Cobalt shift on pricing sets post-Libor trend', 19th November 2013; Josh Noble and Lucy Hornby, 'HKEx enters commodities trade with metals listing plan', 23rd April 2014; Gregory Meyer, 'ICE chief blasts rival's tactics to lure users', 5th November 2014; Philip Stafford, 'Industry strives to find its form', 5th November 2014; Henry Sanderson, 'Regulators prize open London gold market', 13th November 2014; Jeremy Grant, 'SGX targets greater China link with Taiwan', 25th November 2014; Philip Stafford, 'US the dominant derivatives superpower', 9th January 2015; Emiko Terazono, 'Rival exchanges whip up a cocoa war', 24th March 2015; Henry Sanderson, 'Exchange pushes the pedal to the metal', 10th June 2015; Gregory Meyer, 'Global cotton futures contract clears hurdle', 18th June 2015; Henry Sanderson, 'Exchange pushes the pedal to the metal', 10th June 2015; Henry Sanderson, 'London gold trade wrestles with modernity', 5th February 2016; Philip Stafford, 'ICE circles amid D Börse's tie-up talks with LSE', 2nd March 2016; Philip Stafford, 'Bourse tie-ups put clearing risk in spotlight', 5–6th March 2016; Kate Burgess, 'Foreign bidders prepare to climb aboard Baltic Exchange for $100m', 11th March 2016; Gregory Meyer and Philip Stafford, 'Alarm spreads ahead of US algorithm rules', 22nd March 2016; Henry Sanderson and Neil Hume, 'LME faces broker breakaway threat over increase in fees', 14th July 2016; Henry Sanderson and Neil Hume, 'Bullion banks seek alternative to gold exchange', 13th August 2016; Henry Sanderson and Neil Hume, 'Crunch time for increasingly brittle LME', 9th February 2017; David Sheppard and Anjli Raval, 'Plans to upgrade Brent trigger calls for caution', 27th February 2017; Henry Sanderson, 'Ex-LME chief plans to launch rival platform', 2nd March 2017; Henry Sanderson and Neil Hume, 'LME head looks to lure investors by simplifying offering', 26th April 2017; Jennifer Hughes, 'Inspiration from Home Depot for LME owner', 11th May 2017; Henry Sanderson and Neil Hume, 'Ex-Glencore traders to launch metals platform', 5th July 2017; Henry Sanderson, 'Lacklustre launch for LME gold contract as big bullion banks back rival venture', 11th July 2017; Henry Sanderson, 'LME hopes gold futures contract will provide the Midas touch for its reform', 18th July 2017; Neil Hume and David Sheppard, 'London sitting on $300bn worth of bullion', 2nd August 2017; Neil Hume, 'Incoming chief of metals exchange plots evolution not revolution', 7th August 2017; Emiko Terazono, 'Russia's rise shakes up global grain landscape', 17th November 2017; Gregory Meyer and Philip Stafford, 'ICE plots escape from Mifid 2 as it prepares to shift 245 energy contracts to US', 12th January 2018; Emma Dunkley, 'Brexit delays Hong Kong–LME tie up', 25th January 2018; Tom Hancock, 'Shanghai unveils renminbi oil futures to rival WTI and Brent benchmarks', 27th March 2018; Emiko Terazono and Gregory Meyer, 'CME's Black Sea wheat futures contract stirs interest of traders and hedge funds', 4th April 2018; Tom Hancock and Neil Hume, 'China opens iron ore futures trading to foreigners as it seeks pricing clout', 3rd May 2018; Emiko Terazono, 'Resources traders seek data wizards to combat squeeze on margins', 11th July 2018; Henry Sanderson and Neil Hume, 'LME trading volumes soar on price swings and trade war', 8th October 2018; Gregory Meyer and David Sheppard, 'Exchange giants battle over new US oil benchmark', 12th February 2019; Emiko Terazono, 'Blockchain platform Vakt signs majority of North Sea traders', 26th February 2019; Gregory Meyer, 'Nodal Exchange to start trading futures in the cost of hiring freight trucks', 28th

monopolies as underlying changes in technology and products with an integrated global economy exposed them to competition. As Jean-Francois Lambert, former head of commodity trade finance at HSBC admitted in 2019, 'It's become more and more difficult to make money by trading commodities and any means to lower costs and shorten transaction times is welcome.'[29]

Financial Derivatives and the Financial Crisis

Unlike commodity derivatives financial derivatives played a central role in the Global Financial Crisis, both in contributing to the bubble that preceded it and the events that played out in 2007 and 2008. They were then centre stage in the attempts by regulators and central backs to curb the causes of financial instability in the years that followed the crisis. Financial derivatives were viewed by many as novel and dangerous instruments that led to the build-up of risk-taking away from the supervision of regulators and central banks. To others they represented a way of coping with the volatility present in a dynamic and open world economy and covering the risks present in both banks and financial markets. In the wake of the crisis it was the negative perception that dominated, with derivatives being blamed for the crisis and its severity, leading to intervention to prevent the same happening again. Certainly, the rapid growth and the huge size of outstanding derivative contracts prior to the crisis gave cause for concern, with the total reaching $450tn in May 2007. However, most of these were being used to mitigate risk by spreading exposure to losses throughout the financial system and so provide a means of absorbing the impact of small-scale shocks. It was for these reasons that regulators before the crisis had advocated the use of derivatives as a way of avoiding liquidity crises, and minimizing exposure to both volatility and defaults. Little distinction was made between different types of derivatives and whether they were traded on the OTC market, which were customized to suit specific requirements and were illiquid, or on exchanges, where the standardized variety was traded, and were highly liquid. By 2007 the most common derivative was an interest-rate swap in which two banks exchanged exposure to different borrowers, with no payment being made or obligation created. A swap allowed each counterparty to tailor their cash flow to suit their precise requirements, as well as diversifying the risks they took in the event of a default by a borrower.

The invention of credit derivatives contributed to the switch from the lend-and-hold model of banking to the originate-and-distribute one. With credit derivatives the risks attached to lending could be separated out from the underlying assets and sold as a separate contract. In the lend-and-hold model banks made loans that were then retained until maturity. This meant that the bank received the interest paid while accepting the risk that the borrower would default. In the originate-and-distribute model the bank issued stocks and bonds on behalf of borrowers and arranged their sale to investors, including handling subsequent buying and selling in many cases. With credit derivatives a loan could be

March 2019; Emiko Terazono, 'Traders wake up to cost of coffee volatility as farmers down tools', 17th April 2019; Gregory Meyer, 'CME shows how automation is the future of futures trading', 24th April 2019; Henry Sanderson, 'LME appoints first female chairman in its history', 11th May 2019; Henry Sanderson, 'Platinum setback for Shanghai Gold Exchange highlight hazards of reform', 21st May 2019; Gregory Meyer, 'Intercontinental Exchange muscles into New York harbour heating oil futures', 26th June 2019.

29 Emiko Terazono, 'Blockchain platform Vakt signs majority of North Sea traders', 26th February 2019.

repackaged as a bond and sold to an investor accompanied with a contract that guaranteed against a default. This left the investor with a risk-free return as long as the counterparty to the credit derivative could be relied upon. After the introduction of credit derivatives banks were able to repackage loans into bonds and sell these to investors, including fund managers and other banks, because the risks had been greatly reduced. No longer was it necessary for banks to provide permanent intermediation between savers and borrowers, as in the lend-and-hold model, because this could be done transaction by transaction using the originate-and-distribute model. In this way the use of financial derivatives contributed directly to the credit bubble that preceded the crisis as banks were able to obtain additional funds to lend by selling existing loans and keep repeating the process. The ability to transfer the risk of default to others through credit derivatives also encouraged banks to take greater risks when making a loan as they no longer expected to retain it until maturity. As the switch to the originate-and-distribute model gained traction within banking the process of securitization was extended to ever more diverse pools of debt with varying risk profiles, blurring the distinction between credit and capital. By the end of 2007 the value of credit derivatives-contracts outstanding had reached $62tn though that was still dwarfed by interest rate derivatives at $350tn.

These credit derivatives were not traded on exchanges but in the OTC market where the megabanks were the major players. By March 2007 David Oakley and Jim Pickard reported that the OTC credit-derivatives market had 'proved wildly successful'.[30] Underpinning its success was the ability of the OTC market to design derivative contracts tailored to fit exact requirements, unlike the standardized products available from exchanges. It was also the OTC market that drove product innovation in derivatives as the financial community searched for ways of covering even more of the risks they were exposed to. One new product that became very popular prior to the Global Financial Crisis was Credit Default Swaps. In the lend-and-hold model of banking lenders were exposed to the default of a borrower. Helping to drive the take-up of this product among banks was the need to comply with the new Basel 2 capital-adequacy rules, as this encouraged them to reduce the level of default risk they were exposed to. A single name credit default swap, for example, allowed the purchaser to insure against the default of a specific borrower, especially a large company. Another product that was gaining popularity was property derivatives, beginning in the USA but spreading to the UK, France, Germany, Hong Kong, and Australia. Such derivatives could be used either to increase exposure to the property market or to hedge the risks being run by property investors. Prior to the Global Financial Crisis derivative products were being introduced that made risk itself a separate tradeable commodity. Through these derivatives investors could choose to position themselves along the entire spectrum of risk-taking so removing the barriers that had placed restraints on the willingness of savers to invest and the ability of borrowers to obtain the funds they wanted.[31]

[30] David Oakley and Jim Pickard, 'Banks move in on property derivatives', 5th March 2007.

[31] Brian Bollen, 'They created the game—so they invent the rules', 5th March 2007; David Oakley and Jim Pickard, 'Banks move in on property derivatives', 5th March 2007; Paul J. Davies and Richard Beales, 'New players join the credit game', 14th March 2007; Richard Beales, 'Exchanges take the risk plunge', 23rd March 2007; Richard Beales, 'Exchanges attempting to offer instruments that align with OTC credit derivatives', 23rd March 2007; Paul J. Davies, 'Eurex has confidence in credit derivatives', 23rd March 2007; Richard Beales, 'Trading times cut, says ISDA', 20th April 2007; Norma Cohen and Ivar Simensen, 'D Börse lands in the US via ISE', 1st May 2007; Anuj Gangahar, 'Krell swansong fulfils global ambitions', 1st May 2007; John Authers and Gillian Tett, 'Snapping Point', 23rd May 2007; Gillian Tett, 'No turning back the revolution', 28th May 2007; Gillian Tett, 'Swaps soar as investors pile in', 28th May 2007; Gillian Tett, 'Growth brings loss of oversight', 28th May 2007; Martin Wolf, 'The new capitalism', 19th June 2007; Mark Mulligan, 'Enviable BME prepares for next challenge',

Though the first signs of the Global Financial Crisis were apparent in 2007 this did not immediately damage the popularity of financial derivatives, rather the reverse. The risks that had emerged with subprime mortgages increased the demand for derivatives as a way of covering exposure to those who had been extensively engaged in making such loans. The value of outstanding Credit Default Swaps (CDS) grew from $34.2tn in 2006 to $62.2tn by the end of 2007. The seller of a CDS agreed, in return for a premium, to pay the face value of the policy to the buyer in the event of a default. However, no less a person than Bill Gross, the manager of the world's largest bond fund at the time, Pimco, pointed out in January 2008 that those providing CDSs had 'no requirements to hold reserves',[32] leaving holders unprotected if it was the issuer that defaulted. When it collapsed in 2008, Lehman Brothers was counterparty to hundreds of billions of dollars-worth of bilateral OTC derivatives contracts. It was during the course of 2008 that doubts emerged about the value of OTC derivatives as a way of protecting against risk. Especially after the collapse of Lehman Brothers, there was a rush to switch from private bilateral derivatives contracts into exchange-traded ones as the latter included the use of a central counterparty. This shift was backed by regulators which was a reversal of their pre-crisis policy which was to press for the break-up of exchanges that combined trading and clearing, known as the vertical-silo model, because it was anti-competitive. In the wake of the crisis those exchanges that had adopted the vertical-silo pointed out how well it had performed. One example was Fabio Dutra, the director for fixed-income, foreign exchange and derivatives at the Brazilian exchange, BM&F Bovespa, which had adopted the vertical-silo model before the crisis. In 2012 he claimed that 'This integrated model is becoming a reference for other global and foreign regulators…because it minimises systemic risk. It is one of the reasons this market has managed to weather the increase in global volatility that we've seen since the financial crisis.'[33]

A clearing house stood between parties to a trade, stepping in to ensure that a deal went ahead even if one party defaulted. They were often integrated into the service provided by leading commodity exchanges, such as the CME. After the Global Financial Crisis regulators pressed for clearing houses to be used more widely to process OTC derivatives in order to provide greater security to both parties to a trade. However, this was resisted by many market participants because of the additional costs it imposed on their business. A clearing house, or central counterparty, collected a fee each time a trade was cleared and demanded that the parties to a deal posted collateral, which they lent out in the money market and took the income it generated. By not using a clearing house a market participant could avoid this fee and retain the capital for its own use. Market participants, and users of financial derivatives, were also quick to point out that exchange-traded products were not perfect substitutes for the OTC variety, and being forced to use them created new risks. The Wholesale Market Brokers Association warned in 2009 that 'There is a danger that policy decisions are being considered that may attempt to force OTC products on to exchanges, resulting in a dramatic reduction in liquidity and product flexibility in

21st June 2007; Paul J. Davies and Aline van Duyn, 'Collapse of bank shakes foundations of the CDS industry', 16th September 2008; Michael Mackenzie, 'Interest rate swaps dominate dealing', 15th October 2008; Michael Mackenzie, 'Interest rate swaps dominate dealing', 15th October 2008.

[32] Saskia Scholtes and Gillian Tett, 'Shipwrecks and casualties warning for credit markets', 11th January 2008.
[33] Vivianne Rodrigues, 'Sophisticated market drives liquidity', 3rd October 2012.

markets essential for trading and hedging.'[34] The Association of Corporate Treasurers explained that:

> Ordinary non-financial companies use tailored derivatives provided by their banks to hedge the sorts of risks that arise from normal business activity, and not for speculative purposes. Exactly matched hedging can be done for specific risks, amount and timings, using OTC derivatives to eliminate or manage the risk. Prohibiting OTC derivatives might help in minimising risk in the financial sector but could result in additional risk being carried in the non-financial sector with potentially devastating effect.[35]

What they were warning regulators about was that the prohibition of OTC derivatives would merely shift the risks within the financial system. Companies had long used derivatives contracts to hedge against anything from the volatility of currencies to safeguarding future pension liabilities and any obstacles introduced by regulators could have an adverse effect on their ability to manage these risks effectively.

At the time these warnings were ignored, such was the identification of OTC-traded derivative contracts as a prime cause of the crisis. However, it was not easy to convert OTC derivative contracts into a standard form that would lend themselves to trading on exchanges. Also, the use of clearing houses increased costs, especially through the provision of collateral, making the products less attractive to both the banks that issued them and those that bought them. Neither of these solutions offered a quick fix. Less than 4 per cent of derivatives contracts outstanding were listed on exchanges by 2010. In that year the value of derivatives outstanding on the OTC market stood at $615tn, and most of these were not being processed through clearing houses. Of the total $449.8tn were interest-rate contracts and $49.2tn foreign exchange contracts compared to only $32.7tn in Credit Default Swaps (CDSs), which was the category that most concerned regulators. The level for CDS contracts by 2010 had dropped to half the peak it reached during the crisis of 2008, but its continuing size showed the difficulty of moving away from products that had become embedded into the global financial system, and replacing those that remained with either exchange-traded equivalents or making the use of clearing mandatory. Even in 2010, according to Michael Mackenzie and Aline van Duyn, 'Banks tend to trade OTC derivatives such as swaps directly with their customer, by telephone. These trades are then managed with other banks into the bigger and more liquid interbank market. There, trading is done by means of interdealer brokers such as ICAP, Tullett Prebon, GFI and BGC, using voice and electronic trading systems.'[36] The reason for the continued dominance of the OTC market was 'because that has suited the dynamics of an unregulated market dominated by the big dealers'.[37] Kevin McPartland, a senior analyst at the Tabb Group, observed that, 'A good portion of the swaps market activity is dealer to dealer, and the interdealer brokers handle the majority of that volume.'[38] The average size of a swap was $100m but it could reach as high as $1bn, being tailored to meet a specific purpose.

One of the alternatives to the use of derivative exchanges being promoted were Swap Execution Facilities (SEFs). These were described by Michael Mackenzie and Aline van

[34] Jeremy Grant, 'Exchanges and brokers at odds over crisis blame', 20th February 2009.
[35] Jeremy Grant, 'Derivatives reform draws UK warning', 25th July 2009.
[36] Michael Mackenzie and Aline van Duyn, 'Regulators may silence derivative squawk boxes', 22 July 2010.
[37] Michael Mackenzie and Aline van Duyn, 'Regulators may silence derivative squawk boxes', 22 July 2010.
[38] Michael Mackenzie, 'Rate swap traders wait for no man', 20th October 2010.

Duyn in 2010 as 'a facility trading system or platform in which multiple participants have the ability to execute or trade swaps by accepting bids and offers made by other participants that are open to multiple participants in the facility or system'.[39] They observed that several interdealer brokers had built SEFs, either alone or jointly, to complement the bulk of the trading which continued to take place by telephone. Nevertheless, regulators still remained intent on pushing most of the OTC derivatives market onto exchanges, even though that suited only those products that were widely used, simple in structure, and actively traded. Customized derivatives continued to be traded on the OTC market and the solution for them was that they would either have to be processed through a clearing house or collateral provided in case of a default. The effect of this regulatory intervention was to tilt the balance of the derivatives market firmly away from OTC trading, whether it was the large internal markets maintained by banks or the international networks operated by interdealer brokers. As this pressure from regulators was not evenly spread around the world the outcome by 2010, according to Jeremy Grant was 'a growing risk of regulatory arbitrage, where market participants shop around for the most favourable set of rules. The main beneficiaries will be Asian centres only too keen to build up derivatives and clearing businesses of their own.'[40] Less than two years after the collapse of Lehman Brothers divisions and doubts were emerging over the best strategy to be followed in devising a solution to the risks in derivative contracts. The inherent difficulty regulators faced was that OTC-traded derivatives remained a cheap and convenient way of coping with both the volatility of a market-based financial system and the consequences of counterparty default.[41]

At a meeting of the governments of the world's leading economies in 2009 there had been an agreement to shift the bulk of OTC derivatives on to exchanges or other electronic trading platforms and require them to be processed through clearing houses. Following the

[39] Michael Mackenzie and Aline van Duyn, 'Regulators may silence derivative squawk boxes', 22 July 2010.

[40] Jeremy Grant, 'The route to regulation diverges for Europe and America', 12th August 2010.

[41] Saskia Scholtes and Gillian Tett, 'Shipwrecks and casualties warning for credit markets', 11th January 2008; Paul J. Davies and Aline van Duyn, 'Collapse of bank shakes foundations of the CDS industry', 16th September 2008; Gillian Tett, Paul J. Davies, and Aline van Duyn, 'A new formula? Complex finance contemplates a more fettered future', 1st October 2008; Javier Blas and Jeremy Grant, 'Rush to put private commodities contracts on public exchanges', 13th October 2008; Hal Weitzman, 'Exchanges have their eyes on the next opportunity', 21st October 2008; John Plender, 'Originative sin', 5th January 2009; Jeremy Grant, 'Exchanges and brokers at odds over crisis blame', 20th February 2009; Aline van Duyn and Anuj Gangahar, 'Exchanges big winners in OTC overhaul', 15th May 2009; Gillian Tett, Aline van Duyn, and Jeremy Grant, 'Let battle commence', 20th May 2009; Jeremy Grant, 'OTC derivatives plan lifts shares', 2nd June 2009; Jeremy Grant, 'Exchanges warn on OTC clearing', 4th June 2009; Gillian Tett and Aline van Duyn, 'On the march', 9th June 2009; Jeremy Grant, 'NYSE Euronext joint venture to capitalise on rising demand for clearing', 19th June 2009; Michael Mackenzie and Aline van Duyn, 'Costs set to rise amid shake-up in derivatives trading', 19th June 2009; Jeremy Grant, 'Clearing not the cure-all for financial system woes', 26th June 2009; James Wilson, 'More than just a historic trading floor', 30th June 2009; Jeremy Grant and Nikki Tait, 'Eurex and ICE lead clearing race after Liffe setback', 6th July 2009; Jeremy Grant, 'Derivatives reform draws UK warning', 25th July 2009; Jeremy Grant, Richard Milne and Aline van Duyn, 'Collateral damage', 7th October 2009; Aline van Duyn, 'Numbers game', 2nd November 2009; Daniel Thomas, 'Investors begin to return to property derivatives trading', 25th January 2010; Rachel Sanderson, Guy Dinmore, and Gillian Tett, 'An Exposed Position', 9th March 2010; Nikki Tait, Ben Hall, and David Oakley, 'Dilemma over CDS trades policing', 10th March 2010; Aline van Duyn, 'Transparency of derivatives becomes key battleground', 12th March 2010; Hal Weitzman, 'Banks urged to rethink OTC trading', 6th April 2010; Aline van Duyn, 'Derivatives traders search for ways to appease regulators', 23rd April 2010; Aline van Duyn and Francesco Guerrera, 'Dodd–Frank bill is no Glass–Steagall', 28th June 2010; Aline van Duyn, Michael Mackenzie, and Hal Weitzman, 'Derivatives dealers brace for clearing shake-up', 14th July 2010; Michael Mackenzie and Aline van Duyn, 'Regulators may silence derivative squawk boxes', 22 July 2010; Aline van Duyn, 'Derivative Dilemmas', 12th August 2010; Jeremy Grant, 'The route to regulation diverges for Europe and America', 12th August 2010; Philip Stafford, 'Regulators show united front', 20th October 2010; Michael Mackenzie, 'Rate swap traders wait for no man', 20th October 2010; Aline van Duyn, 'New rules aim to bring trading of derivatives more into public view', 17th December 2010.

2009 agreement the US authorities were quick to carry through the measures agreed, followed by the EU. In the USA there was the Dodd–Frank Act, while the EU responded with a combination of the European Market Infrastructure Regulation (Emir) and the Markets in Financial Instruments Directive (Mifid). In 2011, Lee Olesky, the chief executive of Tradeweb, which operated a global multi-dealer-to-client interest-rate derivatives platform, credited the recent upsurge in trading to regulatory intervention: 'Our business model is benefiting from the prospect of swaps trading in a regulated environment and on a platform that is transparent and open to investors.'[42] However, it was not until 2012 that Asian countries put forward regulations to cover derivatives and they were adapted to suit local conditions. By then much had been learnt from the consequences of the US and the EU regulations, which were considered to have damaged the working of the derivatives market. As a consequence Asian countries were reluctant to implement in full the regulations introduced in the USA and the EU. By 2012 the consequence, in the judgement of Mike Bodson, the chief executive, of the US's DTCC, was that 'Asia is well positioned to seize a greater share of the OTC derivatives market, while at the same time having the right tools in place to protect it from the risks that nearly led to the collapse of the global financial system.'[43] What had emerged was that the rules in place in the USA and Europe, which tried to limit the use of derivatives for speculative purposes, had undermined their use for hedging purposes. A CDS, for example, was used both by investors to insure against risk and to speculate on corporate creditworthiness. The former was considered desirable, even though it could mask the underlying risk attached to a particular investment, while the latter was not, but it was not possible to have the one without the other, though that was what regulators wanted to achieve. The result of the intervention was to undermine the CDS market. In response to the combination of new regulations and increased capital requirements, trading in CDSs declined significantly from a weekly volume of $140bn in 2011 to $57bn in 2016. Whereas the value of CDSs outstanding stood at $60tn in 2007 it had fallen to $8tn in 2018. In the absence of such products banks either did not lend, reducing the finance provided to business, or accepted that the failure of a large borrower would result in a large loss, endangering their own solvency.

Revival of Financial Derivatives, 2010–20

As early as 2011 a reaction to the regulatory intervention in the derivatives market was underway in the USA because of the adverse consequences it was having. In that year John Damgard, the president of the Futures Industry Association, warned that one consequence of over-regulation was to drive trading out of the USA: 'Markets are awfully portable, especially derivatives markets, and capital will flow to markets that aren't burdened with oppressive regulation.'[44] One response from US regulators was to try and extend their rules covering derivatives beyond their own shores. Not only were foreign banks operating in the United States forced to comply but also the foreign subsidiaries of US banks. This raised the complex issue of whether regulation implemented by one country could be forced on others. There was a degree of self-interest in the actions taken by US legislators in trying to force trading through regulated derivatives exchanges, as the most important of these were

[42] Michael Mackenzie, 'Market prepares for transparency', 4th November 2011.
[43] Jeremy Grant, 'Asia watches and learns from European and US rule makers', 30th October 2012.
[44] Jeremy Grant and Nikki Tait, 'NYSE link-up faces hurdles', 11th February 2011.

American. On the back of its acquisition of the CBOT and Nymex, approved by US regulators, the CME had become the dominant derivatives exchange in the USA, and with that base it was well positioned to attract trading internationally, as it could offer the most liquid contracts. However, it faced strong competition from the OTC market and this took place largely in London, where so many banks had offices from which they traded directly with each other or through the interdealer brokers. In the OTC market banks constantly swapped commitments they had made to customers, and adjusted their assets and liabilities, to ensure that they maximized returns while minimizing risks. These were customized contracts designed to meet particular needs and so were little traded once in place, being allowed to stand until maturity. Secondary trading in the OTC derivatives market was thus relatively light compared to the high turnover of standard contracts on the exchanges. An estimate made in 2011 suggested that only 3000–3500 interest-rate swaps contracts were traded each day, for example, compared to 2.7m Eurodollar interest-rate futures contracts traded daily on the CME Group. Whereas the amount of derivatives outstanding was far greater on the OTC market than on exchanges, when it came to trading the reverse was the case. For those reasons the exchange-traded and OTC market complemented each other, with the former providing customized contracts and the latter liquidity, so that a mixture of both was employed.

Even without the bias apparent in the USA, regulators favoured the simplicity and liquidity of exchange-traded derivatives, along with the guarantees of clearing houses. Prior to the crisis OTC derivatives were popular based on the assumptions that they were liquid and that counterparties could be trusted to complete their side of the deal. Once the possibility of illiquidity and default was recognized regulators wanted those deals to go through an exchange, or equivalent, and involve the use of collateral. In contrast, both were considered unnecessary and costly by the global banks, and they were responsible for most activity in the OTC derivatives market. If they were forced to comply it would represent a serious constraint on their ability to use swaps to cover risks, considering the fine margins at which the business was done. By matching assets and liabilities through deals with banks in a reverse position, the exposure to risk could be reduced or eliminated without the use of an exchange or the need for collateral. A bank with assets in one currency and liabilities in another, for example, could do a deal with a bank faced with a reverse position, with each gaining from the interest paid on the credit they provided to customers. Faced with the opposition from the banks in being forced to route such business through an exchange, or a SEF, and use the services of a central counterparty, in 2011 the US Treasury agreed to exempt OTC foreign exchange swaps and forward contracts from the derivatives rules proposed under the Dodd–Frank Act. This was symptomatic of the general backlash to the draconian rules covering derivatives that followed the Global Financial Crisis, aimed specifically at the OTC market. Stringent rules covering derivatives harmed the ability of banks to hedge the risks attached to lending or buying bonds and so discouraged them from undertaking all but the safest type of business. The increased costs of swaps made it more expensive for fund managers to cover their exposure to future risks and so discouraged them from financing long-term investment. This had major economic consequences in terms of the provision of both credit and capital. The problem was that there was little support for an OTC derivatives market, operated by a 'cosy club of leading global dealer banks',[45] in the words of Michael Mackenzie and Tracy Alloway in 2012. The new Basel

[45] Michael Mackenzie and Tracy Alloway, 'Swaps profits threatened by Dodd–Frank', 23rd August 2012.

rules raised the level of capital that banks had to hold against uncleared derivatives in a bid to force the use of central counterparties, for example.

However, by 2011 there were emerging worries that the derivatives exchanges were exploiting the monopoly position that the new rules gifted them. Those exchanges that had adopted the vertical-silo model continued to worry regulators in both the USA and the EU, as this had long been regarded as anti-competitive, but no action was taken to force them to split up their business. Instead, regulators increasingly turned to mandatory clearing, greater transparency, and additional collateral as ways to reduce leverage, monitor linkages, and enhance resilience. This made OTC derivatives more expensive while the increased transparency allowed high-frequency traders using super-fast computers running algorithmic programs to generate profits by anticipating the needs of banks and fund managers to reverse their positions. The effect was to either discourage users of financial derivatives from using them to hedge against volatility, as they could find the market stacked against them, or resort to alternatives. As Briton Ryan, at the brokers, Newedge, pointed out in 2011, 'Traders are always looking for new and cheaper ways to hedge.'[46] One alternative that came into vogue were ETFs, indicating that no matter what the regulators did the market would turn to new products or new ways of trading if sufficient demand existed. Outright bans or highly-restrictive rules were effective only in forcing a shift from one product to another, one market to another, or one jurisdiction to another, not in preventing the activity taking place if the demand remained strong.

In an age of continuing volatility the demand for ways of hedging against risk remained, and was even magnified as the Global Financial Crisis exposed new dangers, such as counterparty defaults. Pension funds, for example, looked to swaps as a way of covering their exposure to inflation risk, as they had a commitment to match payments to the price index. Even without regulatory intervention those actively engaged in the derivatives market sought ways of redesigning both the products and the market so as to reduce the risks they ran, while still obtaining the service they wanted in the most simple and cost-effective manner. William Rhode, director of fixed-income research at the Tabb Group, a NY-based capital markets consultancy, observed in 2012, 'that the market response to regulation is product innovation. I think there will be certain CDS products that will have enough liquidity to trade on exchange.'[47] To Jon Kinol, global head of interest-rate swaps at Credit Suisse, in 2011 his bank was 'ready to clear and electronically trade derivatives when the rules are finalised'[48] while the plea from Chris Ferreri, managing director at the interdealer broker, ICAP, was for rules that were 'flexible and can be changed in the future as the market develops.'[49] Though alternatives to the derivative products traded on the OTC market were developed they were not exact copies and also involved additional costs. The demand for more and higher quality collateral to back customized derivatives, for example, meant providers had to hold low yielding government debt or cash deposits, which reduced profitability and made the activity less attractive. This forced those still wanting to use derivatives to switch to standard futures contracts but these did not match their particular requirements.

Though support for the regulatory reform of derivatives trading did falter as the immediacy of the Global Financial Crisis faded it received a boost from the scandals involving

[46] Telis Demos, 'Interest of markets and regulators grows', 4th November 2011.
[47] Philip Stafford, 'ICE plans CDS exchange trading', 17th October 2012.
[48] Michael Mackenzie, 'Market prepares for transparency', 4th November 2011.
[49] Michael Mackenzie, 'Industry hopes longer delays will mean looser rules', 4th November 2011.

market manipulation. That involving Libor brought into doubt the derivative contracts that used it as a benchmark, with around $170tn of these in circulation in 2012. Faced with these scandals regulators approached the task of curbing the use of derivatives, especially those traded on the OTC market, with renewed vigour. Nevertheless, the resistance to forcing derivatives through exchanges or the use of mandatory clearing remained strong, because of the contribution they made to covering financial risks in an age of continuing volatility and the lack of perfect substitutes. Swaps in particular came in so many different types tailored to suit specific conditions and partners that they did not lend themselves to standardization. This meant they could not all be forced to comply with a common set of rules as required by the authorities. For those reasons the OTC derivatives market remained dominant. An estimate for 2014 put the notional value of exchange-listed futures at $30tn globally while the figure for the OTC market stood at $700tn. Banks found OTC trading much more profitable than passing business through exchanges and using clearing houses, and so refused to move most of their business in that direction. Bespoke derivatives provided fund managers with a cheap and flexible method of hedging their exposure to volatility, without moving the market price against themselves, and so were unwilling to move to standardized futures and options.

There were also problems associated with the derivative contracts traded on exchanges such as the popular Volatility Index (Vix) option available on the Chicago Board Options Exchange (Cboe). This allowed investors to speculate on the behaviour of the US stock market. The problem was that trading the derivative products linked to the Vix itself influenced the Vix, so that it was no longer an accurate measure of stock market volatility. Sandy Rattray, who had jointly devised, with Devesh Shah, the formula to trade futures contracts tied to the Vix, pointed this out in 2018: 'I don't think all the people buying these products understand the complex mechanics of it. I think they are terrible products that serve no real purpose. I think the Vix is being used by banks as an important input into models for risk management, credit spreads, bid-ask spreads. The fact that it has been wired into all of these ways of measuring risk is worrying to me.'[50] What worried him was that the Vix was responding to speculative trading in the derivative contracts based on it rather than acting as a neutral measure of volatility. Despite these concerns the Vix continued to be used as a measure of volatility, indicating the continued need to find ways of hedging against the unpredictability present in modern financial markets. It was this underlying need that drove demand for derivatives whether they were of the exchange-traded variety or those found in the OTC market.

By tailoring derivatives to meet customer needs and using electronic technology to stay connected to their clients, those operating in the OTC market were able to resist attempts by exchanges to capture the business. The OTC market had also adopted many of the features of exchanges, such as central clearing, settlement, and confirmation and so remained competitive with exchanges not only on price but also on the service and guarantees they provided. SwapClear, owned by LCH.Clearnet, operated as the central counterparty for bilateral swap trades between banks. Also, it was generally accepted that rather than being competitors much of the activity generated on exchanges was driven by the needs of the OTC market while the reverse was also the case. The growth of the OTC swaps market, for example, benefited from the quoting of short-term interest-rate futures on exchanges. These provided a key building block for valuing and hedging OTC swaps. In turn the

[50] Miles Johnson, 'Volatility derivatives have become tail that wags the dog', 9th February 2018.

growth of OTC swaps helped fuel trading in exchange contracts. The result was a mixture of competition and co-operation between exchanges and the OTC market, with 80 per cent of transactions favouring the latter. Whatever actions regulators took after the Global Financial Crisis to constrain the OTC derivatives market proved ineffective as the underlying need for its products remained. At the same time its success contributed to the increased activity taking place on the exchanges, which, in turn, drove higher OTC volumes.[51]

Derivatives and Exchanges, 2007–20

There was another dimension to the market in financial derivatives that was brought into sharp focus by the crisis of 2008 and that was the rivalry between exchanges. By 2007 the

[51] Jeremy Grant and Nikki Tait, 'NYSE link-up faces hurdles', 11th February 2011; Jeremy Grant, 'Dealers look for answers on US derivatives reform', 17th March 2011; Jeremy Grant, 'Central counterparties eye wave of opportunities', 22nd March 2011; Tom Braithwaite, 'US Treasury to exempt forex swaps from new rules', 30th April 2011; Joshua Chaffin and Hal Weitzman, 'How clearing helped ICE reinforce ties with banks', 30th April 2011; Aline van Duyn, '"ET" stokes fears about sweeping swaps rules', 4th May 2011; Aline van Duyn, 'Battle lines emerge as new rules are created', 31st May 2011; Michael Mackenzie, 'Habits change in anticipation of arrival of electronic trading', 31st May 2011; Jeremy Grant, 'Reform in Europe', 31st May 2011; Jeremy Grant, 'Conduits of contention', 16th June 2011; Hal Weitzman and Telis Demos, 'Ultra-fast trading firms hit headwinds in race to be first', 14th July 2011; Alex Barber, 'EU to ban naked sovereign CDS', 19th October 2011; Michael Mackenzie, 'Market prepares for transparency', 4th November 2011; Hal Weitzman, 'Euro crisis gives clearing a boost', 4th November 2011; Telis Demos, 'Interest of markets and regulators grows', 4th November 2011; Michael Mackenzie, 'Industry hopes longer delays will mean looser rules', 4th November 2011; Alexander Kliment and Vivianne Rodrigues, 'Regulated, representative and popular with investors', 15th November 2011; Jeremy Grant, 'New rules are struggle for industry and regulators', 23rd January 2012; Philip Stafford, 'Changes bring global flurry of innovation', 23rd January 2012; Michael Mackenzie, 'Libor probe shines light on voice brokers', 17th February 2012; Michael Mackenzie, Nicole Bullock, and Telis Demos, 'JPMorgan loss exposes dangers of derivatives', 16th May 2012; Sophia Grene, 'Derivatives rules will bring new demands', 21st May 2012; Brooke Masters, 'UK banks lead world on liquidity rules', 22nd June 2012; Philip Stafford, 'CME puts Europe at the centre of expansion plan', 21st August 2012; Michael Mackenzie and Tracy Alloway, 'Swaps profits threatened by Dodd–Frank', 23rd August 2012; Philip Stafford, 'Battle for derivatives clearing heats up', 11th September 2012; Philip Stafford, 'ICE plans CDS exchange trading', 17th October 2012; Stephen Foley and Michael Mackenzie, 'Derivatives trades on the brink of tough new regime', 18th October 2012; Jeremy Grant, 'Asia watches and learns from European and US rule makers', 30th October 2012; Michael Mackenzie, 'Fight looms over which model is best', 30th October 2012; Philip Stafford, 'Rules covering derivatives built on ground that has yet to settle', 30th October 2012; Michael Mackenzie and Gregory Meyer, 'US swaps shake-up set to boost exchanges', 2nd November 2012; Michael Mackenzie and Stephen Foley, 'High costs to hit made to measure derivatives', 12th December 2012; FT Reporters, 'ICE chief makes his biggest bet with deal', 21st December 2012; Philip Stafford and Arash Massoudi, 'Upstart ICE in $8bn gamble with deal for 208-year-old NYSE Euronext', 21st December 2012; Philip Stafford, 'CME poised for European clearing push', 11th February 2013; Brooke Masters, 'Objective evidence offers better guarantees in a brave new world', 19th March 2013; Michael Mackenzie and Philip Stafford, 'US swaps trading prepares for its big bang', 18th February 2014; Paul Amery, 'ETF giants bet on futures for flows', 2nd February 2015; Philip Stafford, Arash Massoudi, and Anna Nicolaou, 'Virtu's reward could be a valuation of $1.8bn', 6th March 2015; Philip Stafford, 'US swaps market resists futures model', 17th March 2015; David Sheppard and Neil Hume, 'Traders fear new derivatives rules', 26th October 2015; Philip Stafford and Paul McClean, 'Listed options accelerate in the electronic era', 2nd March 2016; Philip Stafford, 'ICE circles amid D Börse's tie-up talks with LSE', 2nd March 2016; Joe Rennison and Mary Childs, 'CDS demise sends traders running for cover', 10th June 2016; Philip Stafford, 'Strains show in over-the-counter dealing', 14th June 2016; Gregory Meyer, 'City retains role as capital of the derivatives industry', 16th December 2016; Philip Stafford, 'European attempts to grab UK clearing house business underlines London's great strength', 16th December 2016; Philip Stafford, 'Clearing houses pose post-crisis challenge', 17th February 2017; Robin Wigglesworth, 'The fearless market', 19th April 2017; John Dizard, 'Arguing over who owns a clearing time bomb', 8th May 2017; Philip Stafford, 'Brexit poses threat to London's role as global hub', 10th October 2017; Miles Johnson, 'Volatility derivatives have become tail that wags the dog', 9th February 2018; Joe Rennison, Robin Wigglesworth, and Miles Johnson, 'Concerns mount over scale of volatility-trading ecosystem', 10th February 2018; Robin Wigglesworth, 'Exchange traded products face scrutiny as worries deepen', 15th February 2018; Robin Wigglesworth, 'The Volatility Virus', 14th April 2018; Joe Rennison, 'Trio sets out plans to launch corporate bond futures', 17th May 2018; Katie Martin and Philip Stafford, 'Banks and insurers slow to switch on as nightfall approaches for Libor', 20th September 2018; Caroline Binham, Philip Stafford, and Jim Brunsden, 'No-deal Brexit threat concentrates minds at London clearing houses', 10th October 2018.

long-established division between stock and derivatives exchanges, and along national boundaries, had broken down leading to competition. Exchanges recognized the loss of the monopoly they once possessed and the need to compete if they were to survive. This was especially so as they were increasingly organized as profit-maximizing businesses rather than member-owned clubs. In this competitive environment there was a strong focus on bringing down costs, as that would allow charges to be reduced and profits expanded, as well as improving the service provided to users. This led inexorably towards the continuing electronification of markets and a desire to expand the volume of trading as that brought huge economies of scale. In 2010 Hal Weitzman reported that financial derivatives had moved from 'floor-based trading to the computer screen, ever-faster trade execution and now co-location facilities enabling lightning-fast algorithmic trading'.[52]

Benefiting from this shift was a new generation of high-frequency traders, such as the Global Electronic Trading Company (Getco), co-founded by Dan Tierney, a former pit trader at the Chicago Board Options Exchange. Firms such as Getco traded derivatives along with equities, fixed income, and commodities on markets around the world, regardless of whether they were provided by exchanges or existed on an OTC basis. To compete, exchanges had to meet the needs of traders like Getco, as they were responsible for a growing share of the trading that took place because of the highly-active strategies they followed. This forced exchanges to invest heavily in the latest electronic technology, expand the product range, multiply the number of markets served, and integrate trading with clearing and settlement so as to provide users with a single package covering the entire process. Integrating clearing with trading was attractive to exchanges as they not only received additional revenue from the fees charged, while employing the collateral posted, but it also gave them an element of protection against competition as users paid a single fee for a bundle of services. This made it difficult for a rival to break into the market served by an established exchange, which was difficult in any case because of the inertia attached to successful derivatives contracts. As Jeremy Grant observed in 2010, 'Shifting liquidity in a single product dominated by a futures exchange in the US has repeatedly proved hard.'[53]

Occupying a dominant position in the US market for financial derivatives was the CME. With the acquisition of the CBOT in 2007, approved by US Department of Justice, the CME became the market for the two leading interest-rate contracts in the USA and combined them with an integrated clearing house. In 2011 the CME had a 95 per cent share of the US interest-rate futures market having seen off competition from an electronic futures exchange, ELX. This had been formed in 2008, and was backed by the likes of JP Morgan, Credit Suisse, Bank of America Merrill Lynch, and Goldman Sachs. When ELX was abandoned in 2011 it had managed to gain only a 3 per cent share of the US derivatives market. The dilemma faced by regulators was that competition between exchanges led to market fragmentation, which eroded liquidity and harmed the price discovery process, while the dominance of a single exchange led to market concentration, allowing an incumbent to exploit a monopoly position. Prior to the Global Financial Crisis regulatory intervention favoured the former as that brought lower charges for users but after it they favoured the latter as that provided greater certainty that transactions would be completed. For reasons of the stability they delivered, the regulators condoned the vertical-silo operated by the CME and market dominance it delivered. Both the NYSE and Nasdaq did contemplate moves into derivatives but realized that this could only be done through an

[52] Hal Weitzman, 'Chicago builds on its reputation for speed', 3rd November 2010.
[53] Jeremy Grant, 'NYSE plans to launch interest rate futures', 7th April 2010.

acquisition, given the inertia attached to derivatives contracts. John Thain, the chief executive of NYSE Euronext, stated as such in 2007: 'I think if we're going to develop a bigger presence in the US in the areas that are currently in existence, I think it has to be by acquisition.'[54] The problem they faced was that there were few obvious targets available and all involved paying a price that might not be justified because of the strong competition coming from the OTC market. One target was the International Securities Exchange (ISE), a New York-based electronic options exchange begun in 2000 by David Krell and Gary Katz, whose initial experience lay with the NYSE. By 2007 the ISE had gained a 30 per cent share of the US options market, compared to 36 per cent by Cboe, the market leader. However, the ISE was acquired by Deutsche Börse in 2007, as it was willing to pay the price demanded by its owners. Deutsche Börse was determined to break into the US derivatives market, as it already controlled the European derivatives exchange, Eurex, and wanted to build up a global operation.

The CME was aware of potential competition, especially from abroad where a growing share of its business came from, and did try to counter that by developing an international network. In 2010 it added to this network by establishing links to the Bolsa Mexicana de Valores (BMV), which had a wholly-owned derivatives subsidiary, MexDer, and Bursa Malaysia. The plan was to create a global alliance of derivatives exchanges trading financial futures, orchestrated by the CME in Chicago. This would counter the threat coming from Eurex and Liffe in London. Liffe was now under the control of the NYSE, which saw it as a way of serving the US market from a London base. This was a strategy already followed successfully in commodity futures by another US derivatives exchange, the Intercontinental Exchange (ICE). ICE had long looked for a way to challenge the CME in financial futures and saw a way of doing so by combining trading in the OTC market with the provision of a clearing house. This already took place with LCH.Clearnet, which provided guarantees against counterparty default for OTC-traded derivatives contracts. Spotting this, ICE offered its clearing facilities to those trading on the OTC market. By 2010 it had emerged as the leading global clearing organization for privately negotiated credit default swaps, which suited the needs of a market that remained unregulated, complex, and opaque. In 2010 Michael Mackenzie observed that 'OTC derivatives are the domain of banks, institutional investors, and corporations looking to hedge interest rate, credit, and currency risk, or to trade these instruments. Unlike the futures and equities markets, OTC derivatives can trade infrequently as many trades are bespoke in nature, and have been manufactured between a dealer and their client to hedge a specific interest-rate or currency risk. Often such trades can be substantial, with notional amounts in the hundreds of millions.'[55] Though regulators sought to make derivatives trading more open and transparent, as a means of preventing abuses and reducing risks, this was an impossible dream as each swap was often a unique contract and was neither simple to price nor easy to trade. The compromise increasingly accepted by regulators was to permit the OTC derivatives market to flourish but to persuade more of it to be processed through clearing houses. The CME itself responded to the challenge posed by the ICE by launching in 2010 a central clearing for OTC-traded interest-rate swaps, which was the most common form of derivative in circulation.

Where the CME possessed an advantage over all others was in its control of the US exchange-traded derivatives market, which was the broadest, deepest, and most liquid in

[54] Anuj Gangahar, 'NYSE races to build derivatives trade', 11th July 2007.
[55] Michael Mackenzie, 'One-size-fits-all approach risks killing flexibility', 3rd November 2010.

the world. For that reason US derivative exchanges attracted a growing international business as their contracts were used to hedge positions often arising from less-liquid OTC-traded swaps. By 2008 the US's leading options exchange, Cboe, was deriving between 15 and 20 per cent of its order flow from outside the USA, particularly from Europe, but also Hong Kong, Singapore, and Australia. In 2012 over 20 per cent of the business passing through the CME group originated abroad. With such a strong base in the USA the CME was under little competitive pressure to expand internationally. It was thus unwilling to pay the asking price for foreign derivative exchanges and so had missed out in taking over Liffe, which fell to the NYSE through its takeover of Euronext, while the LME was bought by Hong Kong Exchange and Clearing. Without foreign acquisitions many remained sceptical that the CME could emerge as the main winner in what Michael Henry, a senior executive in Accenture's Global Capital Markets practice, described in 2008 as 'An ongoing battle for market share between virtually all of the world's largest exchanges.'[56] He predicted that three or four large global players would emerge. Though the CME was expected to be one of these he cautioned that, 'If the CME wants to be a global player, it will have to attempt more challenging strategic moves in the future, such as acquiring a cash market or overseas exchange.'[57] Larry Tabb, an expert on financial markets, expressed similar doubts at the time: 'Will the tightly and vertically integrated CME strategy of being the largest global player in an increasingly global market play out?'[58]

Outside the USA the level of derivatives trading conducted on individual exchanges was much lower, depriving them of emulating the breadth and depth of the CME. Instead, they were forced to contemplate the multiproduct route if they were to enjoy the benefits from economies of scale. In Japan both the Tokyo and Osaka stock exchanges had developed a derivatives business, with the latter being especially successful. In Spain the Bolsas y Mercados Espanoles (BME) was a merger of its stock and futures exchanges in 2002. It controlled the country's equity, fixed-income, and derivatives markets along with their associated clearing and settlement systems. The Korea Exchange was formed in 2005 from a merger of the country's stock and derivatives exchanges. In 2008 Brazil's futures and derivatives exchange, BM&F, merged with Bovespa, the owner of the São Paulo Stock Exchange. As Roberto Teixeira da Costa, former president of the CVM, Brazil's securities commission, explained at the time, 'The world today demands that things be done on a global scale. In a few years there will be just a handful of exchange groups and Brazil's will be among them.'[59] In 2009 the Multi-Commodity Exchange in India launched a platform for trading currencies, futures, and equities. In contrast, the CME stuck to derivatives.[60]

[56] Anuj Gangahar and Hal Weitzman, 'CME–Nymex tie-up sets scene for showdown', 26th August 2008.

[57] Anuj Gangahar and Hal Weitzman, 'CME–Nymex tie-up sets scene for showdown', 26th August 2008.

[58] Anuj Gangahar and Hal Weitzman, 'CME–Nymex tie-up sets scene for showdown', 26th August 2008.

[59] Jonathan Wheatley, 'Brazil exchange executives get into global party mood', 29th February 2008.

[60] Norma Cohen and Ivar Simensen, 'D Börse lands in the US via ISE', 1st May 2007; Anuj Gangahar, 'Krell swansong fulfils global ambitions', 1st May 2007; Mark Mulligan, 'Enviable BME prepares for next challenge', 21st June 2007; Doug Cameron, 'All-Chicago deal is coup for city', 11th July 2007; Anuj Gangahar, 'NYSE races to build derivatives trade', 11th July 2007; Norma Cohen, 'Nasdaq retreat marks triumph for LSE's Furse', 21st August 2007; Doug Cameron and Anuj Gangahar, 'Battle for Nymex on hold after bid talks', 23rd August 2007; Paul J. Davies, 'LiquidityHub launches swaps product', 23rd October 2007; Anuj Gangahar, 'New exchange to shake up futures trading', 27th December 2007; Hal Weitzman and Anuj Gangahar, 'CME casts its eye in Nymex's direction', 29th January 2008; Jonathan Wheatley, 'Brazil exchange executives get into global party mood', 29th February 2008; Hal Weitzman, 'CBOE announces deal with Korea Exchange', 9th June 2008; Anuj Gangahar and Hal Weitzman, 'CME–Nymex tie-up sets scene for showdown', 26th August 2008; Lindsay Whipp, 'Exchange has big plans for its expansion', 12th September 2008; Jeremy Grant, 'Exposure puts Bolsas' long period in the sun at risk', 15th October 2008; Michael Mackenzie, 'Interest rate swaps dominate dealing', 15th October 2008; Hal Weitzman, 'Legend in his own futures is neither shy nor retiring', 21st October 2008; Jeremy Grant, 'New breed of

Among those derivatives exchanges it was those that operated the vertical-silo model that gained most from the Global Financial Crisis and the regulatory reaction against the OTC market that followed it. These included the CME, Deutsche Börse as owner of Eurex, BM&F Bovespa, Hong Kong Exchange and Clearing, and the Singapore Exchange. Among these the CME, referred to by Gregory Meyer in 2015 as 'The Chicago Colossus'[61] appeared to occupy an unassailable position. In 2017 Gregory Meyer and Philip Stafford observed that 'Futures tends to be a winner-takes-all business because the contracts cannot be transferred between exchanges. Once volumes built up on one exchange traders have little reason to go elsewhere.'[62] Gregory Meyer then added in 2018 that 'It is rare for similar future contracts to flourish in more than one venue.'[63] Deutsche Börse had hoped to challenge the CME's dominance of the US derivatives market by acquiring the US options exchange, the International Securities Exchange. This strategy failed and, in 2016, Deutsche Börse sold the international Securities Exchange to Nasdaq. Philip Stafford and Joe Rennison reflected in 2018 that 'It has historically been difficult to move liquidity in actively traded futures contracts from one venue to another. However, Eurex was considered a credible threat to Chicago because it had successfully prised the lucrative Bund contract away from London rival Liffe in the late 1990s. Eurex had a faster electronic system while the CBOT, like Liffe, still relied on trading by humans in noisy pits.'[64] What commentators such as these had not factored in was that the CME was alive to the threat of competition, and invested heavily in moving trading onto an electronic platform employing the latest technology, depriving Deutsche Börse of the advantage that had allowed it to conquer Liffe, when that exchange had been slow to move from floor trading. Automated trading at the CME rose from 46 per cent in 2013 to 66 per cent in 2018 in livestock futures, by which time the figure for currency futures had reached 91 per cent. This led Jean-François Lambert, at Lambert Commodities,

trader heads for Europe', 4th December 2008; Jeremy Grant, 'Exchanges and brokers at odds over crisis blame', 20th February 2009; Jeremy Grant, 'Exchanges hit out at impact of dark pools', 13th March 2009; Daniel Thomas, 'Property platform launch attracts flurry of interest', 26th March 2009; Gillian Tett, Aline van Duyn, and Jeremy Grant, 'Let battle commence', 20th May 2009; Jeremy Grant, 'OTC derivatives plan lifts shares', 2nd June 2009; Jeremy Grant, 'Exchanges warn on OTC clearing', 4th June 2009; Jeremy Grant, 'NYSE Euronext joint venture to capitalise on rising demand for clearing', 19th June 2009; Michael Mackenzie and Aline van Duyn, 'Costs set to rise amid shake-up in derivatives trading', 19th June 2009; Jeremy Grant, 'Clearing not the cure-all for financial system woes', 26th June 2009; James Wilson, 'More than just a historic trading floor', 30th June 2009; Joe Leahy, 'India's MCX-SX stock exchange targets foreign investors', 6th July 2009; Jeremy Grant and Nikki Tait, 'Eurex and ICE lead clearing race after Liffe setback', 6th July 2009; Jonathan Wheatley, 'Exchange gains from caution and strict rules', 7th July 2009; Jeremy Grant, 'Spain's BME to close remaining open outcry pits', 8th July 2009; Jonathan Wheatley, 'Strong growth after slight dip', 5th November 2009; Hal Weitzman, 'Regulation threat to CME dominance', 27th January 2010; Lindsay Whipp, 'Ambitions to recapture its glory days', 8th February 2010; Hal Weitzman, 'CME Group faces twin threats to its long ascendancy', 9th March 2010; Adam Thomson, 'Deal marks turning point in history of the bourse', 31st March 2010; Jeremy Grant, 'NYSE plans to launch interest rate futures', 7th April 2010; Kevin Brown, 'Malaysia bourse plans derivatives boost', 28th April 2010; Hal Weitzman, 'ICE chief backs financial reform', 6th May 2010; Jeremy Grant, 'LSE set for pan-European trading assault on derivatives', 9th June 2010; Michael Mackenzie, 'Frozen in Time', 16th June 2010; Aline van Duyn, Michael Mackenzie and Hal Weitzman, 'Derivatives dealers brace for clearing shake-up', 14th July 2010; Michael Mackenzie and Aline van Duyn, 'Regulators may silence derivative squawk boxes', 22 July 2010; Aline van Duyn, 'Derivative Dilemmas', 12th August 2010; Philip Stafford, 'Regulators show united front', 20th October 2010; Michael Mackenzie, 'Rate swap traders wait for no man', 20th October 2010; Hal Weitzman, 'Co-location set to reap up to $40 million for CME', 29th October 2010; Michael Mackenzie, 'One-size-fits-all approach risks killing flexibility', 3rd November 2010; Hal Weitzman, 'Chicago builds on its reputation for speed', 3rd November 2010; Aline van Duyn, 'New rules aim to bring trading of derivatives more into public view', 17th December 2010.

[61] Gregory Meyer, 'Trading', 19th November 2015.
[62] Gregory Meyer and Philip Stafford, 'Race for bitcoin futures stirs concerns', 16th December 2017.
[63] Gregory Meyer, 'CME pulls ahead in race to control bitcoin derivatives trading', 22nd August 2018.
[64] Philip Stafford and Joe Rennison, 'Judge cancels planned CME hearing', 7th May 2018.

to comment in 2019 that trading at the CME now took place with 'light-speed price movements'.[65] With the attractions provided by this investment in electronic trading, the CME captured the liquidity that came with the concentration of trading in individual products at a single venue and the stability delivered by the use of its own clearing house that acted as a central counterparty to all deals. Though regulators were unhappy with the situation it was tolerated in the aftermath of the Global Financial Crisis as the clearing facilities it provided for both exchange-traded and OTC contracts were guarantees against default. By 2012 exchanges across Asia, such as those in Singapore, Japan, South Korea, and Hong Kong were all already copying the CME in offering clearing facilities for OTC-traded derivative products or working on ways of doing so.

With the CME so dominant in the trading of financial futures in its home market the one challenge it faced was on the international front, with London being seen as a base from which to attack its position. The vast majority of deals in the global derivatives market took place in either Chicago and New York or London. In 2019 Christopher Giancarlo, the chairman of the CFTC, was happy to admit that 'London is, and will remain, a global centre for derivatives trading and clearing',[66] recognizing that US derivatives exchanges included London as a base from which to compete with each other and for international operations. The goal of these exchanges was to provide, as near as possible, twenty-four-hour trading five-days a week in the derivative products they specialized in, and so offer a superior service to both international and US customers compared to the CME, which was reliant on its Chicago base. The exchange most committed to taking on the CME was the Atlanta-based InterContinental Exchange (ICE), established by Jeff Sprecher. In 2012 Jeff Sprecher and the InterContinental Exchange were described as 'The exchange industry's big upstarts'[67] while Jeff Sprecher himself said, 'I like competing and I like competing against incumbents and I like going into markets and seeing where we can effect change.'[68] Using its close relationship with the global banks ICE had already stepped in to provide them with a European clearing service for Credit Default Swaps, when regulators forced them to use a central counterparty in the wake of the Global Financial Crisis. In 2012 ICE then bought NYSE Euronext largely for its futures business, centred on Liffe in London. As the *FT* reported at the time, 'The real prize for ICE is Liffe, the derivatives exchange, and the opportunity to expand into interest-rate derivatives.'[69] In Jeff Sprecher's own words, 'While derivatives markets have become more global... many cash and equity markets have become more regional as major European financial institutions turned their focus to capital efficiency and regulatory reform.'[70] Following this philosophy under the control of ICE, NYSE Euronext disposed of its European stock exchanges, while retaining the NYSE in New York and Liffe in London. Despite this acquisition ICE remained weaker than the CME in derivatives. At the CME investors could trade all along the yield curve whereas Liffe shared that market with Eurex.

Nevertheless, faced with a growing international challenge the CME responded by opening its own clearing house in London in 2011 as a prelude to establishing a London-based

[65] Gregory Meyer, 'CME shows how automation is the future of futures trading', 24th April 2019.
[66] Philip Stafford, 'US and UK strike eleventh-hour accord to minimise no-deal Brexit disruption', 26th February 2019.
[67] *FT* Reporters, 'ICE chief makes his biggest bet with deal', 21st December 2012.
[68] *FT* Reporters, 'ICE chief makes his biggest bet with deal', 21st December 2012.
[69] *FT* Reporters, 'ICE chief makes his biggest bet with deal', 21st December 2012.
[70] Philip Stafford and Arash Massoudi, 'Upstart ICE in $8bn gamble with deal for 208-year-old NYSE Euronext', 21st December 2012.

derivatives exchange in 2013. In 2012 Phupinder Gill, the chief executive of the CME, made clear what lay behind the proposed London-based derivatives exchange: 'This exchange is aimed at a client base that wouldn't trade in the US. It's for clients that are not trading at CME. We will offer whatever our clients want.'[71] It was estimated that around half of derivatives trading in the OTC market took place in London, and the CME's ambition was to capture part of that. The new CME exchange in London began by trading foreign exchange futures, as London was the centre of the forex market. That contract failed to gain traction and the CME closed its London exchange in 2017. The international alliances forged by the CME were also not particularly successful because those it linked up with had their own ambitions. One was with the Brazilian exchange, BM&F Bovespa, which developed its own Latin American network. By 2016 BM&F Bovespa had consolidated its grip on the Brazilian market by acquiring Cetip, the country's largest clearing house, and had bought stakes in the exchanges operating in Chile, Mexico, and Colombia with moves into Argentina and Peru being planned. Its chief executive, Edemir Pinto, made their strategy clear: 'Our competitors are not local but global—we needed to create the infrastructure to strengthen ourselves and compete in a global way.'[72]

With limited success in its international expansion the CME was thrown back on its US base, investing in a new computer centre close to Chicago, which opened in 2012. This met the demands of the high-frequency traders by allowing them to place their computers next to the exchange's matching engine, shaving a millisecond off trade execution times. The CME followed this up in 2018 with a major strategic move, by buying NEX. It was a leading operator of electronic platforms, having emerged from the interdealer broker, ICAP, after it sold its voice-broking operations to Tullet Prebon. In particular NEX ran BrokerTec, the main venue for trading US Treasuries. By buying NEX, CME united the derivatives and cash market so allowing it to meet the needs of customers such as banks and fund managers, along the entire spectrum of financial products. As a result it further consolidated its position as the dominant exchange in the USA, with only equities being a major omission. Though the weakness in equities did leave a major gap in what it could provide, the spread and depth that the CME was able to offer, along with its US base, put it in a commanding position in global financial markets. What competition it faced came from the OTC market, which continued to thrive, and those multiproduct exchanges that served niche markets, defined by either product or geography.[73]

[71] Philip Stafford, 'CME puts Europe at the centre of expansion plan', 21st August 2012.

[72] Samantha Pearson, 'Brazil's exchange chief rejoices at post-impeachment chances', 11th October 2016.

[73] Jeremy Grant and Telis Demos, 'D Börse and NYSE talks stir up rivals', 10th February 2011; Jeremy Grant and Nikki Tait, 'NYSE link-up faces hurdles', 11th February 2011; Hal Weitzman, 'CME now faces foreign and domestic challenges', 11th February 2011; Jeremy Grant, 'Dealers look for answers on US derivatives reform', 17th March 2011; Joshua Chaffin and Hal Weitzman, 'How clearing helped ICE reinforce ties with banks', 30th April 2011; Jeremy Grant, 'Reform in Europe', 31st May 2011; Adam Thomson, 'Changes give vigour to once-somnolent bourse', 24th June 2011; Hal Weitzman, 'NYSE Liffe takes fight to "Fortress Chicago"', 28th June 2011; Hal Weitzman, 'Regulatory uncertainties weigh on CME', 7th July 2011; Philip Stafford, 'CME steps up Asian push with revamp of renminbi futures', 12th July 2011; Hal Weitzman and Telis Demos, 'Ultra-fast trading firms hit headwinds in race to be first', 14th July 2011; Michael Mackenzie, 'Market prepares for transparency', 4th November 2011; Hal Weitzman, 'Euro crisis gives clearing a boost', 4th November 2011; Alexander Kliment and Vivianne Rodrigues, 'Regulated, representative and popular with investors', 15th November 2011; Jeremy Grant, 'Two Argentine exchanges agree to combine forces', 17th December 2011; Hal Weitzman and Gregory Meyer, 'Uncertain futures', 27th January 2012; Jeremy Grant, 'Alliances offer solution for exchanges', 26th March 2012; Jeremy Grant, 'CME puts focus on London as its European beachhead', 17th April 2012; Philip Stafford, 'Failed NYSE/Euronext merger haunts exchange', 11th June 2012; Jeremy Grant, 'SGX eyes organic growth after failing to seal Australian deal', 23rd July 2012; Philip Stafford, 'CME puts Europe at the centre of expansion plan', 21st August 2012; Michael Mackenzie and Tracy Alloway, 'Swaps profits threatened by Dodd–Frank', 23rd August 2012; Philip Stafford, 'CBOE to offer 24-hour Vix futures trading from London', 7th September 2012; Philip

Conclusion

Derivatives had thrived prior to the Global Financial Crisis as they provided both the products and the markets that met the needs of banks and fund managers looking for ways of minimizing risk in the highly-integrated world economy. The Global Financial Crisis both emphasized the need for derivative products that could cope with volatility and defaults and the risks they brought in terms of leverage and links. It was these risks that were foremost in the minds of central banks, regulators, governments, politicians, and the media as they tried to respond to the immediate effects of the crisis and then plan a more stable global financial system. As a consequence derivatives were identified as a serious cause for

Stafford, 'Battle for derivatives clearing heats up', 11th September 2012; Vivianne Rodrigues, 'Sophisticated market drives liquidity', 3rd October 2012; Philip Stafford, 'ICE plans CDS exchange trading', 17th October 2012; Jeremy Grant, 'Asia watches and learns from European and US rule makers', 30th October 2012; Michael Mackenzie, 'Fight looms over which model is best', 30th October 2012; Courtney Weaver, 'Moscow tie-up wins approval from participants', 30th October 2012; Samantha Pearson, 'Foreign rivals join battle for post-trade prize', 30th October 2012; Philip Stafford, 'Rules covering derivatives built on ground that has yet to settle', 30th October 2012; Michael Mackenzie and Gregory Meyer, 'US swaps shake-up set to boost exchanges', 2nd November 2012; Vivianne Rodrigues, 'Derivatives market enjoys solid outlook', 14th November 2012; *FT* Reporters, 'ICE chief makes his biggest bet with deal', 21st December 2012; Philip Stafford and Arash Massoudi, 'Upstart ICE in $8bn gamble with deal for 208-year-old NYSE Euronext', 21st December 2012; Philip Stafford, 'CME poised for European clearing push', 11th February 2013; Philip Stafford, 'Eurex makes push into trading foreign currency derivatives', 22nd August 2013; Michael Mackenzie and Philip Stafford, 'US swaps trading prepares for its big bang', 18th February 2014; Philip Stafford, 'US the dominant derivatives superpower', 9th January 2015; Philip Stafford and Neil Munshi, 'Last shout looms for US options traders', 24th February 2015; Philip Stafford, 'US swaps market resists futures model', 17th March 2015; Lindsay Whipp, 'End of an era for Chicago futures trading', 8th July 2015; Philip Stafford, 'LSE in ambitious push for Europe's futures markets', 17th October 2015; Gregory Meyer, 'Trading', 19th November 2015; Philip Stafford, 'ICE circles amid D Börse's tie-up talks with LSE', 2nd March 2016; Arash Massoudi, 'CBOE snaps up rival in $3.2bn deal', 27th September 2016; Philip Stafford, 'LSE and banks launch derivatives exchange', 27th September 2016; Philip Stafford and Nicole Bullock, 'CBOE–Bats tie-up poised to shake up sector', 28th September 2016; Samantha Pearson, 'Brazil's exchange chief rejoices at post-impeachment chances', 11th October 2016; Gregory Meyer, 'City retains role as capital of the derivatives industry', 16th December 2016; Philip Stafford, 'European attempts to grab UK clearing house business underlines London's great strength', 16th December 2016; Philip Stafford, 'CBOE aims to tap shifting investor demand for structured products with Bats purchase', 22nd December 2016; Robin Wigglesworth, 'The fearless market', 19th April 2017; Philip Stafford, 'Chicago derivatives exchanges do battle to dominate bitcoin futures trading', 5th December 2017; Emma Dunkley, 'Singapore exchange to increase derivatives trading fees as much as tenfold', 12th December 2017; Gregory Meyer and Philip Stafford, 'Race for bitcoin futures stirs concerns', 16th December 2017; Gregory Meyer and Philip Stafford, 'Chicago bourses in bitcoin futures duel', 19th December 2017; Gregory Meyer and Philip Stafford, 'ICE plots escape from Mifid 2 as it prepares to shift 245 energy contracts to US', 12th January 2018; Joe Rennison, Greg Meyer, and Nicole Bullock, 'Vix Vexations', 8th February 2018; Miles Johnson, 'Volatility derivatives have become tail that wags the dog', 9th February 2018; Joe Rennison, Robin Wigglesworth, and Miles Johnson, 'Concerns mount over scale of volatility-trading ecosystem', 10th February 2018; Philip Stafford and Emma Dunkley, 'India exchanges seek to bring equities trading home by halting data supply', 13th February 2018; Philip Stafford, 'CME eyes pole position in Treasury trades with audacious bid for Nex', 28th March 2018; Philip Stafford, 'CME clinches Spencer's Nex in deal set to shake up $500bn Treasuries market', 29th March 2018; Robin Wigglesworth, 'The Volatility Virus', 14th April 2018; Philip Stafford and Joe Rennison, 'Judge cancels planned CME hearing', 7th May 2018; Gregory Meyer, 'CME pulls ahead in race to control bitcoin derivatives trading', 22nd August 2018; Jim Brunsden and Mehreen Khan, 'Brussels to drag UK into court over tax breaks for commodities traders', 24th January 2019; Philip Stafford, 'Intercontinental Exchange working on interest rate benchmark to replace Libor', 25th January 2019; Philip Stafford, 'BoE official warns EU on pitfalls of UK clearing house regulation post-Brexit', 15th February 2019; Philip Stafford, 'US and UK strike eleventh-hour accord to minimise no-deal Brexit disruption', 26th February 2019; John Dizard, 'Grandma will lose in a clearing house crisis, too', 4th March 2019; Joe Rennison, 'Wall Street cuts a deal to clean up $8.2tn credit default swaps trading', 7th March 2019; Joe Rennison and Sujeet Indap, 'Wall Street strives to clean up credit default swaps industry', 14th March 2019; Gregory Meyer, 'CME shows how automation is the future of futures trading', 24th April 2019; Henry Sanderson, 'LME appoints first female chairman in its history', 11th May 2019; Philip Stafford, 'Futures exchanges put faith in "Flash Boys" speed bumps', 30th May 2019; Gregory Meyer, 'Intercontinental Exchange muscles into New York harbour heating oil futures', 26th June 2019.

concern, especially those that were traded on the OTC market rather than in exchanges. A priority among them was to impose order and stability on the OTC derivatives market, suppressing those products held responsible for the events that led to the crisis and introducing much greater resilience to combat the impact of future crises. This meant driving the trading of derivatives through exchanges operating the vertical-silo model, though previously they had wanted to break these up, and forcing what remained to either use clearing houses or post collateral. In that way the contribution made by derivatives to hedging risks would be preserved while the contagion that came from losses and defaults would be contained.

However, achieving this balance was an impossible task as it met the resistance of those who used derivatives in their everyday business and objected to the restrictions and costs imposed. Though the scandals associated with market manipulation did strengthen the hand of those who wanted to curb the use of derivatives, regarding them as more a cause of instability than a way of controlling it, this ran counter to the direction of travel over the previous thirty years. At the same time it was increasingly recognized that the OTC and the exchange-traded derivatives market complemented each other and excessive regulatory intervention could destabilize the delicate and evolving balance that existed between them. Excessive intervention could drive derivatives trading into the hands of the exchanges operating the vertical-silo model, with consequences for monopolistic behaviour, or suppress it completely so that the products were not available. Conversely, intervention to open up the derivatives market to competition and encouraging transparency could encourage fragmentation and drive trading underground. Under the circumstances, the easiest course of action was to maintain prudential oversight and to restrict direct intervention to dealing with major abuses. Under these circumstances the OTC derivatives market continued to flourish ten years after the crisis, despite the intentions of those at the time.

Even though commodity derivatives were relatively untouched by the financial crisis of 2008 they were caught up in its regulatory backlash. This came in the form of the regulations that tried to force trading away from the OTC markets and into exchanges and through clearing houses. That was then followed by the consequences that flowed from the restrictions placed on the global universal banks. These curtailed the trading activity of these banks and also required them to hold much higher levels of capital against the risks that they took, leading a number of them to withdraw or even abandon their involvement in global commodity markets. The next blow to hit commodity derivatives was again a by-product of events elsewhere in the global financial system, which was the exposure of the manipulation of interest and exchange rates. This discredited the whole process through which prices were arrived at unless it was a product of trading on open markets, such as those provided by regulated exchanges. Given the vast variety of commodities much pricing was the product of private information gathering and bilateral negotiation before an agreed price emerged. Though there was no evidence of any manipulation across the commodity markets the outcome was attempts to devise more transparent ways of generating prices. The cumulative effect of all these developments was to undermine the OTC market and boost the position of the regulated exchanges and promote the use of clearing houses. At the same time the way that commodity exchanges were operating was being transformed through the electronic revolution, while there was a growing convergence between the contracts that they traded and other financial instruments, removing the barriers that had once compartmentalized trading into separate floors with specific membership characteristics. The result was growing competition between multiproduct exchanges that were run as global businesses. This was led by the CME, which had secured a dominant position among US commodity exchanges after its acquisition of both the CBOT and Nymex. It had to meet the challenge of its US rival, ICE, which had a strong base in both New York and London and had taken control of the NYSE. Also appearing as a global competitor was the Hong Kong-based HKEx, which had transformed itself into an international powerhouse through the acquisition of the LME.

18
Equities and Exchanges, 2007–20

Introduction

Throughout the Global Financial Crisis and its aftermath the world of equities and stock exchanges operated to its own agenda though it was affected by what was happening to banks and financial markets generally. The focus of those involved in equities and exchanges continued to revolve around the disruptive effects of technological change and globalization, and the actions of regulators motivated by a desire to protect investors and stimulate competition. The effect was to drive the introduction of electronic trading systems that continued to break down national boundaries. Nevertheless, equity trading continued to take place in national pools, as there remained a strong home bias among investors. Integrating these national pools of liquidity were the megabanks and they placed incumbent exchanges under increasing competitive pressure as they had the capacity to internalize transactions or route them through the growing number of electronic platforms. In response stock exchanges increasingly opted for either the horizontal or vertical model or a combination of both. In the horizontal model exchanges merged to create multiproduct platforms, which combined trading in equities with that in derivatives and other financial products. With the vertical model trading in equities was integrated with the processing of transactions, providing users with a single venue covering the placing of an order through to its completion. Increasingly it was the combination of equities and derivatives on the one hand and trading, clearing and settlement on the other that proved to be the winning formula, as it also led exchanges into the lucrative field of data provision. It allowed exchanges to capture multiple earning streams and spread costs widely, while providing them with a degree of protection against competition as it was difficult for a rival to replicate the complete service they could provide. It was also popular among most users as it provided them with a total package from the placing of an order to payment or receipt across a range of different financial instruments and the reassurance of a central counterparty that acted as guarantee against default. However, regulators were opposed to the vertical-silo because it limited the degree of competition, as what was provided was bundled together, making price comparisons difficult and forcing consumers to pay for an entire package. It was considerations such as these that drove developments in the global equity market rather than any directly related to the financial crisis and its legacy.

A Parallel Universe, 2007

Informed observers were aware that the changes already taking place in global equity markets in 2007 were largely a product of internal forces. In February 2007 Anuj Gangahar reported that 'Competition for market share and listings continues to be intense, with more market centres looking to increase business in these areas. These include smaller stock exchanges, as well as broker-dealers giving access to their own order flow and forming alliances with

Banks, Exchanges, and Regulators: Global Financial Markets from the 1970s. Ranald Michie, Oxford University Press (2021).

DOI: 10.1093/oso/9780199553730.003.0018

other banks, posing yet another challenge to the established exchange model.'[1] He followed that up in March when he observed that 'The global exchange landscape is going through unprecedented consolidation.'[2] His views echoed those of Bill Cline, the managing partner of a capital markets consultancy, Acai Solutions, who claimed that 'everyone can trade directly with everyone else. The hub-and-spoke network does not really stand up any longer.'[3] In May Jim Pickard and Norma Cohen commented on 'headlong rush for consolidation among the world's stock exchanges'.[4] The next month Magnus Bocker, the chief executive of the Scandinavian exchange operator, OMX, painted a vision of the future global stock market which would be 'borderless... dependent on technology. It will move at speed. Monopolies are disappearing.'[5] Reflecting on the year that had passed, in November 2007, John Authers pointed out that whereas, 'Traditionally, the concepts of exchanges and financial centres went hand in hand. For markets to work, all the participants needed to gather in the same place, which meant that they would also maintain their offices nearby', adding that 'But that is no longer the case.'[6] At that stage there was little sign that the global equity market was experiencing any consequences from the emerging difficulties in other parts of the financial system. The equities market had not only recovered from the dot.com speculative mania but also grown in response to a global demand for corporate stocks of all types and in all countries. Writing in November 2007 Jonathan Wheatley pointed out that 'The world is awash with liquidity and emerging market assets are offering both high returns and a safe haven.'[7] Towards the end of 2007 investment banks did widen the difference between the prices at which they would buy and sell many stocks, so as to protect themselves in the event of a market downturn. They also reduced the level of trading they did on their own account so as to preserve capital in case of losses made elsewhere in their business, such as subprime mortgages. However, these were little more than precautionary measures. There was no stock market panic at this stage.[8]

As contemporary observers reported there were major changes taking place in the global equity market during 2007, led by developments in the USA, with Regulation NMS (RegNMS) coming into force in March. That was followed six months later by Mifid in the EU, which also had a transformational effect on Europe's equity market. The NYSE also completed its takeover of Euronext in 2007, while Nasdaq made its bid to acquire OMX, the Scandinavian stock exchange operator. It was also in the USA that the most important advances in the electronic trading of stocks were being made, with the EU, again, following in their wake. A pattern was emerging with developments in the USA leading the way, closely followed by the EU. Elsewhere in the world countries were either quick to follow the US example, such as Australia and Canada, or did so only slowly as was the case of Japan. Regardless of the pace, it was the USA that was setting the agenda for the world's stock market.

[1] Anuj Gangahar, 'Unclear course for Greifeld post-LSE bid', 14th February 2007.
[2] Anuj Gangahar, 'Chicago's program for change', 20th March 2007.
[3] Anuj Gangahar, 'Chicago's program for change', 20th March 2007.
[4] Jim Pickard and Norma Cohen, 'Dubai group eyes move for OMX', 28th May 2007.
[5] Mark Mulligan, 'Enviable BME prepares for next challenge', 21st June 2007.
[6] John Authers, 'Nationalism bites the dust', 19th November 2007.
[7] Jonathan Wheatley, 'Bovespa float inspires other exchanges', 19th November 2007.
[8] Mark Odell, 'Aim fatigue emerges on oil and gas', 4th January 2007; Anuj Gangahar, 'Unclear course for Greifeld post-LSE bid', 14th February 2007; Anuj Gangahar, 'Chicago's program for change', 20th March 2007; Jim Pickard and Norma Cohen, 'Dubai group eyes move for OMX', 28th May 2007; Mark Mulligan, 'Enviable BME prepares for next challenge', 21st June 2007; John Authers, 'Nationalism bites the dust', 19th November 2007; Jonathan Wheatley, 'Bovespa float inspires other exchanges', 19th November 2007; Chris Hughes, 'Triple blow sends cost of trading soaring', 24th December 2007.

Driving forward stock market developments in the USA was the increasingly competitive environment within which all participants operated. The breakdown of the binary divide between commercial and investment banks, and the switch from the lend-and-hold to the originate-and-distribute model, brought stocks to the fore. What attracted investors to corporate stocks was their greater liquidity compared to securitized assets, as they were quoted on the leading stock exchanges, notably the NYSE and Nasdaq. Being quoted on the NYSE and Nasdaq provided investors with the confidence that these stocks had passed through quality control and that a secondary market existed. Confidence in stocks among US investors had been shaken by the collapse of the dot.com bubble in 2000 but then steadily recovered. In particular, exchange-traded funds (ETFs) had grown in popularity. ETFs were quoted stocks that replicated a stock market index, and so combined the liquidity and high returns associated with equities with the certainty attached to bonds, through the spread of assets they contained. Despite the overall growth in the US stock market which was, by far, the largest in the world, the problems faced by both the NYSE and Nasdaq was that their share of trading was in serious decline due to the rise of alternative trading venues. A number of factors contributed to this. One was the rapid advance in trading technology that allowed buying and selling to take place directly between owners and purchasers rather than being routed via intermediaries. Richard Evans, head of alternative execution at Citigroup, explained in 2007 that 'Dark liquidity has always been there, among the broker community. Nothing has changed in terms of availability. What has changed is how you access it.'[9] The electronic revolution provided that access.

Another factor was the concentration of stock ownership in the hands of banks and fund managers as that meant that sales and purchases could be more easily matched internally, so avoiding the expense and delay of using an exchange. A number of banks operated their own electronic platforms, or dark pools, in which sales and purchases of corporate stocks were matched. Portfolio trading, for example, involved the sale or purchase of a basket of 15 or more stocks and accounted for 46 per cent of equity trading in the USA. It was usually conducted away from stock exchanges by the likes of Goldman Sachs, Morgan Stanley, or Merrill Lynch contacting potential buyers and sellers directly and then completing the deal before the market became aware of what was happening. At the other end of the scale were hedge funds and high-frequency traders who bought and sold in volume and rapidly, profiting from minute and temporary price differences. Their activities made an important contribution to market liquidity though the regulators and the public regarded them as little better than speculators who made large profits from their socially useless activities. As James Mackintosh observed in 2007, 'It is no surprise that earnings not seen since the Robber Barons of the nineteenth century should lead to resentment from lesser mortals, as well as attracting many of the smartest in the financial industry to set up funds.'[10] As they operated on very fine margins any reduction in transaction costs was welcomed by them, and this is what the new electronic markets, or Electronic Communication Networks (ECNs) provided. ECNs provided an accessible platform through which all participants could buy and sell for a small fee. Among the most successful of these was Bats (Better Alternative Trading System). It was based in Kansas City and had been started in 2006 by Dave Cummings, a computer scientist turned futures trader. His first intention, according to himself, was to 'invent a robot to trade wheat futures'.[11] Instead he turned to trading

9 Norma Cohen, 'Mifid ushers in a new era of trading', 23rd May 2007.
10 James Mackintosh, 'Investors still pile in', 27th April 2007.
11 Norma Cohen, 'Kansas City undercuts NYC', 9th February 2007.

stocks, building TradeBot, an electronic broker that used mathematical models to send trading instructions to electronic markets. That was followed by an electronic communication network that was itself a marketplace.

There was little optimism that Cummings would succeed because the accepted wisdom was that Nasdaq and the NYSE were natural monopolies, as they provided the most liquid markets in the stocks that they quoted. He said himself in 2007 that 'The economics of the trading business are that you lose money until you get to a certain critical mass.'[12] A total of $14m was invested in Bats by its backers, who were mainly banks. They expected to benefit through forcing Nasdaq and the NYSE to reduce their fees, with the eventual success of Bats being a secondary consideration. Those at the NYSE and Nasdaq expected BATS to fail as they had already embraced electronic trading themselves, having bought the most successful of the previous challengers. Jerry Putman, who had founded the ECN acquired by NYSE, namely Archipelago, and then joined the NYSE, considered that BATS 'is not a sustainable business model program.'[13] They were proved wrong because BATS did reach the required critical mass, putting increased pressure on both the NYSE and Nasdaq to respond. Assisting in its success were the rules introduced under RegNMS, as these forced buying and selling orders to be routed to the exchange offering the best price. Another effect of RegNMS was a product of the transparency it forced upon the NYSE and Nasdaq. Investors seeking to deal in large blocks of shares turned to dark pools and other venues, in order to hide their buying and selling from public view until after a deal had been completed. This prevented others from taking a contrary position and profiting from the need of the dealers to complete a sale or purchase. The Block Interest Discovery Service (BIDS) trading system, for example, was an alternative trading system formed by some of the largest US investment banks. It allowed the anonymous electronic trading of 10,000 or more shares in a single company.

By the end of 2007 the combined market share of all dark pools was around 15 per cent of trading in the entire US stock market. Though RegNMS did not take effect until March 2007 it quickly led to competition between exchanges and other trading venues. The use of smart-order routing systems allowed orders to be automatically directed to the best price on the lowest-cost venue. Facilitating competition in the US stock market was the nationwide clearing and settlement system in operation. Unlike the CME, which operated a vertical-silo in derivatives, neither the NYSE nor Nasdaq controlled the clearing and settlement of the stocks that were traded through them. This was in the hands of the Depository Trust and Clearing Corporation (DTCC). Those trading on Bats, for example, had equal access to this service, which allowed them to confirm and match trades, and to send payment instructions to banks and securities to their new owners. This accessible infrastructure allowed direct competition to take place between the NYSE, Nasdaq, and Bats, leading to a price war during 2007. Bats was well positioned to win this war as it had the lowest costs. Bats had only fifty-five employees and a base in Kansas City, compared to the NYSE, which continued to support a trading floor in New York and the specialist system of market-makers. By September 2007 the NYSE's share of trading in NYSE-listed stocks had fallen to 56.1 per cent compared to 69.3 per cent in September 2005. This decline was masked by the volume remaining the same. Nasdaq and the NYSE did attempt to meet the domestic challenge they faced by expanding the range of products they traded, but this was restricted by the dominant position achieved by other exchanges such as the CME in derivatives. The

[12] Norma Cohen, 'Kansas City undercuts NYC', 9th February 2007.
[13] Norma Cohen, 'Kansas City undercuts NYC', 9th February 2007.

NYSE tried bonds while Nasdaq launched Portal, which aimed to provide a liquid market for new issues that were privately placed rather than being sold through an Initial Public Offering. The NYSE initiative in bonds came to little but that of Nasdaq was welcomed by some, such as the retail banks. Michael Cummings, the chief operating officer at the equities division of Wachovia, thought that, 'With the advent of an enhanced private placement market, companies considering a traditional IPO should have an attractive new option to gain faster, simpler, less expensive access to the capital they require.'[14] However, as with the NYSE's move into bonds, Nasdaq's faced strong competition from the investment banks, which had built up a large, successful, and profitable business in these areas. They responded to the challenge of the NYSE and Nasdaq by investing heavily in staff and technology to maintain their position.

This left the NYSE and Nasdaq looking at international expansion as a way of both combating the domestic competition they faced and generating additional sources of revenues. They were in a strong position to do this given their location in the largest equity market in the world and a network of international alliances built up over many years. However, these alliances involving close co-operation in areas such as trading systems, cross listings, regulation, and corporate governance had produced little in the way of tangible benefits. The intention this time was to go a step further by acquiring a foreign stock exchange, with the London Stock Exchange being the favoured target, as it was located in the ideal financial centre from which to serve the global financial system. No less a person than John Thain, head of the NYSE, was of this opinion: 'If for any reason you choose not to enter the US, then for the most part you want to list in London. London does have a great brand.'[15] Encouraging both Nasdaq and the NYSE to look abroad were the regulatory burden they were placed under due to the Sarbanes–Oxley Act of 2002. This made it difficult for them to attract, and even retain, international listings because of the need to comply with US legislative requirements. The LSE and, especially its AIM subsidiary, provided a less-regulated market, and had been a major beneficiary of the switch away from a US listing by non-US companies. By acquiring a European exchange the NYSE and Nasdaq could provide foreign companies with a way of escaping US controls.

Discovering that the LSE was both an unwilling and expensive partner, the NYSE had switched to the Paris-based Euronext, which was desperate to escape coming under the control of the Frankfurt-based Deutsche Börse, while Nasdaq decided to pursue the Scandinavian exchange operator, OMX. In both cases the acquisition gave the US stock exchanges an entry into derivatives, with the London-based Liffe being the real prize. Anuj Gangahar, Richard Beales, and Gillian Tett concluded in 2007 that by taking control of Euronext, the NYSE had gained 'a leading role in the wave of consolidation sweeping the global exchange landscape'[16] while Anuj Gangahar credited John Thain, the chief executive of the NYSE, as being the 'chief architect of consolidation in the exchange business.'[17] John Thain was motivated by the belief that in the future 'There will be a small number of large multiproduct exchange groups and lots of smaller local ones.'[18] He intended the NYSE to be at the forefront of the multiproduct ones. The acquisition of Euronext was a key element in this plan as it delivered both a group of European exchanges and a derivatives market.

[14] Anuj Gangahar, 'Nasdaq Portal opens view on private placings', 3rd August 2007.

[15] John Gapper and David Blackwell, 'NYSE chief says Aim must raise standards', 27th January 2007.

[16] Anuj Gangahar, Richard Beales, and Gillian Tett, 'NYSE on the move as deal with Euronext is completed', 4th April 2007.

[17] Anuj Gangahar, 'Exchanges step up the march east', 12th April 2007.

[18] Anuj Gangahar, 'NYSE Euronext leaves the door open for another deal', 26th April 2007.

With control over Euronext the NYSE could offer those companies seeking to establish an international footprint, such as those from China and India, a listing in either or both Paris and New York, giving them the choice between euros and US$s or multiple currencies. Trading, clearing, and settlement would then be seamless between the two exchanges. The expectation was that this would appeal to both budding multinationals and to global fund managers. Acquiring Euronext was only part of Thain's plan, which included expanding into derivatives by acquiring a US derivatives exchange, as he made clear during 2007: 'I think if we're going to develop a bigger presence in the US in the areas that are currently in existence, I think it has to be by acquisition.'[19] Recognising this vision and ambition Anuj Gangahar considered that John Thain had become 'the main driver of consolidation among exchanges, in the eyes of most observers'.[20]

With the NYSE's focus now on integrating Euronext into its operations, and targeting US derivatives exchanges, Nasdaq was left free to pursue the LSE, which it proceeded to do in 2007. It was in a strong position to do so having already accumulated a near 30 per cent stake by the beginning of the year. The stumbling block was its unwillingness to pay the price that the investors who owned the LSE were demanding. The owners of the LSE saw it as a unique asset which could command a high price. In contrast, those running Nasdaq were aware of the growing competition that stock exchanges faced from dark pools and ECNs and so were reluctant to meet that price. Norma Cohen, writing in February 2007, reported that Bob Greifeld, chief executive of Nasdaq, did not want to overpay for LSE because, though 'It's a monopoly business today. It won't be a monopoly business tomorrow.'[21] In particular, he identified the EU legislation coming in under Mifid as leading to a repeat of what had happened in the USA with RegNMS, bringing in its wake far greater competition for incumbent stock exchanges.

The outcome was that Nasdaq failed to acquire the LSE because it would not meet the price demanded. Instead, it turned to alternative and softer targets but its focus remained on securing a European base. With Euronext now in the hands of the NYSE, and Deutsche Börse an expensive purchase, Nasdaq made a bid for OMX, the operator of exchanges in Sweden, Denmark, Iceland, Finland, and the Baltic states. Once that was accepted it put its stake in the LSE up for sale. What Nasdaq had not expected was a rival bid for OMX but one came from Borse Dubai, though that was soon dropped. Instead, Borse Dubai bought a 20 per cent in the merged group, Nasdaq OMX. The result was that both the leading US stock exchanges had acquired European partners by the end of 2007, having been driven to follow this route by a combination of domestic competition and a particular vision of the future. That vision predicted a world in which a small number of mega exchanges would dominate the world. They would provide integrated electronic platforms through which multiple products in multiple currencies were traded over multiple jurisdictions. Both the NYSE under John Thain and Nasdaq under Bob Griefeld were determined that their exchanges would be numbered among those.[22]

[19] Anuj Gangahar, 'NYSE races to build derivatives trade', 11th July 2007.

[20] Anuj Gangahar, 'New push in Nasdaq's painful global expansion campaign', 21st September 2007.

[21] Norma Cohen, 'Nasdaq chief: LSE faces crucial 18 months', 1st February 2007.

[22] Norma Cohen, 'Marathon LSE bid milestone', 8th January 2007; Francesco Guerrera and John Authers, 'Institutions increase equity stakes', 22nd January 2007; John Gapper and David Blackwell, 'NYSE chief says Aim must raise standards', 27th January 2007; Gillian Tett and Anuj Gangahar, 'Deals on dark pools set to surge', 31st January 2007; Norma Cohen, 'Nasdaq chief: LSE faces crucial 18 months', 1st February 2007; Anuj Gangahar and David Turner, 'Tokyo joins NYSE in strategy for a global market', 1st February 2007; Gillian Tett, 'Dark Liquidity system to launch', 5th February 2007; Norma Cohen, 'Kansas City undercuts NYC', 9th February 2007; Norma Cohen, 'LSE prepares for freedom from Nasdaq bid', 10th February 2007; Anuj Gangahar, 'Unclear course for

Even at the time there were those who doubted the strategy being pursued by the NYSE and Nasdaq. What they pointed to was the fractured nature of the global equity market in particular. While there could be no doubt that growing competition between exchanges was driving down charges and forcing up the search for cost reductions, and the adoption of electronic trading systems promised huge gains from economies of scale, it was not obvious that this would lead to the emergence of mega stock exchanges. One sceptic was Larry Tabb, the chief executive of the Tabb Group, and an expert on financial markets. Early in 2007 he concluded that 'The benefits of these newly-formed global exchanges such as NYSE Euronext are still to be borne out. It remains to be seen whether scale will hurt or help.'[23] Unless NYSE Euronext, and later Nasdaq OMX, could provide internationally integrated trading platforms then there were no benefits to be gained from combining a US and European stock exchange. This integration was unlikely to happen because companies tended to have a natural home, such as Paris for French companies and New York for US ones. There were not many companies whose shares commanded a global following or were extensively traded outside their domestic markets when overseas exchanges were able to provide better access to the investing community. As Charles Jacobs at the corporate lawyers, Linklaters, explained in 2007, 'A company wants to list where its peer group is located. You want to go where you can get the best rating for your shares and where there is a strong analyst community that covers your sector.'[24] Hence the attractions of national exchanges for national companies as that was where the largest pool of likely buyers for their shares were found. There were also a few stock exchanges that had earned a reputation as a good market for specific stocks, where valuations would be higher than domestically. Such was the case with Nasdaq for high-technology companies and the LSE for mining

Greifeld post-LSE bid', 14th February 2007; Chris Hughes, 'Move to lower "ticks" earns exchange top marks from investors', 20th February 2007; Anuj Gangahar, 'Banks back move for block trading', 1st March 2007; Anuj Gangahar, 'New rules to prompt surge in trading', 5th March 2007; Norma Cohen, 'Doors open as industry removes barriers', 30th March 2007; Norma Cohen, 'Competitive age dawns in Europe', 3rd April 2007; Anuj Gangahar, Richard Beales and Gillian Tett, 'NYSE on the move as deal with Euronext is completed', 4th April 2007; Geoff Dyer and Amy Yee, 'NYSE heads for Paris to woo Asia', 10th April 2007; Anuj Gangahar, 'Exchanges step up the march east', 12th April 2007; Norma Cohen, 'OMX up 10% on talk of link', 13th April 2007; Norma Cohen, 'Turquoise reality being fleshed out', 19th April 2007; Norma Cohen, 'Lehman to launch off-bourse product', 20th April 2007; Saskia Scholtes, 'NYSE Euronext unveils bond platform', 23rd April 2007; Anuj Gangahar, 'NYSE Euronext leaves the door open for another deal', 26th April 2007; James Mackintosh, 'Investors still pile in', 27th April 2007; Norma Cohen, 'Mifid ushers in a new era of trading', 23rd May 2007; Norma Cohen, Robert Anderson and Anuj Gangahar, 'Nasdaq goes Nordic with $3.7bn deal for OMX', 26th May 2007; Norma Cohen and Robert Anderson, 'Nasdaq finds its European partner in OMX at last', 26th May 2007; Joanna Chung, 'A capital idea for emerging economies', 30th May 2007; Steve Johnson, 'eBay for portfolio trades debuts', 4th June 2007; Doug Cameron, 'All-Chicago deal is coup for city', 11th July 2007; Anuj Gangahar, 'NYSE races to build derivatives trade', 11th July 2007; Norma Cohen and David Wighton, 'Citi gives London priority', 19th July 2007; Ben White and James Politi, 'Banks join forces on trading platform', 23rd July 2007; Eric Uhlfelder, 'US de-listings changing the landscape for investors', 23rd July 2007; Norma Cohen, 'Middlemen sidelined?', 26th July 2007; Anuj Gangahar, 'Nasdaq Portal opens view on private placings', 3rd August 2007; Norma Cohen, 'Nasdaq retreat marks triumph for LSE's Furse', 21st August 2007; Norma Cohen, 'OMX bid fight puts Greifeld leadership of Nasdaq to test', 3rd September 2007; Anuj Gangahar, 'NYSE to cut fees as rivals move in', 13th September 2007; Ben White, 'Banks join OPU-5 platform', 13th September 2007; Norma Cohen and Robert Anderson, 'Exchange rivalries usher in a new era', 21st September 2007; Anuj Gangahar, 'New push in Nasdaq's painful global expansion campaign', 21st September 2007; Norma Cohen, 'Price war breaks out among US exchanges', 25th October 2007; Michael Mackenzie, 'NYSE Euronext agrees block trading system', 31st October 2007; Saskia Scholtes, 'Best execution encourages alternative venues', 1st November 2007; John Authers, 'Nationalism bites the dust', 19th November 2007; Chris Brown-Humes, 'Fear of business going elsewhere', 19th November 2007; John Authers, 'London blows its trumpet too loudly', 19th November 2007; Bernard Simon and Anuj Gangahar, 'TSX joins consolidation race with Montreal deal', 11th December 2007.

[23] Anuj Gangahar, 'Unclear course for Greifeld post-LSE bid', 14th February 2007.

[24] Joanna Chung, 'Floating along in a sea of global liquidity', 30th May 2007.

companies. Joanna Chung remarked in 2007 that 'London has become a magnet for the natural resources sector while the Nasdaq stock market in New York and the US culture of venture capital investing draws fast-growing technology companies.'[25] However, there were few stock exchanges in the world in this position and then only for a few niche sectors.

As access to national markets was increasingly opened up, institutional investors were able to take their pick of corporate stocks regardless of where they were quoted. This was certainly the view of Tom Ahearne, head of equity origination and syndicate at Credit Suisse, in 2007: 'Many sizeable investors, both long and hedge funds, are unconstrained geographically. Companies do not necessarily have to list in a specific geographic location to have appeal.'[26] Rupert Hume-Kendall, chairman of equity capital markets at Merrill Lynch, echoed this when he said, 'if you are a big French company, you want to list in Paris. If you are a big German company, you will list in Frankfurt.'[27] He did add the caveat that 'If companies feel that local markets have limits in terms of time zone or the ability to be traded by international investors, then companies have to look at listing on a major global stock exchange too.'[28] It was these considerations that continued to underpin the use of global depository receipts (GDRs). A depository receipt represented ownership of a given number of a company's shares and could be listed and traded independently of the underlying stock, in a different jurisdiction. They enabled investors to trade equities of companies listed in markets that were either hard to access, were expensive to use or subjected to regulatory and other restrictions. To Nancy Lissemore, managing director and global head of depository receipt services at Citigroup:

> For emerging market companies, they are a very important security because many investors don't necessarily have the same kind of access to emerging economies as they do to developed ones. Institutional investors can easily buy the ordinary shares sold in western European markets, but it is more difficult and complex to do so in emerging markets. Some companies look at the size of their offering and decide that their home market is too small and too illiquid to absorb a significant amount of the offering. That is one reason you continue to see a trend of emerging market companies doing a dual listing using GDRs.[29]

For those reasons GDRs continued to be issued by companies from the likes of Russia, South Korea, Taiwan, and India, and were listed in New York or London so as to attract international investors.

However, the market for GDRs and ADRs (American Depository Receipts) was in decline as the markets provided by national exchanges improved in terms of liquidity and governance and the attractions of listing in London and New York fell because of increased regulation. Luiz Vaz-Pinto, head of European syndicates at JP Morgan, observed in 2007 that foreign companies were delisting from US exchanges:

> In the past, a US listing could enable an issuer to tap investor demand that would otherwise not be achievable, but many US investors now no longer require an ADR or a dollar-denominated security to invest in a company. On the contrary, they will prefer to trade

[25] Joanna Chung, 'Floating along in a sea of global liquidity', 30th May 2007.
[26] Joanna Chung, 'Floating along in a sea of global liquidity', 30th May 2007.
[27] Joanna Chung, 'Floating along in a sea of global liquidity', 30th May 2007.
[28] Joanna Chung, 'Floating along in a sea of global liquidity', 30th May 2007.
[29] Joanna Chung, 'A capital idea for emerging economies', 30th May 2007.

> where the liquidity is highest, which tends to be the issuer's domestic market. Thus there is little point in doing all the extra work for a US listing if you can list in a domestic market, such as Paris, and still attract the main US investors.[30]

At the very time Nasdaq and the NYSE were positioning themselves as global stock exchange operators the rationale that lay behind it was fading. It was not only the effects of Sarbanes–Oxley that was diminishing the appeal of a US listing but also the improvements made by stock exchanges around the world, especially as they embraced the new trading technology and eased access for global investors. Neither the NYSE nor Nasdaq had much value to add to their European acquisitions as both Euronext and OMX had fully embraced electronic trading and extended membership to global banks. All they were acquiring were a group of European stock exchanges that dominated their domestic markets at a time when Mifid was threatening to break that monopoly in the same way it was happening in the USA. The one exchange whose acquisition could have made a difference to either Nasdaq or the NYSE was the LSE but it escaped their grasp. Like the NYSE and Nasdaq the LSE was located in an international financial centre, offering the potential to create an integrated global stock market, though there were no guarantees that such a project could be accomplished given the obstacles that existed in terms of national rules and regulations. In 2007 the global banks and the global fund managers were already working to create a global stock market without the need for any assistance from institutions such as stock exchanges.[31]

During 2007 developments in Europe undermined the dominance of national stock exchanges through the introduction of Mifid, which copied RegNMS. In the EU the authorities were determined to remove the legal barriers that prevented the creation of an integrated capital market. These legal barriers were held responsible for gifting each national stock exchange a monopoly of its domestic market. Unlike the USA the EU did not possess a single equity market but multiple ones reflecting long-standing national divisions. These were deeply entrenched because of differences of language, culture, laws, regulations, and currency, with even the Euro not being universally used. There were major differences within Europe on the tax levied on share transfers, for example, leading to ways being devised by each national market to limit its effect. In 2007 the tax on share trading was 0.5 per cent in the UK but only 0.15 per cent in France and was not applied in Germany and the Netherlands. The response in the UK was to trade not in shares but in contracts for difference, which acted as proxy for the underlying securities. By 2007 a third of share trading in the UK was based on contracts for difference, as these were tax exempt. Even after the date that Mifid became law there remained variations in the timing, degree, and way that national regulators across the EU implemented it, reflecting the different priorities of individual governments. Smaller stock exchanges feared the competition that might come from the larger ones located in the major financial centres of London, Frankfurt, and Paris, and looked to their national government for a degree of protection. Within the Eurozone there was strong rivalry between the Frankfurt-based Deutsche Börse and the Paris-based Euronext, and this was backed by their respective governments. An American observer,

[30] Joanna Chung, 'A capital idea for emerging economies', 30th May 2007.

[31] Anuj Gangahar, 'Unclear course for Greifeld post-LSE bid', 14th February 2007; Joanna Chung, 'Floating along in a sea of global liquidity', 30th May 2007; Joanna Chung, 'A capital idea for emerging economies', 30th May 2007; Doug Cameron, 'All-Chicago deal is coup for city', 11th July 2007; Eric Uhlfelder, 'US de-listings changing the landscape for investors', 23rd July 2007.

Georges Ugeux, a former executive vice president at the NYSE, picked up on this at the beginning of 2007, 'The Eurozone badly needs deeper and more fungible pools of liquidity if it wants to compete effectively with the US. It is extraordinary that neither the European Commission nor Ecofin, the committee of European finance ministers, have encouraged the European exchanges to get together.'[32]

There was also institutional resistance to an integrated equity market in Europe. The stock exchanges established in the former communist countries in Eastern Europe, for example, resisted attempts to integrate them into pan-European groupings led by either Deutsche Börse, Euronext, or the Vienna Börse, as they valued their independence. Generally, there was limited pressure on European stock exchanges to merge as certain countries banned off-exchange trading while, even in those that did not, such as the UK and Germany, it posed a limited threat. In 2006, for example, the volume of shares traded on private systems owned by investment banks was less than 2 per cent of the total in Europe and ECNs, also known as Multilateral Trading Facilities (MTFs), made only slow progress. Some commentators were optimistic about the impact they would make. Gillian Tett reported in February 2007 that a new electronic trading platform for European equities from the International Technology Group 'will enable large company stocks to be traded anonymously on a continuous basis by matching buy and sell orders using a price set according to the published quotes on the LSE'.[33] However, in the ten years prior to Mifid there had been seven attempts to create rival trading platforms to Europe's established exchanges, including Easdaq in 1996 and Liquidnet Europe in 2001, and none had been successful. As Jonathan Guthrie observed in 2007, 'Fledgling exchanges have an inglorious history of failing to attract sufficient liquidity.'[34] A competitive advantage that the exchanges possessed was that they were the source of current prices for the stocks that they listed and access to this information was crucial in a world where trading increasingly took place at high speed. As Norma Cohen reported in 2007, 'The demand for real-time data is enormous and growing. Without immediate access to real-time prices—the best gauge of aggregate demand for securities—trading would come to a halt. And nothing communicates aggregate demand more immediately and accurately than the actual price a buyer or seller paid a split-second earlier.'[35] As long as European stock exchanges could retain privileged access to this information they enjoyed a degree of protection from competitors.

Nevertheless, there was a growing expectation that Mifid would be very disruptive. This was certainly the view of Norma Cohen: 'Mifid will for the first time form genuine competition for what had been until now a service with monopoly providers: exchanges. Mifid will not only allow new trading platforms to spring up but will also allow existing exchanges to compete for each other's trading volumes.'[36] A similar view was expressed by Steve Wilson, global head of exchange-traded instruments at Reuters: 'Our customers know that Mifid is the biggest regulatory change to hit European markets in the last twenty years.'[37] The greatest threat was expected to come not from other stock exchanges but the ability of banks to make markets either through internal trading or linking up with each other and accessing pools of liquidity wherever they were to be found, including ECNs. This was certainly the intention of Citigroup, as its head of European electronic execution sales, Tony

[32] Georges Ugeux, 'Exchange battles mask Europe's silence', 3rd January 2007.
[33] Gillian Tett, 'Dark Liquidity system to launch', 5th February 2007.
[34] Jonathan Guthrie, 'Online return for regional exchange', 30th March 2007.
[35] Norma Cohen, 'Reuters to join scramble for real-time data', 11th July 2007.
[36] Norma Cohen, 'Reuters to join scramble for real-time data', 11th July 2007.
[37] Norma Cohen, 'Path through the data explosion', 1st November 2007.

Bayliss, made clear: 'We are going to connect to everything with significant liquidity.'[38] No longer could European stock exchanges expect to be the automatic market of choice after Mifid because they would have to compete for the business of the banks and institutional investors, which were now free to match sales and purchases internally or direct them to wherever the best price and the cheapest deal was to be found. In response to this threat European stock exchanges took measures to bolster their defences against competition, including cutting fees and investing in the new technology to create high-capacity, high-speed, low-cost trading systems, especially Deutsche Börse, Euronext, and the LSE.

In the process commentators expected Deutsche Börse to spin off its clearing arm, Clearstream, under pressure from the EU authorities, but that did not happen. The authorities wanted Deutsche Börse to sell Clearstream because it was considered anti-competitive, as the combination of trading and clearing made it difficult for buyers and sellers of German corporate stocks to trade anywhere else. For the same reason Deutsche Börse was not willing to sell Clearstream as it provided it with protection against competition in whatever form it took. Unlike Deutsche Börse neither Euronext nor the LSE had the same protection as they did not directly control their own clearing houses. The SWX Swiss stock exchange (SWX) decided to emulate Deutsche Börse by merging with both its clearing house (SIS) and its payment and data services operator (Telekurs) to create its own vertical-silo, as a way of combating the increased competition coming from technological innovation and regulatory changes. The Spanish stock exchange, Bolsas y Mercados Espanoles (BME) had already done so, being the operator of the country's equity, fixed-income, and derivatives markets and their clearing and settlement systems. The expectation of increased competition after Mifid also encouraged stock exchanges to consider mergers. Deutsche Börse, for example, courted both Euronext and the BME, but could not overcome national opposition. Instead, transatlantic alliances were preferred as they left the European operations intact. The merger with NYSE kept Euronext out of the hands of Deutsche Börse, while the acquisition of OMX by Nasdaq prevented it being absorbed into Euronext. In 2007 Borsa Italiano linked up with the LSE as that forestalled falling under the control of Euronext. To the LSE the attractions of Borsa Italiano was diversification in the products it traded as it gained control of MTS, Europe's largest bond-trading platform. Deutsche Börse and Euronext were already strong in derivatives.[39]

[38] Norma Cohen, 'Citigroup to launch smart ordering', 1st November 2007.

[39] Georges Ugeux, 'Exchange battles mask Europe's silence', 3rd January 2007; Norma Cohen, 'Marathon LSE bid milestone', 8th January 2007; Ivar Simensen, 'Frankfurt Finance is in fear of a drift from "Mainhattan" to marginalisation', 8th February 2007; Gillian Tett and Anuj Gangahar, 'Deals on dark pools set to surge', 31st January 2007; Norma Cohen, 'Nasdaq chief: LSE faces crucial 18 months', 1st February 2007; Gillian Tett, 'Dark Liquidity system to launch', 5th February 2007; Norma Cohen, 'Kansas City undercuts NYC', 9th February 2007; Norma Cohen, 'LSE prepares for freedom from Nasdaq bid', 10th February 2007; Anuj Gangahar, 'Unclear course for Greifeld post-LSE bid', 14th February 2007; Chris Hughes, 'Dealing with a softer touch', 20th February 2007; David Turner and Joanna Chung, 'London and Tokyo combine', 23rd February 2007; Lucy Warwick-Ching, 'The long and the short of it', 6th March 2007; Jonathan Guthrie, 'Online return for regional exchange', 30th March 2007; Anuj Gangahar, Richard Beales, and Gillian Tett, 'NYSE on the move as deal with Euronext is completed', 4th April 2007; Norma Cohen, 'Turquoise reality being fleshed out', 19th April 2007; Norma Cohen, 'Lehman to launch off-bourse product', 20th April 2007; Haig Simonian and Norma Cohen, 'Swiss seek to merge securities operations', 16th May 2007; Norma Cohen, 'Mifid ushers in a new era of trading', 23rd May 2007; Ellen Kelleher, 'Share dealers say tax hampers London', 26th May 2007; Norma Cohen, 'LSE reaches electronic trading target a year early', 9th June 2007; Mark Mulligan, 'Enviable BME prepares for next challenge', 21st June 2007; Norma Cohen, 'LSE agrees in principle to take over Borsa Italiana', 23rd June 2007; Norma Cohen, 'Defensive move with a useful line in attack', 23rd June 2007; Mark Mulligan, 'Bolsa bides its time in midst of merger frenzy', 28th June 2007; Norma Cohen, 'Reuters to join scramble for real-time data', 11th July 2007; James Mackintosh, 'Exchange joins fight to host alternative funds', 12th July 2007; Jamie Chisholm, 'Record quota of shares are in foreign hands', 14th July 2007; Norma Cohen and David Wighton, 'Citi gives London priority', 19th July 2007; Norma Cohen,

Generally in the world in 2007 equity markets boomed, driven by rising wealth and continuing privatization. In response stock exchanges became larger and more sophisticated, incorporating the latest electronic trading technology, as in the case of Vietnam. Others copied the success of the LSE's market catering for small and emerging companies, AIM, and established their own versions, as in Egypt. Nevertheless, most of the world's exchanges continued to lack the depth and breadth of those in London and New York. An exchange such as the Johannesburg Stock Exchange, which was Africa's largest, was dominated by trading in only two companies, Anglo American and BHP Billiton, and had to compete with the LSE in providing a market in their shares. Issues surrounding governance, transparency, and market manipulation also undermined the ability of many smaller stock exchanges to appeal for global investors. For those reasons the likes of the LSE, NYSE, and Nasdaq continued to attract new issues from foreign companies seeking to attract international investors, despite the existence of alternative national exchanges, pressure from governments to favour a domestic institution, the activities of global banks and fund managers, and the regulatory burdens they needed to overcome. Israeli high-technology companies, for example, listed on Nasdaq rather than the Tel Aviv Stock Exchange, as Ester Levanon, its chief executive, acknowledged in 2007: 'For many years, high-tech companies in Israel did their initial public offerings on Nasdaq, because at the time the American market was more receptive. It was easier to get a good valuation there, and in most cases it was the natural market for those companies.'[40]

Even those stock exchanges located in such large and highly-developed economies as Canada and Australia recognized the shallow nature of their domestic equity market and the migration of trading in their largest companies to London and New York. With the decline of the protection provided by national governments the Australian and Canadian stock exchanges took proactive measures to counter the threat they faced, both externally and internally. Canadian stock exchanges were especially vulnerable facing competition from the NYSE and Nasdaq. Canadian banks themselves unveiled in 2007 plans for an alternative trading platform, Project Alpha, which claimed to offer better pricing, speed, and capacity than the stock exchanges, and so meet the needs demanded by high-speed, high-volume algorithmic trading based on computer models. In response the stock exchanges not only spent heavily on a new electronic trading platform but also merged to create a deeper and broader domestic market. The Australian exchanges had already made this move in 2006 and then built on that by continuing to invest in technology and develop

'Nasdaq retreat marks triumph for LSE's Furse', 21st August 2007; David Ibison, 'Borse Dubai suffers double blow in its efforts to take over OMX', 24th August 2007; Norma Cohen, 'The world was our oyster but Project Turquoise has persistently floundered', 24th October 2007; Paul J. Davies, 'NYSE Euronext in dark liquidity plan', 25th October 2007; Norma Cohen, 'Turquoise appoints chief from Morgan Stanley', 25th October 2007; Peter Norman, 'Revolution in EU securities kick off', 29th October 2007; Peter Thal Larsen, 'Institutions prepare for the consequences', 30th October 2007; Norma Cohen, 'Seeking to end a share trading monopoly', 30th October 2007; Philip Stafford, 'Directive to break down barriers', 30th October 2007; Michiyo Nakamoto and Norma Cohen, 'London and Tokyo bring forth Asian cousin for Aim', 31st October 2007; Stacy-Marie Ishmael and John Authers, 'NYSE takes 1% stake in Bovespa', 1st November 2007; Norma Cohen, 'Marching orders in the Mifid revolution', 1st November 2007; Norma Cohen, 'Citigroup to launch smart ordering', 1st November 2007; Norma Cohen, 'Platforms quick to respond to Project Tortoise', 1st November 2007; Norma Cohen, 'Path through the data explosion', 1st November 2007; Jennifer Hughes and Gillian Tett, 'A long road to any Mifid impact', 2nd November 2007; Chris Hughes, 'London poised to cement leading position', 3rd November 2007; Eric Jansson, 'Telecommunism helps power stock market growth', 12th November 2007; Chris Brown-Humes, 'Fear of business going elsewhere', 19th November 2007; Norma Cohen, 'LSE outlines measures to help its biggest customers cut expenses', 24th December 2007.

[40] Tobias Buck, 'Tel Aviv exchange aiming for a bigger league', 18th December 2007.

new products. Similar developments were also taking place in Latin America as a way of bolstering the ability of that region's stock exchanges to compete with New York, where the shares of many of the region's largest companies were traded. In 2007 thirty-two Brazilian companies were listed on the NYSE. That year the São Paulo Stock Exchange, Bovespa, in Brazil, demutualized and became Latin America's first quoted stock exchange, putting it on a better footing to compete with the NYSE. The Mexican stock exchange was also following the same route.[41]

The problem that stock exchanges around the world faced was the inability to overcome national rivalries and establish cross-border institutions capable of delivering markets of the depth and breadth that delivered the liquidity sought by global banks and fund managers. Nowhere was this more apparent than in Asia. The underlying difficulty was that the extreme differences in language, culture, market structure, rules and regulations, trading, clearing and settlement mechanisms, accounting standards and currencies, made it impossible to create an integrated equity market not only for Asia but also for any region within it. All of the stock exchanges were engaged in defending their home market rather than establishing a pan-Asian presence. Matthew Wilson, in Morgan Stanley's Singapore office, expressed the hope in 2007, that 'You never know, you may get a significant merger or link-up of some sort in the next ten years or so... It is all about having many irons in the fire. Some will succeed, other won't.'[42] The one stock exchange that could have been expected to operate on a pan-Asian basis was that in Tokyo. Though secure in its domination of its vast domestic market the Tokyo Stock Exchange (TSE) was weak internationally. Its incoming president, Atsushi Saito, said in 2007 that 'Unless we can plan attractive products, trading will go to London, Shanghai, Singapore, Hong Kong, New York.'[43] Hoping to capitalize on the international weakness of the TSE was the Singapore Exchange (SGX) but it made little headway because of the localized nature of equity markets. China's strict capital controls even prevented the integration of its mainland exchanges in Shanghai and Shenzhen with that in Hong Kong, In India there were still twenty-two separate stock exchanges in operation in 2007, though the two based in Mumbai, namely the National and the Bombay, dominated trading.[44]

[41] Geoff Dyer, 'Concerns at market bubble float over China', 31st January 2007; Amy Kazim, 'Stock market mania grips Vietnam's middle classes', 21st February 2007; Norma Cohen, 'Mifid ushers in a new era of trading', 23rd May 2007; Bernard Simon, 'Breakaway platforms take on Toronto Stock Exchange', 24th May 2007; Ellen Kelleher, 'Share dealers say tax hampers London', 26th May 2007; Joanna Chung, 'A capital idea for emerging economies', 30th May 2007; Andrew England, 'Egypt plans baby bourse', 12th October 2007; William MacNamara, 'Johannesburg listing boom could spawn an African version of Aim', 18th October 2007; Peter Smith and Sundeep Tucker, 'Australia in world first with CFD platform', 22nd October 2007; Stacy-Marie Ishmael and John Authers, 'NYSE takes 1% stake in Bovespa', 1st November 2007; John Authers, 'Nationalism bites the dust', 19th November 2007; Jonathan Wheatley, 'Brazil backwater hits top rank', 19th November 2007; Jonathan Wheatley, 'Bovespa float inspires other exchanges', 19th November 2007; Jonathan Wheatley, 'Brazil backwater hits top rank', 19th November 2007; James Drummond, 'Bubble fears amid liquidity', 10th December 2010; Bernard Simon and Anuj Gangahar, 'TSX joins consolidation race with Montreal deal', 11th December 2007; Tobias Buck, 'Tel Aviv exchange aiming for a bigger league', 18th December 2007.

[42] Joanna Chung and Sundeep Tucker, 'Asia's chain of exchanges keeps adding links', 15th March 2007.

[43] David Turner, 'TSE to launch exotic products to view with other bourses', 2nd June 2007.

[44] Anuj Gangahar and David Turner, 'Tokyo joins NYSE in strategy for a global market', 1st February 2007; David Turner and Joanna Chung, 'London and Tokyo combine', 23rd February 2007; Michiyo Nakamoto, 'Bid reflects a shifting climate', 7th March 2007; Joanna Chung and Sundeep Tucker, 'Asia's chain of exchanges keeps adding links', 15th March 2007; Joe Leahy, 'Local sensitivities may damp foreign ambitions', 15th March 2007; Assif Shameen, 'Malaysia bourse looks overseas', 16th March 2007; Anuj Gangahar, 'Exchanges step up the march east', 12th April 2007; Michiyo Nakamoto, 'Citigroup deal could broker new shake-up', 30th April 2007; Michiyo Nakamoto, 'Market failure', 8th May 2007; Richard McGregor and Sundeep Tucker, 'China looks to fend off pressure by US brokers', 18th May 2007; Norma Cohen, 'Mifid ushers in a new era of trading', 23rd May 2007; Ellen Kelleher, 'Share dealers say tax hampers London', 26th May 2007; Jim Pickard and Norma Cohen, 'Dubai group

Crisis, What Crisis? 2008

By the end of 2007 the emerging Global Financial Crisis had largely bypassed the equity market, and that continued to be the case in 2008. In virtually all countries it remained possible to trade corporate stocks, unlike the position in the OTC markets where securitized assets were bought and sold. The changes taking place in the global equity market continued to be driven by internal considerations. One of the most marked features by 2008 was the continuing switch of trading away from the USA towards activity elsewhere in the world. This switch was driven by the vibrancy of equity markets around the world, as companies turned to stocks to either raise finance or capture the benefits of using the joint-stock form, and investors were attracted by the flexibility, liquidity, and returns of corporate stocks. Whereas in 2001 52 per cent of all money raised through public offerings was raised in the USA, by 2007 that had fallen to 18 per cent. In response the Securities and Exchange Commission (SEC) relaxed a number of its rules to make US equity markets more attractive. This change was being driven by the combination of the Sarbanes–Oxley regulations discouraging foreign companies listing in the USA and an increasing appetite for foreign stocks by US investors. Nevertheless, the US equity market remained the largest and most dynamic, with developments there influencing the rest of the world, such as electronic markets and algorithmic trading.

Within the USA a rapid pace of change in the equity market was a product of regulatory intervention and technological progress. Measures relating to transparency and the routing of orders undermined the protection that the NYSE and Nasdaq had long enjoyed, which partly explained their embrace of an international agenda. Combined with the explosive growth of automated trading, and the use of different types of electronic platforms, the ability of Nasdaq and the NYSE to dominate the market for the stocks that each quoted experienced rapid decline. By 2008 the NYSE's share of trading in NYSE-listed stocks had fallen to 26 per cent, as it was neither the cheapest nor the fastest market in many cases. Conversely, by 2008 Bats Trading, the electronic platform backed by the major banks, had captured 8 per cent of trading in NYSE listed stocks, as well as 11 per cent of that in Nasdaq listed ones. Another platform, Direct Edge, had a 10 per share of trading in all US listed equities. The result was a process of exchange consolidation, as the remaining regional stock exchanges lost their independence, with that in Philadelphia falling to Nasdaq in 2008, and fragmentation, with the emergence of new electronic markets and internal trading systems.

eyes move for OMX', 28th May 2007; David Turner, 'TSE to launch exotic products to view with other bourses', 2nd June 2007; Michiyo Nakamoto, Jack Burton, and Doug Cameron, 'TSE buys stake in SGX for $303m', 16th June 2007; Sundeep Tucker, 'Rival Asian bourses blush at merger talk', 26th June 2007; Sundeep Tucker, 'Tokyo faces an uphill battle in attracting foreign listings', 28th June 2007; Sundeep Tucker, 'Asia seeks its centre', 6th July 2007; David Ibison, 'Borse Dubai bid for OMX faces test over respectability', 18th August 2007; Simeon Kerr, 'Borse Dubai to push ahead in spite of regulatory snag', 24th August 2007; David Turner, 'TSE caught between talk of innovation and natural caution', 28th August 2007; Norma Cohen, 'OMX bid fight puts Greifeld leadership of Nasdaq to test', 3rd September 2007; Norma Cohen and Robert Anderson, 'Exchange rivalries usher in a new era', 21st September 2007; Anuj Gangahar, 'New push in Nasdaq's painful global expansion campaign', 21st September 2007; David Pilling, 'JSDA in talks on selling Jasdaq holding', 28th September 2007; Peter Smith and Sundeep Tucker, 'Australia in world first with CFD platform', 22nd October 2007; Tom Mitchell, 'Integration of bourses is not black and white', 23rd October 2007; Michiyo Nakamoto and Norma Cohen, 'London and Tokyo bring forth Asian cousin for Aim', 31st October 2007; John Authers, 'Nationalism bites the dust', 19th November 2007; Sundeep Tucker, 'Consolidation runs up against expensive buffers', 19th November 2007; Simeon Kerr, 'Bourses at war for business', 20th November 2007; David Ibison and Joanna Chung, 'Qatar bows out of OMX battle', 5th December 2007; John Burton, 'Bursa Malaysia in partnership talks with CME', 11th December 2007.

There were 68 alternative trading systems operating in the USA in 2008, of which thirty-two were dark pools.

What the final outcome would be was, however, unclear to those planning a strategy to cope with what was happening. Bob Greifeld, at Nasdaq, predicted a fragmented equity market whereas Duncan Niederauer at the NYSE thought that a few exchange operators would achieve a dominant position. Both were correct but in different ways. The equity market was continuing to fragment as multiple trading venues appeared, each designed to meet diverse needs. This can be seen in terms of the corporate stocks in circulation. On the one hand there were those issued by companies that were essentially private in nature, as these were closely held and little traded. On the other hand there were those issued by multinational corporations that were widely held and actively traded. The former were bought and sold by negotiation while the latter supported an active market. A similar diversity existed for investors and their needs. Large institutional investors wanted to trade anonymously and opaquely as they needed time to complete their deals before others realized what they were doing, anticipated their need to buy or sell, and turned the market against them. The forced transparency of the new regulations created an opportunity for a trader to take advantage of that need by pushing the price in the reverse direction. These investors turned to the dark pools provided by the investment banks, as these allowed them to complete their deals before the wider market became aware of what they were doing. By 2008 dark pools accounted for 12 per cent of US daily stock trading by volume. Conversely, the new breed of algorithmic traders, such as Getco, Peak6, Tradebot, and RGM, wanted instant access to current prices, sales, and purchases, and to be able to enter and exit the market frequently, quickly, and cheaply. They employed sophisticated trading programs that took advantage of momentary and minute price discrepancies, and wanted to co-locate their computers next to those of the market, so as to eliminate any delay in connection. The new electronic platforms were ideal for them, and their transactions accounted for over 30 per cent of all trading in equities in the USA in 2008. In between were the regulated markets provided by exchanges as these met the needs of the retail investor, but their importance was in terminal decline as stock ownership became dominated by institutional fund managers and buying and selling by the high-frequency traders.

These underlying changes appeared to leave stock exchanges like Nasdaq and the NYSE with a shrinking business. However, with the separation of membership and ownership there was no reason that each could not provide a range of markets to meet different requirements. By reinventing themselves as owners of multiple trading venues at home and abroad both the NYSE and Nasdaq saw a promising future in 2008. As Robert Greifeld, the chief executive of Nasdaq OMX, expressed it in 2008, 'Global customers want to deal with global enterprises.'[45] With a strong base in the world's largest equity market, the USA, and the acquisition of OMX, in the case of Nasdaq, and Euronext for the NYSE, the two leading US stock exchanges positioned themselves to serve fund managers and companies with a range of equity markets in a number of locations. They did face competition in implementing this strategy, as those operating US electronic platforms were also contemplating a global future. In 2008 Seth Merrin, the chief executive officer of one of these, Liquidnet, claimed that it 'is now a global institutional marketplace, which offers large, buy-side investors the ability to source block liquidity from a worldwide community of institutional investment firms, streaming liquidity from the world's largest exchanges and leading

[45] Anuj Gangahar, Jeremy Grant, and Stacy-Marie Ishmael, 'Nasdaq OMX calls for client benefits', 22nd September 2008.

broker-dealers, and strategic access to the open-market'.[46],[47] Though exchanges like Nasdaq and the NYSE envisaged a global future in 2008 the huge advances that had been made in both lowering barriers and increasing the speed and capacity of trading had not made the world into a single integrated global equity market. Numerous divisions remained, not least being regulatory intervention at the national level. It was developing strategies that both coped with these divisions, but also capitalized on the integration that was taking place, that were the over-riding considerations of those operating in the global equity market in 2008. It was only towards the end of that year that the implications of what was happening elsewhere in the global financial system began to make an impact, and then it was those markets lacking depth and breadth that suffered. The Jakarta Stock Exchange lacked the capacity to cope with a rash of selling in October 2008 and had to suspend trading. There was no global stock market panic.

What did take place was growing speculation in bank shares after the collapse of Lehman Brothers. Rather than attribute this speculation to genuine concerns over the ability of particular banks to survive, many blamed the increased volatility on the actions of high-speed traders attempting to make speculative gains by selling bank shares they did not own, and so drive down the price, allowing them to buy at the lower price and then complete the transaction, before repeating the exercise. Though short selling, as this was, was normal market practice by November 2008 seventeen countries had banned or restricted the practice. These included the USA, UK, Germany, France, Switzerland, Australia, Taiwan, and Japan. The one element of the equity market that did experience difficulty due to the crisis was that reliant on OTC trading. Prior to the crisis fund managers traded shares directly with, rather than through, an investment bank. Rather than have to wait to find a counterparty to a complex trade, a fund manager would execute a transaction instantly with an investment bank. The bank would agree a price and then find suitable counterparties later. After the collapse of Lehman Brothers this type of business largely ceased as investment banks pulled back from risky activities, reverting to an agency role. This damaged those equities whose liquidity was most dependent upon the investment banks' willingness to act as a direct counterparty to their clients' trades, confident that they could find a third-party buyer to take on the position afterwards. In contrast, the stocks issued by large corporations, that was widely held by investors and quoted on large and established stock exchanges,

[46] Anuj Gangahar, 'Liquidnet and NYSE Arca link up as exchange dip into dark pools', 25th November 2008.

[47] Anuj Gangahar, 'New York IPOs eclipse LSE for first time in three years', 3rd January 2008; Jeremy Grant, 'SEC eyes cross-border shake-up', 3rd January 2008; Anuj Gangahar, 'Nasdaq chief says sector will fragment', 8th January 2008; Norma Cohen, 'Exchanges appear ready to go over to the dark side', 9th January 2008; Anuj Gangahar, 'Banks throw weight behind BATS', 9th January 2008; Professor John Coffee, 'Regulation-lite belongs to a different age', 21st January 2008; Ross Tieman, 'Algo trading: the dog that bit its master', 19th March 2008; Ross Tieman, 'When microseconds really count', 19th March 2008; Jeremy Grant, 'Upstart Bats heads for Europe', 31st March 2008; Anuj Gangahar, 'Banks to allow dips into liquidity pools', 20th May 2008; Anuj Gangahar, 'NYSE revises trading rules', 14th June 2008; Anuj Gangahar and Jeremy Grant, 'Exchanges moot greater links with dark pools of liquidity', 24th June 2008; Jeremy Grant, 'BATS reveals date for European debut', 15th July 2008; Martin Arnold, 'Secondaries market set for growth', 11th August 2008; Jeremy Grant, 'BATS seeks 15% of FTSE 100 market', 20th August 2008; Jeremy Grant, 'MTF platforms poised to proliferate', 21st August 2008; Jeremy Grant and Anuj Gangahar, 'ISE buys into Direct Edge trading platform', 23rd August 2008; Lindsay Whipp, 'TSE tightens its defences as new era of trading looms', 29th August 2008; Jeremy Grant, 'The fast bowlers arrive: Europe's battle for share dealing business is about to intensify', 1st September 2008; Deborah Brewster, 'US retail investors slump to record low', 2nd September 2008; Anuj Gangahar, Jeremy Grant, and Stacy-Marie Ishmael, 'Nasdaq OMX calls for client benefits', 22nd September 2008; Anuj Gangahar, 'US electronic networks step on exchanges' toes', 21st October 2008; Anuj Gangahar, 'Liquidnet and NYSE Arca link up as exchange dip into dark pools', 25th November 2008; Jeremy Grant and Anuj Gangahar, 'Dark pools are stirred by attention from regulators', 27th November 2008; Anuj Gangahar, 'Algorithmic trades produce snowball effect on volatility', 5th December 2008; Aline van Duyn, 'SecondMarket enters new territory', 11th December 2008.

remained liquid, as it was always able to be bought and sold at close to its market price or capable of being used as collateral for a loan because its current price was publicly available and constantly updated.[48]

Generally in 2008 there was a jockeying for position among the world's stock exchanges, as the removal of the barriers that had previously separated products and countries disappeared, leaving a highly-competitive environment in its wake. Contributing to this environment was the disruptive effects of electronic technology and the interventions of regulators, each of which further contributed to blurring the distinctions between stock exchanges and OTC markets, and removing the protection that incumbency and location had once provided. In May 2008 Anuj Gangahar highlighted that 'winning the battle for liquidity is one of the keys to success for trading venues. Consolidation in the exchange sector in recent years has been driven at least in part by a desire to establish the broadest and deepest pools of public liquidity.'[49] He continued by pointing out that, conversely, the proliferation of trading venues kept fragmenting the liquidity pools: 'These are private inter-bank or intra-bank platforms that are widely used to trade stocks away from exchanges. The pools are used by clients such as hedge funds to buy and sell large blocks of shares in complete anonymity and without the danger of moving the public price of a stock on an exchange as a result of copycatting by other traders.'[50] There was a simultaneous process of concentration and fragmentation. Consolidation came with mergers between existing exchanges as they tried to reach a scale that justified the heavy investment in the most advanced electronic trading technology and allowed them to provide the deep and broad markets demanded by the ever-larger companies that issued stock, and the global fund managers that bought and sold it. Conversely fragmentation was a product of the multiplication of active stock markets around the world, as every country embraced an equity culture, and numerous electronic platforms and internal trading systems were developed. An estimate made in 2008 indicated that there were sixty-eight alternative trading systems in the USA, of which thirty-two were dark pools. As the share of the market taken by alternative platforms grew so did their ability to rival stock exchanges as provider of liquidity. Mamoun Tazi, an analyst at MF Global, highlighted their potential in 2008, 'Once the MTFs can build up core liquidity then liquidity starts to track its own liquidity—and it does so at the expense of another pool of liquidity.'[51]

[48] Anuj Gangahar, 'New York IPOs eclipse LSE for first time in three years', 3rd January 2008; Jeremy Grant, 'SEC eyes cross-border shake-up', 3rd January 2008; Anuj Gangahar, 'Nasdaq chief says sector will fragment', 8th January 2008; Norma Cohen, 'Exchanges appear ready to go over to the dark side', 9th January 2008; Jeremy Grant, Hal Weitzman, Anuj Gangahar, 'Tense Exchanges: Banks wrest trading from the established stock markets', 17th April 2008; Jeremy Grant and Paul J. Davies, 'Exchanges show how to tackle clearing conundrum', 23rd April 2008; Anuj Gangahar, 'Banks to allow dips into liquidity pools', 20th May 2008; Jeremy Grant, 'Bullish LSE fails to convince investors it can make the grade', 23rd May 2008; Jeremy Grant, 'Decision pending on post-trade', 23rd May 2008; Anuj Gangahar and Jeremy Grant, 'Exchanges moot greater links with dark pools of liquidity', 24th June 2008; John Aglionby, 'Jakarta exchange closed indefinitely', 9th October 2008; Michael Mackenzie and Rachel Morarjee, 'Fear reigns as spectre of a global recession looms large', 9th October 2008; Jeremy Grant, 'Time of crisis also gives opportunities', 21st October 2008; Jeremy Grant and Anuj Gangahar, 'Spotlight on role of electronic trading in recent volatility', 30th October 2008; Joe Leahy and Sundeep Tucker, 'Exchanges urged to work together', 5th November 2008; Chris Hughes, 'No more easy money', 11th November 2008; Jeremy Grant and Anuj Gangahar, 'Dark pools are stirred by attention from regulators', 27th November 2008; Abeer Allam, 'Foreign investors key to plans', 28th November 2008; Jeremy Grant, 'New breed of trader heads for Europe', 4th December 2008; Anuj Gangahar, 'Algorithmic trades produce snowball effect on volatility', 5th December 2008.

[49] Anuj Gangahar, 'Banks to allow dips into liquidity pools', 20th May 2008.

[50] Anuj Gangahar, 'Banks to allow dips into liquidity pools', 20th May 2008.

[51] Jeremy Grant, 'Bullish LSE fails to convince investors it can make the grade', 23rd May 2008.

One response among stock exchanges to this growing competition was to embrace the vertical-silo model. In the vertical-silo a stock exchange controlled the whole process from providing a trading platform to handling the subsequent clearing and settlement of transactions. Regulators were opposed to the vertical-silo, regarding it anti-competitive, because it made it difficult for competition to take place on the basis of price alone as users paid for the entire package. Regulators favoured the horizontal-silo in which stock exchanges provided a trading venue, leaving it for others to supply clearing and settlement services. Under this model users could compare prices for each service, purchasing that which was the cheapest, and so stimulating competition, leading to greater efficiency. Despite this clear preference for the horizontal-silo among regulators it was those stock exchanges operating the vertical model that were gaining ground throughout 2008. What regulators never understood was the appeal of the simplicity of the vertical model, as it gave users access to an integrated package from the initial order to final payment or delivery, reducing the internal costs attached to handling these separately. The combination of trading and clearing also limited exposure to counterparty risk, as any default was covered through the use of a central clearer, and this was given a great boost during the financial crisis. Prior to the financial crisis there was room for both stock exchanges and alternative platforms as the global equity market was thriving. The equity culture had established a strong hold and it supported numerous stock exchanges around the world, with virtually every country having at least one.

The problem of this proliferation of stock exchanges was that, individually, none could provide the level of liquidity that large companies and institutional investors sought. Within Africa the one stock exchange that could provide a liquid market was the Johannesburg Stock Exchange (JSE), and it did attempt to create a pan African market. This was rebuffed as none were willing to cede power to the JSE. A similar situation prevailed across the Middle East where no single stock exchange could achieve a dominant position, including the largest, the Istanbul Stock Exchange (ISE). The aim of all these stock exchanges was to retain control of their domestic market, as was the case in both Australia and New Zealand. Liquidity was the magnet that drew trading to a stock exchange from around the world, making it almost impossible to break the stranglehold once established, but only with a continued investment in technology, a willingness to reduce charges, and the acceptance of foreign members. One way of achieving this position was to create a multiproduct exchange as this could support the costs involved. A number of stock exchanges had taken this route. In 2008 it was followed by Bovespa in Brazil, the owner of the São Paulo Stock Exchange, which merged with the country's derivatives exchange, BM&F. The motivation behind the move was explained by Roberto Teixeira da Costa, the former president of Brazil's securities commission, the CVM: 'The world today demands that things be done on a global scale. In a few years there will be just a handful of exchange groups and Brazil's will be among them.'[52] The combination of growing competition and the changing technology of trading was driving exchanges to merge into single units combining stocks and derivatives on the one hand and trading and processing on the other, regardless of the attitude of regulators.[53]

[52] Jonathan Wheatley, 'Brazil exchange executives get into global party mood', 29th February 2008.

[53] Joanna Chung, 'Divide and conquer', 24th January 2008; David Ibison and Simeon Kerr, 'Qataris sell OMX stake to Gulf rival', 14th February 2008; Jonathan Wheatley, 'Brazil exchange executives get into global party mood', 29th February 2008; Ross Tieman, 'When microseconds really count', 19th March 2008; Peter Guest, 'Egypt's stock exchange enjoys revival', 31st March 2008; Jeremy Grant, 'JSE intends to list pan-African stocks', 2nd June 2008; Barney Jopson, 'Rivals query JSE's pan-Africa plan', 9th June 2008; Simeon Kerr and Jeremy

However, there was a limit to how far these mergers would extend as there was a strong resistance among both governments and individual institutions to the surrender of national sovereignty. In many cases national stock exchanges monopolized their domestic market and their priority was to preserve that position. The Tokyo Stock Exchange (TSE) handled 89 per cent of all trading in equities in Japan and alternative trading venues had yet to make much impact in 2008. The difficulty for those stock exchanges located outside countries the size of China, India, Japan, and South Korea was that they lacked the scale to provide the deep and broad markets sought by institutional investors. The Korea Exchange did attempt to widen its appeal as Lee Junghwan, its chairman and chief executive, made clear in 2008: 'We are an international bourse with foreign investors owning about thirty per cent of the shares traded here. We will improve listings procedures and disclosure systems to match global standards.'[54] Similarly a number of smaller Asian countries tried to create a common trading platform in 2008 but this was thwarted by deep-rooted national differences, involving language and culture as well as currency and regulation. The leading contenders to fill a pan-Asian role in 2008 remained the Hong Kong Exchange and the Singapore Exchange. The Hong Kong Exchange tried to capitalize on its status of being both within and outside China by providing a platform through which Chinese companies attracted international investors and global fund managers accessed Chinese stocks, but it faced competition from the stock exchanges within mainland China as well as the inducements that the LSE, Nasdaq, and the NYSE provided to Chinese companies to list with them. The Singapore Exchange lacked Hong Kong's Chinese connection and so tried hard to develop an international business by investing in the latest trading technology and providing a market for the stocks of Asia's high-growth companies, but the results remained limited. Across Asia national governments and individual exchanges continued to throw up barriers to market integration as well as becoming more willing to embrace the latest advances in trading technology themselves, as was the case with the Bombay Stock Exchange.[55]

In contrast to Asia the creation of an integrated equity market was pursued rigorously in Europe in 2008 under pressure from the EU and Mifid. Roland Bellegarde, head of European equity markets at Euronext, said, 'We are adapting to the competitive environment. I am

Grant, 'Qatar's ambition revealed in plans for exchange', 25th June 2008; Isabel Gorst, 'Market comes out of shadows', 2nd July 2008; Peter Smith, 'Australia's ASX warns of tougher climate for equities', 15th August 2008; Andrew England, 'Saudi opens exchange to outsiders', 21st August 2008; Abeer Allam, 'Foreign investors key to plans', 28th November 2008; Jeremy Grant, 'Low transaction fees and an international dimension', 1st December 2008.

[54] Song Jung-a, 'Korea Exchange tries to lure foreign companies', 22nd September 2008.

[55] Sundeep Tucker, 'Revamped Singapore bourse to rival Aim', 28th January 2008; Lindsay Whipp, 'Aim seeks more exposure in Japan', 3rd March 2008; Joe Leahy, 'BSE could list this year to raise global profile', 31st March 2008; Farhan Bokhari, 'Karachi hopes for more open trading', 14th April 2008; Joe Leahy, 'No bull as Mumbai chief focuses on modernisation', 14th April 2008; Michiyo Nakamoto, 'Investors look overseas for wind of change', 21st May 2008; Lindsay Whipp, 'Lehman's dark pools swell', 27th May 2008; Hal Weitzman, 'CBOE announces deal with Korea Exchange', 9th June 2008; Jeremy Grant and Sundeep Tucker, 'SGX is determined to punch above its weight', 12th June 2008; Michiyo Nakamoto and Kate Burgess, 'Dividends To Reap: Shareholder activists begin to make their mark in Japan', 3rd July 2008; Raphael Minder, 'Asian regional platform planned', 9th July 2008; Lindsay Whipp and Jeremy Grant, 'Tokyo and London in small-cap push', 30th July 2008; Lindsay Whipp, 'Tokyo moves to boost foreign listings', 5th August 2008; Joe Leahy, 'India's brokerages face shake-up', 14th August 2008; Lindsay Whipp, 'TSE tightens its defences as new era of trading looms', 29th August 2008; Lindsay Whipp, 'Exchange has big plans for its expansion', 12th September 2008; Lindsay Whipp, 'Fear concentrates aged minds', 12th September 2008; Song Jung-a, 'Korea Exchange tries to lure foreign companies', 22nd September 2008; Sundeep Tucker, 'Deregulation prompts new look at trading monopolies', 1st October 2008; Lindsay Whipp, 'Domestic investors remain wary', 14th October 2008; Patti Waldmeir, 'Liberalisation marches to its own drum', 24th November 2008.

not complacent or non-reactive.'[56] His equivalent at the LSE, Martin Graham, director of equity markets at LSE, said much the same: 'We know that if we want to continue to be the central marketplace we need to ensure that our products and services are second to none.'[57] Not all were so responsive. Frank Gerstenschläger, an executive board member at Deutsche Börse, stressed the advantage an incumbent exchange had, especially one that had already invested heavily in its own electronic trading platform, Xetra: 'It is very difficult to transfer large amounts of liquidity from one platform to another. Xetra has a lot of liquidity due to the expansion of electronic trade, which makes it look pretty good in the European comparison.'[58] However, it was not the trading system that gave him reasons to be confident but the fact that his exchange operated the vertical-silo model while the others did not. Identifying the protection that the vertical-silo provided in 2008 Switzerland adopted it, with the merger of not only the equities and derivatives markets but also the clearing, settlement, and payments systems into a single group, Swiss Financial Services. Even without the vertical-silo model individual governments within the EU continued to use the regulatory power devolved to them in order to prevent cross-border competition. Charlie McCreevy, the EU internal market commissioner responsible for implementing Mifid, expressed his annoyance at the slow rate of progress made a year after its introduction: 'Legal barriers make it much more complex to hold securities cross-border, and lead to higher costs for transactions and credit.'[59] What Mifid did do was expose national stock exchanges to alternative platforms and dark pools. The LSE was the stock exchange most targeted by the alternative trading venues as it was home to so many internationally-held corporate stocks and lacked the protection of the vertical-silo model, while the UK government was reluctant to intervene as it might damage London's standing as an international financial centre. Though the LSE did invest in 2008 in a faster trading system with increased capacity, and offer co-location to those requiring a closer connection, it steadily lost trading in the stocks it quoted to the MTFs, especially Chi-X.[60]

[56] Jeremy Grant, Hal Weitzman, Anuj Gangahar, 'Tense Exchanges: Banks wrest trading from the established stock markets', 17th April 2008.

[57] Jeremy Grant and James Wilson, 'Deutsche Börse unafraid of MTF rivals', 22nd May 2008.

[58] Jeremy Grant and James Wilson, 'Deutsche Börse unafraid of MTF rivals', 22nd May 2008.

[59] Jeremy Grant, 'Brussels calls for ideas on securities trading', 26th August 2008.

[60] Norma Cohen, 'Exchanges appear ready to go over to the dark side', 9th January 2008; Jan Cienski, 'Warsaw's target is to be financial hub', 15th January 2008; Joanna Chung, 'Exchanges in fight over dearth of new issues', 1st March 2008; Ross Tieman, 'Algo trading: the dog that bit its master', 19th March 2008; Jeremy Grant, 'Upstart Bats heads for Europe', 31st March 2008; James Wilson, 'Deutsche Börse lays out strategy to raise gearing', 31st March 2008; Jeremy Grant, 'Settlement slow to follow rapid trades', 4th April 2008; Jeremy Grant, 'NYSE tries to undermine LSE', 14th April 2008; Jeremy Grant, 'BATS chooses Savvis for drive into Europe', 14th April 2008; Clara Furse, 'Speak up to keep clearing houses competitive', 16th April 2008; Jeremy Grant, Hal Weitzman, Anuj Gangahar, 'Tense Exchanges: Banks wrest trading from the established stock markets', 17th April 2008; Jeremy Grant, 'Fortis arm to play key role in new Nasdaq pan-European trading system', 19th May 2008; Jeremy Grant and James Wilson, 'Deutsche Börse unafraid of MTF rivals', 22nd May 2008; Jeremy Grant, 'Bullish LSE fails to convince investors it can make the grade', 23rd May 2008; Jeremy Grant, 'Decision pending on post-trade', 23rd May 2008; The Lex Column, 'Meeting their match', 29th May 2008; Jeremy Grant, 'New platform for Spanish small-caps', 30th May 2008; Jeremy Grant, 'Do exchanges feel blue over Turquoise?', 16th June 2008; Jeremy Grant, 'LSE looks beyond speed in the race to beat upstart rivals', 19th June 2008; Anuj Gangahar and Jeremy Grant, 'Exchanges moot greater links with dark pools of liquidity', 24th June 2008; Jeremy Grant, 'Mifid causing data frustration', 24th June 2008; Jeremy Grant, 'Embarrassed LSE trails in rival's wake', 25th June 2008; Jeremy Grant, 'LSE and Lehman's platform to have dark pool', 26th June 2008; Jeremy Grant, 'LSE hopes Baikal will refresh its fortunes', 27th June 2008; Jeremy Grant, 'Walking in the shadow of global peers', 9th July 2008; Haig Simonian, 'Zurich hopes revamp will help it climb global ranks', 15th July 2008; Jeremy Grant, 'BATS reveals date for European debut', 15th July 2008; Jeremy Grant, 'SWX wins dark pool backers', 21st July 2008; Jeremy Grant, 'Turquoise and Chi-X suffer Italian blow', 30th July 2008; Jeremy Grant, 'Frustration for exchange newcomers', 31st July 2008; James Wilson, 'D Börse running trials for dark pool', 6th August 2008; Jeremy Grant, 'European platforms step into the pool', 9th August 2008; James Wilson and Jeremy Grant, 'Deutsche Börse is reaping the

Collateral Benefits? 2009

Rather than suffering damaging consequences from the collapse of Lehman Brothers and the ensuing financial crisis those operating in the global equity market saw that there were opportunities to be seized. This was firstly in the continuing attractiveness of equities as investments, boosted by the problems associated with securitized assets as a result of the crisis, especially their lack of liquidity and the difficulties of valuing them. More directly stock exchanges expected to gain. Prior to the crisis the combination of high-speed, high capacity, low-cost electronic trading systems had become a real threat to stock exchanges. That situation changed with the Global Financial Crisis as it made regulators change their attitude towards stock exchanges. Before the crisis they had regarded stock exchanges as inefficient monopolies that offered a poor service and over-charged their customers, especially those operating the vertical-silo model. In contrast OTC markets were considered cheap and efficient providing customers with a highly-competitive alternative. What happened in the crisis was that the market in securitized assets froze, with catastrophic results for those that relied upon them for liquidity or collateral. In contrast, the market provided by stock exchanges did not freeze. Where there were problems was in the less liquid stocks but even they had usually been saleable, though at reduced prices, and so they retained a value for collateral purposes. An added bonus was that those exchanges operating the vertical-silo model had been able to reassure buyers and sellers that the use of the integral clearing house covered counterparty risk. In 2009 Reto Francioni, the Swiss-born chief executive of Deutsche Börse, proclaimed the virtues of the vertical-silo: 'Having trading and risk management under one roof meant we could act quickly and efficiently. The liquidity pools were always there, helping build trust in price discovery. We delivered our services at a very high level of quality during the crisis. If you are a service provider and no one is talking about you, you are doing a good job.'[61] In the USA the DTCC, which handled clearing and settlement in the equity market, provided this service for all users. Also in 2009, Bob Greifeld, the chief executive of Nasdaq OMX, summed up the arguments that all

benefits of its diversity', 11th August 2008; Jeremy Grant, 'Chi-X secures share of trading', 14th August 2008; Jeremy Grant, 'Turquoise refreshes exchange landscape', 15th August 2008; Jeremy Grant, 'LSE receives wake-up call as rivals grab market share', 16th August 2008; Jeremy Grant, 'BATS seeks 15% of FTSE 100 market', 20th August 2008; Jeremy Grant, 'MTF platforms poised to proliferate', 21st August 2008; Jeremy Grant, 'Brussels calls for ideas on securities trading', 26th August 2008; James Wilson, 'Deutsche Börse to cut fees for frequent traders', 27th August 2008; Lindsay Whipp, 'TSE tightens its defences as new era of trading looms', 29th August 2008; Jeremy Grant, 'LSE slashes fees as it steps up battle against emerging rivals', 1st September 2008; Jeremy Grant, 'The fast bowlers arrive: Europe's battle for share dealing business is about to intensify', 1st September 2008; Jeremy Grant, 'Nasdaq lifts the stakes in Europe's trading arena', 2nd September 2008; David Blackwell and Philip Stafford, 'Party over as investors walk away from Aim', 3rd September 2008; Jeremy Grant, 'NYSE Euronext fights back', 8th September 2008; Jeremy Grant, 'MTFs begin to encroach on traditional stock exchange territory', 8th September 2008; Stacy-Marie Ishmael and Neil Hume, 'Traders twiddle as London Stock Exchange shuts', 9th September 2008; James Mackintosh and James Wilson, 'D Börse ponders joining trading dogfight', 15th September 2008; Jeremy Grant, 'Competitive UK stock clearing gets the go-ahead', 25th September 2008; Robert Cookson and Chris Hughes, 'CFDs blamed for higher volatility across traditional stock markets', 9th October 2008; Jeremy Grant, 'Exposure puts Bolsas' long period in the sun at risk', 15th October 2008; Jeremy Grant, 'Turquoise plays down need for speed', 21st October 2008; Jeremy Grant, 'Blink and you miss a competitive advantage', 21st October 2008; Jan Cienski, 'Warsaw pays price for world's woes', 21st October 2008; Jeremy Grant, 'Baikal strategy remains unclear', 30th October 2008; Jeremy Grant, 'Mifid opens door to US platforms', 31st October 2008; Haig Simonian and Jeremy Grant, 'SWX Europe moves out of London', 12th November 2008; Jeremy Grant and James Wilson, 'D Börse to launch hybrid dark pool trading facility', 21st November 2008; Jeremy Grant, 'Trading data has deteriorated since Mifid, IMA warns', 25th November 2008.

[61] James Wilson, 'More than just a historic trading floor', 30th June 2009.

stock exchanges had been making: 'As we reflect on the state of the US equity markets, we can take pride in their performance through the tumult of the last year. While investors did not appreciate the direction of the market, at all times the markets were accessible, liquid and transparent.'[62] This contrast between the freezing of OTC market for securitized assets and the liquidity of the equity market operated by stock exchanges presented the latter with an ideal opportunity to persuade regulators that the balance needed to be shifted in their favour. This was especially the case with those exchanges operating the vertical-silo model.

European exchanges operating the vertical-silo did not have the field to themselves as there were a number of independent clearing houses that saw the opportunity of replicating there what the DTCC provided in the USA. These included the European Multilateral Clearing Facility (EMCF), LCH.Clearnet, and Euroclear. As with other aspects of financial regulation EU regulators were closely wedded to US practice, and they remained hesitant to back the vertical-silo model because of its anti-competitive aspects. If stability and resilience could be achieved through independent clearing houses there was no need to provide regulatory backing to stock exchanges, despite their performance during the crisis. During 2009 the share of share trading by incumbent stock exchanges thus continued to fall as the regulatory authorities promoted competition rather than stability by forcing through an agenda of transparency. Electronic platforms attracted trading in the most liquid stocks because of lower fees and superior service, aided by technology that allowed buyers and sellers to identify the best prices, the fastest execution, and the lowest costs. High-frequency traders invested in this technology as it allowed them to generate profits from minute price differences by trading in volume and at speed. In 2009 high-frequency trading accounted for an estimated 70 per cent of trading in the USA and was rising rapidly in Europe.

By September 2009 Jeremy Grant considered that stock exchanges were in 'a technology arms race' to stay competitive.[63] The result was the fragmentation of the equity market, which made each pool of liquidity shallower and more volatile. This exposed large institutional investors to adverse price movements caused by high-frequency traders taking up a reverse position in the expectation that a sale or purchase would have to be made so as to complete a deal. By August 2009 Michael Mackenzie and Jeremy Grant reported that 'Computer systems or algorithms that can break down a large order into tiny slices and execute them all across different trading venues at somewhere near the speed of light has become the new way of doing business.'[64] The effect was to encourage fund managers to bypass public markets, including those provided by stock exchanges, and to direct orders to dark pools where deals could be completed in private before the details were revealed. What asset managers valued more than the cost of doing business was certainty that they could buy or sell when they wanted, in the amounts they wanted and at prices that allowed them to close a deal at a profit, and that was often best done in private. As a result the share of trading handled by the stock exchanges continued to fall. That of Nasdaq dropped from 30 per cent in 2008 to 20 per cent in 2009. In Europe at the LSE a similar pattern was emerging during 2009. By August 2009 Chi-X claimed a 15 per cent share of European equities trading with a further three platforms sharing 10 per cent, and dark pools being responsible for 8 per cent.

During 2009 regulators struggled to achieve a balance between rules that provided the retail investor with a fair market but did not disadvantage the institutional investor by

[62] Bob Greifeld, 'Exchanges should unite to end flash orders', 7th August 2009.
[63] Jeremy Grant, 'Bourses in data arms race', 15th September 2009.
[64] Michael Mackenzie and Jeremy Grant, 'The dash to flash', 6th August 2009.

allowing predatory traders to take advantage of public disclosure, which drove trading into the dark pools operated by the banks. The dilemma they faced in terms of equity markets was summed up in October 2009 by Mary Schapiro, the chairman of the SEC:

> The commission must assure that the public markets and non-public trading venues operate within a balanced regulatory framework. This means that as markets evolve, the commission must continually seek to preserve the essential role of the public markets in promoting efficient price discovery and investor confidence.... Given the growth of dark pools, this lack of transparency could create a two-tiered market that deprives the public of information about stock prices and liquidity.[65]

The question that the SEC failed to address was that of trading being conducted in alternative platforms and dark pools on the basis of publicly available prices, even though those providing the platform and doing the trading neither contributed to the costs of maintaining the market nor the price discovery process. In the past these costs had been borne by the stock exchanges and their members out of the fees they charged their customers for buying and selling costs. With competition driving these fees down there was no longer a willingness to meet the expenses of ensuring that prices accurately reflected the ebb and flow of demand as the results were freely available to all.[66]

[65] Michael Mackenzie, 'SEC plans to illuminate dark pools', 22nd October 2009.

[66] Jeremy Grant, 'Nasdaq OMX's Nordic move highlights post-trade focus', 26th January 2009; Jeremy Grant, 'NYSE Euronext in move to one platform', 17th February 2009; Jeremy Grant, 'Exchanges and brokers at odds over crisis blame', 20th February 2009; Sundeep Tucker, 'Goldman launches dark pool in HK', 2nd March 2009; Anuj Gangahar, 'NYSE opens door to options floor', 2nd March 2009; Jeremy Grant, 'LSE drops central clearing plan', 3rd April 2009; James Wilson and Jeremy Grant, 'D Börse in pan-Europe drive', 17th April 2009; Jeremy Grant, 'Big exchanges come round to multilateral approach', 20th April 2009; Jeremy Grant, 'European trading trails the US in coping with outages', 21st April 2009; Jeremy Grant, 'Streamlining sees Graham resign from LSE', 21st April 2009; Jeremy Grant, 'LSE closes in on pan-European trading', 22nd April 2009; Jeremy Grant, 'LSE takes tough new approach to technology', 27th April 2009; Jeremy Grant, 'Vienna seeks to be architect of East European network', 11th May 2009; Aline van Duyn and Anuj Gangahar, 'Exchanges big winners in OTC overhaul', 15th May 2009; Gillian Tett and Aline van Duyn, 'On the march', 9th June 2009; Jeremy Grant, 'NYSE Euronext joint venture to capitalise on rising demand for clearing', 19th June 2009; Jeremy Grant, 'Regulators keen to shine a light into dark pools', 20th June 2009; Jeremy Grant, 'Tom Trading aims for retail investors', 24th June 2009; James Wilson, 'More than just a historic trading floor', 30th June 2009; Jeremy Grant, 'Spain's BME to close remaining open outcry pits', 8th July 2009; Jeremy Grant, 'Jury still out on benefits of Mifid for the trading arena', 10th July 2009; Jeremy Grant, 'SmartPool signs 14 banks and brokers to dark pool', 13th July 2009; Jeremy Grant and Nikki Tait, 'Trading costs in Europe remain stubbornly high', 17th July 2009; Sophia Grene, 'When cheaper can lead to more expense', 20th July 2009; Jeremy Grant, 'Platforms increase focus on liquidity', 3rd August 2009; Jeremy Grant, 'Europe calm on flash orders', 3rd August 2009; Bob Greifeld, 'Exchanges should unite to end flash orders', 7th August 2009; Michael Mackenzie, 'Nasdaq OMX loses a third of market share in price war', 7th August 2009; David Blackwell, 'SmartPool expansion drive', 17th August 2009; Patrick Jenkins and Adam Jones, 'Turquoise put up for sale after approach', 19th August 2009; Jeremy Grant, 'LSE targeting upgrade to move ahead of rivals', 8th September 2009; Andrew Ward, 'Nasdaq OMX plans to step up Oslo Børs battle', 10th September 2009; Jeremy Grant, 'Bourses in data arms race', 15th September 2009; Peter Smith, 'ASX chief hits at US shake-up', 18th September 2009; Sophia Grene, 'A niche in high-frequency trading', 21st September 2009; Jeremy Grant, 'Exchanges body issues dark pools warning', 23rd September 2009; Jeremy Grant, 'Innovative ideas fail to lighten European mood over dark pools', 25th September 2009; John Authers, 'A risky revival', 26th September 2009; Jeremy Grant, 'ISE to offer more foreign trading', 29th September 2009; Michael Mackenzie and Jeremy Grant, 'Trading co-locate takes root in Essex hangar', 30th September 2009; Jeremy Grant, 'LSE in talks to buy Turquoise', 2nd October 2009; Jeremy Grant, 'Competition is sharper but liquidity fragmented', 21st October 2009; Michael Mackenzie, 'High-frequency trading dominates the debate', 21st October 2009; Michael Mackenzie, 'SEC plans to illuminate dark pools', 22nd October 2009; Haig Simonian, 'Leading banks turn city into a regional hub', 23rd October 2009; Michael Mackenzie and Helen Thomas, 'SEC looks to get to the bottom of dark pools', 28th October 2009; Saskia Scholtes and Aline van Duyn, 'SEC chief seeks new securities laws', 28th October 2009; Aline van Duyn, 'US falls behind rivals in new listings', 31st October–1st November 2009; Jeremy Grant, 'Trading in European dark pools leaps fivefold since start of year', 2nd November 2009; Haig Simonian, 'Aim is to be a significant regional force', 6th November 2009; Jeremy Grant, 'Trading rebates cut into Nasdaq OMX

Even though neither alternative electronic platforms nor dark pools had made much impact outside the USA and the EU before 2009 the threat was there, and drove stock exchanges to respond. In Japan the speed of response was slow because of the dominance that the Tokyo Stock Exchange (TSE) exerted over the domestic market, with 90 per cent of all share trading in 2009. By 2009 the combined share of trading handled by the Proprietary Trading Systems (PTSs) was 1 per cent. Nevertheless, the threat they posed was real as Ron Gould, the chief executive for Asia-Pacific for Chi-X, made clear: 'The high-speed, low-cost and intelligent Chi-X trading platforms have significantly reduced costs and improved execution performance for investors...'[67] This led the TSE to respond in 2009 with a faster trading platform and the offer of co-location to high-frequency traders. In Canada the response to competition was much quicker as the merged Toronto and Montreal stock exchanges (TMX Group) faced strong competition from alternative trading systems (ATSs), especially Alpha, which was backed by Canada's six largest banks. The TMX's share of trading fell from 94 per cent in January 2009 to 80 per cent in November, with Alpha picking up 14 per cent. The TMX was also vulnerable to international competition as it was home to over 55 per cent of the world's listed mining companies in 2009. This forced the TMX to take competition seriously and respond to it. However, most stock exchanges remained national monopolies and were able to ignore competitive threats in 2009. What was most noticeable about developments in the global equity market during 2009, and outside the USA and North America, was how little the financial crisis had disturbed the established pattern. Even by the end of 2009 the Global Financial Crisis had passed the global equity market by.[68]

revenues', 6th November 2009; Jeremy Grant, 'LSE to allow hidden orders', 9th November 2009; Jan Cienski and James Wilson, 'Poland sets conditions on bourse privatisation', 19th November 2009; John Keefe, 'Regulator's torch to light up dark pools', 23rd November 2009; Jeremy Grant, 'Chi-X leaves upstart label behind and looks to the future', 23rd November 2009; Jonathan Guthrie, 'Cluster of firms can handle all but the largest deals', 27th November 2009; Jeremy Grant, 'Traders stuck with LSE in spite of crash', 29th November 2009; Steve Johnson, 'New bond market faces fight', 30th November 2009; Jan Cienski and James Wilson, 'Warsaw calls off D Börse talks over exchange sale', 1st December 2009; Steve Johnson, 'Hidden costs found in dark pools', 7th December 2009; David Blackwell, 'Signs of recovery seen after years of famine', 16th December 2009; Jeremy Grant, 'Eurex and LSE to counter Liffe with equity options trading', 16th December 2009; Jeremy Grant, 'Regulator research sheds more light on dark pools', 18th December 2009; Jeremy Grant, 'Turquoise will bolster the LSE's position', 22nd December 2009; Jeremy Grant, 'Computer-driven trading boom raises meltdown fears', 26th January 2010.

[67] Lindsay Whipp, 'Chi-X global to spearhead Asian push with plans for Japan platform', 1st December 2009.

[68] David Oakley, 'Syria in exchange debut', 10th March 2009; Sundeep Tucker and Peter Smith, 'ASX to develop energy-related futures', 21st May 2009; Mary Watkins, 'Bursa Malaysia plans to expand its appeal', 15th June 2009; Jeremy Grant and Simeon Kerr, 'NYSE Euronext takes Doha stake', 20th June 2009; Robin Kwong, 'New Chinese bourse set to lure domestic flotations', 24th June 2009; Lindsay Whipp, 'Tokyo Aim looks to niche role to get ahead of rivals', 1st July 2009; Jeremy Grant, 'Spain's BME to close remaining open outcry pits', 8th July 2009; Lindsay Whipp, 'Tokyo looks at PTS clearing services', 10th July 2009; Jeremy Grant, 'Canada's bourse up to speed', 30th July 2009; James Fontanella-Khan and Varun Sood, 'Nasdaq closes office in India', 3rd August 2009; John Burton and Lindsay Whipp, 'SGX and Chi-X Global plan dark pool', 13th August 2009; Mary Watkins, 'India's oldest exchange gets an injection of new blood', 25th August 2009; Peter Smith, 'ASX chief hits at US shake-up', 18th September 2009; Mary Watkins, 'Exchange big hitters in battle for market share', 21st September 2009; Delphine Strauss, 'ISE faces test from Turkey's trading past', 22nd September 2009; Delphine Strauss, 'Istanbul and Athens bourses form joint index', 29th September 2009; Lindsay Whipp, 'Tokyo market prepares to move up a gear', 21st October 2009; Jonathan Wheatley, 'São Paulo adopts a more international approach', 21st October 2009; Parselelo Kantai, 'Trouble at old boys club', 29th October 2009; Robert Cookson, 'Demand for "funky" shares swamps new Chinese exchange', 31st October–1st November 2009; Lindsay Whipp, 'Co-location to get Tokyo up to speed', 2nd November 2009; Roel Landingin, 'New blow to reputation of Philippines' exchange', 2nd November 2009; Jonathan Wheatley, 'Strong growth after slight dip', 5th November 2009; Bernard Simon, 'Toronto's trading platforms draw regulatory scrutiny', 20th November 2009; James Fontanella-Khan, 'Bombay Stock Exchange plans listing', 25th November 2009; Lindsay Whipp, 'Chi-X global to spearhead Asian push with plans for Japan platform', 1st December 2009; Song Jung-a and Kevin Brown, 'Citizen traders hooked on Korean derivatives', 10th December 2009; Enid Tsui, 'Taiwan exchange drops plan for IPO', 11th December 2009; Aline van Duyn, Michael Mackenzie and Jeremy Grant, 'That sinking feeling', 2nd June 2010.

Déjà vu or not? 2010

By 2010 the immediate impact of the Global Financial Crisis was beginning to fade but it had left a legacy for many financial markets, especially in terms of regulation. In March 2010 Jennifer Hughes observed that, 'Since the financial crisis, regulators and officials have clamped down on OTC markets, preferring to move trading to more transparent electronic platforms and to force trades to be officially recorded in so-called repositories.'[69] That statement only referred to derivatives and, to an extent, bonds. It did not apply to equities. This was something that Aline van Duyn, Michael Mackenzie, and Jeremy Grant picked up on later in 2010: 'Opacity in privately traded markets, such as in derivatives and complex securitized bonds, is widely seen as having contributed to the meltdown of the financial system in 2008 and the ensuing global economic crisis. Laws are being passed across the globe to force over-the-counter derivatives and other markets into the public eye.' They then drew a contrast with the global equity market: 'In many cases, stock markets have been hailed as the standard to live up to, for the ease with which investors can check stock prices and trade shares even when markets are volatile.'[70] The equity market, and especially that part served by stock exchanges, had proved resilient during the financial crisis. There were a few exceptions, such as Indonesia and Nigeria where speculative bubbles had burst, seriously damaging the functioning of the market, while the stocks of smaller companies had suffered from a lack of liquidity. However, the stocks issued by large companies and traded on the major exchanges had remained liquid, allowing holders to either sell or use them as collateral, proving their worth compared to recently securitized assets. The global equity market then recovered quickly during 2009 and flourished in 2010. The market capitalization of the world's 500 largest quoted companies rose from $15.6tn in 2009 to $23.5tn in 2010, reflecting the attractions of corporate stocks at a time of low interest rates and an absence of alternatives because of the collapse of securitization. About the only tangible legacy of the crisis was a commitment to prevent the short-selling of systemically-important financial stocks, because of fears that it could lead to a crisis of confidence in individual banks. Even that commitment varied over the world and was fading.

It was not the legacy of the crisis that was most relevant to the global equity market by 2010 but the combination of long-term trends, such as the transformation of technology, and the effects of the regulatory changes made before the crisis of 2008, especially RegNMS in the USA and Mifid in the EU. Writing in 2010 Jeremy Grant divided these forces into three, making competition a separate category, rather than a product of the other two:

> Change is being driven by a cocktail of three things: regulation, competition and technology. Regulation has created competition between exchanges and new platforms in cash equities—such as Chi-X and BATS—leading to fragmentation and a battle for market share. At the same time that has led to complexity. Technology is now vital to navigate multiple markets, be they exchanges or 'dark pools', where larger orders are handled with prices posted after trades are done.[71]

Underlying these developments were the forces of global integration and the responses of individual stock exchanges in the face of the challenges and opportunities being created.

[69] Jennifer Hughes, 'Revolution in the cosy world of bonds', 1st March 2010.
[70] Aline van Duyn, Michael Mackenzie and Jeremy Grant, 'That sinking feeling', 2nd June 2010.
[71] Jeremy Grant, 'Market structures face test of trust', 3rd November 2010.

There was no sign that the financial crisis had forced a change of direction, persuaded regulators to adopt different views, or altered the shape of the industry. Instead, what emerged was that the forces for change that pre-dated the crisis were having a cumulative impact by 2010, and one that was not predicted by those who had tried to shape the equity markets.

The forced disclosure of current prices by the stock exchanges, for example, did not lead to competition between them, with the most efficient triumphing, but to the proliferation of alternative electronic platforms. In turn this encouraged the growth of high-frequency traders who used complex mathematical programs and the speed of computer processing to spot profitable opportunities to buy and sell the same stocks on different markets simultaneously, exploiting brief and minute price differences to generate a profit. They relied on the information that was now made publicly available to identify buyers and sellers, anticipate their next moves as they sought to complete a deal, and then adopt a reverse stance and so generate a profit as they bought for a rise or sold for a fall. Though their actions kept prices in line across the different venues, and contributed to liquidity, it also drove volatility because of the selective nature of their activities and the speed and volume at which they traded. These high-frequency traders became expert at slicing up trading into ever-smaller sizes, so as to mask their actions, making it difficult for others to counter their activity. The result was to drive trading away from the regulated exchanges where there was a requirement for immediate transparency. Instead asset managers placed large orders with their brokers, giving them the discretion to carry out the transaction in such a way that their identity was kept secret until completion. This was done using a dark pool, which undermined both the depth of the market and the reliability of the prices that stock exchanges had long provided, as so much buying and selling took place on other venues.

These developments were generally attributed to the transformation of the technology of trading rather than the impact of regulation. The US flash crash, for example, which took place on 6th May 2010, was blamed on technology rather than the regulation. Jeremy Grant described it as the product of 'a technological revolution that has allowed trading at almost the speed of light, combined with fragmentation of trading across multiple kinds of venues'. This had 'produced a sequence of events that turned the US equity markets into a dangerous quagmire last week'.[72] There had certainly been a transformation of the technology of trading which observers were quick to pick up on. Jeremy Grant and Michael Mackenzie had reported in 2010 that 'Advances in technology have been so great in the past five years that markets are now overwhelmingly driven by machines rather than humans punching orders into a keyboard.'[73] Jeremy Grant was also impressed by the fact that 'Today's stock markets are overwhelmingly governed by mathematical algorithms programmed to jump in and out of markets almost at the speed of light, in a frenzied search for trades that yield a quick profit',[74] while for Michael Mackenzie it was the speed of trading that amazed him: 'Today, equities are transacted in microseconds or 1,000 times faster than the human eye can blink.'[75] Sharing their views was Adam Thomson, who reported that 'Algorithmic trading is fast becoming an influential form of trading around the world.'[76] An estimate for 2010 suggested that over 30 per cent of trading on Deutsche Börse and the LSE was accounted for by high-frequency traders while the figure for the USA was twice that, at 60 per cent. As

[72] Jeremy Grant, 'Plunge places focus on safety of the share markets', 11th May 2010.
[73] Jeremy Grant and Michael Mackenzie, 'Ghost in the machine', 18th February 2010.
[74] Jeremy Grant, '"Algo-trading" changes speed of the game on Wall Street', 8th May 2010.
[75] Michael Mackenzie, 'Regulators push technology to track trades in real time', 29th September 2010.
[76] Adam Thomson, 'Mexican Exchange set for IPO surge', 7th May 2010.

Jeremy Grant noted, high-frequency traders (HFT) were able 'to dip automatically in and out of markets hundreds of times faster than the blink of a human eye'.[77]

Important as this impact of technology had been it was not the main cause of the fragmentation of markets and the role that gave to high-frequency traders. The same technology could either direct orders from a single centre to multiple locations or from multiple locations to a single centre. There existed a standard communication language for the financial community making it easier to access markets from a distance, for example. Traditionally, the forces leading to concentration were the stronger, as buyers and sellers favoured those markets where the ability to complete a transaction in the fastest time and at the current price was the greatest. It was these forces that had always drawn trading to those stock exchanges that commanded the deepest pool of liquidity for the stocks that they quoted, even when alternatives were available. For that reason the duopoly of Nasdaq and the NYSE dominated the US equity market as each provided a trading venue for a specific list of stocks. Elsewhere in the world each national stock exchange provided the market for its own country's corporate stocks, as they provided the most liquid market. As the barriers to the international trading of corporate stocks were removed, the technology of trading and communication channelled orders from around the world to these exchanges, because that was where the most liquid market and the most up-to-date prices were found. This can be seen if the example of NYSE Euronext is examined. By 2010 NYSE Euronext was a global business controlling stock exchanges in both the USA and Europe. Rather than merging these into a single electronic platform they operated two, as each served a separate component of the global equity market. The one in Europe catered for the trading in European stocks while that in the USA met the needs of North America. Though the North American one was located in New Jersey, close to the NYSE's head office in Wall Street, that in Europe was not in Paris, from where Euronext was run. Instead it was sited close to the City of London, which was Europe's financial centre, as that was where the greatest concentration of those who used its market were to be found.

Dispersion was driven not by technology but by the location of the cluster of users. Reinforcing this conclusion was the importance of co-location. The high-frequency traders paid to place their computers adjacent to those serving the exchanges, such was the importance of being closest to the most liquid market. Despite the revolution in technology it remained important to be close to the centre of liquidity and this dictated concentration of trading not fragmentation as a single integrated global equity market did not exist. Instead, there were a series of strongly interconnected pools, which were increasingly accessible from around the world by the megabanks and megafunds. The US company, Liquidnet, for example, recognized this and operated separate dark pools in thirty-eight different markets around the world in order to provide trading facilities tailored to meet the specific needs of each. What regulatory intervention did was to split trading in the same corporate stocks to the detriment of liquidity and to the benefit of high-frequency traders who could trade between the different venues. As they traded in the same stocks in the same countries and in the same currencies the only variable that mattered was the price, and by taking advantage of momentary differences, reflecting localized supply and demand conditions, they could buy and sell or sell and buy for an immediate gain and little risk as their exposure was restricted to the milliseconds it took to complete the transaction. This made the activities of high-frequency traders a product of the fragmentation of a single market, which

[77] Jeremy Grant, 'Up Against a Bandsaw', 3rd September 2010.

resulted from regulatory intervention rather than being the inevitable consequence of the revolution in trading technology.

This conclusion is supported by what was happening generally in the world. The removal of protection along national boundaries imperilled the survival of many smaller stock exchanges as trading drained away to those that could provide a more liquid market. This left these smaller exchanges with a number of choices. One was to merge with other exchanges in the same country, and so combine separate pools of liquidity into a single market. This had already been done in many countries around the world but it continued to face obstacles where exchanges retained the mutual structure. When controlled by its members narrow self-interest dictated the policy followed by each exchange, which made mergers difficult as not all gained as a result. Many individual members lost out in a merger, as they lacked economies of scale, while those that were part of larger groups gained, as they could afford the investment in expensive technology and highly-paid staff. By 2010 the momentum behind demutualization was well established, according to Tom Burgis, and this removed a major obstacle to domestic mergers:

> From Brazil's Bovespa to Bursa Malaysia numerous exchanges have either demutualised or are planning to, spurred on by the prospect of a profit-driven exchange investing in better systems and bolstering international credibility. Another temptation is the potentially sizeable windfall for members who convert their mutual ownership into part of the equity in a newly-listed exchange and float the rest.[78]

Even after such a merger many exchanges remained small because of the limited size of their domestic market. Rather than face a slow erosion of trading to a bigger exchange located in a major financial centre, an option was to seek to become bigger by attracting both investors and corporate issues from abroad, with one feeding off the other. One exchange that accomplished this was that in Hong Kong, but it had the advantage of access to the Chinese market. By 2010 Chinese companies accounted for almost 60 per cent of the market capitalization of the Hong Kong Stock Exchange. In the words of Charles Li, the chief executive of Hong Kong Exchanges and Clearing, 'Our market is no longer an isolated one.'[79] Another possibility was for a smaller exchange to link up with one of those located in the likes of New York, London, Tokyo, Frankfurt, or Paris, benefiting from becoming part of an international group able to share technology, expertise, and business. In 2010 both the Warsaw and the Qatar Exchange, for example, adopted NYSE Euronext's 'universal trading platform.'[80] This was all part of what Jeremy Grant described in 2010 as the 'battle between global exchanges.'[81] The likes of NYSE Euronext, Nasdaq OMX, Deutsche Börse, the London and Tokyo stock exchanges all sought to bolster their own position by establishing alliances around the world.

However, what was taking place was much less rivalry between exchanges than competition between each exchange and alternative trading platforms, which Jeremy Grant observed in 2010: 'Exchanges now compete not only with each other for their order flow but also with bank and broker networks, including dark pools.'[82] Regulatory intervention

[78] Tom Burgis, 'Difficulties of listing a prized asset come to the fore', 24th August 2010.
[79] Tom Mitchell, 'HK exchange seeks to align trading hours with mainland', 12th August 2010.
[80] Jeremy Grant, 'Emerging markets dump old trading habits', 9th September 2010.
[81] Jeremy Grant, 'NYSE Euronext to set up clearing houses in London and Paris', 12th May 2010.
[82] Jeremy Grant, 'Up Against a Bandsaw', 3rd September 2010.

not only removed the quasi-official support that stock exchanges had once enjoyed but also undermined their natural immunity from competition. Stock exchanges were forced to cede access to current prices and other trading information that had previously acted as a magnet, drawing in orders from the wider financial community and so creating the liquid markets and reliable prices that attracted further business. To many this concentration of trading in stock exchanges could only be explained by the enforcement of anti-competitive rules and regulations, which benefited the members of exchanges, and later their owners, and disadvantaged their users. By breaking these restrictive practices, competition between different venues, including stock exchanges, would be stimulated, which would bring down charges and make the market more efficient. By 2010 Jeremy Grant reported on the consequences it had, especially high-frequency trading (HFT): 'Such fragmentation has been a driving force behind the growth of HFT, since it produces a variety of trading venues each with slightly different trading systems, speeds and fee schedules. This allows traders to exploit these differences by using computer algorithms to trade back and forth from one platform to another.'[83] In the USA high-frequency trading rose from 21 per cent of equity turnover in 2005 to 61 per cent in 2009.

These US rules were then taken up in Europe, under the Market in Financial Instruments Directive (Mifid). They provided a simple model to be followed by those seeking to replicate for the EU the integrated equity market in operation in the USA. What had happened was that regulations designed to eliminate national barriers in the European equity market had been combined with those introduced in the USA to break the duopoly of Nasdaq and the NYSE. As Michel Barnier, the EU commissioner with responsibility for the internal market, explained in 2010: 'We're not saying that everything that happens in America has to be directly applicable in Europe, but I don't think we should ignore the fact that there is a certain "parallelism".'[84] Under Mifid each member state of the EU was required to remove the barriers that gave each national stock exchange a monopoly of its domestic market. The assumption made was this monopoly was a product of the application of national rules and regulations and not the existence of separate pools of liquidity reflecting investor preference for the stocks of national companies. There was no acceptance that underlying conditions in the EU, let alone within Europe as a whole, did not mirror those of the USA, because of long-standing and fundamental divisions that could only be slowly overcome. Following on from that attitude it was an easy step to copy the other aspects of the US regulations that focused on driving through greater competition in the interests of delivering a better service and lower charges to investors. The consequence of Mifid was thus not the creation of a single European equity market, because trading remained divided along national lines, as that was where the deepest single pools of liquidity were. Instead, the result was the same as in the USA with existing pools of liquidity being fractured. One of the most successful of these was Chi-X, which targeted stocks listed by the LSE, and could undercut its charges because of its lower cost base. In 2010 the LSE employed 150 compliance staff while Chi-X had only five.

The conclusion drawn by Jeremy Grant in 2010 was that in both the USA and Europe, 'the end of exchanges' monopolies has fragmented liquidity, lowered costs and paved the way for "high-frequency" traders'.[85] That left regulators with the problem of how to cope with the reshaping of the global equity market that their own intervention, along with the

[83] Jeremy Grant, 'Up Against a Bandsaw', 3rd September 2010.
[84] Nikki Tait, Jeremy Hall and Javier Blas, 'EU to rein in commodity speculation', 21st September 2010.
[85] Jeremy Grant, 'Chi-X's pan-Asian plans may include HK and Seoul platforms', 13th April 2010.

revolution in technology, had accomplished. Until then regulators had largely relied on stock exchanges to police their own markets under the overall authority of a regulatory agency. The fragmentation of markets and the huge increase in trading, especially from a small number of computer-driven high-speed traders, meant that exchanges could no longer be relied upon to monitor activity and exercise discipline, but the regulatory agencies lacked the staff and the expertise to replace them, including even the SEC in the USA. This was an issue demanding serious attention because of the disappearance of trading into dark pools and the loss of control by exchanges was undermining trust among investors in the quality of the market and the reliability of the publicly available prices. Above all investors required the guarantee that corporate stocks could always be bought and sold, and be valued at prices that could be relied upon. If not, they were no different from securitized assets reliant on OTC markets and the willingness of investment banks to ensure that they could be traded. Though these concerns were confined to regulators in the USA and the EU in 2010 those located elsewhere in the world were conscious that they would have to address them in the near future, because of irresistible tide of alternative platforms and high-frequency traders that had been unleashed.[86]

Driving so many of the changes taking place globally was the example of the USA. It was there that high-frequency trading made a steady advance unaffected by the crisis, reaching a 61 per cent share in 2009. The SEC did not know how to respond to these high-frequency traders as they brought both benefits and disadvantages to the equity market, according to Jeremy Grant in 2010: 'Regulators acknowledge that such traders can improve prices for investors but also question whether their short-term horizons are beneficial in markets still

[86] Michael Mackenzie, Francesco Guerrera, and Gillian Tett, 'A course to chart', 4th January 2010; Sam Jones, 'Alert over short-selling disclosure rules', 9th February 2010; Jeremy Grant and Michael Mackenzie, 'Ghost in the machine', 18th February 2010; Jeremy Grant, 'New tools in race for trading speed', 19th February 2010; Jennifer Hughes, 'Revolution in the cosy world of bonds', 1st March 2010; Michael Mackenzie, 'SEC's new rules threaten liquidity critics warn', 3rd March 2010; Lina Saigol, 'Confidence Rises', 18th March 2010; Jeremy Grant, 'Chi-X's pan-Asian plans may include HK and Seoul platforms', 13th April 2010; Jeremy Grant, 'LSE changes tariffs to attract high-frequency traders', 21st April 2010; Jeremy Grant, 'Africa's first dark pool created on JSE', 22nd April 2010; Adam Thomson, 'Mexican Exchange set for IPO surge', 7th May 2010; Jeremy Grant, '"Algo-trading" changes speed of the game on Wall Street', 8th May 2010; Michael Mackenzie and Jeremy Grant, 'Warnings on systemic market risk', 10th May 2010; Jeremy Grant, 'Plunge places focus on safety of the share markets', 11th May 2010; Jeremy Grant, 'NYSE Euronext to set up clearing houses in London and Paris', 12th May 2010; Michael Mackenzie, '"Flash glitch" fears force SEC hand', 13th May 2010; Kevin Brown and Christian Oliver, 'Seoul warms to naked short selling', 13th May 2010; Jeremy Grant, 'Trust in Dark Pools is dented', 26th May 2010; Jennifer Hughes, 'Europe dithers over adopting Germany's short selling ban', 27th May 2010; Joe Leahy, 'India Plans short-selling move', 28th May 2010; *FT* Global 500, 29th May 2010; Tom Burgis, 'Brokers Resist Nigerian Watchdog', 8th June 2010; Henny Sender, 'Short measures', 9th July 2010; Jeremy Grant, 'Paris dealt blow over London platform', 15th July 2010; Jeremy Grant, 'Emerging markets lure big exchanges', 28th July 2010; Tom Mitchell, 'HK exchange seeks to align trading hours with mainland', 12th August 2010; Tom Burgis, 'Difficulties of listing a prized asset come to the fore', 24th August 2010; Jeremy Grant, 'Dutch lift lid on a high-frequency universe', 26th August 2010; Jeremy Grant, 'Up Against a Bandsaw', 3rd September 2010; Jeremy Grant, 'Emerging markets dump old trading habits', 9th September 2010; Jeremy Grant, 'High-frequency traders battle to make big returns', 10th September 2010; Jeremy Grant, 'OMX plans new platform', 20th September 2010; Nikki Tait, Jeremy Hall and Javier Blas, 'EU to rein in commodity speculation', 21st September 2010; Jeremy Grant, 'Light speed ahead', 27th September 2010; Michael Mackenzie, 'Regulators push technology to track trades in real time', 29th September 2010; Tom Burgis, 'Regulator intends to shake up the bourse', 30th September 2010; Aline van Duyn and Telis Demos, 'Flash Crash: market reforms to be examined', 5th October 2010; Robert Cookson, 'HK eclipses rivals as the place to list', 7th October 2010; Jeremy Grant, 'Call to make dark pools trades public', 28th October 2010; Jeremy Grant, 'Market structures face test of trust', 3rd November 2010; Jeremy Grant, 'Regulators face uphill battle as dark pools grow murkier', 3rd November 2010; Philip Stafford, 'High-speed electronic trading leaves regulator far behind', 3rd November 2010; Jeremy Grant, 'Super-fast traders pose risk to clearers', 1st December 2010; Philip Stafford and Nikki Tait, 'Europe moves against super-fast traders', 9th December 2011; Telis Demos and Aline van Duyn, 'Debate reopens over equity trades', 21st December 2010; Jeremy Grant, 'Liquidnet in talks with stock exchanges', 30th December 2010.

dominated by investors with longer-term views.'[87] Under these circumstances they held back from intervention. Increasingly the stock exchanges were unwilling to police the US equity market because the costs involved and the restrictions imposed made them uncompetitive compared to the alternative platforms. These alternative platforms had no interest in policing the market as they confined themselves to providing a service as cheaply and efficiently as possible. That left the likes of the SEC to regulate the equity market but they could do little more than set out the broad parameters, focusing on investor protection, as they had neither the expertise nor capacity to exercise day-to-day control, which had always been left to the stock exchanges. There did exist the US Financial Industry Regulatory Authority (FINRA), which monitored activity on the smaller stock exchanges, and in 2010 the NYSE turned over market supervision to it, effectively ending the era when each stock exchange regulated itself. By then the NYSE accounted for less than 35 per cent of the trading in NYSE listed stocks. This raised concerns not only over the policing of the market but also over whether there was sufficient depth of liquidity required to ensure that shares could always be bought and sold and whether the publicly available prices were an accurate reflection of supply and demand.[88]

Following closely behind developments in the USA were those in Europe where, in the words of Jeremy Grant in 2010, Mifid had broken 'the national monopolies of Europe's established exchanges and allowed upstart platforms such as Chi-X to emerge. Most were backed by banks and brokers that were the biggest providers of orders to the exchanges. Yet the exchanges' monopoly positions meant that they had little incentive to cut fees or improve trading technology—frustrating the banks.'[89] Bolstering this monopoly position was control over clearing and settlement for those exchanges operating the vertical-silo model. However, the continuing fracturing of the market meant that, according to Jeremy Grant in 2010, 'No single exchange now sees all the activity on any given stock for which they are responsible.'[90] By 2010 Chi-X had captured 25 per cent of trading in the LSE's FTSE 100 stocks and 20 per cent of Deutsche Börse's Dax index stocks though only 1 per cent of the equivalent in Spain. Regulators remained concerned that Europe's 'equities markets are saddled with post-trade costs—mainly clearing and settlement—that can be up to eight times higher than those in the US'[91] in the opinion of Jeremy Grant in 2010. The solution they preferred was the use of the Europe-wide clearing houses along the lines of the DTCC in the USA, but this raised the issue of such an institution abusing its monopoly and imposing high charges, and the question of what would happen if it collapsed. No European

[87] Jeremy Grant, 'High-frequency traders facing tracking reform', 8th April 2010.

[88] Jeremy Grant, 'Computer-driven trading boom raises meltdown fears', 26th January 2010; Jeremy Grant, 'High-speed traders seek bigger profile', 4th February 2010; Michael Mackenzie, 'Getco to become market maker at NYSE', 12th February 2010; Jeremy Grant, 'Smaller orders breed dark pools and higher post-trade costs', 22nd February 2010; Hal Weitzman, 'BATS squeezes into crowded world of US equity options', 26th February 2010; Michael Mackenzie and Jeremy Grant, 'Liffe proves its worth to NYSE', 4th March 2010; Jeremy Grant, 'High-frequency traders facing tracking reform', 8th April 2010; Jeremy Grant, 'LSE changes tariffs to attract high-frequency traders', 21st April 2010; Brooke Masters, 'Finra to watch over NYSE Euronext', 5th May 2010; Jeremy Grant, '"Algo-trading" changes speed of the game on Wall Street', 8th May 2010; Michael Mackenzie and Jeremy Grant, 'Warnings on systemic market risk', 10th May 2010; Jeremy Grant, 'Plunge places focus on safety of the share markets', 11th May 2010; Aline van Duyn, Michael Mackenzie, and Jeremy Grant, 'That sinking feeling', 2nd June 2010; Michael Mackenzie, 'Frozen in Time', 16th June 2010; Michael Mackenzie, 'Flaws in share system are exposed', 18th June 2010; David Gelles, 'New Stock on the Bloc', 29th October 2010; David Gelles and Kara Scannell, 'SEC probes US secondary market', 29th December 2010; Dan McCrum, 'BlackRock trading platform plan set to hit Wall St profit centres', 29th December 2010.

[89] Jeremy Grant, 'BATS seen as likely Chi-X suitor', 25th August 2010.

[90] Jeremy Grant, 'Multiple venues leave Europe "open to abuse"', 7th April 2010.

[91] Jeremy Grant, 'Lack of coherence on clearing reform', 9th April 2010.

central bank was willing to act as lender of last resort to such an institution. Regulators were also having to devise a response to the increasingly important role played by the high-frequency traders, which Petr Koblic, the head of the Prague Stock Exchange, regarded as 'opportunistic cherry-pickers'.[92] Making the task far more difficult than in the USA was the continuing support given to national stock exchanges by national governments despite the introduction of Mifid. Spain's Bolsas y Mercados Espanoles BME) was able to maintain a domestic stranglehold not only because it operated the vertical model but through the Spanish government frustrating the efforts of the EU to apply Mifid in its country.[93]

Though the global equity market continued to lack a single pool of liquidity by 2010, despite the technological advances and regulatory intervention, there was a steady drift of trading in the largest corporate stocks to an exchange located in one of the major financial centres, as that was where the megabanks and megafunds were clustered. The main beneficiaries of this were Nasdaq and the NYSE in the USA, though they continued to suffer from the Sarbanes–Oxley legislation, along with the LSE in the UK. Among mining companies, for example, the TMX in Canada was a magnet for those at the exploration stage. The problem for most stock exchanges was that they continued to lack the depth and breadth that would provide the level of liquidity demanded by the megabanks and megafunds, especially in the wake of the financial crisis. In the Middle East, for example, there was a proliferation of exchanges, often enjoying government support, and each providing a market for the shares of local companies.[94] Latin America was in a similar position with many of the exchanges limited to catering for the shares of a few local companies, which were closely held and

[92] Jeremy Grant, 'Prague Exchange slams speed trades', 21st October 2010.

[93] Masa Serdarevic, 'Sungard offers access to exchanges', 22nd January 2010; William MacNamara, Miles Johnson, and Matthew Kennard, 'Hong Kong vies with London for IPO supremacy', 27th January 2010; Jeremy Grant and Masa Serdarevic, 'LSE contemplates acquiring Dutch clearer to diversify away from the UK', 30th January 2010; Steve Johnson, 'UK plan to open up bond trade', 1st February 2010; Jeremy Grant, 'High-speed traders seek bigger profile', 4th February 2010; Jeremy Grant, 'Nasdaq renews European efforts', 8th February 2010; Jeremy Grant, 'Europe's post trade dilemma', 10th February 2010; Jeremy Grant, 'Chi-X becomes second largest Europe bourse', 11th February 2010; Mark Mulligan, 'Spanish bourse weighs up reform', 16th February 2010; Anousha Sakoui, 'Hunt for yield boosts retail demand', 25th February 2010; Jennifer Hughes, 'Revolution in the cosy world of bonds', 1st March 2010; Jeremy Grant and James Wilson, 'Private investors fail to see benefits of Mifid reform', 8th March 2010; Mark Mulligan, 'Spanish exchange brushes aside fears', 30th March 2010; Jan Cienski, 'Warsaw seeks partner to revamp bourse', 30th March 2010; Jeremy Grant, 'Multiple venues leave Europe "open to abuse"', 7th April 2010; Jeremy Grant, 'Lack of coherence on clearing reform', 9th April 2010; Anousha Sakoui, 'Rising foreign ownership could be good for the Footsie', 10th April 2010; Jeremy Grant, 'Chi-X's pan-Asian plans may include HK and Seoul platforms', 13th April 2010; Nikki Tait and Jeremy Grant, 'Greater clarity on equity trades urged', 14th April 2010; Jeremy Grant, 'Platforms to trade US shares in Europe', 15th April 2010; Jeremy Grant, 'Share trades in blink of an eye just got faster', 20th April 2010; Jeremy Grant, 'LSE changes tariffs to attract high-frequency traders', 21st April 2010; Jeremy Grant, 'Nasdaq OMX to close Europe arm', 29th April 2010; Jeremy Grant, 'Low volumes hurt new trading venues', 4th May 2010; Aline van Duyn, Michael Mackenzie, and Jeremy Grant, 'That sinking feeling', 2nd June 2010; Chris Bryant and Jan Cienski, 'Old Stager has yet to make a comeback', 7th July 2010; Chris Bryant, Jan Cienski, and Jeremy Grant, 'Warsaw and Vienna vie for listings', 16th July 2010; Jeremy Grant, 'Apathy hinders regional exchanges', 26th July 2010; Jeremy Grant and Nikki Tait, 'Europe set for overhaul of rules on share dealing', 30th July 2010; Jeremy Grant, 'LSE's Turquoise heading into profit', 9th August 2010; Jeremy Grant, 'BATS seen as likely Chi-X suitor', 25th August 2010; Victor Mallet, 'Spanish plan to rival BME', 25th August 2010; Jeremy Grant, 'LSE bid to build clearing house', 18th September 2010; Nikki Tait, Jeremy Hall, and Javier Blas, 'EU to rein in commodity speculation', 21st September 2010; Jeremy Grant, 'London "No 1" for trading speed', 12th October 2010; Jeremy Grant, 'Prague Exchange slams speed trades', 21st October 2010; Jeremy Grant, Philip Stafford, and Miles Johnson, 'Police called after LSE platform is knocked out', 4th November 2010; Philip Stafford, 'BATS and Chi-X eye new landscape', 24th December 2010.

[94] Simeon Kerr, 'Nasdaq Dubai blow as DP World looks to London', 7th January 2010; Tobias Buck, 'Push to raise Palestinian bourse's profile', 17th March 2010; Simeon Kerr, Andrew England, and Jeremy Grant, 'Dubai talks to Abu Dhabi over bourse merger', 31st March 2010; Jeremy Grant, Simeon Kerr, and Andrew England, 'Nasdaq and LSE wait for shifting sands to settle', 1st April 2010; Robin Wigglesworth, 'Saudi Bourse poised to exercise more global appeal', 2nd September 2010; Delphine Strauss, 'Istanbul embraces algo trading', 1st November 2010.

little traded. It was only in Brazil and Mexico that the stock exchange was of a size to support liquid stocks.[95] In Africa the Johannesburg Stock Exchange (JSE) struggled to hold onto the market for those stocks most in demand by international investors, especially those of the big mining companies as London, Sydney, and Toronto could provide a more attractive market in terms of liquidity. The JSE was being punished for the legacy of exchange controls and restrictive regulations that had limited outside access and so left its market too small to support trading in the shares of its largest companies.[96]

The smaller countries of South-East Asia did recognize their weakness in an age of global integration and attempted to create a single market for the leading stocks. However, they faced major technical, currency, clearing, and settlement problems. There was also a culture of protectionism across Asia that resisted any challenge to national stock exchanges whether it came from alternative trading platforms and dark pools or external competition. This continued to apply in Japan, where the dominant position it occupied meant there was little pressure on the Tokyo Stock Exchange (TSE) to change. Plans to float the TSE as a public company were delayed yet again in 2010, leaving the members firmly in control.[97] The Australian Stock Exchange (ASX) also had a monopoly of trading in Australian equities but in 2010 the government gave permission for competitors to establish their own operations, with Chi-X, owned by Nomura, quick to seize the opportunity. However, the Australian government also intervened in 2010 to prevent the takeover of ASX by the Singapore Exchange. This protectionist attitude shown by the Australian government towards its national exchange was a general feature of the entire Asia-Pacific region. The Securities and Exchange Board of India made it difficult for the existing stock exchanges to be challenged, for example, especially by alternative platforms and dark pools. In China change was also limited with competition there was being confined to the rivalry between Shanghai and Shenzhen stock exchanges for new listings of Chinese companies.[98] By the

[95] John Paul Rathbone, 'Investors require patience more than nimble financial footwork', 6th April 2010; Adam Thomson, 'Mexican Exchange set for IPO surge', 7th May 2010; Naomi Mapstone, 'Andean trio plan market alliance', 3rd November 2010; Vincent Bevins, 'Caution and tough regulation are all-weather assets', 15th November 2010.

[96] William MacNamara, Miles Johnson, and Matthew Kennard, 'Hong Kong vies with London for IPO supremacy', 27th January 2010; Richard Lapper, 'Jo'burg starts to warm up', 19th March 2010; Bernard Simon, 'Toronto Exchange in drive to attract Chinese investors', 13th April 2010; Richard Lapper, 'Exchange held back by apartheid-era regulations', 21st April 2010; Jeremy Grant, 'Africa's first dark pool created on JSE', 22nd April 2010; Tom Burgis, 'Brokers Resist Nigerian Watchdog', 8th June 2010; Tom Burgis, 'Nigeria plans to take bourse public', 24th August 2010; Tom Burgis, 'Regulator intends to shake up the bourse', 30th September 2010.

[97] Lindsay Whipp, 'TSE seeks boost to trade from launch of new platform', 4th January 2010; Lindsay Whipp, 'Arrowhead will take time to hit target for TSE', 11th January 2010; Lindsay Whipp, 'Japan urged to stimulate IPOs with tax breaks', 8th February 2010; Lindsay Whipp, 'Ambitions to recapture its glory days', 8th February 2010; Kevin Brown, 'Asian Traders warm to dark pool benefits', 4th March 2010; Jeremy Grant, 'Rolet hits at "uneven field"', 30th March 2010; Lindsay Whipp, 'Tokyo weighs up longer trading days', 27th July 2010.

[98] Lindsay Whipp, 'TSE seeks boost to trade from launch of new platform', 4th January 2010; Lindsay Whipp, 'Arrowhead will take time to hit target for TSE', 11th January 2010; Robert Cookson, 'Short selling opens doors in China', 12th January 2010; Joe Leahy, 'Mumbai exchanges join rush for faster trading', 12th January 2010; Lindsay Whipp, 'Japan urged to stimulate IPOs with tax breaks', 8th February 2010; Lindsay Whipp, 'Ambitions to recapture its glory days', 8th February 2010; Kevin Brown, 'Single Asean market a step closer', 9th February 2010; Kevin Brown, 'Asian Traders warm to dark pool benefits', 4th March 2010; Jeremy Grant, 'Rolet hits at "uneven field"', 30th March 2010; Robert Cookson, 'Beijing gears up for key reforms on equity trades', 30th March 2010; Jeremy Grant, 'Chi-X's pan-Asian plans may include HK and Seoul platforms', 13th April 2010; Kevin Brown, 'Move towards single Asean exchange', 23rd April 2010; Kevin Brown, 'Malaysia bourse plans derivatives boost', 28th April 2010; Kevin Brown, 'Tora plans pan-Asian "dark pool"', 2nd June 2010; Jeremy Grant and Kevin Brown, 'Asian Exchanges in competitive overhaul', 4th June 2010; Lindsay Whipp, Kevin Brown and Robert Cookson, 'Asia takes dip in "dark pools"', 9th June 2010; Lindsay Whipp, 'Tokyo weighs up longer trading days', 27th July 2010; Tom Mitchell, 'HK exchange seeks to align trading hours with mainland', 12th August 2010; Joe Leahy, 'Proposed new Indian stock exchange "not fit and proper"', 27th September 2010; Joe Leahy, 'Aspirant Indian

end of 2010 the pace and pattern of developments in the global equity market owed little to what had happened during the financial crisis or even the reaction to it that had followed. Instead, it was a resumption of the changes already set in motion by RegNMS in the USA followed by what had taken place in the EU, which built on it. The effects of these changes had a profound effect of the equity market of both the USA and EU but were only slowly pervading the rest of the world.

Continuity and Change, 2011–20

The legacy of the crisis was to make investors wary, for a time, of assets lacking a liquid market. Increasingly investors looked for assets that combined high returns with liquidity and found it among the range of equities quoted on stock exchanges. Among large asset managers equities retained their popularity, comprising 41 per cent of pension fund holdings in 2011, which was the same as in 1999. What became increasingly popular among retail investors after the crisis were Exchange Traded Funds (ETFs). The most common of these provided investors with access to a diversified portfolio of corporate stocks that matched an index, while possessing the characteristics of an individual holding as they were quoted on a stock exchange where they could be bought and sold. In 2017 ETFs had $4tn under management compared to $0.6tn in 2006. They proved especially popular in the USA where nearly 40 per cent of equity assets under management were in the hands of ETFs and other index-tracking funds. As Chris Flood wrote in 2018 'Exchange-traded funds are revolutionising stock markets, regularly accounting for a third of all US equity trades and growing rapidly in popularity among equity investors in Europe and Asia.'[99] In contrast, the financial crisis made only a limited impact on the structure of the global equity market, as that continued to be dictated by the trends in technology, globalization, and regulatory intervention that predated it. These trends raised issues relating to coping with market fragmentation, the effects of high-frequency trading, and the differing pace and extent of change around the world. As with the situation before the financial crisis it was developments within the USA, followed closely by the EU, that drove change either by example or through competition.[100]

bourse fights regulator', 1st October 2010; Robert Cookson, 'HK eclipses rivals as the place to list', 7th October 2010; Robert Cookson, 'Shenzhen takes over as China's listing hub', 19th October 2010; Peter Smith and Jeremy Grant, 'SGX set to make A$6bn bid for ASX', 23rd October 2010; Jeremy Grant and Peter Smith, 'SGX offers premium for ASX', 25th October 2010; Kevin Brown, Jeremy Grant, and Peter Smith, 'Canberra "key" on SGX bid for ASX', 26th October 2010; Kevin Brown, 'Singapore's offer sparks talk of Asia consolidation', 2nd November 2010; Kevin Brown, 'Region in flux as bourses fragment', 3rd November 2010; Jeremy Grant, 'Market structures face test of trust', 3rd November 2010.

[99] Chris Flood, 'Liquidity enables big ticket trades', 18th June 2018.

[100] David Gelles, 'Approval for Xpert as private company shares exchange', 4th January 2011; James Mawson, 'Fears grow over long-term investment', 9th May 2011; Michael Mackenzie and Nicole Bullock, 'Push-button perils, Richard Milne', 6th June 2011; Jeremy Grant, 'Automation is "strangling" small caps', 30th November 2011; David Oakley, 'Switch to bonds signals end for cult of equity', 20th November 2012; Michael Mackenzie, Dan McCrum, and Tracy Alloway, 'Electronic trading set to muscle in on corporate debt', 4th April 2013; Deborah Fuhr, 'Happy anniversary—but challenges lie ahead', 2nd February 2015; John Authers and Chris Newlands, 'Taking over the markets', 6th December 2016; Robin Wigglesworth, 'Brutal culls ensure the ETF graveyard is full', 15th December 2016; Charles D Ellis, 'Technology and low returns: the end for active investing?', 21st January 2017; Robin Wigglesworth, 'ETFs and index-trackers coin it in with 20% share of US bond market', 6th February 2017; Chris Flood, 'Active management is not dead', 4th September 2017; Jennifer Thompson, 'Regulators descend on booming market', 11th September 2017; Ian Smith, 'Could ETFs survive a sudden downturn in the market?', 14th October 2017; Chris Flood, 'Global assets to sell to $145tn by 2015', 30th October 2017; Chris Flood, 'Global

Among those developments, one of the most significant was the simultaneous concentration and fragmentation of the global equity market. From the perspective of institutional investors they had the world to choose from. The 320,000 Bloomberg terminals spread around the world provided instant information and access to national equity markets. With business becoming increasingly international so did the ownership of the companies conducting it. Global investors chased capital gains and high yields regardless of nationality, but now ever mindful of the importance of liquidity. The most liquid market for most corporate stocks was, in normal circumstances, found in each national stock exchange, as that was where the largest cluster of investors was to be found, even with the increasing diffusion of ownership. Nevertheless, as ownership of the world's largest companies moved into the hands of global fund managers the trading of their stocks had a tendency to concentrate where they were located, once a critical mass was established. This favoured financial centres such as London and New York because they contained the offices of so many of the world's banks and fund managers, from where buying and selling was directed. In turn these centres could provide the deep and broad markets that banks and fund managers looked for after the crisis, due to concerns over liquidity. In dual listed stocks, for example, most trading gravitated to a particular exchange rather than being distributed among all those where they were quoted. Banks and fund managers sought out the most liquid markets and concentrated their buying and selling there, which made them even more liquid and so enhanced their appeal. The technology of communication favoured this clustering of trading as there continued to be a delay in communication, though it was now infinitesimal. As Peter Knapp, the managing director of Interxion, a data management group, stated bluntly in 2011, 'If I have a service which is 2.5 milliseconds and the other guy has 2.6 milliseconds, I will get the deal.'[101]

However, what was taking place within a number of countries was market fragmentation as incumbent exchanges lost out to alternative venues due to regulatory intervention. This fragmentation undermined the quality of the market as it deprived those buying and selling shares of the depth necessary to conduct a trade quickly, without affecting the current price. As Alasdair Haynes, the chief executive of Aquis Exchange, a share trading venue in London, put it in 2019, 'Splitting up liquidity is poor for the end-investor.'[102] This concern for liquidity waxed and waned in the years after 2010, surfacing whenever issues over the resilience of banks and investment funds arose. A false belief grew up that listing corporate securities made them liquid, unlike those assets which lacked a public market. However, there were huge differences between the liquidity of the stocks issued by large companies, and traded on major stock exchanges, compared to those of small enterprises listed on small or moribund exchanges. As Andrew Bailey, the chief executive of the UK's Financial Conduct Authority, pointed out in 2019, 'Listing something on an exchange where trading does not actually happen, as far as I can see, does not actually count as liquidity.'[103]

regulator to launch fresh ETF probe', 4th December 2017; Chris Flood, 'Mifid 2 set to stimulate growth in ETFs', 3rd January 2018; Chris Flood, 'Pension fund assets reach a record $41.3tn, up 13 per cent', 5th February 2018; Robin Wigglesworth, 'Exchange traded products face scrutiny as worries deepen', 15th February 2018; Robin Wigglesworth and Joe Rennison, 'The Future of Trading', 10th May 2018; Chris Flood, 'Liquidity enables big ticket trades', 18th June 2018; Robin Wigglesworth, 'Asset managers seek an entrée to the trillion-dollar club', 26th October 2018; Gregory Davis, 'Index funds are not to blame for market volatility', 31st October 2018; Richard Henderson, 'Landmark for exchange traded bond funds as assets crash through $1tn', 24th April 2019.

[101] Ed Hammond, 'Trading floors live on in data centre', 14th June 2011.

[102] Philip Stafford, 'No-deal Brexit share trade ruling sparks accusations of EU land Grab', 21st March 2019.

[103] Caroline Binham, 'Woodford crisis down to flawed rules', 26th June 2019.

However, because of easy access to finance, listed companies shrank in numbers after 2010. As Robert Buckland, an analyst at Citibank, explained in 2019, 'Stock markets are not competitive places to raise capital or sell companies right now. Public equity markets are shrinking because companies can find cheaper capital elsewhere.'[104] Between 2000 and 2018 the number of listed companies in the USA fell from 7000 to 4000 while those that remained often chose to buy back their own shares. Also, many of the companies, and also many of the ETFs, that were listed outside the USA were on exchanges where little trading took place, making them illiquid. Even for those stocks quoted on the world's largest stock exchanges, there were numerous ones that were little traded. Andras Bohak, head of research at the index compilers, MSCI (formerly Morgan Stanley Capital International), pointed this out in 2019: 'You can have companies listed on the London Stock Exchange, but if they are not traded then they are not much better than a non-listed stock.'[105] The result was to create an illusion of liquidity for many corporate stocks that was absent in reality, though regulators continued to put their faith in listing, regardless of the particular stock exchange used or the precise nature of the company.[106]

For those reasons the drift of trading away from the exchanges alarmed regulators, though it was their intervention that was the prime cause. The fragmentation of the equity market reduced the reliability of the publicly available prices and exposed buyers and sellers to greater volatility and even deliberate manipulation. Jeremy Grant and Alex Barber wrote as early as 2011, that 'The fragmentation of equity trading across multiple venues, the growth of "dark pools"—where shares are traded between institutional investors with prices posted publicly only after deals are done—and of "high-frequency" trading, has led regulators to worry that technology has created dangerous market structures that fall outside their scope.'[107] Unless provided with government support stock exchanges had never monopolized national stock markets, though they occupied a dominant position that was particularly marked for those corporate stocks they quoted. However, beginning with RegNMS in the USA and Mifid in the EU, that dominance was steadily undermined.[108] Stock exchanges were not only forbidden to use their rules and regulations to force trading to take place through them, but they were also required to make available current price and other information that had been the exclusive privilege of their members. Taking a

[104] Richard Henderson, 'Shrinking share listings show radical shift to private sphere', 27th June 2019.

[105] Owen Walker, 'UK funds with small-cap weighting at higher risk of liquidity shock', 22nd July 2019.

[106] Andrew Bailey, 'The Woodford episode raises issues for regulators', 10th June 2019; Caroline Binham, 'Woodford crisis down to flawed rules', 26th June 2019; Richard Henderson, 'Shrinking share listings show radical shift to private sphere', 27th June 2019; Jennifer Thompson, 'Assets in European Ucits funds burst through landmark Euro10tn', 1st July 2019; Merryn Somerset Webb, 'A local exchange: an idea whose time has come', 6th July 2019; John Dizard, 'H20 is an omen: a liquidity crisis lurks', 15th July 2019; Owen Walker, 'UK funds with small-cap weighting at higher risk of liquidity shock', 22nd July 2019; Chris Flood, 'EU regulator rejects FCA's criticism', 16th September 2019.

[107] Jeremy Grant and Alex Barber, 'Mifid's net cast wide to overhaul Europe's trading', 21st October 2011.

[108] Jeremy Grant and Telis Demos, 'Growth in off-exchange trade stokes pricing fears', 26th January 2011; Robert Cookson, 'Doubts on Hong Kong secondary listings', 18th May 2011; Ed Hammond, 'Trading floors live on in data centre', 14th June 2011; Janina Conboye, 'Computers create demand for a different set of skills', 14th July 2011; Jeremy Grant, 'Traders cautious on exchanges tie-up', 1st August 2011; Dan McCrum, Alex Barber, Jennifer Hughes, Richard Milne, Peggy Hollinger, and Matthew Steinglass, 'Short-selling ban attacked by academics and investors', 13th August 2011; Jeremy Grant and Alex Barber, 'Mifid's net cast wide to overhaul Europe's trading', 21st October 2011; Maija Palmer, 'Number of UK-listed tech stock dwindles', 14th November 2011; Sophia Grene, 'Securities lending and its many functions', 6th February 2012; Kate Burgess, 'Big British funds cut UK stocks ownership', 13th March 2012; Elaine Moore, 'Keeping tabs on prices triggers knee-jerk reaction', 24th July 2012; Adam Thomson, 'Trading surge brings region together', 14th November 2012; Philip Stafford, 'US still the first choice for IPOs', 14th February 2013; Philip Stafford, 'Deutsche Börse unfurls plan for European champion', 27–28th February 2016; Gregory Meyer, 'US markets braced for trading tax grab', 11th October 2016; Charles D Ellis, 'Technology and low returns: the end for active investing?', 21st January 2017.

reflective view in 2012 Michael Mackenzie, Arash Massoudi, and Stephen Foley pointed out the consequences of regulatory intervention: 'This fragmentation in US markets is largely by design. Five years ago, the Securities and Exchange Commission introduced rules to encourage greater competition and break the grip of the traditional exchanges, making stock trading cheaper and more democratic'.[109] Drawing a similar conclusion in 2014 was Clive Williams, global head of equity trading at the US asset manager, T. Rowe Price. He attributed the changes to 'an unintended consequence of regulation'.[110]

The consequences of those US decisions had implications for the global equity market, as it was US practice that was followed around the world. Combined with the rapid advances in the technology of trading the result was a huge boost to alternative trading venues. As these electronic platforms proliferated they created ideal conditions for high-frequency trading. Specialist high-frequency traders used computer algorithms to seek out pricing and other discrepancies in different markets and then trade high volumes in millionths of seconds using their own capital. They invested heavily in technology and communications so as to gain even a marginal advantage in the market in terms of speed. Using the fastest transatlantic cable, for example, cost $4m a year while that from Chicago to New York was $2m. They also invested in the staff with the necessary expertise. In 2017, according to one expert on the use of quantum computing techniques, Marcos Lopez de Pado, at Berkeley Lab, 'You need to decode markets and find the invisible patterns. The people that do that best have the best models and the most powerful computers. It gives you an edge.'[111] The result of their activities was that between 2005 and 2012 high-frequency trading rose from 21 per cent of the US equities market, by volume of activity, to 53 per cent, while in Europe it grew from 15 to 37 per cent. As the cost of high-frequency trading fell competition between the firms involved intensified as more entered the business. By 2011 the cost of launching a high-frequency service had fallen to $0.2m or less. Where the fragmentation of markets occurred high-speed traders were quick to exploit the opportunities created.[112]

[109] Michael Mackenzie, Arash Massoudi, and Stephen Foley, 'Rage against the machine', 17th October 2012,

[110] Chris Flood, 'High-frequency trading is "growing cancer"', 14th April 2014,

[111] Robin Wigglesworth, 'Hedge funds seek to park quantum revolution', 2nd November 2017,

[112] Gillian Tett, 'Dark Liquidity system to launch', 5th February 2007; Norma Cohen, 'Kansas City undercuts NYC', 9th February 2007; Anuj Gangahar, 'Chicago's program for change', 20th March 2007; Norma Cohen, 'Doors open as industry removes barriers', 30th March 2007; Norma Cohen, 'Competitive age dawns in Europe', 3rd April 2007; Michael Mackenzie, 'Global trade facilitators behind a 24-hour market', 20th April 2007; Norma Cohen, 'Reuters to join scramble for real-time data', 11th July 2007; Anuj Gangahar, 'Nasdaq chief says sector will fragment', 8th January 2008; Ross Tieman, 'Algo trading: the dog that bit its master', 19th March 2008; Ross Tieman, 'When microseconds really count', 19th March 2008; Jeremy Grant, 'Geeks grow into the kingmakers', 21st October 2008; Jeremy Grant, 'Bourses in data arms race', 15th September 2009; Peter Garnham, 'Net brings power to the people', 29th September 2009; Michael Mackenzie and Jeremy Grant, 'Trading co-locate takes root in Essex hangar', 30th September 2009; Jeremy Grant, 'Screens replacing screams in the dealing room', 2nd October 2009; Jeremy Grant and Michael Mackenzie, 'Ghost in the machine', 18th February 2010; Michael Mackenzie and Jeremy Grant, 'Liffe proves its worth to NYSE', 4th March 2010; Jeremy Grant, 'Plunge places focus on safety of the share markets', 11th May 2010; Michael Mackenzie, '"Flash glitch" fears force SEC hand', 13th May 2010; Aline van Duyn, Michael Mackenzie, and Jeremy Grant, 'That sinking feeling', 2nd June 2010; Jeremy Grant, 'Emerging markets dump old trading habits', 9th September 2010; Jeremy Grant, 'Light speed ahead', 27th September 2010; Jennifer Hughes, 'Innovation drives trading surge', 28th September 2010; Izabella Kaminska, 'Man and machinery in perfect harmony', 28th September 2010; Michael Mackenzie, 'Regulators push technology to track trades in real time', 29th September 2010; Aline van Duyn and Telis Demos, 'Flash Crash: market reforms to be examined', 5th October 2010; Philip Stafford, 'Regulators show united front', 20th October 2010; Hal Weitzman, 'Co-location set to reap up to $40 million for CME', 29th October 2010; Jeremy Grant, 'Market structures face test of trust', 3rd November 2010; Telis Demos and Aline van Duyn, 'Debate reopens over equity trades', 21st December 2010; Gregory Meyer, 'High-speed commodities traders under crash scrutiny', 10th March 2011; Jennifer Hughes, 'Focus on speed blurs big picture', 29th March 2011; Hal Weitzman and Telis Demos, 'Ultra-fast trading firms hit headwinds in race to be first', 14th July 2011; Janina Conboye, 'Computers create demand for a different set of skills', 14th July 2011; Jeremy Grant, 'Barriers higher for Asian dominance in

High-frequency traders added to the liquidity of the equity market by buying when others were selling, and selling whenever others were buying, in the expectation of quickly reversing the deal. However, they also contributed to volatility and instability through a deluge of small orders. In response institutional investors resorted to dark pools where information did not have to be divulged until the trade was completed. As Rob Boardman, a broker, explained in 2015, 'Dark pools are key to secondary trading in small-cap stocks, which cannot operate efficiently if a trader has to tell the market of his intention to trade in the illiquid market.'[113] The other activity of the high-frequency trader was to constantly monitor the different trading venues, being ready to dip in and out whenever an opportunity arose to profit from minute price differences. Again this was done through a deluge of transactions that contributed to keeping prices aligned across the different venues but could also increase volatility as prices were driven up or down. Prior to the crisis the megabanks had performed the role of shock absorbers by acting as counterparties to the buying and selling of others, especially in less-liquid stocks. In the wake of the crisis regulatory intervention forced the retreat of the megabanks from this role, making equity markets more fragile, and undermining the liquidity of the stock of smaller companies. High-frequency traders according to Philip Stafford in 2018, had 'stepped in to support two-way pricing in markets in the past decade as investment banks have retreated'.[114] However, the high-frequency traders lacked both the capital and the portfolios of the megabanks, and so could not take a long position. What they did was dart in and out of markets at lightning speed, using sophisticated programs to interpret or anticipate market signals, and earn profits by exploiting tiny differences thousands of times a day. As well the sudden price dips and spikes this generated, these sophisticated trading programs were vulnerable to programming and execution errors, which could not only result in large losses for the traders using them but also create market volatility through sudden and large buy or sell orders. As Ken Polcari, managing director of ICAP Equities, pointed out in 2012, 'There is no kill switch; the minute you hit the send button on an algo it's running and you can't stop it.'[115]

Nevertheless, by 2012 in the USA conditions were ideal for high-frequency trading as there were over fifty different trading venues, leading Duncan Niederauer, the chief executive of the NYSE, to complain that the 'Market structure has gotten incredibly complex. It's virtually impossible to explain to a policy maker or an investor any more.'[116] By then it could no longer be expected that the likes of the NYSE would supervise and police the entire trading system when they only handled a shrinking share of it. For Mary Schapiro, chairman of the SEC, the response was to place responsibility on those using the market: 'Existing rules make it clear that when broker-dealers with access to our markets use

algo trading', 24th August 2012; Kara Scannell, 'Rise of machines prompts SEC to join the tech war', 6th March 2013; Elaine Moore, 'Humans or machines: who's running the markets?', 16–17th March 2013; Gill Plimmer and Philip Stafford, 'Cable hub gives City edge on Frankfurt', 7th May 2013; Philip Stafford, 'Deutsche Börse unfurls plan for European champion', 27–28th February 2016; Robin Wigglesworth, 'Algorithms bring benefits but fears of accidents grow', 1st June 2016; Gregory Meyer and Nicole Bullock, 'Algo traders look beyond need for speed in quest to gain competitive edge', 31st March 2017; Robin Wigglesworth, 'Hedge funds seek to park quantum revolution', 2nd November 2017; Philip Stafford, 'Selling time to traders: the physicist who measures deals in microseconds', 5th February 2018; Robin Wigglesworth and Stefania Palma, 'Quant funds take creative tack to gain recruitment edge over Silicon Valley', 29th September 2018.

[113] Rob Boardman, 'Shining a light on the importance of dark pools', 23rd February 2015.
[114] Philip Stafford, 'Bloc must find its own path, shorn of British expertise', 17th November 2018.
[115] Michael Mackenzie and Arash Massoudi, 'Ultra-fast traders under fire after US algo glitch', 3rd August 2012.
[116] *FT* Reporters, 'Traders urge action after Knight fiasco', 6th August 2012.

computers to trade, trade fast or trade frequently, they must check those systems to ensure they are operating properly.'[117] The SEC remained committed to the changes it had introduced as its priority was protecting the interests of the users of the equity market, and that was interpreted as promoting greater competition between trading venues. David Shillman, associate director in the Division of Trading and Markets at the SEC, made this clear: 'Advances in technology have allowed for more complex and dispersed markets to develop, but at the same time have provided market participants tools to efficiently monitor market prices and implement routeing strategies to address that complexity.'[118] His colleague, Erozan Kurtas, head of the Quantitative Analysis Unit, was much less optimistic about the control the SEC could exercise: 'The use of quantitative techniques and computer-driven algorithms has changed the market structure and financial world drastically in the past decade. It provides a lot of challenges to regulators and companies.'[119] What this division of opinion reflected was the difficulties regulators in the USA were experiencing with the results of RegNMS, but it was now the model to be followed around the world.

These developments in the equity market forced stock exchanges to respond. They invested heavily in trading technology, which encouraged demutualization in order to finance the costs involved. Then they looked for ways to increase trading volumes in order to generate the revenue required to pay for the investment they made, and generate the profits expected by those who now owned the stock exchanges. One consequence was attempted mergers to achieve economies of scale. As Philip Stafford, Arash Massoudi, and Jeremy Grant observed as early as 2013, 'The once-fragmented, equities-dominated business has been overturned in the past decade by competition, increasing use of automated trading and the growing popularity of derivatives. The industry response was to bulk up via acquisitions.'[120] Intensifying competition in equity trading, driving down the fees that exchanges could charge users, also forced them to diversify into other revenue sources, like clearing and settlement services and selling current prices and other market information. As John Authers noted in 2017, 'Exchanges are no longer a series of protected monopolies. Trading carries on in numerous venues.'[121] Increasingly exchanges identified particular services that they were in control of, such as instant price data and immediate access to the trading system, and so they charged for that to compensate for the low returns generated through providing a market for equities. High-frequency traders, for example, were willing to pay to connect their computers directly to those that controlled the market, as that gave them an advantage over other users.[122]

[117] *FT* Reporters, 'Traders urge action after Knight fiasco', 6th August 2012.

[118] Michael Mackenzie, Arash Massoudi, and Stephen Foley, 'Rage against the machine', 17th October 2012.

[119] Kara Scannell, 'Rise of machines prompts SEC to join the tech war', 6th March 2013.

[120] Philip Stafford, Arash Massoudi, and Jeremy Grant, 'ICE and NYSE go where others fear to tread', 4th October 2013.

[121] John Authers, 'Black Monday anniversary finds new risks and opportunities', 19th October 2017.

[122] Jeremy Grant and Telis Demos, 'Growth in off-exchange trade stokes pricing fears', 26th January 2011; Jeremy Grant and Telis Demos, 'Super-fast traders feel heat from competition', 15th April 2011; Telis Demos and Hal Weitzman, 'Speed will not always bring a bonanza', 10th October 2011; Ajay Makan, 'Academics determine that just being swift is not risky', 10th October 2011; Jeremy Grant, 'Crackdown on high-speed trading', 12th October 2011; Jeremy Grant and Telis Demos, 'Ultra-fast traders braced for tough curbs in Europe', 14th October 2011; Jeremy Grant and Alex Barber, 'Mifid's net cast wide to overhaul Europe's trading', 21st October 2011; Jeremy Grant, 'Automation is "strangling" small caps', 30th November 2011; Jeremy Grant and Telis Demos, 'Superfast traders feel the heat as bourses act', 6th March 2012; Sam Jones, 'Volker Rule', 10th April 2012; Michael Stothard, 'Norway's day traders live to fight the algos', 17th May 2012; Michael Mackenzie and Arash Massoudi, 'Ultra-fast traders under fire after US algo glitch', 3rd August 2012; Philip Stafford, 'High-tech firms reshape dealing', 3rd August 2012; FT Reporters, 'Traders urge action after Knight fiasco', 6th August 2012; Vince Heaney, 'High-frequency traders' claims refuted by studies', 1st October 2012; Philip Stafford, 'Mishaps prompt greater scrutiny

Both market fragmentation, and the high-frequency trading it spawned, advanced most rapidly in the USA after 2010. In 2019 buyers and sellers of corporate stocks in the USA could choose from over a dozen exchanges and thirty alternative trading venues. By then the NYSE's share of the US equity market, by volume, was 24.2 per cent, followed by Nasdaq on 20.5 per cent and Cboe, which had taken over Bats, at 16.75 per cent. For some users the fact that two thirds of trading remained in the hands of three exchanges, NYSE, Nasdaq, and Cboe, was considered unsatisfactory, and so they proposed a new exchange, the Members Exchange (MEMX). There remained a widespread belief, according to Richard Henderson in 2019, that 'The incumbent groups have retained their hegemony and HFTs still threaten to pick off the best prices from slower investors.'[123] He was echoing the view of Brad Katsuyama, whose creation, the IEX exchange, had only gained a 3 per cent share of the market despite being given official approval by the SEC: 'The legacy exchanges have a strong hold on the market.'[124] In 2019 NYSE and Nasdaq, between them, operated six of the thirteen registered US stock exchanges. What such comments ignored were the major changes that had taken place since the introduction of RegNMS in 2005. This included much greater competition for listings between the NYSE and Nasdaq and the established position of the leading electronic platform, Bats, which was now under the control of Cboe, a Chicago-based options exchange. In addition, a third of trading was conducted off-exchange, being either internalized within banks or through the operation of dark pools. As Larry Weiss, head of US trading at Instinet, an agency broker, observed in 2017, 'The more you trade, the more you supply, the more you see the book, the more you can set up your own book.'[125] The result, according to Nicole Bullock in 2019, was that 'Most of the

of high speed traders', 17th October 2012; Michael Mackenzie, Arash Massoudi, and Stephen Foley, 'Rage against the machine', 17th October 2012; Philip Stafford, 'UK report calls for measures to limit risks of high-speed trading', 23rd October 2012; Arash Massoudi, 'Increase in competition raises the stakes', 30th October 2012; Philip Stafford, 'Surge in US dark pools trading highlights fears over regulation', 20th November 2012; Rhodri Price, 'The pros and cons of dark pools of liquidity', 7th January 2013; Philip Stafford and Arash Massoudi, 'US share trading glitches fuel call to revisit rulebook', 23rd January 2013; Arash Massoudi and Michael Mackenzie, 'In search of a fast buck', 20th February 2013; Kara Scannell, 'Rise of machines prompts SEC to join the tech war', 6th March 2013; Elaine Moore, 'Humans or machines: who's running the markets?', 16-17th March 2013; Arash Massoudi and Michael Mackenzie, 'Investors turn to the dark side for trading', 26th April 2013; Stephen Foley, 'HFT platforms facing "speed limits"', 29th April 2013; Tracy Alloway and Arash Massoudi, 'ETFs under scrutiny in market turbulence', 28th June 2013; Arash Massoudi and Tracy Alloway, 'Trading glitch threatens Goldman's image', 23rd August 2013; Philip Stafford, Arash Massoudi, and Jeremy Grant, 'ICE and NYSE go where others fear to tread', 4th October 2013; Ralph Atkins, 'High-speed trading aids efficiency, says ECB report', 5th November 2013; Arash Massoudi, Philip Stafford, and Alex Barber, 'Pressure grows for limits on "dark pools"', 22nd November 2013; Steve Johnson, 'High-speed trading is "bad influence"', 28th April 2014; Martin Arnold and Daniel Schäfer, 'Dark pool allegations a double blow to pledge of "Saint Antony"', 27th June 2014; Nicole Bullock and Philip Stafford, 'The focus moves from speed to safety', 24th September 2014; Rob Boardman, 'Shining a light on the importance of dark pools', 23rd February 2015; Philip Stafford, 'Guessing game over dark pool caps', 24th July 2015; Philip Stafford, 'Regulators put dark pools back in the dock', 13th August 2015; Philip Stafford, 'Deutsche Börse unfurls plan for European champion', 27–28th February 2016; Philip Stafford, 'Bourse tie-ups put clearing risk in spotlight', 5–6th March 2016; Philip Stafford, 'Big bourses curb high-frequency trading', 13th October 2016; Philip Stafford, 'Instinet ensures fairness by offering clients strictly equal cable lengths for trades', 10th October 2017; Philip Stafford, 'Bourses become more than stock exchanges', 10th October 2017; John Authers, 'Black Monday anniversary finds new risks and opportunities', 19th October 2017; Philip Stafford, 'Investors in European stocks look to Mifid 2 rules waiver on dark trading', 7th November 2017; Philip Stafford, 'Europe's exchanges clash with banks and traders over increase in data fees', 28th December 2017; Gregory Meyer, Nicole Bullock and Joe Rennison, 'Trading', 2nd January 2018; Robin Wigglesworth and Joe Rennison, 'The Future of Trading', 10th May 2018; Philip Stafford, 'Bloc must find its own path, shorn of British expertise', 17th November 2018.

[123] Richard Henderson, 'IEX exits listing business after effort to lure trade from NYSE and Nasdaq fails', 24th September 2019.

[124] Richard Henderson, '"Flash Boys" challenger IEX struggles to shake up trading', 11th June 2019.

[125] Philip Stafford and Nicole Bullock, 'High-speed traders fight to keep edge', 26th April 2017.

matching of buyers and sellers happens via sophisticated computers in New Jersey at speeds faster than the blink of an eye.'[126] The two leading high-frequency traders, Virtu Financial and Citadel Securities, accounted for around 40 per cent of daily US trading flow by then.

Facing an increasingly competitive environment neither Nasdaq nor the NYSE could protect themselves by establishing vertical-silos, as clearing and settlement in the USA was under the control of the DTCC. One option was for them to merge and so lower their costs by pushing more business through a single organization. In 2011 Nasdaq combined with ICE to mount a bid for NYSE but it foundered on anti-trust grounds, as the regulators were unwilling to accept the dominant position that the merged institution would occupy. This left the NYSE vulnerable to other approaches, as its merger with Euronext had delivered no tangible benefits. Speaking retrospectively in 2014, Philip Stafford referred to NYSE Euronext as 'an underperforming cross-border conglomeration put together at the height of the 2005–07 financial bubble'.[127] Domestically, the NYSE was a fading force with its share of trading in its own listed stocks in decline. Sensing the difficult situation the NYSE was in, ICE made its own bid, in 2012, unhampered by the monopoly concerns which had led the Nasdaq deal to fail This approach was successful, being completed in 2013. ICE then disposed of the European stock exchanges in 2014, which were resurrected as Euronext. The takeover by ICE did little to arrest the NYSE's declining share of US equity trading, as it lacked the economies of scale benefits that would have stemmed from a tie up with Nasdaq. What it left ICE with was a strong transatlantic derivatives operation, which was central to its strategy.

Nasdaq's response to the growing competition in equity trading, and its falling share, was to broaden the range of financial products for which it provided a market. In 2013 Nasdaq moved into fixed-income securities by buying eSpeed, the electronic bond-trading platform. It followed that in 2015 by taking over SecondMarket, a venue for privately-held securities. In 2016 Nasdaq bought the International Securities Exchange from Deutsche Börse, establishing itself as the largest options exchange in the USA. Nasdaq had also expanded into Canada in 2015, buying Chi-X Canada, that country's largest alternative share trading venue. In addition, both Nasdaq and the NYSE discovered that they could generate a substantial income by charging premium rates for supplying data based on the prices generated on their markets. Under Adena Friedman, who replaced Bob Greifeld at Nasdaq in 2016, the exchange moved from acquiring other exchanges to buying up suppliers of financial data. Despite the loss of market share they remained the source of reference prices upon which all transactions were based. As Brooke Masters observed in 2018, the NYSE and Nasdaq had 'long enjoyed and profited from a privileged position as the aggregators of essential data'.[128] What developments in the US equity market revealed was that each regulatory intervention produced a response as both stock exchanges and their users devised ways to exploit the new situation and survive. This transformation of the US equity market, almost fifteen years after the introduction of RegNMS, did lead to some reflection among the regulators. In 2019 Jay Clayton, the SEC chairman, admitted that:

> My view on Regulation NMS is, in summary: there are many areas that the commission got right, some that may have missed their mark, and some that were positive in 2005 but may no longer be so. As technology and business practices evolve, so must our

[126] Nicole Bullock, 'Top NYSE trader readies for Uber IPO scrum', 9th May 2019.
[127] Philip Stafford, 'Industry strives to find its form', 5th November 2014.
[128] Brooke Masters, 'A fight over data roils Wall Street', 24th October 2018.

regulatory framework. One of our key responsibilities as regulators is to strive to ensure that, as technology changes, our regulations continue to drive efficiency, integrity and resilience.[129]

However, there was little sign that they intended to roll back what they had done.[130]

[129] Richard Henderson and Nicole Bullock, 'SEC head calls for sweeping review of rules underpinning equity transactions', 9th March 2019.

[130] David Gelles, 'Approval for Xpert as private company shares exchange', 4th January 2011; Telis Demos, 'Nasdaq OMX lures trades to platform', 31st January 2011; Jeremy Grant, 'Exchange chiefs seek global powerhouses', 10th February 2011; Jeremy Grant, 'A market to capture', 18th February 2011; Jeremy Grant, 'BATS evolves into the big league with Chi-X merger', 19th February 2011; Jeremy Grant and Helen Thomas, 'Nasdaq is running out of options', 24th February 2011; Philip Stafford and Telis Demos, 'BATS takes on NYSE with new primary listing platform', 30th March 2011; Jeremy Grant, 'Bold move by Nasdaq and ICE', 2nd April 2011; Jeremy Grant, Helen Thomas, Telis Demos, and Hal Weitzman, 'US exchanges in $11bn NYSE bid', 2nd April 2011; Jeremy Grant, 'Börse tie to NYSE focuses cuts on Europe', 8th April 2011; Jeremy Grant, 'Chill wind blows over plans for market mergers', 17th May 2011; Telis Demos, 'Quandary for Nasdaq returns with bid failure', 17th May 2011; Jeremy Grant and Caroline Binham, 'Doubt cast on BATS purchase of Chi-X', 21st June 2011; Jeremy Grant, 'LSE share of Footsie dips below 50%', 19th September 2011; Maija Palmer, 'Number of UK-listed tech stock dwindles', 14th November 2011; Jeremy Grant and Alex Barber, 'D Börse and NYSE Euronext seek to woo Brussels', 14th December 2011; Jeremy Grant, 'Brussels' block points to future of global alliances', 2nd February 2012; Telis Demos, 'Nasdaq upbeat over tie-ups', 2nd February 2012; Jeremy Grant, 'Alliances offer solution for exchanges', 26th March 2012; Michael Stothard, 'Norway's day traders live to fight the algos', 17th May 2012; Philip Stafford, 'High-tech firms reshape dealing', 3rd August 2012; Kate Burgess, 'NYSE aims to show small is beautiful', 6th August 2012; Arash Massoudi, 'Increase in competition raises the stakes', 30th October 2012; Philip Stafford, 'Surge in US dark pools trading highlights fears over regulation', 20th November 2012; Arash Massoudi, 'Professional traders have edge on retail investors, says NYSE', 19th December 2012; FT Reporters, 'ICE chief makes his biggest bet with deal', 21st December 2012; Philip Stafford and Arash Massoudi, 'Upstart ICE in $8bn gamble with deal for 208-year-old NYSE Euronext', 21st December 2012; Philip Stafford and Arash Massoudi, 'US share trading glitches fuel call to revisit rulebook', 23rd January 2013; Arash Massoudi and Michael Mackenzie, 'In search of a fast buck', 20th February 2013; Kara Scannell, 'Rise of machines prompts SEC to join the tech war', 6th March 2013; Michael Mackenzie, Arash Massoudi and Philip Stafford, 'Nasdaq opens new front in fixed income', 3rd April 2013; Philip Stafford, Arash Massoudi and Michael Mackenzie, 'Nasdaq sets stage for HFT in Treasuries', 5th April 2013; Arash Massoudi and Michael Mackenzie, 'Investors turn to the dark side for trading', 26th April 2013; Arash Massoudi, 'Direct-Edge-BATS merger to rival NYSE', 27th August 2013; Philip Stafford, Arash Massoudi and Jeremy Grant, 'ICE and NYSE go where others fear to tread', 4th October 2013; Arash Massoudi, 'Soaring cost of US share dealing risks "investor harm"', 18th October 2013; Michael Mackenzie and Arash Massoudi, 'Traders resist Nasdaq's Treasury Push', 30th January 2014; Arash Massoudi, 'A steward of Wall Street glories', 10th March 2014; Arash Massoudi and Tracy Alloway, 'Goldman says farewell to NYSE floor with sale of market maker', 2nd April 2014; Chris Flood, 'High-frequency trading is "growing cancer"', 14th April 2014; Jonathan Davies, 'High-frequency traders: heroes or hoodlums?', 21st April 2014; Martin Arnold and Daniel Schäfer, 'Dark pool allegations a double blow to pledge of "Saint Antony"', 27th June 2014; Nicole Bullock, Michael Mackenzie and Kara Scannell, 'Prosecutor stares deep into hidden area of stock trading', 27th June 2014; Philip Stafford and Arash Massoudi, 'Dark Pool spotlight falls on US "underdog"', 28th June 2014; Michael Mackenzie, Kara Scannell, and Nicole Bullock, 'Murky Pools', 28th June 2014; Nicole Bullock and Gregory Meyer, 'NYSE chief sees value in the trading floor', 5th November 2014; Philip Stafford, 'Industry strives to find its form', 5th November 2014; Tracy Alloway, 'Legislation to simplify capital raising boosts crowd funding', 5th November 2014; Philip Stafford, Arash Massoudi, and Anna Nicolaou, 'Virtu's reward could be a valuation of $1.8bn', 6th March 2015; Gregory Meyer, 'Trading places', 11th March 2015; Philip Stafford, 'IPO filing provides rare insight into HFT world', 14th April 2015; Philip Stafford and Nicole Bullock, 'SEC probes arcane part of equity market's plumbing', 12th May 2015; Philip Stafford and Nicole Bullock, 'NYSE and Nasdaq in back-up auction plan', 24th July 2015; Nicole Bullock, 'Nasdaq buys Canadian trading venue', 9th December 2015; Philip Stafford, 'Exchange chiefs eye deals to tap new markets', 31st December 2015; Nicole Bullock and Philip Stafford, 'US Exchanges', 8th March 2016; Philip Stafford and Nicole Bullock, 'Options traders prepare for "worst of all worlds"', 17th March 2016; Nicole Bullock, 'IEX presents regulator with a bumper dilemma', 30th March 2016; Nicole Bullock, 'Acquiring a reputation', 13th June 2016; John Plender, 'The Big Bang spawned a dark-trading monster', 13th June 2016; Nicole Bullock, 'US trading upstart IEX is seeking slow progress', 21st June 2016; Robin Wigglesworth, Nicole Bullock, and Gregory Meyer, 'Battle over price of finance data heats up', 6th July 2016; Nicole Bullock, '"Flash Boys" exchange targets level playing field', 16th August 2016; Philip Stafford and Nicole Bullock, 'CBOE–Bats tie-up poised to shake up sector', 28th September 2016; Philip Stafford and Nicole Bullock, 'Radical pilot to boost trade in smallest US stocks begins', 5th October 2016; Charles D Ellis, 'Technology and low returns: the end for active investing?', 21st January 2017; Nicole Bullock and Philip Stafford, 'NYSE prepares to challenge smaller rival IEX with speed bump of its own', 26th January 2017; Gregory Meyer and Nicole Bullock, 'Algo traders look

Tracking developments in the US equity market from 2010 onwards was the progress made in the EU since the introduction of Mifid. However, there were simply too many underlying differences between the nation states of Europe, for a single equity market to appear simply through the removal of barriers and the imposition of regulatory harmonization. Within Europe, including the EU, member states retained sufficient power to slow down and even prevent integration if it appeared to threaten national interests. Each national stock exchange remained the market for the stocks it quoted, which were largely those issued by companies based in that country and mainly owned by investors from that country. These exchanges attracted trading in those stocks as they provided the deepest pool of liquidity. Subjected to the same conditions that had followed RegNMS in the USA, what these European stock exchanges did face was growing competition from electronic platforms, leading to the fragmentation of the market. While the exchanges continued to be the source of reference pricing, under Mifid these were now immediately available, allowing not only dark pools and private bank networks to flourish but also the MTFs to undercut them, as they had none of the regulatory costs to bear. In turn this market fragmentation encouraged the high-frequency traders. Eventually a new version of Mifid emerged, Mifid 2, which was implemented in 2018, but this had many of the flaws of the original. Jeff Sprecher, the chief executive of ICE, referred to Mifid 2 in 2018 as 'the worst piece of legislation I have seen in my career'.[131] What was being attempted was a new set of rules that would allow banks to trade privately while preserving a transparent public market generating reliable prices that was available to all. Many doubted that such an objective was possible and believed that its result would be to further distort the market.[132]

beyond need for speed in quest to gain competitive edge', 31st March 2017; Philip Stafford and Nicole Bullock, 'High-speed traders fight to keep edge', 26th April 2017; Nicole Bullock, 'IEX sticks to principles in battle for presence', 2nd June 2017; Nicole Bullock, 'High-frequency traders adjust to overcapacity and leaner times', 10th March 2017; Nicole Bullock and Philip Stafford, 'Nasdaq pins hopes on shift to tech, data and analytics', 13th October 2017; Nicole Bullock, 'Higher data fees prompt backlash against exchanges', 18th November 2017; Gregory Meyer, Nicole Bullock, and Joe Rennison, 'Trading', 2nd January 2018; Nicole Bullock, 'Tech IPO crown up for grabs as bourses battle intensifies', 24th April 2018; Robin Wigglesworth, 'Liquidity smirk prompts calls for shorter US trading period', 25th April 2018; Gregory Meyer, 'Chicago's sharp traders delve into the turbulent digital currency', 1st October 2018; Brooke Masters, 'A fight over data roils Wall Street', 24th October 2018; Gregory Davis, 'Index funds are not to blame for market volatility', 31st October 2018; Philip Stafford and Nicole Bullock, 'Wall Street big hitters back new exchange to challenge NYSE–Nasdaq dominance', 8th January 2019; Philip Stafford, 'MEMX turns up the heat on US stock exchanges', 10th January 2019; Philip Stafford, 'MEMX turns up the heat on US stock exchanges', 10th January 2019; Nicole Bullock and Philip Stafford, 'NYSE and Nasdaq urge court to block fees cap plan', 16th February 2019; Richard Henderson and Nicole Bullock, 'SEC head calls for sweeping review of rules underpinning equity transactions', 9th March 2019; Philip Stafford, 'Investors angered by mounting cost of vital data from exchanges', 4th April 2019; Nicole Bullock and Philip Stafford, 'Nasdaq chief redoubles drive for data in NYSE dogfight', 3rd May 2019; Nicole Bullock, 'Top NYSE trader readies for Uber IPO scrum', 9th May 2019; Richard Henderson, 'Mifid 2-minded dark pool operator Liquidnet pushes into research', 14th May 2019; Richard Henderson, 'IEX backs regulator's stance on data fees charged by big stock exchange groups', 15th May 2019; Richard Henderson, 'Regulator calls on US stock exchanges to justify increase in data charges', 23rd May 2013; Philip Stafford, 'Futures exchanges put faith in "Flash Boys" speed bumps', 30th May 2019; Richard Henderson, '"Flash Boys" challenger IEX struggles to shake up trading', 11th June 2019; Richard Henderson, 'New York's rival bourses wage fierce fight for IPOs', 10th September 2019; Philip Stafford, 'Exchange operators cut dependence on legacy trading business', 21st September 2019; Richard Henderson, 'IEX exits listing business after effort to lure trade from NYSE and Nasdaq fails', 24th September 2019.

131 Philip Stafford and Peter Smith, 'Europe begins countdown to day of the Mifid', 2nd January 2018.

132 Jeremy Grant, 'Exchange chiefs seek global powerhouses', 10th February 2011; Jeremy Grant, 'Bats and Chi-X to create Europe share trading hub', 18th February 2011; Jeremy Grant, 'BATS evolves into the big league with Chi-X merger', 19th February 2011; Jeremy Grant, 'Bank and broker trading networks come under attack', 8th April 2011; Phil Davis, 'Howls of anguish meet EU proposals on trading reforms', 18th April 2011; Jeremy Grant and Nikki Tait, 'City fortunes in flux as exchanges merge', 12th May 2011; Jeremy Grant and Philip Stafford, 'Savings for investors as Europe acts on trading', 25th May 2011; Jeremy Grant and Caroline Binham, 'Doubt cast

What Mifid had done was intensify a battle for survival among Europe's stock exchanges in the face of the growing challenge from alternative trading forums. This had already begun before the Global Financial Crisis and then continued thereafter, forcing European stock exchanges to search for strategies to ensure survival over and above investing in the latest electronic technology, charging for information and granting favourable access to high-frequency traders. Some exchanges explored potential mergers to achieve economies of scale and a stronger position in the market while others tried to diversify into new products. Where possible the vertical-silo model was used as a form of protection as there was no common provider of clearing and settlement services across Europe or within the EU. These strategies met with varying degrees of success after 2010. Whereas domestic mergers were long established and relatively easy, creating multiproduct exchanges in the process, cross-border ones were not, facing strong opposition from national governments as well as regulatory, technical, and other obstacles. The attempts in 2015 and again in 2017 by Deutsche Börse to acquire the LSE failed, for example, meeting opposition from within both countries as well as on anti-trust grounds. It was also difficult to branch out into other products, such as derivatives, other than through a merger with an existing exchange, which a number had already done, because liquidity tended to remain with the incumbent.

on BATS purchase of Chi-X', 21st June 2011; Vince Heaney, 'Europe takes step closer to a tax on financial transactions', 19th September 2011; Jeremy Grant and Telis Demos, 'Ultra-fast traders braced for tough curbs in Europe', 14th October 2011; Jeremy Grant and Alex Barber, 'Mifid's net cast wide to overhaul Europe's trading', 21st October 2011; Samantha Pearson, 'Brazilian clearing blow for BATS', 14th November 2011; Philip Stafford, 'High-speed trading rules', 23rd December 2011; Jeremy Grant, 'LSE in U-turn on Milan stocks', 19th January 2012; Michael Stothard, 'Norway's day traders live to fight the algos', 17th May 2012; Philip Stafford, 'NYSE Euronext to offer retail service', 15th October 2012; Stephen Foley and Michael Mackenzie, 'Derivatives trades on the brink of tough new regime', 18th October 2012; Philip Stafford, 'UK report calls for measures to limit risks of high-speed trading', 23rd October 2012; Philip Stafford, 'Blizzard of regulation has its effect', 30th October 2012; Philip Stafford, 'Collateral drive puts the focus on settlements', 30th October 2012; Kara Scannell, 'Rise of machines prompts SEC to join the tech war', 6th March 2013; Philip Stafford, 'Netting UK and Irish dealing costs on offer across Europe', 13th August 2013; Philip Stafford, 'European "dark pool" trading surges', 18th October 2013; Philip Stafford, 'Regulation: All eyes on Italy's new rules', 20th February 2013; Ralph Atkins, 'High-speed trading aids efficiency, says ECB report', 5th November 2013; Philip Stafford, 'Battle flares up over future of "dark pools"', 7th November 2013; Arash Massoudi, Philip Stafford, and Alex Barber, 'Pressure grows for limits on "dark pools"', 22nd November 2013; Philip Stafford, 'Guessing game over dark pool caps', 24th July 2015; Vanessa Houlder, 'Exchange survives scandal to trade another day', 5th December 2014; Philip Stafford, 'BATS to target block trades ahead of Mifid 2', 10th August 2016; Hannah Murphy, 'Exchanges line up block trade bonanza', 24th March 2017; Philip Stafford, 'Anxiety over EU regulatory shake-up goes global', 6th July 2017; Philip Stafford, 'Mifid vies with Brexit as City traders' top concern', 11th August 2017; Philip Stafford, 'Investors' Mifid 2 challenges flagged up', 24th August 2017; Philip Stafford, 'EU and US regulators race to seal equivalence deal before Mifid 2 deadline', 21st September 2017; Norma Cohen, 'Mifid 2 will have profound impact on fixed income', 9th October 2017; Philip Stafford, 'Instinet ensures fairness by offering clients strictly equal cable lengths for trades', 10th October 2017; Philip Stafford, 'Clock ticks down on EU's Mifid reform', 10th October 2017; Philip Stafford, 'Investors in European stocks look to Mifid 2 rules waiver on dark trading', 7th November 2017; Philip Stafford and Peter Smith, 'Europe begins countdown to day of the Mifid', 2nd January 2018; Chris Flood, 'Mifid 2 set to stimulate growth in ETFs', 3rd January 2018; Hannah Murphy and Philip Stafford, 'Mifid 2 risks drowning in its own ambition', 4th January 2018; Philip Stafford, 'Mifid 2 brings dark pool trading into the light', 10th January 2018; Philip Stafford, 'Mifid 2 share trading shake-up put on hold', 10th January 2018; Philip Stafford, 'Trading venues play down rift over Mifid 2', 11th January 2018; Philip Stafford, 'Dark pool trading flourishes after Mifid 2 delay', 19th January 2018; Philip Stafford, 'Stock exchanges cast wary eye on threat from big tech groups', 2nd March 2018; The Lex Column, 'Mifid 2/dark pools: shifty shades of grey', 27th March 2018; David Keohane and Philip Stafford, 'Jury still out on Mifid 2 transparency rules', 18th June 2018; Chris Flood, 'Liquidity enables big ticket trades', 18th June 2018; Philip Stafford and Ralph Atkins, 'London worries it will be the EU's next target after Swiss stand-off', 29th June 2018; Pauline Skypala, 'EU rule changes deliver mixed results so far', 10th September 2018; Philip Stafford and Hannah Murphy, 'Mifid 2 starts to weave its influence through markets', 1st October 2018; Philip Stafford, 'Bloc must find its own path, shorn of British expertise', 17th November 2018; Hannah Murphy, Stephen Morris and Attracta Mooney, 'Mifid 2 throws up unintended consequences', 2nd January 2019; Andrea Vismara, 'Mifid 2 drags down an ecosystem along with Europe's banks', 15th May 2019; Philip Stafford, 'Mifid 2 rules tighten Wall Street's grip on Europe', 27th June 2019.

The one option that was successful in repelling competition was the vertical-silo, leading the LSE to move in that direction after years of resisting it.

In 2011 the LSE took the decision to pursue a takeover of LCH.Clearnet, the London-based clearing house, leading to a process of creeping control which reached 80 per cent in 2018. In 2012 Jeremy Grant reported that 'Securing LCH.Clearnet would give the LSE its own clearing house in the UK at a time when the exchange business is dominated by groups that already own their clearing services.'[133] LCH.Clearnet provided the LSE not only with its own clearing house but also a new revenue stream, as clearing was increasingly required by regulators for most financial transactions in the wake of the crisis. In 2017 Philip Stafford claimed that the LSE had been transformed 'from a share-trading venue to a global data and clearing powerhouse.'[134] The LSE built on this position by acquiring Refinitiv in 2019. Refinitiv was one of the leading providers of financial information, with a 22 per cent share compared to Bloomberg with 32 per cent in 2019. The demand for the data it supplied was growing rapidly as Steve Frob, former strategy officer at Ion Fidessa, a UK trading and data group, pointed out: 'Traditional exchange activities like trading have come under severe pressure. Providing data is the major exception as our ability to consume it appears almost limitless.'[135] Refinitiv also had stakes in the electronic platforms used for trading bonds and foreign exchange and the LSE already owned the European bond-trading platform, MTS. The other advantage that the LSE had over all its European rivals was a strong position in the global equity market, courtesy of its location in one of the world's leading financial centres, and home to numerous offices belonging to megabanks and megafunds. LSE-listed corporate stocks were especially popular among international investors because of the liquidity they could provide in the European time zone. As Philip Stafford commented in 2019 'London-listed shares often see much higher volumes of trading than equivalents in Europe, meaning that big trades can be carried out more efficiently.'[136] For those reasons the LSE attracted a wide range of foreign companies eager to have their shares listed on either its main market or the specialist division devoted to smaller enterprises, namely AIM. AIM had continued to flourish after the collapse of the dot.com bubble, while its equivalents across Europe had been closed or faded away.[137]

[133] Jeremy Grant, 'LSE to take lead stake in clearer', 10th March 2012.

[134] Philip Stafford, 'Tough times loom for LSE after Rolet bows out', 20th October 2017.

[135] Philip Stafford, 'LSE has to beat Bloomberg at its own game', 19th August 2019.

[136] Philip Stafford, 'No-deal Brexit share trade ruling sparks accusations of EU land Grab', 21st March 2019.

[137] Jeremy Grant, 'LSE pins outage on "human error"', 12th January 2011; Jeremy Grant, 'Exchange chiefs seek global powerhouses', 10th February 2011; Jeremy Grant and Catherine Belton, 'Bourse tie-up clears logjam in Moscow', 3rd February 2011; Bernard Simon and Javier Blas, 'Mixed emotions as Canadian investors speculate on developments', 10th February 2011; Philip Stafford and Jeremy Grant, 'Inevitability of LSE and TMX deal', 11th February 2011; Jeremy Grant, '"London Stop Exchange"' counts cost of outage', 26th February 2011; Masa Serdarevic and Jeremy Grant, 'Traders stay loyal to LSE despite outage', 5–6th March 2011; David Blackwell, 'Board subtractions leave Plus feeling minus', 6th June 2011; Simon Mundy, 'Birmingham exchange sputters', 6th June 2011; Jeremy Grant and Caroline Binham, 'Doubt cast on BATS purchase of Chi-X', 21st June 2011; Daniel Schäfer, 'Opening up the mid-market', 22nd June 2011; Bernard Simon and Jeremy Grant, 'Decision time looms for TMX shareholders', 27th June 2011; Jeremy Grant, 'Rolet back to earth as TMX–LSE hopes fade', 30th June 2011; Jeremy Grant and Telis Demos, 'Spurned LSE chief looks over shoulder at Nasdaq', 1st July 2011; Jeremy Grant, 'LCH.Clearnet at the centre of bidding war', 7th September 2011; Jeremy Grant, 'LSE share of Footsie dips below 50%', 19th September 2011; Jeremy Grant, 'Every Bourse wants a house of its own', 28th September 2011; Jeremy Grant, 'LSE beats Markit in battle to buy LCH', 28th September 2011; Jeremy Grant and Alex Barber, 'Mifid's net cast wide to overhaul Europe's trading', 21st October 2011; Alison Smith and Michael Stothard, 'Plus has little to show for multiple roles', 9th November 2011; Jeremy Grant, 'Automation is "strangling" small caps', 30th November 2011; Jeremy Grant, 'LSE in U-turn on Milan stocks', 19th January 2012; Jeremy Grant, 'LSE to take lead stake in clearer', 10th March 2012; Kate Burgess, 'Big British funds cut UK stocks ownership', 13th March 2012; Jeremy Grant, 'LSE seeks holy grail of clearing from LCH.Clearnet deal', 20th March 2012; Simon Mundy and Philip Stafford, 'Plus companies expected to sign for new teams', 15th May 2012; Sam Jones, 'Tangled up

In contrast to the LSE the other major European stock exchanges, like Deutsche Börse and Euronext, did not have a global role, though the BME in Spain did cater for Latin American companies. Once the NYSE was taken over by ICE, Euronext was cut adrift, becoming an independent company in 2014, but losing control of Liffe, its London-based derivatives operation. That stayed with ICE. In retrospect the merger between Euronext and the NYSE had proved a failure, leaving Euronext as little more than an expanded Paris Bourse. Apart from acquiring the Irish Stock Exchange in 2018 and attempting to take full control of the Oslo Børs in 2019, Euronext did not attract major European stock exchanges to its network, while its lack of an integral clearing and settlement operation, prevented it from employing the vertical-silo model.[138] Spain's Bolsas y Mercados Espanoles (BME) steered an independent course, secure in its ability to monopolize the entire range of financial products traded in Spain, through the use of the vertical-silo model and the backing of

anew', 30th May 2012; Philip Stafford, 'LSE chief shifts focus with shake-up', 13th June 2012; Philip Stafford, 'Nasdaq OMX to launch derivatives in UK', 22nd June 2012; Elaine Moore, 'Keeping tabs on prices triggers knee-jerk reaction', 24th July 2012; Kate Burgess, 'NYSE aims to show small is beautiful', 6th August 2012; Lina Saigol and Cynthia O'Murchu, 'FTSE has case of free floating anxiety', 11th September 2012; Philip Stafford, 'Blizzard of regulation has its effect', 30th October 2012; Philip Stafford, 'BATS Chi-X Europe in talks to secure UK exchange licence', 7th November 2012; David Oakley and Philip Stafford, 'LSE tries to change terms of Euro 463m LCH. Clearnet deal', 15th December 2012; David Oakley and Philip Stafford, 'New rules hit LSE deal with LCH. Clearnet', 18th December 2012; Philip Stafford, 'LCH deal looms as critical for LSE', 1st April 2013; Philip Stafford, 'Bats Europe given UK exchange status', 10th May 2013; Andrew Bolger, 'UK Share Ownership shifts overseas', 26th September 2013; Philip Stafford, Arash Massoudi, and Jeremy Grant, 'ICE and NYSE go where others fear to tread', 4th October 2013; Philip Stafford, 'European "dark pool" trading surges', 18th October 2013; Claree Barrett, 'Aim-20 years of a few big winners and too many losers', 20th June 2015; Kate Burgess and Scheherazade Daneshkhu, 'LSE hopes brewer's exit will encourage more listings', 14th November 2015; Philip Stafford, 'Clearing capital drives Deutsche Börse-LSE talks', 24th February 2016; Philip Stafford, 'LSE chief sets out plan to win over merger sceptics', 30th March 2016; Philip Stafford, 'LSE and banks launch derivatives exchange', 27th September 2016; Philip Stafford, 'LSE in talks over Paris clearing sale to Euronext', 21st December 2016; James Shotter, Philip Stafford and Patrick Jenkins, 'D Börse dismisses merger HQ fears', 22nd December 2016; Philip Stafford, 'LSE set to sell Paris unit to Euronext', 28th December 2016; Hannah Murphy and Philip Stafford, 'LSE agrees French clearing unit sale in move to placate Brussels', 4th January 2017; Philip Stafford and James Shotter, 'D Börse merger crumbles as tensions boil over', 28th February 2017; Philip Stafford and James Shotter, 'LSE and D Börse consider separate futures', 1st March 2017; Philip Stafford, 'How LSE and D Börse merger unravelled', 4th March 2017; Philip Stafford, 'LSE switches focus as Deutsche Börse deal fails', 30th March 2017; Philip Stafford, 'Bourses become more than stock exchanges', 10th October 2017; Philip Stafford, 'Tough times loom for LSE after Rolet bows out', 20th October 2017; Philip Stafford and John Gapper, 'LSE chief centre stage in bitter public dispute', 18th November 2017; Philip Stafford, 'LSE chief Rolet quits as pressure grows to resolve governance crisis', 30th November 2017; Chris Flood, 'Pension fund assets reach a record $41.3tn, up 13 per cent', 5th February 2018; Philip Stafford, 'LSE springs surprise with choice of chief', 14th April 2018; Philip Stafford and Ralph Atkins, 'London worries it will be the EU's next target after Swiss stand-off', 29th June 2018; Philip Stafford and Hannah Murphy, 'Booming CFD industry faces reckoning under new EU rules', 2nd August 2018; Philip Stafford, 'London Stock Exchange to raise stake in clearing house LCH', 20th October 2018; Philip Stafford, 'Bloc must find its own path, shorn of British expertise', 17th November 2018; Arthur Beesley, 'Sale brings stock exchange into EU-wide network', 31st January 2018; Philip Stafford, 'Investors seek no-deal Brexit assurance on dual listings', 4th February 2019; Philip Stafford, 'No-deal Brexit share trade ruling sparks accusations of EU land Grab', 21st March 2019; *FT* Reporters, 'LSE in talks on $20bn Refinitiv link-up with scale to rival Bloomberg empire', 27th July 2019; Cat Rutter Pooley and Arash Massoudi, 'Tests await LSE when deal euphoria subsides', 2nd August 2019; Adam Samson and Philip Stafford, 'Glitch delays start of trading by nearly two hours at LSE', 17th August 2019; Philip Stafford, 'LSE has to beat Bloomberg at its own game', 19th August 2019; Philip Stafford, 'Cboe to open Dutch hub for trading shares of EU groups amid Brexit uncertainty', 4th September 2019.

[138] Michael Stothard, 'Euronext on the alert for merger fallout', 21st June 2016; Hannah Murphy and Philip Stafford, 'LSE agrees French clearing unit sale in move to placate Brussels', 4th January 2017; Philip Stafford, 'Euronext's Dutch gambit puts pressure on LSE to sell French house', 4th April 2017; Philip Stafford, 'Euronext finalises LSE derivatives deal', 9th August 2017; Arthur Beesley, 'Irish Brokers ring changes as China comes to Kerry', 24th December 2018; Philip Stafford, 'Euronext in 625m Euros offer for Oslo Børs', 15th January 2019; Philip Stafford, 'Euronext grows portfolio as Irish bourse stares down Brexit risk', 13th February 2019.

the government.[139] Following a similar path was Deutsche Börse, with its control of the German stock market, though it retreated from its global ambitions by ending its pursuit of the LSE and selling its US operation, the International Securities Exchange, to Nasdaq. In 2011 Deutsche Börse took full control of Eurex, which rivalled Liffe as the leading derivatives exchange in Europe. Deutsche Börse also proceeded to build upon its vertical-silo model by providing post-trade services, such as clearing and settlement, to the OTC market.[140] For Wiener Börse, which also operated the vertical-silo model, the route to survival was to make itself into a regional hub for share trading, through links to other stock exchanges in central and Eastern Europe. However, it faced the rivalry of the Warsaw Stock Exchange, which saw a similar role for itself, while Nasdaq's control of OMX blocked expansion into Scandinavia and the Baltic. As a result the landscape of European stock exchanges altered little in the wake of both the financial crisis of 2008 or the introduction of Mifid within the EU.[141]

The Swiss stock exchange also remained independent, with Switzerland in an ambiguous position because it was neither fully in the EU nor fully out of it. What the Swiss stock exchange, the SIX Group, attempted to do was plot a middle route which retained control over its domestic market, helped by the vertical-silo model, while attracting trading from international buyers and sellers by complying with the main elements of EU regulations. This position was then threatened by the EU's withdrawal of equivalence recognition as it was determined to protect its internal market rules by withdrawing any concession to countries that did not adhere to them. Under equivalence the shares of EU companies could be traded in Switzerland and Swiss shares traded in the EU. In 2019 the EU refused permission for EU shares to be traded in Switzerland. In retaliation the Swiss banned Swiss shares being traded outside Switzerland. Before the dispute in 2019 72 per cent of trading in Swiss stocks took place on the SIX, the Swiss exchange, and 28 per cent elsewhere in Europe. After the ban trading was repatriated to Switzerland, mainly from London where they were traded on Cboe Europe. As Thomas Zeeb, the chief executive of the Swiss Stock Exchange, noted: 'Investors have benefited from a single pool of liquidity more than a

[139] Miles Johnson, 'Bourse still dominates at home', 5th October 2011; Jeremy Grant, 'Spanish exchange wary of high-speed trading arms race', 26th April 2012.

[140] Haig Simonian, 'Swiss bourse hit by new trading rivals', 16th March 2011; James Wilson, 'Exchange seeks transatlantic boost', 14th June 2011; Jeremy Grant, 'LSE chief fears threat to City voice if rival exchanges merge', 1st August 2011; Jeremy Grant and Alex Barber, 'D Börse and NYSE Euronext seek to woo Brussels', 14th December 2011; Jeremy Grant and Alex Barber, 'D Börse and NYSE face an uphill battle', 12th January 2012; Jeremy Grant, 'Brussels' block points to future of global alliances', 2nd February 2012; Philip Stafford, 'Failed NYSE/Euronext merger haunts exchange', 11th June 2012; Gerrit Wiesmann and Philip Stafford, 'Germany to press ahead with high-speed trading regulation', 26th September 2012; Philip Stafford, 'Deutsche Börse hopes that its philosophy has global appeal', 17th April 2014; Jeevan Vasagar and Philip Stafford, 'Deutsche Börse buys forex platform', 27th July 2015; Philip Stafford, 'Exchange chiefs eye deals to tap new markets', 31st December 2015; Philip Stafford, 'Clearing capital drives Deutsche Börse–LSE talks', 24th February 2016; Philip Stafford, 'LSE chief sets out plan to win over merger sceptics', 30th March 2016; Philip Stafford, 'Bourses become more than stock exchanges', 10th October 2017; Philip Stafford, 'Deutsche Börse makes progress in push to lure derivatives clearing from London', 6th February 2018; Olaf Storbeck, 'Deutsche Börse eyes UK's euro clearing', 22nd February 2018.

[141] Robert Anderson, 'Bourse painstakingly pursues goal to be regional hub', 6th April 2011; Jan Cienski, 'Bourse pursues foreign groups as it vies to lead central Europe', 20th April 2011; Jan Cienski, 'Broker sees city as regional centre', 20th April 2011; Jan Cienski, 'Capitalism has taken root, capital markets not yet', 21st June 2011; Jan Cienski, 'Friends devise set of winning formulas', 21st June 2011; Jeremy Grant, 'ISE banks on technology to strengthen its business', 28th June 2011; Jan Cienski, 'Vienna and Warsaw vie for pre-eminence', 18th May 2012; Jan Cienski, 'Buoyant growth gives city clout', 23rd May 2012; Jan Cienski, 'Bourse promises a sharper eye on small listings', 23rd May 2012; Jan Cienski, 'Sound of overtures in Warsaw and Vienna', 9th May 2013; Kester Eddy, 'Bourse sees privatisation as big opportunity', 31st October 2013; Henry Foy, 'Data—not takeovers—signal bourse's way ahead', 26th June 2015; Olaf Storbeck and Philip Stafford, 'Deutsche Börse in talks to acquire Refinitiv foreign exchange assets', 12th April 2019.

fragmented market.'[142] What he did not mention was that they faced higher charges, reflecting the fact that the likes of Cboe, which had become Europe's largest trading platform, was able to provide a low-cost service using prices generated by Europe's stock exchanges. As Alasdair Haynes, the chief executive of one of these alternative platforms, Aquis Exchange, admitted in 2019, 'Investors don't trade unless the national exchange is open, even when there are alternative markets available.'[143]

What all this added up to was that long after the introduction of rules and regulations within the EU that were designed to remove barriers and encourage integration, the European equity market remained fragmented, with the continuing presence of not only national exchanges but the growth of electronic trading platforms and dark pools as well. Even in the EU transactions remained scattered across dozens of separate national exchanges and other trading venues, each operating in their own way. Across Europe as a whole an estimate for 2019 suggested that there were 200 separate trading venues.[144] Though Asia was less exposed to both electronic platforms and dark pools than Europe, the Asian equity market was also highly fragmented, largely along national boundaries. Attempts to broaden and deepen the markets located in the smaller Asian countries through regional co-operation also failed. What integration there was came from the ability of the biggest banks and brokers in the region to conduct cross-border dealing on behalf of their clients through their internal and external links. However, these banks and brokers encountered problems in conducting cross-border trading as the national exchanges enjoyed a high degree of support from their governments, which insulated them from competitive pressures. In South Korea the exchange, the KRX, enjoyed a monopoly of trading under the financial services act.[145] The result was to slow down technological progress and delay product development. Even where multiple exchanges still operated, as in India, the self-interest of those who controlled them hampered mergers that could have led to more efficient trading platforms and deeper pools of liquidity. Though the two largest stock exchanges, the Bombay and National, had been converted into companies, they long delayed becoming publicly-listed companies, leaving them run in the interests of their members. The result was a market that lacked liquidity because of the slow rate of technological progress and the continuing division between the two exchanges.[146]

[142] Philip Stafford, 'Swiss trading volumes rise but so do costs after EU ends equivalence rules', 25th September 2019.

[143] Adam Samson and Philip Stafford, 'Glitch delays start of trading by nearly two hours at LSE', 17th August 2019.

[144] Haig Simonian, 'Swiss bourse hit by new trading rivals', 16th March 2011; Sam Jones, 'Tangled up anew', 30th May 2012; Philip Stafford and Ralph Atkins, 'London worries it will be the EU's next target after Swiss stand-off', 29th June 2018; Ralph Atkins and Philip Stafford, 'Switzerland's crypto ambitions get boost from digital platform launch by exchange', 7th July 2018; Jim Brunsden and Philip Stafford, 'Brussels set to extend access to Swiss exchanges for another six months', 18th December 2018; Philip Stafford and Philip Georgiadis, 'EU markets regulator abandons no-deal block on big UK stocks', 30th May 2019; Philip Stafford and Mehreen Khan, 'London venues poised to delist Swiss stocks as Bern's EU dispute drags on', 26th June 2019; Philip Stafford, 'Swiss stock trading shifts away from the EU exchanges after Brussels–Bern dispute', 2nd July 2019; Attracta Mooney, 'Could London be Berned like the Swiss?', 8th July 2019; Philip Stafford, 'Brussels eyes payment plan for exchanges' trading data', 12th July 2019; Philip Stafford, 'Cboe to open Dutch hub for trading shares of EU groups amid Brexit uncertainty', 4th September 2019; Philip Stafford, 'Tale of the tape needed for Europe's fragmented trading', 13th September 2019; Philip Stafford, 'Swiss trading volumes rise but so do costs after EU ends equivalence rules', 25th September 2019.

[145] Song Jung-a, 'Seoul SME bourse plan faces scepticism', 11th June 2012; Jeremy Grant and Simon Mundy, 'Chi-X sets sights on South Korea', 9th August 2013; Song Jung-a, 'South Korea's Kosdaq soars but troubles persist', 23rd November 2017.

[146] Mary Watkins, 'NSE shuns mega-mergers', 29th August 2011; James Crabtree, 'India to tighten trading controls after flash crash', 10th October 2012; James Crabtree and Philip Stafford, 'New Exchange opens in India', 11th February 2013; James Crabtree, 'Frustrated investors push for IPOs of Indian stock exchanges', 3rd July 2015;

This fragmentation of the Asian equity market, and the slow pace of progress, continued to encourage a number of Asia's largest companies to list in London or New York rather than using small, illiquid and poorly-regulated local exchanges.[147] What mergers there were between exchanges took place within national boundaries such as that between the Tokyo Stock Exchange (TSE) and Osaka Securities Exchange (OSE). This was announced in 2011 but took until 2013 to complete. In 2012 Atsushi Saito, the TSE chief executive, explained the thinking behind the merger: 'The Japanese market needs to be of a certain size and offer unique services in order not to be left behind by global developments.'[148] Looking for a liquid Asian equity market to complement those of London and New York the megabanks and megafunds increasingly preferred that provided by Singapore and Hong Kong rather than Tokyo.[149] The Hong Kong Stock Exchange and Clearing (HKEX) operated as a multi-asset exchange and employed the vertical-silo model. While acting as the bridge between the Chinese and international equity market it faced competition for the Chinese market from both the Shanghai and Shenzhen stock exchanges.[150] The Singapore Exchange (SGX) lacked a large domestic market and so tried to pick up trading in the shares of Asian companies that had either outgrown their own country or faced restrictions and high taxes in their domestic market. By 2018 the SGX had become a popular way for overseas investors to trade Indian shares because the contracts were dollar

Simon Mundy, 'Investors' wait for Indian listings nears end', 11th October 2016; Philip Stafford and Simon Mundy, 'Indian stock exchange chief quits ahead of public listing', 3rd December 2016; Simon Mundy, 'NSE chief seeks to ditch arrogant approach', 10th October 2017; Philip Stafford and Emma Dunkley, 'India exchanges seek to bring equities trading home by halting data supply', 13th February 2018; Emma Dunkley, 'Mumbai bourse seeks to block Singapore's launch of Indian equity futures contracts', 23rd May 2018.

[147] Jeremy Grant and William MacNamara, 'LSE seeks to grab lead in deal with Mongolian exchange', 9th April 2011; Jeremy Grant, 'LSE signals it will look to Asia for merger', 21st April 2011; Jeremy Grant, 'Asia and LatAm bourses ripe for mergers', 8th August 2011; Robin Wigglesworth, Kevin Brown, and Sarah Mishkin, 'Asia shows growing viability as IPO venue', 19th August 2011; Sarah Mishkin, 'Competition helps to reduce barriers', 10th October 2011; Jeremy Grant and Telis Demos, 'Ultra-fast traders braced for tough curbs in Europe', 14th October 2011; Jeremy Grant and Daniel Dombey, 'Turkish exchanges plan to link', 23rd November 2011; Jeremy Grant, 'LSE and Russian exchanges in race to partner Kazakh bourse', 6th December 2011; Jeremy Grant, 'Drive for Asean exchanges tie-up', 7th January 2013; John Sedgwick, 'Stock exchange link-ups need to prove their worth', 15th June 2015; Michael Peel, 'Myanmar's one company bourse struggles to meet demand', 9th April 2016; Jeevan Vasagar, 'Malaysia's regional ambitions curbed by local problems', 11th October 2016; Steve Johnson, 'Pakistan bourse woes fuel doubts over emerging market status', 17th April 2019.

[148] Ben McLannahan, 'Merger of markets may foreshadow expansion overseas', 9th March 2012.

[149] Lindsay Whipp and Telis Demos, 'TSE looks at joining forces with Osaka exchange', 11th March 2011; Ben McLannahan, 'Japan's leading exchanges to merge', 23rd November 2011; Ben McLannahan, 'Merger of markets may foreshadow expansion overseas', 9th March 2012; Ben McLannahan, 'TSE set to pull plug on Tokyo Aim', 27th March 2012; Ben McLannahan, 'Japan commodities exchange looks for deeper ties with rivals', 28th March 2012; Philip Stafford, Arash Massoudi, and Jeremy Grant, 'ICE and NYSE go where others fear to tread', 4th October 2013; Leo Lewis and Kama Inagaki, 'Tokyo renews push as financial hub', 22nd November 2016,

[150] Robert Cookson, 'HKEx looks to forge links with Shanghai and Shenzhen bourses', 19th August 2011; Jeremy Grant, 'Six emerging market exchanges combine in cross-listing alliance', 13th October 2011; Jeremy Grant, 'LSE aims to revive Delhi exchange', 9th November 2011; Simon Rabinovitch and Robert Cookson, 'China unlikely to impose big bang reforms', 24th February 2012; Josh Noble, 'HKEx unveils plan to be "gateway for China"', 16th January 2013; Jennifer Hughes, 'HK–Shanghai link creates winners and losers', 17th November 2014; John Noble, 'Slow start fails to dim Stock Connect', 25th November 2014; John Sedgwick, 'Stock exchange link-ups need to prove their worth', 15th June 2015; Kiran Stacey, 'Dhaka bourse stake sale sparks tension', 19th February 2018; Emma Dunkley and Tom Hancock, '2018 HKEX move clears path for China biotech challenge to New York hub', 4th April 2018; Emma Dunkley, 'HKEX looks to trading suspensions after string of accounting scandals', 18th October 2018; Louise Lucas and Emma Dunkley, 'China start-ups resist lure of Hong Kong IPO sweeteners', 19th October 2018; James Kynge and Emma Dunkley, 'MSCI hands Chinese stocks a bigger global role', 2nd March 2019; Hudson Lockett, 'Starring role for Shanghai's answer to Nasdaq', 20th July 2019; Hudson Lockett, Wang Xueqiao, and Tom Hancock, 'Investors star-struck by new Shanghai tech exchange', 24th July 2019; Philip Stafford, Owen Walker, Daniel Thomas, and Hudson Lockett, 'London Stock Exchange poised to rebuff £32bn Hong Kong bid', 12th September 2019; Patrick Jenkins and Philip Stafford, 'Exchanges', 14th September 2019.

denominated and subject to lower taxes. However, it continued to lack the depth and breadth required to attract new issues made by companies from outside Singapore.[151] Leng Ng, the director of capital markets, Fidelity International in Singapore, made this clear in 2019: 'New issuers would tend to gravitate towards larger and deeper markets where they believe they can fetch the best valuation.'[152]

What the situation in both Europe and Asia reflected was the lack of integration in the global equity market and the continuing fragmentation that deprived domestic markets of the depth and breadth required to provide a liquid market for the shares of their largest companies. What existed was a collection of markets ranging from the very large to the tiny, without any exchange able to provide a co-ordinating element. That was also the case in the Middle East, for example, with no exchange emerging from the pack, as each focused on its domestic market.[153] A similar situation existed in Africa where individual stock exchanges were much more focused on dominating their domestic market, and expanding beyond equities into options and futures, than in transborder co-operation.[154] All over the world governments intervened to protect their national exchanges from foreign takeover. Jeremy Grant wrote in 2011 that proposed stock exchange mergers 'automatically run up against regulatory, antitrust and nationalist barriers'.[155] In 2019 Niki Beattie, owner of Market Structure Partners, observed that, 'It's proven very difficult for exchanges to get deals done with other exchanges either because of competitive issues or because of protection of perceived national assets.'[156] This was view echoed by David Schwimmer, the chief executive of the LSE: 'Cross-border exchange transactions are pretty challenging. That can be for political or industry reasons.'[157] The Australian authorities, for example, were not willing to countenance any attempt to place the ASX under foreign control, even in the interests of creating a pan-Asia/Pacific equity market. This had been the ambition of the SGX when it made its takeover bid.[158] To many the proposed merger of the UK's LSE and

[151] Jeremy Grant, 'SGX eyes organic growth after failing to seal Australian deal', 23rd July 2012; Jeremy Grant, 'Singapore exchange slips behind Asia rivals', 24th April 2014; Jeremy Grant, 'SGX targets greater China link with Taiwan', 25th November 2014; John Sedgwick, 'Stock exchange link-ups need to prove their worth', 15th June 2015; Philip Stafford and Emma Dunkley, 'India exchanges seek to bring equities trading home by halting data supply', 13th February 2018; Philip Stafford, 'Singapore exchange plans to tighten grip as Asia's largest forex trading hub', 11th June 2019; Mercedes Ruehl and Siddarth Shrikanth, 'Singapore struggles to catch south-east Asian tech boom', 16th July 2019.

[152] Mercedes Ruehl and Siddarth Shrikanth, 'Singapore struggles to catch south-east Asian tech boom', 16th July 2019.

[153] Jeremy Grant, 'ISE banks on technology to strengthen its business', 28th June 2011; Jeremy Grant and Daniel Dombey, 'Turkish exchanges plan to link', 23rd November 2011; Jeremy Grant, 'Ankara weighs in with shake-up of exchanges', 14th December 2011; Simeon Kerr, 'Imbalances keep Gulf region on the sidelines', 29th May 2012; Philip Stafford, 'LSE targets new openings as Borse Dubai bows out', 27th March 2015; David O'Byrne, 'Borsa Istanbul has ambitious expansion plan beyond equities', 13th October 2015; *FT* Reporters, 'Global exchanges vie to lure Aramco IPO', 10th March 2017; Simeon Kerr, 'Riyadh ready to ease Saudi bourse access', 12th May 2017; John Reed, 'Tel Aviv exchange courts high-tech innovators', 11th July 2017; Steve Johnson, 'Saudi exchange takes first step into main global equity benchmarks', 19th March 2019; Steve Johnson, 'Foreign funds shun Saudi Arabia on entry to flagship index', 21st May 2019.

[154] Jeremy Grant, 'ISE banks on technology to strengthen its business', 28th June 2011; Jeremy Grant, 'Exchange: Aiming to build on success', 4th November 2011; Andrew England and William Wallis, 'JSE plan viewed with caution', 6th November 2012; Javier Blas, 'From missing watches to premium boards', 11th October 2013.

[155] Jeremy Grant, 'Brussels' block points to future of global alliances', 2nd February 2012.

[156] Cat Rutter Pooley and Arash Massoudi, 'Tests await LSE when deal euphoria subsides', 2nd August 2019.

[157] Cat Rutter Pooley and Arash Massoudi, 'Tests await LSE when deal euphoria subsides', 2nd August 2019.

[158] Peter Smith and Jeremy Grant, 'Canberra set to reject SGX deal', 6th April 2011; Peter Smith, 'Australia rejects Singapore's bid for rival bourse', 9–10th April 2011; Jeremy Grant, 'LSE signals it will look to Asia for merger', 21st April 2011; Jeremy Grant, 'Asia and LatAm bourses ripe for mergers', 8th August 2011; Peter Smith and Jeremy Grant, 'ASX on the offensive to fend off Chi-X', 16th August 2011; Philip Stafford, 'ASX and Clearstream in talks over outsourcing', 29th August 2011; Sarah Mishkin, 'Competition helps to reduce barriers',

Canada's TMX in 2011 also appeared to have logic on its side. It would have created an exchange with a commanding global position in the stocks of mining companies while bolstering both against the predatory activities of US exchanges, electronic platform operators, and investment banks. Ultimately those opposing the merger triumphed, as TMX fell under the control of the Canadian banks.[159]

Representative of the prevailing position by 2019 was Latin America where an unwillingness to end national rivalries left the region without a dominant stock exchange. What existed was a number of large equity markets, with that of Brazil being the most important, and a host of much smaller ones, some of which were active while others bordered on being moribund. Brazil's BM&F Bovespa tried to emerge as the dominant exchange but foundered in the face of opposition at both the institutional and global level while facing growing competition from electronic trading platforms, often backed by the likes of Direct Edge and Bats from the USA. To Edemir Pinto, the chief executive of BM&F Bovespa, the threat was not these electronic platforms but the likes of the NYSE in 2016 when he stated that, 'Our competitors are not local but global—we needed to create the infrastructure to strengthen ourselves and compete in a global way.' What he was wanted for his exchange was for it to become the hub of the Latin American equity market. This was to be achieved by purchasing minority stakes in exchanges located elsewhere in Latin America, having begun with those in Chile, Mexico, and Colombia. These were to be followed by Argentina and Peru. The intention was to repatriate trading from New York and London, claiming that 'We have to unite because together we can do so much more. What is the point of fighting by ourselves in a globalised world.'[160] His words were almost a rallying cry for most stock exchanges around the world in their battle with those located in the twin global financial centres of London and New York. The fragmentation of the global equity market deprived the largest companies from many countries of the liquid market that both domestic and foreign institutional investors wanted. Combined with the restrictions and taxes imposed on share trading by many governments, the result was to drive companies to London, New York, and Hong Kong, where they found the depth of market that their shares required. They were then followed by the global fund managers looking for liquid markets, though others were willing to purchase less-liquid corporate stocks because of their higher yields and potential capital gains.[161]

10th October 2011; Jeremy Grant and Telis Demos, 'Ultra-fast traders braced for tough curbs in Europe', 14th October 2011; Jeremy Grant and Alex Barber, 'D Börse and NYSE Euronext seek to woo Brussels', 14th December 2011; Jamie Smyth, 'Australia poised to end ASX monopoly on equity clearing', 31st March 2016.

[159] Jeremy Grant, 'Exchange chiefs seek global powerhouses', 10th February 2011; Bernard Simon and Javier Blas, 'Mixed emotions as Canadian investors speculate on developments', 10th February 2011; Philip Stafford and Jeremy Grant, 'Inevitability of LSE and TMX deal', 11th February 2011; Bernard Simon and Jeremy Grant, 'Banks look to counter LSE's TMX deal', 12th May 2011; Jeremy Grant, 'Counterbid for TMX catches the LSE on the hop', 16th May 2011; Bernard Simon, 'Consortium appeals to patriotism', 16th May 2011; Bernard Simon, 'LSE bid for TMX gains support', 18th June 2011; Bernard Simon and Jeremy Grant, 'Decision time looms for TMX shareholders', 27th June 2011; Jeremy Grant, 'Rolet back to earth as TMX–LSE hopes fade', 30th June 2011; Jeremy Grant and Telis Demos, 'Spurned LSE chief looks over shoulder at Nasdaq', 1st July 2011; Bernard Simon, 'Maple's TMX bid faces antitrust hurdle', 1st July 2011; Jeremy Grant, 'LSE chief fears threat to City voice if rival exchanges merge', 1st August 2011; Jeremy Grant, 'Asia and LatAm bourses ripe for mergers', 8th August 2011; Jeremy Grant, 'Merger plan puts spotlight on silos', 1st November 2011; Jeremy Grant and Alex Barber, 'D Börse and NYSE Euronext seek to woo Brussels', 14th December 2011; Nicole Bullock, 'Nasdaq buys Canadian trading venue', 9th December 2015.

[160] Samantha Pearson, 'Brazil's exchange chief rejoices at post-impeachment chances', 11th October 2016.

[161] Jeremy Grant and Catherine Belton, 'Bourse tie-up clears logjam in Moscow', 3rd February 2011; Joe Leahy, 'Shanghai forges Brazil bourse link', 17th February 2011; Adam Thomson, 'Changes give vigour to once-somnolent bourse', 24th June 2011; Naomi Mapstone, 'Cross-border stocks start trading slowly', 21st September 2011; Jeremy Grant and Telis Demos, 'Ultra-fast traders braced for tough curbs in Europe', 14th October 2011; Samantha

Conclusion

From a perspective of more than a decade after the Global Financial Crisis its impact and legacy on stock exchanges and equity market is hard to detect. The situation remained much the same as it had been before. The forces pushing for change, such as those of globalization, convergence, and technology continued to be met by insurmountable barriers revolving around regulation, currency, and harmonization with the question of control being a major factor, especially when it involved loss of sovereignty at both the institutional and governmental level. Governments were equally keen to support the international expansion of their national exchanges and protect them from external competition though the two objectives were incompatible. Faced with a choice, governments chose the latter leaving the global equity market highly fragmented. This continued to be the case, though to a lesser degree, when a supra-national body became involved, as was the case in the European Union, as even there the progress towards a single European equity market remained both slow and halting. The UK's potential departure from the EU, removing as it would the region's most important stock exchange, the LSE, from the block, further jeopardized that progress as attempts were made to cut off trading in London from the pan-European market. The uncertainty that created contributed to the dominance of the US equity market in the world as it left it without serious rivals.

The US equity market was, by far, the world's largest and operated free from internal barriers. The regional stock exchanges had disappeared as a significant element, to be replaced by a duopoly of Nasdaq and the NYSE. In turn that duopoly was being challenged by the Cboe, after taking control of Bats. With its depth and breadth the US equity market could provide the world's banks and fund managers with the combination of liquidity and returns they craved at a time of financial uncertainty. In turn that attracted the largest companies in the world, as a listing in the USA brought with it the profile that attracted these banks and fund managers. This made the US market even broader and deeper, and so the process went on. The only serious challenge to the New York-centred US equity market was that found in London, where the LSE and a number of electronic trading platforms were located as well as Euronext's own market computer. London provided an attractive alternative for companies from outside the USA that wanted liquidity and international exposure but not the draconian regulations that came with a New York listing. The TSE in Tokyo could have occupied a similar position, with an Asian base, combining to form a triumvirate of liquidity pools that circled the globe, but all it could offer was a deep domestic market. Unlike the LSE, Nasdaq, and the NYSE the TSE had failed to make the transition from a domestic to an international exchange in terms of the companies it attracted. Elsewhere in the world the continuing fragmentation of trading into individual pools of liquidity, with varying depths or none, meant that they were not in a position to challenge the LSE,

Pearson, 'Brazilian clearing blow for BATS', 14th November 2011; Samantha Pearson, 'Threat of competition triggers improvements', 15th November 2011; Jeremy Grant, 'Two Argentine exchanges agree to combine forces', 17th December 2011; Jeremy Grant, 'Argentine bourses extend consolidation', 28th December 2011; Samantha Pearson, 'Industry stalemate as rivals clamour for access', 3rd October 2012; Samantha Pearson, 'Foreign rivals join battle for post-trade prize', 30th October 2012; Jude Webber, 'Santiago aims to be hub for global investment', 14th November 2012; Adam Thomson, 'Trading surge brings region together', 14th November 2012; Andres Schipani, 'Uniting to build critical mass', 24th November 2012; Samantha Pearson, 'Change is in the air for stocks', 14th November 2012; Lars Ottersgard, 'Global ambitions can be achieved through a single voice', 14th November 2012; Samantha Pearson, 'Brazil's exchange chief rejoices at post-impeachment chances', 11th October 2016.

Nasdaq, and the NYSE despite the huge advances made around the world in the importance of equity trading.

Complementing the LSE, Nasdaq, and the NYSE were the electronic platforms because they could provide a cheaper and faster alternative, as they operated with a much leaner administrative and regulatory structure. The development of electronic communication networks (ECNs), that matched sales and purchases automatically using powerful computers, challenged the role previously played by stock exchanges. The ability of these alternative trading platforms to compete with stock exchanges was encouraged by regulators, whose mission was to drive competition in the interests of consumers of financial services, not promote strong and stable markets. This intervention in the functioning of the market was particularly marked in the USA, with the Regulation New Market System (RegNMS), and the European Union, where a variant of the same policy was introduced under the Market in Financial Instruments Directive (Mifid). Stock exchanges were forced to respond to the growing competition they faced by fully embracing electronic trading themselves, because of the cost reductions and improved speed of execution it delivered. However, this did not mean that a single global equity market came into existence. Equity trading continued to take place in national pools, as the centre of liquidity lay where the location of shareholders in particular companies was at its most dense. With a home bias among equity investors the market for the shares of most companies was normally found in the stock exchange located in the country where their head office was located and most of their activities were based. As a result the global equity market continued to be comprised of a series of separate though inter-connected pools, reflecting the liquidity generated by the geographical distribution of the ownership of corporate stocks. With access to these individual pools opened up to all, and restrictive practices and high charges abandoned, that was where buying and selling was directed.

Megabanks, for example, bought and sold where the market was most liquid, the charges were lowest, and the speed of execution fastest, or any combination of those that they chose, but with the first being given priority. Commanding the pool of liquidity in individual stocks was now the priority for any stock exchange, or those electronic platforms that wanted to mount a challenge, and that meant responding to the needs of users ranging from megabanks and megafunds to retail investors and high-frequency traders. These placed incumbent exchanges under increasing competitive pressure, encouraging mergers that could deliver economies of scale as trading shifted onto a single electronic platform. Such was the amount of trading in the USA that these mergers could be confined to single categories of financial products, whether they were equities or derivatives. Elsewhere in the world, reaching the volume required to justify the investment in an electronic trading platform could only be achieved across a range of different financial products, including both equities and derivatives, and this is what mainly took place. Deutsche Börse was one of the first stock exchanges to integrate trading in both equities and derivatives and then combine it with clearing and settlement. This was known as the vertical-silo model, and it became standard practice around the world. The alternative was the horizontal model in which trading, clearing, and settlement remained separate whether or not the range of products covered both equities and derivatives. This model prevailed in the USA because of the existence of the DTCC.

19
Regulation and Regulators, 2007–20

Introduction

Of all global financial crises that have taken place over the ages that of 2008 should never have happened. Never was so much known about the way that banks and financial markets operated. Never was the ability of regulators to supervise the financial system so great. Never did central banks possess so much power to intervene if a crisis did occur. Never were governments so committed to the maintenance of financial stability both individually and collectively. Nevertheless, a global financial crisis did occur and its consequences were long lasting. For those reasons the causes and lasting legacy of the Global Financial Crisis of 2008 need to be sought more in the environment within which it took place rather than the actions of individual bankers or the behaviour of particular markets. That environment was the product not only of long-term trends and at the mercy of random events but also an unprecedented level of government intervention in the financial system at both the national and international level. This ranged from attempts to reform equity markets with RegNMS in the USA and Mifid 2 in the EU to the models followed by banks around the world, as dictated by the Basel Committee of banking supervisors at the Bank for International Settlement. These interventions were based on the advice of professional economists, carried out by experienced administrators and reflected expert judgement. They were intended to be in the best interest of all users of the global financial system as well as the operational efficiency of banks and markets.

What they prioritized was competition, investor protection, and stability. Competition was to be achieved by removing internal and external barriers as these distorted the operation of the market and prevented savers, lenders, and investors obtaining the highest returns or borrowers accessing the largest pools of finance at the lowest rates of interest and at the least cost. Investor protection would result from this competition, accompanied by the breakup of monopolies, the ending of restrictive practices, and the enforcement of transparency throughout the financial system, whether it took place within or between countries. Finally, stability could be entrusted to the megabanks as they possessed their own internal mechanisms to supervise the actions of their staff, and the resources necessary to withstand any crisis. These banks were closely supervised by government-appointed regulatory agencies and state-owned central banks, which had the power to compel them to follow the guidelines they laid down, as advised by the Bank for International Settlement. The switch from the lend-and-hold model of banking to the originate-and-distribute one, combined with the existence of markets where liquid assets could always be bought and sold, were considered fully capable of providing sufficient resilience so that these banks could surmount either a liquidity or a solvency crisis. As John Plender reflected in the aftermath of the Global Financial Crisis, 'In the credit bubble, much of the impetus for driving loans off balance sheets into securitised form came from the risk-weighted capital regime introduced by the Basel committee of international bank regulators. By encouraging off-balance sheet activity, the regime turned banking into a shorter-term, more transactional

Banks, Exchanges, and Regulators: Global Financial Markets from the 1970s. Ranald Michie, Oxford University Press (2021).

DOI: 10.1093/oso/9780199553730.003.0019

business.'[1] The final element in providing an environment in which banks could prosper and financial markets flourish was a commitment to monetary stability by central banks. This layered approach to managing the global financial system had evolved since the 1970s and had proved itself resilient during several financial crises around the world, including the speculative bubble associated with the dot.com boom.

On the eve of the crisis there was a genuinely held belief that a way had been discovered that made mankind the master of the financial system and that it could be forced to deliver whatever politicians wanted. That meant a world in which the impossible trilemmas of the past had been replaced by a managed strategy that delivered the magic combination of monetary stability, continuous economic growth, and open financial markets. With hindsight it is obvious that no such world had been discovered. Instead, in the decades leading up to the crisis the world was experiencing a man-made credit bubble that was longer in duration, encompassed more countries, and was more intense than any other in history. When that bubble finally burst in 2008 its consequences brought down the global financial system, and all that saved the world from a disaster that would have replicated the economic depression of the 1930s and the political consequences that had had, was the intervention of governments. These interventions were a reverse of those of the 1930s as governments chose to co-operate rather than compete, maintain open borders rather than close them, and to remain committed to markets rather than replace them with central direction. That was the lesson that had been learnt from the events of the 1930s.

What had not been learnt was why the crisis had occurred in the first place and the contribution made by regulators, central banks, and politicians to causing it. Their actions in preventing a catastrophe stopped them from being accused of creating the conditions that led to it in the first place. Instead, blame was placed on greedy bankers and irrational markets as had been done in the 1930s, though without the added touches of anti-Semitism and nationalist rhetoric that were to have such devastating consequences at the time. The world, at least, escaped those elements. Nevertheless, the result was to generate a belief that the interventions of regulators, central banks, and politicians were capable of framing a new global financial system that could, once again, deliver the impossible trilemmas of the past while escaping the consequences that had led to the crisis of 2008. Prior to the financial crisis there was a widespread belief that a sound financial system could be built around the megabanks, reliant on their inner resilience to eliminate the possibility of a liquidity crisis. With a liquidity crisis no longer a possibility a central bank could concentrate on its monetary policy functions as it would no longer be called upon to intervene. A solvency crisis was always possible though that was also considered unlikely because of the greater professionalism in banking, the management structures in place within the megabanks, and the role played by regulators in monitoring and supervising the financial system.

Even if a solvency crisis did happen such was the overall resilience of the financial system that a bank could be allowed to fail without jeopardizing stability. This solved the central banker's dilemma relating to moral hazard, which was whether to intervene or not. Intervention was justified in the case of a liquidity crisis as that could destroy the entire banking system through the contagious spread of fear. In contrast, a solvency crisis did not justify intervention as it generated the belief that a bank would not be allowed to fail, which encouraged a culture of risk-taking. Under these circumstances central bank intervention in the banking system was no longer required. In turn, this meant that governments could

[1] John Plender, 'Originative sin', 5th January 2009. See also John Plender, 'Re-spinning the web', 22nd June 2009.

devolve responsibility for maintaining monetary stability to the central banks, while leaving financial stability to the megabanks. Prior to the Global Financial Crisis the results appeared successful for all.

After the crisis it was acknowledged that the question of systemic risk should come into focus and that banks had to be treated differently from other financial institutions. With the passage of time it is now possible to examine what role regulators, central banks, and politicians played in the crisis and in shaping the financial system that followed it. Part of this examination has already been touched upon in earlier chapters. The intention of this one is to bring the separate elements together and so provide a comprehensive account that explains why regulators stood aside while the Global Financial Crisis developed and assesses the costs and benefits of their intervention in the financial system both before and after it took place.

Fiddling at the Margins, 2007–8

The financial system that experienced the crisis of 2008 was a man-made creation moulded by the actions of regulators, banks, and governments. Their influence dated from the 1970s and was shaped by the collapse of the control and compartmentalization policies pursued after the Second World War. That was followed by the learning experience delivered by successive financial crises and bouts of monetary instability. The lessons learnt determined the structure of the global financial system with all countries moving in the same direction, especially as the Bank for International Settlement provided a lead which all followed. However, the pace at which change proceeded, and the exact form it took, varied enormously in terms of the precise nature of financial regulation. China, for example, proceeded cautiously with financial regulation especially in the field of derivatives, because of their potential risks as well as benefits. Another tardy participant was Saudi Arabia. Nevertheless, the participation of both in the financial liberalization taking place indicated that none were immune from the process. That variation existed not only between countries but was also present within those with devolved administration, such as Canada. In 2007 thirteen separate authorities oversaw securities trading in Canada, for example, making it difficult to agree national standards. Within the EU national governments were free to interpret and implement rules, regulations, and guidelines as they wished, though convergence and harmonisation was the stated aim. The divergences were even more marked elsewhere in the world where the policies pursued by national governments were not moderated by external agencies, as was the case across Asia. There were gains to be made by not adopting regulations imposed elsewhere in the world. London had gained at the expense of New York by not following the USA down the Sarbanes–Oxley route of legislation. Within the EU London had lost out to Luxembourg and Dublin, which took a more relaxed attitude to regulation, while Qatar and Dubai followed a similar course in the hope of capturing international business. Conversely, Japan's failure to liberalize its highly-restrictive rules, governing the separation of banking and securities, had hampered the development of its financial system to the advantage of Hong Kong and Singapore in Asia.

Within this transformation of the global financial system, what was happening in the USA exerted an enormous influence on developments elsewhere in the world. As the home to the world's largest and most sophisticated financial system it led the process of innovation across products, markets, businesses, and regulation, with the rest of the world either copying, adapting or reacting to what was taking place there. The problem was that much of what took place in the USA was itself driven by conditions unique to that country, and had limited applicability to other countries with different financial systems. Conversely, the USA was often reluctant to adopt regulatory changes made elsewhere, such as following the recommendations made by the accountancy body, the International Financial Reporting Standards, though it was keen to impose its own on the rest of the world. The US regulatory authorities did gradually accept that there were different ways of achieving the same ends as can be seen in the rules governing stock markets. In March 2007 the chairman of the US's Securities and Exchange Commission (SEC) took the view that 'The idea that there can exist more highly-regulated markets with ample disclosure isn't necessarily at odds with the maintenance of very high standards in the main.'[2] His wording indicated the reluctance with which he accepted divergence, as his main concern was that lax regulations and an absence of enforcement outside the USA made his task of enforcement difficult or even impossible, in a world without exchange controls.

This was a perennial US complaint but it had been given an added dimension by the Sarbanes–Oxley legislation as it encouraged US companies to list abroad, such as on the LSE's AIM, where their shares could be bought by US investors even though they were not compliant with US regulations and accounting standards. The SEC had long prohibited foreign exchanges from operating trading facilities in the US without registering with it, because of concerns that this would expose US investors to foreign regulatory regimes operating under weaker disclosure and accounting regimes. Foreign exchanges had been reluctant to comply, as it would impose dual registration on them because they were already regulated in their home country. The solution was for the SEC to recognize foreign regulatory regimes as providing a comparable standard to their own, but the SEC was only slowly coming round to that way of thinking This change was being driven by the increasing appetite for foreign stocks by US investors, with nearly two-thirds of US investors having holdings in non-US companies, the creation of US led cross-border exchanges in the form of NYSE/Euronext, and the convergence of international accounting standards.

The USA itself had its own internal conflicts with multiple agencies responsible for different parts of the financial system, and often taking contradictory approaches to regulation. There were numerous financial regulators in the USA as not only were there Federal agencies but they were often duplicated at the state level. In securities there was the Securities and Exchange Commission, the Commodity Futures Trading Commission, the Financial Industry Regulatory Authority, and various state regulators. For banking there was Office of the Comptroller of the Currency, the Federal Reserve, the Federal Deposit Insurance Corporation, the National Credit Union Administration, and the Office of Thrift Supervision and, again, a variety of state authorities. The judgement of Joanna Chung in 2009 was that 'If it were to start from scratch, the US would not invent the kind of financial regulatory system it has today. Its multi-layered patchwork has well over 100 authorities keeping watch over the banking system and financial marketplace, where the boundaries between financial products and institutions are increasingly blurred.'[3] This system was the product of a division of power between the individual states and the federal government, and was shaped by its response to a succession of largely internal financial crises, market innovations, and flurries of consolidation. The result was to make the US regulatory system very complex and unlike that existing anywhere else in the world, beset by overlaps and inner contradictions. In derivatives, for example, the SEC policed options whereas the

[2] Norma Cohen, David Blackwell, and Jeremy Grant, 'Top SEC official calls Aim a casino', 9th March 2007.
[3] Joanna Chung, 'Complexity has led to cracks in system', 12th June 2009.

CFTC handled futures. The CFTC followed a flexible principles-based approach which was more sympathetic to those wanting to introduce new products. In contrast, the SEC operated a rigid rules-based system which was much stricter. In 2013 Dan Gallagher, at the Securities and Exchange Commission, accepted that 'The complexity of the markets today is in large part due to rational responses by market participants to the requirements, incentives and disincentives—both intended and unintended—arising from laws and regulations.'[4] Despite the uniqueness of the structure of financial regulation in the USA its model was followed around the world, having a major influence on the EU in particular.

Nevertheless, there was also a reaction against the US model of regulation involving multiple and competing agencies, as it was no longer considered adequate when faced with the growing convergence between banks, markets, and products. Instead, there was a growing preference for the UK's approach of using a single regulator, the Financial Services Authority. In June 2007 Jennifer Hughes and Peter Thal Larsen reported that the UK's Financial Services Authority (FSA) had 'In the past year or so... attracted praise from around the world as a model for effective regulation of the financial services industry.'[5] Countries such as South Korea were moving from the US model of separate agencies to a single one covering all financial services. It was not until 2008 that the SEC and the CFTC formally agreed to co-operate. What all regulators faced was the emergence of new and complex challenges, which required them to assess whether they needed to become involved, and then decide the nature and level of any measures they proposed. Regulators were aware that the rapidly-growing OTC markets were more exposed to manipulation and excessive risk-taking than those of exchanges, but they were unsure whether they possessed the power to tackle these and how to do so, if they were called upon to intervene. This was an issue facing the CFTC, for example, in the fast-growing OTC energy derivatives market, and the response in 2007 of its acting chairman, Walt Lukken, illustrates the dilemma faced by all regulators: 'The evolution of these energy markets in recent years requires our agency to address whether the level of regulatory oversight is proper given the importance of energy prices to all Americans.'[6] In 2009 the CFTC did intervene in the energy market in response to sudden spikes in oil prices but trading then shifted to alternative locations, with London, Dubai, Shanghai, and São Paulo all bidding to capture any business driven out of the USA. Given the competitive nature of the various players in the global financial system, legislation to move opaque derivatives into exchanges and clearing houses, along with trading curbs on speculators and banks, had the power to both damage a market and drive it away, and regulators were very conscious of this. John Damgard, the president of the Futures Industry Association, warned regulators in 2011 that 'Markets are awfully portable, especially derivatives markets, and capital will flow to markets that aren't burdened with oppressive regulation.'[7]

What is most evident in the years leading up to the crisis of 2008 was that the focus in most countries, including the USA and the EU, was not on the stability of the financial system, because that was assumed to be under control. There were few concerns that banks had become so big and complex that they posed a threat to the stability of financial systems or that the liquidity of financial markets was dangerously dependent on high levels of leverage. Instead, the assumption was made that the risks lay at the margins. Paul J. Davies

[4] Arash Massoudi, 'Soaring cost of US share dealing risks "investor harm"', 18th October 2013.
[5] Jennifer Hughes and Peter Thal Larsen, 'A light approach and 9,000 page rulebook', 23rd June 2007.
[6] Jeremy Grant, 'OTC energy trades under CFTC spotlight', 3rd August 2007.
[7] Jeremy Grant and Nikki Tait, 'NYSE link-up faces hurdles', 11th February 2011.

commented in March 2007 that 'Leverage levels are part of a complicated pattern of risk that includes uncertain correlations between asset classes—in part created by the operations of wide-ranging, diversified hedge funds—and the speed at which losses can be transmitted between funds, banks and other parts of the financial system.'[8] Since the collapse of Long-Term Capital Management in 1998 financial authorities around the world had concentrated on the risks posed by hedge funds to the banking system. This was tackled by reforms designed to improve the resilience of banks to counterparty risk, through their ability to distribute it to others. Out of this came the official approval of the originate-and-distribute model. As a result banks were considered to be sufficiently resilient to withstand any possible losses because they held assets that could be easily sold. Little thought was given to the ability of markets to provide liquidity to such assets.

New risks to bank stability also emerged through banks' off-balance sheet activities, such as structured investment vehicles, and the inducement the originate-and-distribute model gave them to leverage their capital and reserves. Even when a crisis first emerged that threatened a bank, as in the case of the UK's Northern Rock in August 2007, the regulators failed to act. As Gillian Tett explained in November 2007, 'It is one thing for the different national regulators to co-operate in creating long-term policy reforms; it is quite another for them to act quickly, in a unified manner, when turmoil hits.'[9] That failure to act quickly, decisively, and collectively when a crisis arose was a marked feature of the regulatory system that had been put in place prior to the crisis. It was left to central banks to act as lenders of last resort when a bank got into difficulties, but they were reluctant to intervene because of the issue of moral hazard. Moral hazard arose when intervention to prevent a bank failure encouraged excessive risk-taking in the knowledge that losses would force the central bank to provide support and so save the bank from collapse. What central banks wanted to avoid was assisting an insolvent bank as that would encourage others to follow a policy of increased risk-taking, and the profits that generated, confident that losses would result in intervention in order to prevent failure.

Instead of a focus on ensuring stability the priority of regulators before the crisis was to foster competition. A prime target in this campaign were stock exchanges as they were regarded as anachronistic monopolies that no longer fulfilled a purpose but managed to extract high fees in return for a poor service. This attack on stock exchanges had begun in the USA where RegNMS was designed to introduce a much greater element of competition for the duopoly of Nasdaq and the NYSE. As these exchanges had a stranglehold over the listing of new stocks each then became the centre of liquidity and source of reference pricing, which made it difficult for other venues to compete with them on the basis of providing a cheaper and better service. Various attempts had been made to undermine the commanding position of these two exchanges but that had failed, especially as they acquired leading competitors and responded to competition by lowering their fees and embracing electronic trading. With RegNMS the control exercised by Nasdaq and the NYSE was broken. They had to make available current market data while trades had to be routed to the venue offering the best price. RegNMS was introduced in March 2007 after a delay of two years. The EU followed with its own version, Mifid, which came into force in November 2007. Mifid built on earlier efforts in the EU to remove the protected status of national stock exchanges. The general effect of RegNMS and Mifid was to increase competition between exchanges and encourage the growth of alternative trading platforms and

[8] Paul J. Davies, 'The dangers inherent in imprudent lending', 5th March 2007.
[9] Gillian Tett, 'Regulators weigh up supra-national intervention', 19th November 2007.

dark pools, leading to the fragmentation of the equity market. Under these circumstances the power of established stock exchanges to regulate the securities market was undermined. No longer could stock exchanges spread the costs of policing the market over all participants, and force compliance with the rules and regulations imposed to ensure disciplined buying and selling, prevent price manipulation, and remove counterparty risk. As it was the multiple roles played by stock exchanges were increasingly seen by the regulators as responsibilities that could be left to others, so depriving them of the power that they had used to monopolize the equity market and extract excessive fees from those who used their facilities.

Prior to the crisis markets had become electronic networks open to all subscribers and provided either as standalone businesses or as a customized service to particular users. Markets other than those for corporate stocks had long operated in this way, including ones that were much larger, such as global foreign exchange trading, and so there was no reason why stock exchanges should continue to exist. Regulation had become the responsibility of government-appointed agencies with statutory powers over all who acted as intermediaries in the buying and selling of corporate stocks. Counterparty risk could be dealt with through clearing houses with a number ready to provide a service for the global community. One was LCH.Clearnet with its chairman, Chris Tupker, observing in 2007 that, 'Financial markets have long been global while their infrastructure has remained largely national.'[10] What he was keen to provide was an international clearing service that would replicate that which already existed in the USA. In the USA the Depository Trust and Clearing Corporation (DTCC) provided a single clearing service for all the country's stock exchanges, and also catered for transactions that took place outside through the new electronic platforms. According to Tupker, the DTCC's 'gigantic volumes and scale advantages of its privileged position shut out any European competitor'.[11]

To achieve the same position elsewhere in the world, but beginning in Europe, meant that regulators would have to remove the privileges attached to national clearers. This they were reluctant to do, causing much frustration. Charlie McCreevy, the EU internal market commissioner, complained in 2008 that, 'Legal barriers make it much more complex to hold securities cross-border, and lead to higher costs for transactions and credit.'[12] Regulators would also have to intervene to block the formation of vertical silos and dismantle those that already existed, as they were considered a barrier to competition. A vertical-silo existed when an exchange not only controlled trading but also the subsequent processing of transactions, including clearing. In the judgement of Chris Tupker: 'A clearing house owned by an exchange has every incentive to block competition for its contracts by refusing to give margin offsets to clients who want to trade the same contracts elsewhere.'[13] The problem he faced was that regulators were unwilling to prevent the formation of new vertical-silos let alone dismantle those in existence. In not blocking the CME/CBOT merger the US Department of Justice accepted the reality of the vertical-silo model for derivatives while the EU took no action to force Deutsche Börse to de-merge its clearing house from its equity and derivatives trading platforms. In 2008 Jeremy Grant observed that, 'Ownership of clearing—and, crucially, providing the location where traders' open positions are

[10] Chris Tupker, 'Clearing houses must be free to compete', 21st June 2007.
[11] Chris Tupker, 'Clearing houses must be free to compete', 21st June 2007.
[12] Jeremy Grant, 'Brussels calls for ideas on securities trading', 26th August 2008.
[13] Chris Tupker, 'Clearing houses must be free to compete', 21st June 2007.

kept—has become strategically important for many exchanges since it is a highly lucrative part of the business.'[14]

As providers of reliable market information and price data the assumption was also made that exchanges could easily be replaced by others who already specialized in such a service, such as Reuters. There was nothing that a stock exchange did that could not be better done by others and more cheaply. It was this that Norma Cohen picked up on in July 2007 when she observed 'Mifid will for the first time form genuine competition for what had been until now a service with monopoly providers: exchanges. Mifid will not only allow new trading platforms to spring up but will also allow existing exchanges to compete for each other's trading volumes'[15] Even in supervising daily behaviour in the equity market regulators could turn to the megabanks, as they already took responsibility for transactions in the money, foreign exchange, and bond markets. The megabanks had invested in the technology, staff, and office systems that not only allowed them to comply with new regulations but also provide best execution trading at the lowest price by accessing different electronic platforms. The undermining of exchanges suited the megabanks as they were already developing internal markets in which securitized assets were traded. It was they that provided liquidity through their willingness to act as counterparties by using their reserves to buy when others were selling and to sell from their vast holdings when others were buying. Increasingly it was banks, both individually and collectively, that were becoming the centres of liquidity rather than exchanges. This meant that concerns among regulators that RegNMS or Mifid would fragment the market, by breaking up the power of exchanges, were greatly diminished as the banks could be relied upon to provide liquidity, prevent manipulation, maintain the reliability of pricing, and cover counterparty risk. Regulators supervised banks and that indirect control was considered sufficient for the OTC market. There was no need to channel trading through exchanges rather than OTC markets, which cost less because of lower regulatory expenses. By adopting many of the features of exchanges, such as central clearing, settlement, and confirmation, the distinction between them and the OTC market was fast disappearing in the eyes of the regulators.

What remained a concern for regulators prior to the crisis was investor protection as individuals were still important holders of corporate stocks. Here stock exchanges had a poor record given their focus on the interests of members and later the owners, after demutualization. The solution adopted by regulators was to force through transparency whatever the consequences that had on the ability of the exchanges to generate an income or the interests of the large institutional investors with complex transactions that took time to complete. This enforced transparency had the effect of driving equity trading away from regulated exchanges, where users had to meet the new rules, and into dark pools as there transactions could be completed before the details had to be revealed. As these dark pools involved banks and fund managers dealing with each other regulators could trust them to police their own transactions and take responsibility for counterparty risk. One effect was to blur the distinction between those products that were publicly listed, such as corporate stocks, and those that were not, as was the case of the numerous bonds generated as part of the securitization process. All were seen as equivalent, even though the liquidity of corporate stocks relied upon the collective self-interest of an exchange to ensure that trading could and would take place, as that was how it attracted users and generated fees. Securitized assets depended upon the willingness of an individual bank to make and maintain a

[14] Jeremy Grant, 'Energy platforms in final tussle for clearer advantage', 19th May 2008.

[15] Norma Cohen, 'Reuters to join scramble for real-time data', 11th July 2007.

market. This difference was to prove of enormous importance during the crisis when quoted stocks continued to be bought and sold and generate a price that was of value for collateral purposes, whereas securitized assets became impossible to sell or value. What the crisis revealed was that not all markets were equal when it came to liquidity, but the assumption had been made by regulators that they were. The originate-and-distribute model adopted by banks, after encouragement from the regulators, relied upon that assumption which proved to be a false one.[16]

[16] Gillian Tett, 'Dark Liquidity system to launch', 5th February 2007; Norma Cohen, 'Kansas City undercuts NYC', 9th February 2007; Norma Cohen, 'LSE prepares for freedom from Nasdaq bid', 10th February 2007; Anuj Gangahar, 'New rules to prompt surge in trading', 5th March 2007; Paul J. Davies, 'The dangers inherent in imprudent lending', 5th March 2007; Norma Cohen and Gerrit Wiesmann, 'ECB pledges to consult on settlement system T2S', 9th March 2007; Norma Cohen, David Blackwell and Jeremy Grant, 'Top SEC official calls Aim a casino', 9th March 2007; Jeremy Grant, 'SEC official warns on foreign standards', 27th March 2007; Norma Cohen, 'Doors open as industry removes barriers', 30th March 2007; Norma Cohen, 'Competitive age dawns in Europe', 3rd April 2007; Tom Burgis, 'Canada sets the pace for free trade in securities', 3rd April 2007; Jeremy Grant, 'Regulators play different notes on the same instrument', 17th April 2007; Norma Cohen, 'Turquoise reality being fleshed out', 19th April 2007; Norma Cohen, 'Lehman to launch off-bourse product', 20th April 2007; Norma Cohen, 'Mifid ushers in a new era of trading', 23rd May 2007; Chris Tupker, 'Clearing houses must be free to compete', 21st June 2007; Jennifer Hughes and Peter Thal Larsen, 'A light approach and 9,000 page rulebook', 23rd June 2007; Jennifer Hughes and Peter Thal Larsen, '"Twin peaks" watching duties', 23rd June 2007; Song Jung-a, 'Brokerage sector looks set for consolidation', 26th June 2007; Mark Mulligan, 'Bolsa bides its time in midst of merger frenzy', 28th June 2007; Norma Cohen, 'Reuters to join scramble for real-time data', 11th July 2007; Doug Cameron, 'All-Chicago deal is coup for city', 11th July 2007; Jeremy Grant, 'OTC energy trades under CFTC spotlight', 3rd August 2007; Norma Cohen, 'LCH.Clearnet launches appeal for bourses access', 10th august 2007; Michiyo Nakamoto, 'Call to pull down barriers', 14th September 2007; Peter Thal Larsen, George Parker, Chris Giles and Lina Saigol, 'Recriminations fly at handling of Rock Crisis', 19th September 2007; Peter Norman, 'Revolution in EU securities kick off', 29th October 2007; Peter Thal Larsen, 'Institutions prepare for the consequences', 30th October 2007; Norma Cohen, 'Seeking to end a share trading monopoly', 30th October 2007; Philip Stafford, 'Directive to break down barriers', 30th October 2007; Norma Cohen, 'Marching orders in the Mifid revolution', 1st November 2007; Norma Cohen, 'Path through the data explosion', 1st November 2007; Saskia Scholtes, 'Best execution encourages alternative venues', 1st November 2007; Jennifer Hughes and Gillian Tett, 'A long road to any Mifid impact', 2nd November 2007; Paul J. Davies, 'Bond markets likely to escape strict transparency', 2nd November 2007; Lionel Barber and Jeremy Grant, 'US regulator eyes London as base for Europe office', 2nd November 2007; Jennifer Hughes, 'US stands out on worldwide language', 19th November 2007; Gillian Tett, 'MTS grip under threat', 19th November 2007; Gillian Tett, 'OTC derivatives hold their own', 19th November 2007; Gillian Tett, 'Regulators weigh up supra-national intervention', 19th November 2007; Kate Burgess, 'Luxembourg edges, as London hedges', 19th November 2007; Anuj Gangahar, 'Fewer platforms, faster trading', 19th November 2007; Simeon Kerr, 'Bourses at war for business', 20th November 2007; Bernard Simon and Anuj Gangahar, 'TSX joins consolidation race with Montreal deal', 11th December 2007; Jeremy Grant, 'Regulators' turf battles prompt talk about reform', 5th December 2007; David Ibison, 'Swedish law to stop OMX being Americanised', 19th December 2007; Jeremy Grant, 'SEC eyes cross-border shake-up', 3rd January 2008; Norma Cohen, 'Exchanges appear ready to go over to the dark side', 9th January 2008; Professor John Coffee, 'Regulation-lite belongs to a different age', 21st January 2008; Joanna Chung, 'Exchanges in fight over dearth of new issues', 1st March 2008; Lindsay Whipp, 'Aim seeks more exposure in Japan', 3rd March 2008; Hal Weitzman and Joanna Chung, 'SEC–CFTC liaison deal set to hasten product approval', 12th March 2008; Peter Norman, 'Call to improve plumbing of fund processing', 31st March 2008; Jeremy Grant, 'Liffe in first for options contracts', 31st March 2008; Jeremy Grant, 'Settlement slow to follow rapid trades', 4th April 2008; Jeremy Grant, 'Party mood might elude LCH.Clearnet', 29th April 2008; Jeremy Grant, 'Energy platforms in final tussle for clearer advantage', 19th May 2008; Jeremy Grant, 'Decision pending on post-trade', 23rd May 2008; Jeremy Grant, 'Europe urged to adopt US clearing model', 16th June 2008; Jeremy Grant, 'Turquoise and Chi-X suffer Italian blow', 30th July 2008; Jeremy Grant, 'Frustration for exchange newcomers', 31st July 2008; Jeremy Grant, 'Brussels calls for ideas on securities trading', 26th August 2008; Jeremy Grant, 'The fast bowlers arrive: Europe's battle for share dealing business is about to intensify', 1st September 2008; Jeremy Grant, 'Unsettling facts of post-trading', 8th September 2008; Jeremy Grant, 'Competitive UK stock clearing gets the go-ahead', 25th September 2008; Michael Mackenzie, 'Interest rate swaps dominate dealing', 15th October 2008; Jeremy Grant, 'Clearers step into limelight', 21st October 2008; Jeremy Grant, 'Mifid opens door to US platforms', 31st October 2008; Patti Waldmeir, 'Liberalisation marches to its own drum', 24th November 2008; Jeremy Grant, 'Trading data has deteriorated since Mifid, IMA warns', 25th November 2008; Abeer Allam, 'Foreign investors key to plans', 28th November 2008; Edward Luce, 'New recipe thickens alphabet soup', 12th June 2009; Joanna Chung, 'Complexity has led to cracks in system', 12th June 2009; Gregory Meyer, 'Banks back strict energy-trading limits', 30th July 2009; Gregory Meyer, 'Dilemma over limiting speculation', 4th August 2009; Javier Blas and Gregory Meyer,

By the beginning of 2008 regulators were becoming aware that problems were emerging in the global financial system that threatened to overwhelm the structures they had put in place. These were becoming apparent in the banking system, where, according to Peter Thal Larsen in January 2008, 'In the past few years, the banks' apparent ability to pass on much of their risk meant the scope for creating new credit was almost limitless.'[17] While the banks had been permitted, and even encouraged through the adoption of the originate-and-distribute model, to expand their lending without restraint, the regulators had contented themselves with supervising and reforming other parts of the financial system. The equity market and the stock exchanges had been the focus for reform while it was the risks posed by hedge funds, not banks, that most concerned global regulators. By March 2008 it was clear that highly-regulated banks had been taking huge risks, leaving them with losses that were far bigger than those of the lightly-regulated hedge funds. The regulators were then called upon to respond but failed to do so in a way that helped to avert the crisis taking place. One of the regulatory systems that proved to be among the most incapable of doing so was that of the UK, which had been much admired the year before. In a 2008 review of British banking regulation David Lascelles pointed out the fundamental flaw that had existed at its heart since the formation of the Financial Services Authority (FSA) in 1997/8:

> The Treasury makes decisions about the use of public resources to keep the financial services sector in order, and the Financial Services Authority supervises it day to day. The confusion lies only with the role of the Bank of England, which is neither one thing nor the other?... The Bank is uniquely placed to understand banks and markets, and to provide guidance to both of these.'[18]

The Bank of England's role in banking supervision had been marginalized in the establishment of the FSA, and it then concentrated on advising and implementing monetary policy, despite having the maintenance of financial stability, including acting as lender of last resort, as one of its priorities. This fundamental flaw was used by Adair Turner, the chairman of the FSA, in his defence in 2009 as it left 'the Bank with power without responsibility and the FSA with responsibility without power'.[19] The flaw lay in the design of the regulatory system, not the actions, or lack of them, by those left to carry out the tasks, and that placed responsibility on the politicians and their administrators who had created it, though the consequences were felt ten years later. By then the blame could be placed on the inhabitants of the building not the architects who had designed it.

However, the UK's system of financial regulation was not alone in being found wanting in 2008 as the series of crises that took place around the world testified. Few countries escaped whatever system they had put in place, though there were exceptions such as Australia and Canada. Only government intervention prevented a complete breakdown indicating the inadequacy of the regulatory structures that had been put in place over the previous ten years. Faced with a financial crisis of escalating magnitude during 2008 regulators had little to offer. One response was to reverse their previous recommendation

'Regulators face risk of encouraging traders to migrate', 5th August 2009; Gregory Meyer, 'US natural gas industry fears damage from trading curbs', 13th August 2009; Bernard Simon, 'Toronto's trading platforms draw regulatory scrutiny', 20th November 2009; Gregory Meyer, 'Regulators aim to curb the massive passives', 25th November 2009.

[17] Peter Thal Larsen, 'Payback Time', 7th January 2008.
[18] David Lascelles, 'The Bank needs a stronger role in the City', 16th June 2008.
[19] George Parker and Chris Giles, 'Turner goes in to bat for "whipping boy" FSA', 24th June 2009.

for banks to adopt the originate-and-distribute model over the lend-and-hold one, as that was now seen to have encouraged a policy of excessive lending and increased risk-taking. Another reversal was opposition to vertical-silos. In July 2008 Paul J. Davies and Hal Weitzman reported that 'In the wake of the credit crisis and heightened regulatory attention, exchanges and dealer banks are battling to be at the centre of an electronic, automated and more centralised financial infrastructure'.[20] At that stage of the crisis regulators remained committed to the central role played by the megabanks while turning to exchanges with clearing houses for added reassurance that transactions in financial markets would be completed. As Jeremy Grant observed in October 2008, after the failure of Lehman Brothers, 'The collapse left banks and other institutions with huge trading positions in which Lehman was the counterparty'.[21] The risk that a counterparty to a trade might be unable to meet their side of a bargain and default had become a major concern by the middle of 2008, whereas it had been considered a remote possibility a year before. To counter the risk of counterparty default regulators also pressed for trades to be confirmed and processed on the same day as this reduced the level of exposure. Those more measured responses were accompanied by temporary bans on short-selling by regulators around the world. Speculators were an obvious scapegoat to blame for the turmoil that was affecting financial markets, rather than the fundamental weaknesses in the financial system that the rolling crisis had exposed. Another target for blame were the hedge funds as some did employ short-selling tactics. This was despite the evidence that pointed to investors being responsible for most of the selling of bank shares because of genuine fears that the businesses would not survive. Collectively, none of the actions of regulators during 2008 addressed the immediate issues in the global financial system. These revolved around a collapse of trust in banks as counterparties and the evaporation of liquidity in a number of important markets, especially those involving securitized assets. Other than pointing the finger at speculators and hedge funds regulators appeared to have had no solutions as to what to do in the face of a global financial crisis, whose making they had contributed to. The response was left to central banks and national governments.[22]

First Stage Intervention, 2009

Having played a limited role in the crisis itself the regulators came to the fore in the years that followed. Such was the seriousness of the crisis, and the flaws in the regulatory structures it exposed, that there was a public demand for a new approach. The global financial system that developed prior to the financial crisis had been forged by deregulation underpinned by a belief in free markets. That belief ended with the crisis. Writing in 2009 Brooke Masters highlighted the pressure that regulators were under to act: 'With belief in a

[20] Paul J. Davies and Hal Weitzman, 'CME and Markit launch OTC land grab', 22nd July 2008.

[21] Jeremy Grant, 'Clearers step into limelight', 21st October 2008.

[22] Peter Thal Larsen, 'Payback Time', 7th January 2008; James Mackintosh, 'Hedge funds pose dilemma for regulators', 5th March 2008; David Lascelles, 'The Bank needs a stronger role in the City', 16th June 2008; Gillian Tett, Aline van Duyn, and Paul J. Davies, 'A re-emerging market? Bankers are seeking simpler ways to sell on debt', 1st July 2008; Paul J. Davies and Hal Weitzman, 'CME and Markit launch OTC land grab', 22nd July 2008; Michael Mackenzie and Nicole Bullock, 'Deadline is looming for derivatives clean-up', 22nd July 2008; Joanna Chung, Henry Sender and James Mackintosh, 'Short-selling ban catches funds out', 20th September 2008; James Mackintosh and Deborah Brewster, 'Evidence falls short of talk in assault on speculation', 20th September 2008; Jeremy Grant, Gillian Tett, and Aline van Duyn, 'Calls for derivatives clearing intensify', 15th October 2008; George Parker and Chris Giles, 'Turner goes in to bat for "whipping boy" FSA', 24th June 2009.

self-correcting market shattered by the financial collapse, taxpayers and politicians are angry about the enormous cost of propping up the banking system. Regulators, meanwhile, are under fire for allowing such a catastrophe to occur on their watch. Roundly criticised for their failure to prevent the financial crisis, regulators have become more proactive and intrusive.'[23] Agreement in principle, that action had to be taken, was relatively easy to achieve but not the details of what was to be done, as these were both complex and time-consuming, especially as an international solution was required given the importance of cross-border financial activity. What the crisis had done was focus the minds of regulators on the issue of liquidity, which they had largely ignored before. The assumption they had made, that assets could always be sold when converted into marketable securities, whether they were listed on a public exchange or not, turned out not to be flawed. The lesson from the 2008 crisis was that a liquidity crisis soon became a solvency one when assets were impossible to sell or even to value for collateral purposes. Illiquidity was a temporary situation, which could be met through inter-bank transfers or the intervention of a lender of last resort, as that could diffuse the crisis without having lasting consequences. In contrast, insolvency arose when a bank's liabilities were greater than its assets and could only be met by suspending the business and winding-down its affairs, paying creditors a proportion of what they were owed. The time that would take risked great disruption not only to the financial system but also to the economy. Only as assets were disposed of would it become clear whether a bank was illiquid or insolvent. It was therefore a matter of judgement for a central bank, acting as a lender of last resort, whether to intervene or not so as to prevent a bank failing. If the judgement was that the cause of the crisis was a sudden loss of liquidity then intervention could be justified, as the assistance provided was temporary. Conversely, if the judgement was that the issue was one of solvency then no intervention was justified, as that would risk moral hazard. For regulators the task was how to fashion a financial system that either prevented these crises arising or put in place mechanisms for dealing with them if they did, distinguishing between liquidity and solvency issues.

Framing a new financial system created a problem for regulators for it undermined the reliance they had placed on the megabanks to maintain stability as they had been considered immune from issues of liquidity and solvency. As central banks and governments had been forced to intervene to save a number of these banks from collapse, that position no longer existed. Writing in 2009 Peter Thal Larsen reported that, 'Regulators are set to restrict the amount of risk that banks take on. They may also be tempted to restrict their overall size.'[24] This was echoed by Ben Bernanke, the chair of the Federal Reserve, when he emphasised that 'Any firm whose failure would pose a systemic risk must receive especially close supervisory oversight of its risk-taking, risk management and financial condition, and be held to high capital and liquidity standards,'[25] An immediate response to this new situation was to force banks to hold more capital and reduce the leverage they applied when making loans. This would provide a reserve to cover losses and reduce the build-up of risk. Since the collapse of Long-Term Capital Management in 1998 the banks themselves had applied this strategy to hedge funds, requiring them to provide collateral to support their trading positions, but they did not follow that requirement themselves. Instead, banks had relied heavily on short-term funding through the repurchase (repo) market. In the repo market assets, ranging from Treasury bonds to complex mortgage-backed securities, were

[23] Brooke Masters, 'Long road to regulation', 26th October 2009.
[24] Peter Thal Larsen, 'Too early to declare death of "universal banking"', 15th January 2009.
[25] Peter Thal Larsen, 'A lot to be straightened out', 31st March 2009.

lent out overnight, with the cash received helping finance these holdings. That exposed banks to the classic run caused by a heavy reliance on short-term funds to finance illiquid assets, with insufficient cash and easily-disposed investments being held to cover a temporary shortfall. Around the world the confidence in the originate-and-distribute model had encouraged banks to adopt this strategy in the belief that the assets they held were liquid, only to discover in the crisis that they were not. In the wake of the crisis there was a rapid reassessment of the capital required by banks even without regulatory intervention. The outcome was higher levels of capital, which had serious consequences in terms of the ability of banks to lend or invest in assets that had been regarded as liquid. As the banks withdrew from lending, because of a combination of the risks the crisis exposed, the transparency requirements imposed by regulators, and the pressure to conserve capital, the liquidity of many transferable assets dried up. That left investors holding assets they could no longer sell and businesses unable to raise funds, which made the crisis worse. What had begun as a liquidity crisis, affecting marginal players in 2007, had by 2008 become a solvency crisis endangering the survival of some of the largest banks in the world. By 2009 regulators were forced to recognize the close links between liquidity and solvency and propose measures to address this.[26]

Addressing the issue of liquidity meant that regulators had to reappraise their attitude to markets, including the role played by exchanges. Prior to the crisis the focus of regulators had been on creating a competitive trading environment by removing the monopoly of incumbent exchanges. Writing in 2009 Jeremy Grant hailed this as 'a resounding success'.[27] Both in the USA and the EU, competition for stock exchanges had been provided, driving down fees and improving the service provided. Accompanying this increased competition, however, was market fragmentation in both the USA and the EU. That contributed to undermining both liquidity and the reliability of the prices generated in the equity market, as that had relied upon the concentration of trading through the regulated exchanges. Nevertheless, during the crisis equity markets remained places where corporate stocks could be bought and sold, and reliable prices were generated. In contrast, it was the OTC markets, whose growth the regulators had condoned or promoted, that broke down in 2008, rendering assets impossible to sell or even value, with disastrous consequences for those financial institutions that relied upon their supposed liquidity. Liquidity relied upon confidence in counterparties and this evaporated in the unregulated OTC market, where securitized assets and financial derivatives were traded, but existed in the equity market through the self-regulation of exchanges and the oversight of statutory agencies. The regulators, who had been mounting an attack on stock exchanges prior to the crisis, were forced to recognize this in 2009.

At that stage the response by regulators to the crisis was to push for more trading to be channelled through exchanges. Only on exchanges could those buying and selling financial instruments of any kind be certain of completing a deal at a reliable price, rather than being at the mercy of a small club of dominant banks as in the OTC market. Those exchanges

[26] Peter Thal Larsen, 'Too early to declare death of "universal banking"', 15th January 2009; Jeremy Grant, 'Post-trade services come into their own', 2nd February 2009; James Sassoon, 'Britain deserves a better system of financial regulation', 9th March 2009; Peter Thal Larsen, 'A lot to be straightened out', 31st March 2009; Adrian Cox, 'Multiple threats still loom for the investment banking model', 1st April 2009; Michael Mackenzie and Aline van Duyn, 'Costs set to rise amid shake-up in derivatives trading', 19th June 2009; Hal Weitzman and Jeremy Grant, 'Futures brokers fear new capital rules', 6th July 2009; Steve Johnson, 'How to breathe life back into bonds', 20th July 2009; Steve Johnson, 'Fear for corporate bonds trade', 20th July 2009; David Oakley, 'Europe's ravaged landscape begins to stabilise', 11th September 2009; Brooke Masters, 'Long road to regulation', 26th October 2009.

[27] Jeremy Grant, 'Competition is sharper but liquidity fragmented', 21st October 2009.

most favoured by the switch in the stance of regulators were those that combined clearing and settlement with a trading platform, such as the CME in the USA and Deutsche Börse in the EU. In the USA a nationwide national clearing agency, the Depository Trust and Clearing Corporation (DTCC) already provided a centralized service for equity trading while the Options Clearing Corporation (OCC) did the same for options. In those markets the support given to exchanges in the USA was tempered by the fact that subsequent processing of transactions was not in their hands, but lay with an agency that operated as a utility provider, and so could not be used to block competition. However, that was not the position in the US futures market where the CME combined both trading and clearing and, since its takeover of CBOT and Nymex, was in a totally dominant position. The legislation enacted by the US Congress, designed to force OTC derivatives to be processed through clearing houses, as a way of reducing the counterparty risks associated with defaults, was a gift to the CME. The CME had faced growing competition from the OTC market where swaps were traded between banks or through interdealer brokers. The legislation would force that business to take place through exchanges with the CME the most obvious beneficiary. A further by-product of US legislation would be to enhance the position of a US institution, the CME, through preventing US traders using the OTC market, which was largely located in London. Though the justification for the US move was to improve transparency and eliminate counterparty risk the ulterior motive was to undermine this foreign competition. This use of regulation as way of favouring national institutions and national businesses in the aftermath of the crisis was not confined to the USA. Though regulation was given the appearance of being designed to address the issues uncovered in the crisis it was also used as a cover for national self-interest. In the EU, regulatory intervention after the crisis included an attempt by the German and French governments to favour Frankfurt and Paris as locations for fund managers, so that they could be brought under greater control, as three-quarters of global assets were currently managed in the USA, the UK, and Switzerland.

However, these attempts by regulators to drive financial activity towards exchanges brought a strong resistance from market participants, which built up during 2009 as they became aware of the additional costs and lack of flexibility it would involve. In the case of derivatives the Association of Corporate Treasurers explained that:,

> Ordinary non-financial companies use tailored derivatives provided by their banks to hedge the sorts of risks that arise from normal business activity, and not for speculative purposes. Exactly matched hedging can be done for specific risks, amount and timings, using OTC derivatives to eliminate or manage the risk. Prohibiting OTC derivatives might help in minimising risk in the financial sector but could result in additional risk being carried in the non-financial sector with potentially devastating effect.[28]

Alexander McDonald, the chief executive of the Wholesale Market Brokers' Association, also voiced his members concerns: 'There is a danger that policy decisions are being considered that may attempt to force OTC products on to exchanges, resulting in a dramatic reduction in liquidity and product flexibility in markets essential for trading and hedging.'[29] What they were resisting was being required to obey rules that were neither appropriate nor beneficial. Even some of those running exchanges that could expect to pick up business

[28] Jeremy Grant, 'Derivatives reform draws UK warning', 25th July 2009.
[29] Jeremy Grant, 'Exchanges and brokers at odds over crisis blame', 20th February 2009.

were worried that the actions of regulators would expose them to risks that they could not manage. Adam Kinsley, head of regulation at the LSE, said 'I don't think it's the right way for regulators to force inappropriate products on-exchange.'[30] Most of the contracts entered into in the OTC derivatives markets, for example, were bilateral arrangements between individual buyers and sellers, with each exposed to the counterparty risk of default by the other side. These were unsuitable for trading on exchanges that worked best with standard products. Those involved in the world's largest financial market, that for foreign exchange, were completely opposed to any attempt to force trading through exchanges because of the difficulties it would create. They had devised their own solution to counterparty risk, which involved settling transactions through the CLS Bank, where deals were completed through simultaneous transactions. As the detail of what a shift to exchange trading would involve emerged there was significant backtracking among regulators, because of the costs involved and the loss of useful products and markets. Even without regulatory intervention the crisis had heightened the appreciation of risk, with those involved taking their own measures to reduce it through more care in the selection of products and counterparties.

At the same time as resistance to the use of exchanges for all financial transactions grew so the commitment of regulators to push through such a policy shift waned. This was despite pressure from exchanges, especially those operating vertical-silos, to be made central to any post-crisis solution to counterparty risk. By 2009 the three leading exchange operators in the world all used the vertical-silo model, namely Hong Kong Exchanges and Clearing, CME Group, and Deutsche Börse. Reto Francioni, the Swiss-born chief executive of Deutsche Börse, articulated their case: 'Having trading and risk management under one roof meant we could act quickly and efficiently. The liquidity pools were always there, helping build trust in price discovery. We delivered our services at a very high level of quality during the crisis. If you are a service provider and no one is talking about you, you are doing a good job.'[31] Countering this pressure were the megabanks, as they wanted the freedom to trade in any manner they chose. Fears also resurfaced among regulators that exchanges operating vertical-silos could monopolize markets, stifle innovation, and exploit users. The dilemma regulators faced after the crisis was no different from that they had before, which was how to capture the benefits stemming from the OTC market with the reduced risks and greater transparency provided by exchanges. This had generated different scenarios even in the same country. The virtual monopoly of the CME in US futures trading could be tolerated because it was largely a professionals market, and the alternative of the OTC market was readily available and heavily used, leading to a dynamic situation in which the two elements both complemented each other and competed. In contrast, the OTC equity market was much smaller and largely the domain of the professionals with their dark pools, leaving the incumbent exchanges with a monopoly of trading in those stocks that they quoted, unless regulatory intervention took place. As these concerns began to triumph over those related to counterparty risk, regulators withdrew their support for exchanges, while it was accepted that certain OTC markets, such as those dealing with foreign exchange and complex swaps, were better left to the self-regulation of the participants.

One commitment that continued was that to channel more trading through clearing houses, though this also met resistance during 2009. When a clearing house was involved, providing a guarantee that if either side to a deal defaulted the other party did not lose out, participants were required to provide collateral, which they could not then use for their own

[30] Jeremy Grant, 'Exchanges warn on OTC clearing', 4th June 2009.

[31] James Wilson, 'More than just a historic trading floor', 30th June 2009.

business. This was a major loss to a bank, especially if it did not consider such a guarantee necessary, as in the foreign exchange market with a turnover of $5tn a day. Alexander McDonald, the chief executive of Wholesale Market Brokers' Association, pleaded on behalf of his members in 2009 that, 'We would hope that policymakers are aware of the wide range of OTC products across the financial, energy and commodity markets that are unlikely ever to be considered as eligible for central clearing.'[32] It was also pointed out by Mark Ibbotson, the chief operating officer at the futures division of NYSE Euronext, that, 'It could damage the security of a clearing house to force products on to a clearing house that shouldn't be there.'[33] Many financial products were of a bespoke nature making it impossible for a clearing house to guarantee completion in the event of a default. If they had to provide that guarantee the level of collateral demanded would make the deal unprofitable and so would not be done, leaving banks and others without a cheap and convenient means of covering their risks. For that reason many banks and major users of financial markets preferred a solution generated internally, as had been the case in foreign exchange markets, rather than one imposed by regulators. Chris Willcox, global head of rates trading at JP Morgan, stated in 2009, 'Even the clearing houses themselves agree on the need to ensure only products with sufficient liquidity and price transparency in the market are deemed suitable for clearing.'[34] There was always the problem of applying common rules and regulations to a market comprising numerous and diverse products and participants. This was at its most extreme in the equity market and at its least in that for foreign exchange. Under these circumstances what met the needs of one did not fit the other. Roger Liddell, the chief executive of LCH.Clearnet, did caution regulators in 2009 that 'Clearing houses manage risk; they don't work miracles. In this headlong rush to clearing, we must take care that clearing does not become an end in itself. If it does, there is a danger that we simply transfer, rather than reduce, systemic risk.'[35]

Nevertheless, pressure remained to move as much of the trading as possible through clearing houses as that represented a response of some kind to the crisis from the regulators. All had been impressed by the ability of clearing houses to deal with the vast exposure of outstanding deals between Lehman Brothers and various counterparties in the aftermath of its collapse. Pierre Francotte, the chief executive of Euroclear, claimed in 2009 that:

> The infrastructures most directly involved in managing the impact of the Lehman failure, LCH.Clearnet and Euroclear, incurred no losses and unwound their positions in a way that avoided risk for themselves and disruption to the market. Euroclear Bank and Clearstream continued to provide their customers every day with the intra-day credit necessary to settle cross-border trades smoothly and were able to obtain the liquidity they needed from the banks they use for this purpose.[36]

In the USA the DTCC had worked through $500bn in counterparty exposures resulting from the Lehman failure and had completed the task by 30th October 2008. By June 2009 no less a body than the BIS, the central bankers' central bank, was advocating that bilateral trading between banks should go through central counterparties. In Japan the services of

[32] Jeremy Grant, 'The humdrum has fresh significance', 21st October 2009.
[33] Jeremy Grant, 'Exchanges warn on OTC clearing', 4th June 2009.
[34] Jeremy Grant, 'Clearing up the system', 2nd November 2009.
[35] Jeremy Grant, 'NYSE Euronext joint venture to capitalise on rising demand for clearing', 19th June 2009.
[36] Pierre Francotte, 'Competition and challenges ahead', 2nd February 2009.

Japan Securities Clearing Corporation were being promoted as a solution to the risks inherent in the OTC market. The attraction of a clearing house was that it provided the certainty that if a participant in a market failed all others knew immediately what their exposure to that party was, and that there was a central deposit of collateral to cover money owed on outstanding contracts. If counterparty risk could be addressed by the use of a clearing house then liquidity would return because its absence was attributed to a lack of trust in financial markets. The use of a clearing house would restore that trust as it acted as a buyer for every seller and seller for every buyer in a transaction, helping to virtually eliminate counterparty risk.

That then raised the question of how best to provide central clearing facilities to financial markets. The DTCC in the USA was ready to provide this service to other countries, and attempted to acquire its main international rival, LCH.Clearnet in 2009. The DTCC was owned by the 500 banks, brokers, and others for whom it provided clearing, settlement, and information services across equities, corporate and municipal bonds, government and mortgage-backed securities, money-market instruments, and OTC derivatives. DTCC was also a leading processor of mutual funds and insurance transactions. In 2009 Donald Donahue, the chairman and chief executive of DTCC, explained that 'DTCC is a firewall to stop contagions, in the event of a firm failure, across each of the financial asset classes we support.'[37] Devin Wenig, chief executive of the markets division of Thomson Reuters, was one among many who advocated the DTCC model of clearing in 2009: 'If the regulators are going to mandate clearing, then they should be treated like utilities and we should all have fair and equal access to them.'[38] However, not all were happy with this as the DTCC was considered a monopoly, being able to impose charges and conditions on its users without fear of competition, which could have an adverse impact on those trading in financial markets, especially the banks. National governments were also reluctant to cede control of clearing to the DTCC, as that would give greater power to US authorities to impose their rules and regulations around the world. Even within the EU member states were unwilling to accept the establishment of a single clearing house, with strong opposition coming from those exchanges that operated vertical-silos. As Frederic Perard, global head of fund services products at BNP Paribas Securities Services, said in 2009, 'Europe is still a sum of markets. I don't see how it's going to be possible to offer a global solution.'[39] The best that the EU could come up with was to encourage links between separate clearing houses, though this raised the risk of contagion if one should fail. Clearing was not a universal panacea though regulators regarded it as such.

During 2009 regulators struggled to devise ways of making the financial system more resilient while maintaining its ability to respond to the needs of users. This struggle was articulated in 2009 by Mary Schapiro, the chairman of the SEC:

> The commission must assure that the public markets and non-public trading venues operate within a balanced regulatory framework. This means that as markets evolve, the commission must continually seek to preserve the essential role of the public markets in promoting efficient price discovery and investor confidence.... Given the growth of dark

[37] Michael Mackenzie, 'DTCC paves way for all roads to lead to its warehouse', 1st July 2009.
[38] Jeremy Grant, 'Clearing not the cure-all for financial system woes', 26th June 2009.
[39] Sophia Grene, 'Striving for a one-stop, straight through shop', 2nd February 2009.

pools, this lack of transparency could create a two-tiered market that deprives the public of information about stock prices and liquidity.[40]

The SEC recognized the benefits that came from the OTC market but was also aware of their opaque nature and the risks they posed. Though articulated by Mary Shapiro at the SEC the same issues were to be found around the world as regulators grappled with the complex issues of the degree and nature of intervention in a post-crisis world. Towards the end of 2009 regulators had identified a twin track approach as a way of responding to the issues raised by the crisis. This combined a central role for clearing along with improved oversight of the OTC market. However, that raised subsidiary concerns over the degree of oversight to be extended to banks, exchanges, and OTC markets, and what allowance should be made to suit individual circumstances, such as foreign exchange on the one hand and equities on the other. Even the use of clearing houses raised another set of problems for regulators. In the case of the USA these revolved around the role of the DTCC as a monopoly. For Europe, where a number of different clearing houses competed with each other for business, the issue was whether this encouraged them to require less collateral from users and so risk a collapse if a crisis arose. At the end of 2009 Jeremy Grant raised the prospect of a cascade of clearing house collapses in Europe as one failure led to another: 'Regulators have grown concerned about the risks associated with the inter-clearing house links that this would involve. If one clearer were to fail due to massive customer defaults such links—interoperability—could bring another clearing house down, they fear, with catastrophic results for the wider financial system.'[41] What was evident was that, a year on from the Global Financial Crisis of 2008, regulators were further away from devising a solution to the problems it had revealed, as each proposal was discovered to have flaws and met strong opposition.[42]

[40] Michael Mackenzie, 'SEC plans to illuminate dark pools', 22nd October 2009.

[41] Jeremy Grant, 'Rolet's new broom sweeps LSE', 24th December 2009.

[42] Jeremy Grant, 'LSE faces data-service challenge', 19th January 2009; Jeremy Grant, 'Single platform for settlements', 23rd January 2009; Jeremy Grant, 'Nasdaq OMX's Nordic move highlights post-trade focus', 26th January 2009; Jeremy Grant, 'Post-trade services come into their own', 2nd February 2009; Paul J. Davies, 'Credit derivatives drive hits a wall', 2nd February 2009; Hal Weitzman, 'Humble OTC emerges from shadows', 2nd February 2009; Jeremy Grant, 'Europe's post-trade infrastructure poised at the crossroads', 2nd February 2009; Pierre Francotte, 'Competition and challenges ahead', 2nd February 2009; Sophia Grene, 'Striving for a one-stop, straight through shop', 2nd February 2009; Jeremy Grant, 'Learning from the Lehman catastrophe', 2nd February 2009; Sophia Grene, 'Rules of engagement becoming blurry', 2nd February 2009; Jeremy Grant, 'Icap looks to LCH.Clearnet for growth', 3rd February 2009; Jeremy Grant, 'EMCF in X-Clear tie up', 3rd February 2009; Jeremy Grant, 'Case for change heard loud and clear', 9th February 2009; Jeremy Grant, 'CDS clearing planned for Europe', 17th February 2009; Jeremy Grant, 'Exchanges and brokers at odds over crisis blame', 20th February 2009; Nikki Tait and Jeremy Grant, 'Agreement reached over European CDS clearance', 20th February 2009; Jeremy Grant, 'Why the future for clearer is anything but clear', 5th March 2009; Jeremy Grant, 'LCH aims to buy out investors', 5th March 2009; Jeremy Grant, 'LSE drops central clearing plan', 3rd April 2009; Jeremy Grant, 'Clock ticking over future of LCH.Clearnet', 5th May 2009; Jeremy Grant, 'Competition in Europe toughens', 5th May 2009; Aline van Duyn and Anuj Gangahar, 'Exchanges big winners in OTC overhaul', 15th May 2009; Nikki Tait, 'Europe on the same wavelength as US, but moving more slowly', 15th May 2009; Gillian Tett, Aline van Duyn, and Jeremy Grant, 'Let battle commence', 20th May 2009; Jeremy Grant, 'OTC derivatives plan lifts shares', 2nd June 2009; Jeremy Grant, 'Exchanges warn on OTC clearing', 4th June 2009; Michael Mackenzie, 'OTC markets to get stronger oversight', 18th June 2009; Krishna Guha, 'US seeks safety allied to dynamism', 18th June 2009; Jeremy Grant, 'NYSE Euronext joint venture to capitalise on rising demand for clearing', 19th June 2009; Michael Mackenzie and Aline van Duyn, 'Costs set to rise amid shake-up in derivatives trading', 19th June 2009; Jeremy Grant, 'Clearing not the cure-all for financial system woes', 26th June 2009; Jeremy Grant, 'Origins in Japanese rice and French coffee markets', 26th June 2009; James Wilson, 'More than just a historic trading floor', 30th June 2009; Chris Giles, 'BIS calls for wide global financial reforms', 30th June 2009; Michael Mackenzie, 'DTCC paves way for all roads to lead to its warehouse', 1st July 2009; Hal Weitzman and Jeremy Grant, 'Futures brokers fear new capital rules', 6th July 2009; Jeremy Grant and Nikki Tait, 'Eurex and ICE lead clearing race after Liffe

Tipping Point, 2010

Prior to the financial crisis regulators proceeded on the assumption that there would not be a major financial crisis and, even if there were, the megabanks were too big to fail and markets would remain liquid. Under these circumstances the focus of regulators was on breaking down monopolies and creating competition not on enhancing the resilience of the system. The crisis destroyed those assumptions leading to an immediate search of ways to prevent another taking place. Apart from the more general calls for an end to capitalism, curbing globalization and a return to government direction the more specific recommendations focused on breaking up the megabanks, as they had proved to be too big to be allowed to fail, and restore exchanges to a central position in financial markets, because they had continued to function during the crisis. These recommendations were supported by powerful lobbies in the USA where deregulation had led to the growth of large and powerful banks, with the ending of the prohibition of both universal and inter-state banking, while undermining the power of incumbent exchanges like the NYSE, leading to the rise of unregulated financial markets. It was a natural assumption to link the 2008 crisis to the process of deregulation that had preceded it, despite evidence to the contrary and the global nature of what had taken place. The result was a reversal of policies that had promoted the growth of universal banks and OTC markets. That underpinned demands to break up the largest banks and to curb the OTC market. However, the commitment among governments to break up the megabanks quickly faded in the USA, and had never been well supported in those countries, such as Germany and Switzerland, where that type of banking had been long established. Though aware that some action was required to appease public opinion, greater reflection in the USA brought a recognition that breaking up the biggest US banks would undermine their ability to provide the service demanded by US business and investors and make it difficult for them to compete internationally.

By 2010 it was increasingly accepted that the megabanks were an indispensable part of the global financial system because of their size, scale, and interconnections. The modern financial world was complex, opaque, global, and integrated, comprising numerous independent units that were highly interconnected. Only the megabanks were in a position to provide the micro-management that this world required, including the ability to make and receive payments internationally, provide the credit that underpinned world trade, and the

setback', 6th July 2009; Brooke Masters and Nikki Tait, 'Dodging the Draft', 14th July 2009; Jeremy Grant and Nikki Tait, 'Trading costs in Europe remain stubbornly high', 17th July 2009; Jennifer Hughes, 'FX faces prospect of two-tier pricing', 21st August 2009; Gregory Meyer, 'CFTC and FSA eye London loophole', 21st August 2009; Jennifer Hughes, 'Concern over scope of initiatives', 29th September 2009; Jeremy Grant, 'First steps towards clearing for FX', 6th October 2009; Jeremy Grant, Richard Milne and Aline van Duyn, 'Collateral damage', 7th October 2009; Jeremy Grant, 'Sweeping changes are on the way', 21st October 2009; Jeremy Grant, 'Competition is sharper but liquidity fragmented', 21st October 2009; Hal Weitzman, 'The tectonic plates are shifting', 21st October 2009; Hal Weitzman, 'Clearport is a central part of CME's strategy', 21st October 2009; Michael Mackenzie, 'SEC plans to illuminate dark pools', 22nd October 2009; Michael Mackenzie and Helen Thomas, 'SEC looks to get to the bottom of dark pools', 28th October 2009; Saskia Scholtes and Aline van Duyn, 'SEC chief seeks new securities laws', 28th October 2009; Parselelo Kantai, 'Trouble at old boys club', 29th October 2009; Aline van Duyn, 'Numbers game', 2nd November 2009; Jeremy Grant, 'Clearing up the system', 2nd November 2009; Jennifer Hughes, 'Currency derivatives caught in US clearing net', 20th November 2009; John Keefe, 'Regulator's torch to light up dark pools', 23rd November 2009; Jeremy Grant, 'LCH.Clearnet sees need for a clear path to Washington', 27th November 2009; Lindsay Whipp, 'Chi-X global to spearhead Asian push with plans for Japan platform', 1st December 2009; Steve Johnson, 'Hidden costs found in dark pools', 7th December 2009; Jeremy Grant, 'Eurex and LSE to counter Liffe with equity options trading', 16th December 2009; Jeremy Grant, 'Rolet's new broom sweeps LSE', 24th December 2009; Aline van Duyn and Jeremy Grant, 'Use of clearers to rein in OTC derivatives poses fresh dilemma', 15th January 2010; Masa Serdarevic, 'Sungard offers access to exchanges', 22nd January 2010.

facilities that moved funds around seamlessly. Their contribution also included supervising and policing those who carried out these innumerable tasks on a daily basis. The megabanks were better able to handle these tasks than regulators, who continued to operate on a largely national basis and lacked the expertise and resources required to cope with a system that was neither simple, transparent, nor confined by national boundaries or responsive to centralized direction. Before the crisis these regulators had placed their faith in the megabanks to micro-manage the system under their direction. After the crisis they had little alternative but to return to this position but to combine it with more rules, greater supervision, and a faith in clearing houses to provide a guarantee against counterparty defaults. One who understood this was Adair Turner, the chair of the UK's Financial Services Authority. He pointed out in 2010 that 'Interconnectedness between different categories of financial institution increases the potential impact of a shock in any one sector and increases the danger of feedback loops.'[43] Rather than excusing the inadequacies of his own organization, when faced with the crisis, this was a statement reflecting the inability of regulators to deliver a stable financial system through their own efforts, and the reliance they had to place on the megabanks to undertake the day-to-day supervision of a financial system. That involved continuous judgements of risk and reward and interaction with multiple markets and products as money moved around the financial system and assets and liabilities were constantly matched over space, time, and type.

In contrast to the early impulse to break up the megabanks, which faded quite quickly, that to tackle the vast OTC market, and replace it with regulated exchanges, took longer to die. Even in 2010 Aline van Duyn, Michael Mackenzie, and Jeremy Grant could write that:

> Opacity in privately traded markets, such as in derivatives and complex securitised bonds, is widely seen as having contributed to the meltdown of the financial system in 2008 and the ensuing global economic crisis. Laws are being passed across the globe to force over-the-counter derivatives and other markets into the public eye. In many cases, stock markets have been hailed as the standard to live up to, for the ease with which investors can check stock prices and trade shares even when markets are volatile.[44]

However, by then regulators were retreating from regarding exchanges as the solution to the problems that had beset financial markets in 2008. In the years that followed the crisis it had become clear that exchanges could not cope with the volume and variety of financial transactions that would come their way if the OTC market was suppressed, and were even reluctant to do so because it was so unlike the business they normally handled. In 2010 Michael Mackenzie and Aline van Duyn described the everyday reality of the swaps market, where the average size of a transaction was $100m, but could reach as high as $1bn: 'Banks tend to trade OTC derivatives such as swaps directly with their customer, by telephone. These trades are then managed with other banks into the bigger and more liquid interbank market. There, trading is done by means of interdealer brokers such as ICAP, Tullett Prebon, GFI and BGC, using voice and electronic trading systems.'[45] These deals were negotiated between banks to meet a specific purpose and so were not suited to an exchange where standard contracts were actively traded. An estimate made for December 2009 indicated the total value of derivatives outstanding was $636,431bn, of which only

[43] Paul J. Davies and Izabella Kaminska, 'Banks seek help from new set of institutions', 22nd December 2010.
[44] Aline van Duyn, Michael Mackenzie, and Jeremy Grant, 'That sinking feeling', 2nd June 2010.
[45] Michael Mackenzie and Aline van Duyn, 'Regulators may silence derivative squawk boxes', 22 July 2010.

3.4 per cent was traded on exchanges. It was also recognized that putting exchanges in control could bring with it the anti-competitive behaviour that had led to intervention in the equity market before the crisis. Instead of promoting exchanges, regulatory intervention increasingly switched to favouring pushing as much of the trading as possible through clearing houses to make the financial system less vulnerable to default. These clearing houses possessed their own capital, demanded collateral, and collected up-front payments to ward against possible losses.

Other than the complexity of modern banking and financial markets in a global world, the other constraint faced by regulators in the post-crisis era, was what Jeremy Grant called in 2010, 'Regulatory arbitrage, where market participants shop around for the most favourable set of rules.'[46] As regulators increased the capital requirements on banks, and introduced other controls on what business they could do and how, they responded by discovering ways around the regulatory restrictions, while others quickly moved in to exploit any gaps that the intervention caused. A similar pattern had already emerged in financial markets before the crisis where dark pools and internal trading were used to evade rules and regulations imposed by regulators on the buying and selling conducted through exchanges. The problem with regulation was that it could not be sufficiently fine tuned to distinguish between those aspects of a bank's business, or the trading conducted on financial markets, that was low margin/low risk on the one hand and high margin/high risk on the other. The result was that regulators penalized them all equally, distorting the nature of a bank's business and the trading that took place. Much of a bank's business was routine and had not been disturbed by the crisis, such as the provision of credit and the making of payments that underpinned everyday transactions whether conducted within a country or internationally. The same was true of financial markets as the world's largest, the foreign exchange market, functioned normally throughout the crisis. Michael Mackenzie, writing in 2010, made the point about how different were markets, which, to the outside eye, were identical, such as those involving the trading of derivatives outside exchanges:

> OTC derivatives are the domain of banks, institutional investors and corporations looking to hedge interest rate, credit and currency risk, or to trade these instruments. Unlike the futures and equities markets, OTC derivatives can trade infrequently as many trades are bespoke in nature, and have been manufactured between a dealer and their client to hedge a specific interest-rate or currency risk. Often such trades can be substantial, with notional amounts in the hundreds of millions.[47]

The difficulty that regulators faced was framing rules that applied to all banks and financial markets. If they were too restrictive the inevitable response was to drive trading into the hands of those able to evade it. As one lawyer, whose expertise was in financial services, observed in 2010, 'For every regulatory action, there is an equally opposite reaction by the banks. The high-risk behaviour doesn't go away, it just goes somewhere else.'[48] Boutique and smaller banks gained the business being off-loaded by the megabanks as they could escape the most severe of the regulations. The same was true of financial markets, as Jeremy Grant observed in 2010: 'Dark pools exist to allow institutional investors to do large trades

[46] Jeremy Grant, 'The route to regulation diverges for Europe and America', 12th August 2010.
[47] Michael Mackenzie, 'One-size-fits-all approach risks killing flexibility', 3rd November 2010.
[48] Megan Murphy and Francesco Guerrera, 'Prop-hostile climate throws up some tough calls for banks', 4th August 2010.

away from standard exchanges, where prices are posted for all to see before trades are done. In a dark pool, prices are advertised only after trades are done.'[49] If only the megabanks and the regulated exchanges were covered by regulations then those omitted would be able expand their business, exploiting the restrictions placed on the others. This was a concern of Mario Draghi, the chairman of the BIS's Financial Stability Board in 2010: 'As we strengthen the requirements for banks, we must make sure that we also capture within the regulatory perimeter the sources of systemic risk presently outside it.'[50] The blurring of distinctions between and within banking and financial markets, and the erosion of barriers between countries, made it essential for regulators to take a comprehensive and global approach but they struggled to do this. Nikki Tait and Jeremy Grant talked in 2010 about the need for 'the regulatory framework' to 'keep pace with the changing shape of financial markets.'[51] By 2010 the results were far from perfect as they attempted to fashion a new regulatory system to meet the needs of the post-crisis world.[52] Numerous new rules were introduced but these were not applied evenly around the world. The enforcement of common rules and standards, even when agreed, was largely left to national authorities, creating considerable scope for variations to occur. This was the case within the EU despite the existence of a pan-European regulatory agency, the European Securities and Markets Authority, as supervision remained at the national level. Within the USA regulation remained divided among the different agencies leaving scope for a flexible interpretation of the rules within the same country.

What was most marked was the inability of regulators to predict the consequences of their actions. This had already happened in the equity market where the drive for increased transparency had encouraged the fragmentation of trading venues, the growth of dark pools, the use of complex derivatives, the deterioration in the quality of prices, and the rise of high-frequency trading (HFT). As Jeremy Grant explained in 2010, 'Such fragmentation has been a driving force behind the growth of HFT, since it produces a variety of trading venues each with slightly different trading systems, speeds and fee schedules. This allows traders to exploit these differences by using computer algorithms to trade back and forth from one platform to another.'[53] This had regulatory implications as fragmentation meant that exchanges were in no position to provide the self-regulation of the market that they had been accustomed to do in the past, and so relinquished their responsibilities to statutory agencies. However, these agencies had been used to relying on the exchanges for

[49] Jeremy Grant, 'Regulators face uphill battle as dark pools grow murkier', 3rd November 2010.

[50] Brooke Masters, '"Too big to fail" debate still muddled', 17th September 2010.

[51] Nikki Tait and Jeremy Grant, 'Greater clarity on equity trades urged', 14th April 2010.

[52] Aline van Duyn, Michael Mackenzie, and Jeremy Grant, 'That sinking feeling', 2nd June 2010; Michael Mackenzie and Aline van Duyn, 'Regulators may silence derivative squawk boxes', 22 July 2010; Megan Murphy and Francesco Guerrera, 'Prop-hostile climate throws up some tough calls for banks', 4th August 2010; Aline van Duyn, 'Derivative Dilemmas', 12th August 2010; Jeremy Grant, 'The route to regulation diverges for Europe and America', 12th August 2010; Patrick Jenkins, 'New regulatory standards are the next big unknown', 8th October 2010; Brooke Masters, 'Trade finance may become a casualty', 20th October 2010; Jennifer Hughes, 'Currency markets ready for the next big thing', 20th October 2010; Philip Stafford, 'Regulators show united front', 20th October 2010; Michael Mackenzie, 'Rate swap traders wait for no man', 20th October 2010; Michael Mackenzie, 'One-size-fits-all approach risks killing flexibility', 3rd November 2010; Jeremy Grant, 'Regulators face uphill battle as dark pools grow murkier', 3rd November 2010; Tom Braithwaite and Francesco Guerrera, 'A Garden to Tame', 15th November 2010; Brooke Masters, '"Too big to fail" debate still muddled', 17th September 2010; Javier Blas, 'Regulators extend commodities push', 23rd November 2010; Gregory Meyer and Javier Blas, 'US delays vote on commodity trade', 17th December 2010; *FT* Reporters, 'Before and after: how the investment banks had to change shape post-crisis', 21st December 2010; Paul J. Davies and Izabella Kaminska, 'Banks seek help from new set of institutions', 22nd December 2010.

[53] Jeremy Grant, 'Up Against a Bandsaw', 3rd September 2010.

the detailed supervision of market activity, and the behaviour of participants, confining themselves to establishing rules of conduct and overall policing. What regulatory intervention had achieved was a hollowing out of the system of supervision, removing layers of responsibility that had contributed to the smooth working of a market. One of the reasons that regulatory intervention had these unintended consequences was that it often took its lead from what was happening in the USA, and this reflected the underlying structure of the US financial system. This was different from most other countries with its particular combination of banks and markets and separate regulatory agencies. When this was pointed out to Michel Barnier, the EU Internal Market Commissioner, in 2010 his only response was that, 'We're not saying that everything that happens in America has to be directly applicable in Europe, but I don't think we should ignore the fact that there is a certain "parallelism"'.[54] It was much easier to apply an existing model than design one that met the diversity of experience that existed in the EU, even if that model was the SEC's legalistic approach rather that of the CFTC which was a principles-based one.[55]

What began to take place in 2010 was a rolling back among regulators from the first response to the crisis. Though popular opinion continued to favour breaking the power of the megabanks, those with greater insight were aware of the contribution such banks made to the efficiency and stability of the financial system, and that it was not they that were the weakest links in the chain of interconnections that circled the world. Many of the world's largest banks had proved resilient during the crisis while it was the smaller and more specialized that had failed, spreading a contagion of fear around the globe. It was those banks that had taken excessive risks in their lending, and had retained insufficient liquidity to cover themselves when a crisis arose, that got into difficulties, and they were both large and small, conducting a specialized or general business. Rather than force the break-up of the megabanks there was a a commitment to make banking safer by requiring higher levels of capital and reserves, and reduced levels of leverage along with controls over the degree of risk being taken. As Aline van Duyn and Francesco Guerrera reported in 2010, 'One outcome is broad and almost certain: large financial groups whose failure would put the whole system at risk will have to cut back on risk and set aside more capital than before the

[54] Nikki Tait, Jeremy Hall, and Javier Blas, 'EU to rein in commodity speculation', 21st September 2010,

[55] Robert Cookson, 'Regulators' turf war helps market take root', 25th February 2010; Hal Weitzman, 'BATS squeezes into crowded world of US equity options', 26th February 2010; Michael Mackenzie, 'SEC's new rules threaten liquidity critics warn', 3rd March 2010; Aline van Duyn, 'Transparency of derivatives becomes key battleground', 12th March 2010; Jeremy Grant, 'Multiple venues leave Europe "open to abuse"', 7th April 2010; Jeremy Grant, 'High-frequency traders facing tracking reform', 8th April 2010; Ben Hall, Scheherazade Daneshkhu, and Jeremy Grant, 'France calls on Brussels for US-style CFTC', 14th April 2010; Nikki Tait and Jeremy Grant, 'Greater clarity on equity trades urged', 14th April 2010; Brooke Masters, 'Finra to watch over NYSE Euronext', 5th May 2010; Jeremy Grant and Nikki Tait, 'Europe set for overhaul of rules on share dealing', 30th July 2010; Sophia Grene, 'Pension funds anxious to have their say', 2nd August 2010; Megan Murphy and Francesco Guerrera, 'Prop-hostile climate throws up some tough calls for banks', 4th August 2010; Jean Eaglesham and Brooke Masters, 'No longer a doormat', 27th August 2010; Jeremy Grant, 'Up Against a Bandsaw', 3rd September 2010; Nikki Tait, 'London fears Brussels reform will shift power', 6th September 2010; Sam Jones, 'Dublin entices funds with softer regulation', 6th September 2010; Nikki Tait, Jeremy Hall and Javier Blas, 'EU to rein in commodity speculation', 21st September 2010; Jeremy Grant, 'Light speed ahead', 27th September 2010; Michael Mackenzie, 'Regulators push technology to track trades in real time', 29th September 2010; Javier Blas, 'Speculators at fault for food prices, says poll', 11th October 2010; Gregory Meyer, 'Crackdown hangs over derivatives bets', 14th October 2010; Philip Stafford, 'Competitive market requires deep pockets', 20th October 2010; Jeremy Grant, 'Call to make dark pools trades public', 28th October 2010; Philip Stafford and Nikki Tait, 'Europe moves against super-fast traders', 9th December 2011; Aline van Duyn, 'New rules aim to bring trading of derivatives more into public view', 17th December 2010; Francesco Guerrera, Justin Baer, and Patrick Jenkins, 'A sparser future', 20th December 2010; FT Reporters, 'Before and after: how the investment banks had to change shape post-crisis', 21st December 2010.

crisis.'[56] A particular target of the regulators was to prevent banks trading on their own account as this was considered to be the mechanism through which risks were spread and built up. The intention was to restrict the ability of banks to do this type of business and to move what remained onto regulated markets and through clearing houses so as to reduce the systemic risk posed. The solution devised in 2010 in the USA was to create Swap Execution Facilities (SEFs) to replace the unregulated market through which the large banks traded with each other. A SEF was 'a facility trading system or platform in which multiple participants have the ability to execute or trade swaps by accepting bids and offers made by other participants that are open to multiple participants in the facility or system'.[57] Accompanying this US solution in 2010 was an international agreement among bank regulators to force banks to hold more capital to support this trading activity. There was also growing international agreement that every country would have to adopt a formal resolution scheme for handling failing banks.

These measures were to be implemented and policed by national regulators due to there being considerable opposition to the creation of a supra-national body that would have authority over the world's banks and financial markets. What the regulators were aiming to do, at both the national level with the Dodd–Frank Act in the USA and Basel 3 internationally, was to force banks to withdraw from those activities regarded as being central to the crisis of 2008. However, this intervention was moderated by a concern that it could limit the ability of banks to lend, which would harm smaller companies in particular, as they were more reliant on bank finance than the larger companies that could recycle funds internally or issue stocks and bonds. The end result was that by 2010 the megabanks had escaped any attempt to break them up but they were being subjected to rules and prohibitions that restrained both what they could do and how they could operate. The result was to provide the megabanks with a set of new parameters within which they had to operate that were different from those in place before the crisis. The megabanks then proceeded to adjust their business models to comply with these new rules, shedding certain activities while expanding others. Though smaller and more specialized competitors were able to challenge the megabanks, because of the constraints they were placed under, the enhanced regulatory environment also benefited them as they had the size, scale, and diversification necessary to meet the new requirements. Writing in 2010 Justin Baer concluded that:

> One consequence of the crisis is that it has left the survivors bigger and more powerful than they were before. Institutions such as JP Morgan Chase, Goldman Sachs and Bank of America are almost ubiquitous: from commodities trading and retail brokerage to credit cards and cash management, there are few financial services markets that they do not dominate. The massive scale these banks now enjoy will make it harder than ever for smaller institutions to compete.[58]

This was the complete reverse of what had been expected in 2008.[59]

[56] Aline van Duyn and Francesco Guerrera, 'Dodd–Frank bill is no Glass–Steagall', 28th June 2010.

[57] Michael Mackenzie and Aline van Duyn, 'Regulators may silence derivative squawk boxes', 22 July 2010.

[58] Justin Baer, 'From recession to regulation', 27th September 2010.

[59] Francesco Guerrera and Justin Baer, 'Doubts beset mission to trim giants' girth', 23rd January 2010; *FT* Reporters, 'Proposals fail to forge consensus in Europe', 23rd January 2010; Francesco Guerrera and Megan Murphy, 'Tripped up', 25th January 2010; Patrick Jenkins, 'Poll finds solid support for tougher action', 25th January 2010; Pauline Skypala, 'Advance of the index trackers', 1st February 2010; Jennifer Hughes, 'FSA plays down prop trading impact', 2nd March 2010; Norma Cohen, 'Crisis thrusts debt-financing theorem back under the spotlight', 5th April 2010; Aline van Duyn and Francesco Guerrera, 'Dodd–Frank bill is no Glass–Steagall',

Another issue of immediate concern to regulators during the Global Financial Crisis was the lack of liquidity of securitized assets. A related problem lay with certain derivative contracts as, again, banks had relied upon these as a way of covering the risks they were taking. When the counterparties to these contracts defaulted, those holding them were left without that cover, exposing them to losses. It was for that reason that exchanges were seen as the initial saviours of financial markets as they could provide liquidity for the assets being traded and mechanisms to reduce or eliminate counterparty risk. However, it became increasingly evident that exchanges did not provide a solution to the issue of liquidity. It was true that exchanges did provide the most liquid market for derivatives whereas much of that which was traded outside involved contracts that were hardly traded at all, such as swaps. However, among corporate stocks many of those quoted on exchanges lacked liquidity as that only applied to the issues of the largest companies listed on the likes of Nasdaq, NYSE, LSE, TSE, and Deutsche Börse. Forcing more financial products to be traded on exchanges would not, of itself, provide the liquidity that regulators now recognized as vital if future crises were to be avoided. Conversely, the electronic platforms that had proliferated after RegNMS and Mifid had shown themselves capable of providing active markets in corporate stocks, encouraging regulators to favour them rather than exchanges. According to Jennifer Hughes in 2010, 'Since the financial crisis, regulators and officials have clamped down on OTC markets, preferring to move trading to more transparent electronic platforms and to force trades to be officially recorded in so-called repositories.'[60]

Along with the use of these electronic markets the issue of liquidity was to be addressed through making banks hold more assets whose sale, if required, could be guaranteed, such as the debt of large sovereign states and the stock of major corporations rather than securitized assets and many categories of bonds. Conversely some regulators undermined liquidity by trying to outlaw short-selling because it was seen to cause price volatility. Whereas the contribution of short-selling to liquidity was recognized in the likes of South Korea, regulators in Germany, France, and Spain remained opposed to the practice. The solution here remained the use of clearing houses since they could vet buyers and sellers, require them to possess a minimum level of capital, demand collateral to accompany every deal, and then guarantee that trades were completed even when a default happened. By 2010 regulators across Asia, including Japan, India, China, Hong Kong, Singapore, South Korea, and Taiwan, were turning to clearing houses as a way of dealing with the risks generated in the OTC markets. However, the use of clearing houses as a universal panacea to counterparty risk continued to be resisted by those who did not recognize that as an issue, did not want to pay the fees demanded, and were unwilling to post the collateral required. There were also genuine concerns among regulators that forcing the use of clearing houses could concentrate risk in institutions that lacked resilience and could collapse in the face of mass defaults as they had insufficient capital and collateral to cover losses. In turn that would magnify a crisis as fear spread that other users of that clearing house would be left exposed,

28th June 2010; Michael Mackenzie and Aline van Duyn, 'Regulators may silence derivative squawk boxes', 22 July 2010; Hal Weitzman, 'CME predicts OTC opacity will remain', 30th July 2010; Patrick Jenkins and Brooke Masters, 'The money moves on', 15th September 2010; Brooke Masters, '"Too big to fail" debate still muddled', 17th September 2010; Justin Baer, 'From recession to regulation', 27th September 2010; Brooke Masters and Francesco Guerrera, 'Threat to small business', 27th September 2010; Justin Baer, 'Proprietary traders weigh up new options', 25th October 2010.

[60] Jennifer Hughes, 'Revolution in the cosy world of bonds', 1st March 2010.

leading to a bank run. Governments would then be forced to intervene to save a clearing house from collapse, in the same way as they had been drawn in to support banks during the 2008 crisis.

To some, clearing houses were the ultimate too-big-to-fail financial institutions. They could point to past examples in which clearing houses had failed or governments had been forced to intervene to save them. These included the Caisse de Liquidation in France in 1974 and the Kuala Lumpur Commodity Clearing House in Malaysia in 1983. Only government intervention or emergency funding had prevented failures in Hong Kong and the USA in 1987 and Brazil in 1989. In seeking to address the vulnerability of clearing houses to sudden shocks leading to their collapse regulators faced the same choices as with megabanks and incumbent exchanges. Jeremy Grant reflected this dilemma in 2010. In one piece he wrote that 'regulators have touted the value of clearing houses as a way to safeguard the financial system from the catastrophic effects of another Lehman-style default',[61] while in another he mentioned that 'linkages between clearers could trigger a domino effect if one clearer was to default'.[62] A solution was for governments or central banks to act as lenders of last resort to clearing houses but that raised the issue of moral hazard. Jeremy Grant was also aware of that, as it would lead to 'a situation where clearers would have less incentive to ensure they are robustly capitalised, managed and governed as possible if they know central banks will ride to their rescue'.[63] What could not be agreed was whether this was best done by a supra-national agency backed by the world's central banks or left as a responsibility of national authorities.

Despite the inability of regulators to agree on the best means through which clearing could be provided, and what measures were needed to either prevent the failure of a clearing house or provide it with the equivalent of a lender of last resort, by the end of 2010 their use appeared to deliver a much simpler solution of how to provide a financial system that delivered the resilience required in the post-crisis world. The alternatives involved a break-up of the megabanks and a complete restructuring of the world's financial markets, which were tasks beyond anything regulators could deliver. There were always demands for regulatory intervention whether to dampen down speculative activity, reform the financial system to achieve social, environmental, and political ends or to reduce the risks of another financial crisis. Conversely, these were countered by demands to let the market operate as free from controls as possible, because it was recognized that every intervention had a consequence which was not the one intended. What the Global Financial Crisis did was to tilt the balance back towards the former but by 2010 it was beginning to move in the other direction again. Evidence was emerging that an overly restrictive regime would either drive financial activity away from those banks and markets that were regulated to those that were not, or even prevent it taking place at all with detrimental consequences for the functioning of the economy. Prior to the crisis regulators were focusing on creating increased competition in the market whereas after the crisis the focus was on mitigating risk. By 2010 there was a greater recognition that banks and markets had to be allowed to function with greater freedom.[64]

[61] Jeremy Grant, 'New push to give clearing houses solid foundations', 8th June 2010.
[62] Jeremy Grant, 'Lack of coherence on clearing reform', 9th April 2010.
[63] Jeremy Grant, 'New push to give clearing houses solid foundations', 8th June 2010.
[64] Jeremy Grant, 'Businesses demand OTC exemptions', 6th January 2010; Jeremy Grant, Tom Braithwaite, and Aline van Duyn, 'Cracks are emerging in transatlantic approach to reform', 6th January 2010; Aline van Duyn and Jeremy Grant, 'Use of clearers to rein in OTC derivatives poses fresh dilemma', 15th January 2010; Samantha Pearson, 'US plans threaten LatAm FX', 20th January 2010; Jeremy Grant and Masa Serdarevic, 'LSE

Second Stage Intervention, 2011–20

Though 2010 proved something of a tipping point in terms of the regulatory response to the Global Financial Crisis it was accepted that there could be no return to a world where the megabanks were masters of the universe and markets were left unsupervised. The Global Financial Crisis had been a shock to the regulators, forcing them to frame a response that recognized the risks inherent in any market-based financial system but also one that allowed it to operate relatively free of controls. That meant increasing the financial system's resilience to crises without destroying its ability to function. As early as 2008 regulators from the G20 countries had agreed to co-operate in making the financial system safer through greater regulation, leading to the BIS's Financial Stability Board being upgraded to a global watchdog in 2009, followed in 2010 with systemically-important banks being set minimum capital ratios. That set the scene for the subsequent years with continuing regulatory intervention, which was widely accepted as necessary. Robin Wigglesworth picked up on this in 2012: 'In addition to the institutional curbs imposed by banks, politicians and regulators, memories of the crisis have also acted as a natural brake on the more excessive risk-taking by traders...'[65] Bankers showed little resistance to increased regulation with Peter Sands, the chief executive of Standard Chartered, accepting in 2012 that it had to

contemplates acquiring Dutch clearer to diversify away from the UK', 30th January 2010; Sam Jones, 'Alert over short-selling disclosure rules', 9th February 2010; Jeremy Grant, 'Europe's post trade dilemma', 10th February 2010; Hal Weitzman and Aline van Duyn, 'ICE eyes sovereign CDS clearing', 11th February 2010; Mark Mulligan, 'Spanish bourse weighs up reform', 16th February 2010; Jeremy Grant, 'Icap and Nasdaq in OTC expansion', 18th February 2010; Robert Cookson, 'Asian regulators launch reforms for OTC derivatives', 25th February 2010; Robert Cookson, 'Regulators' turf war helps market take root', 25th February 2010; Hal Weitzman, 'BATS squeezes into crowded world of US equity options', 26th February 2010; Jennifer Hughes, 'Revolution in the cosy world of bonds', 1st March 2010; Aline van Duyn, 'Transparency of derivatives becomes key battleground', 12th March 2010; Gregory Meyer, 'Push for clearing houses fails to move leading oil traders', 12th March 2010; Jeremy Grant, 'Blow to London as LCH.Clearnet launches clearing house in Paris', 29th March 2010; Mark Mulligan, 'Spanish exchange brushes aside fears', 30th March 2010; Jennifer Hughes, 'Worries over threat of "heavy touch"', 30th March 2010; Jeremy Grant, 'Fresh questions raised over regulation of clearing houses', 1st April 2010; Hal Weitzman, 'Banks urged to rethink OTC trading', 6th April 2010; Jeremy Grant, 'Lack of coherence on clearing reform', 9th April 2010; Geraldine Lambe, 'Settlement model aids FX market success', 12th April 2010; Ben Hall, Scheherazade Daneshkhu, and Jeremy Grant, 'France calls on Brussels for US-style CFTC', 14th April 2010; Jeremy Grant, 'LCH.Clearnet warns of loose standards', 16th April 2010; Aline van Duyn, 'Derivatives traders search for ways to appease regulators', 23rd April 2010; Jennifer Hughes, Michael Mackenzie, and Scheherazade Daneshkhu, 'Paris Project recommends central clearing for bonds', 27th April 2010; Hal Weitzman, 'ICE chief backs financial reform', 6th May 2010; Jeremy Grant, 'NYSE Euronext to set up clearing houses in London and Paris', 12th May 2010; Kevin Brown and Christian Oliver, 'Seoul warms to naked short selling', 13th May 2010; Jennifer Hughes, 'Europe dithers over adopting Germany's short selling ban', 27th May 2010; Joe Leahy, 'India Plans short-selling move', 28th May 2010; Jeremy Grant, 'New push to give clearing houses solid foundations', 8th June 2010; Aline van Duyn and Francesco Guerrera, 'Dodd–Frank bill is no Glass–Steagall', 28th June 2010; Aline van Duyn, Michael Mackenzie, and Hal Weitzman, 'Derivatives dealers brace for clearing shake-up', 14th July 2010; Hal Weitzman, 'CME predicts OTC opacity will remain', 30th July 2010; Jeremy Grant, 'Buyside wakes up to impact of legislation', 2nd August 2010; Martha Tirinmanzi and Mike Hemphill, 'Management of risk remains an issue for the buyside user', 2nd August 2010; Jeremy Grant, 'Stoking the boilers for the battle of the clearing houses', 24th August 2010; Victor Mallet, 'Spanish plan to rival BME', 25th August 2010; Jeremy Grant, 'DTCC in talks over European clearing stake', 28–29th August 2010; Jeremy Grant, 'LSE bid to build clearing house', 18th September 2010; Jeremy Grant, 'LCH.Clearnet faces derivatives battle', 28th September 2010; Izabella Kaminska, 'Growth is driven by investors' need for clarity', 28th September 2010; Michael Mackenzie and Hal Weitzman, 'CME wins swap clearing support', 18th October 2010; Jeremy Grant, 'Clearing war set to get hotter', 22nd October 2010; Jeremy Grant and Nikki Tait, 'Brussels eyes faster times for settlement', 25th October 2010; Hal Weitzman, 'Co-location set to reap up to $40 million for CME', 29th October 2010; Aline van Duyn, 'Pressure mounts over derivatives clearing', 3rd November 2010; Philip Stafford, 'Stock exchanges muscle in as clearing houses prepare for shake-up', 3rd November 2010; Norma Cohen and Jeremy Grant, 'Clearers' ownership model under scrutiny', 23rd December 2010.

[65] Robin Wigglesworth, 'Taming the traders', 20th March 2012.

come because 'Some banks did behave recklessly and with extraordinary stupidity.'[66] By 2018 Alex Barber referred to financial services as 'a highly-regulated sector',[67] but that did not mean a return to the controlled and compartmentalized world that had broken down in the 1970s.

By then the weight of expert opinion, though not the public or the media, had generally accepted that the megabanks had not been the prime cause of the crisis, and were less likely to suffer a catastrophic failure than smaller and more specialized banks, because of their size and diversification. In 2012 the eminent international banker, Jacques de Larosière, concluded that, 'The crisis has shown that bank failures are not related to specific structures, but to excessive risk-taking. The institutions that were the hardest hit by the crisis were those that pursued risky operations either in trading or in more traditional activities, be they specialised or not.'[68] The regulators themselves did not escape blame for their contribution to the crisis, as it emerged that they had failed to identify the risks being taken by those banks that had enthusiastically embraced the originate-and-distribute banking model, supporting their lending and repackaging of loans with extensive borrowing in the wholesale market. The average gross leverage in the hedge-fund sector, measured as the sum of long and short exposures divided by net asset value, was only 2.1 in 2007–8 compared with an average of 14.2 for investment banks. Hedge-fund leverage then peaked at 2.6 in June 2007 whereas that of the investment banks rose from 10.4 in June 2007 to a peak of 40.7 in February 2009, the month when the US Treasury took equity positions in several large US banks. Both before and during the crisis regulators had failed to recognize that a number of banks were financing long-term lending with short-term borrowing, without maintaining adequate reserves of cash, capital, and easy-to-sell assets. Such reserves generated low returns, and none in the case of cash, compared to the profits to be made from lending to borrowers, repacking the loans as bonds, and then either selling the resulting securities to investors, including other banks, or retaining them in their own special-purpose investment funds. This was perceived by regulators as a much less risky way of conducting a banking business than either the lend-and-hold model, as that risked a liquidity crisis, or hedge funds taking positions in the market. Regulators had failed to appreciate how the originate-and-distribute model was being used by banks to disguise a move towards highly-leveraged long-term lending, financed by short-term borrowing. By 2014 Patrick Jenkins was one among a number who pointed the finger of blame at 'self-righteous regulators whose own shortcomings helped cause the crisis in the first place.'[69]

The problem facing regulators in the post-crisis world was how to cope with the calls for greater intervention when they lacked the means of doing so. In 2015 the UK's Financial Conduct Authority (FCA), for example, was expected to supervise a financial system comprising 73,000 different companies and generating 18m transactions a day. The complexity they faced led regulators to continue to rely on the megabanks as a means of micro-managing the global financial system. In return, these banks could expect a degree of official support if they got into difficulties. As Simon Samuels, a banking consultant, observed in 2019, 'Today, as in 2008, it will be down to taxpayers in the home country to rescue their own banks.'[70] In the case of Australia, Jamie Smyth was more explicit stating that the largest

[66] Peter Sands, 'The perils of 1970s-style regulation', 29th March 2012.
[67] Alex Barber, 'Brexit talks near deal on financial services', 6th November 2018.
[68] Jacques de Larosière, 'Do not be seduced by the simplicity of ringfencing', 27th September 2012.
[69] Patrick Jenkins, 'It's right for shareholders to share the pain', 13th November 2014.
[70] Simon Samuels, 'The ECB should resist the lure of bigger banks', 31st January 2019.

banks: 'Enjoy lower funding costs than smaller competitors, due in part to an implicit government guarantee to save the banks if they got into trouble.'[71] However, that reliance had to be tempered by the recognition that it could not be based on the uncontrolled self-interest of these banks and the operation of markets unrestrained by even self-regulating bodies such as exchanges. At a global level banking and financial regulators were able to formulate guidelines that dictated the way banks operated through the banking stability committee of the Bank for International Settlement. At the national level the regulators and central bankers could ensure that these guidelines were put into practice, though leaving considerable scope for variation dependent upon individual circumstances and preferences. What remained was how to apply this regulation to the actual working of the financial system, at both the national and international level. This is what the megabanks could provide.

Banks were responsible for the everyday business of managing staff, dealing with customers, balancing assets and liabilities, and responding to the needs of a huge diversity of savers, investors, and borrowers in a world that was complex and international. Only a megabank was in a position to do this in a way that gave regulators and central bankers confidence that the enhanced rules and regulations that followed the Global Financial Crisis were being obeyed and guidelines followed. They could comply with the regulatory demands as they could spread the costs across large income streams so that the burden remained manageable. The unit cost of the staff, information technology, data systems, and risk models required to respond to the new regulatory climate were inversely related to the size of the institution. Though subjected to a greater regulatory oversight, because they were systemically-important financial institutions, these megabanks found ways of compensating for the increased costs and greater restrictions imposed on them compared to smaller rivals, while delivering the supervision of the financial system that regulators and central banks needed. They could, for example, invest in the modelling and advanced systems which generated significant capital savings on risk-weighted assets, so providing them with a competitive advantage over smaller rivals. For that reason Patrick Jenkins argued in 2014 that 'Banks need to be left alone to support the fragile recovery.'[72] It was to the megabanks that regulators turned when the issue of cyber security arose in banking and finance, for example.

What the megabanks possessed was the practical experience of managing a complex financial business, and the connections and insight that came from being in continuous touch with all aspects of the financial system through the deposits they received, the payments they handled, the loans they provided, and the investments they made. They did this through the management of hundreds of subsidiaries; the employment, training, and supervision of thousands of staff; the handling of daily transactions running into the billions; and the control of assets measured in the trillions. Though regulators and central banks were aware that the failure of one of these giant institutions could have catastrophic consequences, they were also conscious that there was no alternative to them if they wanted to engage directly with the global financial system. Central bankers could formulate policy at the BIS, and regulators could oversee national banking systems, but only these megabanks could manage the day-to-day delivery of financial services in ways compliant with the rules, regulations, and guidelines deemed necessary after the crisis. These megabanks provided regulators with both a point of entry and a means of enforcing their authority which

[71] Jamie Smyth, 'Australian regulator pledges to tackle cosy oligopoly of big banks and punish misconduct', 4th February 2019.

[72] Patrick Jenkins, 'It's right for shareholders to share the pain', 13th November 2014.

no other institutions could deliver. Germany's financial regulator, BaFin, was responsible for supervising the activities of 1740 separate banks in 2018, ranging from megabanks to local savings institutions. This meant, according to its president, Felix Hufeld, being 'as flexible and as pragmatic as legally possible.'[73] Reflecting the size and diversity of the US financial system the Dodd–Frank Act of 2010 ended up being 828 pages long with a further 14,000 pages relating to specific rules and technical requirements. It included 882 pages alone devoted to the Volcker Rule, which banned proprietary trading. By working through the megabanks national regulators were able to supervise the key elements within the financial system, including its international dimension. A similar situation existed in financial markets. In the vast US Treasury bill market regulators had little option but to devolve responsibility to the major players, which were the largest banks. A similar situation existed in the global foreign exchange market, with Philip Stafford reporting in 2017 that 'Most currency trading is conducted between banks, away from exchanges, creating a fragmented market that regulators have found difficult to police.'[74] Again, regulators relied on the megabanks to police that market, as it was they that dominated trading.

Providing evidence of the close working relationship between the regulators and the megabanks was the response to the series of scandals that rocked both banks and financial markets between 2010 and 2014. These involved the staff of banks, largely operating out of their London offices, manipulating key benchmark rates in the inter-bank money market and the foreign exchange market. The first revelation concerned the London Inter-Bank Offered Rate (Libor), which was administered by the British Bankers' Association and dated from the 1980s. Libor was not the actual rate of interest paid by banks in the inter-bank money market but measured the rate at which they said they could borrow. Being an artificial construction rather than a product of market activity exposed Libor to manipulation, as it was set by a small group of bankers employed by the world's largest banks. As Gary Gensler, the chairman of the US's Commodity Futures Trading Commission, put it in 2013, 'Having benchmark rates that are not anchored in actual transactions undermines market integrity and leaves the financial system with benchmarks that are prone to misconduct.'[75] His remarks indicated the gulf between someone whose experience lay in stock and commodity exchanges, and the task facing those trying to get a grip on the far larger OTC markets. The OTC market was forced to rely on benchmark rates as indicators because they lacked centralization, as in the inter-bank trading of money and currency. In calculating Libor every day a panel of banks submitted the rate at which they thought they could borrow, in various currencies, for different periods of time. These bids were then passed to an administrator who used them to produce an average. As the number of banks submitting bids was small, and those involved known to each other, the opportunity for collusion was high. Only eighteen banks submitted bids for borrowing in the US$ and eleven for the Swiss franc. There was also a reason to submit false data. During the crisis those submitting rates were under pressure to pitch them as low as possible as a way of suggesting that other banks retained confidence in them as counterparties. This was a time when doubts over the liquidity and even solvency of individual banks were circulating. More generally, Libor was used as a benchmark to price an estimated \$350tn of financial

[73] Olaf Storbeck, 'German regulator makes soft pitch to lure banks after Brexit,' 10th January 2018.

[74] Philip Stafford, 'Fears over "last look" spur tighter FX code,' 20th December 2017.

[75] Brooke Masters, Philip Stafford, and Michael Mackenzie, 'Libor heads for history in hunt for new bank rate,' 24th April 2013.

products. Manipulating Libor could produce a favourable outcome for those trading these products and the megabanks were extensively engaged in this business.

Whereas regulators in the USA, such as those in the SEC and the CFTC, were much more familiar with the working of stock and commodity exchanges, it fell to those in London to cope with the OTC markets, as much of the activity in these was conducted between the London offices maintained by banks from all over the world, and relied heavily on benchmarks to price the products that they traded. One of these was Libor. Subadra Rajappa, head of US rates strategy at Société Generale's New York office, explained in 2019, 'Banks compiling Libor often derive their submissions based on judgement rather than on actual deals.'[76] These markets lacked the institutional structure of the likes of the NYSE and the CME and so could not be regulated in that way. Instead, the only option for regulators was to act through the megabanks, as it was their employees who were involved. In 2015 Andrew Bailey, a deputy governor at the Bank of England, justified this approach:

> In any profession, people who break rules and neglect their duties should face serious consequences.... During the financial crisis, and the subsequent revelations of misconduct, I have often been asked why so few senior bankers have been held to account for their part in the crisis, or for allowing the mis-selling of payment protection or the manipulation of the Libor interest-rate benchmark to happen on their watch.... In practice it has been almost impossible to hold individual senior bankers accountable for serious failures and misdeeds. This was in large part because of the difficulty of establishing who was responsible for the areas where the problems occurred.[77]

With it proving impossible to identify and punish individuals in most cases, and no authority in place to discipline users as with an exchange, regulators had no alternative but to make banks collectively responsible for what had taken place. As Tracey McDermott, the director of enforcement and financial crime at the UK's Financial Conduct Authority (FCA), said in 2014, 'Firms could have been in no doubt, especially after Libor, that failing to take steps to tackle the consequences of a free-for-all culture on their trading floors was unacceptable.'[78] The sanction they applied was large fines. By 2014 the megabanks had been fined \$6bn for their involvement in the Libor scandal. Between 2014 and 2019 they paid a further \$12bn in fines because of their involvement in the manipulation of the currency benchmarks, while being subjected to a voluntary code of conduct introduced in 2016, drawn up under the direction of the BIS. That code was overseen by the Global Foreign Exchange Committee (GFXC), which was composed of central banks and megabanks, indicating where regulatory responsibility lay.

Altogether, it was estimated that collectively banks had paid \$276.8bn in fines by the end of 2019, imposed by authorities around the world for a wide variety of reasons. What this revealed was the breakdown of self-regulation among banks and markets, fuelling demands for statutory intervention. The respected banker, Evelyn de Rothschild, observed in 2013 that it was vital to have 'rules and regulations that are effective detriments of bad behaviour'.[79] The conclusion drawn in 2014 by Carolyn Williams, the technical director at the Institute of Risk Management, was that 'Over the past twenty years banking has moved

[76] Subadra Rajappa, 'Investors have to embrace challenge of Libor's demise', 10th July 2019.
[77] Andrew Bailey, 'Irresponsible conduct carries consequences in British finance', 23rd February 2015.
[78] Caroline Binham and Sam Fleming, 'Record fines carry strong echo of Libor scandal', 13th November 2014.
[79] Evelyn de Rothschild, 'Banking must pursue the holy grail of confidence', 25th June 2013.

away from a profession and this has created an inherent risk. A move away from professional exams in favour of narrow quantitative and sales training has, in my view, created a cultural inability by some banks to recognise and address risk in a holistic manner.'[80] Though she detected a 'resurgence in risk management…driven by regulators',[81] this was considered too little and too late. An alternative to statutory intervention could have been more reliance on the auditing process to expose the risks that banks were running and to identify fraudulent behaviour. This was meant to be the purpose of an audit, according to Natasha Landell-Mills, the head of stewardship at asset manager Sarasin & Partners. In 2018 her view was that 'Auditors are supposed to underpin trust in financial markets. Major stock markets require listed companies to hire auditors to verify their accounts, providing reassurance to shareholders that material matters have been inspected and their capital is protected.'[82] However, so tarnished were the reputation of auditors, by previous failures to spot accounting irregularities, that devolving responsibility to them was not considered an acceptable solution. There was a general feeling that auditors were more responsive to the management of the businesses whose accounts they were examining, including banks, than to the shareholders.

In addition, the application of new auditing standards to banks had contributed to masking the risks they were running before the crisis, which further undermined the trust that regulators were willing to place in them. The new accounting standards introduced in 2005 were meant to make accounts more transparent but in banking they had the reverse effect of making it easier to cover up possible losses as no provision was made for defaults. The new rules allowed banks to hold assets at inflated values and so use them as collateral for loans they obtained, which helped support the switch from the lend-and-hold to originate-and-distribute model of banking. This practice continued after the crisis, allowing central banks to lend to the banking sector under the pretence that the banks were solvent and so only faced a liquidity crisis. As these rules were the international standard auditors had no choice but to follow them when drawing up the accounts for banks. John McDonnell, from Price Waterhouse Coopers (PWC), was the lead auditor for the Bank of Ireland, and he said in 2018 that 'When those rules are in law, you must apply them to give a true and fair view. If you don't apply them, you cannot say the accounts give a true and fair view.'[83] The result was, according to Hans Hoogervorst, the chair of the International Accounting Standards Board, that 'many banks had wafer-thin capital levels and were accidents waiting to happen'. Though this was known, the existing accounting standards 'gave banks too much leeway to delay recognition of inevitable loan losses' which masked the true position they were in.[84] It was only after the crisis that new accounting standards were brought in that forced banks to recognize potential losses and so provide a warning regarding a potential default. However, writing in 2018 he warned that though 'Accounting standards are designed to reflect economic reality as clearly as possible…future losses are notoriously difficult to predict.' He then emphasized the limitations of the accounting profession to provide a solution to the risks present in the financial system through the auditing process:

> Accounting is highly dependent on the exercise of judgement and is therefore more an art than a science. Good standards limit the room for mistakes or abuse, but can never

80 Daniel Schäfer, 'Banks' skills gap forces up pay for talented minority', 28th April 2014.
81 Daniel Schäfer, 'Banks' skills gap forces up pay for talented minority', 28th April 2014.
82 Natasha Landell-Mills, 'Should the Big Four accountancy firms be split up? Yes', 22nd March 2018.
83 Jonathan Ford and Madison Marriage, 'Auditing in Crisis', 30th August 2018.
84 Hans Hoogervorst, 'Do not blame accounting rules for the financial crisis', 4th October 2018.

> entirely eliminate them. The capital markets are full of risks that accounting cannot possibly predict. This is certainly the case now, with markets swimming in debt and overpriced assets. For accounting standards to do their job properly, we need management to own up to the facts—and auditors, regulators and investors to be vigilant.[85]

Nevertheless, like the global banks, auditors did provide regulators with a valuable source of information and insight which they could not otherwise obtain. In 2017 the top four firms of auditors in the world employed 945,000 staff.

In the field of financial markets exchanges had long provided a substitute for statutory regulation. Through the control they exercised over their members or users in the trading of stocks, bonds and derivatives, specialist exchanges were able to police particular markets and enforce discipline that prevented fraudulent behaviour, the manipulation of prices, and dealt with counterparty risk, though the consequences included a range of restrictive practices and a limit to competition. However, the power of exchanges over markets was waning as more and more trading was conducted between the global universal banks as they could either internalize transactions or deal directly with each other and major institutional investors. In addition a number of financial markets had never been conducted through exchanges, most notably foreign exchange and inter-bank borrowing and lending, and they were joined by others where most of the activity took place over-the-counter (OTC) and involved banks as buyers, sellers, and intermediaries. These included the entire range of bonds, including government, corporate and mortgage; all the securitized assets produced by the originate-and-distribute model of banking; and numerous and diverse derivative contracts especially of the swap variety. Even in the markets still in the hands of exchanges, which involved the trading of corporate stocks and standardized futures and options contracts, it was the megabanks that were, again, the major players. They valued the liquidity and certainty that exchange-traded products provided and so used them selectively to complement the dealing they did internally, for themselves and their customers, and with each other. This dwarfed anything that the exchanges could produce. In the global derivatives market, for example, which reached a peak in 2013, when the notional amount outstanding was $734.6tn, only $24.5tn was traded on exchanges, or 3.3 per cent. Despite considerable efforts by regulators to switch the trading of derivatives to exchanges the results were very limited. In 2017, when the amount outstanding stood at the lower figure of $565.6tn, the exchange-traded element was still only $33.7tn or 6 per cent. In terms of turnover the world's largest financial market remained that for foreign exchange, where turnover stood at $8.9.tn a day in 2019, measured on a gross basis, and none of this passed through exchanges.[86]

With exchanges in no position to provide the regulation they had in the past, especially as they were now operating as profit-maximizing businesses, the regulators had, again, little choice but to rely on the services of the megabanks. It was in the self-interest of these banks to police these markets because of the reliance they placed upon them. Through the foreign exchange market a bank could cover its currency risks by swapping its exposure with another facing an equivalent but reverse situation. In the inter-bank money market, banks could lend and borrow amongst each other and so were able to either meet a temporary shortfall or employ a short-term excess without maintaining large idle balances. In the derivatives market the risk of a major borrower failing to repay a counterparty

[85] Hans Hoogervorst, 'Do not blame accounting rules for the financial crisis', 4th October 2018.
[86] For the data see the BIS online statistics database.

defaulting could be shared with other banks so minimizing its effect. In the markets for equities and bonds a bank could either invest in illiquid but high-yielding assets or liquid but low-yielding ones depending upon the returns it wanted to achieve and the risks it was willing to take. At all times banks had to balance assets and liabilities and financial markets provided them with the essential tools for doing so. Hence the preference for the originate-and-distribute model of banking among central banks and regulators prior to the crisis, though that was accompanied by assumptions of market liquidity that turned out to be false. The constant activity taking place in these financial markets was a product of the continuous adjustments that banks had to make as they conducted business in a highly-complex global economy, and their interaction with other major players such as the fund managers and multinational companies. By 2010 regulators had realized that these markets could neither be suppressed nor switched to exchanges but had to be made more liquid. The dilemma faced by regulators was how to achieve that while intervening to make markets more resilient.

This much greater level of intervention created opportunities for national governments to use regulation to tilt the financial system in favour of their own financial centres, banks, markets, and institutions, under the cover of greater oversight to prevent future crises. This had the effect of eroding the operation of the integrated global financial system that had been developing rapidly prior to the crisis. Even within the European Union, which was committed to creating a single market in financial services replicating that of the USA, there was continuing divergence. Faced with a crisis involving the Euro in 2011 member states such as Greece, Belgium, France, Italy, and Spain were quick to introduce bans on short-selling bank shares, for example, with action co-ordinated by the European Securities and Markets Authority. In contrast, Germany and the UK refused to participate, pointing out that analysis showed that such bans had made no contribution to restoring stability in the past, and probably aggravated the situation. There were also attempts to introduce an EU-wide transaction tax but this was opposed by those countries in which the most active markets were located, as it could damage their international competitiveness. Of greater importance for regulatory intervention in the EU was the division between member states resulting from the adoption of the Euro, as the UK had stayed outside, and it hosted Europe's leading financial centre, London. The crisis presented national governments with a legitimate reason to demand increased control over the foreign banks that operated within their boundaries and the markets through which particular financial products were traded. Brooke Masters observed in 2012 that, 'The European Commission is generating reams of financial rules, many aimed at reining in short selling, high-frequency trading, shadow banking and other specific activities.'[87] These rules were then interpreted differently by national governments leading to divergent policies and regulatory barriers.

As London had emerged as the dominant centre in which not only was the Euro traded, but also Euro-denominated financial products, those countries hosting other financial centres and using the Euro, namely Germany with Frankfurt and France with Paris, pressed for the business to be transferred to them. They had been prevented from doing so because of the EU's single market rules but the crisis created another opportunity for pushing forward with this ambition. Writing in 2011 Phil Davis expressed the view that, 'While the process of regulation is ostensibly all about markets, there is a widespread suspicion in London that much of the post-crisis rule-making emanating from the European Union has

[87] Brooke Masters, 'Wariness over EU's level playing field', 10th May 2012.

a political element to it.'[88] Alex Barker, George Parker, and Jeremy Grant followed this up by observing that the European Central Bank (ECB) was attempting to have all euro-denominated transactions cleared in the Eurozone, as a way of better monitoring banks' trading and risk-management divisions in case those activities threatened the stability of the Eurozone banking system. A by-product of this decision would be to prise the business away from London. They reported that 'British diplomats have long feared Paris was trying to rig market rules in an attempt to shift the centre of gravity for financial services to continental Europe.'[89] The UK was in a weak position to resist this pressure as a result of the new regulatory structure introduced for the EU. Though London was the home of the European Banking Authority its regulation over many financial activities was shared with the European Systemic Risk Authority, which was located in Frankfurt, so as to be close to the head office of the ECB, which took responsibility for Eurozone banking. Similarly, the European Securities and Markets Authority was run from Paris even though the greatest concentration of trading in the EU was found in London. Unlike the US where the Federal Reserve was based in Washington, the location of the Federal government, the EU's administrative centre was Brussels while both Frankfurt and Paris had ambitions to rival London as European financial centres and were backed by their national governments in this aim. In the opinion of the experienced banker, Stanislas Yassukovich, the EU lacked the coherence found in US banking and financial markets despite the attempts to foster it. His judgement in 2017 was that in the EU there was 'no banking union, no unified capital market and no European stock exchange' and that 'the regulation of financial services, focused largely on investor protection, is at national not EU level'.[90] This pressure to force the relocation of financial activity away from London and into the Eurozone was intensified after the UK voted to leave the EU in 2016. In 2018 Philip Stafford reported that 'EU politicians have repeatedly called for processing of euro-denominated deals to be relocated to the Eurozone after Brexit.'[91] This was all part of a concerted effort from the French and German governments to persuade as many financial businesses to open offices and branches in Paris and Frankfurt and conduct business from there under the guise of bringing it closer to the appropriate regulatory authorities.

To William Dudley, president of the Federal Reserve Bank of New York, the solution to government interference was that 'We need all national authorities to resist the temptation to favour domestic financial interests over achieving a true level playing field globally.'[92] The US authorities were very keen to prevent other countries exploiting tight US controls by providing an opportunity to evade them. Conversely countries outside the USA resented the imposition of US regulations upon their own banks and exchanges, as well as sensing that opportunities existed for repatriating business that previously went to the USA or even attracting US business to their financial centres. All this made it very difficult to agree global standards let alone a common set of regulations. Even agreeing the equivalence of regulatory regimes was a near impossible task because each had different objectives and so designed rules to suit these. This was the case between the EU and the USA, for example, despite many similarities. Each regulator claimed the superiority of its particular rules and regulations when compared to those of other countries. Tilman Luder, head of the

[88] Phil Davis, 'London feels the force of regulation', 16th May 2011.

[89] Alex Barker, George Parker, and Jeremy Grant, 'Britain to sue ECB over rules on clearing', 15th September 2011.

[90] Stanislas Yassukovich, 'The City has nothing to fear from Brexit', 12th January 2017.

[91] Philip Stafford, 'Record half for LCH despite Brexit uncertainty', 5th July 2018.

[92] Jeremy Grant, 'Industry in the midst of a maelstrom', 10th October 2011.

securities markets unit at the European Commission, observed in 2017 that 'The rest of the world simply doesn't have Mifid...the rest of the world has sometimes, despite the financial crisis, followed a different path.'[93] When Mifid 2 was unveiled in 2018, it had been seven years in the making and was over 1.7m paragraphs long. It replaced the original Mifid which the 2008 financial crisis had 'exposed its flaws',[94] according to Philip Stafford and Peter Smith. Within the EU many member states were reluctant to implement Mifid 2, and were slow to transpose it into local law, considering it too complex and wide-ranging and so requiring numerous exemptions.

Despite agreement among all the world's leading financial regulators in 2010 that the global banking system had to be made more resilient it proved difficult to introduce common regulations that would apply to all, and then follow that up with measures to ensure they were complied with. Each regulatory authority wanted maximum jurisdiction for itself, and so resisted the imposition of rules and regulations imported from outside, especially the USA. Ian Smith, a managing director on the Asia electronic execution team at Citibank, pointed out in 2011 that 'A key challenge is the very distinct markets and regulatory environments that make up Asia, with each implementing a potentially different view of what is practical, efficient and sensible for its own market.'[95] Through a combination of exchange controls and internal regulations China, for example, had insulated itself from the Global crisis and was reluctant to implement the new measures being recommended, even though it was facing financial problems of its own by 2012 that were destabilizing banks and markets. In contrast, the Japanese government continued to push ahead with the removal of the regulations that had long prevented Japanese banks and markets being exposed to foreign competition.

The objectives of regulatory intervention also changed over time. In the immediate aftermath of the crisis the over-riding consideration was to restore stability and make the financial system more resilient. As the memory of the crisis faded other aims were prioritized. One of these was investor protection, which had been a major concern before the crisis and had underpinned both RegNMS and Mifid. By 2012 it was again given increased prominence in both the USA and the EU. In the USA the Dodd–Frank Act of 2010 included provisions for investor protection and these were followed in the EU. Verena Ross, executive director of ESMA, made clear at the end of 2011 that 'The ultimate objective of most of our work is to protect EU investors and consumers of financial products.'[96] Similarly, Jamie Selway, the managing director of the US broker-dealer, ITG, observed in 2018, 'Where there is retail investor pain, regulatory scrutiny follows.'[97] Robert Cohen, a US lawyer and SEC's head of cyber security, admitted as such, even though he emphasized his agency's commitment to helping financial markets develop: 'The key point is that innovative ways to raise capital are a great thing; it's a core part of our mission, to support capital formation. But we also have to protect investors.'[98] However, unlike the pre-crisis years the US authorities had pulled back from a rigid commitment to increasing the level of competition as a way of promoting the interests of consumers of financial services but it remained a priority for

[93] Philip Stafford, 'EU and US regulators race to seal equivalence deal before Mifid 2 deadline', 21st September 2017.
[94] Philip Stafford and Peter Smith, 'Europe begins countdown to day of the Mifid', 2nd January 2018.
[95] Jeremy Grant, 'Industry in the midst of a maelstrom', 10th October 2011.
[96] Brooke Masters, 'EU watchdog issues alert on unregulated forex groups', 6th December 2011.
[97] Robin Wigglesworth, 'Exchange traded products face scrutiny as worries deepen', 15th February 2018.
[98] Ben McLannahan, 'SEC eyes initial coin offerings with suspicion', 15th March 2018.

those in the EU as it served the wider objective of removing barriers to the development of an internal market.[99]

[99] Ralph Atkins, 'Authority aims to give early warnings to avert crises', 5th January 2011; Nikki Tait, 'Traders fear threat of political agendas', 5th January 2011; Nikki Tait and Tony Barber, 'Star-crossed levers', 10th January 2011; Jeremy Grant, 'Derivatives trading platform bypasses intermediary banks', 17th January 2011; Jeremy Grant and Nikki Tait, 'NYSE link-up faces hurdles', 11th February 2011; Jeremy Grant, 'Traders face jump in clearing costs', 11th March 2011; David Oakley, 'Crisis probe puts Libor in spotlight', 16th March 2011; Jeremy Grant, 'Chill wind blows over plans for market mergers', 17th May 2011; Tom Braithwaite, Brooke Masters, and Jeremy Grant, 'A Shield Asunder', 20th May 2011; Jeremy Grant, 'Reform in Europe', 31st May 2011; Jeremy Grant, 'Conduits of contention', 16th June 2011; Jeremy Grant and Philip Stafford, 'London uneasy at potential foreign takeover', 1st July 2011; Philip Stafford, 'Citi plans "dark pool" to link HFTs and smaller investors', 7th July 2011; Larry Tabb, 'Playing ostrich over high-speed trading is not an option', 14th July 2011; Sharlene Goff, 'Risk is the new "sexy" job at the bank', 14th July 2011; Jeremy Grant, 'Avalanche of rulemaking blocks road to OTC clarity', 1st August 2011; Anuj Gangahar, 'Finding a mechanism to save the trades', 1st August 2011; Dan McCrum, Alex Barber, Jennifer Hughes, Richard Milne, Peggy Hollinger, and Matthew Steinglass, 'Short-selling ban attacked by academics and investors', 13th August 2011; Patrick Jenkins and Megan Murphy, 'Again on the edge', 15th August 2011; Jeremy Woolfe, 'London's sway weakens as EU authorities gain power', 15th August 2011; Alex Barker, George Parker, and Jeremy Grant, 'Britain to sue ECB over rules on clearing', 15th September 2011; Vince Heaney, 'Europe takes step closer to a tax on financial transactions', 19th September 2011; Brooke Masters, 'Industry worries about the impact of new rules', 20th September 2011; Brooke Masters and Tom Braithwaite, 'Bankers versus Basel', 3rd October 2011; Brooke Masters, Jeremy Grant, and Chris Bryant, 'Warning of unintended outcomes with Tobin tax plans', 6th October 2011; Jeremy Grant, 'Industry in the midst of a maelstrom', 10th October 2011; Sarah Mishkin, 'Competition helps to reduce barriers', 10th October 2011; Alex Barber, 'Barnier vs the Brits', 9th November 2011; Paul Taylor, 'How to make ready for regulation', 9th November 2011; Jeremy Grant and Alex Barber, 'ECB preference for Eurozone clearers raises ire in London', 24th November 2011; Brooke Masters, 'EU watchdog issues alert on unregulated forex groups', 6th December 2011; Jeremy Grant, 'New rules are struggle for industry and regulators', 23rd January 2012; Philip Stafford, 'Changes bring global flurry of innovation', 23rd January 2012; Patrick Jenkins, 'Banks face a perfect storm that is getting worse', 25th January 2012; Michael Mackenzie, 'Libor probe shines light on voice brokers', 17th February 2012; Simon Rabinovitch and Robert Cookson, 'China unlikely to impose big bang reforms', 24th February 2012; Ben McLannahan, 'Merger of markets may foreshadow expansion overseas', 9th March 2012; FT Reporters, 'A benchmark to fix', 12th March 2012; Nicole Bullock, 'US central counterparty set to clear trades in mortgage debt', 13th March 2012; Robin Wigglesworth, 'Taming the traders', 20th March 2012; Steve Johnson, 'EU shadow banking plan rapped', 26th March 2012; Sam Jones, 'The mood music is about to change', 26th March 2012; Peter Sands, 'The perils of 1970s-style regulation', 29th March 2012; Brooke Masters, 'Conflicting signals', 2nd April 2012; Brooke Masters and David Oakley, 'Financial regulators take aim at repo trading markets', 27th April 2012; Brooke Masters, 'Cities hold firm amid Eurozone upheaval', 10th May 2012; James Pickford, James Wilson, Haig Simonian, 'Big hubs keep the wheels of industry turning', 10th May 2012; Brooke Masters, 'Wariness over EU's level playing field', 10th May 2012; Sophia Grene, 'Derivatives rules will bring new demands', 21st May 2012; Sam Jones, 'Tangled up anew', 30th May 2012; Anousha Sakoui, 'Restructuring could lift M&A market', 30th May 2012; Barbara Ridpath, 'Crisis—and regulation—can breed opportunity', 30th May 2012; Philip Stafford, 'CME puts Europe at the centre of expansion plan', 21st August 2012; Michael Mackenzie and Tracy Alloway, 'Swaps profits threatened by Dodd–Frank', 23rd August 2012; Jeremy Grant, 'Asia fears systemic risk over Dodd–Frank', 7th September 2012; Jacques de Larosière, 'Do not be seduced by the simplicity of ringfencing', 27th September 2012; Andrew Haldane, 'We should go further still in unbundling banks', 3rd October 2012; Philip Stafford, 'ICE plans CDS exchange trading', 17th October 2012; Patrick Jenkins, 'Volker attacks Vickers reforms', 18th October 2012; Brooke Masters, 'Tampering with Libor to become criminal offence', 18th October 2012; Jeremy Grant, 'Asia watches and learns from European and US rule makers', 30th October 2012; Michael Mackenzie, 'Fight looms over which model is best', 30th October 2012; Philip Stafford, 'Rules covering derivatives built on ground that has yet to settle', 30th October 2012; Philip Stafford, 'Collateral drive puts the focus on settlements', 30th October 2012; Jeremy Grant, 'Singapore OTC trades hit by turmoil', 2nd November 2012; Philip Stafford and Michael Mackenzie, 'Interdealer brokers braced for shake-up', 22nd November 2012; Patrick Jenkins and Alex Barber, 'City bankers fret over being on the margins', 5th December 2012; Shahien Nasiripour and Brooke Masters, 'Regulators edge towards "every country for itself"', 10th December 2012; Brooke Masters and Shahien Nasiripour, 'US banks want new liquidity rules eased', 17th December 2012; Brooke Masters and Shahien Nasiripour, 'Basel move aims to stoke recovery', 8th January 2013; Tom Burgis, Brooke Masters, and Lina Saigol, 'Sants warns on foreign branches in UK', 11th January 2013; Tracy Alloway and Nicole Bullock, 'Banks offer debt product to help skirt new liquidity rules', 30th January 2013; Philip Stafford, 'Regulation: All eyes on Italy's new rules', 20th February 2013; John Gapper, 'Europe finally takes its bite from the City of London', 21st February 2013; Tracy Alloway, 'Banks debate liquidity trade-off', 19th March 2013; Michael Mackenzie, Dan McCrum, and Tracy Alloway, 'Electronic trading set to muscle in on corporate debt', 4th April 2013; Daniel Schäfer, 'Regulation threat to global banks', 12th April 2013; Brooke Masters, Philip Stafford, and Michael Mackenzie, 'Libor heads for history in hunt for new bank rate', 24th April 2013; Shahien Nasiripour and Tom Braithwaite, 'Out to break the banks', 1st May 2013; Alex Barber and Kara Scannell, 'Plans to

shift Libor heart to Europe', 7th June 2013; Anne-Sylvaine Chassany and Henny Sender, 'Forced into the shadows', 7th June 2013; Evelyn de Rothschild, 'Banking must pursue the holy grail of confidence', 25th June 2013; Philip Stafford and Brooke Masters, 'Libor deal commences rehabilitation of benchmark', 10th July 2013; Alex Barber, Gregory Meyer, and Philip Stafford, 'US and EU derivatives truce averts rules crunch', 12th July 2013; Philip Stafford, 'Q and A : Algorithms', 23rd August 2013; Philip Stafford, 'US funds transfer trades to London', 18th October 2013; Arash Massoudi, 'Soaring cost of US share dealing risks "investor harm"', 18th October 2013; Chris Flood, 'Regulators stalk secretive financial giants', 24th February 2014; Sam Fleming, 'Foreign banks meet BoE over branch rules', 27th February 2014; Patrick Jenkins and Claire Jones, 'Eurozone bank rules menace City prosperity, warns lobby', 19th March 2014; Chris Flood, 'Hedge funds transmit most risk', 28th April 2014; Philip Stafford, 'Tougher capital rules boost traders' feelings of security', 28th April 2014; Daniel Schäfer, 'Banks' skills gap forces up pay for talented minority', 28th April 2014; Tom Braithwaite, Martin Arnold, and Tracy Alloway, 'Tough choices confront traditional lenders', 18th June 2014; Paul Tucker, 'Financial regulation needs principles as well as rules', 19th June 2014; Sam Fleming and Gina Chon, 'Push begins to put lenders' house in order', 19th June 2014; Sam Fleming and Gina Chon, 'Boutique banks flourish as larger institutions rethink business models', 12th August 2014; Philip Stafford, 'Sense of urgency underpins fresh scrutiny of markets', 16th September 2014; Tom Braithwaite and Vivianne Rodrigues, 'Wall Street's biggest lenders blame bond volatility on tight regulation', 17th October 2014; Gina Chon, 'Regulators wrestle with cross-border strategy', 24th October 2014; Caroline Binham and Sam Fleming, 'Record fines carry strong echo of Libor scandal', 13th November 2014; Patrick Jenkins, 'It's right for shareholders to share the pain', 13th November 2014; Martin Arnold, 'Carney's too big to fail buffer represents clear progress despite doubt', 9th December 2014; Andrew Bailey, 'Irresponsible conduct carries consequences in British finance', 23rd February 2015; Alex Barker and Claire Jones, 'ECB agrees UK clearing houses can work outside currency area', 30th March 2015; Caroline Binham and George Parker, 'Banks increase attacks against wave of regulation', 6th June 2015; Caroline Binham and Jonathan Guthrie, 'FCA', 3rd July 2015; Caroline Binham, 'Zen and the art of cracking down on financial market manipulation', 3rd July 2015; Philip Stafford, 'Banks eye hub to cut swaps trading disputes', 8th July 2015; Miles Johnson, 'Geneva's bright lights lose their allure', 1st August 2015; Philip Stafford, 'Europe to mandate clearing of swaps', 7th August 2015; Philip Stafford, 'Nasdaq steps up dark pools surveillance push', 9th October 2015; Frederic Oudea, 'Europe needs home grown bulge bracket banks', 12th October 2015; Philip Stafford, 'Confidence shaken by violent swings', 13th October 2015; Philip Stafford, 'Markets planning for a world after the day of the Mifid', 13th October 2015; Joe Rennison, 'Policymakers left with problem in the wake of London whale', 13th October 2015; David Sheppard and Neil Hume, 'Traders fear new derivatives rules', 26th October 2015; Philip Stafford, 'Exchange chiefs eye deals to tap new markets', 31st December 2015; Chris Flood, 'Cracking down on "megalomaniacs and bullies"', 28th March 2016; Philip Stafford, 'Europe's regulatory crackdown set to ease', 25th May 2016; Philip Stafford, 'Strains show in over-the-counter dealing', 14th June 2016; Gregory Meyer, 'Trading', 7th July 2016; Philip Stafford, 'City brokers put brave face on Brexit', 20th July 2016; Joe Rennison and Philip Stafford, 'Fears grow that global reforms to derivatives will fragment into a patchwork of local standards', 23rd September 2016; Philip Stafford and Nicole Bullock, 'Radical pilot to boost trade in smallest US stocks begins', 5th October 2016; Philip Stafford, 'ICAP's new direction reflects changing future of derivatives', 6th October 2016; Philip Stafford, 'Brexit brings headache to industry weary of regulation', 11th October 2016; Stanislas Yassukovich, 'The City has nothing to fear from Brexit', 12th January 2017; Eric Platt and Robert Smith, 'Efforts to harmonise risky-loans rules in doubt', 6th June 2017; Philip Stafford, 'Debate over post-Brexit clearing of euro swaps focuses on margin costs', 13th June 2017; Reza Moghadam, 'Branch out to avoid a Brexit capital markets crunch', 20th July 2017; Martin Arnold and Emma Dunkley, 'UK watchdog sounds the death knell for Libor', 28th July 2017; Alexandra Scaggs, 'Demise of Libor is far from a done deal', 3rd August 2017; Philip Stafford, 'Investors' Mifid 2 challenges flagged up', 24th August 2017; Philip Stafford, 'EU and US regulators race to seal equivalence deal before Mifid 2 deadline', 21st September 2017; Philip Stafford, 'Voice brokers fight to survive Europe's shake-up', 10th October 2017; Philip Stafford, 'Clock ticks down on EU's Mifid reform', 10th October 2017; Philip Stafford, 'European Parliament seeks to extend regulatory powers over clearing houses', 29th September 2017; Philip Stafford, 'LSE admits case for tougher EU oversight', 1st November 2017; Ben McLannahan and Jim Brunsden, 'EU plan over bank runs faces US opposition', 2nd November 2017; Joe Rennison, 'Senators press regulators to clarify position over Treasury market reform', 2nd November 2017; Philip Stafford, 'Fears over "last look" spur tighter FX code', 20th December 2017; Philip Stafford and Peter Smith, 'Europe begins countdown to day of the Mifid', 2nd January 2018; Hannah Murphy and Philip Stafford, 'Mifid 2 risks drowning in its own ambition', 4th January 2018; Olaf Storbeck, 'German regulator makes soft pitch to lure banks after Brexit', 10th January 2018; Philip Stafford, 'Trading venues play down rift over Mifid 2', 11th January 2018; Philip Stafford, 'Dark pool trading flourishes after Mifid 2 delay', 19th January 2018; ICMA 50 Years [advertisement], 5th February 2018; Robin Wigglesworth, 'Exchange traded products face scrutiny as worries deepen', 15th February 2018; Owen Walker, 'Spooked fund managers look at rivals to London', 19th February 2018; Philip Stafford, 'Brexit anxieties grow over London's vital market infrastructure', 22nd February 2018; Olaf Storbeck, 'Deutsche Börse eyes UK's euro clearing', 22nd February 2018; Ben McLannahan, 'SEC eyes initial coin offerings with suspicion', 15th March 2018; Natasha Landell-Mills, 'Should the Big Four accountancy firms be split up? Yes', 22nd March 2018; Kadhim Shubber, 'CFTC chairman set to overhaul restrictive Obama-era swaps execution regulations', 27th April 2018; Robin Wigglesworth and Ben McLannahan, 'Liquidity outs leverage as the big worry for investors', 4th May 2018; Philip Stafford, 'Frankfurt narrows gap with London as incentive scheme boosts euro clearing', 13th June 2018; David Keohane and Philip Stafford, 'Jury still out on Mifid

Consequences of Intervention: Banks, 2011–20

By 2011 the core element of the regulatory approach being taken meant making systemically-important banks more resilient so that they could withstand, individually and collectively, a future crisis without calling on central banks to intervene and governments to provide support using public funds. As Jaime Caruana, head of the central banks' central bank, the Bank for International Settlements, said in 2011, 'The lesson of the crisis is that authorities need to pay attention when we see complexity and liquidity and maturity transformation.'[100] Under the new proposals coming from the BIS, and regulators around the world, the most systemically-important banks were to be forced to hold more capital to cover those activities that were considered to pose the highest risk or even stopped from engaging in them. The systemically-important banks were identified as those that were large, complex, and deeply embedded in both national and international financial systems. As it was accepted that these banks were also irreplaceable, because of the contribution they made to the

2 transparency rules', 18th June 2018; Chris Flood, 'Forget passports! Trade must go on', 18th June 2018; Jeff Merkley, 'Avoid past mistakes and preserve key bank safety law', 26th June 2018; Gregory Meyer and Philip Stafford, 'Derivatives traders forced to cut holdings as banks push for Basel clampdown', 3rd July 2018; Philip Stafford, 'Record half for LCH despite Brexit uncertainty', 5th July 2018; Joe Rennison and Philip Stafford, 'Traders find receptive ear among regulators to relax capital rules', 10th July 2018; Philip Stafford, 'Deutsche Bank's Frankfurt move revives City concerns', 31st July 2018; Jonathan Ford and Madison Marriage, 'Setting flawed standards', 2nd August 2018; Chloe Cornish and Hannah Murphy, 'Crypto bubble bursts after brief history of surges and plunges', 21st August 2018; Madison Marriage and Jonathan Ford, 'Close ties of auditors and watch-dogs draw fire', 21st August 2018; Jonathan Ford and Madison Marriage, 'Auditing in Crisis', 30th August 2018; Laura Noonan and Patrick Jenkins, 'Financial Crisis', 13th September 2018; John Gapper, 'My naïve part in the downfall of Lehman', 13th September 2018; Mark Vandevelde, 'Financial Crisis', 20th September 2018; Philip Stafford, 'Fresh risks emerge from the depth', 1st October 2018; Gabriel Wildau, 'Doors to China's markets are creaking open', 1st October 2018; Nicole Bullock, 'Battle intensifies over the costs of using US market data', 1st October 2018; Hans Hoogervorst, 'Do not blame accounting rules for the financial crisis', 4th October 2018; Philip Stafford, 'US threatens EU banks with ban over Brexit clearing plans', 18th October 2018; Philip Stafford, Nicole Bullock, and Kadhim Shubber, 'Shares in US exchanges hit after rebuke from regulator over high data charges', 18th October 2018; Alex Barber, 'Brexit talks near deal on financial services', 6th November 2018; Philip Stafford, 'Bloc must find its own path, shorn of British expertise', 17th November 2018; Claire Jones, Caroline Binham, and Sam Fleming, 'Fed governor to head global finance police', 21st November 2018; Eswar Prasad, 'Central banks' embrace of blockchain remains too timid', 2nd January 2019; Philip Stafford, 'Intercontinental Exchange working on interest rate benchmark to replace Libor', 25th January 2019; Siobhan Riding, 'EU and UK regulators strike fund group Brexit deal', 4th February 2019; Philip Stafford, 'Traders face anxious wait for Brexit guidance', 12th February 2019; Arthur Beesley, 'Cautious Dublin reaps benefits of Brexit exodus', 13th February 2019; Philip Stafford, 'US and UK strike eleventh-hour accord to minimise no-deal Brexit disruption', 26th February 2019; Philip Stafford, 'EU licence boost for investors in Irish assets', 2nd March 2019; Delphine Strauss, Philip Stafford, and Claire Jones, 'BoE and ECB launch swap line to buffer banks in event of post-Brexit turmoil', 6th March 2019; Sarah Gordon, 'Making sense of the City', 9th March 2019; Caroline Binham, David Crow, and Patrick Jenkins, 'Lenders told to triple liquid assets as Brexit protection', 11th March 2019; Oliver Ralph, 'Conduct replaces capital as focus', 25th March 2019; Paul Murphy, 'Cyber-attacks target banks' easy pickings', 25th March 2019; Philip Stafford and Katie Martin, 'Growing pains for rules that rocked European finance', 8th May 2019; Caroline Binham and Patrick Jenkins, 'Bailey signals need for Brexit talks focus on financial services', 8th May 2019; Richard Henderson, 'US fund managers mimic Brussels rules on research', 10th May 2019; Eva Szalay and Rochelle Toplensky, 'Banks look for closure in EU benchmark probe', 11th May 2019; Philip Stafford and Mehreen Khan, 'London venues poised to delist Swiss stocks as Bern's EU dispute drags on', 26th June 2019; Jennifer Thompson, 'Assets in European Ucits funds burst through landmark Euro10tn', 1st July 2019; Philip Stafford, 'Swiss stock trading shifts away from the EU exchanges after Brussels–Bern dispute', 2nd July 2019; Subadra Rajappa, 'Investors have to embrace challenge of Libor's demise', 10th July 2019; Philip Stafford, 'Brussels eyes payment plan for exchanges' trading data', 12th July 2019; Eva Szalay and Jane Croft, 'Five banks face forex-rigging lawsuits in London', 30th July 2019; Nicholas Megaw, 'Sting in the tail for banks caught in PPI scandal', 10th September 2019; Vikram Pandit, 'Outdated rules are holding back financial innovation', 19th September 2019; Colby Smith, Joe Rennison, and Philip Stafford, 'NY Fed head says some institutions are not moving fast enough to cut Libor reliance', 24th September 2019.

[100] Michael Mackenzie and Nicole Bullock, 'Push-button perils, Richard Milne', 6th June 2011.

operation of the financial system at all levels, the only option available to regulators, central banks, and governments was to exercise a degree of control that made them safer. An alternative approach would have been to establish a supra-national lender of last resort to be responsible for those banks that were systemically important on a global scale. Nationally that was what was achieved through a central bank, under government ownership and direction, acting as lender of last resort, ready to intervene in a crisis though mindful of the issue of moral hazard. However, in the case of the megabanks no collective lender of last resort existed. Each central bank took responsibility for those banks based within its own jurisdiction and no other. The BIS, despite being the central banks' central bank, lacked both the mandate and the resources to act as a global lender of last resort. Being in the position of a lender of last resort meant having the ability to provide unlimited quantities of money in the appropriate currency to allow a bank to match its assets and liabilities. The BIS had no power to produce this currency as that belonged, exclusively, to each national central bank. Only the US Federal Reserve could supply US$s, for example, despite that being the currency used as the medium of exchange within the international banking system.

The Federal Reserve had provided support during the Global Financial Crisis through swap arrangements with other central banks, and continued to act closely with other central banks. However, it was not willing to make this a permanent open-ended arrangement, as it had no control over the activities of non-US banks. Conversely, national governments were unwilling to grant this power to the Federal Reserve, as it would mean an end to any pretence of operating an independent economic policy. The Eurozone provided an example where an uneasy compromise existed between a supra-national central bank, the European Central Bank (ECB) located in Frankfurt, and those central banks based in the various member states, as these were under the control of the individual national governments. The result was to cast doubt on the ability of the ECB, and the other Eurozone central banks, to provide the liquidity support in a crisis, because of the restrictions placed on their ability to supply unlimited quantities of euros. Despite the events of 2008, with the failure of a bank as systemically important as Lehman Brothers, the regulatory authorities around the world were also unable to agree on a co-ordinated, cross-border plan of how to deal with a similar situation if it happened again. Six years after the Global Financial Crisis Martin Arnold pointed to the fact that there remained banks that were still 'too big, complex and systemically important to fail'.[101]

Under these circumstances regulators had no option but to try and prevent systemically-important banks from taking the risks that could lead to a liquidity or solvency crisis. A direct approach was to ban them from undertaking those activities considered the most risky. Here there was a particular focus on proprietary trading, where banks used their own money to buy and sell assets rather than confining themselves to acting as intermediaries. This practice was considered to have left banks holding assets, which they could either not sell, or only at greatly reduced prices, precipitating a liquidity crisis followed by a solvency one. Though later evidence suggested that the contribution made by this practice was marginal, compared to the other causes of the crisis, it did lead to it being outlawed in the Dodd–Frank package of financial reforms passed in the USA in 2010. This included the Volcker rule that prevented banks from trading using their own money. Though other countries did not follow the USA in imposing this rule the other measures taken did force

[101] Martin Arnold, 'Carney's too big to fail buffer represents clear progress despite doubt', 9th December 2014.

systemically-important banks to scale back their trading operations. In the Basel 3 proposals coming from the BIS in 2011, to be implemented over the coming years, systemically-important banks were required to build up buffers of equity, cash, and liquid assets to protect themselves against unexpected losses or another financial crisis, and so not require any form of government rescue.

Though the megabanks had escaped the threat of dismemberment, with a repeat of the Glass–Steagall Act but on a global scale, the result of this regulatory intervention was to undermine their business model. The new liquidity requirements meant that the banks had to accurately match the duration of their assets and liabilities, making it hard to offer the ultra-cheap financing that they had been able to do before the crisis. That model relied on their ability to make maximum use of the funds at their disposal while minimizing the risks they ran through a policy of diversification. The intervention by regulators made many aspects of their business unprofitable because of the increased resources they were required to hold, whether in the form of additional capital or low-yielding government debt, and the provision of collateral, whereas in the past none was required. Sharlene Goff reported in 2011 that 'Intricate, efficient funding links developed over decades will be severed. Banks will no longer be able... to tap wholesale markets as diversified businesses—a status that has entitled them to cheaper funding. Tougher capital requirements are likely to mean riskier activities, from loans to lower earners to the most sophisticated fixed-income and derivative-trading products, become more expensive.'[102] As Marc Gilly, global head of prime brokerage at Goldman Sachs admitted in 2012, 'Basel and other regulation is forcing recognition of the true cost of financing. This is something we are welcoming and ready for.'[103] Being ready meant reducing leverage and avoiding high-risk or difficult-to-value assets, which was what they had already begun to do after the crisis. In 2013 Anne-Sylvaine Chassany and Henny Sender reported that, 'To make the banks safer, regulators in the US and Europe regulators require banks to hold more capital. This has made them more reluctant to lend to smaller companies, and they charge more for the money when they do.'[104] When implemented Basel 3 required banks to hold much higher levels of high-quality assets. Basel 3 simultaneously demanded that inter-bank lending, borrowing, and trading be backed by collateral in the shape of high-quality assets. This forced banks to pull back from the lend-and-hold model of banking.

These requirements also led the megabanks to pull back from indirect financing through the issue of bonds on behalf of governments, companies, mortgage lenders, or the securitization and reselling of their own loans, accompanied by the maintenance of a liquid market, which attracted investors to purchase such assets. The regulations meant the megabanks had to hold more capital to support their trading activities, post margin to cover their dealings with counterparties, and provide collateral when transactions were processed through clearing houses. The combination of these increased the costs involved and reduced the profits generated, leading the megabanks to withdraw from the business or reduce their involvement. No longer could the megabanks easily leverage the funds at their disposal, and the portfolio they held, by actively trading assets and acting as counterparties to others in the market, through their ability to absorb what was being sold and supply what was being bought. The effect was to reduce the liquidity in all these markets, making such assets less attractive to investors unless they were sufficiently deep to withstand the withdrawal of the

[102] Sharlene Goff, 'The price of protection', 12th September 2011.
[103] Sam Jones, 'The mood music is about to change', 26th March 2012.
[104] Anne-Sylvaine Chassany and Henny Sender, 'Forced into the shadows', 7th June 2013.

megabanks, as was the case with US Treasury bonds. Writing in 2018, Robin Wigglesworth and Ben McLannahan reflected that 'Since the financial crisis, regulatory changes have aimed to purge leverage, primarily by curtailing the role banks have traditionally played in providing it.'[105] With liquidity drying up the originate-and-distribute model of banking was also undermined by regulatory intervention.

The international aspect of banking was also being eroded by intervention from national governments as they searched for ways of insulating themselves from crises taking place abroad. In the wake of the financial crisis regulators took steps to protect their financial systems from contagion, spread through branches of foreign banks operating in their country. They imposed the stricter requirements regarding capital and business practices required from their own banks on to those foreign banks with significant operations in their own country. The effect of this was to undermine the business models of the megabanks as that relied on treating the world as an integrated unit, with the flexibility to move funds around at will, in response to favourable opportunities to either access cheap funds or lend and invest for the greatest profit. By 2013 regulators around the world were trying to force the megabanks to replace branches and offices with local subsidiaries that possessed their own capital and management structures. These subsidiaries would be more resilient in a crisis and, if they collapsed, they could be wound up more easily compared to an integral unit. Unlike a branch a subsidiary had to conform to local regulations and was subjected to supervision by the host central bank, rather than the central bank of the country in which the bank had its head office. Reza Moghadam, the vice-chair for sovereigns and official institutions at Morgan Stanley, pointed out in 2017 the implications this had for global banks, in response to demand to establish a subsidiary within the EU rather than operate through branches managed from London:

> A subsidiary, as a legally separate entity, is expensive, duplicating not only fixed costs such as management and information systems, but also capital costs. A subsidiary needs more capital since it cannot diversify risk in the small continental market as effectively as in London. The parent needs more capital as loans to the subsidiary from London count as outside exposures. The result: lower bank profitability and return on equity, and so pressure to scale back services or raise prices.[106]

What followed the Global Financial Crisis was not only much stricter regulations at the global level but also an increasing patchwork of regulations that forced megabanks to divide up their operations along national lines and complicated their ability to function as a single businesses. As Philip Stafford observed as early as 2013, 'A difference in regulatory regime can mean a difference in millions of dollars of collateral that investors have to put up to back their derivatives trades.'[107] The implementation of regulatory reform was neither uniform nor harmonized but varied in nature and timing around the world. It was usually initiated in USA, followed by the EU and Japan, while the likes of Singapore lagged behind. Even with the oversight of the BIS there were differences between regulators over important details, such as what constituted liquid assets. If the definition was too strict it undermined the ability of a bank to lend, for example, encouraging it to relocate to a location

[105] Robin Wigglesworth and Ben McLannahan, 'Liquidity outs leverage as the big worry for investors', 4th May 2018.

[106] Reza Moghadam, 'Branch out to avoid a Brexit capital markets crunch', 20th July 2017.

[107] Philip Stafford, 'US funds transfer trades to London', 18th October 2013.

with a more flexible interpretation of the rules. As the interpretation of the rules by national regulators, under the influence of their central banks and governments, was somewhat fluid, as between Switzerland, the EU and USA, the effect was to make it difficult for megabanks to plan a coherent international strategy with a stable distribution of offices and staff. This favoured those from the USA as they controlled the largest domestic market, providing them with the economies of scale those located in other jurisdictions lacked, including France, Germany, Switzerland, Japan, and the UK. The result gave the US megabanks a huge competitive advantage, which they could combine with the added bonus of being able to easily match assets and liabilities in US$s, the vehicle currency of international finance. They could also rely on the support of the Federal Reserve which was the only central bank in a position to act as lender of last resort in that currency. The ten years after the Global Financial Crisis witnessed the eclipse of the likes of UBS, Credit Suisse, Deutsche Bank, and Nomura as megabanks, as they retreated to niche international operations and their domestic bases, leaving only Barclays, through its Lehman Brothers acquisition, and HSBC, with its Asian franchise, still struggling to compete on the world stage. This left a group of US megabanks in a dominant position, namely Bank of America, Citibank, JP Morgan Chase, Goldman Sachs, and Morgan Stanley.

As time passed there were growing doubts among regulators that the rules introduced after the Global Financial Crisis were effective and could even be damaging. The new chairman of the CTFC, Christopher Giancarlo, expressed such views, based on his experience as an executive of interdealer brokerage GFI. His assessment in 2018 was that 'The Obama-era CFTC inadvertently pushed the trading of certain swaps into less-regulated parts of the market by being too specific about how execution platforms should operate.'[108] However, once introduced, regulators were reluctant to repeal any legislation, especially by those tasked with making the financial system safer. In 2018 Martin Gruenberg, the chair of the Federal Deposit Insurance Corporation (FDIC) opposed any changes claiming that the measures had 'served well in addressing the excessive leverage that helped deepen the financial crisis'.[109] Along with this resistance to relaxation the process by which it took place was as haphazard and uneven as the introduction of the rules in the first place. Eric Platt and Robert Smith reported in 2017 that, 'Just as the European Central Bank has finalised the framework of its regulation on leveraged lending, to mirror existing US guidelines, Washington is looking for reverse gear.'[110] Nevertheless, by 2016 it was widely recognized that the regulatory crackdown that had followed the Global Financial Crisis, and then intensified followed the revelations concerning banking and market scandals, had been too draconian and too comprehensive and so needed to be eased. There was a gradual modification of regulations to take into account the practicalities of banking and trading and so allow business to continue. One example was the requirement placed on systemically-important banks to maintain a buffer of cash and easy-to-sell assets in case they faced a liquidity crisis, caused by a depositor run or the freezing of the money market. Initially this liquidity coverage ratio required a bank to hold only cash, sovereign bonds, and top-quality corporate bonds to meet short-term commitments. By imposing a strict ratio, and a restricted range of eligible assets, the regulators had limited the lending that these banks

[108] Kadhim Shubber, 'CFTC chairman set to overhaul restrictive Obama-era swaps execution regulations', 27th April 2018.

[109] Joe Rennison and Philip Stafford, 'Traders find receptive ear among regulators to relax capital rules', 10th July 2018.

[110] Eric Platt and Robert Smith, 'Efforts to harmonise risky-loans rules in doubt', 6th June 2017.

could do, and made it more expensive as there was shortage in the supply of the likes of US Treasury bills and bonds. It also cut off access to finance by many potential borrowers, especially smaller companies. In response the Basel Committee of Banking Supervisors gave banks greater flexibility in the mix of assets they could hold to achieve the required liquidity level. This had the triple effect of allowing banks to increase their lending, lower the interest charged, and revive interest in corporate bonds and securitized assets.

Despite these relaxations the lasting effect of the requirements imposed on the megabanks was to drive business into the hands of the lightly-regulated shadow banking sector. As the host of new regulations aimed at making banks safer also made it more expensive and difficult for them to lend and trade, others were attracted to provide the services from which the megabanks had withdrawn. These shadow banks were able to operate unconstrained by the tough new rules on capital and liquidity that now circumscribed the banks and often hired megabank employees to undertake the business. The Dodd–Frank financial reforms in the USA, which banned banks from proprietary trading in which they used their own money to buy and sell securities, triggered an exodus of senior traders into a less-regulated environment. Whole teams departed from the likes of Goldman Sachs, Deutsche Bank, Morgan Stanley, Barclays, and JP Morgan to establish either their own businesses or join existing independent firms, though still using the prime brokerage units of banks to carry out buying and selling. In the USA, where alternatives to banks had long existed, such as the money-market funds, both established concerns and new entrants were quick to provide a serious challenge. Even without the restrictions the megabanks were already in a weakened position. Prior to the crisis banks had tapped the wholesale market for cheap short-term funds, which were used to make loans. These loans were then securitized and sold on, so releasing funds, which could be used to make new loans and so repeat the process. After the crisis banks were forced to repay this wholesale borrowing as it matured, because replacement funds were no longer available, forcing them to cut back on lending until those who had borrowed from them repaid and the inter-bank market recovered, which took place only slowly. Their place was taken by the likes of private equity funds, flush with funds from institutional investors desperate for yield amid the record low interest rates generated by central bank intervention. Similarly, as banks moved out of commodity finance, because of the increased capital required, lightly-regulated trading firms such as Glencore and Trafigura took their place. Specialist wealth managers also flourished, as they were able to attract the experienced staff by offering them the high rewards that banks could not, because of bonus caps imposed as a result of political pressure. Patrick Jenkins wrote in 2015, that 'While banks have been forced to accept tougher regulatory capital requirements, making much of their core lending more expensive, challengers from outside banking are only lightly regulated.'[111]

One group of institutions that benefited from the forced withdrawal of the megabanks were institutional fund managers. Writing in 2018 Mark Vandevelde observed that 'lightly-regulated asset managers…have filled the void as banks are forced to retreat from risky deals. Unlike banks, which are dependent on deposits and other short-term funding, these funds raise money from long-term investors such as insurance companies and pension funds.'[112] By then the size of those parts of the financial system that performed bank-like functions was estimated at $45tn, and it was beginning to cause regulators serious concern. As early as 2011 Brooke Masters had reported that 'These shadow banks have taken on part

[111] Patrick Jenkins, 'Start-up threat to creaking banks', 14th October 2015.
[112] Mark Vandevelde, 'Financial Crisis', 20th September 2018.

or all of the maturity transformation role of banks—matching short-term depositor funds with long-term lending—and much of the attendant risk, but they do not have the same requirements to hold capital and liquid assets against losses or a rash of customer withdrawals or failures.'[113] What she was picking up on was the warning that year from the likes of Vikram Pandit, the Citigroup chief executive: 'Shifting risk into unregulated or differently regulated sectors won't make the banking system safer. On the contrary, overall risk in the system could actually rise.'[114] The danger posed by the shadow banks was that, as they were largely unmonitored by the regulators, the risks emerging there went undetected even though they were of increasing importance and deeply entwined with the core banking system. Vikram Pandit warned as early as 2012, that 'You cannot address systemic risk unless you tackle things other than banks. We've gravitated from a hub-and-spoke world, where everything used to go through large financial institutions, to a network of millions of points of contact with each other.'[115] As the size of the shadow banking sector grew so did the risks it posed to the entire financial system, including a repeat of the 2008 crisis. One source of such instability was the resurgence of money-market funds. Corporate treasurers and investors turned to them because they offered a better rate of interest than the banks, confident that their investment was both safe and liquid. In 2012 John Gapper warned that, as a result, 'The old-fashioned bank run, with depositors lining up outside banks to withdraw cash, has been updated to corporate treasurers wiring money from money-market funds at any hint of trouble.'[116]

There was an implicit recognition as early as 2014 that regulators had contributed to new risks through the indirect encouragement given to non-bank financial institutions, as these flourished outside their strict controls. In that year Paul Tucker, the former Deputy Governor of the Bank of England, admitted that 'Complex regulations can seem to legitimise the practice of borrowing through the holes they inevitably contain. And rigid rules are of little use when activity moves outside the regulated sector.'[117] By then regulators around the world were struggling to keep pace with a constantly-evolving shadow banking sector, which was able to switch business between countries or, in the case of the USA, between the jurisdictions of the different agencies. The regulators were also torn between conflicting priorities. As the memory of the crisis faded so did the commitment to ensuring stability at all costs, being replaced by a need to stimulate lending to aid economic recovery. Older objectives were also revived, especially encouraging competition, protecting investors and punishing criminal behaviour. There was always a fine balance to be struck by regulators between giving financial institutions the freedom to be innovative, and respond to ever-changing opportunities and challenges, and imposing restrictions and controls that provided safeguards against the build-up of risk and to protect users from exploitation and fraudulent behaviour. These dilemmas had been present before the crisis and came to the fore once the immediate emergency of tackling a potential collapse of the entire financial system disappeared.

Another visible consequence of regulatory intervention by 2014 was the withdrawal of banks from the repo market because of the increased capital requirements imposed on them. Christopher Thompson reported that 'As banks wind down their repo trading much

[113] Brooke Masters, 'A real problem for regulators', 22nd March 2011.
[114] Brooke Masters and Jeremy Grant, 'Shadow boxes', 3rd February 2011.
[115] Patrick Jenkins, Tom Braithwaite and Brooke Masters, 'New force emerges from the shadows', 10th April 2012.
[116] John Gapper, 'Don't leave the financial system resting on quicksand', 30th August 2012.
[117] Paul Tucker, 'Financial regulation needs principles as well as rules', 19th June 2014.

repo business is set to migrate to the less-regulated "shadow" banking sector, such as hedge funds.'[118] These hedge funds lacked the resources of the megabanks, depriving the repo market of its depth and breadth and so exposing it to the greater possibility of a liquidity crisis. Acting in his capacity as chairman of the BIS's Financial Stability Board, Mark Carney, made clear in 2014 that 'The goal is to replace a shadow banking system prone to excess and collapse with one that contributes to strong, sustainable balanced growth of the world economy.'[119] However, that was easier said than done because regulatory intervention continued to restrain the ability of the banks to lend and to trade, creating opportunities for others to undertake the business instead. Patrick Jenkins and Sam Fleming reported in 2014 that 'The risks posed by the escalating size and complexity of the shadow banking market are a big concern for global regulators.'[120] These concerns were greatest in the USA where shadow banks were, collectively, almost twice the size of all the deposit-taking banks in 2012, measured by assets, whereas in most other countries the reverse was the case by a wide margin. In Japan the deposit-taking banks were seven times bigger than the shadow banks, four times bigger in Germany and twice the size in the UK. By 2016 regulators had become aware of the growing private debt market because of the rising risks it posed to financial stability. Though in the form of bonds that were nominally transferable they lacked either a public market or the support of a major bank committed to providing liquidity. The bank-capital rules introduced after the global financial crisis had shifted the balance of power from banks to asset managers. What had changed was that those making long-term loans to businesses, purchasing the bonds issued by small- and medium-sized companies or absorbing sales of securitized assets were pension funds, insurance companies, and other holders of collective assets.

The immediate response to the crisis by regulators was to force banks to hold more capital and restrict their lending. The effect of that was to cut back on the loans available to small- and medium-sized enterprises as banks concentrated on lending to their largest and safest customers where the risk of default was lowest. In turn that led those borrowers unable to obtain finance to seek alternatives, which they found within the shadow banking sector such as the fund managers. Attracted by the higher returns obtained from direct lending to businesses compared to the lower yields and increased volatility attached to stocks, bonds, and property, fund managers responded to the demand. Gradually regulators became aware of the risks to the stability of the financial system they were attempting to control by restricting bank lending, which had shifted leverage to the shadow banks. The verdict of Laura Noonan in 2018 was that 'Regulations have in effect banned them from once lucrative activities such as trading stocks on their own behalf and co-investing in funds with clients. Areas including trading structured products have all but dried up as clients balked at the collapse in value of some instruments and revelations of widespread manipulation of others, especially mortgage-backed bonds.'[121] As these consequences became recognized the reaction from regulators was not to significantly reduce the restrictions placed on banks, so that they could resume lending to the customers they knew and understood best and in ways that they were long familiar with in terms of risks and rewards. Instead, regulators sought to extend their restrictions to those elements of the shadow banking system they could easily identify and police. However, as long as the demand from

[118] Christopher Thompson, 'Basel 3 rules to hit repo trading', 7th February 2014.
[119] Mark Carney, 'The need to focus a light on shadow banking is nigh', 16th June 2014.
[120] Patrick Jenkins and Sam Fleming, 'Alternative finance steps out of the shadow', 16th June 2014.
[121] Laura Noonan, 'Financials', 12th June 2018.

business for finance was there sources of supply would find mechanisms through which flows from the latter to the former could take place. The choice facing regulators was how to regulate the banking system in such a way and to such a degree that it could continue to meet the demands of borrowers, and so remove the need for alternative providers who escaped regulation entirely as these posed a far greater risk to financial stability because their activities took place away from the public gaze. What evidence there was suggested that regulators failed to find that balance.[122]

[122] Ralph Atkins, 'Authority aims to give early warnings to avert crises', 5th January 2011; Nikki Tait, 'Traders fear threat of political agendas', 5th January 2011; Nikki Tait and Tony Barber, 'Star-crossed levers', 10th January 2011; Aline van Duyn, 'Regulator set to rule on Wall Street's swaps power', 13th January 2011; Jeremy Grant, 'Derivatives trading platform bypasses intermediary banks', 17th January 2011; Brooke Masters and Jeremy Grant, 'Shadow boxes', 3rd February 2011; Sam Jones, 'Hedge funds are wary of taking on more risk', 24th February 2011; David Oakley, 'Crisis probe puts Libor in spotlight', 16th March 2011; Brooke Masters, 'A real problem for regulators', 22nd March 2011; Michael Mackenzie and Nicole Bullock, 'Push-button perils, Richard Milne', 6th June 2011; Brooke Masters, 'League battle over bank risk will end in tiers', 21st June 2011; David Oakley, 'Collateral demand rises for interbank lending', 4th July 2011; Sharlene Goff, 'Risk is the new "sexy" job at the bank', 14th July 2011; Patrick Jenkins and Megan Murphy, 'Again on the edge', 15th August 2011; Jeremy Woolfe, 'London's sway weakens as EU authorities gain power', 15th August 2011; Megan Murphy, 'Search for new approaches has begun', 9th September 2011; Brooke Masters, Henny Sender, and Dan McCrum, '"Shadow banks" move in amid regulatory push', 9th September 2011; Sharlene Goff, 'The price of protection', 12th September 2011; Phillip Stephens, 'Vickers hands victory to the bankers' shop steward', 13th September 2011; Sharlene Goff, 'Vickers Report', 13th September 2011; Brooke Masters, 'Industry worries about the impact of new rules', 20th September 2011; Brooke Masters and Tom Braithwaite, 'Bankers versus Basel', 3rd October 2011; Tracy Alloway, 'Counterparty risk makes an anxious return', 27th October 2011; Paul Taylor, 'How to make ready for regulation', 9th November 2011; Tracy Alloway, 'Higher capital demands and dearer funding bring a dual burden', 2nd December 2011; Tanya Powley, 'FSA sees "common sense" on mortgage overhaul', 19th December 2011; Nicole Bullock and Ajay Makan, 'Reform debate swirls in the CLO sector', 23rd December 2011; Patrick Jenkins, 'Banks face a perfect storm that is getting worse', 25th January 2012; Michael Mackenzie, 'Libor probe shines light on voice brokers', 17th February 2012; FT Reporters, 'A benchmark to fix', 12th March 2012; Brooke Masters, 'Shadow banking poses threat to broader stability, FSA head warns', 15th March 2012; Peter Sands, 'The perils of 1970s-style regulation', 29th March 2012; Brooke Masters, 'Conflicting signals', 2nd April 2012; Patrick Jenkins, Tom Braithwaite, and Brooke Masters, 'New force emerges from the shadows', 10th April 2012; Sam Jones, 'Volker Rule', 10th April 2012; James Wilson and Daniel Schäfer, 'Double entry at Deutsche', 13th April 2012; Brooke Masters and David Oakley, 'Financial regulators take aim at repo trading markets', 27th April 2012; Javier Blas and Jack Farchy, 'Trafigura plans trade funding drive', 2nd May 2012; Anousha Sakoui, 'Restructuring could lift M&A market', 30th May 2012; Barbara Ridpath, 'Crisis—and regulation—can breed opportunity', 30th May 2012; Michael Mackenzie and Tracy Alloway, 'Swaps profits threatened by Dodd–Frank', 23rd August 2012; John Gapper, 'Don't leave the financial system resting on quicksand', 30th August 2012; Philip Stafford, 'Battle for derivatives clearing heats up', 11th September 2012; Sharlene Goff, 'Taxpayers left in queue as old brand shuts up shop', 13th September 2012; Jacques de Larosière, 'Do not be seduced by the simplicity of ringfencing', 27th September 2012; Andrew Haldane, 'We should go further still in unbundling banks', 3rd October 2012; Patrick Jenkins, 'Volker attacks Vickers reforms', 18th October 2012; Brooke Masters, 'Tampering with Libor to become criminal offence', 18th October 2012; Stephen Foley and Michael Mackenzie, 'Derivatives trades on the brink of tough new regime', 18th October 2012; Ralph Atkins, Philip Stafford, and Brooke Masters, 'Collateral Damage', 25th October 2012; Daniel Schäfer, 'Once-neglected segment is now banking's belle of the ball', 30th October 2012; Brooke Masters, 'Regulators peer into financial shadows', 19th November 2012; Shahien Nasiripour and Brooke Masters, 'Regulators edge towards "every country for itself"', 10th December 2012; Brooke Masters and Shahien Nasiripour, 'US banks want new liquidity rules eased', 17th December 2012; Brooke Masters and Shahien Nasiripour, 'Basel move aims to stoke recovery', 8th January 2013; Tom Burgis, Brooke Masters, and Lina Saigol, 'Sants warns on foreign branches in UK', 11th January 2013; Tracy Alloway and Nicole Bullock, 'Banks offer debt product to help skirt new liquidity rules', 30th January 2013; Brooke Masters, 'Safety net plans raise industry ire', 19th March 2013; Tracy Alloway, 'Banks debate liquidity trade-off', 19th March 2013; Michael Mackenzie, Dan McCrum, and Tracy Alloway, 'Electronic trading set to muscle in on corporate debt', 4th April 2013; Daniel Schäfer, 'Regulation threat to global banks', 12th April 2013; Brooke Masters, Philip Stafford, and Michael Mackenzie, 'Libor heads for history in hunt for new bank rate', 24th April 2013; Shahien Nasiripour and Tom Braithwaite, 'Out to break the banks', 1st May 2013; Anne-Sylvaine Chassany and Henny Sender, 'Forced into the shadows', 7th June 2013; Evelyn de Rothschild, 'Banking must pursue the holy grail of confidence', 25th June 2013; Philip Stafford and Brooke Masters, 'Libor deal commences rehabilitation of benchmark', 10th July 2013; Patrick Jenkins and Daniel Schäfer, 'Banks suffer as derivatives trade shifts to the "shadows"', 12th September 2013; Tracy Alloway, 'Buyers struggle to find a safe landing', 21st November 2013; Christopher Caldwell, 'The Volcker rule is a gift to banks and excludes the rest', 14th December 2013; Christopher Thompson, 'Basel 3 rules to hit repo trading', 7th February 2014; Chris Flood,

'Regulators stalk secretive financial giants', 24th February 2014; Tracy Alloway and Arash Massoudi, 'Non-bank lending steps out of the shadows', 26th February 2014; Sam Fleming, 'Foreign banks meet BoE over branch rules', 27th February 2014; Patrick Jenkins and Claire Jones, 'Eurozone bank rules menace City prosperity, warns lobby', 19th March 2014; Chris Flood, 'Hedge funds transmit most risk', 28th April 2014; Daniel Schäfer, 'Banks' skills gap forces up pay for talented minority', 28th April 2014; Mark Carney, 'The need to focus a light on shadow banking is nigh', 16th June 2014; Patrick Jenkins and Sam Fleming, 'Alternative finance steps out of the shadow', 16th June 2014; Tom Braithwaite, Martin Arnold, and Tracy Alloway, 'Tough choices confront traditional lenders', 18th June 2014; Paul Tucker, 'Financial regulation needs principles as well as rules', 19th June 2014; Sam Fleming and Gina Chon, 'Push begins to put lenders' house in order', 19th June 2014; Sam Fleming and Gina Chon, 'Boutique banks flourish as larger institutions rethink business models', 12th August 2014; Tom Braithwaite and Vivianne Rodrigues, 'Wall Street's biggest lenders blame bond volatility on tight regulation', 17th October 2014; Gina Chon, 'Regulators wrestle with cross-border strategy', 24th October 2014; Caroline Binham and Sam Fleming, 'Record fines carry strong echo of Libor scandal', 13th November 2014; Patrick Jenkins, 'It's right for shareholders to share the pain', 13th November 2014; Philip Stafford, 'Fall in value of LCH.Clearnet interest rate swaps', 28th November 2014; Martin Arnold, 'Carney's too big to fail buffer represents clear progress despite doubt', 9th December 2014; Andrew Bailey, 'Irresponsible conduct carries consequences in British finance', 23rd February 2015; Philip Stafford, 'IPO filing provides rare insight into HFT world', 14th April 2015; Caroline Binham and George Parker, 'Banks increase attacks against wave of regulation', 6th June 2015; Joe Rennison, 'Fitch warns of growing repo threat', 18th June 2015; Philip Stafford, 'Banks eye hub to cut swaps trading disputes', 8th July 2015; Frederic Oudea, 'Europe needs home grown bulge bracket banks', 12th October 2015; Philip Stafford, 'Confidence shaken by violent swings', 13th October 2015; Patrick Jenkins, 'Start-up threat to creaking banks', 14th October 2015; Philip Stafford, 'Exchange chiefs eye deals to tap new markets', 31st December 2015; Thomas Hale, 'Non-banks rebuild UK home loan landscape', 4th February 2016; Philip Stafford, 'ICE circles amid D Börse's tie-up talks with LSE', 2nd March 2016; Philip Stafford, 'LSE combination spawns derivatives doubts', 6th April 2016; Henry Sanderson, 'Regulator says banks back plan for more transparency in London's gold trade', 19th August 2016; Joe Rennison and Robin Wigglesworth, 'Outsiders struggle to shake up Treasury trade', 31st August 2016; Harriet Agnew and Patrick Jenkins, 'What's next for the City', 3rd September 2016; Attracta Mooney, 'Fund houses take on banks over lending', 5th September 2016; Philip Stafford, 'LSE and banks launch derivatives exchange', 27th September 2016; Joe Rennison, 'Bond trading platform muscles in as banks retreat', 29th September 2016; Philip Stafford and Nicole Bullock, 'Radical pilot to boost trade in smallest US stocks begins', 5th October 2016; Philip Stafford and Hannah Murphy, 'Clearing houses benefit from rule change', 6th April 2017; Eric Platt and Gregory Meyer, 'Exchanges jump on index data as banks beat a retreat', 3rd June 2017; Eric Platt and Robert Smith, 'Efforts to harmonise risky-loans rules in doubt', 6th June 2017; Reza Moghadam, 'Branch out to avoid a Brexit capital markets crunch', 20th July 2017; Philip Stafford, 'Voice brokers fight to survive Europe's shake-up', 10th October 2017; Philip Stafford, 'LSE admits case for tougher EU oversight', 1st November 2017; Ben McLannahan and Jim Brunsden, 'EU plan over bank runs faces US opposition', 2nd November 2017; Miles Johnson, 'Mifid 2 poised to hasten slow death of analysts', 25th January 2018; Robin Wigglesworth and Ben McLannahan, 'Liquidity outs leverage as the big worry for investors', 4th May 2018; Laura Noonan, 'Financials', 12th June 2018; Jeff Merkley, 'Avoid past mistakes and preserve key bank safety law', 26th June 2018; Joe Rennison and Philip Stafford, 'Traders find receptive ear among regulators to relax capital rules', 10th July 2018; Laura Noonan and Patrick Jenkins, 'Financial Crisis', 13th September 2018; John Gapper, 'My naïve part in the downfall of Lehman', 13th September 2018; Mark Vandevelde, 'Financial Crisis', 20th September 2018; Philip Stafford, 'Fresh risks emerge from the depth', 1st October 2018; Hans Hoogervorst, 'Do not blame accounting rules for the financial crisis', 4th October 2018; Caroline Binham, Philip Stafford, and Jim Brunsden, 'No-deal Brexit threat concentrates minds at London clearing houses', 10th October 2018; Robin Wigglesworth and Joe Rennison, 'New credit ecosystem blossoms as portfolio trades surge', 11th October 2018; Caroline Binham, 'BoE warns over rapid growth of high-risk corporate lending', 18th October 2018; Philip Stafford, Nicole Bullock, and Kadhim Shubber, 'Shares in US exchanges hit after rebuke from regulator over high data charges', 18th October 2018; Claire Jones, Caroline Binham, and Sam Fleming, 'Fed governor to head global finance police', 21st November 2018; Caroline Binham, 'Ringfence rules come into effect for UK banks', 2nd January 2019; Kate Allen and Philip Stafford, 'EU sovereign debt costs at risk if access to City banks ends with no-deal Brexit', 4th January 2019; Laura Noonan, 'Ex-bankers embrace adrenalin ride of fintech', 9th January 2019; Lindsay Fortado and Laura Noonan, 'Banks bet on hedge fund prime broking fees', 10th January 2019; Nicholas Megaw, 'Challenger banks struggle to smash glass ceiling', 14th January 2019; Simon Samuels, 'The ECB should resist the lure of bigger banks', 31st January 2019; Jamie Smyth, 'Australian regulator pledges to tackle cosy oligopoly of big banks and punish misconduct', 4th February 2019; Jo Johnson, 'Politicians must stand up for the City after EU exit', 21st February 2019; Eva Szalay, 'Fears over forex trading going bump in the night', 6th March 2019; Delphine Strauss, Philip Stafford, and Claire Jones, 'BoE and ECB launch swap line to buffer banks in event of post-Brexit turmoil', 6th March 2019; Caroline Binham, David Crow, and Patrick Jenkins, 'Lenders told to triple liquid assets as Brexit protection', 11th March 2019; Paul Murphy, 'Cyber-attacks target banks' easy pickings', 25th March 2019; David Crow, 'Banks strain to effect a post-crisis funding fix', 25th March 2019; Tommy Stubbington, 'Investor alarm sounded over amazing disappearing Bunds', 12th July 2019; Philip Stafford, 'BGC signs trio of high-frequency trading firms to boost European equity options', 25th July 2019; Caroline Binham, 'BoE presses banks for living wills to limit bailout damage', 31st July 2019; Robert Armstrong, 'Warnings sounded over watered-down Volcker', 23rd August 2019; Joe Rennison and Philip

Consequences of Intervention: Markets, 2011–20

Regulators faced an even more difficult task than they encountered with banks in tackling the risks inherent in financial markets, because of the volume and variety of transactions and the fact that the markets were extensively used both to cover risks and to speculate for gain. In 2015 Michael Bodson, the chief executive of the US clearing house, DTCC, doubted that regulators could get to grips with even US financial markets, as that involved 100,000 separate participants generating 12bn messages a year with $1,600,000bn of assets transferred annually: 'There is a naiveté from some regulators. They felt pressure to get rules done but—because it's the first time they had tried this—I don't think they understood what they were asking for.'[123] Nevertheless, this was the task they had taken on. In 2012 Michel Barnier, EU commissioner for the internal market, stated that, 'No player, no market and no instruments must escape appropriate regulation and efficient supervision.'[124] Though some markets had an institutional structure, through the use of exchanges, which provided regulators with a mechanism through which a degree of control could be exercised, most did not. Most transactions involved currencies, swaps, bonds, and other financial instruments, and trading in these took place directly between banks, through the intermediation of interdealer brokers, or on electronic communication networks. Products that were bespoke and arranged bilaterally between trusted counterparties, as was the case in the market for swaps, did not require the services of an exchange, especially when contact could be made over the telephone or the Internet. Neither were exchanges required in the high-volume trading of standardized products, such as currencies, when it also took place between a small number of trusted counterparties, which was the case in the foreign exchange market.

Though once important in the trading of bonds, when that trading consisted of standard products bought and sold between numerous investors, exchanges no longer played a role in that market. Bonds were either of a bespoke nature, issued in small quantities, and closely held, as was the case with numerous corporate and mortgage issues, or large, standardized issues from governments and multinational corporations. In the case of the former, private deals, arranged bilaterally met the needs of the market while, in the latter, those involved were trusted counterparties who traded directly with each other or through specialist intermediaries and electronic platforms. In the securitization boom that preceded the crisis it was banks that made the market in the products they created, acting as counterparties to the buying and selling of both to each other and their own customers. Writing in 2016 Philip Stafford explained why OTC markets were so popular:

> Deregulation ended fixed commissions, ushering in electronic trading. It also kicked off a boom in risk management. Big companies going global needed complex tools to hedge their risk to adverse interest-rate or currency moves. For that they needed big investment banks and with it was born the modern global derivatives market. Banks transacted

Stafford, 'Rise of MarketAxess mirrors demise of traders on Wall Street', 30th August 2019; Attracta Mooney, 'Liquidity crunches heat up debate over capital buffers', 16th September 2019; Nicholas Megaw, 'Challenger banks struggle against big four', 30th September 2019; *FT* Reporters, 'Fed analyses regulation's role in sudden rates jump', 2nd October 2019.

[123] Joe Rennison, 'Policymakers left with problem in the wake of London whale', 13th October 2015.

[124] Steve Johnson, 'EU shadow banking plan rapped', 26th March 2012.

> interest rates, corporate bonds, currencies and credit deals and hedged their own risks in futures markets.[125]

That left exchanges to cater for the market in corporate stocks and standardized derivatives as these were best suited to the facilities they could provide, being uniform financial products bought and sold in volume between a large number of diverse participants. Trading in these could support the costs involved in providing the human and physical infrastructure of a dedicated market, such as an exchange. In turn, the existence of an exchange attracted those who looked for liquidity and transparency from financial products, such as banks and large institutional investors. An exchange generated confidence that those financial products, for which it provided a market, could always be easily and quickly bought and sold and at prices that could be relied upon to reflect current conditions. What attracted regulators to exchanges was their ability to concentrate trading and so produce deep and liquid markets, detect and eliminate abuses including price manipulation, and enforce discipline on those who used their market so as to remove counterparty risk and generate reliable prices. The existence of exchanges also gave regulators a mechanism through which the rules they devised could be enforced. An exchange possessed the power to discipline its members by banning access to the trading system that it provided. Agencies such as the SEC and the CFTC had been created to police self-regulating organizations, like exchanges, rather than undertake the task themselves. In 2012 the CME employed 200 staff at an annual cost of $40m to carry out its duties as a self-regulatory body. Writing in 2018 Philip Stafford, Nicole Bullock and Kadhim Shubber were of the opinion that exchanges 'are usually treated as quasi-governmental entities charged with ensuring markets are clean and fair',[126] and were of the same opinion in 2019.[127] While recognizing that the task they faced had become much more difficult, because of the major changes that had taken place in the structure of markets, many running the regulatory agencies remained confident that they were up to the challenge. One was David Shillman, associate director in the Division of Trading and Markets at the SEC, who claimed in 2012 that 'Advances in technology have allowed for more complex and dispersed markets to develop, but at the same time have provided market participants tools to efficiently monitor market prices and implement routeing strategies to address that complexity.'[128] In contrast, Gregory Meyer was much more sceptical in 2016 because, 'Markets have become increasingly placeless, regulated by national laws but open in any time zone.'[129]

There were international organizations that provided a degree of regulatory co-ordination. One was the International Organization of Securities Commissions (IOSC), which dated from 1983 and by 2016 had 207 members from 115 jurisdictions. However, it largely confined itself to corporate stocks and had little control over national authorities. Pre-dating IOSC was the International Capital Markets Association (ICMA) which had begun in 1968 as the Association of International Bond Dealers (AIBD). By 2018 it had a membership of 530 organizations located in over sixty countries. It claimed to be

> Active in all segments of the international debt capital markets, representing the views of market users, from the issuers raising capital, the banks which act as intermediaries, to

[125] Philip Stafford, 'ICAP's new direction reflects changing future of derivatives', 6th October 2016.

[126] Philip Stafford, Nicole Bullock, and Kadhim Shubber, 'Shares in US exchanges hit after rebuke from regulator over high data charges', 18th October 2018.

[127] Nicole Bullock and Philip Stafford, 'NYSE and Nasdaq urge court to block fees cap plan', 16th February 2019.

[128] Michael Mackenzie, Arash Massoudi, and Stephen Foley, 'Rage against the machine', 17th October 2012.

[129] Gregory Meyer, 'Trading', 7th July 2016.

> the institutions who are investors, and the central banks, exchanges, clearing houses and law firms which support market activity. ICMA's conventions, standard documentation, rules and recommendations provide the framework of market practice which has facilitated the growth and orderly functioning of the cross-border market—the world's largest market for international capital—for fifty years.[130]

What was absent from that list was any regulatory functions as these lay with the national authorities. The financial markets lacked any equivalent to the BIS and its Basel committee of banking regulators, who not only drew up internationally-recognized rules and regulations but also had the power to see these carried through into national legislation, as they were backed by government owned central banks. Making the difficult task of regulating these vast and diverse financial markets even harder was that they were in a constant state of flux, forever changing in composition and structure. Larry Tabb, a leading US expert on financial markets, warned regulators in 2011 of the complicated task they faced. In his words these markets were

> Living and breathing things that grow and change over time, reacting to external pressures slowly but surely.... With new rules, come new loopholes and new exploitation methodologies. Each regulatory initiative is followed by unintended consequences and greater technology investment both to take advantage of temporal opportunities, and subsequently to defend against opportunities. The more stable the rules, the better market participants can react, invest, and respond. A constant stream of rules means a constant stream of loopholes, creating constant opportunities, requiring constant investment, which crowds out the weak and creates greater exploitation incentives...Not all regulation is bad. However regulators need to weigh the risks of new rules against the costs and unintended consequences of change.

His parting advice was that 'While regulation may provide a veil of protection, we must be careful that new rules don't create a market worse than where we started.'[131]

With the experience of the Global Financial Crisis behind them regulators did press for a switch from the OTC market, especially in derivatives, to one that was more institutional and more centralized, and so lent itself to greater control. In both the Dodd–Frank Act in the USA and the European Market Infrastructure Regulation (Emir), the intention was to shift the bulk of OTC derivatives trading onto either exchanges or their equivalent, namely Swap Execution Facilities (SEFs) in the USA and Organized Execution Facilities (OEFs) in the EU. Such an intention was implicit in the EU's revision of the Market in Financial Instruments Directive (Mifid), which was finally delivered in 2019. According to David Keohane and Philip Stafford in 2018, 'The vast Mifid rules were designed to make European markets safer, more efficient and transparent, and discourage trading away from stock exchanges. Banks were banned from trading customers' orders via their internal trading desks.'[132] By then US regulators were already retreating from the backing they had provided to exchanges after the crisis. Robert Jackson, an SEC commissioner, announced in 2018 that 'We at the SEC have far too often continued to treat exchanges with the same kid

[130] ICMA 50 Years [advertisement], 5th February 2018.
[131] Larry Tabb, 'Playing ostrich over high-speed trading is not an option', 14th July 2011.
[132] David Keohane and Philip Stafford, 'Jury still out on Mifid 2 transparency rules', 18th June 2018.

gloves we applied to their not-for-profit ancestors.'[133] In the wake of the financial crisis the SEC had placed restrictions on banks while being supportive of exchanges. It was now changing that policy in response to exchanges, as profit-seeking companies, trying to maximize earnings by exploiting their ability to monopolize the delivery of data by charging users high fees for access to such information. Banks, in particular, objected to paying these fees as they considered that it was their collective buying and selling that generated the data in the first place. This was part of an ongoing war between banks and exchanges for control over financial markets. Jeremy Grant and Alex Barber noted in 2011 that exchanges 'compete fiercely with banks.'[134] This had intensified by 2018 because, according Stafford, Bullock, and Shubber, 'Banks need to lower costs but exchanges need to find ways to boost revenues.'[135] Gaining the support of regulators was a key weapon in the armoury of each as it could tip the balance in favour of one side or the other. Before the crisis it was banks that had persuaded regulators to back them against exchanges. That position was then reversed with the crisis but it had changed again ten years later.

The motivation behind the drive among regulators to move derivatives trading onto exchanges or Swap Execution Facilities (SEFs)/Organized Trading Facilities (OTFs) was to reduce the risks that such contracts involved, as revealed in the crisis. The results were, however, very limited as the trading of derivatives continued to strongly favour the OTC market because that suited the needs of the vast majority of users. Most wanted the customized products and known counterparties available in the OTC market, rather than standard contracts and anonymity provided by exchanges. Another problem with exchanges and SEFs/OTFs was that prices had to be displayed publicly, which exposed a buyer or seller's position to its competitors, and so revealed either their strategy or exposed their vulnerability. This made many unwilling to use either exchanges or the new facilities, preferring dark pools instead. There was also a reluctance among exchanges to step in and provide an alternative market for products that came in so many different types and were often little traded. In 2011 only 3000–3500 interest-rate swaps contracts were traded each day compared to 2.7m Eurodollar interest-rate futures contracts traded daily on the CME Group. Foreign exchange swaps, for example, were direct arrangements between participating banks designed to cover their short-term exposure to currency risks by matching it with the reverse position of another bank. As such there was little in the way of a secondary market while counterparty risk had been met through the use of the CLS Bank, set up by the banks themselves for precisely that purpose. Businesses did shift from bespoke products traded on the OTC market to standardized products traded on exchanges, but only to a limited degree.

The dilemma facing regulators in choosing between exchanges and the OTC markets was that both had features that they considered unacceptable. In the OTC market prices were opaque and unreliable, counterparty risk was rife, users lacked protection, and liquidity could suddenly evaporate because trading was fragmented between different venues. Conversely, regulators disliked the ability of exchanges to use their monopoly position to benefit those who controlled them at the expense of the wider public through high charges and restrictive practices. This had driven the intervention before the crisis that had undermined the role played by stock exchanges. In contrast, the unregulated markets could

[133] Nicole Bullock, 'Battle intensifies over the costs of using US market data', 1st October 2018.

[134] Jeremy Grant and Alex Barber, 'Mifid's net cast wide to overhaul Europe's trading', 21st October 2011.

[135] Philip Stafford, Nicole Bullock, and Kadhim Shubber, 'Shares in US exchanges hit after rebuke from regulator over high data charges', 18th October 2018.

provide users with a cheap, flexible, and convenient service that was highly responsive to changes in products and technology. Conscious of the needs to balance the advantages and disadvantages of each type of market there was a reluctance among regulators to make the use of exchanges mandatory after the crisis or return to a pre-crisis position which endorsed OTC trading. Even in Japan, which had long provided the Tokyo and Osaka stock exchanges with a degree of regulatory protection, there was a move to lessen the support provided once the two agreed to merge in 2011. Similarly, in Australia the regulator pushed to open up the domestic equity market, which was dominated by a single exchange, while in the EU there was continuing pressure to generate more competition among exchanges. Philip Stafford observed in 2018 that in the EU 'Policymakers do not want to eliminate dark pools and accept that institutional investors want to be able to trade large blocks of shares without moving the market price against them.'[136] Regulators had to devise a solution that combined the flexibility and competitiveness of the OTC market with the guarantees provided by exchanges in terms of the reliability of prices, the certainty that deals would be completed, and the confidence that sales and purchases could be made. As Greg Medcraft, the chairman of the International Organization of Securities Commissions, emphasized in 2015, 'If a market is going to work effectively, it's important that participants have trust and confidence in it.'[137]

The problem for regulators seeking a means of controlling markets was that the more the exchanges and the megabanks responded to the restrictions, the more trading migrated to alternatives such as dark pools, electronic platforms, and intermediaries who connected buyers and sellers. This was already the case in equity markets where the likes of RegNMS and Mifid had driven trading away from regulated exchanges and into a variety of OTC markets. After the crisis the regulatory intervention had the same effects on a range of established OTC markets. The result was to undermine, in the words of Jeremy Grant in 2011, 'the efficiencies that single pools of liquidity bring.'[138] Whereas in 2011 the senior economist at the IMF, Manmohan Singh, was expressing the view that 'These regulatory steps seem unlikely to adequately reduce systemic risk from OTC derivatives and the likelihood of future taxpayer bailouts appears to remain significant, '[139] by 2016 Philip Stafford warned that the 'regulatory crackdown from policy makers' was affecting the role played by the megabanks in providing financial markets:

> New rules on leverage have made it more expensive for banks to use their balance sheets to hold inventory or trade and finance positions in OTC derivatives markets. Not helping banks navigate a more costly world of doing business has been the suppression of bond yields and market volatility due to central bank policy, reducing the need among companies and portfolio managers to use derivatives for hedging risk.[140]

There was a difficult balance between rules that were too lax, and thus permitted the build-up of risk leading to another crisis, and those that were too restrictive, leading to the suppression of trading activity. By 2016 tougher prudential and capital rules so restricted the ability of banks to trade profitably that they had abandoned certain market-making

[136] Philip Stafford, 'Mifid 2 brings dark pool trading into the light', 10th January 2018.
[137] Philip Stafford, 'Confidence shaken by violent swings', 13th October 2015.
[138] Jeremy Grant, 'Industry in the midst of a maelstrom', 10th October 2011.
[139] Jeremy Grant, 'Conduits of contention', 16th June 2011.
[140] Philip Stafford, 'ICAP's new direction reflects changing future of derivatives', 6th October 2016.

activities. In 2019 Robin Wigglesworth reported that, 'Since the financial crisis, stricter regulations and commercial pressures have forced many banks to pare back or close their once-vast proprietary and market-making desks.'[141] The leverage rule introduced under Basel 3 in 2014 had forced banks to hold more capital and post more collateral as they had to cover not only their own positions but also those of their customers, such as hedge funds, so that any failure did not spread through the market. This reduced trading, made markets less liquid, increased volatility, and increased the risks attached to particular financial instruments, which discouraged their use. Though the rules were relaxed as regulators became aware of their impact the priority remained making the banks as resilient as possible, regardless of the wider consequences. In 2018 Joe Rennison and Philip Stafford reported that 'Banks have retreated from their traditional roles of providing two-way prices for investors in listed futures and over-the-counter arenas for equities, bonds and foreign exchange.' The consequence was that these markets had 'become increasingly electronic with market-making activity gravitating towards high-speed trading firms, which by their nature do not extend support for prices once volatility heats up'. The effect was 'far more volatile swings in asset prices'.[142] With banks no longer acting as shock absorbers, buying when others were selling and selling when others were buying, a number of OTC financial markets were left short of liquidity. That put them at the mercy of the High-frequency Traders whose horizons were very short term as they lacked the resources of the megabanks. The intervention of regulators created instability in the financial markets, driving trading into the hands of those less able to counter sudden spikes in buying and selling.

This left regulators searching for a permanent solution that would bring greater stability and certainty to financial markets, and so avoid a repetition of the problems experienced in 2008. That solution could not involve any major relaxation on the requirement of the megabanks to hold more capital, reduce the level of leverage they applied, and supply more collateral to support deals. Such a course would not be countenanced by governments as it risked a repeat of the 2008 crisis while it also ran counter to public opinion, which continued to put these banks in the frame for what had happened in 2008. Nor could the solution include banning the use of derivatives, whatever the risks they posed through exposure to losses and counterparty default, though such action would be popular among many members of the public, as they had been demonized during the crisis. It was increasingly recognized that these products were an essential means through which banks, fund managers, and multinational businesses covered the risks they ran in a world of volatile prices, interest rates, and exchange rates and in diffusing the consequences of counterparty default. The solution could also not lie in restricting derivatives to those traded on exchanges, as that would hand a monopoly to the likes of the CME in the USA, which would create their own problems for regulators. The merger between the CME and the CBOT had made the resulting institution into a near-monopoly provider of exchange-traded futures contracts in the USA, with only the OTC market able to provide alternative products. In the EU concerns from regulators that a Deutsche Börse/Euronext merger would place the Continent's two dominant futures exchanges, namely Eurex and Liffe, under the control of a single institution, had led to it being blocked.

With those avenues not available the only remaining solution acceptable to regulators was an even greater reliance on clearing houses, which had already risen to prominence in

[141] Robin Wigglesworth, 'IMF warns of "tip of the iceberg" threat over volatility', 12th April 2019.

[142] Joe Rennison and Philip Stafford, 'Traders find receptive ear among regulators to relax capital rules', 10th July 2018.

the crisis. Prior to the crisis OTC derivatives like swaps were traded between banks on the basis that each counterparty could be trusted to complete their side of the deal. The crisis made such a position unacceptable, because defaults had occurred, and so regulators had turned to clearing houses. In 2019 Philip Stafford wrote that 'Clearing houses stand between the counterparties to a trade and, given their role in helping to manage the wider risk if one side defaults, have grown in systemic importance since the financial crisis.'[143] Later that year Jim Brunsden and Philip Stafford reported that 'Regulators see clearing houses as a critical part of the financial infrastructure, since they act as central counterparties between sellers and buyers of shares and derivatives.'[144] Philip Stafford then praised clearing houses as 'pillars of global stability, standing between parties in a deal and managing the risk of contagion if one side defaults'.[145] A clearing house took on the financial risk if a party to a deal defaulted. It used both its own funds and those collected from users as collateral to ensure deals could be completed in the event of a default. This already took place on the CME and Eurex, as these exchanges had their own clearing houses, but the intention was to make the use of Central Clearing Parties (CCPs) mandatory for all derivatives trading, unless there were compelling reasons why it could not be used.

By 2011 Jeremy Grant had concluded that, 'Ultimately, central bankers are relying on CCPs to maintain the highest possible risk-management standards to help avoid the need for bailouts.'[146] This reliance on clearing houses then intensified. Writing in 2012 Nicole Bullock made clear that 'Since the financial crisis global regulators are intent on having the majority of derivatives transactions cleared.'[147] In 2017 Philip Stafford observed that, 'To safeguard the financial system, regulators have sought to ensure that more derivative deals are processed through clearing houses which sit between counterparties and ensure trades are completed even if one side defaults on payment.'[148] He repeated the same observation in 2018 when he reflected that, 'The financial crisis made the clearing industry a priority for regulators keen to contain the threat of contagion in the derivatives market. Entities from companies to banks use derivatives to manage their exposure to interest rate risks, and clearing houses sit between the two counterparties of a trade.'[149] Even without this regulatory push banks and institutional investors had turned to clearing houses as a way of addressing counterparty risk, combining it with shortening the delay in completing transactions. By closing deals more quickly counterparties were less exposed to default. As Michael Bodson, the chief executive of the Depository Trust and Clearing Corporation (DTCC), explained in 2012, 'Post-2008, there has been a lot of emphasis on looking at sources of systemic risk and on how to control it. Risk can appear very quickly and shortening the settlement cycle is something we can do that will improve our risk-management capabilities.'[150]

[143] Philip Stafford, 'European customers handed clearing house access to contain Brexit fallout', 19th February 2019.

[144] Jim Brunsden and Philip Stafford, 'UK clearing houses face threat of pressure to move to EU', 14th March 2019.

[145] Philip Stafford, 'LSE shrugs off Brexit worries to gain boost from clearing', 2nd May 2019.

[146] Jeremy Grant, 'Conduits of contention', 16th June 2011.

[147] Nicole Bullock, 'US central counterparty set to clear trades in mortgage debt', 13th March 2012.

[148] Philip Stafford, 'European Parliament seeks to extend regulatory powers over clearing houses', 29th September 2017.

[149] Philip Stafford, 'Frankfurt narrows gap with London as incentive scheme boosts euro clearing', 13th June 2018.

[150] Stephen Foley and Michael Mackenzie, 'Derivatives trades on the brink of tough new regime', 18th October 2012.

Clearing houses not only held capital and reserves against possible losses caused by the default of one party to a deal, but also required users of their services to provide collateral in the form of cash or assets that were both secure and liquid, such as US treasury bonds. Throughout the world there was a general move by regulators towards the mandatory use of central clearing in order to make the global financial system safer, with Asia following the USA and the EU. Though the process took time and happened in different ways and speeds, by 2014 it was well established. Whereas only 24 per cent of interest-rate swaps, for example, were centrally cleared in 2009 by 2017 the figure had reached 62 per cent. Even parts of the foreign exchange market were being driven towards the use of centralized clearing houses by 2018. As the rules under Basel 3, along with national regulations, forced banks to set aside larger and larger amounts of collateral when trading derivatives, foreign exchange and bonds, it became a cheaper option to have the deals processed through clearing houses than provide ever larger quantities of high quality collateral that was expensive to obtain and in short supply. The alternative was to abandon the business, which a number of banks, fund managers and insurance companies did, because the risks no longer justified the profits to be made. Thus, an indirect effect of mandatory clearing was to shrink trading in a number of financial markets.

Another consequence of mandatory clearing was that the profits to be made attracted new entrants to the business. While unwilling to provide a new home for many of the products found in the OTC market, exchanges spotted that providing clearing facilities offered profitable prospects. Clearing worked most effectively when vast amounts of trades were pooled together, with losses and gains across the market for equities, swaps, and repo cancelling each other out. Under these circumstances those exchanges operating the vertical-silo model identified profitable openings in extending their clearing services to participants in the OTC market. This is what ICE, CME, Deutsche Börse, the Singapore Exchange, the Hong Kong Exchange, and the KRX exchange in South Korea did. Though regulators continued to regard vertical-silos as anti-competitive they took no action to break them up, despite complaints that they were exploiting their position. There was also a grudging acceptance among regulators that vertical-silos did have some merits as they provided users with a single package covering the entire transaction. Nevertheless, the clearing model that regulators preferred was that operating in the US equity market. The USA provided an example of a low-cost and highly-efficient clearing service in the form of the DTCC. The DTCC cleared all transactions in the US equity market, and also extended its services to other financial markets. 'Having a trade guarantor for this market will reduce operational and systemic risk... It makes it much more efficient if there is a member failure' was the claim of Murray Pozmanter, the managing director of the DTCC, when they started clearing mortgage bonds in 2012.[151] The US model was also used in Japan where the Japan Securities Clearing Corporation serviced all the country's stock exchanges and was owned by them. In contrast, clearing in the EU was split between fourteen separate clearing houses resulting in a much more expensive operation and the lock-up of collateral, as users were unable to gain the benefits of netting as they could through a single institution. Despite efforts by the European Commission to deal with the fragmentation of clearing or, at least, force those providing the service to co-operate, it remained. This encouraged exchanges in Europe to merge and offer their customers a single clearing service through the vertical-silo model.

[151] Nicole Bullock, 'US central counterparty set to clear trades in mortgage debt', 13th March 2012.

By concentrating business in a single clearing house, traders could economize on the amount of collateral they had to post to guarantee deals, so encouraging them to route all their orders to multiplatform exchanges owning their own clearing houses. Through a process known as netting, positions in the same clearing house could be offset against each other, cutting the amount of collateral that traders had to provide. The type, amount, and cost of collateral had become a serious concern because of the Basel rules as it affected profitability. The quantitative easing practised by central banks had diminished the supply of the high-quality assets demanded by clearing houses as collateral, so any steps to reduce the amount needed would be of benefit. The proposed merger between Deutsche Börse/ NYSE Euronext in 2011 promised users of the clearing house a collective annual saving of around $4bn as transactions on Eurex and Liffe would all be cleared through a single institution. Nevertheless it was blocked by the EU regulatory authorities. The 2017 merger between Deutsche Börse and the LSE was also blocked though it would have combined the in-house clearing of the contracts traded at Eurex with those on the OTC market cleared by the LCH, which was controlled by the LSE. In contrast, the merger between ICE and NYSE Euronext in 2013 was approved, despite having to pass twenty-five separate regulatory authorities before it could proceed, as it did not pose any issues relating to clearing, and could even lead to competition for the CME.

This triumph of the vertical-silo left those exchanges without their own clearing houses at a disadvantage and so there was a scramble for them to acquire their own. By 2011 Martin Abbott, the chief executive of LME, considered that 'the horizontal clearing model is being steadily eroded'[152] as he revealed plans for his exchange to establish its own clearing house. In 2012 NYSE Euronext decided to supply the futures exchange it owned, Liffe, with its own clearing house. There were a number of independent clearing houses, with the LCH in London being the most important. These became a target for exchanges with the LCH being pursued by NYSE Euronext, Nasdaq OMX, and the LSE. This contest was won by the LSE which not only gave it an integral clearing house but one that serviced the global OTC interest-rate swaps market, SwapClear. 'Securing LCH.Clearnet would give the LSE its own clearing house in the UK at a time when the exchange business is dominated by groups that already own their clearing services' was the verdict of Jeremy Grant in 2012.[153] LCH. Clearnet cleared nearly half the world's $400tn global interest-rate swap market and was the second largest clearer of bonds and repos in the world. This left Euronext without a vertical-silo, so in 2017 it tried to buy Clearnet from LCH.Clearnet, as that would have provided it with a clearing service. Speaking in 2017 Stephane Boujnah, the chief executive officer of Euronext, explained the importance of the deal: 'This acquisition is an opportunity for Euronext to secure long-term control of clearing activities for the Euronext market, both in cash and derivatives.'[154] However, the deal fell through forcing Euronext to consider setting up its own clearing house, which it was only prevented from doing by being given a stake in Clearnet. What that indicated was how important it was by 2018 for an exchange to operate a vertical-silo model in the light of the regulatory intervention that had made the use of a central clearer essential across all financial markets.

Though regarded as a solution to the counterparty risks posed by systemically-important banks and financial markets, whether operated by exchanges or through OTC trading, the

[152] Philip Stafford, 'LME eyes its own metals clearing for earnings boost', 4th May 2011.

[153] Jeremy Grant, 'LSE to take lead stake in clearer', 10th March 2012.

[154] Hannah Murphy and Philip Stafford, 'LSE agrees French clearing unit sale in move to placate Brussels', 4th January 2017.

use of clearing houses also raised concerns which regulators were either reluctant or unable to address. When Ben Bernanke, the chairman of the Federal Reserve, endorsed the use of clearing houses in 2011, observing how they had 'generally performed well in the highly-stressed financial environment of the recent crisis' he had added the warning that 'We should not take for granted that we will be as lucky in the future.'[155] What he and many others were already well aware of was that pushing responsibility for guaranteeing the completion of deals onto clearing houses made them into systemically-important institutions, whose failure could lead to or intensify a future financial crisis. There were repeated warnings that the failure of a clearing house could have catastrophic consequences for the stability of the global financial system, and calls to ensure that they were sufficiently resilient to withstand the default of one or two big members, to avoid triggering a systemic crisis. These concerns, and demands for action to be taken, included William Dudley, the president of the Federal Reserve Bank of New York, who wrote in 2012 that, 'Stability demands that central counterparties themselves be subject to tough rules and appropriate oversight to ensure they can withstand any wider financial stresses.'[156] It also included Jean-Pierre Mustier, head of investment banking at UniCredit and a former board member at LCH-Clearnet. He wrote in 2013, 'We're moving from a set-up where banks were interconnected because they had transactions between them, to a system where very lowly capitalised entities, the clearing houses, are supposed to protect the banks from a problem.'[157] In 2015 Ana Arsov, an associate managing director at the rating agency, Moody's, passed judgement on clearing houses: 'We believe these institutions have always had a very elevated systemic risk profile. But now with the mandatory clearing of OTC derivatives their profile is even more elevated.'[158] Picking up on these concerns John Dizard concluded in 2017 that 'There is a good argument to be made that forcing bilateral derivatives contracts on to clearing platforms has concentrated rather than reduced systemic risk.'[159] The following year he repeated that point: 'A favourite post-crisis fix, mandatory clearing of derivatives contracts, has concentrated rather than dissipated financial risk.'[160] Forcing the use of clearing houses reduced the consequences stemming from the failure of an individual bank but had magnified the threat to the entire system if the clearing house itself should collapse. In 2019 Philip Stafford went so far as to say that the failure of a key clearing 'could threaten the stability of the US financial system.'[161] In turn that would have serious consequences for the global financial system.

In dealing with this problem regulators faced a conflict between placing clearing in the hands of a few large institutions or encouraging competition between different providers. The former risked creating an inefficient monopoly in a position to overcharge users and demand large amounts of high-quality collateral, but it would be resilient in the face of defaults. The latter would drive up efficiency and drive down charges but lead to less resilient institutions as they demanded less collateral and accepted lower quality. It was this latter option that gradually came to the fore. Philip Stafford observed in 2018 that 'Banks quote clients specialised prices and spreads—or the difference at what the bank will buy

[155] Jeremy Grant, 'Conduits of contention', 16th June 2011.
[156] Brooke Masters and Philip Stafford, 'Clearing houses face tougher capital rules by end of the year', 17th April 2012.
[157] Patrick Jenkins, Philip Stafford, and Tom Braithwaite, 'Bankers voice concerns over risks posed by clearing houses', 8th July 2013.
[158] Joe Rennison, 'Moody's sets out shake-up for clearing houses', 24th June 2015.
[159] John Dizard, 'Arguing over who owns a clearing time bomb', 8th May 2017.
[160] John Dizard, 'Brexit could be a toy train crash for derivatives', 8th October 2018.
[161] Philip Stafford, 'Chicago's Options Clearing Corp hones plan to shore up its balance sheet', 19th July 2019.

and sell at—depending on the clearing house.'[162] What it proved impossible to create was a single global central counterparty supported by collective central bank liquidity. Opposition included Mark Carney, while governor of the Bank of Canada, despite his role on the BIS's Financial Stability Board. Financial markets were vital components of national financial systems and so were seen by central banks as a critical mechanism for transmitting monetary policy. For these reasons governments wanted control over national clearing houses as they might be called upon to provide guarantees if they were overwhelmed by defaults. Conversely, national central banks did not want to accept liabilities over which they had no control. Even in the EU such co-operation could not be achieved. Britain's decision in 2016 to leave the EU thrust the question of responsibility for clearing houses into the political spotlight. Governments of countries in the Eurozone, such as Germany and France, insisted the clearing of euro-based transactions took place in either Frankfurt or Paris, rather than London, where most was currently done. The UK was not a member of the Eurozone but in 2017 London-based clearing houses processed about 90 per cent of the world's euro-denominated derivatives transactions and around half of European banks' repo business. Relocating that business to other centres ran counter to the interests of most banks as they wanted it to remain in London, and not fragmented over different locations, as that allowed them to concentrate their portfolios, net down exposures, and save billions of dollars in collateral and associated capital charges each year. There was also a division of opinion among regulators over what to do about the risks posed by clearing houses. Banking regulators did not want banks exposed to losses stemming from a failure of a clearing house while market regulators wanted clearing houses to be able to call in support from banks to prevent their collapse. Each was concerned by the systemic risk posed by a clearing house failure and so wanted to protect either the banking system or the market from its consequences.

What the issue over clearing houses revealed were the machinations that went on behind regulatory proposals with the outcome not determined by concerns for either efficiency or stability but national interest. Each regulatory authority worked to its own agenda, which made reaching agreement on equivalence so difficult, even within the EU, between the EU and Switzerland, and between the EU and the USA, which were all at much the same stage of development and heading in the same direction at the same speed. For global markets this was an impossible position as Christopher Giancarlo, the chairman of the CFTC, pointed out in 2018 when he said that it was a 'completely untenable position of having to choose between violating domestic laws and regulations or violating foreign laws and regulations.'[163] He threatened that US regulators would intervene to force compliance with their laws and regulations including banning US banks from using EU clearing houses and EU banks from using US ones. The effect was to leave clearing houses confused over what support and from whom they could expect it in a crisis. Daniel Maguire, the chief executive of LCH made this clear in 2019: 'Clearing houses are generally only in the spotlight during crises. We need to be able to operate in those scenarios. One of the key ingredients is everybody knowing what they can do, what they need to do and when.'[164] Central banks were also unclear over what their precise role would be as David Bailey, director of markets

[162] Philip Stafford, 'Deutsche Börse makes progress in push to lure derivatives clearing from London', 6th February 2018.

[163] Philip Stafford, 'US threatens EU banks with ban over Brexit clearing plans', 18th October 2018.

[164] Philip Stafford, 'BoE official warns EU on pitfalls of UK clearing house regulation post-Brexit', 15th February 2019.

infrastructure at the Bank of England admitted in 2019: 'The last thing you want in a crisis is potentially overlapping or conflicting requirements being placed on systemically-important institutions.'[165] The impression was generated that those tasked with providing a more resilient financial system in the wake of the Global Financial Crisis were no further towards achieving that objective after a decade of effort. In 2019 Philip Stafford reported that 'Global regulators are growing concerned that their push to mandate more clearing of assets in markets is creating more linkages between banks and clearing houses... such linkages could destabilise markets under certain circumstances.'[166]

In contrast to the alacrity with which national regulators responded to protect national issues, there remained an inability to apply the same speed and focus to more general concerns, despite the huge increase in the cost, extent, and invasiveness of regulation since the crisis. One such example comes from the Central Bank of Ireland where the regulatory staff grew from 369 in 2008 to over 1000 in 2019, justified by the greatly increased importance of regulation. As Edward Sibley, the deputy governor for financial regulation explained in 2019: 'Appropriately strong regulatory and supervisory frameworks have an important role in delivering a resilient financial system that can support the economy and its consumers in good times and bad.... Our gatekeeping role is hugely important in mitigating financial stability risks, and protecting market integrity and customers in Ireland and across Europe.'[167] At the same time the Irish regulatory authorities were involved in using regulation in a bidding war as they attempted to attract financial activities from London in the wake of the UK's decision to leave the EU. If successful this would break up the slowly emerging single market in financial services in the EU, much to the disappointment of those who were engaged in it. In 2019 Staffan Ahlner, head of collateral management at BNY Mellon complained that, 'As the EU political situation is evolving, the risk of fragmented liquidity pools emerging across European financial markets is a real concern.'[168] Vincent Dessard, the senior regulatory adviser at the European Fund and Asset Management Association, pleaded on behalf of their members that, 'We urge the European Commission to... grant equivalence to all UK recognised trading venues and for all types of financial instruments.'[169] What they wanted was a smooth and transparent way of trading stocks across Europe not markets where barriers had been erected for political reasons. One European banker, Andrea Vismara, chief executive of Equita, an Italian investment bank, suggested that despite the time regulators had spent 'analysing and promoting regulatory changes' they 'have failed so far to understand the intricacies of the European investment banking landscape'.[170] Another regulator, Robert Ophele, chairman of France's Autorité des Marches Financiers, considered that 'Being so rule-based... is something which is detrimental to the efficiency, the agility, the capability of the European regulation to give the appropriate answer to any challenge.'[171] What this reflected was the degree to which the EU was following the structure and practice of what had already been put in place in the USA. Throughout the world there was a strong temptation to adopt the financial

[165] Philip Stafford, 'BoE official warns EU on pitfalls of UK clearing house regulation post-Brexit', 15th February 2019.

[166] Philip Stafford, 'Vix volatility spike prompts shake-up at leading equity options clearing house', 20th March 2019.

[167] Laura Noonan and Claire Jones, 'Central bank has bigger stick to win respect at home and abroad', 13th February 2019.

[168] Philip Stafford, 'Liquidity fears trigger European repo shift to Paris', 7th May 2019.

[169] Philip Stafford, 'No-deal Brexit share trade ruling sparks accusations of EU land Grab', 21st March 2019.

[170] Andrea Vismara, 'Mifid 2 drags down an ecosystem along with Europe's banks', 15th May 2019.

[171] David Keohane and Philip Stafford, 'French regulator calls for flexible market rules', 15th July 2019.

regulations devised in the USA in the belief that they offered a tried and tested solution, regardless of either their applicability or effectiveness.

Ten years on from the Global Financial Crisis there was growing evidence that regulatory intervention had been no more successful in removing the risks present to financial markets, and putting in place coping mechanisms, than it had been in banking. One example was the crypto-currency bubble, which left participants with large losses. The Basel Committee on Banking Supervision (BCBS) viewed crypto assets, according to Madison Darbyshire, in 2019, as not providing 'the standard functions of money and are unsafe to rely on as a medium of exchange or store of value. Crypto assets are not legal tender and are not backed by any government or public authority.'[172] In 2018 Chloe Cornish and Hannah Murphy reported that 'The cryptocurrency bubble has burst.'[173] The value in circulation had risen from $18bn in January 2017 to $800bn by January 2018 and then fell to $200bn by August 2018. Another financial market posing a threat to financial stability by then was that in leveraged loans, according to Gavin Jackson: 'Regulators across the world have flagged leveraged loans as an area of concern, pointing to declining lending standards and falling protections for investors as a possible indicator of financial risk.'[174] Judith Evans highlighted a speculative bubble in the property market through the use of 'lightly regulated and opaque debt funds.'[175] More generally, the operations of the shadow banking sector were leading to a potential liquidity crisis. In 2019 Steven Maijoor, chairman of the European Securities and Market Authority (Esma) admitted that 'The resilience of the fund sector is of growing importance, as it accounts for an increasing part of the EU's financial system. Therefore, it is crucial to ensure that the fund industry is resilient and is able to absorb economic shocks.'[176] Funds of all kinds had grown in popularity since the crisis, benefiting from the climate of low interest rates and the restrictions placed on the banks. As Sam Fleming, Joe Rennison, and Robert Armstrong pointed out in 2019, 'While post-crisis regulation forced traditional banks to have larger amounts of capital and more resilient liquidity backstops, the non-banking sector is much more loosely supervised.'[177]

Regulatory intervention had shifted risk from the megabanks to the megafunds and clearing houses, but both were less well placed to cope with a crisis if one did take place. The megafunds and the clearing houses lacked the close links to the central banks that the megabanks had. In a crisis, as in 2008, the megabanks could call on the assistance of the central banks to act as lenders of last resort. The US Federal Reserve did act as lender of last resort to the inter-bank money market, for example, though in 2019 it was still learning what this required in practice. As home to the world's dominant megabanks and the only source of the international currency, the US$, it was only the Federal Reserve that was in a position to undertake this task, however reluctant it might be to assume it. In contrast, neither the megafunds nor the clearing houses could call on central banks, including the Federal Reserve, to act as lender of last resort in a crisis. John Dizard pointed out in 2019 that the asset management industry 'does not have systemic oversight by bank regulators

[172] Madison Darbyshire, 'Basel watchdog adopts tougher line after urging banks to be wary of risks', 14th March 2019.

[173] Chloe Cornish and Hannah Murphy, 'Crypto bubble bursts after brief history of surges and plunges', 21st August 2018.

[174] Gavin Jackson, 'Bank of England plays down surge in risky corporate loans', 24th January 2019.

[175] Judith Evans, 'Building a real estate bubble', 19th June 2019.

[176] Chris Flood, 'Esma warns on bond fund liquidity risk', 9th September 2019.

[177] Sam Fleming, Joe Rennison and Robert Armstrong, 'Non-bank lenders under scrutiny after taking big share in US mortgage market', 10th April 2019.

and central banks'.[178] What was becoming of growing concern by then was an emerging liquidity crisis in the fund management industry. In certain funds investors had been promised either immediate repayment or the ability to sell out even though the assets of the fund were largely illiquid. As long as redemptions and sales were matched by receipts and purchases, then liquidity was not an issue. However, in a crisis the reverse would occur, as such funds would be able to liquidate their holdings and certainly not at prices sufficient to meet outflows. The BIS's Financial Stability Board was tasked with spotting risks such as these, and then proposing measures that would either defuse them or prevent a crisis escalating out of control if one did take place. However, its focus was on banking not the global financial system as a whole. In 2019 Vikram Pandit, who had run Citibank, pointed out that 'Politicians still worry about banks that are too big to fail, regulators struggle to supervise such big institutions.'[179] With that focus since the crisis, measures had been put in place that made banking much less exposed to a liquidity crisis. However, as the memory of the crisis faded the effect had been to transfer liquidity risks to other parts of the financial system, which was much less familiar with it and much less able to cope if a crisis took place. As Caroline Binham and Siobhan Riding noted in 2019 there were 'divergent positions of central bankers and securities regulators over the direction of fund liquidity rules'.[180] However, the two activities were completely intertwined and so required a co-ordinated approach that recognized the changes that had taken place since 2008. One organization that should have been able to take this overview, and so be in a position to act if a crisis did occur, was the Federal Reserve Bank of the USA. The verdict of Gillian Tett in 2019 was that 'Neither the Fed nor investors completely understand how the cogs of the modern financial machine mesh.'[181] If true this had serious implications for the entire global financial system.[182]

178 John Dizard, 'H20 is an omen: a liquidity crisis lurks', 15th July 2019.

179 Vikram Pandit, 'Outdated rules are holding back financial innovation', 19th September 2019.

180 Caroline Binham and Siobhan Riding, 'Iosco fires back at BoE in spat over fund rules', 22nd July 2019.

181 Gillian Tett, 'Repo markets mystery reminds us we are flying blind', 20th September 2019.

182 David Gelles, 'Approval for Xpert as private company shares exchange', 4th January 2011; Jeremy Grant, 'Deutsche Börse in talks with rivals over joint clearing', 6th January 2011; Aline van Duyn, 'Regulator set to rule on Wall Street's swaps power', 13th January 2011; Jeremy Grant, 'Derivatives trading platform bypasses intermediary banks', 17th January 2011; Jeremy Grant and Telis Demos, 'Growth in off-exchange trade stokes pricing fears', 26th January 2011; Jeremy Grant and Nikki Tait, 'NYSE link-up faces hurdles', 11th February 2011; Jeremy Grant, 'Brussels casts shadow over exchanges' plan', 4th March 2011; Jeremy Grant, 'Traders face jump in clearing costs', 11th March 2011; David Oakley, 'Crisis probe puts Libor in spotlight', 16th March 2011; Jeremy Grant, 'Dealers look for answers on US derivatives reform', 17th March 2011; Jeremy Grant, 'Central counterparties eye wave of opportunities', 22nd March 2011; Jeremy Grant, 'Industry pleads its case against rules forged in heat of crisis', 29th March 2011; Aline van Duyn, 'IMF raises concern over US reforms to derivatives trading', 30th March 2011; Philip Stafford, 'Euroclear adds to "vertical silo" fears over Deutsche Börse deal', 31st March 2011; Jeremy Grant, 'Dealers warn against spread of derivatives clearing houses', 14th April 2011; Phil Davis, 'Howls of anguish meet EU proposals on trading reforms', 18th April 2011; Tom Braithwaite, 'US Treasury to exempt forex swaps from new rules', 30th April 2011; Joshua Chaffin and Hal Weitzman, 'How clearing helped ICE reinforce ties with banks', 30th April 2011; Aline van Duyn, '"ET" stokes fears about sweeping swaps rules', 4th May 2011; Philip Stafford, 'LME eyes its own metals clearing for earnings boost', 4th May 2011; Jeremy Grant and Nikki Tait, 'City fortunes in flux as exchanges merge', 12th May 2011; Jeremy Grant and Philip Stafford, 'Savings for investors as Europe acts on trading', 25th May 2011; Jeremy Grant, 'Three stock exchanges enter battle for control of London clearing house', 28th May 2011; Aline van Duyn, 'Battle lines emerge as new rules are created', 31st May 2011; Michael Mackenzie, 'Habits change in anticipation of arrival of electronic trading', 31st May 2011; Jeremy Grant, 'Reform in Europe', 31st May 2011; Aline van Duyn, 'Proposals would widen competition', 31st May 2011; Jeremy Grant, 'Drive for consolidation leaves clock ticking for LCH.Clearnet', 13th June 2011; Jeremy Grant, 'Conduits of contention', 16th June 2011; Bernard Simon, 'TMX battle homes in on derivatives', 23rd June 2011; Hal Weitzman, 'NYSE Liffe takes fight to "Fortress Chicago"', 28th June 2011; David Oakley, 'Collateral demand rises for interbank lending', 4th July 2011; Philip Stafford, 'Citi plans "dark pool" to link HFTs and smaller investors', 7th July 2011; Tracy Alloway, 'Avoiding collateral damage for derivatives', 12th July 2011; Jeremy Grant, 'London steers clear of ECB settlement platform plan', 22nd July 2011; Larry Tabb, 'Playing ostrich over high-speed trading is not an option', 14th July

2011; Jeremy Grant, 'Traders cautious on exchanges tie-up', 1st August 2011; Jeremy Grant, 'Avalanche of rulemaking blocks road to OTC clarity', 1st August 2011; John Rivett, 'Collateral will be key in shake-up for derivatives', 1st August 2011; Anuj Gangahar, 'Finding a mechanism to save the trades', 1st August 2011; Jeremy Grant and Alex Barber, 'Brussels to probe exchanges merger', 5th August 2011; Peter Smith and Jeremy Grant, 'ASX on the offensive to fend off Chi-X', 16th August 2011; Philip Stafford, 'Chi-X European clearing deal takes on established bourses', 17th August 2011; Philip Stafford, 'ASX and Clearstream in talks over outsourcing', 29th August 2011; Jeremy Grant, 'LCH.Clearnet at the centre of bidding war', 7th September 2011; Jeremy Grant, 'Europe closer to settlement system', 12th September 2011; Jeremy Grant, 'Deutsche Börse-NYSE tie-up to save extra $1bn for customers', 15th September 2011; Jeremy Grant, 'LSE beats Markit in battle to buy LCH', 28th September 2011; Jeremy Grant, 'Every Bourse wants a house of its own', 28th September 2011; Jeremy Grant, 'Industry in the midst of a maelstrom', 10th October 2011; Sarah Mishkin, 'Competition helps to reduce barriers', 10th October 2011; Jeremy Grant, 'Regulators and industry unsure about rules', 10th October 2011; Philip Stafford, 'Divisions over audit trails as G20 deadline approaches', 10th October 2011; Jeremy Grant, 'Uncertainty over detail of clearing reforms', 10th October 2011; Gregory Meyer, 'CFTC approves caps on speculation', 19th October 2011; Alex Barber, 'EU to ban naked sovereign CDS', 19th October 2011; Jeremy Grant and Alex Barber, 'Mifid's net cast wide to overhaul Europe's trading', 21st October 2011; Tracy Alloway, 'Counterparty risk makes an anxious return', 27th October 2011; Michael Mackenzie, 'Market prepares for transparency', 4th November 2011; Gregory Meyer, 'An example for regulators to study', 4th November 2011; Hal Weitzman, 'Euro crisis gives clearing a boost', 4th November 2011; Jeremy Grant, 'New trading venues aim to provide choice of structures', 4th October 2011; Michael Mackenzie, 'Industry hopes longer delays will mean looser rules', 4th November 2011; Jeremy Grant and Alex Barber, 'ECB preference for Eurozone clearers raises ire in London', 24th November 2011; Jeremy Grant, 'X-clear lifts share of LSE clearing', 1st December 2011; Brooke Masters, 'EU watchdog issues alert on unregulated forex groups', 6th December 2011; Greg Meyer and Michael Mackenzie, 'Wall Street takes on derivatives watchdog', 6th December 2011; Philip Stafford, 'High-speed trading rules', 23rd December 2011; Jeremy Grant, 'New rules are struggle for industry and regulators', 23rd January 2012; Philip Stafford, 'Changes bring global flurry of innovation', 23rd January 2012; Hal Weitzman and Gregory Meyer, 'Uncertain futures', 27th January 2012; Jeremy Grant, 'Brussels' block points to future of global alliances', 2nd February 2012; Telis Demos, Philip Stafford, and Jeremy Grant, 'London clearing a priority for NYSE', 11th February 2012; Michael Mackenzie, 'Libor probe shines light on voice brokers', 17th February 2012; Jack Farchy and Jeremy Grant, 'Prospect of LME's sale puts clearing in focus', 23rd February 2012; Simon Rabinovitch and Robert Cookson, 'China unlikely to impose big bang reforms', 24th February 2012; Ben McLannahan, 'Merger of markets may foreshadow expansion overseas', 9th March 2012; Jeremy Grant, 'LSE to take lead stake in clearer', 10th March 2012; *FT* Reporters, 'A benchmark to fix', 12th March 2012; Nicole Bullock, 'US central counterparty set to clear trades in mortgage debt', 13th March 2012; Robin Wigglesworth, 'Taming the traders', 20th March 2012; Jeremy Grant, 'LSE seeks holy grail of clearing from LCH. Clearnet deal', 20th March 2012; Steve Johnson, 'EU shadow banking plan rapped', 26th March 2012; Philip Stafford, 'NYSE Euronext to start full derivatives clearing in London', 29th March 2012; Brooke Masters, 'Conflicting signals', 2nd April 2012; Jeremy Grant, 'CME eyes London as European springboard', 10th April 2012; Jeremy Grant, 'CME puts focus on London as its European beachhead', 17th April 2012; Jack Farchy, 'LME eyes renminbi move for metals', 17th April 2012; Brooke Masters and Philip Stafford, 'Clearing houses face tougher capital rules by end of the year', 17th April 2012; James Pickford, James Wilson, Haig Simonian, 'Big hubs keep the wheels of industry turning', 10th May 2012; Brooke Masters, 'Wariness over EU's level playing field', 10th May 2012; Sophia Grene, 'Derivatives rules will bring new demands', 21st May 2012; Philip Stafford, 'Deutsche Börse to clear rate swaps', 1st June 2012; Alice Ross and Philip Stafford, 'Rage against the machine as forex traders fight back', 12th July 2012; Hal Weitzman, 'ICE shifts OTC energy swaps to futures', 1st August 2012; Philip Stafford, 'CME puts Europe at the centre of expansion plan', 21st August 2012; Michael Mackenzie and Tracy Alloway, 'Swaps profits threatened by Dodd–Frank', 23rd August 2012; Jeremy Grant, 'Barriers higher for Asian dominance in algo trading', 24th August 2012; Jeremy Grant, 'Asia fears systemic risk over Dodd–Frank', 7th September 2012; Philip Stafford, 'Battle for derivatives clearing heats up', 11th September 2012; Gerrit Wiesmann and Philip Stafford, 'Germany to press ahead with high-speed trading regulation', 26th September 2012; Philip Stafford, 'ICE plans CDS exchange trading', 17th October 2012; Michael Mackenzie, Arash Massoudi, and Stephen Foley, 'Rage against the machine', 17th October 2012; Stephen Foley and Michael Mackenzie, 'Derivatives trades on the brink of tough new regime', 18th October 2012; Philip Stafford, 'Blizzard of regulation has its effect', 30th October 2012; Arash Massoudi, 'Increase in competition raises the stakes', 30th October 2012; Jeremy Grant, 'Asia watches and learns from European and US rule makers', 30th October 2012; Michael Mackenzie, 'Fight looms over which model is best', 30th October 2012; Philip Stafford, 'Rules covering derivatives built on ground that has yet to settle', 30th October 2012; Philip Stafford, 'Collateral drive puts the focus on settlements', 30th October 2012; Jeremy Grant, 'Singapore OTC trades hit by turmoil', 2nd November 2012; Michael Mackenzie and Gregory Meyer, 'US swaps shake-up set to boost exchanges', 2nd November 2012; Philip Stafford, 'BATS Chi-X Europe in talks to secure UK exchange licence', 7th November 2012; Philip Stafford, 'Surge in US dark pools trading highlights fears over regulation', 20th November 2012; Philip Stafford and Michael Mackenzie, 'Interdealer brokers braced for shake-up', 22nd November 2012; Michael Mackenzie and Stephen Foley, 'High costs to hit made to measure derivatives', 12th December 2012; David Oakley and Philip Stafford, 'LSE tries to change terms of Euro 463m LCH.Clearnet deal', 15th December 2012; David Oakley and Philip Stafford, 'New rules hit LSE deal with LCH. Clearnet', 18th December 2012; Arash Massoudi, 'Professional traders have edge on retail investors, says NYSE',

19th December 2012; Philip Stafford and Arash Massoudi, 'US share trading glitches fuel call to revisit rulebook', 23rd January 2013; Arash Massoudi and Philip Stafford, 'NYSE deal drew interest from Buffett, David Gelles', 29th January 2013; Philip Stafford, 'JPX seeks to expand OTC alliances with rivals in Asia', 6th February 2013; Philip Stafford, 'CME poised for European clearing push', 11th February 2013; Arash Massoudi and Michael Mackenzie, 'In search of a fast buck', 20th February 2013; Michael Mackenzie, Dan McCrum, and Tracy Alloway, 'Electronic trading set to muscle in on corporate debt', 4th April 2013; Brooke Masters, Philip Stafford, and Michael Mackenzie, 'Libor heads for history in hunt for new bank rate', 24th April 2013; Arash Massoudi and Michael Mackenzie, 'Investors turn to the dark side for trading', 26th April 2013; Stephen Foley, 'HFT platforms facing "speed limits"', 29th April 2013; Patrick Jenkins, Philip Stafford, and Tom Braithwaite, 'Bankers voice concerns over risks posed by clearing houses', 8th July 2013; Alex Barber, Gregory Meyer, and Philip Stafford, 'US and EU derivatives truce averts rules crunch', 12th July 2013; Tracy Alloway, 'Collateral Management', 17th September 2013; Philip Stafford, 'The new heart of a safer system', 17th September 2013; Michael Mackenzie, 'Rivals angle for custom in changing world of swaps', 17th September 2013; Sam Fleming and Philip Stafford, 'Regulators warn on boom-era debt', 16th October 2013; Philip Stafford, 'US funds transfer trades to London', 18th October 2013; Arash Massoudi, 'Soaring cost of US share dealing risks "investor harm"', 18th October 2013; Philip Stafford, 'Fears grow over rules on derivatives trading', 19th December 2013; Philip Stafford and Alex Barber, 'Europe agrees biggest securities overhaul since 2008', 16th January 2014; Jonathan Davies, 'High-frequency traders: heroes or hoodlums?', 21st April 2014; Philip Stafford, 'Tougher capital rules boost traders' feelings of security', 28th April 2014; Philip Stafford, 'Sense of urgency underpins fresh scrutiny of markets', 16th September 2014; Tom Braithwaite and Vivianne Rodrigues, 'Wall Street's biggest lenders blame bond volatility on tight regulation', 17th October 2014; Philip Stafford, 'Industry strives to find its form', 5th November 2014; Philip Stafford, 'Members fear they may have to stump up in case of a failure', 5th November 2014; Philip Stafford, 'Fall in value of LCH.Clearnet interest rate swaps', 28th November 2014; Philip Stafford, 'Too big to fail fears reach clearing houses', 3rd December 2014; Philip Stafford, 'US the dominant derivatives superpower', 9th January 2015; Tom Braithwaite and Philip Stafford, 'US banks urge action on clearing houses', 13th January 2015; Philip Stafford, 'Insurance for clearing houses underwritten', 12th March 2015; Philip Stafford, 'US swaps market resists futures model', 17th March 2015; Kara Scannell, Nicole Bullock, and Gregory Meyer, 'CME faces questions over missed red flags on trades', 24th April 2015; Philip Stafford and Nicole Bullock, 'SEC probes arcane part of equity market's plumbing', 12th May 2015; Philip Stafford, 'Swiss broker to set up London repo venue', 19th May 2015; Joe Rennison, 'Moody's sets out shake-up for clearing houses', 24th June 2015; Philip Stafford, 'Europe to mandate clearing of swaps', 7th August 2015; Philip Stafford, 'Markets planning for a world after the day of the Mifid', 13th October 2015; Joe Rennison, 'Policymakers left with problem in the wake of London whale', 13th October 2015; David Sheppard and Neil Hume, 'Traders fear new derivatives rules', 26th October 2015; Philip Stafford, 'Clearing capital drives Deutsche Börse-LSE talks', 24th February 2016; Philip Stafford, 'ICE circles amid D Börse's tie-up talks with LSE', 2nd March 2016; Philip Stafford, 'Bourse tie-ups put clearing risk in spotlight', 5-6th March 2016; Nicole Bullock and Philip Stafford, 'US Exchanges', 8th March 2016; Lindsay Fortado and Katie Martin, 'SFO drops forex fraud probe', 16th March 2016; Chris Flood, 'Cracking down on "megalomaniacs and bullies"', 28th March 2016; Nicole Bullock, 'IEX presents regulator with a bumper dilemma', 30th March 2016; Philip Stafford, 'LSE combination spawns derivatives doubts', 6th April 2016; John Plender, 'The Big Bang spawned a dark-trading monster', 13th June 2016; Philip Stafford, 'Strains show in over-the-counter dealing', 14th June 2016; Gregory Meyer, 'Trading', 7th July 2016; Joe Rennison and Robin Wigglesworth, 'Outsiders struggle to shake up Treasury trade', 31st August 2016; Joe Rennison and Philip Stafford, 'Fears grow that global reforms to derivatives will fragment into a patchwork of local standards', 23rd September 2016; Philip Stafford, 'Brexit brings headache to industry weary of regulation', 11th October 2016; Philip Stafford, 'LSE set to sell Paris unit to Euronext', 28th December 2016; Hannah Murphy and Philip Stafford, 'LSE agrees French clearing unit sale in move to placate Brussels', 4th January 2017; Robin Wigglesworth, 'Capital Group targets HFTs with rules push', 1st February 2017; Philip Stafford, 'Derivatives Big Bang catches traders off guard', 2nd February 2017; Philip Stafford, 'Clearing houses pose post-crisis challenge', 17th February 2017; Hannah Murphy, 'Exchanges line up block trade bonanza', 24th March 2017; Philip Stafford, 'LSE switches focus as Deutsche Börse deal fails', 30th March 2017; Philip Stafford, 'Euronext's Dutch gambit puts pressure on LSE to sell French house', 4th April 2017; Philip Stafford and Hannah Murphy, 'Clearing houses benefit from rule change', 6th April 2017; Philip Stafford and Zoskia Wasik, 'LSE faces strong demand to use clearing house', 27th April 2017; John Dizard, 'Arguing over who owns a clearing time bomb', 8th May 2017; Philip Stafford, 'Debate over post-Brexit clearing of euro swaps focuses on margin costs', 13th June 2017; Philip Stafford, 'Anxiety over EU regulatory shake-up goes global', 6th July 2017; Martin Arnold and Emma Dunkley, 'UK watchdog sounds the death knell for Libor', 28th July 2017; Alexandra Scaggs, 'Demise of Libor is far from a done deal', 3rd August 2017; Philip Stafford, 'Euronext finalises LSE derivatives deal', 9th August 2017; Philip Stafford, 'Mifid vies with Brexit as City traders' top concern', 11th August 2017; Philip Stafford, 'Investors' Mifid 2 challenges flagged up', 24th August 2017; Gregory Meyer and Philip Stafford, 'Derivatives watchdog eyes swaps trading reform', 13th September 2017; Philip Stafford, 'EU and US regulators race to seal equivalence deal before Mifid 2 deadline', 21st September 2017; Barney Jopson and Joe Rennison, 'Brexit spurs call for more clearing house regulation', 7th October 2017; Norma Cohen, 'Mifid 2 will have profound impact on fixed income', 9th October 2017; Philip Stafford, 'Voice brokers fight to survive Europe's shake-up', 10th October 2017; Philip Stafford, 'Clock ticks down on EU's Mifid reform', 10th October 2017; Alexandra Scaggs, 'Money-market funds lift repo deals', 20th October 2017; Philip Stafford, 'Brexit unleashes a three-way battle over clearing', 25th October 2017; Philip Stafford, 'European Parliament seeks to extend regulatory powers over clearing houses', 29th September 2017; Philip Stafford, 'LSE admits case for tougher EU oversight', 1st November 2017; Philip Stafford, 'Deutsche Börse draws allies in swaps fight', 21st November 2017; Joe Rennison, 'Senators press regulators to clarify position over Treasury market reform', 2nd November 2017; Philip Stafford, 'Fears over "last look" spur tighter FX code', 20th December 2017; Gregory Meyer, Nicole Bullock, and Joe Rennison, 'Trading', 2nd January 2018; Philip Stafford and Peter Smith, 'Europe begins countdown to day of the Mifid', 2nd January 2018; Chris Flood, 'Mifid 2 set to stimulate growth in ETFs', 3rd January 2018; Hannah Murphy and Philip Stafford, 'Mifid 2 risks drowning in its own ambition', 4th January 2018; Philip Stafford, 'Exchanges seek Mifid review as Brexit looms', 9th January 2018; Philip Stafford, 'Mifid 2 brings dark pool trading into the light', 10th January 2018; Philip Stafford, 'Mifid 2 share trading shake-up put on hold', 10th January 2018; Philip Stafford, 'Trading venues play down rift over Mifid 2', 11th January 2018; Philip Stafford, 'Dark pool trading flourishes after Mifid 2 delay', 19th January 2018; Emma Dunkley, 'Brexit delays Hong Kong–LME tie up', 25th January 2018; ICMA 50 Years [advertisement], 5th February 2018; Philip Stafford, 'Deutsche Börse makes progress in push to lure derivatives clearing from London', 6th February 2018; Robin Wigglesworth, 'Exchange traded products face scrutiny as worries deepen', 15th February 2018; Ben McLannahan, 'SEC eyes initial coin offerings with suspicion', 15th March 2018; Natasha Landell-Mills, 'Should the Big Four accountancy firms be split up? Yes', 22nd March 2018; The Lex Column, 'Mifid 2/dark pools: shifty shades of grey', 27th March 2018; Kadhim Shubber, 'CFTC chairman set to overhaul restrictive Obama-era swaps execution regulations', 27th April 2018; Robin Wigglesworth and Ben McLannahan, 'Liquidity outs leverage as the big worry for investors', 4th May 2018; Philip Stafford, 'Frankfurt narrows gap with London as incentive scheme boosts euro clearing', 13th June 2018; David Keohane and Philip Stafford, 'Jury still out on Mifid 2 transparency rules', 18th June 2018; Chris Flood, 'Liquidity enables big ticket trades', 18th June 2018; Gregory Meyer and Philip Stafford, 'Derivatives traders forced to cut holdings as banks push for Basel clampdown', 3rd July 2018; Philip Stafford, 'Record half for LCH despite Brexit uncertainty', 5th July 2018; Joe Rennison and Philip Stafford, 'Traders find receptive ear among regulators to relax capital rules', 10th July 2018; Philip Stafford, 'Deutsche Bank's Frankfurt move revives City concerns', 31st July 2018; Jonathan Ford and Madison Marriage, 'Setting flawed standards', 2nd August 2018; Caroline Binham, 'Regulators praise post-crisis derivatives rules', 8th August 2018; Madison Marriage and Jonathan Ford, 'Close ties of auditors and watchdogs draw fire', 21st August 2018; Pauline Skypala, 'EU rule changes deliver mixed results so far', 10th September 2018; Philip Stafford, 'Fresh risks emerge from the depth', 1st October 2018; Gabriel Wildau, 'Doors to China's markets are creaking open', 1st October 2018; Nicole Bullock, 'Battle intensifies over the costs of using US market data', 1st October 2018; Philip Stafford and Hannah Murphy, 'Mifid 2 starts to weave its influence through markets', 1st October 2018; John Dizard, 'Brexit could be a toy train crash for derivatives', 8th October 2018; Caroline Binham, Philip Stafford, and Jim Brunsden, 'No-deal Brexit threat concentrates minds at London clearing houses', 10th October 2018; Robin Wigglesworth and Joe Rennison, 'New credit ecosystem blossoms as portfolio trades surge', 11th October 2018; Philip Stafford, 'US threatens EU banks with ban over Brexit clearing plans', 18th October 2018; Emma Dunkley, 'HKEX looks to trading suspensions after string of accounting scandals', 18th October 2018; Louise Lucas and Emma Dunkley, 'China start-ups resist lure of Hong Kong IPO sweeteners', 19th October 2018; Philip Stafford, 'ABN Amro's clearing business seeks London licences to prepare for Brexit', 22nd November 2018; Philip Stafford, 'Corners of Wall Street remain undeterred by crypto crash', 28th November 2018; Jim Brunsden and Philip Stafford, 'Brussels set to extend access to Swiss exchanges for another six months', 18th December 2018; Hannah Murphy, Stephen Morris and Attracta Mooney, 'Mifid 2 throws up unintended consequences', 2nd January 2019; Eva Szalay, 'Yen traders wrongfooted as flash crash strikes during Asia's witching hour', 4th January 2019; Gavin Jackson, 'Bank of England plays down surge in risky corporate loans', 24th January 2019; Philip Stafford and Sarah Provan, 'LSE takes Euroclear stake as regulators look to tighten rules on use of collateral', 31st January 2019; Laura Noonan and Claire Jones, 'Central bank has bigger stick to win respect at home and abroad', 13th February 2019; Philip Stafford, 'BoE official warns EU on pitfalls of UK clearing house regulation post-Brexit', 15th February 2019; Nicole Bullock and Philip Stafford, 'NYSE and Nasdaq urge court to block fees cap plan', 16th February 2019; Philip Stafford, 'European customers handed clearing house access to contain Brexit fallout', 19th February 2019; Siobhan Riding, 'Supermancos, the fund businesses that are winning big from Brexit', 25th February 2019; John Dizard, 'Grandma will lose in a clearing house crisis, too', 4th March 2019; Sam Fleming, 'Global regulator starts leveraged loans scrutiny', 8th March 2019; Richard Henderson and Nicole Bullock, 'SEC head calls for sweeping review of rules underpinning equity transactions', 9th March 2019; Jim Brunsden and Philip Stafford, 'UK clearing houses face threat of pressure to move to EU', 14th March 2019; Madison Darbyshire, 'Basel watchdog adopts tougher line after urging banks to be wary of risks', 14th March 2019; Jim Brunsden and Claire Jones, 'ECB attacks EU proposals for boosting clearing house oversight', 18th March 2019; Philip Stafford, 'Vix volatility spike prompts shake-up at leading equity options clearing house', 20th March 2019; Siobhan Riding, 'Watchdogs probe systemic risks of passive fund growth', 1st April 2019; Sam Fleming, Joe Rennison and Robert Armstrong, 'Non-bank lenders under scrutiny after taking big share in US mortgage market', 10th April 2019; Robin Wigglesworth, 'IMF warns of "tip of the iceberg" threat over volatility', 12th April 2019; Eva Szalay and Philip Stafford, 'Citigroup calls for burden of managing risky trades to be shared more widely', 17th April 2019; Philip Stafford, 'LSE shrugs off Brexit worries to gain boost from clearing', 2nd May 2019; Nicole Bullock and Philip Stafford, 'Nasdaq chief redoubles drive for data in NYSE dogfight', 3rd May 2019; Philip Stafford, 'Liquidity fears trigger European repo shift to Paris', 7th May 2019; Richard Henderson, 'IEX backs regulator's stance on data fees charged by big stock exchange groups', 15th May

Conclusion

In 2012 Philip Stafford had warned that 'The changing of market structures often leads to unintended consequences.'[183] Taking a more reflective view in 2018 he considered that:

> Ten years on from the height of the financial crisis it is tempting to look back at the havoc precipitated by the collapse of Lehman Brothers and think we have come a long way. Waves of overlapping reforms, such as the Dodd–Frank Act, Basel 3 and Mifid 2, have been passed to make financial institutions and markets safer. Banks have to set aside more capital for trading, and clearing houses—which sit between parties in a deal to manage credit risk—have become the biggest crash barriers. Banks now cannot leverage their own balance sheets and hold inventory and positions in the market on behalf of clients quite as aggressively as they once did. However, the last decade has also seen rapid technological changes. Trading is increasingly performed by machines using automated systems that fire off trades in fractions of a second without human intervention. Artificial intelligence is also beginning to creep into markets, as some participants explore whether computers can 'learn' from huge amounts of markets data. Regulators now view these twin trends with some trepidation.[184]

His view that much had changed was endorsed by Charles Himmelberg, a Goldman Sachs strategist. Also writing in 2018 he concluded that 'Financial markets have changed pretty dramatically since the crisis.'[185] What can be concluded is that much had changed on the regulatory front but that the world had yet to discover a way of coping with potential liquidity crises that extended beyond a small group of very large banks and pervaded the entire global financial system. In the past that role of global stabilizer in the event of a liquidity crisis had been performed by central banks operating on a national basis and restricting themselves to those banks that were considered systemically important.

2019; Andrea Vismara, 'Mifid 2 drags down an ecosystem along with Europe's banks', 15th May 2019; Richard Henderson, 'Regulator calls on US stock exchanges to justify increase in data charges', 23rd May 2013; Philip Stafford, 'Futures exchanges put faith in "Flash Boys" speed bumps', 30th May 2019; Philip Stafford and Philip Georgiadis, 'EU markets regulator abandons no-deal block on big UK stocks', 30th May 2019; Judith Evans, 'Building a real estate bubble', 19th June 2019; Eva Szalay, 'UK watchdog lends teeth to currency trading code', 28th June 2019; John Dizard, 'Eyes front, fund bosses, it's Carney's army now', 1st July 2019; Jennifer Thompson, 'French fail to capitalise on Brexit as number of Paris funds falls', 8th July 2019; Attracta Mooney, 'Could London be Berned like the Swiss?', 8th July 2019; John Dizard, 'H20 is an omen: a liquidity crisis lurks', 15th July 2019; David Keohane and Philip Stafford, 'French regulator calls for flexible market rules', 15th July 2019; Philip Stafford, 'Chicago's Options Clearing Corp hones plan to shore up its balance sheet', 19th July 2019; Caroline Binham and Siobhan Riding, 'Iosco fires back at BoE in spat over fund rules', 22nd July 2019; Owen Walker, 'UK funds with small-cap weighting at higher risk of liquidity shock', 22nd July 2019; Philip Stafford, 'Global regulators delay big bang rules by a year to stop last minute scramble', 24th July 2019; Siobhan Riding, 'Europe bickers over passporting future', 5th August 2019; Chris Flood, 'Esma warns on bond fund liquidity risk', 9th September 2019; Siobhan Riding, 'Luxembourg watchdog eyes tougher liquidity rule', 9th September 2019; Don Weinland, 'Euroclear plans link with China allowing global use of renminbi debt as collateral', 10th September 2019; Chris Flood, 'EU regulator rejects FCA's criticism', 16th September 2019; Joe Rennison and Brendan Greeley, 'Soaring repo rate puts spotlight on Fed policy', 19th September 2019; Vikram Pandit, 'Outdated rules are holding back financial innovation', 19th September 2019; Gillian Tett, 'Repo markets mystery reminds us we are flying blind', 20th September 2019; Joe Rennison and Brendan Greeley, 'New York Fed defends response to turmoil', 25th September 2019; Tommy Stubbington, 'Eurozone bailout fund ditches English law for bonds in fresh Brexit hit to UK', 27th September 2019; John Dizard, 'Fed standing repo facility comes into view', 30th September 2019.

[183] Philip Stafford, 'Blizzard of regulation has its effect', 30th October 2012.
[184] Philip Stafford, 'Fresh risks emerge from the depth', 1st October 2018.
[185] Robin Wigglesworth and Ben McLannahan, 'Liquidity outs leverage as the big worry for investors', 4th May 2018.

Such was the confidence placed in these megabanks before the Global Financial Crisis that central banks had shed much of their lender-of-last-resort responsibilities. The scale and diversification of a megabank provided it with the resilience necessary to cope with a liquidity crisis on its own, along with its peers, through the inter-bank markets. Shorn of this responsibility central banks could focus on the other roles expected from them by governments, relating to the operation of monetary policy and the management of the economy. Markets could also be left to look after themselves and operate normally regardless of circumstances and without self-regulation, because the megabanks were there to provide a constant supply of liquidity. Such beliefs ended with the Global Financial Crisis. In the aftermath of the crisis systemically-important banks were forced to hold more capital, reduce leverage, and provide collateral to support their trading operations. This made them more resilient but only by transferring risks onto others, leading to the growth of an expanding shadow financial sector. Within this shadow sector new risks appeared relating to the activities of high-frequency traders that contributed to volatility not stability and investment funds that were highly exposed to a liquidity crisis. Neither of these possessed the experience or the support network that the megabanks had. To cover counterparty risk, for example, heavy reliance was placed on clearing houses, but they lacked the implicit support of a lender of last resort if faced with multiple defaults. The response to the failure of a systemically-important clearing house or a systemically-important megafund were issues still awaiting a response from regulators more than ten years after the Global Financial Crisis.

20
Conclusion
Retrospect, Hindsight, and Foresight

Context

In the aftermath of the Global Financial Crisis of 2008 the world of finance became totally discredited. However, despite the views of the media, what happened between 2007 and 2009 was not the product of a few rogue bankers or a sudden crisis of capitalism but the result of a combination of powerful forces stretching back to the end of the Second World War, including decisions made by governments, central banks, and regulators that had far-reaching consequences. Financial crises are ever present but their causes, frequency, magnitude, nature, and consequences vary. Each time is different. Some crises arise in asset markets driven by irrational exuberance as investors chase illusory gains. Some are found within banks as the emphasis switches from the avoidance of risk to the pursuit of high returns. Some are confined to individual businesses whereas others consume entire countries and infect the global financial system. Fluctuations characterize economic activity no matter the desire of individuals for certainty and stability or the attempts by governments to suppress the market. Given the inevitability of crises of one kind or another, it is important to identify both the general and unique forces at work, the steps taken to avoid or minimize them, and the ways of coping with their consequences. Suggesting that a future can be created in which crises do not occur is as foolish as politicians claiming that they have the means and the power to abolish boom and bust in the economy. Like death itself crises will continue to occur, especially financial ones, given the complexities and interconnections of a global market economy.

The Global Financial Crisis that took place in 2007–9 was the product of both long-term trends and a specific set of circumstances. In particular, the thirty years preceding that crisis had witnessed a refashioning of the global financial system, which was, itself, a reaction to that which had emerged after the Second World War. At the end of the Second World War there was no desire, among those wielding political power, to return to the financial markets of the type that had prevailed in the past. The bursting of speculative bubbles and accompanying bank collapses between the wars fostered an acceptance of government control and restriction rather than competition and freedom, especially after the experience of the Second World War. This manifested itself both through barriers to international flows of credit and capital and intervention by governments to either abolish banks and markets, exercise direct ownership and control, or closely regulate them. This system eventually broke down in the early 1970s. Between 1971 and 1973 the system of fixed but adjustable exchange rates, which had been operated by central bankers through the 1950s and 1960s collapsed, with March 1973 being seen as the end of the post-war Bretton Woods System. With the demise of the Bretton Woods system the international monetary system was, increasingly, left to find its own solution to the problems caused by financial imbalances that were both temporary and permanent. The outcome of the events that took place in the

Banks, Exchanges, and Regulators: Global Financial Markets from the 1970s. Ranald Michie, Oxford University Press (2021).

DOI: 10.1093/oso/9780199553730.003.0020

1970s was a transformation of the global financial system through the progressive removal of barriers to international financial flows. There was a gathering momentum of exchange rate liberalization around the world accompanied by the ending of restrictions on capital flows.

Over the next thirty years competitive markets gradually replaced governments and central banks in determining the volume and direction of international financial flows. Whereas governments had sought to restrict or impede financial inflows and outflows over the previous fifty years, so as to bolster the control they exercised over the national economy, this gradually ceased to be the case. Though this was accompanied by volatility in terms of such variables as exchange and interest rates compared to the past, what it also meant was a great increase in the ability of economies to adjust to each other in response to changing circumstances. This adjustment took place on a daily basis through the markets for short-term credit, long-term loans, foreign exchange, securities, and a growing array of ever more complex financial instruments that allowed risks to be hedged whether in terms of interest rates, currencies, exposure to counterparties, or other variables. This was a period of great innovation as an array of new financial instruments were created in order to match the needs of lenders for high returns, certainty, and stability and those of borrowers for low-cost finance and flexibility in terms of the amount, currency, and timing of repayment. This change represented something of a return to the pre-1914 era when money and capital flowed around the world in response to the best combination available of risk and return across a range of assets.

Unlike that pre-1914 era governments remained highly influential, especially in the domestic regulation of banks and financial markets. What replaced the era of control and compartmentalization was not a return to freedom and integration. Instead, governments exercised a major influence on shaping the new world of finance. There remained a reluctance to trust financial markets which came to the fore after every financial crisis, leading to intervention designed to make them safer as well as encourage greater competition in the interests of the user. It was for these reasons that regulators promoted the adoption of the originate-and-distribute method of banking in place of the lend-and-hold. In the latter a bank's funds became locked up in loans, leaving them vulnerable to a liquidity crisis, forcing central banks to act as lenders of last resort which, in turn, could encourage greater risk under the assumption that it would always happen if a bank got into difficulties. With the originate-and-distribute model of banking loans were converted into transferable assets which could be subsequently sold, and so represented a liquid asset. What was not recognized by regulators was the use of the originate-and-distribute model, unlike the lend-and-hold one, allowed a bank to expand lending without limit as the repackaging and sale of loans released funds which could then be lent out, and so the process could be repeated time and again. The originate-and-distribute model was given the backing of no less an authority than the Bank for International Settlement, which acted as the central banks' central bank, which meant its recommendation were implemented throughout the world.

The other difference between this new world and that of the pre-First World War era was the importance of a small number of banks whose activities extended across the entire range of financial activities and took place around the world. Banks of this type had long existed within particular countries in Continental Europe, especially Austria, Germany, and Switzerland, and had briefly developed in the USA in the 1920s. However, many of them suffered badly during the severe economic difficulties of the early 1930s and had to be rescued by the state, as in the Austrian and German cases. In the USA the actions of these banks were blamed for the Wall Street Crash of 1929 and so they were subjected to government controls, as with the Glass–Steagall Act of 1933. This banned US banks from combining commercial and investment banking operations. After the Second World War this type of banking reappeared in Continental Europe, especially Germany, as a way of providing business in these countries with the finance they required. Within the USA the barriers that prevented banks combining an investment and a commercial business were progressively relaxed between 1987 and 1997 before being finally repealed in 1999. With the removal of barriers to international finance banks of this kind took the opportunity to place their activities on a global basis, unlike the position in the past where they were largely national businesses. The result was the emergence of a group of megabanks deemed too big to fail not because of the support they could expect from national governments or central banks acting as lenders of last resort but because their scale and diversification made them highly resilient to any kind of crisis, including both liquidity and solvency ones. These megabanks provided the means through which an integrated and borderless global financial system could operate without the need for the intervention of a matching global regulator or global lender of last resort to prevent both the build-up of risk and to act as a backstop in the event of a crisis.

In the 1970s the world had turned to uncontrolled competitive markets in response to the financial, monetary, and economic crises of that decade. This worked well until 2007 despite such events as a banking crisis in Asia, a corporate scandal in the USA, or the worldwide collapse of the dot.com speculative bubble. However, in 2008 the financial edifice that had been built up collapsed, threatening the stability of entire economies. Across Continental Europe and in the USA governments were forced to intervene on a scale not seen since the 1930s, while for Britain there was no precedent for what took place. The result was a reaction in which restrictions were placed on the freedom of banks and markets to operate, but there was no return to the highly-restrictive regimes that had characterized the pre-1970s era. Under the influence of governments, central banks, and regulators, a new global financial system gradually took shape that was to be more stable than the one that collapsed in 2008, but without returning to the era of control and compartmentalization that had failed in the 1970s. The problem with intervention of this kind was that it presupposed a definite and final outcome whereas financial systems were fluid and flexible, forever adapting to changing circumstances. A financial system with too many rigidities breaks, as had happened in the 1970s. Conversely, a financial system lacking in layers of resilience also proves vulnerable to crises as had happened in 2007–8. What was required was a global financial system that was simultaneously flexible and resilient but achieving that was an impossible task given the divergent aims of all involved in achieving such an outcome.

Though the changes to the financial system after the 1970s owed much to government intervention across the world, either through removing barriers or forcing change, once begun it had developed a momentum of its own, outpacing efforts by governments to either slow it down or direct it. Banks and financial markets needed to devise instant remedies to current problems as they could not wait for the deliberations of regulators and the long drawn out process of law making, driven by the poorly informed verdict of public opinion and the instant conclusions of the media. The same situation prevailed after the Global Financial Crisis of 2008. Governments, central banks, and regulators all had their own agenda which focused on preventing another crisis of such magnitude ever taking place again, and making the financial system more resilient to any that did occur. In contrast, the priority of those in the financial sector was to conduct a profitable business and that was best achieved by responding to the needs of savers and investors on the one hand and borrowers on the other as well as satisfying the requirements of buyers and sellers and those making and receiving payments. All these were functions that had to be performed by the financial system and demands for them continued regardless of the actions of governments, central banks, and regulators. As a consequence the evolving shape of the global financial system after the crisis included a response to these basic requirements. Any intervention designed to make the financial system more resilient, that also prevented it from performing the functions required of it, eventually led to the appearance of alternative, such as shadow banks or dark pools because they functioned beyond the reach of governments, central banks, and regulators. The more oppressive the intervention the greater the stimulus given to those components of the financial system that existed on the margins and this had been the case before the 1970s and became so again after 2008.

Trends and the Global Financial Crisis

The world within which banks, exchanges, and regulators operated was transformed from the 1970s onwards, and this forced fundamental changes on the way each operated and their relationship to one another. The certainties that had built up since the Second World War ended in the 1970s. However, the changes that took place were not only the product of the wider political, economic, and monetary environment but were also a consequence of forces acting directly upon banks, exchanges, and regulators. A combination of globalization and a revolution in both information technology and business structures forced a reshaping of banks and financial markets. Throughout the world the removal of barriers to financial flows destroyed local monopolies through the simultaneous operation of centrifugal and centripetal forces that had long been subdued because of government intervention. The result was to integrate all engaged in the provision of financial services into global networks rather than being confined within national boundaries. Accompanying the removal of barriers to global integration was a process of deregulation that steadily undermined the compartmentalization of financial activity within countries and encouraged its replacement by fluid structures and active competition. One outcome was the creation of financial markets that transcended not only national boundaries but also time zones to provide a global 24/7 operation. Another was the growth and operation of multinational and multidivisional businesses that could internalize functions once performed by individual banks and financial markets. These included banks themselves, which had the effect of unbalancing the relationship between financial markets and their largest users. What lagged behind this process of change were regulatory regimes that could cope with borderless and timeless markets and supervise banks whose activities spanned the globe.

The direction of travel among the world's banks after the Second World War was towards megabanks. The growing size of business enterprise forced banks to grow in scale if they were to provide the financial services required. A similar development was taking place with the growing importance of institutions that managed savings and investment on a collective basis, as they also required banks to be bigger and more diversified. Finally, the emergence of an increasingly integrated global economy drove banks to expand internationally not only to participate in the new opportunities but also protect the business they did domestically from those who had access to a wider range of services. The result from the 1970s onwards was the growth of a small number of megabanks that covered the entire range of financial activity and had a presence in all major financial centres around the world. However, this direction of travel was interrupted by the Global Financial Crisis. In its wake these megabanks faced attack from different directions. The first came from regulators as they blamed the banks for causing the crisis and so wanted to prevent another crisis occurring and, if one did, remove the need for intervention using taxpayer funds. The initial solution was to press for the break-up of these banks but that policy faded as it was recognized how integral they were to the operation of an integrated global economy and the role they played in providing the means of monitoring, supervising, and regulating the everyday conduct of financial activity. The eventual solution adopted was to restrict the range of activities these megabanks could engage in either directly or through capital, reserve, and liquidity requirements.

The effect was to narrow the range of activities undertaken by these megabanks and to encourage them to withdraw from countries they considered marginal. That created opportunities for smaller and more specialized banks to pick up the business that was being abandoned, whether it was in specific activities or countries. This rolled back the advance of the megabanks that had been gathering pace since the 1970s. That advance had been favoured by the conditions prevailing since then, as this rewarded the scale and scope they possessed. It was the megabanks that were best placed to profit from globalization and the desire by governments to deal with banks that were too big to fail and possessed the internal supervisory structures favoured by regulators. However, the Global Financial Crisis and its aftermath reversed that position favouring more specialist banks and those operating on a national rather than international basis. The reversal in the fortunes of the megabanks was not permanent in the case of those from the USA that survived the crisis intact. They emerged stronger than before, benefiting from domestic mergers and the ability to operate nationwide and engage in virtually all types of financial activities. US megabanks dominated their domestic market, which was the world's largest, while operating on the basis of the US$, the world's international currency. They could also all look to the Federal Reserve Bank of the USA for support, which was the only central bank able to provide an endless supply of liquidity in the form of US$s. In contrast, the European market remained fragmented, despite the use of the Euro, which was reflected in the national basis on which the continent's banks operated. The same was true for Asia while in Japan there continued to be a major divide between the different types of banks, limiting their ability to compete with those from the USA. The restrictions imposed by central banks and regulators since the crisis made these megabanks safer, as they shed a number of peripheral activities, without damaging their ability to function. A small core of largely US megabanks remained at the core of the world's financial system and governments, central banks, and regulators were aware of both the risks this posed to stability and the essential benefits they delivered. However, in making the megabanks safer as a way of preventing a repeat of the 2008 crisis, this intervention shifted risks to other parts of the financial system, especially the large and rapidly growing shadow banking sector. In place of the threat to stability coming from the megabanks a new one was emerging from the megafunds as they acquired the liquidity exposure once the exclusive property of banks.

After the Second World War exchanges had either ceased to exist because the markets they had served no longer operated or were subjected to a high degree of control by governments, central banks, and regulators. The institutional nature of exchanges provided governments with a ready-made apparatus through which control over financial markets could be exercised. However, there were many markets that operated without the need for exchanges, and they continued to thrive in an unregulated state, while the controls imposed on exchanges rendered them less attractive to many users, driving business away as a result. In the 1970s the revival of markets, whether for commodities or financial instruments, stimulated a growth of trading on existing exchanges and the formation of new ones. As this coincided with growing investor interest in corporate stocks, stock exchanges, in particular, once again became central to financial activity. Subsequently, the collapse of centrally-planned economies created opportunities for new exchanges in these countries because of the need for markets for the stocks issued by state enterprises after conversion into companies. Finally, emerging economies also embraced the idea of corporate capitalism and so required stock exchanges on which locally issued stocks could be traded. The result was an explosion of stock exchange formation in the late twentieth century along with greatly increased trading activity. Speculative bubbles even reappeared as with the dot. com boom around 2000. Beginning in the 1970s the demarcation between exchanges, whether by product or locality, not only broke down but also disappeared in some cases. In their place developed multiproduct exchanges dominating their national market.

Despite the revival in the fortunes of exchanges from the 1970s the main developments in financial markets took place elsewhere. OTC markets assumed gigantic proportions being conducted by and between banks operating global networks from the world's leading financial centres. It is a mistake to treat financial markets as a series of separate compartments catering for distinct segments of lenders and borrowers. In reality there was always only a single market with each distinct segment shading into its neighbours. This included banks and markets as they not only complemented each other but were also rivals for the same business. From the 1970s onwards the interaction of multiple forces transformed the operation of these financial markets. The growth of gigantic companies facilitated both the internalization of market activity within individual businesses, including banks, and direct trading between banks, as they possessed the size and permanence to act as reliable counterparties to each other. The growth of a new species of intermediary, the interdealer broker, epitomized this change, as they provided banks with a network of connections that was previously only obtainable through an exchange. This trend towards trading gravitating to the OTC markets was greatly facilitated by the increasingly important regulatory role played by statutory agencies, as they supplanted the self-regulating authority that was once the exclusive privilege of an exchange.

The desire to bypass the exchanges had grown prior to 1970s as they had exercised the power they possessed to limit the number able to participate in the markets they controlled and to increase the charges levied on users. During and after the 1970s the ability to create alternative market structures was also transformed through a technological revolution. The combination of near-instantaneous communication networks and the processing power of ever-faster computers with almost infinite capacity eventually produced a serious rival to the trading floor that had been the focus of every exchange. With the dematerialization of trading and the rise of megabanks the exchanges lost control over those financial markets they had once almost monopolized. As this took place against a background in which government-imposed barriers, that compartmentalized markets both internally and internationally, were removed, the result was the emergence of global OTC markets, successfully challenging exchanges for business. Alone none of the forces at work from the 1970s would have transformed the world's financial markets to the degree and with the pace that actually took place over the last thirty years, but together their effect was revolutionary. The Global Financial Crisis threatened to resurrect the importance of exchanges as regulators turned to them as a safer alternative to OTC markets. Whereas a number of OTC markets had frozen during the crisis, including those for securitized assets and certain derivatives, it remained possible to buy and sell the stock of major companies if quoted on stock exchanges. However, this reversal of attitude among regulators proved brief. It was recognized that a number of the largest OTC markets continued to function normally during the crisis, including that for foreign exchange and US Treasury bonds. It was also recognized that many financial products were unsuited to exchanges, such as the vast and diverse swaps market that was conducted directly between banks or through the negotiations conducted by interdealer brokers. Finally, the increasing reliance placed on electronic trading, and its ability to deliver both capacity and speed, marginalized both the interdealer brokers and the exchanges as trading could be conducted automatically between computers that matched sales and purchases.

What had also emerged after 1945 was a much greater degree of government regulation of banks and markets. Prior to the 1970s the way that regulation was conducted was to treat the financial system as a series of separate compartments. This worked when governments were able to exercise a significant degree of control through erecting barriers between national economies and dictating to both exchanges and banks what they were permitted to do. Conventional wisdom separated banks from capital markets or went even further in focusing on particular types of banks or on specific financial markets, ignoring the links that existed between them and the degree of overlap. However, as national barriers disappeared with the ending of exchange and capital controls, and governments themselves fostered competition in order to appease complaints from investors and savers over low returns and borrowers because of a shortage of finance, it was no longer possible to regulate through the principle of divide and rule. In their place there was a reliance upon government-appointed regulatory agencies who found it easiest to operate through the banks, as they already possessed internal controls. The regulators wanted banks to take responsibility for day-to-day activities and that was best achieved by megabanks as they had the scale and resources to train and pay for the appropriate staff unlike small banks. Increasingly it was the megabanks that became the trusted gatekeepers of the financial system under the overall supervision of statutory regulatory authorities.

With the Global Financial Crisis regulators retreated from relying on the megabanks but soon returned because of the lack of any obvious alternatives. However, safeguards were put in place designed to ensure that the megabanks took fewer risks and would be more resilient in a future crisis. As with regulatory intervention in the past the effect was to shift risk-taking to other parts of the financial system. The incentive to shift was magnified by central bank intervention under the policy of quantitative easing as this drove down interest rates. In a climate of low interest rates and a rising appetite for higher yields among investors there was a growing willingness to sacrifice liquidity for returns. From this emerged megafunds that invested in less-liquid assets, such as property and stocks and bonds lacking an active market, while promising investors that holdings could be immediately liquidated. There was also a return of securitization and highly-leveraged loans which also posed liquidity issues as the assets involved lacked the marketability of either the quoted stock of major corporations or the bonds issued by large and stable countries. The result was to shift the liquidity and solvency risks usually associated with banks to other components of the financial system. Intervention reduced the exposure of banks to a liquidity crisis but increased it elsewhere in the financial system.

An Uncertain Future?

Though governments, central banks, and regulators were largely blind to the risks emerging in the global financial system before 2007, that was not the case ten years after the Global Financial Crisis. The problem they faced was that they were trapped by the policies followed in the aftermath of the crisis as they acted to prevent the repeat of an economic crisis on the scale of that which took place in the 1930s. Governments the world over were keen to avoid that happening again, and so backed intervention at a number of levels. At the macro level intervention took the form of quantitative easing which involved pumping liquidity into the financial system not only to stimulate economic recovery but also forestall a liquidity crisis. However, this policy not only depressed interest rates, with consequences for savers and investors, but also fostered expectations that it would always take place in the face of any hint of any tightening of credit. The dilemma posed by moral hazard, where intervention to prevent a crisis encourages greater risk-taking leading to an even greater crisis, had been abandoned. In the interests of protecting the world economy from a catastrophic collapse a credit bubble had been promoted in the wake of the Global Financial Crisis. Over time that risked repeating the conditions that had led to the Global Financial Crisis in the first place. However, the epicentre of any future crisis would not be the megabanks as action had also been taken to make them more resilient. These megabanks had withdrawn from certain trading activities while increasing their capital and reserves while reducing their leverage. The problem was that others took their place. As the megabanks withdrew and retrenched, but the demand for the services they had previously provided remained, alternatives appeared eager to replace them because of the profits to be made despite the risks involved. One group were the megafunds which, like the megabanks before them, appeared too big to fail because of their scale and diversification, despite them becoming more exposed to liquidity issues through the promises they made to savers and investors. Unlike the megabanks these megafunds, and others that copied their practices, were unpractised in the balancing of assets and liabilities in order to reduce exposure to a liquidity crisis or able to call on the support of central banks to act as lenders of last resort if difficulties did arise.

Recognizing the emerging risks present in the refashioned global financial system regulators had turned to clearing houses, as the solution. These clearing houses guaranteed the completion of any transaction that was processed by them through holding reserves and requiring collateral from counterparties. By providing this service clearing houses would contribute to preventing a liquidity crisis as there would be no collapse in confidence; all involved would be paid for what they had sold and receive what they had bought, whether it was stocks, bonds, currencies, or the results of a derivatives contract. Clearing houses constituted a form of universal insurance for the global financial system and one that was paid for not by governments or the actions of central banks but by participants themselves, related to the risks that they were taking. However, many transactions did not go through clearing houses being either of a highly-customized nature or because the charges made and the amount of collateral demanded did not justify doing so. Also, though regulators increasingly mandated that transactions did pass through clearing houses there was no universal policy to ensure that they were in a position to withstand a high level of default in terms of the amount of collateral they held and their own reserves. There was also no agreement on what should happen if a clearing house should fail, and thus be in no position to cover those parties relying upon it to cover their losses. The international nature of many transactions, and the vast volume of commitments, made all central banks reluctant to provide an open commitment to act as lender of last resort to a clearing house located within its jurisdiction. Whereas the megabanks could look to government-owned central banks for support in the event of a crisis, and access to their lender-of-last-resort facility, the clearing houses could not. Some were standalone organizations while others were integral parts of exchanges, and each had an individual risk profile which made it difficult to assess their exposure or take steps to curtail it. It had taken around fifty years, from the Overend Gurney Crisis in England in 1866 to the establishment of the Federal Reserve in the USA in 1913, for the lender-of-last-resort facility to be developed. Ten years after the Global Financial Crisis of 2008 that process of learning was still taking place because it needed to meet the needs of a highly-integrated global financial system and the liquidity needs of both megafunds and clearing houses in addition to those of the megabanks. Until that wider remit was undertaken the global financial system remained exposed to a repeat of the Global Financial Crisis of 2008 but with even fewer adequate safeguards in place.

Afterword

Continuity versus Change

Introduction

Important as it is to draw conclusions about what happened in the aftermath of the Global Financial Crisis of 2008, not least to put in place a more resilient system, the results cannot be definitive. Global financial markets are always in a constant state of flux, continually evolving in response to the challenges and opportunities they face, including the ever-growing importance of regulatory intervention at both the national and international level. This makes it difficult to provide a concluding assessment based on a combination of past developments, the current situation, and predictions about the future. Without the benefit of hindsight it is impossible to know whether the evidence available supports a prediction of a coming disaster or that deeper forces of resilience, including the willingness of central banks to intervene to prevent a global financial crisis, will prevent one taking place. However, hindsight itself presents a distorted picture. Reliance on hindsight tends to stress the inevitability of what has taken place, as it selects and then emphasizes the evidence that points towards that event rather than recognizing that it was dependent upon particular decisions that could have tipped the balance in an alternative direction. In contrast, immersion in the minute details of daily occurrences throws up innumerable possibilities, making it very difficult, or even impossible, to identify those which, in the end, played a dominant role. It is possible to establish the path of causality by eliminating alternatives. In a world as diverse and complex as that of global financial markets it is impossible to establish with certainty which action had the greatest impact, and what the precise reaction to it was. There are simply too many variables.[1]

[1] 7th October 2019 UK Watchdog eyes liquidity reforms, Siobhan Riding; 7th October 2019 US fund houses manage more than a third of global assets, Chris Flood; 7th October 2019 Are retail investors missing out on the message? Rebecca Hampson; 8th October 2019 Hong Kong and Shanghai battle to be China's main gateway, Philip Stafford and Hudson Lockett; 8th October 2019 Beware of distortions caused by monetary policy innovation, Philip Lowe; 9th October 2019 Questions swirl over Hong Konk's failed LSE bid, Philip Stafford and Henry Sender; 11th October 2019 Fed rules out liquidity gauge for foreign banks, Kiran Stacey and Laura Noonan; 11th October 2019 Better data on shadow banking reveals uncomfortable truths, Gillian Tett; 16th October 2019 Peer-to-peer forex services aim to bypass Wall St banks, Eva Szalay; 17th October 2019 Hedge funds are happy to let the machines take over, Robin Wigglesworth; 17th October 2019 IMF warns low rates are fuelling risk-taking, Chris Giles; 18th October 2019 Payment for order flow is a good deal for investors, Larry Tabb; 21st October 2019 London set to keep its crown, says head of Citi Europe, Stephen Morris; 21st October 2019 Bond bubble puts global financial system at risk, Chris Flood; 22nd October 2019 All about data: LSE bid show exchanges' new priorities, Philip Stafford; 22nd October 2019 US regulators take a closer look at data fees, Richard Henderson; 22nd October 2019 Clearing reforms set to upend asset management industry, Eva Szalay; 22nd October 2019 Popularity of passive investing changes rules of the game, Chris Flood; 25th October 2019 Clearing houses are ripe for reform, Gillian Tett; 25th October 2019 Blackrock and Vanguard push for clearing reforms, Philip Stafford; 29th October 2019 ICE launches ETF platform specialising in bonds, Philip Stafford; 31st October 2019 Lime liquidity issues spark contagion feeas at South Korea hedge funds, Song Jung-A;31st October 2019 Citigroup outlines plan to withdraw from two-thirds of foreign exchange platforms, Eva Szalay; 1st November 2019 The

Banks, Exchanges, and Regulators: Global Financial Markets from the 1970s. Ranald Michie, Oxford University Press (2021).

DOI: 10.1093/oso/9780199553730.003.0021

attraction of staying private, Richard Henderson and Miles Kruppa; 1st November 2019 Mobile-savvy Kenyans will soon be able to buy shares on phones, Tom Wilson; 2nd November 2019 Virtu backed bourse MEMX clears vital regulatory hurdle, Richard Henderson; 4th November 2019 Growth of private capital funds accelerates while ETFs slow, Robin Wigglesworth; 4th November 2019 Hybrid funds smooth path between active and passive strategies, Andrew Whiffin; 6th November 2019 Germany will consider EU-wide bank deposit reinsurance, Olaf Scholz; 7th November 2019 Lack of volatility lines up Niederhoffer hedge fund for near annual loss, Laurence Fletcher; 7th November 2019 Repo ructions call attention to failure of post-crisis policy, Karen Petrou; 9th November 2019 Trading looks to tackle its long-hours culture, Philip Stafford and Eva Szalay; 11th November 2019 London is top renminbi trading hub outside China despite Brexit wobbles, Eva Szalay; 13th November 2019 Nasdaq agrees sale of commodities futures business to German exchange, Philip Stafford; 13th November 2019 Sun threatens to set on foreign companies' Japanese listings, Leo Lewis; 15th November 2019 EU targeted reform of Mifid 2 rules after backlash, Philp Stafford; 15th November 2019 Russia makes fresh effort to take control of its oil price using electronic platform, Nastassia Astrasheuskava; 16th November 2019 Nasdaq raises listing fees to funs swanky new showroom, Philip Stafford and Richard Henderson; 16th November 2019 Time is ripe for block cheeses futures and options at CME, Philip Stafford; 18th November 2019 The pension house is on fire, Josephine Cumbo and Robin Wigglesworth; 18th November Dangers lurk in the design of junk bond ETFs, David Tuckwell; 19th November 2019 Safe assets in short supply as central banks buy big, Tommy Stubbington; 19th November 2019 SIX makes Euro2.8bn Madrid exchange move to fend off Euronext interest, Philip Stafford; 19th November 2019 Rivals battle for Madrid bourse owner, Philip Stafford; 19th November 2019 Hong Kong's GEN tarnished by back door listings and drab returns, Daniel Shane; 22nd November 2019 ETF pioneer Ross decides to call it a day at State Street, Robin Wigglesworth; 22nd November 2019 Investors pile into US corporate bond funds as Fed warns on credit quality, Jennifer Ablan and Joe Rennison; 23rd November 2019 Stockpickers bide their time on clash with Quant challengers, Laurence Fletcher and Ortenca Aliaj; 25th November 2019 CEOs quit London amid Brexit tumult, Siobhan Riding; 25th November 2019 Ireland to review fund rules after Woodford, Siobhan Riding; 28th November 2019 Bond ETFs are no menace to financial system, Jennifer Kim; 29th November 2019 Overhaul for Japanese stock trading as regulator unveils premium segment, Robin Harding and Leo Lewis; 29th November 2019 European investors back UK call for shorter trading day to improve liquidity, Philip Stafford; 29th November 2019 HK riots put boardrooms in holding position, George Hammond, Leo Lewis and Don Weinland; 2nd December 2019 QE sows seeds of next crisis, funds warn, Jennifer Thompson; 2nd December 2019 Bond ETFs outshine equity rivals, Chris Flood; 2nd December 2019 Baselheads are crushing EU project finance, John Dizzard; 3rd December 2019 Investors secure New York Fed loans with cash crunch worries lingering, Joe Rennison; 6th December 2019 Ultra low interest rates spur euro to become world's new carry trade, Eva Szalay; 7th December 2019 Year-end repo rates surge despite Fed attempts to ease the funding strain. Joe Rennison and Colby Smith; 9th December 2019 Cash-hungry hedge funds deepened recent repo market turmoil finds BIS, Tommy Stubbington and Joe Rennison; 13th December 2019 Brussels lines up one-year access to UK clearing houses in event of no-deal Brexit, Joe Rennison and Philip Stafford; 14th December 2019 Fed gears up to double its repo interventions, Colby Smith and Joe Rennison; 20th December 2019 Bank of Japan acts to avert liquidity squeeze for exchange traded funds, Robin Harding; 20th December 2019 Global watchdog warns on rising risk of shocks in leveraged loans, Tommy Stubbington; 24th December 2019 Bermuda, Oliver Ralph; 2nd January 2020 Germany's Scope take the long view as it aims to break stranglehold of US rating agencies, Olaf Storbeck; 2nd January 2020 Lanquid fore trading due a wake-up call, Eva Szalay; 3rd January 2020 Fed aims to stop another year of grim repo, Colby Smith and Joe Rennison; 7th January 2020 Banks back computing revolution, Richard Waters; 7th January 2020 Momentum grows for shorter days on European exchanges, Philip Stafford; 10th January 2020 Fed signals exit from repo market this year, Colby Smith and Joe Rennison; 10th January 2020 Arrival of passive fund leader Vanguard rattles UL investment advice industry, Madison Darbyshire; 11th January 2020 Traders across Europe face up to cost of failure on transactions, Philip Stafford; Michael Howell, Rising tide of liquidity lifters many boats, but keep an eye on the horizon, 17th January 2020; Caroline Binham, Shadow banking sector shifts into decline, 20th January 2020; Philip Stafford and Peggy Hollinger, Airbus plans exchange to hedge airline fare vitality, 20th January 2020; Colby Smith and Robin Wigglesworth, Boom in EM corporate debt stirs liquidity fears, 20th January 2020; Eva Szalay, India seeks to lure rupee trading back onshore, 22nd January 2020; Joe Rennison, Robert Armstrong and Robin Wigglesworth, Meet the new bond kings, 23rd January 2020; Philip Stafford, European regulator steps up dark pools campaign, 5th February 2020; Daniel Thomas and David Crow, City grandees fear EU will extract high price for Johnson's hard line on trade, 6th February 2020; Philip Stafford, Investors question logic behind ICE's mooted deal for eBay, 6th February 2020;Philip Stafford, EU dashes hopes for failed trade rules phase-in, 6th February 2020; Siobhan Riding, Singapore challenges Hong Kong, 10th February 2020; Sam Fleming, Philip Stafford, Matthew Vincent and George Parker, EU rules out permanent access deal for City of London, 12th February 2020; Matthew Vincent, City sets out proposals for equivalence with EU 13th February 2020; Laura Noonan, European capital markets not fit for purpose, 17th February 2020; Siobhan Riding, How will the EU reshape regulations after Brexit? 17th February 2020; Siobhan Riding and Chris Flood, Wall St's index trackers make strides in UK, 18th February 2020; Philip Stafford, JP Morgan and Goldman Sachs throw weight behind stock exchange start-up, 21st February 2020; Don Weinland, China reopens bond futures trading to big local banks, 22nd February 2020; Norman Blackwell, Britain should diverge on domestic financial services rules, 25th February 2020; Laura Noonan, A Retreat from Wall street, 3rd March 2020; John Plender, The seeds of the Next Crisis, 5th March 2020;

It is this complexity and lack of transparency that makes the work of regulators so difficult, and the consequences of central bank intervention impossible to assess with any precision. Regulators have little choice but to deal with the world as they find it. The decisions that they take might solve one problem while creating others of greater magnitude, requiring further measures in the future. Similarly, central banks have to err on the side of caution, and so respond to every perceived threat to financial stability, because the alternative is to court economic disaster. Whereas before the Global Financial Crisis the choice of non-intervention was available to both regulators and central banks that option no longer exists. Both regulators and central banks are well aware that the media will castigate them for failing to intervene, as that is what the public and democratically elected governments expect, even though careful reflection and deep analysis might suggest that events in the market need to be allowed to take their course. Global financial markets need to be exposed to a learning curve through which they become, simultaneously, more efficient and more resilient. Both regulators and central banks have important roles to play in that learning process but excessive intervention, by either or both, prevents the market evolving, and so able to devise solutions to its own problems. That is the lesson that needs to be learned from the causes, course, and consequences of the Global Financial Crisis.

The shock to the global financial system in 2020, caused by the coronavirus, provides a test for the measures taken since the Global Financial Crisis of 2008. As with the events of 2008 the outcome of the 2020 crisis is not dependent upon irresistible forces leading to an inevitable result, but the decisions taken by governments, central banks, and regulators throughout the world. These decisions need to be informed by what happened in 2008 but also responsive to what is different about the 2020 crisis. The coronavirus has caused a shock to the global economic system, disrupting both supply and demand, and this demands more direct government intervention than central banks are able to provide. Whereas the 2008 crisis was one centred on the global banking system that of 2020 was an event akin to a war, natural disaster, or a political revolution. In turn that had implications for the global financial system as it contained the potential to destabilize banks by threatening the solvency of those to whom they had made loans and extended credit, creating fears leading to a liquidity crisis. To forestall such an event central banks are called upon to act as lenders of last resort, particularly the Federal Reserve, as it was the only one capable of supplying the US$s on which all banks relied when making and receiving payments, and borrowing and lending, among themselves. From the outset that response appears to have learned lessons from the mistakes of the 2008 crisis, in terms of speed, scale, and

Robin Wigglesworth, Virus mayhem reflects danger of shock-led trading, 7th March 2020; Philip Stafford, Regulators to review pricing of trading data and benchmarks, 10th March 2020; Robin Wiggleworth, Philip Stafford, and Eva Szalay, Trading stability begins to fray as oil slum piles on pain, 10th March 2020; Colby Smith and Brendan Greeley, Fed seeks to limit fallout by boosting repo injections, 10th March 2020; Vivek Bommi, Drop in hedging costs makes US high yield bonds a bargain, 12th March 2020; Joe Rennison and Colby Smith, Cracks in US Treasuries spell trouble for financial system, 13th March 2020; *FT* Reporters, Homeworking prompts biggest test for trading since 9/11 14th March 2020; Colby Smith and Brendan Greeley, Fed looks to accelerate purchase of US Treasuries in wake of virus disruptions, 14th March 2020; Tommy Stubbington and Colby Smith, Investors flag up worries over limits of monetary policy to end turmoil, 14th March 2020; Robin Wigglesworth, Covid-19 tips markets into week of chaos as central banks play catch-up with new reality, 14th March 2020; Peter Smith, Vanguard, BlackRock and State Street asset shrinkage spells end of golden era, 16th March 2020; Rana Foroohar, How the virus became a credit run, 16th March 2020; *FT* Reporters, Bank acts to ease liquidity strains, 17th March 2020; Brendan Greeley, Joe Rennison, and Colby Smith, Fed Swoops to buy commercial paper, 18th March 2020; Philip Stafford, Watchdogs weigh up costs and benefits of exchange shutdowns, 18th March 2020; Eva Szalay and Colby Smith, Bank hoarding and fears over Covid-19 push dollar higher, 18th March 2018; Philip Stafford and David Keohane, France, Spain, Italy and Belgium ban short selling in effort to restore calm. 18th March 2020.

co-ordination, while the global banking system is far more resilient. Nevertheless, concerns exist over other components of the global financial system and the longer-term implications of the intervention.

Continuity

Important as was the Global Financial Crisis it left much untouched. More than a decade after the Global Financial Crisis of 2008 the hierarchy of financial centres was undisturbed. Neither the crisis itself nor subsequent events, such as the UK's decision to leave the EU or political upheaval in Hong Kong, appear to have produced any major changes. Singapore did benefit from Hong Kong's difficulties while Britain's departure left London vulnerable to political and regulatory attack from elsewhere in Europe, but the consequences were limited. In Asia the commitment of the Chinese government to independent monetary policy and exchange controls continued to restrict the ability of Shanghai to compete with Hong Kong for the role as the country's international financial centre. More generally, throughout Asia the policies followed by governments continued to fragment financial markets along national lines, leaving the likes of Tokyo, Mumbai, and Seoul able to dominate domestically but failing to play an international role. That left a gap to be filled by Hong Kong and Singapore within Asia, and London and New York outside. In terms of foreign exchange, for example, London had emerged as a major centre for trading both the Chinese renminbi and the Indian rupee. In 2019 London was responsible for 44 per cent of renminbi transactions outside China, having overtaken Hong Kong. In the case of the Indian rupee whereas $35bn was traded daily in Mumbai a total of $79bn was done elsewhere in the world, of which $47bn was done in London. The ability of global banks and brokers to access markets around the world instantly, removed the advantages possessed by national financial centres, especially when they were hampered by restrictions and taxes, and lacked the depth and breadth of the markets found in London and New York.

Despite pressure from the European Commission to create an integrated EU-wide market, European financial markets remained fragmented along national lines, preventing the emergence of a serious rival to London, even in Euro-denominated products. As Germany's finance minister, Olaf Scholz, admitted at the end of 2019, 'European financial markets are still fragmented, and barriers to the free flow of capital and financial liquidity still exist.' He pointed to the distorting effects of differential taxation and 'the need to deepen and complete European banking union'.[2] His views were echoed in 2020 by Luis de Guindos, Vice-President of the European Central Bank (ECB), when he observed that 'European capital markets are too small and fragmented.'[3] The EU remained far short of replicating the degree of financial integration achieved in the USA, that made New York such a powerful financial centre. Colm Kelleher, ex-President of Morgan Stanley, pointed out in 2020 that New York's only rival was London. 'The City of London is the world-class portal through which global capital enters and exits the EU. No other EU country has had to think about the requisite legal and physical infrastructure.'[4] London, in particular, was able to occupy a commanding position within global financial markets as it could span a large part of the

[2] 6th November 2019 Germany will consider EU-wide bank deposit reinsurance, Olaf Scholz.
[3] Laura Noonan, European capital markets not fit for purpose, 17th February 2020.
[4] Laura Noonan, European capital markets not fit for purpose, 17th February 2020.

trading day, because of its geographic position and the depth and breadth of its facilities. As Jorg Ambrosius, at the US fund manager, State Street, observed in November 2019, 'As of now I have no reason to doubt London's pre-eminent position. It is still the natural base for the European head of a global financial institution.'[5] Under these circumstances the fundamental forces that had long supported the concentration of trading activity in a few global financial centres remained undiminished after the crisis.[6]

The Global Financial Crisis also left untouched the consequences stemming from the relentless improvement in the speed of communications, the capacity to process information, and the sophistication of the mathematical models employed while costs were driven down. As the markets expert Larry Tabb, commented in October 2019, 'The problem with providing liquidity in markets that move in microseconds is that you either need to be very fast or very smart.'[7] The use of Quantum computing introduced ways of making algorithmic programs more flexible and less deterministic, and so able to respond to a greater variety of variables and possible outcomes. These allowed banks, for example, to respond better and more quickly to the risks they were running and then take positions to cover them. There was a growing reliance on computers not only to conduct trades following algorithmic models designed by programmers, but also to develop these models by extrapolating from the data. As Michael Kharitonov, chief executive of the San Francisco hedge fund, Voleon, explained in October 2019, 'Quants automate decisions that used to be made by humans.'[8] Though there were risks associated with the automation of trading, the speed at which it took place and the volumes involved, through a sudden spike in activity, there were also benefits in terms of the ability to anticipate and mitigate risks. Nevertheless, despite the dominance of trading by computers what the coronavirus revealed was continuing contribution of human intervention to the liquidity of markets and the contribution made by the concentration of activity in particular locations. Coronavirus led to more traders working from home creating problems for the regulation of behaviour, the speed of communication, and the nature of interaction, which had consequences for liquidity. As Kevin McPartland, head of market structure and technology research, at Greenwich Associates observed, 'If you are no longer sitting in the trading room and you don't hear that old-fashioned market colour that comes across the desk, that has the potential to

[5] 25th November 2019 CEOs quit London amid Brexit tumult, Siobhan Riding.

[6] 8th October 2019 Hong Kong and Shanghai battle to be China's main gateway, Philip Stafford and Hudson Lockett; 21st October 2019 London set to keep its crown, says head of Citi Europe, Stephen Morris; 6th November 2019 Germany will consider EU-wide bank deposit reinsurance, Olaf Scholz; 7th November 2019 Europe's traders call for shorter working day, Philip Stafford; 9th November 2019 Trading looks to tackle its long=hours culture, Philip Stafford and Eva Szalay; 11th November 2019 London is top renminbi trading hub outside China despite Brexit wobbles, Eva Szalay; 13th November 2019 Sun threatens to set on foreign companies' Japanese listings, Leo Lewis; 25th November 2019 CEOs quit London amid Brexit tumult, Siobhan Riding; 29th November 2019 European investors back UK call for shorter trading day to improve liquidity, Philip Stafford; 29th November 2019 HK riots put boardrooms in holding position, George Hammond, Leo Lewis and Don Weinland; 13th December 2019 Brussels lines up one-year access to UK clearing houses in event of no-deal Brexit, Joe Rennison and Philip Stafford; 24th December 2019 Bermuda, Oliver Ralph; 7th January 2020 Momentum grows for shorter days on European exchanges, Philip Stafford; Eva Szalay, India seeks to lure rupee trading back onshore, 22nd January 2020; Daniel Thomas and David Crow, City grandees fear EU will extract high price for Johnson's hard line on trade, 6th February 2020; Siobhan Riding, Singapore challenges Hong Kong, 10th February 2020; Sam Fleming, Philip Stafford, Matthew Vincent, and George Parker, EU rules out permanent access deal for City of London, 12th February 2020; Matthew Vincent, City sets out proposals for equivalence with EU 13th February 2020; Laura Noonan, European capital markets not fit for purpose, 17th February 2020; Siobhan Riding, How will the EU reshape regulations after Brexit? 17th February 2020; Norman Blackwell, Britain should diverge on domestic financial services rules, 25th February 2020.

[7] 18th October 2019 Payment for order flow is a good deal for investors, Larry Tabb.

[8] 17th October 2019 Hedge funds are happy to let the machines take over, Robin Wigglesworth.

change the dynamics of the market.'[9] This tempted regulators to consider closing down financial markets as Philip Stafford reported in March 2020. 'They fear that swings in prices have become disorderly and institutions with depleted workforces cannot cope with heavy volumes.' [10] However, they were also aware that there could be future shocks when markets re-opened as prices had not been able to adjust to changing conditions. [11]

Another area of continuity was continuing innovation in the use of derivatives, despite these financial instruments being regarded as central to the Global Financial Crisis of 2008. In markets where price volatility continued to be of major concern, new derivative products were designed and introduced to cover the risks involved. These products ranged from markets in oil through cheese to airline fares. Internationally, oil was priced using Brent Crude but Russian producers were unhappy with the results, and so pressed for a contract that better reflected supply and demand for their product and was traded domestically. A similar motivation drove the attempt to introduce a new cheese contract in the USA, as Tim Andriesen, managing director of agricultural products at CME, explained at the end of 2019. 'Our clients continue to look for tools to manage their price exposure in physical cheese markets, including food manufacturers and processors of cheese.'[12] Among the most ambitious among the new derivative products being developed at the beginning of 2020 was one to protect against volatility in the price of air travel. The uncertainty surrounding future fares was causing unease among aircraft manufacturers that airlines could collapse and so default on payments for the planes they had ordered. The solution was a derivatives contract that allowed airlines to hedge the risks they were running, so giving them the confidence to continue updating and expanding their fleet, and manufacturers the assurance that orders placed would be paid for. Christine Rovelli, head of treasury at Finnair, wanted 'a risk management instrument tailor-made for the air-travel industry that will help us manage our exposure to ticket price volatility more efficiently'.[13] What this reflected was the role played by derivatives as an essential risk management tool employed by producers, consumers, and those that provided short- and long-term loans to all involved. In 2020 Chinese banks were permitted to trade domestic bond futures, despite the risks involved, as regulators recognized the contribution that would make to the liquidity and transparency of a market. They were keen to promote the bond market as a way widening sources of credit to businesses.[14]

Exchanges had expected to benefit from the Global Financial Crisis as they provided regulated and resilient markets unlike a number of the OTC variety. That turned out not to be the case and so exchanges remained confined to providing trading facilities for corporate stocks and standardized derivative contracts. There they were able to monopolize the

[9] *FT* reporters, Homeworking prompts biggest test for trading since 9/11 14th March 2020.

[10] Philip Stafford, Watchdogs weigh up costs and benefits of exchange shutdowns, 18th March 2020.

[11] 17th October 2019 Hedge funds are happy to let the machines take over, Robin Wigglesworth; 18th October 2019 Payment for order flow is a good deal for investors, Larry Tabb; 22nd October 2019 All about data: LSE bid show exchanges' new priorities, Philip Stafford; 22nd October 2019 US regulators take a closer look at data fees, Richard Henderson; 7th January 2020 Banks back computing revolution, Richard Waters; Joe Rennison, Robert Armstrong, and Robin Wigglesworth, Meet the new bond kings, 23rd January 2020; Robin Wigglesworth, Virus mayhem reflects danger of shock-led trading, 7th March 2020; FT reporters, Homeworking prompts biggest test for trading since 9/11 14th March 2020; Philip Stafford, Watchdogs weigh up costs and benefits of exchange shutdowns, 18th March 2020.

[12] 16th November 2019 Time is ripe for block cheeses futures and options at CME, Philip Stafford.

[13] Philip Stafford and Peggy Hollinger, Airbus plans exchange to hedge airline fare vitality, 20th January 2020.

[14] 15th November 2019 Russia makes fresh effort to take control of its oil price using electronic platform, Nastassia Astrasheuskava; 16th November 2019 Time is ripe for block cheeses futures and options at CME, Philip Stafford; Philip Stafford and Peggy Hollinger, Airbus plans exchange to hedge airline fare vitality, 20th January 2020; Don Weinland, China reopens bond futures trading to big local banks, 22nd February 2020.

market being the centre of liquidity and reference pricing. As Philip Stafford noted for derivatives markets in November 2019, 'Direct competition between futures exchanges is rare, as different venues tend to dominate in their chosen market.' [15] It was only at the stage of an initial public offering that stock exchanges, for example, competed. Once the market was established it did not move. Philip Stafford and Richard Henderson reported in November 2019 that the NYSE and Nasdaq were 'locked in a fierce rivalry to secure initial public offerings as they are the only exchanges that launch companies on to the US stock market'.[16] This position left the OTC market to cater for all other financial instruments, ranging from the most active, such as foreign exchange, to the least active, like many corporate bonds. What continued to take place was a blurring of the distinctions between exchanges, including ICE, CME, and the LSE; trading platforms like MarketAxess and Tradeweb; and information providers such as Bloomberg. There was a continuing process of diversification and consolidation taking place as each strived to cover not only stocks, bonds, and derivatives but expand into the provision of real-time price and other data to their customers and offer clearing, settlement, and other services following the vertical-silo model. This was taking place not only at the level of the largest exchanges but also among the smallest as each attempted to cover the costs associated with electronic trading platforms and reduce charges in the face of demands from users and pressure from regulators. The income generated by exchanges from selling data rose from $1bn in 2005 to $6bn in 2019. This compensated them from the low return obtained from providing the market infrastructure, as the charges they could impose were driven down by alternative platforms and dark pools.

No longer could exchanges monopolize the market in corporate stocks. Rob Arnott, chairman of the fund mangers, Research Affiliates, observed in November 2019 that, 'The appeal of being a public company has been eviscerated. The pressure is overwhelming.' [17] A corporate stock could be traded without the need for an official quotation which could bring additional scrutiny from the regulatory authorities in any case. By the end of 2019 the high frequency traders, Virtu and Citadel, accounted for 40 per cent of US stock trading, and they were looking for alternatives to routing business through the established stock exchanges, in order to bypass the charges imposed and the regulations they were forced to comply with. Even on established stock exchanges many of the small capitalization stocks were little traded and so lacked liquidity, making them similar to unquoted ones. In the USA high-grade corporate bonds were increasingly traded on electronic platforms provided by MarketAxess and Tradeweb, so providing them with a recognized market, indicative of the potential threat faced by stock exchanges when it came to the stock issued by smaller companies. There was growing criticism of the Tokyo Stock Exchange, as many of the corporate stocks it quoted were illiquid. Faced with these pressures exchanges considered mergers as a way of expanding the volume of business handled on a single platform and so reduce their costs. However, completing such mergers remained difficult, as with Hong Kong's failed attempt at a take-over of the London Stock Exchange in late 2019. Easier to accomplish were bolt-on acquisitions such as Euronext buying the Oslo Bors, to expand its European coverage, and Deutsche's Borse's purchase from Nasdaq of NFX, an oil and

[15] 13th November 2019 Nasdaq agrees sale of commodities futures business to German exchange, Philip Stafford.

[16] 16th November 2019 Nasdaq raises listing fees to funs swanky new showroom, Philip Stafford and Richard Henderson.

[17] 1st November 2019 The attraction of staying private, Richard Henderson and Miles Kruppa.

freight futures platform, in order to bulk up in trading in this area. Much more ambitious was the bid by the SIX group, owner of the Swiss Exchange, for Spain's BME, as a means of countering Euronext's ambition to consolidate all continental European exchanges under its control. Developments of this kind had been taking place before the Global Financial Crisis and then resumed after a brief pause.[18]

Change

The area of finance where the Global Financial Crisis made the greatest impact, with a lasting legacy, was on the operations of the megabanks. Whereas before the crisis they had been left relatively free to pursue their own agenda, that was no longer considered acceptable. Their size made them a threat to the stability of the entire financial system if one should collapse. Beginning in the USA, but followed to a lesser or greater extent around the world, restrictions were placed on the operation of the megabanks, along with higher and stricter requirements regarding capital and reserves. The priority was to force the megabanks to be in a position to be able to withstand the pressures of another major liquidity crisis without being forced to rely on central bank support and government intervention. Though the accompanying threat to break up the megabanks was not proceeded with, the result was to curtail their ability to pursue the aggressive lending and trading strategies that they had employed before the crisis. The effect of this regulatory intervention was to undermine the competiveness of the megabanks and either allow rivals to undercut them or lead to a shortage of specific types of finance. One casualty was project finance according to John Dizzard in December 2019. 'Bank regulators have been deeply suspicious of the project finance model, particularly since the financial crisis.'[19] The reason was that banks funded the construction phase of a project, with insurers and pension funds only becoming involved once completed. This left banks with an asset that could be difficult to sell, and so running the risk of a liquidity crisis if disposal took a long time or proved impossible. The response from regulators after the crisis was to require banks to set aside capital and reserves to cover this situation, which made the business financially unattractive to them. Other financial institutions were reluctant to step in because, in Dizzard's judgement

[18] 9th October 2019 Questions swirl over Hong Kong's failed LSE bid, Philip Stafford and Henry Sender; 22nd October 2019 All about data: LSE bid show exchanges' new priorities, Philip Stafford; 22nd October 2019 US regulators take a closer look at data fees, Richard Henderson; 31st October 2019 Citigroup outlines plan to withdraw from two-thirds of foreign exchange platforms, Eva Szalay; 1st November 2019 The attraction of staying private, Richard Henderson and Miles Kruppa; 1st November 2019 Mobile-savvy Kenyans will soon be able to buy shares on phones, Tom Wilson; 2nd November 2019 Virtu backed bourse MEMX clears vital regulatory hurdle, Richard Henderson; 13th November 2019 Nasdaq agrees sale of commodities futures business to German exchange, Philip Stafford; 16th November 2019 Nasdaq raises listing fees to funs swanky new showroom, Philip Stafford and Richard Henderson; 19th November 2019 SIX makes Euro2.8bn Madrid exchange move to fend off Euronext interest, Philip Stafford; 19th November 2019 Rivals battle for Madrid bourse owner, Philip Stafford; 19th November 2019 Hong Kong's GEM tarnished by back door listings and drab returns, Daniel Shane; 23rd November 2019 Stockpickers bide their time on clash with Quant challengers, Laurence Fletcher and Ortenca Aliaj; 29th November 2019 Overhaul for Japanese stock trading as regulator unveils premium segment, Robin Harding and Leo Lewis; Joe Rennison, Robert Armstrong, and Robin Wigglesworth, Meet the new bond kings, 23rd January 2020; Philip Stafford, European regulator steps up dark pools campaign, 5th February 2020; Philip Stafford, Investors question logic behind ICE's mooted deal for eBay, 6th February 2020; Philip Stafford, JP Morgan and Goldman Sachs throw weight behind stock exchange start-up, 21st February 2020; Philip Stafford, Regulators to review pricing of trading data and benchmarks, 10th March 2020.

[19] 2nd December 2019 Baselheads are crushing EU project finance, John Dizzard.

'Project finance is not especially well suited for public markets, with its lack of ready liquidity and technical complexity.'[20]

A more general effect was to force the megabanks to withdraw from market-making, where they had leveraged their capital and reserves to act as counterparties to buyers and sellers. Where they were prevented from doing this, or found the business less profitable and more risky, their response was to wind down their operations. As secondary market trading shrank so did the popularity of many of the financial instruments that had been in demand before the crisis, encouraging a shift away from their use. Sarah Bayer, a managing director for equity capital at Citigroup, observed in November 2019 that 'There are more alternatives today for companies to raise capital privately from a larger swath of investors than there were 20 years ago.' [21] Similarly, Jim Cooney, head of equity capital markets for the Americas at Bank of America, concluded that 'Companies are staying private for longer and getting funded longer.'[22] Another market where the withdrawal of the megabanks was having an effect, despite its growing size, was that for corporate debt issued in emerging economies. Robert Koenigsberger, chief investment officer at Gramercy Funds Management, a US fund manager with assets of $5.5bn, pointed out in January 2020 that 'The size of the market is bigger, the liquidity promise of the underlying vehicles has become much shorter and, because of the regulatory environment in the post-2008 world, there are just fewer banks with less balance sheets.' [23] By 2019 this type of debt in circulation had reached $2.3tn but the market lacked liquidity because the banks held only $16bn in inventories, so reducing their ability to act as counterparties. The reason for the change, according to Colby Smith and Robin Wigglesworth in 2020, was that, 'Regulatory changes have forced banks' trading desks to scale back their holdings, hampering their ability to cushion any turmoil.'[24]

An unintentional consequence of regulatory intervention had been to increase the risks present in the bond market by depriving it of the liquidity that the megabanks had previously provided. As Chris Flood reported in December 2019:

> Regulatory reforms introduced after the financial crisis have led to significant reductions in the inventories of bonds held by banks and broker-dealers, some of the most important liquidity providers in fixed income markets. As a result, constructing and running fixed income strategies with individual bonds has become more expensive and less efficient than in the past, encouraging investors to employ low-cost ETFs as portfolio building blocks.[25]

There were also elements of this in the stock market contributing to increased volatility. Though the megabanks continued to occupy a supreme position within the global financial system they no longer enjoyed the freedom that had made them so powerful in the years before the Global Financial Crisis. As Sam Fleming, Philip Stafford, Matthew Vincent, and George Parker reflected in 2020, 'Since the financial crisis, policymakers worldwide have been working out the best way to supervise and punish global institutions that trade and

[20] 2nd December 2019 Baselheads are crushing EU project finance, John Dizzard.
[21] 1st November 2019 The attraction of staying private, Richard Henderson and Miles Kruppa.
[22] 1st November 2019 The attraction of staying private, Richard Henderson and Miles Kruppa.
[23] Colby Smith and Robin Wigglesworth, Boom in EM corporate debt stirs liquidity fears, 20th January 2020.
[24] Colby Smith and Robin Wigglesworth, Boom in EM corporate debt stirs liquidity fears, 20th January 2020.
[25] 2nd December 2019 Bond ETFs outshine equity rivals, Chris Flood.

move vast amounts of money across borders.'[26] One effect of that regulatory onslaught was to leave the field to a small group of US banks secure in their command of their vast domestic market. The only exception was the British bank, Barclays, whose acquisition of Lehman Brothers at the time of the Global Financial Crisis, had provided it with sufficient US credentials to compete, but only as a minor player.[27]

Profiting from the regulatory restraints placed on the megabanks were a host of other financial institutions and markets, as they moved in to take their place. Though difficult to define, let alone measure, what evidence there is indicates a significant expansion of the shadow banking sector in the years after the Global Financial Crisis. By 2020 the Financial Stability Board of the Bank for International Settlements calculated that the assets within the global shadow banking sector had reached $183.7tn in 2018, or almost half of all financial assets, which stood at $378.9tn. Writing in January 2020, Michael Howell, the managing director of the investment advisory firm, CrossBorder Capital, observed that:

> For some years now, the wholesale money markets have been fuelled by vast inflows from corporate and institutional cash pools, such as those controlled by cash-rich companies, asset managers and hedge funds, the cash-collateral business of derivatives traders, sovereign wealth funds and foreign exchange reserve managers Today, these pools probably exceed $30tn and have outgrown the banking system.[28]

One prominent group among these were fund managers who grew to a size and importance that rivalled the megabanks among the world's financial institutions. As with the banks it was again a small number from the United States that occupied the top spots, benefiting from the scale and integrated nature of their domestic market as that provided a secure base from which to launch their international operations. By 2019 the twenty largest US fund managers controlled 35 per cent of global assets under management. Among the most successful products handled by these megafunds in the post-crisis era were passive funds that sought only to replicate a particular index. These appeared to provide the desired combination of yield, security, and liquidity that the megabanks had been able to offer in the past. The assets held in passive funds rose from $2.3tn in 2009 to $11tn in 2019.

The most prominent of these passive funds were Exchange Traded Funds (ETFs). Robin Wigglesworth reflected at the end of 2019 that 'The ETF market has exploded in size and diversity over the past decade, seizing market share from traditional, active fund managers thanks to the funds' cheapness. These listed, benchmark mimicking vehicles offer investors exposure to a wide range of securities. They have also become a vital tool for other managers who use them as building blocks for their trades.' [29] ETFs attracted investors

[26] Sam Fleming, Philip Stafford, Matthew Vincent, and George Parker, EU rules out permanent access deal for City of London, 12th February 2020.

[27] 11th October 2019 Fed rules out liquidity gauge for foreign banks, Kiran Stacey and Laura Noonan; 11th October 2019 Better data on shadow banking reveals uncomfortable truths, Gillian Tett; 16th October 2019 Peer-to-peer forex services aim to bypass Wall St banks, Eva Szalay; 18th October 2019 Payment for order flow is a good deal for investors, Larry Tabb; 31st October 2019 Citigroup outlines plan to withdraw from two-thirds of foreign exchange platforms, Eva Szalay; 2nd December 2019 Bond ETFs outshine equity rivals, Chris Flood; 2nd December 2019 Baselheads are crushing EU project finance, John Dizzard; Colby Smith and Robin Wigglesworth, Boom in EM corporate debt stirs liquidity fears, 20th January 2020; Sam Fleming, Philip Stafford, Matthew Vincent, and George Parker, EU rules out permanent access deal for City of London, 12th February 2020; Laura Noonan, A Retreat from Wall street, 3rd March 2020.

[28] Michael Howell, Rising tide of liquidity lifters many boats, but keep an eye on the horizon, 17th January 2020.

[29] 22nd November 2019 ETF pioneer Ross decides to call it a day at State Street, Robin Wigglesworth.

worldwide because of their low cost, simplicity, and their tax-efficient nature. Grant Engelbart, director of research at CLS Investment, a fund manager, explained their tax advantages. 'ETFs have always been a more tax efficient way to package an investment strategy. Unlike traditional mutual funds structures, they can avoid capital gains taxes as the sale of instruments takes place outside the fund itself.'[30] At a time of persistently low interest rates ETFs provided investors with higher returns than could be obtained from banks while offering liquidity as well, as they could be bought and sold in the same way as corporate stocks. Between 2009 and 2019 $3.5tn flowed into ETFs, and the total reached $5.8tn. Nevertheless, there were risks attached to ETFs. Certain ETFs were vulnerable to a sudden increase in redemptions as they held illiquid assets. As Lee Spelman, head of US equity for JP Morgan Asset Management, explained in November 2019, 'A lot of private equity investments don't work out. It's absolutely risky for the end investor.'[31] Many trades of exchange-listed stocks failed because it proved impossible to find a willing counterparty to a proposed sale or purchase. Varghese Thomas, chief operating officer at technology provider Trading-Screen, noted that 'Dark trading exists due to strong demand from investors to trade larger volumes of stock especially in less liquid smaller and mid-cap stocks, where at times it can be difficult to do so on an exchange.' [32]

As bonds were not traded on stock exchanges the underlying value of bond-based ETFs relied on the ratings applied by the US trio of Standard and Poor's, Moody's, and Fitch, and the subsequent pricing generated on markets that could be lacking in both liquidity and transparency. For those reasons considerable effort was made to improve the liquidity and transparency of corporate bond markets, especially in the USA, where they provided a major alternative to bank finance. By January 2020 Joe Rennison, Robert Armstrong, and Robin Wigglesworth claimed that 'Hundreds of bond trades can be electronically priced as one and executed simultaneously with a single counterparty.' [33] Nevertheless, pricing remained dependent on complex computer programs and the ability of high-frequency-traders to make and maintain two-way markets across a range of bonds. In the coronavirus crisis of 2020 a number of these bond markets froze as shadow banks pulled back. This forced companies to turn back to banks for funding as alternative sources dried up, activating the credit lines they had established but did not expect to use. In turn that led the banks to turn to central banks as lenders of last resort. In March 2020 the Federal Reserve intervened to support the commercial paper market in the USA, which had frozen, replicating action last taken during the Global Financial Crisis. To a degree the liquidity risks always present when short-term funds were used to purchase difficult-to-sell assets still existed but had been displaced from the banks to the shadow banks since the Global Financial Crisis

Of particular concern by 2019 were the number and size of open-ended funds, which held hard-to-sell assets while promising investors instant withdrawal. Gerry Cross, director of policy and risk at the Central Bank of Ireland, pointed out in November 2019 that 'It is important there should not be a mismatch between investors' expectations and what a fund is able to deliver in terms of daily redemptions, particularly in times of stress.' [34] As Dublin was the second largest fund management centre in the EU, he had reasons for concern. Investors had been drawn into these funds because of their ability to provide better yields

[30] 4th November 2019 Hybrid funds smooth path between active and passive strategies, Andrew Whiffin.
[31] 1st November 2019 The attraction of staying private, Richard Henderson and Miles Kruppa.
[32] Philip Stafford, European regulator steps up dark pools campaign, 5th February 2020.
[33] Joe Rennison, Robert Armstrong. and Robin Wigglesworth, Meet the new bond kings, 23rd January 2020.
[34] 25th November 2019 Ireland to review fund rules after Woodford, Siobhan Riding.

despite the greater risks involved, encouraged by the lack of returns elsewhere. As Chris Giles reported in October 2019, 'Persistently low interest rates encouraged investors to take dangerous risks in a quest to maintain their financial returns.'[35] This was echoed by Chris Flood, when he referred to 'Mounting fears that a dangerous pricing bubble has developed in fixed income markets.' In his assessment, 'Many bond fund managers have reduced their holdings of cash and other liquid assets which provide little or no income in an effort to improve returns.' Instead, they had invested in 'lower quality assets that could prove more difficult to sell if market conditions deteriorate'. [36] What these journalists were picking up on were reports by the likes of the International Monetary Fund (IMF). One of the advisors to the IMF, Tobias Adrian, stated that, 'Declines in holdings of liquid assets raise questions about fixed income funds' ability to absorb redemption shocks.' [37] If bond funds were unable to meet redemption requests this could spark fire sales where managers dumped assets to raise cash, which would inflict losses on other investors and so spread the crisis throughout the financial system.

The most exposed of these were those funds offering daily redemptions while investing in assets that could take weeks or months to sell in an orderly way. Stephen Tu, senior credit officer at Moody's, referred to the 'structural mismatch between the assets they hold and their liabilities to investors'. [38] Marc Oswald, the chief economist at the brokers, ADM Investor Services, explained the predicament faced by fund managers at the end of 2019. 'Central banks have crowded out private sector fixed income investors from government bond markets. Zero-interest rate policies have also forced investors into riskier bond investments in a reach for yield.' [39] Some fund managers expressed concerns that large-scale redemptions, followed by the large-scale sale of assets into markets lacking the ability to absorb them, would amplify price moves, and so transmit stress to other parts of the financial system. One of those was Pascal Blanque, chief investment officer at Amundi, Europe's largest asset manager. 'As the share of assets held by central banks rises, there is an increased scarcity of bonds available for investors to purchase, squeezing liquidity in some markets.' [40] In contrast, others took an optimistic view, such as Jennifer Kim, co-head of ETF capital markets for the Americas at Invesco, believing funds would prove resilient in a crisis. Regulators and central banks were aware of the situation that had arisen in the years since the Global Financial Crisis but none could predict how serious it was or what action to take to reduce the threat posed. The one piece of comfort they could take was that these fund managers did not pose the same systemic risk as banks as they were much less exposed to liquidity issues. Instead, it would be investors that would have to bear the losses inflicted in a crisis and the collapse in the value of hard-to-sell corporate stocks and bonds.

By January 2020 the world's three biggest fund managers, BlackRock, Vanguard, and State Street, were responsible for assets that, collectively, had reached $16.7 trillion on the strength of the huge increase in passive investing. In the wake of the stock market collapse precipitated by the coronavirus epidemic, the value of their holdings fell to $13.9tn by the middle of March 2020, or by $2.8 tn (17 per cent). To Tim Buckley, chief executive of

[35] 17th October 2019 IMF warns low rates are fuelling risk-taking, Chris Giles.
[36] 21st October 2019 Bond bubble puts global financial system at risk, Chris Flood.
[37] 21st October 2019 Bond bubble puts global financial system at risk, Chris Flood.
[38] 21st October 2019 Bond bubble puts global financial system at risk, Chris Flood.
[39] 21st October 2019 Bond bubble puts global financial system at risk, Chris Flood.
[40] 21st October 2019 Bond bubble puts global financial system at risk, Chris Flood.

Vanguard, such 'Repricings are inevitable, sometimes violent, but never predictable.'[41] What he was reflecting on was that there had been major stock market crashes in 1987, 1997/8, and 2008 but it was only that one associated with the Global Financial Crisis that had produced devastating consequences. Stock markets rose and fell but it was the consequences of these events for the rest of the financial system that created systemic crises, and that depended upon the resilience of banks. In 2008 in the USA and Western Europe banks were not resilient and central banks had lost sight of their role as lenders of last resort. In 2020 banks were resilient and central banks were aware of their need to act as lenders of last resort both individually and collectively. Nevertheless, there were weaknesses in the global financial system, especially the shadow banks that had grown in importance because of the restrictions placed on the megabanks, reducing their ability to act as reliable counterparties under all conditions.[42]

One solution adopted to meet the emerging risks in financial markets was a greater reliance on clearing houses or central counterparties (CCPs). This included promoting their use in markets where they had not been considered necessary in the past, such as foreign exchange trading. Philip Stafford wrote at the end of 2019 that,

> In the past decade, global authorities have turned to clearing houses such as LCH and ICE Futures US as pillars of stability. These institutions stand between two parties in a trade and help manage the impact to the market if one defaults. But this has raised

[41] Peter Smith, Vanguard, BlackRock and State Street asset shrinkage spells end of golden era, 16th March 2020.

[42] 7th October 2019 UK Watchdog eyes liquidity reforms, Siobhan Riding; 7th October 2019 US fund houses manage more than a third of global assets, Chris Flood; 7th October 2019 Are retail investors missing out on the message? Rebecca Hampson; 11th October 2019 Better data on shadow banking reveals uncomfortable truths, Gillian Tett; 16th October 2019 Peer-to-peer forex services aim to bypass Wall St banks, Eva Szalay; 17th October 2019 IMF warns low rates are fuelling risk-taking, Chris Giles; 18th October 2019 Payment for order flow is a good deal for investors, Larry Tabb; 21st October 2019 Bond bubble puts global financial system at risk, Chris Flood; 22nd October 2019 Popularity of passive investing changes rules of the game, Chris Flood; 29th October 2019 ICE launches ETF platform specialising in bonds, Philip Stafford; 31st October 2019 Lime liquidity issues spark contagion feeas at South Korea hedge funds, Song Jung-A; 1st November 2019 The attraction of staying private, Richard Henderson and Miles Kruppa; 4th November 2019 Growth of private capital funds accelerates while ETFs slow, Robin Wigglesworth; 4th November 2019 Hybrid funds smooth path between active and passive strategies, Andrew Whiffin; 18th November 2019 The pension house is on fire, Josephine Cumbo and Robin Wigglesworth; 18th November Dangers lurk in the design of junk bond ETFs, David Tuckwell; 19th November 2019 Safe assets in short supply as central banks buy big, Tommy Stubbington; 22nd November 2019 ETF pioneer Ross decides to call it a day at State Street, Robin Wigglesworth; 22nd November 2019 Investors pile into US corporate bond funds as Fed warns on credit quality, Jennifer Ablan and Joe Rennison; 23rd November 2019 Stockpickers bide their time on clash with Quant challengers, Laurence Fletcher and Ortenca Aliaj; 25th November 2019 Ireland to review fund rules after Woodford, Siobhan Riding; 28th November 2019 Bond ETFs are no menace to financial system, Jennifer Kim; 2nd December 2019 Bond ETFs outshine equity rivals, Chris Flood; 20th December 2019 Bank of Japan acts to avert liquidity squeeze for exchange traded funds, Robin Harding; 20th December 2019 Global watchdog warns on rising risk of shocks in leveraged loans, Tommy Stubbington; 2nd January 2020 Germany's Scope take the long view as it aims to break stranglehold of US rating agencies, Olaf Storbeck; 10th January 2020 Arrival of passive fund leader Vanguard rattles UL investment advice industry, Madison Darbyshire; Michael Howell, Rising tide of liquidity lifters many boats, but keep an eye on the horizon, 17th January 2020; Caroline Binham, Shadow banking sector shifts into decline, 20th January 2020; Colby Smith and Robin Wigglesworth, Boom in EM corporate debt stirs liquidity fears, 20th January 2020; Joe Rennison, Robert Armstrong, and Robin Wigglesworth, Meet the new bond kings, 23rd January 2020.; Philip Stafford, EU dashes hopes for failed trade rules phase-in, 6th February 2020; Siobhan Riding and Chris Flood, Wall St's index trackers make strides in UK, 18th February 2020; John Plender, The seeds of the Next Crisis, 5th March 2020; Robin Wigglesworth, Covid-19 tips markets into week of chaos as central banks play catch-up with new reality, 14th March 2020; Peter Smith, Vanguard, BlackRock and State Street asset shrinkage spells end of golden era, 16th March 2020; *FT* Reporters, Bank acts to ease liquidity strains, 17th March 2020; Brendan Greeley, Joe Rennison and Colby Smith, Fed Swoops to buy commercial paper, 18th March 2020.

> concerns that clearing houses are too important to fail. Rules that formally cover what happens if clearers run into financial trouble are yet to be finalised in the US and EU.[43]

Regulators were trying to push responsibility onto the owners of clearing houses, such as the exchanges, or their members, especially the banks, or their main users, such as fund managers. In response banks and fund managers wanted clearing houses to hold more capital to cover losses but this would increase their costs and limit their profitability and, as they operated as businesses, they were reluctant to do that. Without 'better default buffers, disclosure and corporate governance', Gillian Tett warned that there was a risk that a clearing house could collapse, and that 'Even as the trading risks were being concentrated into the clearing houses, regulators did not spell out what would happen if a CCP itself collapsed.'[44] There was no lender of last resort facility in place for the world's clearing houses. In the wake of the crisis posed by the coronavirus John Plender posed the question of 'Whether the regulatory response to the great financial crisis has been sufficient to rule out another systemic crisis and whether the increase in banks' capital will provide an adequate buffer against the losses that will result from widespread mispricing of risk.'[45] The answer to that question lies sometime in the future.

Without doubt the most important change that came about as a result of the Global Financial Crisis was the much greater intervention by regulatory authorities and central banks in global financial markets. This was not confined to the years that immediately followed the crisis or to particular levels of operation, as it continued into the 2020s, and extended from influencing the operation of entire markets through quantitative easing, the behaviour of banks because of the Basel Rules, and the relationship between participants dictated by regulatory intervention. As late as 2020 concerns over a build-up of risk, for example, led regulators to impose rules limiting delays in the completion of sales and purchases rather than allowing those involved to deal with these issues through bilateral negotiations. There was also intervention by a number of regulators to prevent the short-selling of particular stocks at the time of the coronavirus epidemic, as well as plans to close entire financial markets in order to suppress volatility. Whereas before the crisis there was a presumption that the megabanks could be trusted to police the markets and maintain stability, in its aftermath only the agencies of government were considered able to carry out that task. The need for such intervention had also grown because of the withdrawal of the megabanks from providing liquidity to markets ranging all the way from corporate stocks to government debt. Even in the US Treasury Bond market, which was regarded as one of the most liquid in the world, intervention by the Federal Reserve was required at the time of the coronavirus epidemic. Much of the trading had fallen into the hands of the hedge funds, and they lacked the resources to act as reliable counterparties at times of major stress. It was not that regulators and central banks had not intervened prior to the crisis, as with earlier versions of the Basel Rules followed by the megabanks, but the level at which this took place became much more intrusive. By 2020 the consequences of this intervention was visible to all, leading to questions over whether the results were to make the global financial system more or less resilient. Where intervention did appear to have been successful was to strengthen the ability of the megabanks to withstand a future crisis, by forcing them to focus much more on liquidity than profitability. However, that had the effect

[43] 25th October 2019 Blackrock and Vanguard push for clearing reforms, Philip Stafford.
[44] 25th October 2019 Clearing houses are ripe for reform, Gillian Tett.
[45] John Plender, The seeds of the Next Crisis, 5th March 2020.

of displacing financial activity to other parts of the financial system where the ability to withstand the impact of a future crisis was untested. There was no lender of last resort to the shadow banking system, including the megafunds.

In the wake of the Global Financial Crisis central banks were credited with preventing it becoming a world depression as had happened in the 1930s, following the Wall Street Crash of 1929. This had been achieved by pumping liquidity into the global financial system through a policy known as monetary easing (QE). However, by the end of 2019 central bankers were ready to accept that this policy had consequences for the operation of global financial markets. In October of that year, Philip Lowe, the Governor of the Reserve Bank of Australia and chair of the Committee on the Global Financial System at the Bank for International Settlements, acknowledged that monetary policy intervention by central banks have 'introduced some distortions in the capital markers'.[46] Their concerns were over not only the consequences of what they had done already but also those that would be caused when central banks eventually withdrew the liquidity that they had been providing since the crisis. Global financial markets had become dependent upon central banks for liquidity rather than it being generated from within, as banks with surplus funds lent short-term to those in deficit on a continuous basis. Amin Rajan, chief executive of Create Research, noted that, 'As a crisis-era measure, QE has worked. But its unintended side-effects have undermined its overall effectiveness.'[47] What he was pointing out was that QE had stabilized markets after the collapse of Lehman Brothers but then underpinned an asset bubble through a policy of ultra-low interest rates and central bank purchases of government debt. Another expressing similar concerns in 2020 was Michael Howell, the managing director of the advisory firm, CrossBorder Capital. He highlighted the fact that, 'In the absence of public sector instruments such as treasury bills, the private sector has had to step in by creating short-term vehicles known as repurchase agreements and asset backed commercial paper'. [48] Since the crisis the provision of liquidity had moved from being the preserve of a small number of megabanks, acting collectively for the entire banking sector, to a much more dispersed grouping of financial institutions playing a more limited role, leaving central banks to take up the slack.

Another consequence of monetary easing was that it had absorbed government debt and forced down interest rates to historically low levels. This deprived banks of access to the risk-free liquid assets where they employed temporarily idle funds or were used as collateral when they lent and borrowed among each other. The effect was to reduce daily liquidity in the wholesale money market leading to sudden shortages. In turn that forced central bank intervention to alleviate a liquidity crisis. As these markets operated on the basis of the US$ the only central bank able to provide this liquidity was the Federal Reserve. As one financial markets expert, Karen Petrou, explained in November 2019, 'The central bank was once supposed to be lender of last resort, backing banks which had no other way of funding... But after 2008, the Fed became market-maker of last resort, lowering rates whenever equities trembled. Now it is market lender of last resort, too.'[49] In particular, the Federal Reserve had become the main support of the repo market, where banks borrowed and lent between each other, using ultra-safe securities such as US government debt, as collateral.

[46] 8th October 2019 Beware of distortions caused by monetary policy innovation, Philip Lowe.

[47] 2nd December 2019 QE sows seeds of next crisis, funds warn, Jennifer Thompson.

[48] Michael Howell, Rising tide of liquidity lifters many boats, but keep an eye on the horizon, 17th January 2020.

[49] 7th November 2019 Repo ructions call attention to failure of post-crisis policy, Karen Petrou.

'The Fed didn't just stabilise the repo market; now it is the repo market.'[50] This was a position that the Federal Reserve was reluctant to occupy on a permanent basis as doing so meant becoming the lender of last resort to the global financial system. This exposed it to the liquidity risks of the global banking system while lacking the authority to impose discipline upon it.

There was also the question of moral hazard. The more certain banks were that the Federal Reserve would intervene to provide liquidity the less they were willing to hold cash and low yielding assets because of the poor returns they generated. In the words of Tommy Stubbington and Colby Smith in March 2020:

> Since the financial crisis of 2008–9, investors have relied on central bankers to step in with interest rate cuts and asset purchases during periods of market stress and policy-makers have often delivered. But as the spread of coronavirus sent stocks into a bear market in record time this week and as strains emerged in the all important US Treasury market, that dependency appears to have been tested to breaking point.[51]

Faced by an emergency, such as the increased volatility and the hoarding of $s that accompanied the coronavirus epidemic, the Federal Reserve was left with no choice but to greatly increase the liquidity it provided both within the USA and globally, through concerted action with the central banks of the EU, UK, Canada, Japan, and Switzerland. Drawing on evidence from around the world the *Financial Times* reported that, 'The US Federal Reserve has taken a number of aggressive steps to help financial markets keep moving and aid banks to deal sympathetically with borrowers.'[52] What this suggests is that central bankers had learned the lesson of the Global Financial Crisis, which was that liquidity was of paramount importance to the global banking system and prompt action was required to maintain it.[53]

[50] 7th November 2019 Repo ructions call attention to failure of post-crisis policy, Karen Petrou.

[51] Tommy Stubbington and Colby Smith, Investors flag up worries over limits of monetary policy to end turmoil, 14th March 2020.

[52] *FT* Reporters, Bank acts to ease liquidity strains, 17th March 2020.

[53] 8th October 2019 Beware of distortions caused by monetary policy innovation, Philip Lowe; 11th October 2019 Fed rules out liquidity gauge for foreign banks, Kiran Stacey and Laura Noonan; 17th October 2019 IMF warns low rates are fuelling risk-taking, Chris Giles; 18th October 2019 Payment for order flow is a good deal for investors, Larry Tabb; 21st October 2019 Bond bubble puts global financial system at risk, Chris Flood; 22nd October 2019 All about data: LSE bid show exchanges' new priorities, Philip Stafford; 22nd October 2019 Clearing reforms set to upend asset management industry, Eva Szalay; 22nd October 2019 Popularity of passive investing changes rules of the game, Chris Flood; 25th October 2019 Clearing houses are ripe for reform, Gillian Tett; 25th October 2019 Blackrock and Vanguard push for clearing reforms, Philip Stafford; 7th November 2019 Repo ructions call attention to failure of post-crisis policy, Karen Petrou; 15th November 2019 EU targeted reform of Mifid 2 rules after backlash, Philip Stafford; 18th November Dangers lurk in the design of junk bond ETFs, David Tuckwell; 19th November 2019 Safe assets in short supply as central banks buy big, Tommy Stubbington; 25th November 2019 Ireland to review fund rules after Woodford, Siobhan Riding; 2nd December 2019 QE sows seeds of next crisis, funds warn, Jennifer Thompson; 2nd December 2019 Bond ETFs outshine equity rivals, Chris Flood; 3rd December 2019 Investors secure New York Fed loans with cash crunch worries lingering, Joe Rennison; 6th December 2019 Ultra low interest rates spur euro to become world's new carry trade, Eva Szalay; 7th December 2019 Year-end repo rates surge despite Fed attempts to ease the funding strain. Joe Rennison and Colby Smith; 9th December 2019 Cash-hungry hedge funds deepened recent repo market turmoil finds BIS, Tommy Stubbington and Joe Rennison; 14th December 2019 Fed gears up to double its repo interventions, Colby Smith and Joe Rennison; 2nd January 2020 Lanquid fore trading due a wake-up call, Eva Szalay; 3rd January 2020 Fed aims to stop another year of grim repo, Colby Smith and Joe Rennison; 10th January 2020 Fed signals exit from repo market this year, Colby Smith and Joe Rennison; 11th January 2020 Traders across Europe face up to cost of failure on transactions, Philip Stafford; Michael Howell, Rising tide of liquidity lifters many boats, but keep an eye on the horizon, 17th January 2020; Caroline Binham, Shadow banking sector shifts into decline, 20th January 2020; Sam Fleming, Philip Stafford, Matthew Vincent, and George Parker, EU rules out permanent

Conclusion

Dramatic as the Global Financial Crisis had been, its consequences for large parts of the world's financial system were limited. Continuity not change was its legacy in many areas. Where its consequences were both major and long-lasting was when accompanied by outside intervention. The most marked of these were the quantitative easing programmes adopted by central banks in order to prevent a liquidity crisis becoming a solvency one and then leading to a world economic depression. Successful as that programme was it left an enduring legacy from which it appeared impossible to escape even as late as the beginning of the 2020s. Intervention had stabilized the banking system and made it more resilient but at the expense of shifting financial activity elsewhere. As the Global Financial Crisis of 2008 had centred on the banking system, and led to a rediscovery of the importance of liquidity, a focus on making banks more resilient was the right call at the time. The problem was that it drew central banks into the moral hazard dilemma where the banking system came to rely upon intervention as a source of both liquidity and stability. Restraining the ability of banks to take advantage of the situation were the Basel Rules as these were applied to the megabanks and enforced by national authorities. However, that left other parts of the financial system free to exploit the opportunities created through the restraints placed on the megabanks, as these were subject to much less rigorous supervision and control. The result was the expansion of the shadow banking system that increasingly acquired a number of the liquidity characteristics of banks themselves. Most obvious of these were funds that promised instant redemption but lacked the means of delivering it because of the nature of their investments. The outstanding question was whether those components of the shadow banking system with a high liquidity exposure were of sufficient size and connectivity to destabilize the global financial system in the event of a failure of one or more of them, bringing down banks as a consequence In turn, would the destabilizing effects spread to markets where clearing houses provided guarantees that transactions would be completed even in the face of multiple defaults by participants? Finally, if a clearing house itself failed what would the consequences be or would central banks, acting collectively, be forced to intervene to prevent such an event taking place?

By 2020 a new set of uncertainties were present in global financial markets with a number being direct results of what had happened in 2008 and the response that had produced among regulators and central banks. What had happened was an acceptance that global financial markets needed to be allowed to evolve and find their own way of coping with issues of both liquidity and solvency while avoiding the perennial question of moral hazard. The global pandemic caused by the coronavirus, and its economic and financial consequences, was the first real test for the arrangements put in place since 2008. The strength of

access deal for City of London, 12th February 2020; John Plender, The seeds of the Next Crisis, 5th March 2020; Robin Wigglesworth, Virus mayhem reflects danger of shock-led trading, 7th March 2020; Robin Wiggleworth, Philip Stafford, and Eva Szalay, trading stability begins to fray as oil slum piles on pain, 10th March 2020; Colby Smith and Brendan Greeley, Fed seeks to limit fallout by boosting repo injections, 10th March 2020; Vivek Bommi, Drop in hedging costs makes US high yield bonds a bargain, 12th March 2020; Joe Rennison and Colby Smith, Cracks in US Treasuries spell trouble for financial system, 13th March 2020; Colby Smith and Brendan Greeley, Fed looks to accelerate purchase of US Treasuries in wake of virus disruptions, 14th March 2020; Tommy Stubbington and Colby Smith, Investors flag up worries over limits of monetary policy to end turmoil, 14th March 2020; Robin Wigglesworth, Covid-19 tips markets into week of chaos as central banks play catch-up with new reality, 14th March 2020; Rana Foroohar, How the virus became a credit run, 16th March 2020; *FT* Reporters, Bank acts to ease liquidity strains, 17th March 2020; Eva Szalay and Colby Smith, Bank hoarding and fears over Covid-19 push dollar higher, 18th March 2018; Philip Stafford and David Keohane, France, Spain, Italy and Belgium ban short selling in effort to restore calm. 18th March 2020.

these arrangements was the resilience of the megabanks and the co-ordinated action of the central banks, led by the Federal Reserve. The weakness was the size of the shadow banking system and its connections to other parts of the financial system. However, what needs to be remembered is that stock markets rise and fall with remarkable regularity, but it takes a banking collapse to produce a full scale financial crisis. In that way the events of 2020 were much more akin to the bursting of a stock market bubble combined with the impact of an external shock than a systemic weakness within the global banking system and an inadequate response from the world's central banks, as had been the case in 2008.

Bibliography

Note: All articles are from the *Financial Times*.

Ablan, Jennifer and Rennison, Joe, 'Investors pile into US corporate bond funds as Fed warns on credit quality', 22nd November 2019
Abrahams, Paul, 'State sales are likely to keep the ball rolling', 17th December 1999
Adam, Nigel, 'Tough competition', 24th May 1991
Adam, Nigel, 'New lending cut short', 27th March 1992
Adams, Christopher, 'Promise of greater liquidity welcomed', 8th July 1998
Adams, Richard, 'An artificial and antiquated straightjacket', 5th December 1996
Adams, Richard, 'Market developed out of a disaster', 9th April 1997
Adams, Richard, 'Voice-brokers are lapsing into silence', 18th April 1997
Adams, Richard, 'Brokers alter shape of things to come', 25th June 1999
Adams, Richard and Jack, Andrew, 'Matif invites bets on EMU', 22nd March 1997
Adonis, Andrew, '6,000km under the seas', 17th August 1993
Adonis, Andrew, 'Lines open for the global village', 17th September 1994
Aglionby, John, 'Jakarta exchange closed indefinitely', 9th October 2008
Aglionby, John, 'Purple tea tipped for place at Kenya auction', 2nd June 2017
Agnew, Harriet, 'City fears loss of access and influence in event of Brexit', 9th February 2015
Agnew, Harriet, 'City urges open philosophy on immigration', 5th October 2016
Agnew, Harriet and Jenkins, Patrick, 'What's next for the City', 3rd September 2016
Alden, Edward, 'Canadian exchanges act to stem listings losses', 6th November 1998
Alden, Edward, 'An unsettling performance', 25th May 1999
Alden, Edward, 'Gains for US houses', 25th May 1999
Alden, Edward, 'TSE members set to vote for restructuring', 10th June 1999
Alden, Edward, 'Fierce struggle with the giant next door', 31st March 2000
Alden, Edward and Morrison, Scott, 'Canada's stock dealing reputation takes a knock', 25th May 1998
Alexander, Lord, 'Bring it all under one roof', 28th February 1997
Ali, Omar, 'Dublin is top destination for financial groups post-Brexit', 9th May 2017
Allam, Abeer, 'Foreign investors key to plans', 28th November 2008
Allen, Kate, 'Canary Wharf set to double workforce', 19th August 2013
Allen, Kate and Fray, Keith, 'Central banks' balance sheets start to shrink', 28th August 2018
Allen, Kate and Stafford, Philip, 'EU sovereign debt costs at risk if access to City banks ends with no-deal Brexit', 4th January 2019
Allen, Robert, 'Control held behind closed doors', 8th November 1996
Allen, Robin, 'Private sector hopes rise', 11th April 2000
Allen, Robin, 'New Floor sets scene for growth', 9th April 2001
Alloway, Tracy, 'Avoiding collateral damage for derivatives', 12th July 2011
Alloway, Tracy, 'Collateral Rush spells challenges for Europe's banks', 20th October 2011
Alloway, Tracy, 'Counterparty risk makes an anxious return', 27th October 2011
Alloway, Tracy, 'Financial system creaks as loan lubricant dries up', 29th November 2011
Alloway, Tracy, 'Higher capital demands and dearer funding bring a dual burden', 2nd December 2011
Alloway, Tracy, 'Traditional lenders shiver as shadow banking grows', 29th December 2011
Alloway, Tracy, 'BlackRock moves in as banks retreat', 2nd October 2012
Alloway, Tracy, 'Banks debate liquidity trade-off', 19th March 2013
Alloway, Tracy, 'Buyers struggle to find a safe landing', 21st November 2013
Alloway, Tracy, 'Collateral Management', 17th September 2013
Alloway, Tracy, 'The debt penalty', 11th September 2013

Alloway, Tracy, 'Goldman promotes its bond platform', 23rd August 2013
Alloway, Tracy, 'Big investors replace banks in $4tn repo market', 30th May 2014
Alloway, Tracy, 'Call for reforms to broker-dealing', 14th August 2014
Alloway, Tracy, 'Legislation to simplify capital raising boosts crowd funding', 5th November 2014
Alloway, Tracy and Bullock, Nicole, 'Banks offer debt product to help skirt new liquidity rules', 30th January 2013
Alloway, Tracy and Mackenzie, Michael, 'Big banks back digital venue for bond traders', 25th November 2013
Alloway, Tracy and Mackenzie, Michael, 'Default swaps face risk of extinction', 16th October 2013
Alloway, Tracy and Mackenzie, Michael, 'Goldman restructures electronic bond trading platform', 23rd September 2013
Alloway, Tracy and Mackenzie, Michael, 'Bond Traders dealt a new hand', 24th September 2014
Alloway, Tracy and Massoudi, Arash, 'ETFs under scrutiny in market turbulence', 28th June 2013
Alloway, Tracy and Massoudi, Arash, 'Non-bank lending steps out of the shadows', 26th February 2014
Alloway, Tracy and Stafford, Philip, 'Protocol plan to boost bond liquidity', 25th November 2014
Amery, Paul, 'ETF giants bet on futures for flows', 2nd February 2015
Anderlini, Jamil, 'China's corporate bonds come of age', 15th June 2007
Anderson, Robert, 'Bourse painstakingly pursues goal to be regional hub', 6th April 2011
Anderson, Robert and Andress, Mark, 'Slovakia bourse to go private', 10th June 2005
Andress, Mark, 'Prague SE sees future in IPOs', 2nd November 2004
Andress, Mark, 'Sleepy laggard shows signs of life', 1st November 2004
Andress, Mark, Anderson, Robert and Cienski, Jan, 'Vienna plans local consolidation', 16th June 2005
Andrews, James, 'Gearing up fast to meet Tokyo trading volume', 10th November 1988
Andrews, James, 'Regulation on way out', 29th June 1988
Andrews, James, 'Trading likely to rise by a quarter this year', 15th July 1988
Andrews, James, 'The latecomer has potential', 20th February 1989
Andrews, James, 'Reforms at hand', 13th March 1989
Andrews, James, 'Sphere of influence', 13th March 1989
Armstrong, Robert, 'Warnings sounded over watered-down Volcker', 23rd August 2019
Arnold, Martin, 'Secondaries market set for growth', 11th August 2008
Arnold, Martin, 'Carney's too big to fail buffer represents clear progress despite doubt', 9th December 2014
Arnold, Martin, 'Barclays admits rigging the market', 21st May 2015
Arnold, Martin, 'Birmingham banks on appeal as financial centre', 26th March 2015
Arnold, Martin, 'SocGen to merge Kleinwort with Hambros', 16th March 2016
Arnold, Martin, 'Brexit relocation threats surge in City', 9th May 2017
Arnold, Martin, 'How US banks took over the financial world', 17th September 2018
Arnold, Martin, 'JP Morgan head warns of tough Brexit effect', 11th July 2018
Arnold, Martin and Dunkley, Emma, 'UK watchdog sounds the death knell for Libor', 28th July 2017
Arnold, Martin and Hall, Camilla, 'Big banks are giving up on global ambitions', 19th October 2014
Arnold, Martin, Jenkins, Patrick and Noonan, Laura, 'Banking', 12th July 2018
Arnold, Martin and Noonan, Laura, 'Finance capitals face low-cost challengers', 10th June 2016
Arnold, Martin and Noonan, Laura, 'US banks warn of fund fragmentation if hard Brexit throws up high barriers', 21st June 2017
Arnold, Martin and Schäfer, Daniel, 'Dark pool allegations a double blow to pledge of "Saint Antony"', 27th June 2014
Arnold, Martin, Walker, Owen and Keohane, David, 'BlackRock and Citi succumb to allure of Paris after Macron vows less red tape', 9th July 2018
Ashurst, Mark, 'Foreigners spark feeling of euphoria', 25th March 1997
Asokan, Shyamantha, 'UK leads in sowing seeds for a sector', 19th July 2008
Astrasheuskava, Nastassia, 'Russia makes fresh effort to take control of its oil price using electronic platform', 15th November 2019
Atkins, Ralph, 'More join the risk business', 15th July 1988

Atkins, Ralph, 'A sterling drama at the money theatre', 15th July 1988
Atkins, Ralph, 'Zurich's precious tradition', 19th December 1988
Atkins, Ralph, 'Authority aims to give early warnings to avert crises', 5th January 2011
Atkins, Ralph, 'High-speed trading aids efficiency, says ECB report', 5th November 2013
Atkins, Ralph, 'With the volume turned down', 12th February 2013
Atkins, Ralph, 'The decline of the Swiss private bank', 12th December 2017
Atkins, Ralph and Stafford, Philip, 'Switzerland's crypto ambitions get boost from digital platform launch by exchange', 7th July 2018
Atkins, Ralph, Stafford, Philip and Masters, Brooke, 'Collateral Damage', 25th October 2012
Atkins, Ralph and Stothard, Michael, 'A change of gear', 1st July 2013
Atkins, Ralph and Watkins, Mary, 'Eurozone crisis forces funding rethink for banks', 15th March 2013
Augar, Philip and McFall, John, 'Is it time to strip the banks of their clutter?', 18th June 2010
Authers, John, 'Merging Nasdaq with the LSE makes real strategic sense and creates deep liquidity', 11th March 2006
Authers, John, 'NYSE plans to diversify after Archipelago merger finalised', 6th March 2006
Authers, John, 'Revenues rise at CBOT', 20th April 2006
Authers, John, 'Spread of derivatives reshapes the markets', 25th January 2006
Authers, John, 'Wall Street's mergermeister', 27th May 2006
Authers, John, 'London blows its trumpet too loudly', 19th November 2007
Authers, John, 'Nationalism bites the dust', 19th November 2007
Authers, John, 'Model of sophistication offers brighter future', 1st October 2009
Authers, John, 'A risky revival', 26th September 2009
Authers, John, 'Black Monday anniversary finds new risks and opportunities', 19th October 2017
Authers, John, 'In nothing we trust', 6th October 2018
Authers, John, 'Time to confess that I hushed up Wall St's scariest day', 8th September 2018
Authers, John, 'Trust', 6th October 2018
Authers, John and Childs, Mary, 'Overpriced, underperforming', 25th May 2016
Authers, John and Cohen, Norma, 'Clearing the floor: how a regulatory overhaul is helping rivals to close in on the Big Board', 14th September 2006
Authers, John and Cohen, Norma, 'An end to the old order', 28th November 2006
Authers, John and Cohen, Norma, 'Exchange merger poses question of liquidity', 19th June 2006
Authers, John and Gangahar, Anuj, 'Euronext integration no bar to success', 23rd May 2006
Authers, John and Gangahar, Anuj, 'In-house clearing threat to NYSE', 9th August 2006
Authers, John and Grant, Jeremy, 'NYSE says it could set up London exchange', 27th June 2006
Authers, John and Mackenzie, Michael, 'Technology endures in spite of Nasdaq fall', 10th March 2010
Authers, John and Newlands, Chris, 'Taking over the markets', 6th December 2016
Authers, John and Postelnicu, Andrei, 'NYSE members vote for merger', 7th December 2005
Authers, John and Tett, Gillian, 'Snapping Point', 23rd May 2007
Baer, Justin, 'From recession to regulation', 27th September 2010
Baer, Justin, 'Proprietary traders weigh up new options', 25th October 2010
Bailey, Andrew, 'Irresponsible conduct carries consequences in British finance', 23rd February 2015
Bailey, Andrew, 'The Woodford episode raises issues for regulators', 10th June 2019
Bailey, Nick, 'We live in a bubble in financial services', 15th September 2018
Baker, Gerard, 'Regional rivals hot on its heels', 19th October 1994
Baker, Gerard, 'Ripple effect of Tokyo's Big Bang', 24th November 1994
Baker, Russell, 'ASX set to control its own destiny', 23rd September 1998
Balls, Edward, 'Tentative recovery stalls', 22nd July 1991
Balls, Edward, 'No advantage in pseudo-scientific futurology', 21st February 1994
Bank for International Settlement *see* BIS
Barber, Alex, 'Barnier vs the Brits', 9th November 2011
Barber, Alex, 'EU to ban naked sovereign CDS', 19th October 2011
Barber, Alex, 'Brexit talks near deal on financial services', 6th November 2018
Barber, Alex, Meyer, Gregory and Stafford, Philip, 'US and EU derivatives truce averts rules crunch', 12th July 2013

Barber, Alex and Scannell, Kara, 'Plans to shift Libor heart to Europe', 7th June 2013
Barber, Lionel, 'How gamblers broke the banks', 16th December 2008
Barber, Lionel, 'The world in focus', 13th February 2013
Barber, Lionel and Grant, Jeremy, 'US regulator eyes London as base for Europe office', 2nd November 2007
Barber, Tony, 'A tale of two complementary cities', 12th June 2002
Barber, Tony, 'Börse's innovative chief strikes the right note', 23rd March 1999
Barber, Tony, 'Celebrations turn to sober reflection', 2nd December 1999
Barber, Tony, 'DBC strives for pivotal role', 9th July 1999
Barber, Tony, 'Young guns take slice of the action', 31st March 2000
Barchard, David, 'Buyers have the whip hand', 23rd April 1988
Barchard, David, 'Good times are deceptive', 26th September 1988
Barchard, David, 'Competing on all fronts', 11th February 1989
Barchard, David, 'Putting down provincial roots', 27th January 1989
Barchard, David, 'A slack year', 12th July 1989
Barchard, David, 'Supervisors' eye on the ball', 11th February 1989
Barchard, David, 'Cut-throat business', 24th May 1991
Barchard, David, 'House in need of repair', 24th July 1991
Barchard, David, 'Investors go elsewhere', 21st May 1992
Barchard, David and Lapper, Richard, 'Seeking a unified system', 18th December 1991
Barham, John, 'Argentine dealers glimpse the future', 1st March 1991
Barham, John, 'Lenient but lopsided', 7th February 1994
Barham, John, 'Designs on neighbours', 6th December 1996
Barham, John, 'Chaotic yet successful', 24th March 1998
Barham, John, 'Crisis causes investors to turn their eyes away', 23rd March 1999
Barker, Alex, 'Brussels forces BoE to rethink banks lifeline', 11th April 2014
Barker, Alex and Jones, Claire, 'ECB agrees UK clearing houses can work outside currency area', 30th March 2015
Barker, Alex, Parker, George and Grant, Jeremy, 'Britain to sue ECB over rules on clearing', 15th September 2011
Barker, Alex and Schäfer, Daniel, 'Scandal-wracked City braced for closer scrutiny', 30th June 2012
Barnes, Hilary, 'Drift of trade to London causes concern', 7th April 1994
Barrett, Claree, 'Aim—20 years of a few big winners and too many losers', 20th June 2015
Bartz, Tim and Bauer, Ina, 'Neuer Markt prepares for foreign influx', 31st July 2000
Batchelor, Charles, 'Over-the-counter market set for expansion', 12th March 1984
Batchelor, Charles, 'Popularity matches that of future exchanges', 12th September 1984
Batchelor, Charles, 'Stock Exchange launches its white paper on single-capacity trading', 20th July 1984
Batchelor, Charles, 'Wider range of contracts urged', 14th February 1984
Batchelor, Charles, 'BT helps to seal the future', 5th March 1985
Batchelor, Charles, 'Concern expressed over electronic equity dealing', 18th November 1985
Batchelor, Charles, 'Smaller players carve out niches', 27th October 1986
Batchelor, Charles, 'Enterprise looks for a way out', 22nd December 1992
Batchelor, Charles, 'A trading headache revealed by a bomb', 5th April 1993
Batchelor, Charles, 'Essential, controversial, popular and profitable', 5th November 2003
Batchelor, Charles, 'Basel 2 favours high quality borrowers', 3rd November 2004
Batchelor, Charles, 'A brief jargon buster', 29th November 2004
Batchelor, Charles, 'EuroMTS launches European T-bill platform', 16th March 2004
Batchelor, Charles, 'Future income protecting the present', 23rd March 2004
Batchelor, Charles, 'Joining Europe's mainstream', 29th November 2004
Batchelor, Charles, 'London leads in trading volumes', 23rd September 2004
Batchelor, Charles, 'Long pedigree of the clearing house for short-term funds', 23rd July 2004
Batchelor, Charles, 'Restructuring at risk from CDSs', 19th October 2004
Batchelor, Charles, 'Taking the mystery out of securitisation', 28th September 2004

Batchelor, Charles, 'Don't get carried away by the lure of cheap borrowing', 28th May 2005
Batchelor, Charles and Fuller, Jane, 'Inland revenue in talks on securitisation', 22nd December 2004
Batchelor, Charles and Skorecki, Alex, 'German banks sign up for true sale', 10th July 2003
Batchelor, Charles and Skorecki, Alex, 'Banks look to create one index', 30th January 2004
Baxter, Andrew, 'Liquidity poses the greatest problem', 21st June 1989
Beales, Richard, 'Fed receives commitments on CDS', 6th October 2005
Beales, Richard, 'New CD electronic broker goes live', 6th December 2005
Beales, Richard, 'Boom time for derivatives markets', 16th March 2006
Beales, Richard, 'New instruments call the tune', 20th October 2006
Beales, Richard, 'Regulator warns on trading backlogs', 26th January 2006
Beales, Richard, 'Exchanges attempting to offer instruments that align with OTC credit derivatives', 23rd March 2007
Beales, Richard, 'Exchanges take the risk plunge', 23rd March 2007
Beales, Richard, 'ICE plans to set up clearing unit', 1st May 2007
Beales, Richard, 'Trading times cut, says ISDA', 20th April 2007
Beales, Richard and Tett, Gillian, 'Hedge funds rival banks for share of US Treasury market', 9th March 2007
Beales, Richard and Wighton, David, 'Concerns mount over risky lending in US market', 14th February 2007
Beattie, Alan, '"Barrow boys" at risk as the currency markets switch on', 6th July 1999
Beattie, Alan, 'Fighting spirit seeps into dried-up markets', 25th June 1999
Beattie, Alan, 'Floor presence thins out', 25th June 1999
Beattie, Alan, 'Knocking spots into the background', 25th June 1999
Beattie, Alan, 'Tullett and Bloomberg plan new broking system', 5th July 1999
Beattie, Alan, Jacob, Rahul and Baker, Gerard, 'Regulators alarmed over high-tech mania', 16th March 2000
Beesley, Arthur, 'Dublin on a high as China aviation sector surges', 6th November 2017
Beesley, Arthur, 'Irish Brokers ring changes as China comes to Kerry', 24th December 2018
Beesley, Arthur, 'Sale brings stock exchange into EU-wide network', 31st January 2018
Beesley, Arthur, 'Cautious Dublin reaps benefits of Brexit exodus', 13th February 2019
Behr, Rafael, 'Beefing up for the battle of the Baltics', 8th March 2001
Beioley, Kate, 'Woodford lifts the lid on open-ended funds', 22nd June 2019
Benoit, Bertrand, 'Steely nerves are an asset for investors', 22nd May 2000
Benoit, Bertrand, 'Testing times for a once solid market', 23rd October 2000
Benoit, Bertrand, 'Tough lessons for the Neuer Markt', 4th October 2000
Benoit, Bertrand, 'Frankfurt has muscle to upstage Brussels', 2nd April 2001
Benoit, Bertrand, 'Gloomy fifth birthday for ailing Neuer Markt', 8th March 2002
Benoit, Bertrand, 'Long-held dream has proved to be unrealistic', 10th June 2003
Benoit, Bertrand and Skorecki, Alex, 'The market has been burnt badly... retail investing has been wiped out for a whole generation', 27th November 2002
Bergstrom, Rupini, 'OMX goal of integrated marketplace a step nearer', 16th November 2004
Bergstrom, Rupini, 'Icelandic exchange considers merger', 28th July 2005
Bergstrom, Rupini, 'OMX planning a rival to AIM', 6th October 2005
Betts, Paul, 'Banks rush to buy French brokers', 9th December 1987
Betts, Paul, 'Market half the size it should be', 10th December 1997
Betts, Paul, 'Stemming the Gucci Trail', 10th December 1997
Betts, Paul, 'Year of reckoning for the ugly caterpillar', 28th February 1997
Betts, Paul, 'Italian bourse plans new segment', 26th June 1998
Bevins, Vincent, 'Caution and tough regulation are all-weather assets', 15th November 2010
Bickerton, Ian, 'Dutch bourse in survival struggle', 28th March 2006
Bickerton, Ian, 'Euronext takes its time to reflect on merger options', 24th May 2006
Binham, Caroline, 'Zen and the art of cracking down on financial market manipulation', 3rd July 2015
Binham, Caroline, 'BoE warns over rapid growth of high-risk corporate lending', 18th October 2018
Binham, Caroline, 'Regulators praise post-crisis derivatives rules', 8th August 2018

Binham, Caroline, 'Shadow banking grows beyond $45tn', 6th March 2018
Binham, Caroline, 'BoE presses banks for living wills to limit bailout damage', 31st July 2019
Binham, Caroline, 'Ringfence rules come into effect for UK banks', 2nd January 2019
Binham, Caroline, 'Woodford crisis down to flawed rules', 26th June 2019
Binham, Caroline, 'Shadow banking sector shifts into decline', 20th January 2020
Binham, Caroline, Crow, David and Jenkins, Patrick, 'Lenders told to triple liquid assets as Brexit protection', 11th March 2019
Binham, Caroline and Fleming, Sam, 'Record fines carry strong echo of Libor scandal', 13th November 2014
Binham, Caroline and Guthrie, Jonathan, 'FCA', 3rd July 2015
Binham, Caroline and Jenkins, Patrick, 'Regulators plan to internationalise UK regime', 12th June 2015
Binham, Caroline and Jenkins, Patrick, 'Bailey signals need for Brexit talks focus on financial services', 8th May 2019
Binham, Caroline and Parker, George, 'Banks increase attacks against wave of regulation', 6th June 2015
Binham, Caroline and Riding, Siobhan, 'Iosco fires back at BoE in spat over fund rules', 22nd July 2019
Binham, Caroline, Stafford, Philip and Brunsden, Jim, 'No-deal Brexit threat concentrates minds at London clearing houses', 10th October 2018
Birchall, Jonathan, 'Caution the watchword in the birth of Vietnamese securities', 26th June 1998
BIS, Financial Derivative Instruments, 1993–2017
BIS, Online Statistics Database
BIS, Triennial Bank Survey, 2019
BIS, Triennial Central Bank survey, 2016
Black, George, 'Challenges for Swift', 15th November 1994
Blackwell, David, 'Moving house broadens LCE's options', 22nd May 1987
Blackwell, David, 'Brighter prospects for a revival', 28th June 1988
Blackwell, David, 'London builds up lead in white sugar contest', 2nd February 1988
Blackwell, David, 'Overlap must be cut', 10th March 1988
Blackwell, David, 'Going for a "buzz" at the Baltic Exchange', 16th February 1990
Blackwell, David, 'Price-fixing volatility attacked', 25th October 1990
Blackwell, David, 'A ring of confidence in the market', 29th November 1990
Blackwell, David, 'London raw sugar to trade on screen from Friday', 9th January 1991
Blackwell, David, 'Market hooked on hedging', 22nd June 1992
Blackwell, David, 'Fox tries to dig itself out of a hole', 1st December 1992
Blackwell, David, 'Fox tries to make up lost ground', 16th January 1992
Blackwell, David, 'Junior market must learn to play by the new rules', 2nd October 2006
Blackwell, David, 'Scattering of seedlings turns into a forest', 30th March 2006
Blackwell, David, 'Signs of recovery seen after years of famine', 16th December 2009
Blackwell, David, 'SmartPool expansion drive', 17th August 2009
Blackwell, David, 'Board subtractions leave Plus feeling minus', 6th June 2011
Blackwell, David and Stafford, Philip, 'Party over as investors walk away from Aim', 3rd September 2008
Blair, Sheila, 'Congress should stay out of new bank rules for loan losses', 5th August 2006
Blanden, Michael, 'Leading players take the plunge', 2nd October 1986
Blanden, Michael, 'A chance to move in on the stock market', 21st September 1987
Blas, Javier, 'Commodities players bid to close the gap on big two', 28th November 2008
Blas, Javier, 'Nymex to offer steel futures contract', 5th August 2008
Blas, Javier, 'Worldwide credit squeeze triggers changes in commodities trading', 14th October 2008
Blas, Javier, '"Beginning of the end" for gold miner hedging', 14th September 2009
Blas, Javier, 'BHP shocks sector on iron ore spot prices', 30th July 2009
Blas, Javier, 'How it all came about', 25th November 2009
Blas, Javier, 'Price critical to global inflation', 30th July 2009

Blas, Javier, 'Sweet taste of success for Cargill as sugar market soars higher', 22nd October 2009
Blas, Javier, 'Wall Street and miners to gain as benchmark system is left behind', 30th July 2009
Blas, Javier, 'Annual contract system collapses', 31st March 2010
Blas, Javier, 'Geneva set to trump London in oil trading', 23rd November 2010
Blas, Javier, 'Into the spotlight', 9th July 2010
Blas, Javier, 'Regulators extend commodities push', 23rd November 2010
Blas, Javier, 'Speculators at fault for food prices, says poll', 11th October 2010
Blas, Javier, 'UBS prioritises agriculture in new division', 1st December 2010
Blas, Javier, 'Battle for cereals derivatives heats up', 20th October 2011
Blas, Javier, 'Glencore trading empire unveiled', 15th April 2011
Blas, Javier, 'Switzerland sees inflow of Russian oil traders at expense of London', 8th February 2011
Blas, Javier, 'Unfashionable actor takes centre stage', 21st December 2011
Blas, Javier, 'Veil slowly lifts on a secretive profession', 24th May 2011
Blas, Javier, 'From missing watches to premium boards', 11th October 2013
Blas, Javier, 'Tougher times for the trading titans', 15th April 2013
Blas, Javier and Farchy, Jack, 'Trafigura plans trade funding drive', 2nd May 2012
Blas, Javier and Farrell, Greg, 'Food producers hedge their way through wheat turmoil', 13th August 2010
Blas, Javier and Grant, Jeremy, 'Rush to put private commodities contracts on public exchanges', 13th October 2008
Blas, Javier and Makan, Ajay, 'Commodities credit crunch eases', 6th February 2013
Blas, Javier and Meyer, Gregory, 'Regulators face risk of encouraging traders to migrate', 5th August 2009
Blas, Javier and Meyer, Gregory, 'All you can eat', 19th May 2010
Blas, Javier and Tait, Nikki, 'France leads the charge on commodities rules reform', 9th September 2010
Blas, Javier and Whipp, Lindsay, 'Asia accepts the need for commodities exchange hub', 22nd October 2008
Blitz, James, 'Forex dealers can buy time', 12th August 1992
Blitz, James, 'A top-hat tradition in the balance', 22nd June 1992
Blitz, James, 'All change in foreign exchanges', 2nd April 1993
Blitz, James, 'Banks gag on money market illiquidity', 15th October 1993
Blitz, James, 'ERM crisis quicken activity', 20th October 1993
Blitz, James, 'Foreign exchange dealers enter the 21st century', 13th September 1993
Blitz, James, 'An insurance or a threat to stability?', 26th May 1993
Blitz, James, 'New anxieties for the banks', 26th May 1993
Blitz, James, 'Stamp Duty on non-resident exchange traded funds to go', 30th November 2006
Blitz, James, Burns, Tom, Cramb, Gordon and McIvor, Greg, 'New axis stirs mixed feelings across Europe', 8th July 1998
Blitz, Roger, 'City launches Brussels office to boost EU clout', 19th January 2004
Blitz, Roger and Stafford, Philip, 'BATS plans to open UK forex platform', 25th March 2015
Blum, Patrick, 'Market in the doldrums', 4th March 1992
Boardman, Rob, 'Shining a light on the importance of dark pools', 23rd February 2015
Bobinski, Christopher, 'Warsaw exchange proves to be a robust youngster', 30th October 1996
Bobinski, Christopher and Robinson, Anthony, 'Warsaw exchange opens with bubbly and braces', 17th April 1991
Bodgener, Jim, 'Immaturity exposed', 21st November 1990
Bokhari, Farhan, 'Spurred on by foreign investors', 28th November 1994
Bokhari, Farhan, 'Karachi hopes for more open trading', 14th April 2008
Bokhari, Farhan and de Silva, Mervyn, 'Foreign buyers cast a spell', 7th February 1994
Boland, Vincent, 'Floor needed to keep prices in Czech', 13th March 1995
Boland, Vincent, 'Greater transparency on the way', 2nd June 1995
Boland, Vincent, 'Consolidation process under way', 26th April 1996
Boland, Vincent, 'Liffe and DTB vie for supremacy', 5th August 1997

Boland, Vincent, 'Reforms promised', 14th May 1997
Boland, Vincent, 'ASX set to demutualise next month', 22nd September 1998
Boland, Vincent, 'Chastened but resurgent', 17th July 1998
Boland, Vincent, 'Easdaq's aim is to break down the barriers', 24th March 1998
Boland, Vincent, 'Europe's exchanges meet to bolster alliance', 18th December 1998
Boland, Vincent, 'Logical development in a fast-changing world', 13th October 1998
Boland, Vincent, 'A place in the holy trinity', 26th March 1998
Boland, Vincent, 'Stock exchange has taken steps to protect its position', 26th March 1998
Boland, Vincent, 'Why Tokyo's bankers are definitely not for tennis', 26th March 1998
Boland, Vincent, 'Bourse alliance squabbles may delay trading harmonisation', 31st August 1999
Boland, Vincent, 'Bourses may face rival single system', 14th September 1999
Boland, Vincent, 'Dealers opt for the alternative', 23rd March 1999
Boland, Vincent, 'Deutsche and ABN in Tradepoint move', 24th September 1999
Boland, Vincent, 'Euro.NM seeks London presence, but is uncertain about AIM', 8th January 1999
Boland, Vincent, 'European exchanges divided on technology platform', 21st September 1999
Boland, Vincent, 'Exchanges broaden their global appeal', 11th June 1999
Boland, Vincent, 'Frankfurt and London put on a brave face', 1st March 1999
Boland, Vincent, 'Frankfurt to seek global investor base', 7th December 1999
Boland, Vincent, 'Italian clearer seeks links', 14th September 1999
Boland, Vincent, 'London SE to change share trading', 6th October 1999
Boland, Vincent, 'Milan joins bourses alliance', 12th March 1999
Boland, Vincent, 'Nasdaq concentrates European minds', 8th November 1999
Boland, Vincent, 'A pan-European enthusiast', 23rd March 1999
Boland, Vincent, 'Pan-European exchange moves closer', 5th May 1999
Boland, Vincent, 'Plan for single Europe bourse shelved', 24th September 1999
Boland, Vincent, 'Race to save the superbourse speeds up', 7th June 1999
Boland, Vincent, 'Sets wins over investors', 18th August 1999
Boland, Vincent, 'Super bourse takes place slowly', 23rd March 1999
Boland, Vincent, '"Superbourse" faces competition', 23rd August 1999
Boland, Vincent, 'Alliances heighten need for clearing unity', 20th July 2000
Boland, Vincent, 'Anglo-Swiss merger yields a new market', 14th November 2000
Boland, Vincent, 'Collapse of exchange merger must not derail cost-cutting', 19th September 2000
Boland, Vincent, 'Debt on the net', 28th January 2000
Boland, Vincent, 'Dotcom venture to aid recovery', 31st March 2000
Boland, Vincent, 'Euronext puts pressure on European markets', 22nd March 2000
Boland, Vincent, 'Exchange chairman rejects link with Liffe', 4th October 2000
Boland, Vincent, 'Frankfurt pushes exchange link nearer break-up', 1st March 2000
Boland, Vincent, 'FSA to commence alternative exchanges inquiry', 24th January 2000
Boland, Vincent, 'Heat is on to create pan-regional market', 31st March 2000
Boland, Vincent, 'Heavyweights attracted by promise of anonymity', 31st March 2000
Boland, Vincent, 'Jiway sets fee of 7 euros per contract', 31st May 2000
Boland, Vincent, 'LSE and Deutsche Börse clear merger obstacle', 22nd April 2000
Boland, Vincent, 'LSE to go-it-alone for trading shares in Europe', 20th October 2000
Boland, Vincent, 'LSE to phase in central counterparty service', 9th March 2000
Boland, Vincent, 'Market shows greater value and maturity', 28th June 2000
Boland, Vincent, 'Merged European bourse plans to expand into London and US', 21st March 2000
Boland, Vincent, 'Merger reshapes the financial landscape', 31st March 2000
Boland, Vincent, 'The next big market force', 10th November 2000
Boland, Vincent, 'Proposed exchange merger looks set for a rocky ride', 20th April 2000
Boland, Vincent, 'A revolution just waiting to happen', 31st March 2000
Boland, Vincent, 'Selling the appliance of alliance', 11th November 2000
Boland, Vincent, 'Shadow over new talks on potential Frankfurt merger', 6th April 2000
Boland, Vincent, 'A share in the future', 18th January 2000
Boland, Vincent, 'Swiss exchange set to move blue chip trading to London base', 11th July 2000

Boland, Vincent, 'System breakdown a boost for alternative trading', 7th April 2000
Boland, Vincent, 'Tentative steps towards greater accountability', 28th June 2000
Boland, Vincent, 'Time for the faint-hearted to beware', 19th May 2000
Boland, Vincent, 'Tradepoint and SWX seal Virt-x merger', 24th October 2000
Boland, Vincent, 'Waiting time for groups with an eye on the LSE', 17th October 2000
Boland, Vincent, 'World's bourses jostle for position as upstarts elbow in', 31st March 2000
Boland, Vincent, 'All bets on hold as market waits out crisis', 25th September 2001
Boland, Vincent, 'Bid for Liffe would be icing on the cake for LSE', 15th August 2001
Boland, Vincent, 'A buying opportunity for the LSE', 24th May 2001
Boland, Vincent, 'Cash conduit that secures London's reputation', 12th September 2001
Boland, Vincent, 'Clearstream set for takeover battle', 31st October 2001
Boland, Vincent, 'D-Day for a stock market migrant', 25th June 2001
Boland, Vincent, 'Deutsche Börse puts sentiment on new issues market to the test', 2nd February 2001
Boland, Vincent, 'Euro gives spur for updating', 21st June 2001
Boland, Vincent, 'European settlement systems under fire', 22nd March 2001
Boland, Vincent, 'Failure to achieve victory puts LSE in the line of fire', 31st October 2001
Boland, Vincent, 'A healthy appetite for Liffe', 29th September 2001
Boland, Vincent, 'Liffe back in the black after reinventing itself', 22nd March 2001
Boland, Vincent, 'Liffe chairman denies LSE bid talks', 23rd August 2001
Boland, Vincent, 'LSE chairman calls for a split in exchange activities', 26th April 2001
Boland, Vincent, 'LSE revamps trading structure', 26th February 2001
Boland, Vincent, 'Nasdaq's lacklustre European launch leaves executives talking of long term', 16th July 2001
Boland, Vincent, 'Nasdaq-Easdaq negotiations to take weeks longer', 1st March 2001
Boland, Vincent, 'Progress of alliances is slow', 28th March 2001
Boland, Vincent, 'RepoClear to include UK gilts service', 22nd August 2001
Boland, Vincent, 'Rift opens between LSE and Europe', 27th April 2001
Boland, Vincent, 'Securing a future', 5th March 2001
Boland, Vincent, 'World's bourses look to find a new role', 28th March 2001
Boland, Vincent, 'Nasdaq falls foul of bear market', 9th August 2002
Boland, Vincent, 'Next step for Nasdaq marked by challenges', 19th December 2002
Boland, Vincent, 'Trading Up', 27th May 2002
Boland, Vincent, 'US markets face up to technology gap', 6th June 2002
Boland, Vincent, 'Banks find a way to spread their risk', 18th February 2003
Boland, Vincent, 'Could a probe of trading practices trigger reform of the New York Stock Exchange?', 12th May 2003
Boland, Vincent, 'Enthusiasm is growing for direct access in US and European securities markets', 24th May 2003
Boland, Vincent, 'Nasdaq halts IPO and pulls out of Europe', 27th June 2003
Boland, Vincent, 'Capital's ecosystem offers fertile ground for growth', 24th January 2017
Boland, Vincent and Barber, Tony, 'Seifert draws close to the summit', 18th April 2000
Boland, Vincent and Buckley, Neil, 'Europe exchanges to merge', 16th March 2000
Boland, Vincent and Davies, Simon, 'Amsterdam SE chief seeks to join alliance', 30th July 1998
Boland, Vincent and Dombey, Daniel, 'The changing face of Europe's markets', 2nd January 2002
Boland, Vincent and Grant, Jeremy, 'Mergers likely amid exchange turmoil', 1st December 2003
Boland, Vincent and Iskandar, Samer, 'Nine into one will just not go', 20th November 1998
Boland, Vincent and Iskandar, Samer, 'Paris deal sets up pact on continental trading', 20th November 1998
Boland, Vincent and Labate, John, 'UK and Germany consider Nasdaq deal', 28th April 2000
Boland, Vincent and Labate, John, 'Sell, sell, sell as exchanges eye consolidation', 30th January 2002
Boland, Vincent and Luce, Edward, 'Electronic bond trading system to expand range', 26th July 1999
Boland, Vincent and Postelnicu, Andrei, 'Specialist firms hit by fall-out at NYSE', 26th September 2003

Boland, Vincent, Postelnicu, Andrei and Barber, Lionel, 'I am a revolutionary. But we need a careful, deliberative process. There is only one New York Stock Exchange', 13th November 2003

Boland, Vincent and Pretzlik, Charles, 'How the LSE managed to miss an open goal', 3rd November 2001

Boland, Vincent and Skorecki, Alex, 'Time called on 24-hour marketplace', 27th June 2003

Boland, Vincent and van Duyn, Aline, 'Investor moods prove difficult to interpret', 21st June 2001

Boland, Vincent and Wassener, Bettina, 'Deutsche Börse takes the cautious approach', 11th May 2001

Boland, Vincent and Wassener, Bettina, 'LSE to select chief amid fears on rivals' IPOs', 23rd January 2001

Bolger, Andrew, 'LSE poised to confirm float plans', 21st May 2001

Bolger, Andrew, 'Still open after Wall Street shuts', 25th May 2001

Bolger, Andrew, 'Big players in the European game', 12th October 2005

Bolger, Andrew, 'UK Share Ownership shifts overseas', 26th September 2013

Bolger, Andrew, 'Corporate loans rise above pre-crisis levels', 11th February 2015

Bollen, Brian, 'Nightmare for harmonisers', 28th October 1993

Bollen, Brian, 'Baby with a big future', 1st March 1996

Bollen, Brian, 'Europe takes to tri-party', 1st March 1996

Bollen, Brian, 'They created the game—so they invent the rules', 5th March 2007

Bollen, Brian, 'The sector stays aloft in a risky climate', 8th September 2008

Bose, Kunal, 'Regional exchanges fail screen test', 10th March 1997

Boulton, Leyla, 'Soviet oil and gas exchange opens this month', 11th June 1991

Boulton, Leyla, 'Birth of a hundred markets', 23rd February 1993

Boulton, Leyla, 'Going from one extreme to the other', 23rd March 1999

Bounds, Andrew, 'Liverpool takes title as second city of wealth management', 29th March 2010

Bounds, Andrew, 'Liverpool's legacy strengthens the fabric of global cotton trading', 9th April 2012

Bounds, Andrew, 'Alternative financials fill gap left by banks', 12th September 2013

Bowen, Christopher, 'Upstarts upset the applecart', 6th June 2002

Bowley, Graham, 'At the heart of everyday life', 16th November 1995

Bowley, Graham, 'New breed of exotics thrives', 16th November 1995

Bowley, Graham, 'Bankers ponder whether to seize the day', 19th November 1996

Bowley, Graham, 'Forex houses sanguine despite possibility of single currency', 6th December 1996

Bowley, Graham, 'Repos may keep City on top', 6th November 1996

Bowley, Graham, 'Troubled road to reform', 1st March 1996

Bowley, Graham, 'UK pushes for equal access to Target', 17th December 1996

Bowley, Graham, 'German, Austrian exchanges in talks', 25th September 1997

Bowley, Graham, 'Historic day for way Bank goes to work', 3rd March 1997

Bowley, Graham, 'MG to move metal trading to London', 1st May 1997

Bowley, Graham, 'Montreal exchange given reprieve', 12th November 1999

Bowley, Graham and Lapper, Richard, 'Gilt-edged opportunities', 19th June 1996

Boxell, James, 'Oil in the workings of high finance', 20th December 2004

Braithwaite, Tom, 'Financial chiefs pay tribute to City-minded practitioner', 18th October 2005

Braithwaite, Tom, 'US Treasury to exempt forex swaps from new rules', 30th April 2011

Braithwaite, Tom, Arnold, Martin and Alloway, Tracy, 'Tough choices confront traditional lenders', 18th June 2014

Braithwaite, Tom and Guerrera, Francesco, 'A Garden to Tame', 15th November 2010

Braithwaite, Tom and Jenkins, Patrick, 'Balance sheet battles', 15th August 2013

Braithwaite, Tom, Mackenzie, Michael, Alloway, Tracy and Chon, Gina, 'Dust starts to settle on the derivatives revolution', 12th September 2013

Braithwaite, Tom, Masters, Brooke and Grant, Jeremy, 'A Shield Asunder', 20th May 2011

Braithwaite, Tom and Rodrigues, Vivianne, 'Wall Street's biggest lenders blame bond volatility on tight regulation', 17th October 2014

Braithwaite, Tom and Stafford, Philip, 'US banks urge action on clearing houses', 13th January 2015

Bream, Rebecca, 'Corporate sector embraces credit swaps', 9th March 2000

Bream, Rebecca, 'Healthy pipeline of deals is emerging', 19th May 2000

Bream, Rebecca, 'Neighbours get too close for comfort', 31st March 2000
Bream, Rebecca, 'Profusion of platforms looking for a niche', 28th June 2000
Bream, Rebecca, 'Surge in M&A comes to the rescue', 19th May 2000
Bream, Rebecca, 'A form of protection for the rising risk of defaults', 25th September 2001
Bream, Rebecca, 'Market participants react to regulatory straitjacket', 25th September 2001
Bream, Rebecca, 'Signs of progress in a volatile market', 21st June 2001
Bream, Rebecca, 'Fixed-income business stays in the limelight', 22nd February 2002
Bream, Rebecca, 'More debt and equity mergers on the cards', 9th September 2002
Bream, Rebecca, 'Plenty of bad news for a market to thrive on', 7th October 2002
Bream, Rebecca, 'Unified approach increases efficiency', 22nd February 2002
Bream, Rebecca and Morrison, Kevin, 'Miners move to London to tap a cash stream', 21st November 2003
Brewster, Deborah, 'US retail investors slump to record low', 2nd September 2008
Brice, Martin, 'Four years of explosive growth for GDR's', 10th November 1994
Brice, Martin, 'Receipts valued at $10bn', 8th November 1994
Brice, Martin, 'Mexican crisis makes its mark', 14th September 1995
Brooker, Nathan, 'How the crash created one global city', 17th March 2018
Brown, David, 'Strategy for a single entity', 29th October 1996
Brown, David, 'Capital market in those of big changes', 30th June 1988
Brown, Jeffrey, 'Major players in their own right', 27th May 1986
Brown, Jeffrey, 'More Players respond as volatility falls', 8th March 1989
Brown, Jeffrey, 'Bells and whistles count', 9th March 1990
Brown, Jeffrey, 'From slow start to relentless build-up', 1st January 2000
Brown, Kevin, 'A gateway to Asia and the Pacific', 5th June 1990
Brown, Kevin, 'Asian Traders warm to dark pool benefits', 4th March 2010
Brown, Kevin, 'Malaysia bourse plans derivatives boost', 28th April 2010
Brown, Kevin, 'Move towards single Asean exchange', 23rd April 2010
Brown, Kevin, 'Region in flux as bourses fragment', 3rd November 2010
Brown, Kevin, 'SGX to offer OTC derivatives clearing', 21st September 2010
Brown, Kevin, 'Singapore's offer sparks talk of Asia consolidation', 2nd November 2010
Brown, Kevin, 'Single Asean market a step closer', 9th February 2010
Brown, Kevin, 'Tora plans pan-Asian "dark pool"', 2nd June 2010
Brown, Kevin, Grant, Jeremy and Smith, Peter, 'Canberra "key" on SGX bid for ASX', 26th October 2010
Brown, Kevin and Oliver, Christian, 'Seoul warms to naked short selling', 13th May 2010
Brown, Kevin and Tucker, Sundeep, 'A high-flying rivalry', 26th April 2010
Brown-Humes, Chris, 'Fear of business going elsewhere', 19th November 2007
Brown-Humes, Christopher, 'CrestCo to pay maiden dividend, give rebates', 23rd September 1998
Brown-Humes, Christopher, 'CrestCo unveils pan-European network for share settlement', 14th September 1998
Brown-Humes, Christopher, 'Cocky OM decides to play David and Goliath', 28th August 2000
Brown-Humes, Christopher, 'Glory days have faded since OM's audacious LSE bid', 24th August 2001
Brown-Humes, Christopher, 'Consolidation is fevered but all bets are still on', 28th November 2006
Brown-Humes, Christopher, 'A grown-up Brady bunch? Why returns in emerging markets are vigorous—for now', 1st March 2006
Bruce, Peter, 'The aim is to get it right on the night', 21st June 1989
Bruce, Peter, 'A patient approach to a near impossible job', 21st June 1989
Bruce, Peter, 'Downside emerges after fairy-tale beginning', 23rd October 1991
Brunsden, Jim and Barker, Alex, 'City to be sidelined by capital markets plan', 30th June 2016
Brunsden, Jim and Jones, Claire, 'ECB attacks EU proposals for boosting clearing house oversight', 18th March 2019
Brunsden, Jim and Khan, Mehreen, 'Brussels to drag UK into court over tax breaks for commodities traders', 24th January 2019

Brunsden, Jim and Stafford, Philip, 'Brussels set to extend access to Swiss exchanges for another six months', 18th December 2018
Brunsden, Jim and Stafford, Philip, 'UK clearing houses face threat of pressure to move to EU', 14th March 2019
Bryant, Chris, 'Welcome to the plumbing capital of the world wide web', 17th April 2014
Bryant, Chris and Cienski, Jan, 'Old Stager has yet to make a comeback', 7th July 2010
Bryant, Chris, Cienski, Jan and Grant, Jeremy, 'Warsaw and Vienna vie for listings', 16th July 2010
Buchan, David, 'Brussels spreads the pain of tax on savers', 9th February 1989
Buchan, David, 'Big Bang switch in 1999', 10th December 1996
Buchan, David, 'Investors take note', 2nd June 1997
Buck, Tobias, 'Dealing costs must be cut, says Brussels', 13th September 2005
Buck, Tobias, 'Competition absent in clearing: EU', 25th May 2006
Buck, Tobias, 'Tel Aviv exchange aiming for a bigger league', 18th December 2007
Buck, Tobias, 'Push to raise Palestinian bourse's profile', 17th March 2010
Buck, Tobias and Cohen, Norma, 'Call to break up exchanges', 20th February 2006
Buck, Tobias and Tett, Gillian, 'Battle heats up over Europe's bond markets', 30th November 2006
Bullock, Nicole, 'Credit easing but cost of debt remains expensive', 21st October 2008
Bullock, Nicole, 'US central counterparty set to clear trades in mortgage debt', 13th March 2012
Bullock, Nicole, 'Nasdaq buys Canadian trading venue', 9th December 2015
Bullock, Nicole, 'Acquiring a reputation', 13th June 2016
Bullock, Nicole, '"Flash Boys" exchange targets level playing field', 16th August 2016
Bullock, Nicole, 'IEX presents regulator with a bumper dilemma', 30th March 2016
Bullock, Nicole, 'US trading upstart IEX is seeking slow progress', 21st June 2016
Bullock, Nicole, 'High-frequency traders adjust to overcapacity and leaner times', 10th March 2017
Bullock, Nicole, 'Higher data fees prompt backlash against exchanges', 18th November 2017
Bullock, Nicole, 'IEX sticks to principles in battle for presence', 2nd June 2017
Bullock, Nicole, 'Battle intensifies over the costs of using US market data', 1st October 2018
Bullock, Nicole, 'Tech IPO crown up for grabs as bourses battle intensifies', 24th April 2018
Bullock, Nicole, 'Top NYSE trader readies for Uber IPO scrum', 9th May 2019
Bullock, Nicole, Mackenzie, Michael and Scannell, Kara, 'Prosecutor stares deep into hidden area of stock trading', 27th June 2014
Bullock, Nicole, Mackenzie, Michael and van Duyn, Aline, 'Fed exit looms over US mortgages', 26th March 2010
Bullock, Nicole and Makan, Ajay, 'Reform debate swirls in the CLO sector', 23rd December 2011
Bullock, Nicole and Meyer, Gregory, 'NYSE chief sees value in the trading floor', 5th November 2014
Bullock, Nicole and Stafford, Philip, 'The focus moves from speed to safety', 24th September 2014
Bullock, Nicole and Stafford, Philip, 'US Exchanges', 8th March 2016
Bullock, Nicole and Stafford, Philip, 'Nasdaq pins hopes on shift to tech, data and analytics', 13th October 2017
Bullock, Nicole and Stafford, Philip, 'NYSE prepares to challenge smaller rival IEX with speed bump of its own', 26th January 2017
Bullock, Nicole and Stafford, Philip, 'Nasdaq chief redoubles drive for data in NYSE dogfight', 3rd May 2019
Bullock, Nicole and Stafford, Philip, 'NYSE and Nasdaq urge court to block fees cap plan', 16th February 2019
Bunker, Nick, 'Escalating the war', 2nd October 1986
Bunker, Nick, 'Still evolving from the cartel', 2nd October 1986
Bunker, Nick, 'Watch Taurus toss out paper', 27th October 1986
Bunker, Nick, 'Electronic stock market takes a leap nearer', 13th February 1989
Burgess, Kate, 'Discord stirs in a polite world', 18th January 2005
Burgess, Kate, 'Regulators test hedge funds' formula', 11th March 2005
Burgess, Kate, 'Luxembourg edges, as London hedges', 19th November 2007
Burgess, Kate, 'Credit crunch: a final twist in rocky road for ex-mutual', 29th September 2008
Burgess, Kate, 'Big British funds cut UK stocks ownership', 13th March 2012

Burgess, Kate, 'NYSE aims to show small is beautiful', 6th August 2012
Burgess, Kate, 'Foreign bidders prepare to climb aboard Baltic Exchange for $100m', 11th March 2016
Burgess, Kate, Authers, John, Cohen, Norma and Jenkins, Patrick, 'End of the phoney war as global consolidation nears', 13th April 2006
Burgess, Kate and Binham, Caroline, 'BBA sets out plans to monitor standards', 16th January 2013
Burgess, Kate and Cohen, Norma, 'Controversial LSE plan raises fears of a Balkanised market', 13th November 2004
Burgess, Kate and Daneshkhu, Scheherazade, 'LSE hopes brewer's exit will encourage more listings', 14th November 2015
Burgess, Kate and Postelnicu, Andrei, 'Why Aim is foreign target of choice', 3rd September 2005
Burgis, Tom, 'Canada sets the pace for free trade in securities', 3rd April 2007
Burgis, Tom, 'Brokers Resist Nigerian Watchdog', 8th June 2010
Burgis, Tom, 'Difficulties of listing a prized asset come to the fore', 24th August 2010
Burgis, Tom, 'Nigeria plans to take bourse public', 24th August 2010
Burgis, Tom, 'Regulator intends to shake up the bourse', 30th September 2010
Burgis, Tom, Masters, Brooke and Saigol, Lina, 'Sants warns on foreign branches in UK', 11th January 2013
Burke, John, 'Tensions beneath the surface', 14th February 1984
Burns, Tom, 'Why bank beats Bolsa', 30th November 1989
Burns, Tom, 'Divided Meffsa looks both ways', 4th June 1992
Burns, Tom, 'Domestic volumes dominate', 20th June 1994
Burns, Tom, 'Timing of launch was fortunate', 11th February 1997
Burns, Tom, 'Foreign funds in a fever', 28th March 2001
Burt, Tim, 'Alliances are just the beginning', 24th March 1998
Burt, Tim, 'Special partners sought', 14th April 1998
Burt, Tim, 'Bloomberg in forex challenge to Reuters', 21st May 2003
Burt, Tim, 'A new vision of finance beckons as rivals prepare for court battle', 12th July 2003
Burt, Tim, 'Reuters loses market share', 28th April 2005
Burton, John, 'Eyeing EC systems', 3rd July 1990
Burton, John, 'Stockholm bourse Sax opens on a sour note', 2nd August 1990
Burton, John, 'The web spreads', 9th March 1990
Burton, John, 'Sax, Sox, tax moves widen interest', 17th October 1991
Burton, John, 'Protectionist policy', 7th February 1994
Burton, John, 'City-state may need more than stability to become leader', 12th April 2006
Burton, John, 'Malaysia relaxes short-selling ban', 24th March 2006
Burton, John, 'Bursa Malaysia in partnership talks with CME', 11th December 2007
Burton, John and Whipp, Lindsay, 'SGX and Chi-X Global plan dark pool', 13th August 2009
Bush, Janet, 'Calm follows squeezed margins', 3rd June 1987
Bush, Janet, 'Pressure grows for freer markets', 3rd June 1987
Bush, Janet, 'A fragile monopoly', 17th February 1988
Bush, Janet, 'Low post crash volumes the major problem', 15th July 1988
Bush, Janet, 'Portfolio insurance loses its appeal', 10th March 1988
Bush, Janet, 'Strategists were a factor but not the cause', 10th March 1988
Bush, Janet, 'Wall Street wants to deal wholesale', 30th August 1988
Bush, Janet, 'Arguments intensify in the regulatory minefield', 26th June 1989
Bush, Janet, 'Five banks with universal plans', 2nd May 1989
Bush, Janet, 'US gears up to meet the challenges of globalisation', 20th December 1989
Bush, Janet, 'Enforcement of securities law remains politically popular', 7th February 1990
Bush, Janet, 'Magic ingredients for an outdated market', 23rd April 1990
Bush, Janet, 'New rule will clear path', 2nd July 1990
Bush, Janet, 'A pointer from New York', 9th March 1990
Bush, Janet, 'Referee tries to be fair to investors large and small', 16th August 1990
Butler, Rick, 'Where the rubber meets a regulatory road', 6th July 2001
Butler, Steven, 'Simex is on target', 19th March 1987

Butler, Steven, 'Investment banks cash in on volatile oil prices', 1st July 1988
Butler, Steven, 'Oil traders braced for the onset of regulation', 10th February 1988
Butler, Steven, 'London's crude oil traders look to the futures', 25th January 1989
Butler, Steven, 'IPE budgets $1m in oil futures launch', 13th June 1990
Butler, Steven, 'Mixed reviews for London oil futures late show', 19th January 1990
Buxton, James, 'Action south of the border', 2nd October 1986
Buxton, James, 'Regional strategy for a second-tier alliance', 16th May 1991
Byland, Terry, 'Wall Street dismayed at ADR levy', 25th March 1986
Byland, Terry, 'Contracts take a fivefold leap', 19th March 1987
Caddy, Peter, Schofield, Mark and Johnson, Chris, 'How the consumer outweighs Opec', 3rd February 1987
Caldwell, Christopher, 'The Volcker rule is a gift to banks and excludes the rest', 14th December 2013
Cameron, Doug, 'Currenex to form exchange', 26th November 2001
Cameron, Doug, 'Ways to enhance voice-broking services', 3rd April 2002
Cameron, Doug, 'Chicago Board Options Exchange sets ball rolling for market listing', 28th June 2006
Cameron, Doug, 'Chicago rises to the European challenge', 15th March 2006
Cameron, Doug, 'Chicago takes the top spot in derivatives', 18th October 2006
Cameron, Doug, 'CME damps speculation of LSE bid', 17th March 2006
Cameron, Doug, 'CME lifts profile in Europe via acquisition', 6th July 2006
Cameron, Doug, 'CME's over-the-counter drive to continue', 25th October 2006
Cameron, Doug, 'CME-CBOT deal set to come under increased scrutiny', 22nd November 2006
Cameron, Doug, 'Futures exchanges' role under review', 30th May 2006
Cameron, Doug, 'ICE announces plans for first coal futures', 1st June 2006
Cameron, Doug, 'Introspection succeeded by internationalism', 26th September 2006
Cameron, Doug, 'NYSE pulls rug from under Chicago Mercantile's feet', 30th May 2006
Cameron, Doug, 'The price was right', 28th November 2006
Cameron, Doug, 'Rivals' rude health spells out merger potential', 28th June 2006
Cameron, Doug, 'All-Chicago deal is coup for city', 11th July 2007
Cameron, Doug and Gangahar, Anuj, 'Banks plan to take CHX minority stake', 22nd June 2006
Cameron, Doug and Gangahar, Anuj, 'Battle for Nymex on hold after bid talks', 23rd August 2007
Cameron, Doug and Hughes, Jennifer, 'Citigroup to join online currency platform', 8th April 2002
Campbell, Katharine, 'Ifox set date for electronic trading', 3rd May 1989
Campbell, Katharine, 'Liffe and the Matif bare their knuckles', 21st April 1989
Campbell, Katharine, 'Liffe dilemma for German banks', 19th January 1989
Campbell, Katharine, 'London traded options seeks to go it alone', 23rd May 1989
Campbell, Katharine, 'They may kick the puppy-dog', 8th March 1989
Campbell, Katharine, 'OM seeks clearance to set up London subsidiary', 2nd June 1989
Campbell, Katharine, 'OTC derivatives take up the running in equities', 9th February 1989
Campbell, Katharine, 'Protection for the portfolio', 8th March 1989
Campbell, Katharine, 'Still no substitute for skill', 26th October 1989
Campbell, Katharine, 'Suspicion lingers in the pit', 8th March 1989
Campbell, Katharine, 'Technology wars ravage Chicago', 21st March 1989
Campbell, Katharine, 'US-UK deal on futures agreed', 24th April 1989
Campbell, Katharine, 'Anxious parents await DTB birth', 26th January 1990
Campbell, Katharine, 'A call for support', 19th June 1990
Campbell, Katharine, 'German banks search for support for futures market', 19th December 1990
Campbell, Katharine, 'New Exchanges on trial', 9th March 1990
Campbell, Katharine, 'No recipe for long-term success', 9th March 1990
Campbell, Katharine, 'Conservative investors find a taste for adventure', 17th July 1991
Campbell, Katharine, 'DTB announces launch of two options contracts', 16th August 1991
Campbell, Katharine, 'German bourses bid for technological heights', 12th June 1991
Campbell, Katharine, 'German exchanges agree to Ibis system', 9th September 1991
Campbell, Katharine, 'Late starter tries to catch up', 13th March 1991

Campbell, Katharine, 'Plans to centralise provoke old squabbles', 11th October 1991
Campbell, Katharine, 'Risks and rewards of change in Frankfurt', 7th January 1991
Campbell, Katharine, 'Roles are reversed for city of bankers', 28th October 1991
Campbell, Katharine, 'Easdaq seeks new chief as rival threatens', 11th December 1998
Campbell, Katharine and Hargreaves, Deborah, 'Chicago ready to give the go-ahead for Globex', 2nd February 1989
Campbell, Katharine and Hargreaves, Deborah, 'Liffe plans to put open-outcry pits on the screen', 2nd February 1989
Campbell, Katharine and Hargreaves, Deborah, 'Bund futures force pace of change', 4th May 1990
Campbell, Katharine and Hargreaves, Deborah, 'Frankfurt fights to regain bunds', 26th November 1990
Campbell Smith, D, 'Hunting for the gig game', 28th November 1983
Cane, Alan, 'Information systems play an integral role', 14th February 1984
Cane, Alan, 'A screen test for the City's dealers', 19th November 1984
Cane, Alan, 'Big need to integrate front and back offices', 16th October 1986
Cane, Alan, 'Expectations are now more realistic', 16th October 1986
Cane, Alan, 'How they screened the biggest game', 27th October 1986
Cane, Alan, 'Increasing quality and speed in dealing rooms', 27th May 1986
Cane, Alan, 'London Stock Exchange spells out its plans for automated trading', 10th April 1986
Cane, Alan, 'Market makers seek bells and whistles for competitive edge', 9th April 1986
Cane, Alan, 'Rapid data: a vital commodity', 24th March 1986
Cane, Alan, 'Sleepers awake to a Big Bang scramble', 13th February 1986
Cane, Alan, 'Systems tailored to market-makers', 16th October 1986
Cane, Alan, 'A Talisman for the future', 12th August 1986
Cane, Alan, 'Unsettled by Big Bang', 12th August 1986
Cane, Alan, 'Advantage from the third phase', 3rd June 1987
Cane, Alan, 'Big-hearted visions of integrated trading', 28th October 1987
Cane, Alan, 'The electronic route to equity', 21st October 1987
Cane, Alan, 'From here to maturity', 30th October 1987
Cane, Alan, 'Pioneers pay a high price', 3rd December 1987
Cane, Alan, 'Deals system wins praise', 15th July 1988
Cane, Alan, 'Outlook bullish for the electronic market', 2nd May 1989
Cane, Alan, 'Rivalry delays progress', 6th November 1995
Cane, Alan, 'Why talk today is relatively cheap', 23rd December 1996
Carnegy, Hugh, 'Two dynamic exchanges', 20th June 1996
Carnegy, Hugh, 'Speculation about mergers', 28th February 1997
Carney, Mark, 'The need to focus a light on shadow banking is nigh', 16th June 2014
Casassus, Barbara, 'Top-slot turnover has quadrupled', 27th May 1986
Casassus, Barbara, 'Report likely to allay anxiety', 10th March 1988
Cecchetti, Stephen, 'A legal challenge for Europe's markets', 17th August 2000
Chaffin, Joshua, 'Bankers emerging from cover after crisis', 12th November 1999
Chaffin, Joshua, 'Banks scatter over Manhattan', 27th November 2001
Chaffin, Joshua, 'Recovery from rare default is taking time', 21st June 2001
Chaffin, Joshua and Weitzman, Hal, 'How clearing helped ICE reinforce ties with banks', 30th April 2011
Chassany, Anne-Sylvaine and Sender, Henny, 'Forced into the shadows', 7th June 2013
Cheeseright, Paul, 'The competition intensifies', 12th July 1989
Chisholm, Jamie, 'Record quota of shares are in foreign hands', 14th July 2007
Chon, Gina, 'Regulators wrestle with cross-border strategy', 24th October 2014
Chung, Joanna, 'EU securitisation may have passed peak', 7th December 2005
Chung, Joanna, 'Derivatives spotlight on Russian companies', 29th November 2006
Chung, Joanna, 'Middle Eastern businesses are looking towards the City for investors and to raise their profiles', 3rd February 2006
Chung, Joanna, 'A capital idea for emerging economies', 30th May 2007

Chung, Joanna, 'Floating along in a sea of global liquidity', 30th May 2007
Chung, Joanna, 'MTS goes for investor order driven trading', 3rd October 2007
Chung, Joanna, 'Tradeweb expands into Asian trade hours', 7th March 2007
Chung, Joanna, 'Divide and conquer', 24th January 2008
Chung, Joanna, 'Exchanges in fight over dearth of new issues', 1st March 2008
Chung, Joanna, 'Complexity has led to cracks in system', 12th June 2009
Chung, Joanna and Arnold, Martin, 'European worries do not make sense', 19th October 2006
Chung, Joanna, Sender, Henry and Mackintosh, James, 'Short-selling ban catches funds out', 20th September 2008
Chung, Joanna and Tett, Gillian, 'MTS chief hedges bets on global expansion', 19th October 2006
Chung, Joanna and Tett, Gillian, 'MTS plans to broaden trading beyond banks', 27th September 2007
Chung, Joanna and Tett, Gillian, 'Trading suspension raises eyebrows', 24th January 2007
Chung, Joanna and Tucker, Sundeep, 'Asia's chain of exchanges keeps adding links', 15th March 2007
Chung, Mary, 'IPE stays calm over New York challenge on Brent contracts', 22nd August 2001
Cicutti, Nic, 'Derivatives' terms made easy', 26th October 2002
Cienski, Jan, 'Warsaw says farewell to the lean years', 21st October 2003
Cienski, Jan, 'Warsaw pays price for world's woes', 21st October 2008
Cienski, Jan, 'Warsaw's target is to be financial hub', 15th January 2008
Cienski, Jan, 'Warsaw seeks partner to revamp bourse', 30th March 2010
Cienski, Jan, 'Bourse pursues foreign groups as it vies to lead central Europe', 20th April 2011
Cienski, Jan, 'Broker sees city as regional centre', 20th April 2011
Cienski, Jan, 'Capitalism has taken root, capital markets not yet', 21st June 2011
Cienski, Jan, 'Friends devise set of winning formulas', 21st June 2011
Cienski, Jan, 'Bourse promises a sharper eye on small listings', 23rd May 2012
Cienski, Jan, 'Buoyant growth gives city clout', 23rd May 2012
Cienski, Jan, 'Vienna and Warsaw vie for pre-eminence', 18th May 2012
Cienski, Jan, 'Sound of overtures in Warsaw and Vienna', 9th May 2013
Cienski, Jan and Skorecki, Alex, 'Warsaw exchange at crossroads', 3rd September 2004
Cienski, Jan and Wilson, James, 'Poland sets conditions on bourse privatisation', 19th November 2009
Cienski, Jan and Wilson, James, 'Warsaw calls off D Börse talks over exchange sale', 1st December 2009
Cifuentes, Arturo, 'Credit of the big three rating agencies under fire', 12th September 2007
Clover, Charles, 'Kazakh bourse awaits helping hand from privatisations', 26th June 1998
Clow, Robert, 'Dull but reliable business wins respect', 22nd February 2002
Cochrane, William, 'A worldwide acceleration', 13th November 1986
Coffee, John, 'Regulation-lite belongs to a different age', 21st January 2008
Coggan, Philip, 'Corporations are chary', 3rd June 1987
Coggan, Philip, 'Lobbying clout grows', 3rd June 1987
Coggan, Philip, 'A more flexible way to manage interest rates', 19th March 1987
Coggan, Philip, 'New players speed trade', 21st April 1987
Coggan, Philip, 'Regulators cramp market's growth', 21st April 1987
Coggan, Philip, 'Regulators take an interest', 3rd June 1987
Coggan, Philip, 'A worldwide stratagem', 19th March 1987
Coggan, Philip, 'Horses for bourses in the world race', 28th November 1988
Coggan, Philip, 'Just a simple idea', 29th June 1988
Coggan, Philip, 'Exchange faces a Catch-22 situation', 20th November 1991
Coggan, Philip, 'Some brokers remain uneasy about reform package', 20th November 1991
Coggan, Philip, 'It's just a small problem', 8th February 1996
Coggan, Philip, 'Nominee comes to the aid of the Clob', 8th February 1996
Coggan, Philip, 'Obstacles to integration', 16th February 1996
Coggan, Philip, 'Bourses fight for supremacy', 24th April 1997
Coggan, Philip, 'City of London no newcomer to upheaval', 4th May 2000
Coggan, Philip, 'High-tech stock slide hits Europe', 16th March 2000
Coggan, Philip, 'Competition intensifies among rival exchanges', 31st October 2001
Coggan, Philip, 'Market slide provokes a new deal for shares', 28th September 2002

Coggan, Philip, 'Swiss caught out as the 1990s bubble burst', 10th December 2003
Coggan, Philip, 'Arguments persist over assessing valuations', 10th October 2005
Coggan, Philip, 'If they all rush for the exit at the same time', 28th May 2005
Cohen, Edi, 'Amsterdam trading buoyant', 12th June 1990
Cohen, Edi, 'A change for the better', 12th June 1990
Cohen, Edi, 'An early stage of development', 12th June 1990
Cohen, Edi, 'Interest reappears', 4th September 1991
Cohen, Norma, 'The bad apple in the other guy's barrel', 8th March 1989
Cohen, Norma, 'A debate intensified by fear', 22nd May 1989
Cohen, Norma, 'A home-loan hurdle', 27th March 1990
Cohen, Norma, 'Clients move from global to local services', 24th September 1991
Cohen, Norma, 'Institutional investors flex their settlement muscles', 10th October 1991
Cohen, Norma, 'Exploiting the differences', 30th April 1993
Cohen, Norma, 'Cash-generating practice', 29th November 1994
Cohen, Norma, 'A City flea waits to draw blood', 4th September 1995
Cohen, Norma, 'Competition comes to market', 23rd June 1995
Cohen, Norma, 'NYSE reviews non-US share trading', 15th June 1995
Cohen, Norma, 'Learning lessons from the US', 1st March 1996
Cohen, Norma, 'Exchange set to announce deals changes', 25th May 1998
Cohen, Norma, 'Industry joins the information age', 12th March 1999
Cohen, Norma, 'Merger of bourses prompts Crest to cut fees', 24th April 2000
Cohen, Norma, 'The remarkable fall and rise of Canary Wharf', 21st October 2000
Cohen, Norma, 'Square mile faces growing threat from the east', 8th September 2001
Cohen, Norma, 'A compelling case for joining forces', 13th December 2004
Cohen, Norma, 'Concerns over competition and governance', 14th December 2004
Cohen, Norma, 'Deutsche Börse chief's overture to the world', 8th November 2004
Cohen, Norma, 'Euronext plan for UK trades', 22nd March 2004
Cohen, Norma, 'Eurosets Dutch Trading Service captures 30% of equity trading', 25th May 2004
Cohen, Norma, 'Exchange in competition spotlight', 15th December 2004
Cohen, Norma, 'LSE a target for bid battle as it spurns Deutsche Börse', 14th December 2004
Cohen, Norma, 'Seeking an all-share formula to merge Europe's stock exchanges', 26th October 2004
Cohen, Norma, 'Big banks and listed companies welcome referral of LSE bids', 30th March 2005
Cohen, Norma, 'Börse left rudderless at crucial moment', 10th May 2005
Cohen, Norma, 'Börse still in the running to buy LSE', 4th August 2005
Cohen, Norma, 'A chance to reform capital markets', 7th March 2005
Cohen, Norma, 'Commission calls for end to European vertical silo model', 30th July 2005
Cohen, Norma, 'Europe to contend with stronger rival', 22nd April 2005
Cohen, Norma, 'Frankfurt body faces post-trade services hurdle', 28th January 2005
Cohen, Norma, 'LSE the key to European domination', 10th January 2005
Cohen, Norma, 'The race to buy the LSE has become an endurance contest', 12th February 2005
Cohen, Norma, 'Borsa Italiana aims for pan-European exchange', 13th October 2006
Cohen, Norma, 'Brussels to act on securities', 10th July 2006
Cohen, Norma, 'A clash of titans: why big banks are wading into the stock exchange fray', 24th November 2006
Cohen, Norma, 'Club of bankers has come full circle', 16th November 2006
Cohen, Norma, 'D Börse facing fresh calls to expose Eurex to competition', 15th September 2006
Cohen, Norma, 'Deutsche Börse woos Euronext', 12th May 2006
Cohen, Norma, 'EU securities code receives mixed review', 12th July 2006
Cohen, Norma, 'Euronext in state of flux over future', 17th May 2006
Cohen, Norma, 'Euronext risks investor wrath', 4th April 2006
Cohen, Norma, 'Funds hint at price for LSE deal', 11th October 2006
Cohen, Norma, 'Goldman to begin off-exchange trades', 13th November 2006
Cohen, Norma, 'Headlong scramble for speed', 28th November 2006
Cohen, Norma, 'Hopes recede for merger of European exchanges', 16th October 2006

Cohen, Norma, 'Level playing fields', 28th November 2006
Cohen, Norma, 'LSE awaits new suitor as Nasdaq pulls bid', 31st March 2006
Cohen, Norma, 'LSE scorns final Nasdaq bid', 21st November 2006
Cohen, Norma, 'LSE shrugs off threat to listings', 5th June 2006
Cohen, Norma, 'LSE's secret software weapon meets traders' need for speed', 24th February 2006
Cohen, Norma, 'Merger talks stall over Euronext, D Börse HQ', 12th January 2006
Cohen, Norma, 'Nasdaq bids £2.4bn for LSE', 11th March 2006
Cohen, Norma, 'Nasdaq goes back on the offensive', 13th December 2006
Cohen, Norma, 'Nasdaq's hunter sees an end to the chase', 21st November 2006
Cohen, Norma, 'Nasdaq's market share of NYSE stocks soars', 16th August 2006
Cohen, Norma, 'NYSE pressed to beat D Börse', 30th August 2006
Cohen, Norma, 'Rivals race to finalise bids for Euronext', 22nd May 2006
Cohen, Norma, 'Shareholders sceptical about LSE proposals', 20th December 2006
Cohen, Norma, 'Special relationship on the horizon', 30th January 2006
Cohen, Norma, 'Swiss exchange to cut its tariffs', 4th September 2006
Cohen, Norma, 'SWX reduces its Virt-x trading fees', 5th September 2006
Cohen, Norma, 'TSE chief promises to strengthen infrastructure', 17th July 2006
Cohen, Norma, 'UK stockbrokers seek clarification from Nasdaq', 12th May 2006
Cohen, Norma, 'Worried Italian banks to discuss Borsa offering', 17th May 2006
Cohen, Norma, 'Citigroup to launch smart ordering', 1st November 2007
Cohen, Norma, 'Competitive age dawns in Europe', 3rd April 2007
Cohen, Norma, 'Defensive move with a useful line in attack', 23rd June 2007
Cohen, Norma, 'Doors open as industry removes barriers', 30th March 2007
Cohen, Norma, 'Kansas City undercuts NYC', 9th February 2007
Cohen, Norma, 'LCH.Clearnet launches appeal for bourses access', 10th august 2007
Cohen, Norma, 'Lehman to launch off-bourse product', 20th April 2007
Cohen, Norma, 'LSE agrees in principle to take over Borsa Italiana', 23rd June 2007
Cohen, Norma, 'LSE outlines measures to help its biggest customers cut expenses', 24th December 2007
Cohen, Norma, 'LSE prepares for freedom from Nasdaq bid', 10th February 2007
Cohen, Norma, 'LSE reaches electronic trading target a year early', 9th June 2007
Cohen, Norma, 'Marathon LSE bid milestone', 8th January 2007
Cohen, Norma, 'Marching orders in the Mifid revolution', 1st November 2007
Cohen, Norma, 'Middlemen sidelined?', 26th July 2007
Cohen, Norma, 'Mifid ushers in a new era of trading', 23rd May 2007
Cohen, Norma, 'Nasdaq chief: LSE faces crucial 18 months', 1st February 2007
Cohen, Norma, 'Nasdaq retreat marks triumph for LSE's Furse', 21st August 2007
Cohen, Norma, 'OMX bid fight puts Greifeld leadership of Nasdaq to test', 3rd September 2007
Cohen, Norma, 'OMX up 10% on talk of link', 13th April 2007
Cohen, Norma, 'Path through the data explosion', 1st November 2007
Cohen, Norma, 'Platforms quick to respond to Project Tortoise', 1st November 2007
Cohen, Norma, 'Price war breaks out among US exchanges', 25th October 2007
Cohen, Norma, 'Reuters to join scramble for real-time data', 11th July 2007
Cohen, Norma, 'Seeking to end a share trading monopoly', 30th October 2007
Cohen, Norma, 'Turquoise appoints chief from Morgan Stanley', 25th October 2007
Cohen, Norma, 'Turquoise reality being fleshed out', 19th April 2007
Cohen, Norma, 'The world was our oyster but Project Turquoise has persistently floundered', 24th October 2007
Cohen, Norma, 'Exchanges appear ready to go over to the dark side', 9th January 2008
Cohen, Norma, 'Bank lists obstacles on path to stability', 18th December 2009
Cohen, Norma, 'System remains vulnerable to shocks', 26th June 2009
Cohen, Norma, 'Crisis thrusts debt-financing theorem back under the spotlight', 5th April 2010
Cohen, Norma, 'Lenders warned over profit and bonus pay-outs', 2nd December 2011
Cohen, Norma, 'Mifid 2 will have profound impact on fixed income', 9th October 2017

Cohen, Norma and Anderson, Robert, 'Exchange rivalries usher in a new era', 21st September 2007
Cohen, Norma and Anderson, Robert, 'Nasdaq finds its European partner in OMX at last', 26th May 2007
Cohen, Norma, Anderson, Robert and Gangahar, Anuj, 'Nasdaq goes Nordic with $3.7bn deal for OMX', 26th May 2007
Cohen, Norma and Authers, John, 'LSE investors are holding out for another bidder to emerge', 21st February 2006
Cohen, Norma and Authers, John, 'Nasdaq increases LSE stake to 18.7%', 4th May 2006
Cohen, Norma and Authers, John, 'Nasdaq prepares for price war if NYSE cuts tariffs', 21st August 2006
Cohen, Norma and Authers, John, 'New Deutsche Börse bid to lure Euronext from NYSE', 20th June 2006
Cohen, Norma and Authers, John, 'NYSE stock offering lifts exchanges', 6th May 2006
Cohen, Norma, Authers, John and Grant, Jeremy, 'NYSE says it could set up London exchange', 19th June 2006
Cohen, Norma, Blackwell, David and Grant, Jeremy, 'Top SEC official calls Aim a casino', 9th March 2007
Cohen, Norma and Cameron, Doug, 'Participants get ready for realignment', 22nd May 2006
Cohen, Norma and Gangahar, Anuj, 'Nasdaq looks at Europe growth via Sweden', 14th September 2006
Cohen, Norma and Grant, Jeremy, 'Clearers' ownership model under scrutiny', 23rd December 2010
Cohen, Norma, Grant, Jeremy and Postelnicu, Andrei, 'Leading exchanges consider their moves in the race to consolidate', 11th March 2005
Cohen, Norma and Jenkins, Patrick, 'LSE suitors face bid constraints', 30th July 2005
Cohen, Norma and O'Murchu, Cynthia, 'Owners risked homes as crash neared', 19th December 2011
Cohen, Norma, Saigol, Lina and Hume, Neil, 'Nasdaq in early talks to acquire OMX', 11th September 2006
Cohen, Norma and Simensen, Ivar, 'D Börse lands in the US via ISE', 1st May 2007
Cohen, Norma and Smith, Alison, 'Heat turned on self-regulation', 28th July 1995
Cohen, Norma and Tett, Gillian, 'Icap sets sights on MTS platform', 25th June 2007
Cohen, Norma and White, Ben, 'LSE remains a bid target for stateside suitors', 31st March 2006
Cohen, Norma and Wiesmann, Gerrit, 'ECB pledges to consult on settlement system T2S', 9th March 2007
Cohen, Norma and Wighton, David, 'Citi gives London priority', 19th July 2007
Cohen, Ronald, 'Special care for young companies', 8th March 1994
Colchester, Nicholas, 'A heavyweight sheds pounds', 8th April 1986
Coles, Adrian, 'UK home ownership typical of EU', 10th July 1995
Colitt, Leslie, 'Face to face with reality', 1st July 1992
Conboye, Janina, 'Computers create demand for a different set of skills', 14th July 2011
Considine, Jill, 'Let the customers decide on European clearing', 21st January 2004
Cooke, Kieran, 'Offshore Labuan hits snags', 19th September 1995
Cooke, Kieran, 'Rising hub of global trading', 6th June 1995
Cookson, Clive, '24-hour traders', 9th November 1989
Cookson, Robert, 'Demand for "funky" shares swamps new Chinese exchange', 31st October-1st November 2009
Cookson, Robert, 'Asian regulators launch reforms for OTC derivatives', 25th February 2010
Cookson, Robert, 'Beijing gears up for key reforms on equity trades', 30th March 2010
Cookson, Robert, 'HK eclipses rivals as the place to list', 7th October 2010
Cookson, Robert, 'Regulators' turf war helps market take root', 25th February 2010
Cookson, Robert, 'Shenzhen takes over as China's listing hub', 19th October 2010
Cookson, Robert, 'Short selling opens doors in China', 12th January 2010
Cookson, Robert, 'Doubts on Hong Kong secondary listings', 18th May 2011
Cookson, Robert, 'HKEx looks to forge links with Shanghai and Shenzhen bourses', 19th August 2011

Cookson, Robert and Hughes, Chris, 'CFDs blamed for higher volatility across traditional stock markets', 9th October 2008
Cookson, Robert, O'Connor, Sarah and Davies, Paul J., 'Painful lessons to be learnt for CDSs', 11th January 2008
Cornish, Chloe and Murphy, Hannah, 'Crypto bubble bursts after brief history of surges and plunges', 21st August 2018
Corrigan, Tracy, 'Investors attracted by firmer currency', 2nd July 1990
Corrigan, Tracy, 'The syndicate disbands', 13th December 1990
Corrigan, Tracy, 'Borrowers rush to tap newly-opened Paris market', 13th March 1991
Corrigan, Tracy, 'A broader tool found for hedging', 3rd April 1991
Corrigan, Tracy, 'Competition helps cut costs', 29th April 1991
Corrigan, Tracy, 'Ecu swaps market grows despite drawbacks', 24th October 1991
Corrigan, Tracy, 'Europeans edge forward', 19th June 1991
Corrigan, Tracy, 'Finland opens doors to foreign investment', 11th January 1991
Corrigan, Tracy, 'Fox orders review of structure by year-end', 19th November 1991
Corrigan, Tracy, 'The heat is on for Italian bond futures', 19th September 1991
Corrigan, Tracy, 'Liffe aims for ECU contract success', 6th March 1991
Corrigan, Tracy, 'Liffe merger improves outlook for equity options', 29th October 1991
Corrigan, Tracy, 'London Fox', 16th August 1991
Corrigan, Tracy, 'Specialist alive and well in nascent market', 19th June 1991
Corrigan, Tracy, 'Treasurers learn to hedge their bets', 28th March 1991
Corrigan, Tracy, 'Uncertain future for stock option trading', 17th December 1991
Corrigan, Tracy, 'Where innovation prevails', 13th March 1991
Corrigan, Tracy, 'Currency upheaval wins converts', 8th December 1992
Corrigan, Tracy, 'Diversification is the spur', 19th March 1992
Corrigan, Tracy, 'End of rapid growth', 20th July 1992
Corrigan, Tracy, 'Europe takes a bigger share', 19th March 1992
Corrigan, Tracy, 'An innovative way of raising money', 20th July 1992
Corrigan, Tracy, 'Liffe and market makers resolve argument', 23rd March 1992
Corrigan, Tracy, 'A marriage made in the market place', 15th January 1992
Corrigan, Tracy, 'A new Liffe together', 4th February 1992
Corrigan, Tracy, 'Small markets stock up', 19th March 1992
Corrigan, Tracy, 'Techniques find new markets', 19th March 1992
Corrigan, Tracy, 'US pioneers lured to new frontier by rich packages', 8th December 1992
Corrigan, Tracy, 'Volatility demands ingenuity', 8th December 1992
Corrigan, Tracy, 'Divisions hazy in OTC derivatives clearing battle debate', 13th September 1993
Corrigan, Tracy, 'DTB and Matif in co-operation agreement', 14th January 1993
Corrigan, Tracy, 'Dull can be dynamic', 27th May 1993
Corrigan, Tracy, 'Europe waits for floodgates to open', 20th October 1993
Corrigan, Tracy, 'Exchanges fight for the future across Europe', 15th January 1993
Corrigan, Tracy, 'Light at the end of the tunnel', 11th November 1993
Corrigan, Tracy, 'Moving on to centre stage', 20th October 1993
Corrigan, Tracy, 'Quirky offshoots gain respect', 20th October 1993
Corrigan, Tracy, 'A short cut to domination', 20th October 1993
Corrigan, Tracy, 'Swaps market may be bigger than estimated', 16th November 1993
Corrigan, Tracy, 'Traditional split in derivatives is less clear-cut', 25th January 1993
Corrigan, Tracy, 'Volume rises to record levels', 24th September 1993
Corrigan, Tracy, 'Banks chase new business', 26th May 1994
Corrigan, Tracy, 'Mood is sombre as bears spoil the fun', 26th May 1994
Corrigan, Tracy, 'On trial for dangerous dealing', 21st March 1994
Corrigan, Tracy, 'Privatisation the driving force', 26th May 1994
Corrigan, Tracy, 'Securitisation: a viable financing option', 22nd August 1994
Corrigan, Tracy, 'The tail still wags the dog', 26th May 1994
Corrigan, Tracy, 'Funds ready if the price is right', 14th September 1995

Corrigan, Tracy, 'Daunting price but high rewards', 1st May 1997
Corrigan, Tracy, 'Nasdaq's new regime', 13th January 1997
Corrigan, Tracy and Byland, Terry, 'Stock market tail wags vigorously', 3rd May 1994
Corrigan, Tracy and Harris, Clay, 'Thundering herd comes storming in out of the blue', 20th November 1997
Corrigan, Tracy and Harverson, Patrick, 'Ever more complex', 8th December 1992
Corrigan, Tracy and Morse, Laurie, 'A global game for allies and rivals', 8th December 1992
Corrigan, Tracy and Morse, Laurie, 'Trouble after hours', 3rd June 1993
Corrigan, Tracy and Waters, Richard, 'Japan turns to securitisation', 20th March 1991
Corzine, Robert, 'Energy Groups set to tender for IPE stake after merger talks fail', 10th May 1999
Corzine, Robert, 'Executives attempt to stretch Swift's wings', 4th December 1991
Corzine, Robert, 'Prospect of UK competition sparks gas trading plans', 9th June 1995
Costello, Evelyn, 'The big engine shows its capacity', 3rd December 1987
Cowper, Richard, 'Struggling to spread its wings', 10th May 2000
Cox, Adrian, 'Multiple threats still loom for the investment banking model', 1st April 2009
Coyle, Dominick, 'Europeans challenge the capital place for business', 17th June 1989
Crabtree, James, 'India to tighten trading controls after flash crash', 10th October 2012
Crabtree, James, 'Frustrated investors push for IPOs of Indian stock exchanges', 3rd July 2015
Crabtree, James and Stafford, Philip, 'New Exchange opens in India', 11th February 2013
Cramb, Gordon, 'Aiming to be both liquid and transparent', 21st October 1987
Cramb, Gordon, 'Unthinkable achieved', 18th November 1993
Cramb, Gordon, 'Two pioneers are extending the frontiers', 28th February 1997
Cramb, Gordon, 'Benelux markets form trading link', 25th November 1998
Crawford, Leslie, 'Kenyans go on equity buying spree', 31st December 1994
Crawford, Leslie and Cohen, Norma, 'BME unveils plan to seek a public listing', 28th April 2005
Croft, Jane, 'Brokers talk up the positive', 22nd November 2002
Croft, Jane, 'Bite-size former building societies turn heads of investors', 1st April 2006
Croft, Jane, 'Profits in the billions underline the vital role of banking in the economy', 18th February 2006
Croft, Jane, 'Bid spotlight once again falls on A&L', 28th May 2007
Croft, Jane, 'Lucrative market may yet prove house of cards', 20th February 2007
Croft, Jane, 'B&B poised for state ownership', 29th September 2008
Croft, Jane, 'A long and winding road to recovery: the banks', 13th September 2008
Croft, Jane, 'The danger of relying too much on only one tool', 22nd March 2011
Croft, Jane and Daneshkhu, Scheherazade, 'Bank warns on risks of property lending', 13th December 2004
Croft, Jane and Giles, Chris, 'Fury over Rock Nationalisation', 18th February 2008
Croft, Jane and Jenkins, Patrick, 'Mutual suspicion', 3rd September 2009
Crooks, Ed, 'Capital keeps its prominence as European finance centre', 8th February 2002
Crooks, Ed, 'Bank owes much to the loyalty of "Steady Eddie"', 28th June 2003
Crooks, Ed and Grant, Jeremy, 'Nasdaq to launch UK power market', 27th November 2008
Crow, David, 'Banks strain to effect a post-crisis funding fix', 25th March 2019
Crow, David, 'The last man in European investment banking', 23rd August 2019
Crow, David and Morris, Stephen, 'The battle for Barclays', 21st January 2019
Cruickshank, Don, 'Clearing away inefficiency', 16th May 2001
Cumbo, Josephine and Wigglesworth, Robin, 'The pension house is on fire', 18th November 2019
Curry, Lynne, 'Heavy demand for shares', 16th June 1992
Daneshkhu, Scheherazade, 'Demand for professional expertise nets trade surplus', 12th September 2005
Daneshkhu, Scheherazade and Giles, Chris, 'King acts to avoid nightmare scenario', 17th January 2005
Daneshkhu, Scheherazade and Giles, Chris, 'City becomes undeniable engine of growth', 27th March 2006
Daneshkhu, Scheherazade and Giles, Chris, 'Warning of risks in over-valued markets', 18th January 2006

Daniel, Caroline, 'As mania grows, prices are leaping ahead', 10th March 2000
Daniel, Patrick, 'B&C cliff-hanger still runs', 15th July 1988
Darbyshire, Madison, 'Basel watchdog adopts tougher line after urging banks to be wary of risks', 14th March 2019
Darbyshire, Madison, 'Arrival of passive fund leader Vanguard rattles UL investment advice industry', 10th January 2020
Davey, Emma, 'Slow but steady convergence', 16th November 1995
Davies, Howard, 'We need urgently to rationalise the rules on capital', 25th September 2009
Davies, Jonathan, 'High-frequency traders: heroes or hoodlums?', 21st April 2014
Davies, Paul J., 'Raising the roof with covered bonds', 2nd November 2005
Davies, Paul J., 'A brouhaha over best execution', 18th July 2006
Davies, Paul J., 'Concerns over rapid growth of CMBS deals among banks', 24th March 2006
Davies, Paul J., 'Failure of LBOs a risk to debt markets', 1st December 2006
Davies, Paul J., 'FSA backing for UK bond markets', 6th July 2006
Davies, Paul J., 'Markit to launch trade finance and index service', 30th November 2006
Davies, Paul J., 'Securitisation enters a fresh phase of life', 25th April 2006
Davies, Paul J., 'Securitisations set to keep on robust growth path', 3rd February 2006
Davies, Paul J., 'Bond markets likely to escape strict transparency', 2nd November 2007
Davies, Paul J., 'The dangers inherent in imprudent lending', 5th March 2007
Davies, Paul J., 'Eurex has confidence in credit derivatives', 23rd March 2007
Davies, Paul J., 'Europe's hottest trades', 28th May 2007
Davies, Paul J., 'LiquidityHub launches swaps product', 23rd October 2007
Davies, Paul J., 'NYSE Euronext in dark liquidity plan', 25th October 2007
Davies, Paul J., 'RMBS register hot first quarter', 3rd April 2007
Davies, Paul J., 'Armageddon fears ease, but lending needs to begin again', 16th October 2008
Davies, Paul J., 'Effort to bring credit ratings into clearer focus gathers pace', 5th August 2008
Davies, Paul J., 'High noon chimes for collateral with no name', 10th October 2008
Davies, Paul J., 'Moody's reviews six SIVs for downgrade', 25th April 2008
Davies, Paul J., 'Securitisation provides liquidity', 26th November 2008
Davies, Paul J., 'Credit derivatives drive hits a wall', 2nd February 2009
Davies, Paul J., 'NY insurance market on horizon', 5th March 2010
Davies, Paul J., 'Lack of experience restrains investment in liquidity swaps', 3rd October 2011
Davies, Paul J., 'Banks look to insurers for lessons', 16th April 2012
Davies, Paul J. and Beales, Richard, 'New players join the credit game', 14th March 2007
Davies, Paul J. and Kaminska, Izabella, 'Banks seek help from new set of institutions', 22nd December 2010
Davies, Paul J. and Scholtes, Saskia, 'Interbank rate easing drives liquidity hopes', 3rd January 2008
Davies, Paul J. and van Duyn, Aline, 'Collapse of bank shakes foundations of the CDS industry', 16th September 2008
Davies, Paul J. and Weitzman, Hal, 'CME and Markit launch OTC land grab', 22nd July 2008
Davies, Rachel, 'Invasion of the City increases', 15th July 1985
Davies, Simon, 'When the bubble had to burst', 18th September 1992
Davies, Simon, 'Focus on a dynamic present', 20th October 1993
Davies, Simon, 'Taking a position in the market', 28th June 1994
Davies, Simon, 'IPE may switch to electronic trading', 25th September 1997
Davies, Simon, 'Vital role in restructuring', 8th December 1997
Davies, Simon, 'Battle of the bourses', 14th May 1998
Davies, Simon, 'Cost cuts fuel mergers', 17th July 1998
Davies, Simon, 'Equity culture growing fast', 23rd January 1998
Davies, Simon, 'Futures trade in the balance', 8th July 1998
Davies, Simon, 'Junk bonds are back in fashion', 1st May 1998
Davies, Simon, 'Myriad possibilities', 1st May 1998
Davies, Simon, 'Powerful forces for change', 30th April 1998
Davies, Simon, 'Stock exchanges get down to details of European alliance', 9th July 1998

Davies, Simon, 'Success masks market turmoil', 24th March 1998
Davies, Simon and Graham, George, 'Europe's Big Bang', 8th July 1998
Davis, Gregory, 'Index funds are not to blame for market volatility', 31st October 2018
Davis, Phil, 'The search is now on for new ideas', 11th October 2004
Davis, Phil, 'Howls of anguish meet EU proposals on trading reforms', 18th April 2011
Davis, Phil, 'London feels the force of regulation', 16th May 2011
Dawkins, William, 'Expansion from a broader base', 12th March 1984
Dawkins, William, 'Boisterous youngster has come of age', 30th January 1985
Dawkins, William, 'USM growth matched by that of its smaller rival', 30th January 1985
Dawkins, William, 'Buy-outs bring benefits', 2nd October 1986
Dawkins, William, 'Block trading review on the way', 9th September 1991
Dawkins, William, 'Bourse regulators back plan for reforms', 10th July 1991
Dawkins, William, 'France presses on with liberalisation', 26th September 1991
Dawkins, William, 'French bourse heads for second wave of reforms', 9th September 1991
Dawkins, William, 'French brokers call for reforms', 18th July 1991
Dawkins, William, 'Small bang fall-out', 12th December 1991
Dawkins, William, 'A big bang in slow motion', 10th December 1996
Dawkins, William, 'Last chance to catch up', 25th March 1997
de Jacquelot, Patrick, 'London's irresistible lure', 22nd October 1990
de Jonquières, Guy, 'Trusting the market', 16th September 1987
de Jonquières, Guy, '1992: countdown to reality', 19th February 1988
de Jonquières, Guy, 'Risk, opportunities and arduous negotiations', 18th May 1988
de Jonquières, Guy, 'Single EU securities market at risk', 16th May 1995
de Jonquières, Guy, 'Happy end to a cliff hanger', 15th December 1997
de Jonquières, Guy, 'WTO risk to financial markets', 16th October 1997
de Larosière, Jacques, 'Do not be seduced by the simplicity of ringfencing', 27th September 2012
de Larosière, Jacques and Lebegue, Daniel, 'Bringing harmony to Europe's markets', 14th September 2000
de Rothschild, Evelyn, 'Banking must pursue the holy grail of confidence', 25th June 2013
Demos, Telis, 'Interest of markets and regulators grows', 4th November 2011
Demos, Telis, 'Nasdaq OMX lures trades to platform', 31st January 2011
Demos, Telis, 'Quandary for Nasdaq returns with bid failure', 17th May 2011
Demos, Telis, 'Nasdaq upbeat over tie-ups', 2nd February 2012
Demos, Telis, Stafford, Philip and Grant, Jeremy, 'London clearing a priority for NYSE', 11th February 2012
Demos, Telis and van Duyn, Aline, 'Debate reopens over equity trades', 21st December 2010
Demos, Telis and Weitzman, Hal, 'Speed will not always bring a bonanza', 10th October 2011
Dempsey, Judy, 'The Börse finally wakes up', 16th May 1989
Dempsey, Judy, 'Bulgaria enters the bourse business', 28th November 1991
Dempsey, Judy, 'Legislative fillip sought', 30th March 1992
Dempsey, Judy, 'Germany unveils plan to boost stock market competitiveness', 20th July 1996
Dempsey, Judy, 'Tel Aviv mulls tax reforms', 8th May 2000
Dempsey, Michael, 'Trend-setters of the financial world', 2nd July 1997
Denton, Nicholas, 'Budapest's first year disappoints investors', 15th June 1991
Denton, Nicholas, 'Banks plan clearing house for trade in emerging market debt', 10th June 1996
Devi, Sharmila, 'Battle is on to acquire listings', 23rd March 1999
Dickson, Martin, 'Now the Swiss call the shots', 17th December 1990
Dickson, Martin, 'NYSE seeks unified circuit breakers', 13th June 1990
Dickson, Martin, 'New York has a fresh champion', 2nd January 1991
Dickson, Martin, 'Helpless infant grows into mature part of the financial framework', 27th March 1998
Dickson, Martin, 'Don Cruickshank's problems are only just beginning', 16th September 2000
Dickson, Martin, 'Entering the endgame with a badly weakened position', 3rd November 2001
Dickson, Martin, 'The market is another country for City's go-between', 7th April 2001

Dickson, Martin, 'Capital Gain: how London is thriving and taking on the global competition', 27th March 2006
Dickson, Tim, 'Antwerp polishes up diamond sales', 22nd February 1989
Dickson, Tim, 'Brussels braced for little bang reforms', 28th November 1990
Dickson, Tim, 'Coming soon, the Euro pension', 12th July 1990
Dickson, Tim, 'Exposed by the market's transparency', 12th December 1991
Dinmore, Guy, 'Slow progress made in Zagreb', 28th May 1997
Dixon, Hugo, 'Men of mutuality look to profits', 14th February 1987
Dixon, Hugo, 'The phone redraws map of the world', 8th June 1990
Dixon, Hugo, 'Reconnecting charges with costs', 3rd April 1990
Dixon, Hugo and Staple, Greg, 'New perspective on patterns of power', 7th October 1991
Dizard, John, 'Arguing over who owns a clearing time bomb', 8th May 2017
Dizard, John, 'Brexit could be a toy train crash for derivatives', 8th October 2018
Dizard, John, 'Baselheads are crushing EU project finance', 2nd December 2019
Dizard, John, 'Eyes front, fund bosses, it's Carney's army now', 1st July 2019
Dizard, John, 'Fed standing repo facility comes into view', 30th September 2019
Dizard, John, 'Grandma will lose in a clearing house crisis, too', 4th March 2019
Dizard, John, 'H20 is an omen: a liquidity crisis lurks', 15th July 2019
Dodsworth, Terry, 'Master of the game no longer', 27th May 1986
Dodwell, David, 'Now for silver linings and tight rules', 10th March 1988
Dombey, Daniel, 'Lack of growth signals need for reinvention', 7th June 2001
Dombey, Daniel, 'Transatlantic invasion keeps industry thriving', 7th June 2001
Dombey, Daniel and Skorecki, Alex, 'LSE reaches deal on Euroclear', 13th December 2001
Dombey, David, 'Call for lead EU financial supervisor', 16th June 2004
Donaldson, William, 'A simple new rule that gives investors priority', 8th April 2005
Done, Kevin, 'Concern over corporate disclosure', 26th April 1996
Donnan, Shawn, 'Ebbs and capital flows', 22nd August 2017
Drexel Burnham Lambert, Advertisement, 27th October 1986
Drummond, James, 'The attraction is still there', 27th January 2005
Drummond, James, 'Raft of bourses crowds market', 24th July 2007
Drummond, James, 'Bubble fears amid liquidity', 10th December 2010
Drummond, Lachland, 'Closer Overseas Ties', 5th March 1985
Dullforce, William, 'Tax cuts urged to revive Swiss market', 14th March 1986
Dullforce, William, 'Share registration rules under fire', 28th June 1988
Dullforce, William, 'Soffex will eschew the ring's hurly burly', 10th March 1988
Dullforce, William, 'Prices ignore good forecasts', 19th December 1989
Dullforce, William, 'How Geneva is still holding its ground', 9th October 1990
Dullforce, William, 'Squalls in a safe haven', 13th December 1990
Dullforce, William, 'Swiss under pressure', 29th March 1990
Dullforce, William, 'Outlook fair but uncertain', 17th December 1991
Dunkley, Emma, 'Challenger banks branch out into business loans', 5th November 2015
Dunkley, Emma, 'Challengers fail to loosen big four's grip', 5th January 2015
Dunkley, Emma, 'Singapore exchange to increase derivatives trading fees as much as tenfold', 12th December 2017
Dunkley, Emma, 'Brexit delays Hong Kong-LME tie up', 25th January 2018
Dunkley, Emma, 'HKEX looks to trading suspensions after string of accounting scandals', 18th October 2018
Dunkley, Emma, 'Mainland's curbs spell downside for HK bourse in contest for listings', 21st July 2018
Dunkley, Emma, 'Mumbai bourse seeks to block Singapore's launch of Indian equity futures contracts', 23rd May 2018
Dunkley, Emma and Hancock, Tom, '2018 HKEX move clears path for China biotech challenge to New York hub', 4th April 2018
Dunne, Nancy, 'A bright spot in the gloom', 11th December 1985

Dunne, Nancy, 'Innovation becomes basis for expansion', 5th March 1985
Dunne, Nancy, 'London scores sweet victory', 28th July 1987
Durr, Barbara, 'Chicago lines up a link with Japan', 13th June 1990
Durr, Barbara, 'Comex chief talking himself out of a job', 22nd March 1990
Durr, Barbara, 'Japanese derivatives approved by CBOT', 21st June 1990
Durr, Barbara, 'Moscow marketeers stampede to Chicago', 13th June 1990
Durr, Barbara, 'Nymex pipes in its natural gas contract', 4th April 1990
Durr, Barbara, 'Open outcry from Chicago's pits', 27th June 1990
Durr, Barbara, 'Potentially crippling attack', 25th June 1990
Durr, Barbara, 'US exchanges fight dual trading ban', 18th July 1990
Durr, Barbara, 'US exchanges race for 24-hour trading', 27th June 1990
Durr, Barbara, 'CBOT to launch first insurance futures', 26th February 1991
Durr, Barbara, 'Competition grows fiercer and spawns new alliances', 22nd July 1991
Durr, Barbara, 'New futures exchange in US', 27th February 1991
Durr, Barbara, 'Nymex plans 1992 launch for electronic trading', 8th November 1991
Durr, Barbara, 'Plea for a level playing field', 13th June 1991
Durr, Barbara, 'World market share shrinks', 13th March 1991
Durr, Barbara, 'Exchange stakes out fresh index territory', 12th February 1992
Durr, Barbara, 'Expansion planned by Chicago Mercantile Exchange', 22nd June 1992
Durr, Barbara, 'New products to hold the line', 19th March 1992
Durr, Barbara, 'Options exchanges worried by over-the-counter trading', 15th May 1992
Durr, Barbara, 'A shrinking share of a larger pie', 11th June 1992
Durr, Barbara, 'Talent capsized by money wave', 19th March 1992
Durr, Barbara and Corrigan, Tracy, 'The future comes into focus on screen', 25th June 1992
Dyer, Geoff, 'Family-run companies in search of finance', 10th June 1997
Dyer, Geoff, 'Drive for liquidity continues', 19th March 2001
Dyer, Geoff, 'Cosmopolis dreams large', 12th April 2006
Dyer, Geoff, 'Concerns at market bubble float over China', 31st January 2007
Dyer, Geoff and Yee, Amy, 'NYSE heads for Paris to woo Asia', 10th April 2007
Eaglesham, Jean, 'Important long-term effects for the small investor', 17th October 1997
Eaglesham, Jean, 'Tight timetable turned to rare working success', 9th July 1999
Eaglesham, Jean and Masters, Brooke, 'No longer a doormat', 27th August 2010
Eddy, Kester, 'Bourse sees privatisation as big opportunity', 31st October 2013
Edgecliffe-Johnson, Andrew, 'Glocer needs to be clearer to get growth message across on Reuters', 24th February 2006
Edwards, John, 'Readiness to change becomes the most vital commodity', 12th September 1984
Edwards, John, 'Broader base and wider choice', 5th March 1985
Edwards, John, 'Fight ahead to maintain growth', 5th March 1985
Edwards, John, 'Steps to improve competitiveness', 5th March 1985
Edwards, John, 'Why the future may not work', 26th July 1985
Edwards, John, 'New rules will help private clients', 27th October 1986
Edwards, John, 'London's rival', 30th April 1988
Edwards, John, 'Profiting from a small outlay', 20th August 1988
Ehrlich, Everett and Mann, Michael, 'One size does not fit all', 16th October 2000
El-Erian, Mohamed, 'Relying on liquidity runs risk of leaving investors in hot water', 6th August 2019
Elliot, John, 'Share dealing returns to Shanghai', 19th December 1990
Elliot, John, 'Old tune is heard again', 24th April 1991
Ellis, Charles D, 'Technology and low returns: the end for active investing?', 21st January 2017
Elstob, P M, 'UK links with Tokyo houses', 14th February 1984
Elstob, Peter, 'Anxious to become the Ecu centre', 29th November 1990
Endt, Friso, 'The debate intensifies', 30th June 1988
Endt, Friso, 'Takeover defences come under heavy fire', 30th June 1988
England, Andrew, 'Egypt plans baby bourse', 12th October 2007
England, Andrew, 'Saudi opens exchange to outsiders', 21st August 2008

England, Andrew and Wallis, William, 'JSE plan viewed with caution', 6th November 2012
Evans, Judith, 'Building a real estate bubble', 19th June 2019
Evers, Sean, 'Cairo becomes a hot favourite', 8th November 1996
Evers, Sean, 'Cairo sets a busy timetable for privatisation', 4th October 1996
Farchy, Jack, 'Tide turns against annual contracts for raw materials', 10th August 2010
Farchy, Jack, 'Metdist owners poised to reap benefits of LME bidding tussle', 3rd October 2011
Farchy, Jack, 'Potential credit crunch risks hobbling raw materials trade', 6th December 2011
Farchy, Jack, 'Sticklers for tradition rule roost when it comes to sale of LME', 16th December 2011
Farchy, Jack, 'Deal would aid path to China growth', 18th June 2012
Farchy, Jack, 'LME eyes renminbi move for metals', 17th April 2012
Farchy, Jack, 'Cobalt shift on pricing sets post-Libor trend', 19th November 2013
Farchy, Jack and Cookson, Robert, 'LME chief set for £10m after agreeing £1.4bn sale to HKEx', 16th June 2012
Farchy, Jack and Grant, Jeremy, 'LME has already seen a "raft of interest" ', 29th September 2011
Farchy, Jack and Grant, Jeremy, 'Prospect of LME's sale puts clearing in focus', 23rd February 2012
Fidler, Stephen, 'Deregulate or risk being left behind', 21st October 1987
Fidler, Stephen, 'Deregulation aids fledgling markets', 21st April 1987
Fidler, Stephen, 'In the eye of the storm', 18th November 1987
Fidler, Stephen, 'Loan market emerges from twilight', 21st May 1987
Fidler, Stephen, 'Minefields await the unprepared', 21st April 1987
Fidler, Stephen, 'More than a mere slogan', 7th May 1987
Fidler, Stephen, 'Rising demand for sterling CP', 2nd December 1987
Fidler, Stephen, 'Where British brokers rule world', 7th July 1987
Fidler, Stephen, 'A broader and safer market in a storm', 18th May 1988
Fidler, Stephen, 'Don't throw out the baby', 29th June 1988
Fidler, Stephen, 'Europe slower to lighten balance sheets', 17th February 1988
Fidler, Stephen, 'A force more respected than loved', 11th May 1988
Fidler, Stephen, 'Great leap forward', 29th June 1988
Fidler, Stephen, 'A trickle of issues', 29th June 1988
Fidler, Stephen, 'US stock exchanges wage listings war abroad', 20th April 1988
Fidler, Stephen, 'Amex to launch options in fixed-income securities', 24th May 1989
Fidler, Stephen, 'Europe falls behind in the securities race', 25th January 1989
Fidler, Stephen, 'Bank points to blurred boundaries', 8th February 1990
Fidler, Stephen, 'A franchise under stress', 2nd July 1990
Fidler, Stephen, 'Money brokers step into the financial limelight', 22nd November 1990
Fidler, Stephen, 'W Germany may suffer withholding tax legacy', 18th May 1990
Fidler, Stephen, 'When family loyalties are placed under severe strain', 28th December 1990
Fidler, Stephen, 'Covering risks of global volatility', 21st February 1991
Fidler, Stephen, 'Basel 2 boosts Europe's repo market', 29th November 2005
Fidler, Stephen, 'How the Square Mile defeated the prophets of doom', 10th December 2005
Fifield, Anna, 'Swimmer breathes new life into NZSE', 6th May 2003
Fifield, Anna, 'Korea Exchange seeks foreign capital', 18th March 2005
Fifield, Anna, 'S Korea steps up its efforts to become a hub', 12th April 2006
Fifield, Anna, 'Seoul looks to echo London big bang', 26th June 2007
Financial Times *see FT*
Fisher, Andrew, 'City flexes financial muscle', 1st July 1992
Fisher, Andrew, 'Fewer bourses offer more for the investor', 10th May 1995
Fisher, Andrew, 'German stock market seeks ambitious revamp', 1st June 1995
Fisher, Andrew, 'New rules benefit Frankfurt', 17th May 1995
Fisher, Andrew, 'Germany's stock answer', 22nd October 1996
Fisher, Andrew, 'The market that comes to you', 16th February 1996
Fisher, Andrew, 'Bigger is better in bourses' brave euro world', 15th July 1997
Fisher, Andrew, 'Börse bonus', 4th March 1997
Fisher, Andrew, 'Euro likely to start equities ball rolling', 18th November 1997

Fisher, Andrew, 'European bourses may get lift on back of Emu', 15th April 1997
Fisher, Andrew, 'Frankfurt exchange adds new dimension', 28th November 1997
Fisher, Andrew, 'New era dawns in Germany', 28th February 1997
Fisher, Andrew, 'Sights are set on overtaking Paris', 9th June 1997
Fisher, Andrew, 'London link offers way into top tier', 8th July 1998
Fisher, Andrew, 'Looking over borders', 24th March 1998
Fisher, Andrew, 'Exchanges set for a global shake-out', 13th January 1999
Fisher, Andrew and Frey, Eric, 'Frankfurt and Vienna SEs to co-operate', 6th April 1998
Fisher, Andrew and Jack, Andrew, 'German, French bourses in link-up talks', 21st June 1997
FitzSimons, Alastair, 'EC Directives change securities markets', 15th February 1990
Flanders, Stephanie, 'Market bears revive Tobin's ratio', 13th January 1997
Fleming, Ian, Stafford, Philip and Brunsden, Jim, 'Iran sanctions pose dilemma for Swift', 18th May 2018
Fleming, Sam, 'Foreign banks meet BoE over branch rules', 27th February 2014
Fleming, Sam, 'Global regulator starts leveraged loans scrutiny', 8th March 2019
Fleming, Sam and Chon, Gina, 'Boutique banks flourish as larger institutions rethink business models', 12th August 2014
Fleming, Sam and Chon, Gina, 'Push begins to put lenders' house in order', 19th June 2014
Fleming, Sam and Gray, Alistair, 'Fed research points to risk from non-banks', 9th March 2018
Fleming, Sam and Hume, Neil, 'City regulators to police more benchmarks', 26th September 2014
Fleming, Sam, Rennison, Joe and Armstrong, Robert, 'Non-bank lenders under scrutiny after taking big share in US mortgage market', 10th April 2019
Fleming, Sam and Stafford, Philip, 'Regulators warn on boom-era debt', 16th October 2013
Fletcher, Laurence, 'Lack of volatility lines up Niederhoffer hedge fund for near annual loss', 7th November 2019
Fletcher, Laurence, 'Tumbling yields see debt securitisation hit pre-crisis levels', 17th September 2019
Fletcher, Laurence and Aliaj, Ortenca, 'Stockpickers bide their time on clash with quant challengers', 23rd November 2019
Flood, Chris, 'LME clears the way for consolidation', 31st May 2006
Flood, Chris, 'LME sees sharp rise in turnover', 18th July 2006
Flood, Chris, 'Hedge funds transmit most risk', 28th April 2014
Flood, Chris, 'High-frequency trading is "growing cancer"', 14th April 2014
Flood, Chris, 'Regulators stalk secretive financial giants', 24th February 2014
Flood, Chris, 'Side pockets: a curiosity shop of esoteric assets', 21st April 2014
Flood, Chris, 'Cracking down on "megalomaniacs and bullies"', 28th March 2016
Flood, Chris, 'Market leaders face pressure from upstarts', 12th December 2016
Flood, Chris, 'Active management is not dead', 4th September 2017
Flood, Chris, 'European regulators move to mitigate Brexit threat', 11th December 2017
Flood, Chris, 'Global assets to sell to $145tn by 2015', 30th October 2017
Flood, Chris, 'Global regulator to launch fresh ETF probe', 4th December 2017
Flood, Chris, 'BlackRock and Vanguard pull in 57% of global fund flows', 18th February 2018
Flood, Chris, 'Bond liquidity issues prompt investors to turn to ETFs', 17th September 2018
Flood, Chris, 'Forget passports! Trade must go on', 18th June 2018
Flood, Chris, 'Global debt pile creates new chances in nascent market', 5th November 2018
Flood, Chris, 'Liquidity enables big ticket trades', 18th June 2018
Flood, Chris, 'Mifid 2 set to stimulate growth in ETFs', 3rd January 2018
Flood, Chris, 'Pension fund assets reach a record $41.3tn, up 13 per cent', 5th February 2018
Flood, Chris, 'Bond bubble puts global financial system at risk', 21st October 2019
Flood, Chris, 'Bond ETFs outshine equity rivals', 2nd December 2019
Flood, Chris, 'Bond funds head for $1tn landmark', 1st April 2019
Flood, Chris, 'Esma warns on bond fund liquidity risk', 9th September 2019
Flood, Chris, 'EU regulator rejects FCA's criticism', 16th September 2019
Flood, Chris, 'Popularity of passive investing changes rules of the game', 22nd October 2019
Flood, Chris, 'The $14tn debt challenge', 5th August 2019

Flood, Chris, 'US fund houses manage more than a third of global assets', 7th October 2019
Flood, Chris and Brown-Humes, Christopher, 'LME plans to see off challenges with dual expansion moves', 5th January 2007
Foley, Stephen, 'Battle is on to make bonds more transparent', 2nd May 2013
Foley, Stephen, '*HFT* platforms facing "speed limits"', 29th April 2013
Foley, Stephen, 'How to stay on top of the wave', 19th October 2013
Foley, Stephen and Mackenzie, Michael, 'Derivatives trades on the brink of tough new regime', 18th October 2012
Fontanella-Khan, James, 'Bombay Stock Exchange plans listing', 25th November 2009
Fontanella-Khan, James and Sood, Varun, 'Nasdaq closes office in India', 3rd August 2009
Ford, Jonathan and Marriage, Madison, 'Auditing in Crisis', 30th August 2018
Ford, Jonathan and Marriage, Madison, 'Setting flawed standards', 2nd August 2018
Fortado, Lindsay and Martin, Katie, 'SFO drops forex fraud probe', 16th March 2016
Fortado, Lindsay and Noonan, Laura, 'Banks bet on hedge fund prime broking fees', 10th January 2019
Fossli, Karen, 'Liberalisation helps to fuel interest', 30th March 1989
Foster, Angus, 'Crusaders tighten their grip', 20th November 1991
Foster, Angus, 'Fear beneath the optimism', 20th November 1991
Foster, Angus, 'Future of stock exchange comes to a head', 16th August 1991
Foster, Angus, 'Two bourses go on trial but development will be orderly', 20th November 1991
Foster, Angus, 'Stock market soars to dizzy heights', 7th February 1994
Foy, Henry, 'Data—not takeovers—signal bourse's way ahead', 26th June 2015
Francotte, Pierre, 'Competition and challenges ahead', 2nd February 2009
Fraser, Damian, 'Propelled into a new financial age', 20th October 1993
Fraser, Damian, 'Edging closer to US standards', 7th February 1994
Freeland, Chrystia, 'Capitalism's capital fears being caught out as London booms', 4th November 2006
Freeman, Andrew, 'Bankers resolve to drive settlement back to the back office', 22nd December 1989
Freeman, Andrew, 'A business that has to perform', 2nd May 1989
Freeman, Andrew, 'London waits for Taurus', 20th February 1989
Freeman, Andrew, 'Spurred by the Americans', 20th February 1989
Freeman, Andrew, 'When clients ask for more', 20th February 1989
Freeman, Andrew, 'AIBD rule fuels bond clearers row', 25th January 1990
Freeman, Andrew, 'Eurobonds ride crest of a wave', 2nd August 1990
Freeman, Andrew, 'Many will struggle to meet the improvement timetable', 2nd July 1990
Freeman, Andrew, 'Rethinking the package', 3rd September 1990
Freeman, Andrew, 'Secondary market moves into first place', 7th June 1990
Freeman, Andrew, 'Tokyo institutions build up derivatives expertise', 25th July 1990
Freeman, Andrew, 'Weakness of Tokyo equities punishes Eurobond market', 2nd July 1990
Freeman, Andrew, 'Cross-border lending now big business', 24th September 1991
Frey, Eric, 'Luring the local saver', 22nd May 1992
Frey, Eric, 'Vienna Bourse looks to the east', 15th July 2004
Friedman, Alan, 'Merger wave continues amid hopes for interstate reform', 20th May 1992
FT Global 500, 29th May 2010
FT Euromarkets Staff, 'Big reforms face bond dealers' association', 22nd May 1985
FT Euromarkets Staff, 'Irish futures market subscriptions on target', 30th September 1987
FT Lex Column, 'Cracking the City Club', 6th February 1995
FT Lex Column, 'Meeting their match', 29th May 2008
FT Lex Column, 'Mifid 2/dark pools: shifty shades of grey', 27th March 2018
FT Reporters, 'City well placed to benefit from banking trend', 10th July 1985
FT Reporters, 'Australian SE to start automated trading system', 26th September 1990
FT Reporters, 'A superficial culture', 3rd November 1994
FT Reporters, 'Surviving in the free world', 21st March 1996
FT Reporters, 'Investing in bonds: now back in favour', 9th November 1998
FT Reporters 'Sweden's platform must prove itself on the global stage', 31st August 2000

FT Reporters 'Euronext snubs latest D Börse offer', 21st June 2006
FT Reporters 'Solid capital has the upper hand', 23rd September 2008
FT Reporters 'Before and after: how the investment banks had to change shape post-crisis', 21st December 2010
FT Reporters 'Proposals fail to forge consensus in Europe', 23rd January 2010
FT Reporters 'A benchmark to fix', 12th March 2012
FT Reporters 'Daily fix that spiralled out of control', 20th December 2012
FT Reporters 'ICE chief makes his biggest bet with deal', 21st December 2012
FT Reporters 'Regions boosted by bank plans to move 3,000 jobs out of City', 10th December 2012
FT Reporters 'Traders urge action after Knight fiasco', 6th August 2012
FT Reporters 'Europe plots a bank heist', 1st July 2016
FT Reporters 'Global exchanges vie to lure Aramco IPO', 10th March 2017
FT Reporters 'Fed analyses regulation's role in sudden rates jump', 2nd October 2019
FT Reporters 'LSE in talks on $20bn Refinitiv link-up with scale to rival Bloomberg empire', 27th July 2019
FT Special Correspondent, 'Poised for a comeback after 27 years', 12th April 1996
Fuhr, Deborah, 'Happy anniversary—but challenges lie ahead', 2nd February 2015
Furse, Clara, 'Sox is not to blame—London is just better as a market', 18th September 2006
Furse, Clara, 'Speak up to keep clearing houses competitive', 16th April 2008
Galang, Jose, 'Watchdog vigilant', 7th February 1994
Gangahar, Anuj, 'Banks begin to dip into "dark pools"', 19th October 2006
Gangahar, Anuj, 'Chairman of the Amex gains focus', 6th July 2006
Gangahar, Anuj, 'Europe banks mirror US trading strategy', 17th November 2006
Gangahar, Anuj, 'Exchanges wait on new rules', 5th May 2006
Gangahar, Anuj, 'Fund managers do their maths', 31st May 2006
Gangahar, Anuj, 'ISE to launch stock exchange', 20th April 2006
Gangahar, Anuj, 'Nanoseconds matter as traders prepare for a shake-up', 14th September 2006
Gangahar, Anuj, 'Nasdaq's man of action', 16th October 2006
Gangahar, Anuj, 'Seismic shift looms for trading', 21st April 2006
Gangahar, Anuj, 'Sox effect hits US exchanges', 28th November 2006
Gangahar, Anuj, 'Threat of duopoly increases pools of dark liquidity', 28th November 2006
Gangahar, Anuj, 'Volumes increase by the month', 28th November 2006
Gangahar, Anuj, 'Banks back move for block trading', 1st March 2007
Gangahar, Anuj, 'Chicago's program for change', 20th March 2007
Gangahar, Anuj, 'Exchanges step up the march east', 12th April 2007
Gangahar, Anuj, 'Fewer platforms, faster trading', 19th November 2007
Gangahar, Anuj, 'Krell swansong fulfils global ambitions', 1st May 2007
Gangahar, Anuj, 'Nasdaq Portal opens view on private placings', 3rd August 2007
Gangahar, Anuj, 'New exchange to shake up futures trading', 27th December 2007
Gangahar, Anuj, 'New push in Nasdaq's painful global expansion campaign', 21st September 2007
Gangahar, Anuj, 'New rules to prompt surge in trading', 5th March 2007
Gangahar, Anuj, 'NYSE Euronext leaves the door open for another deal', 26th April 2007
Gangahar, Anuj, 'NYSE races to build derivatives trade', 11th July 2007
Gangahar, Anuj, 'NYSE to cut fees as rivals move in', 13th September 2007
Gangahar, Anuj, 'Unclear course for Greifeld post-LSE bid', 14th February 2007
Gangahar, Anuj, 'Weight behind LiquidityHub grows', 9th May 2007
Gangahar, Anuj, 'Algorithmic trades produce snowball effect on volatility', 5th December 2008
Gangahar, Anuj, 'Banks throw weight behind BATS', 9th January 2008
Gangahar, Anuj, 'Banks to allow dips into liquidity pools', 20th May 2008
Gangahar, Anuj, 'Boomtime for derivatives as investors bet on volatility', 25th April 2008
Gangahar, Anuj, 'Liquidnet and NYSE Arca link up as exchange dip into dark pools', 25th November 2008
Gangahar, Anuj, 'Nasdaq chief says sector will fragment', 8th January 2008
Gangahar, Anuj, 'New York IPOs eclipse LSE for first time in three years', 3rd January 2008

Gangahar, Anuj, 'NYSE revises trading rules', 14th June 2008
Gangahar, Anuj, 'US electronic networks step on exchanges' toes', 21st October 2008
Gangahar, Anuj, 'NYSE opens door to options floor', 2nd March 2009
Gangahar, Anuj, 'Finding a mechanism to save the trades', 1st August 2011
Gangahar, Anuj, Beales, Richard and Tett, Gillian, 'NYSE on the move as deal with Euronext is completed', 4th April 2007
Gangahar, Anuj and Brewster, Deborah, 'Hedging industry resents taking blame for turmoil', 20th September 2008
Gangahar, Anuj and Cohen, Norma, 'Traders fear fee increase in wake of $8bn link-up', 19th October 2006
Gangahar, Anuj and Cohen, Norma, 'Three named as Nymex merger talks starts', 16th June 2007
Gangahar, Anuj and Grant, Jeremy, 'Exchanges moot greater links with dark pools of liquidity', 24th June 2008
Gangahar, Anuj, Grant, Jeremy and Ishmael, Stacy-Marie, 'Nasdaq OMX calls for client benefits', 22nd September 2008
Gangahar, Anuj and Turner, David, 'Tokyo joins NYSE in strategy for a global market', 1st February 2007
Gangahar, Anuj and Weitzman, Hal, 'CME-Nymex tie-up sets scene for showdown', 26th August 2008
Gapper, John, 'The equation that didn't add up', 2nd February 1993
Gapper, John, 'IMF study warns in $8,000bn derivatives market', 24th September 1993
Gapper, John, 'Transatlantic lesson on passing on risks', 22nd October 1993
Gapper, John, 'Lending climate tightens banking disciplines', 4th March 1994
Gapper, John, 'More alert and questioning', 27th July 1994
Gapper, John, 'Uncertainty over expansion plans', 29th November 1994
Gapper, John, 'Bankers support role of Old Lady', 25th July 1995
Gapper, John, 'Big is beautiful once again', 6th October 1995
Gapper, John, 'Cold logic wins out at Warburg', 10th January 1995
Gapper, John, 'Contest to guard the nest-egg', 7th February 1995
Gapper, John, 'Crisis at liquidity leader', 16th February 1996
Gapper, John, 'New rules, new rivals, new order', 16th February 1996
Gapper, John, 'Painful struggle back to centre of world markets', 25th October 1996
Gapper, John, 'Tradepoint loss rises to £5.7m', 15th August 1996
Gapper, John, 'World banking and securities watchdogs aim to co-operate', 21st May 1996
Gapper, John, 'A concentration of firepower', 31st January 1997
Gapper, John, 'Harmony after a turbulent period', 28th February 1997
Gapper, John, 'Out with the old, in with the new', 28th February 1997
Gapper, John, 'When the smile is wiped off', 8th March 1997
Gapper, John, 'What price information', 20th July 1998
Gapper, John, 'The Big Board must end its costly costume drama', 11th November 2003
Gapper, John, 'Stock exchanges go peer-to-peer', 28th April 2005
Gapper, John, 'The last gasp of the broker-dealer', 16th September 2008
Gapper, John, 'Don't leave the financial system resting on quicksand', 30th August 2012
Gapper, John, 'Europe finally takes its bite from the City of London', 21st February 2013
Gapper, John, 'There is no such thing as the banking profession', 13th February 2014
Gapper, John, 'My naïve part in the downfall of Lehman', 13th September 2018
Gapper, John and Blackwell, David, 'NYSE chief says Aim must raise standards', 27th January 2007
Gapper, John and Cohen, Norma, 'Not yet the death knell', 10th December 1994
Gapper, John and Cohen, Norma, 'They've really got a hold on EU', 20th April 1994
Gapper, John and Corrigan, Tracy, 'Formidable rivals on a shifting battleground', 4th March 1994
Gapper, John and Lapper, Richard, 'Warburg breaks the bond', 11th January 1995
Gapper, John and Lapper, Richard, 'Europe unlocked for dealers', 2nd January 1996
Gapper, John and Wighton, David, 'A squeeze too far in the City', 4th May 1995
Garner, Roy, 'Larger companies lead the way', 24th March 1986

Garnham, Peter, 'Currencies establish themselves as asset class', 5th March 2007
Garnham, Peter, 'London's dominance of global forex grows', 27th September 2007
Garnham, Peter, 'Quant techniques drive volumes ever higher', 19th November 2007
Garnham, Peter, 'Forex market soars with little sign of change in trading system', 15th October 2008
Garnham, Peter, 'Keeping its head as others lost theirs', 29th September 2009
Garnham, Peter, 'Net brings power to the people', 29th September 2009
Garnham, Peter, 'Fears rise for future of dollar carry trade', 24th February 2010
Garrett, Terry, 'Giants head the broking league', 14th February 1984
Garrett, Terry, 'European markets are a step in right direction', 3rd December 1985
Gawith, Philip, 'Remarkable rehabilitation', 30th August 1991
Gawith, Philip, 'New leader for a new era', 3rd June 1992
Gawith, Philip, 'Technology on the march', 2nd June 1994
Gawith, Philip, 'Brokers lose their voices on the small screen', 15th December 1995
Gawith, Philip, 'Forex market growth startles exchanges', 20th September 1995
Gawith, Philip, 'Forex surge masks maturing market', 24th October 1995
Gawith, Philip, 'Exotic but not for faint hearts', 15th May 1996
Gawith, Philip, 'Gilt repo may hasten change', 1st March 1996
Gawith, Philip, 'Service central to Paribas forex move', 2nd February 1996
Gawith, Philip and Lapper, Richard, 'The new kid in the City', 1st March 1996
Gawith, Philip and Lapper, Richard, 'A step away from City tradition', 2nd January 1996
Gelles, David, 'New Stock on the Bloc', 29th October 2010
Gelles, David, 'Approval for Xpert as private company shares exchange', 4th January 2011
Gelles, David and Scannell, Kara, 'SEC probes US secondary market', 29th December 2010
Genillard, Ariane, 'Prague plods on towards a regulated stock market', 15th May 1992
George, Nicholas, 'Baltic exchanges battle for dominance', 7th September 1999
George, Nicholas, 'Consolidation will be a reality in May', 23rd March 1999
George, Nicholas, 'Northern lights lead way for neighbours', 26th July 1999
George, Nicholas, 'Niche player relishes a new role on world stage', 29th August 2000
George, Nicholas, 'Stockholm legend has tough battle ahead', 31st August 2000
George, Nicholas, 'OMX in talks with Danish stock exchange', 4th October 2004
Giles, Chris, 'Old Lady forced to adapt as world has grown more complex and risky', 18th October 2005
Giles, Chris, 'Bank stresses actions are not unusual', 22nd August 2007
Giles, Chris, 'Conceptual issues at heart of reform', 10th October 2008
Giles, Chris, 'Into the storm', 14th November 2008
Giles, Chris, 'BIS calls for wide global financial reforms', 30th June 2009
Giles, Chris, 'King's faded realm', 16th February 2009
Giles, Chris, 'The bank that roared', 14th July 2012
Giles, Chris, 'BoE bows to pressure for probes into crisis', 22nd May 2012
Giles, Chris, 'BoE loosens regulations on liquid asset holdings', 30th June 2012
Giles, Chris, 'Ill-prepared Treasury did not see dangers brewing', 30th March 2012
Giles, Chris, 'King admits he should have shouted about risk', 3rd May 2012
Giles, Chris, 'Mervyn King', 5th May 2012
Giles, Chris, 'Carney tears up rule book on help for struggling banks', 25th October 2013
Giles, Chris, 'The Old Lady is right that prudential policy is not everything', 19th June 2014
Giles, Chris, 'IMF warns low rates are fuelling risk-taking', 17th October 2019
Giles, Chris and Guha, Krishna, 'Liquidity shortages appear to ease', 16th January 2008
Giles, Chris and Thal Larsen, Peter, 'Week that shook the banking world', 22nd September 2007
Giles, Chris and Walker, Owen, 'BoE head urges stricter rules for funds', 27th June 2019
Gimbel, Florian, 'Electronic swap systems set to go live', 20th December 2000
Gimbel, Florian, 'Exchange tries to stay ahead of the pack', 28th October 2002
Gimbel, Florian and Minder, Raphael, 'Bleak outlook for high-growth sectors', 11th January 2001
Glover, Hannah, 'Spotlight turns to the mechanics of securities lending', 8th September 2008
Goff, Sharlene, 'Building Societies refuse to roll over', 6th September 2010

Goff, Sharlene, 'Near-death experience has left deep scars', 22nd March 2011
Goff, Sharlene, 'The price of protection', 12th September 2011
Goff, Sharlene, 'Report dismisses merger U-turn', 2–3rd April 2011
Goff, Sharlene, 'Risk is the new "sexy" job at the bank', 14th July 2011
Goff, Sharlene, 'Vickers Report', 13th September 2011
Goff, Sharlene, 'The middle is still the safest bet', 25th June 2012
Goff, Sharlene, 'Policymakers recognise SMEs need more funding options', 16th April 2012
Goff, Sharlene, 'Taxpayers left in queue as old brand shuts up shop', 13th September 2012
Goff, Sharlene, 'Challenger leaders square up to the big four', 25th January 2014
Goff, Sharlene, 'Scrutiny puts free banking in question', 19–20th July 2014
Goff, Sharlene, Hughes, Jennifer and Jenkins, Patrick, 'Mortgage-backed securities market gathering steam', 16th September 2010
Goodhart, Charles and Demos, Antonis, 'The Asian surprise in the forex markets', 2nd September 1991
Goodhart, David, 'Hastening the revolution', 19th November 1986
Goodhart, David, 'Economy's world standing given a frank assessment', 25th May 1994
Gooding, Kenneth, 'A boost for the market', 13th June 1988
Gooding, Kenneth, 'Dangerous times at the metal exchange', 6th July 1988
Gooding, Kenneth, 'Global regulation provides the immediate challenge', 2nd October 1989
Gooding, Kenneth, 'LME prepares for tin's rehabilitation', 12th April 1989
Gooding, Kenneth, 'LME zinc restrictions spark row', 22nd December 1989
Gooding, Kenneth, 'Shortage of stocks may threaten the return of tin', 1st June 1989
Gooding, Kenneth, 'London Metal Exchange chairman resigns his post', 20th July 1990
Gooding, Kenneth, 'Financial engineering tames the gold market', 26th July 1991
Gooding, Kenneth, 'Metal traders start their mating season', 8th October 1991
Gooding, Kenneth, 'Bagri sees wider horizons for LME', 17th December 1992
Gooding, Kenneth, 'From Calcutta clerk to metals magnate', 10th December 1992
Gooding, Kenneth, 'Havens of inertia', 22nd June 1992
Gooding, Kenneth, 'London traders sceptical about US merger', 27th January 1993
Gooding, Kenneth, 'Metals business booms', 5th May 1994
Gooding, Kenneth, 'Former LME chairman defends clearing system', 19th July 1996
Gooding, Kenneth, 'LME prepares to celebrate after a difficult year', 4th October 1996
Gooding, Kenneth, 'The LME bites the bullet of change', 13th June 1997
Gooding, Kenneth, 'LME may act on ring membership', 7th October 1997
Gooding, Kenneth, 'LME changes rules to halt short-sell manipulations', 28th October 1998
Gooding, Kenneth and Wagstyl, Stefan, 'SIB calls for big changes at metal exchange', 20th December 1996
Gordon, Sarah, 'Edinburgh more upbeat on Brexit than London', 20th November 2017
Gordon, Sarah, 'Making sense of the City', 9th March 2019
Gorst, Isabel, 'Market comes out of shadows', 2nd July 2008
Gorton, Gary, 'Banking must not be left to lurk in the shadows', 21st November 2012
Gourlay, Richard, 'Pan-Europe stock market planned', 16th November 1994
Gourlay, Richard and Price, Christopher, 'Capital idea for the small investor', 17th June 1995
Gowers, Andrew, 'International tin trading slows down to a trickle', 2nd December 1985
Gowers, Andrew, 'Lost business not yet returning', 23rd July 1986
Gowers, Andrew, 'Island of integrity', 29th March 1993
Gowers, Andrew, 'Planning blight in the City', 20th May 1997
Graham, George, 'The cost conscious competitor', 27th January 1986
Graham, George, 'Hopes of an end to O'Brien Rules', 27th May 1986
Graham, George, 'Mercurial times in the market', 27th May 1986
Graham, George, 'Rowing with the tide', 22nd May 1986
Graham, George, 'Faster growth than London's', 20th January 1987
Graham, George, 'Matif forges ahead', 19th March 1987
Graham, George, 'Paris adds to continuous market', 20th January 1987

Graham, George, 'Paris sugar market under siege', 13th August 1987
Graham, George, 'In need of ratings', 17th February 1988
Graham, George, 'Major reforms under way', 29th September 1988
Graham, George, 'Change unsettles small investors', 3rd May 1989
Graham, George, 'France launches search for new financial centre', 10th January 1989
Graham, George, 'A rapid developer', 8th March 1989
Graham, George, 'Trading shows signs of renewed vitality', 3rd April 1989
Graham, George, 'Year of quiet change', 2nd November 1989
Graham, George, 'A battle with London', 22nd October 1990
Graham, George, 'Creating a modern system', 22nd October 1990
Graham, George, 'Doubts about tax burden', 22nd October 1990
Graham, George, 'Foreign investment doubles', 22nd October 1990
Graham, George, 'New weapons for the global fray', 5th June 1990
Graham, George, 'Paris takes on London', 26th June 1990
Graham, George, 'Sanctioned to protect', 22nd October 1990
Graham, George, 'A tale of two sugar markets', 16th February 1990
Graham, George, 'Tuffier collapse highlights decline in commission rates', 22nd October 1990
Graham, George, 'Worries over imbalances', 22nd October 1990
Graham, George, 'In the front rank in Europe', 17th June 1991
Graham, George, 'An unusual path', 19th June 1991
Graham, George, 'BIS outlines forex settlement risk strategy', 28th March 1996
Graham, George, 'Blood on the road to the promised land', 5th March 1996
Graham, George, 'Emerging markets lift global securities trade', 16th February 1996
Graham, George, 'Foreign exchange groups plan merger', 9th December 1996
Graham, George, 'Forex dealers move to limit settlement risk', 5th June 1996
Graham, George, 'New chief sent to the Tower', 15th June 1996
Graham, George, 'Stockbrokers to urge end of stamp duty on deals', 21st February 1996
Graham, George, 'All change at the exchange', 20th October 1997
Graham, George, 'Bank bows to outcry on derivatives', 7th June 1997
Graham, George, 'BIS weighs expanded role', 9th June 1997
Graham, George, 'Chase plans new forex derivative', 29th April 1997
Graham, George, 'Global payments bodies to merge', 1st October 1997
Graham, George, 'Much more a small fizz than a Big Bang', 17th October 1997
Graham, George, 'New forex bank to cut risk', 9th June 1997
Graham, George, 'Order-driven system will bring London into line', 17th October 1997
Graham, George, 'Radical changes may lie ahead', 9th April 1997
Graham, George, 'Banks settle down to action', 5th June 1998
Graham, George, 'Beyond the storm, small will be beautiful', 19th October 1998
Graham, George, 'CrestCo wins gilt and money market settlement', 19th September 1998
Graham, George, 'Electronic book settling down', 24th March 1998
Graham, George, 'Exchange lobbied on behalf of small investors', 11th July 1998
Graham, George, 'French banker hits at stock exchange alliance', 24th July 1998
Graham, George, 'Mixed fortunes in banking's second tier', 2nd March 1998
Graham, George, 'Partnership must aim for common rules and systems', 8th July 1998
Graham, George, 'Stark Staring Bankers', 5th October 1998
Graham, George, 'Stock Exchange poised to fine tune the trading system that went electric', 30th March 1998
Graham, George, 'Cottages consolidate', 6th December 1999
Graham, George, 'Forex trading system planned', 15th September 1999
Graham, George, 'Weighing up the risks', 4th June 1999
Graham, George and Cohen, Norma, 'Investment experts spurn reforms', 22nd February 1996
Graham, George and Martinson, Jane, 'Handful of firms set for a dominant role', 20th November 1997
Graham, George and Tett, Gillian, 'City fears profit loss by missing Target', 6th July 1996
Grande, Carlos, 'Heavy dealing stretches systems to limit', 6th April 2000

Grant, Jeremy, 'CME gambles on electronic success', 17th June 2002
Grant, Jeremy, 'Battle looms between CBOT and Eurex', 31st October 2003
Grant, Jeremy, 'CBOT starts battle for market share', 13th January 2003
Grant, Jeremy, 'CME reduces fees for European customers', 11th November 2003
Grant, Jeremy, 'Eurex faces vote on clearing house', 20th October 2003
Grant, Jeremy, 'Euronext-Liffe and CBOT mull further links', 11th January 2003
Grant, Jeremy, 'From strangle to straddle in a few seconds', 5th November 2003
Grant, Jeremy, 'Hedging with options in vogue as bourses decline', 27th May 2003
Grant, Jeremy, 'Landscape altered by earthquake', 5th November 2003
Grant, Jeremy, 'LME considers steel futures', 21st March 2003
Grant, Jeremy, 'Trading volumes buoyed by rise in markets', 5th November 2003
Grant, Jeremy, 'Board looks beyond frozen orange juice', 30th November 2004
Grant, Jeremy, 'CBOT retaliates in Eurex battle', 4th February 2004
Grant, Jeremy, 'CCX takes Chicago by storm', 16th November 2004
Grant, Jeremy, 'Chicago enters electronic future', 10th August 2004
Grant, Jeremy, 'Chicago exchanges look to Asia', 15th June 2004
Grant, Jeremy, 'CHX considers a partnership to boost volume', 19th May 2004
Grant, Jeremy, 'CME seeks to broaden its business', 10th June 2004
Grant, Jeremy, 'New exchange shakes up pricing', 4th February 2004
Grant, Jeremy, 'NQLX listing of Eurodollar future on hold', 2nd November 2004
Grant, Jeremy, 'A single-product boutique is not the way: is one-stop shopping coming to US exchanges?', 14th September 2004
Grant, Jeremy, 'Traders consider their options', 27th April 2004
Grant, Jeremy, 'Archipelago ahead in race for early trades', 18th January 2005
Grant, Jeremy, 'Merger will bring mutual benefits', 22nd April 2005
Grant, Jeremy, 'Capital, traders and fraudsters are all completely mobile', 28th November 2006
Grant, Jeremy, 'Flat out: why regulators are rushing to keep up with mergers by exchanges', 13th July 2006
Grant, Jeremy, 'Hurdles appear in the race for exchange consolidation', 15th June 2006
Grant, Jeremy, 'Man Group nabs 70% of Eurex US', 28th July 2006
Grant, Jeremy, 'Man injects life into dying Börse arm', 31st July 2006
Grant, Jeremy, 'Market revived to instil a dose of competition', 28th November 2006
Grant, Jeremy, 'Nymex's long road to the electronic age', 17th February 2006
Grant, Jeremy, 'Regulators face uncharted waters if deal goes ahead', 9th June 2006
Grant, Jeremy, 'Regulators' boundaries may soon start to blur', 19th June 2006
Grant, Jeremy, 'SEC set to relax margin rules in move to cut trading costs', 16th October 2006
Grant, Jeremy, 'Self-regulation to oversee US broker-dealers', 11th November 2006
Grant, Jeremy, 'US looks to regain edge by relaxing margin rules', 20th October 2006
Grant, Jeremy, 'McGraw-Hill forced to reveal energy trading data', 1st May 2007
Grant, Jeremy, 'OTC energy trades under CFTC spotlight', 3rd August 2007
Grant, Jeremy, 'Regulators play different notes on the same instrument', 17th April 2007
Grant, Jeremy, 'Regulators' turf battles prompt talk about reform', 5th December 2007
Grant, Jeremy, 'SEC official warns on foreign standards', 27th March 2007
Grant, Jeremy, 'Baikal strategy remains unclear', 30th October 2008
Grant, Jeremy, 'BATS chooses Savvis for drive into Europe', 14th April 2008
Grant, Jeremy, 'BATS reveals date for European debut', 15th July 2008
Grant, Jeremy, 'BATS seeks 15% of FTSE 100 market', 20th August 2008
Grant, Jeremy, 'Blink and you miss a competitive advantage', 21st October 2008
Grant, Jeremy, 'Brussels calls for ideas on securities trading', 26th August 2008
Grant, Jeremy, 'Bullish LSE fails to convince investors it can make the grade', 23rd May 2008
Grant, Jeremy, 'Chi-X secures share of trading', 14th August 2008
Grant, Jeremy, 'Clearers step into limelight', 21st October 2008
Grant, Jeremy, 'Competitive UK stock clearing gets the go-ahead', 25th September 2008
Grant, Jeremy, 'Decision pending on post-trade', 23rd May 2008

Grant, Jeremy, 'Do exchanges feel blue over Turquoise?', 16th June 2008
Grant, Jeremy, 'Embarrassed LSE trails in rival's wake', 25th June 2008
Grant, Jeremy, 'Energy platforms in final tussle for clearer advantage', 19th May 2008
Grant, Jeremy, 'Europe urged to adopt US clearing model', 16th June 2008
Grant, Jeremy, 'European platforms step into the pool', 9th August 2008
Grant, Jeremy, 'Exposure puts Bolsas' long period in the sun at risk', 15th October 2008
Grant, Jeremy, 'The fast bowlers arrive: Europe's battle for share dealing business is about to intensify', 1st September 2008
Grant, Jeremy, 'Fortis arm to play key role in new Nasdaq pan-European trading system', 19th May 2008
Grant, Jeremy, 'Frustration for exchange newcomers', 31st July 2008
Grant, Jeremy, 'Geeks grow into the kingmakers', 21st October 2008
Grant, Jeremy, 'Imarex to launch shipping contract', 12th June 2008
Grant, Jeremy, 'JSE intends to list pan-African stocks', 2nd June 2008
Grant, Jeremy, 'Liffe in first for options contracts', 31st March 2008
Grant, Jeremy, 'Low transaction fees and an international dimension', 1st December 2008
Grant, Jeremy, 'LSE and Lehman's platform to have dark pool', 26th June 2008
Grant, Jeremy, 'LSE hopes Baikal will refresh its fortunes', 27th June 2008
Grant, Jeremy, 'LSE looks beyond speed in the race to beat upstart rivals', 19th June 2008
Grant, Jeremy, 'LSE receives wake-up call as rivals grab market share', 16th August 2008
Grant, Jeremy, 'LSE slashes fees as it steps up battle against emerging rivals', 1st September 2008
Grant, Jeremy, 'Mifid causing data frustration', 24th June 2008
Grant, Jeremy, 'Mifid opens door to US platforms', 31st October 2008
Grant, Jeremy, 'MTF platforms poised to proliferate', 21st August 2008
Grant, Jeremy, 'MTFs begin to encroach on traditional stock exchange territory', 8th September 2008
Grant, Jeremy, 'Nasdaq lifts the stakes in Europe's trading arena', 2nd September 2008
Grant, Jeremy, 'New breed of trader heads for Europe', 4th December 2008
Grant, Jeremy, 'New platform for Spanish small-caps', 30th May 2008
Grant, Jeremy, 'NYSE Euronext fights back', 8th September 2008
Grant, Jeremy, 'NYSE tries to undermine LSE', 14th April 2008
Grant, Jeremy, 'Party mood might elude LCH.Clearnet', 29th April 2008
Grant, Jeremy, 'Planned merger comes at crucial time for industry', 14th August 2008
Grant, Jeremy, 'SEC eyes cross-border shake-up', 3rd January 2008
Grant, Jeremy, 'Settlement slow to follow rapid trades', 4th April 2008
Grant, Jeremy, 'SWX wins dark pool backers', 21st July 2008
Grant, Jeremy, 'Time of crisis also gives opportunities', 21st October 2008
Grant, Jeremy, 'Trading data has deteriorated since Mifid, IMA warns', 25th November 2008
Grant, Jeremy, 'Turquoise and Chi-X suffer Italian blow', 30th July 2008
Grant, Jeremy, 'Turquoise plays down need for speed', 21st October 2008
Grant, Jeremy, 'Turquoise refreshes exchange landscape', 15th August 2008
Grant, Jeremy, 'Unsettling facts of post-trading', 8th September 2008
Grant, Jeremy, 'Upstart Bats heads for Europe', 31st March 2008
Grant, Jeremy, 'Walking in the shadow of global peers', 9th July 2008
Grant, Jeremy, 'Big exchanges come round to multilateral approach', 20th April 2009
Grant, Jeremy, 'Bourses in data arms race', 15th September 2009
Grant, Jeremy, 'Canada's bourse up to speed', 30th July 2009
Grant, Jeremy, 'Case for change heard loud and clear', 9th February 2009
Grant, Jeremy, 'CDS clearing planned for Europe', 17th February 2009
Grant, Jeremy, 'Chi-X leaves upstart label behind and looks to the future', 23rd November 2009
Grant, Jeremy, 'Clearing not the cure-all for financial system woes', 26th June 2009
Grant, Jeremy, 'Clearing up the system', 2nd November 2009
Grant, Jeremy, 'Clock ticking over future of LCH.Clearnet', 5th May 2009
Grant, Jeremy, 'Competition in Europe toughens', 5th May 2009
Grant, Jeremy, 'Competition is sharper but liquidity fragmented', 21st October 2009

Grant, Jeremy, 'Derivatives reform draws UK warning', 25th July 2009
Grant, Jeremy, 'EMCF in X-Clear tie up', 3rd February 2009
Grant, Jeremy, 'Eurex and LSE to counter Liffe with equity options trading', 16th December 2009
Grant, Jeremy, 'Europe calm on flash orders', 3rd August 2009
Grant, Jeremy, 'Europe's post-trade infrastructure poised at the crossroads', 2nd February 2009
Grant, Jeremy, 'European data service poses threat to LSE', 12th January 2009
Grant, Jeremy, 'European trading trails the US in coping with outages', 21st April 2009
Grant, Jeremy, 'Exchanges and brokers at odds over crisis blame', 20th February 2009
Grant, Jeremy, 'Exchanges body issues dark pools warning', 23rd September 2009
Grant, Jeremy, 'Exchanges hit out at impact of dark pools', 13th March 2009
Grant, Jeremy, 'Exchanges warn on OTC clearing', 4th June 2009
Grant, Jeremy, 'First steps towards clearing for FX', 6th October 2009
Grant, Jeremy, 'The humdrum has fresh significance', 21st October 2009
Grant, Jeremy, 'Icap looks to LCH.Clearnet for growth', 3rd February 2009
Grant, Jeremy, 'Innovative ideas fail to lighten European mood over dark pools', 25th September 2009
Grant, Jeremy, 'Interdealer brokers join forces on OTC issues', 9th March 2009
Grant, Jeremy, 'ISE to offer more foreign trading', 29th September 2009
Grant, Jeremy, 'Jury still out on benefits of Mifid for the trading arena', 10th July 2009
Grant, Jeremy, 'LCH aims to buy out investors', 5th March 2009
Grant, Jeremy, 'LCH.Clearnet sees need for a clear path to Washington', 27th November 2009
Grant, Jeremy, 'Learning from the Lehman catastrophe', 2nd February 2009
Grant, Jeremy, 'LSE closes in on pan-European trading', 22nd April 2009
Grant, Jeremy, 'LSE drops central clearing plan', 3rd April 2009
Grant, Jeremy, 'LSE faces data-service challenge', 19th January 2009
Grant, Jeremy, 'LSE in talks to buy Turquoise', 2nd October 2009
Grant, Jeremy, 'LSE takes tough new approach to technology', 27th April 2009
Grant, Jeremy, 'LSE targeting upgrade to move ahead of rivals', 8th September 2009
Grant, Jeremy, 'LSE to allow hidden orders', 9th November 2009
Grant, Jeremy, 'Nasdaq OMX's Nordic move highlights post-trade focus', 26th January 2009
Grant, Jeremy, 'NYSE Euronext in move to one platform', 17th February 2009
Grant, Jeremy, 'NYSE Euronext joint venture to capitalise on rising demand for clearing', 19th June 2009
Grant, Jeremy, 'Origins in Japanese rice and French coffee markets', 26th June 2009
Grant, Jeremy, 'OTC derivatives plan lifts shares', 2nd June 2009
Grant, Jeremy, 'Platforms increase focus on liquidity', 3rd August 2009
Grant, Jeremy, 'Post-trade services come into their own', 2nd February 2009
Grant, Jeremy, 'Regulator research sheds more light on dark pools', 18th December 2009
Grant, Jeremy, 'Regulators keen to shine a light into dark pools', 20th June 2009
Grant, Jeremy, 'Rolet's new broom sweeps LSE', 24th December 2009
Grant, Jeremy, 'Screens replacing screams in the dealing room', 2nd October 2009
Grant, Jeremy, 'Single platform for settlements', 23rd January 2009
Grant, Jeremy, 'SmartPool signs 14 banks and brokers to dark pool', 13th July 2009
Grant, Jeremy, 'Spain's BME to close remaining open outcry pits', 8th July 2009
Grant, Jeremy, 'Streamlining sees Graham resign from LSE', 21st April 2009
Grant, Jeremy, 'Sweeping changes are on the way', 21st October 2009
Grant, Jeremy, 'Tom Trading aims for retail investors', 24th June 2009
Grant, Jeremy, 'Traders stuck with LSE in spite of crash', 29th November 2009
Grant, Jeremy, 'Trading in European dark pools leaps fivefold since start of year', 2nd November 2009
Grant, Jeremy, 'Trading rebates cut into Nasdaq OMX revenues', 6th November 2009
Grant, Jeremy, 'Tullett predicts rebound for OTC derivatives', 5th August 2009
Grant, Jeremy, 'Turquoise will bolster the LSE's position', 22nd December 2009
Grant, Jeremy, 'US clearing proposal fuels tension', 23rd October 2009
Grant, Jeremy, 'Vienna seeks to be architect of East European network', 11th May 2009
Grant, Jeremy, 'Why the future for clearer is anything but clear', 5th March 2009

Grant, Jeremy, 'Africa's first dark pool created on JSE', 22nd April 2010
Grant, Jeremy, '"Algo-trading" changes speed of the game on Wall Street', 8th May 2010
Grant, Jeremy, 'Apathy hinders regional exchanges', 26th July 2010
Grant, Jeremy, 'Back office in leading role', 20th October 2010
Grant, Jeremy, 'BATS seen as likely Chi-X suitor', 25th August 2010
Grant, Jeremy, 'Blow to London as LCH.Clearnet launches clearing house in Paris', 29th March 2010
Grant, Jeremy, 'Businesses demand OTC exemptions', 6th January 2010
Grant, Jeremy, 'Buyside wakes up to impact of legislation', 2nd August 2010
Grant, Jeremy, 'Call to make dark pools trades public', 28th October 2010
Grant, Jeremy, 'Chi-X becomes second largest Europe bourse', 11th February 2010
Grant, Jeremy, 'Chi-X's pan-Asian plans may include HK and Seoul platforms', 13th April 2010
Grant, Jeremy, 'Clearing war set to get hotter', 22nd October 2010
Grant, Jeremy, 'Computer-driven trading boom raises meltdown fears', 26th January 2010
Grant, Jeremy, 'DTCC in talks over European clearing stake', 28–29th August 2010
Grant, Jeremy, 'Dutch lift lid on a high-frequency universe', 26th August 2010
Grant, Jeremy, 'Emerging markets dump old trading habits', 9th September 2010
Grant, Jeremy, 'Emerging markets lure big exchanges', 28th July 2010
Grant, Jeremy, 'Europe's post trade dilemma', 10th February 2010
Grant, Jeremy, 'Fresh questions raised over regulation of clearing houses', 1st April 2010
Grant, Jeremy, 'High-frequency traders battle to make big returns', 10th September 2010
Grant, Jeremy, 'High-frequency traders facing tracking reform', 8th April 2010
Grant, Jeremy, 'High-speed traders seek bigger profile', 4th February 2010
Grant, Jeremy, 'Icap and Nasdaq in OTC expansion', 18th February 2010
Grant, Jeremy, 'Lack of coherence on clearing reform', 9th April 2010
Grant, Jeremy, 'LCH.Clearnet faces derivatives battle', 28th September 2010
Grant, Jeremy, 'LCH.Clearnet warns of loose standards', 16th April 2010
Grant, Jeremy, 'Light speed ahead', 27th September 2010
Grant, Jeremy, 'Liquidnet in talks with stock exchanges', 30th December 2010
Grant, Jeremy, 'London "No 1" for trading speed', 12th October 2010
Grant, Jeremy, 'Low volumes hurt new trading venues', 4th May 2010
Grant, Jeremy, 'LSE bid to build clearing house', 18th September 2010
Grant, Jeremy, 'LSE changes tariffs to attract high-frequency traders', 21st April 2010
Grant, Jeremy, 'LSE set for pan-European trading assault on derivatives', 9th June 2010
Grant, Jeremy, 'LSE's Turquoise heading into profit', 9th August 2010
Grant, Jeremy, 'Market structures face test of trust', 3rd November 2010
Grant, Jeremy, 'Multiple venues leave Europe "open to abuse"', 7th April 2010
Grant, Jeremy, 'Nasdaq OMX to close Europe arm', 29th April 2010
Grant, Jeremy, 'Nasdaq renews European efforts', 8th February 2010
Grant, Jeremy, 'New push to give clearing houses solid foundations', 8th June 2010
Grant, Jeremy, 'New tools in race for trading speed', 19th February 2010
Grant, Jeremy, 'NYSE Euronext to set up clearing houses in London and Paris', 12th May 2010
Grant, Jeremy, 'NYSE plans to launch interest rate futures', 7th April 2010
Grant, Jeremy, 'OMX plans new platform', 20th September 2010
Grant, Jeremy, 'Paris dealt blow over London platform', 15th July 2010
Grant, Jeremy, 'Platforms to trade US shares in Europe', 15th April 2010
Grant, Jeremy, 'Plunge places focus on safety of the share markets', 11th May 2010
Grant, Jeremy, 'Prague Exchange slams speed trades', 21st October 2010
Grant, Jeremy, 'Regulators face uphill battle as dark pools grow murkier', 3rd November 2010
Grant, Jeremy, 'Rolet hits at "uneven field"', 30th March 2010
Grant, Jeremy, 'The route to regulation diverges for Europe and America', 12th August 2010
Grant, Jeremy, 'Share trades in blink of an eye just got faster', 20th April 2010
Grant, Jeremy, 'Smaller orders breed dark pools and higher post-trade costs', 22nd February 2010
Grant, Jeremy, 'Stoking the boilers for the battle of the clearing houses', 24th August 2010
Grant, Jeremy, 'Super-fast traders pose risk to clearers', 1st December 2010

Grant, Jeremy, 'Trust in Dark Pools is dented', 26th May 2010
Grant, Jeremy, 'Up Against a Bandsaw', 3rd September 2010
Grant, Jeremy, 'Ankara weighs in with shake-up of exchanges', 14th December 2011
Grant, Jeremy, 'Argentine bourses extend consolidation', 28th December 2011
Grant, Jeremy, 'Asia and LatAm bourses ripe for mergers', 8th August 2011
Grant, Jeremy, 'Automation is "strangling" small caps', 30th November 2011
Grant, Jeremy, 'Avalanche of rulemaking blocks road to OTC clarity', 1st August 2011
Grant, Jeremy, 'Bank and broker trading networks come under attack', 8th April 2011
Grant, Jeremy, 'Bats and Chi-X to create Europe share trading hub', 18th February 2011
Grant, Jeremy, 'BATS evolves into the big league with Chi-X merger', 19th February 2011
Grant, Jeremy, 'Bold move by Nasdaq and ICE', 2nd April 2011
Grant, Jeremy, 'Börse tie to NYSE focuses cuts on Europe', 8th April 2011
Grant, Jeremy, 'Brussels casts shadow over exchanges' plan', 4th March 2011
Grant, Jeremy, 'Central counterparties eye wave of opportunities', 22nd March 2011
Grant, Jeremy, 'Chill wind blows over plans for market mergers', 17th May 2011
Grant, Jeremy, 'Conduits of contention', 16th June 2011
Grant, Jeremy, 'Counterbid for TMX catches the LSE on the hop', 16th May 2011
Grant, Jeremy, 'Crackdown on high-speed trading', 12th October 2011
Grant, Jeremy, 'D Börse-NYSE merger "bad for markets" ', 5th July 2011
Grant, Jeremy, 'Dealers look for answers on US derivatives reform', 17th March 2011
Grant, Jeremy, 'Dealers warn against spread of derivatives clearing houses', 14th April 2011
Grant, Jeremy, 'Derivatives trading platform bypasses intermediary banks', 17th January 2011
Grant, Jeremy, 'Deutsche Börse in talks with rivals over joint clearing', 6th January 2011
Grant, Jeremy, 'Deutsche Börse-NYSE tie-up to save extra $1bn for customers', 15th September 2011
Grant, Jeremy, 'Drive for consolidation leaves clock ticking for LCH.Clearnet', 13th June 2011
Grant, Jeremy, 'Europe closer to settlement system', 12th September 2011
Grant, Jeremy, 'Every Bourse wants a house of its own', 28th September 2011
Grant, Jeremy, 'Exchange: Aiming to build on success', 4th November 2011
Grant, Jeremy, 'Exchange chiefs seek global powerhouses', 10th February 2011
Grant, Jeremy, 'Industry in the midst of a maelstrom', 10th October 2011
Grant, Jeremy, 'Industry pleads its case against rules forged in heat of crisis', 29th March 2011
Grant, Jeremy, 'ISE banks on technology to strengthen its business', 28th June 2011
Grant, Jeremy, 'LCH.Clearnet at the centre of bidding war', 7th September 2011
Grant, Jeremy, 'London steers clear of ECB settlement platform plan', 22nd July 2011
Grant, Jeremy, ' "London Stop Exchange' counts cost of outage', 26th February 2011
Grant, Jeremy, 'LSE aims to revive Delhi exchange', 9th November 2011
Grant, Jeremy, 'LSE and Russian exchanges in race to partner Kazakh bourse', 6th December 2011
Grant, Jeremy, 'LSE beats Markit in battle to buy LCH', 28th September 2011
Grant, Jeremy, 'LSE chief fears threat to City voice if rival exchanges merge', 1st August 2011
Grant, Jeremy, 'LSE pins outage on "human error" ', 12th January 2011
Grant, Jeremy, 'LSE share of Footsie dips below 50%', 19th September 2011
Grant, Jeremy, 'LSE signals it will look to Asia for merger', 21st April 2011
Grant, Jeremy, 'A market to capture', 18th February 2011
Grant, Jeremy, 'Merger plan puts spotlight on silos', 1st November 2011
Grant, Jeremy, 'New trading venues aim to provide choice of structures', 4th October 2011
Grant, Jeremy, 'Reform in Europe', 31st May 2011
Grant, Jeremy, 'Regulators and industry unsure about rules', 10th October 2011
Grant, Jeremy, 'Rolet back to earth as TMX-LSE hopes fade', 30th June 2011
Grant, Jeremy, 'Six emerging market exchanges combine in cross-listing alliance', 13th October 2011
Grant, Jeremy, 'Three stock exchanges enter battle for control of London clearing house', 28th May 2011
Grant, Jeremy, 'Traders cautious on exchanges tie-up', 1st August 2011
Grant, Jeremy, 'Traders face jump in clearing costs', 11th March 2011
Grant, Jeremy, 'Two Argentine exchanges agree to combine forces', 17th December 2011

Grant, Jeremy, 'Uncertainty over detail of clearing reforms', 10th October 2011
Grant, Jeremy, 'X-clear lifts share of LSE clearing', 1st December 2011
Grant, Jeremy, 'Alliances offer solution for exchanges', 26th March 2012
Grant, Jeremy, 'Asia fears systemic risk over Dodd-Frank', 7th September 2012
Grant, Jeremy, 'Asia watches and learns from European and US rule makers', 30th October 2012
Grant, Jeremy, 'Barriers higher for Asian dominance in algo trading', 24th August 2012
Grant, Jeremy, 'Brussels' block points to future of global alliances', 2nd February 2012
Grant, Jeremy, 'CME eyes London as European springboard', 10th April 2012
Grant, Jeremy, 'CME puts focus on London as its European beachhead', 17th April 2012
Grant, Jeremy, 'LSE in U-turn on Milan stocks', 19th January 2012
Grant, Jeremy, 'LSE seeks holy grail of clearing from LCH.Clearnet deal', 20th March 2012
Grant, Jeremy, 'LSE to take lead stake in clearer', 10th March 2012
Grant, Jeremy, 'New rules are struggle for industry and regulators', 23rd January 2012
Grant, Jeremy, 'SGX eyes organic growth after failing to seal Australian deal', 23rd July 2012
Grant, Jeremy, 'Singapore OTC trades hit by turmoil', 2nd November 2012
Grant, Jeremy, 'Spanish exchange wary of high-speed trading arms race', 26th April 2012
Grant, Jeremy, 'To take on Shanghai and Hong Kong: specialise', 27th July 2012
Grant, Jeremy, 'Drive for Asean exchanges tie-up', 7th January 2013
Grant, Jeremy, 'SGX in talks on Asian trading platform for corporate bonds', 17th November 2014
Grant, Jeremy, 'SGX targets greater China link with Taiwan', 25th November 2014
Grant, Jeremy, 'Singapore exchange slips behind Asia rivals', 24th April 2014
Grant, Jeremy, 'Singapore eyes Hong Kong's financial crown', 17th October 2014
Grant, Jeremy and Barber, Alex, 'Brussels to probe exchanges merger', 5th August 2011
Grant, Jeremy and Barber, Alex, 'D Börse and NYSE Euronext seek to woo Brussels', 14th December 2011
Grant, Jeremy and Barber, Alex, 'ECB preference for Eurozone clearers raises ire in London', 24th November 2011
Grant, Jeremy and Barber, Alex, 'Mifid's net cast wide to overhaul Europe's trading', 21st October 2011
Grant, Jeremy and Barber, Alex, 'D Börse and NYSE face an uphill battle', 12th January 2012
Grant, Jeremy and Belton, Catherine, 'Bourse tie-up clears logjam in Moscow', 3rd February 2011
Grant, Jeremy and Binham, Caroline, 'Doubt cast on BATS purchase of Chi-X', 21st June 2011
Grant, Jeremy and Blas, Javier, 'Singapore fights for commodities trade supremacy', 23rd May 2012
Grant, Jeremy and Boland, Vincent, 'Chicago is their kinda town: but how long can the city's futures traders keep Eurex's electronic exchange at bay?', 16th October 2003
Grant, Jeremy, Braithwaite, Tom and van Duyn, Aline, 'Cracks are emerging in transatlantic approach to reform', 6th January 2010
Grant, Jeremy and Brown, Kevin, 'Asian Exchanges in competitive overhaul', 4th June 2010
Grant, Jeremy and Cameron, Doug, 'Lords of the Windy City', 21st October 2006
Grant, Jeremy and Davies, Paul J., 'Exchanges show how to tackle clearing conundrum', 23rd April 2008
Grant, Jeremy and Demos, Telis, 'D Börse and NYSE talks stir up rivals', 10th February 2011
Grant, Jeremy and Demos, Telis, 'Growth in off-exchange trade stokes pricing fears', 26th January 2011
Grant, Jeremy and Demos, Telis, 'Spurned LSE chief looks over shoulder at Nasdaq', 1st July 2011
Grant, Jeremy and Demos, Telis, 'Super-fast traders feel heat from competition', 15th April 2011
Grant, Jeremy and Demos, Telis, 'Ultra-fast traders braced for tough curbs in Europe', 14th October 2011
Grant, Jeremy and Demos, Telis, 'Super-fast traders feel the heat as bourses act', 6th March 2012
Grant, Jeremy and Dombey, Daniel, 'Turkish exchanges plan to link', 23rd November 2011
Grant, Jeremy and Farchy, Jack, 'LME receives offers of interest', 24th September 2011
Grant, Jeremy and Freeland, Chrystia, 'Brokering change: how Cox is building a consensus as regulation goes global', 4th August 2006
Grant, Jeremy and Gangahar, Anuj, 'Dark pools are stirred by attention from regulators', 27th November 2008
Grant, Jeremy and Gangahar, Anuj, 'ISE buys into Direct Edge trading platform', 23rd August 2008

Grant, Jeremy and Gangahar, Anuj, 'Spotlight on role of electronic trading in recent volatility', 30th October 2008
Grant, Jeremy and Garnham, Peter, 'LCH.Clearnet looks at forex markets', 16th October 2008
Grant, Jeremy and Kerr, Simeon, 'NYSE Euronext takes Doha stake', 20th June 2009
Grant, Jeremy, Kerr, Simeon and England, Andrew, 'Nasdaq and LSE wait for shifting sands to settle', 1st April 2010
Grant, Jeremy, Kirchgässner, Stephanie and Guerrera, Francesco, 'Panel calls for regulatory loosening', 1st December 2006
Grant, Jeremy and Mackenzie, Michael, 'Ghost in the machine', 18th February 2010
Grant, Jeremy and MacNamara, William, 'LSE seeks to grab lead in deal with Mongolian exchange', 9th April 2011
Grant, Jeremy and Masters, Brooke, 'Brokers set out to fight backlash against OTC trade', 28th April 2009
Grant, Jeremy, Milne, Richard and van Duyn, Aline, 'Collateral damage', 7th October 2009
Grant, Jeremy and Mundy, Simon, 'Chi-X sets sights on South Korea', 9th August 2013
Grant, Jeremy and Serdarevic, Masa, 'LSE contemplates acquiring Dutch clearer to diversify away from the UK', 30th January 2010
Grant, Jeremy and Skorecki, Alex, 'Electronic trading is dealt a double blow', 12th July 2002
Grant, Jeremy and Skorecki, Alex, 'Chicago plans for Eurex attack', 19th September 2003
Grant, Jeremy and Skorecki, Alex, 'Eurex makes inroads into US', 28th May 2003
Grant, Jeremy and Skorecki, Alex, 'Software vendors globalise pit', 3rd March 2004
Grant, Jeremy and Smith, Peter, 'SGX offers premium for ASX', 25th October 2010
Grant, Jeremy and Stafford, Philip, 'London uneasy at potential foreign takeover', 1st July 2011
Grant, Jeremy and Stafford, Philip, 'Savings for investors as Europe acts on trading', 25th May 2011
Grant, Jeremy, Stafford, Philip and Johnson, Miles, 'Police called after LSE platform is knocked out', 4th November 2010
Grant, Jeremy and Tait, Nikki, 'Eurex and ICE lead clearing race after Liffe setback', 6th July 2009
Grant, Jeremy and Tait, Nikki, 'Trading costs in Europe remain stubbornly high', 17th July 2009
Grant, Jeremy and Tait, Nikki, 'Brussels eyes faster times for settlement', 25th October 2010
Grant, Jeremy and Tait, Nikki, 'Europe set for overhaul of rules on share dealing', 30th July 2010
Grant, Jeremy and Tait, Nikki, 'City fortunes in flux as exchanges merge', 12th May 2011
Grant, Jeremy and Tait, Nikki, 'NYSE link-up faces hurdles', 11th February 2011
Grant, Jeremy, Tett, Gillian and van Duyn, Aline, 'Calls for derivatives clearing intensify', 15th October 2008
Grant, Jeremy and Thomas, Helen, 'Nasdaq is running out of options', 24th February 2011
Grant, Jeremy, Thomas, Helen, Demos, Telis and Weitzman, Hal, 'US exchanges in $11bn NYSE bid', 2nd April 2011
Grant, Jeremy and Tucker, Sundeep, 'SGX is determined to punch above its weight', 12th June 2008
Grant, Jeremy, Weitzman, Hal, Gangahar, Anuj, 'Tense Exchanges: Banks wrest trading from the established stock markets', 17th April 2008
Grant, Jeremy and Wilson, James, 'D Börse to launch hybrid dark pool trading facility', 21st November 2008
Grant, Jeremy and Wilson, James, 'Deutsche Börse unafraid of MTF rivals', 22nd May 2008
Grant, Jeremy and Wilson, James, 'Private investors fail to see benefits of Mifid reform', 8th March 2010
Grass, Doris, 'Stock exchanges attack proposed EU rule changes', 29th August 2003
Gray, Alistair, 'Tullett hangs on to phone trading', 9th March 2010
Greenberg, Maurice, 'Shake up the NYSE specialist system or drop it', 10th October 2003
Greene, Megan and Scott, Dwight, 'Do leveraged loans pose a threat to the US economy?', 12th February 2019
Greifeld, Bob, 'Exchanges should unite to end flash orders', 7th August 2009
Grene, Sophia, 'A niche in high-frequency trading', 21st September 2009
Grene, Sophia, 'Rules of engagement becoming blurry', 2nd February 2009
Grene, Sophia, 'Striving for a one-stop, straight through shop', 2nd February 2009

Grene, Sophia, 'Taking the sting out of fluctuation', 6th October 2009
Grene, Sophia, 'When cheaper can lead to more expense', 20th July 2009
Grene, Sophia, 'Pension funds anxious to have their say', 2nd August 2010
Grene, Sophia, 'Derivatives rules will bring new demands', 21st May 2012
Grene, Sophia, 'Securities lending and its many functions', 6th February 2012
Grene, Sophia, 'Non-banks colonise former bank territory', 2nd June 2014
Griffith, Victoria, 'S. American trading agreement', 17th December 1991
Groom, Brian, 'Lenders confident of riding out crisis thanks to low risk appetite', 18th November 2010
Groom, Brian, 'Access denied', 31st May 2012
Groom, Brian, 'London powers ahead of regions as north-south divide grows wider', 12th December 2013
Grossman, Richard, *Unsettled Account: The Evolution of Banking in the Industrialized World since 1800* (Princeton: Princeton UP, 2010)
Guerrera, Francesco, 'Brussels plans share trading shake-up', 27th September 2002
Guerrera, Francesco, 'Clearing the air after integration', 6th June 2002
Guerrera, Francesco, 'Outsiders are eager to take the spoils', 12th April 2006
Guerrera, Francesco, 'Region weighs the need for a one-stop shop', 12th April 2006
Guerrera, Francesco, 'Top dog at home but needs to appeal abroad', 12th April 2006
Guerrera, Francesco and Authers, John, 'Institutions increase equity stakes', 22nd January 2007
Guerrera, Francesco and Baer, Justin, 'Doubts beset mission to trim giants' girth', 23rd January 2010
Guerrera, Francesco, Baer, Justin and Jenkins, Patrick, 'A sparser future', 20th December 2010
Guerrera, Francesco and Boland, Vincent, 'Pitfalls lurk in drawing up new trading rules', 28th September 2002
Guerrera, Francesco and Murphy, Megan, 'Tripped up', 25th January 2010
Guerrera, Francesco and Postelnicu, Andrei, 'A not so foreign exchange: China shuns the west as a location for its big corporate share offers', 18th November 2005
Guest, Peter, 'Egypt's stock exchange enjoys revival', 31st March 2008
Guha, Krishna, 'India's NSE shrugs off satellite failure', 10th October 1997
Guha, Krishna, 'Poser for Paulson', 13th September 2008
Guha, Krishna, 'US seeks safety allied to dynamism', 18th June 2009
Guha, Krishna and Sender, Henny, 'No bail-out this time around', 13th September 2008
Guha, Malini and Gangahar, Anuj, 'Accelerating flow from US', 10th October 2006
Guild, Alistair, 'Clearing in line for development', 11th December 1985
Guthrie, Jonathan, 'Sighs of relief as Exco takeover get nod of approval', 27th October 1998
Guthrie, Jonathan, 'Online return for regional exchange', 30th March 2007
Guthrie, Jonathan, 'Cluster of firms can handle all but the largest deals', 27th November 2009
Guthrie, Jonathan, 'A doomed golden age for UK plc', 31st May 2012
Hague, Helen, 'Facing up to a cultural challenge', 9th January 1987
Haldane, Andrew, 'We should go further still in unbundling banks', 3rd October 2012
Hale, David, 'Rebuilt by Wall Street', 25th January 2000
Hale, David, 'The world's banking superpower', 18th June 2003
Hale, Thomas, 'Riskier RMBS sales to double last year's total', 9th October 2015
Hale, Thomas, 'Bypassing the banks', 28th December 2016
Hale, Thomas, 'Non-banks rebuild UK home loan landscape', 4th February 2016
Hale, Thomas, 'Shadow banks step into the spotlight', 5th April 2017
Hall, Ben and Daneshkhu, Scheherazade, 'Overarching ambition', 24th July 2009
Hall, Ben, Daneshkhu, Scheherazade and Grant, Jeremy, 'France calls on Brussels for US-style CFTC', 14th April 2010
Hall, Camilla, 'Citi unveils pricing tool for block trades', 24th April 2014
Hall, William, 'Concentrating on the domestic market', 28th November 1983
Hall, William, 'Delays have plagued electronic bourse', 28th October 1996
Hall, William, 'EBS doubters shaken off', 28th February 1997
Hall, William, 'New chief executive injects a fresh sense of purpose', 13th October 1998
Hall, William, 'Swiss exchange aims to lick stamp duty', 26th October 1998

Hall, William, 'Bold Vienna tries to shed its coy image', 27th October 1999
Hall, William, 'Global shares face a long uphill battle', 31st May 2000
Hall, William and Skorecki, Alex, 'Swiss exchange in move to control blue chips', 20th December 2002
Hamilton Fazey, Ian, 'The manager still matters', 1st April 1986
Hamilton Fazey, Ian, 'The message is getting across', 2nd October 1986
Hamilton Fazey, Ian, 'Sharper eye kept on progress', 2nd October 1986
Hamilton Fazey, Ian, 'Capital keeps grip on HQs', 3rd August 1992
Hamilton Fazey, Ian, 'Leeds to join network of Europe finance centres', 5th October 1993
Hamilton Fazey, Ian, 'Regional finance centres need a lift', 25th November 1993
Hamlin, Kevin, 'New contracts started', 19th March 1987
Hammond, Ed, 'Trading floors live on in data centre', 14th June 2011
Hammond, Ed, 'Pressure on banks' real estate loans', 6th January 2012
Hammond, Ed, 'Change of inhabitants transforms City', 10th June 2013
Hammond, Ed and Masters, Brooke, 'FSA clampdown on mortgage-backed loans sparks friction', 17th January 2013
Hammond, George, Lewis, Leo and Weinland, Don, 'HK riots put boardrooms in holding position', 29th November 2019
Hampson, Rebecca, 'Are retail investors missing out on the message?', 7th October 2019
Han, Alice, 'Shanghai needs resilience if it is to challenge London', 8th May 2018
Hancock, Tom, 'Shanghai unveils renminbi oil futures to rival WTI and Brent benchmarks', 27th March 2018
Hancock, Tom and Hume, Neil, 'China opens iron ore futures trading to foreigners as it seeks pricing clout', 3rd May 2018
Harding, James, 'Farmers face challenge of futures', 16th November 1995
Harding, James, 'Mating season arrives for futures markets', 11th July 1995
Harding, James, 'Mammon comes to Shanghai', 18th March 1997
Harding, James, 'First steps on the ladder', 19th May 1998
Harding, James, 'Contradiction in markets', 23rd March 1999
Harding, James and Morse, Laurie, 'New York tests the water in global village', 10th July 1995
Harding, Robin, 'Bank of Japan acts to avert liquidity squeeze for exchange traded funds', 20th December 2019
Harding, Robin and Lewis, Leo, 'Overhaul for Japanese stock trading as regulator unveils premium segment', 29th November 2019
Hargreaves, Deborah, 'Hybrids fight to escape regulation', 9th December 1987
Hargreaves, Deborah, 'Mixed response to black box trading', 23rd October 1987
Hargreaves, Deborah, 'Black box is on trial', 10th March 1988
Hargreaves, Deborah, 'Brave new products', 14th October 1988
Hargreaves, Deborah, 'Hopes fade of Liffe-CBOT link', 22nd March 1988
Hargreaves, Deborah, 'Less risk and back to basics', 10th March 1988
Hargreaves, Deborah, 'Regulators seek to protect retail customer in battle of look-alikes', 10th March 1988
Hargreaves, Deborah, 'Sharp rise expected', 13th June 1988
Hargreaves, Deborah, 'Chicago faces a strengthening challenge', 13th December 1989
Hargreaves, Deborah, 'In need of a strong leader', 10th April 1989
Hargreaves, Deborah, 'International regulators slow to tame the machines', 22nd December 1989
Hargreaves, Deborah, 'Matif to join Globex electronic trading', 9th November 1989
Hargreaves, Deborah, 'The new player arrives at work', 30th November 1989
Hargreaves, Deborah, 'OML opens London branch', 15th December 1989
Hargreaves, Deborah, 'Philly's fancy turns to thoughts of merger', 25th July 1989
Hargreaves, Deborah, 'Supremacy battle hots up for on-screen trading', 10th November 1989
Hargreaves, Deborah, 'Tighter regulation feared', 10th April 1989
Hargreaves, Deborah, 'A yoke for Japan's bull', 8th March 1989
Hargreaves, Deborah, 'ADRs refuse to bow out gracefully', 20th July 1990
Hargreaves, Deborah, 'Appeal ruling fails to restore certainty', 9th March 1990

Hargreaves, Deborah, 'Chicago exchanges at variance', 9th March 1990
Hargreaves, Deborah, 'Chicago giants fight to keep their share', 2nd July 1990
Hargreaves, Deborah, 'Collars suit the UK', 2nd July 1990
Hargreaves, Deborah, 'CSFB to integrate European share trading', 8th February 1990
Hargreaves, Deborah, 'Derivatives exchanges seeks tax reform', 12th December 1990
Hargreaves, Deborah, 'An exchange by any other name', 29th June 1990
Hargreaves, Deborah, 'In pole position for Europe', 29th November 1990
Hargreaves, Deborah, 'Liffe aims at one exchange', 7th June 1990
Hargreaves, Deborah, 'LTOM upgrades system', 18th May 1990
Hargreaves, Deborah, 'Marriage plan surprises the guests', l Times 4th April 1990
Hargreaves, Deborah, 'More join the bandwagon', 9th March 1990
Hargreaves, Deborah, 'Race to create a Euro-share index', 21st June 1990
Hargreaves, Deborah, 'Screens stretch time', 9th March 1990
Hargreaves, Deborah, 'SEC delays full opening of options competition', 11th January 1990
Hargreaves, Deborah, 'Sydney FE to set up own clearing house', 14th December 1990
Hargreaves, Deborah, 'Time for players to take their pick', 12th December 1990
Hargreaves, Deborah, 'Turbulence keeps global issues on the ground', 2nd July 1990
Hargreaves, Deborah, 'Value of Cedel deposits surges', 2nd January 1990
Hargreaves, Deborah, 'Derivatives come of age', 13th March 1991
Hargreaves, Deborah, 'Cutting raw material risks', 20th October 1993
Hargreaves, Deborah, 'Future looks brighter for EU farm futures', 18th November 1996
Hargreaves, Deborah, 'Liffe may take on olive oil futures', 29th October 1996
Hargreaves, Deborah, 'Price rises put spotlight on hedging', 6th November 1996
Hargreaves, Deborah, 'Consolidation remains top of the agenda', 8th March 2005
Hargreaves, Deborah, Cohen, Norma and Jopson, Barney, 'Europe looks to new law on securities', 26th January 2005
Hargreaves, Deborah and Durr, Barbara, 'Computers threaten the futures pits', 29th May 1990
Harington, Henry, 'Testing times for fund managers', 16th November 1995
Harington, Henry, 'Vanilla the flavour of the times', 16th November 1995
Harington, Henry, 'Behind the remote reality', 16th February 1996
Harnischfeger, Uta and Boland, Vincent, 'Dispute hits London-Frankfurt link', 24th February 1999
Harrington, Charles, 'Global custodians are bullish about Taurus', 3rd September 1990
Harrington, Charles, 'London is now expected to re-emerge as the centre', 3rd September 1990
Harris, Clay, '"Trailblazer" with vision for London's future', 8th November 1997
Harris, Clay, 'The network solution', 5th November 1998
Harris, Clay, 'Bid to set up biggest wholesale money broker', 10th June 1999
Harris, Clay, 'Brokers agree merger terms', 16th February 1999
Harris, Clay, 'Garban and Intercapital in £300m merger', 3rd July 1999
Harris, Clay, Graham, George and Labate, John, 'Small deal backs big plans for Tradepoint', 7th May 1999
Harrison, Barbara, 'Exchanges defend their world title', 1st December 1992
Harverson, Patrick, 'Profit matters most now', 2nd May 1989
Harverson, Patrick, 'When gilts are sick there is a remedy', 8th March 1989
Harverson, Patrick, 'Leningrad exchange planned', 12th December 1990
Harverson, Patrick, 'Stormy days for securities firms', 7th December 1990
Harverson, Patrick, 'Back to normal after scares over prepayment risks', 19th June 1991
Harverson, Patrick, 'Big Board takes an after-hours gamble', 10th June 1991
Harverson, Patrick, 'Brokers appeal against SEC ruling on small-order system', 24th October 1991
Harverson, Patrick, 'NASD wins early-trading approval from SEC', 11th October 1991
Harverson, Patrick, 'NYSE wakes up to the problem of early trading', 5th August 1991
Harverson, Patrick, 'SEC decision on NASD trading system expected shortly', 9th October 1991
Harverson, Patrick, 'Unhappy new year greets NASD', 13th February 1991
Harverson, Patrick, 'A welcome tonic', 22nd July 1991
Harverson, Patrick, 'The competitive edge', 11th June 1992

Harverson, Patrick, 'It's time to know what's going on', 8th December 1992
Harverson, Patrick, 'The NYSE begins to show its age', 15th May 1992
Harverson, Patrick, 'Daimler's arrival marks new spirit at US securities agency', 1st April 1993
Harverson, Patrick, 'Integration top of the agenda', 20th October 1993
Harverson, Patrick, 'SEC study could bring equities trading shake-up', 15th June 1993
Harverson, Patrick, 'Temperature has cooled markedly', 20th October 1993
Harverson, Patrick, 'Exco staff suffer as world markets slow', 24th November 1995
Harverson, Patrick and Corrigan, Tracy, 'The threat of regulation stirs an unfettered giant', 11th August 1992
Harverson, Patrick and Sharpe, Antonia, 'Market stopped in its tracks', 26th May 1994
Hawkins, Tony, 'Buy-and-hold persists', 14th September 1992
Hayward, Dal, 'Computer dealing shows its value', 19th March 1987
Heaney, Vince, 'Europe takes step closer to a tax on financial transactions', 19th September 2011
Heaney, Vince, 'High-frequency traders' claims refuted by studies', 1st October 2012
Heath, Sean, 'City's stability appreciated', 26th September 1988
Heath, Sean, 'Solution to settlement', 7th November 1990
Heathcote, Edwin, 'Creative tension: City absorbs the new and adapts the old', 4th December 2013
Henderson, Richard, 'Regulator calls on US stock exchanges to justify increase in data charges', 23rd May 2013
Henderson, Richard, '"Flash Boys" challenger IEX struggles to shake up trading', 11th June 2019
Henderson, Richard, 'IEX backs regulator's stance on data fees charged by big stock exchange groups', 15th May 2019
Henderson, Richard, 'IEX exits listing business after effort to lure trade from NYSE and Nasdaq fails', 24th September 2019
Henderson, Richard, 'Landmark for exchange traded bond funds as assets crash through $1tn', 24th April 2019
Henderson, Richard, 'Mifid 2-minded dark pool operator Liquidnet pushes into research', 14th May 2019
Henderson, Richard, 'New York's rival bourses wage fierce fight for IPOs', 10th September 2019
Henderson, Richard, 'Shrinking share listings show radical shift to private sphere', 27th June 2019
Henderson, Richard, 'US fund managers mimic Brussels rules on research', 10th May 2019
Henderson, Richard, 'US regulators take a closer look at data fees', 22nd October 2019
Henderson, Richard, 'Virtu backed bourse MEMX clears vital regulatory hurdle', 2nd November 2019
Henderson, Richard and Bullock, Nicole, 'SEC head calls for sweeping review of rules underpinning equity transactions', 9th March 2019
Henderson, Richard and Kruppa, Miles, 'The attraction of staying private', 1st November 2019
Hermann, A H, 'Lessons from the ITC debacle', 13th March 1986
Hill, Andrew, 'Brussels Bourse takes stock of its finances', 16th August 1991
Hill, Andrew, 'Little Bang a blow to small brokers', 25th October 1991
Hill, Andrew, 'Impact of "little bang" is slightly muted', 3rd December 1992
Hill, Andrew, 'Belfox thrives in the gentleman's club', 25th November 1993
Hill, Andrew, 'More sell-offs expected next year', 24th November 1994
Hill, Andrew, 'Borsa link may usher new era for Milan', 18th October 1996
Hill, Andrew, 'Time to solve problems', 26th November 1996
Hill, Andrew, 'Financial inventors underpin success', 27th March 2006
Hobson, Dominic, 'Four banks dominate the market', 25th July 1988
Hobson, Dominic, 'How the Continentals beat London on its home ground', 17th February 1988
Hobson, Dominic, 'Wide appeal', 17th February 1988
Hobson, Dominic, 'Goal: trades that never touch the sides', 6th July 2001
Hodgson, Godfrey, 'The race is on for the universal terminal', 28th November 1984
Holberton, Simon, 'How hedging can help to trim the risk', 28th November 1988
Holberton, Simon, 'Return of the large private player', 15th July 1988
Holberton, Simon, 'Two ways to shield profits', 10th March 1988

Holberton, Simon, 'Mining a wider seam of shareholder loyalty and enhancing financial clout', 20th April 1990
Holberton, Simon, 'Foreigners join the queue for Shenzhen flotations', 3rd April 1992
Holberton, Simon, 'Regulators battle to catch up', 18th November 1993
Holberton, Simon, 'Shares and the Chinese', 27th April 1994
Holler, Christian, 'Bourses agree alliance', 16th August 2004
Hollinger, Peggy, 'Pensions Tensions', 27th May 2010
Holman, Michael, 'Continent of hazard and opportunity', 7th February 1994
Holman, Michael, 'Reforms ease business climate', 4th August 1995
Hoogervorst, Hans, 'Do not blame accounting rules for the financial crisis', 4th October 2018
Hook, Leslie, 'Ambition to build China's futures', 29th October 2010
Hook, Leslie, 'Beijing seeks to widen gold trading', 4th August 2010
Hook, Leslie, 'Rapid growth but influence stunted by restrictions', 30th November 2010
Hope, Kerin, 'Small investors desert bourse', 20th May 1991
Hope, Kerin, 'Regulations become stricter', 20th May 1994
Hope, Kerin, 'Soaring volumes strain the stock exchange system', 20th May 1994
Hope, Kerin, 'Scandal prompts tighter rules', 28th February 1997
Hope, Kerin, 'Progress is slow but steady', 6th April 1998
Hope, Kerin, 'Greek ship owners likely to set course back to Athens', 12th February 2008
Hope, Kerin, 'Greek shipping chiefs prepare to abandon UK after tax crackdown', 12th February 2008
Houlder, Vanessa, 'Market makers missed', 6th February 1989
Houlder, Vanessa, 'FOX attempts to build on property futures', 10th May 1991
Houlder, Vanessa, 'Many hurdles for Fox to jump', 8th February 1991
Houlder, Vanessa, 'Meat and potatoes row', 11th August 1992
Houlder, Vanessa, 'A mountain of debt', 7th August 1992
Houlder, Vanessa, 'Buildings take on new air of respectability', 25th May 1993
Houlder, Vanessa, 'Expensive vote of confidence', 3rd June 1993
Houlder, Vanessa, 'Weighed down with debts', 5th March 1993
Houlder, Vanessa, 'Financial services' tax out of proportion', 7th November 2005
Houlder, Vanessa, 'Trouble abroad for the City?', 10th September 2013
Houlder, Vanessa, 'Exchange survives scandal to trade another day', 5th December 2014
Houlder, Vanessa and Peel, Michael, 'Harbours of resentment', 1st December 2008
Housego, David, 'A bull market far from being tamed', 20th December 1988
Howell, Michael, 'Rising tide of liquidity lifts many boats, but keep an eye on the horizon', 17th January 2020
Hu, Fred, 'Staying ahead of the game', 24th October 2006
Huband, Mark, 'Egyptian groups take the public road', 27th March 1997
Huband, Mark, 'Firing industry's engine', 12th May 1998
Huband, Mark, 'Expansion is just weeks away', 11th April 2000
Huband, Mark, 'Spread the message to the masses', 31st March 2000
Hughes, Chris, 'Concerns grow for rules as global deals loom', 1st December 2006
Hughes, Chris, 'A controversial investment choice', 5th September 2006
Hughes, Chris, 'Lehman sets record on LSE', 14th August 2006
Hughes, Chris, 'Dealing with a softer touch', 20th February 2007
Hughes, Chris, 'London poised to cement leading position', 3rd November 2007
Hughes, Chris, 'Move to lower "ticks" earns exchange top marks from investors', 20th February 2007
Hughes, Chris, 'Triple blow sends cost of trading soaring', 24th December 2007
Hughes, Chris, 'No more easy money', 11th November 2008
Hughes, Chris and Cohen, Norma, 'Loss of light touch poses threat to LSE', 14th June 2006
Hughes, Chris and Cohen, Norma, 'Thain is attracted by all the right things in London', 20th June 2006
Hughes, Chris and Grant, Jeremy, 'City Limits', 21st January 2008
Hughes, Chris and Guerrera, Francesco, 'A week that shook the system to its core', 20th September 2008

Hughes, Jennifer, 'Traders set to take the forex challenge', 22nd May 2003
Hughes, Jennifer, 'History goes full circle as volume is king', 27th May 2004
Hughes, Jennifer, 'Investor appetite for paper shows few signs of abating', 29th November 2004
Hughes, Jennifer, 'The mouse takes over the floor', 27th May 2004
Hughes, Jennifer, 'Taking their law into their own hands', 27th May 2004
Hughes, Jennifer, 'A veteran with a proud record of service', 27th May 2004
Hughes, Jennifer, 'Where money talks very loudly', 27th May 2004
Hughes, Jennifer, 'Currency futures trading record', 25th August 2005
Hughes, Jennifer, 'Customising risk in Chicago', 28th October 2005
Hughes, Jennifer, 'Eurex issues a challenge to CME', 17th June 2005
Hughes, Jennifer, 'Interbank online action set to soar', 25th February 2005
Hughes, Jennifer, 'Securitisation gets security conscious', 2nd March 2005
Hughes, Jennifer, 'Bankers divided on need for backstop', 4th May 2006
Hughes, Jennifer, 'FX firebrand dream of revolution', 9th May 2006
Hughes, Jennifer, 'Guide to make fails safer', 28th March 2006
Hughes, Jennifer, 'Jury out on NYSE trade plan', 24th March 2006
Hughes, Jennifer, 'Lava Platform to challenge duopoly', 25th April 2006
Hughes, Jennifer, 'NYBOT to offer electronic trading', 26th January 2006
Hughes, Jennifer, 'Securities bodies prepare to merge', 29th June 2006
Hughes, Jennifer, 'US stands out on worldwide language', 19th November 2007
Hughes, Jennifer, 'Bankers seek to detoxify the alphabet soup', 13th October 2009
Hughes, Jennifer, 'Concern over scope of initiatives', 29th September 2009
Hughes, Jennifer, 'Currency derivatives caught in US clearing net', 20th November 2009
Hughes, Jennifer, 'Doubt for safety of bundling up loans', 18th December 2009
Hughes, Jennifer, 'FX faces prospect of two-tier pricing', 21st August 2009
Hughes, Jennifer, 'A lesson in how to run a smooth global settlement system', 21st August 2009
Hughes, Jennifer, 'Currency markets ready for the next big thing', 20th October 2010
Hughes, Jennifer, 'Europe dithers over adopting Germany's short selling ban', 27th May 2010
Hughes, Jennifer, 'Fooled again', 19th March 2010
Hughes, Jennifer, 'FSA plays down prop trading impact', 2nd March 2010
Hughes, Jennifer, 'Greek drama darkens mood', 25th February 2010
Hughes, Jennifer, 'Innovation drives trading surge', 28th September 2010
Hughes, Jennifer, 'Paris targets a French revolution in bond trading', 26th January 2010
Hughes, Jennifer, 'Post-crisis wrangle over the best way to measure value', 11th February 2010
Hughes, Jennifer, 'Private Placement deals find favour in search for funding', 24th August 2010
Hughes, Jennifer, 'Revolution in the cosy world of bonds', 1st March 2010
Hughes, Jennifer, 'S&P warns on UK mortgage securities', 10th September 2010
Hughes, Jennifer, 'Worries over threat of "heavy touch"', 30th March 2010
Hughes, Jennifer, 'Focus on speed blurs big picture', 29th March 2011
Hughes, Jennifer, 'So where do they make their money?', 29th March 2011
Hughes, Jennifer, 'HK-Shanghai link creates winners and losers', 17th November 2014
Hughes, Jennifer, 'Singapore-Hong Kong battle heats up', 29th July 2016
Hughes, Jennifer, 'Inspiration from Home Depot for LME owner', 11th May 2017
Hughes, Jennifer and Authers, John, 'Taking the floor: how a screen role will challenge New York's market debutant', 7th March 2006
Hughes, Jennifer, Beales, Richard and Tett, Gillian, 'The yield conundrum: as bond returns drift downwards, is risk soaring for investors', 17th June 2005
Hughes, Jennifer and Gangahar, Anuj, 'CBOT soon to go electronic on agri-trades', 27th April 2006
Hughes, Jennifer and Guha, Krishna, 'World foreign exchange trading soars to a peak of $1,900bn a day', 29th September 2004
Hughes, Jennifer, Mackenzie, Michael and Daneshkhu, Scheherazade, 'Paris Project recommends central clearing for bonds', 27th April 2010
Hughes, Jennifer and Stafford, Philip, 'MTS to expand into corporate debt', 16th November 2010
Hughes, Jennifer and Tett, Gillian, 'A long road to any Mifid impact', 2nd November 2007

Hughes, Jennifer and Thal Larsen, Peter, 'A light approach and 9,000 page rulebook', 23rd June 2007
Hughes, Jennifer and Thal Larsen, Peter, '"Twin peaks" watching duties', 23rd June 2007
Hughes, Margaret, 'Quest for new sources of finance', 29th May 1984
Hughes, Margaret, 'Sector receives fresh lease of life', 29th May 1984
Hume, Neil, 'London unveils bullion futures platform', 9th August 2016
Hume, Neil, 'Grain traders reap few rewards from record crops due to intense competition', 9th August 2017
Hume, Neil, 'Incoming chief of metals exchange plots evolution not revolution', 7th August 2017
Hume, Neil, Rice, Xan and Schäfer, Daniel, 'Gold fix on the spot after Barclays fine', 24th May 2014
Hume, Neil and Sheppard, David, 'London sitting on $300bn worth of bullion', 2nd August 2017
Ibison, David, 'Market feels effects of uncertainty', 5th May 2000
Ibison, David, 'Banks lose hope sun will rise on Japan's Big Bang', 14th February 2003
Ibison, David, 'OMX open to transatlantic deal', 20th July 2006
Ibison, David, 'Stockholm plots course as financial centre', 12th July 2006
Ibison, David, 'Borse Dubai bid for OMX faces test over respectability', 18th August 2007
Ibison, David, 'Borse Dubai suffers double blow in its efforts to take over OMX', 24th August 2007
Ibison, David, 'Swedish law to stop OMX being Americanised', 19th December 2007
Ibison, David and Chung, Joanna, 'Qatar bows out of OMX battle', 5th December 2007
Ibison, David and Kerr, Simeon, 'Qataris sell OMX stake to Gulf rival', 14th February 2008
ICMA, 50 Years [advertisement], 5th February 2018
Irving, Richard, 'Shock-absorbing models', 16th November 1995
Ishmael, Stacy-Marie, 'Fall-out from subprime crisis spreads', 27th November 2007
Ishmael, Stacy-Marie, 'Victoria woes rock SIV sector', 9th January 2008
Ishmael, Stacy-Marie and Authers, John, 'NYSE takes 1% stake in Bovespa', 1st November 2007
Ishmael, Stacy-Marie and Hume, Neil, 'Traders twiddle as London Stock Exchange shuts', 9th September 2008
Ishmael, Stacy-Marie, Scholtes, Saskia and van Duyn, Aline, 'Time to address counterparty risk', 8th April 2008
Iskandar, Samer, 'Exchanges go into battle', 22nd November 1996
Iskandar, Samer, 'Exchanges square up for a fight', 17th December 1996
Iskandar, Samer, 'Unrelenting flow of funds boost region', 8th November 1996
Iskandar, Samer, 'Definitions of a new financial instrument', 5th December 1997
Iskandar, Samer, 'Euro set to shrink volumes', 28th February 1997
Iskandar, Samer, 'Fierce battle rages for market share', 27th June 1997
Iskandar, Samer, 'Great expectations of a promising future', 27th June 1997
Iskandar, Samer, 'Management by mathematics', 31st March 1997
Iskandar, Samer, 'Safer lending of securities', 5th December 1997
Iskandar, Samer, 'Survey sees Liffe dominant in Europe', 7th October 1997
Iskandar, Samer, 'Electronic trading system for Eurobonds', 23rd January 1998
Iskandar, Samer, 'Market explodes into life', 17th July 1998
Iskandar, Samer, 'The search for growth', 1st May 1998
Iskandar, Samer, 'E-advantage has yet to make mark', 14th May 1999
Iskandar, Samer, 'Paris Bourse enjoys a long hot summer', 7th September 1999
Iskandar, Samer, 'Shaped for a common platform', 20th September 1999
Iskandar, Samer, 'Turning point for SBF's chairman', 23rd March 1999
Iskandar, Samer, 'Paris bids for Europe's crown', 10th November 2000
Iskandar, Samer, 'Technology overtakes tradition', 1st January 2000
Iskandar, Samer and Boland, Vincent, 'French move to harmonise settlements', 28th February 2000
Iskandar, Samer and Luce, Edward, 'Big issue for Europe', 4th February 1998
Iskandar, Samer and Luce, Edward, 'Liffe grasps the nettle of electronic trading', 10th March 1998
Iskandar, Samer and Luce, Edward, 'Move to a life less ordinary', 11th March 1998
Jack, Andrew, 'The Matif success story', 14th November 1994
Jack, Andrew, 'Local bourse shuts as Paris calls the tune', 8th November 1995
Jack, Andrew, 'The French revolution', 16th February 1996

Jack, Andrew, 'Matif celebrates 10 speculative years', 22nd February 1996
Jack, Andrew, 'Miracle helps birthday celebrations', 10th December 1996
Jack, Andrew, 'More liquid than London', 1st March 1996
Jack, Andrew, 'Paris market opens doors to wheat futures trading', 5th July 1996
Jack, Andrew, 'Dreaming of an alliance', 28th February 1997
Jack, Andrew, 'French Bourse seeking European collaboration', 13th February 1997
Jack, Andrew, 'SBF, Matif join forces ahead of German link', 18th September 1997
Jack, Andrew, 'SBF plans equities exchanges link', 10th July 1997
Jack, Andrew, 'News takes Paris exchange by surprise', 8th July 1998
Jack, Andrew, Cohen, Norma, Gapper, John, Urry, Maggie and Hamilton Fazey, Ian, 'Angry City takes stock of lost money and time', 12th March 1993
Jack, Andrew and Lapper, Richard, 'Volumes drop by 31 per cent', 16th November 1995
Jackson, Dominique, 'Futures scramble triggers global gold rush', 28th October 1988
Jackson, Dominique, 'Liffe and LTOM fall into step', 12th October 1988
Jackson, Dominique, 'Private investors are regaining confidence', 20th August 1988
Jackson, Dominique, 'Swaps keep in step with the regulators', 10th August 1988
Jackson, Gavin, 'Bank of England plays down surge in risky corporate loans', 24th January 2019
Jacob, Rahul, 'Modernisation plan sparks recovery', 28th April 2000
Jacob, Rahul and Nakamae, Naoko, 'Prospects promising in year of the deal', 19th May 2000
Jacomb, Martin, 'Fine-tuning the London market', 19th April 1988
Jacques, Bruce, 'Sydney sheds the casino image', 19th March 1987
Jacques, Bruce, 'Bonds shortage whets appetites', 17th February 1988
Jacques, Bruce, 'Slimming programme', 10th December 1990
James, Canute, 'Securities exchange set up in Santo Domingo', 16th December 1991
James, Canute, 'Taking stock of the Caribbean', 26th February 1991
James, Canute, 'Boost for Caribbean Exchange plan', 4th February 2003
Jansson, Eric, 'Telecommunism helps power stock market growth', 12th November 2007
Jenkins, Patrick, 'Commissions on German share deals to decline', 2nd September 2000
Jenkins, Patrick, 'How to find the best price', 8th April 2000
Jenkins, Patrick, 'Another shot at his London prize', 14th December 2004
Jenkins, Patrick, 'Germany's exchanges fight for survival', 14th July 2004
Jenkins, Patrick, 'Faltering financial centre sees bright lights amid gloom', 6th December 2005
Jenkins, Patrick, 'Visionary who fell foul of investors', 10th May 2005
Jenkins, Patrick, 'Germany's innovative streak', 28th March 2006
Jenkins, Patrick, 'Investment banks enjoy companies' bond boom', 14th September 2009
Jenkins, Patrick, 'Mutuals seek means to adapt and survive', 6th September 2010
Jenkins, Patrick, 'New regulatory standards are the next big unknown', 8th October 2010
Jenkins, Patrick, 'Poll finds solid support for tougher action', 25th January 2010
Jenkins, Patrick, 'Banks face a perfect storm that is getting worse', 25th January 2012
Jenkins, Patrick, 'Volker attacks Vickers reforms', 18th October 2012
Jenkins, Patrick, 'Humbled financiers reassess their culture', 17th March 2014
Jenkins, Patrick, 'It's right for shareholders to share the pain', 13th November 2014
Jenkins, Patrick, 'Banker bashing is back as public resentment returns', 8th May 2015
Jenkins, Patrick, 'Start-up threat to creaking banks', 14th October 2015
Jenkins, Patrick and Arnold, Martin, 'Lenders struggle to weather storms on all sides', 11th November 2015
Jenkins, Patrick and Barber, Alex, 'City bankers fret over being on the margins', 5th December 2012
Jenkins, Patrick and Binham, Caroline, 'City financiers struggle to unite on post-Brexit regulation', 5th July 2018
Jenkins, Patrick, Braithwaite, Tom and Masters, Brooke, 'New force emerges from the shadows', 10th April 2012
Jenkins, Patrick and Cameron, Doug, 'D Börse sticks with plan for Eurex in US', 10th January 2006
Jenkins, Patrick and Cohen, Norma, 'A determined player', 18th December 2004

Jenkins, Patrick and Cohen, Norma, 'Deutsche Börse courts LSE for European exchange union', 14th December 2004
Jenkins, Patrick and Cohen, Norma, 'Seifert's downfall: how a shareholder revolt sent his plans for Deutsche Börse up in smoke', 25th May 2005
Jenkins, Patrick and Cohen, Norma, 'Timely decision to resurrect Deutsche Börse small-cap index', 18th October 2005
Jenkins, Patrick and Cohen, Norma, 'Bourses attack bank moves to upset trading structures', 21st February 2006
Jenkins, Patrick and Fleming, Sam, 'Alternative finance steps out of the shadow', 16th June 2014
Jenkins, Patrick and Fleming, Sam, 'Taking another path', 17th June 2014
Jenkins, Patrick and Hughes, Jennifer, 'Big Gaps to fill in', 9th December 2010
Jenkins, Patrick and Jones, Adam, 'Turquoise put up for sale after approach', 19th August 2009
Jenkins, Patrick and Jones, Claire, 'Eurozone bank rules menace City prosperity, warns lobby', 19th March 2014
Jenkins, Patrick and Masters, Brooke, 'The money moves on', 15th September 2010
Jenkins, Patrick and Masters, Brooke, 'Banks test CDO-style finance for trade', 9th April 2012
Jenkins, Patrick and Masters, Brooke, 'London's precarious position', 30th July 2012
Jenkins, Patrick, Masters, Brooke and Braithwaite, Tom, 'Hunt for a common front', 8th September 2011
Jenkins, Patrick and Milne, Richard, 'Caught in the grip', 2nd December 2011
Jenkins, Patrick and Morris, Stephen, 'Paris set to be post-Brexit trading hub as UK defends City's global credentials', 1st October 2018
Jenkins, Patrick and Murphy, Megan, 'Again on the edge', 15th August 2011
Jenkins, Patrick, Parker, George and Barker, Alex, 'UK refuses to give up on post-Brexit plan for City', 24th July 2018
Jenkins, Patrick, Sanderson, Rachel and Johnson, Miles, 'Banks Contemplate shrunken future', 14th October 2011
Jenkins, Patrick and Schäfer, Daniel, 'New York is a tall order for Europeans', 4th October 2012
Jenkins, Patrick and Schäfer, Daniel, 'Banks suffer as derivatives trade shifts to the "shadows"', 12th September 2013
Jenkins, Patrick and Stafford, Philip, 'Exchanges', 14th September 2019
Jenkins, Patrick, Stafford, Philip and Braithwaite, Tom, 'Bankers voice concerns over risks posed by clearing houses', 8th July 2013
Jenkins, Patrick and Wassener, Bettina, 'Wake-up call to corporate Germany', 10th May 2005
John, Peter, 'LCH provides crisis cover for derivatives', 6th August 1996
John, Peter, 'Foreign ownership drives expansion in the City', 19th March 1998
John, Peter, 'Fat Finger syndrome can be bad for financial health', 9th December 2001
John, Peter, George, Nicholas and Boland, Vincent, 'Stock Exchanges start talks on synchronising hours in Europe', 1st March 1999
Johnson, Jo, 'Ringfence and regulate in haste, repent at leisure', 13th September 2011
Johnson, Jo, 'Politicians must stand up for the City after EU exit', 21st February 2019
Johnson, Miles, 'Bourse still dominates at home', 5th October 2011
Johnson, Miles, 'Geneva's bright lights lose their allure', 1st August 2015
Johnson, Miles, 'Mifid 2 poised to hasten slow death of analysts', 25th January 2018
Johnson, Miles, 'Volatility derivatives have become tail that wags the dog', 9th February 2018
Johnson, Rachel, 'Reuters triumphs in the derivatives jungle', 21st December 1989
Johnson, Steve, 'Fears rise on change to regime', 27th May 2004
Johnson, Steve, 'London rules new wave of FX deals', 18th July 2006
Johnson, Steve, 'eBay for portfolio trades debuts', 4th June 2007
Johnson, Steve, 'Concerns over risks sharpens the focus', 6th April 2009
Johnson, Steve, 'Fear for corporate bonds trade', 20th July 2009
Johnson, Steve, 'Hidden costs found in dark pools', 7th December 2009
Johnson, Steve, 'How to breathe life back into bonds', 20th July 2009

Johnson, Steve, 'A little oasis of calm for currencies', 2nd February 2009
Johnson, Steve, 'New bond market faces fight', 30th November 2009
Johnson, Steve, 'UK plan to open up bond trade', 1st February 2010
Johnson, Steve, 'Securities owners keen to lend again but income falls', 21st March 2011
Johnson, Steve, 'EU shadow banking plan rapped', 26th March 2012
Johnson, Steve, 'High-speed trading is "bad influence"', 28th April 2014
Johnson, Steve, 'Foreign funds shun Saudi Arabia on entry to flagship index', 21st May 2019
Johnson, Steve, 'Pakistan bourse woes fuel doubts over emerging market status', 17th April 2019
Johnson, Steve, 'Saudi exchange takes first step into main global equity benchmarks', 19th March 2019
Jones, Claire, Binham, Caroline and Fleming, Sam, 'Fed governor to head global finance police', 21st November 2018
Jones, Claire and Morris, Stephen, 'ECB to test how long banks can last without fresh funds', 7th February 2019
Jones, Matthew and Wassener, Bettina, 'March date set for EEX derivatives', 31st January 2001
Jones, Sam, 'Alert over short-selling disclosure rules', 9th February 2010
Jones, Sam, 'Dublin entices funds with softer regulation', 6th September 2010
Jones, Sam, 'Customers cast a more critical eye on the field', 21st March 2011
Jones, Sam, 'Hedge funds are wary of taking on more risk', 24th February 2011
Jones, Sam, 'Big spending clients keep providers on their toes', 26th March 2012
Jones, Sam, 'Hedge funds feel pinch from new banking rules', 18th April 2012
Jones, Sam, 'The mood music is about to change', 26th March 2012
Jones, Sam, 'Tangled up anew', 30th May 2012
Jones, Sam, 'Volker Rule', 10th April 2012
Jones, Sam and Ishmael, Stacy-Marie, 'No relief in sight for CDO investors', 11th January 2008
Jones, Sheila, 'The market moves ahead', 25th November 1993
Jones, Sheila, 'SE edges towards full automation', 2nd June 1995
Jones, Sheila, 'Manchester seeks virtual stock market for Europe', 26th January 2000
Jopson, Barney, 'European regulators learn to sing in harmony', 17th November 2005
Jopson, Barney, 'Financial watchdog eager to show its cuddly side after years of growling', 11th August 2005
Jopson, Barney, 'City institutions perform double act in risk alerts', 21st August 2006
Jopson, Barney, 'Countries follow UK in merging regulators', 7th February 2006
Jopson, Barney, 'Regulatory overhaul brings rising hope', 16th February 2006
Jopson, Barney, 'Regulatory reform not going by the book', 16th January 2006
Jopson, Barney, 'Rivals query JSE's pan-Africa plan', 9th June 2008
Jopson, Barney, 'Delicate art of tea pricing in Mombasa', 2nd September 2009
Jopson, Barney and Rennison, Joe, 'Brexit spurs call for more clearing house regulation', 7th October 2017
Joubert, Michelle, 'South African companies head for the open door', 22nd March 1999
JP Morgan, advertisement, 8th December 1992
Jung-a, Song, 'Brokerage sector looks set for consolidation', 26th June 2007
Jung-a, Song, 'Korea Exchange tries to lure foreign companies', 22nd September 2008
Jung-a, Song, 'Seoul SME bourse plan faces scepticism', 11th June 2012
Jung-a, Song, 'South Korea's Kosdaq soars but troubles persist', 23rd November 2017
Jung-a, Song, 'Lime liquidity issues spark contagion fears at South Korea hedge funds', 31st October 2019
Jung-a, Song and Brown, Kevin, 'Citizen traders hooked on Korean derivatives', 10th December 2009
Jung-a, Song and Sanchanta, Mariko, 'TSE and Korea exchange move towards link-up', 7th July 2006
Jung-a, Song and Turner, David, 'Tokyo may take stake as Korea Exchange plans IPO', 18th November 2006
Kaletsky, Anatole, 'Passing their book round the world', 21st October 1987
Kaletsky, Anatole, 'Big decisions ahead', 24th June 1988
Kaletsky, Anatole, 'It's time to get to grips with the tough universal game', 18th May 1988
Kaminska, Izabella, 'Growth is driven by investors' need for clarity', 28th September 2010

Kaminska, Izabella, 'Man and machinery in perfect harmony', 28th September 2010
Kantai, Parselelo, 'Trouble at old boys club', 29th October 2009
Kapner, Fred, 'Borsa to adopt a contrarian stance', 28th March 2001
Kapner, Fred, 'Nuovo Mercato enters blue-chip era', 14th October 2003
Karmali, Naazneen, 'Early bird catches worm', 13th March 1995
Kavanagh, Michael, 'Beyond the bean counters', 31st May 2012
Kay, John, 'Big Bang shows the power of competition to surprise', 24th October 2006
Kay, John, 'A realm dismal in its rituals of rigor', 26th August 2011
Kazim, Amy, 'Stock market mania grips Vietnam's middle classes', 21st February 2007
Keefe, John, 'Regulator's torch to light up dark pools', 23rd November 2009
Kellaway, Lucy, 'Attractions stretch to the US', 27th January 1986
Kellaway, Lucy, 'The costs of entry', 27th January 1986
Kellaway, Lucy, 'Rapid rise to maturity', 27th January 1986
Kellaway, Lucy, 'Stock Exchange plans to bring in OTC as third tier', 1st April 1986
Kellaway, Lucy, 'Futures contract proves popular', 3rd February 1987
Kellaway, Lucy, 'Need and firmness brighten the year', 3rd February 1987
Kellaway, Lucy, 'Opec hang on to control', 3rd February 1987
Kellaway, Lucy, 'EC member states prepare law to protect against insider trading', 7th February 1990
Kellaway, Lucy, 'Many moves on the way to market', 21st November 1990
Kellaway, Lucy and Dickson, Tim, 'Painful birth of single market', 19th December 1990
Kellaway, Lucy and Waters, Richard, 'Brittan pledges flexibility in EC financial services rules', 6th February 1990
Kelleher, Colm, 'The EU misses the point on finance after Brexit', 24th April 2019
Kelleher, Ellen, 'Share dealers say tax hampers London', 26th May 2007
Kelleher, Ellen, 'Obscure property vehicle could carry Armageddon-style risk', 18th November 2013
Kelleher, Ellen and Ross, Alice, 'Run unlikely', 9th July 2008
Kelly, Jim, 'Auditors face up to the future', 27th June 1997
Kelly, Jim, 'World accounting wins more converts', 9th June 1997
Kelly, Jim, 'Standard procedures', 17th July 1998
Kenchington, John, 'Investors are being urged to stress test fixed income funds', 3rd November 2014
Kent, Pen and Fox, Darren, 'Why providers should merge', 28th March 2001
Keohane, David, 'SocGen buys Commerzbank's EMC business', 4th July 2018
Keohane, David and Stafford, Philip, 'Jury still out on Mifid 2 transparency rules', 18th June 2018
Keohane, David and Stafford, Philip, 'French regulator calls for flexible market rules', 15th July 2019
Kerr, Simeon, 'Borse Dubai to push ahead in spite of regulatory snag', 24th August 2007
Kerr, Simeon, 'Bourses at war for business', 20th November 2007
Kerr, Simeon, 'Dubai dazzles but Riyadh is the big prize', 19th November 2007
Kerr, Simeon, 'Qatar's 10-year financial plan', 21st September 2007
Kerr, Simeon, 'Nasdaq Dubai blow as DP World looks to London', 7th January 2010
Kerr, Simeon, 'Imbalances keep Gulf region on the sidelines', 29th May 2012
Kerr, Simeon, 'Riyadh ready to ease Saudi bourse access', 12th May 2017
Kerr, Simeon, England, Andrew and Grant, Jeremy, 'Dubai talks to Abu Dhabi over bourse merger', 31st March 2010
Kerr, Simeon and Grant, Jeremy, 'Qatar's ambition revealed in plans for exchange', 25th June 2008
Khalaf, Roula, 'Bourse starts to modernise', 28th November 1995
Khalaf, Roula, 'Appetite survives political turmoil', 8th November 1996
Khalaf, Roula, 'Casablanca hopes for index funds', 8th November 1996
Khalaf, Roula, 'Private sector is quick to adjust', 8th November 1996
Khalaf, Roula, 'Keeping the foreigners happy', 10th May 2000
Kibazo, Joel, 'A step back to yesterday', 5th November 1996
Kim, Jennifer, 'Bond ETFs are no menace to financial system', 28th November 2019
Kingman, John, 'Doors thrown open to the world', 28th March 1996
Kingman, John, 'Painful jolt ends bull run', 28th March 1996
Kingsley, Stephen, 'Quest for a new role and a new strategy', 23rd March 1999

Kingsley, Stephen, 'A blueprint for the new exchange', 19th September 2000
Kliment, Alexander and Rodrigues, Vivianne, 'Regulated, representative and popular with investors', 15th November 2011
Kuper, Simon, 'Bleak days ahead for forex traders', 24th December 1996
Kuper, Simon, 'Banks trade places as race for foreign exchange intensifies', 20th May 1997
Kuper, Simon, 'Dealers on the spot as margins narrow', 18th April 1997
Kuper, Simon, 'Merrill makes up for lost time on forex', 14th July 1997
Kuper, Simon, 'Reuters falls behind EBS in electronic broking', 30th June 1997
Kuper, Simon, 'Information on the button', 5th June 1998
Kuper, Simon, 'Old divide is starting to crumble', 23rd January 1998
Kuper, Simon, 'Old order gives way to the new', 5th June 1998
Kwong, Robin, 'New Chinese bourse set to lure domestic flotations', 24th June 2009
Kynge, James, 'Sime Darby delists from London exchange', 15th October 1996
Kynge, James, 'Battle is on for the hub role', 19th May 1997
Kynge, James, 'Exotics reach the major league', 9th May 1997
Kynge, James, 'Ingenious new ideas for futures', 9th May 1997
Kynge, James, 'Singapore to ease SE listing requirements', 10th March 1997
Kynge, James, 'China may form cotton exchange', 17th December 1998
Kynge, James and Dunkley, Emma, 'MSCI hands Chinese stocks a bigger global role', 2nd March 2019
Labate, John, 'Wall Street feels the tremors', 23rd March 1999
Labate, John, 'Hoping to leapfrog the regulators', 31st March 2000
Labate, John, 'Market visionary and architect of change', 31st March 2000
Labate, John, 'US plan for electronic exchange', 15th March 2000
Labate, John, 'Wall starts to crack as pressure intensifies', 31st March 2000
Labate, John, 'Wall Street takes a long, hard look at its (e-) future', 3rd March 2000
Labate, John, 'Decentralised exchange the hot topic of debate', 27th November 2001
Labate, John, 'Fragmented trading boosts their worth', 26th January 2001
Labate, John, 'Master of the cautious, careful approach', 28th March 2001
Labate, John, 'Nasdaq faces challenge from smaller exchanges', 7th November 2001
Labate, John, 'Nasdaq falls in second quarter', 22nd August 2001
Labate, John, 'Nasdaq receives platform approval', 11th January 2001
Labate, John, 'NYSE costs lower than Nasdaq', 9th January 2001
Labate, John, 'NYSE poised for concerted push on ETFs', 12th July 2001
Labate, John, 'Seamless, smooth and secure', 28th March 2001
Labate, John, 'Failure is not an option', 6th June 2002
Labate, John, 'High-tech systems jolt old markets into action', 6th June 2002
Labate, John, 'Instinet plan could deal a blow to Nasdaq', 13th February 2002
Labate, John, 'Selling Nasdaq's strengths to the market', 10th April 2002
Labate, John, 'Terrorist threats a constant concern', 6th June 2002
Labate, John and Boland, Vincent, 'Nasdaq attempts to lure London exchange', 17th December 2000
Labate, John and Harris, Clay, 'Fighting for a share', 26th May 1999
Labate, John and Hill, Andrew, 'Ringing the exchanges', 6th March 2000
Labate, John and Leahy, Joseph, 'Trading system is set to start pilot scheme', 8th June 2001
Labate, John and Merchant, Khozem, 'Mixed results for ADRs as issuance slows down', 23rd March 1999
Labate, John and van Duyn, Aline, 'Nasdaq dispels any doubts over its European ambitions', 31st March 2001
Laitner, Sarah, 'Demand for debt puts swaps at the cutting edge', 25th September 2001
Laitner, Sarah, 'Euronext set for Liffe', 28th December 2001
Lamb, Christina, 'Brazil moves toward a single stock exchange', 17th September 1991
Lambe, Geraldine, 'FX markets ride wave of widening appeal', 4th October 2010
Lambe, Geraldine, 'Settlement model aids FX market success', 12th April 2010
Lambert, Richard, 'The lessons Wall Street can teach London', 18th April 1984
Lambert, Richard, 'Questions for the Gilt-Edged Market', 18th April 1984

Lambert, Richard, 'Capturing the market's mood', 1st July 1985
Lambert, Richard, 'More protection for investors', 21st December 1985
Lambert, Richard, 'More products now need round-the-clock trading', 27th October 1986
Lambert, Richard, 'A stain not easy to wash out', 17th October 1987
Lambert, Richard, 'The new toys were fallible', 14th October 1988
Lambert, Richard, 'Finance grows into a threat to the City', 1st June 1989
Lambert, Richard, 'Investment firms at mercy of single-passport talks', 9th October 1989
Lambert, Richard, 'Wider horizons beckon New York Exchange', 24th September 1997
Landell-Mills, Natasha, 'Should the Big Four accountancy firms be split up? Yes', 22nd March 2018
Landingin, Roel, 'New blow to reputation of Philippines' exchange', 2nd November 2009
Lane, David, 'Curing a bad name', 20th February 1989
Lane, David, 'Final curtain now in sight', 19th November 1990
Lane, David, 'Big Bang looms', 6th June 1991
Lapper, Richard, 'Alliances with a future', 7th September 1995
Lapper, Richard, 'Innovation in swaps and oranges', 23rd May 1995
Lapper, Richard, 'Liffe may list Matif products switched from open outcry', 17th May 1995
Lapper, Richard, 'Liffe to take trading space at stock exchange', 12th December 1995
Lapper, Richard, 'New generation takes over', 16th November 1995
Lapper, Richard, 'Regulators aim to gird the globe', 10th July 1995
Lapper, Richard, 'Revival of the floor show', 27th July 1995
Lapper, Richard, 'A rosy future for futures spells a charmed Liffe', 14th January 1995
Lapper, Richard, 'Strategic global electronic connections', 16th November 1995
Lapper, Richard, 'Strong growth in volume', 17th May 1995
Lapper, Richard, 'Clarifying a complicated subject', 1st March 1996
Lapper, Richard, 'An important new frontier is opening', 22nd November 1996
Lapper, Richard, 'New deal fuels price rises', 7th March 1996
Lapper, Richard, 'No longer the new kid', 21st March 1996
Lapper, Richard, 'Pace of state sell-offs stepped up', 14th June 1996
Lapper, Richard, 'A slice of NY's pie', 7th June 1996
Lapper, Richard, 'A tale of two cities', 12th June 1996
Lapper, Richard, 'Traders starting to catch on', 1st March 1996
Lapper, Richard, 'Brokers need volumes', 25th March 1997
Lapper, Richard, 'Restrictions set to ease', 25th March 1997
Lapper, Richard, 'Exchange held back by apartheid-era regulations', 21st April 2010
Lapper, Richard, 'Jo'burg starts to warm up', 19th March 2010
Lapper, Richard and Cohen, Norma, 'Liffe to extend automated trading', 13th September 1995
Lapper, Richard and Gawith, Philip, 'Forex market growth slowing, says BIS', 31st May 1996
Lapper, Richard and Gawith, Philip, 'London braces itself for a repo revolution', 2nd January 1996
Lapper, Richard and Jack, Andrew, 'Aiming for a meeting of markets', 24th November 1995
Lapper, Richard and Middelmann, Conner, 'Risks of a concrete proposal', 21st August 1996
Lapper, Richard and Mulligan, Mark, 'Picture continues to darken', 28th March 2001
Large, Andrew, 'Save us from Section 62', 29th September 1987
Lascelles, David, 'Big business but competition keen', 14th February 1984
Lascelles, David, 'Huge changes in progress', 21st May 1984
Lascelles, David, 'System more accessible to outsiders', 19th March 1984
Lascelles, David, 'UK mergers bring a conflict of interest', 29th May 1984
Lascelles, David, 'Wall St lures UK merchant banks', 27th February 1985
Lascelles, David, 'The backroom gets ready for Big Bang', 15th January 1986
Lascelles, David, 'The battle to keep tabs in the face of rapid change', 21st April 1986
Lascelles, David, 'A Bill to launch a new regime', 2nd October 1986
Lascelles, David, 'The competition will get tougher', 2nd October 1986
Lascelles, David, 'An enigma with a shrewd view of how to use capital', 15th December 1986
Lascelles, David, 'An established profit centre', 27th May 1986
Lascelles, David, 'Global wrestling match hots up', 11th April 1986

Lascelles, David, 'Green light for market in UK commercial paper', 30th April 1986
Lascelles, David, 'A magnet for foreign banks', 27th October 1986
Lascelles, David, 'Morgan takes a flyer', 18th June 1986
Lascelles, David, 'A New York-Tokyo-London axis', 7th April 1986
Lascelles, David, 'Now it's the Big Five', 2nd October 1986
Lascelles, David, 'A propitious moment for the Bang', 27th October 1986
Lascelles, David, 'Rich field for bright ideas', 8th February 1986
Lascelles, David, 'Round-the-clock bankers', 9th April 1986
Lascelles, David, 'Selectivity, not size', 2nd October 1986
Lascelles, David, 'Shift is mixed blessing', 28th November 1986
Lascelles, David, 'Sidestepping the Big Bang', 15th January 1986
Lascelles, David, 'The stampede to become global players', 2nd April 1986
Lascelles, David, 'A time to map new strategies', 22nd May 1986
Lascelles, David, 'When the walls come down', 23rd July 1986
Lascelles, David, 'After the rush, the shakeout', 8th May 1987
Lascelles, David, 'Another flurry in money brokers' world', 19th August 1987
Lascelles, David, 'Banking on an international status', 3rd November 1987
Lascelles, David, 'Clearers look overseas', 21st September 1987
Lascelles, David, 'Earnings continue to increase', 3rd June 1987
Lascelles, David, 'Foundations laid, but plans still vague', 23rd June 1987
Lascelles, David, 'Grave doubts about the rule books', 21st October 1987
Lascelles, David, 'New strengths and a ticket to the City's turf', 21st September 1987
Lascelles, David, 'Pressure mounts for global consistency', 21st April 1987
Lascelles, David, 'Regulator of the robust', 21st September 1987
Lascelles, David, 'Swaps market likely to last, says Bank', 12th February 1987
Lascelles, David, 'Thrive, merge or specialise', 21st September 1987
Lascelles, David, 'Through the pain barrier', 21st September 1987
Lascelles, David, 'Trying to end the City paperchase', 22nd September 1987
Lascelles, David, 'Why the transatlantic deal must be extended', 7th May 1987
Lascelles, David, 'City sticks to a paper standard', 3rd August 1988
Lascelles, David, 'How Midland was struck by a Californian earthquake', 25th January 1988
Lascelles, David, 'Less like a father-figure', 26th September 1988
Lascelles, David, 'Midland storm-troopers fight to stem soaring losses', 27th January 1988
Lascelles, David, 'Specialise if you're not a global player', 26th September 1988
Lascelles, David, 'Trusting in local judgement', 15th July 1988
Lascelles, David, 'Anything but dull', 25th September 1989
Lascelles, David, 'The barriers are falling', 2nd May 1989
Lascelles, David, 'Calls to bring watchdogs into line', 14th August 1989
Lascelles, David, 'City bank branch costs £3m to set up', 24th April 1989
Lascelles, David, 'Euromarkets face uncertain fate', 1st March 1989
Lascelles, David, 'Important transformation', 7th November 1989
Lascelles, David, 'New services in UK high streets', 2nd May 1989
Lascelles, David, 'Order in the marketplace', 25th September 1989
Lascelles, David, 'Pitching for a share of London's work', 5th July 1989
Lascelles, David, 'A potential financial capital for the EC', 25th September 1989
Lascelles, David, 'Questions over the City's future', 22nd December 1989
Lascelles, David, 'Rules permit local leeway', 2nd May 1989
Lascelles, David, 'Single market faces further delay', 16th June 1989
Lascelles, David, 'Banks seem set to move cautiously', 2nd July 1990
Lascelles, David, 'Cautious steps in the merchant bank forest', 2nd January 1990
Lascelles, David, 'Discreet charm of the Bank', 5th March 1990
Lascelles, David, 'Fortunes vary as recession bites', 29th November 1990
Lascelles, David, 'The London cavern is the hub for Europe', 5th June 1990
Lascelles, David, 'London is the springboard', 15th March 1990

Lascelles, David, 'No room for complacency', 29th November 1990
Lascelles, David, 'Prospects look less certain', 29th November 1990
Lascelles, David, 'Reforms progressing slowly', 9th July 1990
Lascelles, David, 'Reforms fail to keep pace with changes in the markets', 24th May 1991
Lascelles, David, 'The Bank needs a stronger role in the City', 16th June 2008
Lascelles, David and Fidler, Stephen, 'Morgan Stanley sticks to equities', 29th February 1987
Lascelles, David, Hall, William and Montagnon, Peter, 'The Fed weighs the risks', 22nd January 1986
Lascelles, David and Nicoll, Alexander, 'An oddly quiet revolution', 4th February 1987
Lascelles, David and Oram, Roderick, 'Key link added to a global chain', 3rd March 1987
Lascelles, David and Waters, Richard, 'New market disappointment for Citicorp', 17th January 1990
Lawson, Nigel, 'Side effects of deregulation', 27th January 1992
Lawson, Nigel, 'We must not take London's success for granted', 23rd October 2006
Leahy, Joe, 'Regional alliance is long overdue', 28th March 2001
Leahy, Joe, 'Thirst grows for capital pools', 6th June 2002
Leahy, Joe, 'Farewell to the old family brokers' club', 10th October 2006
Leahy, Joe, 'Local sensitivities may damp foreign ambitions', 15th March 2007
Leahy, Joe, 'BSE could list this year to raise global profile', 31st March 2008
Leahy, Joe, 'India's brokerages face shake-up', 14th August 2008
Leahy, Joe, 'No bull as Mumbai chief focuses on modernisation', 14th April 2008
Leahy, Joe, 'India's MCX-SX stock exchange targets foreign investors', 6th July 2009
Leahy, Joe, 'Ambani makes a play for stake in ICEX', 19th August 2010
Leahy, Joe, 'Aspirant Indian bourse fights regulator', 1st October 2010
Leahy, Joe, 'India Plans short-selling move', 28th May 2010
Leahy, Joe, 'Mumbai exchanges join rush for faster trading', 12th January 2010
Leahy, Joe, 'Proposed new Indian stock exchange "not fit and proper"', 27th September 2010
Leahy, Joe, 'Shanghai forges Brazil bourse link', 17th February 2011
Leahy, Joe and Tucker, Sundeep, 'Exchanges urged to work together', 5th November 2008
Lee, John Paul, 'Technology demonstrates its worth', 18th May 1988
Lee, Ruben, 'Why regulators must let markets decide', 20th June 1995
Lee, Ruben, 'In good faith', 17th December 1996
Lee, Ruben, 'Get the stock exchange sale right', 14th December 2005
Levitt, Joshua, 'Taking stock of futures market', 21st October 2003
Lewin, Joel, 'Exchange traded fund assets top $3tn', 6th May 2015
Lewis, Leo, 'Sun threatens to set on foreign companies' Japanese listings', 13th November 2019
Lewis, Leo and Inagaki, Kama, 'Tokyo renews push as financial hub', 22nd November 2016
Lieven, Anatol, 'Past few months have been bumpy', 9th December 1997
Lockett, Hudson, 'Starring role for Shanghai's answer to Nasdaq', 20th July 2019
Lockett, Hudson and Lewis, Leo, 'Japanese watchdog calls for Citigroup to be fined for spoofing bond orders', 27th March 2019
Lockett, Hudson, Xueqiao, Wang and Hancock, Tom, 'Investors star-struck by new Shanghai tech exchange', 24th July 2019
Lodge, Oliver, 'Not waving but drowning in regulation', 7th March 2005
London, Simon, 'Secretive market set to enter the spotlight', 26th September 1990
London, Simon, 'Captains of industry search for impeccable ratings', 9th January 1991
London, Simon, 'Cedel's rise in turnover confirms trend', 5th February 1991
London, Simon, 'The "credit crunch": hard fact or financial fiction', 24th May 1991
London, Simon, 'Recession spurs bonds', 11th November 1991
London, Simon, 'A squeeze in the interbank loans market', 16th October 1991
London, Simon, 'Structures under stress', 22nd July 1991
London, Simon, 'Total amount in issue reaches £10bn', 19th June 1991
London, Simon, 'Banks take expansive view', 19th March 1992
London, Simon, 'Centre of European operations', 27th March 1992
London, Simon, 'More call for change', 27th March 1992
London, Simon, 'Muted cheers for the single market', 11th June 1992

London, Simon, 'Profits are still flowing', 27th March 1992
London, Simon, 'Slower pace pleases dealers', 27th March 1992
Lowe, Philip, 'Beware of distortions caused by monetary policy innovation', 8th October 2019
Lucas, Louise, 'Growth plan may not be so smooth', 27th April 1994
Lucas, Louise, 'Watchdogs do their best', 27th April 1994
Lucas, Louise, 'Small brokers on the rack in HK', 1st August 1996
Lucas, Louise, 'Capital raisers fly high', 9th May 1997
Lucas, Louise, 'Doors are swinging open', 9th May 1997
Lucas, Louise, 'Lessons from the crash', 24th March 1998
Lucas, Louise, 'Esoteric products tap door', 17th December 1999
Lucas, Louise, 'Exchange prepare for wedding bells', 11th August 1999
Lucas, Louise, 'Softer requirements attract start-ups', 17th December 1999
Lucas, Louise, 'Exchange expands at home so it can make its mark abroad', 6th September 2006
Lucas, Louise and Dunkley, Emma, 'China start-ups resist lure of Hong Kong IPO sweeteners', 19th October 2018
Luce, Edward, 'Philippine SE moves toward self-regulation', 29th October 1996
Luce, Edward, 'Euro fever starts scramble', 27th June 1997
Luce, Edward, 'Split in ratings', 25th August 1997
Luce, Edward, 'Agencies to target Europe's burgeoning bond market', 17th December 1998
Luce, Edward, 'Bankers and Brussels at odds over impact on London', 9th December 1998
Luce, Edward, 'A cloud over Frankfurt's ambitions', 24th June 1998
Luce, Edward, 'Discount market follows the top hat into history', 23rd December 1998
Luce, Edward, 'Emu to make Europe more like America', 18th December 1998
Luce, Edward, 'Eurex set to address complaints', 20th November 1998
Luce, Edward, 'The future of futures', 30th June 1998
Luce, Edward, 'Liffe blow as German contract is dropped', 5th March 1998
Luce, Edward, 'Liffe finds little comfort in tie-up with Frankfurt', 11th July 1998
Luce, Edward, 'Liffe to focus on forging new alliances and changing rules', 3rd November 1998
Luce, Edward, 'Liffe will open share ownership to non-members', 18th December 1998
Luce, Edward, 'Liffe's limited reform plan fails to impress critics', 23rd April 1998
Luce, Edward, 'Bonding together', 6th August 1999
Luce, Edward, 'Breathing a second lease of life into Liffe', 27th July 1999
Luce, Edward, 'Central trading cushion cleared for take-off', 9th February 1999
Luce, Edward, 'Clearers settle on continent', 9th July 1999
Luce, Edward, 'Deutsche Börse may demutualise', 3rd December 1999
Luce, Edward, 'Exchanges in world flux', 20th September 1999
Luce, Edward, 'Future is uncertain after frantic year', 23rd March 1999
Luce, Edward, 'Hard global pressure on Liffe', 20th September 1999
Luce, Edward, 'Hoist by their own petard', 20th September 1999
Luce, Edward, 'Hub and spokes proposal for root and branch reform', 14th May 1999
Luce, Edward, 'LCH introduces real-time settlement on Euro-MTS', 14th December 1999
Luce, Edward, 'LSE moves towards anonymous trading', 25th August 1999
Luce, Edward, 'New Technology is driving mating dances', 23rd March 1999
Luce, Edward, 'A step towards a leaner forum for liquidity', 4th October 1999
Luce, Edward, 'Too many cooks', 30th July 1999
Luce, Edward, 'New recipe thickens alphabet soup', 12th June 2009
Luce, Edward and Boland, Vincent, 'Paris seethes at offer of second class berth', 18th July 1998
Luce, Edward and Boland, Vincent, 'Nasdaq goes global', 6th November 1999
Luce, Edward and Guha, Krishna, 'DTB plans challenge to Liffe', 10th July 1997
Luce, Edward and Iskandar, Samer, 'Exchanges walk the thin line that separates rivalry and war', 14th July 1997
Luce, Edward and Iskandar, Samer, 'Liffe or death struggle', 19th September 1997
Luce, Edward and Labate, John, 'The trading bell tolls', 26th July 1999
Luce, Edward and Merchant, Khozem, 'Cantor launches electronic trading for bonds', 2nd July 1999

Luce, Edward and Tait, Nikki, 'Exchanges struggle with costs', 5th September 1997
Lukken, Walt, 'Exchange regulation in a world without borders', 1st November 2006
MacCarthy, Claire, 'Team spirit brings gains all round', 31st October 2000
Macdonald, Neil, 'Iraq exchange set to spur recovery', 5th December 2005
Machlis, Avi, 'All eyes are on Netanyahu', 8th November 1996
Mackenzie, Michael, 'Activists focus on battle for eSpeed', 20th April 2007
Mackenzie, Michael, 'Global trade facilitators behind a 24-hour market', 20th April 2007
Mackenzie, Michael, 'NYSE Euronext agrees block trading system', 31st October 2007
Mackenzie, Michael, 'Equities rally as optimists discount credit crunch', 20th May 2008
Mackenzie, Michael, 'Interest rate swaps dominate dealing', 15th October 2008
Mackenzie, Michael, 'London interbank lending rates ease', 14th October 2008
Mackenzie, Michael, 'Mixed response to SEC selected protectionism', 17th July 2008
Mackenzie, Michael, 'Money markets hope for autumn thaw', 1st September 2008
Mackenzie, Michael, 'Repo sector scramble', 16th September 2008
Mackenzie, Michael, 'Changes welcomed for crucial area of finance', 13th March 2009
Mackenzie, Michael, 'DTCC paves way for all roads to lead to its warehouse', 1st July 2009
Mackenzie, Michael, 'High-frequency trading dominates the debate', 21st October 2009
Mackenzie, Michael, 'Nasdaq OMX loses a third of market share in price war', 7th August 2009
Mackenzie, Michael, 'Network of companies designed to help central bank manage liquidity', 16th July 2009
Mackenzie, Michael, 'OTC markets to get stronger oversight', 18th June 2009
Mackenzie, Michael, 'Push to reduce risks in short-term funding', 22nd June 2009
Mackenzie, Michael, 'Ranks of US primary dealers growing once more', 16th July 2009
Mackenzie, Michael, 'Run on banks left repo sector highly-exposed', 11th September 2009
Mackenzie, Michael, 'SEC plans to illuminate dark pools', 22nd October 2009
Mackenzie, Michael, '"Flash glitch" fears force SEC hand', 13th May 2010
Mackenzie, Michael, 'Flaws in share system are exposed', 18th June 2010
Mackenzie, Michael, 'Frozen in Time', 16th June 2010
Mackenzie, Michael, 'Getco to become market maker at NYSE', 12th February 2010
Mackenzie, Michael, 'One-size-fits-all approach risks killing flexibility', 3rd November 2010
Mackenzie, Michael, 'Rate swap traders wait for no man', 20th October 2010
Mackenzie, Michael, 'Regulators push technology to track trades in real time', 29th September 2010
Mackenzie, Michael, 'Repo market faces struggle to pull back from slump', 15th April 2010
Mackenzie, Michael, 'SEC's new rules threaten liquidity critics warn', 3rd March 2010
Mackenzie, Michael, 'Habits change in anticipation of arrival of electronic trading', 31st May 2011
Mackenzie, Michael, 'Industry hopes longer delays will mean looser rules', 4th November 2011
Mackenzie, Michael, 'Market prepares for transparency', 4th November 2011
Mackenzie, Michael, 'Fight looms over which model is best', 30th October 2012
Mackenzie, Michael, 'Libor probe shines light on voice brokers', 17th February 2012
Mackenzie, Michael, 'Rivals angle for custom in changing world of swaps', 17th September 2013
Mackenzie, Michael, 'Search for liquidity tests firms' talent for innovation', 5th November 2014
Mackenzie, Michael, 'Swap traders resist moves to increase use of platforms', 16th September 2014
Mackenzie, Michael and Alloway, Tracy, 'Swaps profits threatened by Dodd-Frank', 23rd August 2012
Mackenzie, Michael and Bullock, Nicole, 'Deadline is looming for derivatives clean-up', 22nd July 2008
Mackenzie, Michael and Bullock, Nicole, 'Push-button perils, Richard Milne', 6th June 2011
Mackenzie, Michael, Bullock, Nicole and Demos, Telis, 'JPMorgan loss exposes dangers of derivatives', 16th May 2012
Mackenzie, Michael, Bullock, Nicole and Tett, Gillian, 'Big Bang arrives for credit default swaps industry', 8th April 2009
Mackenzie, Michael and Foley, Stephen, 'High costs to hit made to measure derivatives', 12th December 2012
Mackenzie, Michael and Grant, Jeremy, 'The dash to flash', 6th August 2009

Mackenzie, Michael and Grant, Jeremy, 'Trading co-locate takes root in Essex hangar', 30th September 2009
Mackenzie, Michael and Grant, Jeremy, 'Liffe proves its worth to NYSE', 4th March 2010
Mackenzie, Michael and Grant, Jeremy, 'Warnings on systemic market risk', 10th May 2010
Mackenzie, Michael, Guerrera, Francesco and Tett, Gillian, 'A course to chart', 4th January 2010
Mackenzie, Michael and Massoudi, Arash, 'Ultra-fast traders under fire after US algo glitch', 3rd August 2012
Mackenzie, Michael and Massoudi, Arash, 'Traders resist Nasdaq's Treasury Push', 30th January 2014
Mackenzie, Michael, Massoudi, Arash and Foley, Stephen, 'Rage against the machine', 17th October 2012
Mackenzie, Michael, Massoudi, Arash and Stafford, Philip, 'Nasdaq opens new front in fixed income', 3rd April 2013
Mackenzie, Michael, McCrum, Dan and Alloway, Tracy, 'Electronic trading set to muscle in on corporate debt', 4th April 2013
Mackenzie, Michael, McCrum, Dan and Milne, Richard, 'Investors warn on the impact of S&P's US move', 20th April 2011
Mackenzie, Michael and Meyer, Gregory, 'US swaps shake-up set to boost exchanges', 2nd November 2012
Mackenzie, Michael and Morarjee, Rachel, 'Fear reigns as spectre of a global recession looms large', 9th October 2008
Mackenzie, Michael, Scannell, Kara and Bullock, Nicole, 'Murky Pools', 28th June 2014
Mackenzie, Michael and Scholtes, Saskia, 'Regulators issue a warning at bond trading's wild frontier', 13th November 2006
Mackenzie, Michael and Scholtes, Saskia, 'Subprime securitisation threat', 7th March 2007
Mackenzie, Michael and Stafford, Philip, 'US swaps trading prepares for its big bang', 18th February 2014
Mackenzie, Michael and Tett, Gillian, 'Libor remarks fail to put unease to rest', 2nd June 2008
Mackenzie, Michael and Thomas, Helen, 'SEC looks to get to the bottom of dark pools', 28th October 2009
Mackenzie, Michael and van Duyn, Aline, 'Costs set to rise amid shake-up in derivatives trading', 19th June 2009
Mackenzie, Michael and van Duyn, Aline, 'Regulators may silence derivative squawk boxes', 22 July 2010
Mackenzie, Michael and Weitzman, Hal, 'CME wins swap clearing support', 18th October 2010
Mackintosh, James, 'Brokers reach merger agreement', 12th October 1997
Mackintosh, James, 'Bright lights, big City', 3rd July 1999
Mackintosh, James, 'Electronic network planned to bypass stock exchanges', 30th July 1999
Mackintosh, James, 'Global computer network may be a recipe for disaster', 23rd March 1999
Mackintosh, James, 'Balance of Power may be changing', 26th May 2000
Mackintosh, James, 'Old timers start to play catch-up', 31st March 2000
Mackintosh, James, 'Share trade tax revenue doomed, says regulator', 10th January 2000
Mackintosh, James, 'Watchdogs draft rules for new stock markets', 26th September 2000
Mackintosh, James, 'Financial police prepare for a firmer hand', 6th July 2001
Mackintosh, James, 'Venerable names will disappear', 26th January 2001
Mackintosh, James, 'Exchange joins fight to host alternative funds', 12th July 2007
Mackintosh, James, 'Investors still pile in', 27th April 2007
Mackintosh, James, 'Hedge funds pose dilemma for regulators', 5th March 2008
Mackintosh, James and Brewster, Deborah, 'Evidence falls short of talk in assault on speculation', 20th September 2008
Mackintosh, James and Hughes, Jennifer, 'New York steals UK hedge funds business', 17th October 2008
Mackintosh, James and Wilson, James, 'D Börse ponders joining trading dogfight', 15th September 2008
MacNamara, William, 'Johannesburg listing boom could spawn an African version of Aim', 18th October 2007

MacNamara, William, Johnson, Miles and Kennard, Matthew, 'Hong Kong vies with London for IPO supremacy', 27th January 2010
MacRae, Desmond, 'How depositories raise efficiency', 3rd September 1990
Maheshwari, Vijai, 'Baltic states prepare to join Nordic alliance', 15th June 2000
Maitland, Allison, 'Slow steps in the paper chase', 21st October 1987
Major, Tony, 'When good things come in small investors', 9th February 2000
Makan, Ajay, 'Academics determine that just being swift is not risky', 10th October 2011
Makan, Ajay, 'Search is on for a new gas pricing benchmark', 10th May 2013
Makan, Ajay and Blas, Javier, 'Price probe ripples across oil world', 18–19th May 2013
Makinson, John, 'London reflects scale of international flows', 23rd November 1983
Makinson, John, 'Prime area for diversification', 7th December 1984
Makinson, John, 'Advance of the Euroequity', 2nd November 1985
Mallet, Victor, 'Curbs on a casino', 3rd December 1991
Mallet, Victor, 'Manipulators targeted', 7th February 1994
Mallet, Victor, 'On the move to electronic settlement', 23rd March 1999
Mallet, Victor, 'Rainbow colours of the future', 20th September 1999
Mallet, Victor, 'Spanish plan to rival BME', 25th August 2010
Manchester, Philip, 'An aid to better investment decisions', 5th June 2002
Manchester, Philip, 'Powerful incentives for trading in real time', 3rd April 2002
Manchester, Philip, 'Why collaboration will be crucial', 3rd April 2002
Manchester, Philip, 'Driving change in ways of trading in markets', 5th November 2003
Mandel-Campbell, Andrea, 'Mexican stock exchange at loggerheads with brokers', 20th March 2001
Mandel-Campbell, Andrea, 'Not just a traditional market for shares', 19th March 2001
Mann, Michael, 'Watch out, the rivalry is beginning to hot up', 6th June 2002
Mapstone, Naomi, 'Andean trio plan market alliance', 3rd November 2010
Mapstone, Naomi, 'Cross-border stocks start trading slowly', 21st September 2011
Marozzi, Justin, 'Lure of the lion city', 18th February 1997
Marozzi, Justin, 'Philippine derivatives planned', 10th March 1997
Marriage, Madison, 'Scandalous past still haunts forex industry', 12th December 2016
Marriage, Madison and Ford, Jonathan, 'Close ties of auditors and watchdogs draw fire', 21st August 2018
Marsh, David, 'Higher profile being taken', 5th March 1985
Marsh, David, 'Cocoa butter melts away', 23rd July 1986
Marsh, David, 'Expansion seen for new French financial futures market', 28th February 1986
Marsh, David, 'Powerhouse holds its ground', 4th March 1994
Marsh, Peter, 'They're breathing down London's neck', 26th May 1993
Marsh, Virginia, 'ASX, NZ exchange spell out objectives', 20th December 2000
Marsh, Virginia, 'Australia, NZ consider stock exchange deal', 15th August 2000
Marsh, Virginia, 'Cultural barriers impede progress', 28th April 2000
Marsh, Virginia, 'Markets taking stock of the future', 4th July 2000
Marsh, Virginia, 'NZ Stock exchange in talks on merger', 8th May 2000
Marsh, Virginia, 'Australian futures market calls it a day', 29th March 2001
Marsh, Virginia, 'NZSE accuses ASX for failure of merger talks', 23rd February 2001
Marsh, Virginia and Cameron, Doug, 'Australian exchanges team up to regain lost ground', 29th March 2006
Marsh, Virginia and Dawkins, William, 'ASX seeks to extend links with London', 10th March 2000
Martin, Katie, 'City secures hold on offshore renminbi trade as daily volume soars to £69bn', 27th September 2018
Martin, Katie, 'Trading data show tougher rule book improves banks' forex behaviour', 4th September 2018
Martin, Katie, 'Funds face trade-off between liquidity and performance, warns Amundi chief', 6th August 2019
Martin, Katie, 'Swiss franc hit by mini-flash crash during Asian session', 12th February 2019
Martin, Katie and Stafford, Philip, 'Banter banned as forex traders clean up act', 23rd May 2015

Martin, Katie and Stafford, Philip, 'Banks and insurers slow to switch on as nightfall approaches for Libor', 20th September 2018
Martin, Peter, 'Bank feel the electronic impulse', 13th December 1990
Martin, Peter, 'Debate centres on powers of supervision', 29th November 1990
Martin, Peter, 'As independent as they feel', 25th January 1993
Martin, Peter, 'Exchange to look at US option for trading system', 23rd April 1993
Martin, Peter, 'Trading places', 2nd July 1998
Martin, Peter, 'Multinationals come into their own', 6th December 1999
Martin, Peter, 'The end of Liffe as we know it', 30th October 2001
Martin, Peter, 'Trading on dangerous ground', 12th February 2002
Martineau, Lisa, 'Hedging helps the boom', 3rd June 1987
Martineau, Lisa, 'The rules need to be eased', 17th February 1988
Martinson, Jane, 'Slow burn before Big Bang 2', 6th October 1997
Martinson, Jane, 'No Sets please, we're large institutions', 8th August 1998
Mason, Christopher and Simon, Bernard, 'Canada bank prove envy of the world', 20th February 2009
Massey, Katy, 'New house rules for exchanges', 27th June 1997
Massoudi, Arash, 'Increase in competition raises the stakes', 30th October 2012
Massoudi, Arash, 'Professional traders have edge on retail investors, says NYSE', 19th December 2012
Massoudi, Arash, 'Direct-Edge-BATS merger to rival NYSE', 27th August 2013
Massoudi, Arash, 'Soaring cost of US share dealing risks "investor harm"', 18th October 2013
Massoudi, Arash, 'A steward of Wall Street glories', 10th March 2014
Massoudi, Arash, 'Cboe snaps up rival in $3.2bn deal', 27th September 2016
Massoudi, Arash and Alloway, Tracy, 'Trading glitch threatens Goldman's image', 23rd August 2013
Massoudi, Arash and Alloway, Tracy, 'Goldman says farewell to NYSE floor with sale of market maker', 2nd April 2014
Massoudi, Arash and Mackenzie, Michael, 'In search of a fast buck', 20th February 2013
Massoudi, Arash and Mackenzie, Michael, 'Investors turn to the dark side for trading', 26th April 2013
Massoudi, Arash and Stafford, Philip, 'NYSE deal drew interest from Buffett, David Gelles', 29th January 2013
Massoudi, Arash, Stafford, Philip and Barber, Alex, 'Pressure grows for limits on "dark pools"', 22nd November 2013
Masters, Brooke, 'Set apart by Englishness', 14th August 2008
Masters, Brooke, 'Banks move to Belfast and Bournemouth', 19th March 2009
Masters, Brooke, 'Long road to regulation', 26th October 2009
Masters, Brooke, 'Finra to watch over NYSE Euronext', 5th May 2010
Masters, Brooke, 'New York vies with City for finance crown', 12th March 2010
Masters, Brooke, '"Too big to fail" debate still muddled', 17th September 2010
Masters, Brooke, 'Trade finance may become a casualty', 20th October 2010
Masters, Brooke, 'Banks learn the liquidity lessons from tough rules', 30th December 2011
Masters, Brooke, 'EU watchdog issues alert on unregulated forex groups', 6th December 2011
Masters, Brooke, 'Industry worries about the impact of new rules', 20th September 2011
Masters, Brooke, 'League battle over bank risk will end in tiers', 21st June 2011
Masters, Brooke, 'A real problem for regulators', 22nd March 2011
Masters, Brooke, 'Reveal leverage ratio ahead of rivals banks told', 2nd December 2011
Masters, Brooke, 'Cities hold firm amid Eurozone upheaval', 10th May 2012
Masters, Brooke, 'Conflicting signals', 2nd April 2012
Masters, Brooke, 'Regulators peer into financial shadows', 19th November 2012
Masters, Brooke, 'Shadow banking poses threat to broader stability, FSA head warns', 15th March 2012
Masters, Brooke, 'Tampering with Libor to become criminal offence', 18th October 2012
Masters, Brooke, 'UK banks lead world on liquidity rules', 22nd June 2012
Masters, Brooke, 'Wariness over EU's level playing field', 10th May 2012
Masters, Brooke, 'Objective evidence offers better guarantees in a brave new world', 19th March 2013
Masters, Brooke, 'Safety net plans raise industry ire', 19th March 2013

Masters, Brooke, 'A fight over data roils Wall Street', 24th October 2018
Masters, Brooke and Braithwaite, Tom, 'Bankers versus Basel', 3rd October 2011
Masters, Brooke and Grant, Jeremy, 'Shadow boxes', 3rd February 2011
Masters, Brooke, Grant, Jeremy and Bryant, Chris, 'Warning of unintended outcomes with Tobin tax plans', 6th October 2011
Masters, Brooke and Guerrera, Francesco, 'Threat to small business', 27th September 2010
Masters, Brooke and Nasiripour, Shahien, 'US banks want new liquidity rules eased', 17th December 2012
Masters, Brooke and Nasiripour, Shahien, 'Basel move aims to stoke recovery', 8th January 2013
Masters, Brooke and Oakley, David, 'Financial regulators take aim at repo trading markets', 27th April 2012
Masters, Brooke, Saigol, Lina and Farrell, Greg, 'Closing door: bankers' bonuses', 30th October 2008
Masters, Brooke, Sender, Henny and McCrum, Dan, '"Shadow banks" move in amid regulatory push', 9th September 2011
Masters, Brooke and Stafford, Philip, 'Clearing houses face tougher capital rules by end of the year', 17th April 2012
Masters, Brooke, Stafford, Philip and Mackenzie, Michael, 'Libor heads for history in hunt for new bank rate', 24th April 2013
Masters, Brooke and Tait, Nikki, 'Dodging the Draft', 14th July 2009
Masters, Brooke and Thompson, Jennifer, 'Smaller banks face "glass ceiling"', 11th February 2013
Mawson, James, 'Fears grow over long-term investment', 9th May 2011
McCallum, Jim, 'Big three battle it out', 29th April 1991
McCallum, Jim, 'End of controls provides a lift', 11th November 1991
McCallum, Jim, 'Few tears shed for open outcry', 25th April 1991
McCallum, Jim, 'Footsie futures steps out', 15th February 1991
McCallum, Jim, 'Institutional interest quickens after tax changes', 13th March 1991
McCallum, Jim and Corrigan, Tracy, 'Outcry over screen trading plan', 14th June 1991
McCarthy, Sir Callum, 'Europe's financial regulators must exploit existing ties', 22nd August 2005
McCloskey, Gerard, 'Coal trading settles in UK', 23rd August 2000
McCrum, Dan, 'BlackRock trading platform plan set to hit Wall St profit centres', 29th December 2010
McCrum, Dan, 'Hybrid model eyed for money market funds', 10th April 2012
McCrum, Dan, Barber, Alex, Hughes, Jennifer, Milne, Richard, Hollinger, Peggy and Steinglass, Matthew, 'Short-selling ban attacked by academics and investors', 13th August 2011
McDermott, Anthony, 'More will own shares', 18th November 1992
McGregor, Richard, 'China sets its sights on stock market efficiency', 26th January 2001
McGregor, Richard, 'Seriously out of step with the economy', 16th December 2003
McGregor, Richard, 'Dalian overtakes CBOT on soya', 18th June 2004
McGregor, Richard and Tucker, Sundeep, 'China looks to fend off pressure by US brokers', 18th May 2007
McIvor, Greg, 'Finnish bourse aims to feed off pulp volatility', 16th August 1996
McIvor, Greg, 'Swedish group to launch London pulp futures', 30th August 1996
McIvor, Greg, 'Helsinki offers hedge against pulp volatility', 4th February 1997
McIvor, Greg, 'Old perceptions are swept aside', 11th March 1997
McIvor, Greg, 'Smoothing out the peaks and troughs', 8th December 1997
McIvor, Greg, 'Sweden and Denmark to link bourses', 12th June 1997
McIvor, Greg, 'Choice between merging or being marginalised', 27th October 1998
McLannahan, Ben, 'Japan's leading exchanges to merge', 23rd November 2011
McLannahan, Ben, 'Japan commodities exchange looks for deeper ties with rivals', 28th March 2012
McLannahan, Ben, 'Merger of markets may foreshadow expansion overseas', 9th March 2012
McLannahan, Ben, 'TSE set to pull plug on Tokyo Aim', 27th March 2012
McLannahan, Ben, 'SEC eyes initial coin offerings with suspicion', 15th March 2018
McLannahan, Ben and Brunsden, Jim, 'EU plan over bank runs faces US opposition', 2nd November 2017
McMeeken, Roxane, 'Dublin closing the gap in race for hottest investments', 7th June 2001

McSheedy, Will and Hughes, Jennifer, 'Dubai sticks to electronic trading', 18th January 2007
Mead, Gary, 'Outpost that refuses to die', 16th November 1990
Mead, Gary, 'Exchange of copper bottomed guarantees', 6th October 1997
Mead, Gary, 'IPE in outcry over options for reform', 3rd December 1997
Mead, Gary, 'OMLX prepares pulp contract', 7th May 1997
Mead, Gary, 'Foundations upon which bullion trading is built', 22nd June 1998
Mead, Gary, 'IPE forms link with Norwegian exchange', 2nd July 1998
Megaw, Nicholas, 'High-speed trading masts face slowdown', 28th March 2016
Megaw, Nicholas, 'Challenger banks struggle against big four', 30th September 2019
Megaw, Nicholas, 'Challenger banks struggle to smash glass ceiling', 14th January 2019
Megaw, Nicholas, 'Sting in the tail for banks caught in PPI scandal', 10th September 2019
Merchant, Khozem, 'Avalanche of change hits Alpine retreat', 14th September 1999
Merchant, Khozem, 'Market for ECP opens up via Trax', 7th September 1999
Merchant, Khozem, 'Maverick market gains credibility', 20th September 1999
Merchant, Khozem, 'Straight on for global market', 5th May 2000
Merchant, Khozem, 'Mumbai exchange could fetch $650m', 17th March 2006
Merchant, Khozem, 'Towering ambitions, masses of capital but let down by its poor infrastructure', 12th April 2006
Merchant, Khozem and Ibison, David, 'Slowly, the net begins to close in', 5th May 2000
Meredith, Mark, 'Heed the southern giants', 2nd July 1986
Merkley, Jeff, 'Avoid past mistakes and preserve key bank safety law', 26th June 2018
Metcalfe, Richard, 'Forex options in the long term', 22nd November 1996
Meyer, Gregory, 'Banks back strict energy-trading limits', 30th July 2009
Meyer, Gregory, 'CFTC and FSA eye London loophole', 21st August 2009
Meyer, Gregory, 'Dilemma over limiting speculation', 4th August 2009
Meyer, Gregory, 'Regulators aim to curb the massive passives', 25th November 2009
Meyer, Gregory, 'US natural gas industry fears damage from trading curbs', 13th August 2009
Meyer, Gregory, 'Bunge rides on volatility of food markets', 29th December 2010
Meyer, Gregory, 'Crackdown hangs over derivatives bets', 14th October 2010
Meyer, Gregory, 'Push for clearing houses fails to move leading oil traders', 12th March 2010
Meyer, Gregory, 'US bans insider trading on official commodities data', 23rd July 2010
Meyer, Gregory, 'An example for regulators to study', 4th November 2011
Meyer, Gregory, 'CFTC approves caps on speculation', 19th October 2011
Meyer, Gregory, 'High-speed commodities traders under crash scrutiny', 10th March 2011
Meyer, Gregory, 'Nymex floor loses its voice to electronics', 1st June 2011
Meyer, Gregory, 'Backlash brews over longer trading day for grain futures', 16th May 2012
Meyer, Gregory, 'Grain trade feels need for speed in longer day', 12th June 2012
Meyer, Gregory, 'BP joins banks as US Swaps dealer', 12th July 2013
Meyer, Gregory, 'Trading houses sow the seeds of change', 19th September 2013
Meyer, Gregory, 'ICE chief blasts rival's tactics to lure users', 5th November 2014
Meyer, Gregory, 'Oil price swings come too late for banks who made desk cutbacks', 5th November 2014
Meyer, Gregory, 'Global cotton futures contract clears hurdle', 18th June 2015
Meyer, Gregory, 'Sun sets for trading pioneer Phibro as prices tumble', 3rd February 2015
Meyer, Gregory, 'Trading', 19th November 2015
Meyer, Gregory, 'Trading places', 11th March 2015
Meyer, Gregory, 'City retains role as capital of the derivatives industry', 16th December 2016
Meyer, Gregory, 'Trading', 7th July 2016
Meyer, Gregory, 'US markets braced for trading tax grab', 11th October 2016
Meyer, Gregory, 'From ranchers to fund managers, algos cause a stir', 10th October 2017
Meyer, Gregory, 'Chicago's sharp traders delve into the turbulent digital currency', 1st October 2018
Meyer, Gregory, 'CME pulls ahead in race to control bitcoin derivatives trading', 22nd August 2018
Meyer, Gregory, 'DRW unit joins top rank of traders with nearly $1bn revenues over two years', 16th January 2018

Meyer, Gregory, 'CME shows how automation is the future of futures trading', 24th April 2019
Meyer, Gregory, 'Intercontinental Exchange muscles into New York harbour heating oil futures', 26th June 2019
Meyer, Gregory, 'Nodal Exchange to start trading futures in the cost of hiring freight trucks', 28th March 2019
Meyer, Gregory and Blas, Javier, 'US delays vote on commodity trade', 17th December 2010
Meyer, Gregory and Bullock, Nicole, 'Algo traders look beyond need for speed in quest to gain competitive edge', 31st March 2017
Meyer, Gregory, Bullock, Nicole and Rennison, Joe, 'Trading', 2nd January 2018
Meyer, Gregory and Farchy, Jack, 'Farmers left short-changed by a margin call squeeze', 23rd November 2010
Meyer, Gregory and Farchy, Jack, 'Wall Street falls out of love with commodities trading business', 5th August 2013
Meyer, Gregory and Hume, Neil, 'Goldman thrives in commodities as rivals melt away', 16th July 2014
Meyer, Gregory and Mackenzie, Michael, 'Wall Street takes on derivatives watchdog', 6th December 2011
Meyer, Gregory and Sheppard, David, 'Exchange giants battle over new US oil benchmark', 12th February 2019
Meyer, Gregory and Stafford, Philip, 'Alarm spreads ahead of US algorithm rules', 22nd March 2016
Meyer, Gregory and Stafford, Philip, 'Chicago bourses in bitcoin futures duel', 19th December 2017
Meyer, Gregory and Stafford, Philip, 'Derivatives watchdog eyes swaps trading reform', 13th September 2017
Meyer, Gregory and Stafford, Philip, 'Race for bitcoin futures stirs concerns', 16th December 2017
Meyer, Gregory and Stafford, Philip, 'Derivatives traders forced to cut holdings as banks push for Basel clampdown', 3rd July 2018
Meyer, Gregory and Stafford, Philip, 'ICE plots escape from Mifid 2 as it prepares to shift 245 energy contracts to US', 12th January 2018
Michaels, Adrian and Cohen, Norma, 'Borsa Italiana to study public offering', 19th January 2006
Michaels, Adrian and Wiggins, Jenny, 'Regulators plan overhaul', 31st March 2004
Michie, R. C., 'Nature or Nurture: The British financial system since 1688', in Matthew Hollow, Folarin Akinbami &, Ranald Michie (eds), *Complexity and Crisis: Critical perspectives on the evolution of American and British Banking* (Cheltenham: Edward Elgar, 2016)
Middelmann, Conner, 'Merits of open-outcry challenged', 14th July 1994
Middelmann, Conner, 'Comet burns out', 13th March 1995
Middelmann, Conner, 'Shift to a higher gear', 19th September 1995
Middelmann, Conner, 'Step closer to becoming a well-rounded market', 16th November 1995
Middelmann, Conner, 'Domestic market is struggling', 1st March 1996
Millham, Colin, 'Caution is entering the market', 27th May 1986
Milne, Richard, 'Money for nothing-and the debt is (almost) for free', 25th May 2011
Milne, Richard, Cameron, Doug and Gangahar, Anuj, 'D Börse might be in danger of losing again', 3rd June 2006
Minder, Raphael, 'Flotation by Euronext to raise Euro700m', 5th July 2001
Minder, Raphael, 'Asian regional platform planned', 9th July 2008
Mishkin, Sarah, 'Competition helps to reduce barriers', 10th October 2011
Mishkin, Sarah, 'Asian lenders step up their push into trade finance', 12th April 2012
Mitchell, Tom, 'Integration of bourses is not black and white', 23rd October 2007
Mitchell, Tom, 'HK exchange seeks to align trading hours with mainland', 12th August 2010
Moghadam, Reza, 'Branch out to avoid a Brexit capital markets crunch', 20th July 2017
Moir, Christine, 'A drift towards experience', 16th November 1995
Moir, Christine, 'Matchbook trading matures', 6th November 1995
Moir, Christine, 'Consolidation on the cards', 1st March 1996
Moir, Christine, 'Once more unto a breach?', 16th February 1996
Moir, Christine, 'Barriers go up in Europe', 28th February 1997

Moir, Christine, 'Mirror on a domestic scene', 27th June 1997
Moir, Christine, 'New rules in changed world', 24th March 1998
Montagnon, Peter, 'International powerhouse', 21st May 1984
Montagnon, Peter, 'Novel offerings bring fresh edge to competition', 14th February 1984
Montagnon, Peter, 'Profound changes in culture', 19th March 1984
Montagnon, Peter, 'Caution at the top end', 2nd October 1986
Montagnon, Peter, 'Across the threshold of credibility', 28th November 1986
Montagnon, Peter, 'Downgrading of Libor', 22nd May 1986
Montagnon, Peter, 'A need for banks to watch extent of commitment', 17th March 1986
Montagnon, Peter, 'Pragmatic approach to City rules', 27th October 1986
Montagnon, Peter, 'Securitisation can often be the key to the future', 18th May 1988
Montagnon, Peter, 'Reforms with a muted bang', 31st March 1998
Montagnon, Peter, 'Nanny state loosens its grip', 28th April 2000
Montagnon, Peter and Murthy, R C, 'Bombay regulators again in the dock', 21st March 1995
Mooney, Attracta, 'Managers turn to dark pools to carry out trades', 2nd March 2015
Mooney, Attracta, 'Fund houses take on banks over lending', 5th September 2016
Mooney, Attracta, 'Passive funds hit new highs on wave of investor approval', 10th September 2018
Mooney, Attracta, 'Could London be Berned like the Swiss?', 8th July 2019
Mooney, Attracta, 'Liquidity crunches heat up debate over capital buffers', 16th September 2019
Mooney, Attracta and Smith, Peter, 'Deal of the decade: how BlackRock buying BGI changed the industry', 6th May 2019
Mooney, Richard, 'Unrivalled sector for volatility', 28th October 1987
Mooney, Richard, 'Members of Fox vote for restructuring', 20th July 1990
Mooney, Richard, 'At the tip of an iceberg', 22nd June 1992
Moore, Elaine, 'Uncertainty in an evolving landscape', 21st March 2011
Moore, Elaine, 'Keeping tabs on prices triggers knee-jerk reaction', 24th July 2012
Moore, Elaine, 'Humans or machines: who's running the markets?', 16–17th March 2013
Moore, Elaine, 'Post Office moves to expand banking', 18th January 2014
Moore, John, 'Uncertain time ahead for London houses', 28th November 1983
Moore, John, 'The fight to win back foreign business', 9th April 1984
Moore, John, 'Ultimate target is broad band of financial services', 14th February 1984
Moore, John, 'Goodison to outline foreign links plan', 31st October 1985
Moore, John, 'Pension fund involvement will become commonplace', 5th March 1985
Moore, John, 'SE firms urged to adapt in face of change', 21st November 1985
Moore, John, 'Single main board envisaged to regulate services of 15,000 City concerns', 20th December 1985
Moore, John, 'Discount houses face up to radical change', 20th March 1986
Moore, John and Graham, George, 'The City digests a setback on the road to reform', 7th June 1985
Moran, Nuala, 'Not a moment too soon', 3rd July 1996
Moran, Nuala, 'Savings financed new system', 4th September 1996
Moran, Nuala, 'Strategic IT development by the securities industry', 3rd July 1996
Morarjee, Rachel, 'Merger creates market less prone to squabbling', 4th October 2011
Morgan, Michael, 'Investors dive in', 11th April 1997
Morgan, Michael, 'Reforms boost Vienna', 28th February 1997
Morris, Stephen, 'London easily tops league of best-paid European financiers', 12th March 2019
Morris, Stephen, 'London set to keep its crown, says head of Citi Europe', 21st October 2019
Morris, Stephen and Crow, David, 'Axe swings at European banks after lamentable fourth quarter', 22nd February 2019
Morris, Stephen, Crow, David and Storbeck, Olaf, 'Deutsche is all downside while Barclays blooms', 25th October 2018
Morris, Stephen and Storbeck, Olaf, 'Humbled giant struggles to silence doubters', 9th July 2019
Morrison, Kevin, 'IPE might delay electronic move', 19th December 2003
Morrison, Kevin, 'IPE set to move towards ending open outcry trade', 6th October 2003
Morrison, Kevin, 'LME steeled to broaden its base', 13th November 2003

Morrison, Kevin, 'Mixed response to LME upgrade', 2nd December 2003
Morrison, Kevin, 'Dublin debut for Nymex gets muted reception', 2nd November 2004
Morrison, Kevin, 'Energy exchanges turn up the heat', 1st November 2004
Morrison, Kevin, 'Nybot sees future in pulp trading', 22nd December 2004
Morrison, Kevin, 'Nymex eyes future in Europe', 15th October 2004
Morrison, Kevin, 'Private buyers fill bullion vaults', 16th April 2004
Morrison, Kevin, 'APX wants slice of gas trading pie', 3rd February 2005
Morrison, Kevin, 'Changing their old image', 22nd November 2005
Morrison, Kevin, 'Dubai moves into gold futures', 18th November 2005
Morrison, Kevin, 'Dubai to launch gold futures', 29th June 2005
Morrison, Kevin, 'Emissions and ethanol join the newcomers', 22nd November 2005
Morrison, Kevin, 'ICE to make waves with flotation', 18th October 2005
Morrison, Kevin, 'LME bets on future in plastics', 26th May 2005
Morrison, Kevin, 'LME nears a decision on steel futures', 28th October 2005
Morrison, Kevin, 'Nymex feels an unwelcome pinch', 11th October 2005
Morrison, Kevin, 'Open outcry as futures exchange opens in London', 13th September 2005
Morrison, Kevin, 'Open outcry moves closer to silence', 8th March 2005
Morrison, Kevin, 'Steel Futures next on LME list', 27th May 2005
Morrison, Kevin, 'Driven by a blistering rise in metal prices', 10th March 2006
Morrison, Kevin, 'An exodus from floor to screen', 7th April 2006
Morrison, Kevin, 'ICE goes online with West Texas', 3rd February 2006
Morrison, Kevin, 'ICE keen on forming LCH.Clearnet partnership', 20th November 2006
Morrison, Kevin, 'LME eyes profit-making option', 17th May 2006
Morrison, Kevin, 'LME reacts to Nymex challenge', 3rd July 2006
Morrison, Kevin, 'LME steps on to a long and winding road', 18th May 2006
Morrison, Kevin, 'Nybot set to accept $1bn offer from ICE', 14th September 2006
Morrison, Kevin, 'Nymex and LME go head to head', 1st December 2006
Morrison, Kevin, 'Nymex clears path to IPO', 4th August 2006
Morrison, Kevin, 'Nymex disadvantaged by futures rules', 15th April 2006
Morrison, Kevin, 'Nymex relents and allows electronic trade', 12th June 2006
Morrison, Kevin, 'Nymex restricts voting rights', 17th March 2006
Morrison, Kevin, 'Nymex within days of Comex deal', 12th June 2006
Morrison, Kevin, 'OFT refuses to lift trading ban on LME', 3rd March 2006
Morrison, Kevin, 'Pits stop proves a winning formula', 9th November 2006
Morrison, Kevin, 'Realignment of Futures', 28th November 2006
Morrison, Kevin and Braithwaite, Tom, 'Nymex aims to take on IPE with London trading floor', 15th February 2005
Morrison, Kevin and Cameron, Doug, 'CME grapples with possible metals conflict', 19th October 2006
Morrison, Kevin and Pretzlik, Charles, 'Standard changes as Rothschild leaves gold business', 15th April 2004
Morse, Iain, 'Market jostling sees ownership rise', 9th October 2006
Morse, Laurie, 'After-hours Globex has yet to live up to its promise', 1st December 1992
Morse, Laurie, 'New law lifts uncertainty', 8th December 1992
Morse, Laurie, 'CBOT aims to boost its international appeal', 18th June 1993
Morse, Laurie, 'Chicago and New York exchanges plan merger', 26th January 1993
Morse, Laurie, 'Chicago returns to its 19th century origins', 15th May 1993
Morse, Laurie, 'Consolidating for the futures', 27th January 1993
Morse, Laurie, 'Derivatives industry scrambles to find some kind of infrastructure', 12th July 1993
Morse, Laurie, 'European futures links encounter local opposition', 21st July 1993
Morse, Laurie, 'New York exchange makes time for night shift', 18th June 1993
Morse, Laurie, 'Quest for definitive answers', 20th October 1993
Morse, Laurie, 'Swaps trade dodges issue', 20th October 1993
Morse, Laurie, 'A two-pronged development', 20th October 1993

Morse, Laurie, 'CBOT to assist Poland with new futures exchange', 10th November 1994
Morse, Laurie, 'CME seeks strength through harmonisation', 23rd August 1994
Morse, Laurie, 'Both sides benefit from London-Chicago link', 16th March 1995
Morse, Laurie, 'Flow of capital slows down', 16th November 1995
Morse, Laurie, 'LCE in talks on Chicago futures link', 20th July 1995
Morse, Laurie, 'New York exchange merger proposal expected today', 13th July 1995
Morse, Laurie, 'Rappaport takes long view after NY exchange merger', 12th April 1995
Morse, Laurie, 'CME seen to get something for nothing', 22nd November 1996
Morse, Laurie, 'Crisis control proves difficult', 22nd November 1996
Morse, Laurie, 'Futures shake-out tops conference agenda', 21st October 1996
Morse, Laurie, 'Liffe sets its sights on the No 1 spot', 22nd November 1996
Morse, Laurie, 'Nymex switches on to an electric future', 24th December 1996
Morse, Laurie, 'US exchanges seek to stem fall in volumes', 2nd July 1996
Morse, Laurie, 'CBOT warming to the computer', 6th March 1997
Morse, Laurie, 'Futures trading slackens', 31st March 1997
Morse, Laurie, 'London could become global swaps centre', 27th March 1997
Morse, Laurie, 'Regulators to voice fears for US futures', 10th March 1997
Morse, Laurie, 'Traders turn credit risks into profits', 23rd May 1997
Morse, Laurie and Corrigan, Tracy, 'Derivatives no threat to banking system, say experts', 22nd July 1993
Morse, Laurie and Corrigan, Tracy, 'European futures trade comes of age', 31st December 1993
Morse, Laurie and Corzine, Robert, 'London oil market reaches out to Asia', 9th June 1995
Morse, Laurie and Iskandar, Samer, 'Rivals unite in a marriage of convenience', 6th May 1997
Mulligan, Mark, 'Bolsa bides its time in midst of merger frenzy', 28th June 2007
Mulligan, Mark, 'Enviable BME prepares for next challenge', 21st June 2007
Mulligan, Mark, 'Spanish bourse weighs up reform', 16th February 2010
Mulligan, Mark, 'Spanish exchange brushes aside fears', 30th March 2010
Mundy, Simon, 'Birmingham exchange sputters', 6th June 2011
Mundy, Simon, 'S Korea to tax derivatives will hit volumes, bankers warn', 9th August 2012
Mundy, Simon, 'Investors' wait for Indian listings nears end', 11th October 2016
Mundy, Simon, 'NSE chief seeks to ditch arrogant approach', 10th October 2017
Mundy, Simon, 'Investors in India spooked by the shadow financiers', 22nd February 2019
Mundy, Simon and Stafford, Philip, 'Plus companies expected to sign for new teams', 15th May 2012
Munter, Päivi, 'Protection becomes more desirable', 5th November 2003
Munter, Päivi, 'Flair keeps deficit in check', 29th November 2004
Munter, Päivi, 'Bonds trading needs clarity', 29th April 2005
Munter, Päivi, 'ESpeed increases its offer for MTS', 16th June 2005
Munter, Päivi, 'ESpeed leads bidding for MTS', 4th May 2005
Munter, Päivi, 'European group wins bid for MTS', 2nd July 2005
Munter, Päivi, 'Italian Exchange aims to partner up', 10th August 2005
Munter, Päivi and Batchelor, Charles, 'Citigroup coup stirs up emotions', 11th August 2004
Murphy, Hannah, 'Exchanges line up block trade bonanza', 24th March 2017
Murphy, Hannah, 'Mifid spoils the mood at junior market party', 13th October 2018
Murphy, Hannah, 'TP Icap names Paris as its EU base after Brexit', 8th August 2018
Murphy, Hannah, Morris, Stephen and Mooney, Attracta, 'Mifid 2 throws up unintended consequences', 2nd January 2019
Murphy, Hannah and Stafford, Philip, 'LSE agrees French clearing unit sale in move to placate Brussels', 4th January 2017
Murphy, Hannah and Stafford, Philip, 'Mifid 2 risks drowning in its own ambition', 4th January 2018
Murphy, Megan, 'Search for new approaches has begun', 9th September 2011
Murphy, Megan and Guerrera, Francesco, 'Prop-hostile climate throws up some tough calls for banks', 4th August 2010
Murphy, Paul, 'Cyber-attacks target banks' easy pickings', 25th March 2019
Murray Brown, John, 'The Irish stock exchange's special role', 8th November 2004

Murray Brown, John, 'Desmond surprises with ISTC bond deal', 3rd November 2007
Murray Brown, John, 'Cardiff seeks to rebrand itself as a centre for financial services', 31st December 2012
Murthy, R C, 'Economic fundamentals augur well', 11th September 1989
Myners, Paul, 'The Square Mile must fight to stay successful', 30th March 2006
Nagel, Joe, 'The Neuer Markt meltdown', 18th July 2001
Nairn, Geoff, 'IT is still changing the face of trading', 24th March 1998
Nairn, Geoffrey, 'Braced for big upheavals', 1st July 1998
Nairn, Geoffrey, 'Bourse rivalries overshadowed by single currency's arrival', 6th October 1999
Nairn, Geoffrey, 'Internet fails to transform the foreign exchange world', 5th June 2002
Nakamae, Naoko, 'Appetite for Samurais grows', 17th December 1999
Nakamae, Naoko, 'Deregulation opens doors slowly to investors', 23rd March 1999
Nakamae, Naoko, 'Steady progress with JGBs', 21st June 1999
Nakamae, Naoko, 'Prices still resilient despite jitters', 8th May 2000
Nakamae, Naoko, 'Racing along the comeback trail', 8th May 2000
Nakamae, Naoko, 'Rivals agree to bury the hatchet', 31st March 2000
Nakamoto, Michiyo, 'Domestic market loses out', 13th March 1989
Nakamoto, Michiyo, 'Portfolio-power provides lift-off', 25th May 1989
Nakamoto, Michiyo, 'Bid reflects a shifting climate', 7th March 2007
Nakamoto, Michiyo, 'Call to pull down barriers', 14th September 2007
Nakamoto, Michiyo, 'Citigroup deal could broker new shake-up', 30th April 2007
Nakamoto, Michiyo, 'Market failure', 8th May 2007
Nakamoto, Michiyo, 'Investors look overseas for wind of change', 21st May 2008
Nakamoto, Michiyo and Burgess, Kate, 'Dividends to Reap: Shareholder activists begin to make their mark in Japan', 3rd July 2008
Nakamoto, Michiyo, Burton, Jack and Cameron, Doug, 'TSE buys stake in SGX for $303m', 16th June 2007
Nakamoto, Michiyo and Cohen, Norma, 'London and Tokyo bring forth Asian cousin for Aim', 31st October 2007
Nakamoto, Michiyo and Jenkins, Patrick, 'Bowed by over-ambition', 2nd August 2012
Nasiripour, Shahien and Braithwaite, Tom, 'Out to break the banks', 1st May 2013
Nasiripour, Shahien and Masters, Brooke, 'Regulators edge towards "every country for itself"', 10th December 2012
Nasiripour, Shahien, McCrum, Dan and Watkins, Mary, 'Regulators want end of money fund fixed price', 21st February 2013
Nicholson, Mark, 'Venture still in its infancy', 27th September 1989
Nicholson, Mark, 'Law stifles more than it enables', 22nd April 1993
Nicholson, Mark, 'Two busy years of regulatory power', 13th March 1995
Nicholson, Mark, 'India poised to begin electronic share trading', 6th September 1996
Nicholson, Mark and Nicoll, Alexander, 'First take an aspirin', 13th March 1995
Nicholson, Mark and Whittington, James, 'Magic carpet not ready for take-off', 7th February 1994
Nicoll, Alexander, 'A boon for the corporate treasurer', 11th December 1985
Nicoll, Alexander, 'Fast growth on back of market volatility', 11th December 1985
Nicoll, Alexander, 'A global defensive strategy', 11th December 1985
Nicoll, Alexander, 'Hesitant steps on road to success', 11th December 1985
Nicoll, Alexander, 'International moves before Big Bang', 29th August 1985
Nicoll, Alexander, 'A new option for the corporate treasurer', 1st August 1985
Nicoll, Alexander, 'Potential begins to be fulfilled', 11th December 1985
Nicoll, Alexander, 'Round-the-clock trading brings a new challenge', 5th November 1985
Nicoll, Alexander, 'Big Board's ambitions reach towards London', 13th February 1986
Nicoll, Alexander, 'Dealers worry about fallout from Big Bang', 28th February 1986
Nicoll, Alexander, 'Electronic Bridge boosts global equities trading', 23rd April 1986
Nicoll, Alexander, 'Europe is watching American programmes', 28th November 1986
Nicoll, Alexander, 'Global distribution should be good for share prices', 27th October 1986

Nicoll, Alexander, 'London hopes for sterling paper market', 14th March 1986
Nicoll, Alexander, 'Market wakes up early to competition', 17th April 1986
Nicoll, Alexander, 'The new market has an electronic heart', 27th October 1986
Nicoll, Alexander, 'Risks yet to be tested', 17th March 1986
Nicoll, Alexander, 'Set to play a prime role in markets', 8th February 1986
Nicoll, Alexander, 'The sour taste of success', 16th December 1986
Nicoll, Alexander, 'Swiss connection is prominent', 17th March 1986
Nicoll, Alexander, 'Ticklish issue of share stabilisation', 11th July 1986
Nicoll, Alexander, 'Time-span suits futures', 27th October 1986
Nicoll, Alexander, 'Trend towards globalisation', 17th March 1986
Nicoll, Alexander, 'UK commercial paper market on the way', 20th January 1986
Nicoll, Alexander, 'Agreement among rivals', 19th March 1987
Nicoll, Alexander, 'A banker rather than a regulator', 20th January 1987
Nicoll, Alexander, 'The big investors go global', 17th March 1987
Nicoll, Alexander, 'Borrowers' confidence grows', 21st April 1987
Nicoll, Alexander, 'Everything to play for', 21st October 1987
Nicoll, Alexander, 'Firms seek benefits of automation', 8th January 1987
Nicoll, Alexander, 'The heart of the world game', 21st October 1987
Nicoll, Alexander, 'Liffe in search of greater liquidity', 30th September 1987
Nicoll, Alexander, 'London's global ambitions signal aggressive mood', 5th February 1987
Nicoll, Alexander, 'Markets to pay heavy price for regulation', 19th May 1987
Nicoll, Alexander, 'The rocky road to a global village', 27th May 1987
Nicoll, Alexander, 'Underpinning the market's liquidity', 19th March 1987
Nicoll, Alexander, 'Volumes rocket after Big Bang', 19th March 1987
Nicoll, Alexander, 'Warning signs in global game', 21st April 1987
Nicoll, Alexander, 'Bittersweet birthday celebrations for options', 12th April 1988
Nicoll, Alexander, 'Confidence is growing though snags remain', 17th February 1988
Nicoll, Alexander, 'Higher risk, greater reward', 17th February 1988
Nicoll, Alexander, 'New class of seat may appeal to locals', 10th March 1988
Nicoll, Alexander, 'A pendulum over the pit', 10th March 1988
Nicoll, Alexander, 'Profit for the few', 17th February 1988
Nicoll, Alexander, 'Regulation a tough task for the board', 16th September 1991
Nicoll, Alexander, 'Learning from misfortune', 7th February 1994
Nisse, Jason, 'US projects are ahead by two years', 16th October 1986
Noble, John, 'Slow start fails to dim Stock Connect', 25th November 2014
Noble, Josh, 'HKEx unveils plan to be "gateway for China"', 16th January 2013
Noble, Josh, 'UK's share of renminbi trade leaps', 9th October 2013
Noble, Josh and Hornby, Lucy, 'HKEx enters commodities trade with metals listing plan', 23rd April 2014
Noonan, Laura, 'Relocation threat for thousands of London investment bank staff', 7th January 2016
Noonan, Laura, 'Wall Street deal fees eclipse European rivals', 10th June 2016
Noonan, Laura, 'Banks look to route business via HK', 23rd October 2017
Noonan, Laura, 'Banks scale back on plans for City jobs exodus', 14th December 2017
Noonan, Laura, 'Dublin emerges as top choice for post-Brexit bases in EU', 11th July 2017
Noonan, Laura, 'Financials', 12th June 2018
Noonan, Laura, 'City has power to lure business without Brexit', 13th February 2019
Noonan, Laura, 'Ex-bankers embrace adrenalin ride of fintech', 9th January 2019
Noonan, Laura, 'Goldman to wield axe on bond unit as peers sit tight', 8th February 2019
Noonan, Laura, 'Transaction work is fastest growth area for big banks', 8th March 2019
Noonan, Laura, 'Weak margins drag on safe banks' ambitions', 13th February 2019
Noonan, Laura and Armstrong, Robert, 'Earnings reveal true picture of hard-hit banks', 14th January 2019
Noonan, Laura, Binham, Caroline and Arnold, Martin, 'Investment banks face baptism of fire after City watchdog's opening salvo', 20th February 2015

Noonan, Laura and Jenkins, Patrick, 'Financial Crisis', 13th September 2018
Noonan, Laura and Jones, Claire, 'Central bank has bigger stick to win respect at home and abroad', 13th February 2019
Noonan, Laura, Norris, Stephen and Crow, David, 'City's top lenders hold fire on Brexit exodus', 2nd April 2019
Noonan, Laura, Rennison, Joe and Hale, Thomas, 'Lenders trim budgets for maths and models', 24th May 2016
Norman, Peter, 'Highs and lows of a dizzy decade', 23rd June 1993
Norman, Peter, 'Payments and settlements', 8th August 1994
Norman, Peter, 'European SEC plan spurned', 16th September 2000
Norman, Peter, 'Securities watchdog sharpens its teeth', 25th October 2004
Norman, Peter, 'Revolution in EU securities kick off', 29th October 2007
Norman, Peter, 'Call to improve plumbing of fund processing', 31st March 2008
Norman, Peter and Boland, Vincent, 'Caution over pace of market regulation', 16th February 2001
Norman, Peter and Hargreaves, Deborah, 'Long haul for Lamfalussy on securities markets' regulation', 28th December 2000
Norman, Peter and Lambert, Richard, 'A steady hand at the tiller', 1st July 1993
Nowinski, Richard and Brooks, Robin, 'UK financial services face new and important EC Council directives', 12th April 1990
Nusbaum, Alexandra, 'Mothers planning to be nimble', 17th December 1999
O'Byrne, David, 'Borsa Istanbul has ambitious expansion plan beyond equities', 13th October 2015
O'Connor, Gillian, 'Credit given for change to London listing', 15th December 1999
O'Dea, Christopher, 'Financial instruments hold sway', 5th March 1985
Oakley, David, 'European repo trading grows Euro 500bn in year', 2nd March 2007
Oakley, David, 'Record repurchase volumes for Europe', 29th August 2007
Oakley, David, 'Square Mile fears losing its edge', 1st October 2007
Oakley, David, 'Austria gives nod to MTS Eurozone rival', 1st July 2008
Oakley, David, 'Banks' reluctance to part with cash keeps the heat on Libor', 23rd May 2008
Oakley, David, 'Search for safety sparks record flows into money market funds', 21st October 2008
Oakley, David, 'Europe's ravaged landscape begins to stabilise', 11th September 2009
Oakley, David, 'Lenders are slow to regain lost confidence', 10th September 2009
Oakley, David, 'Syria in exchange debut', 10th March 2009
Oakley, David, 'European repo trading bounces back', 16th September 2010
Oakley, David, 'Collateral demand rises for interbank lending', 4th July 2011
Oakley, David, 'Crisis probe puts Libor in spotlight', 16th March 2011
Oakley, David, 'Switch to bonds signals end for cult of equity', 20th November 2012
Oakley, David, 'Asset managers fill the gap as banks retreat', 4th March 2013
Oakley, David, 'Shadow banks fill infrastructure debt void', 1st February 2013
Oakley, David and Blas, Javier, 'Explosive rise in iron ore derivatives trading forecast over next 10 years', 31st March 2010
Oakley, David and Gangahar, Anuj, 'Volatility fears fuel equity derivative surge', 23rd May 2007
Oakley, David and Mackenzie, Michael, 'Interbank credit lines dry up', 16th September 2008
Oakley, David and Pickard, Jim, 'Banks move in on property derivatives', 5th March 2007
Oakley, David, Pickard, Jim and Burgess, Kate, 'No silver bullet to end City short-termism', 24th July 2012
Oakley, David and Scholtes, Saskia, 'Flurry of activity in banks for CDSs', 3rd April 2007
Oakley, David and Stafford, Philip, 'LSE tries to change terms of Euro 463m LCH.Clearnet deal', 15th December 2012
Oakley, David and Stafford, Philip, 'New rules hit LSE deal with LCH.Clearnet', 18th December 2012
Oakley, David and Tett, Gillian, 'European bond market puts US in the shade', 15th January 2007
Odell, Mark, 'Aim fatigue emerges on oil and gas', 4th January 2007
Oram, Roderick, 'Banks fight for share of oldest market's growth', 28th November 1986
Oram, Roderick, 'Further transatlantic links on the way', 12th October 1987
Oram, Roderick, 'Innovators to cut global risk', 19th March 1987

Oram, Roderick, 'Japanese established as traders', 21st April 1987
Oram, Roderick, 'Time to level with volatility', 19th March 1987
Oram, Roderick, 'Volatility spurs cross-trading', 3rd June 1987
Oram, Roderick, 'Merrill Lynch joins Manhattan exodus', 29th June 1989
Orr, Robert, 'Founder of Icap is new chairman of Numis', 30th April 2003
Orton, Ian, 'A small world may be a riskier home', 24th February 2001
Ostrovsky, Arkady, 'Back-office emerges from shadows', 23rd March 1999
Ostrovsky, Arkady, 'Clearers jostle for dominance', 20th September 1999
Ostrovsky, Arkady, 'JP Morgan targets e-trading', 25th October 1999
Ostrovsky, Arkady, 'The odds are good on future growth', 20th September 1999
Ostrovsky, Arkady, 'Securities leaders lift Easdaq', 30th July 1999
Ostrovsky, Arkady, 'Technology drives the markets', 19th May 2000
Ostrovsky, Arkady, 'Working towards a seamless link', 28th June 2000
Ostrovsky, Arkady, 'From chaos to capitalist triumph', 9th October 2003
Ostrovsky, Arkady, 'Russia's IPO rush: companies touch down in London seeking growth and status', 20th July 2005
Ostrovsky, Arkady and van Duyn, Aline, 'Volumes rise as investors seek security amid turmoil', 7th October 2002
Ostrovsky, Arkady and Wendlandt, Astrid, 'Tradepoint wins backing of clearing houses', 11th February 2000
Ottersgard, Lars, 'Global ambitions can be achieved through a single voice', 14th November 2012
Oudea, Frederic, 'Europe needs home grown bulge bracket banks', 12th October 2015
Owen, David, 'Exchanges look to diversification', 23rd July 1986
Owen, David, 'Farm futures in the shade', 23rd July 1986
Owen, David, 'Chicago exchange to re-launch gold futures', 28th May 1987
Owen, David, 'Chicago trading livens up', 27th May 1987
Owen, David, 'Expansion is the keynote', 19th March 1987
Owen, David, 'Experience wins over Chicago', 3rd February 1987
Owen, David, 'Over the counter, round the law', 19th March 1987
Owen, David, 'Pros and cons in WTI contract', 3rd February 1987
Owen, David, 'Banks close the gap', 17th February 1988
Owen, David, 'In place of the pit', 23rd May 1991
Owen, David, 'Old credit routes are back', 23rd May 1991
Owen, David, 'Regionals seek new role', 23rd May 1991
Owen, Edward, 'Keeping the young at home', 2nd October 1986
Ozanne, Julian, 'Symptom of change', 6th June 1995
Palmer, Maija, 'Number of UK-listed tech stock dwindles', 14th November 2011
Pandit, Vikram, 'Outdated rules are holding back financial innovation', 19th September 2019
Parker, George and Burns, Jimmy, 'Modern precedents for public ownership', 18th February 2008
Parker, George and Giles, Chris, 'Turner goes in to bat for "whipping boy" FSA', 24th June 2009
Parker, George, Mai, Christine and Cohen, Norma, 'EU issues deadline to exchanges on charges', 7th March 2006
Parkes, Christopher and Waller, David, 'Politics comes to the Finanzplatz', 24th January 1992
Parkin, Benjamin, 'Mutual funds in India seek to restore faith of skittish investor', 2nd July 2019
Parry, John H, 'Threat from over-complexity', 5th March 1985
Pearson, Clare, 'Demand disappoints enthusiasts', 27th May 1986
Pearson, Clare, 'Leaping ahead on a nice greasy breakfast', 21st October 1987
Pearson, Clare, 'Overcrowding inhibits new issues', 21st April 1987
Pearson, Clare, 'Transfer of Euroyen bond centre to Tokyo suggested', 22nd May 1987
Pearson, Clare, 'Wholesale success by Halifax', 15th July 1987
Pearson, Clare, 'A healthy niche operation', 17th February 1988
Pearson, Clare, 'Less fashionable, still useful', 17th February 1988
Pearson, Clare, 'October's storm produces ideal trading weather', 10th March 1988
Pearson, Samantha, 'US plans threaten LatAm FX', 20th January 2010

Pearson, Samantha, 'Brazilian clearing blow for BATS', 14th November 2011
Pearson, Samantha, 'Threat of competition triggers improvements', 15th November 2011
Pearson, Samantha, 'Change is in the air for stocks', 14th November 2012
Pearson, Samantha, 'Foreign rivals join battle for post-trade prize', 30th October 2012
Pearson, Samantha, 'Industry stalemate as rivals clamour for access', 3rd October 2012
Pearson, Samantha, 'Brazil's exchange chief rejoices at post-impeachment chances', 11th October 2016
Peel, Michael, 'Myanmar's one company bourse struggles to meet demand', 9th April 2016
Peel, Quentin, 'Financial integration makes slow progress', 4th June 1985
Persaud, Avinash, 'The Basel plan must get back to market basics', 3rd September 2003
Persaud, Avinash, 'Lehman had to fall to save the financial system', 16th September 2008
Peston, Robert, 'Enforcer rides into town', 3rd November 1992
Peston, Robert, 'Invisible threats sighted to City's international status', 8th July 1992
Peston, Robert, 'Loans that change their spots', 19th July 1993
Peston, Robert, 'The risks of regulating', 25th January 1993
Peston, Robert, 'Silent launch of the lifeboat', 19th October 1993
Peston, Robert, 'Nasdaq plans European exchange', 5th November 1999
Peston, Robert and Cohen, Norma, 'Country gent in exchange of fire', 15th January 1994
Petrou, Karen, 'Repo ructions call attention to failure of post-crisis policy', 7th November 2019
Phillips, Stephen, 'System suppliers in a state of high flux', 3rd April 2002
Pickard, Jim, 'CMBS demand set to increase', 13th January 2006
Pickard, Jim, 'Number of buy-to-let mortgages rises 30-fold in past decade', 15th February 2007
Pickard, Jim, 'Ominous signs for students of history', 28th September 2007
Pickard, Jim and Cohen, Norma, 'Dubai group eyes move for OMX', 28th May 2007
Pickford, James, 'The capital's unique selling point', 4th December 2013
Pickford, James, 'The global city with a gift for reinvention', 11th June 2013
Pickford, James, Wilson, James, Simonian, Haig, 'Big hubs keep the wheels of industry turning', 10th May 2012
Pilling, David, 'Big Bang for Chile capital markets', 27th January 1994
Pilling, David, 'New sparkle to market image', 7th February 1994
Pilling, David, 'JSDA in talks on selling Jasdaq holding', 28th September 2007
Pimlott, Daniel, 'Retreat on idea that big lenders need to be split', 18th December 2009
Piramal, Gita, 'Indian stock market reform gathers pace', 5th March 1992
Pitt, Harvey, 'Sarbanes-Oxley is an unhealthy export', 21st June 2006
Pitt, John, 'Storm gathers from the east', 16th February 1996
Platt, Eric, 'Wall St banks join forces to form debt platform', 18th June 2018
Platt, Eric and Meyer, Gregory, 'Exchanges jump on index data as banks beat a retreat', 3rd June 2017
Platt, Eric and Smith, Robert, 'Efforts to harmonise risky-loans rules in doubt', 6th June 2017
Plender, John, 'Deregulation gains that add up to zero', 29th August 1985
Plender, John, 'Hard to pull off gracefully', 20th December 1985
Plender, John, 'The risk of conglomerates slipping through the net', 25th September 1985
Plender, John, 'Capital loosens its bonds', 8th May 1986
Plender, John, 'The dangers of deregulation', 9th May 1986
Plender, John, 'An omelette yet to be tasted', 27th October 1986
Plender, John, 'Watchdogs follow the sun', 27th October 1986
Plender, John, 'Cries of foul from the maze', 23rd September 1987
Plender, John, 'A homing instinct', 14th November 1987
Plender, John, 'Cocktail of liberalisation', 17th November 1988
Plender, John, 'A rocky boat in the City', 22nd February 1990
Plender, John, 'Uncertainty in a stable world', 22nd July 1992
Plender, John, 'Through a market, darkly', 27th May 1994
Plender, John, 'The box that can never be shut', 28th February 1995
Plender, John, 'City plays growing role in drawing investors', 2nd October 1995
Plender, John, 'Stock market splits', 16th August 1997
Plender, John, 'Crisis in the making', 12th April 1999

Plender, John, 'Out of sight, not out of mind', 20th September 1999
Plender, John, 'Exchange values', 3rd September 2000
Plender, John, 'Too close for comfort', 21st March 2000
Plender, John, 'The limits of ingenuity', 17th May 2001
Plender, John, 'Shock of the new: a changed financial landscape may be eroding resistance to systemic risk', 16th February 2005
Plender, John, 'Homeward Bound', 30th April 2009
Plender, John, 'Originative sin', 5th January 2009
Plender, John, 'Re-spinning the web', 22nd June 2009
Plender, John, 'Shame gene has disappeared from the financial system', 17th August 2009
Plender, John, 'The Big Bang spawned a dark-trading monster', 13th June 2016
Plender, John and Fisher, Andrew, 'No end to the wave of buying', 16th June 1995
Plews, Tim, 'The "Balls clauses" are a mixed blessing for the City', 29th November 2006
Plimmer, Gill, 'Financial sector rescues off-set sell-offs', 13th August 2012
Plimmer, Gill and Stafford, Philip, 'Cable hub gives City edge on Frankfurt', 7th May 2013
Politi, James, 'Changing hopes boost volumes', 7th October 2002
Pooler, Michael, 'New York and London vie for financial crown', 2nd October 2014
Postelnicu, Andrei, 'Easy trades thrive on a complex platform', 25th September 2001
Postelnicu, Andrei, 'Invisible trades come under scrutiny', 6th June 2002
Postelnicu, Andrei, 'Sprightly operator defies the market's gloom', 6th June 2002
Postelnicu, Andrei, 'A card game in which one player sees all the hands', 12th May 2003
Postelnicu, Andrei, 'A little breathing space', 7th July 2003
Postelnicu, Andrei, 'A once endangered species still roams the floor', 17th April 2003
Postelnicu, Andrei, 'Fast market proposals might spell danger for NYSE traders', 24th February 2004
Postelnicu, Andrei, 'Listing chief sets sights abroad', 23rd August 2004
Postelnicu, Andrei, Barber, Lionel and Wighton, David, 'A great part of America: John Thain sets out to restore trust in the New York Stock Exchange', 2nd April 2004
Postelnicu, Andrei and Wighton, David, 'NYSE members keep listing question afloat', 8th March 2004
Powers, John, 'Doors open for pin-striped pork bellies', 5th March 1985
Powley, Tanya, 'FSA sees "common sense" on mortgage overhaul', 19th December 2011
Prasad, Eswar, 'Central banks' embrace of blockchain remains too timid', 2nd January 2019
Prest, Michael, 'Fear of "cats" results in new products', 27th June 1997
Prest, Michael, 'Pressure on rule-makers', 27th June 1997
Prest, Michael, 'Time for a new exchange', 24th March 1998
Pretzlik, Charles, 'Euro gives a boost to bond markets', 26th May 2000
Pretzlik, Charles, 'US banks take Europe by storm', in *Europe Reinvented: The new rules of the game* (London: Financial Times, 2000)
Pretzlik, Charles, 'LSE set to face competition in move for Liffe', 13th October 2001
Pretzlik, Charles, 'LSE talking to four potential partners', 7th November 2001
Pretzlik, Charles, 'Benefits to City would be only marginal at best, report concludes', 10th June 2003
Pretzlik, Charles, 'The financial revolution that never was', 9th May 2003
Pretzlik, Charles, 'Maintaining a resilience to risk—and shocks', 1st October 2003
Pretzlik, Charles and Boland, Vincent, 'LSE in new talks on merger', 26th April 2002
Pretzlik, Charles, Croft, Jane and Burgess, Kate, 'The Financial Services Authority has been reactive, not aggressive. It must go out and make the market work', 20th September 2003
Pretzlik, Charles, Jenkins, Patrick and Skorecki, Alex, 'New LSE chairman ready for action', 18th September 2003
Pretzlik, Charles and Silverman, Gary, 'Investment bank job cuts reach 25,000', 13th August 2001
Pretzlik, Charles and Silverman, Gary, 'City partnerships that were forced to grow up', 8th January 2002
Pretzlik, Charles and Skorecki, Alex, 'LSE plays down US merger talk', 24th May 2002
Price, Christopher, 'Braced for radical changes', 9th December 1993
Price, Christopher, 'LSE sets the pace', 17th May 1996

Price, Christopher, 'Cool reception for new exchanges', 28th February 1997
Price, Christopher, 'Juniors gather strength', 30th May 1997
Price, Christopher, 'Wider market's sideshow', 29th September 1999
Price, Rhodri, 'The pros and cons of dark pools of liquidity', 7th January 2013
Pritchard, Stephen, 'A race to stay ahead of fraudsters', 5th June 2002
Purton, Peter, 'Glass is at the heart of a revolution', 7th October 1991
Quek, Joyce, 'A blessing in disguise', 9th August 1990
Quek, Joyce, 'Profits of big four leap by 30%', 9th August 1990
Quek, Joyce, 'Singapore's Clob wins rapid acceptance', 18th January 1990
Quek, Joyce, 'A revolution in the wings', 30th April 1991
Rabinovitch, Simon and Cookson, Robert, 'China unlikely to impose big bang reforms', 24th February 2012
Rachman, Gideon, 'How the Square Mile fell out of love with Brussels', 12th December 2006
Rahman, Bayan, 'Disclosure and liquidity will be key', 31st March 2000
Rahman, Bayan, 'Global players enjoy feast', 8th May 2000
Rahman, Bayan, 'Troubled times for Mothers', 8th May 2000
Rahman, Bayan, 'TSE members vote for privatisation', 27th September 2001
Rahman, Bayan, 'Japan's bourses face an uncertain future', 12th December 2003
Rahman, Bayan and Pretzlik, Charles, 'Merrill set to cut 20 brokerages', 28th December 2001
Rajan, Amin, 'Illiquidity will amplify the magnitude of a bear market', 5th August 2019
Rajappa, Subadra, 'Investors have to embrace challenge of Libor's demise', 10th July 2019
Ralph, Oliver, 'Universal banks', 30th March 2015
Ralph, Oliver, 'Future Risks', 26th May 2016
Ralph, Oliver, 'Singapore moves in on catastrophe bonds', 2nd November 2017
Ralph, Oliver, 'Slip in market share knocks London role in reinsurance', 9th May 2017
Ralph, Oliver, 'Bermuda', 24th December 2019
Ralph, Oliver, 'Conduct replaces capital as focus', 25th March 2019
Ralph, Oliver, 'Insurers warned over vulnerability to risky debt after stretch for yield', 22nd February 2019
Ratcliffe, Alice, 'Banking on an outsider status', 13th October 1998
Rathbone, John Paul, 'Investors require patience more than nimble financial footwork', 6th April 2010
Ratner, Juliana, 'Nasdaq looks to strike deal with Easdaq', 31st January 2001
Raun, Laura, 'Gold contract initiative', 5th March 1985
Raun, Laura, 'Amsterdam bourse to test block trading', 13th March 1986
Raun, Laura, 'Campaign to lead in Europe', 14th April 1986
Raun, Laura, 'Exchange answers its critics', 19th March 1987
Raun, Laura, 'Loss of business stemmed', 21st April 1987
Raun, Laura, 'Amsterdam drops gold relaunch plan', 10th February 1988
Raun, Laura, 'Oldest bourse sets sights on full automation', 29th June 1988
Raun, Laura, 'Amsterdam SE set to cut fees', 15th December 1989
Raun, Laura, 'Dutch aim to get in on the act', 25th January 1989
Raun, Laura, 'Dutch master plan', 28th March 1989
Raun, Laura, 'Rotterdam oil futures challenge to London's IPE', 31st October 1989
Raun, Laura, 'Moves to recoup business', 12th June 1990
Raun, Laura, 'A new mood of realism', 12th June 1990
Raval, Anjli, 'China launch aims to create first Asian benchmark for oil deals', 10th February 2018
Rawsthorn, Alice, 'Intermediaries' buy out', 27th May 1986
Rawsthorn, Alice, 'A liquidity test for the smaller exchanges', 27th October 1986
Rawsthorn, Alice, 'Saving companies from erratic swings', 27th May 1986
Rawsthorn, Alice, 'Criteria for the young and small', 20th January 1987
Rawsthorn, Alice, 'Hazards of a new role', 20th January 1987
Rawsthorn, Alice, 'French plan relaunch of second-tier market', 20th March 1992
Rawsthorn, Alice, 'Re-engineering the Paris stock market', 24th March 1992
Rawsthorn, Alice, 'Tomorrow will be better', 13th October 1992

Reed, John, 'Under the magnifying glass', 13th May 2016
Reed, John, 'Tel Aviv exchange courts high-tech innovators', 11th July 2017
Reed, John, Anderson, Robert and Eddy, Kester, 'Unified trading faces battle to justify worth', 2nd November 2000
Reed, Nick, 'Investors seek wider horizons', 22nd November 1996
Rennison, Joe, 'Bond traders grow nervous over glitch potential', 2nd July 2015
Rennison, Joe, 'Fitch warns of growing repo threat', 18th June 2015
Rennison, Joe, 'HFT's role in Treasuries give regulators pause', 2nd September 2015
Rennison, Joe, 'Moody's sets out shake-up for clearing houses', 24th June 2015
Rennison, Joe, 'Policymakers left with problem in the wake of London whale', 13th October 2015
Rennison, Joe, 'Treasury trading swept up in rapid change', 10th July 2015
Rennison, Joe, 'US Treasuries hit by liquidity concerns', 30th July 2015
Rennison, Joe, 'BGC set for Treasuries trading push', 1st December 2016
Rennison, Joe, 'Bond trading platform muscles in as banks retreat', 29th September 2016
Rennison, Joe, 'Transparency beckons for US Treasury trade', 18th February 2016
Rennison, Joe, 'Lutnick makes Treasury trading comeback', 16th May 2017
Rennison, Joe, 'Pace of reform in bond market slows to a crawl under Trump', 10th October 2017
Rennison, Joe, 'Senators press regulators to clarify position over Treasury market reform', 2nd November 2017
Rennison, Joe, 'Bloomberg snatches corporate bond trade data partner from rival Thomson Reuters', 26th July 2018
Rennison, Joe, 'High-speed traders have their say on Treasury data', 2nd April 2018
Rennison, Joe, 'Hunt for yield drives stronger demand for riskier slices of US mortgage securities', 31st August 2018
Rennison, Joe, 'Trio sets out plans to launch corporate bond futures', 17th May 2018
Rennison, Joe, 'BIS sounds alarm on risk of corporate debt fire sale', 6th March 2019
Rennison, Joe, 'Investors flock to CLOs with ghost of previous loan vehicles left in the past', 29th January 2019
Rennison, Joe, 'Investors secure New York Fed loans with cash crunch worries lingering', 3rd December 2019
Rennison, Joe, 'MarketAxess muscles into ETFs with Virtu tie-up', 8th April 2019
Rennison, Joe, 'Repo pressure eases despite fears over bank lending at end of quarter', 1st October 2019
Rennison, Joe, 'Wall Street cuts a deal to clean up $8.2tn credit default swaps trading', 7th March 2019
Rennison, Joe, Armstrong, Robert and Wigglesworth, Robin, 'Meet the new bond kings', 23rd January 2020
Rennison, Joe and Childs, Mary, 'CDS demise sends traders running for cover', 10th June 2016
Rennison, Joe and Greeley, Brendan, 'New York Fed defends response to turmoil', 25th September 2019
Rennison, Joe and Greeley, Brendan, 'Soaring repo rate puts spotlight on Fed policy', 19th September 2019
Rennison, Joe and Indap, Sujeet, 'Wall Street strives to clean up credit default swaps industry', 14th March 2019
Rennison, Joe, Meyer, Greg and Bullock, Nicole, 'Vix Vexations', 8th February 2018
Rennison, Joe and Noonan, Laura, 'Week of repo turbulence rattles Wall Street traders', 21st September 2019
Rennison, Joe and Scaggs, Alexandra, 'US Treasury dealers accused of collusion', 17th November 2017
Rennison, Joe and Smith, Colby, 'Debt machine risks running out of control', 22nd January 2019
Rennison, Joe and Smith, Colby, 'Year-end repo rates surge despite Fed attempts to ease the funding strain', 7th December 2019
Rennison, Joe and Stafford, Philip, 'Complexity clouds the case for repo clearing', 19th June 2015
Rennison, Joe and Stafford, Philip, 'Fears grow that global reforms to derivatives will fragment into a patchwork of local standards', 23rd September 2016

Rennison, Joe and Stafford, Philip, 'Traders find receptive ear among regulators to relax capital rules', 10th July 2018
Rennison, Joe and Stafford, Philip, 'Brussels lines up one-year access to UK clearing houses in event of no-deal Brexit', 13th December 2019
Rennison, Joe and Stafford, Philip, 'Rise of MarketAxess mirrors demise of traders on Wall Street', 30th August 2019
Rennison, Joe and Wigglesworth, Robin, 'Outsiders struggle to shake up Treasury trade', 31st August 2016
Rennison, Joe, Wigglesworth, Robin and Johnson, Miles, 'Concerns mount over scale of volatility-trading ecosystem', 10th February 2018
Report, Reuter, 'Slow start for Manila currency futures', 6th March 1991
Reuters, 'Toronto exchange to automate', 14th February 1992
Rice, Robert, 'Legislative shortcomings in post-Big Bang era lead to calls for reform', 7th February 1990
Rice, Robert, 'No certainties about securities', 21st November 1995
Rice, Xan, 'In search of a new standard', 15th April 2014
Rice, Xan, 'New Solver price strips away cloak of secrecy', 17th July 2014
Rice, Xan, 'Thomson Reuters and CME win bid to set silver price', 12th July 2014
Riddell, Peter and Hargreaves, Deborah, 'Chicago protests over planned futures tax', 31st January 1990
Ridding, John, 'Investors pay high price for exposure', 27th November 1989
Ridding, John, 'New set of much-needed hedging instruments', 13th March 1989
Ridding, John, 'Second fiddle's new tunes', 13th March 1989
Ridding, John, 'Prising an opening', 29th October 1991
Ridding, John, 'Rival markets battle for the top spot', 27th April 1998
Ridding, John, 'A way out of the crisis', 1st May 1998
Riding, Siobhan, 'CEOs quit London amid Brexit tumult', 25th November 2019
Riding, Siobhan, 'EU and UK regulators strike fund group Brexit deal', 4th February 2019
Riding, Siobhan, 'Europe bickers over passporting future', 5th August 2019
Riding, Siobhan, 'Ireland to review fund rules after Woodford', 25th November 2019
Riding, Siobhan, 'Luxembourg watchdog eyes tougher liquidity rule', 9th September 2019
Riding, Siobhan, 'Supermancos, the fund businesses that are winning big from Brexit', 25th February 2019
Riding, Siobhan, 'UK Watchdog eyes liquidity reforms', 7th October 2019
Riding, Siobhan, 'Watchdogs probe systemic risks of passive fund growth', 1st April 2019
Ridpath, Barbara, 'Crisis—and regulation—can breed opportunity', 30th May 2012
Rigby, Elizabeth, 'Collins Stewart eyes Prebon', 27th May 2004
Rigby, Elizabeth, 'The bankers' new best friends', 22nd July 2004
Rigby, Elizabeth, 'FSA examines a burgeoning industry', 22nd May 2004
Rigby, Elizabeth, 'Windy City rivals may feel fresh blast of competition', 2nd April 2004
Riley, Barry, 'Equities develop global market', 23rd November 1983
Riley, Barry, 'Well-placed centre with advantages', 28th November 1983
Riley, Barry, 'Cross-border phenomenon', 7th December 1984
Riley, Barry, 'The fight for Liffe', 12th September 1984
Riley, Barry, 'Gower, after the City upheaval', 30th April 1984
Riley, Barry, 'Increased emphasis placed on taking a global view', 7th December 1984
Riley, Barry, 'Living by their wits without privileges', 29th May 1984
Riley, Barry, 'City regulator gets into gear', 20th July 1985
Riley, Barry, 'Concentration of talent bolsters prominent role', 18th November 1985
Riley, Barry, 'A costly question for the futures markets', 19th August 1985
Riley, Barry, 'Design stands test of time', 1st July 1985
Riley, Barry, 'More aggression shown on a broader front', 18th November 1985
Riley, Barry, 'Regulatory framework for City takes shape', 31st October 1985
Riley, Barry, 'SEC urges controls on international securities trading', 22nd May 1985

Riley, Barry, 'Selling self-regulation to the City', 2nd December 1985
Riley, Barry, 'A tough battle for survival', 10th July 1985
Riley, Barry, 'Where the Stock Exchange draws the line', 7th October 1985
Riley, Barry, 'Why global traders are stepping up pressure', 21st February 1985
Riley, Barry, 'A big leap predicted', 27th October 1986
Riley, Barry, 'The City Revolution', 27th October 1986
Riley, Barry, 'Foreign banks attracted by open policy', 8th January 1986
Riley, Barry, 'It's going to be like New York', 3rd July 1986
Riley, Barry, 'London's the third leg of our stool', 27th October 1986
Riley, Barry, 'The Stock Exchange extends its reach', 17th April 1986
Riley, Barry, 'Strangers at the gilt-edged gate', 28th July 1986
Riley, Barry, 'A unique global background', 3rd July 1986
Riley, Barry, 'Bourses respond to London threat', 6th November 1987
Riley, Barry, 'Critical mass works in the City's favour', 16th November 1987
Riley, Barry, 'Hedging lifts the five-date contract', 19th March 1987
Riley, Barry, 'Seaq stretches the day', 21st October 1987
Riley, Barry, 'The exposure of a club', 26th October 1988
Riley, Barry, 'Home looked safest', 14th October 1988
Riley, Barry, 'More interdealer brokers to open', 28th March 1988
Riley, Barry, 'New regulations, new faces', 14th October 1988
Riley, Barry, 'A question of survival', 26th October 1988
Riley, Barry, 'Reciprocity worries London', 29th June 1988
Riley, Barry, 'Regulators are balancing on a tightrope', 8th November 1989
Riley, Barry, 'A bridge between New York and Tokyo', 29th November 1990
Riley, Barry, 'A formidable task', 29th March 1990
Riley, Barry, 'Beginnings of a flight to safety', 24th July 1991
Riley, Barry, 'Big three join battle for supremacy', 4th July 1991
Riley, Barry, 'Individualists seek a niche', 16th May 1991
Riley, Barry, 'Move to join Swift is slow', 9th December 1992
Riley, Barry, 'Securities Institute sallies forth into the world', 16th September 1992
Riley, Barry, 'The world as portfolio', 25th November 1992
Riley, Barry, 'On the way to speedier settlements', 9th December 1993
Riley, Barry, 'Empty vaults will bring new opportunities', 29th November 1994
Riley, Barry, 'A new asset class created', 7th February 1994
Riley, Barry, 'Caught off balance by Wall Street', 4th December 1995
Riley, Barry, 'The honeymoon is over', 4th December 1995
Riley, Barry, 'Free flow of finance', 27th September 1996
Riley, Barry, 'Growth on a grand scale', 24th April 1997
Riley, Barry, 'Aim for bourse without borders', 18th May 1998
Riley, Barry, 'Free float presented with a bumpy ride', 5th April 2000
Ritson, Marjorie, 'Some may prefer Europe', 26th September 1988
Rivett, John, 'Collateral will be key in shake-up for derivatives', 1st August 2011
Roberts, Adrienne, 'Dotcom deals expected', 28th March 2001
Roberts, Adrienne, 'Exchanges trading on an uncertain future', 25th September 2001
Roberts, Adrienne, 'IPE searching for technology partner', 11th January 2001
Roberts, Adrienne, 'IPE split over digital future', 23rd March 2001
Roberts, Adrienne, 'Soft commodity traders find the going hard', 3rd July 2001
Roberts, Adrienne, 'ABS debt thrives on innovation', 22nd October 2003
Robinson, Anthony, 'Creating capitalism without capital', 7th February 1994
Robinson, Anthony, 'An enviable reputation', 28th February 1997
Robinson, Gwen, 'Japanese go straight to markets to raise cash', 15th October 1996
Robinson, Gwen, 'Backward in coming forward', 27th June 1997
Robinson, Gwen, 'Another milestone nears', 24th March 1998
Robinson, Gwen, 'Screen test looms', 17th July 1998

Robinson, Gwen, 'SFE in push to go fully electronic', 6th April 1998
Robinson, Gwen, 'Cry goes out for screen trading', 16th April 1999
Robinson, Gwen, 'Record trading as merger talks go on', 23rd March 1999
Robinson, Gwen, 'A revolutionary in a changing world', 26th July 1999
Rodger, Ian, 'Overshadowed by Zurich', 21st November 1991
Rodger, Ian, 'Successful Soffex', 17th December 1991
Rodger, Ian, 'This difficult year', 17th December 1991
Rodger, Ian, 'London is now a banker bet for the Swiss', 2nd December 1992
Rodger, Ian, 'A painful period', 13th November 1992
Rodger, Ian, 'Soffex gets the real thing', 17th December 1992
Rodger, Ian, 'Switzerland suffers setback over financial proposals', 29th January 1992
Rodger, Ian, 'Worrying outflow of funds', 7th May 1992
Rodger, Ian, 'Brisk activity on most fronts', 18th November 1993
Rodger, Ian, 'Electronic trading approaches reality', 18th November 1993
Rodger, Ian, 'Private banking provides fuel', 2nd December 1993
Rodger, Ian, 'The real time breakthrough', 6th December 1994
Rodger, Ian, 'Bugs balk Switzerland's big bang', 22nd June 1995
Rodger, Ian, 'December date set for start-up', 26th October 1995
Rodrigues, Vivianne, 'Derivatives market enjoys solid outlook', 14th November 2012
Rodrigues, Vivianne, 'Groups prepare to play catch-up', 14th November 2012
Rodrigues, Vivianne, 'Sophisticated market drives liquidity', 3rd October 2012
Rosling, Hans, *Factfulness: Ten reasons we're wrong about the world—and why things are better than you think* (London: Sceptre/Flatiron Books, 2018)
Ross, Alice, 'Reversal of euro carry trade inflicts global pain', 30th January 2013
Ross, Alice, 'Business coups help raise profile', 17th April 2014
Ross, Alice and Stafford, Philip, 'Rage against the machine as forex traders fight back', 12th July 2012
Roubini, Nouriel, 'The shadow banking system is unravelling', 22nd September 2006
Roubini, Nouriel, 'Nouriel Roubini calls for radical reforms for the broken financial system', 2nd November 2009
Ruehl, Mercedes and Shrikanth, Siddarth, 'Singapore struggles to catch south-east Asian tech boom', 16th July 2019
Rule, David, 'Time is nigh to rethink basis of floating rate debt', 10th April 2008
Rutter Pooley, Cat and Massoudi, Arash, 'Tests await LSE when deal euphoria subsides', 2nd August 2019
Saigol, Lina, 'LSE left exposed by bid failure', 30th October 2001
Saigol, Lina, 'Confidence Rises', 18th March 2010
Saigol, Lina, 'New money put City's reputation at risk', 18th May 2013
Saigol, Lina and O'Murchu, Cynthia, 'FTSE has case of free floating anxiety', 11th September 2012
Sakoui, Anousha, 'More UK companies turn to asset-based borrowing', 8th September 2008
Sakoui, Anousha, 'New Powers create legal uncertainty', 15th September 2008
Sakoui, Anousha, 'Stability possible for leveraged loan pricing as backlog declines', 9th July 2008
Sakoui, Anousha, 'Hunt for yield boosts retail demand', 25th February 2010
Sakoui, Anousha, 'Rising foreign ownership could be good for the Footsie', 10th April 2010
Sakoui, Anousha, 'Restructuring could lift M&A market', 30th May 2012
Sakoui, Anousha and Masters, Brooke, 'UK businesses' finance options undergo rethink', 21st January 2010
Samson, Adam and Stafford, Philip, 'Glitch delays start of trading by nearly two hours at LSE', 17th August 2019
Samuels, Simon, 'The ECB should resist the lure of bigger banks', 31st January 2019
Samuelson, Maurice, 'International fur trade scurries away from the City', 7th August 1989
Sanderson, Henry, 'Global metals trading challenges regulators', 25th November 2014
Sanderson, Henry, 'ICE to run electronic gold benchmark', 8th November 2014
Sanderson, Henry, 'Regulators prize open London gold market', 13th November 2014
Sanderson, Henry, 'Chinese banks stake their claim on the LME', 11th February 2015

Sanderson, Henry, 'Exchange pushes the pedal to the metal', 10th June 2015
Sanderson, Henry, 'Traders warn on gold liquidity as banks stay away', 19th May 2015
Sanderson, Henry, 'LME vows to keep open outcry trading floor', 19th February 2016
Sanderson, Henry, 'London gold trade wrestles with modernity', 5th February 2016
Sanderson, Henry, 'Regulator says banks back plan for more transparency in London's gold trade', 19th August 2016
Sanderson, Henry, 'Ex-LME chief plans to launch rival platform', 2nd March 2017
Sanderson, Henry, 'Gold market ready to reveal how much bullion is deposited in London's vaults', 6th February 2017
Sanderson, Henry, 'Lacklustre launch for LME gold contract as big bullion banks back rival venture', 11th July 2017
Sanderson, Henry, 'LME hopes gold futures contract will provide the Midas touch for its reform', 18th July 2017
Sanderson, Henry, 'LME appoints first female chairman in its history', 11th May 2019
Sanderson, Henry, 'Platinum setback for Shanghai Gold Exchange highlight hazards of reform', 21st May 2019
Sanderson, Henry and Hume, Neil, 'LME chief to meld metals with electronic age', 4th February 2015
Sanderson, Henry and Hume, Neil, 'Bullion banks seek alternative to gold exchange', 13th August 2016
Sanderson, Henry and Hume, Neil, 'LME faces broker breakaway threat over increase in fees', 14th July 2016
Sanderson, Henry and Hume, Neil, 'Crunch time for increasingly brittle LME', 9th February 2017
Sanderson, Henry and Hume, Neil, 'Ex-Glencore traders to launch metals platform', 5th July 2017
Sanderson, Henry and Hume, Neil, 'LME head looks to lure investors by simplifying offering', 26th April 2017
Sanderson, Henry and Hume, Neil, 'LME trading volumes soar on price swings and trade war', 8th October 2018
Sanderson, Rachel, Dinmore, Guy and Tett, Gillian, 'An Exposed Position', 9th March 2010
Sands, Peter, 'The perils of 1970s-style regulation', 29th March 2012
Sassoon, James, 'Britain deserves a better system of financial regulation', 9th March 2009
Saunders, Emma, 'Finance chiefs aim to raise debt', 11th October 2010
Sawton, Elizabeth, 'City unclear on Big Bang', 21st October 1985
Scaggs, Alexandra, 'Demise of Libor is far from a done deal', 3rd August 2017
Scaggs, Alexandra, 'Money-market funds lift repo deals', 20th October 2017
Scaggs, Alexandra and Rennison, Joe, 'Investors seek cover against fire sales as headwinds approach', 26th July 2018
Scannell, Kara, 'Rise of machines prompts SEC to join the tech war', 6th March 2013
Scannell, Kara, Bullock, Nicole and Meyer, Gregory, 'CME faces questions over missed red flags on trades', 24th April 2015
Schäfer, Daniel, 'Opening up the mid-market', 22nd June 2011
Schäfer, Daniel, 'A small slice of the action', 30th May 2012
Schäfer, Daniel, 'Once-neglected segment is now banking's belle of the ball', 30th October 2012
Schäfer, Daniel, 'Fragmented business offers huge potential for mergers', 7th May 2013
Schäfer, Daniel, 'Regulation threat to global banks', 12th April 2013
Schäfer, Daniel, 'Banks' skills gap forces up pay for talented minority', 28th April 2014
Schäfer, Daniel, 'Capital gains from foreign money and time zone', 10th June 2014
Schäfer, Daniel, 'Shrinking margins and higher costs drive down returns', 5th November 2014
Schäfer, Daniel and Braithwaite, Tom, 'Lawyers comb details for way round the rules', 1st March 2013
Schäfer, Daniel and Fleming, Sam, 'Forex probe poised to eclipse Libor cases', 10th March 2014
Schäfer, Daniel and Fleming, Sam, 'Scandal puts city's reputation on the line', 6th March 2014
Schäfer, Daniel and Strauss, Delphine, 'Moves into forex etrading speed up', 4th March 2014
Schipani, Andres, 'Uniting to build critical mass', 24th November 2012
Schmertz, Alexandra, 'JGB market in scramble to introduce electronic trading', 25th October 2000
Scholtes, Saskia, 'Atlantic divide over e-trading', 5th December 2006

Scholtes, Saskia, 'Electronic battle heats up', 28th July 2006
Scholtes, Saskia, 'Fitch unveils new agency', 19th October 2006
Scholtes, Saskia, 'A spectacular parting of the ways', 23rd August 2006
Scholtes, Saskia, 'Best execution encourages alternative venues', 1st November 2007
Scholtes, Saskia, 'Deutsche files subprime writs', 1st May 2007
Scholtes, Saskia, 'Nymex to launch first uranium contract', 17th April 2007
Scholtes, Saskia, 'NYSE Euronext unveils bond platform', 23rd April 2007
Scholtes, Saskia and Tett, Gillian, 'Does it all add up?', 28th June 2007
Scholtes, Saskia and Tett, Gillian, 'Shipwrecks and casualties warning for credit markets', 11th January 2008
Scholtes, Saskia and van Duyn, Aline, 'SEC chief seeks new securities laws', 28th October 2009
Scholz, Olaf, 'Germany will consider EU-wide bank deposit reinsurance', 6th November 2019
Sedacca, Boris, 'Advanced system comes on stream', 10th November 1988
Sedacca, Boris, 'New trade-matching system launched', 10th November 1988
Sedgwick, John, 'Stock exchange link-ups need to prove their worth', 15th June 2015
Sender, Henny, 'Lehman creditors in fight to recover disputed collateral', 22nd June 2009
Sender, Henny, 'Short measures', 9th July 2010
Sender, Henny, 'US retreat from global system lets China in', 5th April 2017
Serdarevic, Masa, 'Sungard offers access to exchanges', 22nd January 2010
Serdarevic, Masa and Grant, Jeremy, 'Traders stay loyal to LSE despite outage', 5–6th March 2011
Shameen, Assif, 'Malaysia bourse looks overseas', 16th March 2007
Shane, Daniel, 'Hong Kong's GEM tarnished by back door listings and drab returns', 19th November 2019
Sharpe, Antonia, 'Floating the Sims', 9th December 1991
Sharpe, Antonia, 'Monte Titoli's hidden vaults', 9th December 1991
Sharpe, Antonia, 'Stocks clear first hurdle', 9th December 1991
Sharpe, Antonia, 'New magnet for funds', 6th April 1992
Sharpe, Antonia, 'Flexible friend for lenders', 28th October 1993
Sharpe, Antonia, 'Hedge against stock swings', 20th October 1993
Sharpe, Antonia, 'Unsung hero is unique', 20th October 1993
Sharpe, Antonia, 'Amsterdam prepares to fight back', 16th June 1994
Sharpe, Antonia, 'Cash haven lures investors', 26th May 1994
Sharpe, Antonia, 'Latest tool to manage risks', 16th November 1995
Sharpe, Antonia, 'A shift in the balance of power', 5th July 1995
Sharpe, Antonia, 'The haves and the have-nots', 1st March 1996
Sharpe, Antonia, 'New issues end dry spell', 12th April 1996
Sharpe, Antonia, 'Opportunities to make money in Europe', 10th June 1996
Shelley, Toby, 'Baltic Exchange seeks to fill a gap', 5th July 2002
Shelley, Toby, 'Oil groups eye LSE's emerging market skill', 14th October 2003
Sheppard, David and Hume, Neil, 'Traders fear new derivatives rules', 26th October 2015
Sheppard, David and Raval, Anjli, 'Plans to upgrade Brent trigger calls for caution', 27th February 2017
Sherwell, Chris, 'Many teething troubles', 5th March 1985
Sherwell, Chris, 'Quality counts now', 14th October 1988
Sherwell, Chris, 'A storm mars September', 8th March 1989
Sherwell, Chris, 'It's open all hours for Sydney futures', 23rd November 1989
Shibata, Yoko, 'Early setback for Tokyo bond futures', 11th December 1985
Shillingford, Joia, 'The number of exchanges can only become smaller', 5th November 1998
Short, Eric, 'Unit trusts gear up for a European challenge', 12th November 1988
Shotter, James, Noonan, Laura and Arnold, Martin, 'Top brass set to advise against full exit from retail operations', 24th April 2015
Shotter, James, Stafford, Philip and Jenkins, Patrick, 'D Börse dismisses merger HQ fears', 22nd December 2016
Shubber, Kadhim, 'CFTC chairman set to overhaul restrictive Obama-era swaps execution regulations', 27th April 2018

Sieghart, Mary Ann, 'Increasing reliance on innovation as market declines', 19th March 1984
Sieghart, Mary Ann, 'Kick-off for US-style sport of financial futures trading', 3rd May 1984
Sieghart, Mary Ann, 'Rapid rise to prominence', 19th March 1984
Silverman, Gary, 'Bottom line is always in sight', 26th January 2001
Silverman, Gary, 'Grand vision of the future client', 28th January 2001
Silverman, Gary, 'Level playing field still elusive', 22nd February 2002
Silverman, Gary, 'NYSE chief's $139m deal rubs salt into the wounds', 29th August 2003
Silverman, Gary, Crooks, Ed and Boland, Vincent, 'The hunt for yield hots up: investors and pension funds plunge deeper into illiquid and riskier assets', 22nd July 2003
Silverman, Gary and Pretzlik, Charles, 'Bankers suffer an identity crisis as hard times hit', 22nd February 2002
Simensen, Ivar, 'Branching out from their German roots', 29th November 2004
Simensen, Ivar, 'Inaugural issuer back after 40 years', 27th May 2004
Simensen, Ivar, 'A roller-coaster ride at Welcome Break', 29th November 2004
Simensen, Ivar, 'UK regulator warned over transparency', 6th December 2005
Simensen, Ivar, 'Exchange looks east for new partnerships', 16th November 2006
Simensen, Ivar, 'Frankfurt fights back', 19th November 2007
Simensen, Ivar, 'Frankfurt Finance is in fear of a drift from "Mainhattan" to marginalisation', 8th February 2007
Simensen, Ivar and Tucker, Sundeep, 'Iceland raises key interest rate as vulnerable currencies are hit', 31st March 2006
Simkins, John, 'Milan bourse ready for EU reforms', 2nd February 1996
Simon, Bernard, 'Obstacles yet to be surmounted', 28th November 1986
Simon, Bernard, 'Pension boost to expansion hopes', 19th March 1987
Simon, Bernard, 'Hard times hit Toronto brokers', 5th February 1991
Simon, Bernard, 'Breakaway platforms take on Toronto Stock Exchange', 24th May 2007
Simon, Bernard, 'Making capital from strong financial base', 13th October 2009
Simon, Bernard, 'Toronto's trading platforms draw regulatory scrutiny', 20th November 2009
Simon, Bernard, 'Toronto Exchange in drive to attract Chinese investors', 13th April 2010
Simon, Bernard, 'Consortium appeals to patriotism', 16th May 2011
Simon, Bernard, 'LSE bid for TMX gains support', 18th June 2011
Simon, Bernard, 'Maple's TMX bid faces antitrust hurdle', 1st July 2011
Simon, Bernard, 'TMX battle homes in on derivatives', 23rd June 2011
Simon, Bernard, 'Open wheat market takes root in Canada', 2nd February 2012
Simon, Bernard and Blas, Javier, 'Mixed emotions as Canadian investors speculate on developments', 10th February 2011
Simon, Bernard and Gangahar, Anuj, 'TSX joins consolidation race with Montreal deal', 11th December 2007
Simon, Bernard and Grant, Jeremy, 'Banks look to counter LSE's TMX deal', 12th May 2011
Simon, Bernard and Grant, Jeremy, 'Decision time looms for TMX shareholders', 27th June 2011
Simon, Bernard and Tett, Gillian, 'Restructuring for ABCP market', 27th December 2007
Simonian, Haig, 'No early end to differences', 28th November 1986
Simonian, Haig, 'Banking growth bolsters demand', 3rd June 1987
Simonian, Haig, 'Dealers welcome rise in volatility', 15th July 1988
Simonian, Haig, 'Liffe eyes D-Mark business', 18th February 1988
Simonian, Haig, 'Liffe hijacks the Bund-wagon', 21st September 1988
Simonian, Haig, 'Thwarted by the tax', 17th February 1988
Simonian, Haig, 'A computer-based market', 8th March 1989
Simonian, Haig, 'European stock exchanges close ranks', 13th April 1989
Simonian, Haig, 'Liffe accelerates the tempo in technology race', 23rd February 1989
Simonian, Haig, 'Quiet revolution for German securities', 13th September 1989
Simonian, Haig, 'West German futures face tough debut', 23rd February 1989
Simonian, Haig, 'A new breed of institution in Milan', 14th December 1990
Simonian, Haig, 'Playing a waiting game in Milan', 11th July 1990

Simonian, Haig, 'Barrage of criticism for Italy's latest CGT', 6th February 1991
Simonian, Haig, 'Counting the cost of technological change', 9th October 1991
Simonian, Haig, 'Italian derivatives look towards a new future', 2nd August 1991
Simonian, Haig, 'Milan calculates costs of new technology', 26th July 1991
Simonian, Haig, 'Nerves on edge as the Milan bourse gears up for reform', 19th July 1991
Simonian, Haig, 'Battle looms over Italy's new securities law', 14th February 1992
Simonian, Haig, 'Italians chase a futures fast track', 20th March 1992
Simonian, Haig, 'Seeking a starring role in the new EU', 25th October 2004
Simonian, Haig, 'Swiss look outside their borders', 25th May 2006
Simonian, Haig, 'SWX to plot its strategic options', 4th July 2006
Simonian, Haig, 'Vienna exchange's quiet expansion', 14th June 2006
Simonian, Haig, 'Zurich hopes revamp will help it climb global ranks', 15th July 2008
Simonian, Haig, 'Aim is to be a significant regional force', 6th November 2009
Simonian, Haig, 'Leading banks turn city into a regional hub', 23rd October 2009
Simonian, Haig, 'A vault unlocked', 24th March 2009
Simonian, Haig, 'Swiss bourse hit by new trading rivals', 16th March 2011
Simonian, Haig and Cohen, Norma, 'Swiss seek to merge securities operations', 16th May 2007
Simonian, Haig and Frey, Eric, 'Regional ambitions thwarted', 16th May 2012
Simonian, Haig and Grant, Jeremy, 'SWX Europe moves out of London', 12th November 2008
Skold, Valeria and Burt, Tim, 'Oslo set to join Nordic bourse tie-up', 11th December 1998
Skorecki, Alex, 'Euro.NM alliance to cease by year-end', 5th October 2000
Skorecki, Alex, 'London holds back from opening all hours', 20th April 2000
Skorecki, Alex, 'Newcomers face reality as euphoria fades', 23rd March 2000
Skorecki, Alex, 'Pension moves may boost equity flows', 30th June 2000
Skorecki, Alex, 'Unfortunate few caught in steps of giants', 17th February 2000
Skorecki, Alex, 'Banks form platform for short-sellers', 22nd March 2001
Skorecki, Alex, 'The line becomes blurred', 18th July 2001
Skorecki, Alex, 'Seamless market opens up', 16th November 2001
Skorecki, Alex, 'Turnover on bourses hits record levels', 3rd January 2001
Skorecki, Alex, 'Virt-X might merge to survive', 28th December 2001
Skorecki, Alex, 'Virt-x off to brisk start with UK trades', 26th June 2001
Skorecki, Alex, 'Bigger share of derivatives for exchanges', 2nd October 2002
Skorecki, Alex, 'Europe's bourse masters play game with no rules', 30th May 2002
Skorecki, Alex, 'Exchange glory in their listed status', 23rd February 2002
Skorecki, Alex, 'Forex system that takes the waiting out of wanting', 4th January 2002
Skorecki, Alex, 'Happy end nears for a tale of two cities', 4th September 2002
Skorecki, Alex, 'Investors track down a hybrid source of income', 28th October 2002
Skorecki, Alex, 'Italian market most liquid', 26th February 2002
Skorecki, Alex, 'London Clearing House mulls link with Clearnet', 15th February 2002
Skorecki, Alex, 'LSE buying time while it searches for a new chief', 26th November 2002
Skorecki, Alex, 'LSE milestone for Sets trade', 9th July 2002
Skorecki, Alex, 'Securities lending joins the internet age', 22nd October 2002
Skorecki, Alex, 'Stock exchanges play for a winning position', 8th July 2002
Skorecki, Alex, 'T+1 pipedream is close to reality', 6th June 2002
Skorecki, Alex, 'Time for London to pull off a deal', 6th June 2002
Skorecki, Alex, 'Virt-X fails to meet European market share target', 26th June 2002
Skorecki, Alex, 'Waiting to play kingmaker', 31st October 2002
Skorecki, Alex, 'All eyes are on Euronext', 8th December 2003
Skorecki, Alex, 'Chicago meets electronic challenge', 4th December 2003
Skorecki, Alex, 'Derivatives sector faces up to Eurex's assault on the US', 9th June 2003
Skorecki, Alex, 'Deutsche Börse mystery tests loyalty', 11th November 2003
Skorecki, Alex, 'Deutsche Börse offers deal to Dutch', 10th September 2003
Skorecki, Alex, 'Deutsche Börse rejects calls for clearing reform', 28th May 2003
Skorecki, Alex, 'Dubai pins hope on shares', 23rd September 2003

Skorecki, Alex, 'Electronic trading "cuts costs"', 4th June 2003
Skorecki, Alex, 'European exchanges slash fees', 1st October 2003
Skorecki, Alex, 'Exchanges divided by more than time zones', 6th November 2003
Skorecki, Alex, 'Global future forecast for covered bonds', 13th November 2003
Skorecki, Alex, 'How London lost the battle of the Bund', 16th October 2003
Skorecki, Alex, 'How to make a banker's heart race', 5th November 2003
Skorecki, Alex, 'ISE takes battle to Chicago', 18th June 2003
Skorecki, Alex, 'Latecomer presses its advantage', 5th November 2003
Skorecki, Alex, 'London exchange goes into derivatives', 30th July 2003
Skorecki, Alex, 'London explores alternatives', 26th June 2003
Skorecki, Alex, 'Markets braced for ISD changes', 22nd May 2003
Skorecki, Alex, 'A returning hero with eyes set on the west', 16th January 2003
Skorecki, Alex, 'Rivals vie for Amsterdam blue chips', 12th November 2003
Skorecki, Alex, 'Unexpected choice could prove ideal fit for LSE's missing piece', 9th April 2003
Skorecki, Alex, 'Voice-broked bond trading holds its own', 19th March 2003
Skorecki, Alex, 'Will Williamson fly even higher now he has finished with Liffe?', 15th April 2003
Skorecki, Alex, 'Bank of England lights a fuse', 30th November 2004
Skorecki, Alex, 'Bold vision demands a response', 14th December 2004
Skorecki, Alex, 'Cantor split off bucks the trend', 18th August 2004
Skorecki, Alex, 'CBOT in move to hit back at Eurex', 16th April 2004
Skorecki, Alex, 'Complex, opaque and risky—yet popular', 29th November 2004
Skorecki, Alex, 'Deutsche Börse softens its stance', 3rd March 2004
Skorecki, Alex, 'Electronic trading of CDSs expands', 3rd November 2004
Skorecki, Alex, 'Euro bond traders get back on phone', 27th August 2004
Skorecki, Alex, 'Euronext plans to hit back at rival LSE', 20th March 2004
Skorecki, Alex, 'From the scream to the screen', 10th March 2004
Skorecki, Alex, 'Gilts still stuck in 17th century', 29th January 2004
Skorecki, Alex, 'Icap forms bond trading alliance with MarketAxess', 22nd March 2004
Skorecki, Alex, 'Icap says phone broking rules market', 4th June 2004
Skorecki, Alex, 'IPE sees future in electricity', 2nd June 2004
Skorecki, Alex, 'Liffe goes to war with CME', 16th March 2004
Skorecki, Alex, 'Liffe tops SGX in Eurodollar contracts', 6th October 2004
Skorecki, Alex, 'Lithuania joins Baltic collection', 1st April 2004
Skorecki, Alex, 'LSE tries the smart order route', 25th May 2004
Skorecki, Alex, 'Market is making switch to electronic', 8th October 2004
Skorecki, Alex, 'NYSE rivals focus on costs', 21st April 2004
Skorecki, Alex, 'Old stock exchange buildings never die, they're just rented out to hair salons', 28th July 2004
Skorecki, Alex, 'Reuters takes battle to Bloomberg', 23rd November 2004
Skorecki, Alex, 'Steps taken to tackle share trade barriers', 14th April 2004
Skorecki, Alex, 'Tax advantage drives CFD growth', 23rd September 2004
Skorecki, Alex, 'Trading without stamp duty', 13th November 2004
Skorecki, Alex, 'Vertical Expansion under fire', 20th January 2004
Skorecki, Alex, 'Web power helps smaller customers', 27th May 2004
Skorecki, Alex, 'Cantor wrestles to stay Treasury heavyweight', 8th February 2005
Skorecki, Alex, 'Carbon emissions trading fires up', 14th January 2005
Skorecki, Alex, 'Citi trades broke gentleman's deal', 3rd February 2005
Skorecki, Alex, 'Europe's paperless trail', 25th January 2005
Skorecki, Alex and Arnold, Martin, 'Euronext in talks to buy MTS trading platform', 5th January 2005
Skorecki, Alex and Davies, Paul J., 'Clearing houses set for £800m marriage', 26th June 2003
Skorecki, Alex and Dombey, Daniel, 'Crest is to merge with Euroclear', 5th July 2002
Skorecki, Alex and Munter, Päivi, 'Sea change for Eurozone bonds', 9th November 2004
Skorecki, Alex and Politi, James, 'LCH offers new cash and repo gilts service', 5th August 2002
Skypala, Pauline, 'Pressure on banks raising risk to buyers', 26th September 2003

Skypala, Pauline, 'Rethink under way as some securities lending suspended', 6th April 2009
Skypala, Pauline, 'Advance of the index trackers', 1st February 2010
Skypala, Pauline, 'EU rule changes deliver mixed results so far', 10th September 2018
Smith, Alison and Stothard, Michael, 'Plus has little to show for multiple roles', 9th November 2011
Smith, Ben, 'London sees rise in hedge funds', 17th April 2007
Smith, Charles, 'The pulse is weak', 28th March 1996
Smith, Charles, 'Banking parent provides strength', 21st June 1999
Smith, Charles, 'Opportunities to ease the pain', 21st June 1999
Smith, Claire, 'Fastest-growing risk protector', 19th May 2000
Smith, Claire, 'Synthetic deals take on natural growth curve', 25th September 2001
Smith, Colby, 'Borrowers want dollars—some more than others', 20th September 2018
Smith, Colby, 'Systemic risk fears intensify over leveraged loan boom', 30th October 2018
Smith, Colby and Rennison, Joe, 'Fed gears up to double its repo interventions', 14th December 2019
Smith, Colby and Rennison, Joe, 'Fed aims to stop another year of grim repo', 3rd January 2020
Smith, Colby and Rennison, Joe, 'Fed signals exit from repo market this year', 10th January 2020
Smith, Colby, Rennison, Joe and Stafford, Philip, 'NY Fed head says some institutions are not moving fast enough to cut Libor reliance', 24th September 2019
Smith, Colby and Wigglesworth, Robin, 'Boom in EM corporate debt stirs liquidity fears', 20th January 2020
Smith, Henry, 'Reverberations from volatility in the real economy', 6th October 2009
Smith, Ian, 'Could ETFs survive a sudden downturn in the market?', 14th October 2017
Smith, Michael, 'Core of growing influence', 31st March 1998
Smith, Peter, 'Australia's ASX warns of tougher climate for equities', 15th August 2008
Smith, Peter, 'ASX chief hits at US shake-up', 18th September 2009
Smith, Peter, 'Australia rejects Singapore's bid for rival bourse', 9–10th April 2011
Smith, Peter and Grant, Jeremy, 'SGX set to make A$6bn bid for ASX', 23rd October 2010
Smith, Peter and Grant, Jeremy, 'ASX on the offensive to fend off Chi-X', 16th August 2011
Smith, Peter and Grant, Jeremy, 'Canberra set to reject SGX deal', 6th April 2011
Smith, Peter and Tucker, Sundeep, 'Australia in world first with CFD platform', 22nd October 2007
Smith, Robert, 'Big buyers pull back from US debt', 18th June 2018
Smyth, Jamie, 'Australia poised to end ASX monopoly on equity clearing', 31st March 2016
Smyth, Jamie, 'Australian regulator pledges to tackle cosy oligopoly of big banks and punish misconduct', 4th February 2019
Snoddy, Raymond, 'An information revolution', 24th March 1986
Solman, Paul, 'No time to be complacent', 17th July 1998
Solman, Paul, 'IPE and Nymex to step up talks', 22nd January 1999
Solman, Paul, 'Trading in old methods', 3rd September 1999
Solman, Paul, 'Gold delivers a hard lesson', 28th June 2000
Solman, Paul, 'Liffe to end open outcry dealing', 9th March 2000
Solman, Paul, 'LME to consult on mutual status', 11th May 2000
Solman, Paul, 'Online trading set to grow at metal exchange', 20th June 2000
Solman, Paul and Tait, Nikki, 'Last shout for open outcry', 9th March 2000
Somerset Webb, Merryn, 'A local exchange: an idea whose time has come', 6th July 2019
Sowton, Elizabeth, 'Demand for a faster settlement process', 3rd December 1987
Spikes, Sarah, 'Icap chief caps a 20-year rise to the stars', 22nd April 2006
Spikes, Sarah, 'Icap snaps up EBS for £464m', 22nd April 2006
Spikes, Sarah and Cohen, Norma, 'It's still good to talk on the cutting edge', 10th May 2007
Spikes, Sarah and Thal Larsen, Peter, 'Interdealer broking behind rapid growth', 19th December 2006
Stacey, Kiran, 'Dhaka bourse stake sale sparks tension', 19th February 2018
Stacey, Kiran and Noonan, Laura, 'Fed rules out liquidity gauge for foreign banks', 11th October 2019
Stafford, Philip, 'Selling without making waves', 23rd November 2005
Stafford, Philip, 'Directive to break down barriers', 30th October 2007
Stafford, Philip, 'BATS and Chi-X eye new landscape', 24th December 2010
Stafford, Philip, 'Competitive market requires deep pockets', 20th October 2010

Stafford, Philip, 'High-speed electronic trading leaves regulator far behind', 3rd November 2010
Stafford, Philip, 'Regulators show united front', 20th October 2010
Stafford, Philip, 'Stock exchanges muscle in as clearing houses prepare for shake-up', 3rd November 2010
Stafford, Philip, 'ASX and Clearstream in talks over outsourcing', 29th August 2011
Stafford, Philip, 'Chi-X European clearing deal takes on established bourses', 17th August 2011
Stafford, Philip, 'Citi plans "dark pool" to link HFTs and smaller investors', 7th July 2011
Stafford, Philip, 'CME steps up Asian push with revamp of renminbi futures', 12th July 2011
Stafford, Philip, 'Divisions over audit trails as G20 deadline approaches', 10th October 2011
Stafford, Philip, 'Euroclear adds to "vertical silo" fears over Deutsche Börse deal', 31st March 2011
Stafford, Philip, 'High-speed trading rules', 23rd December 2011
Stafford, Philip, 'LME eyes its own metals clearing for earnings boost', 4th May 2011
Stafford, Philip, 'BATS Chi-X Europe in talks to secure UK exchange licence', 7th November 2012
Stafford, Philip, 'Battle for derivatives clearing heats up', 11th September 2012
Stafford, Philip, 'Blizzard of regulation has its effect', 30th October 2012
Stafford, Philip, 'Cboe to offer 24-hour Vix futures trading from London', 7th September 2012
Stafford, Philip, 'Changes bring global flurry of innovation', 23rd January 2012
Stafford, Philip, 'CME puts Europe at the centre of expansion plan', 21st August 2012
Stafford, Philip, 'Collateral drive puts the focus on settlements', 30th October 2012
Stafford, Philip, 'Deutsche Börse to clear rate swaps', 1st June 2012
Stafford, Philip, 'Failed NYSE/Euronext merger haunts exchange', 11th June 2012
Stafford, Philip, 'High-tech firms reshape dealing', 3rd August 2012
Stafford, Philip, 'ICE plans CDS exchange trading', 17th October 2012
Stafford, Philip, 'LSE chief shifts focus with shake-up', 13th June 2012
Stafford, Philip, 'Mishaps prompt greater scrutiny of high speed traders', 17th October 2012
Stafford, Philip, 'Nasdaq OMX to launch derivatives in UK', 22nd June 2012
Stafford, Philip, 'NYSE Euronext to offer retail service', 15th October 2012
Stafford, Philip, 'NYSE Euronext to start full derivatives clearing in London', 29th March 2012
Stafford, Philip, 'Rules covering derivatives built on ground that has yet to settle', 30th October 2012
Stafford, Philip, 'Surge in US dark pools trading highlights fears over regulation', 20th November 2012
Stafford, Philip, 'UK report calls for measures to limit risks of high-speed trading', 23rd October 2012
Stafford, Philip, 'Bats Europe given UK exchange status', 10th May 2013
Stafford, Philip, 'Battle flares up over future of "dark pools"', 7th November 2013
Stafford, Philip, 'CME poised for European clearing push', 11th February 2013
Stafford, Philip, 'Eurex makes push into trading foreign currency derivatives', 22nd August 2013
Stafford, Philip, 'European "dark pool" trading surges', 18th October 2013
Stafford, Philip, 'Fears grow over rules on derivatives trading', 19th December 2013
Stafford, Philip, 'JPX seeks to expand OTC alliances with rivals in Asia', 6th February 2013
Stafford, Philip, 'LCH deal looms as critical for LSE', 1st April 2013
Stafford, Philip, 'MTS prepares US push to tap into institutional demand', 2nd May 2013
Stafford, Philip, 'Netting UK and Irish dealing costs on offer across Europe', 13th August 2013
Stafford, Philip, 'The new heart of a safer system', 17th September 2013
Stafford, Philip, 'Q and A : Algorithms', 23rd August 2013
Stafford, Philip, 'Regulation: All eyes on Italy's new rules', 20th February 2013
Stafford, Philip, 'Settlement a blow to Spencer', 26th September 2013
Stafford, Philip, 'US funds transfer trades to London', 18th October 2013
Stafford, Philip, 'US still the first choice for IPOs', 14th February 2013
Stafford, Philip, 'Colourful world of interdealers faces deep structural changes', 3rd June 2014
Stafford, Philip, 'Deutsche Börse hopes that its philosophy has global appeal', 17th April 2014
Stafford, Philip, 'Fall in value of LCH.Clearnet interest rate swaps', 28th November 2014
Stafford, Philip, 'Industry strives to find its form', 5th November 2014
Stafford, Philip, 'Members fear they may have to stump up in case of a failure', 5th November 2014
Stafford, Philip, 'Sense of urgency underpins fresh scrutiny of markets', 16th September 2014
Stafford, Philip, 'Too big to fail fears reach clearing houses', 3rd December 2014

Stafford, Philip, 'Tougher capital rules boost traders' feelings of security', 28th April 2014
Stafford, Philip, 'Banks eye hub to cut swaps trading disputes', 8th July 2015
Stafford, Philip, 'Confidence shaken by violent swings', 13th October 2015
Stafford, Philip, 'Europe to mandate clearing of swaps', 7th August 2015
Stafford, Philip, 'Exchange chiefs eye deals to tap new markets', 31st December 2015
Stafford, Philip, 'Exchanges seek slice of $5tn forex pie', 7th August 2015
Stafford, Philip, 'Guessing game over dark pool caps', 24th July 2015
Stafford, Philip, 'Insurance for clearing houses underwritten', 12th March 2015
Stafford, Philip, 'IPO filing provides rare insight into HFT world', 14th April 2015
Stafford, Philip, 'LSE in ambitious push for Europe's futures markets', 17th October 2015
Stafford, Philip, 'LSE targets new openings as Borse Dubai bows out', 27th March 2015
Stafford, Philip, 'Markets planning for a world after the day of the Mifid', 13th October 2015
Stafford, Philip, 'Nasdaq steps up dark pools surveillance push', 9th October 2015
Stafford, Philip, 'Regulators put dark pools back in the dock', 13th August 2015
Stafford, Philip, 'Swiss broker to set up London repo venue', 19th May 2015
Stafford, Philip, 'US swaps market resists futures model', 17th March 2015
Stafford, Philip, 'US the dominant derivatives superpower', 9th January 2015
Stafford, Philip, 'BATS to target block trades ahead of Mifid 2', 10th August 2016
Stafford, Philip, 'Big bourses curb high-frequency trading', 13th October 2016
Stafford, Philip, 'Bourse tie-ups put clearing risk in spotlight', 5–6th March 2016
Stafford, Philip, 'Brexit brings headache to industry weary of regulation', 11th October 2016
Stafford, Philip, 'Cboe aims to tap shifting investor demand for structured products with Bats purchase', 22nd December 2016
Stafford, Philip, 'City brokers put brave face on Brexit', 20th July 2016
Stafford, Philip, 'Clearing capital drives Deutsche Börse-LSE talks', 24th February 2016
Stafford, Philip, 'Deutsche Börse unfurls plan for European champion', 27–28th February 2016
Stafford, Philip, 'Europe's regulatory crackdown set to ease', 25th May 2016
Stafford, Philip, 'European attempts to grab UK clearing house business underlines London's great strength', 16th December 2016
Stafford, Philip, 'ICAP chief prepares for radical change of direction', 26th February 2016
Stafford, Philip, 'ICAP's new direction reflects changing future of derivatives', 6th October 2016
Stafford, Philip, 'ICE circles amid D Börse's tie-up talks with LSE', 2nd March 2016
Stafford, Philip, 'LSE and banks launch derivatives exchange', 27th September 2016
Stafford, Philip, 'LSE chief sets out plan to win over merger sceptics', 30th March 2016
Stafford, Philip, 'LSE combination spawns derivatives doubts', 6th April 2016
Stafford, Philip, 'LSE in talks over Paris clearing sale to Euronext', 21st December 2016
Stafford, Philip, 'LSE set to sell Paris unit to Euronext', 28th December 2016
Stafford, Philip, 'Strains show in over-the-counter dealing', 14th June 2016
Stafford, Philip, 'US eyes prize if swaps shift from London', 20th October 2016
Stafford, Philip, 'Voice brokers answer call for liquidity', 12th August 2016
Stafford, Philip, 'Watchdog raises ICE-Trayport worries', 17th August 2016
Stafford, Philip, 'Amsterdam chosen as Tradeweb's EU base', 4th August 2017
Stafford, Philip, 'Anxiety over EU regulatory shake-up goes global', 6th July 2017
Stafford, Philip, 'Bourses become more than stock exchanges', 10th October 2017
Stafford, Philip, 'Brexit poses threat to London's role as global hub', 10th October 2017
Stafford, Philip, 'Brexit unleashes a three-way battle over clearing', 25th October 2017
Stafford, Philip, 'Central banks warned on repo volatility', 13th April 2017
Stafford, Philip, 'Chicago derivatives exchanges do battle to dominate bitcoin futures trading', 5th December 2017
Stafford, Philip, 'City confident of keeping infrastructure edge', 23rd March 2017
Stafford, Philip, 'City traders put Brexit back-up plans into action', 2nd August 2017
Stafford, Philip, 'Clearing houses pose post-crisis challenge', 17th February 2017
Stafford, Philip, 'Clock ticks down on EU's Mifid reform', 10th October 2017
Stafford, Philip, 'Data centres help London retain cachet', 24th February 2017

Stafford, Philip, 'Debate over post-Brexit clearing of euro swaps focuses on margin costs', 13th June 2017
Stafford, Philip, 'Derivatives Big Bang catches traders off guard', 2nd February 2017
Stafford, Philip, 'Deutsche Börse draws allies in swaps fight', 21st November 2017
Stafford, Philip, 'EU and US regulators race to seal equivalence deal before Mifid 2 deadline', 21st September 2017
Stafford, Philip, 'Euronext finalises LSE derivatives deal', 9th August 2017
Stafford, Philip, 'Euronext's Dutch gambit puts pressure on LSE to sell French house', 4th April 2017
Stafford, Philip, 'Europe's exchanges clash with banks and traders over increase in data fees', 28th December 2017
Stafford, Philip, 'European Parliament seeks to extend regulatory powers over clearing houses', 29th September 2017
Stafford, Philip, 'Fears over "last look" spur tighter FX code', 20th December 2017
Stafford, Philip, 'How LSE and D Börse merger unravelled', 4th March 2017
Stafford, Philip, 'Instinet ensures fairness by offering clients strictly equal cable lengths for trades', 10th October 2017
Stafford, Philip, 'Investors in European stocks look to Mifid 2 rules waiver on dark trading', 7th November 2017
Stafford, Philip, 'Investors' Mifid 2 challenges flagged up', 24th August 2017
Stafford, Philip, 'LSE admits case for tougher EU oversight', 1st November 2017
Stafford, Philip, 'LSE chief Rolet quits as pressure grows to resolve governance crisis', 30th November 2017
Stafford, Philip, 'LSE switches focus as Deutsche Börse deal fails', 30th March 2017
Stafford, Philip, 'Mifid vies with Brexit as City traders' top concern', 11th August 2017
Stafford, Philip, 'Personal touch critical as banks trim brokers', 29th June 2017
Stafford, Philip, 'Tough times loom for LSE after Rolet bows out', 20th October 2017
Stafford, Philip, 'Voice brokers fight to survive Europe's shake-up', 10th October 2017
Stafford, Philip, 'ABN Amro's clearing business seeks London licences to prepare for Brexit', 22nd November 2018
Stafford, Philip, 'Amsterdam is biggest winner as trading groups set up plans for Europe bases', 4th July 2018
Stafford, Philip, 'Bloc must find its own path, shorn of British expertise', 17th November 2018
Stafford, Philip, 'Bloomberg picks Amsterdam for EU trade base', 9th May 2018
Stafford, Philip, 'Brexit anxieties grow over London's vital market infrastructure', 22nd February 2018
Stafford, Philip, 'CME clinches Spencer's Nex in deal set to shake up $500bn Treasuries market', 29th March 2018
Stafford, Philip, 'CME expects no asset sales after Nex purchase', 3rd April 2018
Stafford, Philip, 'CME eyes pole position in Treasury trades with audacious bid for Nex', 28th March 2018
Stafford, Philip, 'Corners of Wall Street remain undeterred by crypto crash', 28th November 2018
Stafford, Philip, 'Dark pool trading flourishes after Mifid 2 delay', 19th January 2018
Stafford, Philip, 'Departure of TP ICAP chief eposes tensions at top', 11th July 2018
Stafford, Philip, 'Deutsche Bank's Frankfurt move revives City concerns', 31st July 2018
Stafford, Philip, 'Deutsche Börse makes progress in push to lure derivatives clearing from London', 6th February 2018
Stafford, Philip, 'Electronic trading pioneer throws down gauntlet to BrokerTec on Treasuries', 8th June 2018
Stafford, Philip, 'European regulators to rewrite share trading rules after fears of Brexit hit', 14th July 2018
Stafford, Philip, 'Exchanges seek Mifid review as Brexit looms', 9th January 2018
Stafford, Philip, 'Fintech alley cat gets the cream with £670bn CME deal', 31st March 2018
Stafford, Philip, 'Frankfurt narrows gap with London as incentive scheme boosts euro clearing', 13th June 2018
Stafford, Philip, 'Fresh risks emerge from the depth', 1st October 2018

Stafford, Philip, 'Key London markets in the lurch under a no-deal Brexit', 1st October 2018
Stafford, Philip, 'London Stock Exchange to raise stake in clearing house LCH', 20th October 2018
Stafford, Philip, 'LSE springs surprise with choice of chief', 14th April 2018
Stafford, Philip, 'Mifid 2 brings dark pool trading into the light', 10th January 2018
Stafford, Philip, 'Mifid 2 share trading shake-up put on hold', 10th January 2018
Stafford, Philip, 'Record half for LCH despite Brexit uncertainty', 5th July 2018
Stafford, Philip, 'Selling time to traders: the physicist who measures deals in microseconds', 5th February 2018
Stafford, Philip, 'Spencer considers a financial future without Nex', 17th March 2018
Stafford, Philip, 'Stock exchanges cast wary eye on threat from big tech groups', 2nd March 2018
Stafford, Philip, 'Thomson to move forex derivatives out of London', 16th May 2018
Stafford, Philip, 'Trading venues play down rift over Mifid 2', 11th January 2018
Stafford, Philip, 'US threatens EU banks with ban over Brexit clearing plans', 18th October 2018
Stafford, Philip, 'All about data: LSE bid show exchanges' new priorities', 22nd October 2019
Stafford, Philip, 'BGC signs trio of high-frequency trading firms to boost European equity options', 25th July 2019
Stafford, Philip, 'BlackRock and Vanguard push for clearing reforms', 25th October 2019
Stafford, Philip, 'BoE official warns EU on pitfalls of UK clearing house regulation post-Brexit', 15th February 2019
Stafford, Philip, 'Brussels eyes payment plan for exchanges' trading data', 12th July 2019
Stafford, Philip, 'Cboe to open Dutch hub for trading shares of EU groups amid Brexit uncertainty', 4th September 2019
Stafford, Philip, 'Chicago's Options Clearing Corp hones plan to shore up its balance sheet', 19th July 2019
Stafford, Philip, 'EU licence boost for investors in Irish assets', 2nd March 2019
Stafford, Philip, 'EU targeted reform of Mifid 2 rules after backlash', 15th November 2019
Stafford, Philip, 'Euronext grows portfolio as Irish bourse stares down Brexit risk', 13th February 2019
Stafford, Philip, 'Euronext in 625m Euros offer for Oslo Børs', 15th January 2019
Stafford, Philip, 'Europe's traders call for shorter working day', 7th November 2019
Stafford, Philip, 'European customers handed clearing house access to contain Brexit fallout', 19th February 2019
Stafford, Philip, 'European investors back UK call for shorter trading day to improve liquidity', 29th November 2019
Stafford, Philip, 'Exchange operators cut dependence on legacy trading business', 21st September 2019
Stafford, Philip, 'Futures exchanges put faith in "Flash Boys" speed bumps', 30th May 2019
Stafford, Philip, 'Global regulators delay big bang rules by a year to stop last minute scramble', 24th July 2019
Stafford, Philip, 'ICE launches ETF platform specialising in bonds', 29th October 2019
Stafford, Philip, 'Intercontinental Exchange working on interest rate benchmark to replace Libor', 25th January 2019
Stafford, Philip, 'Investors angered by mounting cost of vital data from exchanges', 4th April 2019
Stafford, Philip, 'Investors seek no-deal Brexit assurance on dual listings', 4th February 2019
Stafford, Philip, 'Liquidity fears trigger European repo shift to Paris', 7th May 2019
Stafford, Philip, 'LSE has to beat Bloomberg at its own game', 19th August 2019
Stafford, Philip, 'LSE shrugs off Brexit worries to gain boost from clearing', 2nd May 2019
Stafford, Philip, 'MEMX turns up the heat on US stock exchanges', 10th January 2019
Stafford, Philip, 'Mifid 2 rules tighten Wall Street's grip on Europe', 27th June 2019
Stafford, Philip, 'Nasdaq agrees sale of commodities futures business to German exchange', 13th November 2019
Stafford, Philip, 'No-deal Brexit share trade ruling sparks accusations of EU land Grab', 21st March 2019
Stafford, Philip, 'Rivals battle for Madrid bourse owner', 19th November 2019
Stafford, Philip, 'Singapore exchange plans to tighten grip as Asia's largest forex trading hub', 11th June 2019

Stafford, Philip, 'SIX makes Euro2.8bn Madrid exchange move to fend off Euronext interest', 19th November 2019

Stafford, Philip, 'Swiss stock trading shifts away from the EU exchanges after Brussels-Bern dispute', 2nd July 2019

Stafford, Philip, 'Swiss trading volumes rise but so do costs after EU ends equivalence rules', 25th September 2019

Stafford, Philip, 'Tale of the tape needed for Europe's fragmented trading', 13th September 2019

Stafford, Philip, 'Time is ripe for block cheeses futures and options at CME', 16th November 2019

Stafford, Philip, 'Traders face anxious wait for Brexit guidance', 12th February 2019

Stafford, Philip, 'US and UK strike eleventh-hour accord to minimise no-deal Brexit disruption', 26th February 2019

Stafford, Philip, 'Vix volatility spike prompts shake-up at leading equity options clearing house', 20th March 2019

Stafford, Philip, 'Momentum grows for shorter days on European exchanges', 7th January 2020

Stafford, Philip, 'Traders across Europe face up to cost of failure on transactions', 11th January 2020

Stafford, Philip and Atkins, Ralph, 'London worries it will be the EU's next target after Swiss stand-off', 29th June 2018

Stafford, Philip and Barber, Alex, 'Europe agrees biggest securities overhaul since 2008', 16th January 2014

Stafford, Philip and Blitz, Roger, 'Battle intensifies over London's euro clearing role', 5th July 2016

Stafford, Philip and Blitz, Roger, 'Undersea cables boost euro trading', 6th July 2017

Stafford, Philip and Brunsden, Jim, 'Concerns mount for European banks over positions in UK clearing houses', 11th December 2018

Stafford, Philip and Bullock, Nicole, 'NYSE and Nasdaq in back-up auction plan', 24th July 2015

Stafford, Philip and Bullock, Nicole, 'SEC probes arcane part of equity market's plumbing', 12th May 2015

Stafford, Philip and Bullock, Nicole, 'Cboe-Bats tie-up poised to shake up sector', 28th September 2016

Stafford, Philip and Bullock, Nicole, 'Options traders prepare for "worst of all worlds"', 17th March 2016

Stafford, Philip and Bullock, Nicole, 'Radical pilot to boost trade in smallest US stocks begins', 5th October 2016

Stafford, Philip and Bullock, Nicole, 'High-speed traders fight to keep edge', 26th April 2017

Stafford, Philip and Bullock, Nicole, 'Bond platform Tradeweb joins IPO rush in windfall for investment banks', 8th March 2019

Stafford, Philip and Bullock, Nicole, 'Wall Street big hitters back new exchange to challenge NYSE-Nasdaq dominance', 8th January 2019

Stafford, Philip, Bullock, Nicole and Shubber, Kadhim, 'Shares in US exchanges hit after rebuke from regulator over high data charges', 18th October 2018

Stafford, Philip and Demos, Telis, 'BATS takes on NYSE with new primary listing platform', 30th March 2011

Stafford, Philip and Dunkley, Emma, 'India exchanges seek to bring equities trading home by halting data supply', 13th February 2018

Stafford, Philip, Dunkley, Emma and Brunsden, Jim, 'Financial services groups go Dutch to ensure EU access', 5th August 2017

Stafford, Philip and Gapper, John, 'LSE chief centre stage in bitter public dispute', 18th November 2017

Stafford, Philip and Georgiadis, Philip, 'EU markets regulator abandons no-deal block on big UK stocks', 30th May 2019

Stafford, Philip and Grant, Jeremy, 'Inevitability of LSE and TMX deal', 11th February 2011

Stafford, Philip and Henderson, Richard, 'Nasdaq raises listing fees to fund swanky new showroom', 16th November 2019

Stafford, Philip and Hollinger, Peggy, 'Airbus plans exchange to hedge airline fare vitality', 20th January 2020

Stafford, Philip and Khan, Mehreen, 'London venues poised to delist Swiss stocks as Bern's EU dispute drags on', 26th June 2019

Stafford, Philip and Lockett, Hudson, 'Hong Kong and Shanghai battle to be China's main gateway', 8th October 2019
Stafford, Philip and Mackenzie, Michael, 'Interdealer brokers braced for shake-up', 22nd November 2012
Stafford, Philip and Martin, Katie, 'Growing pains for rules that rocked European finance', 8th May 2019
Stafford, Philip and Massoudi, Arash, 'Upstart ICE in $8bn gamble with deal for 208-year-old NYSE Euronext', 21st December 2012
Stafford, Philip and Massoudi, Arash, 'US share trading glitches fuel call to revisit rulebook', 23rd January 2013
Stafford, Philip and Massoudi, Arash, 'Dark Pool spotlight falls on US "underdog"', 28th June 2014
Stafford, Philip, Massoudi, Arash and Grant, Jeremy, 'ICE and NYSE go where others fear to tread', 4th October 2013
Stafford, Philip, Massoudi, Arash and Mackenzie, Michael, 'Nasdaq sets stage for HFT in Treasuries', 5th April 2013
Stafford, Philip, Massoudi, Arash and Nicolaou, Anna, 'Virtu's reward could be a valuation of $1.8bn', 6th March 2015
Stafford, Philip and Masters, Brooke, 'Libor deal commences rehabilitation of benchmark', 10th July 2013
Stafford, Philip and McClean, Paul, 'Listed options accelerate in the electronic era', 2nd March 2016
Stafford, Philip, Morris, Stephen and Brunsden, Jim, 'Banks look at exit from UK derivatives', 1st October 2018
Stafford, Philip and Mundy, Simon, 'Icap nets exchange licence in deal for Plus unit', 19th May 2012
Stafford, Philip and Mundy, Simon, 'Indian stock exchange chief quits ahead of public listing', 3rd December 2016
Stafford, Philip and Munshi, Neil, 'Last shout looms for US options traders', 24th February 2015
Stafford, Philip and Murphy, Hannah, 'Clearing houses benefit from rule change', 6th April 2017
Stafford, Philip and Murphy, Hannah, 'Booming CFD industry faces reckoning under new EU rules', 2nd August 2018
Stafford, Philip and Murphy, Hannah, 'City of London agonises over jumping on crypto bandwagon', 26th May 2018
Stafford, Philip and Murphy, Hannah, 'Mifid 2 starts to weave its influence through markets', 1st October 2018
Stafford, Philip, Noonan, Laura and Murphy, Hannah, 'Banks seek reprieve on key part of Mifid 2 rules', 14th December 2017
Stafford, Philip and Provan, Sarah, 'LSE takes Euroclear stake as regulators look to tighten rules on use of collateral', 31st January 2019
Stafford, Philip and Rennison, Joe, 'Judge cancels planned CME hearing', 7th May 2018
Stafford, Philip and Sender, Henry, 'Questions swirl over Hong Kong's failed LSE bid', 9th October 2019
Stafford, Philip and Shotter, James, 'D Börse merger crumbles as tensions boil over', 28th February 2017
Stafford, Philip and Shotter, James, 'LSE and D Börse consider separate futures', 1st March 2017
Stafford, Philip and Smith, Peter, 'Europe begins countdown to day of the Mifid', 2nd January 2018
Stafford, Philip and Szalay, Eva, 'London pulls away from New York in forex and swaps as it shrugs off Brexit', 17th September 2019
Stafford, Philip and Szalay, Eva, 'Trading looks to tackle its long-hours culture', 9th November 2019
Stafford, Philip and Tait, Nikki, 'Europe moves against super-fast traders', 9th December 2011
Stafford, Philip, Walker, Owen, Thomas, Daniel and Lockett, Hudson, 'London Stock Exchange poised to rebuff £32bn Hong Kong bid', 12th September 2019
Stafford, Philip and Wasik, Zoskia, 'LSE faces strong demand to use clearing house', 27th April 2017
Steadman, Anne, 'A chance to manage risk', 23rd November 1990
Steele, Tim, 'Markets bent on shortening the cycle', 14th July 2000
Steil, Benn, 'Europe's security markets need new plumbing', 11th August 2005

Steil, Benn, 'Derivatives exchanges owe much to wise regulation', 28th November 2006
Steinbruck, Peer, 'A tax on trading to share the costs of the crisis', 25th September 2009
Stephens, Phillip, 'Living with turbulence', 3rd June 1987
Stephens, Phillip, 'Vickers hands victory to the bankers' shop steward', 13th September 2011
Stoermer, Torsten, 'Sectors gain as country funds lose appeal', 27th July 1999
Stone, Jeremy, 'Yardstick by which to gauge success', 1st July 1985
Storbeck, Olaf, 'Deutsche Börse eyes UK's euro clearing', 22nd February 2018
Storbeck, Olaf, 'German regulator makes soft pitch to lure banks after Brexit', 10th January 2018
Storbeck, Olaf, 'Germany eyes looser labour laws to woo banks', 21st February 2018
Storbeck, Olaf, 'Germany's Scope take the long view as it aims to break stranglehold of US rating agencies', 2nd January 2020
Storbeck, Olaf and Stafford, Philip, 'Deutsche Börse in talks to acquire Refinitiv foreign exchange assets', 12th April 2019
Stothard, Michael, 'Norway's day traders live to fight the algos', 17th May 2012
Stothard, Michael, 'Euronext on the alert for merger fallout', 21st June 2016
Strauss, Delphine, 'ISE faces test from Turkey's trading past', 22nd September 2009
Strauss, Delphine, 'Istanbul and Athens bourses form joint index', 29th September 2009
Strauss, Delphine, 'Istanbul embraces algo trading', 1st November 2010
Strauss, Delphine, 'Five big banks extend their domination of forex trading', 9th May 2014
Strauss, Delphine, Stafford, Philip and Jones, Claire, 'BoE and ECB launch swap line to buffer banks in event of post-Brexit turmoil', 6th March 2019
Stubbington, Tommy, 'Eurozone bailout fund ditches English law for bonds in fresh Brexit hit to UK', 27th September 2019
Stubbington, Tommy, 'Global watchdog warns on rising risk of shocks in leveraged loans', 20th December 2019
Stubbington, Tommy, 'Investor alarm sounded over amazing disappearing Bunds', 12th July 2019
Stubbington, Tommy, 'Safe assets in short supply as central banks buy big', 19th November 2019
Stubbington, Tommy and Rennison, Joe, 'Cash-hungry hedge funds deepened recent repo market turmoil finds BIS', 9th December 2019
Sullivan, Ruth, 'Metal exchange loses reforming chief executive', 6th January 2001
Sullivan, Ruth, 'Metal exchange takes jump into electronic trading', 22nd January 2001
Sullivan, Ruth, 'Anxiety grows over new powers for ESMA', 19th July 2010
Swann, Christopher, 'Big banks play game of brinkmanship', 25th June 1999
Swann, Christopher, 'Dawning of the age of European equity', 15th December 1999
Swann, Christopher, 'Paris is Europe's top dog, but for how long', 11th November 1999
Swann, Christopher and Cameron, Doug, 'FXall set to intensify battle in online currency trading', 10th May 2001
Sychrava, Juliet, 'Electricity forward market is world first', 23rd October 1991
Symon, Fiona, 'How to maintain momentum', 7th December 2005
Szalay, Eva, 'Asset managers scramble to cut banks out of forex dealing', 18th April 2019
Szalay, Eva, 'Banks resist demand to shed more daylight on forex charges', 16th May 2019
Szalay, Eva, 'Citigroup outlines plan to withdraw from two-thirds of foreign exchange platforms', 31st October 2019
Szalay, Eva, 'Clearing reforms set to upend asset management industry', 22nd October 2019
Szalay, Eva, 'Fears over forex trading going bump in the night', 6th March 2019
Szalay, Eva, 'Jump in London rupee trades rings alarms', 18th September 2019
Szalay, Eva, 'London charm offensive pays off in race for renminbi', 9th February 2019
Szalay, Eva, 'London gains ground in renminbi trading drive', 30th January 2019
Szalay, Eva, 'London is top renminbi trading hub outside China despite Brexit wobbles', 11th November 2019
Szalay, Eva, 'Offshore currency trade poses challenge for India's central bank', 6th March 2019
Szalay, Eva, 'Peer-to-peer forex services aim to bypass Wall St banks', 16th October 2019
Szalay, Eva, 'UK watchdog lends teeth to currency trading code', 28th June 2019
Szalay, Eva, 'Ultra low interest rates spur euro to become world's new carry trade', 6th December 2019

Szalay, Eva, 'Yen traders wrongfooted as flash crash strikes during Asia's witching hour', 4th January 2019
Szalay, Eva, 'India seeks to lure rupee trading back onshore', 22nd January 2020
Szalay, Eva and Croft, Jane, 'Five banks face forex-rigging lawsuits in London', 30th July 2019
Szalay, Eva and Stafford, Philip, 'Citigroup calls for burden of managing risky trades to be shared more widely', 17th April 2019
Szalay, Eva and Toplensky, Rochelle, 'Banks look for closure in EU benchmark probe', 11th May 2019
Tabb, Larry, 'Playing ostrich over high-speed trading is not an option', 14th July 2011
Tabb, Larry, 'Payment for order flow is a good deal for investors', 18th October 2019
Tait, Nikki, 'Tested to the limit', 12th September 1994
Tait, Nikki, 'ASX members consider future of their club', 17th October 1996
Tait, Nikki, 'ASX members vote to demutualise exchange', 19th October 1996
Tait, Nikki, 'Sydney exchange sees future in commodities', 3rd January 1997
Tait, Nikki, 'Changes create new risks', 17th July 1998
Tait, Nikki, 'Uncertain futures ahead', 23rd March 1998
Tait, Nikki, 'US leaves foreigners out in the cold', 30th October 1998
Tait, Nikki, 'US proposes stiff tests for foreign futures exchanges', 20th July 1998
Tait, Nikki, 'Electronic threat prompts action', 23rd March 1999
Tait, Nikki, 'Exchanges look to their electronic futures', 22nd March 1999
Tait, Nikki, 'LCH expects go-ahead for swaps clearing', 22nd March 1999
Tait, Nikki, 'LCH seeks twin in the US', 11th November 1999
Tait, Nikki, 'Marriage proposals dominate the sector', 23rd March 1999
Tait, Nikki, 'Nymex feels the draught', 27th October 1999
Tait, Nikki, 'Older birds can still fly', 13th January 1999
Tait, Nikki, 'Pit in the dumps', 20th September 1999
Tait, Nikki, 'Regulators reach over the counter', 20th September 1999
Tait, Nikki, 'Exchange President keeps his options open', 28th February 2000
Tait, Nikki, 'Fierce battle to take lead', 28th June 2000
Tait, Nikki, 'The floor is going electronic', 28th June 2000
Tait, Nikki, 'ISE takes another step closer to launch', 25th May 2000
Tait, Nikki, 'There's life in the old bourses yet', 31st March 2000
Tait, Nikki, 'Americans poised to be offered contracts', 21st June 2001
Tait, Nikki, 'Catalogue of woes starts to take a toll', 28th March 2001
Tait, Nikki, 'Chicago traders stay entrenched in the bull-pit', 25th September 2001
Tait, Nikki, 'ICE to offer facility via London Clearing House', 30th August 2001
Tait, Nikki, 'Technology spawns new range of rivals', 28th March 2001
Tait, Nikki, 'Europe on the same wavelength as US, but moving more slowly', 15th May 2009
Tait, Nikki, 'London fears Brussels reform will shift power', 6th September 2010
Tait, Nikki, 'Traders fear threat of political agendas', 5th January 2011
Tait, Nikki and Barber, Tony, 'Star-crossed levers', 10th January 2011
Tait, Nikki and Denton, Nicholas, 'ASX to offer fund raising on internet', 12th June 1997
Tait, Nikki and Grant, Jeremy, 'Agreement reached over European CDS clearance', 20th February 2009
Tait, Nikki and Grant, Jeremy, 'Greater clarity on equity trades urged', 14th April 2010
Tait, Nikki, Hall, Ben and Oakley, David, 'Dilemma over CDS trades policing', 10th March 2010
Tait, Nikki, Hall, Jeremy and Blas, Javier, 'EU to rein in commodity speculation', 21st September 2010
Targett, Simon, 'Low-cost track for all indices', 5th May 2000
Targett, Simon, 'Preparing for invasion by the Spider men', 3rd March 2000
Targett, Simon, 'It's the liquidity that matters', 28th March 2001
Targett, Simon, 'Time to open up Europe's money centre', 26th May 2003
Targett, Simon, 'Pension gloom is lifting', 19th January 2004
Tassell, Tony, 'Pepper futures exchange for India', 16th October 1996
Tassell, Tony, 'Culture change on Dalal Street', 24th June 1997
Tassell, Tony, 'Domestic debt shapes up', 10th March 1997
Tassell, Tony, 'End of the paper chase in sight', 10th March 1997

Tassell, Tony, 'Risk business lures entrepreneurs', 10th March 1997
Tassell, Tony, 'Smaller centres offer a more exotic allure', 1st March 2006
Taylor, Paul, 'Major banks spearhead era of massive re-organisation', 21st May 1984
Taylor, Paul, 'Bankers Trust breaks ranks-again', 15th July 1985
Taylor, Paul, 'Blow, not knockout', 28th September 1988
Taylor, Paul, 'Consolidation worries the smaller firms', 22nd March 1991
Taylor, Paul, 'How to make ready for regulation', 9th November 2011
Taylor, Robert, 'Sweden to axe bond turnover tax', 26th January 1990
Taylor, Robert, 'Swedish investors' group applauds bourse tax move', 11th October 1991
Taylor, Robert, 'All change for Stockholm bourse', 25th February 1992
Taylor, Roger, 'Shift in power accompanies a move westwards', 29th September 1999
Temple, Peter, 'Easdaq set for listings surge', 19th April 1997
Terazono, Emiko, 'Japanese futures activity soars', 17th December 1991
Terazono, Emiko, 'Fears of new restrictions', 19th March 1992
Terazono, Emiko, 'JGB futures stir bad memories', 20th October 1993
Terazono, Emiko, 'Known for know-how', 24th March 1993
Terazono, Emiko, 'Patience is running out', 26th May 1994
Terazono, Emiko, 'Long road back to Tokyo', 28th March 1996
Terazono, Emiko, 'Move to create a new market', 1st March 1996
Terazono, Emiko, 'The worst may be over', 28th March 1996
Terazono, Emiko, 'Rival exchanges whip up a cocoa war', 24th March 2015
Terazono, Emiko, 'Russia's rise shakes up global grain landscape', 17th November 2017
Terazono, Emiko, 'Banks and energy traders back blockchain launches', 20th September 2018
Terazono, Emiko, 'Resources traders seek data wizards to combat squeeze on margins', 11th July 2018
Terazono, Emiko, 'Blockchain platform Vakt signs majority of North Sea traders', 26th February 2019
Terazono, Emiko, 'Traders wake up to cost of coffee volatility as farmers down tools', 17th April 2019
Terazono, Emiko and Blas, Javier, 'Swiss question role of commodities traders in economy', 27th March 2013
Terazono, Emiko and Meyer, Gregory, 'CME's Black Sea wheat futures contract stirs interest of traders and hedge funds', 4th April 2018
Tett, Gillian, 'A bang or a whimper?', 1st April 1998
Tett, Gillian, 'Big Bang calls for some swift reforms', 24th March 1998
Tett, Gillian, 'Big Bang or just a whimper?', 26th March 1998
Tett, Gillian, 'Complex timetable for reforms package', 26th March 1998
Tett, Gillian, 'No longer a Cinderella', 1st May 1998
Tett, Gillian, 'Rivalry to replace cosy collaboration', 26th March 1998
Tett, Gillian, 'Traders gamble on an anomaly', 17th July 1998
Tett, Gillian, 'Wave of corporate flirting', 26th March 1998
Tett, Gillian, 'Facing up to a wave of foreign competitors', 21st June 1999
Tett, Gillian, 'Fresh education heralds a shift', 21st June 1999
Tett, Gillian, 'Retail defences may start to fall', 21st June 1999
Tett, Gillian, 'Visitors grab some juicy prizes', 21st June 1999
Tett, Gillian, 'Crunch brings some benefits', 8th May 2000
Tett, Gillian, 'Silence conceals significant tale', 8th May 2000
Tett, Gillian, 'The City struggles to escape from European Union red tape', 1st July 2005
Tett, Gillian, 'Déjà vu as markets face new challenge', 16th November 2006
Tett, Gillian, 'Driven faster by low rates, more users and technology', 18th November 2006
Tett, Gillian, 'FOA worried by US regulatory aspirations', 14th June 2006
Tett, Gillian, 'Dark Liquidity system to launch', 5th February 2007
Tett, Gillian, 'Dominant role of MTS could be undermined', 2nd November 2007
Tett, Gillian, 'Doomed to repeat it?', 27th August 2007
Tett, Gillian, 'Funds are ousting the banks', 27th April 2007
Tett, Gillian, 'Growth brings loss of oversight', 28th May 2007
Tett, Gillian, 'MTS grip under threat', 19th November 2007

Tett, Gillian, 'No turning back the revolution', 28th May 2007
Tett, Gillian, 'OTC derivatives hold their own', 19th November 2007
Tett, Gillian, 'Regulators weigh up supra-national intervention', 19th November 2007
Tett, Gillian, 'Sub-prime in its context', 19th November 2007
Tett, Gillian, 'Swaps soar as investors pile in', 28th May 2007
Tett, Gillian, 'Complex system built on flimsy foundations', 2nd October 2008
Tett, Gillian, 'Pressures for a rethink are on the rise', 23rd January 2008
Tett, Gillian, 'A year that shook faith in finance', 4th August 2008
Tett, Gillian, 'When the world held its breath', 1st September 2018
Tett, Gillian, 'Better data on shadow banking reveals uncomfortable truths', 11th October 2019
Tett, Gillian, 'Clearing houses are ripe for reform', 25th October 2019
Tett, Gillian, 'Repo markets mystery reminds us we are flying blind', 20th September 2019
Tett, Gillian and Buck, Tobias, 'Trade body seeks talks on future of MTS', 14th March 2007
Tett, Gillian and Chung, Joanna, 'Hedge funds are at the gates of the eurozone's cosy bond club', 13th March 2007
Tett, Gillian and Chung, Joanna, 'MTS to decide on hedge fund access', 20th April 2007
Tett, Gillian and Davies, Paul J., 'What's the damage', 5th November 2007
Tett, Gillian and Davies, Paul J., 'Battle-scarred bankers lapse into a hoarding habit', 8th May 2008
Tett, Gillian, Davies, Paul J. and van Duyn, Aline, 'A new formula? Complex finance contemplates a more fettered future', 1st October 2008
Tett, Gillian and Gangahar, Anuj, 'Surge in equity derivatives trade', 11th July 2006
Tett, Gillian and Gangahar, Anuj, 'Deals on dark pools set to surge', 31st January 2007
Tett, Gillian and Mackenzie, Michael, 'Debate over Libor breeds a crisis of confidence', 22nd April 2008
Tett, Gillian and Oakley, Daniel, 'European banks in chase for dollars', 10th June 2008
Tett, Gillian and Tassell, Tony, 'A swing into bonds: why equities are losing their allure for global investors', 10th October 2005
Tett, Gillian, Thal Larsen, Peter and Hume, Neil, 'Barclays Capital banker quits', 24th August 2007
Tett, Gillian and van Duyn, Aline, 'On the march', 9th June 2009
Tett, Gillian and van Duyn, Aline, 'Under restraint', 7th July 2009
Tett, Gillian, van Duyn, Aline and Davies, Paul J., 'A re-emerging market? Bankers are seeking simpler ways to sell on debt', 1st July 2008
Tett, Gillian, van Duyn, Aline and Grant, Jeremy, 'Let battle commence', 20th May 2009
Thal Larsen, Peter, 'Heading for the trenches', 22nd February 2002
Thal Larsen, Peter, 'How long can good times last?', 8th November 2005
Thal Larsen, Peter, 'One shocking bank failure deposited a stern warning in the history books', 19th February 2005
Thal Larsen, Peter, 'Action may be needed to maintain competitive advantage', 26th March 2006
Thal Larsen, Peter, 'Banks switch view of Mifid', 16th November 2006
Thal Larsen, Peter, 'Hats off: Big Bang still brings scale and innovation to finance in London', 26th October 2006
Thal Larsen, Peter, 'Many are miffed at the costly Mifid', 26th October 2006
Thal Larsen, Peter, 'FSA concedes that rules only go so far', 20th December 2007
Thal Larsen, Peter, 'Global, universal, unmanageable? Why many are wary of bank mega-mergers', 29th March 2007
Thal Larsen, Peter, 'Institutions prepare for the consequences', 30th October 2007
Thal Larsen, Peter, 'Investment banking has fresh attraction', 14th March 2007
Thal Larsen, Peter, 'Number behind the M&A boom', 30th May 2007
Thal Larsen, Peter, 'Regulators face global challenge', 23rd March 2007
Thal Larsen, Peter, 'Never become too dependent on your bank', 1st October 2008
Thal Larsen, Peter, 'Payback Time', 7th January 2008
Thal Larsen, Peter, 'Withdrawal unavailable', 6th December 2008
Thal Larsen, Peter, 'A lot to be straightened out', 31st March 2009
Thal Larsen, Peter, 'Reviving flow of credit will take greater intervention', 17th January 2009

Thal Larsen, Peter, 'Too early to declare death of "universal banking"', 15th January 2009
Thal Larsen, Peter and Batchelor, Charles, 'Credit derivatives go through "pain process"', 24th February 2005
Thal Larsen, Peter and Drummond, James, 'Regulator's radar hunts for approach to hedge funds', 24th June 2005
Thal Larsen, Peter and Farrell, Greg, 'Landscape shifts for investment banks', 23rd September 2008
Thal Larsen, Peter and Guerrera, Francesco, 'Investment banks' future questioned', 16th September 2008
Thal Larsen, Peter and Jopson, Barney, 'Cost analysis of Mifid rules confirms FSA chief's doubts', 25th November 2006
Thal Larsen, Peter and Jopson, Barney, 'Good behaviour key to regulator's remit', 28th March 2006
Thal Larsen, Peter, Parker, George, Giles, Chris and Saigol, Lina, 'Recriminations fly at handling of Rock Crisis', 19th September 2007
Thal Larsen, Peter, Pretzlik, Charles and Hughes, Chris, 'Big Bang celebrants find party has moved on', 28th October 2006
Thal Larsen, Peter and Wighton, David, 'Record earning as sector recovers', 27th January 2005
Thomas, Daniel, 'Property platform launch attracts flurry of interest', 26th March 2009
Thomas, Daniel, 'Vacant Possessions', 7th December 2009
Thomas, Daniel, 'Investors begin to return to property derivatives trading', 25th January 2010
Thomas, Daniel, 'London tops Europe property list', 11th October 2010
Thomas, Daniel, Minder, Rachel, Pimlott, Daniel, Rappeport, Alan and Nakamoto, Michiyo, 'Market is shaken to its foundations', 22nd January 2009
Thomas, Simon and Collingwood, Chris, 'Clearers at the crossroads', 3rd September 1990
Thompson, Barney, 'Banks seen as better run than newspapers', 26th March 2015
Thompson, Barney, 'Brexit puts legal hub at risk, City warns', 23rd November 2017
Thompson, Christopher, 'Basel 3 rules to hit repo trading', 7th February 2014
Thompson, Jennifer, 'Regulators descend on booming market', 11th September 2017
Thompson, Jennifer, 'China and Latin America help send assets towards $80tn', 23rd July 2018
Thompson, Jennifer, 'Assets in European Ucits funds burst through landmark Euro10tn', 1st July 2019
Thompson, Jennifer, 'French fail to capitalise on Brexit as number of Paris funds falls', 8th July 2019
Thompson, Jennifer, 'Liquidity risk moves centre stage', 1st July 2019
Thompson, Jennifer, 'QE sows seeds of next crisis, funds warn', 2nd December 2019
Thompson, Jennifer, Jenkins, Patrick and Schäfer, Daniel, 'MPs to probe London job losses', 9th November 2012
Thomson, Adam, 'Deal marks turning point in history of the bourse', 31st March 2010
Thomson, Adam, 'Mexican Exchange set for IPO surge', 7th May 2010
Thomson, Adam, 'Changes give vigour to once-somnolent bourse', 24th June 2011
Thomson, Adam, 'Trading surge brings region together', 14th November 2012
Thomson, Robert, 'High hopes demolished', 24th March 1993
Thornhill, John, 'Helping to oil the market's wheels', 27th April 1994
Thornhill, John, 'Reining in wild expansion', 11th April 1996
Thornhill, John, 'Strange beast is eye-catching', 28th February 1997
Thornhill, John and Jenkins, Patrick, 'Ties that bind', 2nd April 2013
Thwaites, Christian, 'I have become extremely suspicious about an industry I have worked in since 1981', 15th September 2018
Tieman, Ross, 'Algo trading: the dog that bit its master', 19th March 2008
Tieman, Ross, 'When microseconds really count', 19th March 2008
Tieman, Ross, 'Knowledge and old-fashioned skill are back in favour', 22nd June 2009
Tieman, Ross, 'Second tier focuses on specialised approach', 10th May 2012
Tirinmanzi, Martha and Hemphill, Mike, 'Management of risk remains an issue for the buyside user', 2nd August 2010
Tomkins, Richard, 'Cost justification is deterrent', 27th January 1986
Tomkins, Richard, 'No rush to seize opportunity created', 27th January 1986
Tsui, Enid, 'Taiwan exchange drops plan for IPO', 11th December 2009

Tucker, Emma, 'The Square Mile stays out in front', 29th May 1992
Tucker, Emma, 'Not the bustling place it used to be', 22nd April 1993
Tucker, Paul, 'Financial regulation needs principles as well as rules', 19th June 2014
Tucker, Sundeep, 'A battle for hearts and wallets', 24th October 2006
Tucker, Sundeep, 'Deal flows spur change of tactic', 10th October 2006
Tucker, Sundeep, 'Asia seeks its centre', 6th July 2007
Tucker, Sundeep, 'Consolidation runs up against expensive buffers', 19th November 2007
Tucker, Sundeep, 'Merrill evolves a strategy for survival in the Asian climate', 15th March 2007
Tucker, Sundeep, 'Rival Asian bourses blush at merger talk', 26th June 2007
Tucker, Sundeep, 'Rivals to HK and Singapore emerge', 19th November 2007
Tucker, Sundeep, 'Tokyo faces an uphill battle in attracting foreign listings', 28th June 2007
Tucker, Sundeep, 'Deregulation prompts new look at trading monopolies', 1st October 2008
Tucker, Sundeep, 'Revamped Singapore bourse to rival Aim', 28th January 2008
Tucker, Sundeep, 'Goldman launches dark pool in HK', 2nd March 2009
Tucker, Sundeep and Smith, Peter, 'ASX to develop energy-related futures', 21st May 2009
Tuckwell, David, 'Dangers lurk in the design of junk bond ETFs', 18th November 2019
Tupker, Chris, 'Clearing houses must be free to compete', 21st June 2007
Turnbull, John, 'On a quest to boost financial flows', 11th April 2001
Turner, David, 'International dimension is missing link', 12th April 2006
Turner, David, 'Japan needs derivatives to compete', 10th August 2006
Turner, David, 'Still a cosy and cosseted world', 28th November 2006
Turner, David, 'Tokyo exchange chief seeks tie-up with foreign bourse', 8th April 2006
Turner, David, 'Tokyo exchange ready for Chinese listings', 26th April 2006
Turner, David, 'Tokyo exchange sets timetable for 2009 listing', 27th June 2006
Turner, David, 'TSE and NYSE in talks over alliance', 28th October 2006
Turner, David, 'TSE would like to meet suitors with view to friendship but not marriage', 7th November 2006
Turner, David, 'TSE caught between talk of innovation and natural caution', 28th August 2007
Turner, David, 'TSE to launch exotic products to view with other bourses', 2nd June 2007
Turner, David and Chung, Joanna, 'London and Tokyo combine', 23rd February 2007
Turner, David, Chung, Joanna and Postelnicu, Andrei, 'Tokyo exchange undone by lack of investment', 23rd January 2006
Turner, David and Cohen, Norma, 'Nomura to buy broker Instinet', 3rd November 2006
Turner, David, Marsh, Virginia and Lau, Justine, 'TSE keeps close eye on battle for bourse', 24th May 2006
Turner, David and Suzuki, Kaori, 'TSE considers anti-takeover measures', 29th November 2006
Tyler, Christian, 'First shoots of huge growth', 21st October 1987
Ugeux, Georges, 'Exchange battles mask Europe's silence', 3rd January 2007
Uhlfelder, Eric, 'US de-listings changing the landscape for investors', 23rd July 2007
Underwood, Sarah, 'IT evolution meeting demand for speed, efficiency and accuracy', 16th October 2006
Urry, Maggie, 'Profitability on the horizon', 12th September 1984
Urry, Maggie, 'The round the clock future', 7th December 1984
Urry, Maggie, 'Pru-Bache opens up a swaps warehouse', 16th December 1985
Urry, Maggie, 'Advantage to lending opportunities', 8th February 1986
Urry, Maggie, 'Ingenuity of structures seems unlimited', 17th March 1986
Urry, Maggie, 'A subtle equation between risk and return', 28th November 1986
Urry, Maggie, 'Two good years, now the crunch', 2nd October 1986
Urry, Maggie, 'New structures that keep the stags at bay', 22nd June 1992
Urry, Maggie, 'A question of sink or swim on the main market', 4th March 1993
Urry, Maggie, 'Nasdaq operator unveils proposals to calm critics', 22nd March 1995
Urry, Maggie, 'Questions over youth's behaviour', 23rd August 1995
Urry, Maggie, 'SEC clears the final T+3 hurdle', 17th May 1995
Urry, Maggie, 'Success could bring extinction', 1st February 1996

Urry, Maggie, 'Trio battle for foreign issuers' favour', 1st February 1996
van de Krol, Ronald, 'Confronting overseas competition', 4th October 1991
van de Krol, Ronald, 'Merger pace accelerates', 4th September 1991
van de Krol, Ronald, 'Volumes need to rise', 4th November 1992
van de Krol, Ronald, 'Action plan lifts Amsterdam's status', 12th September 1994
van de Krol, Ronald, 'The EOE will be humming in 1996', 12th September 1994
van de Krol, Ronald, 'Poised for a shake-up', 12th September 1994
van de Krol, Ronald, 'Dutch challenge London', 16th February 1996
van Duyn, Aline, 'Bond markets extend to smaller firms', 19th May 2000
van Duyn, Aline, 'Cash bond trading explored', 8th September 2000
van Duyn, Aline, 'Coredeal signs up two new backers', 5th March 2000
van Duyn, Aline, 'Euro helps prompt a shift to equities', 19th May 2000
van Duyn, Aline, 'European clearers urged to merge', 20th June 2000
van Duyn, Aline, 'A future of opportunity', 4th October 2000
van Duyn, Aline, 'In search of efficiency', 28th June 2000
van Duyn, Aline, 'Liffe battles with Eurex hots up', 11th September 2000
van Duyn, Aline, 'Liffe plans a push into equity markets', 7th September 2000
van Duyn, Aline, 'Sets may be scrapped early next year', 4th May 2000
van Duyn, Aline, 'Trading costs reach unacceptable levels', 8th September 2000
van Duyn, Aline, 'Why closer links with Europe could lead to US costs', 1st September 2000
van Duyn, Aline, 'Bond market has operators on the line', 21st June 2001
van Duyn, Aline, 'Hopes for unity are diminished', 28th March 2001
van Duyn, Aline, 'Looking to an electronic future', 23rd February 2001
van Duyn, Aline, 'Only the best will survive', 28th March 2001
van Duyn, Aline, 'UK companies embrace cashflow securitisation', 12th July 2001
van Duyn, Aline, 'Investors in bonds ask companies for a little respect', 13th May 2002
van Duyn, Aline, 'Banks could adopt derivatives code', 30th May 2003
van Duyn, Aline, 'Credit derivatives unmasked', 21st March 2003
van Duyn, Aline, 'Uncertainty hits derivatives use', 10th April 2003
van Duyn, Aline, 'SecondMarket enters new territory', 11th December 2008
van Duyn, Aline, 'Securitisation sector braced for a long, painful haul', 5th December 2008
van Duyn, Aline, 'Numbers game', 2nd November 2009
van Duyn, Aline, 'US falls behind rivals in new listings', 31st October-1st November 2009
van Duyn, Aline, 'Worries remain even after CDS clean-up', 11th March 2009
van Duyn, Aline, 'Derivative Dilemmas', 12th August 2010
van Duyn, Aline, 'Derivatives traders search for ways to appease regulators', 23rd April 2010
van Duyn, Aline, 'New rules aim to bring trading of derivatives more into public view', 17th December 2010
van Duyn, Aline, 'Pressure mounts over derivatives clearing', 3rd November 2010
van Duyn, Aline, 'SEC backs new trade disclosure rules', 25th February 2010
van Duyn, Aline, 'Sector resized and reshaped', 28th October 2010
van Duyn, Aline, 'Transparency of derivatives becomes key battleground', 12th March 2010
van Duyn, Aline, 'Battle lines emerge as new rules are created', 31st May 2011
van Duyn, Aline, '"ET" stokes fears about sweeping swaps rules', 4th May 2011
van Duyn, Aline, 'IMF raises concern over US reforms to derivatives trading', 30th March 2011
van Duyn, Aline, 'Proposals would widen competition', 31st May 2011
van Duyn, Aline, 'Regulator set to rule on Wall Street's swaps power', 13th January 2011
van Duyn, Aline, Benoit, Bertrand and Major, Tony, 'Members likely to welcome merger', 4th May 2000
van Duyn, Aline and Boland, Vincent, 'Industry flourishes in bear market turmoil', 7th October 2002
van Duyn, Aline, Brewster, Deborah and Tett, Gillian, 'The Lehman Legacy', 13th October 2008
van Duyn, Aline and Bullock, Nicole, 'Ruling on Lehman creates new CDO doubts', 9th February 2010
van Duyn, Aline and Demos, Telis, 'Flash Crash: market reforms to be examined', 5th October 2010

van Duyn, Aline and Gangahar, Anuj, 'Exchanges big winners in OTC overhaul', 15th May 2009
van Duyn, Aline and Grant, Jeremy, 'Use of clearers to rein in OTC derivatives poses fresh dilemma', 15th January 2010
van Duyn, Aline and Guerrera, Francesco, 'Dodd-Frank bill is no Glass-Steagall', 28th June 2010
van Duyn, Aline and Labate, John, 'GEM and iX choose different paths', 8th June 2000
van Duyn, Aline, Labate, John and Marsh, Virginia, 'Bid may reignite interest from other bourses', 28th August 2000
van Duyn, Aline, Mackenzie, Michael and Grant, Jeremy, 'That sinking feeling', 2nd June 2010
van Duyn, Aline, Mackenzie, Michael and Weitzman, Hal, 'Derivatives dealers brace for clearing shake-up', 14th July 2010
van Duyn, Aline and Milne, Richard, 'Arbiters under fire', 25th July 2011
van Duyn, Aline and Munter, Päivi, 'How Citigroup shook Europe's bond markets with two minutes of trading', 10th September 2004
van Duyn, Aline and Pretzlik, Charles, 'Deutsche Börse ready to defend merger with LSE', 28th August 2000
van Duyn, Aline, Rahman, Bayan and Labate, John, 'Ten exchanges plan global market', 8th June 2000
van Duyn, Aline and Tait, Nikki, 'Liffe plans futures on single stocks', 8th September 2000
van Duyn, Aline and Wassener, Bettina, 'Deutsche Börse in deal to boost US trading', 1st June 2001
Vandevelde, Mark, 'Financial Crisis', 20th September 2018
Vasagar, Jeevan, 'Malaysia's regional ambitions curbed by local problems', 11th October 2016
Vasagar, Jeevan and Stafford, Philip, 'Deutsche Börse buys forex platform', 27th July 2015
Viermetz, Kurt, 'No need to tinker with the integrated clearing model', 13th April 2006
Vincent, Bob, 'Intent on expanding its services', 17th December 1991
Vincent, Bob, 'Market impetus drives through the credit crunch', 19th June 1991
Virtanen, Olli, 'Finnish options exchanges to merge', 18th January 1988
Vismara, Andrea, 'Mifid 2 drags down an ecosystem along with Europe's banks', 15th May 2019
Wagstyl, Stefan, 'Living in the shadow of an avalanche', 21st November 1985
Wagstyl, Stefan, 'Ultimate seal of approval', 30th January 1985
Wagstyl, Stefan, 'Glint of change in the gold market', 5th December 1986
Wagstyl, Stefan, 'Paying the price of the market's collapse', 12th March 1986
Wagstyl, Stefan, 'LME plans dollar switch for silver contract', 28th May 1987
Wagstyl, Stefan, 'Reforms on the way', 22nd June 1987
Wagstyl, Stefan, 'Firm rules bolster stability', 14th October 1988
Wagstyl, Stefan, 'Japanese decide to hedge bets', 19th December 1988
Wagstyl, Stefan, 'Risk of missing the global bus', 2nd December 1988
Wagstyl, Stefan, 'Signposts to expansion', 8th March 1989
Wagstyl, Stefan, 'Suffering from insecurity', 13th March 1989
Wagstyl, Stefan, 'Banks welcome Tokyo's infant', 9th March 1990
Wagstyl, Stefan, 'A testing time for equities', 2nd July 1990
Wagstyl, Stefan, 'Rival market gives Bombay impetus to reform', 23rd November 1993
Wagstyl, Stefan, 'Avalanche of paper threatens investment in India', 1st February 1994
Wagstyl, Stefan, 'Wrong perception and harsh reality', 27th October 1998
Wagstyl, Stefan and Gooding, Kenneth, 'Not such a shining example', 6th October 1997
Waldmeir, Patti, 'Big four still recruiting', 13th March 1989
Waldmeir, Patti, 'Most continue to take long view', 13th March 1989
Waldmeir, Patti, 'Liberalisation marches to its own drum', 24th November 2008
Walker, Owen, 'Fintech targets fund managers with securities lending platform', 5th November 2018
Walker, Owen, 'New rules will shine a light on securities lending', 30th July 2018
Walker, Owen, 'Spooked fund managers look at rivals to London', 19th February 2018
Walker, Owen, 'BlackRock warns of Brexit break', 23rd September 2019
Walker, Owen, 'EU27 nations change laws to help UK fund groups survive no deal', 11th February 2019
Walker, Owen, 'Regulators have been slow to see liquidity risk', 5th August 2019

Walker, Owen, 'Small is beautiful for big fund groups', 4th March 2019
Walker, Owen, 'UK funds with small-cap weighting at higher risk of liquidity shock', 22nd July 2019
Walker, Owen and Flood, Chris, 'Amundi will backstop funds in a crunch', 5th August 2019
Walker, Tony, 'On the road to reform in Cairo's markets', 22nd October 1991
Walker, Tony, 'Big ideas on dance floor', 2nd June 1993
Walker, Tony, 'Dragon with an eye on its futures', 2nd April 1994
Waller, David, 'Three-way benefits', 17th February 1988
Waller, David, 'Reuters chases a forex scoop', 15th March 1989
Waller, David, 'Not all gloom and doom', 12th June 1990
Waller, David, 'Fragile but promising', 23rd April 1991
Waller, David, 'Bank chief's sights set on central role for Germany', 10th June 1992
Waller, David, 'Bonn has a change of heart', 26th October 1992
Waller, David, 'German bourses combine to take on Europe', 8th October 1992
Waller, David, 'Going for the lion's share', 1st July 1992
Waller, David, 'Lack of regulator stalls DTB expansion', 12th February 1992
Waller, David, 'Germany takes stock', 7th May 1993
Waller, David, 'Technology is the weapon against London', 1st July 1993
Waller, David, 'Frankfurt's role consolidated', 31st May 1994
Waller, David, 'Resisting the bait of equity ownership', 14th July 1994
Waller, David, 'A tightening of the rules', 31st May 1994
Ward, Andrew, 'Nasdaq OMX plans to step up Oslo Børs battle', 10th September 2009
Warn, Ken, 'Buenos Aires exchange links with the LSE', 14th April 2000
Warn, Ken, 'Rival plan for Argentine stocks', 22nd February 2000
Warwick-Ching, Lucy, 'Offshore industry faces gathering storm', 27th November 2004
Warwick-Ching, Lucy, 'The long and the short of it', 6th March 2007
Wassener, Bettina, 'Driving ambition for a listed Deutsche Börse', 22nd January 2001
Wassener, Bettina, 'Fed rate cut boosts call for extended trading', 17th January 2001
Wassener, Bettina, 'High hopes come down to earth', 25th November 2002
Wassener, Bettina, 'Doing well in troubled times', 10th June 2003
Wassener, Bettina and Boland, Vincent, 'Deutsche Börse chief awaits chance to test the market', 18th January 2001
Waters, Richard, 'Finding a role for the Exchange', 4th October 1989
Waters, Richard, 'Paperless deals', 9th November 1989
Waters, Richard, 'Stock Exchange may face US 24-hour trading', 10th June 1989
Waters, Richard, 'Taurus plan enters critical phase', 9th October 1989
Waters, Richard, 'Towards Europe's super-league', 11th September 1989
Waters, Richard, 'Banks compete for a share', 19th June 1990
Waters, Richard, 'Bourse battle for pride of place in Europe', 17th May 1990
Waters, Richard, 'Drexel's fall may spur the talking-shop', 2nd July 1990
Waters, Richard, 'A Grand Vision of the way to leave the maze', 27th February 1990
Waters, Richard, 'In the shadow of Big Bang', 29th November 1990
Waters, Richard, 'Making the stock market relevant to its members', 19th February 1990
Waters, Richard, 'A new deal for the survival of the Stock Exchange', 1st February 1990
Waters, Richard, 'Pipe brings dream of Euro-bourse closer to reality', 19th April 1990
Waters, Richard, 'Rivals may yet collaborate', 2nd July 1990
Waters, Richard, 'Stalemate in the marketplace', 15th November 1990
Waters, Richard, 'Warning on European capital market', 14th December 1990
Waters, Richard, 'Bourses build up defences', 24th September 1991
Waters, Richard, 'Brokers learn the value of money', 4th November 1991
Waters, Richard, 'Delays to Taurus keep costs high', 11th November 1991
Waters, Richard, 'Elusive international solution', 22nd July 1991
Waters, Richard, 'Europe extends the fuse leading to Big Bang', 29th May 1991
Waters, Richard, 'Farewell to the trading floor as markets plan automation', 22nd July 1991
Waters, Richard, 'Frankfurt gains a foothold', 4th October 1991

Waters, Richard, 'Fundamental questions', 12th November 1991
Waters, Richard, 'Heated dispute', 18th December 1991
Waters, Richard, 'Intermediaries warned of tough challenges', 24th April 1991
Waters, Richard, 'Level playing field may not be open to all-comers', 14th February 1991
Waters, Richard, 'Life in the shadow of deregulation', 19th March 1991
Waters, Richard, 'Liverpool Stock Exchange finally laid to rest', 23rd March 1991
Waters, Richard, 'The local traders fight back', 19th March 1991
Waters, Richard, 'Making sure SEAQ stays at the centre of cross-border share trading', 8th November 1991
Waters, Richard, 'Man with a bull by the horns', 18th September 1991
Waters, Richard, 'Matif in Italian contract move', 11th October 1991
Waters, Richard, 'Revolution at a cosy British club', 21st October 1991
Waters, Richard, 'Securities firms look across borders', 7th January 1991
Waters, Richard, 'Survival of the biggest', 11th December 1991
Waters, Richard, 'Unbundling the City's top club', 5th March 1991
Waters, Richard, 'US, UK stock markets call off talks on link-up', 20th June 1991
Waters, Richard, 'Barings' transatlantic leap', 3rd July 1992
Waters, Richard, 'Gaps in information on markets', 11th November 1992
Waters, Richard, 'Higher return, no extra risk', 8th December 1992
Waters, Richard, 'International stock trading falls at the LSE', 12th February 1992
Waters, Richard, 'Light at the end of the tunnel', 10th November 1992
Waters, Richard, 'Markets start to multiply', 10th November 1992
Waters, Richard, 'Parliament approves Taurus changes', 12th February 1992
Waters, Richard, 'Progress seen in world settlement systems says G30', 17th December 1992
Waters, Richard, 'Salutary September', 8th December 1992
Waters, Richard, 'Securities industry capital rules move closer', 30th January 1992
Waters, Richard, 'A tune-up for City trades', 9th April 1992
Waters, Richard, 'An upheaval waiting to happen', 30th January 1992
Waters, Richard, 'Vision of a grand strategy fades', 26th February 1992
Waters, Richard, 'Easy option or unnecessary risk', 22nd July 1993
Waters, Richard, 'New box of risk-management tricks', 20th October 1993
Waters, Richard, 'The plan that fell to earth', 12th March 1993
Waters, Richard, 'Survival through a part-exchange', 22nd April 1993
Waters, Richard, 'The price of a share of the cake', 31st January 1994
Waters, Richard, 'Talk of mergers is in the air', 12th August 1996
Waters, Richard, 'A share in Nasdaq's future', 22nd January 1998
Waters, Richard, 'A tale of two trade cultures', 24th March 1998
Waters, Richard, 'The view from Wall Street', 8th July 1998
Waters, Richard, 'From Netscape to the Next Big Thing: how a dot.com decade change our lives', 5th August 2005
Waters, Richard, 'Banks back computing revolution', 7th January 2020
Waters, Richard and Cane, Alan, 'Sudden death of a runaway bull', 19th March 1993
Waters, Richard and Graham, George, 'Birth of a market needs burial of differences', 28th November 1990
Watkins, Mary, 'Bursa Malaysia plans to expand its appeal', 15th June 2009
Watkins, Mary, 'Exchange big hitters in battle for market share', 21st September 2009
Watkins, Mary, 'India's oldest exchange gets an injection of new blood', 25th August 2009
Watkins, Mary, 'NSE shuns mega-mergers', 29th August 2011
Weaver, Courtney, 'Moscow tie-up wins approval from participants', 30th October 2012
Webb, Sara, 'Creating a true Nordic market', 30th March 1989
Webb, Sara, 'Give the infants time', 29th May 1990
Webb, Sara, 'International investors find a silver lining', 22nd July 1991
Webb, Sara, 'Poll names top three banks in swaps market', 17th September 1991
Webb, Sara, 'Repo traders fight their corner', 24th July 1991

Webb, Sara, 'Analysts sceptical', 18th November 1992
Webb, Sara, 'Going gets tough', 18th November 1992
Webb, Sara, 'South Korean securities houses target City', 5th March 1992
Webb, Sara, 'Limited scope for development', 20th October 1993
Webb, Sara, 'Tackling the ghost of Black Wednesday', 23rd December 1993
Webb, Sara, 'Dutch win back state debt trade', 16th May 1994
Webb, Sara and Montagnon, Peter, 'Losing its lustre', 27th November 1991
Webber, Jude, 'Santiago aims to be hub for global investment', 14th November 2012
Weinberg, Peter, 'How London can close the gap on Wall Street', 30th March 2006
Weinland, Don, 'Banks race to launch blockchain trade platforms', 9th November 2018
Weinland, Don, 'Beijing set to open up bond futures trading to local banks', 23rd May 2019
Weinland, Don, 'Euroclear plans link with China allowing global use of renminbi debt as collateral', 10th September 2019
Weitzman, Hal, 'Cboe announces deal with Korea Exchange', 9th June 2008
Weitzman, Hal, 'Exchanges have their eyes on the next opportunity', 21st October 2008
Weitzman, Hal, 'Hunt is stepped up for the rogue traders', 21st October 2008
Weitzman, Hal, 'Legend in his own futures is neither shy nor retiring', 21st October 2008
Weitzman, Hal, 'Clearport is a central part of CME's strategy', 21st October 2009
Weitzman, Hal, 'Humble OTC emerges from shadows', 2nd February 2009
Weitzman, Hal, 'The tectonic plates are shifting', 21st October 2009
Weitzman, Hal, 'Banks urged to rethink OTC trading', 6th April 2010
Weitzman, Hal, 'BATS squeezes into crowded world of US equity options', 26th February 2010
Weitzman, Hal, 'Chicago builds on its reputation for speed', 3rd November 2010
Weitzman, Hal, 'CME Group faces twin threats to its long ascendancy', 9th March 2010
Weitzman, Hal, 'CME predicts OTC opacity will remain', 30th July 2010
Weitzman, Hal, 'CME to launch cheese futures', 6th May 2010
Weitzman, Hal, 'Co-location set to reap up to $40 million for CME', 29th October 2010
Weitzman, Hal, 'ICE chief backs financial reform', 6th May 2010
Weitzman, Hal, 'Regulation threat to CME dominance', 27th January 2010
Weitzman, Hal, 'CME now faces foreign and domestic challenges', 11th February 2011
Weitzman, Hal, 'Euro crisis gives clearing a boost', 4th November 2011
Weitzman, Hal, 'NYSE Liffe takes fight to "Fortress Chicago"', 28th June 2011
Weitzman, Hal, 'Regulatory uncertainties weigh on CME', 7th July 2011
Weitzman, Hal, 'ICE shifts OTC energy swaps to futures', 1st August 2012
Weitzman, Hal and Chung, Joanna, 'SEC-CFTC liaison deal set to hasten product approval', 12th March 2008
Weitzman, Hal and Demos, Telis, 'Ultra-fast trading firms hit headwinds in race to be first', 14th July 2011
Weitzman, Hal and Gangahar, Anuj, 'CME casts its eye in Nymex's direction', 29th January 2008
Weitzman, Hal and Grant, Jeremy, 'Futures brokers fear new capital rules', 6th July 2009
Weitzman, Hal and Meyer, Gregory, 'Uncertain futures', 27th January 2012
Weitzman, Hal and van Duyn, Aline, 'ICE eyes sovereign CDS clearing', 11th February 2010
Wells, David, 'New NYSE chief seeks to restore a ring of confidence', 15th January 2004
Wells, David, Wighton, David and Postelnicu, Andrei, 'Archipelago shares gain 60% on NYSE deal', 22nd April 2005
Wendlandt, Astrid, 'Fragments in need of piecing together', 31st March 2000
Wendlandt, Astrid, 'Settlement books set to double', 14th July 2000
Wendlandt, Astrid, 'Urgent need for consolidation', 14th July 2000
Wendlandt, Astrid, 'Winner gets to rule the world', 31st March 2000
Wheatley, Jonathan, 'Ready for foreign flows', 27th June 1997
Wheatley, Jonathan, 'Small victory for exchange', 10th June 1997
Wheatley, Jonathan, 'The time has come, the analysts say', 10th June 1997
Wheatley, Jonathan, 'Warmer international reception for paper', 10th June 1997
Wheatley, Jonathan, 'Bovespa float inspires other exchanges', 19th November 2007

Wheatley, Jonathan, 'Brazil backwater hits top rank', 19th November 2007
Wheatley, Jonathan, 'Brazil exchange executives get into global party mood', 29th February 2008
Wheatley, Jonathan, 'Exchange gains from caution and strict rules', 7th July 2009
Wheatley, Jonathan, 'São Paulo adopts a more international approach', 21st October 2009
Wheatley, Jonathan, 'Strong growth after slight dip', 5th November 2009
Wheatley, Jonathan, Warn, Ken and Mulligan, Mark, 'Latin American brokers face home truths on local problems', 3rd March 2000
Whiffin, Andrew, 'BoJ's dominance raises concern on distorting influence', 1st April 2019
Whiffin, Andrew, 'Hybrid funds smooth path between active and passive strategies', 4th November 2019
Whipp, Lindsay, 'Aim seeks more exposure in Japan', 3rd March 2008
Whipp, Lindsay, 'Domestic investors remain wary', 14th October 2008
Whipp, Lindsay, 'Exchange has big plans for its expansion', 12th September 2008
Whipp, Lindsay, 'Fear concentrates aged minds', 12th September 2008
Whipp, Lindsay, 'Lehman's dark pools swell', 27th May 2008
Whipp, Lindsay, 'Tokyo moves to boost foreign listings', 5th August 2008
Whipp, Lindsay, 'TSE tightens its defences as new era of trading looms', 29th August 2008
Whipp, Lindsay, 'Chi-X global to spearhead Asian push with plans for Japan platform', 1st December 2009
Whipp, Lindsay, 'Co-location to get Tokyo up to speed', 2nd November 2009
Whipp, Lindsay, 'Tokyo Aim looks to niche role to get ahead of rivals', 1st July 2009
Whipp, Lindsay, 'Tokyo looks at PTS clearing services', 10th July 2009
Whipp, Lindsay, 'Tokyo market prepares to move up a gear', 21st October 2009
Whipp, Lindsay, 'Ambitions to recapture its glory days', 8th February 2010
Whipp, Lindsay, 'Arrowhead will take time to hit target for TSE', 11th January 2010
Whipp, Lindsay, 'Japan urged to stimulate IPOs with tax breaks', 8th February 2010
Whipp, Lindsay, 'Tokyo weighs up longer trading days', 27th July 2010
Whipp, Lindsay, 'TSE seeks boost to trade from launch of new platform', 4th January 2010
Whipp, Lindsay, 'End of an era for Chicago futures trading', 8th July 2015
Whipp, Lindsay, Brown, Kevin and Cookson, Robert, 'Asia takes dip in "dark pools"', 9th June 2010
Whipp, Lindsay and Demos, Telis, 'TSE looks at joining forces with Osaka exchange', 11th March 2011
Whipp, Lindsay and Grant, Jeremy, 'Tokyo and London in small-cap push', 30th July 2008
White, Ben, 'Banks join OPU-5 platform', 13th September 2007
White, Ben, 'Buoyant Bear Stearns shrugs off subprime woes', 16th March 2007
White, Ben, 'London's rise concentrates minds in US', 26th May 2007
White, Ben, 'Lehman shares slide on fears over results', 20th August 2008
White, Ben and Politi, James, 'Banks join forces on trading platform', 23rd July 2007
Whittington, James, 'The market wakes up', 15th May 1995
Whittington, James, 'New system will multiply deals', 9th June 1995
Wicks, John, 'A world leader must not be left behind', 25th April 1989
Wiesmann, Gerrit, Milne, Richard and Wallmeyer, Andrew, 'Deutsche Börse hints at sweeter Euronext offer', 25th May 2006
Wiesmann, Gerrit and Stafford, Philip, 'Germany to press ahead with high-speed trading regulation', 26th September 2012
Wiggins, Jenny, 'Electronic bond trading still has a future', 6th September 2002
Wiggins, Jenny, 'History catches up with deals', 7th October 2002
Wiggins, Jeremy, 'US commercial banks' holding of derivatives climb by 9%', 9th June 2003
Wigglesworth, Robin, 'Saudi Bourse poised to exercise more global appeal', 2nd September 2010
Wigglesworth, Robin, 'Bonds find favour over syndicated lending', 13th April 2012
Wigglesworth, Robin, 'Rising Expectations', 25th June 2012
Wigglesworth, Robin, 'Taming the traders', 20th March 2012
Wigglesworth, Robin, 'Asset manager calls for more regulation', 19th June 2015
Wigglesworth, Robin, 'Maturity mismatch sparks fears of financial drought', 19th June 2015
Wigglesworth, Robin, 'Algorithms bring benefits but fears of accidents grow', 1st June 2016

Wigglesworth, Robin, 'Brutal culls ensure the ETF graveyard is full', 15th December 2016
Wigglesworth, Robin, 'Capital Group targets HFTs with rules push', 1st February 2017
Wigglesworth, Robin, 'ETFs and index-trackers coin it in with 20% share of US bond market', 6th February 2017
Wigglesworth, Robin, 'The fearless market', 19th April 2017
Wigglesworth, Robin, 'Hedge funds seek to park quantum revolution', 2nd November 2017
Wigglesworth, Robin, 'Asset managers seek an entrée to the trillion-dollar club', 26th October 2018
Wigglesworth, Robin, 'Exchange traded products face scrutiny as worries deepen', 15th February 2018
Wigglesworth, Robin, 'Liquidity smirk prompts calls for shorter US trading period', 25th April 2018
Wigglesworth, Robin, 'Passive Attack: The story of a Wall Street revolution', 22nd December 2018
Wigglesworth, Robin, 'The Volatility Virus', 14th April 2018
Wigglesworth, Robin, 'ETF pioneer Ross decides to call it a day at State Street', 22nd November 2019
Wigglesworth, Robin, 'Growth of private capital funds accelerates while ETFs slow', 4th November 2019
Wigglesworth, Robin, 'Hedge funds are happy to let the machines take over', 17th October 2019
Wigglesworth, Robin, 'IMF warns of "tip of the iceberg" threat over volatility', 12th April 2019
Wigglesworth, Robin, 'Markets: Volatile Times', 10th January 2019
Wigglesworth, Robin, 'Negative yields force investors to snap up riskier debt', 16th August 2019
Wigglesworth, Robin, 'Non-bank lending surge stirs painful subprime memories', 5th February 2019
Wigglesworth, Robin, Brown, Kevin and Mishkin, Sarah, 'Asia shows growing viability as IPO venue', 19th August 2011
Wigglesworth, Robin, Bullock, Nicole and Meyer, Gregory, 'Battle over price of finance data heats up', 6th July 2016
Wigglesworth, Robin and McLannahan, Ben, 'Liquidity outs leverage as the big worry for investors', 4th May 2018
Wigglesworth, Robin and Palma, Stefania, 'Quant funds take creative tack to gain recruitment edge over Silicon Valley', 29th September 2018
Wigglesworth, Robin, Pickard, Jim and Parker, George, 'Big project finance hit by squeeze on banks', 3rd May 2012
Wigglesworth, Robin and Rennison, Joe, 'Goldman expands algo bond trading programme as investors look to cut costs', 17th August 2017
Wigglesworth, Robin and Rennison, Joe, 'Algos blaze trail in odd lots segment of US corporate bonds', 15th June 2018
Wigglesworth, Robin and Rennison, Joe, 'The Future of Trading', 10th May 2018
Wigglesworth, Robin and Rennison, Joe, 'New credit ecosystem blossoms as portfolio trades surge', 11th October 2018
Wighton, David, 'NYSE fights to retain its dominance', 12th June 2004
Wighton, David, 'Goldman buy-out lending soars', 17th July 2006
Wighton, David, 'Nasdaq's marathon man', 25th November 2006
Wighton, David, 'Selling the attractions of Euronext', 22nd May 2006
Wighton, David, 'Prince shows his daring with move for Nikko', 7th March 2007
Wighton, David and Grant, Jeremy, 'Thain forces pace of change to maintain market share', 22nd April 2005
Wighton, David and Postelnicu, Andrei, 'UBS bets on exchange listing', 18th October 2004
Wighton, David and Wells, David, 'NYSE clients demand independent units', 28th April 2005
Wild, Jane, 'Central banks eye digital money', 2nd November 2016
Wildau, Gabriel, 'Doors to China's markets are creaking open', 1st October 2018
Wildau, Gabriel, 'China struggling to quit debt addiction', 25th March 2019
Wilkes, Giles, 'Wanted: bankers to electrify the British economy', 7th March 2015
Williams, Elaine, 'Banking's unifying force', 16th October 1986
Williams, Frances, 'New rules for a trillion-dollar game', 15th December 1997
Williams, Frances, 'The Savile Row of asset management', 31st October 1997
Williamson, Hugh, 'New regime takes root', 12th June 2002
Willman, John, 'Bank backs changes in accounting', 26th June 2000

Willman, John, 'Banking on borrowed time', 6th November 2000
Willman, John, 'Newly rich press for service', 26th January 2001
Willman, John, 'US giants throw down gauntlet', 26th January 2001
Wilson, James, 'D Börse running trials for dark pool', 6th August 2008
Wilson, James, 'Deutsche Börse lays out strategy to raise gearing', 31st March 2008
Wilson, James, 'Deutsche Börse to cut fees for frequent traders', 27th August 2008
Wilson, James, 'More than just a historic trading floor', 30th June 2009
Wilson, James, 'Exchange seeks transatlantic boost', 14th June 2011
Wilson, James and Grant, Jeremy, 'Deutsche Börse is reaping the benefits of its diversity', 11th August 2008
Wilson, James and Grant, Jeremy, 'D Börse in pan-Europe drive', 17th April 2009
Wilson, James and Schäfer, Daniel, 'Double entry at Deutsche', 13th April 2012
Wilson, Tom, 'Mobile-savvy Kenyans will soon be able to buy shares on phones', 1st November 2019
Wine, Elizabeth, 'Mutual funds can breathe again as new threat recedes', 31st May 2000
Wine, Elizabeth, 'Sidelined cash may stay out of stocks', 4th January 2002
Wine, Elizabeth, 'NYSE competitors step up reform calls', 20th October 2003
Wise, Peter, 'Depression after the comet', 30th April 1990
Wise, Peter, 'Lisbon shapes up for change', 7th February 1994
Wise, Peter, 'Outlook for growth remains bright', 22nd February 1994
Wise, Peter, 'Rescued from a life of obscurity', 4th May 2001
Wolf, Martin, 'Why banks are dangerous', 6th January 1998
Wolf, Martin, 'Painful lessons from a turbulent century', 6th December 1999
Wolf, Martin, 'This stable isle: how Labour has steered an economy going global', 18th September 2006
Wolf, Martin, 'The new capitalism', 19th June 2007
Wolkoff, Neal, 'America's regulations are scaring the Sox off small caps', 1st August 2006
Wolman, Clive, 'Investor protection safety net remains', 16th December 1985
Wolman, Clive, 'Tax exemption for Euro and US bond dealers', 16th December 1985
Wolman, Clive, 'Costs under scrutiny', 19th November 1986
Wolman, Clive, 'Gains in efficiency but monopoly risk', 27th October 1986
Wolman, Clive, 'Pace of game quickens', 8th February 1986
Wolman, Clive, 'A shake-up in gilts', 2nd October 1986
Wolman, Clive, 'Cuts and vigilance reduce appeal of secret money', 12th June 1987
Wolman, Clive, 'Market hypothesis gains support', 21st October 1987
Wolman, Clive, 'Out of shape for the paper chase', 14th August 1987
Wolman, Clive, 'Small deals suffer', 21st October 1987
Wolman, Clive, 'An empty space at the market's heart', 22nd November 1988
Wolman, Clive, 'London's weakness', 14th October 1988
Wolman, Clive, 'Shearson bounces back after its Big Bang shake-out', 8th November 1988
Wolman, Clive, 'The battle of the paper mountain', 3rd April 1989
Wong, Douglas, 'Former Morgan Grenfell man heads SGX', 20th January 2003
Woolfe, Jeremy, 'London's sway weakens as EU authorities gain power', 15th August 2011
Wyles, John, 'European financiers consider plans for joint stock exchange', 13th November 1980
Yassukovich, Stanislas, 'Single market for equities', 26th January 1998
Yassukovich, Stanislas, 'The City has nothing to fear from Brexit', 12th January 2017
Yeager, Holly, 'Vulnerable industry learns lessons from the disaster', 22nd February 2002
Yuan, Yang, Shepherd, Christian, Li, Wan, Hornby, Lucy, Hume, Neil, 'China's speculators rattle raw materials traders', 7th May 2016

Index